To Clare
Christmas 2002
From Scott

D1571171

AUTHOR'S PREFACE

A VERY remarkable resemblance has always been observed between the Book of Daniel and the Book of Revelation. Whatever view may be taken of the proper interpretation of these books, it is difficult to write a Commentary on one of them without carefully studying the other, and without practically furnishing to a considerable extent an exposition of the other. There is no evidence, indeed, that John, in the Book of Revelation, intended to imitate Daniel, and yet there is so strong a resemblance in the manner in which the Divine disclosures respecting the future were made to the two writers; there is so clear a reference to the same great events in the history of the world; there is so much similarity in the symbols employed, that no commentator can well write on the one without discussing many points, and making use of many illustrations, which would be equally appropriate in an exposition of the other.

The following Notes on the Book of Daniel were mostly written before I commenced the preparation of Notes on the Book of Revelation, though the latter book is published first. It has thus happened that many inquiries have been started, and many subjects discussed, in connection with this book, which would otherwise have found a place

in the Notes on the Book of Revelation, and that in the exposition of
the latter, I have, in many places, to avoid needless repetition, done
little more than refer to corresponding places in the Notes on Daniel.
While I have endeavoured to make each work a complete exposition in
itself, it is nevertheless true that the two are designed, in some measure, to go together, and that the one is necessary to the full understanding of the other.

PHILADELPHIA, *December* 26, 1851.

EDITOR'S PREFACE

WE send forth these volumes on Daniel, in perfect confidence that they will be hailed with acceptance by the author's numerous admirers in this country.

The book of Daniel possesses charms alike for the susceptible mind of youth, and the mature mind of the advanced student. Who has not hung with delight in the days of his childhood over the wondrous stories of the captive prophet, regarding the judgment of God on the haughty Nebuchadnezzar, Belshazzar's impious feast and awful doom, the three children in the burning fiery furnace, and Daniel in the lions' den? No Eastern tales, no *Arabian Nights' Entertainments*, have so fascinated us as these. Here, assuredly, truth is more wonderful than fiction. And what student of Scripture has not been arrested and detained by the sublime visions of Daniel, and has not felt all his powers tasked in the interpretation of them? The vision of the colossal statue; of the four beasts from the sea; of the ram and the he-goat; of the seventy weeks, and the final resurrection scene, presenting a kind of epitomized history of the successive empires of the world, and of the varying condition of the church, as existing in them, or affected by them, have all along excited deep interest, and formed the subject of prolonged inquiry to the most gifted minds. Sir Isaac Newton was as anxious to penetrate into these prophetic depths, as into those depths of heaven, where he sought the starry worlds, whose laws he expounded.

Of the Author's commentary the reader will judge for himself. It seems to us to be characterized by his usual thoroughness of research, and solidity of judgment. We do not say that we can accord with him on all points, or that his book is likely to satisfy any student of prophecy on all points; but inasmuch as what may be called the Protestant scheme of exposition is presented with more clearness and fulness, and with more advantages from the new lights of modern history

and research, than in any other English work of the kind, we should anticipate for it a very high, if not the highest place, among English commentaries on Daniel. We doubt not a brief outline or analysis of the
exposition will be acceptable to our readers. We shall, therefore, present it here, noting, when it may seem necessary, the points where our
author diverges from the usual course of exposition, or differs from those
who have been regarded as authorities.

We say nothing of the historical part, but pass at once to the prophetic. The vision of the colossal statue (chap. ii.) is interpreted in
the usual way of the four great monarchies ; and "the stone cut out of
the mountain without hands," is the kingdom of the Messiah, superhuman in its origin, feeble in its beginnings, but ultimately supplanting
all other kingdoms, and filling the earth. The vision of the four beasts,
the lion, the bear, the leopard, and the nondescript animal, "dreadful and
terrible," (chap. vii.) presents the four monarchies again, under another
form or different set of symbols. The ten horns in the head of this last
monster (which represents the Roman empire) are the ten kingdoms
into which the Western empire was divided ; and the little horn springing up among the ten, and destroying three of them, the horn with
"eyes of man, and mouth speaking great things," is the Papacy, not
Antiochus Epiphanes, as Eichhorn, Bertholdt, Bleek, Stuart, and others,
maintain. The Author's defence (vol. ii. p. 76–82), of this interpretation, seems to us not only able, but triumphant. The time of this little
horn, or Papal power (vii. 25), is $3\frac{1}{2}$ prophetic years, or 1260 prophetic
days, that is, years, beginning, A.D. 752 (vol. ii. p. 96), when Pepin,
king of France, gave a grant to Pope Stephen of the exarchate of Ravenna, and the Pentapolis. The year A.D. 2012 is, of course, the termination of the period.

We have next the vision of the ram and the he-goat, interpreted of
the Medo-Persian and Greek empires, of which these animals were respectively the well-known emblems (chap. viii.) The "notable horn"
(ver. 5) of the goat is Alexander the Great. The "four notable ones"
that come up afterwards are his successors ; and the "little horn out of
one of them" is Antiochus Epiphanes. The time in this vision is 2300
days, which our author interprets literally of a period of six years and
110 days ; and applies to the whole period of the Antiochian persecution, from B.C. December, 25, 165, when the sanctuary was cleansed

under Judas Maccabeus, and the persecution of course ended, backwards to B.C. August 5, 171, when the aggressions on the part of Antiochus began. It may not be practicable to make out the precise number of days, but this calculation brings us to the year which is necessary to make out the 2300 days. So Mr. Barnes. The two Newtons, on the other hand, in strict consistency with their Year-day principle, expound the little horn of Rome, and calculate the time from B.C. 334, the date of Alexander's invasion of Asia, or from the vision of the he-goat, and thus they make it end with the world's sixth millennium. Scott, following Faber, expounds of the Mahometan delusion, and dates from somewhere in the time of the ram or Persian empire; that is, somewhere between B.C. 536 and B.C. 330, and maintains, of course, the Year-day principle.

Next we have the famous vision of the seventy weeks. This general period, explained of 490 years, is calculated by our author from the 20th of Artaxerxes Longimanus, that is, from B.C. 454: it is divided into three parts; first, a period of seven weeks or forty-nine years to the rebuilding of the city, which, counting from the *terminus a quo* as above, brings us to B.C. 405, the time when Nehemiah had completely finished his undertaking (vol. ii. p. 175); second, a period of sixty-two weeks, or 434 years, *after* which Messiah would appear and be cut off, which brings us to A.D. 29; and third, a period of one week, or seven years, which was occupied in confirming the covenant with many, through the ministry of Christ and his apostles; in the midst of this week Jesus, in accordance with the prediction, died, and the sacrifice and oblation for ever ceased! (vol. ii. p. 182). A more remarkable prophecy, and one whose fulfilment can be more distinctly traced, never was uttered ; and our author's full and lucid exposition, after his happiest manner, makes this one of the most interesting portions of his book.

The prophecy next passes, at chap. xi., to the wars between the kings of the north and the south, that is, between Syria and Egypt, or the Seleucidæ and the Ptolemies. The introductory part (vers. 1-4) presents an epitome of previous history—noticing the three successors of Cyrus, viz., Cambyses, Smerdis, and Darius Hystaspis; also the fourth and rich king, viz., Xerxes; and the mighty king, whose kingdom should be divided to the four winds of heaven, viz., Alexander the Great and his four generals, who, at his death, partitioned the kingdom among them.

After this introductory part, the wars between the north and the south, or the long succession of hostilities between two parts of Alexander's dominions, Syria, and Egypt, immediately follow (vers. 5-20). At this place (ver. 21) Antiochus Epiphanes, king of Syria, is again introduced, under the character of a " vile person." Mr. Barnes applies the whole chapter, from this verse onwards to the end, to him alone. There is, however, difference of opinion among interpreters in regard to the passage beginning at verse 31, where, according to many, the Romans or Antichrist must be understood. See the application to this last power ably defended in Elliott's *Horæ Apoc.*, vol. iv. p. 7, 4th edition. The argument of Birks, Elliott, and others, in favour of a change of subject at verse 31, from the translation of the first clause, " arms shall stand up *from* or *after* him," seemingly indicating some *new* prince or power, has been overlooked by our author; and on other grounds the entire application to Antiochus seems not very tenable, though argued with very great learning and ingenuity. At verse 40 occurs another indication of change of subject. Certain events are said to take place at "the time of the end," that is, of the period to which the vision refers. But as no such events as those described happened towards the *close* of the reign of Antiochus, Mr. Barnes has recourse to a theory of recapitulation on the part of the prophet, which, to say the best of it, is but an ingenious conjecture. This enables him to find events in the history of Antiochus corresponding with the prophetic description.

The prophecy concludes with a sublime vision of the resurrection (ch. xii.), which is indeed but a continuation of the vision commenced in ch. x. According to our author, the primary reference is to the restoration of the temple worship, and deliverance of the Jews by Judas Maccabeus and his compatriots; while the mind of the prophet is supposed to rest ultimately, by the law of prophetic association, on the general resurrection at the last day. The various notices of time in this chapter are thus treated; the 1260 (verse 7) has a primary reference to the three and a half years' persecution under Antiochus, and an ultimate reference to the downfall of the Papacy, as in vii. 25; the 1290 and the 1335 are not to be known till the event, and conjecture is useless. Newton, Scott, and the school to which they belong, suppose that, when at the close of the well-known 1260, Antichrist shall be subverted—thirty years more may be occupied in *totally* extirpating that power, while forty-five years more still may serve to completely introduce the millennium.

Such is a very brief sketch of our author's work on Daniel. We add a sentence or two on his mode of interpreting the Danielic times. It will be seen, from the above analysis, that he does not rigidly adhere to the Year-day principle. He seems very much to adopt or reject it as the exigency of the particular passage under consideration may require. The time, times, and dividing of a time, in ch. vii. 25, is interpreted on that principle, and accordingly is explained of the 1260 years of Antichrist; while the 2300 days of ch. viii. 13, 14, are interpreted on the Literal-day principle, and explained of the duration of the Antiochian persecution. Again, the Year-day theory is adopted in the vision of the seventy weeks in ch. ix.; while in ch. xii. 7, the three-and a half years, are both literal and prophetic, in order to answer the primary reference to Antiochus, and the ultimate one to Antichrist. Possibly, this varying principle of interpretation may be the true one. It *may* be, that in many cases the shorter period is typical of the longer, and that, therefore both may be understood in the same passages. Yet if this be so in many passages, or in any, why not in all? We could wish to see all interpretations of prophetic times preceded by some *clear* observations on the *principles* by which the author professes to be guided. We confess, therefore, a strong partiality for that system of interpretation which carries the Year-day principle consistently out; of course the merit of consistency belongs equally to those who carry out any other well-understood principle. In the author's note on ch. vii. 25, and other places where notices of time occur, very able defences of the Year-day principle may be found, to which, as the Notes on Daniel were written first, there is constant reference in the Notes on the times of the Apocalypse; and we have only to regret the want of some hints to guide us in regard to the mode of its application.

To do justice to the author and to himself, the reader, moreover, must remember that the Commentary on Daniel, and that on the Apocalypse, form together but one work. The author, in an advertisement, informs us, that the two may, without impropriety, be considered as parts of one whole. The two books, according to the views taken in the exposition, refer to a considerable extent to the same events;

and the intention was, that they should be published as nearly simultaneously as possible. Many important points, therefore, which are merely glanced at in the Commentary on Revelation, will be found more fully elucidated in the Notes on Daniel, which, though last in point of publication, were first composed.

Of the general character of these volumes, we must say again, that we cannot speak too highly. They form, we think, take them all in all, our best English Commentary on Daniel. The author has made himself familiar with the more ancient expositions; with the rich stores of Germany—of Eichhorn, Bertholdt, and Hengstenberg, from whom he has drawn with that nice discrimination which the admixture of good and bad in these works required at his hands; with the views of his own great countrymen, Stuart and Bush; and with those of our own Newtons and Wintles; and, in fine, with all that has been written worthily on the subject—and the result is a most satisfying fulness. Another result of the author's labours will be to confirm public confidence more completely in that system of interpretation of prophecy which has so long prevailed amongst us, and to destroy which so many attempts have recently been made. The cry against it originating in Germany, and echoed in America by Professor Moses Stuart, has been adopted and defended by eminent scholars at home. But in the author of the Notes on Daniel and the Apocalypse, we have a man of no mean learning and research adhering to the old, though much maligned principles, and willing to hazard his reputation by following such a guide as the despised Bishop Newton. When we read such sneering assaults as the following, from the pen of one who may be styled the chief of the New School, we will be better able to appreciate the boldness with which our author, in spite of it, has taken up his position. We introduce the quotation by simply remarking that Bishop Newton has long maintained his place, and is likely to maintain it for a long while to come ; and that something more is necessary to an expounder of the Word of God, than a knowledge of historico-grammatical interpretation. The profoundest scholars may prove the poorest exegetes, as witness Grotius and the great man who writes:—

" As to the book of Daniel itself, I believe that no other of the scriptural books, the Apocalypse excepted, has called forth such a variety of discrepant opinions and interpretations. How can I agree with all of them? And yet the great mass of readers are ready to say, each one for himself, that I ought to agree with him. But why? my friend. You take the liberty to differ from others; and why should you refuse the same liberty to me? Besides, I have to ask, On what grounds have you based your opinion? Have you studied the book in its original languages; sought for light on every side, from history, and from antiquities; and above all, have you thoroughly and simply applied to it, irrespective of any favourite and preconceived notions about it, the established principles of historico-grammatical exegesis? And do you even know, with any certainty, what those principles are? If not, how much is your opinion worth, even in your own eyes, when you look candidly at such a difficult matter as the interpretation of the book before us?

" If here and there a self-complacent critic of my Commentary on the Apocalypse, had asked himself such questions, before he sat down to write his *diatribe*, the public would have been spared a deal of *à priori* interpretation and spider-web theories. Some had written their book, on the same work of John, and mine disagreed with it. *Hinc illae lacrymae.* Some had read that *profound* work of Bishop Newton on the Prophecies; and because I did not agree with him, I must be in the wrong. The most confident of my condemning judges were, of course, those who could not read a word of the original, and would not be able to form any idea what one means, who talks about historico-grammatical interpretation. I have no defence to make against any such assailants."

In taking leave of this latest work of our author, we must not omit to advert to the reappearance of an admirable feature in his earliest publications. We have very full and pointed practical reflections at the close of each chapter, onward to the sixth inclusive. In the remaining portions of the work, such reflections are more sparingly introduced.

Of this edition we can only say, that the text has been subjected to careful revision; that very many errors have been corrected; and that the illustrations have everywhere been greatly improved, while in some instances the original ones have been rejected, and others more appropriate substituted in their room. We had intended to enlarge the Essay on the Year-day principle which is prefixed to our edition of the author's Notes on the Apocalypse, with the view of giving it a place here. But the rapidity with which the work has gone through the press, allowed no time for the necessary labour. We can, therefore, in the meantime, only refer to that Essay in the imperfect form in which it already exists. In the first volume will be found one or two Appendices, from the Commentary of Professor Stuart, on such points as his learning and scholarship eminently qualified him to discuss. In the second volume there is an Appendix, consisting of part of the first and second books of the Maccabees, which we were induced to insert from a conviction that in an exposition of a prophecy, where Antiochus Epiphanes and the Maccabees figure so conspicuously, it would be for the reader's convenience to have the original history at hand, to which reference is made in almost every page.

N.B.—The copyright of the Notes on Daniel for Great Britain and Ireland, has been assigned by the author to Messrs. Knight and Hawkes; and this edition is now published under arrangement with them.

INTRODUCTION

§ I.—THE LIFE OF DANIEL.

Of Daniel little more is known, or can now be ascertained, than is recorded in this book. There are two other persons of this name mentioned in the Bible — a son of David (1 Chron. iii. 1); and a Levite of the race of Ithamar (Ezra viii. 2; Neh. x. 6). The latter has been sometimes confounded with the prophet, as he is in the apocryphal addenda to the Septuagint.

Daniel, supposed commonly to be the same person as the author of this book, is twice mentioned by Ezekiel, once as deserving to be ranked with Noah and Job, and once as eminent for wisdom. "Though these three men, Noah, Daniel, and Job, were in it, they should deliver but their own souls by their righteousness, saith the Lord God" (Ezek. xiv. 14). "Behold, thou art wiser than Daniel; there is no secret that they can hide from thee" (Ezek. xxviii. 3). Whether this is the Daniel who is the author of this book, however, or whether this was some ancient patriarch whose name had been handed down by tradition, and whose name was *assumed* by the author of this book in later times, has been a question among recent critics, and will properly come up for examination under the next section in this Introduction.

Assuming now that the book is genuine, and that it was written by him whose name it bears, all that is known of Daniel is substantially as follows:—

He was descended from one of the highest families in Judah, if not one of royal blood (Notes on ch. i. 3; Josephus' *Ant.* b. x. ch. x. § 1). His birthplace was probably Jerusalem (comp. ch. ix. 24), though it is not absolutely certain that this passage would demonstrate it.

Of his first years nothing is recorded. At an early age we find him in Babylon, among the captive Hebrews whom Nebuchadnezzar had carried away at the first deportation of the people of Judah, in the fourth year of Jehoiakim. He is mentioned in connection with three

other youths, apparently of the same rank, Hananiah, Mishael, and
Azariah, who, with him, were selected for the purpose of being
instructed in the language and literature of the Chaldeans, with a
view to their being employed in the service of the court (Dan. i. 3, 4).
His age at that time it is impossible to determine with accuracy, but
it is not improbable that it was somewhere about twelve or fifteen
years. In ch. i. 4, he and his three friends are called " children "
(יְלָדִים). " This word properly denotes the period from the age of
childhood up to manhood, and might be translated *boys*, *lads*, or
youth."—(Professor Stuart on Daniel, p. 373). Ignatius (*Ep. ad
Magn.*) says that Daniel was twelve years of age when he went into
exile; Chrysostom says that he was eighteen (*Opp.* vi. p. 423);
Epiphanius says, ἔτι νήπιος ὤν; Jerome calls him *admodum puer*.
These are, of course, mere conjectures, or traditions, but they are
probably not far from the truth.   Such was the age at which persons
would be most *likely* to be selected for the training here referred to.
The design of this selection and training is not mentioned, but in the
circumstances of the case it is perhaps not difficult to conjecture it.
The Hebrews were a captive people.   It was natural to suppose that
they would be restless, and perhaps insubordinate, in their condition,
and it was a matter of policy to do all that could be done to conciliate them.   Nothing would better tend to this than to select some
of their own number who were of their most distinguished families;
to place them at court; to provide for them from the royal bounty;
to give them the advantages of the best education that the capital
afforded; to make an arrangement that contemplated their future
employment in the service of the state, and to furnish them every
opportunity of promotion.   Besides, in the intercourse of the government with the captive Hebrews, of which, from the nature of the case,
there would be frequent occasion, it would be an advantage to have
native-born Hebrews in the confidence of the government, who could
be employed to conduct that intercourse.

In this situation, and with this view, Daniel received that thorough
education which Oriental etiquette makes indispensable in a courtier
(comp. Plato, *Alcib.* § 37), and was more especially instructed in the
science of the Chaldeans, and in speaking and writing their language.
He had before evidently been carefully trained in the Hebrew learning,
and in the knowledge of the institutions of his country, and was
thoroughly imbued with the principles of the religion of his fathers.
An opportunity soon occurred of putting his principles to the test.
Trained in strict religious principles, and in the sternest rules of temperance in eating and drinking, and fearing the effect of the luxurious
living provided for him and his companions by the royal bounty, he
resolved, with them, to avoid at once the danger of conforming to the
habits of idolaters; of "polluting" himself by customs forbidden by
his religion, and of jeoparding his own health and life by intemperate

indulgence. He aimed, also, to secure the utmost vigour of body, and the utmost clearness of mind, by a course of strict and conscientious temperance. He obtained permission, therefore, to abstain from the food provided for him, and to make an experiment of the most temperate mode of living (ch. i. 8–14). "His prudent proceedings, wise bearing, and absolute refusal to comply with such customs, were crowned with the Divine blessing, and had the most splendid results."

After the lapse of three years spent in this course of discipline, Daniel passed the examination which was necessary to admit him to the royal favour, and was received into connection with the government, to be employed in the purposes which had been contemplated in this preparatory training (ch. i. 18–20). One of his first acts was an interpretation of a dream of Nebuchadnezzar, which none of the Chaldeans had been able to interpret, the result of which was that he was raised at once to that important office, the governorship of the province of Babylon, and the head inspectorship of the sacerdotal caste (ch. ii.)

Considerably later in the reign of Nebuchadnezzar, we find Daniel interpreting another dream of his, to the effect that, in consequence of his pride, he would be deprived for a time of his reason and his throne, and would be suffered to wander from the abodes of men, and to live among wild beasts, but that after a time he would be again restored. The record which we have of this is found in a proclamation of the king himself, which is preserved by Daniel (ch. iv.) In the interpretation of this remarkable dream, and in stating to the king—the most proud and absolute monarch of the earth at that time — what would come upon him, Daniel displays the most touching anxiety, love, and loyalty for the prince, and shows that he was led to this interpretation only by the conviction of the truth. In view of a calamity so great, he exhorted the monarch yet to humble himself and to repent of his sins, and to perform acts of charity, with the hope that God might be merciful, and avert from him a doom so humiliating—so much to be dreaded (ch. iv. 19–27).

Under the immediate successor of Nebuchadnezzar—Evil-Merodach —Daniel appears to have been forgotten, and his talents and his former services seem to have passed away from the recollection of those in power. His situation at court appears to have been confined to an inferior office (ch. viii. 27), and it would seem also that this led him occasionally, if not regularly, away from Babylon to some of the provinces to attend to business there. (Comp. Notes on ch. viii. 2). This was not strange. On the death of a monarch, it was not unusual to discharge the officers who had been employed in the government, as, at the present time, on the death of a king, or a change of dynasty, the members of the cabinet are changed ; or as the same thing happens in our own country when a change occurs in the chief magistracy of the nation.* Sir John Chardin, in his MS. Notes on Persia, says that, in his time, on the death of a Shah or king, all the soothsayers and physicians attached to the court were at once dismissed from office; the former because they did not *predict* his death, and the latter because they did not *prevent* it. It is to be remembered also, that Daniel was raised to power by the will of Nebuchadnezzar alone, and that the offices which he held were, in part, in consequence of the service which he had rendered that prince; and it is not strange, therefore, that on a change of the government, he, with perhaps the other favourites of the former sovereign, should be suffered to retire. We find consequently no mention made of Daniel during the reign of Evil-Merodach, or in the short reign of his successor; we lose sight of him until the reign of Belshazzar, the last king of Babylon, and then he is mentioned only in connection with the closing scene of his life (ch. v.) In consequence of a remarkable vision which Belshazzar had of a handwriting on the wall, and of the inability of any of the wise men of the Chaldeans to read and interpret it, Daniel, at the instance of the queen-mother, who remembered his former services at court, was called in, and read the writing, and announced to the king the impending destiny of himself and his empire. For this service he was again restored to honour, and the purpose was formed to raise him to an exalted rank at court—a purpose which was, however, frustrated by the fact that Babylon was that very night taken, and that the government passed into the hands of the Medes and Persians. It was under this king, however, that Daniel had two of his most remarkable visions (ch. vii., viii.) respecting future events— visions which, perhaps, more definitely than any other in the Scriptures, disclose what is to occur in the ages to come.

After the conquest of Babylon by the united arms of the Medes and Persians, under the reign of Darius or Cyaxares, Daniel was raised again to an exalted station. The whole kingdom was divided into one hundred and twenty provinces, and over these three presidents or chief governors were appointed, and of these Daniel had the first rank (ch. vi. 1—3). The *reasons* of this appointment are not stated, but they were doubtless found in such circumstances as the following : that it was desirable for Darius to employ some one who was familiar with the affairs of the Babylonian empire ; that Daniel probably had knowledge on that subject equal or superior to any other one that could be found ; that he had long been employed at court, and was familiar with the laws, usages, and customs that prevailed there ; that he knew better

---

* Since this was written, a remarkable illustration of what is here said has occurred in our own country (United States), on the death of the late president, General Zachary Taylor. It will be recollected that on the very night of his death, all the members of the cabinet tendered their resignation to his constitutional successor, and all of them in fact ceased to hold office, and retired to private life.

than any one else, perhaps, what would secure the tranquillity of that portion of the empire; that, being himself a foreigner, it might be supposed better to employ him than it would be a native Chaldean, for it might be presumed that he would be less inimical to a foreign dominion. Under these circumstances he was again raised to a high rank among the officers of the government; but his elevation was not beheld without malice and envy. Those who might have expected this office for themselves, or who were dissatisfied that a foreigner should be thus exalted, resolved, if possible, to bring him into such a situation as would ruin him (ch. vi. 4). To do this, they determined to take advantage of a principle in the government of the Medes and Persians, that a law having once received the royal sanction could not be changed; and by securing the passing of such a law as they knew Daniel would not obey, they hoped to humble and ruin him. They, therefore, under plausible pretences, secured the passing of a law that no one in the realm should be allowed for a certain time to offer any petition to any God or man, except the king, on penalty of being thrown into a den of lions. Daniel, as they anticipated, was the first to disregard this law, by continuing his regular habit of worshipping God, praying, as he had been accustomed, three times a-day, with his window open. The consequence was, that the king, there being no way to prevent the execution of the law, allowed it to be executed. Daniel was cast into the den of lions, but was miraculously preserved; and this new proof of his integrity, and of the Divine favour, was the means of his being raised to more exalted honour (ch. vi.)

In this situation at court, and with these advantages for promoting the interests of his people, he employed himself in seriously and diligently securing the return of the exiles to their own country, though it does not appear that he himself returned, or that he contemplated a return. It is probable that he supposed that at his time of life it would not be wise to attempt such a journey; or that he supposed he could be of more use to his countrymen in Babylon in favouring their return than he could by accompanying them to their own land. His position at the court of the Medo-Persian government gave him an opportunity of rendering material aid to his people, and it is not improbable that it was through his instrumentality that the decree was obtained from Cyrus which allowed them to return. One of the designs of Providence in raising him up was, doubtless, that he might exert that influence at court, and that he might thus be the means of restoring the exiles. He had at last the happiness to see his most ardent wishes accomplished in this respect.

In the third year of Cyrus, he had a vision, or a series of visions (ch. x.—xii.), containing minute details respecting the history and sufferings of his nation to the time of Antiochus Epiphanes, concluding with a more general representation (ch. xii.) of what would occur in the last days of the world's history.

Beyond this, nothing certain is known of Daniel. The accounts respecting him are vague, confused, and strange. How long he lived, and when and where he died, are points on which no certain information can now be obtained. Josephus gives no account of his latter days, or of his death, though he says respecting him, " he was so happy as to have strange revelations made to him, and those as to one of the greatest of the prophets, insomuch that while he was alive he had the esteem and applause both of kings and of the multitude ; and now he is dead, he retains a remembrance that will never fail." (*Ant.* b. x. ch. xi). It is commonly believed that he died in Chaldea, having been detained there by his employments in the Persian empire. Epiphanius says that he died in Babylon, and this has been the commonly received opinion of historians. This opinion, however, has not been universal. Some suppose that he died at Shushan or Susa. Josephus (*Ant.* b. x. ch. xi.) says that, " on account of the opinion which men had that he was beloved of God, he built a tower at Ecbatana in Media, which was a most elegant building and wonderfully made," and that it was still remaining in his day. Benjamin of Tudela says that his monument was shown at Chuzestan, which is the ancient Susa. As Benjamin of Tudela professes to record what he saw and heard, and as his *Itinerary* is a book which has been more frequently transcribed and translated than almost any other book, except the *Travels* of Maundeville, it may be of some interest to copy what he has said of the tomb of Daniel. It is a record of the traditions of the East—the country where Daniel lived and died, and it is not improbably founded in essential truth. At any rate, it will show what has been the current tradition in the East respecting Daniel, and is all that can now be known respecting the place of his death and burial. Benjamin of Tudela was a Jewish Rabbi of Spain, who travelled through Europe, Asia, and Africa, from Spain to China, between A.D. 1160 and 1173. His *Itinerary* was first printed in 1543. It was a work in wide circulation in the thirteenth, fourteenth, and fifteenth centuries, and has been translated from the original Hebrew into Latin, English, French, Dutch, and Jewish German, and in these languages has passed through not less than twenty-two editions. I quote from the London and Berlin edition of 1840. " Four miles from hence begins Khuzestan, Elam of Scripture, a large province which, however, is but partially inhabited, a portion of it lying in ruins. Among the latter are the remains of Shushan, the metropolis and palace of king Achashverosh, which still contains very large and handsome buildings of ancient date. Its seven thousand Jewish inhabitants possess fourteen synagogues, in front of one of which is the tomb of Daniel, who rests in peace. The river Ulai divides the parts of the city, which are connected with a bridge ; that portion of it which is inhabited by the Jews contains the markets ; to it all trade is confined, and there dwell all the rich ; on the other side of the river they are poor, because they are deprived of the above-named advantages, and have even no gardens nor orchards. These circumstances gave rise to jealousy, which was fostered by the belief that all honour and riches originated from the possession of the remains of the prophet Daniel, who rests in peace, and who was buried on their side. A request was made *by the poor* for permission to remove the sepulchre to the other side, but it was rejected; upon which a war arose, and was carried on between the two parties for a length of time. This strife lasted ' until their souls became loath' (Numb. xxi. 4, 5 ; Judg. xvi. 16), and they came to a mutual agreement, by which it was stipulated that the coffin which contained Daniel's bones should be deposited alternately every year on either side. Both parties faithfully adhered to this arrangement, which was, however, interrupted by the interference of Sanjar Shah Ben Shah, who governs all Persia, and holds supreme power over forty-five of its kings.

" When this great emperor Sanjar, king of Persia, came to Shushan, and saw that the coffin of Daniel was removed from side to side, he crossed the bridge with a very numerous retinue, and accompanied by Jews and Mahometans, inquired into the nature of these proceedings. Upon being told what we have related above, he declared that it was derogatory to the honour of Daniel, and recommended that the distance between the two banks should be exactly measured ; that Daniel's coffin should be deposited in another coffin, made of glass, and that it should be suspended from the very middle of the bridge, fastened by chains of iron. A place of public worship was erected on the very spot, open to every one who desired to say his prayers, whether he be Jew or Gentile, and the coffin of Daniel is suspended from the bridge unto this very day."—(Vol. i. pp. 117—120).

This story, trifling as it is in some of its details, may be admitted as evidence of a tradition in the East that Daniel died and was buried at Shushan. This tradition, moreover, is very ancient. In a note on this passage (vol. ii. p. 152), A. Asher, the publisher of the *Itinerary* of Benjamin, says : " Aasim of Cufah, a venerable historian, who preceded Ibn Haukel by two hundred years (for he died 735), mentions the discovery of Daniel's coffin at Sus. Ibn Haukel, who travelled in the tenth century, speaks of it, and ascribes to the possession of the bones of Daniel the virtue of dispelling all sorts of distress, particularly that of famine from want of rain." It has been a matter of much controversy whether the place now known as Chouck, Chouz, or Sous- is the ancient Shushan (lat. 31° 55′, long. 83° 40′), or the place now called Shuster (lat. 31° 30′, long. 84° 30′). The former opinion is maintained by Rennel, Ouseley, Barbié du Bocage, Kinneir, and Hoek ; the latter by d'Herbelot, d'Anville, Vincent, Mannert, and Hammer. Major Rawlinson, who has furnished the most recent account of this place, maintains that " Shushan the palace" is the present Susan on the Kulan or Eulaeus, the Ulai of Scripture. (See vol. ix. of the *Journal of the Royal Geographical Society*).

§ II.—GENUINENESS AND AUTHENTICITY OF THE BOOK OF DANIEL.

Consideration of Objections.

Until a comparatively recent period, with some slight exceptions, the genuineness and authenticity of the book of Daniel have been regarded as settled, and its canonical authority was as little doubted as that of any other portion of the Bible. The ancient Hebrews never called its genuineness or authenticity in question (Lengerke, *Das Buch Daniel*, Königsberg, 1835, p. 6; Hengstenberg, *Die Authentie des Daniel*, Berlin, 1831, p. 1). It is true that in the *Talmud* (*Tract. Baba Bathra*, Fol. 15, Ed. Venet.) it is said that "the men of the Great Synagogue wrote—כתבו the קדינג K. D. N. G.—that is, portions (eleven chapters) of the book of Ezekiel, the prophet Daniel, and the book of Esther ;'' but this, as Lengerke has remarked (p. v.), does not mean that they had introduced this book into the canon, as Bertholdt supposes, but that, partly by tradition, and partly by inspiration, they revised it anew. But whatever may be the truth in regard to this, it does not prove that the ancient Jews did not consider it canonical. It is true that much has been said about the fact that the Jews did not class this book among the prophets, but placed it in the *Hagiographa* or *Kethubim*, כְּתוּבִים. It has been inferred from this, that they believed that it was composed a considerable time after the other prophetic books, and that they did not deem it worthy of a place among their prophetic books in general. But, even if this were so, it would not prove that they did not regard it as a genuine production of Daniel; and the fact that it was not placed among the prophetic books may be accounted for without the supposition that they did not regard it as genuine. The usual statement on that subject is, that they placed the book there because they say that Daniel lived the life of a courtier in Babylon, rather than the life of a prophet ; and the Jews further assert that, though he received Divine communications, they were only by dreams and visions of the night, which they regard as the most imperfect kind of revelations.—(Horne, *Intro.* iv. 188). The place which Daniel should occupy in the Sacred Writings probably became a matter of discussion among the Hebrews only after the coming of the Saviour, when Christians urged so zealously his plain prophecies (ch. ix. 24–27) in proof of the Messiahship of the Lord Jesus.

The first open and avowed adversary to the genuineness and authenticity of the book of Daniel was Porphyry, a learned adversary of the Christian faith in the third century. He wrote fifteen books against Christianity, all of which are lost, except some fragments preserved by Eusebius, Jerome, and others. His objections against Daniel were made in his twelfth book, and all that we have of these objections has been preserved by Jerome in his commentary on the book of Daniel. A full account of Porphyry, and of his objections against the Christians and the sacred books of the Old and New Testament, so far as can now be known, may be seen in Lardner, *Jewish and Heathen Testimonies*, vol. vii. pp. 390–470, of his works, Ed. London, 1829. In regard to the book of Daniel, he maintained, according to Jerome (*Pr.* and *Explan.* in Daniel), "that the book was not written by him whose name it bears, but by another who lived in Judea in the time of Antiochus, surnamed Epiphanes; and that the book of Daniel does not foretell things to come, but relates what had already happened. In a word, whatever it contains to the time of Antiochus is true history; if there is anything relating to after-times it is falsehood; forasmuch as the writer could not see things future, but at the most only could make some conjectures about them. To him several of our authors have given answers of great labour and diligence—in particular, Eusebius, bishop of Cæsarea, in three volumes, the 18th, the 19th, and the 20th; Apollinarius, also, in one large book, that is, the 26th; and before them, in part, Methodius. 'As it is not my design,' says Jerome, 'to confute the objections of the adversary, which would require a long discourse; but only to explain the prophet to our own people, that is, to Christians, I shall just observe that none of the prophets have spoken so clearly of Christ as Daniel, for he not only foretells his coming, as do others likewise, but he also teaches the time when he will come, and mentions in order the princes of the intermediate space, and the number of the years, and the signs of his appearance. And because Porphyry saw all these things to have been fulfilled, and could not deny that they had actually come to pass, he was compelled to say as he did; and because of some similitude of circumstances, he asserted that the things foretold as to be fulfilled in Antichrist at the end of the world happened in the time of Antiochus Epiphanes:—which kind of opposition is a testimony of truth; for such is the plain interpretation of the words, that to incredulous men the prophet seems not to foretell things to come, but to relate things already past; and though, as before said, it is not my intention to confute all his objections, I shall, as occasion offers, take notice of some of his weak arguments. And it may be proper for us, among other things, to observe now, that Porphyry argued that the book of Daniel was not genuine, because it was written in Greek, and, therefore, was not the work of any Jew, but the forgery of some Greek writer. This he argued from some Greek words which are in the fable of Susanna, to which both Eusebius and Apollinarius returned the same answer, that the fabulous stories of Susanna, and Bel and the Dragon, are not in the Hebrew, but are said to have been composed by a person of the tribe of Levi; whereas the sacred Scriptures assure us that Daniel and the three children, his companions, were of the tribe of Judah. And they said they were not accountable for what was not received by the Jews, nor was a part of the sacred Scriptures.' " A few of the objections which Porphyry makes to the credibility of certain parts of Daniel, Jerome has quoted in his commentary on the particular passages referred to. These have been collected by Dr. Lardner, and may be seen in his works, vol. vii. pp. 402–415. It is not necessary to transcribe them here, as they will come up for consideration in the notes on the particular chapters.

Dr. Lardner (vol. vii. p. 401) remarks respecting Porphyry, " that Porphyry's work against the Christians was much laboured, and that in this argument he displayed all his learning, which was very considerable. Hence we can perceive the difficulty of undertaking an answer to him, for which very few were fully qualified; in which none of the apologists for Christianity seem to have answered expectations." We cannot now form a correct opinion of the argument of Porphyry, for we have only the few fragments of his work which Jerome and others have seen proper to preserve. We are in danger, therefore, of doing injustice to what may have been the real force of his argument, for it *may* have been stronger than would be indicated by those fragments that remain. It is impossible to recover his main objections; and all that can now be said is, that, as far as is known, he did not make any converts to his opinions, and that his objections produced no change in the faith of the Christian world.

No further attack on the genuineness and authenticity of Daniel seems to have been made, and no further doubt entertained, until the time of Spinoza. Spinoza was by birth a Jew; was born at Amsterdam in 1632; became professedly converted to Christianity in consequence of supposing that his life was in danger among the Jews, but was probably indifferent to all religions. He gave himself up to philosophical inquiries, and is commonly understood to have been a pantheist. He maintained (*Tractat. Theol. Politicus*, c. 10, t. i. p. 308, Ed. Paulus), that the last five chapters of Daniel were written by Daniel himself, but that the seven previous chapters were collected about the time of the Maccabees from the chronological writings of the Chaldeans, and that the whole was arranged by some unknown hand. Edward Wells, who lived in the first part of the eighteenth century, maintained that the work was composed by some one soon after the death of Daniel. Antony Collins, one of the British Deists, maintained also that it was not written by Daniel. In more recent times, the genuineness of the book has been doubted or denied, in whole or in part, by Corrodi, Gesenius, Lüderwald, Dereser, Scholl, Lengerke, Eichhorn, De Wette, Griesenger, Bertholdt, Bleek, Ewald, Hitzig, and Kirms; it has been defended by the English writers generally, and among the Germans by Staudlin, Beekhaus, Jahn, Hävernick, Hengstenberg, and others. The general ground taken by those who have denied its genuineness and authenticity is, that the book was written, at or about the time of the Maccabees, by some Jew, who, in order to give greater authority and importance to his work, wrote under the assumed name of Daniel, and laid the scene in Babylon in the time of the captivity.

The various arguments urged against the genuineness of the book may be seen in Bertholdt, Eichhorn, Lengerke, Kirms (*Commentatio*

Historico Critica, Jenae, 1828), and De Wette. The best defence of
its authenticity, probably, is the work of Hengstenberg (*Die Authentie
des Daniel*, Berlin, 1831). The examination of the objections alleged
against the particular chapters, and particular portions of chapters, it
will be most convenient to examine in the introductions to the respective chapters. I propose, in this general Introduction, merely to examine the objections of a general character which have been made to
the work. These have been concisely arranged and stated by De Wette
(*Lehrbuch der Historisch-kritischen, Einleitung*, &c., Berlin, 1845, pp.
382-389), and in the examination of the objections I shall consider
them in the order in which he has stated them.

The view which De Wette entertains of the book is stated in
the following manner:—"That in the time of Antiochus Epiphanes,
when the spirit of prophecy among the Jews had been a long time
extinct, a Jewish friend of his country endeavoured to encourage and
strengthen his contemporary sufferers, and those who were contending
for their liberty, through these apocalyptic prophecies respecting the
future ascendency of the theocratic principle, which, in order to give
the work greater reputation and authority, he ascribed to an ancient
Seer of the name of Daniel, of whom probably something had been
handed down by tradition. Designedly he suffered the promises to
extend to a great length of time, in order to make them appear the
more certain. After the manner of the ancient prophets also, he inwove
much that was historical, and especially such as would be fitted to excite
and arouse the martyr spirit of his own people."—(*Lehrbuch*, p. 390).

I. The first objection which is urged against the genuineness of the
book is derived from what is denominated *the fabulous contents—*
Mährchenhaften Inhalte—*of its narrative parts.* This objection, in the
words of De Wette, is, that "the book is full of improbabilities (ii. 3,
ff. 46, f. iii. 1, 5, f. 20, 22, 28, f. 31, ff. iv. 31, f. v. 11, f. 18, ff. 29,
vi. 8, ff. 26, ff.); of wonders (ii. 28, iii. 23, ff. v. 5, vi. 23, 25); its historical inaccuracies are such as are found in no prophetic book of the
Old Testament, and are founded on the same type (comp. ii. 2-11, with
iv. 4, v. 8; iii. 4-12, 26-30, with vi. 8-18, 21-24).* This seeking
after wonders and strange things, and the religious fanaticism nourished
through these persecutions, which it breathes, place the book in the
same condition as the second book of the Maccabees, as a production
of the time of Antiochus Epiphanes, and the similarity of the former
of the two books betrays the fictitious character (*Dichtung*) of the
book."—(*Lehrbuch*, pp. 382, 383).

In reference to this objection, which turns on the marvellous character of the book, and the improbable historical statements in it, the
following remarks may be made:—

---

* These references of De Wette's are according to the chapters and verses of
the Hebrew Bible.

(*a*) These objections are noticed in detail in the introductions to the respective chapters where the historical events here objected to are stated, and the question whether they are fabulous, or are in accordance with true history, is there fully considered. This will make it needless to notice them here particularly. In the introduction to the respective chapters, I have noticed, and have endeavoured to answer, all the objections which I have found of this character in the works of Eichhorn, Bertholdt, Bleek, and Lengerke. This will make it the less necessary to dwell on this point in this general Introduction.

(*b*) But as to the alleged contradiction between Daniel and the historical accounts which we have of the affairs to which he refers, it may be proper to observe in general—(1.) That, for anything that appears, Daniel may be as accurate an historian as any of the heathen writers of those times. There is, in the nature of the case, no reason why we should put implicit confidence in Berosus, Abydenus, Xenophon, and Herodotus, and distrust Daniel; nor why, if a statement is omitted by them, we should conclude at once that, if mentioned by Daniel, it is false. It is an unhappy circumstance, that there are many persons who suppose that the fact that a thing is mentioned by a profane historian is presumptive evidence of its truth; if mentioned by a sacred writer, it is presumptive evidence of its falsehood. Under the influence of the same feeling, it is inferred, that if an event is mentioned by a sacred writer which is omitted by a profane historian, it is regarded as demonstrative that the work in which it is found is fabulous. It is unnecessary to show that this feeling exists in many minds; and yet nothing can be more unjust—for the mere fact that an author writes on sacred subjects, or is the professed friend of a certain religion, *should not* be allowed to cast a suspicion on his testimony. That testimony must depend, in regard to its value, on his credibility as a historian, and not on the subject on which he writes. In the nature of things, there is no more reason why a writer on sacred subjects should be unworthy of belief, than one who is recording the ordinary events of history. (2.) Daniel, according to the account which we have of him, had opportunities of ascertaining the truth of the facts which he narrates, which no profane historian had. He spent the greater part of a long life in Babylon, in the very midst of the scenes which he describes; he was intimately acquainted with the affairs of the government; he enjoyed, in a remarkable degree, the confidence of those in authority, and he was himself deeply concerned in most of these transactions, and could have adopted the language of Æneas—*et quorum magna pars fui.* (3.) It is to be remembered, also, in regard to these events and times, that we have few fragments of history remaining. We have fragments of the writings of Berosus, a Chaldean, indeed, who wrote in Greece; and of Abydenus, a Greek, who wrote in Chaldea; we have some historical statements in Xenophon, and a few in Herodotus: but the Chaldean history, if ever written, is lost; the public documents are destroyed; the means of an accurate and full knowledge of the Chaldean or Babylonish power in the time when Daniel lived, have disappeared for ever. Under these circumstances, it would not be strange if we should not be able to clear up all the difficulties of a historical nature that may be suggested respecting these fragmentary accounts, or be able to verify the statements which we find in the sacred books by the explicit testimony of contemporary writers.

(c) As a matter of fact, the investigations of history, as far as they can be made, go to confirm the authority of Daniel. Instances of this will occur in the examination of the particular chapters in this book, and all that can now be done is merely to refer to them, particularly to the introductions to ch. i., iv.–vi. In general, it may be said here, that none of the historical authorities *contradict* what is stated by Daniel, and that the few fragments which we have go to confirm what he has said, or at least to make it probable.

(d) As to the objections of De Wette and others, derived from the miraculous and marvellous character of the book, it may be observed further, that the same objection would lie against most of the books of the Bible, and that it is, therefore, not necessary to notice it particularly in considering the book of Daniel. The Bible is a book full of miracles and marvels; and he who would have any proper understanding of it must regard and treat it as such. It is impossible to understand or explain it without admitting the possibility and the reality of miraculous events; and in a book which *claims* to be founded on miracles, it does not prove that it is not authentic or genuine simply to say that it assumes that miracles are possible. To destroy the credibility of the book, it is necessary to show that *all* claims of a miraculous character are unfounded, and *all* miracles impossible and absurd; and this objection would not lie against the book of Daniel peculiarly, but equally against the whole Bible. Two remarks here may be made, however, of a more particular character: (1), that the statements in Daniel are not more marvellous than those which occur in other parts of the Bible, and if *they* may be believed, those occurring in Daniel may be also; and (2), that it would rather be an argument against the genuineness and authenticity of the book if *no* miraculous and marvellous statements were found in it. It would be *so* unlike the other books of the Bible, where miracles abound, that we should feel that there was wanting in its favour the evidence of this nature, which would show that it had the same origin as the other portions of the volume. The particular objections in regard to the statements in Daniel of this nature are considered in the notes on the book.

II. A second objection to the genuineness of the book of Daniel relates to the *prophecies* which are found in it. This objection is derived from the peculiar character of these prophecies; from the minuteness of the detail; the exact designation of the order of events;

the fact that they seem to be a summary of history written *after* the events occurred; and that in these respects they are essentially unlike the other prophecies in the Bible. This objection, we have seen, is as old as Porphyry; and this was, in fact, with him the *principal* argument against the authenticity of the book. This objection is summed up and stated by De Wette in the following manner (§ 255 *b*, pp. 384, 385): "The ungenuineness (Unächtheit) appears further from the prophetic contents of the same, which is to a remarkable extent different from that of all the remaining prophetic books, (*a*) through its apocalyptic character, or through this—that the coming of the kingdom of the Messiah is mentioned and determined according to certain definite periods of time, or specified periods, and that the representation of it occurs so much in the form of visions; (*b*) that the circumstances of the distant future, and the fortune of the kingdoms which were not yet in existence, even down to the time of Antiochus Epiphanes, are described with so much particularity and accuracy (viii. 14, ix. 25, ff. xii. 11, ff.) that the account must have been written after the event; (*c*) and that, if Daniel was a prophet, he must have lived in the times of Ezekiel and Zechariah, and we must suppose that his prophecies would have borne the general character of the prophecies of those times, but that in fact we find in them the spirit of a later age—the spirit that ultimately developed itself in the Sibylline books, to which these prophecies bear a strong resemblance."

In reply to this it may be remarked:—

(1.) That all that is said in Daniel is *possible:* that is, it is possible that prophetic intimations of the future should be given with as much particularity as are found in Daniel. No one can demonstrate, or even affirm, that God could not, if he chose, inspire a prophet to predict in detail the occurrences of the most remote times, and the fall of kingdoms not yet in being. All this knowledge must be with him; and for anything that appears, it would be as easy to inspire a prophet to predict *these* events as any other. The sole inquiry, therefore, is in regard to a fact; and this is to be settled by an examination of the evidence, that the prophet lived and prophesied *before* the events predicted occurred.

(2.) The prophecies in Daniel are not, in their structure and character, *so* unlike those whose genuineness is undisputed as to make it certain, or even probable, that the latter are genuine and those of Daniel not. Dreams and visions were common methods of communicating the Divine will to the prophets—see Introduction to Isaiah, § 7, (2), (4)—and who will undertake from any internal evidence to determine between those of Isaiah, Jeremiah, Ezekiel, and Daniel?

(3.) As to the allegation respecting the details in Daniel of future events—the particularity with which he describes them—all is to be admitted that is affirmed on the subject. It *is* a fact that there is such particularity and minuteness of detail as could be founded only on truth, and that the delineations of Alexander and his conquests, and the statements of the events that would succeed his reign down to the time of Antiochus Epiphanes (ch. xi.), are drawn with as much accuracy of detail as they would be by one writing after the events had occurred. No one can doubt this who attentively examines these remarkable prophecies. Porphyry was undoubtedly right in affirming, that in regard to their minuteness and accuracy, these prophecies appeared to be written *after* the events; and if it can be shown, therefore, that they were written *before* the events referred to, the testimony of Porphyry is a strong evidence of the fact that Daniel was inspired; for no one will maintain that man, by any natural sagacity, could describe events before they occur with the exactness of detail and the minute accuracy which is found in this part of Daniel.

But is not what is here said of Daniel as to the accuracy and minuteness of detail true also, in the main, of other prophecies in the Old Testament? Are there not many prophecies that are as accurate, and in some respects as minute, as they would have been if they were written after the events referred to? Is not this true of the predictions respecting the destruction of Tyre and of Babylon, and the carrying away of the Jews into captivity? Is not Cyrus expressly mentioned by Isaiah, and is not the work which he would perform in the conquest of Babylon drawn out in exact detail? (See Isa. xlv. 1, *seq.*) So in Jeremiah (l., li.), there is a prophetic account of the destruction of Babylon, as minute in many respects as the predictions of Daniel, and as exact and minute as it would have been if written after the events had occurred, and the author had been making a historical record instead of uttering a prediction. But on this point I must content myself with referring to the argument of Hengstenberg, *Authentie des Daniel*, pp. 173-195. It may be added, however, that it is on this accuracy of detail in Daniel that we ground one of the strong arguments for his inspiration. It will be admitted on all hands—it cannot be denied —that no one could foresee those events, and describe them with such accuracy of detail, by any natural sagacity; but no one who believes in the fact of inspiration at all, can doubt that it would be as easy for the Divine Spirit to present future events in this accuracy of detail as in a more general manner. At all events, this accuracy and minuteness of detail removes the prophecies from the region of conjecture, and is an answer to the usual objections that they are obscure and ambiguous. No one can pretend this of the writings of Daniel; and if it can be shown that the book was written before the events occurred, the conclusion cannot be avoided that the author was inspired.

III. A third objection to the genuineness and authenticity of the book of Daniel is thus stated by De Wette (§ 255, b. 3, p. 385): "Grounds of objection lie further in the repeated mention of Daniel himself in so honourable a manner (ch. i. 17, 19, f. v. 11, f. vi. 4, ix. 23, x. 11, *et al.*)"

This objection cannot be regarded as having any great degree of force, or as contributing much to set aside the direct evidence of the authority of the book:—for (*a*) it is possible that all these honours were conferred on him. This is, in itself, no more incredible or remarkable than that Joseph should have reached the honours in Egypt, which are attributed to him in Genesis; and no one can show that if the account had been written by another, it would have been unworthy of belief. (*b*) If it were a fact that he was thus honoured, it was not improper to state it. If Daniel was the historian of those times, and kept the records of the events of his own life, and actually obtained those honours, there was no impropriety in his making a record of those things. He has done no more than what Cæsar did in the mention of himself, his plans, his conquests, his triumphs. In the record of Daniel there is no unseemly parading of his wisdom, or the honours conferred on him; there is no praise for the mere sake of praise; there is no language of panegyric on account of his eminent piety. The account is a mere record of facts as they are said to have occurred—that Daniel was successful in his early studies, and his preparation for the examination through which he and his companions were to pass (ch. i.); that on more than one occasion he succeeded in interpreting a dream or vision which no one of the Chaldeans could do; that in consequence of this he was raised to an exalted rank; that he was enabled to maintain his integrity in the midst of extraordinary temptations; and that he was favoured with the Divine protection when in extraordinary danger. I presume that no one who has read the book of Daniel with an unprejudiced mind ever received an impression that there was any want of modesty in Daniel in these records, or that there was any unseemly or unnecessary parading of his own virtues and honours before the world.

IV. A fourth objection which has been urged against the genuineness of Daniel is derived from the *language* in which it is written. This objection, as stated by De Wette (§ 235, b. 4, p. 385), is founded on "the corrupt Hebrew and Chaldee, and the intermingling of Greek words in the composition." The objection is urged more at length in Bertholdt (p. 24, *seq.*), and by Bleek, Kirms, and others. The objection, as derived from the language of the book, is properly divided into three parts :—(*a*) that it is written in Hebrew and Chaldee; (*b*) that in each part of it there is a want of purity of style, indicating a later age than the time of the captivity; and (*c*) that there is an intermingling of Greek words, such as it cannot be presumed that one who wrote in the time of the exile, and in Babylon, would have employed, and such as were probably introduced into common use only by a later intercourse with the Greeks, and particularly by the Macedonian conquest.

(*a*) As to the first of these, little stress can be laid on it, and indeed it is rather an argument *for* the genuineness of the work than against it. It is well known that from the fourth verse of the second chapter to the end of the seventh chapter, the work is written in the Chaldee language, while the remainder is pure Hebrew. The only way in which this fact could be regarded as an objection to the genuineness of the book, would be that it is an indication that it is the production of two different authors. But this would be an objection only on the supposition that the author could write and speak only one language, or that, supposing he was acquainted with two, there were no circumstances which could account for the use of both. But neither of these suppositions applies here. There is every reason to believe that Daniel was acquainted with both the Hebrew and the Chaldee; and there is no improbability in the supposition that he wrote in both with equal case. And, on the other hand, it may be remarked, that the very circumstance here referred to is a confirmation of the genuineness of the book; for (1.) it accords with all that is known of Daniel. He was a youth when he left his native country, and there is every probability that he was familiar with the Hebrew in early life, and that he would never forget it, though it might be true that he would ordinarily use the language of Chaldea. He was still familiar with the Hebrew books, and it is to be presumed that the language used by the Hebrews in exile was their native tongue. In all his intercourse with his own countrymen, therefore, it is every way probable that he would use his native language, and would thus through life retain his knowledge of it. (2.) It is equally clear that he was familiar with the Chaldee language. He was early, in connection with three other Hebrew youths (ch. i. 3, 4), placed under the best instruction in Babylon, for the express purpose of acquiring, with other branches of learning, a knowledge of the "tongue of the Chaldeans;" and he speedily made such acquisitions as to pass with honour the examination appointed before he was admitted to public employment (ch. i. 18-20). He was, moreover, employed at court during a considerable part of his long life, and no one, therefore, can doubt that he was entirely familiar with the language used in Babylon, and that he could compose in it with ease. (3.) It is evident that the work must, if it is the production of one author, have been composed by some person who was, in this respect, in the circumstances of Daniel; that is, by one who was familiar with both the languages: and the circumstances bear on their face evidence that the work was written by one in the condition in which Daniel was known to be; that is, one who had been early trained in the Hebrew, and who had lived in Chaldea. No native-born Hebrew who had not lived in Chaldea would be likely to be so well acquainted with the two languages that he could use either with equal facility; and it may be presumed that no native-born Chaldean could evince so intimate an acquaintance with the Hebrew. The direct evidence that it *is* the production of one author will be adduced in another part of this Introduction. (4.) It is by no means probable that one who lived so late as the time of Antiochus Epiphanes *could* have written the book as it is written; that is, that he would have been so familiar with the two languages, Hebrew and Chaldee,

that he could use them with equal ease.   It is an uncommon thing for
a man to write in two different languages in the same work, and he
never does it without some special design—a design for which there
would not be likely to be occasion if one were writing in the time of
Antiochus Epiphanes.   It was perfectly *natural* that Daniel should
write in this manner, and perfectly *unnatural* that any one should do it
in a later age, and in different circumstances.   If the book had been
forged by a Hebrew in the time of Antiochus Epiphanes, there is every
reason to believe that he would have been careful to write it in as pure
Hebrew as possible, for that was the language in which the canonical
books were written, and if he had endeavoured to gain credit for the
book as one of Divine authority, he would not have intermingled so
much of a foreign language.   If he were a Chaldean, and could write
Hebrew at all, as it is certain that the author of this book could, then,
for the reason just given, he would have been careful to write the whole
book in as pure Hebrew as possible, and would not have jeoparded its
credit by so large an infusion of a foreign tongue.   (5.) This reasoning
is conclusive, unless it be supposed that the author *meant* to represent
it as a composition of some Hebrew in the time of the exile, and that
in order to give it the greater verisimilitude he adopted this device—
to make it *appear* as if written by one who was a native Hebrew, but
who had become familiar with a foreign language.   But this device
would be too refined to be likely to occur, and, for the reasons given
above, would be difficult of execution if it should occur.   Even in such
a case, the writer would be much more likely to represent its author as
writing in the sacred language of the prophets, in order to procure for
himself the credit of employing the language used in all the Divine
communications to men.   The language in which the book is written,
therefore, is just such as it would be on the supposition that it is
genuine, and just such as it would *not* be on the supposition that it is
a forgery of a later age.

(*b*) As to the statement that the language is *corrupt* Hebrew and
Chaldee—in der Verderbten sowohl Hebräischen als Chaldäishen
Sprache (De Wette)—it may be remarked that this position has never
been satisfactorily made out, nor has it been shown that it is not such
as might be employed, or would be employed, by one who resided in
Babylon in the time of the exile.   That the language would not be the
purest kind of Hebrew, or the purest Chaldee, might be possible, in the
circumstances of the case ; but it could be shown that it was not such
as might be employed there, in case there are words and forms of speech
which did not come into use until a later period of the world.   This
has not been shown.   It is true that there are Persian words ; but this
is not unnatural in the circumstances of the case—bordering as Chaldea
did on Persia, and during a part of the time referred to in the book,
being actually subject to Persia.   It is true that there are Greek words ;
but under the next specification I shall endeavour to show that this

does not militate against the supposition that the book may have been written in Babylon in the time of the exile. It is true that there are words and forms of speech which were not in use in the earlier periods of Hebrew literature, but which became common in the later periods of their literature ; but this does not prove that they may not have been in use as early as the exile. A specimen of the words referred to— indeed all on which the argument is founded—may be seen in De Wette, p. 385, note (e). They are few in number, and in respect to none of these can it be *proved* that they were not in existence in the time of Daniel. They are of Persian, of Syriac, or of Chaldee origin, and are such words as would be *likely* to come into use in the circumstances of the case. In regard to this objection it may be added, that it has been abandoned by some of the objectors to the genuineness of the book of Daniel themselves. Bleek is candid enough to give it up entirely. He says : " We have, in general, too few remains of the different centuries after the exile to draw any conclusions as to the gradual depreciation of the language, and to determine with any certainty to what particular period any writer belongs."—(*Zeitschr.* p. 213). " Daniel," says Prof. Stuart, "in the judgment of Gesenius (*Geschich. Heb. Sprach.* p. 35), has decidedly a purer diction than Ezekiel ; in which opinion," says he, " as far as I am able to judge, after much time spent upon the book, and examining minutely every word and phrase in it many times over, I should entirely coincide."—(*Com.* p. 465).

(c) A more material objection is derived from the use of *Greek* words in the composition of the book. That there *are* such words is undeniable, though they are by no means numerous. Bertholdt (pp. 24, 25) has enumerated *ten* such words ; De Wette has referred to *four* (p. 386). The words enumerated by Bertholdt are פרתמים—προτιμοι ; פתגם — φθεγμα ; כרוזא—κηρυξ ; כרז—κηρυσσειν ; קיתרס—κιθαρις ; סבכא— סמבוכא; סומפניא—συμφωνια ; פסנטר—ψαλτηριον ; פטיש—πετασος; נבזבה—νομισμα.

In regard to this objection, it may be remarked, in general, that it does not assert that the structure of the book of Daniel is fashioned after the Greek manner, or that the Greek style pervades it ; it asserts only that a few Greek words have been incorporated into the book. The question then is, whether even all these words are of Greek origin; and whether, if they are, or if only a part of them are, their use in the book can be accounted for on the supposition that it was written in the time of the captivity, or rather, whether their occurrence in the book is a proof that the book could not have been written at that time.

The first point is the question, whether these words are of undoubted Greek origin ; and this question will require us to examine them in detail.

(1.) The first word specified is פַּרְתְּמִים *partemim*, rendered *princes* (ch. i. 3), which it is alleged is the same as the Greek προτιμοι, protimoi. The word used by Daniel occurs only in two other places in the

Old Testament (Esth. i. 3, vi. 9), where it is rendered *nobles*, and *most noble ;* and it is obvious to remark, that the fact that it is found in Esther *might* be urged in proof that the book of Daniel was written at the time in which it is commonly believed to have been, since the antiquity and genuineness of the book of Esther is not called in quest:on. But apart from this, there is no evidence that the word is of Greek origin. Gesenius, who may be considered as impartial authority on the subject, says, "It is of Persian origin, 1—9. Pehlvi, *pardom*, the first, see Anquetil du perron Zendavesta, ii. p. 468. Comp. Sanscr. *prathama* the first. In the Zend dialect the form is *peoerim*. Comp. Sanscr. *pura* prius, antea, purâna, antiquus. From the former comes the Greek πρῶτος, and from the latter the Latin *primus.*"—(*Lex.*) The same account of the origin of the word is given by Jahn, De Wette, Bleek, and Kirms. This word, then, may be set aside. It is, indeed, objected by Bertholdt, that, though the word had a Persian origin, yet there is no evidence that it would be used in Babylon in the time of the exile. But this objection can have no force. Babylon and Persia were neighbouring kingdoms, and there is no presumption that Persian words might not find their way to Babylon, and as a matter of fact such words occur in Jeremiah, and probably in Isaiah, and in Nahum. (See Hengstenberg, pp. 11, 12). The truth was, that the Assyrians and the Medo-Persians were originally all of the same stem or stock, and there is no presumption against the supposition that the same words might be found in each of the languages spoken by them.

(2.) The next word referred to is פִּתְגָם *pithgham* (Dan. iii. 16, iv. 17, rendered *matter*), which it is alleged is the same as the Greek φθεγμα, *phthegma*. The word occurs, besides these places in Daniel, in Ezra iv. 17, v. 11, rendered *answer ;* v. 7, rendered *letter ;* and vi. 11, rendered *word.* In Hebrew it occurs in Esth. i. 20, rendered *decree*, and in Eccles. viii. 11, rendered *sentence.* In respect to this word, also, Gesenius says, "The origin of the word is to be sought in the Persian, in which *pedam* is *word, edict, mandate.*"—(*Lex.*) The fact, also, it may be added, that it is found in Esther, in Ezra, and the book of Ecclesiastes, is sufficient to destroy the objection that its use proves that the book of Daniel was written later than the time of the exile. It was brought, probably, into the Greek language from the common origin of the Persian and the Greek.

(3, 4.) The next words referred to, are כָּרוֹז *kâhroz* (a herald), ch. iii. 4, and כָּרַז *kârăz*, to cry out, to make proclamation, which it is alleged are the same as the Greek κηρυξ, *kerux*, and κηρυσσειν, *kerussein.* Of these words, also, Gesenius remarks, "The root is widely diffused in the Indo-European languages, *e.g.* Sansc. *krus*, to cry out ; Zenda. *khresio*, crying out, a herald ; Pers. to cry out; Gr. κηρύσσω, also κρίζω, κραζω ; Germ. *kreischen, kreissen ;* Eng. to cry."—(*Lex.*) Among the Christian Arabs, Gesenius remarks, it means to preach. Jahn and Dereser say that the word is related to the Zendish word *khresio*, which means to tread behind, and to scream out, to screech, *kreischen*. Hengstenberg (p. 13) remarks of this word, that its use is spread abroad not only in Chaldee, but in Syriac, and that this circumstance makes it probable that it had a Semitish origin. The probability is, that this word and the Greek had a common origin, but its use is so far spread in the world that it cannot be argued that the fact of its being found in the book of Daniel, demonstrates that the book had a later origin than the period of the exile.

(5.) The next word mentioned as of Greek origin is קִיתָרֹס *kitharos* (ch. iii. 5, 7, 10, 15), *cithara*, *harp*, *lyre* (rendered in each place *harp*), which it is said is the same as the Greek κιθαρις, *citharis*. In regard to this word, which is the name of a musical instrument, it is to be admitted that it is the same as the Greek word. It occurs nowhere else in the Old Testament, and its origin is unknown. *As* a Greek word, it will be considered in connection with the three others of the same class, in the sequel. It cannot be affirmed, indeed, that it has a Greek *origin*, but its origin cannot be found in the Chaldee, Persian, or Sanscrit languages. But, although it is admitted that it is a Greek word, and denotes an instrument that was well known in Greece, this does not *demonstrate* that it is of Greek *origin*. It is admitted on all hands, that the names of Greek instruments of music were mostly of foreign derivation; and there is nothing to lead to the supposition that this was of *Greek* origin, unless it be that the word κιθάρα, or κιθάρος, means, in the Doric dialect, the *breast*, and that this instrument *might* have received its name either because it was played by being placed against the breast, like the violin with us, or because its form resembled the human breast. This is the opinion of Isidorus, Origg. i. 2, 21. But there is great uncertainty in regard to this.

(6.) The next word specified is סַבְּכָא *sabbeka* (ch. iii. 5), and the similar word, שַׂבְּכָא (ch. iii. 7, 10, 15), in each case rendered *sackbut*. Of this word it is alleged that it is the same as the Greek σαμβύκη, *sambuca*, a stringed instrument well known in Greece. But in regard to this word, also, the remark of Gesenius may be quoted : " Strabo affirms," says he, " that the Greek word σαμβύκη (*sambuca*) is of barbarian, *i. e.*, of Oriental origin, and if so, the name might have allusion to the interweaving of the strings—from the root שָׂבַךְ"—*to interweave, to entwine, to plait*. Gesenius, however, remarks that in this place it is joined with a word (symphony) which is manifestly of Greek origin ; and he *seems* to infer that this word also may have had a Greek origin. The direct affirmation of Strabo is (lib. x.) that the names of the Greek instruments of music were of foreign origin ; and in reference to this particular instrument, Athenæus (i. iv.) affirms that it was of *Syrian* origin. So Clemens Alex. expressly declares that the sambuca had a foreign origin.—(*Strom.* lib. i. p. 307). Even Bleek admits this in regard to this particular instrument. (See Hengstenberg, p. 15).

(7.) The next word for which a Greek origin is claimed is סוּמְפֹּנְיָא

symphony, Greek συμφωνια (ch. iii. 5, 10, 15), rendered in the text, in each place, *dulcimer,* and in the margin *symphony,* or *singing.* Gesenius remarks, in regard to this word, that "it is the Greek word adopted into the Chaldee tongue, just as at the present day the same instrument is called in Italy *zampogna,* and in Asia Minor *zambouja.*" It cannot be denied that the word is the same as the Greek word, though it is to be remarked that among the Greeks it was not used to denote the name of an instrument of music; yet, as it is compounded of two Greek words— σύν and φωνή —its Greek origin cannot well be doubted. With the Greeks, the word meant properly harmony, or concert of sounds (*Passow*); and it was then readily given to an instrument that was fitted to produce harmony, or that was distinguished for its sweet sounds. The word is found in Syriac, as applied to a musical instrument; but the evidence seems to be strong that the *word* had a Greek origin, though there is no evidence that the Greeks ever applied it to a musical instrument.

(8.) The next word for which a Greek origin is claimed is פְּסַנְטֵרִין and פְּסַנְתֵּרִין *pesanterin* (ch. iii. 7, 5, 10, 15, rendered *psaltery* in each place), which, it is said, is the same as the Greek ψαλτήριον, *psaltery.* "This word," says Gesenius (*Lex.*), "was adopted from the Greek into Chaldee, ל and נ being interchanged." The origin of the word is, however, wholly uncertain. That it is found in Greek is undoubtedly true; but, as has been before-remarked, as it is admitted that the names of the Greek instruments of music had mostly a foreign origin, it is impossible to demonstrate that this may not have been true in regard to this word. Baxtorf (*Lex. Chald.*) says, that it is a word " corrupted from the Greek."

(9.) The next word is פַּטִּישׁ *pattish* (ch. iii. 21, rendered *hosen*), which it is said is the same as the Greek πετασος, *petasos.* But there is no reason to believe that this word had an original Greek origin. It is found in Syriac, and the root פָּטַשׁ *patash,* Gesenius remarks, " is widely found in the Indo-European languages. The primary form," says he, " is *batt, patt,* whence later Lat. *battere ;* French, *battre ;* Dutch, *bot ;* Swed. *batsch,*" &c. The Greek word has undoubtedly had the same origin, and it cannot be maintained that the Chaldee word is *derived* from the Greek.

(10.) The remaining word, which is alleged to be of Greek origin, is נְבִזְבָּה *nebizbah* (ch. ii. 6, v. 17), rendered in both cases in the text *rewards,* and in the margin *fee.* It does not elsewhere occur in the Old Testament. It is maintained by Bertholdt and others, that this is the same word as the Greek νόμισμα, *money.* But there is no evidence that the word is of Greek origin. Gesenius says (*Lex.*) that the word *may* have a Chaldee origin, though he prefers to assign to it a Persian origin, and he says that the idea of *money* (implied in the Greek word) is foreign to the context here. Bohlen, Winer, and Hengstenberg agree in assigning the word to a Persian origin. (See Hengs. *Authen.* p. 12).

The result, then, to which we have come in regard to the objection that words of Greek origin, and indicating an age later than the time of the exile, are found in Daniel, is, that the number alleged to be of such an origin is very few at best, and that of those which have been referred to, there are not *more* than four (marked 5, 6, 7, and 8, in the enumeration above) to which the objection can be supposed to apply with any degree of probability. These are the words actually selected by De Wette (p. 386) as those on which he relies.

In regard to these *four* words, then, we may make the following general observations :—

(*a*) They are all names of musical instruments said to have been used in Babylon.

(*b*) The general remark of Strabo above referred to may be called to recollection here, that the names of musical instruments among the Greeks were mostly of foreign origin. In itself considered, therefore, there is no improbability in the supposition that the same words should be applied to musical instruments in Greece and in Chaldea.

(*c*) The languages in which these words are found belong to the same great family of languages—the Indo-European; that is, the Persian, the Greek, the Latin, &c. They had a common origin, and it is not strange if we find the same words spread extensively through these languages.

(*d*) There was sufficient intercourse between Persia, Chaldea, Asia Minor, and Greece, before and at the time of the Hebrew captivity, to make it not improbable that the names of musical instruments, and the instruments themselves, should be borne from one to the other. There is, therefore, no improbability in supposing that such instruments may have been carried to Babylon from Greece, and may have retained their Greek names in Babylon. Curtius (b. iv. c. 12) says, that in the Persian host that came out to meet Alexander the Great, there were many persons found of Greek origin who had become subject to the authority of Media. For further historical proofs on this subject, see Hengs. *Authen.* pp. 16, 17. Indeed, little proof is needed. It is known that the Greeks were in the habit of visiting foreign lands, and particularly of travelling into the region of the East, for the purpose of obtaining knowledge; and nothing is, in itself, more probable than that in this way the names of a few musical instruments, in common use among themselves, should have been made known to the people among whom they travelled, and that those names should have been incorporated into the languages spoken there.

V. A fifth objection, or *class* of objections, is derived from the alleged reference to usages, opinions, and customs, *later* than the time of the exile. This objection, which embraces several subordinate points, is thus summed up by De Wette : " The remarkable later representations on the subject of angels (der Angelologie, iv. 14, ix. 21, x. 13, 21; of Christology, vii. 13, f. xii. 1-3; of dogmatics [or doctrines, Dogmatik],

xii. 2, f.; of morals [Sittenlehre] or customs, iv. 24, comp. Tobit, iv. 11, xii. 9; and of asceticism [Askese], i. 8–16, comp. Apoc. Esth. iv. 17, 2 Mac. v. 27, vi. 11, furnish at least an additional argument [einen Hülfsbeweis] against the genuineness of the book."—§ 255, c. (5.)

This objection, it will be observed, divides itself into several parts or portions, though coming under the same *general* description. The general statement is, that there is an allusion to customs and opinions which were found among the Jews *only at a later period* than the captivity, and that, therefore, the book could not have been composed at the time alleged. The specifications relate to angelology, or the representations respecting angels; to Christology, or the views of the Messiah; to the doctrines stated, particularly to those respecting the resurrection of the dead and the final judgment; to the customs that prevailed, and to the ascetic views expressed, particularly on the effect of abstinence from rich kinds of diet. It will be convenient to notice them in their order, so far as to furnish a *general* answer. Most of them will be noticed more particularly in the notes on the passages as they occur; and for a full and complete answer the reader may be referred, in general, to Hengstenberg, *Authentie des Daniel*, pp. 137–173.

A. The first specification is derived from the statements which occur respecting angels, ch. iv. 17; ix. 21; x. 13, 21. These, it is affirmed, indicate a state of opinion which prevailed among the Hebrews *only* at a later age than the time of the exile, and consequently the book could not have been written at that time. This objection, as urged by Bertholdt and others, refers to two points: first, that the statements respecting the opinions of the Chaldeans on the subject are not in accordance with the opinions in the time when the book is said to have been written; and, secondly, that the statements respecting angels, considered as Hebrew opinions, are those which belong to a later age. It will be proper to notice these in their order.

I. The first is, that the statements which occur as representing the opinions of the Chaldeans express sentiments which did not prevail among them. The objections on this point relate to two statements in the book: one, that the Son of God, or *a* Son of God, is spoken of by Nebuchadnezzar; the other, to what is said (ch. iv. 17) of the "decree of *the Watchers.*"

The former objection is thus stated by Bertholdt:—In ch. iii. 25, "Nebuchadnezzar speaks of a Son of God ['and the form of the fourth is like the Son of God']; and although the Chaldeans, and most of the dwellers in Upper Asia were polytheists, yet there is no evidence that anything was known at the time of the views which prevailed among the Greeks on this subject, but that such views became known in the time of Seleucus Nicator" (p. 29). It is hence inferred that the book could not have been written before the time of Seleucus.

In regard to the *objection*, it may be observed, in addition to what is said in the notes on the passage (ch. iii. 25) where the expression occurs, that the objection is so vague and indefinite that it scarcely needs a reply. The opinions which prevailed in the East on the subject of the gods is so little known now, that it is impossible to demonstrate that such an opinion as this might not have existed in the time of Nebuchadnezzar, and impossible to prove that such views as would have suggested this expression did *not* prevail before the time of Seleucus Nicator. Indeed, it is not easy to show that such language as is here ascribed to Nebuchadnezzar would have been more likely to have been suggested by the views of mythology that prevailed in Greece, and that were spread abroad in consequence of the diffusion of Greek opinions in the East, than by the views which prevailed in Babylon in the time of the exile. But it may be more particularly observed in reply to the objection,

(*a*) That according to Gesenius (*Thes.* p. 237), this language, as used by Nebuchadnezzar, is such as would properly denote merely *one* of the gods, or one in the form of the gods ; that is, one who resembled the gods—in the same way as the phrase "son of man" denotes a man, or one in the form and appearance of a man. Perhaps this was all that was meant by Nebuchadnezzar ; at least, that is all that can be demonstrated to have been his meaning, or all that is necessarily implied in his words. See notes on the passage. But,

(*b*) There were opinions which prevailed in Chaldea on the subject of the gods which would fully justify the use of such language. That they regarded one portion of the gods as descended from another, or as begotten by another ; that they looked upon them as constituting *families*, in a way similar to the Greeks, and, particularly, that they regarded Bel, their supreme god, always accompanied by the goddess Mylitta, as the father of the gods, has been abundantly demonstrated. On this point, see Gesenius, *Com. zu.* Isa. ii. 332, *seq.* (Beylage § 2, *Gottheiten der Chaldäer*), and Creuzer, *Symbolik*, on the word *Mylitta*, vol. i. p. 231; vol. ii. pp. 331, 333, 350, 460. The idea of derivation, descent, or birth among the gods, was one that was quite familiar to the Chaldeans, perhaps as much so as to the Greeks : in fact, this has been so common an opinion among all polytheists, that it is rather to be presumed that it would be found everywhere among the heathen than otherwise.

The other objection on this point is derived from what is said of the Watchers, ch. iv. 13, 17. The objection is, that there are betrayed here traces of a later Parsish-Jewish representation ; that is, that this indicates that the book was composed in later times.

In regard to the *meaning* of this language, see notes on ch. iv. 13. Perhaps a reference to this note, where the probability that such a term would be used in Babylon is shown, is all that is necessary in answering the objection. But, in addition to this, an observation of Diodorus Siculus may be introduced here. I copy it as I find it in Gesenius,

Com. zu. Isa. vol. ii., pp. 333, 334. Diodorus is speaking of the sun, moon, and five planets as adored by the Chaldeans, and adds, "To the course of these stars there are, as they say, thirty others that are subordinate, which are represented as *divine counsellors* (θεοὶ βουλαῖοι —*consulting gods*, as we would say), of whom one-half has the supervision of the regions under the earth; the other half has the supervision of things on the earth, among men, and in heaven. Every ten days is one of them sent as a messenger of the stars from those above to those below, and from those below to those above." This quotation will render it unnecessary to say anything more as to the question whether it is improbable that such language would be used by one residing in Babylon in the time of the exile. It is to be remembered that this is language which is represented in *a dream* as having been addressed to Nebuchadnezzar; and the quotation proves that it is such language as would be likely to occur to the king of Babylon in the visions of the night. It was such language as he must have been accustomed to; and so far is the use of this language from being an *objection* to the genuineness of Daniel, that it might rather have been urged as a *proof* of it, since it is not probable that it would have been used by one who was not familiar with the customary ideas of the Chaldeans.

(2.) The other form of the objection derived from the statements respecting the *angels* in the book of Daniel, refers to the opinions held among the Hebrews themselves. The general objection is, that these are representations respecting the ranks, and orders, and names of the angels which pertain only to later times in the history of Jewish opinions, and which did not exist in the period of the exile. This objection divides itself into several specifications, which it may be proper to notice briefly in their order.

(*a*) One is, that there is in the book, and particularly in ch. viii. 16, an allusion to the Persian doctrine of the seven Amhaspands, or angels that stand before God, and that this idea is found only in times later than the exile.—Bertholdt, p. 528.

To this the answer is obvious: (1.) That there is no *manifest* allusion to that Persian doctrine in the book, and no statement which would not as readily have been made if that doctrine had no existence—since it is a mere representation of angels with certain names, and with no particular reference to the number seven; and (2.) if this were so, it is certain that this representation occurs in the Zendavesta, and the Zendavesta was composed in a distant antiquity, probably long before the time of the exile, and certainly before the time of Alexander the Great. See Creuzer, *Symbolik*, i. 183, *seq.*, and the authorities there referred to. This, then, if it were true that the doctrine of the seven Amhaspands is found in the book of Daniel, and was derived from the Zendavesta, or the Persian, would remove the objection so far as to show that the book was composed *before* the time of Alexander the Great, or at least that there is no reason, from this quarter, to suppose that it was written *afterwards*. But the truth is, that the doctrine respecting angels and intermediate beings was so prevalent a doctrine all over the East, that this objection can have no solid foundation.

(*b*) It is objected, that there are found in this book representations of the angels, in reference to their ranks and orders, which are opinions of the Jews of a later age, and which did not exist in the time of the exile; and that, therefore, the book had a later origin than the captivity. —Bertholdt.

To this it is sufficient to reply, (1,) that such a representation of ranks and orders of angels is implied in Isa. vi. 1, *seq.*, in the account of the Seraphim, a representation which supposes that there are angels of exalted rank and names; (2,) that there are traces of such an opinion in much earlier ages, as in Psal. ciii. 20 ; lxviii. 17 ; (3,) that this representation of differences in the ranks of angels is one that *prevails* in the Old Testament; and (4,) that, for anything that appears, all that is implied in Daniel may have been a matter of common belief in his time. There is nothing in the book which would indicate any very definite arrangement of the angels into orders, though it is evidently implied that there *are* different degrees in the ranks of the angelic hosts (ch. x. 5, 13 ; xii. 1) ; but this was a common opinion in the East, and indeed has been a common sentiment where a belief in the existence of angels has prevailed at all.

(*c*) It is objected that *names* are given to the angels—the name of *Gabriel* and *Michael*—and that this is indicative of a later age. To this, also, it may be replied (1,) that long before this we find the name *Satan* given to the leader of evil angels (Job i. 6), and there is no presumption against the belief that names may have been given to good angels also; (2,) that even if the practice had *not* prevailed before, no reason can be assigned why the angels who appeared to Daniel may not have assumed names, or been mentioned under appropriate titles to designate them as well as those who appeared in after times ; and (3,) that, for anything that appears, the fact that names were given to the angels among the Jews of later times may have had its origin in the time of Daniel, or may have occurred from the fact that he actually mentioned them under specific names.

(*d*) A similar objection is, that the statement in ch. vii. 10, that "thousand thousands ministered unto him, and ten thousand times ten thousand stood before him," is also a statement that had its origin in the representation of a Persian court—in the numbers that stood round the throne of a Persian monarch, and that *this* indicates a later age, or a Persian origin. To this objection it is sufficient to refer to Isa. vi., and to the notes on this passage. But we have other representations of the same kind abounding in the Scriptures, in which God is described as a magnificent monarch, attended and surrounded by hosts of angels, and the same objection would lie against them which is urged against the account in Daniel. See particularly Deut. xxxiii. 2; 1 Kings xxii. 19–22; Job ii. 1; Psal. lxviii. 17.

(c) Another objection, from the representations of the angels, is derived from what is said of their interposition in human affairs, and their appearing particularly as the guardians and protectors of nations, in ch. x. 12–20; xii. 1; which it is said indicates opinions of a later age. In reply to this, all that is necessary is to refer to the copious notes on these passages, where the foundation of that opinion is examined, and to add that no one can demonstrate that that opinion may not have had an existence as early as the time of the exile : indeed it was a common opinion in ancient times—an opinion whose origin no one now can determine—an opinion whose correctness no one can disprove. That this was a *prevailing* opinion in ancient times is admitted by Bertholdt himself, pp. 32, 33, 705–707.

In general, therefore, it may be remarked respecting the objections derived from the angelology of the book of Daniel, (a) that there *may* be things occurring in the book which were suggested by opinions prevailing in Babylon and the East; (b) that the statements in Daniel— the revelations made to him as an eminent prophet—may have been the *germ* of the opinions which prevailed among the Jews in later times, developments of which we have in the books of the Apocrypha, and in the later Rabbinical writings : if so, the objection derived from the angelology of the book is entirely unfounded.

B. The second objection derived from the alleged reference to later customs and opinions, is founded on the *Christology* of the book, or the doctrine relating to the Messiah. The objection is, that the opinions which are found in the book belong to a later age; or that in the time of the exile no such views exist in the genuine writings of the prophets, and that consequently the book must have been composed when those later views had come to prevail. The views referred to as the ground of the objection are found in ch. vii. 13, 14, and xii. 1–3. This objection, thus stated by De Wette, has been expanded by Bertholdt and others, and properly embraces, as stated by them, *four* specifications which it will be convenient to notice in their order.

(1.) The first is, that in the time of the exile, the doctrine of the Messiah had not become so developed that it was expected that he would appear in glory and majesty, and set up a kingdom upon the earth, as is implied in ch. vii. 13, 14. See Bertholdt, p. 31.

In reply to this, all that is necessary to be said is, to refer to the prophecies in the other portions of the Old Testament, whose antiquity and genuineness are undoubted. In the prophecies of Isaiah, there are predictions of the Messiah as clear, as definite, as distinct, as any that occur in Daniel; and no one can compare the prophecies found in other parts of the Old Testament with those found in Daniel, and determine, by any internal evidence, that one class must have been written before, and another after, the time of the exile. Besides, why may not the predictions, under the Spirit of inspiration, have been more clearly communicated to one prophet than to another—to Daniel than to Isaiah? And why may not some circumstances respecting the Messiah and his reign have been made to one rather than to another? If it be admitted that all that occurs in the first part of Isaiah (ch. i.–xxxix.) was actually revealed to him, and recorded by him, previous to the exile, there can be no difficulty in admitting that what is found in Daniel may have been communicated and recorded *at* the time of the exile. In proof of what is here said, it is only necessary to refer to Hengstenberg's *Christology*, vol. i. The Messianic prophecies there collected and illustrated, Gen. iii. 14, 15; ix. 26, 27; xlix. 10; Num. xxiv. 17; Deut. xviii. 15–18; Psal. ii., xvi., xxii., xlv., cx.; Isa. ii.–iv, vii., xi., xii, furnish statements *as* clear, in many respects, respecting the Messiah as anything in Daniel, and of many of these statements it might as well be alleged that they are couched in the language of later times, as anything that occurs in the book before us.

(2.) It is alleged further, of the Christology of Daniel, that the ideas respecting the kingdom of the Messiah are stated in the language of later times.—Bertholdt, p. 31. In proof of this, Bertholdt refers to ch. ii. 44; vii. 13, *seq.*

This is the same objection in another form. The reply to it is obvious: (*a*) If Daniel is admitted to be a true prophet, there is no presumption against the supposition that some ideas may have been imparted to him which might not be found in other prophets—any more than that circumstances respecting the power and kingdom of the Messiah may have been communicated to Isaiah which were not to the earlier prophets; and (*b*) as a matter of fact, as before stated, many of the prophecies of Isaiah are as minute and as clear in regard to the kingdom of the Messiah as those in Daniel. Comp. Isa. ix. 6, 7. No one could place *that* prediction by the side of the prediction in Daniel vii. 13, 14, and determine from any internal evidence that the one was written before the exile, and that the other was couched in the language of later times.

(3.) It is objected (Bertholdt, p. 31), that the sentiment found in Daniel (ch. xii. 1), that the setting up of the kingdom of the Messiah would be preceded by times of trouble, is a doctrine of the Rabbinical writings of later times, and savours of a later origin than the times of the exile. To this, also, the reply is obvious. (*a*) It is to be admitted that this idea occurs in the Rabbinical writings, and that it was a common doctrine among the Jews; but can any one demonstrate that the doctrine had not its origin in this very passage in Daniel? It is quite *as* philosophical to suppose that this language may have been found in the genuine language of the prophets, and that the doctrine may have sprung up from that cause, as to suppose that it was first originated by uninspired men among the Jews, and then embodied in a pretended prophecy. (*b*) It was natural that Daniel, if a real prophet, should connect the two things together not *in time*, but *in the range of vision*. See Intro. to Isa. § 7, iii. (5). Placing himself in prophetic vision in the midst of foreseen trouble coming upon his country, it was natural that the mind should be directed to brighter days, and that he should endeavour to cheer his own heart, and to comfort his afflicted countrymen, by dwelling on happier scenes when, under the Messiah, these troubles would cease. (*c*) As a matter of fact, the same thing elsewhere occurs. Thus Isaiah (ch. xl. and onward) describes the coming of the kingdom of the Messiah, by connecting it with the deliverance from the calamities that would come upon the Jewish people in the time of their captivity. He seeks to comfort them in their troubles by the assurance of better days ; and in describing their return to their own land, the mind of the prophet insensibly glides on to the coming of the Messiah—to the happier times that would occur under him—to the deliverance from the bondage of sin, and to the setting up of a kingdom of peace and truth in the world ; and the description which *began* with the troubles of the exile, and the return to their own land, *ends* with a sublime and glorious view of the times of the Messiah, and of the happiness of the world under his reign. And it may be added, that this is in accordance with a general principle laid down in the Bible : "But the Lord shall judge his people, and repent himself for his servants, when he seeth that their power is gone, and there is none shut up, or left" (Deut. xxxii. 36). Comp. Isa. xi. 11, and the Notes of Gesenius on that place. See also Hos. iii. 5 ; Amos ix. 14, 15 ; Mic. iv. 6, 7 ; Joel iii. 16, 17 ; Zeph. iii. 19, 20 ; Jer. xxiii. 8 ; xxxiii. 7 ; Ezek. xxxvi. 36.

(4.) A fourth specification respecting the Christology in the book of Daniel, is derived from the reference to the doctrine of the resurrection (chap. xii. 2). It is objected that this is a doctrine of later times, and that it could not have been known in the age when Daniel is said to have lived.

That the doctrine of the resurrection of the dead is referred to in that passage, or that what is there said is *based* on the belief of that doctrine, and implies that the doctrine was so commonly believed as to make it proper to refer to it as such, seems plain from the passage itself. See notes on the passage.

But in regard to the objection derived from this fact, it may be remarked :—

(*a*) That there is evidence elsewhere that the doctrine *was* known as early as the time of the exile, and was assumed to be true in the same manner in which it is here. Thus in Isa. xxvi. 19, it is referred to in the same manner, for the remark of the prophet is *based* on that, and cannot be explained except on the supposition that this was an article of common belief. See notes on that passage. See also Gesenius, who says, "that this place actually contains the doctrine of the resurrection of the dead, and that in these words the doctrine of the resurrection is undoubtedly implied." The same thing seems also to be true in the vision of the valley of dry bones (Ezek. xxxvii. 1-14). Though that passage does not refer *primarily* to the resurrection of the dead, and is not intended directly to teach it, yet it is difficult, if not impossible, to explain it, except on the supposition that this doctrine was understood, and was believed to be true. It is just such an illustration as would be used now in a community where that doctrine is understood and believed.

(*b*) It is undoubtedly true that, in the passage under consideration (Dan. xii. 2), the design is not directly to *teach* the doctrine of the resurrection of the dead, but that it refers, as the primary thought, to the restoration and recovery of the Jewish people, *as if* they were raised from the dead ; but still, as in the passages in Isaiah and Ezekiel above referred to, the doctrine of the resurrection is assumed, and the illustration is derived from that, and, as Jerome has remarked on the passage, such an illustration would not be employed unless the doctrine were believed, for "no one would attempt to confirm an uncertain or doubtful thing by that which had no existence." But the same design exists in each of the cases in Daniel, Isaiah, and Ezekiel. The doctrine is alluded to in the same manner, and in each case is assumed to be true in the same way—as a doctrine that was known, and that might be employed for *illustration*. This is one of the best proofs that there could be that it was a common article of belief ; and as it is used by these three writers in the same manner, if it proves that one of them lived in a later age, it proves the same of all. But as the genuineness of that portion of Isaiah where the passage occurs, and of Ezekiel is not called in question, it follows that the objection has no force as alleged against the genuineness of Daniel.

(*c*) It may be added, that on the supposition that there *is* no allusion to this doctrine in any of the prophets that lived in the time of the exile, or before it, that would furnish no evidence that it might not be found in a book written by Daniel. The belief undoubtedly sprang up at *some* time among the Jews, for it is admitted by those who object to the genuineness of Daniel on this account, that it *did* exist in the time in which they allege that the book was written—in the time of Antiochus Epiphanes; and it undoubtedly *somehow* gained so much currency among the Jews as to lay the foundation of the peculiar belief of the Pharisees on the subject. But no one can show that this doctrine could not have had its origin in Daniel himself; or that *he*, living in the time of the exile, might not have made such statements on the subject as to lay the foundation for the general belief of the doctrine in later times. Even on the supposition that he was not inspired, this might have been ; much more on the supposition that he *was* inspired —for he was one of the latest of the prophets of the Old Testament, and one of those who were most eminently favoured of God. In itself considered, there is no improbability in supposing that God might have honoured Daniel, by making him the instrument of first distinctly announcing the doctrines of the resurrection and the future judgment of the world.

C. A third objection, from the alleged reference to later customs and opinions in the book of Daniel, is derived from the fact stated in ch. vi. 10, that Daniel in his prayer is said to have turned his face towards Jerusalem. This objection as urged by Bertholdt and others, is, that the custom of turning the face towards Jerusalem in prayer was one that was originated after the building of the second temple, and that no traces of it are found while the first temple was standing. It is admitted, indeed, that the custom of turning the face towards a temple or place of worship prevailed extensively in Oriental countries —as among the Mahometans at present—but it is alleged that this had its origin among the Jews *after* the captivity, and after the second temple was built. It is further added that it is improbable that Daniel would turn his face towards *Jerusalem* on that occasion, for the city and temple were destroyed, and the Shekinah, the symbol of the divine presence there, had disappeared. See Bertholdt, p. 30.

To this objection the following remarks may be made in reply :—

(1.) The custom of turning the face in worship towards a temple or shrine, was one that existed early in the world, and has prevailed in almost all countries. It is one that would naturally spring up, even if there were no positive commands on the subject, for this would seem to be demanded by respect for the god who was worshipped, and who was supposed to have his residence in a particular temple. If Jehovah, therefore, was supposed to have his dwelling in the temple; if the symbols of his presence were believed to be there; if that was his *house*, just in proportion as that was believed would the custom be likely to prevail of turning the face towards that place in worship, just as we now naturally turn the face towards heaven, which we regard as the peculiar place of his abode. It would have been unnatural, therefore, if Daniel had *not* turned his face towards Jerusalem in his devotions.

(2.) The custom is, in fact, far-spread in the East, and goes back, in its origin, beyond any period we can now assign to it. It prevails everywhere among the Mahometans; it was found by Mungo Park among the negroes in Africa (Rosenmüller, *Morgenland*, iv. 361); and it may be said to be the general custom of the East. No one can determine its origin, and probably, for the reason above stated, it existed in the first periods of the history of the world.

(3.) The custom is mentioned in the Psalms as existing *before* the time of Daniel. Thus, in Psal. v. 7, " As for me, I will come into thy house in the multitude of thy mercy; and in thy fear will I worship toward thy holy temple." Psal. cxxxviii. 2, " I will worship toward thy holy temple," &c. Comp. Psal. cxxi. 1. So Psal. xxviii. 2, " Hear the voice of my supplications—when I lift up my hands toward thy holy oracle."

(4.) The custom was sanctioned by what Solomon said at the dedication of the temple. In his prayer, on that occasion, it is implied that the custom *would* prevail, and what was said at that time could not but be regarded as giving a sanction to it. Thus, in the prayer offered at the dedication of the temple, he seems to have supposed just such a case as that before us : " If they sin against thee, and thou be angry with them, and deliver them to the enemy, so that they carry them away captive unto the land of the enemy, far or near; if they shall bethink themselves in the land whither they were carried captives, and repent, and pray unto thee toward their land which thou gavest unto their fathers, the city which thou hast chosen, and the house which I have built for thy name, then hear thou their prayer," &c. (1 Kings viii. 44–49. Comp. also vers. 33, 35, 38, 42).

(5.) It may be added, that nothing was more natural than for Daniel to do this. It is not said that he turned his face toward the "*temple*," but toward "Jerusalem." It was true that the temple was in ruins; true that the ark was removed, and that the Shekinah had disappeared. It was true also that Jerusalem was in ruins. But it is to be remembered that Jerusalem had been long regarded as the city of God, and his dwelling-place on the earth; that this was the place where his worship had been celebrated for ages, and where he had manifested himself by visible symbols; that this was the place where the ancestors of Daniel had lived and worshipped, and where he believed the temple of God would be built again, and where God would again dwell—a place sacred in the recollections of the past and in the anticipations of the future—a place where Daniel had himself been taught to worship God when a child, and where he anticipated that they who should be delivered from the long captivity would again offer sacrifice and praise; and nothing, therefore, was more natural than for him, in his prayer, to turn his face to a spot hallowed by so many sacred associations.

D. A fourth objection designed to show that the book betrays a later origin than the time of the captivity is, that Daniel is represented (ch. vi. 10), as entering into his chamber, or "upper room" (ὑπερῷον), when he prayed, and that the custom of setting apart a chamber in a house for private devotion sprang up in a later age among the Jews, as one of the results of formalism and ostentation in religion.—(*Bertholdt*, p. 30.)

In regard to this custom among the later Jews, see the notes on the passage referred to. But there are two remarks to be made, showing conclusively that this objection has no force :—

(*a*) There is no evidence that it was such an "upper room " (ὑπερῷον), as is here referred to. All that is fairly implied in the word in this passage (עִלִּית) might be applied to any house, and at any time. It denotes, indeed, an upper room, upper story, or loft; but not necessarily *such* an upper room as was built by the Jews in later times, and designated by the word ὑπερῷον. It is not improbable that Daniel would retire to such a part of his house to pray, but it is not necessarily implied in this word that the chamber referred to had been specifically constructed *as* a place of prayer.

(*b*) But even supposing that this was the case, it is impossible to prove that such a custom may not have prevailed in the time of the captivity. We cannot now trace the origin of that custom among the Jews; and though it undoubtedly prevailed in a later age, yet no one can demonstrate that it did not exist also at a time as early as that of the exile. Indeed, there is some evidence that it *did* prevail at an earlier period among the Hebrews. Thus, in 2 Sam. xviii. 33, it is said of David on the death of Absalom, "And the king was much moved, and went up to *the chamber over the gate*, and wept," &c. So in the case of the prophet Elijah, during his residence with the widow of Zarephath, an upper chamber or loft was assigned the prophet (1 Kings xvii. 19), called "a *loft* where he abode"—עֲלִיָּה—the very word which is used in Daniel. The same word occurs again in Judg. iii. 20, 23, 24, 25, in each case rendered *parlour*, and referring to a private room where one might retire, and, as the word implies, to an *upper room*, doubtless a small room built on the flat roof of the house, as being more retired and cool. And again, in 2 Kings i. 2, it is said of Ahaziah that "he fell down through a lattice in his *upper chamber* that was in Samaria." And again, in 2 Kings iv. 10, the Shunamitess proposes to her husband to make for the prophet Elisha "a little *chamber* on the wall"—עֲלִיַּת־קִיר—a place of retirement for him. These passages show that the custom of constructing a chamber, or upper room for the purpose of retirement or devotion, prevailed long before the time of Daniel; and, therefore, the fact that he is represented as having such a place in his house in Babylon, if that *be* the fact referred to here, cannot be alleged as evidence that the book was written at a later period than the captivity.

E. It is alleged, as an evidence that the book was written at a period later than the exile, that Daniel is represented (in the same passage, ch. vi. 10) as praying three times a-day, a custom, it is said, which originated in later times.

But the reply to this is obvious. (*a*) The custom of praying three times a-day in sacred devotion is one of which there are traces in earlier times. Thus the Psalmist (Psa. lv. 17), "Evening, and morning, and at noon, will I pray, and cry aloud: and he shall hear my voice." (*b*) Daniel may have had such a custom, without supposing that he derived it from any one. (*c*) These are the *natural* times of prayer; times that devout persons will be *likely* to select as seasons of devotion; the morning, when one just enters upon the duties and trials of the day, when it is appropriate to give thanks for preservation, and to ask of God that he will guide, direct, and sustain us; the evening, when, having finished the toils of the day, it is appropriate to render thanksgiving, to pray for the remission of the sins of the day, and to seek the blessing and protection of God as we lie down to rest; and noon, when we feel the propriety of dividing the labours of the day by an interval of rest and devotion; thus keeping up, amidst the cares of the world, the life of religion in the soul. (*d*) There is no certain evidence that this became a regular and settled usage in later times among the Jews, any more than that it was of a former age.

F. It is alleged that what is said in ch. iv. 27, of the efficacy of almsgiving in averting the judgments of God, is an opinion that had its origin in later times, and proves that the book must have been written at a period subsequent to the captivity. The passage is, "Let my counsel be acceptable unto thee, and break off thy sins by righteousness, *and thine iniquities by showing mercy to the poor ;* it may be a lengthening of thy tranquillity." This, it is said, could have been written only at a time when great merit was attributed to almsgiving, and when such acts, it was supposed, would avert Divine vengeance from the guilty; and this opinion, it is alleged, sprang up at a period subsequent to the captivity. That the sentiment here adverted to prevailed in later times there can be no doubt, but there is no proof that it is used in the passage before us in the sense in which it prevailed in the time when the books of the Apocrypha were written; and, in reference to the objection here urged, all that is necessary, it seems to me, is to refer to the notes on the passage, where its true meaning is fully considered. The short answer is, that the passage does not teach any such peculiar doctrine on the subject of almsgiving, as prevailed in later times among the Jews, but only the *general* doctrine, which is found everywhere in the Bible, and which accords with all just notions on the subject, that if a sinner will abandon the error of his ways, and perform acts of righteousness, it will conduce to his happiness, and, in all probability, to the lengthening out of his days.

G. One other objection, under the general head now under consideration, remains. It is derived from what are called the *ascetic* customs referred to in the book. On this point De Wette refers to ch. i. 8–16, as compared with 2 Macc. v. 27, and with the apocryphal portion of the book of Esther.

In regard to this objection, also, perhaps all that is necessary is to refer to the notes on the passage. The reason which Daniel gave for not partaking of the food and wine furnished by the king of Babylon, is not such as would be derived from any ascetic or monastic opinions, but such as would be given by any Jew of that age who was conscientious. It was "that he might not defile himself with the portion of the king's meat, nor with the wine which he drank" (ch. i. 8); that is, he purposed to keep himself clear from all participation in idolatry, and to save himself from the temptations to which one would be exposed if he indulged freely in the luxuries in eating and drinking which were practised at the royal table. As this solution explains the passage on principles that would be likely to influence a pious Jew, and which would be proper in young men everywhere, it is unnecessary to seek any other, and improper to suppose that there is an allusion here to superstitious customs which prevailed among the Jews in later times.

VI. A sixth objection to the authenticity and genuineness of the book is derived from the place assigned it in the canon. This objection is urged by Bertholdt, Bleek, Eichhorn, Kirms, and De Wette, and is substantially this, as stated by Bertholdt:—It is well known that the Jews, in the time when the *Talmud* was composed, divided their sacred books into three parts—the Law, the Prophets, and the Hagiographa. The latter class embraced the Psalms, Job, Proverbs, Song of Solomon, Ruth, Lamentations, Ecclesiastes, Esther, Daniel, Ezra, Nehemiah, and the two books of the Chronicles. This classification also existed in the time of Jerome, who obtained it evidently from the Jews in Palestine. The objection is, that in collecting and arranging the books of the Old Testament, Daniel was assigned to this latter class, and was not placed among the Prophets. The book professes to be, in a great part, prophetical, and if genuine, its true place, it is argued, would be among the prophets; and, it is said, it would have been placed in that class if it had been in existence at the time when the collection of the sacred books was made. It is argued, therefore, that it must have had a later origin, and that when it was written it was assigned a place in that *general* collection of writings where all those books were arranged which could not be placed with either of the other classes. This objection is summarily stated by Prof. Stuart (*Critical History and Defence of the Old Testament Canon*, p. 266) in the following words:—"The argument runs thus: 'No reason can be assigned, except the *lateness* of the composition, why Daniel and the Chronicles should be placed among the Kethubim or Hagiographa, since the first belongs to the class of the later prophets, and the second, like Samuel, Kings, &c., to the class of the former prophets. The fact, then, that Daniel and the Chronicles are joined with the Kethubim, shows that they were written after the second class of the Scriptural books, viz., the Prophets, was fully defined and completed; now, as this class comprises Haggai, Zechariah, and Malachi, so we have conclusive evidence that Daniel and Chronicles must have been composed, or at all events introduced into the canon, at a period subsequent to Nehemiah and Malachi, which was about 430–420 B.C.'"

In reference to this objection, perhaps all that would be necessary for me would be to refer to the very full and satisfactory argument of Prof. Stuart on the Canon in the work just named, § 9-13, pp. 214–298. A few remarks, however, on two or three points, seem to be demanded to show the results which have been reached by a careful investigation of the subject, and how entirely without foundation is the objection.

A. The objection, then, takes for granted the following things, which it is impossible now to prove: (1.) That the division of the books of the Old Testament found in the *Talmud*, and prevailing among the Jews in the time of Jerome, in which Daniel is placed in the third class, the

Kethubim, or Hagiographa, is the ancient and original division; for if this is not so, then Daniel *may* have been placed among the prophets, and of course the objection would not then exist. There is the strongest reason to believe that this was *not* the arrangement that prevailed at an earlier period, but that it was made long after the time of Josephus; at any rate it cannot be *proved* to have been the original arrangement. (2.) It takes for granted that the main reason for inserting Daniel and the books of the Chronicles in the Hagiographa was the *recent* origin of these books, or the fact that they were composed *after* the second class —the Prophets—was completed and collected together, for the whole weight of the objection rests on this. If any of these books in the Hagiographa were in fact written at an earlier period than some in the second class—the Prophets—or if any other reason existed for referring them to the class of the Hagiographa than the *lateness* of their composition, then the objection would have no force. But this difficulty of itself would be fatal to the objection, for there is every reason to suppose that the lateness of the composition was *not* the reason why these books were placed in the Hagiographa, and that this was never supposed or implied by those who made the arrangement; for, not to speak of the book of Job, which is found in that class, and which is probably one of the oldest compositions in the Bible, if not the very oldest, what shall we say of the Psalms, and the book of Proverbs, and the book of Ecclesiastes, and the Canticles, which are also found in that class? Assuredly it could not have been pretended that these writings belonged to the Maccabean age, and that they were inserted in the Hagiographa because they were supposed to have had a *later* origin than the Prophets; for, in all ages, the Jews have regarded the book of Proverbs, the book of Ecclesiastes, and the Canticles, as the genuine productions of Solomon. Why, then, were they put into the Hagiographa?—for there the Psalms, and the book of Proverbs, and Ecclesiastes, and the Song of Solomon, have always been, in every triplex division of the books of the Old Testament which has ever been made. (3.) The objection takes for granted that the two classes, the Prophets and the Hagiographa, have been fixed and uniform, like the first, the Law, as to the number of books in each, ever since the division was made; that the same number of books, and the same arrangement, has been found which existed in the time of Josephus; and that no causes have ever operated since to produce a change in the arrangement; for if this is not so, it would be fatal to the objection. But this can never be shown to be true; indeed, there is every reason to believe that the contrary is true—and if it cannot be demonstrated to be true, the objection is without force. But,

B. There are strong positive arguments to show that the fact that Daniel, in the later divisions of the Hebrew books, is placed in the list of the Hagiographa or Kethubim, is no argument against the genuineness and authenticity of the book.

(1.) There is every presumption that in the earliest arrangement of the books of the Old Testament, the book of Daniel, with several that now occupy the same place in the Talmudical arrangement, was ranked with the *second* class—the Prophets. This presumption is founded, mainly, on what is said of the division of the books of the Old Testament by Josephus. It is true that he has not enumerated the books of the Old Testament, but he has mentioned the division of the books in his time, and, of course, in earlier times, in such a way as to make it morally certain that Daniel was not in the third class, but in the second class—the Prophets. His account of this division (*Against Apion*, b. 1, § 8) is as follows : "We have not a countless number of books, discordant and arranged against each other, but only two and twenty books, containing the history of every age, which are justly accredited as Divine [the old editions of Josephus read merely, 'which are justly accredited'—θεῖα (divine) comes from Eusebius' translation of Josephus, in *Ecc. Hist.* iii. 10]; and of these, five belong to Moses, which contain both his laws and the history of the generations of men until his death. This period lacks but little of 3000 years. From the death of Moses, moreover, until the reign of Artaxerxes, king of the Persians after Xerxes, the prophets who followed Moses have described the things which were done during the age of each one respectively, in *thirteen* books. The remaining *four* contain hymns to God and rules of life for men. From the time of Artaxerxes, moreover, till our present period, all occurrences have been written down; but they are not regarded as entitled to the like credit with those which precede them, because there was no certain succession of prophets. Fact has shown what confidence we place in our own writings; for, although so many ages have passed away, no one has dared to add to them, nor to take anything from them, nor to make alterations. In all Jews it is implanted, even from their birth, to regard them as being the instructions of God, and to abide steadfastly by them, and, if it be necessary, to die gladly for them." —(Prof. Stuart's translation, *ut supra*, pp. 430, 431).

Now, in this extract from Josephus, stating the number and order of the sacred books in his time, it is *necessarily* implied that the book of Daniel was then included in the *second* part, or among the "Prophets." For (*a*) it is clear that it was not in the third division, or the Hagiographa. Of that division Josephus says, "The remaining *four* contain hymns to God, and rules of life for men." Now, we are not able to determine with exact certainty, indeed, what these four books were, for Josephus has not mentioned their names; but we can determine with certainty that Daniel was *not* of the number, for his book does not come under the description of "hymns to God," or "rules of life for men." If we *cannot*, therefore, make out what these books were, the argument would be complete on that point; but although Josephus has not enumerated them, they *can* be made out with a good degree of probability. That the "hymns to God" would embrace the Psalms there can be no doubt; and there can be as little doubt that, in the books containing "rules of life for men," the Proverbs would be included. The other books that would more properly come under this designation than any other are Ecclesiastes and the Song of Solomon (see the full evidence of this in Prof. Stuart, *ut supra*, pp. 256-264); at all events, it is clear that *Daniel* would not be included in that number. (*b*) There is evidence, then, that Daniel *was* included at that time in the second division—that of the Prophets. Josephus says that that division comprised "*thirteen* books," and that Daniel was included among them is evident from the rank which Josephus gives to him as one of the greatest of the prophets. Thus he says of him (*Ant.* b. x. chap. xi.) : "He was so happy as to have strange revelations made to him, and those as to one of the greatest of the prophets; insomuch that while he was alive he had the esteem and applause both of kings and of the multitude, and now he is dead he retains a remembrance that will never fail. For the several books that he wrote and left behind him are still read by us till this time, and from them we believe that he conversed with God; for he not only prophesied of future events, as did the other prophets, but he also determined the time of their accomplishment. And while prophets used to foretell misfortunes, and on that account were disagreeable both to the kings and the multitude, Daniel was to them a prophet of good things, and this to such a degree, that, by the agreeable nature of his predictions, he procured the good-will of all men; and by the accomplishment of them he procured the belief of their truth, and the opinion of a sort of divinity for himself among the multitude. He also wrote and left behind him what evinced the accuracy and the undeniable veracity of his predictions." From this it is clear that Josephus regarded Daniel as worthy to be ranked among the greatest of the prophets, and that he considered his writings as worthy to be classed with those of the other eminent prophets of his country. This is such language as would be used in speaking of *any* ancient prophet; and, as we have seen that the book of Daniel could not have been of the number mentioned by him in the third class—those containing "hymns to God and rules of life for men"—it follows that it must have been ranked by Josephus in the second division—that of *the prophets*. It does not seem easy to suppose that there could be clearer proof than this, short of direct affirmation. The proof that he regarded Daniel as belonging to this division of the books, is as clear as can be made out from his writings in favour of Isaiah, Jeremiah, or Ezekiel.

(2.) If Daniel had this rank in the time of Josephus, then it would follow that, in the division of the books of the Old Testament, as referred to by the Saviour (Luke xxiv. 44), he must have had this rank also. There can be no doubt that Josephus expresses not his own private judgment in the matter, but the prevailing opinion of his countrymen on the subject. Josephus was born A.D. 37, and consequently he must have uttered what was the general sentiment in the time of the Saviour and the apostles—for it cannot be supposed that any change had occurred in that short time among the Jews, by which Daniel had been transferred from the *third* division to the *second*. If *any* change had occurred in the arrangement of the books, it would have been, for reasons which are obvious, just the reverse—since the predictions of Daniel were at this time much relied on by Christians, in their arguments against the Jews, to prove that Jesus was the Messiah. We may regard it as morally certain, therefore, that in the time of the Saviour, Daniel was ranked among the prophets. It may be added here, also, that if Daniel had this rank in the estimation of Josephus, it may be presumed that he had the same rank when the division of the sacred books is referred to in the only other two instances among the Jews, previous to the composition of the *Talmud*. In both these cases there is mention of the *triplex* division ; in neither are the *names* of the books recorded. One occurs in the " Prologue of the Wisdom of Jesus, the Son of Sirach," in the Apocrypha. This Prologue was probably written about 130 B.C.; the book itself probably about 180 B.C. In this Prologue the writer mentions the divisions of the sacred books three times in this manner : " Since so many and important things have been imparted to us by *the Law, the Prophets, and other* [*works*] *of the like kind* which have followed, for which one must needs praise Israel on account of learning and wisdom ; and inasmuch as not only those who read ought to be well-informed, but those who are devoted to learning should be able to profit, both in the way of speaking and writing, such as are foreigners, my grandfather, Jesus, having devoted himself very much to the reading of *the Law, the Prophets, and the other books of his country*, and having acquired a great degree of experience in these things, was himself led on to compose something pertaining to instruction and wisdom, so that those desirous of learning, being in possession of these things, might grow much more by a life conformed to the law. Ye are invited, therefore, with good will and strict attention to make the perusal, and to take notice whenever we may seem to lack ability, in respect to any of the words which we have laboured to translate. Not only so, but *the Law itself, and the Prophets, and the remaining books*, exhibit no small diversity among themselves as to the modes of expression."

The other reference of the same kind occurs in Philo Judæus. He flourished about A.D. 40, and in praising a contemplative life, and giving examples of it, he comes at last to the *Therapeutæ*, or *Essenes*, and in speaking of their devotional practices, he uses this language : " In every house is a sanctuary, which is called *sacred place* or *monastery*, in which, being alone, they perform the mysteries of a holy life ; introducing nothing into it, neither drink, nor bread-corn, nor any of the other things which are necessary for the wants of the body, but *the Laws, and Oracles predicted by the prophets, and Hymns, and other writings, by*

which knowledge and piety are increased and perfected." There can be
no reasonable doubt that precisely the same division of the books of the
Old Testament is referred to in each of these cases which is mentioned
by Josephus. If so, then Daniel was at that time reckoned among the
prophets.

(3.) He certainly had this rank among the early Christians, alike in
their estimation of him, and in the order of the sacred books. It happens that, although Josephus, the Son of Sirach, and Philo have given
no *list* of the names and order of the sacred books, yet the early Christians *have*, and from these lists it is easy to ascertain the rank which
they assigned to Daniel. "Melito places Daniel among the Prophets,
and *before* Ezekiel. The same does Origen. The Council of Laodicea
places Daniel next after Ezekiel, and, of course, among the Prophets.
The same do the *Canones Apostol.*, Cyrill of Jerusalem, Gregory
Nazianzen, Athanasius, *Synopsis Scripturæ in Athan.* The Council of
Hippo, like Melito and Origen, place it *before* Ezekiel, as also does
Hilary; and Rufinus places it next after Ezekiel. Jerome alone, in
giving an account of the Rabbinical usage in his day, puts Daniel among
the Hagiographa; and after it he puts Chronicles, Ezra (with Nehemiah),
and Esther."—(Prof. Stuart, *ut supra*, p. 284).* The *Talmud* thus stands
alone, with the exception of Jerome, in placing Daniel among the books
constituting the Hagiographa; and Jerome, in doing this, merely gives
an account of what was customary in his time among the Jewish
Rabbins, without expressing any opinion of his own on the subject.
These testimonies are sufficient to show that Daniel was *never* placed in
the division composing the Hagiographa, so far as can be proved by
the Son of Sirach, by Philo, by Josephus, by the Jews in the time of
the Saviour, or by the Christian writers of the first four centuries; and
of course, until it can be demonstrated that he *was* thus classified, this
objection must fall to the ground. But,

(4.) The fact that Daniel occupied this place in the divisions made
of the books by the later Jews can be accounted for in a way perfectly
consistent with the supposition that he wrote at the time when the book
is commonly believed to have been composed. For,

(*a*) The reason which they themselves give for this arrangement is,
not that his writings were of later *date*, but some fanciful view which
they had about the *degrees* of inspiration of the prophets. They say
that the books of Moses take the precedence above all others, because
God spake with him mouth to mouth; that the prophets who came
after him were such as, whether sleeping or waking when they received
revelations, were deprived of all the use of their senses, and were spoken
to by a voice, or saw prophetic visions in ecstasy; and that the third
and lowest class of writers were those who, preserving the use of their

---

* The lists of the books, as given by these writers and councils, may be seen
at length in Prof. Stuart, *ut supra*, Appendix, pp. 431–452.

senses, spake like other men, and yet in such a way that, although not
favoured with dreams or visions in ecstacy, they still perceived a Divine
influence resting upon them, at whose suggestion they spake or wrote
what they made public. For the proof of this, see Prof. Stuart, *ut supra*,
p. 269. Agreeably to this fanciful opinion, they made the arrangement
of the sacred books which is found in the *Talmud;* and on this principle
they placed Daniel in the list of the Hagiographa. But assuredly this
fanciful opinion, and the mistake of the Jews consequent on it, can be
no reason for supposing that the book of Daniel was written in the time
of the Maccabees; and especially as they who made this arrangement
never pretended this, and never could have made the arrangement on
this ground. And,

(*b*) There is great reason for supposing, after all, that Daniel was
not assigned to the place which he has in the Talmudic divisions of the
sacred books, on the ground that he was properly classed there, even
on their arbitrary and fanciful opinion as to the degrees of inspiration
among the prophets, but because, in the disputes between Christians
and Jews about the Messiah, in the first three and a half centuries, the
Jews felt themselves to be so pressed by the prediction in Dan. ix.,
respecting the seventy weeks, that they sought to give the book a lower
place than it had occupied before, and thus to remove it somewhat from
an association with the other prophets, and to diminish the force of the
argument in proof that Jesus of Nazareth was the Christ.

(5.) To all this it may be added, that it would have been impossible
to have foisted a book into the canon that was composed in the time
of the Maccabees, and that was not regarded as of Divine inspiration.
We have, as above, the express testimony of Josephus, that for some
four hundred years before his time they had no prophets who wrote
inspired books, or who could be regarded as sacred writers. The canon,
according to him, was closed at the time of Artaxerxes, and afterward
they had books in which " all occurrences were written down; but these
were not regarded as of like credit with those that preceded them,
because there was no certain succession of prophets," that is, the canon
of inspired books was then closed, in the apprehension of the Jews, or
they had a definite number which they regarded as of Divine origin,
and as distinguished from all others.

Now, supposing this to have been, as no doubt it was, a prevailing
opinion among the Jews, it would have been impossible to have foisted
in a book written in the time of the Maccabees—or after the time of
Antiochus Epiphanes, as the objection supposes the book of Daniel to
have been—in such a way that it would be regarded as entitled to a
place among the sacred writings. If this book was written at that time,
it must have been known that it was not the genuine production of
the Daniel of the captivity; and by whom could it be introduced into
the canon? On what pretence could it be done? What claim could
have been urged for a spurious book of this kind to a place by the side

of Isaiah and Ezekiel? It is well known that the Hebrews have been, in all ages, most careful of their sacred books; that they have transcribed them with the greatest possible attention; that they have counted the words and the letters; that they have marked and preserved every variety, irregularity, and anomaly, even every unusual shape and position of a letter in the manuscript; and it may be asked with emphasis, In what way it would be possible to introduce a book which was known and admitted to be spurious—a book falsely ascribed to one who was said to have lived long before—among those which they regarded as of Divine origin, and whose purity they guarded with so much care? Scarcely any greater literary absurdity can be imagined than this.

VII. A seventh objection which has been urged to the genuineness of the book of Daniel is derived from the silence of the Son of Sirach in regard to it. This objection is urged by De Wette, Bleek, Eichhorn, Kirms, and Bretschneider, and is substantially this:—That in the book of Ecclesiasticus (ch. xlix.), the author of that book, Jesus, the Son of Sirach, undertakes to give a list of the personages in the Jewish history who had been eminent for virtue, piety, and patriotism; and that the circumstances of the case are such that it is to be presumed that if he had known anything of Daniel and his writings, he would have been mentioned among them. Thus he mentions David, Hezekiah, Josiah, Jeremiah, Ezekiel, the twelve Prophets, Zorobabel, Jesus the son of Josedec, Nehemiah, Enoch, Joseph, Shem, Seth, and Adam. The particular *point*, however, of the objection seems to be, that he mentions men who were eminent in securing the return of the Hebrews to their own country, as Nehemiah and Zorobabel, and that if Daniel had lived then in Babylon, and had had the important agency in effecting the return of the captives which is ascribed to him in this book, or had had the influence at the court of Persia attributed to him, it is unaccountable that his name was not mentioned.

To this objection we may reply: (1.) That the *argumentum a silentio* is admitted not to be a conclusive kind of reasoning. So long as there *may* have been other reasons why the name was omitted in such a list, it is unfair and inconclusive to infer that he had not then an existence, or that there was no such man. It is necessary, in order that this reasoning should have any force, to show that this is the *only* cause which could have led to this omission, or that this *alone* could account for it. But it is easy to conceive that there may have been many reasons why the name was omitted in this rapid enumeration, consistently with the belief that Daniel then lived in Babylon, and that he occupied the position, and rendered the services, which it may be supposed from the account in this book he would render. In such a rapid enumeration, it cannot be supposed that the writer mentioned all the eminent men among the Hebrews, and therefore it is in no way remarkable that the name of Daniel should have been omitted. This is conceded even by Kirms. (See his work, *Commentatio Historico-Critica*, &c., p. 9.) (2.) The objection, if of any value, would prove that no such person as Daniel existed at that time, or even at any time previous to the age of the Son of Sirach ; for he did not mention these persons as authors of books, but as eminent persons—as distinguished not by their *writings*, but by their *lives*. But the existence of Daniel, as a historical personage, is as clear as that of any of the eminent men mentioned in the Jewish history, and is even conceded by the objectors themselves. (See § I. of this Introduction.) 3. As a matter of fact, the Son of Sirach has omitted the names of others whom he would be at least as *likely* to refer to as the name of Daniel. He has wholly omitted the name of Ezra. Would not his agency be as likely to occur to such a writer as that of Daniel ? He has omitted the names of Mordecai and Esther— personages whose agency would be as likely to be remembered in such a connection as that of Daniel. He has omitted also the whole of the minor prophets ; for the passage in ch. xlix. 10, which in the common version makes mention of them, is shown by Bretschneider (*in loc.*) to be clearly spurious, it having been copied verbatim from ch. xlvi. 12, with merely the substitution of the words " the twelve prophets" for the word " their." (See Prof. Stuart, *Com.* p. 463.) How can such an omission be accounted for, if the objection derived from the omission of the name of Daniel has any force?   And if the mere *silence* of the Son of Sirach be allowed to be an argument against the existence of prominent persons in the Jewish history, and the genuineness of the books which they wrote, who will determine the limit to which the objection will go ?   How small a portion of the patriarchs and prophets—how small a portion of the writings of the Old Testament would be spared! And, after all, why should so much weight be allowed to the mere silence of the Son of Sirach—an author comparatively unknown—as to set aside the positive testimony of all antiquity, and change the faith of the world ?

§ III.—CONTINUATION OF THE ARGUMENT FOR THE GENUINENESS AND
AUTHENTICITY OF THE BOOK OF DANIEL.

B. *Positive Proofs of its Genuineness and Authenticity.*

Having thus examined at length the objections which have been made to the genuineness and authenticity of the book of Daniel, I proceed now to notice the positive proofs that it was written at the time when it is alleged to have been, and by the author whose name it bears. This need not detain us long; for if the objections which are made to the genuineness of the book are not well founded, there will be little difficulty in showing that the common sentiment in the church in regard to its authorship and authenticity is correct.   It has undeniably for a long time had a place in the sacred canon ; it has been received by the Christian church at all times as a sacred book, on the same level with the other inspired books; it has had a place among the books regarded by the Jews as inspired; and if it cannot be *displaced* from the position which it has so long occupied, the conclusion would seem to be fair that that is its proper position. We have seen, in the previous discussion, that it was ranked by Josephus among the prophetic books; that it was held in high estimation among the Jews as one of their sacred books; that the canon of Scripture was closed some four hundred years before the time of the Saviour; and that, from the nature of the case, it would have been impossible to foist a book of doubtful origin, or an acknowledged fiction, into that canon in a later age.

In looking now at the *positive* evidence of the genuineness and canonical authority of the book, the only points that are really necessary to be made out are two : that it is the work of one author, and that that author was the Daniel of the captivity. If these two points can be established, its right to a place in the canon will be easily demonstrated. My object, then, will be to establish these two points, and then to show how, if these points are admitted, it follows that the book is inspired, and has a right to a place in the canon.

I. It is the work of one author. That is, it is not made up of fragments from different hands,- and composed at different times. It is a book by itself, every part of which is entitled to credit if any part of it is, and entitled to the same credit on the ground of being the composition of the same author.

The *evidence* of this lies in such circumstances as the following :—

(1.) It is apparent on the face of the book that the design is to represent it as the production of one author. If the book is a forgery, this was no doubt the intention of its author; if it is genuine, it was of course the design. No one, on reading the book, it is presumed, could fail to perceive that the design of the author was to leave the impression that it is the work of one hand, and that it was intended to represent what occurred in the lifetime of one man, and that one man had committed it to writing. This is apparent, because the same name occurs throughout ; because there is substantially one series of transactions; because the transactions are referred to as occurring in one place—Babylon; and because the same languages, customs, usages, and times are referred to. All the *internal* marks which can go to demonstrate that any work is by one hand would be found to be applicable to this; and all the *external* marks will be found also to agree with this supposition.

There are two things, indeed, to be admitted, which have been relied on by some to prove that the work is the composition of different authors.

(*a*) The one is, that it is divided into two parts : the one (ch. i.-vi.), in the main historical ; the other (ch. vii.-xii.), in the main prophetical. But this is no argument against the identity of the authorship, for the same intermingling of history with prophecy occurs in most of the prophetic books; and it is no objection that these occur in separate continuous portions, instead of being irregularly intermingled. In fact, the same thing occurs in Isaiah, where the first part (ch. i.-xxxix.), is made up, in a considerable degree, of historic allusions mingled with prophecy; and where the second part (ch. xl.-lxvi.), is wholly prophetic. Besides, any one must admit, that on the supposition that Daniel was the sole author of the book, nothing would be more natural than this very arrangement. What objection could there be to the supposition that one part of his book might relate to historic incidents mainly— though even these have a strong prophetic character—and that the other should be composed of prophecies? What would there be in his condition or character that would forbid such a supposition?

(*b*) The other circumstance is, that, between these two parts, there is a change in the *person* of the writer; that in the first portion (ch. i.-vi.), he uses the third person when speaking of Daniel, and in the other (ch. vii.-xii.), the first person. This is, in the main, true, though it is true also that in the second part the third person is sometimes used when speaking of himself, ch. vii. 1 ; x. 1. But in regard to this it may be observed (1.) That it is no uncommon thing for an author to speak of himself in the third person. This is uniformly done by Cæsar in his *Commentaries*, and this fact is never urged now as an argument against the genuineness of his work. (2.) This is often done by the prophets. See Isa. ii. 1; vii. 3; xiii. 1; Ezek. i. 3. So Hosea, throughout the first chapter of his book, speaks uniformly of himself in the third person, and in ch. ii. and iii. in the first person; and so Amos, ch. vii. 1, 2, 4, 5, 7, 8, speaks of himself in the first person, and again, vers. 12, 14, in the third person. It may be added that it is the uniform method, also, of the evangelist John, to speak of himself in the third person; and, in fact, this is so common in authors that it can constitute no argument against the genuineness of any particular book.

It may be observed also that, in general, those who have denied the genuineness and authenticity of the book of Daniel have admitted that it is the work of one author. This is expressly admitted by Lengerke, p. ci., who says, " The identity of the author appears from the unifor- mity of the plan, and the relations which the different parts bear to each other; that the historical and prophetic parts are related to each other; that there is a certain uniform gradation (Stufenfolge) of the oracles from the uncertain to the certain; that there is a remarkable similarity of ideas, images, and forms of speech; and that, in the respective parts of the Hebrew and Chaldee, there is great similarity of style." The same opinion is maintained by Dereser, Gesenius, Bleek, De Wette, Kirms, Hoffmann, and Hengstenberg; though nearly all of these authors suppose that it was written in the time of the Maccabees. They admit, however, that it is the work of a single author. Eichhorn and Bertholdt appear to have been the only authors of distinction who have denied it.

(2.) The identity of the book appears from the manner in which it

is written in respect to language. We have already seen that a part
of it is written in Hebrew, and a part in Chaldee. From the beginning to ch. ii. 4 it is Hebrew, then from ch. ii. 4 to the end of ch. vii.
it is Chaldee, and the remainder (ch. viii.–xii.), is Hebrew. Now, it
may be admitted, that if the historical part (ch. i.–vi.) had been wholly
in either of these languages, and the prophetical part (ch. vii.–xii.) had
been wholly in the other, it *might* have constituted a plausible argument
against the identity of the book. But the present arrangement is one
that furnishes no such argument. It cannot well be conceived that,
if the work were the production of two authors, one would begin his
portion in one language and end it in another, and that the other would
just reverse the process in regard to languages. Such an arrangement
would not be likely to occur in two independent compositions professedly treating of the same general subjects, and intended to be
palmed off as the work of one author. As it is, the arrangement is
natural, and easy to be accounted for; but the other supposition would
imply an artifice in composition which would not be likely to occur,
and which would be wholly unnecessary for any purpose which can be
imagined.

(3.) The identity of the book appears from the fact that it refers to
the same series of subjects; that the same great design is pursued
through the whole. Thus, in the two parts, though the first is mainly
historical and the last prophetical, there is a remarkable parallelism
between the predictions in ch. ii. and in ch. vii. The same great series
of events is referred to, though in different forms; and so throughout
the book, as remarked above in the quotation from Lengerke, we meet
with the same ideas, the same modes of speech, the same symbols, the
same imagery, the operations of the same mind, and the manifestation
of the same character in the authors. The Daniel of the first part is
the Daniel of the last; and, in this respect, the similarity is so great
as to leave the irresistible impression on the mind that he is *the* personage of the whole book, and that his own hand is apparent throughout.

(4.) The identity of the book appears from the fact that the objections made to it pertain alike to every part of it, and in reference to
the different parts are substantially the same. By referring to the
objections which have, in the previous section, been examined at length,
it will be seen that they all suppose the identity of the book, or that
they are drawn from the book considered as a whole, and not from any
particular part. Whatever difficulty there is in regard to the book
pertains to it as a whole, and difficulties of precisely the same kind lie
scattered through the entire volume. This fact proves that the book
has such an identity as appertains to one and the same author; and this
fact would not be likely to occur in a book that was made up of the
productions of different authors.

(5.) It may be added, that whenever Daniel is spoken of by Josephus,
by the Saviour, or by the early Christian writers, it is always done as

if the book was the production of one author.   Just such language is
used as would be used on the supposition that the book is the composition of one man; nor is there an intimation that there were two Daniels,
or that there was even any doubt about the identity of the authorship.
The fact that the book of Daniel is the production of one author
may be regarded as established; indeed, there is no ancient work, concerning which, the evidence is more direct and clear.

II. The second point to be made out is, that the author was the
Daniel of the captivity.   The evidences on this point will be adduced
in the order, not of *time*, but of what seems due to them in value and
importance.

(1.) I refer, first, to the testimony of the writer himself.   In ch.
vii. 28; viii. 1, 15, 27; ix. 2; x. 2; xii. 5, the writer speaks of himself as "*I Daniel;*" that is, the same Daniel whose history is given in
ch. i.   This cannot be, indeed, regarded as conclusive evidence; for
the forger of a book might insert the name of another person as the
author, and be constant in maintaining it to be so.   All that is affirmed
is, that this is *primâ facie* evidence, and is good evidence until it is set
aside by substantial reasons.   We assume this in regard to any book,
and the evidence should be admitted unless there are satisfactory reasons
for supposing that the name is assumed for purposes of deception.   It
cannot be doubted that the book bears on its face the *appearance* and
the *claim* of having been written by the Daniel of the captivity, and
that, in this respect, it is altogether such as it would be on that supposition.   There is certainly an air of simplicity, honesty, and sincerity
about it which we expect to find in a genuine production.

(2.) I refer, secondly, to the fact that the book of Daniel was
received into the canon of the Old Testament as an authentic work of
the Daniel of the captivity, and as entitled to a place among the inspired
books of Scripture.

(*a*) It has been shown above, that the canon of Scripture was regarded
as complete long before the time of the Maccabees; or that, according
to the testimony of Josephus, there were three classes of books among
the Hebrews, all regarded as *sacred* books, and all, in this respect, differing from certain *other* books which they had, as containing the record
of affairs subsequent to the time of Artaxerxes.   These classes of books
were known as the Law, the Prophets, and the "Kethubim"—the
"other writings," or the "Hagiographa;" and these books together
constituted what, in the New Testament, are called *the Scriptures*, or
Scripture: the *Scripture* in Mark xii. 10; xv. 28; Luke iv. 21; John
ii. 22; vii. 38, 42; x. 35; xix. 37; Rom. iv. 3; ix. 17; Gal. iii. 8, 22;
2 Tim. iii. 16; 1 Pet. ii. 6; 2 Pet. i. 20;—the *Scriptures* in Matt.
xxi. 42; xxii. 29; xxvi. 54; Luke xxiv. 27, 32, 45; John v. 39; Acts
xvii. 2, 11; xviii. 24, 28; Rom. i. 2; xv. 4; xvi. 26; 1 Cor. xv. 3, 4;
2 Tim. iii. 15; 2 Pet. iii. 16.   These constituted a *collection* of writings which were distinct from all others, and the use of the word

Scripture, or *Scriptures*, at once suggested them, and no others, to the mind.

(*b*) The book of Daniel was found in *that* list of writings, and would be suggested by that term as belonging to the general collection; that is, in order to adduce his authority, or to mention a prophecy *in* that book, it would be done as readily as a part of the Scriptures, and would be as well understood as in quoting a declaration of Moses or Isaiah. This is apparent (1) from the fact seen above, that Josephus must have regarded Daniel as having a rank among the Prophets; and (2), mainly, from the fact that Daniel has *always*, from the earliest knowledge which we have of the book, had a place in the canon. The book has *never*, so far as we have any knowledge, been placed among the apocryphal writings. It was evidently regarded by Josephus, speaking the common sentiment of his countrymen, as having a place in the canonical writings; it was *certainly* so regarded by the authors of the *Talmud*, though they assigned it a place in the third division, or Kethubim; it is expressly so mentioned by Jerome, by Melito, bishop of Sardis (A.D. 170), by Origen, by the Council of Laodicea (A.D. 360–364), by Cyril of Jerusalem (A.D. 350), by Gregory Nazianzen (A.D. 370), by Athanasius of Alexandria (A.D. 326), and by the author of the *Synopsis Scripturæ Sacræ*, who lived in the time of Athanasius. See Prof. Stuart on the Old Testament, Appendix. From that time onward it is needless to show that the book of Daniel has *always* had a place in the canon of Scripture, and been regarded as on a level with the other writings of the sacred volume: indeed, it has never had, so far as we have any historical information, any *other* place than that, but wherever known, and wherever mentioned, it has always been as a portion of the sacred writings.

(*c*) It is morally certain that it could not have been introduced into that canon if it was the work of a later age, and if it was not believed, at the time when the canon of the Old Testament was completed, or when the books of the Old Testament were collected and arranged, by whomsoever this was done, to have been the genuine work of Daniel. This point has been considered already. The Jews were the most cautious of all people in regard to their sacred books, and at an early period of their history the contending sects of the Pharisees and Sadducees arose, and from the very nature of their opinions, and the vigilance of the one against the other, it was impossible that a book could be introduced into the sacred canon which was not universally regarded as genuine and authentic. The exact period, indeed, when these sects arose has not been determined, and cannot now be; but it is put beyond a doubt that it was before the time of the Maccabees. Josephus first mentions them (*Ant.* xiii. 5, 9) under the high priest Jonathan (B.C. 159–144); but he mentions them, together with the Essenes, as sects already fully and definitely formed. Winer thinks that the spirit of Judaism, soon after the return from the exile, gave rise to a feeling which led to the formation of the party of the Pharisees; and that this very naturally called forth an opposition, which embodied itself in the party of the Sadducees. In the time of John Hyrcanus, nephew of Judas Maccabæus, Josephus speaks of the Pharisees as having such influence with the common people that "they would be believed even if they uttered anything against the king or high priest." The Sadducees were always opposed to them; always watched all their movements, opinions, and aims with jealousy; always contended with them for power, and always embodied in their own ranks no small part of the learning, the wealth, and the influence of the nation. The main subject of division between them was one that pertains to the very point before us. It was not the question about the existence of angel or spirit, or the question of predestination, as has been sometimes said, but it was *whether the Scriptures are to be regarded as the only rule of faith and practice.* The Pharisees insisted on the authority of tradition, and claimed that the oral or unwritten law was of equal authority with the written ; while the Sadducees rejected all traditions and ordinances of men not expressly sanctioned by the Scriptures. So Josephus says expressly : "Their custom was to regard nothing except the Laws [that is, the written Laws—the Old Testament]; for they reckon it as a virtue to dispute against the doctors in favour of the wisdom (σοφίας) which they follow."—*Ant.* xviii. 1, 4. Again, in *Ant.* xiii. 10, 6, he says. "The Pharisees inculcated many rules upon the people, received from the fathers, which are not written in the Law of Moses; and on this account the sect of the Sadducees reject them, alleging that those things are to be regarded as rules which are written " [in the Scriptures], " but that the traditions of the fathers are not to be observed."

The rise of these contending sects must, at all events, be referred to a time which preceded the Maccabees—the time when it is pretended by objectors that the book of Daniel was composed. But the moment when these two parties were formed, the *extent* of the Jewish Scriptures was, of course, a matter that was fully and permanently decided. It is impossible to suppose that the Sadducees would concede to their antagonists the right to introduce new books into the canon, or that a new book could be introduced without producing controversy. This would have been giving up the very point in dispute. No book could be introduced, or could be recognised as entitled to a place there, which was not acknowledged by both parties as having been written by a true prophet, and as being believed to be Divinely inspired. If the book of Daniel, then, was the work of that age, and was falsely attributed to the Daniel of the exile, it is impossible that it could have been introduced into the canon.

(*d*) It may be asked, in addition, why, if the book of Daniel was written in the time of the Maccabees, and was then introduced into the canon, the book of Ecclesiasticus, and other books of the Apocrypha, were not also introduced? If the book of Daniel was spurious, what was there that should entitle *that* to a place in the canon which could not have been urged in favour of the *Book of Wisdom*, or of some of the other books of the Apocrypha? Yet these books never found a place in the canon, and were never regarded as belonging to it; and there was, therefore, some reason why Daniel had a place there which could not be applied to them. The only reason must have been that the book of Daniel was regarded as the genuine work of the Daniel of the exile, and therefore written by a prophet before the times of inspiration ceased.

(3.) I refer, thirdly, in proof of the genuineness and authenticity of the book of Daniel, to the New Testament.

Daniel is *expressly* mentioned in the New Testament but once, and that is by the Saviour, in Matt. xxiv. 15, and in the parallel passage in Mark xiii. 14. In the former passage the Saviour says, " When ye, therefore, shall see the abomination of desolation, spoken of by Daniel the prophet, stand in the holy place (whoso readeth let him understand), then let them which be in Judea flee into the mountains." In the latter place—the same passage reported by another writer—" But when ye shall see the abomination of desolation spoken of by Daniel the prophet, standing where it ought not (let him that readeth understand), then let them which be in Judea," &c.

These, it must be admitted, are the only places in the New Testament where Daniel is directly quoted, though it cannot be denied that there are others which seem to imply that the book was known, and that it was intended to be referred to. Compare the argument in Hengstenberg, *Authentie des Daniel*, pp. 273-277. The passages of this nature referred to by De Wette, § 255, (3), and commonly relied on, are the following :—

1 Pet. i. 10, scq., compared with Dan. xii. 8, seq.
2 Thess. ii. 3.   „   „ vii. 8, 25.
1 Cor. vi. 2.   „   „ vii. 22.
Heb. xi. 33.   „   „ vi.

In regard to these passages, however, it may be doubted of some of them (2 Thess. ii. 3; 1 Cor. vi. 2) whether there is in them any designed allusion to *any* prophet of the Old Testament; and of 1 Pet. i. 10, that the allusion is so general that it cannot be demonstrated that Peter had his eye on Daniel rather than on the other prophets, or that he necessarily included Daniel in the number; and of the other passage (Heb. xi. 33), " Stopped the mouths of lions," that, from anything that appears in the passage, it cannot be demonstrated that Paul meant to refer to Daniel, or, if he did, all that is there implied *may* have been founded on a traditional report of Daniel, and it cannot be adduced as proof that he meant to refer to the *book* of Daniel. It cannot be denied that there is, in some respects, a very strong resemblance between the book of Daniel and the book of Revelation, and that the book of Daniel was familiar to the author of the Apocalypse; but still, as Daniel is not expressly quoted or referred to, it cannot be demonstrated with certainty that John meant to recognise the book as inspired. The argument, then, rests mainly, if not exclusively, on the testimony of the Saviour.

And here it is proper to say that, in this country, we may lay out of view, as not worthy of attention, the remark of De Wette, that "Christ neither *would* (*wollte*) nor *could* (*konnte*), from the nature of the case, be *a critical authority*," § 255, (3). In this argument it must be assumed, that if a book of the Old Testament can be shown to have *his* sanction, it is to be regarded as belonging to the inspired canon. Or, to state the proposition in a form which cannot, on any account, be regarded as objectionable, the point of inquiry is, to ascertain whether Christ did, or did not, regard the book of Daniel as belonging to the canon of the inspired writings, and as coming within the class which he, in John v. 39, and elsewhere, calls "the Scriptures."

Now, in regard to this reference to Daniel by the Saviour, considered as an argument for the genuineness and authenticity of the book, the following remarks may be made :—

(*a*) There is a distinct recognition of Daniel as an historical personage—as a man. This is plain on the face of the quotation, for he refers to him as he would to Moses, Isaiah, or Jeremiah. No one can believe that he regarded Daniel as a fictitious or fabulous personage, or that, in this respect, he meant to speak of him as different from the most eminent of the ancient prophets. Indeed, in all the doubts that have been expressed about the genuineness of the book of Daniel, it has never been maintained that the Lord Jesus did not mean to be understood as referring to Daniel as a real historical personage.

(*b*) He refers to him as a prophet : "When ye shall see the abomi· nation of desolation, spoken of by Daniel *the prophet*"—τοῦ προφήτου. This word he uses evidently, in its ordinary signification, as meaning one who predicted future events, and as entitled to a rank among the true prophets. It is the very word which Josephus, in a passage quoted above, employs in relation to Daniel, and is manifestly used in the same sense. The Saviour assigns him no inferior place among the prophets ; regards him as having uttered a true prediction, or a prediction which was to be fulfilled at a period subsequent to the time when he was then speaking ; and refers to him, in this respect, as he would have done to any one of the ancient inspired writers.

(*c*) He refers to him as the author of *a book*, and, by his manner of speaking of him, and by the quotation which he makes, gives his sanction to some well-known book of which he regarded Daniel as the author. This, which if true settles the question about the testimony of the Saviour, is apparent from the following considerations :—(1.) From the very use of the word *prophet* here, it is evident, on the face of the passage, that he refers to him in the use of this word, not as having *spoken* the prediction, but as having *recorded* it ; that the language is used as it would have been of any other of the "prophets," or of those who had this appellation *because* they had made a record predicting future events. It is clear that the word among the Jews had so far a technical signification, that this would at once be suggested on its use. (2.) Because he quotes the *language* found in the book of Daniel—βδέλυγμα τῆς ἐρημώσεως. This very phrase occurs in the Greek translation, in ch. xii. 11, and a similar expression (βδέλυγμα τῶν ἐρημώσεων) occurs in ch. ix. 27 ; and another similar expression (βδέλυγμα ἠφανισμένον) occurs in ch. xi. 31. The phrase, therefore, may be regarded as belonging to Daniel, not only by the express mention of his name, but by the fact that it does not elsewhere occur in the sacred Scriptures. (3.) The same thing is apparent from the parenthetical expression, " Whoso readeth, let him understand." The point of this remark is in the word " *readeth*," as referring to some written record. There has been, indeed, much difference of opinion in regard to this phrase, whether it is to be considered as the command of the Saviour that they who read the words of Daniel should pay attention to its meaning; or whether it is the remark of the evangelist, designed to call attention to the meaning of the prophecy, and to the words of the Saviour. In my notes on the passage in Matt. xxiv. 15, the opinion is expressed that these are the words of the evangelist. It is proper now to say, that on a more careful consideration of that passage, this seems to me to be very doubtful; but whether correct or not, it would only vary the force of the argument by making Matthew the speaker instead of the Saviour. It would still be an inspired testimony that, at the time when Matthew wrote, there was a book which was understood to be the production of Daniel, and that it was the intention of the evangelist to rank him among the prophets, and to call particular attention to what he had *written*. The interpretation of the parenthesis, it must be admitted, however, is so uncertain that no argument can be founded on it to demonstrate that *Christ* meant to call attention to the words of Daniel ; but the passage does prove that such words to be " *read*" were found in the book, and that in order to determine their exact sense there was need of close attention. Olshausen agrees with the interpretation of the parenthesis expressed in my notes on Matthew, regarding it as the declaration of the evangelist. The older expositors generally regard the parenthesis as the words of the Saviour ; more recent ones generally as the words of the evangelist. The former opinion is defended by Hengstenberg.—*Authen.* pp. 259, 260.

Whichever interpretation is adopted, it seems clear, from the above remarks, that the Saviour meant to refer to Daniel as a real historical personage, and to a well-known book bearing his name, as a genuine production of the Daniel of the exile. If so, then the testimony of Christ is expressly in favour of its canonical authority.

(4.) I refer, fourthly, in proof of the genuineness and authenticity of the book, or in proof that it was written by the Daniel of the captivity, to the fact that it had an existence *before* the times of the Maccabees, and was referred to then as among the books having a Divine authority. This might, indeed, be regarded as already demonstrated, if it had a place in the canon of Scripture, as I have endeavoured to show that it had ; but there is other proof of this that will go further to confirm the point. It will be recollected that one of the main positions of those who deny its genuineness is, that it was written in the time of the Maccabees by some one who assumed the name of Daniel. The point now to be made out is, that there is direct evidence that it had an existence *before* that time. In proof of this, I refer,

(*a*) To the testimony of Josephus. His statement is found in his *Antiquities*, b. xi. ch. viii., in the account which he gives of the interview between Alexander and the high-priest Jaddua, in Jerusalem : "And when he went up into the temple he offered sacrifices to God, according to the high-priest's directions ; and magnificently treated both the high-priest and the priests. And when the book of Daniel was shown to him, wherein Daniel declared that one of the Greeks should destroy the empire of the Persians, he supposed that himself was the person intended. And as he was then glad, he dismissed the multitude for the present ; but the next day he called them to him, and bade them ask what favours they pleased of him." The genuineness of this narrative has been examined at length by Hengstenberg, *Authen.* pp. 277–288. In reference to that testimony the following remarks may be made :—(1.) The authority of Josephus is entitled to great credit, and his testimony may be regarded as good proof of a historical fact. (2.) There is here express mention of "the book of Daniel" as a book existing in the time of Alexander, and as shown to him, in which he was so manifestly referred to that he at once recognised the allusion. The passages referred to are the following: ch. vii. 6 ; viii. 3–8, 21, 22 ; xi. 3, 4. For the evidence that these passages relate to Alexander, the reader is referred to the notes on them respectively. It is clear that if they were read to Alexander, and if he regarded them as applying to himself, he could not doubt that his victory over the Persians would be certain. (3.) There is every probability in the circumstances of the case, that, if the Jewish high-priest was in possession of the book of Daniel at that time, with so clear a reference to a Grecian conqueror, he would show those passages to him, for nothing would be more likely to appease his wrath, and to obtain protection for the Jews in Jerusalem, and for those who were scattered in the lands where it was manifest that he purposed to extend his conquests. And (4) it may be presumed that, as a consequence of this, Alexander would grant to the Jews all that Josephus says that he did. The best way of accounting for the favour which Josephus says he did show to the Jews, is the fact which he states, that these predictions were read to him announcing his success in his projected wars. Thus Josephus says, as a consequence of these predictions being shown to him (*Ant. ut supra*), "And as he was then glad, he dismissed the multitude for the present; but the next day he called them to him, and bade them ask what favours they pleased of him. Accordingly the high-priest desired that they might enjoy the laws of their forefathers, and might pay no tribute the seventh year. This was readily granted. And when they entreated that he would permit the Jews in Babylon and Media to enjoy their own laws also, he willingly promised to do hereafter what they desired. And when he said to the multitude, that if any of them would enlist themselves in his army, on the condition that they should continue under the laws of their forefathers, and live according to them, he was willing to take them with him, many were ready to accompany him in his wars."

There is intrinsic probability that this account in Josephus is true, and the main historical facts, as stated by Josephus, are vouched for by other writers. "That Alexander was personally in Judea, Pliny testifies, *Hist. Nat.* xii. 26. That Palestine voluntarily surrendered to him is testified in Arrian's *History of Alexander*, ii. 25. That he was met by the high-priest and his brethren dressed in turbans, is testified by Justin (xi. 10), who says: Obvios cum *infulis* multos orientis regis habuit."—(See Stuart on Daniel, p. 408.)

There is, therefore, the highest degree of probability that this narrative of Josephus is true; and if this is a correct historical narrative, then it is clear that the book of Daniel, containing, in respect to the conquests of Alexander, the same passages that are now applied to him, was in existence long before the time of the Maccabees. This occurred in 332 B.C.; and if this account is correct, then "the book of Daniel, as it now exists, was current among the Jews as a sacred book at least some 168–170 years before the time when, according to the critics of the sceptical school, the book could be written."

(b) The same thing may be inferred from a passage in the Apocrypha. In 1 Macc. ii. 49–68, the dying Mattathias is said, in an exhortation to his sons to be "zealous for the law, and to give their lives for the covenant of their fathers," to have referred to the ancient examples of piety and fortitude among the Hebrews, mentioning, among others, Abraham, "found faithful in temptation;" Joseph, who "in a time of distress kept the commandments, and was made lord of Egypt;" Joshua, who, "for fulfilling the word was made a judge in Israel; Caleb, who for "bearing witness before the congregation received the heritage of the land;" David, Elias, Ananias, Azarias, and Misael, and then (ver. 60) he mentions Daniel in these words: "Daniel, for his innocency, was delivered from the mouth of lions. Here is an evident reference to the history of Daniel as we have it (ch. vi.); and although it is true that such an account *might* be handed down by tradition, and that such a reference as this might be made if there were nothing more than mere tradition, yet it is also true that this is such a reference as would be made if the book were in existence then as it is now, and true also that the other references are, mostly at least, to written accounts of the worthies who are there mentioned. If there were no positive evidence to the contrary, the *primâ facie* proof in this quotation would be, that Mattathias referred to some well-known written record of Daniel.

(*c*) The fact of the existence of the book before the time of the Maccabees, may be inferred from its translation by the authors of the Septuagint. The fact that the book was translated with the other Hebrew and Chaldee books of the Old Testament, is a proof that it had an existence at an early period, and that it was worthy, in the estimation of the translators, of a place among the sacred books of the Jews.

(5.) I refer, fifthly, in proof of the genuineness and authenticity of the book, to the *language* in which it is written. We have already seen that it is written partly in Hebrew and partly in Chaldee. The argument to which I refer from this fact, in proof of the genuineness of the book, consists of the following things :—

(*a*) The language is such as it might be expected it *would* be on the supposition that Daniel was the real author. Daniel was by birth a Hebrew. He was probably born in Jerusalem, and remained there until he was about twelve or fifteen years of age (see § 1.), when he was removed to Babylon. In his youth, therefore, he had used the Hebrew language, and his early education had been in that language. In Babylon he was instructed in the language and literature of the Chaldeans, and probably became as familiar with the language of the Chaldeans, as he was with his native tongue. Both these languages he undoubtedly spoke familiarly, and probably used them with the same degree of ease. That the book, therefore, is written in both these languages accords with this representation; and, if written by one man, it must have been composed by one who was thus familiar with both. It is true that the fact that Daniel could thus speak the two languages is in itself no proof that *he* was the author, but the fact that it was so written accords with the circumstances of the case. His early training, and the fact that the book is written in the two languages with which it is known he was familiar, furnish a coincidence, such as would occur on the supposition that he was the author; and a coincidence, like those adverted to by Dr. Paley in his argument in favour of the genuineness of the New Testament (*Horæ Paulinæ*), the more valuable because it is clear that it was undesigned.

But *why* the book was written in two languages is a question that is not so easily solved, and which it is not necessary to solve. No reason is given in the book itself; none appears from anything in the design of the portions written respectively in Hebrew and Chaldee. There is nothing apparent in these portions of the book which would lead us to suppose that one was designed to be read by the Hebrews and the other by the Chaldeans, or, as it is often affirmed (comp. Horne, *Introduction*, vol. iv. p. 193), that one portion " treats of the Chaldean or Babylonish affairs." There is no particular " treatment" of the Chaldean or Babylonish affairs, for example, in the seventh chapter, where the Chaldean portion ends, any more than in the eighth, where the Hebrew is resumed, and, in fact, no internal reason can be assigned why one of those chapters should have been written in Chaldee or Hebrew rather than the other or both. The same remark is applicable to the first and second chapters, and indeed to every portion of the book; and the reason which induced the author to write different portions of it in different languages must be for ever unknown. This does not, however, affect the force of the argument which I am suggesting.

(*b*) The circumstance now adverted to may be regarded as of some force in showing that it is not probable that the book was forged, and especially that it was not forged in the time of the Maccabees. It is an unusual thing for a man to attempt to forge a book in two languages; and though cases have occurred in great numbers where a man could so familiarly write in two languages that he could do this, yet this would not be likely to occur in the time of the Maccabees. It was probably a very uncommon thing at that time that a man was so familiar with the two languages that he could write readily in each, for there are no writings extant in either of these languages in that age; and it is well known that the Hebrew language became greatly adulterated by foreign admixtures soon after the return from the exile, and never regained the purity which it had in the early periods of its history.

(*c*) To these considerations it may be added, that if the book was written in the times of the Maccabees, or at a later period, there is every reason to suppose that it would have been written in the *Greek* language. This appears from the fact that all the books which we have of that age are written in Greek, and that the Greek at that time had become so prevalent that it would be natural that it should be used. Thus all the books of the Apocrypha, and those parts which profess to be additions to the book of Daniel, as the Song of the Three Holy Children, the History of Susanna, and the Destruction of Bel and the Dragon, are found only in Greek, and there is no evidence that they were ever written in Hebrew or Chaldee. (See § IV. of this Introduction.) If the book of Daniel itself was written in that age, why was not it also written in Greek? Or why should the book, as we have it now, if it were a forged book, have been written in Hebrew and Chaldee, and those other portions, which the author seems to have designed should be regarded as belonging to the book, have been written in Greek? There are none of the books of the Apocrypha of which there is any evidence that they were written in Hebrew or Chaldee. The only one of those books for which such a claim has been set up is the book of Ecclesiasticus. That is affirmed by the Son of Sirach (see the Prologue) to have been written originally by his grandfather in Hebrew, and to have been translated by himself into Greek. But the Hebrew original is not in existence; nor is there any certain evidence that it ever was. It is an additional circumstance, showing that a book of the Maccabæan age would have been written in Greek, that even Berosus, who was himself a Chaldean, wrote his history of Chaldea in Greek. (See Intro. to ch. iv. § 1.)

To all these considerations, which seem to me of themselves to settle the question, I may be permitted to add a very ingenious argument of Prof. Stuart, in his own words; an argument which, I think, no one can answer. (*Com. on Daniel*, pp. 438–449) :—

"The accurate knowledge which the writer of the book of Daniel displays, of ancient history, manners, and customs, and Oriental Babylonish peculiarities, shows that he must have lived at or near the time and place when and where the book leads us to suppose that he lived.

"A great variety of particulars might be adduced to illustrate and confirm this proposition; but I aim only to introduce the leading and more striking ones.

"(*a*) In drawing the character of Nebuchadnezzar, and giving some brighter spots to it, Daniel agrees with hints of the like nature in Jer. xlii. 12; xxxix. 11. If a writer in the Maccabæan age had undertaken, as is asserted, to symbolize Antiochus Epiphanes by drawing the character of Nebuchadnezzar, it would be difficult to conceive how he would have been persuaded to throw into the picture these mellower tints.

"(*b*) In drawing the portrait of Belshazzar, the last king of Babylon, Daniel agrees very strikingly with Xenophon. In this latter writer, he appears as a debauched, pleasure-loving, cruel, and impious monarch. *Cyrop.* (iv. v.) represents him as killing the son of Gobryas, one of his nobles, because he had anticipated him, while hunting, in striking down the game. When the father remonstrated, he replied, that he was sorry only that he had not killed him also. In lib. v. 2, he is styled *haughty* and *abusive*. One of his concubines spoke in praise of Gadates, a courtier, as a handsome man. The king invited him to a banquet, and there caused him to be seized and unmanned. It is all in keeping with this, when he appears in Dan. v. In his intoxication and pride, he orders the sacred vessels of the Jerusalem temple to be profaned; and Daniel is so disgusted with his behaviour, that he does not, as in the case of Nebuchadnezzar (ch. iv.) disclose any strong sympathy for him, but denounces unqualified destruction. Xenophon calls this king ανόσιος.

"(*c*) Cyaxares (*Darius the Mede*) in Dan. is drawn by Xenophon as devoted to wine and women (*Cyrop.*. iv.) In Dan. vi. 18, it is mentioned of Darius, as an extraordinary thing, that after he saw the supposed ruin of Daniel, he neither approached his table nor his harem. Xenophon speaks of him as indolent, averse to business, of small understanding, vain, without self-restraint, and easily thrown into tears ; and then, moreover, as subject to violent outbursts of passion (iv. v.) In Daniel he appears as wholly governed by his courtiers; they flatter his vanity, and obtain the decree intended to destroy Daniel. Daniel's supposed impending fate throws him into lamentation, and he betakes himself to fasting and vigils; and when he learns the safety of his Hebrew servant, he sentences his accusers, with all their wives and children, to be thrown into the lions' den, vi. 18–24.

"Now as there was no history of these times and kings among the Hebrews, and none among the Greeks that gave any minute particulars, in what way did a *late* writer of the book of Daniel obtain his knowledge?

"(*d*) When in Dan. i. 21, it is stated that Daniel continued until the *first year of Cyrus*, without any specification when this was, the writer seems plainly to suppose his readers to be familiar with this period. It is true, that from the book of Ezra a knowledge of that time, the period of Jewish liberation, might be gained; but the familiar manner of the reference to it indicates that the writer feels himself to be addressing those who were cognizant of matters pertaining to the period.

"(*e*) In ch. i. and ii. we are told that *king* Nebuchadnezzar besieged Jerusalem, took it, and sent Daniel and his companions to Babylon. There they were taken under the care and instruction of learned men among the Chaldees, and trained up for the personal service of the king. The period of training was *three* years. At the close of this, they were examined and approved by the king; and soon after this occurred Nebuchadnezzar's first dream, which Daniel was summoned to interpret. This dream is said to be in the *second* year of Nebuchadnezzar's reign. Here, then, is an apparent *parachronism*. How could Daniel have been taken and sent into exile by *king* Nebuchadnezzar, educated *three* years, and then be called to interpret a dream in the *second* year of Nebuchadnezzar's reign? The solution of this difficulty I have already exhibited in an *Exc.* at the end of the commentary on ch. i. I need not repeat the process here. It amounts simply to this, viz., that Nebuchadnezzar is called *king* in Dan. i. 1, *by way of anticipation;* a usage followed by Kings, Chronicles, and Jeremiah. Before he quitted Judea he became actual king by the death of his father; and the Jews, in speaking of him as commanding the invading army, always called him *king*. But in Dan ii. 1, Nebuchadnezzar is spoken of in the Chaldee mode of reference to his actual reign. This leaves some *four* years for Daniel's discipline and service. But to those who were not familiar with the Jewish mode of speaking in respect to Nebuchadnezzar, it would naturally and inevitably appear like a parachronism, or even a downright contradiction of dates. Yet the writer has not a word of explanation to make. He evidently feels as if all were plain to his readers (as doubtless it was). But a writer of the Maccabæan age would plainly have seen and avoided the difficulty.

"(*f*) In Dan. v. 30, it is stated that Belshazzar was slain; but not a word is said descriptive of the manner in which this was brought about, nor even that the city of Babylon was taken. The next verse simply mentions that Darius the Mede took the kingdom. All this brevity seems to imply, that the writer supposed those whom he was addressing to be cognizant of the whole matter. Had he lived in the Maccabæan age, would he have written thus respecting events so interesting and important? In like manner Daniel (x. 1, *seq.*) tells us, that in the third year of Cyrus, Daniel mourned and fasted three weeks. But not a word is said to explain the occasion of this peculiar and extraordinary humiliation. If we turn now to Ezra iv. 1-5, we shall find an account of a combination among the enemies of the Jews to hinder the building of the city walls, which was successful, and which took place in the *third* year of Cyrus' reign, *i.e.*, the same year with Daniel's mourning. There can scarcely be a doubt that this was the occasion of that mourning; for certainly it was no ritual, legal, or ordinary fast. The manner now in which ch. x. is written plainly imports that the writer feels no need of giving explanations. He takes it for granted that his readers will at once perceive the whole extent of the matter. But how, in the Maccabæan age, could a writer suppose this knowledge within the grasp of his readers?

" (*g*) In Dan. ii., the dream is interpreted as indicating the destruction of the Babylonish empire by the Medo-Persians. Abydenus, in his singular account of Nebuchadnezzar's last hours (given on p. 122 above), represents this king as wrapped into a kind of prophetic ecstasy, and in this state as declaring his fearful anticipations of the Medo-Persian conquest. How came such a coincidence?

" (*h*) In Dan. iv. 30, Nebuchadnezzar is introduced as saying, Is not this *great* Babylon which I have built? Recent critics allege this to be a mistake. 'Ctesias,' they tell us, 'attributes the building of Babylon to Semiramis (*Bähr Ctes.* p. 397, *seq.*), and Herodotus (i. 181, *seq.*) ascribes it to Semiramis and Nitocris.' My answer is, that Ctesias follows the Assyrian tradition, and Herodotus the Persian. But Berosus and Abydenus give us the *Babylonian* account; which is, that Nebuchadnezzar added much to the old town, built a magnificent royal palace, surrounded the city with new walls, and adorned it with a vast number of buildings. Well and truly might he say that he had built it, meaning (as he plainly did) its magnificent structures. It was not any falsehood in his declaration which was visited with speedy chastisement, but the pride and vain-glory of his boasting gave offence to Heaven. But how came a writer of the *Maccabæan* period to know of all this matter? No Greek writer has told anything about Nebuchadnezzar or his doings. To Berosus and Abydenus, a writer of the Maccabæan age could hardly have had access. Herodotus and Ctesias told another and different story. Whence, then, did he get his knowledge of the part which Nebuchadnezzar had acted in the building of the city? And yet the account of it in Daniel accords entirely with both Berosus and Abydenus. Even the account of Nebuchadnezzar's madness is virtually adverted to in these writers: see above, p. 122, *seq.*

" (*i*) In Dan. v. 10-12 is introduced a personage styled the *queen,* not because she was Belshazzar's wife, for the latter was already in the banqueting-room (v. 3, 23), but probably because she was a queen-mother. Not improbably this was the Nitocris of Herodotus; and Berosus, *Diod. Sic.* (ii. 10), and Alex. Polyhist (in *Chron. Armen.*), all say that Nitocris was a wife of Nebuchadnezzar. If so, she might have had much to do with ornamenting the city both before and after Nebuchadnezzar's death; and this will account for the great deference paid to her by Belshazzar, as related in ch. v. 10–12. It is one of those accidental circumstances which speaks much for the accordance of Daniel with the narrations of history. It is, moreover, a circumstance about which a writer of the Maccabæan age cannot well be supposed to have known anything.

"And since we are now examining ch. v., it may be proper to note another circumstance. We have seen, that at *Babylon* the wives and concubines of the king were, without any scruple, present at the feast. But in Esth. i. we have an account of the positive refusal of queen Vashti to enter the guest-chamber of Ahasuerus. In other words, this was, and is, against the general custom of the East. How came a writer of the Maccabæan period to know this distinction between the customs of Babylon and of Persia? The author of the Sept. Version, a contemporary of this period, knows so little of such a matter that he even leaves out the passage respecting the presence of women at the feast. Why? Plainly because he thought this matter would be deemed incredible by his readers. In Xen. *Cyrop.* (v. 2, 28,) is an account of a feast of Belshazzar, where his concubines are represented as being present. Not only so, but we have elsewhere, in Greek and Roman writers, abundant testimony to usages of this kind, in their accounts of the Babylonish excesses. But how comes it about, that the forger of the book of Daniel, whose familiarity with those writings is not credible, should know so much more of Babylonish customs than the Sept. translator?

"(*j*) Of the manner in which Babylon was taken, and Belshazzar slain, Daniel has not given us any minute particulars. But he has told us that the *Medes* and *Persians* acquired the dominion of Babylon (v. 28), and that *Darius the Mede* succeeded Belshazzar. The manner in which he announces the slaying of Belshazzar (v. 30) shows that the event was altogether sudden and unexpected. Now Herodotus (I. 190) and Xenophon (*Cyrop.* VII.) have told us, that Cyrus diverted the waters of the Euphrates, and marched in its channel into the heart of Babylon, and took the city in a single night. They tell us that the Babylonians were in the midst of feast-rioting that night, and were unprepared to meet the enemy, who were not expected in the city. How entirely all this harmonizes with Daniel is quite plain. Gesenius himself acknowledges that this is *sehr auffallend*, i.e., very striking. He has even acknowledged, in a moment of more than usual candour and concession, that Isa. xliv. 27 has a definite reference to the stratagem of Cyrus in taking the city. In connection with a prediction concerning Cyrus, Jehovah is here represented as saying to the deep, '*Be dry;* yea, I will *dry up thy rivers.*' So in Jer. l. 38, 'A drought is upon her waters, and they shall be dried up;' and again, li. 36, 'I will dry up her sea [river], and make her springs dry.' If the book of Daniel is to be cast out as a late production, and as spurious, because it seems to predict the sudden capture of Babylon in one night, by the Medes and Persians, what is to be done with these passages of Isaiah and Jeremiah? Even the Neologists, although they maintain a later composition in respect to those parts of the prophets which have just been cited, still do not venture to place that composition *post eventum.* If not, then there is *prediction;* and this, too, of a strange event, and one so minute and specific, that *guessing* is out of question. If, then, Isaiah and Jeremiah *predicted,* why might not a Daniel also *predict?*

"Another circumstance there is also in which all three of these prophets are agreed. According to Dan. v., Babylon was feasting and carousing on the night of its capture. In Isa. xxi. 5, we have the like: 'Prepare the table. . . . . Eat, drink; arise, ye princes, and anoint the shield,' *i.e.*, rise up from your feast-table, and make ready for assault. So Jer. li. 39, 'I will prepare their feasts, and I will make them drunken, that they may rejoice, and sleep a perpetual sleep, and not wake, saith the Lord.'

"If now a writer of the Maccabæan period had undertaken to write the story of the capture of Babylon, is there any probability that he would have hit upon all these circumstances, so peculiar and so concordant? Conversant with the native Greek historians we cannot well suppose him to have been; for Greek literature was regarded as reproachful by the Jews of that period, and even down to the time of Josephus, who speaks strongly on this subject.

"(*k*) Daniel (v. 30) relates the *violent death* of Belshazzar when the city was taken. In this particular he is vouched for by Xenophon, *Cyrop.* VII. v. 24, 30. So do Isa. xiv. 18—20 ; xxi. 2—9 ; Jer. l. 29—35 ; li. 57, declare the same thing. But here Berosus and Abydenus dissent, both of them representing the Babylonish king as surrendering, and as being treated humanely by Cyrus. How comes it, if the forger of the book of Daniel wrote about B.C. 160, that he did not consult those authors on Babylonish affairs? Or if (as was surely the fact in regard to most Jewish writers at that period) he had no familiarity with Greek authors, then where did he obtain his views about the death of Belshazzar? For a full discussion of this matter, see p. 147, *seq.*, above. There can scarcely be a doubt that the account of Daniel and Xenophon is the true one.

"Xenophon relates, that the party which assailed the palace, who were led on by Gobryas and Gadates, fell upon the guards who were carousing, πρὸς φῶς πολύ, *i.e.*, *at broad daylight* :* (*Cyrop.* VII. 5, 27). In other words, the Persians did not accomplish their onset upon the palace until the night was far spent, and daylight was dawning. How now are matters presented in the book of Daniel ? First, there is the feast (of course in the evening); then the quaffing of wine; then the handwriting on the wall; then the assembling of all the Magi to interpret it; then the introduction of Daniel, whose interpretation was followed by his being clothed with the *insignia* of nobility, and being proclaimed the third ruler in the kingdom. All this must of course have taken up most of the night. Here, then, one writer confirms and illustrates the other. A pseudo-Daniel would not have risked such a statement as the true one has made ; for, at first view, the matter seems incredible, and it is charged upon the book as such. But Xenophon has freed it from all difficulties.

"Daniel (v.) also declares that Belshazzar was a son, *i.e.*, a descendant, of Nebuchadnezzar. An appeal is made to Berosus and Megasthenes, to show that this was not true. Yet they do not so testify, but only that Belshazzar was *not of the regular line* of heirs of the throne. He might still have been a younger son of Nebuchadnezzar, or a son of Nebuchadnezzar's daughter. Now Herodotus agrees with Daniel, i. 188, i. 74. So does Xenophon. And as the other authors have not in reality contradicted this, what reason is there for refusing to believe ? See the discussion of this topic at large, p. 144, *seq.*

" It certainly deserves to be noted, that, in part, the book of Daniel is on the side of the Greek writers, and against Berosus and Abydenus, where the representations of the latter may be justly regarded as designed to save the honour and credit of the Babylonians ; in part also is Daniel on the side of the latter, and against the Greek writers, *i.e.*, in cases where there is no reason to suppose the native historians to be partial. The *media via* appears in this case to be hit upon, by the simple pursuit of historical truth in the narratives of the book before us.

"Again, in Dan. v. 31, we have an assurance that *Darius* the *Mede* assumed the throne of Babylon. Here Herodotus and Ctesias are silent ; but here Xenophon fully confirms the account given by Daniel. Herodotus himself states (i. 95) that there were two other modes of telling the story of Cyrus besides that which he follows ; and that of Xenophon and Daniel is probably one of these. This is confirmed by Isa. xiii. 17, where the *Mede* is declared to be the leading nation in destroying Babylon, and the same is also said in Jer. li. 11, 28. In Isa. xxi. 2, both Media and Persia are mentioned. The *silence* of Herodotus and

* " Singular, that in a critical edition and commentary on Xenophon, now before me, this is rendered *before a good fire.* First, the Greek words do not allow this. Secondly, the Babylonians need and have no fires for warmth. Thirdly, Cyrus would not have drained the Euphrates, and marched his army in its channel, at a time when fires were needed for warmth."

Ctesias cannot disprove a matter of this kind. See a full discussion of the topic, p. 148, *seq.*

"Daniel (vi. 1) states that Darius set over his kingdom 120 satraps. Xenophon (*Cyrop.* VIII. 6, 1, *seq.*) relates that satraps were set over all the conquered nations, when Cyrus was in Babylon. He speaks of the appointments as made by Cyrus; and doubtless they were, since he was the only *acting* governor of Babylon, and *vicegerent* of the king. No less true is it, that to Darius also, as supreme, may the appointment be attributed. How came the alleged *late* writer of Daniel to know this? Xenophon mentions no express number. The book of Esther (i. 1) mentions 127 satraps. Why did not our late writer copy that number in order to remove suspicion as to so great a number of those high officers? And how is it that 120 in Daniel is objected to as an incredible number, when the empire was actually as large at the time of their appointment, as it was in the time of Xerxes, as exhibited in Esth. i. 1? The Septuagint translator of Daniel, who belonged to the Maccabæan age, did not venture to write 120, as it seems, but 127 (so in *Cod. Chis.*), thus according with Esth. i. 1, and leaning upon that passage. He seems evidently to have felt that the story of so many satrapies must be supported by the book of Esther, in order to be believed. He even, in his ignorance of history, translates ver. 31 thus: 'And Artaxerxes, the Mede, took the kingdom,' probably meaning the Persian Artaxerxes Longimanus.

"(*l*) It is worthy of remark, that the order of the two nations, *Medes and Persians*, is to be found in strict accordance with the idiom of the times. Thus in vi. 8, 12, 15, we have the *Medes and Persians;* but after Cyrus comes to the throne, the order is invariably *Persians and Medes.* So in the book of Esther, *the law of the Persians and Medes* shows the same change of *usus loquendi.* Would a Pseudo-Daniel have been likely to note such a small circumstance?

"It is also noted (Dan. 5. 31), that when Darius took the kingdom, he was threescore and two years old. From his history, his reign, and his descent from Ahasuerus (ix. 1), this seems altogether probable. But no other author states his age. The fact that it is done in Daniel betokens a familiarity of the writer with the *minutiæ* of his history. So does the mention that in the *first* year of his reign Daniel took into most serious consideration the prophecy of Jeremiah respecting the seventy years' exile of the Hebrews.

"Thus far, then, all is well. All seems to be in conformity with true history, so far as we can ascertain it. It is not upon one or two particulars that we would lay stress. We acknowledge that these might have been traditionally known, and accurately reported. It is on the *tout ensemble* of the historical matters contained in the book that stress is to be laid. And certainly it would be very singular if all these circumstances should be true and consistent, and yet the book be written in the Maccabæan period.

" How is it with the best historical books of that period? The first book of the Maccabees is, in the main, a trustworthy and veracious book. But how easy it is to detect errors in it, both in respect to geography and history! In viii. 7, it is related that the Romans took Antiochus the Great prisoner alive. But this never happened. They gained a great victory over him, and took away many of his provinces; but he himself escaped their grasp. In viii. 8, it is said that they took from him the land of *India, Media,* and Lydia. But neither India nor Media ever belonged to him. The efforts to show that Mysia was originally written instead of Media, are of course but mere guesses; and if true, *India* still remains. More likely is it that the author himself put Media for Mysia, and if so, then this does not mend the matter. In viii. 9, 10, it is related, that 'the Greeks resolved to send an army to Rome and destroy it; but that the Romans learning this, sent forth an army, who slew many, carried away numerous captives of their women and children, laid hold of their strong places, and took possession of their lands, and reduced the people of Syria to servitude *unto this day.*' Now nothing of all this ever happened. There was indeed a fracas between the Ætolians and the Romans at that period; but it was soon made up, without any ravages of war, or any servitude. Further, the author, in viii. 15, represents the Roman Senate as consisting of 320 members, continually administering the government. He goes on to state (ver. 16), that they choose a ruler annually, and that all obey this one. Every tyro in Roman history knows how unfounded all this is. And what shall we say of the very first sentence in the book, which tells us that Alexander, the son of Philip, smote Darius, king of the Persians and Medes, and then reigned *in his stead* over Greece? In i. 6, he states that the same Alexander, about to die, made a partition of his empire among his chiefs—a thing that took place some considerable time afterwards, partly by mutual agreement, and partly by force. In vi. 1, he makes Elymais a *town* instead of a province.

" Such are some of the specimens of this writer's errors in geography and history. That he was a grave, enlightened, and veracious writer, in the main, is conceded by all. But if in things so plain, and transactions so recent, he commits so many errors as have been specified, what would he have done if the scene had been shifted from near countries to the remote places where the book of Daniel finds its circle of action?

" As to the *second* book of the Maccabees, it is so notorious for errors and mistakes, that very little credit has been attached to it on the part of intelligent critics. It is not once to be named in comparison with the book of Daniel. It must have been written when a knowledge of historical events was confused, and at a very low ebb. The book of Tobit, which originated in or near the Maccabæan period, exhibits not only a romantic, and, as it were, fairy tale, but contains historical and geographical difficulties incapable of solution; also physical phenomena are brought to view which are incredible. It is needless to specificate them here. De Wette's *Einleit.* presents them, § 309.

"We have dwelt hitherto, under our 5th head, mainly on things of a *historical* nature, *i.e.*, events and occurrences. Let us now examine a number of things that are of a miscellaneous nature, which it would be somewhat difficult, if not useless, to classify throughout, but most of which are connected with manners, customs, demeanour, &c.

"(*m*) Daniel makes no mention in his book of prostration before the king in addressing him. *O king, live for ever!* was the usual greeting. Arrian (iv.) testifies that the story in the East was, that Cyrus was the first before whom prostration was practised. It is easy to see how this came about. With the Persians, the king was regarded as the *representative of Ormusd*, and therefore entitled to adoration. Nebuchadnezzar was high enough in claims to submission and honour; but not a word of exacting adoration from those who addressed him. How could a Pseudo-Daniel know of this nice distinction, when all the Oriental sovereigns of whom he had any knowledge had, at least for four centuries, exacted prostration from all who approached them?

"(*n*) In mere prose (Dan. i. 2) Babylon is called by the old name, *Shinar* (Gen. xi. 2; xiv. 1); and as an old name, it is poetically used once by Isaiah (xi. 11), and once by Zechariah (v. 11). Now *Shinar* was the vernacular name of what foreigners called *Babylonia;* and it was easy and natural for Daniel to call it so. But *how* or *why* came a Pseudo-Daniel to such a use of the word? *Babylon* he would naturally, and almost with certainty, call it.

"(*o*) Daniel (i. 5) tells us that the Hebrew lads were to be fed from the king's table. Such a custom, even in respect to royal prisoners, Jeremiah (lii. 33, 34) discloses. Among the Persians this was notorious, and extended to the whole *corps d'elites* of the soldiery. Ctesias tells us that the king of Persia daily fed 15,000 men. How came the *late* writer of Daniel to be acquainted with a minute circumstance of the nature of that before us?

"(*p*) Daniel and his companions received Chaldee names, some of which are compounded of the names of their false gods. In 2 Kings xxiv. 17, Nebuchadnezzar is reported to have changed the name of king Mattaniah into *Zedekiah*. How did the late forger of the book come by the notion of assigning to his Hebrew heroes the names of idol-gods? The rigorous attachment to all that was Jewish, and the hearty hatred of heathenism by all the pious in the time of the Maccabees, makes it difficult to account for his course.

"(*q*) In Dan. ii. 1, the Babylonish mode of reckoning time is introduced, viz., the second year of Nebuchadnezzar. Where else, unless in Ezek. i. 1, is this employed? How came the late interpolator of the sacred books to betake himself to this mode of reckoning, and especially since it apparently contradicts i. 1, and ver. 18? See the solution of the difficulty, in *Exc.* I. [See App. I. to this Vol.]

"(r) In Dan. ii. 5, and iii. 29, one part of the threatened punishment is, that the houses of the transgressors should be turned into a *dung-hill*, or rather a *morass-heap*. Here an intimate acquaintance with the Babylonish mode of building is developed. The houses were mostly constructed of *sun-baked* bricks, or with those slightly burned; and when once demolished, the rain and dew would soon dissolve the whole mass, and make them sink down, in that wet land near the river, into a miry place of clay, whenever the weather was wet.

"(s) In Dan. iii. 1, the plain of *Dura* is mentioned; a name found nowhere else, yet mentioned here as a place familiar to the original readers of the book, inasmuch as no explanation is added. Whence did the *Pseudo-Daniel* derive this name?

"(t) In Dan. ii. 5, and iii. 6, we find the punishment of hewing to pieces and burning in ovens mentioned. Testimony to such modes of punishment may be found in Ezek. xvi. 40; xxiii. 25; and Jer. xxix. 22. But such a mode of punishment could not exist among the Persians, who were *fire-worshippers;* and accordingly, in ch. vi. we find casting into a den of lions as substituted for it.

"(u) In Dan. iii. we find not only a huge idol (in keeping with the Babylonish taste), but also a great variety of musical instruments employed at the dedication of it. Quintus Curtius has told us, that when Alexander the Great entered Babylon, 'there were in the procession singing Magi...and artists playing on stringed instruments of a peculiar kind, accustomed to chant the praises of the king' (lib. v. 3).

"(v) According to Herod. I. 195, the Babylonish costume consisted of three parts—first, the wide and long pantaloons for the lower part of the person; secondly, a woollen shirt; and, thirdly, a large mantle with a girdle round it. On the cylinder rolls found at Babylon, Münter (*Relig. d. Bab.* s. 96) discovered the same costume. In Dan. iii. 21, the same three leading and principal articles of dress are particularized. Other parts of clothing are merely referred to, but not specificated; but these garments being large and loose, and made of delicate material, are mentioned in order to show how powerless the furnace was, since they were not even singed. How did a Pseudo-Daniel obtain such particulars as these?

"(w) Daniel (v. 16) shows that the regal token of honour bestowed was a collet or golden chain put round the neck. Brissonius, in his work on the Persian dominion, has shown the same custom among the Persian kings, who, not improbably, borrowed it from the Babylonians.

"(x) In Dan. vi. 8, 'the laws of the Medes which change not' are mentioned. In Esth. i. 19, and viii. 8, we have repeated mention of this same peculiar custom. The reason of this probably was, that the king was regarded as the impersonation of Ormusd, and therefore as infallible.

"(y) In Dan. vii. 9, we have a description of the Divine throne as placed upon *movable wheels*. The same we find in Ezek. i. and x.;

which renders it quite probable that the Babylonian throne was constructed in this way, so that the monarch might move in processions,
with all the insignia of royalty about him.

"(z) It deserves special remark, that Daniel has given individual
classifications of priests and civilians, such as are nowhere else given
in Scripture, and the knowledge of which must have been acquired from
intimate acquaintance with the state of things in Babylon. In Dan. ii.
2, 10, 27, the various classes of diviners and literati are named. In Dan.
iii. 2, 3, the different classes of magistrates, civilians, and rulers are
specifically named. On this whole subject, I must refer the reader to
Exc. III. *on the Chaldees* [See App. III. to this Vol.] Whence a *Maccabæan* writer could have derived such knowledge it would be difficult to
say. It is one of those circumstances which could not well be feigned.
Several of the names occur nowhere else in the Heb. Bible, and some
of them are evidently derivates of the Parsi or Median language; *e.g.*,
פַּרְסִין in Dan. vi. 3, a name unknown in the Semitic. On the other hand,
several of them are exclusively Chaldean; *e.g.*, Dan. iii. 3, אֲדַרְגָּזְרַיָּא, תִּפְתָּיֵא
—of which no profane writer has given the least hint. How came the
Pseudo-Daniel to a knowledge of such officers?"

The evidence that the book is a genuine production of the Daniel of
the captivity may be summed up now in few words. There is (1), on
the face of the book, the testimony of the writer himself to his own
authorship—good evidence in itself, unless there is some reason for
calling it in question or setting it aside. There is (2) the fact that it
was early received into the canon as a part of the inspired Scriptures,
and that it has always been, both by Jews and Christians, regarded as
entitled to a place there. There is (3) the express testimony of the
Saviour that Daniel was a prophet, and a clear reference to a part of
the prophecy by him, as we have it now in the book of Daniel. There
is (4) express testimony that the book was in existence before the time
of the Maccabees, and was then regarded as a genuine production of
Daniel, particularly (*a*) the testimony of Josephus; (*b*) of the author of
the book of *Maccabees*, and (*c*) of the authors of the Septuagint translation. There is (5) the fact that the book was so written in two different languages that we cannot well attribute it to a writer of the
Maccabæan period. And there is (6) "the accurate knowledge which
the writer of the book of Daniel displays of ancient history, manners,
and customs, and Oriental-Babylonish peculiarities, which shows that
he must have lived at or near the time and place when and where the
book leads us to suppose that he lived." For the genuineness and
authenticity of what other book can more clear and decisive testimony
be brought? These considerations seem to make it clear that the book
could not have been a forgery of the time of the Maccabees, and that
every circumstance combines to confirm the common belief that it was
written in the time of the exile, and by the author whose name it bears.
But if this is so, then its canonical authority is established: for we have

all that can be urged in favour of the canonical authority of any of the books of the Old Testament. Its place in the canon from the earliest period; the testimony of Christ; the testimony of Josephus and the Jews in all ages to its canonical authority; the testimony of the early Christian fathers; its prophetic character; and the strong internal probabilities that it was written at the time and in the manner in which it professes to have been, all go to confirm the opinion that it is a genuine production of the Daniel of the captivity, and worthy to be received and accredited as a part of the inspired oracles of truth. On *one* of these points, which has not been insisted on in this Introduction—its *prophetic* character—the evidence can be appreciated only by an examination of the particular prophecies; and that will be seen as the result of the exposition of those parts of the book which refer to future events. It may be said in general, however, that if it is proved to have been written in the time of the captivity, there will be no hesitation in admitting its inspiration. Porphyry maintained, as we have seen, that the pretended prophecies were so clear that they *must* have been written after the events; and this, as we have seen also, is one of the leading objections urged against the book in more modern times. If this is so, then, apart from all the evidence which will be furnished of the fulfilment of the prophecies of Daniel in the course of the exposition, it may be properly inferred, that if the book was written in the time in which it professes to have been, it furnishes the highest evidence of inspiration, for no one can pretend that the predictions occurring in it, pertaining to future events, are the results of any mere natural sagacity.

§ IV.—NATURE, DESIGN, AND GENERAL CHARACTER OF THE BOOK OF DANIEL.

The book of Daniel is not properly a *history* either of the Jews or Babylonians, nor is it a biography of the writer himself. It is not continuous in its structure, nor does it appear to have been written at one time. Though the work, as we have seen, of one author, it is made up of portions, written evidently on different occasions, in two different languages, and having, to a considerable extent, different objects in view. Though the author was a Jewish exile, and surrounded by his own countrymen as exiles, yet there is almost no reference to the past history of these people, or to the causes of their having been carried into captivity, and no description of their condition, struggles, and sufferings in their exile; and though written by one who resided through the greatest part of a very long life in a land of strangers, and having every opportunity of obtaining information, there is no distinct reference to *their* history, and no description of their manners and customs. And although his own career while there was eventful, yet the allusions to himself are very few; and of the largest portion of that long life in Babylon—probably embracing more than seventy years—we have no information whatever. In the book there are few or no allusions to the condition of the exiles there; but two of the native kings that reigned there during that long period are even mentioned; one of those—Nebuchadnezzar—only when Daniel interpreted two of his dreams, and when the colossal idol was set up on the plain of Dura; and the other—Belshazzar—only on the last day of his life. The book is not regular in its structure, but consists of an intermixture of history and prophecy, apparently composed as occasion demanded, and then united in a single volume. Yet it has a unity of authorship and design, as we have seen, and is evidently the production of a single individual.

In considering the nature, design, and general character of the book, the attention may be properly directed to the following points :—

I. The portions containing incidents in the life of the author, and of his companions in Babylon, of permanent value.

II. The prophetic portions.

III. The language and style of the book.

I. *The portions containing incidents in the life of the author, and of his companions in Babylon, of permanent value.*

As already remarked, the allusions to his own life, and to the circumstances of his companions in exile, are few in number ; and it may be added, that where there are such allusions they are made apparently rather to illustrate their principles, and the nature of their religion, than to create an interest in them personally. We could make out but little respecting their biography from this volume, though that little is sufficient to give us decided views of their *character*, and of the value and power of the religion which they professed.

The few personal incidents which we have relate to such points as the following :—The selection of Daniel, and three other captives, when young, with a view to their being trained in the language and science of the Chaldeans, that they might be employed in the service of the government, ch. i. ; the fact that Daniel was called, when all the skill of the Chaldeans failed, to interpret a dream of Nebuchadnezzar, and that he was enabled to give an explanation that was so satisfactory that the king promoted him to exalted honour, ch. ii. ; the narrative respecting the three friends of Daniel—Shadrach, Meshach, and Abednego—who refused to fall down and adore the golden image that Nebuchadnezzar erected in the plain of Dura, and who for their disobedience were cast into the fiery furnace, ch. iii. ; Daniel's interpretation of a second dream of Nebuchadnezzar, and the fulfilment of the interpretation of that dream on the monarch, ch. iv. ; his interpretation of the handwriting on the wall at the feast of Belshazzar, ch. v. ; and the attempt of the enemies of Daniel to destroy his influence and his life by taking advantage of his known piety, and the firmness of his attachment to God, ch. vi.

These must have been but a few of the incidents that occurred to

Daniel in the course of a long life spent in Babylon, and they were probably selected as furnishing valuable illustrations of character; as evincing the nature of true piety; as proofs of Divine inspiration; and as showing that God has control over kings and nations. All that is here stated occurred at distant intervals in a long life, and this fact should be remembered in reading the book. For the practical lessons taught by these portions of the book, I may be permitted to refer to the remarks at the close of ch. i., ii., iii., vi.

II. The prophetic portions of the book.

The prophecies of the book of Daniel may be arranged under two great classes :—those relating to the Babylonian monarchs; and those of more general interest pertaining to the future history of the world.

(A.) The former are confined to the calamities that would come upon the two monarchs who are mentioned in the book—Nebuchadnezzar and Belshazzar. Of the former of these kings, Nebuchadnezzar, his derangement as a judgment of heaven, on account of his pride, is predicted, ch. iv. ; and of the latter, Belshazzar, the termination of his reign, and the taking of his kingdom, are predicted on account of his impiety, ch. v. The object did not seem to be to state what farther would occur to the kingdom of the Chaldeans, except as it should be lost in the great kingdom of the Medes and Persians, in which it would be absorbed.

(B.) Those of general interest pertaining to future times. Of these there are several classes :—

(a) The prospective history of the revolutions in the great kingdoms of the world; or a *general glance* at what would happen in relation to the empires that were then playing their part in human affairs, and of those which would grow out of the kingdoms existing in the time of Daniel.

These may be arranged under the following general heads :—

(1.) A description of the great kingdoms or empires that would properly grow out of the Babylonian or Chaldean monarchy, ch. ii. That kingdom was, in the time of Daniel, the great, and almost the single, sovereignty of the earth ; for, in the time of Nebuchadnezzar, this had absorbed all others. From this, however, were to spring other great dynasties that were to rule over the world, and that might properly, in some sense, be represented as the successors of this. These great revolutions are represented in the dream of Nebuchadnezzar respecting the golden image, ch. ii., and they are described by Daniel as (a) the great monarchy of which Nebuchadnezzar was the head—Babylon—represented in the image by the head of gold (ch. ii. 38); (b) as another kingdom inferior to this, represented in the image by the breast and arms of silver (ch. ii. 32, 39)—the Medo-Persian empire, that would succeed that of Babylon ; (c) as a third kingdom that would succeed this, represented in the image by the belly and the thighs of brass, (ch. ii. 32, 39); (d) as a fourth kingdom more mighty than either, subduing all nations under it, and crushing the powers of the earth, yet made of discordant materials, so as never firmly to adhere as one—represented by the legs of iron, and the feet and toes partly of iron and partly of clay in the image (ch. ii. 33, 41–43), denoting the mighty Roman power ; and (e) as another kingdom that would spring up under this fourth kingdom, and that would ultimately supplant it, and become the permanent kingdom on the earth (ch. ii. 44, 45).

Substantially the same representation occurs again in ch. vii., under the image of a succession of formidable beasts that were seen by Daniel in a dream. These four great kingdoms, represented successively by a lion, by a bear, by a leopard, and by a nondescript monster, were also succeeded by a great and permanent kingdom on the earth—the reign of God. In this representation, Daniel goes more into detail in respect to the last great empire than he does in interpreting the dream of Nebuchadnezzar. Indeed, the design of this latter representation seems to be, to give a more full account of the changes which would occur in this last great kingdom on the earth—the kingdom of the saints—than had been before given.

(2.) A particular prophecy of the conquests of the king of Grecia—Alexander the Great—extending down to the time of Antiochus Epiphanes, and to the calamities and desolations which he would bring upon the holy land (ch. viii). This occurs in a vision which Daniel had at Shushan, in the province of Elam, and consisted of a representation of a ram with two horns, " pushing" in every direction, as if to extend its conquests everywhere. From the West, however, there came a goat, with a single horn between its eyes, that attacked and overcame the ram. This single horn on the head of the goat is subsequently represented as broken, and in its place there came up four other horns, and out of one of them a little horn that became great, and that magnified itself particularly against " the prince of the host," and that took away the daily sacrifice, or that closed the sacred services of religion in the temple.

A part of this is explained by Gabriel, as referring to the king of Grecia ; and there can be no difficulty in understanding that Alexander the Great is referred to, and that by the four horns that sprang up out of the one that was broken, the four kingdoms into which that of Alexander was divided at his death are meant, and that by the little horn that sprang up Antiochus Epiphanes is designated.

(3.) A particular and minute prophecy respecting the wars between two of the kingdoms that sprang out of the empire of Alexander—Syria and Egypt—so far especially as they affected the holy land, and the services in the sanctuary of God (ch. x., xi). This vision occurred in the third year of the reign of Cyrus, and on an occasion when Daniel had been fasting three full weeks. The prediction was imparted to him by an angel that appeared to him by the river Hiddekel, or Tigris, and contains a detailed account of what would occur for a long period in the conflicts which would exist between the sovereigns of Syria and Egypt. In these wars the Hebrew people were to be deeply interested, for their country lay between the two contending kingdoms; their land would be taken and re-taken in those conflicts; not a few of the great battles that would be fought in these conflicts would be fought on their territory; and deep and permanent disasters would occur to them in consequence of the manner in which the Hebrew people would regard and treat one or both of the contending parties. This prophetic history is conducted onward, with great particularity, to the death of Antiochus Epiphanes, the most formidable enemy that the Hebrew people would have to encounter in the future, and then (ch. xii.) the vision terminates with a few unconnected *hints* of what would occur in future periods, to the end of the world.

It was from this portion of the book particularly that Porphyry argued that the whole work must have been written *after* the events had occurred, and that, therefore, it must be a forgery of a later age than the time of the exile in Babylon.

(4.) A particular and minute prophecy respecting the time when the Messiah would appear (ch. ix). This was imparted to Daniel when, anxious about the close of the long captivity of his countrymen, and supposing that the predicted time of the return to the land of their fathers drew on, he gave himself to an earnest and careful study of the books of Jeremiah. At the close of the solemn prayer which he offered on that occasion (ch. ix. 4–19), the angel Gabriel appeared to him (ch. ix. 20, 21) to assure him that his prayer was heard, and to make an important communication to him respecting future times (ch. ix. 22, 23). He then proceeded to inform him how long a period was determined, in respect to the holy city, before the great work should be accomplished of making an end of sin, and of making reconciliation for iniquity, and of bringing in everlasting righteousness; when, that great work having been accomplished, the oblations at the temple would cease, and the overspreading of abomination would occur, and desolation would come upon the temple and city (ch. ix. 24-27). This celebrated prophecy of the "seventy weeks" is among the most important, and, in some respects, among the most difficult parts of the sacred volume. If the common interpretation [and the one that is adopted in these Notes] is correct, it is the most definite prediction of the time when the Messiah would appear to be found in the Old Testament.

(5.) Particular prophecies respecting events that would occur *after* the coming of the Messiah. These relate to two points :—

A. Prophecies relating to the church (ch. vii. 7–27).

(*a*) The rise of ten kingdoms out of the great fourth monarchy which would succeed the Babylonian, the Medo-Persian, and the Macedonian —to wit, the *Roman* power (ch. vii. 24).

(*b*) The rise of another power after them, springing out of them, and subduing three of those powers—to wit the *Papal* power (ch. vii. 24).

(*c*) The characteristics of that new power—as arrogant, and perse-cuting, and claiming supreme legislation over the world (ch. vii. 25).

(*d*) The duration of this power (ch. vii. 25).

(*e*) The manner in which it would be terminated (ch. vii. 26).

(*f*) The permanent establishment of the kingdom of the saints on the earth (ch. vii. 27).

B. Prophecies relating to the final judgment and the end of all things (ch. xii).

This portion (ch. xii.) is made up of *hints* and *fragments*—broken thoughts and suggestions, which there was no occasion to fill up. What is said is not communicated in a direct form *as* a revelation of new truths, but is rather based *on* certain truths as already known, and employed here for the illustration of others. It is *assumed* that there will be a resurrection of the dead and a judgment, and the writer employs the language based on this assumption to illustrate the point immediately before him (ch. xii. 2-4, 9, 13). There is also a very obscure reference to the times when certain great events were to occur in the future (ch. xii. 11, 12); but there is nothing, in this respect, that can enable us certainly to determine when these events will take place.

In reference to these prophetic portions of the book of Daniel, a few illustrative remarks may now be made :—

(1.) They relate to most momentous events in the history of the world. If the views taken of these portions of the book are correct, then the eye of the prophet rested on those events in the future which would enter most deeply into the character of coming ages, and which would do more than any other to determine the final condition of the world.

(2.) The prophecies in Daniel are more *minute* than any others in the Bible. This is particularly the case in respect to the four great kingdoms which would arise; to the conquests of Alexander the Great; to the kingdoms which would spring out of the one great empire that would be founded by him; to the wars that would exist between two of those sovereignties ; to the time when the Messiah would appear ; to the manner in which he would be cut off; to the final destruction of the holy city; and to the rise, character, and destiny of the Papacy. Of these great events there are no other so minute connected descrip-tions anywhere else in the Old Testament; and even, on many of these points, the more full disclosures of the New Testament receive important light from the prophecies of Daniel.

(3.) There is a remarkable resemblance between many of the predic-tions in Daniel and in the book of Revelation. No one can peruse the two books without being satisfied that, in many respects, they were designed to refer to the same periods in the history of the world, and to the same events, and especially where *time* is mentioned. There is, indeed—as is remarked in the Preface to these Notes—no express allu-sion in the Apocalypse to Daniel. There is no direct quotation from the book. There is no certain evidence that the author of the Apocalypse ever saw the book of Daniel, though no one can doubt that he did. There is nothing in the Apocalypse which might not have been written if the book of Daniel had not been written, or if it had been entirely unknown to John. Perhaps it may be added, that there is nothing in the book of Revelation which might not have been as easily explained if the book of Daniel had not been written. And yet it is manifest, that in most important respects the authors of the two books refer to the same great events in history; describe the same important changes in human affairs; refer to the same periods of duration; and have in their eye the same termination of things on the earth. No other two books in the Bible have the same relation to each other; nor are there any other two in which a commentary on the one will introduce so many topics which must be considered in the other, or where the explanations in the one will throw so much light on the other.

III. The language and style of the book.

(1.) The language of the book of Daniel is nearly half Chaldee and half Hebrew. In ch. i. ii. 1–3, it is Hebrew; from ch. ii. 4, to the end of ch. vii., it is Chaldee; and the remainder of the book is Hebrew. The book of Ezra also contains several chapters of Chaldee, exhibiting the same characteristics as the part of the book of Daniel written in that language.

As Daniel was early trained in his own country in the knowledge of the Hebrew, and as he was carefully instructed, after being carried to Babylon, in the language and literature of the Chaldees (see § 1.), it is certain that he was capable of writing in either language; and it is probable that he would use either, as there might be occasion, in his intercourse with his own countrymen, or with the Chaldeans. There is the highest probability that the captive Hebrews would retain the knowledge of their own language in a great degree of purity, during their long captivity in Babylon, and that this would be the language which Daniel would employ in his intercourse with his own countrymen; while from his own situation at court, and the necessity of his intercourse with the Chaldeans, it may be presumed that the language which he would perhaps most frequently employ would be the Chaldean.

That there were reasons why one portion of this book was written in Chaldee, and another in Hebrew, there can be no doubt, but it is now utterly impossible to ascertain what those reasons were. The use of one language or the other *seems* to be perfectly arbitrary. The portions written in Hebrew have no more relation to the Jews, and would have no more interest to them, than those written in Chaldee; and, on the other hand, the portions written in Chaldee have no special relation to the Chaldeans. But while the reasons for this change must for ever remain a secret, there are two obvious suggestions which have often been made in regard to it, and which have already been incidentally adverted to, as bearing on the question of the authorship of the book.

(1.) The first is, that this fact accords with the account which we have of the education of the author, as being instructed in both these languages—furnishing thus an undesigned proof of the authenticity of the book; and (2) the other is, that this would not have occurred if the work was a forgery of a later age; for (a) it is doubtful whether, in the age of the Maccabees, there were any who could write with equal ease in both languages, or could write both languages with purity; (b) if it could be done, the device would not be one that would be likely to occur to the author, and he would have been likely to betray the design if it had existed; and (c) as the apocryphal additions to Daniel (see § v.) were written in Greek, the presumption is, that if the book had been forged in that age it would have been wholly written in that language. At all events, the *facts* of the case, in regard to the languages in which the book was written, accord with all that we know of Daniel.

(2.) The book abounds with symbols and visions. In this respect it resembles very closely the writings of Ezekiel and Zechariah. One of these was his cotemporary, and the other lived but little after him, and it may be presumed that this style of writing prevailed much in that age. All these writers, not improbably, "formed their style, and their manner of thinking and expression, in a foreign land, where symbol, and imagery, and vision, and dreams, were greatly relished and admired. The ruins of the Oriental cities recently brought to the light of day, as well as those which have ever remained exposed to view, are replete with symbolic forms and images, which once gave a play and a delight to the fancy."—Prof. Stuart on Daniel, p. 393. Perhaps none of the other sacred writers abound so much in symbols and visions as Daniel, except John in the book of Revelation; and in these two, as before suggested, the resemblance is remarkable. The interpretation of either of these books involves the necessity of studying the nature of symbolic language; and on the views taken of that language must depend, in a great degree, the views of the truths disclosed in these books.

(3.) The book of Daniel, though not written in the *style* of poetry, yet abounds much with the *spirit* of poetry—as the book of Revelation does. Indeed, the Apocalypse may be regarded as, on the whole, the most *poetic* book in the Bible. We miss, indeed, in both these books, the usual *forms* of Hebrew poetry; we miss the *parallelism* (comp. Intro. to Job, § v.); but the *spirit* of poetry pervades both the book of Daniel and the book of Revelation, and the latter, especially if it were a mere human production, would be ranked among the highest creations of genius. Much of Daniel, indeed, is simple prose—alike in structure and in form; but much also in his visions deserves to be classed among the works of imagination. Throughout the book there are frequent bursts of feeling of a high order (comp. ch. ii. 19-23); there are many passages that are sublime (comp. ch. ii. 27-45; iv. 19-27; v. 17-28); there is a spirit of unshaken fidelity and boldness— as in the passages just referred to; there is true grandeur in the prophetic portions (comp. ch. vii. 9–14; x. 5–9; xi. 41–45; xii. 1–3, 5–8; and there is, throughout the book, a spirit of humble, sincere, firm, and devoted piety, characterizing the author as a man eminently prudent and wise, respectful in his intercourse with others, faithful in every trust, unceasing in the discharge of his duties to God; a man who preferred to lose the highest offices which kings could confer, and to subject himself to shame and to death, rather than shrink, in the slightest degree, from the discharge of the proper duties of religion.

§ V.—THE APOCRYPHAL ADDITIONS TO THE BOOK OF DANIEL.

These additions are three in number:—

(1.) "The Song of the Three Holy Children;" that is, the song of Shadrach, Meshach, and Abednego, who were cast into the burning furnace by Nebuchadnezzar (ch. iii). This "Song," as it is called, is inserted in the Greek copies, in ch. iii., between the twenty-third and twenty-fourth verses, and contains sixty-eight verses, making the whole chapter, in the Greek, to contain an hundred verses. The "Song" consists properly of three parts: I. A hymn of "Azariah," or of "Ananiah, Azariah, and Misael"—Ἀνανίας καὶ Ἀζαρίας καὶ Μισαήλ—of whom Azariah is the speaker, in which praise is given to God, and a prayer is offered that they may be accepted, preserved, and delivered (vers. 1–22). These are the *Hebrew* names of the three persons that were cast into the fiery furnace (Dan. i. 6, 7), but why these names are inserted here rather than the names given them in Babylon by the "prince of the eunuchs" (ch. i. 7), and which are used in the Chaldee in this chapter, is not known; and the circumstance that they *are* so used furnishes a strong presumption that this addition in Greek is spurious, since, in the other portions of the chapter (vers. 12–14, 16, 19, marked in *Codex Chisian.* in brackets), the same names occur which are found in the original Chaldee. II. A statement, that the king's servants added fuel to the flame, or kept up the intensity of the heat by putting in rosin, pitch, tow, and small wood, making the furnace so hot that the flame rose above it to the height of forty-nine cubits, and so hot as to consume the Chaldeans that stood around it, but that the angel of the Lord came down, and smote the flame of fire out of the oven, and made the midst of the furnace like a moist, whistling wind, so that the three "children" were safe (vers. 23–27). III. A hymn of praise, calling on all things to praise God, uttered by "the three, as out of one mouth," (vers. 28–68). The narrative then proceeds, in the Greek translation, as it is in the Chaldee, and as it now stands in our common translation of the book of Daniel.

(2.) The second addition is what is called *The History of Susanna.* This is a story the design of which is to honour Daniel. A man in Babylon, of great wealth, by the name of Joacim, marries Susanna, a Jewess, who had been brought up in the fear of the Lord. The house of Joacim was a place of much resort, and particularly by two men of advanced life, who were appointed judges of the people. Susanna was a woman of great beauty, and each one of the two judges, ignorant of the feelings of the other, fell violently in love with her. They both observed that at a certain time of the day she walked in the garden, and both, unknown to each other, resolved to follow her into the garden. They proposed, therefore, to each other to return to their own homes; and both, after having gone away, returned again, and then, surprised at this, they each declared their love for Susanna, and agreed to watch for the time when she should enter the garden, and then to accomplish their purpose. She entered the garden as usual for the purpose of bathing, and the elders, having hid themselves, suddenly came upon her, and threatened her with death if she would not gratify their desires. She, rather than yield, calmly made up her mind to die, but gave the alarm by crying aloud, and the elders, to save themselves, declared that they found a young man with her in the garden, and the matter coming before the people, she was condemned to death, and was led forth to be executed. At this juncture, Daniel appeared, who proposed to examine the elders anew, and to do it separately. In this examination, one of them testified that what he had seen occurred under a mastick or lentisk tree, the other that it was under a holm tree. The consequence was, that Susanna was discharged, and the two elders themselves put to death.

This story is said, in the common version of the Apocrypha, to be "set apart from the beginning of Daniel because it is not in the Hebrew." It is found only in the Apocrypha, and is not incorporated in the Greek translation of Daniel.

(3.) The third addition is what is called "The History of the Destruction of Bel and the Dragon, cut off from the end of Daniel."

This is a story in two parts. The first relates to Bel, the idol-god of the Babylonians. A large quantity of food was daily placed before the idol in the temple, which it was supposed the idol consumed. The inquiry was made of Daniel by Cyrus, king of Persia, why he did not worship the idol. Daniel replied that he was permitted by his religion to worship only the living God. Cyrus asked him whether Bel was not a living God; and, in proof of it, appealed to the large quantity of food which he daily consumed. Daniel smiled at the simplicity of the king, and affirmed that the god was only brass and clay, and could devour nothing. The king, enraged, called for the priests of Bel, and insisted on being informed who ate the large quantity of food that was daily placed before the idol. They, of course, affirmed that it was the idol, and proposed that a test should be applied by placing the food before him, as usual, and by having the temple carefully closed and sealed with the signet of the king. Under the table they had, however, made a private entrance, and in order to detect them, Daniel caused ashes to be sprinkled on the floor, which, on the following day, revealed the footprints of men, women, and children, who had secretly entered the temple, and consumed the food. The consequence was, that they were put to death, and Bel and his temple were delivered to Daniel, who destroyed them both.

The other part of the story relates to a great dragon which was worshipped in Babylon. The king said that it could not be affirmed that this dragon was made of brass, or that he was not a living being, and required Daniel to worship him. Daniel still declared that he would worship only the living God, and proposed to put the dragon to death. This he did by making a ball of pitch, and fat, and hair, and putting it into the mouth of the dragon, so that he burst asunder. A tumult, in consequence of the destruction of Bel and the Dragon, was excited against the king, and the mob came and demanded Daniel, who had been the cause of this. Daniel was delivered to them, and was thrown into the den of lions, where he remained six days; and, in order that the lions might at once devour him, their appetites had been sharpened by having been fed each day with " two carcasses"—in the margin, " two slaves " — and two sheep. At this juncture, it is said that there was in Jewry a prophet, by the name of Habbacuc, who had made pottage, and was going with it into a field to carry it to the reapers. He was directed by an angel of the Lord to take it to Babylon to Daniel, who was in the lions' den. The prophet answered that he never saw Babylon, and knew not where the den was. So the angel of the Lord took him by the crown, and bare him by the hair of his head, and placed him in Babylon over the den. He gave Daniel the food, and was immediately restored to his own place in Judea. On the seventh day the king went to bewail Daniel; found him alive; drew him out, and threw in those who had caused him to be placed there, who were, of course, at once devoured.

This foolish story is said, in the title, in the common version of the Apocrypha, to have been " cut off from the end of Daniel." Like the Prayer of the Three Children, and the History of Susanna, it is found only in Greek, in which language it was undoubtedly written.

In respect to these additions to the book of Daniel, and the question whether they are entitled to be regarded as a part of his genuine work, and to have a place in the inspired writings, the following remarks may now be made :—

(a) Neither of them, and no portion of them, is found in the Hebrew or the Chaldee, nor is there the slightest evidence that they had a Hebrew or Chaldee original. There is no historical proof that they ever existed in either of these languages, and, of course, no proof that they ever formed a part of the genuine work of Daniel. If they were written originally in Greek, and if the evidence above adduced that the book of Daniel was written in the time of the exile is conclusive, then it is clear that these additions were *not* written by Daniel himself, and of course that they are not entitled to a place among the inspired records. For the Greek language was not understood in Babylon to any considerable extent, if at all, until the time of Alexander the Great, and his conquests in the East; and it is every way certain, that a book written in Babylon in the time of the exile would *not* have been written in Greek. The evidence is conclusive that these additions were never any part of the genuine book of Daniel; and, of course, that they have no claim to a place in the canon. Moreover, as they constituted no part of that book, *none* of the evidence urged in favour of the canonical authority of that book can be urged in behalf of these stories, and any claim that they may have must rest on their own merits.

(*b*) They have no claim, on their own account, to a place in the canon. Their authors are unknown. The time of their composition is unknown. They were never recognised by the Jews as canonical, and never had the sanction of the Saviour and the apostles, as they are never quoted or alluded to in the New Testament. And they have no internal evidence that they are of Divine origin. There is no evidence which could be urged in favour of their claims to a place in the canonical Scriptures which could not be urged in favour of the whole of the Apocrypha, or which could not be urged in favour of *any* anonymous writings of antiquity. The only ground of claim which *could* be urged for the admission of these stories into the sacred canon would be, that they were a part of the genuine book of Daniel ; but this claim *never* can be made out by any possibility.

(*c*) In common with the other books of the Apocrypha, these books were rejected by the early Christian writers, and were not admitted into the canon of Scripture during the first four centuries of the Christian church. (See Horne's *Introduction*, i. 628.) Some of the books of the Apocrypha were indeed quoted by some of the fathers with respect (Lardner, iv. 331), particularly by Ambrose (who lived A. D. 340-397), but they are referred to by Jerome only to be censured and condemned (Lardner, iv. 424, 440, 466-472), and are mentioned only with contempt by Augustine (Lardner, iv. 499).

It is seldom that these additions to Daniel in the Apocrypha are quoted or alluded to at all by the early Christian writers, but when they are it is only that they may be condemned. Origen, indeed, refers to the story of Susanna as a true history, and, in a letter to Africanus, says of it, " That the story of Susanna being dishonourable to the Jewish elders, it was suppressed by their great men; and that there were many things kept, as much as might be, from the knowledge of the people, some of which, nevertheless, were preserved in some apocryphal books."
—Lardner, ii. 466. Origen, indeed, in the words of Dr. Lardner, "Says all he can think of to prove the history [of Susanna] true and genuine, and affirms that it was made use of in Greek by all the churches of Christ among the Gentiles ; yet he owns that it was not received by the Jews, nor to be found in their copies of the book of Daniel."—
Lardner, ii. 541, 542. (Comp. also Dupin, *Dissertation Préliminaire sur*

la Bible, Liv. i. ch. i. § 5, p. 15, note (*e*). To the arguments of Origen on the subject, Africanus replies, that he "wondered that he did not know that the book was spurious, and says it was a piece lately forged." —Lardner, ii. 541. The other books, the Prayer of the Three Children, and the Story of Bel and the Dragon—we do not find, from Lardner, to have been quoted or referred to at all by the early Christian writers.

(*d*) The foolishness and manifest fabulousness of the Story of Bel and the Dragon may be referred to as a proof that that cannot be a part of the genuine book of Daniel, or entitled to a place among books claiming to be inspired. It has every mark of being a fable, and is wholly unworthy a place in any volume claiming to be of Divine origin, or any volume of respectable authorship whatever.

(*e*) Little is known of the origin of these books, and little importance can be attached to them; but it may be of some use to know the place which they have commonly occupied in the Bible by those who have received them as a part of the canon, and the place where they are commonly found in the version of the Scriptures.

"The Song of the Three Children" is placed in the Greek version of Daniel, and also in the Latin Vulgate, between the twenty-third and twenty-fourth verses of the third chapter. "It has always been admired," says Horne (*Intro.* iv. 217, 218), "for the piety of its sentiments, but it was never admitted to be canonical, until it was recognised by the Council of Trent. The fifteenth verse ['Neither is there at this time prince, or prophet, or leader, or burnt-offering, or sacrifice, or oblation, or incense, or place to sacrifice before thee, and to find mercy'] contains a direct falsehood; for it asserts that there was no prophet at that time, when it is well known that Daniel and Ezekiel both exercised the prophetic ministry in Babylon. This apocryphal fragment is, therefore, most probably the production of a Hellenistic Jew. The Hymn (ver. 29, *seq.*) resembles the hundred and forty-eighth Psalm, and was so approved of by the compilers of the Liturgy, that in the first Common Prayer Book of Edward VI. they appointed it to be used instead of the *Te Deum* during Lent."

"The History of Susanna has always been treated with some respect, but has never been considered as canonical, though the Council of Trent admitted it into the number of the sacred books. It is evidently the work of some Hellenistic Jew, and in the Vulgate version it forms the thirteenth chapter of the book of Daniel. In the Septuagint version it is placed at the beginning of that book."—Horne, iv. 218.

"The History of the Destruction of Bel and the Dragon was always rejected by the Jewish church; it is not extant either in the Hebrew or the Chaldee language. Jerome gives it no better title than The Fable of Bel and the Dragon; nor has it obtained more credit with posterity, except with the fathers of the Council of Trent, who determined it to be a part of the canonical Scriptures. This book forms the fourteenth chapter of the book of Daniel in the Latin Vulgate; in the Greek, it

was called the Prophecy of Habakkuk, the son of Jesus, of the tribe of
Levi. There are two Greek texts of this fragment—that of the Septuagint, and that found in Theodotion's Greek version of Daniel. The
former is the most ancient, and has been translated into Syriac. The
Latin and Arabic versions, together with another Syriac translation,
have been made from the text of Theodotion."—Horne, iv. 218. These
additions to Daniel may be found in Greek, Arabic, Syriac, and Latin,
in Walton's *Polyglott*, tom. iv.

§ VI.—THE ANCIENT VERSIONS OF THE BOOK OF DANIEL.

(1.) Of these, the oldest, of course, is the Septuagint. For a general
account of this version, see Intro. to Isaiah, § VIII. I. (1.) Of the *author*
of that portion of the Septuagint version which comprised the book
of Daniel—for no one can doubt that the Septuagint was the work of
different authors—we have now no information. The translation of
Daniel was among the least faithful, and was the most erroneous, of the
whole collection; and, indeed, it was so imperfect that its use in the
church was early superseded by the version of Theodotion—the version
which is now found in the editions of the Septuagint.

The Septuagint translation of the book of Daniel was for a long time
supposed to be lost, and it is only at a comparatively recent period that
it has been recovered and published. For a considerable period before
the time of Jerome, the version by the LXX. had been superseded by
that of Theodotion, doubtless on account of the great imperfection of
the former, though it is probable that its disuse was gradual. Jerome,
in his Preface to the Book of Daniel, says, indeed, that it was not known
to him on what ground this happened—"Danielem prophetam juxta
LXX. interpretes ecclesiæ non legunt, *et hoc cur acciderit, nescio*,"—but
it is in every way probable that it was on account of the great imperfection of the translation; for Jerome himself says, "Hoc unum affirmare,
quod multum a veritate discordet et recto judicio repudiata sit." He
adds, therefore, that though Theodotion was understood to be an *unbeliever*—"post adventum Christi incredulus fuit"—yet that his translation was preferred to that of the LXX. "Illud quoque lectorem admoneo,
Danielem non juxta LXX. interpretes, sed juxta Theodotionem ecclesias legere, qui utique post adventum Christi incredulus fuit. Unde
judicio magistrorum ecclesiæ editio eorum in hoc volumine repudiata
est, et Theodotionis vulgo legitur, quæ et Hebræo et ceteris transla-
toribus congruit."

From this cause it happened that the translation of Daniel by the
LXX. went into entire disuse, and was for a long time supposed to have
been destroyed. It has, however, been recovered and published, though
it has not been substituted in the editions of the Septuagint in the
place of the version by Theodotion. A copy of the old version by the
LXX. was found in the Chisian library at Rome, in a single manuscript

(Codex Chisianus), and was published in Rome, in folio, in the year 1772, under the title, Daniel Secundum LXX. ex tetraplis Origenis nunc primum editus e singulari Chisiano Codice annorum supra DCCC.—*Romæ*, 1772. fol. This was republished at Gœttingen, in 1773, and again in 1774. These editions were prepared by J. D. Michaelis, the former containing the text only, the latter with the text of the LXX., the version of Theodotion, the interpretation of Hippolytus, a Latin version, and the annotations of the Roman editor.

These editions were published from one manuscript, and without any attempt to correct the text by a comparison with other versions. The text is supposed to have been corrupted, so that, as Hahn says, no one can believe that this codex exhibits it as it was when the version was made. "This corruption," says he, "exists not only in particular words and phrases, but in the general disarrangement and disorder of the whole text, so that those parts are separated which ought to be united, and those parts united which ought to be kept distinct. Besides this, there was entire inattention to the *signs* which Origen had used in his edition of the Septuagint."—Pref. to Daniel, κατα τους Εβδομηκοντα. As there was but one manuscript, all hope of correcting the text in the way in which it has been done in the other parts of the Septuagint, and in other versions, by a comparison of manuscripts, was, of course, out of the question.

After four editions of the work had been published, it happened that, in the Ambrosian Library at Milan, Cajetan Bugati discovered a Syriac Hexaplar manuscript, written in the year 616 or 617, after Christ, which embraced the Hagiographa and the prophetic books, and, among others, "Daniel, according to the Septuagint translation." The title of this Syriac version, as translated by Hahn, is as follows : "Explicit liber Danielis prophetæ, qui conversus est ex traditione *τῶν* Septuaginta, duorum, qui in diebus Ptolemæi regis Ægypti ante adventum Christi annis centum plus minus verterunt libros sanctos de lingua Hebræorum, in Græcum, in Alexandria civitate magna. Versus est autem liber iste etiam de Græco in Syriacum, in Alexandria civitate mense Canun posteriori anni nongentesimi vicesimi octavi Alexandri indictione quinta (*i.e.* a 617, p. ch.)." This professes, therefore, to be a Syriac translation of the Septuagint version of Daniel. This version was found to be in good preservation, and the signs adopted by Origen to determine the value of the text were preserved, and a new edition of the Greek translation was published, corrected by this, under the title, "Daniel secundum editionem LXX. interpretum ex tetraplis desumptum. Rom., 1788." This Syriac version enabled the editor to correct many places that were defective, and to do much towards furnishing a more perfect text. Still the work was, in many respects, imperfect; and, from all the aids within his reach, and probably all that can now be hoped for, Hahn published a new edition of the work, corrected in many more places (see them enumerated in his Preface, p. ix.), under the following title, " ΔΑΝΙΗΛ κατα τους Εβδομηκοντα. E Codice Chisiano post Segaarium edidit secundum versionem Syriaco-Hexaplarem recognovit annotationibus criticis et philologicis illustravit Henricus Augustus Hahn, Philosophiæ Doctor et Theologiæ candidatus. Lipsiæ, CIƆIƆCCCXLV." This is now the most perfect edition of the Septuagint version of Daniel, but still it cannot be regarded as of great critical value in the interpretation of the book. It has been used in the preparation of this commentary. An account of the instances in which it departs from the Hebrew and Chaldee original may be seen at length in Lengerke, Das Buch Daniel, Einleitung, pp. cix.–cxiv. It has the Prayer of the Three Children, inserted in the usual place (ch. iii. 23, 24), and the History of Susanna, and the Destruction of Bel and the Dragon, as separate pieces, at the end.

(2.) The translation of Theodotion. That is, that which has been substituted in the Septuagint for the version above referred to, and which is found in the various editions of the Septuagint, and in the Polyglott Bibles. Theodotion was a native of Ephesus, and is termed by Eusebius an Ebionite, or semi-Christian. Jerome, as we have seen above, regarded him as an unbeliever—post adventum Christi incredulus fuit : that is, he *remained* an unbeliever after the coming of Christ ; probably meaning that he was a Jew by birth, and remained unconvinced that Jesus was the Messiah. He was nearly contemporary with Aquila, who was the author of a Greek translation of the Old Testament, and who was also of Jewish descent. The Jews were dissatisfied with the Septuagint version as being too paraphrastic, and Aquila undertook to make a literal version, but without any regard to the genius of the Greek language. We have only some fragments of the version by Aquila. The version of Theodotion is less literal than that of Aquila —holding a middle rank between the servile closeness of Aquila, and the freedom of Symmachus. This version is cited by Justin Martyr, in his *Dialogue with Tryphon the Jew*, which was composed about the year 160. The version of Theodotion is a kind of revision of the Septuagint, and supplies some deficiencies in the Septuagint, but the author shows that he was indifferently skilled in Hebrew. It is evident, that in his translation Theodotion made great use of both the previous versions, that by the LXX. and that of Aquila; that he followed sometimes the diction of the one, and sometimes that of the other ; that he often mingled them together in the compass of the same verse; and that he adapted the quotations from the two versions to his own style. As his style was similar to that of the LXX., Origen, in his *Hexapla*, perhaps for the sake of uniformity, supplied the additions which he inserted in his work chiefly from this version. There are but few fragments of these versions now remaining. See Horne, *Intro.* iv. 171–176. Lengerke supposes that Theodotion was a Christian, p. cxv. From this translation of Theodotion, a version was made in Arabic, in the tenth century, Lengerke, p. cxv.

(3.) The Syriac versions. For the general character of these versions, see Intro. to Isaiah, § viii. (3.) There is nothing remarkable in these versions of Daniel. For an account of a later Syriac version of the Septuagint, see the remarks above. " As Daniel has no Targum or Chaldee version, the Syriac version performs a valuable service in the explanation of Hebrew words."—Stuart, p. 491.

(4.) The Latin Vulgate. For the general character of this, see Intro. to Isaiah, § viii. (2.) As this contains the apocryphal portions, the Prayer of the Three Children, the History of Susanna, and the Destruction of Bel and the Dragon, and as the Latin Vulgate was declared canonical by the Council of Trent, of course those fragments have received the sanction of the Roman Catholic church as a part of the inspired records. This version, as a whole, is superior to any of the other ancient versions, and shows a more thorough knowledge than any of them of the tenor and nature of the book. " An invaluable service has Jerome done, by the translation of Daniel, and by his commentary on the book."—Prof. Stuart, p. 491.

(5.) The Arabic version. For an account of the Arabic versions, see Intro. to Isaiah, § viii. (4.) There is nothing peculiar in the Arabic version of Daniel.

§ VII.—EXEGETICAL HELPS TO THE BOOK OF DANIEL.

Besides the versions above referred to, I have made use of the following exegetical helps to the book of Daniel, in the preparation of these Notes. The order in which they are mentioned is not designed to express anything in regard to their value, but is adopted merely for the sake of convenience :—

Critici Sacri. Tom. iv.

Calvin, Prælectiones in Daniel. Works, vol. v., ed. Amsterdam, 1667.

Jerome, Commentary on Daniel. Works, tom. iv., ed. Paris, 1623.

The Pictorial Bible (Dr. Kitto). London, 1836.

Bush's Illustrations of Scripture. Brattleboro, 1836.

Dr. Gill, Commentaries. Vol. vi., ed. Philadelphia, 1819.

Hengstenberg's Christology, translated by the Rev. Reuel Keith, D.D. Alexandria, 1836.

Newton on the Prophecies. London, 1832.

Einleitung in das Alte Testament. Von Johann Gottfried Eichhorn, Vierter Band, § 612-619.

Daniel aus dem Hebräisch-Aramäischen neu übersetzt und erklärt mit einer vollständigen Einleitung, und einigen historischen und exegetischen Excursen, Von Leonhard Bertholdt. Erlangen, 1806.

Das Buch Daniel Verdeutscht und Ausleget Von Dr. Cæsar von Lengerke, Professor der Theologie zu Königsburg in Pr. Königsberg, 1835.

Commentarius Grammaticus in Vetus Testamentum in usum maxime

Gymnasiorum et Academiarum adornatus. Scripsit Franc. Jos. Valent. Dominic. Maurer. Phil. Doct. Soc. Historico-Theol. Lips. Sod. Ord. Volumen Secundum. Lipsiæ, 1838.

Isaaci Newtohi ad Danielis Profetæ Vaticinia. Opuscula, tom. iii. 1744.

Lehrbuch der Historisch-Kritischen Einleitung in die kanonischen und Apokryphischen Bücher des Alten Testamentes. Von Wilhelm Martin Leberecht De Wette, § 253–259. Berlin, 1845.

In Danielem Prophetam Commentarius editus a Philippo Melan- thone, Anno MDXLIII. Corpus Reformatorum, Bretschneider, vol. xiii., 1846.

Ueber Verfasser und Zweck des Buches Daniel. Theologische Zeitschrift. Drittes Heft. Berlin, 1822, pp. 181–294. By Dr. Fried. Lücke.

Commentatio Historico-Critica Exhibens descriptionem et censuram recentium de Danielis Libro Opinionum, Auctore Henrico Godofredo Kirmss, Saxone Seminarii Theologici Sodali. Jenæ, 1828.

Die Authentie des Daniel. Von Ernst Wilhelm Hengstenberg. Berlin, 1831.

The Season and Time, or an Exposition of the Prophecies which relate to the two periods of Daniel subsequent to the 1260 years now recently expired. By W. Ettrick, A.M. London, 1816.

An Essay towards an Interpretation of the Prophecies of Daniel. By Richard Amner. London, 1776.

Neue Kritische Untersuchungen über des Buch Daniel. Von Heinrich Hävernick, der Theologie Doctor und A. O. Professor an der Univer- sität Rostock. Hamburgh, 1838.

An Exposition of such of the Prophecies of Daniel as receive their accomplishment under the New Testament. By the late Rev. Magnus Frederic Roos, A.M., Superintendent and Prelate in Lustnau and Anhausen. Translated from the German, by Ebenezer Henderson. Edinburgh, 1811.

A Description accompanying an Hieroglyphical Print of Daniel's Great Image. London.

Daniel, his Chaldie Visions and his Ebrew : both translated after the original, and expounded both, by the reduction of heathen most famous stories, with the exact proprietie of his wordes (which is the surest certaintie what he must meane) : and joining all the Bible and learned tongues to the frame of his Worke. London, 1596. By Hugh Broughton.

Observations intended to point out the application of Prophecy in the eleventh chapter of Daniel to the French Power. London, 1800. Author unknown.

An Apologie in Briefe Assertions defending that our Lord died in the time properly foretold to Daniel. For satisfaction to some studentes in both Universities. By H. Broughton. London, 1592.

An Essay in Scripture Prophecy, wherein it is endeavoured to explain the three periods contained in the twelfth chapter of the Prophet Daniel, with some arguments to make it probable that the *first* of the *periods* did expire in the year 1715. Printed in the year 1715. Author and place unknown.

Daniel, an improved Version Attempted, with a Preliminary Dissertation, and Notes, critical, historical, and explanatory. By Thomas Wintle, B.D., Rector of Brightwall, in Berkshire, and Fellow of Pembroke College. Oxford, 1792.

Hermanni Venema Commentarius, ad Danielis cap. xi. 4-45, et xii. 1-3. Leovardiæ, 1752.

A Chronological Treatise upon the Seventy Weeks of Daniel. By Benjamin Marshall, M.A., Rector of Naunton, in Gloucestershire. London, 1725.

The Times of Daniel, Chronological and Prophetical, examined with relation to the point of contact between Sacred and Profane Chronology. By George, Duke of Manchester. London, 1845.

Prof. Stuart's Commentary on Daniel (Boston, 1850) was not published until after the "Notes" or Commentary in this work had been written. I have consulted it carefully in revising the manuscript for the press.

Besides these works, which I have consulted freely, in proportion to what seemed to me their respective worth, and such collateral exegetical helps in addition as I have access to in my own library, the following works are referred to by De Wette, Lehrbuch, pp. 378, 379, as valuable aids in interpreting Daniel :—

Ephræm, d. S. Auslcg. des Proph. Daniel, Opp. ii. 203, *seq.*

Theodoret, Comment. in Visiones Dan. Proph. Opp. ed. Sculz. ii. 1053, *seq.*

Paraph. Josephi Jachidæ in Dan. c. Vers. et Annotatt. Const. l'Empereur. Amst. 1633.

Prælectt. Acad. in Dan. Proph. habitæ a Mart. Geir. Lips. 1667, cd. corr. 84.

H. Venem. Dissertatt. ad Vatice. Danielis, c. ii. vii. et viii. Leov. 1745.

Chr. B. Michæl. Annotatt. in Dan. in J. H. Michæl. Ueberr. Annotatt. in Hagiogr. iii. 1, *seq.*

Rosenmüller schol.

THE BOOK OF DANIEL

CHAPTER I.

FOR the general argument in favour of the genuineness and authenticity of the book of Daniel, see Intro. §§ II., III. To the genuineness and authenticity of each particular chapter in detail, however, objections, derived from something peculiar in each chapter, have been urged, which it is proper to meet, and which I propose to consider in a particular introduction to the respective chapters. These objections it is proper to consider, not so much because they have been urged by distinguished German critics — De Wette, Bertholdt, Bleek, Eichhorn, and others —for their writings will probably fall into the hands of few persons who will read these Notes—but (*a*) because it may be presumed that men of so much learning, industry, acuteness, and ingenuity, have urged all the objections which can, with any appearance of plausibility, be alleged against the book ; and (*b*) because the objections which they have urged may be presumed to be felt, to a greater or less degree, by those who read the book, though they might not be able to express them with so much clearness and force. There are numerous objections to various portions of the Scriptures floating in the minds of the readers of the Bible, and many difficulties which occur to such readers which are not expressed, and which it would be desirable to re-

move, and which it is the duty of an expositor of the Bible, if he can, to remove. Sceptical critics, in general, but collect and embody in a plausible form difficulties which are felt by most readers of the Scriptures. It is for this reason, and with a view to remove what *seems* to furnish plausible arguments against the different portions of this book, that the objections which have been urged, principally by the authors above referred to, will be noticed in special sections preceding the exposition of each chapter.

The only objection to the genuineness and authenticity of the first chapter which it seems necessary to notice is, that the account of Daniel in the chapter is inconsistent with the mention of Daniel by Ezekiel. The objection substantially is, that it is improbable that the Daniel who is mentioned by Ezekiel should be one who was a cotemporary with himself, and who at that time lived in Babylon. Daniel is three times mentioned in Ezekiel, and in each case as a man of eminent piety and integrity ; as one so distinguished by his virtues as to deserve to be classed with the most eminent of the patriarchs. Thus in Ezek. xiv. 14, "Though these three men, Noah, Daniel, and Job, were in it, they should deliver but their own souls by their righteousness, saith the Lord God." So again, ver. 20, "Though Noah, Daniel, and Job, were in it, as I live, saith the Lord God, they shall deliver neither son nor daughter, they shall deliver but their own souls by their righteousness." And again, ch. xxviii. 3, speaking of the prince of Tyre, "Behold thou art wiser than Daniel." The objection urged in respect to the mention of Daniel in these passages is substantially this—that if the account in the book of Daniel is true, he must have been a cotemporary with Ezekiel, and must have been, when Ezekiel prophesied, a young man; that it is incredible that he should have gained a degree of reputation which would entitle him to be ranked with Noah and Job; that he could not have been so well known as to make it natural or proper to refer to him in the same connection with those eminent men; and *especially* that he could not have been thus known to the prince of Tyre, as is supposed of those mentioned by Ezekiel in the passages referred to, for it cannot be presumed that a man so young had acquired such a fame abroad as to make it proper to refer to him in this manner in an address to a heathen prince. This objection was urged by Bernstein (über das Buch Hiob, in den Analekten von Keil und Tzschirner, i. 3, p. 10), and it is found also in Bleek, p. 284, and De Wette, *Einl.* p. 380. De Wette says that it is probable that the author of the book of Daniel used the name of "an ancient mythic or poetic person falsely," in order to illustrate his work.

Now, in regard to this objection, it may be remarked (a) that, according to all the accounts which we have in the Bible, Ezekiel and Daniel *were* cotemporary, and were in Babylon at the same time. As Daniel, however, lived a long time in Babylon after this, it is to be admitted, also, that at the period referred to by Ezekiel, he must have been comparatively a young man. But it does not follow that he might not then have had a well-known character for piety and integrity, which would make it proper to mention his name in connection with the most eminent saints of ancient times. If the account in the book of Daniel *itself* is a correct account of him, this will not be doubted, for he soon attracted attention in Babylon; he soon evinced that extraordinary piety which made him so eminent as a man of God, and that extraordinary wisdom which raised him to the highest rank as an officer of state in Babylon. It was very soon after he was taken to Babylon that the purpose was formed to train him, and the three other selected youths, in the learning of the Chaldeans (ch. i. 1–4), and that Daniel showed that he was qualified to pass the examination, preparatory to his occupying an honourable place in the court (ch. i. 18–21); and it was only in the second year of the reign of Nebuchadnezzar that the remarkable dream occurred, the interpretation of which gave to Daniel so much celebrity (ch. ii.). According to a computation of Hengstenberg (*Authentie des Daniel,* p. 71), Daniel was taken to Babylon full ten years before the prophecy of Ezekiel, in which the first mention of him was made; and if so, there can be no real ground for the objection referred to. In that time, if the account of his extraordinary wisdom is true; if he evinced the character which it is said that he did evince—and against this there is no intrinsic improbability; and if he was exalted to office and rank, as it is stated that he was, there can be no improbability in what Ezekiel says of him, that he had a character which made it proper that he should be classed with the most eminent men of the Jewish nation. (b) As to the objection that the name of Daniel could not have been known to the king of Tyre, as would seem to be implied in Ezek. xxviii. 3, it may be remarked, that it is not necessary to suppose that these prophecies were ever known to the king of Tyre, or that they were ever designed to influence him. The prophecies which were directed against the ancient heathen kings were uttered and published among the Hebrew people, primarily for *their* guidance, and were design d to furnish to them, and to others i . future times, arguments for the truth of religion, though they assumed the form of direct addresses to the kings themselves. Such an imaginary appeal may have been made in this case by Ezekiel to the king of Tyre; and, in speaking of him, and of his boasted wisdom, Ezekiel may have made the comparison which would then naturally occur to him, by mentioning him in connection with the most eminent man for wisdom of that age. But it should be said, also, that there can be no certain evidence that the name of Daniel was *not* known to the king of Tyre, and no intrinsic improbability in the supposition that it was. If Daniel had at that time evinced the remarkable wisdom at the court of Babylon which it is said in this book that he had ; if he had been raised to that high rank which it is affirmed he had reached, there is no improbability in supposing that so remarkable a circumstance should have been made known to the king of Tyre. Tyre was taken by Nebuchadnezzar, B.C. 572, after a siege of thirteen years, and it is in no way improbable that the king of Tyre would be made acquainted with what occurred at the court of the Chaldeans. The prophecy in Ezekiel, where Daniel is mentioned (ch. xxviii. 3), could not have been uttered long before Tyre was taken, and, in referring to what was to occur, it was not unnatural to mention the

man most distinguished for wisdom at the court of Babylon, and in the councils of Nebuchadnezzar, with the presumption that his name and celebrity would not be unknown to the king of Tyre. (c) As to the objection of Bernstein, that it would be improbable, if Daniel lived there, and if he was comparatively a young man, that his name would be placed *between* that of Noah and Job (Ezek. xiv. 14), as if he had lived *before* Job, it may be remarked, that there might be a greater similarity between the circumstances of Noah and Daniel than between Noah and Job, and that it was proper to refer to them in this order. But the mere circumstance of the *order* in which the names are mentioned cannot be adduced as a proof that one of the persons named did not exist at that time. They may have occurred in this order to Ezekiel, because in his apprehension, that was the order in which the degree of their piety was to be estimated.

To this objection thus considered, that the mention of Daniel in connection with Noah and Job, proves that Ezekiel referred to some one of ancient times, it may be further replied, that, if this were so, it is impossible to account for the fact that no such person is mentioned by any of the earlier prophets and writers. How came his name to be known to Ezekiel ? And if there had been a patriarch so eminent as to be ranked with Noah and Job, how is it to be accounted for that all the sacred writers, up to the time of Ezekiel, are wholly silent in regard to him ? And why is it that, when *he* mentions him, he does it as of one who was well known ? The mere mention of his name in this manner by Ezekiel, proves that his character was well known to those for whom he wrote. Noah and Job were thus known by the ancient records ; but how was *Daniel* thus known ? He is nowhere mentioned in the ancient writings of the Hebrews ; and if he was so well known that he could be referred to in the same way as Noah and Job, it must be either because there was some *tradition* in regard to him, or because he was then living, and his character was well understood by those for whom Ezekiel wrote. But there is no evidence that there was any such tradition, and no probability that there was ; and the conclusion, then, is inevitable, that he was then so well known to the Hebrews in exile, that it was proper for Ezekiel to mention him just as he did Noah and Job. If so, this furnishes the highest evidence that he actually lived in the time of Ezekiel ; that is, in the time when this book purports to have been written.

§ II.—ANALYSIS OF THE CHAPTER.

This chapter is entirely historical, the prophetic portions of the book commencing with the second chapter. The *object* of this chapter seems to be to state the way in which Daniel, who subsequently acted so important a part in Babylon, was raised to so distinguished favour with the king and court. It was remarkable that a Jewish captive, and a young man, should be so honoured ; that he should be admitted as one of the principal counsellors of the king, and that he should ultimately become the prime-minister of the realm ; and there was a propriety that there should be a preliminary statement of the steps of this extraordinary promotion. This chapter contains a record of the way in which the future premier and prophet was introduced to the notice of the reigning monarch, and by which his wonderful genius and sagacity were discovered. It is a chapter, therefore, that may be full of interest and instruction to all, and especially to young men. The chapter contains the record

of the following points, or steps, which led to the promotion of Daniel :—

I. The history of the Jewish captivity, as explanatory of the reason why those who are subsequently referred to were in Babylon. They were exiles, having been conveyed as captives to a foreign land, vers. 1, 2.

II. The purpose of the king, Nebuchadnezzar, to bring forward the principal talent to be found among the Jewish captives, and to put it under a process of training, that it might be employed at the court, vers. 3, 4. In carrying out this purpose, a confidential officer of the court, Ashpenaz, was directed to search out among the captives the most promising youths, whether by birth or talent, and to put them under a process of training, that they might become fully instructed in the science of the Chaldeans. What were the reasons which led to this cannot be known with certainty. They may have been such as these : (1.) The Chaldeans had devoted themselves to science, especially to those sciences which promised any information respecting future events, the secrets of the unseen world, &c. Hence they either originated or adopted the science of astrology ; they practised the arts of magic; they studied to interpret dreams ; and, in general, they made use of all the means which it was then supposed could be employed to unlock the secrets of the invisible world, and to disclose the future. (2.) They could not have been ignorant of the fact, that the Hebrews claimed to have communications with God. They had doubtless heard of their prophets, and of their being able to foretell what was to occur. This kind of knowledge would fall in with the objects at which the Chaldeans aimed, and if they could avail themselves of it, it would enable them to secure what they so ardently sought. It is probable that they considered this as a sort of *permanent* power which the Hebrew prophets had, and supposed that at all times, and on all subjects, they could interpret dreams, and solve the various questions about which their own magicians were so much engaged. It is not to be presumed that they had any very accurate knowledge of the exact character of the Hebrew prophecies, or the nature of the communication which the prophets had with God; but it was not unnatural for them to suppose that this spirit of prophecy or divination would be possessed by the most noble and the most talented of the land. Hence Ashpenaz was instructed to select those of the royal family, and those in whom there was no blemish, and who were handsome, and who were distinguished for knowledge, and to prepare them, by a suitable course, for being presented to the king. (3.) It may have been the purpose of the Chaldean monarch to bring forward all the talent of the realm, whether native or foreign, to be employed in the service of the government. There is no reason to suppose that there was any jealousy of foreign talent, or any reluctance to employ it in any proper way, in promoting the interests of the kingdom. As the Chaldean monarch had now in his possession the Hebrew royal family, and all the principal men that had been distinguished in Judea, it was not unnatural to suppose that there might be valuable talent among them of which he might avail himself, and which would add to the splendour of his own court and cabinet. It might have been naturally supposed, also, that it would tend much to conciliate the captives themselves, and repress any existing impatience, or insubordination, to select the most noble and the most gifted of them, and to employ them in the service of the government; and in any questions that might arise between the government and the captive nation, it would be an advantage for the government to be able to employ native-born Hebrews in making known the wishes and purposes of the government. It was, moreover, in accordance with the proud spirit of Nebuchadnezzar (see ch. iv.) to surround himself with all that would impart splendour to his own reign.

III. The method by which this talent was to be brought forward, vers. 5–7. This was by a course of living in the manner of the royal household, with the presumption that at the end of three years, in personal appearance, and in the knowledge of the language of the Chaldeans (ver. 4), they would be prepared to appear at court, and to be employed in the service to which they might be appointed.

IV. The resolution of Daniel not to corrupt himself with the viands which had been appointed for him and his brethren, ver. 8. He had heretofore been strictly temperate; he had avoided all luxurious living; he had abstained from wine; and, though now having all the means of luxurious indulgence at command, and being unexpectedly thrown into the temptations of a splendid Oriental court, he resolved to adhere stedfastly to his principles.

V. The apprehension of the prince of the eunuchs that this would be a ground of offence with his master, the king, and that he would himself be held responsible, vers. 9, 10. This was a very natural apprehension, as the command seems to have been positive, and as an Oriental monarch was entirely despotic. It was not unreasonable for him to whom this office was intrusted to suppose that a failure on his part to accomplish what he had been directed to do would be followed by a loss of place or life.

VI. The experiment, and the result,

CHAPTER I.

IN the third year of the reign of
Jehoiakim king of Judah came

a Nebuchadnezzar king of Babylon
unto Jerusalem, and besieged it.

a 2 Ki. 24. 1, 2; 2 Chr. 36. 6, 7.

vers. 11–17. Daniel asked that a trial
might be made of the effects of temperance in preparing him and his companions for presentation at court. He
requested that they might be permitted,
even for a brief time, yet long enough
to make a fair experiment, to abstain
from wine, and the other luxuries of
the royal table, and that then it might
be determined whether they should be
allowed to continue the experiment.
The result was as he had anticipated.
At the end of ten days, on a fair comparison with those who had indulged
in luxurious living, the benefit of their
course was apparent, and they were
permitted to continue this strict abstinence during the remainder of the time
which was deemed necessary for their
preparation to appear at court.

VII. The presentation at court, vers.
18–21. At the end of the time appointed
for preparation, Daniel and his selected
companions were brought into the royal
presence, and met with the most favourable reception which could have been
hoped for. They were distinguished,
it would seem, for beauty and manly
vigour, and as much distinguished for
wisdom as they were for the beauty and
healthfulness of their bodily appearance. They at once took an honourable station, greatly surpassing in true
wisdom and knowledge those at the
court who were regarded as skilled in
the arts of divination and astrology.
These years of preparation we are not
to suppose were spent in merely culti-
vating the beauty of their personal
appearance, but they were doubtless
employed, under all the advantages of
instruction which could be afforded
them, in the careful cultivation of their
mental powers, and in the acquisition

of all the knowledge which could be
obtained under the best masters at the
court of the Chaldeans. Comp. ver. 4.

1. *In the third year of the reign of
Jehoiakim king of Judah came Nebuchadnezzar king of Babylon unto Jerusalem.* This event occurred, according
to Jahn (*History of the Hebrew Commonwealth*), in the year 607 B.C., and
in the 368th year after the revolt of the
ten tribes. According to Usher, it was
in the 369th year of the revolt, and 606
B.C. The computation of Usher is the
one generally received, but the difference of a year in the reckoning is
not material. Comp. Michaelis, An-
merkung, zu 2 Kön. xxiv. 1. Jehoiakim was a son of Josiah, a prince
who was distinguished for his piety,
2 Ki. xxii. 2 ; 2 Chron. xxxv. 1–7.
After the death of Josiah, the people
raised to the throne of Judah Jehoahaz,
the youngest son of Josiah, probably
because he appeared better qualified
to reign than his elder brother, 2 Ki.
xxiii. 30 ; 2 Chron. xxxvi. 1. He was
a wicked prince, and after he had been
on the throne three months, he was
removed by Pharaoh-nechoh, king of
Egypt, who returned to Jerusalem from
the conquest of Phœnicia, and placed
his elder brother, Eliakim, to whom
he gave the name of Jehoiakim, on
the throne, 2 Ki. xxiii. 34 ; 2 Chron.
xxxvi. 4. Jehoahaz was first impri-
soned in Riblah, 2 Ki. xxiii. 33, and
was afterwards removed to Egypt,
2 Chron. xxxvi. 4. Jehoiakim, an
unworthy son of Josiah, was, in reality,
as he is represented by Jeremiah, one
of the worst kings who reigned over
Judah. His reign continued eleven
years, and as he came to the throne
B.C. 611, his reign continued to the
year 600 B.C. In the third year of
his reign, after the battle of Megiddo,
Pharaoh-nechoh undertook a second
expedition against Nabopolassar, king
of Babylon, with a numerous army,
drawn in part from Western Africa,
Lybia, and Ethiopia. —Jahn's *Hist.*

2 And the Lord gave Jehoiakim king of Judah into his hand, with

part of the vessels of the house of God, which he carried into the land

---

Heb. Commonwealth, p. 134. This Nabopolassar, who is also called Nebuchadnezzar I., was at this time, as Berosus relates, aged and infirm. He therefore gave up a part of his army to his son Nebuchadnezzar, who defeated the Egyptian host at Carchemish (Circesium) on the Euphrates, and drove Nechoh out of Asia. The victorious prince marched directly to Jerusalem, which was then under the sovereignty of Egypt. After a short siege Jehoiakim surrendered, and was again placed on the throne by the Babylonian prince. Nebuchadnezzar took part of the furniture of the temple as booty, and carried back with him to Babylon several young men, the sons of the principal Hebrew nobles, among whom were Daniel and his three friends referred to in this chapter. It is not improbable that one object in conveying them to Babylon was that they might be hostages for the submission and good order of the Hebrews in their own land. It is at this time that the Babylonian sovereignty over Judah commences, commonly called the Babylonian captivity, which, according to the prophecy of Jeremiah, (xxv. 1–14 ; xxix. 10), was to continue seventy years. In Jer. xxv. 1, and xlvi. 2, it is said that this was in the *fourth* year of Jehoiakim ; in the passage before us it is said that it was the *third* year. This difference, says Jahn, arises from a different mode of computation : "Jehoiakim came to the throne at the end of the year, which Jeremiah reckons as the first (and such a mode of reckoning is not uncommon), but Daniel, neglecting the incomplete year, numbers one less." For a more full and complete examination of the objection to the genuineness of Daniel from this passage, I would refer to Prof. Stuart on Daniel, *Excursus* I. [See App. I. to this Vol.] ¶ *And besieged it.* Jerusalem was a strongly-fortified place, and it was not easy to take it, except as the result of a siege. It was, perhaps, never carried by direct and immediate assault. Comp. 2 Ki. xxv. 1–3, for an account of a siege of Jerusalem a second time

by Nebuchadnezzar. At that time the city was besieged about a year and a half. How long the siege here referred to continued is not specified.

2. *And the Lord gave Jehoiakim king of Judah into his hand.* Jehoiakim was taken captive, and it would seem that there was an intention to convey him to Babylon (2 Chron. xxxvi. 6), but that for some cause he was not removed there, but died at Jerusalem (2 Ki. xxiv. 5, 6), though he was not honourably buried there, Jer. xxii. 19 ; xxxvi. 30. In the second book of Chronicles (xxxvi. 6), it is said that "Nebuchadnezzar king of Babylon came up, and bound Jehoiakim in fetters, to take him to Babylon." Jahn supposes that an error has crept into the text in the book of Chronicles, as there is no evidence that Jehoiakim was taken to Babylon, but it appears from 2 Ki. xxiv. 1, 2, that Jehoiakim was continued in authority at Jerusalem under Nebuchadnezzar three years, and then rebelled against him, and that then Nebuchadnezzar sent against him "bands of the Chaldees, and bands of the Syrians, and bands of the Moabites, and bands of the children of Ammon, and sent them against Judah to destroy it." There is no necessity of supposing an error in the text in the account in the book of Chronicles. It is probable that Jehoiakim was taken, and that the *intention* was to take him to Babylon, according to the account in Chronicles, but that, from some cause not mentioned, the purpose of the Chaldean monarch was changed, and that he was placed again over Judah, under Nebuchadnezzar, according to the account in the book of Kings, and that he remained in this condition for three years till he rebelled, and that then the bands of Chaldeans, &c., were sent against him. It is probable that at this time, perhaps while the siege was going on, he died, and that the Chaldeans dragged his dead body out of the gates of the city, and left it unburied, as Jeremiah had predicted, Jer. xxii. 19 ; xxxvi. 30. ¶ *With part of the vessels of the house of God.* 2 Chron. xxxvi. 7. Another portion of the

of Shinar, to the house of his god ; and he brought the vessels into the treasure-house of his god.

3 ¶ And the king spake unto

Ashpenaz the master of his eunuchs, that he should bring *certain* of the children *a* of Israel, and of the king's seed, and of the princes;

a Foretold, 2 Ki. 20. 17, 18; Is. 39. 7.

vessels of the temple at Jerusalem was taken away by Nebuchadnezzar, in the time of Jehoiachin, the successor of Jehoiakim, 2 Chron. xxxvi. 10. On the third invasion of Palestine, the same thing was repeated on a more extensive scale, 2 Ki. xxiv. 13. At the fourth and final invasion, under Zedekiah, when the temple was destroyed, all its treasures were carried away, 2 Ki. xxv. 6–20. A part of these treasures were brought back under Cyrus, Ezra i. 7; the rest under Darius, Ezra vi. 5. Why they were not *all* taken away at first does not appear, but perhaps Nebuchadnezzar did not then intend wholly to overthrow the Hebrew nation, but meant to keep them tributary to him as a people. The temple was not at that time destroyed, but probably he allowed the worship of Jehovah to be celebrated there still, and he would naturally leave such vessels as were absolutely necessary to keep up the services of public worship. ¶ *Which he carried into the land of Shinar.* The region around Babylon. The exact limits of this country are unknown, but it probably embraced the region known as Mesopotamia—the country between the rivers Tigris and Euphrates. The derivation of the name *Shinar* is unknown. It occurs only in Gen. x. 10; xi. 2; xiv. 1, 9; Josh. vii. 21; Isa. xi. 11; Dan. i. 2; Zech. v. 11. ¶ *To the house of his god.* To the temple of Bel, at Babylon. This was a temple of great magnificence, and the worship of Bel was celebrated there with great splendour. For a description of this temple, and of the god which was worshipped there, see Notes on Isa. xlvi. 1. These vessels were subsequently brought out at the command of Belshazzar, at his celebrated feast, and employed in the conviviality and revelry of that occasion. See Dan. v. 3. ¶ *And he brought the vessels into the treasure-house of his god.* It would seem rom this that the vessels had been taken to the temple of Bel, or Belus, in

Babylon, not to be used in the worship of the idol, but to be laid up among the valuable treasures there. As the temples of the gods were sacred, and were regarded as inviolable, it would be natural to make them the repository of valuable spoils and treasures. Many of the spoils of the Romans were suspended around the walls of the temples of their gods, particularly in the temple of Victory. Compare Eschenberg, *Manual of Class. Lit.* pt. iii. § 149, 150.

3. *And the king spake unto Ashpenaz the master of his eunuchs.* On the general reasons which may have influenced the king to make the selection of the youths here mentioned, see the analysis of the chapter. Of Ashpenaz, nothing more is known than is stated here. Eunuchs were then, as they are now, in constant employ in the harems of the East, and they often rose to great influence and power. A large portion of the slaves employed at the courts in the East, and in the houses of the wealthy, are eunuchs. Comp. Burckhardt's *Travels in Nubia*, pp. 294, 295. They are regarded as the guardians of the female virtue of the harem, but their situation gives them great influence, and they often rise high in the favour of their employers, and often become the principal officers of the court. "The chief of the black eunuchs is yet, at the court of the Sultan, which is arranged much in accordance with the ancient court of Persia, an officer of the highest dignity. He is called Kislar-Aga, the overseer of the women, and is the chief of the black eunuchs, who guard the harem, or the apartments of the females. The Kislar-Aga enjoys, through his situation, a vast influence, especially in regard to the offices of the court, the principal Agas deriving their situations through him." See Jos. von Hammers *des Osmanischen Reichs Staatsverwalt,* Th. i. s. 71, as quoted in Rosenmüller's *Alte und neue Morgenland,* ii. 357, 358.

[The figures in the annexed engravings are from the Nimroud sculptures, and represent two *eunuchs* holding high official rank in the royal

household of the Assyrian monarch. The one is the royal sceptre-bearer, and the other the

royal cup-bearer, the office of each being designated by the insignia he bears.]

That it is common in the East to desire that those employed in public service should have vigorous bodies, and beauty of form, and to train them for this, will be apparent from the following extract: —"Curtius says, that in all barbarous or uncivilized countries, the stateliness of the body is held in great veneration ; nor do they think him capable of great services or action to whom nature has not vouchsafed to give a beautiful form and aspect. It has always been the custom of eastern nations to choose such for their principal officers, or to wait on princes and great personages. Sir Paul Ricaut observes, 'That the youths that are designed for the great offices of the Turkish empire must be of admirable features and looks, well shaped in their bodies, and without any defect of nature ; for it is conceived that a corrupt and sordid soul can scarcely inhabit in a serene and ingenuous aspect ; and I have observed, not only in the seraglio, but also in the courts of great men, their personal attendants have been of comely lusty youths, well habited, deporting themselves with singular modesty and respect in the presence of their masters ; so that when a Pascha Aga Spahi travels, he is always attended with a comely equipage, followed by flourishing youths, well clothed, and mounted, in great numbers.' "—Burder. This may serve to explain the reason of the arrangement made in respect to these Hebrew youths. ¶ *That he should bring* certain *of the children of Israel.* Heb., "of the *sons* of Israel." Nothing can with certainty be determined respecting their *age* by the use of this expression, for the phrase means merely the descendants of Jacob, or Israel, that is, *Jews,* and it would be applied to them at any time of life. It would seem, however, from subsequent statements, that those who were selected were young men. It is evident that young men would be better qualified for the object contemplated — to be *trained* in the language and the sciences of the Chaldeans (ver. 4) — than those who were at a more advanced period of life. ¶ *And of the king's seed, and of the princes.* That the most illustrious, and the most promising of them were to be selected ; those who would be most adapted to accomplish the object which he had in view. Compare the analysis of the chapter. It is probable that the king presumed, that among the royal youths

4 Children in whom *was* no blemish, but well-favoured, and skilful

in all wisdom, and cunning in knowledge, and understanding science,

who had been made captive there would be found those of most talent, and of course those best qualified to impart dignity and honour to his government, as well as those who would be most likely to be qualified to make known future events by the interpretation of dreams, and by the prophetic intimations of the Divine will.

4. *Children in whom* was *no blemish.* The word rendered *children* in this place (וִילָדִים) is different from that which is rendered *children* in ver. 3— בָּנִים. That word denotes merely that they were *sons,* or *descendants,* of Israel, without implying anything in regard to their age ; the word here used would be appropriate only to those who were at an early period of life, and makes it certain that the king meant that those who were selected should be youths. Comp. Gen. iv. 23, where the word is rendered "a young man." It is sometimes, indeed, used to denote a son, without reference to age, and is then synonymous with בֵּן *bĕn, a son.* But it properly means *one born ;* that is, *recently born ;* a child, Gen. xxi. 8 ; Exod. i. 17 ; ii. 3 ; and then one in early life. There can be no doubt that the monarch meant to designate youths. So the Vulgate, *pueros,* and the Greek, νεανίσκους, and so the Syriac. All these words would be applicable to those who were in early life, or to young men. Compare Intro. to Daniel, § I. The word *blemish* refers to bodily defect or imperfection. The object was to select those who were most perfect in form, perhaps partly because it was supposed that beautiful youths would most grace the court, and partly because it was supposed that such would be likely to have the brightest intellectual endowments. It was regarded as essential to personal beauty to be without blemish, 2 Sam. xiv. 25 : "But in all Israel there was none to be so much praised as Absalom for beauty ; from the sole of his foot even to the crown of his head there was no blemish in him." Canticles iv. 7 : "Thou art all fair, my love ; there is no spot in thee."

The word is sometimes used in a moral sense, to denote corruption of heart or life (Deut. xxxii. 5 ; Job xi. 15 ; xxxi. 7), but that is not the meaning here. ¶ *But well-favoured.* Heb., "good of appearance ;" that is, beautiful. ¶ *And skilful in all wisdom.* Intelligent, wise—that is, in all that was esteemed wise in their own country. The object was to bring forward the most talented and intelligent, as well as the most beautiful, among the Hebrew captives. ¶ *And cunning in knowledge.* In all that could be known. The distinction between the word here rendered *knowledge* (דַּעַת) and the word rendered *science* (מַדָּע) is not apparent. Both come from the word יָדַע *to know,* and would be applicable to any kind of knowledge. The word rendered *cunning* is also derived from the same root, and means *knowing,* or *skilled in.* We more commonly apply the word to a particular kind of knowledge, meaning artful, shrewd, astute, sly, crafty, designing. But this was not the meaning of the word when the translation of the Bible was made, and it is not employed in that sense in the Scriptures. It is always used in a good sense, meaning intelligent, skilful, experienced, well-instructed. Comp. Gen. xxv. 27 ; Exod. xxvi. 1 ; xxviii. 15 ; xxxviii. 23 ; 1 Sam. xvi. 16 ; 1 Chron. xxv. 7 ; Psal. cxxxvii. 5 ; Isa. iii. 3. ¶ *And understanding science.* That is, the sciences which prevailed among the Hebrews. They were not a nation distinguished for *science,* in the sense in which that term is now commonly understood — embracing astronomy, chemistry, geology, mathematics, electricity, &c. ; but their science extended chiefly to music, architecture, natural history, agriculture, morals, theology, war, and the knowledge of future events ; in all which they occupied an honourable distinction among the nations. In many of these respects they were, doubtless, far in advance of the Chaldeans ; and it was probably the purpose of the Chaldean monarch to avail himself of what they knew.

and such as *had* ability in them to stand in the king's palace, and whom

¶ *And such as* had *ability in them to stand in the king's palace.* Heb., "had strength" — כֹּחַ. Properly meaning, who had strength of body for the service which would be required of them in attending on the court. "A firm constitution of body is required for those protracted services of standing in the hall of the royal presence."— Grotius. The word *palace* here (הֵיכָל) is commonly used to denote the temple (2 Kings xxiv. 13 ; 2 Chron. iii. 17 ; Jer. l. 28 ; Hag. ii. 15. Its proper and primitive signification, however, is a large and magnificent building—a palace—and it was given to the temple as *the palace* of Jehovah, the abode where he dwelt as king of his people. ¶ *And whom they might teach.* That they might be better qualified for the duties to which they might be called. The purpose was, doubtless (see analysis), to bring forward their talent, that it might contribute to the splendour of the Chaldean court ; but as they were, doubtless, ignorant to a great extent of the language of the Chaldeans, and as there were sciences in which the Chaldeans were supposed to excel, it seemed desirable that they should have all the advantage which could be derived from a careful training under the best masters. ¶ *The learning* — סֵפֶר. Literally, *writing* (Isa. xxix. 11, 12). Gesenius supposes that this means the *writing* of the Chaldeans ; or that they might be able to read the language of the Chaldeans. But it, doubtless, included *the knowledge* of what was written, as well as the ability *to read* what was written ; that is, the purpose was to instruct them in the sciences which were understood among the Chaldeans. They were distinguished chiefly for such sciences as these : (1.) Astronomy. This science is commonly supposed to have had its origin on the plains of Babylon, and it was early carried there to as high a degree of perfection as it attained in any of the ancient nations. Their mild climate, and their employment as shepherds, leading them to pass much

they might teach the learning and the tongue of the Chaldeans.

of their time at night under the open heavens, gave them the opportunity of observing the stars, and they amused themselves in marking their positions and their changes, and in mapping out the heavens in a variety of fanciful figures, now called constellations. (2.) Astrology. This was at first a branch of astronomy, or was almost identical with it, for the stars were studied principally to endeavour to ascertain what influence they exerted over the fates of men, and especially what might be predicted from their position, on the birth of an individual, as to his future life. Astrology was then deemed a science whose laws were to be ascertained in the same way as the laws of any other science ; and the world has been slow to disabuse itself of the notion that the stars exert an influence over the fates of men. Even Lord Bacon held that it was a science to be "*reformed*," not wholly rejected. (3.) Magic ; soothsaying ; divination ; or whatever would contribute to lay open the future, or disclose the secrets of the invisible world. Hence they applied themselves to the interpretation of dreams ; they made use of magical arts, probably employing, as magicians do, some of the ascertained results of science in producing optical illusions, impressing the vulgar with the belief that they were familiar with the secrets of the invisible world ; and hence the name *Chaldean* and *magician* became almost synonymous terms (Dan. ii. 2 ; iv. 7 ; v. 7. (4.) It is not improbable that they had made advances in other sciences, but of this we have little knowledge. They knew little of the true laws of astronomy, geology, chemistry, electricity, mathematics ; and in these, and in kindred departments of science, they may be supposed to have been almost wholly ignorant. ¶ *And the tongue of the Chaldeans.* In regard to the *Chaldeans*, see Notes on Job i. 17 ; and Isa. xxiii. 13. The kingdom of Babylon was composed mainly of Chaldeans, and that kingdom was called "the realm of the Chaldeans" (Dan. ix. 1). Of that realm, or kingdom, Babylon was the capital. The origin of the Chaldeans has been a subject of great perplexity, on which there is still a considerable variety of opinions. According to Heeren, they came from the North; by Gesenius they are supposed to have come from the mountains of Kurdistan; and by Michaelis, from the steppes of Scythia. They seem to have been an extended race, and probably occupied the whole of the region adjacent to what became Babylonia. Heeren expresses his opinion as to their origin in the following language: "It cannot be doubted that, at some remote period, antecedent to the commencement of historical records, *one mighty race* possessed these vast plains, varying in character according to the country which they inhabited; in the deserts of Arabia, pursuing a nomad life; in Syria, applying themselves to agriculture, and taking up settled abodes; in Babylonia, erecting the most magnificent cities of ancient times; and in Phœnicia, opening the earliest ports, and constructing fleets, which secured to them the commerce of the known world." There exists at the present time, in the vicinity of the Bahrein Islands, and along the Persian Gulf, in the neighbourhood of the Astan River, an Arab tribe, of the name of the *Beni Khaled*, who are probably the same people as the *Gens Chaldei* of Pliny, and doubtless the descendants of the ancient race of the Chaldeans. On the question when they became a kingdom, or realm, making Babylon their capital, see Notes on Isa. xxiii. 13. Compare, for an interesting discussion of the subject, Forster's *Historical Geography of Arabia*, vol. i. pp. 49–56. The language of the Chaldeans, in which a considerable part of the book of Daniel is written (see the Intro. § iv., III.), differed from the Hebrew, though it was a branch of the same Aramean family of languages. It was, indeed, very closely allied to the Hebrew, but was so different that those who were acquainted with only one of the two languages could not understand the other. Compare Neh. viii. 8. Both were the offspring of the original Shemitish language. This original language may be properly reduced to three great branches: (1.) The Aramean, which prevailed in Syria, Babylonia, and Mesopotamia; and which may, therefore, be divided into the Syriac or West-Aramean, and the Chaldee or East-Aramean, called after the Babylonish Aramean. (2.) The Hebrew, with which the fragments of the Phœnician coincide. (3.) The Arabic, under which belongs the Ethiopic as a dialect. The Aramean, which, after the return from the Babylonish captivity, was introduced into Palestine, and which prevailed in the time of the Saviour, is commonly called the Syro-Chaldaic, because it was a mixture of the Eastern and Western dialects. The Chaldee, or East Aramean, and the Hebrew, had in general the same stock of original words, but they differed in several respects, such as the following: (*a*) Many words of the old primitive language which had remained in one dialect had been lost in the other. (*b*) The same word was current in both dialects, but in different significations, because in the one it retained the primitive signification, while in the other it had acquired a different meaning. (*c*) The Babylonian dialect had borrowed expressions from the Northern Chaldeans, who had made various irruptions into the country. These expressions were foreign to the Shemitish dialects, and belonged to the Japhetian language, which prevailed among the Armenians, the Medes, the Persians, and the Chaldeans, who were probaby related to these. Traces of these foreign words are found in the names of the officers of state, and in expressions having reference to the government. (*d*) The Babylonian pronunciation was more easy and more sonorous than the Hebrew. It exchanged the frequent sibilants of the Hebrew, and the other consonants which were hard to pronounce, for others which were less difficult: it dropped the long vowels which were not essential to the forms of words; it preferred the more sonorous *a* to the long *o*, and assumed at the end of nouns, in order to lighten the pronunciation, a prolonged auxiliary vowel (the so-called emphatic א); it admitted

5 And the king appointed them a daily provision of the king's meat, and of the wine ¹ which he drank ;

1 *Of his drink.*

so nourishing them three years, that at the end thereof they might stand before the king.

6 Now among these were of the

---

contractions in pronouncing many words, and must have been, as the language of common life, far better adapted to the sluggish Orientals than the harsher Hebrew. See an article "On the Prevalence of the Aramean Language in Palestine in the age of Christ and the Apostles," by Henry F. Pfannkuche, in the *Biblical Repository*, vol. i. pp. 318, 319. On this verse also, comp. Notes on Isa. xxxix. 7.

5. *And the king appointed them.* Calvin supposes that this arrangement was resorted to in order to render them effeminate, and, by a course of luxurious living, to induce them gradually to forget their own country, and that with the same view their names were changed. But there is no evidence that this was the object. The purpose was manifestly to train them in the manner in which it was supposed they would be best fitted, in bodily health, in personal beauty, and in intellectual attainments, to appear at court; and it was presumed that the best style of living which the realm furnished would conduce to this end. That the design was not to make them effeminate, is apparent from ver. 15. ¶ *A daily provision.* Heb., "The thing of a day in his day ;" that is, he assigned to them each day a portion of what had been prepared for the royal meal. It was not a permanent provision, but one which was made each day. The word rendered "provision"—פת *path* —means *a bit, crumb, morsel*, Gen. xviii. 5 ; Judg. xix. 5 ; Psa. cxlvii. 17. ¶ *Of the king's meat.* The word *meat* here means *food*, as it does uniformly in the Bible, the old English word having this signification when the translation was made, and not being limited then, as it is now, to animal food. The word in the original—בג *băg*—is of Persian origin, meaning *food*. The two words are frequently compounded —פתבג *path-bag* (Dan. i. 5, 8, 13, 15, 16 ; xi. 26) ; and the compound means delicate food, dainties ; literally, food

of the father, *i.e.*, the king ; or, according to Lorsbach, in *Archiv. f. Morgenl. Litt.* II.ᵥ 313, food for idols, or the gods ; — in either case denoting delicate food ; luxurious living.—Gesenius, *Lex.* ¶ *And of the wine which he drank.* Marg., *of his drink.* Such wine as the king was accustomed to drink. It may be presumed that this was the best kind of wine. From anything that appears, this was furnished to them in abundance ; and with the leisure which they had, they could hardly be thrown into stronger temptation to excessive indulgence. ¶ *So nourishing them three years.* As long as was supposed to be necessary in order to develop their physical beauty and strength, and to make them well acquainted with the language and learning of the Chaldeans. The object was to prepare them to give as much dignity and ornament to the court as possible. ¶ *That at the end thereof they might stand before the king.* Notes, ver. 4. On the arrangements made to bring forward these youths, the editor of the *Pictorial Bible* makes the following remarks, showing the correspondence between these arrangements and what usually occurs in the East :— "There is not a single intimation which may not be illustrated from the customs of the Turkish seraglio, till some alterations were made in this, as in other matters, by the present sultan [Mahmoud]. The pages of the seraglio, and officers of the court, as well as the greater part of the public functionaries and governors of provinces, were originally Christian boys, taken captive in war, or bought or stolen in time of peace. The finest and most capable of these were sent to the palace, and, if accepted, were placed under the charge of the chief of the white eunuchs. The lads did not themselves become eunuchs ; which we notice, because it has been erroneously inferred, that Daniel and the other Hebrew youths *must* have been made eunuchs, *because* they were committed to the care of the

children of Judah, Daniel, Hananiah, Mishael, and Azariah ;

chief eunuch. The accepted lads were brought up in the religion of their masters ; and there were schools in the palace where they received such complete instruction in Turkish learning and science as it was the lot of few others to obtain. Among their accomplishments we find it mentioned, that the greatest pains were taken to teach them to speak the Turkish language (a foreign one to them) with the greatest purity, as spoken at court. Compare this with ' Teach them the learning and tongue of the Chaldeans.' The lads were clothed very neatly, and well, but temperately dieted. They slept in large chambers, where there were rows of beds. Every one slept separately ; and between every third or fourth bed lay a white eunuch, who served as a sort of guard, and was bound to keep a careful eye upon the lads near him, and report his observations to his superior. When any of them arrived at a proper age, they were instructed in military exercises, and pains taken to make them active, robust, and brave. Every one, also, according to the custom of the country, was taught some mechanical or liberal art, to serve him as a resource in adversity. When their education was completed in all its branches, those who had displayed the most capacity and valour were employed about the person of the king, and the rest given to the service of the treasury, and the other offices of the extensive establishment to which they belonged. In due time the more talented or successful young men got promoted to the various high court offices which gave them access to the private apartments of the seraglio, so that they at almost any time could see and speak to their great master. This advantage soon paved the way for their promotion to the government of provinces, and to military commands ; and it has often happened that favourite court officers have stepped at once into the post of grand vizier, or chief minister, and other high offices of state, without having previously been abroad in the world as pashas and military

7 Unto whom the prince of the eunuchs gave names : for he gave

commanders. How well this agrees to, and illustrates the usage of the Babylonian court, will clearly appear to the reader without particular indication. See Habesci's *Ottoman Empire;* Tavernier's *Relation de l'Intérieur du Sérail du Grand Seigneur.*"

6. *Now among these were of the children of Judah.* That is, these were a part of those who were selected. They are mentioned because they became so prominent in the transactions which are subsequently recorded in this book, and because they evinced such extraordinary virtue in the development of the principles in which they had been trained, and in the remarkable trials through which they were called to pass. It does not appear that they are mentioned here particularly on account of any distinction of birth or rank ; for though they were among the noble and promising youth of the land, yet it is clear that others of the same rank and promise also were selected, ver. 3. The phrase "the children of Judah" is only another term to denote that they were Hebrews. They belonged to the tribe, or the kingdom of Judah. ¶ *Daniel.* This name (דָּנִיֵּאל) means properly *judge of God;* that is, one who acts as judge in the name of God. Why this name was given to him is not known. We cannot, however, fail to be struck with its appropriateness, as the events of his life showed. Nor is it known whether he belonged to the royal family, or to the nobles of the land, but as the selection was made from that class it is probable. Those who were at first carried into captivity were selected exclusively from the more elevated classes of society, and there is every reason to believe that Daniel belonged to a family of rank and consequence. The Jews say that he was of the royal family, and was descended from Hezekiah, and cite his history in confirmation of the prophecy addressed by Isaiah to that monarch, " Of thy sons which shall issue from thee, which thou shalt beget, shall they take away ; and they shall be eunuchs in the palace of the king of

unto Daniel *the name* of Belteshaz-zar ; *a* and to Hananiah, of Sha-

drach ; and to Mishael, of Meshach ; and to Azariah, of Abed-nego.

Babylon," Isa. xxxix. 7. Comp. Intro. § I. ¶ *Hananiah, Mishael, and Aza-riah.* Of the rank and early history of these young men nothing is known. They became celebrated for their refu-sal to worship the golden image set up by Nebuchadnezzar, ch. iii. 12, *seq.* 7. *Unto whom the prince of the eunuchs gave names.* This practice is common in Oriental courts. "The captive youths referred to in the notes on ver. 5, in the Turkish court also receive new names, that is, Mahometan names, their former names being Chris-tian."—*Pict. Bible.* It is *possible* that this changing of their names may have been designed to make them forget their country, and their religion, and to lead them more entirely to identify themselves with the people in whose service they were now to be employed, though nothing of this is intimated in the history. Such a change, it is easy to conceive, might do much to make them feel that they were identi-fied with the people among whom they were adopted, and to make them forget the customs and opinions of their own country. It is a circumstance which may give some additional probability to this supposition, that it is quite a common thing now at missionary sta-tions to give new names to the chil-dren who are taken into the boarding-schools, and especially the names of the Christian benefactors at whose ex-pense they are supported. Compare also Gen. xli. 45. Another reason, of the same general character, for this change of names may have been, that the name of the true God constituted a part of their own names, and that thus they were constantly reminded of him and his worship. In the new names given them, the appellation of some of the idols worshipped in Baby-lon was incorporated, and this might serve as remembrancers of the divinities to whose service it was doubtless the intention to win them. ¶ *For he gave unto Daniel* the name *of Belteshazzar.* The name Belteshazzar (בֵּלְטְשַׁאצַּר) is compounded of two words, and means,

according to Gesenius, *Bel's prince ;* that is, he whom Bel favours. *Bel* was the principal divinity worshipped at Babylon (Notes, Isa. xlvi. 1), and this name would, therefore, be likely to impress the youthful Daniel with the idea that he was a favourite of this divinity, and to attract him to his ser-vice. It was a flattering distinction that he was one of the favourites of the principal god worshipped in Baby-lon, and this was not improbably de-signed to turn his attention from the God whose name had been incorporated in his own. The giving of this name seemed to imply, in the apprehension of Nebuchadnezzar, that the spirit of the gods was in him on whom it was conferred. See ch. iv. 8, 9. ¶ *And to Hananiah, of Shadrach.* The name *Hananiah* (חֲנַנְיָה) means, "whom Je-hovah has graciously given," and is the same with Ananias (Gr., Ἀνανίας), and would serve to remind its possessor of the name of *Jehovah,* and of his mercy. The name *Shadrach* (שַׁדְרַךְ), according to Lorsbach, means *young friend of the king ;* according to Boh-len, it means *rejoicing in the way,* and this last signification is the one which Gesenius prefers. In either significa-tion it would contribute to a forgetful-ness of the interesting significancy of the former name, and tend to obliterate the remembrance of the early training in the service of Jehovah. ¶ *And to Mishael, of Meshach.* The name *Mishael* (מִישָׁאֵל) means, *who is what God is ?*—from מִי *who,* שׁ *what,* and אֵל *God.* It would thus be a remembrancer of the greatness of God ; of his supre-macy over all his creatures, and of his *incomparable* exaltation over the uni-verse. The signification of the name *Meshach* (מֵישַׁךְ) is less known. The Persian word means *ovicula,* a little sheep (Gesenius), but why this name was given we are not informed. Might it have been on account of his beauty, his gentleness, his lamb-like disposi-tion? If so, nothing perhaps would be better fitted to turn away the thoughts

8 ¶ But Daniel purposed in his heart that he would not defile him- self with the portion *a* of the king's

a De. 32. 38; Eze. 4. 13; Ho. 9. 3.

from the great God and his service to himself. ¶ *And to Azariah, of Abed-nego.* The name *Azariah* (עֲזַרְיָה) means, *whom Jehovah helps,* from עָזַר *to help,* and יָהּ, the same as *Jehovah.* This name, therefore, had a striking significancy, and would be a constant remembrancer of the true God, and of the value of his favour and protection. The name *Abed-nego* (עֲבֵד נְגוֹ) means, *a servant of Nego,* or perhaps of *Nebo* —נְבוֹ. This word *Nebo,* among the Chaldeans, probably denoted the planet Mercury. This planet was worshipped by them, and by the Arabs, as the celestial scribe or writer. See Notes on Isa. xlvi. 1. The Divine worship paid to this planet by the Chaldeans is attested, says Gesenius, by the many compound proper names of which this name forms a part; as Nebuchadnezzar, Nebushasban, and others mentioned in classic writers; as Nabonedus, Nabonassar, Nabonabus, &c. This change of name, therefore, was designed to denote a consecration to the service of this idol-god, and the change was eminently adapted to make him to whom it was given forget the true God, to whom, in earlier days, he had been devoted. It was only extraordinary grace which could have kept these youths in the paths of their early training, and in the faithful service of that God to whom they had been early consecrated, amidst the temptations by which they were now surrounded in a foreign land, and the influences which were employed to alienate them from the God of their fathers.

8. *But Daniel purposed in his heart.* Evidently in concurrence with the youths who had been selected with him. See vers. 11-13. Daniel, it seems, formed this as a *decided* purpose, and *meant* to carry it into effect, as a matter of principle, though he designed to secure his object, if possible, by making a request that he might be *allowed* to pursue that course (ver. 12), and wished not to give offence, or to provoke opposition. What would have been the result if he had not obtained permission

we know not; but the probability is, that he would have thrown himself upon the protection of God, as he afterwards did (ch. vi.), and would have done what he considered to be duty, regardless of consequences. The course which he took saved him from the trial, for the prince of the eunuchs was willing to allow him to make the experiment, ver. 14. It is always better, even where there is decided principle, and a settled purpose in a matter, to obtain an object by a peaceful request, than to attempt to secure it by violence. ¶ *That he would not defile himself with the portion of the king's meat.* Notes, ver. 5. The word which is rendered *defile himself*—יִתְגָּאָל from גָּאַל—is commonly used in connection with *redemption,* its first and usual meaning being to redeem, to ransom. In later Hebrew, however, it means, to be defiled; to be polluted, to be unclean. The *connection* between these significations of the word is not apparent, unless, as redemption was accomplished with the shedding of blood, rendering the place where it was shed defiled, the idea came to be permanently attached to the word. The defilement here referred to in the case of Daniel probably was, that by partaking of this food he might, in some way, be regarded as countenancing idolatry, or as lending his sanction to a mode of living which was inconsistent with his principles, and which was perilous to his health and morals. The Syriac renders this simply, *that he would not eat,* without implying that there would be defilement. ¶ *Nor with the wine which he drank.* As being contrary to his principles, and perilous to his morals and happiness. ¶ *Therefore he requested of the prince of the eunuchs that he might not defile himself.* That he might be permitted to abstain from the luxuries set before him. It would seem from this, that he represented to the prince of the eunuchs the real danger which he apprehended, or the real cause why he wished to abstain—that he would regard the use of these viands as contrary to the habits which he had formed, as a violation of the principles of his

meat, nor with the wine which he drank : therefore he requested of the prince of the eunuchs that he might not defile himself.

religion; and as, in his circumstances, wrong as well as perilous. This he presented as a *request*. He asked it, therefore, as a favour, preferring to use mild and gentle means for securing the object, rather than to put himself in the attitude of open resistance to the wishes of the monarch. What *reasons* influenced him to choose this course, and to ask to be permitted to live on a more temperate and abstemious diet, we are not informed. Assuming, however, what is apparent from the whole narrative, that he had been educated in the doctrines of the true religion, and in the principles of temperance, it is not difficult to conceive what reasons *would* influence a virtuous youth in such circumstances, and we cannot be in much danger of error in suggesting the following : (1.) It is not improbable that the food which was offered him had been, in some way, connected with idolatry, and that his participation in it would be construed as countenancing the worship of idols.—Calvin. It is known that a part of the animals offered in sacrifice was sold in the market ; and known, also, that splendid entertainments were often made in honour of particular idols, and on the sacrifices which had been offered to them. Compare 1 Cor. viii. Doubtless, also, a considerable part of the food which was served up at the royal table consisted of articles which, by the Jewish law, were prohibited as unclean. It was represented by the prophets, as one part of the evils of a captivity in a foreign land, that the people would be under a necessity of eating that which was regarded as unclean. Thus, in Ezek. iv. 13 : "And the Lord said, Even thus shall the children of Israel eat their defiled bread among the Gentiles, whither I will drive them." Hos. ix. 3 : "They shall not dwell in the Lord's land, but Ephraim shall return to Egypt ; and shall eat unclean things in Assyria." Rosenmüller remarks on this passage (*Alte u. neue Morgenland*, 1076), "It was customary among the ancients to bring a portion of that which was eaten and drank as an offering to

the gods, as a sign of thankful recognition that all which men enjoy is their gift. Among the Romans these gifts were called *libamina*, so that with each meal there was connected an act of offering. Hence Daniel and his friends regarded that which was brought from the royal table as food which had been offered to the gods, and therefore as impure." (2.) Daniel and his friends were, doubtless, restrained from partaking of the food and drink offered to them by a regard to the principles of temperance in which they had been educated, and by a fear of the consequences which would follow from indulgence. They had evidently been trained in the ways of strict temperance. But now new scenes opened to them, and new temptations were before them. They were among strangers. They were noticed and flattered. They had an opportunity of indulging in the pleasures of the table, such as captive youth rarely enjoyed. This opportunity, there can be no doubt, they regarded as a temptation to their virtue, and as in the highest degree perilous to their principles, and they, therefore, sought to resist the temptation. They were captives—exiles from their country—in circumstances of great depression and humiliation, and they did not wish to forget that circumstance.—Calvin. Their land was in ruins ; the temple where they and their fathers had worshipped had been desecrated and plundered ; their kindred and countrymen were pining in exile ; everything called them to a mode of life which would be in accordance with these melancholy facts, and they, doubtless, felt that it would be in every way inappropriate for them to indulge in luxurious living, and revel in the pleasures of a banquet. But they were also, doubtless, restrained from these indulgences by a reference to the dangers which would follow. It required not great penetration or experience, indeed, to perceive that in their circumstances —young men as they were, suddenly noticed and honoured — compliance would be perilous to their virtue ; but

9 Now God had brought Daniel into favour *a* and tender love with the prince of the eunuchs.

10 And the prince of the eunuchs

a Ge. 39. 21 ; Pr. 16. 7.

said unto Daniel, I fear my lord the king, who hath appointed your meat and your drink : for why should he see your faces ¹worse liking than

1 *sadder.*

it did require uncommon strength of principle to meet the temptation. Rare has been the stern virtue among young men which could resist so strong allurements ; seldom, comparatively, have those who have been unexpectedly thrown, in the course of events, into the temptations of a great city in a foreign land, and flattered by the attention of those in the higher walks of life, been sufficiently firm in principle to assert the early principles of temperance and virtue in which they may have been trained. Rare has it been that a youth in such circumstances would form the steady purpose not to "defile himself" by the tempting allurements set before him, and that, at all hazards, he would adhere to the principles in which he had been educated.

9. *Now God had brought Daniel into favour.* Comp. Gen. xxxix. 21 ; Prov. xvi. 7. By what means this had been done is not mentioned. It may be presumed, however, that it was by the attractiveness of his person and manners, and by the evidence of promising talent which he had evinced. Whatever were the means, however, two things are worthy of notice : (1.) The effect of this on the subsequent fortunes of Daniel. It was to him a great advantage, that by the friendship of this man he was enabled to carry out the purposes of temperance and religion which he had formed, without coming in conflict with those who were in power. (2.) God was the author of the favour which was thus shown to Daniel. It was by a controlling influence which he exerted, that this result had been secured, and Daniel traced it directly to him. We may hence learn that the favour of others towards us is to be traced to the hand of God, and if we are prospered in the world, and are permitted to enjoy the friendship of those who have it in their power to benefit us, though it may be on account of our personal qualifications, we should learn to attribute it all to God. There

would have been great reason to apprehend beforehand, that the refusal of Daniel and his companions to partake of the food prepared for them would have been construed as an affront offered to the king, especially if it was understood to be on the ground that they regarded it as *defilement* or *pollution* to partake of it ; but God overruled it all so as to secure the favour of those in power.

10. *And the prince of the eunuchs said unto Daniel, I fear my lord the king.* He was apprehensive that if Daniel appeared less healthful, or cheerful, or beautiful, than it was supposed he would under the prescribed mode of life, it would be construed as disobedience of the commands of the king on his part, and that it would be inferred that the wan and emaciated appearance of Daniel was caused by the fact that the food which had been ordered had not been furnished, but had been embezzled by the officer who had it in charge. We have only to remember the strict and arbitrary nature of Oriental monarchies to see that there were just grounds for the apprehensions here expressed. ¶ *For why should he see your faces worse liking.* Marg., *sadder.* The Hebrew word (זֹעֲפִים) means, pro-

perly, angry ; and then morose, gloomy, sad. The primary idea seems to be, that of *any* painful, or unpleasant emotion of the mind which depicts itself on the countenance—whether anger, sorrow, envy, lowness of spirits, &c. Greek, *σκυθρωπὰ*—stern, gloomy, sad, Matt. vi. 16 ; Luke xxiv. 17. Here the reference is not to the expression of angry feelings in the countenance, but to the countenance as fallen away by fasting, or poor living. ¶ *Than the children.* The youths, or young men. The same word is here used which occurs in ver. 4. Comp. Notes on that verse. ¶ *Which* are *of your sort.* Marg., *term,* or *continuance.* The Hebrew word here used (גִּיל) means,

the children which *are* of your ¹ sort?
then shall ye make *me* endanger my
head to the king.

11 Then said Daniel to ² Melzar,
whom the prince of the eunuchs

1 or, *term*, or *continuance.*　2 or, *the steward.*

had set over Daniel, Hananiah
Mishael, and Azariah,

12 Prove thy servants, I beseech
thee, ten days; and let them give
us ³ pulse to eat, and water to drink.

3 *of pulse that we may eat.*

---

properly, a circle, or circuit; hence an
age, and then the men of an age, a
generation.—*Gesenius.* The word is
not used, however, in the Scriptures
elsewhere in this sense. Elsewhere it
is rendered *joy,* or *rejoicing,* Job iii. 22;
Psa. xliii. 4; xlv. 15; lxv. 12; Prov.
xxiii. 24; Isa. xvi. 10; xxxv. 2; lxv.
18; Jer. xlviii. 33; Hos. ix. 1; Joel
i. 16. This meaning it has from the
usual sense of the verb גִּיל *to exult,*
or *rejoice.* The verb properly means,
to move in a circle; then to *dance* in a
circle; and then to exult or rejoice.
The word "*circle,*" as often used now
to denote those of a certain class, rank,
or character, would accurately express
the sense here. Thus we speak of those
in the *religious* circles, in the *social*
circles, &c. The reference here is to
those of the same class with Daniel; to
wit, in the arrangements made for presenting them before the king. Greek,
συνήλικα ὑμῶν, *of your age.* ¶ *Then
shall ye make* me *endanger my head
to the king.* As if he had disregarded
the orders given him, or had embezzled
what had been provided for these youths,
and had furnished them with inferior
fare. In the arbitrary courts of the
East, nothing would be more natural
than that such an apparent failure in
the performance of what was enjoined
would peril his life. The word here
used, and rendered *make me endanger*—
חוב—occurs nowhere else in the Bible.
It means, in Piel, to make guilty; to
cause to forfeit. Greek, καταδικάσητε
—you will condemn, or cause me to be
condemned.

11. *Then said Daniel to Melzar, whom
the prince of the eunuchs had set over
Daniel,* &c. Marg., or, *the steward.*
It is not easy to determine whether the
word here used (מֶלְצַר *Meltzar*) is to be
regarded as a proper name, or the name
of an office. It occurs nowhere else,
except in ver. 16 of this chapter, applied
to the same person. Gesenius regards

it as denoting the name of an office in
the Babylonian court—master of the
wine, chief butler. Others regard it
as meaning a treasurer. The word is
still in use in Persia. The Vulgate
renders it as a proper name—*Malasar;*
and so the Syriac—*Meshitzar;* and so
the Greek—'Αμελσάδ, *Amelsad.* The
use of the *article* in the word (הַמֶּלְצַר)
would seem to imply that it denoted
the name of an *office,* and nothing would
be more probable than that the actual
furnishing of the daily portion of food
would be intrusted to a steward, or to
some incumbent of an office inferior to
that sustained by Ashpenaz, ver. 3.

12. *Prove thy servants, I beseech thee,
ten days.* A period which would indicate the probable result of the entire
experiment. If during that period
there were no indications of diminished
health, beauty, or vigour, it would not
be unfair to presume that the experiment in behalf of temperance would be
successful, and it would not be improper then to ask that it might be continued longer. ¶ *And let them give us
pulse to eat.* Marg., *of pulse that we
may eat.* Heb., "Let them give us of
pulse, and we will eat." The word
pulse with us means leguminous plants
with thin seeds; that is, plants with a
pericarp, or seed-vessel, of two valves,
having the seeds fixed to one suture
only. In popular language the *legume*
is called a *pod;* as a *pea-pod,* or *bean-
pod,* and the word is commonly applied
to pease or beans. The Hebrew word
(זֵרֹעִים) would properly have reference
to seeds of any kind—from זָרַע *zárá,*
to disperse, to scatter seed, to sow.
Then it would refer to plants that bear
seed, of all kinds, and would be by no
means limited to pulse—as pease or
beans. It is rendered by Gesenius,
" *seed-herbs, greens, vegetables; i. e.,*
vegetable food, such as was eaten in a
half-fast, opposed to meats and the
more delicate kinds of food." The word

13 Then let our countenances be looked upon before thee, and the countenance of the children that eat of the portion of the king's meat; and as thou seest, deal with thy servants.

14 So he consented to them in this matter, and proved them ten days.

15 And at the end of ten days their countenances appeared fairer and fatter in flesh than all the chil-

---

occurs only here and in ver. 16. It is rendered in the Vulgate, *legumina ;* and in the Greek, ἀπὸ τῶν σπερμάτων — "from seeds." It is not a proper construction to limit this to *pulse,* or to suppose that Daniel desired to live solely on pease or beans ; but the fair interpretation is to apply it to that which grows up from *seeds*—such, probably, as would be sown in a garden, or, as we would now express it, *vegetable diet.* It was designed as an experiment—and was a very interesting one—to show the legitimate effect of such a diet in promoting beauty and health, and the result is worthy of special notice as contrasted with a more luxurious mode of life. ¶ *And water to drink.* This, also, was a most interesting and important experiment, to show that wine was not necessary to produce healthfulness of appearance, or manly strength and beauty. It was an experiment to illustrate the effect of *cold water* as a beverage, made by an interesting group of young men, when surrounded by great temptations, and is, therefore, worthy of particular attention.

13. *Then let our countenances be looked upon.* One of the *objects* to be secured by this whole trial was to promote their personal beauty, and their healthful appearance (vers. 4, 5), and Daniel was willing that the trial should be made with reference to that, and that a judgment should be formed from the observed effect of their temperate mode of life. The Hebrew word rendered *countenance* (מַרְאֵה) is not limited to *the face,* as the word countenance is with us. It refers to the whole appearance, the form, the "*looks ;*" and the expression here is equivalent to, "*Then look on us,* and see what the result has been, and deal with us accordingly." The Greek is, αἱ ἰδέαι ἡμῶν—*our appearance.* ¶ *Of the children.* Youths ; young men. Notes,

ver. 4. The reference is, probably, to the Chaldean youths who were trained up amidst the luxuries of the court. It is possible, however, that the reference is to Hebrew youths who were less scrupulous than Daniel and his companions. ¶ *And as thou seest, deal with thy servants.* As the result shall be. That is, let us be presented at court, and promoted or not, as the result of our mode of living shall be. What the effect would have been if there had been a failure, we are not informed. Whether it would have endangered their lives, or whether it would have been merely a forfeiture of the proffered honours and advantages, we have no means of determining. It is evident that Daniel had no apprehension as to the issue.

14. *So he consented to them in this matter.* Heb., "he *heard* them in this thing." The experiment was such, since it was to be for so short a time, that he ran little risk in the matter, as at the end of the ten days he supposed that it would be easy to change their mode of diet if the trial was unsuccessful.

15. *And at the end of ten days their countenances appeared fairer.* Heb., "*good ;*" that is, they appeared more beautiful and healthful. The experiment was successful. There was no diminution of beauty, of vigour, or of the usual indications of health. One of the results of a course of temperance appears in the countenance, and it is among the wise appointments of God that it should be so. He has so made us, that while the other parts of the body may be protected from the gaze of men, it is necessary that the *face* should be exposed. Hence he has made the countenance the principal seat of expression, for the chief muscles which indicate expression have their location there. See the valuable work of Sir Charles Bell on *the Anatomy of Expression,* London, 1844. Hence there are certain marks of guilt and

dren which did eat the portion of the king's meat.

16 Thus Melzar took away the portion of their meat, and the wine that they should drink, and gave them pulse.

---

vice which always are indicated in the countenance. God has so made us that the drunkard and the glutton must proclaim their own guilt and shame. The bloated face, the haggard aspect, the look of folly, the "heaviness of the eye, the disposition to squint, and to see double, and a forcible elevation of the eyebrow to counteract the dropping of the upper eyelid, and preserve the eyes from closing," are all marks which God has appointed to betray and expose the life of indulgence. "Arrangements are made for these expressions in the very anatomy of the face, and no art of man can prevent it."—Bell on the *Anatomy of Expression*, p. 106. God meant that if man *would* be intemperate he should himself proclaim it to the world, and that his fellow-men should be apprised of his guilt. This was intended to be one of the safeguards of virtue. The young man who will be intemperate *knows* what the result must be. He is apprised of it in the loathsome aspect of every drunkard whom he meets. He knows that if he yields himself to indulgence in intoxicating drink, he must soon proclaim it himself to the wide world. No matter how beautiful, or fresh, or blooming, or healthful, he may now be; no matter how bright the eye, or ruddy the cheek, or eloquent the tongue; the eye, and the cheek, and the tongue will soon become indices of his manner of life, and the loathsomeness and offensiveness of the once beautiful and blooming countenance must pay the penalty of his folly. And in like manner, and for the same reason, the countenance is an indication of temperance and purity. The bright and steady eye, the blooming cheek, the lips that eloquently or gracefully utter the sentiments of virtue, proclaim the purity of the life, and are the natural indices to our fellow-men that we live in accordance with the great and benevolent laws of our nature, and are among the rewards of temperance and virtue.*

* "In reviewing the disclosures made by the

16. *Thus Melzar took away the portion of their meat*, &c. Doubtless permanently. The experiment had been satisfactory, and it was inferred that if the course of temperance could be practised for ten days without unhappy results, there would be safety in suffering it to be continued. We may remark on this : I. That the experiment was a most important one, not only for the object then immediately in view, but for furnishing lessons of permanent instruction adapted to future times. It was worth one such trial, and it was desirable to have one such illustration of the effect of temperance recorded. There are so strong propensities in our nature to indulgence ; there are so many temptations set before the young ; there is so much that allures in a luxurious mode of life, and so much of conviviality and happiness is supposed to be connected with the social glass, that it was well to have a fair trial made, and that the result should be recorded for the instruction of future times. II. It was especially desirable that the experiment should be made of the effect of strict abstinence from the use of *wine*. Distilled liquors were indeed then unknown ; but alcohol, the intoxicating principle in all ardent spirits, then

narrative contained in verses 12-17, it seems plain, that the writer meant to exhibit the thriving state of the lads upon their slender diet, as a special blessing of Providence upon their *pious resolution* ; for so, in the view of the Mosaic prescriptions, it would seem that it ought to be called. Yet it is not certain that the writer intends their thrift to be regarded by his readers as strictly *miraculous.* Certainly, in a climate so excessively hot as that of Babylon, a vegetable diet, for many months in the year, would be better adapted to occasion fairness of countenance and fulness of flesh than a luxurious diet of various highly-seasoned meats. That the God of heaven *rewarded* the pious resolution and the persevering abstinence of the Jewish lads, lies upon the face of the narrative; and this is a truth adapted to useful admonition, specially to the Jews who dwelt among the heathen, and were under strong temptations to transgress the Mosaic laws. The uncommon and extraordinary powers which were conferred upon these young Hebrews are placed in such a light, as to show that their peculiar gifts were the consequence of their pious resolution and firmness."—Stuart.

existed, as it does now, in wine, and was then, as it is now, of the same nature as when found in other substances. It was in the use of wine that the principal danger of intemperance then lay ; and it may be added, that in reference to a very large class of persons of both sexes, it is in the use of wine that the principal danger always lies. There are multitudes, especially of young men, who are in little or no danger of becoming intemperate from the use of the stronger kinds of intoxicating drinks. They would never *begin* with them. But the use of *wine* is so respectable in the view of the upper classes of society ; it is deemed so essential to the banquet ; it constitutes so much, apparently, a mark of distinction, from the fact that ordinarily only the rich can afford to indulge in it ; its use is regarded extensively as so proper for even refined and delicate females, and is so often sanctioned by their participating in it ; it is so difficult to frame an argument against it that will be decisive ; there is so much that is plausible that may be said in favour or in justification of its use, and it is so much sanctioned by the ministers of religion, and by those of influence in the churches, that one of the principal dangers of the young arises from the temptation to indulgence in wine, and it was well that there should be a fair trial of the comparative benefit of total abstinence. A trial could scarcely have been made under better circumstances than in the case before us. There was every inducement to indulgence which is ever likely to occur ; there was as much to make it a mere matter of *principle* to abstain from it as can be found now in any circumstances, and the experiment was as triumphant and satisfactory as could be desired. III. The result of the experiment. (*a*) It was complete and satisfactory. *More* was accomplished in the matter of the trial by abstinence than by indulgence. Those who abstained were more healthful, more beautiful, more vigorous than the others. And there was nothing miraculous— nothing that occurred in that case which does not occur in similar cases. Sir J. Chardin remarks, respecting those whom he had seen in the East, "that the countenances of the kechicks [monks] are in fact more rosy and smooth than those of others ; and that those who fast much, I mean the Armenians and the Greeks, are, notwithstanding, very beautiful, sparkling with health, with a clear and lively countenance." He also takes notice of the very great abstemiousness of the Brahmins in the Indies, who lodge on the ground, abstain from music, from all sorts of agreeable smells, who go very meanly clothed, are almost always wet, either by going into water, or by rain ; "yet," says he, "I have seen also many of them very handsome and healthful."—Harmer's *Observa.* ii. pp. 112, 113. (*b*) The experiment has often been made, and with equal success, in modern times, and especially since the commencement of the temperance reformation, and an opportunity has been given of furnishing the most decisive proofs of the effects of temperance in contrast with indulgence in the use of wine and of other intoxicating drinks. This experiment has been made on a wide scale, and with the same result. It is demonstrated, as in the case of Daniel, that "MORE" will be secured of that which men are so anxious usually to obtain, and of that which it is desirable to obtain, than can be by indulgence. (1.) There will be " more " beauty of personal appearance. Indulgence in intoxicating drinks leaves its traces on the countenance— the skin, the eye, the nose, the whole expression—as God *meant* it should. See Notes on ver. 15. No one can hope to retain beauty of complexion or countenance who indulges freely in the use of intoxicating drinks. (2.) "More" clearness of mind and intellectual vigour can be secured by abstinence than by indulgence. It is true that, as was often the case with Byron and Burns, stimulating drinks may excite the mind to brilliant temporary efforts ; but the effect soon ceases, and the mind makes a compensation for its over-worked powers by sinking down below its proper level as it had been excited above. It will demand a penalty in the exhausted energies, and in the incapacity for even its usual efforts, and unless

17 ¶ As for these four children, God gave them knowledge and skill in all learning and wisdom : and

the exhausting stimulus be again applied, it cannot rise even to its usual level, and when often applied the mind is divested of *all* its elasticity and vigour ; the physical frame loses its power to endure the excitement ; and the light of genius is put out, and the body sinks to the grave. He who wishes to make the most of his mind *in the long run*, whatever genius he may be endowed with, will be a temperate man. His powers will be retained uniformly at a higher elevation, and they will maintain their balance and their vigour longer. (3.) The same is true in regard to everything which requires vigour of body. The Roman soldier, who carried his eagle around the world, and who braved the dangers of every clime—equally bold and vigorous, and hardy, and daring amidst polar snows, and the burning sands of the equator—was a stranger to intoxicating drinks. He was allowed only vinegar and water, and his extraordinary vigour was the result of the most abstemious fare. The wrestlers in the Olympic and Isthmian games, who did as much to give suppleness, vigour, and beauty to the body, as could be done by the most careful training, abstained from the use of wine and all that would enervate. Since the temperance reformation commenced in this land, the experiment has been made in every way possible, and it has been *settled* that a man will do more work, and do it better; that he can bear more fatigue, can travel farther, can better endure the severity of cold in the winter, and of toil in the heat of summer, by strict temperance, than he can if he indulges in the use of intoxicating drinks. Never was the result of an experiment more uniform than this has been ; never has there been a case where the testimony of those who have had an opportunity of witnessing it was more decided and harmonious ; never was there a question in regard to the effect of a certain course on health in which the testimony of physicians has been more uniform ; and never has there been a question in

1 Daniel had understanding in all visions and dreams.

1 or, *he made Daniel understand.*

regard to the amount of labour which a man could do, on which the testimony of respectable farmers, and master mechanics, and overseers of public works, could be more decided. (4.) The full force of these remarks about temperance in general, applies to the use of *wine*. It was in respect to *wine* that the experiment before us was made, and it is this which gives it, in a great degree, its value and importance. Distilled spirits were then unknown, but it was of importance that a fair experiment should be made of the effect of abstinence from wine. The great danger of intemperance, taking the world at large, has been, and is still, from the use of wine. This danger affects particularly the upper classes in society and young men. It is by the use of wine, in a great majority of instances, that the peril commences, and that the habit of drinking is formed. Let it be remembered, also, that the intoxicating principle is the same in wine as in any other drink that produces intemperance. It is *alcohol*—the same substance precisely, whether it be driven off by heat from wine, beer, or cider, and condensed by distillation, or whether it remain in these liquids without being distilled. It is neither more nor less intoxicating in one form than it is in the other. It is only more condensed and concentrated in one case than in the other ; better capable of preservation, and more convenient for purposes of commerce. Every *principle*, therefore, which applies to the temperance cause at all, applies to the use of wine ; and every consideration derived from health, beauty, vigour, length of days, reputation, property, or salvation, which should induce a young man to abstain from ardent spirits at all should induce him to abstain, as Daniel did, from the use of wine.

17. *As for these four children.* On the word *children*, see Notes on ver. 4. Comp. ver. 6. ¶ *God gave them knowledge and skill.* See Notes on ver. 9. There is no reason to suppose that in

18 Now at the end of the days | that the king had said he should

the "knowledge and skill" here referred to, it is meant to be implied that there was anything miraculous, or that there was any direct inspiration. Inspiration was evidently confined to Daniel, and pertained to what is spoken of under the head of "visions and dreams." The fact that *all* this was to be attributed to God as his gift, is in accordance with the common method of speaking in the Scriptures; and it is also in accordance with *fact*, that *all* knowledge is to be traced to God. See Exod. xxxi. 2, 3. God formed the intellect; he preserves the exercise of reason; he furnishes us instructors; he gives us clearness of perception; he enables us to take advantage of bright thoughts and happy suggestions which occur in our own minds, as much as he sends rain, and dew, and sunshine on the fields of the husbandman, and endows him with skill. Comp. Isa. xxviii. 26, "For his God doth instruct him." The knowledge and skill which we may acquire, therefore, should be as much attributed to God as the success of the farmer should. Comp. Job xxxii. 8, "For there is a spirit in man, and the inspiration of the Almighty giveth them understanding." In the case before us, there is no reason to doubt that the natural powers of these young men had been diligently applied during the three years of their trial (ver. 5), and under the advantages of a strict course of temperance; and that the knowledge here spoken of was the result of such an application to their studies. On the meaning of the words "knowledge" and "skill" here, see Notes on ver. 4. ¶ *In all learning and wisdom.* See also Notes on ver. 4. ¶ *And Daniel had understanding.* Showing that in that respect there was a special endowment in his case; a kind of knowledge imparted which could be communicated only by special inspiration. The margin is, *he made Daniel understand.* The margin is in accordance with the Hebrew, but the sense is the same. ¶ *In all visions.* On the word rendered *visions*—חֲזוֹן—see Notes on Isa. i. 1, and Intro. to Isaiah, § VII.

(4). It is a term frequently employed in reference to prophecy, and designates the usual method by which future events were made known. The prophet was permitted to see those events *as if* they were made to pass before the eye, and to describe them *as if* they were objects of sight. Here the word seems to be used to denote all supernatural appearances; all that God permitted him to see that in any way shadowed forth the future. It would seem that men who were not inspired were permitted occasionally to behold such supernatural appearances, though they were not able to interpret them. Thus their attention would be particularly called to them, and they would be prepared to admit the truth of what the interpreter communicated to them. Comp. ch. iv.; ch. v. 5, 6; Ge. xl. 5; xli. 1–7. Daniel was so endowed that he could interpret the meaning of these mysterious appearances, and thus convey important messages to men. The same endowment had been conferred on Joseph when in Egypt. See the passages referred to in Genesis. ¶ *And dreams.* One of the ways by which the will of God was anciently communicated to men. See Intro. to Isaiah, § VII. (2), and Notes on Job xxxiii. 14–18. Daniel, like Joseph before him, was supernaturally endowed to explain these messages which God sent to men, or to unfold these pre-intimations of coming events. This was a kind of knowledge which the Chaldeans particularly sought, and on which they especially prided themselves; and it was important, in order to "stain the pride of all human glory," and to make "the wisdom of the wise" in Babylon to be seen to be comparative "folly," to endow one man from the land of the prophets in the most ample manner with this knowledge, as it was important to do the same thing at the court of Pharaoh by the superior endowments of Joseph (Gen. xli. 8).

18. *Now at the end of the days,* &c. After three years. See ver. 5. ¶ *The prince of the eunuchs brought them in.* Daniel, his three friends, and the others who had been selected and trained for the same purpose.

bring them in, then the prince of
the eunuchs brought them in before
Nebuchadnezzar.

19 And the king communed with
them ; and among them all was

a 1 Ki. 10. 1, 3 ; Ps. 119. 99.

19. *And the king communed with
them.* Heb., "spake with them." Probably he conversed with them on the
points which had constituted the principal subjects of their studies ; or he
examined them. It is easy to imagine
that this must have been to these young
men a severe ordeal. ¶ *And among
them all was found none like Daniel,*
&c. Daniel and his three friends had
pursued a course of strict temperance ;
they had come to their daily task with
clear heads and pure hearts—free from
the oppression and lethargy of surfeit,
and the excitement of wine ; they had
prosecuted their studies in the enjoyment of fine health, and with the buoy-
ousness and elasticity of spirit produced
by temperance, and they now showed
the result of such a course of training.
Young men of temperance, other things
being equal, will greatly surpass others
in their preparation for the duties of life
in any profession or calling. ¶ *Therefore stood they before the king.* It is
not said, indeed, that the others were
not permitted also to stand before the
monarch, but the object of the historian
is to trace the means by which *these
youths* rose to such eminence and virtue.
It is clear, however, that whatever may
have been the result on the others, the
historian means to say that these young
men rose to higher eminence than they
did, and were permitted to stand nearer
the throne. The phrase "stood before
the king," is one which denotes elevated
rank. They were employed in honourable offices at the court, and received
peculiar marks of the royal favour.

20. *And in all matters of wisdom
and understanding.* Marg., "*of.*"
The Hebrew is, "Everything of wisdom of understanding." The Greek,
"In all things of wisdom *and* knowledge." The meaning is, in everything
which required peculiar wisdom to understand and explain it. The points
submitted were such as would appropriately come before the minds of the

found none like Daniel, Hananiah,
Mishael, and Azariah : therefore
stood they before the king.

20 And in *a* all matters of wisdom
1 *and* understanding, that the king

1 *of.*

sages and magicians who were employed
as counsellors at court. ¶ *He found
them ten times better.* Better counsellors, better informed. Heb., "ten
hands above the magicians ;" that is,
ten *times,* or *many* times. In this
sense the word *ten* is used in Gen.
xxxi. 7, 41 ; Numb. xiv. 22 ; Neh. iv.
12 ; Job xix. 3. They greatly surpassed
them. ¶ *Than all the magicians.* Gr.,
τοὺς ἰπαοιδοὺς. The Greek word means,
those singing to ; then those who propose to heal the sick by singing ; then
those who practise magical arts or incantations—particularly with the idea
of charming with songs ; and then those
who accomplish anything surpassing
human power by mysterious and supernatural means.—Passow. The Hebrew
word (הַרְטֻמִּים *hhărtŭmmim*), occurs
only in the following places in the
Scriptures, in all of which it is rendered *magicians :*—Gen. xli. 8, 24 ;
Exod. vii. 11, 22 ; viii. 7 (3), 18 (14),
19 (15) ; ix. 11 ; Dan. i. 22 ; ii. 2. From
this it appears that it applied only to
the magicians in Egypt and in Babylon,
and doubtless substantially the same
class of persons is referred to. It is
found only in the plural number, *perhaps* implying that they formed companies, or that they were always associated together, so that different persons performed different parts in their
incantations. The word is defined by
Gesenius to mean, "Sacred scribes,
skilled in the sacred writings or hiero-
glyphics — ἱερογραμματεῖς — a class of
Egyptian priests." It is, according to
him (*Lex.*), of Hebrew origin, and is
derived from חָרֵט *hheret, stylus*—an instrument of writing, and ־ָ—formative.
It is not improbable, he suggests, that
the Hebrews with these letters imitated
a similar Egyptian word. Prof. Stuart
(*in loc.*) says that the word would be
correctly translated *pen-men,* and supposes that it originally referred to those
who were "busied with books and writ-

inquired of them, he found them ing, and skilled in them." It is evident that the word is not of Persian origin, since it was used in Egypt long before it occurs in Daniel. A full and very interesting account of the Magians and their religion may be found in Creuzer, *Mythologie und Symbolik*, i. pp. 187–234. Herodotus mentions the *Magi* as a distinct people, i. 101. The word *Mag* or *Mog* (whence the μάγοι —*magoi* —of the Greeks, and the *magi* of the Romans) means, properly, *a priest ;* and at a very early period the names *Chaldeans* and *Magi* were interchangeable, and both were regarded as of the same class.—Creuzer, i. 187, note. They were doubtless, at first, a class of priests among the Medes and Persians, who were employed, among other things, in the search for wisdom ; who were connected with heathen oracles ; who claimed acquaintance with the will of the gods, and who professed to have the power, therefore, of making known future events, by explaining dreams, visions, preternatural appearances, &c. The Magi formed one of the six tribes into which the Medes were formerly divided (Herodotus, i. 101), but on the downfall of the Median empire they continued to retain at the court of the conqueror a great degree of power and authority. "The learning of the Magi was connected with astrology and enchantment, in which they were so celebrated that their name was applied to all orders of magicians and enchanters." —Anthon, *Class. Dic.* These remarks may explain the reason why the word *magician* comes to be applied to this class of men, though we are not to suppose that the persons referred to in Genesis and Exodus, under the appellation of the Hebrew name there given to them (חַרְטֻמִּים), or those found in Babylon, referred to in the passage before us, to whom the same name is applied, were of that class of priests. The name *magi*, or *magician*, was so extended as to embrace *all* who made pretensions to the kind of knowledge for which the magi were distinguished, and hence came also to be synonymous with the *Chaldeans*, who were also celebrated for this. Compare Notes on

ten times better than all the magi- ch. ii. 2. In the passage before us it cannot be determined with certainty, that the persons were of *Magian* origin, though it is possible, as in ch. ii. 2, they are distinguished from the Chaldeans. All that is certainly meant is, that they were persons who laid claim to the power of diving into future events ; of explaining mysteries ; of interpreting dreams ; of working by enchantments, &c.

[The subjoined figure represents a priest or magician with a gazelle, and is taken to be a diviner, one of the four orders of Chaldeans named in Dan. ii. 2, and the last of the three mentioned in v. 7. From these persons it was

the custom of the kings of Assyria to require the interpretation of dreams and the prediction of future events. This is the only perfect piece of sculpture found by Botta in one of the large courts of Khorsabad.]

¶ *And astrologers* — הָאַשָּׁפִים. This word is rendered by the LXX., μάγους, *magians.* So also in the Vulgate, *magos.* The English word *astrologer* denotes "one who professes to foretell future events by the aspects and situation of the stars." — Webster. The Hebrew word—אַשָּׁפִים—according to Gesenius, means *enchanters, magicians.* It is derived, probably, from the obsolete root אָשַׁף *to cover, to con-*

cians *and* astrologers that *were* in all his realm.

a ch. 6. 28; 10. 1.   He lived to see that glorious time of the return of his people from the Baby-

ceal, and refers to those who were devoted to the practice of occult arts, and to the cultivation of recondite and cabalistic sciences. It is supposed by some philologists to have given rise, by dropping the initial א to the Greek σοφος, *wise, wise man*, and the Persian *sophi*, an epithet of equivalent import. See Gesenius on the word, and compare Bush on Dan. ii. 2. The word is found only in Daniel, ch. i. 20; ii. 2, 10, 27; iv. 7 (4); v. 7, 11, 15, in every instance rendered *astrologer* and *astrologers*. There is no evidence, however, that the science of astrology enters into the meaning of the word, or that the persons referred to attempted to practise divination by the aid of the stars. It is to be regretted that the term *astrologer* should have been employed in our translation, as it conveys an intimation which is not found in the original. It is, indeed, in the highest degree probable, that a part of their pretended wisdom consisted in their ability to cast the fates of men by the conjunctions and opposition of the stars, but this is not necessarily implied in the word.   Prof. Stuart renders it *enchanters*.   ¶ *In all his realm*. Not only in the capital, but throughout the kingdom. These arts were doubtless practised extensively elsewhere, but it is probable that the most skilful in them would be assembled at the capital.

21. *And Daniel continued* even *unto the first year of king Cyrus*. When the proclamation was issued by him to rebuild the temple at Jerusalem, Ezra i. 1. That is, he continued in influence and authority at different times during that period, and, of course, during the whole of the seventy years' captivity. It is not necessarily implied that he did not *live* longer, or even that he ceased then to have influence and authority at court, but the object of the writer is to show that, during that long and eventful period, he occupied a station of influence until the captivity was accomplished, and the royal order was issued for rebuilding the temple   He was

21 And Daniel continued *a even* unto the first year of king Cyrus.

Ionian captivity, though he did not die then.   So *till* is used, Ps. 110. 1; 112. 8.

among the first of the captives that were taken to Babylon, and he lived to see the end of the captivity—"the joyful day of Jewish freedom."—Prof. Stuart. It is commonly believed that, when the captives returned, he remained in Chaldea, probably detained by his high employments in the Persian empire, and that he died either at Babylon or at Shushan.   Comp. the Intro. § I.

PRACTICAL REMARKS.

In view of the exposition given of this chapter, the following remarks may be made:—

(1.) There is in every period of the world, and in every place, much obscure and buried talent that might be cultivated and brought to light, as there are many gems in earth and ocean that are yet undiscovered.   Notes on vers. 1–4.   Among these captive youths—prisoners of war—in a foreign land, and as yet unknown, there was most rich and varied talent—talent that was destined yet to shine at the court of the most magnificent monarchy of the ancient world, and to be honoured as among the brightest that the world has seen.   And so in all places and at all times, there is much rich and varied genius which might shine with great brilliancy, and perform important public services, if it were cultivated and allowed to develope itself on the great theatre of human affairs.   Thus, in obscure rural retreats there may be bright gems of intellect; in the low haunts of vice there may be talent that would charm the world by the beauty of song or the power of eloquence; among slaves there may be mind which, if emancipated, would take its place in the brightest constellations of genius.   The great endowments of Moses as a lawgiver, a prophet, a profound statesman, sprang from an enslaved people, as those of Daniel did ; and it is not too much to say that the brightest talent of the earth has been found in places of great obscurity, and where, but for some remarkable dispensation of Providence, it might have remained for ever unknown. This thought has been immortalized by Gray :—

" Full many a gem of purest ray serene,
    The dark unfathomed caves of ocean bear ;
Full many a flower is born to blush unseen,
    And waste its sweetness on the desert air.

" Some village Hampden, that with dauntless
        breast
    The little tyrant of his fields withstood ;
Some mute inglorious Milton here may rest,
    Some Cromwell, guiltless of his country's
        blood."

There is at any time on the earth talent enough created for all that there is to be done in any generation ; and there is always enough for talent to accomplish if it were employed in the purposes for which it was originally adapted. There need be at no time any wasted or unoccupied mind ; and there need be no great and good plan that should fail for the want of talent fitted to accomplish it, if that which actually exists on the earth were called into action.

(2.) He does a great service to the world who seeks out such talent, and gives it an opportunity to accomplish what it is fitted to, by furnishing it the means of an education, ver. 3. Nebuchadnezzar, unconsciously, and doubtless undesignedly, did a great service to mankind by his purpose to seek out the talent of the Hebrew captives, and giving it an opportunity to expand and to ripen into usefulness. Daniel has taken his place among the prophets and statesmen of the world as a man of rare endowments, and of equally rare integrity of character. He has, under the leading of the Divine Spirit, done more than most

other prophets to lift the mysterious veil which shrouds the future ; more than *could* have been done by the penetrating sagacity of all the Burkes, the Cannings, and the Metternichs of the world. So far as human appearances go, all this might have remained in obscurity, if it had not been for the purpose of the Chaldean monarch to bring forward into public notice the obscure talent which lay hid among the Hebrew captives. He always does a good service to mankind who seeks out bright and promising genius, and who gives it the opportunity of developing itself with advantage on the great theatre of human affairs.

(3.) We cannot but admire the arrangements of Providence by which this was done. Notes on vers. 1–4. This occurred in connection with the remarkable purpose of a heathen monarch—a man who, perhaps more than any other heathen ruler, has furnished an illustration of the truth that "the king's heart is in the hand of the Lord." *That purpose was, to raise to eminence and influence the talent that might be found among the Hebrew captives.* There can be no doubt that the hand of God was in this ; that there was a secret Divine influence on his mind, unknown to him, which secured this result ; and that, while he was aiming at one result, God was designing to secure another. There was thus a double influence on his mind : (1) that which arose from the purpose of the monarch himself, originated by considerations of policy, or contemplating the aggrandizement and increased splendour of his court ; and (2) the secret and silent influence of God, shaping the plans of the monarch to the ends which *He* had in view. Comp. Notes on Isa. x. 5, *seq.*

(4.) As it is reasonable to suppose that these young men had been trained up in the strict principles of religion and temperance (vers. 8–12), the case before us furnishes an interesting illustration of the temptations to which those who are early trained in the ways of piety are often exposed. Every effort seems to have been made to induce them to abandon the principles in which they had been educated, and there was a strong probability that those efforts would be successful. (a) They were among strangers, far away from the homes of their youth, and surrounded by the allurements of a great city. (b) Everything was done which could be done to induce them to *forget* their own land and the religion of their fathers. (c) They were suddenly brought into distinguished notice; they attracted the attention of the great, and had the prospect of associating with princes and nobles in the most magnificent court on earth. They had been selected on account of their personal beauty and their intellectual promise, and were approached, therefore, in a form of temptation to which youths are commonly most sensitive, and to which they are commonly most liable to yield. (d) They were far away from the religious institutions of their country; from the public services of the sanctuary; from the temple; and from all those influences which had been made to bear upon them in early life. It was a rare virtue which could, in these circumstances, withstand the power of such temptations.

(5.) Young men, trained in the ways of religion and in the habits of temperance, are often now exposed to similar temptations. They visit the cities of a foreign country, or the cities in their own land. They are surrounded by strangers. They are far away from the sanctuary to which in early life they were conducted by their parents, and in which they were taught the truths of religion. The eye of that unslumbering vigilance which was upon them in their own land, or in the country neighbourhood where their conduct was known to all, is now withdrawn. No one will know it if they visit the theatre; no one will see them who will make report if they are found in the gambling room, or the place of dissipation. In those new scenes new temptations are around them. They may be noticed, flattered, caressed. They may be invited to places by the refined and the fashionable, from which, when at home, they would have recoiled. Or, it may be, prospects of honour and affluence may open upon them, and in the whirl of business or pleasure, they may be under the strongest temptations to forget the lessons of early virtue, and to abandon the principles of the religion in which they were trained. Thousands of young men are ruined in circumstances similar to those in which these youths were placed in Babylon, and amidst temptations much less formidable than those which encompassed them; and it is a rare virtue which makes a young man safe amidst the temptations to which he is exposed in a great city, or in a distant land.

(6.) We have in this chapter an instructive instance of the value of early training in the principles of religion and temperance. There can be no doubt that these young men owed their safety and their future success wholly to this. Parents, therefore, should be encouraged to train their sons in the strictest principles of religion and virtue. Seed thus sown will not be lost. In a distant land, far away from home, from a parent's eye, from the sanctuary of God; in the midst of temptations, when surrounded by flatterers, by the gay and by the irreligious, such principles will be a safeguard to them which nothing else can secure, and will save them when otherwise they would be engulphed in the vortex of irreligion and dissipation. The best service which a parent can render to a son, is to imbue his mind thoroughly with the principles of temperance and religion.

(7.) We may see the value of a purpose of entire abstinence from the use of *wine*, ver. 8. Daniel resolved that he would not make use of it as a beverage. His purpose, it would seem, was decided, though he meant to accomplish it by mild and persuasive means if possible. There were good reasons for the formation of such a purpose then, and those reasons are not less weighty now. He never had occasion to regret the formation of such a purpose ; nor has any one who has formed a similar resolution ever had occasion to regret it. Among the reasons for the formation of such a resolution, the following may be suggested :—(1.) A fixed resolution in regard to the course which one will pursue ; to the kind of life which he will live ; to the principles on which he will act, is of inestimable value in a young man. Our confidence in a man is just in proportion as we have evidence that he has formed a steady purpose of virtue, and that he has sufficient strength of resolution to keep it. (2.) The same reasons exist for adopting a resolution of abstinence in regard to the use of wine, which exist for adopting it in relation to the use of ardent spirits ; for (a) the intoxicating principle in wine or other fermented liquors is precisely the same as in ardent spirits. It is the result of *fermentation*, not of *distillation*, and undergoes no change by distillation. The only effect of that chemical process is to drive it off by heat, condense, and collect it in a form better adapted to commerce or to preservation, but the

alcoholic principle is precisely the same in wine as in distilled liquors. (b) Intoxication itself is the same thing, whether produced by fermented liquors or by distilled spirits. It produces the same effect on the body, on the mind, on the affections. A man who becomes intoxicated on wine—as he easily may —is in precisely the same condition, so far as intoxication is produced, as he who becomes intoxicated on distilled liquors. (c) There is the same kind of *danger* of becoming intemperate in the use of the one as of the other. The man who habitually uses wine is as certainly in danger of becoming a drunkard as he who indulges in the use of distilled liquors. The danger, too, arises from the same source. It arises from the fact that he who indulges once will feel induced to indulge again ; that a strong and peculiar craving is produced for stimulating liquors ; that the body is left in such a state that it demands a repetition of the stimulus ; that it is a law in regard to indulgence in this kind of drinks, that an increased *quantity* is demanded to meet the exhausted state of the system ; and that the demand goes on in this increased ratio until there is no power of control, and the man becomes a confirmed inebriate. All these laws operate in regard to the use of wine as really as to the use of any other intoxicating drinks ; and, therefore, there is the same reason for the adoption of a resolution to abstain from all alike. (d) The temptations are often *greater* in relation to wine than to any other kind of intoxicating drinks. There is a large class of persons in the community who are in comparatively little danger of becoming intemperate from any other cause than this. This remark applies particularly to young men of wealth ; to those who move in the more elevated circles ; to those who are in college, and to those who are preparing for the learned professions. They are in peculiar danger from this quarter, because it is regarded as genteel to drink a glass of wine ; because they are allured by the example of professed Christians, of ministers of the gospel, and of ladies ; and because they are often in circumstances in which it would not be regarded as respectable or respectful to decline it. (3.) A third reason for adopting such a resolution is, that it is the ONLY SECURITY that any one can have that he will not become a drunkard. No one who indulges at all in the use of intoxicating liquors can have any *certainty* that he will not yet become a confirmed inebriate. Of the great multitudes who have been, and who are drunkards, there are almost none who *meant* to sink themselves to that wretched condition. They have become intemperate by indulging in the social glass when they thought themselves safe, and they continued the indulgence until it was too late to recover themselves from ruin. He who is in the habit of drinking at all can have no *security* that he may not yet be all that the poor drunkard now is. But he *will* be certainly safe from this evil if he adopts the purpose of total abstinence, and steadfastly adheres to it. Whatever other dangers await him, he will be secure against this ; whatever other calamities he may experience, he is sure that he will escape all those that are caused by intemperance.

(8.) We have in this chapter a most interesting illustration of the *value* of temperance in *eating*, vers. 9–17. There are laws of our nature relating to the quantity and quality of food which can no more be violated with impunity than any other of the laws of God ; and yet those laws are probably more frequently violated than any other. There are

more persons intemperate in the use of food than in the use of drink, and probably more diseases engendered, and more lives cut short, by improper indulgence in eating than in drinking. At the same time it is a more base, low, gross, and beastly passion. A drunkard is very often the wreck of a generous and noble-minded nature. He was large-hearted, open, free, liberal, and others took advantage of his generosity of disposition, and led him on to habits of intoxication. But there is nothing noble or generous in the gourmand. He approximates more nearly to the lowest forms of the brutal creation than any other human being ; and if there is any man who should be looked on with feelings of unutterable loathing, it is he who wastes his vigour, and destroys his health, by gross indulgence in eating. There is almost no sin that God speaks of in tones of more decided abhorrence than the sin of *gluttony.* Comp. Deut. xxi. 20, 21 ; Psal. cxli. 4 ; Prov. xxiii. 1–3, 20, 21 ; Luke xvi. 19 ; xxi. 34.

(9.) We have, in the close of the chapter before us, a most interesting illustration of the effect of an early course of strict temperance on the future character and success in life, vers. 17–21. The trial in the case of these young men was fairly made. It was continued through three years ; a period long enough for a *fair* trial ; a period long enough to make it an interesting example to young men who are pursuing a course of literary studies, who are preparing to enter one of the learned professions, or who are qualifying themselves for a life of mechanical or agricultural pursuits. In the case of these young men, they were strictly on *probation*, and the result of their probation was seen in the success which attended them when they passed the severe examination before the monarch (ver. 19), and in the honours which they reached at his court, vers. 19–21. To make this case applicable to other young men, and useful to them, we may notice two things : the fact that every young man is on probation ; and the effect of an early course of temperance in securing the object of that probation.

(a) Every young man is on probation; that is, his future character and success are to be determined by what he is when a youth. (1.) All the great interests of the world are soon to pass into the hands of the young. They who now possess the property, and fill the offices of the land, will pass away. Whatever there is that is valuable in liberty, science, art, or religion, will pass into the hands of those who are now young. They will preside in the seminaries of learning ; will sit down on the benches of justice ; will take the vacated seats of senators ; will occupy the pulpits in the churches ; will be intrusted with all the offices of honour and emolument; will be ambassadors to foreign courts ; and will dispense the charities of the land, and carry out and complete the designs of Christian benevolence. There is not an interest of liberty, religion, or law, which will not soon be committed to them. (2.) The world is favourably disposed towards young men, and they who are now intrusted with these great interests, and who are soon to leave them, are ready calmly to commit them to the guardianship of the rising generation, as soon as they have the assurance that they are qualified to receive the trust. They, therefore, watch with intense solicitude the conduct of those to whom so great interests are so soon to be committed (3.) Early virtue is indispensable to a favourable result of the probation of young men. A merchant demands evidence of integrity and industry in a young man before he will admit him to share his business, or will give him credit ; and the same thing is true respecting a farmer, mechanic, physician, lawyer, or clergyman. No young man can hope to have the confidence of others, or to succeed in his calling, who does not give evidence that he is qualified for success by a fair probation or trial. (4.) Of no young man is it *presumed* that he is qualified to be intrusted with these great and momentous interests until he has had a fair trial. There is no such confidence in the integrity of young men, or in their tendencies to virtue, or in their native endowments, that the world is *willing* to commit great interests to them without an appropriate probation. No advantage of birth or blood can secure this ; and no young man should presume that the world will be ready to confide in him until he has shown that he is qualified for the station to which he aspires. (5.) Into this probation, through which every young man is passing, the question of *temperance* enters perhaps more deeply than anything else respecting character. With reference to his habits on this point, every young man is watched with an eagle eye, and his character is well understood, when perhaps he least suspects it. The public cannot be deceived on this point, and every young man may be assured that there is an eye of unslumbering vigilance upon him.

(b) The effect of an early course of temperance on the issue of this probation. This is seen in the avoidance of a course of life which would certainly blast every hope ; and in its positive influence on the future destiny.

1. The avoidance of certain things which would blast every hope which a young man could cherish. There are certain evils which a young man will

certainly avoid by a course of strict temperance, which would otherwise certainly come upon him. They are such as these : (*a*) Poverty, as arising from this source. He may, indeed, be poor if he is temperate. He may lose his health, or may meet with losses, or may be unsuccessful in business ; but he is certain that he will never be made poor from intemperance. Nine-tenths of the poverty in the community is caused by this vice ; nine-tenths of all who are in almshouses are sent there as the result of it ; but from all this he will be certain that *he* will be saved. There is a great difference, if a man *is* poor, between being such as the result of a loss of health, or other Providential dispensations, and being such as the result of intemperance. (*b*) He will be saved from committing *crime* from this cause. About nine-tenths of the crimes that are committed are the results of intoxicating drinks, and by a course of temperance a man is certain that he will be saved from the commission of all those crimes. Yet if *not* temperate, no man has any security that he will not commit any one of them. There is nothing in himself to save him from the very worst of them ; and every young man who indulges in the intoxicating cup should reflect that he has no security that he will not be led on to commit the most horrid crimes which ever disgrace humanity. (*c*) He will certainly be saved from the drunkard's death. He will indeed die. He may die young ; for, though temperate, he may be cut down in the vigour of his days. But there is all the difference imaginable between dying as a drunkard, and dying in the ordinary course of nature. It would be a sufficient inducement for any one to sign a temperance pledge, and to adhere to it, if there were no other, that he might avoid the horrors of a death by *delirium tremens*, and be saved from the loathsomeness of a drunkard's grave. It is much for a young man to be able to say as he enters on life, and looks out on the future with solicitude as to what is to come, " Whatever may await me in the unknown future, of this one thing I am certain ; I shall never be poor, and haggard, and wretched, as the drunkard is. I shall never commit the crimes to which drunkenness prompts. I shall never experience the unutterable horrors of *delirium tremens*. I shall never die the death of unequalled wretchedness caused by a *mania a potu*. Come what may, I see, on the threshold of life, that I am to be free from the *worst* evils to which man is ever exposed. If I am poor, I will not be poor as the victim of intemperance is. If I die early, the world will not feel it is benefited by my removal, and my friends will not go forth to my grave with the unutterable anguish which a parent has who follows a drunken son to the tomb."

2. A course of temperance will have a direct and positive effect on the issue of such a probation. So it had in the case of the young men in the chapter before us ; and so it will have in every case. Its effect will be seen in the beauty, and healthfulness, and vigour of the bodily frame ; in the clearness of the intellect, and the purity of the heart ; in habits of industry, in general integrity of life, and in rendering it more probable that the soul will be saved. In no respect whatever will a steadfast adherence to the principles of temperance injure any young man ; in every respect, it may be the means of promoting his interests in the present life, and of securing his final happiness in the world to come. Why, then, should *any* young man hesitate about forming such a resolution as Daniel

did (ver. 8), and about expressing, in every proper way, in the most decided manner, his determined purpose to adhere through life to the strictest principles of temperance?

CHAPTER II.

§ I.—AUTHENTICITY OF THE CHAPTER.

The objections to the authenticity and credibility of this chapter are not numerous or important.

I. The first that is alleged, by Bertholdt (*Com.* pp. 192, 193), is substantially this : "that if the account here is true, the records of ancient times could not exhibit a more finished tyrant than Nebuchadnezzar was, if he doomed so many persons to death, on so slight and foolish an occasion, ver. 5. This cruelty, it is said, is wholly contrary to the general character of Nebuchadnezzar as it is reported to us, and wholly incredible. It is further said, that, though it was common in the East to trust in dreams, and though the office of interpreting them was an honourable office, yet no one was so unreasonable, or could be, as to require the interpreter to reveal the dream itself when it was forgotten. The proper office of the interpreter, it is said, was to interpret the dream, not to tell what the dream was."

To this objection, which seems to have considerable plausibility, it may be replied :—

(1.) Much reliance was placed on *dreams* in ancient times, alike among the Hebrews and in the heathen world. The case of Pharaoh will at once occur to the mind ; and it need not be said that men everywhere relied on dreams, and inquired earnestly respecting them, whether they *might* not be the appointed means of communication with the spiritual world, and of disclosing what was to occur in the future. There can

be no objection, therefore, to the supposition that this heathen monarch, Nebuchadnezzar, felt all the solicitude which he is reported to have done respecting the dream which he had. It may be further added, that in the dream itself there is nothing improbable as a dream, for it has all the characteristics of those mysterious operations of the mind ; and, if God ever communicated his will by a dream, or made known future events in this way, there is no absurdity in supposing that he would thus communicate what was to come, to him who was at that time at the head of the empires of the earth, and who was the king over the first of those kingdoms which were to embrace the world's history for so many ages.

(2.) There is no improbability in supposing that a dream would vanish from the distinct recollection, or that if it had vanished, the mind would be troubled by some vague recollection or impression in regard to it. This often occurs in our dreams now, as in the indistinct recollection that we have had a pleasant or a frightful dream, when we are wholly unable to recal the dream itself. This often occurs, too, when we would be *glad* to recover the dream if we could, but when no effort that we can make will recal its distinct features to our minds.

(3.) There was, really, nothing that was unreasonable, absurd, or tyrannical in the demand which Nebuchadnezzar made on the astrologers, that they should recal the dream itself, and then interpret it. Doubtless he could recollect it if they would suggest it, or at least he could so far recollect it as to prevent their imposing on him : for something like this constantly occurs in the operation of our own minds. When we have forgotten a story, or a piece of history, though we could not ourselves recal it, yet when it is repeated to us, we can then distinctly recollect it, and can perceive that that is the same narrative, for it agrees with all our impressions in regard to it. Furthermore, though it was not understood to be a part of the office of an interpreter of dreams to *recal* the dream if it had vanished from the mind, yet Nebuchadnezzar reasoned correctly, that if they could *interpret* the dream they ought to be presumed to be able to tell what it was. The one required no more sagacity than the other : and if they were, as they pretended to be, under the inspiration of the gods in interpreting a dream, it was fair to presume that, under the same inspiration, they could tell what it, was. Comp. Notes on ver. 5. No objection, then, can lie against the authenticity of this chapter from any supposed absurdity in the demand of Nebuchadnezzar. It was not only strictly in accordance with all the just principles of reasoning in the case, but was in accordance with what might be expected from an arbitrary monarch who was accustomed to exact obedience in all things.

(4.) What is here said of the threatening of Nebuchadnezzar (ver. 5), accords with the general traits of his character as history has preserved them. He had in him the elements of cruelty and severity of the highest order, especially when his will was not immediately complied with. In proof of this, we need only refer to his cruel treatment of the king Zedekiah, when Jerusalem was taken : " So they took the king, and brought him to the king of Babylon to Riblah : and they gave judgment upon him. And they slew the sons of Zedekiah before his eyes, and put out the eyes of Zedekiah, and bound him with fetters of brass, and brought him to Babylon," 2 Ki. xxv. 6, 7 : compare also, in vers. 18–21 of the same chapter, the account of his slaying the large number of persons that were taken by Nebuzar-adan, captain of the guard, and brought by him to the king in Babylon. These were slain in cold blood by order of Nebuchadnezzar himself. These facts make it every way probable that, in a fit of passion, he would not hesitate to threaten the astrologers with death if they did not comply at once with his will. Comp. Jer. xxxix. 5, *seq.* ; lii. 9–11. The truth was, that though Nebuchadnezzar had some good qualities, and was religious *in his way*, yet he had all the usual characteristics of an Oriental despot. He was a man of strong passions, and was a man who would never hesitate in carrying out the purposes of an arbitrary, a determined, and a stubborn will.

II. A second objection made by Bertholdt, which may demand a moment's notice, is, substantially, that the account bears the mark of a later hand, for the purpose of conferring a higher honour on Daniel, and making what he did appear the more wonderful : pp. 62, 63, 193–196. The supposition of Bertholdt is, that the original account was merely that Nebuchadnezzar required of the interpreter to explain the sense of the dream, but that, in order to show the greatness of Daniel, the author of this book, long after the affair occurred, added the circumstance that Nebuchadnezzar required of them to make the *dream* known as well as the *interpretation*, and that the great superiority of Daniel was shown by his being able at once to do this.

As this objection, however, is not based on any historical grounds, and as it is throughout mere conjecture, it is not necessary to notice it further. Nothing is gained by the conjecture ; no difficulty is relieved by it ; nor is there any real difficulty *to be* relieved by any such supposition. The narrative, as we have it, has, as we have seen, no intrinsic improbability, nor is there anything in it which is contrary to the well-known character of Nebuchadnezzar.

III. A third objection to the authenticity of the chapter, which deserves to be noticed, is urged by Lüderwald, p. 40, seq., and Bleek, p. 280, that this whole narrative has a strong resemblance to the account of the dreams of Pharaoh, and the promotion of Joseph at the court of Egypt, and was apparently made up from that, or copied from it.

But to this we may reply, (a) that, if either happened, there is no more improbability in supposing that it should happen to Daniel in Babylon than to Joseph in Egypt; and, taken as separate and independent histories, neither of them is improbable. (b) There is so much diversity in the two cases as to show that the one is not copied from the other. They agree, indeed, in several circumstances :—in the fact that the king of Egypt and the king of Babylon had each a dream; in the fact that Joseph and Daniel were enabled to interpret the dream; in the fact that they both ascribed the ability to do this, not to themselves, but to God; and in the fact that they were both raised to honour, as a consequence of their being able to interpret the dream. But in nothing else do they agree. The dreams themselves; the occasion; the explanation; the result; the bearing on future events—in these, and in numerous other things, they differ entirely. It may be added, also, that if the one had been copied from the other, it is probable that there would have been some undesigned allusion by which it could be known that the writer of the one had the other before him, and that he was framing his own narrative from that. But, as a matter of fact, there are no two records in history that have more the marks of being independent and original narratives of real transactions, than the account of Joseph in Egypt, and of Daniel in Babylon.

IV. A fourth objection to the account in this chapter arises from an alleged error in *chronology*. For a consideration of this, see Notes on ver. 1.

§ II.—ANALYSIS OF THE CHAPTER.

The subjects of this chapter are the following :—

I. The dream of Nebuchadnezzar, ver. 1. In accordance with the common belief among the ancients, he regarded this as a Divine message. The dream, too, was of such a character as to make a deep impression on his mind, though its distinct features and details had gone from him.

II. The demand of Nebuchadnezzar that the Chaldeans should recal the dream to his recollection, and expound its meaning, vers. 2-9. He ordered those whose business it was professedly to give such interpretations, to come into his presence, and to make known the dream and its meaning. But it would seem that their pretensions went no further than to explain a dream when it was known, and hence they asked respectfully that the king would state the dream in order that they might explain it. The king, in anger, threatened death, if they did not first recal the dream, and then make known the interpretation, promising at the same time ample rewards if they were able to do this. As all this, under Divine direction, was designed to communicate important information of future events, it was so ordered that the dream should be forgotten, thus entirely confounding the art of the Chaldeans, and giving an opportunity to Daniel to make the dream and its interpretation known, thus exalting a man from the land of the prophets, and showing that it was not by the skill of the pretended interpreters of dreams that future events could be made known, but that it was only by those who were inspired for that purpose by the true God.

III. The acknowledged failure of the power of the astrologers and Chaldeans, vers. 10, 11. They admitted that they could not do what was demanded of them. Whatever might be the consequence, they could not even *attempt* to recal a forgotten dream. And as, though we may be unable to recal such a dream distinctly ourselves, we could easily *recognize* it if it were stated to us ; and as we could not be imposed on by something else that any one should undertake to make us believe was the real dream, the magicians saw that it was hopeless to attempt to palm a story of their own invention on him, as if that were the real dream, and they therefore acknowledged their inability to comply with the demand of the king.

IV. The decree that they should die, vers. 12, 13. In this decree, Daniel and his three friends who had been trained with him at court (ch. i.) were involved, not because they had failed to comply with the demand of the king, for there is the fullest evidence that the subject had not been laid before them, but because they came under the general class of wise men, or counsellors, to whom the monarch looked to explain the prognostics of coming events.

V. Daniel, when apprised of the decree, and the cause of it, went to the king and requested a respite in the execution of the sentence, vers. 14–16. It would seem that he had the privilege of access to the king at pleasure. We may presume that he stated that the thing had not in fact been laid before him, though he had become involved in the general sentence, and it is no unreasonable supposition that the king was so much troubled with the dream, that he was so anxious to know its signification, and that he saw so clearly that if the decree was executed, involving Daniel and his friends, *all* hope of recalling and understanding it would be lost, that he was ready to grasp at *any* hope, however slender, of being made acquainted with the meaning of the vision. He was willing, therefore, that Daniel should be spared, and that the execution of the decree should be suspended.

VI. In these interesting and solemn circumstances, Daniel and his friends gave themselves to prayer, vers. 17, 18. Their lives were in danger, and the case was such that they could not be rescued but by a direct Divine interposition. There was no power which they had of ascertaining by any human means what was the dream of the monarch, and yet it was indispensable, in order to save their lives, that the dream should be made known. God only, they knew, could communicate it to them, and he only, therefore, could save them from death ; and in these circumstances of perplexity they availed themselves of the privilege which all the friends of God have—of carrying their cause at once before his throne.

VII. The secret was revealed to Daniel in a night vision, and he gave utterance to an appropriate song of praise, vers. 19–23. The occasion was one which demanded such an expression of thanksgiving, and that which Daniel addressed to God was every way worthy of the occasion.

VIII. The way was now prepared for Daniel to make known to the king the dream and the interpretation. Accordingly he was brought before the

CHAPTER II.

AND in the second year of the reign of Nebuchadnezzar,

king, and he distinctly disclaimed any power of himself to recal the dream, or to make known its signification, vers. 24–30.

IX. The statement of the dream and the interpretation, vers. 31–45.

X. The effect on Nebuchadnezzar, vers. 46–49. He recognized the dream; acknowledged that it was only the true God who could have made it known ; and promoted Daniel to distinguished honour. In his own honours, Daniel did not forget the virtuous companions of his youth (ch. i.), and sought for them, now that he was elevated, posts of honourable employment also, ver. 49.

1. *And in the second year of the reign of Nebuchadnezzar.* There is an apparent chronological difficulty in this statement which has given some perplexity to expositors. It arises mainly from two sources. (1.) That in Jer. xxv. 1, it is said that the first year of the reign of Nebuchadnezzar corresponded with the fourth year of Jehoiakim, king of Judah, and as the captivity was in the third year of the reign of Jehoiakim (Dan. i. 1), the time here would be the *fourth* year of the reign of Nebuchadnezzar, instead of the second. (2.) That we learn from ch. i. 5, 18, that Daniel and his three friends had been in Babylon already three years, under a process of training preparatory to their being presented at court, and as the whole narrative leads us to suppose that it was *after* this that Daniel was regarded as enrolled among the wise men (comp. ch. ii. 13, 14), on the supposition that the captivity occurred in the first year of the reign of Nebuchadnezzar, this would bring the time of the dream into the fourth year of his reign. This difficulty is somewhat increased from the fact that when Nebuchadnezzar went up to besiege Jerusalem he is called "king," and it

Nebuchadnezzar dreamed dreams, wherewith [a] his spirit was troubled, and his sleep brake from him.

a ch. 4. 5; Gen. 41. 8; Job 33. 15–17.

is evident that he did not go as a lieutenant of the reigning monarch ; or as a general of the Chaldean forces under the direction of another. See 2 Ki. xxiv. 1, 11. Various solutions of this difficulty have been proposed, but the true one probably is, that Nebuchadnezzar reigned some time conjointly with his father, Nabopolassar, and, though the title *king* was given to him, yet the reckoning here is dated from the time when he began to reign alone, and that this was the year of his sole occupancy of the throne. Berosus states that his father, Nabopolassar, was aged and infirm, and that he gave up a part of his army to his son Nebuchadnezzar, who defeated the Egyptian host at Carchemish (Circesium) on the Euphrates, and drove Necho out of Asia. The victorious prince then marched directly to Jerusalem, and Jehoiakim surrendered to him; and this was the beginning of the seventy years, captivity. See Jahn's *History of the Hebrew Commonwealth*, p. 134. Nabopolassar probably died about two years after that, and Nebuchadnezzar succeeded to the throne. The period of their reigning together was two years, and of course the second year of his single reign would be the fourth of his entire reign ; and a reckoning from either would be proper, and would not be misunderstood. Other modes of solution have been adopted, but as this meets the whole difficulty, and is founded on truth, it is unnecessary to refer to them. Comp. Prof. Stuart, on Daniel, Excursus I. and Excursus II. [See App. I. and II. to this Vol.] ¶ *Nebuchadnezzar dreamed dreams.* The plural is here used, though there is but one dream mentioned, and probably but one is referred to; for Nebuchadnezzar, when speaking of it himself (ver. 3), says, " I have dreamed *a dream.*" In the Latin Vulgate, and in the Greek, it is also in the singular. It is probable that this is a popular use of words, as if one should say, "I had strange dreams last night," though

perhaps but a single dream was intended. — Prof. Bush.   Among the
methods by which God made known
future events in ancient times, that by
dreams was one of the most common.
See Notes on ch. i. 17; Intro. to Isaiah,
§ vii. (2); comp. Gen. xx. 3, 6; xxxi.
11; xxxvii. 5, 6; xl. 5; xli. 7, 25; 1 Ki.
iii. 5; Numb. xii. 6; Joel ii. 28; Job
xxxiii. 14–16.   The belief that the will
of heaven was communicated to men
by means of dreams, was prevalent
throughout the world in ancient times.
Hence the striking expression in
Homer, *Il.* i. 63—καὶ γάρ τ᾽ ὄναρ ἐκ Διός
ἐστιν, *the dream is of Jove.*   So in the
commencement of his second Iliad, he
represents the will of Jupiter as conveyed to Agamemnon by Ὄνειρος, or *the
dream.*   So Diogenes Laertius makes
mention of a dream of Socrates, by
which he foretold his death as to happen in three days.   This method of
communicating the Divine will was
adopted, not only in reference to the
prophets, but also to those who were
strangers to religion, and even to wicked
men, as in the case of Pharaoh, Abimelech, Nebuchadnezzar, the butler and
baker in Egypt, &c.   In every such
instance, however, it was necessary, as
in the case before us, to call in the aid
of a true prophet to interpret the dream;
and it was only when thus interpreted
that it took its place among the certain predictions of the future.   One
object of communicating the Divine
will in this manner, seems to have been
to fix the attention of the person who
had the dream on the subject, and to
prepare him to receive the communication which God had chosen to make
to him.   Thus it cannot be doubted
that by the belief in dreams entertained
by Pharaoh and Nebuchadnezzar, as
disclosing future events, and by the
anxiety of mind which they experienced
in regard to the dreams, they were
better prepared to receive the communications of Joseph and Daniel in reference to the future than they could
have been by any other method of
making known the Divine will.   They
had no doubt that some important
communication had been made to them
respecting the future, and they were
anxious to know what it was.   They

were prepared, therefore, to welcome
any explanation which commended itself to them as true, and in this way
the servants of the true God had a
means of access to their hearts which
they could have found in no other way.
By what laws it was so regulated that
a dream should be *known* to be a pre-
intimation of coming events, we have
now no means of ascertaining.   That
it is *possible* for God to have access
to the mind in sleep, and to communicate his will in this manner, no one
can doubt.   That it was, so far as
employed for that purpose, a safe and
certain way, is demonstrated by the
results of the predictions thus made in
the case of Abimelech, Gen. xx. 3, 6; of
Joseph and his brethren, Gen. xxxvii.
5, 6; of Pharaoh, Gen. xli. 7, 25; and
of the butler and baker, Gen. xl. 5.   It
is not, however, to be inferred that the
same reliance, or that any reliance, is
now to be placed on dreams; for were
there no other consideration against
such reliance, it would be sufficient
that there is no authorized interpreter
of the wanderings of the mind in sleep.
God now communicates his truth to the
souls of men in other ways.   ¶ *Wherewith his spirit was troubled.*   Alike by
the unusual nature of the dream, and
by the impression which he undoubtedly
had that it referred to some important
truths pertaining to his kingdom and
to future times.   See vers. 31–36   The
Hebrew word here rendered *troubled*
(פָּעַם) means, properly, *to strike, to beat,
to pound;* then, in Niph., to be moved,
or agitated; and also in Hithpa., to be
agitated, or troubled.   The proper signification of the word is that of striking
as on an anvil, and then it refers to any
severe stroke, or anything which produces agitation.   The *verb* occurs only
in the following places: Judg. xiii. 25,
where it is rendered *move;* and Psa.
lxvii. 4, (5); Gen. xli. 8; Dan. ii. 1, 3,
where it is rendered *troubled.*   The *noun*
is of frequent occurrence.   ¶ *And his
sleep brake from him.*   Heb. נִהְיְתָה עָלָיו
שְׁנָתוֹ.   Literally, "His sleep was upon
him."   The Greek is, *his sleep was from
him; i.e.* left him.   The Vulgate, *his
sleep fled* (fugit) *from him.*   But it may
be doubted whether the Hebrew will

2 Then the king commanded to call the magicians, and the astro-

logers, and the sorcerers, and the Chaldeans, for to show the king his

bear this construction. Probably the literal construction is the true one, by which the sense of the Hebrew—‫עַל‬ *upon* —will be retained. The meaning then would be, that this remarkable representation occurred when he was *in* a profound sleep. It was *a dream*, and not *an open vision*. It was such a representation as passes before the mind when the senses are locked in repose, and not such as was made to pass before the minds of the prophets when they were permitted to see visions of the future, though awake. Comp. Numb. xxiv. 4, 16. There is nothing in the words which conveys the idea that there was anything preternatural in the sleep that had come upon Nebuchadnezzar, but the thought is, that all this occurred when he *was* sound asleep. Prof. Stuart, however, renders this, "his sleep failed him," and so does also Gesenius. Winer renders it, "his sleep went away from him." But it seems to me that the more natural idea is that which occurs in the literal translation of the words, that this occurred as a dream, in a state of profound repose.

2. *Then the king commanded.* That is, when he awoke. The particle rendered *then*, does not imply that this occurred immediately. When he awoke, his mind was agitated; he was impressed with the belief that he had had an important Divine communication; but he could not even recal the dream distinctly, and he resolved to summon to his presence those whose business it was to interpret what were regarded as prognostics of the future. ¶ *The magicians, and the astrologers.* These are the same words which occur in ch. i. 20. See Notes on that place. ¶ *And the sorcerers.* Heb. ‫מְכַשְּׁפִים‬. Vulgate, *malefici*—sorcerers. Gr., φαρμακούς. Syriac, *magician.* The Hebrew word is derived from ‫כָּשַׁף‬ *kâshăph*—meaning, in Piel, to practise magic; to use magic formulas, or incantations; to mutter; and it refers to the various arts by which those who were addicted to magic practised their deceptions. The particular idea in this word would seem to be, that

on such occasions some forms of prayers were used, for the word in Syriac means to offer prayers, or to worship. Probably the aid of idol gods was invoked by such persons when they practised incantations. The word is found only in the following places: once as a *verb*, 2 Chron. xxxiii. 6, and rendered *used witchcraft;* and as a *participle*, rendered *sorcerers*, in Exod. vii. 11; Dan. ii. 2; Mal. iii. 5; and *witch*, in Exod. xxii. 18 (17); Deut. xviii. 10. The *noun* (‫כְּשָׁפִים‬ and ‫כְּשָׁפִים‬) is used in the following places, always with reference to sorcery or witchcraft: Jer. xxvii. 9; 2 Kings ix. 22; Isa. xlvii. 9; Mic. v. 12 (11); Nah. iii. 4. It may not be easy to specify the exact sense in which this word is used as distinguished from the others which relate to the same general subject, but it would seem to be that some form of *prayer* or *invocation* was employed. The persons referred to did not profess to interpret the prognostics of future events by any original skill of their own, but by the aid of the gods. ¶ *And the Chaldeans.* See Notes on ch. i. 4. The Chaldeans appear to have been but one of the tribes or nations that made up the community at Babylon (comp. Notes on Isa. xxiii. 13), and it would seem that at this time they were particularly devoted to the practice of occult arts, and secret sciences. It is not probable that the other persons referred to in this enumeration were Chaldeans. The Magians, if any of these were employed, were Medians (Notes on ch. i. 20), and it is not improbable that the other classes of diviners might have been from other nations. The purpose of Nebuchadnezzar was to assemble at his court whatever was remarkable throughout the world for skill and knowledge (see analysis of ch. i.), and the wise men of the Chaldeans were employed in carrying out that design. The Chaldeans were so much devoted to these secret arts, and became so celebrated for them, that the name came, among the Greek and Roman writers, to be used to denote all those who laid claim to extraordinary powers in this department. Diodorus Siculus

dreams. So they came and stood before the king.

3 And the king said unto them, I have dreamed a dream, and my spirit was troubled to know the dream.

4 Then spake the Chaldeans to the king in Syriac, O king, live ᵃfor

a 1 Ki. 1. 31.

(lib. ii.) says of the Chaldeans in Babylon, that "they sustain the same office there that the priests do in Egypt; for being devoted to the worship of God through their whole lives, they give themselves to philosophy, and seek from astrology their highest glory." Cicero also remarks (*De Divin.*, p. 3), that "the Chaldeans, so named, not from their art, but their nation, are supposed, by a prolonged observation of the stars, to have wrought out a science by which could be predicted what was to happen to every individual, and to what fate he was born." Juvenal likewise (*Sat.* vi., vers. 552–554), has this passage : "Chaldaeis sed major erit fiducia ; quidquid dixerit astrologus, credent a fonte relatum Ammonis.—But their chief dependence is upon the Chaldeans ; whatever an astrologer declares, they will receive as a response of [Jupiter] Ammon." Horace refers to the *Babylonians* as distinguished in his time for the arts of magic, or divination :

"nec Babylonios,
Tentâris numeros."—*Car.* lib. i., xi.

It is not probable that the whole nation of Chaldeans was devoted to these arts, but as a people they became so celebrated in this kind of knowledge that it was their best known characteristic abroad. [See also appendix to this volume, No. III.] ¶ *For to show the king his dreams.* To show him what the dream was, and to explain its import. Comp. Gen. xli. 24 ; Judg. xiv. 12 ; 1 Kings x. 3. That it was common for kings to call in the aid of interpreters to explain the import of dreams, appears from Herodotus. When Astyages ascended the throne, he had a daughter whose name was Mandane. She had a dream which seemed to him so remarkable that he called in the "magi," whose interpretation, Herodotus remarks, was of such a nature that it "terrified him exceedingly." He was so much influenced by the dream and the interpretation, that it produced an entire change in his determination re-

specting the marriage of his daughter. —Book i., cvii. So again, after the marriage of his daughter, Herodotus says (book i., cviii.): "Astyages had another vision. A vine appeared to spring from his daughter which overspread all Asia. On this occasion, also, he consulted his interpreters ; the result was, that he sent for his daughter from Persia, when the time of her delivery approached. On her arrival, he kept a strict watch over her, intending to destroy her child. The magi had declared the vision to intimate that the child of his daughter should supplant him on the throne." Astyages, to guard against this, as soon as Cyrus was born, sent for Harpagus, a person in whom he had confidence, and commanded him to take the child to his own house, and put him to death. These passages in Herodotus show that what is here related of the king of Babylon, demanding the aid of magicians and astrologers to interpret his dreams, was by no means an uncommon occurrence.

3. *And the king said unto them, I have dreamed a dream, and my spirit was troubled to know the dream.* That is, clearly, to know all about it ; to recollect distinctly what it was, and to understand what it meant. He was agitated by so remarkable a dream ; he probably had, as Jerome remarks, a shadowy and floating impression of what the dream was—such as we often have of a dream that has agitated our minds, but of which we cannot recal the distinct and full image ; and he desired to recal that distinctly, and to know exactly what it meant. See ver. 1.

4. *Then spake the Chaldeans to the king.* The meaning is, either that the Chaldeans spoke in the name of the entire company of the soothsayers and magicians (Notes, ch. i. 20; ii. 2), because they were the most prominent among them, or the name is used to denote the collective body of sooth-

ever: tell thy servants the dream, and we will show the interpretation.

sayers, meaning that this request was made by the entire company. ¶ *In Syriac.* In the original—אֲרָמִית—in *Aramean.* Gr., Συριστί — *in Syriac.* So the Vulgate. The Syriac retains the original word. The word means *Aramean,* and the reference is to that language which is known as East Aramean—a general term embracing the Chaldee, the Syriac, and the languages which were spoken in Mesopotamia. See Notes on ch. i. 4. This was the vernacular tongue of the king and of his subjects, and was that in which the Chaldeans would naturally address him. It is referred to here by the author of this book, perhaps to explain the reason why he himself makes use of this language in explaining the dream. The use of this, however, is not confined to the statement of what the magicians said, but is continued to the close of the seventh chapter. Comp. the Intro. § IV. III. The language used is that which is commonly called Chaldee. It is written in the same character as the Hebrew, and differs from that as one dialect differs from another. It was, doubtless, well understood by the Jews in their captivity, and was probably spoken by them after their return to their own land. ¶ *O king, live for ever.* This is a form of speech quite common in addressing monarchs. See 1 Sam. x. 24; 1 Kings i. 25 (margin); ch. iii. 9; v. 10. The expression is prevalent still, as in the phrases, "Long live the king," "*Vive l' empereur,*" "*Vive le roi,*" &c. It is founded on the idea that long life is to be regarded as a blessing, and that we can in no way express our good wishes for any one better than to wish him length of days. In this place, it was merely the usual expression of respect and homage, showing their earnest wish for the welfare of the monarch. They were willing to do anything to promote his happiness, and the continuance of his life and reign. It was especially proper for them to use this language, as they were about to make a rather unusual request, which might be construed as an act of disrespect, implying that the king had not

given them all the means which it was equitable for them to have in explaining the matter, by requiring them to interpret the dream when he had not told them what it was. ¶ *Tell thy servants the dream, and we will show the interpretation.* The claim which they set up in regard to the future was evidently only that of *explaining* what were regarded as the prognostics of future events. It was not that of being able to recal what is forgotten, or even to *originate* what might be regarded as pre-intimations of what is to happen. This was substantially the claim which was asserted by all the astrologers, augurs, and soothsayers of ancient times. Dreams, the flight of birds, the aspect of the entrails of animals slain for sacrifice, the positions of the stars, meteors, and uncommon appearances in the heavens, were supposed to be intimations made by the gods of what was to occur in future times, and the business of those who claimed the power of divining the future was merely to interpret these things. When the king, therefore, required that they should recal the dream itself to his own mind, it was a claim to something which was not involved in their profession, and which they regarded as unjust. To that power they made no pretensions. If it be asked why, as they were mere jugglers and pretenders, they did not *invent* something and state *that* as his dream, since he had forgotten what his dream actually was, we may reply, (1.) that there is no certain evidence that they were not sincere in what they professed themselves able to do—for we are not to suppose that all who claimed to be soothsayers and astrologers were hypocrites and intentional deceivers. It was not at that period of the world certainly determined that nothing could be ascertained respecting the future by dreams, and by the positions of the stars, &c. Dreams *were* among the methods by which the future was made known; and whether the knowledge of what is to come could be obtained from the positions of the stars, &c., was a question which was at that time unsettled. Even Lord Bacon maintained that the

5 The king answered and said to the Chaldeans, The thing is gone

science of astrology was not to be *rejected*, but to be *reformed*. (2.) If the astrologers had been disposed to attempt to deceive the king, there is no probability that they could have succeeded in palming an invention of their own on him as his own dream. We may not be able distinctly to recollect a dream, but we have a sufficient impression of it—of its outlines—or of some striking, though disconnected, things in it, to know what it is *not*. We might instantly recognize it if stated to us; we should see at once, if any one should attempt to deceive us by palming an invented dream on us, that *that* was not what we had dreamed.

5. *The king answered and said to the Chaldeans, The thing is gone from me.* The Vulgate renders this, *Sermo recessit à me*—"The word is departed from me." So the Greek, 'Ο λόγος ἀπ' ἐμοῦ ἀπέστη. Luther, *Es ist mir entfallen*—"It has fallen away from me," or has departed from me. Coverdale, "It is gone from me." The Chaldee word rendered "the thing"—מִלְּתָה—means, properly, *a word, saying, discourse* — something which is *spoken*; then, like דָּבָר and the Greek ῥῆμα, a *thing*. The reference here is to the matter under consideration, to wit, the dream and its meaning. The fair interpretation is, that he had forgotten the dream, and that if he retained *any* recollection of it, it was only such an imperfect outline as to alarm him. The word rendered "is gone"—אַזְדָּא—which occurs only here and in ver. 8, is supposed to be the same as אֲזַל—*to go away, to depart.* Gesenius renders the whole phrase, "The word has gone out from me; *i.e.*, what I have said is ratified, and cannot be recalled;" and Prof. Bush (*in loc.*) contends that this is the true interpretation, and this also is the interpretation preferred by J. D. Michaelis, and Dathe. A construction somewhat similar is adopted by Aben Ezra, C. B. Michaelis, Winer, Hengstenberg, and Prof. Stuart, that it means, "My decree is firm, or steadfast;" to wit, that if they did not fur-

from me: if ye will not make known unto me the dream, with the inter-

nish an interpretation of the dream, they should be cut off. The question as to the true interpretation, then, is between two constructions: whether it means, as in our version, that the dream had departed from him—that is, that he had forgotten it—or, that a decree or command had gone from him, that if they could not interpret the dream they should be destroyed. That the former is the correct interpretation seems to me to be evident. (1.) It is the natural construction, and accords best with the meaning of the original words. Thus no one can doubt that the word מִלָּה, and the words דָּבָר and ῥῆμα, are used in the sense of *thing*, and that the natural and proper meaning of the Chaldee verb אֲזַד is, *to go away, depart.* Comp. the Hebrew (אָזַל) in Deut. xxxii. 36, "He seeth that their power *is gone*;" 1 Sam. ix. 7, "The bread *is spent* in our vessels;" Job xiv. 11, "The waters *fail* from the sea;" and the Chaldee (אָזַל) in Ezra iv. 23. "They *went up* in haste to Jerusalem;" v. 8, "We *went* into the province of Judea;" and Dan. ii. 17, 24; vi. 18 (19), 19 (20). (2.) This interpretation is sustained by the Vulgate of Jerome, and by the Greek. (3.) It does not appear that any such command had at that time gone forth from the king, and it was only when they came before him that he promulgated such an order. Even though the word, as Gesenius and Zickler (*Chaldaismus Dan. Proph.*) maintain, is a feminine participle present, instead of a verb in the preterit, still it would then as well apply to the *dream* departing from him, as the command or edict. We may suppose the king to say, "The thing leaves me; I cannot recal it." (4.) It was so understood by the magicians, and the king did not attempt to correct their apprehension of what he meant. Thus, in ver. 7, they say, "Let the king tell his servants the dream, and we will show the interpretation thereof." This shows that they understood that the dream had gone from him, and that they could not be

pretation thereof, ye shall be ¹ cut

1 *made.*   *a* ch. 3. 29.   *b* Ezr. 6. 11.

expected to interpret its meaning until they were apprised what it was. (5.) It is not necessary to suppose that the king retained the memory of the dream himself, and that he meant merely to try them ; that is, that he told them a deliberate falsehood, in order to put their ability to the test. Nebuchadnezzar was a cruel and severe monarch, and such a thing would not have been entirely inconsistent with his character ; but we should not needlessly charge cruelty and tyranny on any man, nor should we do it unless the evidence is so clear that we cannot avoid it. Besides, that such a test should be proposed is in the highest degree improbable. There was no need of it ; and it was contrary to the established belief in such matters. These men were retained at court, among other reasons, for the very purpose of explaining the prognostics of the future. There was confidence in them; and they were retained *because* there was confidence in them. It does not appear that the Babylonian monarch had had any reason to distrust their ability as to what they professed ; and why should he, therefore, on *this* occasion resolve to put them to so unusual, and obviously so unjust a trial ? For these reasons, it seems clear to me that our common version has given the correct sense of this passage, and that the meaning is, that the dream had actually so far departed from him that he could not repeat it, though he retained such an impression of its portentous nature, and of its appalling outline, as to fill his mind with alarm. As to the objection derived from this view of the passage by Bertholdt to the authenticity of this chapter, that it is wholly improbable that any man would be so unreasonable as to doom others to punishment because they could not recal his dream, since it entered not into their profession to be able to do it (*Comm.* i. p. 192), it may be remarked, that the character of Nebuchadnezzar was such as to make what is stated here by Daniel by no means improbable. Thus it is said respecting him

in pieces, *a* and your houses *b* shall be made a dunghill :

(2 Kings xxv. 7), " And they slew the sons of Zedekiah *before his eyes,* and put out the eyes of Zedekiah, and bound him with fetters of brass, and carried him to Babylon." Comp. 2 Kings xxv. 18–21; Jer. xxxix. 5, *seq.*; lii. 9–11. See also Dan. iv. 17, where he is called " the basest of men." Comp. Hengstenberg, *Die Authentie des Daniel,* pp. 79–81. On this objection, see Intro. to the chapter, § 1. I. ¶ *If ye will not make known unto me the dream, with the interpretation thereof.* Whatever may be thought as to the question whether he had actually forgotten the dream, there can be no doubt that he demanded that they should state what it was, and then explain it. This demand was probably as unusual as it was in one sense unreasonable, since it did not fall fairly within their profession. Yet it was not unreasonable in this sense, that if they really had communication with the gods, and were qualified to explain future events, it might be supposed that they would be enabled to recal this forgotten dream. If the gods gave them power to explain what was to *come,* they could as easily enable them to recal *the past.* ¶ *Ye shall be cut in pieces.* Marg., *made.* The Chaldee is, " Ye shall be made into pieces ;" referring to a mode of punishment that was common to many ancient nations. Compare 1 Sam. xv. 33: "And Samuel hewed Agag in pieces before the Lord in Gilgal." Thus Orpheus is said to have been torn in pieces by the Thracian women ; and Bessus was cut in pieces by order of Alexander the Great. ¶ *And your houses shall be made a dunghill.* Compare 2 Ki x. 27. This is an expression denoting that their houses, instead of being elegant or comfortable mansions, should be devoted to the vilest of uses, and subjected to all kinds of dishonour and defilement. The language here used is in accordance with that which is commonly employed by Orientals. They imprecate all sorts of indignities and abominations on the objects of their dislike, and it is not uncommon for them to smear over with filth what is

6 But *a* if ye show the dream, and the interpretation thereof ye shall receive of me gifts, and [1] rewards,

a ch. 5. 16.   1 or. *fee*, ver. 48; ch. 5. 17.

the object of their contempt or abhorrence. Thus when the caliph Omar took Jerusalem, at the head of the Saracen army, after ravaging the greater part of the city, he caused dung to be spread over the site of the sanctuary, in token of the abhorrence of all Mussulmans, and of its being henceforth regarded as the refuse and offscouring of all things.—Prof. Bush. The Greek renders this, "And your houses shall be plundered ;" the Vulgate, " And your houses shall be confiscated." But these renderings are entirely arbitrary. This may seem to be a harsh punishment which was threatened, and some may, perhaps, be disposed to say that it is improbable that a monarch would allow himself to use such intemperate language, and to make use of so severe a threatening, especially when the magicians had as yet shown no inability to interpret the dream, and had given no reasons to apprehend that they would be unable to do it. But we are to remember (1) the cruel and arbitrary character of the king (see the references above); (2) the nature of an Oriental despotism, in which a monarch is accustomed to require all his commands to be obeyed, and his wishes gratified promptly, on pain of death ; (3) the fact that his mind was greatly excited by the dream; and (4) that he was certain that something portentous to his kingdom had been prefigured by the dream, and that this was a case in which all the force of threatening, and all the prospect of splendid reward, should be used, that they might be induced to tax their powers to the utmost, and allay the tumults of his mind.

6. *But if ye show the dream.* If you show what the dream was.   ¶ *And the interpretation thereof.* What it signifies. That is, they were so to state the dream that Nebuchadnezzar would recognise it ; and they were to give such an explanation of it as would commend itself to his mind as the true one. On this last point he would doubtless rely much on their supposed wisdom in per-

and great honour : therefore show me the dream and the interpretation thereof.

7 They answered again, and said

forming this duty, but it would seem clear, also, that it was necessary that the interpretation should be seen to be a *fair* interpretation, or such as would be *fairly* implied in the dream. Thus, when Daniel made known the interpretation, he saw at once that it met all the features of the dream, and he admitted it to be correct. So also when Daniel explained the handwriting on the wall to Belshazzar, he admitted the justness of it, and loaded him with honours, Dan. v. 29. So when Joseph explained the dreams of Pharaoh, he at once saw the appropriateness of the explanation, and admitted it to be correct (Gen. xli. 39–45) ; and so in the case above referred to (notes on ver. 2), of Astyages respecting the dreams of his daughter (Herod. 1, cvii., cviii.), he at once saw that the interpretation of the dreams proposed by the Magi accorded with the dreams, and took his measures accordingly.   ¶ *Ye shall receive of me gifts, and rewards, and great honour.* Intending to appeal to their highest hopes to induce them, if possible, to disclose the meaning of the dream.   He specifies no particular rewards, but makes the promise general ; and the evident meaning is, that, in such a case, he would bestow what it became a monarch like him to give. That the usual rewards in such a case were such as were adapted to stimulate to the most vigorous exertions of their powers, may be seen from the honour which he conferred on Daniel when he made known the dream (ver. 48), and from the rewards which Belshazzar conferred on Daniel for making known the interpretation of the writing on the wall (ch. v. 29) : " Then commanded Belshazzar, and they clothed Daniel with scarlet, and put a chain of gold about his neck, and made a proclamation concerning him, that he should be the third ruler in the kingdom." Comp. Esth. v. 11; vi. 7–9.

7. *They answered again, and said, Let the king tell his servants the dream, and we will show the interpretation of*

Let the king tell his servants the dream, and we will show the interpretation of it.

8 The king answered and said, I know of certainty that ye would

it. Certainly not an unreasonable request, in any circumstances, and especially in theirs. They did not profess, evidently, to be able to recal a dream that was forgotten, but the extent of their profession on this subject appears to have been, that they were able to *explain* what was commonly regarded as a prognostic of a future event. 8. *The king answered and said, I know of certainty that ye would gain the time.* Marg., *buy.* The Chaldee word זְבַנִין (from זְבַן) means, to get for one's self, buy, gain, procure. Greek, ἐξαγοράζετε—"*that ye redeem* time ;" and so the Vulgate—*quod tempus redimitis.* The idea is, that they saw that they could not comply with his requisition, and that their asking him (ver. 7) to state the dream was only a pretext for delay, in the hope that in the interval some device might be hit on by them to appease him, or to avert his threatened indignation. It would be natural to suppose that they might hope that on reflection he would become more calm, and that, although they *might* not be able to recal the dream and explain it, yet it would be seen to be unreasonable to expect or demand it. The king seems to have supposed that some such thoughts were passing through their minds, and he charges on them such a project. The argument of the king seems to have been something like this : "They who can explain a dream correctly can as well tell what it is as what its interpretation is, for the one is as much the result of Divine influence as the other ; and if men can hope for Divine help in the one case, why not in the other? As you cannot, therefore, recal the dream, it is plain that you cannot interpret it ; and your only object in demanding to know it is, that you may ward off as long as possible the execution of the threatened sentence, and, if practicable, escape it altogether." It is not improbable that what they said

gain [1] the time, because ye see the thing is gone from me.

9 But if ye will not make known unto me the dream, *there is but* one

1 or, *buy,* Ep. 5. 1;

was more than the simple request recorded in ver 7. They would naturally enlarge on it, by attempting to show how unreasonable was the demand of the king in the case, and their arguments would give a fair pretext for what he here charges on them. ¶ *Because ye see the thing is gone from me.* According to the interpretation proposed in ver. 5, *the dream.* The meaning is, "You see that I have forgotten it. I have made a positive statement on that point. There can be no hope, therefore, that it *can* be recalled, and it is clear that your only object *must be* to gain time. Nothing can be gained by delay, and the matter may therefore be determined at once, and your conduct be construed as a confession that you cannot perform what is required, and the sentence proceed without delay." This makes better sense, it seems to me, than to suppose that he means that a sentence had gone forth from him that if they could not recal and interpret it they should be put to death.

9. *But if ye will not make known unto me the dream,* there is but *one decree for you.* That is, you shall share the same fate. You shall all be cut to pieces, and your houses reduced to ruin, ver. 5. There shall be no favour shown to any class of you, or to any individual among you. It seems to have been supposed that the responsibility rested on them individually as well as collectively, and that it would be right to hold each and every one of them bound to explain the matter. As no difference of obligation was recognized, there would be no difference of criminality. It should be said, however, that there is a difference of interpretation here. Gesenius, and some others, render the word translated *decree*—דָּת—*counsel, plan, purpose,* and suppose that it means, "this only is your counsel, or plan ;" that is, to prepare lying words, and to gain time. So Prof. Stuart renders the verse, "If ye will not make known to me the

decree for you; for ye have prepared lying and corrupt words to speak before me, till the time be changed: therefore tell me the dream, and I *a* shall know that ye can show me the interpretation thereof.

10 ¶ The Chaldeans answered

a Is. 41. 23.

dream, one thing is your purpose, both a false and deceitful word have ye agreed to utter before me, until the time shall have changed; therefore tell me the dream, and then I shall know that you can show me the interpretation thereof." The original word, however, is most commonly used in the sense of *law* or *decree.* See Deut. xxxiii. 2; Esth. i. 8, 13, 15, 19; ii. 8; iii. 8, 14, 15; iv. 3, 8, 11, 16; viii. 13, 14, 17; ix. 1, 13, 14; and there seems to be no necessity for departing from the common translation. It contains a sense according to the truth in the case, and is in accordance with the Greek, Latin, and Syriac versions. ¶ *For ye have prepared lying and corrupt words to speak before me.* That is, "You have done this in asking me to state the dream (vers. 4, 7), and in the demand that the dream should be made known to you, in order that you may interpret it. I shall know by your inability to recal the dream that you have been acting a false and deceitful part, and that your pretensions were all false. Your wish, therefore, to have me state the dream will be shown to be a mere pretence, an artifice for delay, that you might put off the execution of the sentence with the hope of escaping altogether." ¶ *Till the time be changed.* That is, till a new state of things shall occur; either until his purpose might change, and his anger should subside, or till there should be a change of government. It was natural for such thoughts to pass through the mind of the king, since, as matters could be no *worse* for them if the subject was delayed, there was a possibility that they might be *better*—for any change would be likely to be an advantage. There does not appear to have been any great confidence or affection on either side. The king suspected that they were influenced by bad motives, and they cer-

before the king, and said, There is not a man upon the earth that can show the king's matter: therefore *there is* no king, lord, nor ruler, *that* asked such things at any magician, or astrologer, or Chaldean.

11 And *it is* a rare thing that

tainly had no strong reasons for attachment to him. Comp. notes on ver. 21, and ch. vii. 25.

10. *The Chaldeans answered before the king, and said.* Perhaps the *Chaldeans* answered because they were the highest in favour, and were those in whom most confidence was usually reposed in such matters. See Notes on ver. 2. On such an occasion, those would be likely to be put forward to announce their inability to do this who would be supposed to be able to interpret the dream, if any could, and on whom most reliance was usually placed. ¶ *There is not a man upon the earth that can show the king's matter.* Chald., אַרְעָא עַל־יַבֶּשְׁתָּא —"*upon the dry ground.*" Comp. Gen. i. 10. The meaning is, that the thing was utterly beyond the power of man. It was what none who practised the arts of divining laid claim to. They doubtless supposed that as great proficients in that art as the world could produce might be found among the wise men assembled at the court of Babylon, and if they failed, they inferred that all others would fail. This was, therefore, a decided confession of their inability in the matter; but they meant to break the force of that mortifying confession, and perhaps to appease the wrath of the king, by affirming that the thing was wholly beyond the human powers, and that no one could be expected to do what was demanded. ¶ *Therefore there is no king, lord, nor ruler, that asked such things.* No one has ever made a similar demand. The matter is so clear, the incompetency of man to make such a disclosure is so manifest, that no potentate of any rank ever made such a request. They designed, undoubtedly, to convince the king that the request was so unreasonable that he would not insist on it. They were urgent, for

the king requireth : and there is
none other that can show it before
a ver. 28.

their life depended on it, and they apprehended that they had justice on
their side.

11. *And it is a rare thing that the
king requireth.* Chald., יַקִּירָה —meaning, *choice, valuable, costly;* then,
heavy, hard, difficult. Greek, βαρύς.
Vulgate, *gravis—heavy, weighty.* The
idea is not so much that the thing demanded by the king was *uncommon* or
rarely made—though that was true, as
that it was so difficult as to be beyond
the human powers. They would not
have been likely on such an occasion
to say that the requirement was absolutely unjust or unreasonable. The
term which they used was respectful,
and yet it implied that no man could
have any hope of solving the question
as it was proposed by him. ¶ *And
there is none other that can show it
before the king except the gods, whose
dwelling is not with flesh.* This was
clearly true, that a matter of that
kind could not be disclosed except by
Divine assistance. It would seem
from this that these persons did not
claim to be inspired, or to have communication with the gods ; or, at least,
that they did not claim to be inspired
by the Supreme God, but that they
relied on their own natural sagacity,
and their careful and long study of the
meaning of those occurrences which
prefigured future events, and perhaps
on the mystic arts derived from their
acquaintance with science as then understood. The word *gods* here—אֱלָהִין
Elahin [the same as the Heb. *Elohim*]
—is in the plural number, but might
be applied to the true God, as the
Hebrew Elohim often is. It is by no
means certain that they meant to use
this in the plural, or to say that it was
an admitted truth that the gods worshipped in Babylon did not dwell with
men. It was, undoubtedly, the common opinion that they did ; that the
temples were their abode ; and that
they frequently appeared among men,
and took part in human affairs. But
it was a very early opinion that the
Supreme God was withdrawn from

the king, except *a* the gods, whose
dwelling *b* is not with flesh.
b Is. 66. 1,

human affairs, and had committed the
government of the world to intermediate beings—*internuncii*—demons, or
æons : beings of power far superior to
that of men, who constantly mingled in
human affairs. Their power, however,
though great, was limited ; and may not
the Chaldeans here by the word אֱלָהִין —
Elahin — have meant to refer to the
Supreme God, and to say that *this* was
a case which pertained to him alone ;
that no inferior divinity could be competent to do such a thing as he demanded; and that as the Supreme God
did *not* dwell among men it was hopeless to attempt to explain the matter ?
Thus understood, the result will convey
a higher truth, and will show more im-
pressively the honour put on Daniel.
The phrase, *whose dwelling is not with
flesh,* means *with men — in human
bodies.* On the supposition that this
refers to the Supreme God, this undoubtedly accords with the prevailing
sentiment of those times, that however
often the inferior divinities might appear to men, and assume human forms,
yet the Supreme God was far removed,
and never thus took up his abode on the
earth. They could hope, therefore, for
no communication from Him who alone
would be competent to the solution of
such a secret as this. This may be regarded, therefore, as a frank confession
of their entire failure in the matter under consideration. They acknowledged
that *they* themselves were not competent to the solution of the question,
and they expressed the opinion that
the ability to do it could not be obtained from the help which the inferior
gods rendered to men, and that it was
hopeless to expect the Supreme God—
far withdrawn from human affairs—to
interpose. It was a public acknowledgment that their art failed on a most
important trial, and thus the way was
prepared to show that Daniel, under
the teaching of the true God, was able
to accomplish what was wholly beyond
all human power. The trial had been
fairly made. The wisest men of the
Chaldean realm had been applied to.

12 For this cause the king was angry and very furious, and commanded to destroy all [a]the wise men of Babylon.

a Mat. 2. 16.

They on whom reliance had been placed in such emergencies; they who professed to be able to explain the prognostics of future events; they who had been assembled at the most important and magnificent court of the world—the very centre of Pagan power; they who had devoted their lives to investigations of this nature, and who might be supposed to be competent to such a work, if any on earth could, now openly acknowledged that their art failed them, and expressed the conviction that there was no resource in the case.

12. *For this cause the king was angry.* Because they failed in explaining the subject which had been referred to them. It is true that his anger was unjust, for their profession did not imply that they would undertake to explain what he demanded, but his wrath was not unnatural. His mind was alarmed, and he was troubled. He believed that what he had seen in his dream foreboded some important events, and, as an arbitrary sovereign, unaccustomed to restrain his anger or to inquire into the exact justice of matters which excited his indignation, it was not unnatural that he should resolve to wreak his vengeance on all who made any pretensions to the arts of divining. ¶ *And very furious.* Wrought up to the highest degree of passion. Chaldee, "Much enraged." It was not a calm and settled purpose to execute his threat, but a purpose attended with a high degree of excitement. ¶ *And commanded to destroy all the wise* men *of Babylon.* That is, all who made pretensions to this kind of wisdom; all who came under the well-known denomination of *wise men*, or *sages.* He had called that class before him (ver. 2); he had demanded of them an explanation of his dream; he had been assured by the leading men among them, the Chaldeans (verses 10, 11), that they could not recall his dream; and, as he supposed that all who could be relied on in such a case had failed, he resolved to cut them off as impostors.

[The cruelty of Asiatic despots, and their in-

fliction of extreme and agonizing punishment on the most frivolous pretences, are proverbial. The fury and anger of Nebuchadnezzar would, no doubt, result in a sentence of death against

13 And the decree went forth that the wise *men* should be slain; and they sought Daniel and his fellows to be slain.

1 *returned.*

14 ¶ Then Daniel [1] answered with counsel and wisdom to Arioch the [2] captain of the king's guard,

2 *chief of the executioners,* or *slaughter-men,* or *chief marshal;* Ge. 37. 36; Jer. 52. 12, 14.

the wise men, accompanied by the most excruciating tortures. And we may probably learn its nature from the engraving, which represents the chief of the slayers commencing the operation of flaying alive, whilst the miserable culprit seems to be deprecating the monarch's wrath. This group forms part of the sculptures in the Hall of Judgment in the interior of the palace at Khorsabad.]

Where Daniel was at this time is not known. It would seem, however, that from some reason he had not been summoned before the king with the others, probably because, although he had shown himself to be eminently endowed with wisdom (ch. i. 20), he had not yet made any pretensions to this kind of knowledge, and was not numbered with the Magi, or Chaldeans. When, however, the decree went forth that *all* the "wise men of Babylon" should be slain, the exhibition of wisdom and knowledge made by him (chap. i. 18–20) was recollected, and the executioners of the sentence supposed that he and his companions were included in the general instructions. Whether the word *Babylon* here relates to the city of Babylon, or to the whole realm, there is no certain way of determining. Considering, however, the character of Oriental despotisms, and the cruelty to which absolute sovereigns have usually been transported in their passion, there would be no improbability in supposing that the command included the whole realm, though it is probable that most of this class would be found in the capital.

13. *And the decree went forth that the wise* men *should be slain.* The original here will bear a somewhat different translation, meaning, "the decree went forth, *and* the wise men were slain;" that is, the execution of the sentence was actually commenced. So the Vulgate : *Et egressâ sententiâ, sapientes interficiebantur.* So also the Greek version : καὶ οἱ σοφοὶ ἀπεκτέννοντο —"and the wise men were slain." This seems to me to be the more probable inter-

pretation, and better to suit the connection. Then it would mean that they had actually begun to execute the decree, and that in the prosecution of their bloody work they sought out Daniel and his companions, and that by his influence with Arioch the execution of the sentence was arrested. ¶ *And they sought Daniel and his fellows to be slain.* His three companions (ch. i. 6), who probably had not been among those who were summoned to court to explain the matter. Had they been consulted at first, the issuing of the decree would have been prevented, but it seems to have been the design of Providence to give the fairest trial of the ability of these sages, and to allow matters to come to a crisis, in order to show that what was done was wholly beyond human power.

14. *Then Daniel answered.* Marg., *returned.* The original literally is, "returned counsel and wisdom," meaning, that he returned an answer which was replete with wisdom. It would seem probable that Arioch had communicated to Daniel the decree of the king, and had stated to him that he was involved in that decree, and must prepare to die. ¶ *Counsel and wisdom.* That is, *wise counsel.* He evinced great prudence and discretion in what he said. He made such a suggestion to Arioch as, if acted on, would stay the execution of the sentence against all the wise men, and would secure the object which the king had in view. What was the exact nature of this answer is not mentioned. It is probable, however, that it was that he might be enabled to disclose the dream, and that he made this so plausible to Arioch, that he was disposed to allow him to make the trial. It is evident that Arioch would not have consented to arrest the execution of the sentence, unless it had appeared to him to be in the highest degree probable that he would be able to relieve the anxiety of the king. Knowing that the *main* object of the king was to

which was gone forth to slay the wise *men* of Babylon :

---

obtain the interpretation of his dream, and seeing that this object was not any the more likely to be secured by the execution of this stern decree, and knowing the high favour with which Daniel had been received at court (ch. i. 19–21), he seems to have been willing to assume some measure of responsibility, and to allow Daniel to make his own representation to the king. ¶ *To Arioch the captain of the king's guard.* Marg., "*chief of the executioners,* or *slaughter-men,* or *chief marshal.*" Greek, ἀρχιμαγείρῳ τοῦ βασιλέως —*chief cook of the king.* The Vulgate renders this, "Then Daniel inquired respecting the law and the sentence of Arioch, the commander of the royal army." The Chaldee word rendered *guard* is טַבָּחַיָּא. It is derived from טְבַח *tâbăhh,* to slaughter ; to kill animals ; and then to kill or slay men. The *noun,* then, means a slaughterer or slayer ; a cook ; an executioner, or one who kills men at the will of a sovereign, or by due sentence of law. There can be no doubt that the word here refers to Arioch, as sent out to execute this sentence ; yet we are not to regard him as a *mere* executioner, or as we would a hangman, for undoubtedly the king would entrust this sentence to one who was of respectable, if not of high rank. It is probable that one of the principal officers of his body-guard would be entrusted with the execution of such a sentence. In 1 Sam. viii. 13, the word is rendered *cooks.* It does not elsewhere occur. That he was not a *mere* executioner is apparent from the title given him in the next verse, where he is called "the king's *captain.*" ¶ *Which was gone forth to slay,* &c. He had gone to execute the decree, and its execution had already commenced.

15. *He answered and said to Arioch the king's captain.* The word *captain* —a different word from that which occurs in ver. 14, שַׁלִּיטָא—denotes one who has rule or dominion ; one who is powerful or mighty ; and it would be applied only to one who sustained a

post of honour and responsibility. See the use of the word שְׁלַט, as meaning *to rule,* in Neh. v. 15 ; Eccles. ii. 19 vi. 2 ; viii. 9 ; Esth. ix. 1 ; Psa. cxix. 133. The word here used is the same which occurs in ver. 10, where it is rendered *ruler.* It doubtless denotes here an officer of rank, and designates one of more honourable employment than would be denoted by the word *executioner.* It should be said on these verses (14, 15), however, that the office of executioner in the East was by no means regarded as a dishonourable office. It was entrusted to those high in rank, and even nobles considered it an honour, and often boasted of it as such, that among their ancestors there were those who had in this way been entrusted with executing the commands of their sovereign. Hanway and Abdul-Kerim both say that this office conferred honour and rank. Tournefort says, that in Georgia "the executioners are very rich, and men of standing undertake this employment ; far different from what occurs in other parts of the world, in that country this gives to a family a title of honour. They boast that among their ancestors there were many who were executioners ; and this they base on the sentiment, that nothing is more desirable than justice, and that nothing can be more honourable than to be engaged in administering the laws." See Rosenmüller, *Morgenland,* 1079. ¶ *Why is the decree so hasty from the king?* Implying that all the effort had not been made which it was possible to make to solve the mystery. The idea is, that a decree of such a nature, involving so many in ruin, ought not to have proceeded from the king without having taken all possible precautions, and having made all possible efforts to find those who might be able to disclose what the king desired. It was to Daniel a just matter of surprise that, after the favour and honour with which he had been received at court (ch. i. 19, 20), and the confidence which had been reposed in him, a command like this should have been issued,

the decree *so* hasty from the king?
Then Arioch made the thing known
to Daniel.

16 Then Daniel went in, and
desired of the king that he would
give him time, and that he would
show the king the interpretation.

17 Then Daniel went to his
house, and made the thing known
to Hananiah, Mishael, and Azariah,
his companions;

18 That *a* they would desire
mercies ¹ of the God of heaven

a ch. 3. 17; 1 Sa. 17. 37; 2 Ti. 4. 17, 18.
¹ *from before.*

---

so comprehensive as to embrace him
and his friends, when they had done
nothing to deserve the displeasure of
the king. ¶ *Then Arioch made the
thing known to Daniel.* The statement
respecting the dream ; the trouble of
the king ; the consultation of the magicians ; their inability to explain the
dream, and the positive command to
put all the pretenders to wisdom to
death. It is clear that Daniel had not
before been informed of these things.
16. *Then Daniel went in,* &c. Either
by himself, or through the medium of
some friend. Perhaps all that is meant
is, not that he actually went into the
presence of the monarch, but that he
went into the palace, and through the
interposition of some high officer of
court who had access to the sovereign,
desired of him that he would give him
time, and that he would make it known.
It would rather appear, from vers. 24,
25, that the first direct audience which he
had with the king was after the thing was
made known to him in a night vision,
and it would scarcely accord with established Oriental usages that he should
go immediately and unceremoniously
into the royal presence. A petition,
presented through some one who had
access to the king, would meet all the
circumstances of the case. ¶ *That he
would give him time.* He did not specify *why* he desired time, though the
reason why he did it is plain enough.
He wished to lay the matter before
God, and to engage his friends in earnest prayer that the dream and the
interpretation might be made known
to him. This request was granted to
him. It may seem remarkable, as no
time was allowed to the Chaldeans that
they might make inquiry (ver. 8), that
such a favour should have been granted
to Daniel, especially after the execution
of the sentence had been commenced ;
but we are to remember (1) that the

king would recollect the favour which
he had already shown Daniel on good
grounds, and the fact that he regarded
him as endowed with great wisdom,
ch. i. 19, 20. (2.) Daniel did not ask,
as the Chaldeans did, that the king
should tell the dream before he undertook to explain it, but he proposed
evidently to unfold the whole matter.
(3.) It could not but occur to the king
that Daniel had not yet been consulted,
and that it was but reasonable that he
should have a fair trial now, since it
appeared that he was involved in the
general sentence. (4.) The anxiety of
the king to understand the dream was
so great that he was willing to grasp
at *any* hope in order that his perplexities might be relieved ; and (5) it is not
improper to suppose that there may
have been a Divine influence on the
mind of this monarch, making him
willing to do so simple an act of justice as this, in order that it might be
seen and acknowledged that the hand
of God was in the whole matter.
17. *Then Daniel went to his house.*
It is quite evident that he had obtained
the object of his request, though this is
not expressly mentioned. The king
was undoubtedly, for the reasons above
stated, willing that he should have a
fair opportunity to try his skill in disclosing the mysterious secret. ¶ *And
made the thing known to Hananiah,*
&c. Made the whole matter known
—the perplexity respecting the dream ;
the failure of the Chaldeans to interpret it ; the decree ; and his own petition to the king. They had a common
interest in knowing it, as their lives
were all endangered.
18. *That they would desire mercies
of the God of heaven concerning this
secret.* That they would implore of
God that he would show his mercy to
them in revealing this secret, that their
lives might be spared. In the margin,

concerning this secret, that [1] Daniel and his fellows should not perish with the rest of the wise *men* of Babylon.

19 ¶ Then was the secret revealed unto Daniel in a night

[1] or, *they should not destroy Daniel.*

vision.[a] Then Daniel blessed the God of heaven.

20 Daniel answered and said, Blessed [b] be the name of God for ever and ever; for wisdom [c] and might are his:

a Nu. 12. 6.   *b* Ps. 50. 23.   *c* Je. 32. 19.

as in the Chaldee, this is "*from before* the God of heaven." All depended now on God. It was clear that human skill was exhausted, and that no reliance could be placed on any ability which man possessed. The art of the Chaldeans had failed, and Daniel, as well by this failure as by the promptings of his own feelings, must now have perceived that the only hope was in God, and that his favour in the case was to be obtained only by prayer. As his three friends were equally interested in the issue, and as it was an early principle of religion, and one found in all dispensations (comp. Matt. xviii. 19), that *united* prayer has special power with God, it was natural and proper to call on his friends to join with him in asking this favour from Him who alone could grant it. It was the natural and the last resource of piety, furnishing an example of what all may do, and should do, in times of perplexity and danger. ¶ *That Daniel and his fellows should not perish.* Marg., "or, *they should not destroy Daniel.*" The leading in the margin is most in accordance with the Chaldee, though the sense is substantially the same. The word *fellows* is the same which is before rendered *companions.* ¶ *With the rest of the wise* men *of Babylon.* It seems to have been certain that the decree would be executed on the Chaldeans, soothsayers, &c. And, indeed, there was no reason *why* the decree should not be executed. They had confessed their inability to comply with the king's command, and whatever Daniel could now do could not be construed in their favour as furnishing any reason why the decree should not be executed on them. It was presumed, therefore, that the law, severe as it seemed to be, would be carried into effect on them, and we may suppose that this was probably done. The only hope of their escaping from the common lot was in the belief

that the God whom they served would now interpose in their behalf.

19. *Then was the secret revealed,* &c. To wit, the dream and the interpretation. The thing which had been *hidden* was disclosed. We may suppose that this occurred after a suitable time had been given to prayer. ¶ *In a night vision.* A representation made to him at night, but whether when he was asleep or awake does not appear. Comp. Notes on ch. i. 17 ; Isa. i. 1 ; Job iv. 13 ; xxxiii. 15. ¶ *Then Daniel blessed the God of heaven.* Nothing would be more natural than that he should burst forth in a song of grateful praise for disclosing a secret by means of which his life, and the lives of his companions, would be preserved, and by which such signal honour would redound to God himself, as alone able to reveal coming events.

20. *Daniel answered and said.* The word "answer," in the Scriptures, often occurs substantially in the sense of *speak* or *say.* It does not always denote a reply to something that has been said by another, as it does with us, but is often used when a speech is commenced, as if one were replying to something that *might* be said in the case, or as meaning that the circumstances in the case gave rise to the remark. Here the meaning is, that Daniel responded, as it were, to the goodness which God had manifested, and gave utterance to his feelings in appropriate expressions of praise. ¶ *Blessed be the name of God for ever and ever.* That is, blessed be God— the *name,* in the Scriptures, being often used to denote the person himself. It is common in the Bible to utter ascriptions of praise to God in view of important revelations, or in view of great mercies. Comp. the song of Moses after the passage of the Red Sea, Exod. xv. ; the song of Deborah after the overthrow of Sisera, Judg. v. ; Isa.

21 And he changeth the *ᵃ* times
and the seasons : he *ᵇ* removeth

a Ps. 31. 14, 15.   b Ps. 75. 6, 7.

kings, and setteth up kings: he
giveth *ᵃ* wisdom unto the wise, and

c Pr. 2. 6, 7.

xii.   ¶ *For wisdom and might are
his.* Both these were manifested in a
remarkable manner in the circumstances of this case, and therefore these
were the beginnings of the song of
praise : *wisdom,* as now imparted to
Daniel, enabling him to disclose this
secret, when all human skill had failed ;
and *might,* as about to be evinced in
the changes of empire indicated by the
dream and the interpretation. Comp.
Jer. xxxii. 19, " Great in counsel, and
mighty in work."

21. *And he changeth the times and
the seasons.* The object of this is to
assert the general control of God in
reference to all changes which occur.
The assertion is made, undoubtedly, in
view of the revolutions in empire which
Daniel now saw, from the signification
of the dream, were to take place under
the Divine hand. Foreseeing now
these vast changes denoted by different parts of the image (vers. 36—45),
stretching into far-distant times, Daniel
was led to ascribe to God the control
over *all* the revolutions which occur
on earth. There is no essential difference between the words *times* and *seasons.* The words in Chaldee denote
stated or appointed seasons ; and the
idea of times *appointed, set, determined,* enters into both. Times and
seasons are not under the control of
chance, but are bounded by established
laws ; and yet God, who appointed
these laws, has power to change them,
and all the changes which occur under
those laws are produced by his agency.
Thus the changes which occur in regard
to day and night, spring and summer,
autumn and winter, clouds and sunshine, health and sickness, childhood
and youth, manhood and age, are under his control. Such changes, being
in accordance with certain laws, may
be regarded as *appointed,* or *set,* and
yet the laws and the revolutions consequent on them are all under his control. So in regard to the revolutions
of empire. By the arrangements of
his providence he secures such revolutions as he shall see it to be best should

occur, and in all of them his high hand
should be regarded. The words *seasons* and *times* are of frequent occurrence in Daniel, and are sometimes
used in a peculiar sense (see Notes on
ch. vii. 12, 25), but they seem here to
be employed in their usual and general signification, to denote that *all* the
revolutions which occur on earth are
under his control. ¶ *He removeth
kings, and setteth up kings.* He has
absolute control over all the sovereigns
of the earth, to place on the throne
whom he will, and to remove them
when he pleases. This was doubtless
suggested to Daniel, and was made the
foundation of this portion of his hymn
of praise, from what he was permitted
to see in the disclosures made to him
in the interpretation of the dream. He
then saw (compare vers. 37-45) that
there would be most important revolutions of kingdoms under the hand of
God, and being deeply impressed with
these great prospective changes, he
makes this general statement, that it
was the prerogative of God to do this
at pleasure. Nebuchadnezzar was
brought to feel this, and to recognize
it, when he said (ch. iv. 17), "The
Most High ruleth in the kingdom of
men, and giveth it to whomsoever he
will ;" "he doeth according to his will
in the army of heaven, and among the
inhabitants of the earth : none can stay
his hand, or say unto him, What doest
thou ?" ch. iv. 32, 35. This claim is
often asserted for God in the Scriptures as a proof of his supremacy and
greatness. "For promotion cometh
neither from the east, nor from the
west, nor from the south : but God is
the judge ; he putteth down one, and
setteth up another," Psa. lxxv. 6, 7.
Comp. 1 Sam. ii. 7, 8. Thus he claimed
absolute control over Sennacherib to
employ him at his pleasure in executing his purposes of punishment on the
Hebrew nation (Isa. x. 5–7), and thus
over Cyrus to execute his purposes on
Babylon, and to restore his people to
their land, Isa. xlv. 1, *seq.* See also
Isa. xlvi. 10, 11. In this manner, all

knowledge to them that know understanding.

22 He revealeth *a* the deep and

a Ps. 25. 14.　　　*b* Ps. 139. 11, 12; He. 4. 13.

secret things: he knoweth *b* what
is in the darkness, and the light
dwelleth *c* with him.

c 1 Ti. 6. 16; 1 Jn. 1. 5.

the kings of the earth may be regarded as under his control ; and if the Divine plan were fully understood it would be found that each one has received his appointment under the Divine direction, to accomplish some important part in carrying forward the Divine plans to their fulfilment. A history of human affairs, showing the exact purpose of God in regard to each ruler who has occupied a throne, and the exact object which God designed to accomplish by placing *him* on the throne at the time when he did, would be a far more important and valuable history than any which has been written. Of many such rulers, like Cyrus, Sennacherib, Pilate, Henry VIII., Edward VI., and the Elector of Saxony, we can see the reason why they lived and reigned when they did ; and doubtless God has had some important end to accomplish in the development of his great plans in the case of every one who has ever occupied a throne. ¶ *He giveth wisdom unto the wise,* &c. He is the source of all true wisdom and knowledge. This is often claimed for God in the Scriptures. Comp. Prov. ii. 6, 7 :

"For the Lord giveth wisdom ;
Out of his mouth cometh knowledge and understanding.
He layeth up sound wisdom for the righteous ;
He is a buckler to them that walk uprightly."

See also 1 Kings iii. 9–12 ; Exod. xxxi. 3. God claims to be the source of all wisdom and knowledge. He originally formed each human intellect, and made it what it is ; he opens before it the paths of knowledge ; he gives to it clearness of perception ; he preserves its powers so that they do not become deranged ; he has power to make suggestions, to direct the laws of association, to fix the mind on important thoughts, and to open before it new and interesting views of truth. And as it would be found, if the history could be written, that God has placed each monarch on the throne with a distinct reference to some important purpose in the development of his great plans, so

probably it would be seen that each important work of genius which has been written ; each invention in the arts ; and each discovery in science has been, for a similar purpose, under his control. He has created the great intellect just at the time when it was needful that such a discovery or invention should be made, and having prepared the world for it by the course of events, the discovery or invention has occurred just at the time when, on the whole, it was most desirable that it should.

22. *He revealeth the deep and secret things.* Things which are too profound for man to fathom by his own power, and which are concealed or hidden until he makes them known. What is said here is an advance on what was affirmed in the previous verse, and relates to another kind of knowledge. *That* related to such knowledge as was not properly beyond the grasp of the human intellect when unaided in any supernatural manner, and affirmed that even then all discoveries and inventions are to be traced to God ; *this* refers to a species of knowledge which lies beyond any natural compass of the human powers, and in which a supernatural influence is needed—such things as the Chaldeans and astrologers claimed the power of disclosing. The assertion here is, that when the highest human wisdom showed itself insufficient for the exigency, God was able to disclose those deep truths which it was desirable for man to understand. Applied generally, this refers to the truths made known by revelation—truths which man could never have discovered by his unaided powers. ¶ *He knoweth what is in the darkness.* What appears to man to be involved in darkness, and on which no light seems to shine. This may refer not only to what is concealed from man in the literal darkness of night, but to all that is mysterious ; all that lies beyond the range of human inquiry ; all that pertains to unseen worlds. An immensely large portion of the universe

23 I thank thee, and praise thee, O thou God of my fathers, who hast given me wisdom and might, and hast made known unto me now what we desired of thee: for thou

hast *now* made known unto us the king's matter.

24 ¶ Therefore Daniel went in unto Arioch, whom the king had ordained to destroy the wise *men*

---

lies wholly beyond the range of human investigation at present, and is, of course, dark to man. ¶ *And the light dwelleth with him.* The word rendered *dwelleth* (שְׁרֵא) means, properly, to loose, to unbind, to solve, as *e. g.* hard questions, Dan. v. 16; and is then applied to travellers who unbind the loads of their beasts to put up for the night, and then it comes to mean to put up for the night, to lodge, to dwell. Hence the meaning is, that the light abides with God; it is there as in its appropriate dwelling-place; he is in the midst of it: all is light about him; light when it is sent out goes from him; when it is gathered together, its appropriate place is with him. Comp. Job xxxviii. 19, 20:—

'Where is the way where light dwelleth?
And as for darkness, where is the place thereof?
That thou shouldest take it to the bound thereof,
And that thou shouldest know the paths to the house thereof?"

See Notes on that passage. Comp. also 1 Tim. vi. 16: "Dwelling in the light which no man can approach unto." 1 John i. 5: "God is light, and in him is no darkness at all."

23. *I thank thee, and praise thee, O thou God of my fathers.* By his "fathers" here, Daniel refers doubtless to the Jewish people in general, and not to his own particular ancestors. The meaning of the phrase "God of my fathers" is, that he had been their protector; had regarded them as his people; had conferred on them great favours. The particular ground of thanksgiving here is, that the same God who had so often revealed himself to the Hebrew people by the prophets in their own land, had now condescended to do the same thing to one of their nation, though a captive in a strange country. The favour thus bestowed had an increased value, from the fact that it showed that the Hebrew people were not forgotten, though far from the land of their birth, and that, though in cap-

tivity, they might still hope for the benign interposition of God. ¶ *Who hast given me wisdom and might.* The word "wisdom" here undoubtedly refers to the ability which had now been given him to declare the nature and purport of the dream, imparting to him a degree of wisdom far superior to those pretenders to whom the matter had been at first submitted. The word "*might*" (Chald., *strength*—גְּבוּרְתָא) does not probably differ materially from "*wisdom.*" It means *ability* to interpret the dream —implying that it was a task beyond natural human ability. ¶ *For thou hast now made known unto us the king's matter.* That is, it had been made known to him and his friends. He joins himself with them; for, although it was particularly made known to *him*, yet, as they had united with him in prayer that the secret might be disclosed, and as they shared common dangers, he regarded it as in fact made known to them all.

24. *Therefore Daniel went in unto Arioch.* In view of the fact that the matter was now disclosed to him, he proposed to lay it before the king. This, of course, he did not do directly, but through Arioch, who was intrusted with the execution of the decree to slay the wise men of Babylon. That officer would naturally have access to the king, and it was proper that a proposal to arrest the execution of the sentence should be made through his instrumentality. The Chaldee (כָּל־קְבֵל דְּנָה) is, properly, "on this whole account"— or, "on this whole account because" —in accordance with the usually full and pleonastic mode of writing particles, similar to the German *alldieweil*, or the compound English *forasmuch as.* The meaning is, that in view of the whole matter, he sought to lay the case before the king. ¶ *Destroy not the wise men of Babylon.* That is, "Stay the execution of the sentence on them. Though they have failed to furnish the

of Babylon: he went and said thus unto him, Destroy not the wise *men* of Babylon: bring me in before the king, and I will show unto the king the interpretation.

25 Then Arioch brought in Daniel before the king in haste, and said

1 *That I.*

thus unto him, [1] I have found a man of the [2] captives of Judah that will make known unto the king the interpretation.

26 The king answered, and said to Daniel, whose name *was* Belteshazzar, Art thou able to make

2 *children of the captivity.*

interpretation demanded, yet, as it *can* now be given, there is no occasion for the exercise of this severity." The ground of the sentence was that they could not interpret the dream. As the execution of the sentence involved Daniel and his friends, and as the reason why it was passed at all would now cease by his being able to furnish the required explanation, Daniel felt that it was a matter of mere justice that the execution of the sentence should cease altogether. ¶ *Bring me in before the king.* It would seem from this that Daniel did not regard himself as having free access to the king, and he would not unceremoniously intrude himself into his presence. This verse confirms the interpretation given of ver. 16, and makes it in the highest degree probable that this was the first occasion on which he was personally before the king in reference to this matter.

25. *Then Arioch brought in Daniel before the king in haste.* The Chaldee word used here implies *in tumultuous haste,* as of one who was violently excited, or in a state of trepidation, from בְּהַל—*to tremble, to be in trepidation.* The trepidation in this case may have arisen from one or both of two causes: (1) exultation, or joy, that the great secret was discovered; or (2) joy that the effusion of blood might be stayed, and that there might be now no necessity to continue the execution of the sentence against the wise men. ¶ *I have found a man.* Marg., as in Chaldee, "That I have found a man." It is not to be supposed that Arioch had known anything of the application which Daniel had made to the king to delay the execution of the sentence (ver. 16), and, for anything that appears, he had suspended that execution on his own responsibility. Ignorant as he was, therefore, of any

such arrangement, and viewing only his own agency in the matter, it was natural for him to go in and announce this as something entirely new to the king, and without suggesting that the execution of the sentence had been at all delayed. It was a most remarkable circumstance, and one which looks like a Divine interposition, that he should have been disposed to delay the execution of the sentence at all, so that Daniel could have an opportunity of showing whether he could not divulge the secret. All the circumstances of the case seem to imply that Arioch was not a man of a cruel disposition, but was disposed, as far as possible, to prevent the effusion of blood. ¶ *Of the captives of Judah.* Marg., as in Chald., "of the children of the captivity." The word *Judah* here probably refers to the *country* rather than to the *people,* and means that he was among those who had been brought from the land of Judah. ¶ *That will make known unto the king the interpretation.* It is clear, from the whole narrative, that Arioch had great confidence in Daniel. All the *evidence* which he could have that he would be able to make this known, must have been from the fact that Daniel *professed* to be able to do it; but such was his confidence in him that he had no doubt that he would be able to do it.

26. *The king answered, and said to Daniel, whose name was Belteshazzar.* Notes on ch. i. 7. The *king* may have addressed him by this name, and probably did during this interview. This was the name, it would seem, by which he was known in Babylon—a name which implied honour and respectability, as being conferred on one whom it was supposed the principal Babylonian divinity favoured. ¶ *Art thou able to make known unto me the dream?* One

known unto me the dream which I have seen, and the interpretation thereof?

27 Daniel answered in the presence of the king, and said, The secret which the king hath demanded,

a Is. 47. 13, 14.   *b* Ge. 40. 8; 41. 16.

cannot *a* the wise *men*, the astrologers, the magicians, the soothsayers show unto the king;

28 But *b* there is a God in heaven that revealeth secrets, and ¹ maketh known to the king Nebuchadnezzar.

1 *hath made.*

of the first points in the difficulty was to recal *the dream itself*, and hence this was the first inquiry which the king presented. If he could not recal that, of course the matter was at an end, and the law would be suffered to take its course.

27. *Daniel answered in the presence of the king, and said, The secret which the king hath demanded, cannot the wise* men, &c., *show unto the king.* Daniel regarded it as a settled and indisputable point that the solution could not be hoped for from the Chaldean sages. The highest talent which the realm could furnish had been applied to, and had failed. It was clear, therefore, that there was no hope that the difficulty would be removed by human skill. Besides this, Daniel would seem also to intimate that the thing, from the necessity of the case, was beyond the compass of the human powers. Alike in reference to the question whether a forgotten dream could be *recalled*, and to the actual *signification* of a dream so remarkable as this, the whole matter was beyond the ability of man. ¶ *The wise* men, *the astrologers*, &c. On these words, see Notes on ch. i. 20. All these words occur in that verse, except גָּזְרִין *Gozrin*—rendered *soothsayers*. This is derived from גְּזַר—*to cut, to cut off;* and then *to decide, to determine;* and it is thus applied to those who decide or determine the fates or destiny of men; that is, those who "by casting nativities from the place of the stars at one's birth, and by various arts of computing and divining, foretold the fortunes and destinies of individuals." See Gesenius, *Com. z. Isa.* ii. 349–356, § 4, Von den Chaldern und deren Astrologie. On p. 555, he has given a figure, showing how the heavens were cut up, or *divided*, by astrologers in the practice of their art. Comp. the phrase *numeri Babylonii*, in Hor. *Carm.* I. xi. 2. The Greek

is γαζαρηνῶν—the Chaldee word in Greek letters. This is one of the words—not very few in number—which the authors of the Greek version did not attempt to translate. Such words, however, are not useless, as they serve to throw light on the question how the Hebrew and Chaldee were pronounced before the vowel points were affixed to those languages.

28. *But there is a God in heaven that revealeth secrets.* One of the principal objects contemplated in all that occurred respecting this dream and its interpretation was, to direct the mind of the monarch to the true God, and to secure the acknowledgment of his supremacy. Hence it was so ordered that those who were most eminent for wisdom, and who were regarded as the favourites of heaven, were constrained to confess their entire inability to explain the mystery. The way was thus prepared to show that he who *could* do this must be the true God, and must be worthy of adoration and praise. Thus prepared, the mind of the monarch was now directed by this pious Hebrew youth, though a captive, to a truth so momentous and important. His whole training, his modesty and his piety, all were combined to lead him to attribute whatever skill he might evince in so difficult a matter to the true God alone: and we can scarcely conceive of a more sublime object of contemplation than this young man, in the most magnificent court of the world, directing the thoughts of the most mighty monarch that then occupied a throne, to the existence and the perfections of the true God. ¶ *And maketh known to the king Nebuchadnezzar.* Margin, *hath made.* The translation in the text is more correct, for it was not true that he had as yet actually made these things known to the king. He had furnished intimations of what was to occur, but he had not yet been permitted to under-

zar what shall be in the latter days. Thy dream, and the visions of thy head upon thy bed, are these;

29 As for thee, O king, thy thoughts 1 came *into thy mind* upon

1 *came up.*

---

stand their signification. ¶ *What shall be in the latter days.* Gr. ἰπ' ἐσχάτων τῶν ἡμερῶν—"in the last days." Vulg., *in novissimis temporibus*—"in the last times." Chald., בְּאַחֲרִית יוֹמַיָּא — "in the after days ;" or, as Faber expresses it, *in the afterhood of days.* The phrase means what we should express by saying, *hereafter—in future times—in time to come.* This phrase often has special reference to the times of the Messiah, as the last dispensation of things on the earth, or as that under which the affairs of the world will be wound up. Comp. Notes on Isa. ii. 2. It does not appear, however, to be used in that sense here, but it denotes merely *future* times. The phrase "the latter days," therefore, does not exactly convey the sense of the original. It is *future* days rather than *latter* days. ¶ *Thy dream, and the visions of thy head upon thy bed.* The phrase "visions of thy head" means conceptions or notions formed by the brain. It would seem from this, that, even in the time of Daniel, the brain was regarded as, in some sense, the organ of thinking, or that *thought* had its seat in the head. We are not to suppose that by the use of these different expressions Daniel meant to describe two things, or to intimate that Nebuchadnezzar had had visions which were distinct. What he saw might be described as a dream or a vision ; it, in fact, had the nature of both. ¶ *Are these.* "These which I now proceed to describe."

29. *As for thee, O king, thy thoughts came* into thy mind *upon thy bed.* Margin, *up;* that is, thy thoughts ascended. The Chaldee is, " thy thoughts ascended"—סְלִקוּ. So the Greek: "Thy thoughts ascended (ἀνέβησαν) upon thy couch." There is, evidently, some allusion to the thoughts *ascending,* or *going up;* and perhaps the idea is, that they were employed on important subjects—an idea which we now express

thy bed, what should come to pass hereafter ; and *a* he that revealeth secrets maketh known to thee what shall come to pass.

30 But as for me, this secret is

a Amos 4. 13.

---

by saying that one's thoughts are *elevated,* as contrasted with those which are *low* and *grovelling.* ¶ *What should come to pass hereafter.* It would seem most probable from this, that the thoughts of Nebuchadnezzar were occupied with this subject in his waking moments on his bed, and that the dream was grafted on this train of thought when he fell asleep. Nothing is more probable than that his thoughts might be thus occupied. The question respecting his successor; the changes which might occur; the possibility of revolutions in other kingdoms, or in the provinces of his own vast empire, all were topics on which his mind would probably be employed. As God designed, too, to fix his thoughts particularly on that general subject — the changes which were to occur in his empire—such an occasion, when his attention was greatly engrossed with the subject, would be very suitable to impart the knowledge which he did by this vision. Daniel refers to this, probably, because it would do much to confirm the monarch in the belief of his inspiration, if he referred to the train of thought which had preceded the dream ; as it is not improbable that the king would remember his *waking* thoughts on the subject, though his *dream* was forgotten.

30. *But as for me.* So far as I am concerned in this matter, or whatever skill or wisdom I may evince in the interpretation, it is not to be traced to myself. The previous verse commences with the expression "*as for thee ;*" and in this verse, by the phrase "as for *me,*" Daniel puts himself in strong contrast with the king. The way in which this was done was not such as to flatter the vanity of the king, and cannot be regarded as the art of the courtier, and yet it was such as would be universally adopted to conciliate his favour, and to give him an elevated idea of the modesty and piety of the youthful Daniel.

not revealed to me for *any* wisdom *a* that I have more than any living, but for ¹ *their* sakes that shall make

a Ac. 3. 12.

1 or, *the intent that the interpretation may be made known.*

In the previous verse he says, that, as to what pertained to the king, God had greatly honoured him by giving him important intimations of what was yet to occur. Occupying the position which he did, it might be supposed that it would not be wholly unnatural that he should be thus favoured, and Daniel does not say, as in his own case, that it was *not* on account of anything in the character and rank of the king that this had been communicated to him. But when he comes to speak of himself —a youth; a captive; a stranger in Babylon; a native of another land— nothing was more natural or proper than that he should state distinctly that it was not on account of anything in him that this was done. ¶ *This secret is not revealed to me for any wisdom that I have more than any living.* That is, "it is not *by* any wisdom which I have above others, nor is it *on account of* any previous wisdom which I have possessed or manifested." There is an absolute and total disclaimer of the idea that it was in any sense, or in any way, on account of his own superiority in wisdom. All the knowledge which he had in the case was to be traced entirely to God. ¶ *But for their sakes that shall make known the interpretation to the king.* Marg., " or, *the intent that the interpretation may be made known.*" The margin is the more correct rendering, and should have been admitted into the text. The *literal* translation is, " but (לְהֵין) on account of the thing that they might make known the interpretation to the king." The word rendered "make known" is indeed in the plural, but it is evidently used in an impersonal sense, meaning that the interpretation would be made known. " It was to the intent that they might make it known;" that is, that somebody might do it, or that it might be done. Would not modesty and delicacy lead to the choice of such an expression here, inclining Daniel to avoid,

known the interpretation to the king, and that thou mightest know the thoughts of thy heart.

31 ¶ Thou, O king, ² sawest, and,

2 *wast seeing.*

as far as possible, all mention of himself? The main thought is, that the grand object to be secured was not to glorify Daniel, or any other human being, but to communicate to this heathen monarch important truths respecting coming events, and through him to the world. ¶ *And that thou mightest know the thoughts of thy heart.* In reference to this matter; that is, that he might be able to recal the thoughts which passed through his mind in the dream. This (vers. 27–30) is the introduction to the important disclosure which Daniel was about to make to the king. This entire disclaimer of the honour of having originated the interpretation by his own wisdom, and the ascribing of it to God, are worthy here of special attention. It is probable that the magicians were accustomed to ascribe to their own skill and sagacity the ability to interpret dreams and the other prognostics of the future, and to claim special honour on that account. In opposition to this, Daniel utterly disclaims any such wisdom himself, and attributes the skill which he has entirely to God. This is a beautiful illustration of the nature of modesty and piety. It places before us a young man, having now the prospect of being elevated to great honours; under every temptation to arrogate the possession of extraordinary wisdom to himself; suddenly exalted above all the sages of the most splendid court on earth, disclaiming all merit, and declaring in the most solemn manner that whatever profound wisdom there might be in the communication which he was about to make, it was not in the slightest degree to be traced to himself. See the remarks at the end of the chapter, (6.)

31. *Thou, O king, sawest.* Marg., *wast seeing.* The margin is in accordance with the Chaldee. The language is properly that which denotes a prolonged or attentive observation. He was in an attitude favourable to vision, or was looking with intensity, and there

behold, a great image. This great image, whose brightness *was* excellent, stood before thee, and the form thereof *was* terrible.

---

appeared before him this remarkable image. Comp. ch. vii. 1, 2, 4, 6. It was not a thing which appeared for a moment, and then vanished, but which remained so long that he could contemplate it with accuracy. ¶ *And, behold, a great image.* Chald., *one image that was grand*—צְלֵם חַד שַׂגִּיא. So the Vulgate—*statua una grandis.* So the Greek —εἰκὼν μία. The object seems to be to fix the attention on the fact that there was but *one* image, though composed of so different materials, and of materials that seemed to be so little fitted to be worked together into the same statue. The idea, by its being represented as *one,* is, that it was, in some respects, *the same kingdom* that he saw symbolized: that is, that it would extend over the same countries, and could be, in some sense, regarded as a prolongation of the same empire. There was so much of *identity,* though different in many respects, that it could be represented as *one.* The word rendered *image* (צְלֵם) denotes properly *a shade,* or *shadow,* and then anything that *shadows forth,* or that represents anything. It is applied to man (Gen. i. 27) as shadowing forth, or representing God; that is, there was something in man when he was created which had so far a resemblance to God that he might be regarded as an *image* of him. The word is often used to denote idols—as supposed to be a *representation* of the gods, either in their forms, or as shadowing forth their character as majestic, stern, mild, severe, merciful, &c. Numb. xxxiii. 52; 1 Sam. vi. 5; 2 Kings xi. 18; 2 Chron. xxiii. 17; Ezek. vii. 20; xvi. 17; xxiii. 14; Amos, v. 26. This image is not represented as an idol to be worshipped, nor in the use of the word is it to be supposed that there is an allusion, as Prof. Bush supposes, to the fact that these kingdoms would be idolatrous, but the word is used in its proper and primitive sense, to denote something which would *represent,* or *shadow forth,* the kingdoms which would exist. The exact *size* of the image **is** not mentioned. It is only suggested that it was *great*—

a proper characteristic to represent the *greatness* of the kingdoms to which it referred. ¶ *This great image.* The word here rendered *great* (רַב) is different from that used in the previous clause, though it is not easy to determine the exact difference between the words. Both denote that the image was of gigantic dimensions. It is well remarked by Prof. Bush, that "the monuments of antiquity sufficiently evince that the humour prevailed throughout the East, and still more in Egypt, of constructing enormous statues, which were usually dedicated to some of their deities, and connected with their worship. The object, therefore, now presented in the monarch's dream was not, probably, entirely new to his thoughts." ¶ *Whose brightness was excellent.* "Whose brightness *excelled,* or was unusual and remarkable." The word rendered *brightness* (זִיו) is found only in Daniel. It is rendered *brightness* in ch. ii. 31, iv. 36, and in the margin in ch. v. 6, 9; and *countenance* in ch. v. 6 (*text*), in vers. 9, 10, ch. vii. 28. From the places where it is found, particularly ch. iv. 36, it is clear that it is used to denote a certain beauty, or majesty, shining forth in the countenance, which was fitted to impress the beholder with awe. The term here is to be understood not merely of the face of the image, but of its entire aspect, as having something in it signally splendid and imposing. We have only to conceive of a colossal statue whose head was burnished gold, and a large part of whose frame was polished silver, to see the force of this language. ¶ *Stood before thee.* It stood over against him in full view. He had an opportunity of surveying it clearly and distinctly. ¶ *And the form thereof was terrible.* Vast, imposing, grand, fearful. The sudden appearance of such an object as this could not but fill the mind with terror. The design for which this representation was made to Nebuchadnezzar is clearly unfolded in the explanation which Daniel gives. It may be remarked here, in general, that such an appearance of a gigantic image

32 This image's head *was* of fine gold, his breast and his arms of sil-

ver, his belly and his ¹thighs of brass,

---

was well adapted to represent successive kingdoms, and that the representation was in accordance with the spirit of ancient times. "In ancient coins and medals," says the editor of the *Pictorial Bible*, "nothing is more common than to see cities and nations represented by human figures, male or female. According to the ideas which suggested such symbols, a vast image in the human figure was, therefore, a very fit emblem of sovereign power and dominion; while the materials of which it was composed did most significantly typify the character of the various empires, the succession of which was foreshown by this vision. This last idea, of expressing the condition of things by metallic symbols, was prevalent before the time of Daniel. Hesiod, who lived about two centuries before Daniel, characterizes the succession of ages (four) by the very same metals—gold, silver, brass, and iron."

32. *This image's head* was *of fine gold*. Chaldee, *good gold*—דְּהַב טָב—that is, fine, pure, unalloyed. The whole head of the figure, colossal as it was, appeared to be composed wholly of this. Had the *whole* image been made of gold, it would not have been so striking—for it was not uncommon to construct vast statues of this metal. Comp. ch. iii. 1. But the remarkable peculiarity of this image was, that it was composed of different materials, some of which were seldom or never used in such a structure, and all of which had a peculiar significancy. On the significancy of this part of the figure, and the resemblance between this head of gold and Nebuchadnezzar himself, see Notes on vers. 37, 38. ¶ *His breast and his arms of silver*. The word rendered *breast* (חֲדִין) is in the plural number, in accordance with a common usage in the Hebrew, by which several members of the human body are often expressed in the plural; as פָּנִים—*faces*, &c. There is a foundation for such a usage in nature, in the two-fold form of many of the por-

tions of the human body. The portion of the body which is here represented is obviously the upper portion of the front part—that which is prominently visible when we look at the human frame. Next to the head it is the most important part, as it embraces most of the vital organs. Some degree of inferiority, as well as the idea of succession, would be naturally represented by this. "The inferior value of silver as compared with gold will naturally suggest some degree of decline or degeneracy in the character of the subject represented by the metal; and so in other members, as we proceed downward, as the material becomes continually baser, we naturally infer that the subject deteriorates, in some sense, in the like manner."—Professor Bush, *in loc*. On the kingdom represented by this, and the propriety of this representation, see Notes on ver. 39. ¶ *His belly and his thighs of brass*. Marg., *sides*. It is not necessary to enter minutely into an examination of the words here used. The word *belly* denotes, unquestionably, the regions of the abdomen as externally visible. The word rendered *thighs* in the text is rendered *sides* in the margin. It is, like the word *breast* in the previous verse, in the plural number, and for the same reason. The Hebrew word (יָרֵךְ) is commonly rendered *thigh* in the Scriptures (Gen. xxiv. 2, 9; xxxii. 25 (26), 31, 32 (32, 33), *et al*.), though it is also frequently rendered *side*, Exod. xxxii. 27; xl. 22, 24; Lev. i. 11; Num. iii. 29, *et al*. According to Gesenius, it denotes "the thick and double fleshy member which commences at the bottom of the spine, and extends to the lower legs." It is that part on which the sword was formerly worn, Exod. xxxii. 27; Judg. iii. 16, 21; Psal. xlv. 3 (4). It is also that part which was smitten, as an expression of mourning or of indignation, Jer. xxxi. 19; Ezek. xxi. 12 (17). Comp. Hom. *Il*. xii. 162, xv. 397; *Od*. xiii. 198; Cic. cl. *Orat*. 80: *Quinc*. xi. 3. It is not improperly

33 His legs of iron, his feet part of iron and part of clay.

1 or, *which was not in hands.*

here rendered *thighs,* and the portion of the figure that was of brass was that between the breast and the lower legs, or extended from the breast to the knees. The word is elsewhere employed to denote the shaft or main trunk of the golden candlestick of the tabernacle, Exod. xxv. 31; xxxvii. 17; Num. viii. 4. ¶ *Of brass.* An inferior metal, and denoting a kingdom of inferior power or excellence. On the kingdom represented by this, see Notes on ver. 39.

33. *His legs of iron.* The portion of the lower limbs from the knees to the ankles. This is undoubtedly the usual meaning of the English word *legs,* and it as clearly appears to be the sense of the original word here. Iron was regarded as inferior to either of the other metals specified, and yet was well adapted to denote a kingdom of a particular kind—less noble in some respects, and yet hardy, powerful, and adapted to tread down the world by conquest. On the application of this, see Notes on ver. 40. ¶ *His feet part of iron and part of clay.* As to his feet; or in respect to his feet, they were partly of iron and partly of clay —a mixture denoting great strength, united with that which is fragile and weak. The word rendered *clay* in this place (חֲסַף) is found nowhere else except in this chapter, and is always rendered *clay,* ch. ii. 33–35, 41 (twice), 42, 43 (twice), 45. In some instances (vers. 41, 43), the epithet *miry* is applied to it. This would seem to imply that it was *not* "burnt or baked clay," or "earthenware," as Professor Bush supposes, but clay in its natural state. The idea would seem to be, that the framework, so to speak, was iron, with clay worked in, or filling up the interstices, so as to furnish an image of strength combined with that which is weak. That it would be well adapted - represent a kingdom that had many elements of permanency in it, yet that was combined with things that made it weak—a mixture of that which was

34 Thou sawest till that a stone was cut out [1] without [a] hands, which

a Zec. 4. 6; Jn. 1. 13.

powerful with that which was liable to be crushed; capable of putting forth great efforts, and of sustaining great shocks, and yet having such elements of feebleness and decay as to make it liable to be overthrown. For the application of this, see Notes on vers. 41–43.

34. *Thou sawest.* Chaldee, "Thou wast seeing;" that is, thou didst continue to behold, implying that the vision was of somewhat long continuance. It did not appear and then suddenly vanish, but it remained so long that he had an opportunity of careful observation. ¶ *Till that a stone was cut out without hands.* That is, from a mountain or hill, ver. 45. This idea is *expressed* in the Latin and the Greek version. The vision appears to have been that of a colossal image *standing on a plain* in the vicinity of a mountain, standing firm, until, by some unseen agency, and in an unaccountable manner, a stone became detached from the mountain, and was made to impinge against it. The margin here is, *which was not in his hands.* The more correct rendering of the Chaldee, however, is that in the text, literally, "a stone was cut out which was not by hands"—בִּידַיִן: or perhaps still more accurately, "a stone was cut out which was not *in* hands," so that the fact that it was not in or by *hands* refers rather to its not being projected by hands than to the manner of its being detached from the mountain. The essential idea is, that the agency of hands did not appear at all in the case. The stone seemed to be self-moved. It became detached from the mountain, and, as if instinct with life, struck the image and demolished it. The word rendered *stone* (אֶבֶן) determines nothing as to the *size* of the stone, but the whole statement would seem to imply that it was not of large dimensions. It struck upon *the feet* of the image, and it *became* itself a great mountain (ver. 35) —all which would seem to imply that it was at first not large. What increased

smote the image upon his feet *that were* of iron and clay, and brake them to pieces.

35 Then was the iron, the clay, the brass, the silver, and the gold, broken to pieces together, and be-

the astonishment of the monarch was, that a stone of such dimensions should have been adequate to overthrow so gigantic a statue, and to grind it to powder. The points on which it was clearly intended to fix the attention of the monarch, and which made the vision so significant and remarkable, were these : (*a*) the colossal size and firmness of the image ; (*b*) the fact that a stone, not of large size, should be seen to be self-detached from the mountain, and to move against the image ; (*c*) the fact that it should completely demolish and pulverize the colossal figure ; and (*d*) the fact that then this stone of inconsiderable size should be itself mysteriously augmented until it filled the world. It should be added, that the vision appears not to have been that of a stone detached from the side of a hill, and rolling *down* the mountain by the force of gravitation, but that of a stone detached, and then *moving off* toward the image as if it had been thrown from a hand, though the hand was unseen. This would very strikingly and appropriately express the idea of something, apparently small in its origin, that was impelled by a cause that was unseen, and that bore with mighty force upon an object of colossal magnitude, by an agency that could not be explained by the causes that usually operate. For the application and pertinency of this, see Notes on vers. 44, 45. ¶ *Which smote the image upon his feet.* The word here used (מְחָא) means, *to strike, to smite,* without reference to the question whether it is a single blow, or whether the blow is often repeated. The Hebrew word (מָחָא) is uniformly used as referring to *the clapping of the hands ;* that is, smiting them together, Ps. xcviii. 8 ; Isa. lv. 12 ; Ezek. xxv. 6. The Chaldee word is used only here and in ver. 35, referring to the smiting of the image, and in ch. iv. 35 (32), where it is rendered "*stay*"—"none can *stay* his hand." The connection here, and the whole statement, would seem to

demand the sense of a continued or prolonged smiting, or of repeated blows, rather than a single concussion. The great image was not only thrown down, but there was a subsequent process of *comminution,* independent of what would have been produced by the fall. A fall would only have broken it into large blocks or fragments ; but this continued smiting reduced it to powder. This would imply, therefore, not only a single shock, or violent blow, but some cause continuing to operate until that which had been overthrown was effectually destroyed, like a vast image reduced to impalpable powder. The *first concussion* on the feet made it certain that the colossal frame would fall ; but there was a longer process necessary before the whole effect should be accomplished. Compare Notes on vers. 44, 45. ¶ *And brake them to pieces.* In ver. 35, the idea is, "they became like the chaff of the summer threshing-floors." The meaning is not that the image was broken to *fragments,* but that it was *beaten fine*—reduced to powder—so that it might be scattered by the wind. This is the sense of the Chaldee word (דְּקַק), and of the Hebrew word also (דָּקַק). See Exod. xxxii. 20 : "And he took the calf which they had made, and burned it in the fire, *and ground it to powder.*" Deut. ix. 21 : "And I took your sin, the calf which ye had made, and burnt it with fire, and stamped it, and ground it very small, even until it was *as small* as dust." Isa. xli. 15 : "Thou shalt thresh the mountains and beat them *small,* and shalt make the hills as chaff." 2 Kings xxiii. 15 : "He burnt the high place, and *stamped* it *small* to powder." 2 Chron. xxxiv. 4 : "And they brake down the altars, &c., and *made dust* of them, and strewed it upon the graves of them that had sacrificed unto them." Compare Exod. xxx. 36 ; 2 Chron. xxxiv. 7 ; 2 Kings xxiii. 6. From these passages it is clear that the general meaning of the word is that of reducing anything to fine dust

came like the *a* chaff of the summer threshing-floors; and the wind carried them away, that no *b* place was found for them: and the stone that smote the image became a great

a Ps. 1. 4; Ho. 13. 3.   b Ps. 37. 36.

mountain, *c* and filled *d* the whole earth.

36 ¶ This *is* the dream; and we will tell the interpretation thereof before the king.

c Is. 2. 2, 3.   d 1 Co. 15. 25.

or powder, so that it may be easily blown about by the wind.

35. *Then was the iron, the clay, the brass, the silver, and the gold broken to pieces together, and became like the chaff of the summer threshing-floor.* The word rendered *together* (כַּחֲדָה) our translators would seem to have understood as referring to *time;* to its being done simultaneously. The more literal interpretation, however, is, "*as one;*" that is, "they were beaten small *as one,*" referring to *identity of condition.* They were all reduced to one indiscriminate mass; to such a mass that the original materials could no longer be distinguished, and would all be blown away together. The literal meaning of the word (חַד used and חֲדָה) is, *one,* or *first.* Ezra iv. 8, "wrote *a* letter;" v. 13, "in the *first* year of Cyrus;" vi. 2, "*a* roll;" Dan. ii. 9; "there is but *one* decree for you;" iii. 19, "heat the furnace *one* seven times hotter," &c. United with the conjunction (כ) it means *as one,* like the Heb. כְּאֶחָד—Eccles. xi. 6; 2 Chron. v. 13; Ezra ii. 64; iii. 9; Isa. lxv. 25. The phrase "chaff of the summer threshing-floors" refers to the mode of winnowing grain in the East. This was done in the open air, usually on an elevated place, by throwing the grain, when thrashed, into the air with a shovel, and the wind thus drove away the chaff. Such chaff, therefore, naturally became an emblem of anything that was light, and that would be easily dissipated. See Notes on Isa. xxx. 24; Matt. iii. 12. ¶ *And the wind carried them away, that no place was found for them.* They were entirely dissipated like chaff. As that seems to have no longer any place, but is carried we know not where, so the figure here would denote an entire annihilation of the power to which it refers. ¶ *And the stone that smote the image became a great mountain, and filled the whole*

earth. The vision which was before the mind of the king as here represented was, that the stone which was cut out of the mountain was at first small, and that while he contemplated it, it swelled to larger dimensions, until it became an immense mountain—a mountain that filled the whole land. It was this which, perhaps more than anything else, excited his wonder, that a stone, at first of so small dimensions, should of itself so increase as to surpass the size of the mountain from which it was cut, until it occupied every place in view. Everything about it was so remarkable and unusual, that it was no wonder that he could not explain it. We have now gone over a description of the literal vision as it appeared to the mind of the monarch. Had it been left here, it is clear that it would have been of difficult interpretation, and possibly the true explanation might never have been suggested. We have, however, an exposition by Daniel, which leaves no doubt as to its design, and which was intended to carry the mind forward into some of the most important and remarkable events of history. A portion of his statement has been fulfilled; a part remains still unaccomplished, and a careful exposition of his account of the meaning of the vision will lead our thoughts to some of the most important historical events which have occurred in introducing the Christian dispensation, and to events still more important in the statement of what is yet to come.

36. *This* is *the dream; and we will tell the interpretation thereof before the king.* Daniel here speaks in his own name, and in the name of his companions. Hence he says, "*we* will tell the interpretation." It was in answer to their united supplications (ver. 18), that this meaning of the vision had been made known to him; and it would not only have been a violation of the

37 Thou, O King, *art* a king *a* of kings: for *b* the God of heaven hath

a Ezr. 7. 12; Is. 47. 5; Eze. 26. 7; Ho. 8. 10.
b Ezr. 1. 2.

rules of modesty, but an unjust assumption, if Daniel had claimed the whole credit of the revelation to himself. Though he was the only one who addressed the king, yet he seems to have desired that it might be understood that he was not alone in the honour which God had conferred, and that he wished that his companions should be had in just remembrance. Comp. ver. 49.

37. *Thou, O King,* art *a king of kings.* The phrase "king of kings" is a Hebraism, to denote a supreme monarch, or one who has other kings under him as tributary, Ezra vii. 12; Ezek. xxvi. 7. As such it is applied by way of eminence to the Son of God, in Rev. xvii. 14; xix. 16. As here used, it means that Nebuchadnezzar ruled over tributary kings and princes, or that he was the most eminent of the kings of the earth. The sceptre which he swayed was, in fact, extended over many nations that were once independent kingdoms, and the title here conferred on him was not one that was designed to flatter the monarch, but was a simple statement of what was an undoubted truth. Daniel would not withhold any title that was in accordance with reality, as he did not withhold any communication in accordance with reality that was adapted to humble the monarch. ¶ *For the God of heaven hath given thee a kingdom,* &c. At the same time that Daniel gave him a title which might in itself have ministered to the pride of the monarch, he is careful to remind him that he held this title in virtue of no wisdom or power of his own. It was the true God who had conferred on him the sovereignty of these extensive realms, and it was one of the designs of this vision to show him that he held his power at his will, and that at his pleasure he could cause it to pass away. It was the forgetfulness of this, and the pride resulting from that forgetfulness, which led to the melancholy calamity which befel this haughty monarch, as recorded in ch. iv.

38. *And wheresoever the children of*

given thee a kingdom, power, and strength, and glory.

38 And wheresoever the children of men dwell, the beasts of the field,

men dwell, the beasts of the field, and the fowls of the heaven, hath he given into thy hand. This is evidently general language, and is not to be pressed literally. It is designed to say that he ruled over the whole world; that is, the world as then known. This is common language applied in the Scriptures to the Babylonian, Persian, Grecian, and Roman kingdoms. Thus in ver. 39, the third of these kingdoms, the Grecian, was to "bear rule over all the earth." Comp. ch. viii. 5: "And, as I was considering, behold, an he-goat came from the west on the face of the whole earth." So of the Roman empire, in ch. vii. 23: "The fourth beast shall devour the whole earth." The declaration that his kingdom embraced the beasts of the field and the fowls of the air is a strong expression, meaning that he reigned over the whole world. A somewhat similar description of the extent of the empire of the king of Babylon occurs in Jer. xxvii. 4-8: "And command them to say unto their masters, Thus saith the Lord of hosts, the God of Israel, Thus shall ye say unto your masters; I have made the earth, the man and the beast that are upon the ground, by my great power, and by my outstretched arm, and have given it unto whom it seemed meet unto me. And now I have given all these lands into the hand of Nebuchadnezzar, the king of Babylon, my servant; and the beasts of the field I have given him also to serve him. And all nations shall serve him, and his son, and his son's son, until the very time of his land come: and then many nations and great kings shall serve themselves of him. And it shall come to pass, that the nation and kingdom which will not serve the same Nebuchadnezzar, the king of Babylon, and that will not put their neck under the yoke of the king of Babylon, that nation will I punish, saith the Lord, with the sword, and with the famine, and with the pestilence, until I have consumed them by his hand." At the time referred to by

and the fowls of the heaven, hath he given *a* into thine hand, and hath

a Je. 27. 6.

made thee ruler over them all Thou *art* this head of gold.

Daniel, the sceptre of Nebuchadnezzar extended over all these realms, and the world was, in fact, placed substantially under one head. "All the ancient Eastern histories," says Bishop Newton, "almost are lost; but there are some fragments even of heathen historians yet preserved, which speak of this mighty conqueror and his extended empire. Berosus, in Josephus (*Contra Apion*, 1. i. § 19), says that he held in subjection Egypt, Syria, Phœnicia, Arabia, and by his exploits surpassed all the Chaldeans and Babylonians who reigned before him. Strabo asserts that this king among the Chaldeans was more celebrated than Hercules; that he proceeded as far as to the pillars of Hercules, and led his army out of Spain into Thrace and Pontus. But his empire, though of great extent, was not of long duration; for it ended in his grandson Belshazzar, not seventy years after the delivery of this prophecy, nor above twenty-three years after the death of Nebuchadnezzar." — Newton on the *Prophecies*, pp. 186, 187. ¶ *Thou art this head of gold.* The head of gold seen in the image represents thee as the sovereign of a vast empire. Compared with the other monarchs who are to succeed thee, thou art like gold compared with silver, and brass, and iron; or, compared with thy kingdom, theirs shall be as silver, brass, and iron compared with gold. It was common, at an early period, to speak of different ages of the world as resembling different metals. Comp. Notes on ver. 31. In reference to the expression before us, "*Thou* art this head of gold," it should be observed, that it is not probably to be confined to the monarch himself, but is rather spoken of him as the head of the empire; as representing the state; as an impersonation of that dynasty. The meaning is, that the Babylonian empire, as it existed under him, in its relation to the kingdoms which should succeed, was like the head of gold seen in the image as compared with the inferior metals that made up the remaining portions of the image. Daniel, as

an interpreter, did not state in what the resemblance consisted, nor in what respects his empire could be likened to gold as compared with those which should follow. In the scanty details which we now have of the life of that monarch, and of the events of his reign, it may not be possible to see as clearly as would be desirable in what that resemblance consisted, or the full propriety of the appellation given to him. So far as may now be seen, the resemblance appears to have been in the following things :—(I.) In respect to the empire itself of which he was the sovereign, as standing at the head of the others—the first in the line. This was not indeed the first kingdom, but the design here was not to give an account of *all* the empires on earth, but to take the world *as it was then*, and to trace the successive changes which would occur preparatory to the establishment of the kingdom which should finally spread over the earth. Viewed in reference to this design, it was undoubtedly proper to designate the empire of Babylon as *the head*. It not only stood before them in the order of time, but in such a relation that the others might be regarded as in some sort its successors; that is, *they would succeed it in swaying a general sceptre over the world.* In this respect they would resemble also the Babylonian. At the time here referred to, the dominion over which Nebuchadnezzar swayed his sceptre was at the head of the nations; was the central power of the Pagan world; was the only empire that could claim to be universal. For a long period the kingdom of Babylon had been dependent on that of Assyria; and while Nineveh was the capital of the Assyrian empire, Babylon was the head of a kingdom, in general subordinate to that of Assyria, until Nabopolassar, the immediate predecessor of Nebuchadnezzar, rendered the kingdom of Babylon independent of the Assyrians, and transferred the seat of empire to Babylon. This was about the year 626 before the Christian era. See *Universal History*, vol. iii.

156   DANIEL.   [B.C. 603.

pp. 412-415. Nebuchadnezzar, receiving this mighty kingdom, had carried his own arms to distant lands ; had conquered India, Tyre, and Egypt ; and, as would appear, all Northern Africa, as far as the pillars of Hercules, and, with quite unimportant exceptions, all the known world was subject to him. (II.) The appellation "head of gold" may have been given him on account of the splendour of his capital, and the magnificence of his court. In Isa. xiv. 4, Babylon is called "the golden city." See Notes on that place. In Isa. xiii. 19, it is called "the glory of kingdoms, the beauty of the Chaldees' excellency." In Isa. xlvii. 5, it is called "the lady of kingdoms." In Jer. li. 13, it is spoken of as "abundant in treasures," and in ver. 41, as "the praise of the whole earth." So in profane writers, Babylon has similar appellations. Thus in Æsch. *Per.* 51, mention is made of Βαβυλὼν ἡ πολύχρυ-σος—*Babylon abounding in gold.* The conquests of Nebuchadnezzar enabled him to bring to his capital the spoils of nations, and to enrich his capital above any other city on the earth. Accordingly, he gave himself to the work of adorning a city that should be worthy to be the head of universal empire, and succeeded in making it so splendid as to be regarded as one of the wonders of the world. His great work in adorning and strengthening his capital consisted, first, of the building of the immense walls of the city; second, of the tower of Belus ; and third, of the hanging gardens. For a full description of these, see Prideaux's *Connexions*, vol. i. p. 232, *seq.* (III.) The appellation may have been given him by *comparison* with the kingdoms which were to succeed him. In *some* respects—in extent and power—some one or more of them, as the Roman, might surpass his ; but the appellation which was appropriate to them was not *gold*, but they would be best denoted by the inferior metals. Thus the Medo-Persian kingdom was less splendid than that of Babylon, and would be better represented by silver ; the Macedonian, though more distinguished by its conquests, was less magnificent, and would be better represented by brass ; and the

Roman, though ultimately still more extensive in its conquests, and still more mighty in power, was less remarkable for splendour than strength, and would be better represented by iron. In magnificence, if not in power, the Babylonian surpassed them all; and hence the propriety of the appellation, "*head of gold.*" (IV.) It is possible that in this appellation there then may have been some reference to the character of the monarch himself. In Jer. xxvii. 6, he is spoken of as the "servant of God," and it is clear that it was designed that a splendid mission was to be accomplished by him as under the Divine control, and in the preparation of the world for the coming of the Messiah. Though he was proud and haughty as a monarch, yet his own personal character would compare favourably with that of many who succeeded him in these advancing kingdoms. Though his conquests were numerous, yet his career as a conqueror was not marked with cruelty, like that of many other warriors. He was not a mere conqueror. He loved also the arts of peace. He sought to embellish his capital, and to make it in outward magnificence and in the talent which he concentrated there, truly the capital of the world. Even Jerusalem he did not utterly destroy ; but having secured a conquest over it, and removed from it what he desired should embellish his own capital, he still intended that it should be the subordinate head of an important province of his dominions, and placed on the throne one who was closely allied to the king who reigned there when he took the city. But the appellation here, and the reign of Nebuchadnezzar, are to be contemplated chiefly, like the kingdoms that succeeded, in their relation to redemption. It is in this aspect that the study of history becomes most interesting to a mind that regards all events as embraced in the eternal counsels of God, and it is undoubtedly with reference to this that the history of these kingdoms becomes in any way introduced into the inspired writings. All history may be contemplated under two aspects : in its secular bearing ; and in its relation to the redemption of the world. In the

39 And after thee shall arise ano- | ther kingdom inferior *a* to thee, and

a ch. 5. 28.

former aspect, it has great and important uses. As furnishing lessons to statesmen ; as showing the progress of society ; as illustrating the effects of vice and immorality, and the evils of anarchy, ambition, and war ; as recording and preserving the inventions in the arts, and as showing what are the best methods of civil government, and what conduces most to the happiness of a people, its value cannot well be overestimated. But it is in its relations to the work of redeeming man that it acquires its chief value, and hence the sacred volume is so much occupied with the histories of early nations. The rise and fall of every nation ; the conquests and defeats which have occurred in past times, may all have had, and perhaps may yet be seen to have had, an important connection with the redemption of man—as being designed to put the world in a proper position for the coming of the Prince of Peace, or in some way to prepare the way for the final triumph of the gospel. This view gives a new and important aspect to history. It becomes an object in which all on earth who love the race and desire its redemption, and all in heaven, feel a deep concern. Every monarch ; every warrior ; every statesman ; every man who, by his eloquence, bravery, or virtue, has contributed anything to the progress of the race, or who has in any way played an important part in the progress of the world's affairs, becomes a being on whom we can look with intense emotion ; and in reference to every man of this character, it would be an interesting inquiry what he has done that has contributed to prepare the way for the introduction of the Mediatorial scheme, or to facilitate its progress through the world. In reference to this point, the monarch whose character is now before us seems to have been raised up, under an overruling Providence, to accomplish the following things :—(1.) To inflict *punishment* on the revolted people of God for their numerous idolatries. See the book of Jeremiah, *passim.* Hence, he led his armies to the land of Palestine ;

he swept away the people, and bore them into captivity ; he burned the temple, destroyed the capital, and laid the land waste. (2.) He was the instrument, in the hand of God, of effectually purifying the Jewish nation from the sin of idolatry. It was for that sin eminently that they were carried away ; and never in this world have the ends of punishment been better secured than in this instance. The chastisement was effectual. The Jewish nation has never since sunk into idolatry. If there have been individuals of that nation—of which, however, there is no certain evidence—who have become idolaters, yet as a people they have been preserved from it. More than two thousand five hundred years have since passed away ; they have been wanderers and exiles in all lands ; they have been persecuted, ridiculed, and oppressed on account of their religion ; they have been placed under every possible inducement to conform to the religion around them, and yet, as professed worshippers of Jehovah, the God of their fathers, they have maintained their integrity, and neither promises nor threatenings, neither hopes nor fears, neither life nor death, have been sufficient to constrain the Hebrew people to bow the knee to an idol god. (3.) Another object that seems to have been designed to be accomplished by Nebuchadnezzar in relation to Redemption was, to gather the nations under one head preparatory to the coming of the Messiah. It will be seen in the remarks which will be made on the relation of the Roman empire to this work (Notes on vers. 40–43), that there were important reasons why this should be done. Preparatory to that, a succession of such kingdoms each swayed the sceptre over the whole world, and when the Messiah came, the way was prepared for the easy and rapid propagation of the new religion to the remotest parts of the earth.

39. *And after thee.* This must mean *subsequently* to the reign, but it does not mean that the kingdom here referred to would *immediately* succeed his own reign, for that would not be true. The

another third kingdom of brass, | which ^ashall bear rule over all the
a ch. 7. 6.

which ^ashall bear rule over all the earth.

Medo-Persian empire did not come into the ascendency until many years after the death of Nebuchadnezzar. This occurred during the reign of Belshazzar, a grandson of Nebuchadnezzar, between whose reign and that of his grandfather there had intervened the reigns of Evil-merodach and Neriglissar ; besides, as the remainder of the prophecy relating to the image refers to *kingdoms*, and not to individual monarchs, it is clear that this also relates not primarily to Nebuchadnezzar as an individual, but as the head of a kingdom. The meaning is, that a kingdom would succeed that over which he reigned, so far inferior that it might be represented by silver as compared with gold. ¶ *Shall arise another kingdom.* Chaldee, "shall *stand up* (תְּקוּם) another kingdom." This is language which would denote something different from a succession in the same dynasty ; for that would be a mere *continuance of the same kingdom.* The reference is evidently to a change of empire ; and the language implies that there would be some revolution or conquest by which the existing kingdom would pass away, and another would succeed. Still there would be so much of sameness in respect to its occupying essentially the same territory, that it would be symbolized in the same image that appeared to Nebuchadnezzar. The kingdom here referred to was undoubtedly the Medo-Persian, established by Cyrus in the conquest of Babylon, which continued through the reigns of his successors until it was conquered by Alexander the Great. This kingdom succeeded that of Assyria or Babylon, 538 years B.C., to the overthrow of Darius Codomanus, 333 years B.C. It extended, of course, through the reigns of the Persian kings, who acted so important a part in the invasion of Greece, and whose defeats have given immortality to the names of Leonidas, Aristides, Miltiades, and Themistocles, and made the names of Salamis, Thermopylæ, Marathon, and Leuctra so celebrated. For a general account of Cyrus, and the founding of the Medo-Persian empire,

the reader is referred to the Notes on Isa. xli. 2. ¶ *Inferior to thee.* And therefore represented by silver as compared with gold. In what respects it would be inferior, Daniel does not specify, and this can only be learned from *the facts* which occurred in relation to that kingdom. All that is necessary to confirm the truth of the prophetic description is, that it was to be so far inferior as to make the appellation *silver* applicable to it in comparison with the kingdom of Babylon, represented by *gold.* The expression would denote that there was a general decline or degeneracy in the character of the monarchs, and the general condition of the empire. There have been different opinions as to the inferiority of this kingdom to the Babylonian. Calvin supposes that it refers to degeneracy. Geir supposes that it relates to the duration of the kingdom—this continuing not more than two hundred and forty years ; while the other, including the Assyrian, embraced a period of one thousand five hundred years. Polanus supposes that the meaning is, that the Babylonian had more rest and tranquillity ; while Junius, Willett, and others understand it of a milder and more humane treatment of the Jews by the Babylonians than the Persians. Perhaps, however, none of these opinions meet the circumstances of the case, for they do not furnish as full an account of the reasons of this inferiority as is desirable. In regard to this, it may be observed, (*a*) that it is not to be supposed that this kingdom was to be in *all respects* inferior to the Babylonian, but only that it would have certain characteristics which would make it more appropriate to describe it as *silver* than as *gold.* In certain *other* respects it might be far superior, as the Roman, though in the same general line of succession, was in extent and power superior to either, though there was still a reason why that should be represented by *iron* rather than by gold, by silver, or by brass. (*b*) The inferiority did not relate to the power, the riches, or the territorial extent of the Medo-Persian empire, for it embraced, so far as appears, all that was comprehended in the Babylonian empire, and all in addition which was added by the conquests of Cyrus. In his proclamation to rebuild the temple (Ezra i. 2), Cyrus speaks of the extent of his empire in language strongly resembling that which is applied to the kingdom of Nebuchadnezzar. "Thus saith Cyrus, king of Persia, The Lord God of heaven hath given me all the kingdoms of the earth." Thus also it is said of Ahasuerus or Astyages, king of Media—a kingdom that constituted a part of the Medo-Persian empire under Cyrus and his successors, that he "reigned from India even unto Ethiopia, over an hundred and twenty and seven provinces." To the kingdom of Babylon, as he found it when he conquered it, Cyrus of course added the kingdoms of Media and Persia, to the crowns of which he was the heir (see Notes on Isa. xli. 2), and also the various provinces which he had conquered before he came to the throne ; that is, Cappadocia, the kingdom of Lydia, and almost the whole of Asia Minor. (c) Nor can it be supposed that the kingdom was inferior in regard to *wealth*, for, in addition to all the wealth that Cyrus found in Babylon, he brought the spoils of his victories ; the treasures in the possession of the crowns of Persia and Media, and all the wealth of Crœsus, the rich king of Lydia, of which he had become possessor by conquest. In considering the *inferiority* of this kingdom, which made it proper that it should be represented by silver rather than by gold, it is to be borne in mind that the representation should embrace *the whole kingdom* in all the successive reigns, and not merely the kingdom as it was under the administration of Cyrus. Thus regarded, it will comprehend the succession of Persian monarchs until the time of the invasion and conquest of the East by Alexander the Great. The reign of Cyrus was indeed splendid ; and if *he* alone, or if the kingdom during his administration, were contemplated, it would be difficult to assign a reason why an appellation should have been given to it implying any inferiority to that of Nebuchadnezzar. The *infe-*

riority of the kingdom, or that which made it proper to represent it by silver rather than by gold, as compared with the kingdom of Babylon, may have consisted in the following particulars :— (1.) In reference to the succession of kings who occupied the Persian throne. It is true that the character of Cyrus is worthy of the highest commendation, and that he was distinguished not only as a brave and successful conqueror, but as a mild, able, and upright civil ruler. Xenophon, who wished to draw the character of a model prince, made choice of Cyrus as the example ; and though he has not improbably embellished his character by ascribing to him virtues drawn from his own fancy in some degree, yet there can be no doubt that in the main his description was drawn from the life. "The true reason," says Prideaux (*Connexions*, vol. i. p. 252, Ed. Charlestown, 1815), "why he chose the life of Cyrus before all others for the purpose above mentioned " [that of giving a description of what a worthy and just prince ought to be] " seemeth to be no other but that he found the true history of that excellent and gallant prince to be, above all others, the fittest for those maxims of right policy and true princely virtue to correspond with, which he grafted upon it." But he was succeeded by a madman, Cambyses, and by a race of kings eminent among princes for folly and crime. "The kings of Persia," says Prideaux, "were the worst race of men that ever governed an empire." (2.) The kingdom was inferior in reference to the remarkable *defeats* in the military campaigns which were undertaken. The Assyrian or Babylonian empire was distinguished for the victories by which it carried its arms around the then known world. The Medo-Persian empire, after the reign of Cyrus, was almost as remarkable for the succession of defeats which have made the period of the world during which the empire continued, so well known in history. It is probable that no kingdom ever undertook so many foolish projects in reference to the conquests of other nations—projects so unwisely planned, and that resulted in so signal failures. The successor of Cyrus, Cambyses, invaded Egypt, and his conduct there in carrying on the war was such as to make him be regarded as a madman. Enraged against the Ethiopians for an answer which they gave him when, under pretence of friendship, he sent spies to examine their country, he resolved to invade their territory. Having come to Thebes, in Upper Egypt, he detached from his army fifty thousand men to go against the Hammonians, with orders to destroy their country, and to burn the temple of Jupiter Hammon that stood in it. After marching a few days in the desert, they were overwhelmed in the sands by a strong south wind, and all perished. Meantime Cambyses marched with the rest of his army against the Ethiopians, though he wanted all the means of subsistence for his army, until, having devoured all their beasts of burden, they were constrained to designate every tenth man of the army to be killed and eaten. In these deplorable circumstances, Cambyses returned to Thebes, having lost a great part of his army in this wild expedition.— Prideaux's *Con.* i. 328. It was also during the continuance of this kingdom, that the ill-starred expeditions to Greece occurred, when Mardonius and Xerxes poured the millions of Asia on the countries of Greece, and met such signal overthrows at Platea, Marathon, and Salamis. Such a series of disasters never before had occurred to invading armies, or made those who repelled invasion so illustrious. In this respect there was an evident propriety in speaking of this as an inferior or degenerate kingdom. (3.) It was inferior in respect to the growing degeneracy and effeminacy of character and morals. From the time of Xerxes (B.C. 479) "symptoms of decay and corruption were manifest in the empire; the national character gradually degenerated; the citizens were corrupted and enfeebled by luxury; and confided more in mercenary troops than in native valour and fidelity. The kings submitted to the control of their wives, or the creatures whom they raised to posts of distinction; and the satraps, from being civil functionaries, began to usurp military authority."—Lyman, *Hist. Chart.*

(4.) The kingdom was inferior by the gradual weakening of its power from internal causes. It was not only defeated in its attempts to invade others, and weakened by the degeneracy of the court and people, but, as a natural consequence, by the gradual lessening of the power of the central government, and the growing independence of the provinces. From the time of Darius Nothus (B.C. 423)—a weak, effeminate, and indolent prince—"the satraps of the distant provinces paid only a nominal obedience to the king. Many of them were, in fact, sovereigns over the countries over which they presided, and carried on wars against each other."—Lyman. It was from causes such as these that the power of the kingdom became gradually weakened, and that the way was prepared for the easy conquests of Alexander the Great. Their successive defeats, and this gradual degeneracy and weakening of the kingdom, show the propriety of the description given of the kingdom in the vision and the interpretation—that it would be an "inferior kingdom," a kingdom which, in comparison with that of Babylon, might be compared with silver as compared with gold. Still it sustained an important relation to the progress of events in regard to the history of religion in the world, and had an important bearing on the redemption of man. As this is the most important bearing of history, and as it was doubtless with reference to this that the mention of it is introduced into the sacred Scriptures, and as it is, in fact, often alluded to by Isaiah, and in the books of Ezra, Nehemiah, Esther, and some of the minor prophets, it may be proper, in the most summary way, to allude to some of those things which pertain to the bearing of this kingdom on the great events connected with redemption, or to what was done during the continuance of this kingdom for the promotion of the true religion. A full account may be found in Prideaux's *Connexions*, part 1, books iii. – vii. Compare Edwards' *History of Redemption*, Period I, part vi. The particular things which occurred in connection with this kingdom bearing on the progress of religion, and favourable to its advancement, were these : (a) The over-throw of Babylon, so long the formid-able enemy of the ancient people of God. (b) The restoration of the exiles to their own land under the auspices of Cyrus, Ezra i. 1. (c) The rebuilding of the temple under the same auspices, and with the favour of the successors of Cyrus. (d) The preparation of the world for the coming of the Messiah, in the agitations that took place during the continuance of the Persian monar-chy ; the invasion of Greece ; the de-feats there ; the preparation by these defeats for the coming of Him who was so long promised as the "desire of all nations." Compare Hag. ii. 7 : "And I will shake all nations, and the desire of all nations shall come ; and I will fill this house" [the temple erected under the auspices of Cyrus and his succes-sors] "with glory, saith the Lord of hosts." There was a propriety, there-fore, that this kingdom should receive a distinct notice in the sacred Scrip-tures, for some of the most important events connected with the history of true religion in the world occurred un-der the auspices of Cyrus and his suc-cessors, and perhaps at no period has there been more occasion to recognize the hand of God than in the influences exerted on the minds of those heathen princes, disposing them to be favour-able to the long-oppressed children of God. ¶ And another third kingdom of brass. See notes on ver. 32. The parts of the image which were of brass were the belly and thighs, denoting inferio-rity not only to the head, but to the part which immediately preceded it—the breast and the arms of silver. It is not, indeed, specified, as in the for-mer case, that this kingdom would be inferior to the former, and it is only from the position assigned to it in the image, and the inferior quality of the metal by which it is represented, that it is implied that there would be any inferiority. There can be no reason-able doubt that by this third kingdom is denoted the empire founded by Alexander the Great—the Macedonian empire. It is known to all that he over-threw the Persian empire, and estab-lished a kingdom in the East, embrac-ng substantially the same territory

which had been occupied by the Medo-Persian and the Babylonian empire. While there can be no doubt that that kingdom is referred to, there can be as little that the reference is not merely to the empire during the reign of Alexan-der himself, but that it embraced the whole empire as founded and arranged by him, until it was succeeded by an-other universal empire—here denomi-nated the fourth kingdom. The reasons for supposing that the Macedonian em-pire is referred to here are almost too obvious to require that they should be specified. They are such as these : (1.) This kingdom actually succeeded that of Medo-Persia, covering the same territory, and, like that, was then un-derstood to be a universal monarchy. (2.) The empire of Alexander is else-where more than once referred to by Daniel in the same order, and in such a manner that the sense cannot be mis-taken. Thus, in ch. viii. 21 : "And the rough goat is the king of Grecia : and the great horn that is between his eyes is the first king. Now that being broken, whereas four stood up for it, four kingdoms shall stand up out of the nation, but not in his power." Ch. x. 20 : "And now," said the man that appeared in vision to Daniel (ver. 5), "will I re-turn to fight with the prince of Persia : and when I am gone forth, lo, the prince of Grecia shall come." Ch. xi. 2–4 : "And now will I show thee the truth. Behold there shall stand up yet three kings in Persia ; and the fourth shall be far richer than they all ; and by his strength through his riches he shall stir up all against the realm of Grecia. And a mighty king shall stand up, that shall rule with great dominion, and do ac-cording to his will. And when he shall stand up, his kingdom shall be broken, and shall be divided toward the four winds of heaven ; and not to his pos-terity, nor according to the kingdom that he ruled : for his kingdom shall be plucked up, even for others beside those." Since this kingdom is thus referred to elsewhere by Daniel in the same order, and as destined to act an important part in the affairs of the world, it is reasonable to suppose that there is a reference to it here. (3.) It is a circum-stance of some importance that the emblem here by which this kingdom is represented, *brass*, is one that is peculiarly appropriate to the Greeks, and one that could not be applied to any other nation with equal propriety. The Greeks were distinguished for their *brazen armour*, and the appellation, *the brazen-coated Greeks*—χαλκοχιτώνες 'Αχαιοὶ— is that by which they were designated most commonly by the ancients.— *Il.* i. 371; ii. 47; *Od.* i. 286. In accordance with this, Josephus says (*Ant.* b. x. c. 10, § 4), τὴν δὲ ἐκείνων ἕτερος τις ἀπὸ δύσεως καθαιρήσει χαλκὸν ἠμφιεσμένος —"*their empire another shall come from the West,* CLOTHED WITH BRASS, *shall destroy.*" These considerations leave no doubt that the kingdom here referred to was that Grecian or Macedonian, which, under Alexander, obtained dominion over all the East. ¶ *Which shall bear rule over all the earth.* In a sense similar to that of the Assyrian, the Babylonian, and the Medo-Persian empire. This is the common description of the empire of Alexander. He himself commanded that he should be called *the king of all the world. Accepto deinde imperio, regem se terrarum omnium ac mundi appellari jussit* (Justin. l. 12, c. 16, § 9)—"Having received the empire, he ordered himself to be called the king of all lands and of the world." Diodorus Siculus says that he received ambassadors from all countries; κατὰ δὲ τοῦτον τὸν χρόνον ἐξ ἁπάσης σχεδὸν τῆς οἰκουμένης ἧκον πρέσβεις, κ. τ. λ.—"At which time, legates came to him from almost the whole habitable world."—L. 17, c. 113. So Arrian (*Expedi. Alex.* l. 7, c. 15) remarks, that "Alexander then appeared to himself, and to those around him, *to be lord of all the earth and of the sea*—γῆς τε ἁπάσης καὶ θαλάσσης κύριον. The author of the book of Maccabees gives a similar account of the extent of this kingdom: "And it came to pass, after that Alexander, the son of Philip the Macedonian, who first reigned in Greece, had overthrown Darius, the king of the Persian and Medes, he fought many battles, and took the strongholds of all, and slew the kings of the earth; and he went through even to the ends of the earth; and took the spoil of many nations; and the earth was quiet before

him," 1 Macc. i. 1–3. The propriety of saying that this "kingdom bore rule over all the earth" is, therefore, apparent. It embraced, of course, all that was anciently included in the Assyrian and Babylonian empires; all that had been added to that empire by the conquests of Cyrus, and also all that Alexander had added to it by his hereditary dominions, and by his conquests in other places. Nearly or quite all the known world, except that which was then subject to the Romans, then just a rising power, was under the sway of Alexander. A question has been started whether this refers merely to the kingdom of Alexander during his own life, or whether it embraced also the succession of dynasties until the conquests of the Romans. That the latter is the correct opinion seems clear from the following considerations:— (1.) It was true, as we have seen, of the two previous kingdoms specified—the Babylonian and the Medo-Persian— that they embraced, not merely the kingdom under any one reigning monarch, but during its entire continuance until it was overthrown by one that had also pretensions to a universal empire—the former by the Medo-Persian, and the latter by the Macedonian. It is to be presumed that the same principles of interpretation are to be applied also to the Macedonian kingdom itself—especially as that was also actually succeeded by one that in a still higher sense laid claim to universal empire. (2.) This was, in fact, one kingdom. It is true that, on the death of Alexander, the empire which he founded was divided among four of his generals, and also that from that sprung the two reigns, the Seleucidæ in Syria, and of the Lagidæ who reigned in Egypt; but, as Newton has remarked, "their kingdom was no more a different kingdom from that of Alexander, than the parts differ from the whole. It was the same government still continued. Those who governed were still Macedonians. All ancient authors spoke of the kingdom of Alexander and of his successors as one and the same kingdom. The thing is implied in the very name by which they are usually called, *the successors of Alexander.* 'Alexander being dead,' says Josephus (*Ant.* b. xi. ch. 8, § 7), 'the empire was divided among his successors.' 'After the death of Alexander,' says Justin (lib. xli. c. 4, § 1), 'the kingdoms of the East were divided among his successors;' and he still denominates them Macedonians, and their empire the Macedonian."— Newton *on the Prophecies*, pp. 189, 190. In regard to the point before adverted to in reference to the kingdoms of Babylon and of Medo-Persia—the relation which they sustained to religion, or the methods in which they were made to contribute to its progress in the world, making it proper that they should be noticed in the volume of inspiration, it may be remarked that the Macedonian kingdom was also designed, undoubtedly, under an overruling Providence, to contribute to the progress of the great work of human redemption, and to prepare the way for the coming of the Messiah. A full statement of what was done under this reign in respect to religion—the most interesting aspect of history—may be seen in Edwards' *History of Redemption*, pp. 271–275, and in Prideaux's *Connexions*, vol. ii. p. 279, *seq.* The kingdom here referred to—the Macedonian, represented here by the portion of the image that was of brass, and in the vision of the four beasts (ch. vii.) by a leopard that had on its back the wings of a fowl, and in ch. viii. 21, by the rough goat—continued from the overthrow of Darius Codomanus by Alexander (B.C. 333), to the conquest of Syria, and the East, by the Romans under Pompey, about sixty-six years before the birth of the Saviour. The principal events during this period affecting the interests of religion, and preparing the way for the coming of the Messiah, were the following:—I. The extensive diffusion of the knowledge of the Greek language. The army of Alexander was mainly composed of Greeks. The Greek language was, of course, that which was spoken by the court, and in the cities which he founded; the despatches were in Greek; that language would be extensively cultivated to gratify those in power; and the successors of Alexander were those who used the Greek tongue. The consequence was, that

the Greek language was extensively spread over the countries which were subdued by Alexander, and which were governed by his successors. That language became the popular tongue; a sort of universal language understood by the great mass of the people, in a manner not unlike the French in Europe at the present day. The effect of this, in preparing for the introduction of the gospel, was seen in two respects: (*a*) In facilitating the *preaching* of the gospel. It is true that the apostles had the gift of tongues, and that there was, notwithstanding the prevalence of the Greek language, occasion for this. But there is no evidence that this was conferred on *all* the early preachers of the gospel, nor is it certain that those on whom it *was* conferred were able to make use of it on all occasions. It is not improbable that, in their ordinary labours, the apostles and others were left to rely on their natural endowments, and to use the language to which they had been most accustomed. As there was, therefore, a common language in most of the countries in which the gospel would be proclaimed, it is evident that the propagation of religion would be greatly facilitated by this, and there can be no doubt that it was *one* of the designs of Providence in permitting the Macedonian conquest thus to prepare the way for the more easy and rapid diffusion of the new religion. (*b*) In like manner, this conquest prepared the way *for the permanent record* of the history of the Saviour's life, and the doctrines of religion in the writings of the New Testament. It was evidently desirable, on many accounts, that the records should be made in one language rather than in many, and of all the languages then spoken on the earth, the *Greek* was the best adapted to such a purpose. It was not only the most polished and cultivated, but it was the most copious; and it was the best fitted to express abstract ideas, and accurate distinctions. Probably with all the improvements since made in the copious Arabic language, and in the languages of modern times, there never has been one that was so well fitted for the purposes of a Divine revelation as the Greek. It may have been one design of Providence, in the extensive and accurate cultivation of that language in Greece itself, as well as in its diffusion over the world, that there should be at the time of the introduction of the Christian revelation a medium of permanent record that should be as free from imperfection as language could be ; a medium also in which there should be so much permanent and valuable literature that, even after it should cease to be a spoken language, it would be cultivated by the whole literary world, thus furnishing the means of an accurate knowledge of the meaning of the sacred writings. II. The translation of the Old Testament into the same language was another important event, which took place during the continuance of this kingdom, which greatly facilitated the introduction and spread of Christianity. The Hebrew language was understood by comparatively few. It ceased to be spoken in its purity after the time of the captivity. In that language the Scriptures of the Old Testament would have been but little diffused in the world. By their being translated, however, into Greek, they became extensively known, and furnished a ready and an intelligible ground of appeal to the preachers of the new religion when they referred to the prophecies of the Old Testament, and the recorded predictions of the Messiah. For a full account of the history of this version, the reader may consult Prideaux's *Connexions,* vol. iii. p. 53, *seq.* It was made according to Archbishop Usher, about 277 B.C. The probability is, that it was made at different periods, and by different hands, as it is executed with very various degrees of ability. See Intro. to Isaiah, § VIII. I. (1), for a more extended account of this version and its value. There can be no doubt that it contributed much to the diffusion of the knowledge of the Holy Scriptures, and was an important instrument in preparing the world for the reception of the revelation that should be made by the Messiah. III. Events of great importance occurred during the continuance of this kingdom in preserving the Jewish people in times of persecution, and saving their city and temple from ruin, and their nation from extinction.

(a) The destruction of Jerusalem and the temple was threatened by Alexander himself. After the siege and capture of Tyre, he became enraged at the Jews for refusing to furnish supplies for his army during the siege, under the plea that they were bound to show allegiance to Darius, and he marched to Jerusalem with an intention to take and destroy it. In order to appease him, it is said that Jaddua, the high-priest, went out to meet him in his pontifical robes, at the head of a procession of priests, and accompanied by the people in white garments. Alexander was so impressed with the scene that, to the surprise of all, he spared the city and temple ; and on being asked by Parmenio the reason of this clemency, said that he had seen this person in vision, who had directed him to lay aside all anxiety about his contemplated expedition to Asia, and that he had promised that God would give him the empire of the Persians. According to the story, Jaddua showed him the prophecies of Daniel, and confirmed him by those prophecies in the confident expectation of conquering the East ; and in view of this, Alexander offered sacrifices in the temple, and granted to the Hebrews the freedom of their country, and the exercise of their laws and religion. See Prideaux, vol. ii. p. 302, *seq.*; Josephus, *Ant.* b. xi. ch. 8. Whatever of fable there may be in this account, it is certain that this city and temple were not destroyed by Alexander, but that in his ravages in the East, he was led, by some cause, to deal with the capital of the Hebrew nation in a manner different from what he did with others. (b) A remarkable preservation of the Jewish people, of a somewhat similar character, and evincing the protection of God, occurred during the great persecution under Antiochus Epiphanes, one of the successors of Alexander, in the time of the Maccabees. See Prideaux, vol. iii. p. 230, and 2 Macc. v. 11–27. In the times of that celebrated persecution, multitudes of the Jews were slain by Antiochus himself; the city was taken, and the temple defiled. Three years after it was taken by Antiochus (B.C. 168), Apollonius was directed by him to march against the city to vent his

40 And the fourth kingdom shall | be strong as iron: forasmuch as iron

wrath on the Jews; and when the people were assembled in their synagogues for worship, he let loose his forces on them, with a command to slay all the men, and to take all the women and children captives to be sold as slaves. After this, he plundered the city, demolished the houses, and pulled down the walls, and then with the ruins of the demolished city built a strong fortress on the top of an eminence in the city of David, in a place which overlooked the temple, and placed a strong garrison within. From this place attacks were made on all who went up to the temple to worship; and the temple was defiled with all manner of pollutions, until it was deserted, and the daily sacrifices ceased. From these calamities and persecutions, the city and the Jewish nation were delivered by the valour of Judas Maccabeus, in the manner detailed in the first book of Maccabees.

40. *And the fourth kingdom.* Represented in the image by the legs of iron, and the feet "part of iron, and part of clay," ver. 33. The first question which arises here is, what kingdom is referred to by this? In regard to this, there have been two leading opinions: one, that it refers to the Roman empire; the other, that it refers to the kingdoms or dynasties that immediately succeeded the reign of Alexander the Great; embracing the kingdoms of the Seleucidæ and Lagidæ, Syria, and Egypt—in the language of Prof. Stuart, who adopts this opinion, "that the legs and feet were symbols of that intermingled and confused empire which sprung up under the Grecian chiefs who finally succeeded him," [Alexander the Great].—*Com. on Daniel*, p. 173. For the reasoning by which this opinion is supported, see Prof. Stuart, pp. 173–193. The common opinion has been, that the reference is to the Roman empire, and in support of this opinion the following conditions may be suggested: (1.) The obvious design of the image was to symbolize the succession of great monarchies, which would precede the setting up of the kingdom of the Redeemer, and which would have an important agency in preparing the world for that.

The Roman empire was in itself too important, and performed too important an agency in preparing the world for that, to be omitted in such an enumeration. (2.) The kingdom here referred to was to be in existence at the time symbolized by the cutting of the stone out of the mountain; for, during the continuance of that kingdom, or under it, "the God of heaven was to set up a kingdom which should never be destroyed," ver. 44. But the kingdoms of the Seleucidæ and the Lagidæ—the "intermingled and confused empires that sprang up" after Alexander the Great—had ceased before that time, being superseded by the Roman. (3.) Unless the Roman power be represented, the symmetry of the image is destroyed; for it would make what was, in fact, one kingdom represented by two different metals—brass and iron. We have seen above that the Babylonian empire was represented appropriately by gold; the Medo-Persian by silver; and the Macedonian by brass. We have seen also, that in fact the empire founded by Alexander, and continued through his successors in Syria and Egypt, was in fact *one* kingdom, so spoken of by the ancients, and being in fact a *Greek* dynasty. If the appellation of *brass* belonged to that kingdom *as* a Greek kingdom, there is an obvious incongruity, and a departure from the method of interpreting the other portions of the image, in applying the term *iron* to any portion of that kingdom. (4.) By the application of the term *iron*, it is evidently implied that the kingdom thus referred to would be distinguished for *strength*— strength greater than its predecessors —as iron surpasses brass, and silver, and gold, in that quality. But this was *not* true of the confused reigns that immediately followed Alexander. They were unitedly weaker than the Babylonian and the Medo-Persian, and weaker than the empire of Alexander, out of which they arose. Comp. ch. viii. 21, 22. It *was* true, however, of the Roman power, that it was so much superior to all its predecessors in power, that it might well be represented by

breaketh in pieces and subdueth all *things:* and as iron that breaketh

iron in comparison with brass, silver, and gold. (5.) The fourth monarchy represented in Nebuchadnezzar's dream is evidently the same which is represented by the fourth beast in Dan. vii. 7, 8, 23, 25. But it will appear, from the exposition of that chapter, that the reference there is to the Roman empire. See Notes on these passages. There can be no well-founded objection to this view on the ground that this kingdom was not properly a *succession* of the kingdom of Alexander, and did not occupy precisely the same territory. The same was true of each of the other kingdoms—the Medo-Persian and Macedonian. Yet while they were not, in the usual sense of the term, in the *succession,* they did, in fact, follow one after the other ; and with such accessions as were derived from conquest, and from the hereditary dominions of the conquerors, they did occupy the same territory. The design seems to have been to give a representation of a series of great monarchies, which would be, in an important sense, universal monarchies, and which should follow each other before the advent of the Saviour. The Roman, in addition to what it possessed in the West, actually occupied in the East substantially the same territory as the Babylonian, the Medo-Persian, and the Macedonian, and, like them, it had all the claims which any ancient sovereignty had to the title of a universal monarchy; indeed no kingdom has ever existed to which this title could with more justice be applied. ¶ *Shall be strong as iron.* It is scarcely necessary to observe that this description is applicable to the Roman power. In nothing was it more remarkable than its *strength ;* for that irresistible power before which all other nations were perfectly weak. This characteristic of the Roman power is thus noticed by Mr. Gibbon : "The arms of the Republic, sometimes vanquished in battle, always victorious in war, advanced with rapid steps to the Euphrates, the Danube, the Rhine, and the ocean; and the images of gold, or silver, or brass, that might serve to represent

all these, shall it break in pieces and bruise.

the nations and their kings, were successively broken by the *iron* monarchy of Rome."—*Dec. and Fall,* p. 642, Lond. ed. 1830, as quoted by Prof. Bush. ¶ *Forasmuch as iron breaketh in pieces and subdueth all* things. Iron is the metal which is used, and always has been used, for the purpose here suggested. In the form of hammers, sledges, and cannon-balls, and, in general, in reference to the accomplishment of any purpose, by beating or battering, this has been found to be the most valuable of the metals. It is heavy, is capable of being easily wrought into desired shapes; is abundant; is susceptible of being made hard so as not to be itself bruised, and has, therefore, all the properties which could be desired for purposes like this. ¶ *And as iron that breaketh all these.* That is, all these things ; to wit, everything. Nothing is able to stand before it ; there is nothing which it cannot reduce to powder. There is some repetition here, but it is for the sake of emphasis. ¶ *Shall it break in pieces and bruise.* Nothing could better characterize the Roman power than this. Everything was crushed before it. The nations which they conquered ceased to be kingdoms, and were reduced to provinces, and as kingdoms they were blotted out from the list of nations. This has been well described by Mr. Irving : "The Roman empire did beat down the constitution and establishment of all other kingdoms ; abolishing their independence, and bringing them into the most entire subjection ; humbling the pride, subjecting the will, using the property, and trampling upon the power and dignity of all other states. For by this was the Roman dominion distinguished from all the rest, that it was the work of almost as many centuries as those were of years ; the fruit of a thousand battles in which millions of men were slain. It made room for itself, as doth a battering-ram, by continual successive blows ; and it ceased not to beat and bruise all nations, so long as they continued to offer any resistance."—*Discourse on Daniel's Visions,* p. 180.

41 And whereas thou sawest the feet and toes, part of potters' clay and part of iron, the kingdom shall be divided; but there shall be in

41. *And whereas thou sawest the feet and toes, part of potters' clay and part of iron.* Ver. 33. The Chaldee is, "of them clay of the potter, and of them iron;" that is, part was composed of one material and part of the other. The sense is, not that the feet were composed entirely of one, and the toes of the other, but that they were intermingled. There was no homogeneousness of material; nothing in one that would coalesce with the other, or that could be permanently united to it, as two metals might be fused or welded together and form one solid compound. Iron and clay cannot be welded; and the idea here clearly is, that in the empire here referred to there would be two main elements which could never be made to blend. ¶ *The kingdom shall be divided.* That is, divided as the iron and clay were in the image. It does not necessarily mean that there would be an open rupture—an actual separation into two parts; but that there would be *such a diversity in the internal constitution* that, while there would be the element of great power, there would be also an element of weakness; there would be something which could never be blended with the element of strength, so as to produce one harmonious and homogeneous whole. ¶ *But there shall be in it of the strength of the iron, forasmuch as thou sawest the iron mixed with miry clay.* The principal idea in this part of the description is, that there would be great *power;* that whatever elements of weakness there might be, yet the *power* of the empire would be apparent. No one can fail to perceive how this applies to the Roman empire; a mighty power which, through all its long history, was distinguished for the vigour with which it carried forward its plans, and pressed on to universal dominion. As to the element of *weakness* symbolized too by the clay, it may not be possible to determine, with absolute certainty, what is referred to. *Any* internal source of weakness; anything in the constitution of the state, whether originally existing

it of the strength of the iron, forasmuch as thou sawest the iron mixed with miry clay.

42 And *as the* toes of the feet *were*

and constituting heterogeneous material, or whether springing up in the empire itself, or whether arising from the intermingling of foreign elements that never amalgamated themselves with the state, any one of these suppositions would meet all that is fairly implied in this language. From ver. 43, "they shall mingle themselves with the seed of men," it would seem, however, that the reference is to some *foreign* admixture—like the intermingling of nations of other languages, laws, and customs, which were never truly amalgamated with the original materials, and which constantly tended to weaken and divide the kingdom. It is to be remarked, in the exposition of the passage, that in the previous three kingdoms there was comparative homogeneousness. In the fourth kingdom, there was to be something of a peculiar character in this respect by which it should be distinguished from the others. As a matter of fact, the other three kingdoms were comparatively homogeneous in their character. The predominant feature was *Oriental;* and though there were different nations and people intermingled in the Babylonian, the Medo-Persian, and the Macedonian kingdoms, yet there was the same general prevailing character in each; there was not such an intermingling of foreign nations as to produce disturbing elements, or to mar the symmetry and strength of the whole. It was not thus with Rome. In that empire there was the intermingling of all nations and tongues, and though the essential element of the empire remained always—*the Roman*—yet there was an intermingling of other influences under the same general government, which could be appropriately compared with clay united with iron, and which ultimately contributed to its fall (see Notes on ver. 43).

42. *And as the toes of the feet* were *part of iron and part of clay, so the kingdom shall be partly strong, and partly broken.* Marg., *brittle.* The margin is the more correct rendering of the

part of iron and part of clay, so the kingdom shall be partly strong, and partly [1] broken.

1 *brittle.*

Chaldee word (תְּבִירָה). It means *frail, fragile*—easily broken, but not necessarily that it was *actually* broken. That did not occur until the stone cut out of the mountain impinged on it. It has been commonly supposed (comp. Newton *on the Prophecies*), that the ten toes on the feet refer to the ten kingdoms into which the Roman empire was ultimately broken up, corresponding with the ten horns seen in the vision of Daniel, in ch. vii. 7. In regard to the *fact* that the Roman empire was ultimately broken up into *ten* such kingdoms, see the extended Notes on ch. vii. 24. The thing which struck the monarch in the vision, and Daniel in the interpretation, as remarkable, was that the feet and toes *were composed partly of iron and partly of clay.* In the upper portion of the image there had been uniformity in the different parts, and had been no intermingling of metals. Here a new feature was seen —not only that a new metal was employed, but that there was intermingled with that, in the same portion of the image, a different substance, and one that had no affinity with the iron, and that could never be made to blend with it. In the latter part of this verse, the original word for "*partly*" is not the same in each clause. In the former it is מִן־קְצָת—properly *from the end,* sc., of the kingdom. Comp. Dan. xii. 13, "*At the end* of the days ;" i. 15, "*At the end* of ten days ;" and vers. 5, 18. The word *might* be employed to denote the *end* or *extremity* of anything, *e.g.*, in respect to *time,* and some have supposed that there is a reference here to the later periods of the Roman empire. See Poole's *Synopsis.* But the word is also used to denote *the sum,* or *the whole number ;* and then the phrase is equivalent to *a part*—as *e.g.*, in the phrase מִקְצָת כְּלֵי בֵית הָאֱלֹהִים—*from the sum of the vessels of the house of God* (Dan. i. 2); that is, a portion of the whole number, or a part. Comp. Neh. vii. 70, "from the sum of the heads of the

43 And whereas thou sawest iron mixed with miry clay, they shall mingle themselves with the seed of

fathers ;" that is, a part of them. In the latter part of the clause it is מִנֵּהּ — *from it ;* that is, a part of it ; partly. The entire phrase means that one part of the whole would be strong, and one part would be fragile. The reference is not to the *time* when this would occur, but to the *fact* that it would be so. The idea in this verse does not vary materially from that in the former, except that in that, the prominent thought is, that there would be *strength* in the kingdom : in this, the idea is, that while there would be strength in the kingdom, there would be also the elements of weakness.

43. *And whereas thou sawest iron mixed with miry clay, they shall mingle themselves with the seed of men.* Various explanations have been given of this verse, and it certainly is not of easy interpretation. The phrase "seed of men," would properly denote something different from the original stock that was represented by iron ; some foreign admixture that would be so unlike that, and that would so little amalgamate with it, as to be properly represented by clay as compared with iron. Prof. Stuart interprets this of matrimonial alliances, and supposes that the idea expressed is, that, "while the object of such alliances was union, or at least a design to bring about a peaceable state of things, that object was, in a peculiar manner, defeated." The word rendered *men* (אֲנָשָׁא) is employed in Hebrew and in Chaldee to denote men of an inferior class—the lower orders, the common herd — in contradistinction from the more elevated and noble classes, represented by the word אִישׁ. See Isa. ii. 9 ; v. 15 ; Prov. viii. 4. The word here used also (from אָנַשׁ—to be sick, ill at ease, incurable), would properly denote feebleness or inferiority, and would be aptly represented by clay as contrasted with iron. The expression "seed of men," as here used, would therefore denote some intermingling of an inferior race

men: but they shall not cleave [1] one to another, even as iron is not mixed
with clay.

[1] *this with this.*

---

with the original stock; some union or alliance under the one sovereignty, which would greatly weaken it as a whole, though the original strength still was great. The language would represent a race of mighty and powerful men, constituting the stamina—the bone and the sinew of the empire—mixed up with another race or other races, with whom, though they were associated in the government, they could never be blended; could never assimilate. This foreign admixture in the empire would be a constant source of weakness, and would constantly tend to division and faction, for such elements could never harmonize. It is further to be remarked, that this would exist to a degree which would not be found in either of the three previous kingdoms. In fact, in these kingdoms there was no such intermingling with foreign nations as to destroy the homogeneousness of the empire. They were, in the main, Orientals; with the language, the manners, the customs, the habits of Orientals; and in respect to energy and power—the point here under consideration—there was no marked distinction between the subjected provinces and the original materials of the monarchy. By the act of subjection, they became substantially one people, and readily blended together. This remark will certainly apply to the two first of these monarchies—the Babylonian and the Medo-Persian; and though with less force to the Macedonian, yet it was not true of that that it became so intermingled with foreign people as to constitute heterogeneous elements as it was of the Roman. In that monarchy, the element of *strength* was *infused* by Alexander and his Greeks; all the elements of weakness were in the original materials of the empire. In the Roman, the element of strength—*the iron*—was in the original material of the empire; the weak, the heterogeneous element—*the clay*—was that which was introduced from the foreign nations. This consideration may perhaps do something to show that the

opinion of Grotius, Prof. Stuart, and others, that this fourth monarchy was that which immediately succeeded Alexander is not well founded. The only question then is, whether, in the constitution of the Roman empire, at the time when it became the successor of the other three as a universal monarchy, there was such an intermingling of a foreign element, as to be properly represented by clay as contrasted with the original and stronger material *iron.* I say, "at the time when it became the successor of the other three as a universal monarchy," because the only point of view in which Daniel contemplated it was that. He looked at this, as he did at the others, as already such a universal dominion, and not at what it was before, or at the steps by which it rose to power. Now, on looking at the Roman empire at that period, and during the time when it occupied the position of the universal monarchy, and during which the "stone cut out of the mountain" grew and filled the world, there is no difficulty in finding such an intermingling with other nations—"the seed of men"—as to be properly described by "iron and clay" in the same image that could never be blended. The allusion is, probably, to that intermingling with other nations which so remarkably characterized the Roman empire, and which arose partly from its conquests, and partly from the inroads of other people in the latter days of the empire, and in reference to both of which there was no proper amalgamation, leaving the original vigour of the empire substantially in its strength, but introducing other elements which never amalgamated with it, and which were like clay intermingled with iron. (1.) From their conquests. Tacitus says, "*Dominandi cupido cunctis affectibus flagrantior est*"—the lust of ruling is more ardent than all other desires; and this was eminently true of the Romans. They aspired at the dominion of the world; and, in their strides at universal conquest, they brought nations under their subjection, and admitted them to the rights of citizenship, which had no affinity with the original material which composed the Roman power, and which never really amalgamated with it, any more than clay does with iron. (2.) This was true, also, in respect to the hordes that poured into the empire from other countries, and particularly from the Scandinavian regions, in the latter periods of the empire, and with which the Romans were compelled to form alliances, while, at the same time, they could not amalgamate with them. "In the reign of the emperor Caracalla," says Mr. Gibbon, "an innumerable swarm of Suevi appeared on the banks of the Mein, and in the neighbourhood of the Roman provinces, in quest of food, or plunder, or glory. The hasty army of volunteers gradually coalesced into a great and permanent nation, and as it was composed of so many different tribes, assumed the name of Allemanni, or allmen, to denote their various lineage, and their common bravery." No reader of the Roman history can be ignorant of the invasions of the Goths, the Huns, and the Vandals, or of the effects of these invasions on the empire. No one can be ignorant of the manner in which they became intermingled with the ancient Roman people, or of the attempts to form alliances with them, by intermarriages and otherwise, which were always like attempts to unite iron and clay. "Placidia, daughter of Theodosius the Great, was given in marriage to Adolphus, king of the Goths; the two daughters of Stilicho, the Vandal, were successively married to Honorius; and Genseric, another Vandal, gave Eudocia, a captive imperial princess, to his son to wife." The effects of the intermingling of foreign people on the character and destiny of the empire cannot be stated perhaps in a more graphic manner than is done by Mr. Gibbon, in the summary review of the Roman history, with which he concludes his seventh chapter, and at the same time there could scarcely be a more clear or expressive commentary on this prophecy of Daniel. "During the four first ages," says he, "the Romans, in the laborious school of poverty, had acquired the virtues of war and govern-

ment: by the vigorous exertion of those virtues, and by the assistance of fortune, they had obtained, in the course of the three succeeding centuries, an absolute empire over many countries of Europe, Asia, and Africa. The last three hundred years had been consumed in apparent prosperity and internal decline. The nation of soldiers, magistrates, and legislators, who composed the thirty-five tribes of the Roman people, was dissolved into the common mass of mankind, and confounded with the millions of servile provincials who had received the name without adopting the spirit of Romans. A mercenary army, levied among the subjects and barbarians of the frontier, was the only order of men who preserved and abused their independence. By their tumultuary election, a Syrian, a Goth, or an Arab was exalted to the throne of Rome, and invested with despotic power over the conquests and over the country of the Scipios. The limits of the Roman empire still extended from the Western Ocean to the Tigris, and from Mount Atlas to the Rhine and the Danube. To the undiscerning eye of the vulgar, Philip appeared a monarch no less powerful than Hadrian or Augustus had formerly been. The form was still the same, but the animating health and vigour were fled. The industry of the people was discouraged and exhausted by a long series of oppression. The discipline of the legions, which alone, after the extinction of every other virtue, had propped the greatness of the state, was corrupted by the ambition, or relaxed by the weakness of the emperors. The strength of the frontiers, which had always consisted in arms rather than in fortifications, was insensibly undermined, and the fairest provinces were left exposed to the rapaciousness or ambition of the barbarians, who soon discovered the decline of the Roman empire."—Vol. i. pp. 110, 111; Harper's Edit. (N. Y.) 1829. Comp. Notes on Rev. vi. 1–8. The agency of the Roman empire was so important in preparing the world for the advent of the Son of God, and in reference to the establishment of his kingdom, that there was an obvious propriety that it should be made a distinct subject of prophecy. We have seen that each of the other three kingdoms had an important influence in preparing the world for the introduction of Christianity, and was designed to accomplish an important part in the "History of Redemption." The agency of the Roman empire was more direct and important than any one or all of these; for (a) that was the empire which had the supremacy when the Son of God appeared; (b) that kingdom had performed a more direct and important work in preparing the world for his coming; (c) it was under authority derived from that sovereignty that the Son of God was put to death; and (d) it was by that that the ancient dispensation was brought to an end; and (e) it was under that that the new religion was spread through the world. It may be of use, therefore, in an exposition of this prophecy, to refer, with some particularity, to the things that were accomplished by this "fourth kingdom" in furthering the work of redemption, or in introducing and establishing the kingdom that was to be "set up, and which was never to be destroyed." That agency related to the following points:—(1.) The establishment of a universal dominion ; the fact that the world was brought under one sceptre greatly favoured the propagation of the Christian religion. We have seen, under the previous dynasties —the Babylonian, Persian, and Macedonian—that such an universal empire was important in earlier ages to *prepare* the world for the advent of the Messiah. This was still more important when he was about actually to appear, and his religion was to be spread over the world. It greatly favoured the diffusion of the new system that there was one empire ; that the means of communication from one part of the world to another had been so extended by the Romans; and that one who was entitled to the privileges of citizenship could claim protection in nearly every part of the world. (2.) The prevalence of universal peace. The world had become subject to the Roman power, and conquest was at an end. The world at last, after so long agitations and strifes,

was at peace. The distant provinces quietly submitted to the Roman control; the civil dissensions which had reigned so long at the capital were hushed ; Augustus, having triumphed over all his rivals, quietly occupied the imperial throne, and, as a symbol of the universal peace, the temple of Janus was closed. Rarely in their history had that temple been closed before ;* and yet there was an obvious propriety that when the "Prince of Peace" should come, the world should be at rest, and that the clangour of arms should cease. It was a beautiful emblem of the nature of his reign. A world that had been always in conflict before rested on its arms ; the tumult of battle had died away ; the banners of war were furled ; the legions of Rome paused in their career of conquest, and the world tranquilly waited for the coming of the Son of God. (3.) The Roman power accomplished an important agency in the great transaction which the Son of God came to perform in his making an atonement for the sins of the world. It was so arranged, in the Divine counsels, that he should be put to death, not by the hands of his own kindred and countrymen, but by the hands of foreigners, and under their authority. The necessity and the certainty of this was early predicted by the Saviour (Matt. xx. 19 ; Mark x. 33 ; Luke xviii. 32), and it is clear that there were important reasons why it should be thus done ; and doubtless one design of bringing Judea and the rest of the world under the Roman yoke was, that it might be accomplished in this way. Among the *reasons* for this may be suggested such as the following : (a) The heathen world, as well as the Jewish community, thus had a part in the great transaction. He died for the whole world—Jews and Gentiles—and it was important that that fact should be referred to in the manner of his death, and that the two great

* This temple was built, or finished at least, by Numa. It was closed, first, in his reign; secondly, at the close of the first Punic war, B.C. 241; three times in the reign of Augustus, the last time near the epoch of the birth of the Saviour; and three times afterwards, once under Nero, once under Vespasian, and once under Constantius, A.D. 350.—Eschenburg, *Class. Lit.,* p. 18.

44 And in [1] the days of these | kings shall the God [a] of heaven set

| *a* Mi. 4. 7 ; Lu. 1. 32. 33.

divisions of the human family should be united in the great transaction. It thus became not a *Jewish* affair only ; not an event in which Judea alone was interested, but an affair of the world ; a transaction in which the representatives of the world took their part. (*b*) It was thus made a matter of publicity. The account of the death of the Saviour would thus, of course, be transmitted to the capital, and would demand the attention of those who were in power. When the gospel was preached at Rome, it would be proper to allege that it was a thing in which Rome itself had had an important agency, from the fact that under the Roman authority the Messiah had been put to death. (*c*) The agency of the Romans, therefore, established the certainty of the death of Jesus, and consequently the certainty of his having risen from the dead. In order to demonstrate the latter, it was indispensable that the former should be made certain, and that all questions in regard to the reality of his death should be placed beyond a doubt. This was done by the agency of Pilate, a Roman governor. His death was certified to him, and he was satisfied of it. It became a matter of record ; a point about which there could be no dispute. Accordingly, in all the questions that came up in reference to the religion of Christ, it was never made a matter of doubt that he had been really put to death under Pilate, the Roman governor, whatever question may have arisen about the fact of his resurrection. (*d*) Equally important was the agency of the Romans in establishing the *innocence* of the Saviour. After patient and repeated trials before himself, Pilate was constrained to say that he was innocent of the charges alleged against him, and that no fault could be found in him. In proclaiming the gospel, it was of immense importance to be able to affirm this throughout the world. It could never be alleged against the gospel that its Author had violated the laws ; that he deserved to be put to death as a malefactor, for the records of the Roman governor himself showed the con-

trary. The agency of the Romans, therefore, in the great work of the atonement, though undesigned on their part, was of inestimable importance in the establishment of the Christian religion ; and it may be presumed that it was for this, in part at least, that the world was placed under their control, and that it was so ordered that the Messiah suffered under authority derived from them. (4.) There was another important agency of the Romans in reference to the religion that was to fill the earth. It was in destroying the city of Jerusalem, and bringing to a final end the whole system of Hebrew rites and ceremonies. The ancient sacrifices lost their efficacy really when the atonement was made on the cross. Then there was no need of the temple, and the altar, and the ancient priesthood. It was necessary that the ancient rites should cease, and that, having now lost their efficacy, there should be no possibility of perpetuating them. Accordingly, within the space of about thirty years after the death of the Saviour, when there had been time to perceive the bearing of the atonement on their temple rites ; when it was plain that they were no longer efficacious, significant, or necessary, the Romans were suffered to destroy the city, the altar, and the temple, and to bring the whole system to a perpetual end. The place where the ancient worship had been celebrated was made a heap of ruins ; the altar was overturned, never to be built again ; and the pomp and splendour of the ancient ritual passed away for ever. It was the design of God that that system should come to a perpetual end ; and hence, by his providence, it was so arranged, that ruin should spread over the city where the Lord was crucified, and that the Jewish people should never build an altar or a temple there again. To this day it has never been in their power to kindle the fire of sacrifice there, or to cause the smoke of incense to ascend in a temple consecrated to the worship of the God of their fathers. The agency of this fourth kingdom, therefore, was exceed-

up a kingdom which shall never be destroyed: and the ¹kingdom shall not be left to other people, *but it*

1 *kingdom thereof.*

shall break *a* in pieces and consume all these kingdoms, and it shall stand for ever.

a Ps. 2. 9.

ingly important in the introduction and establishment of that kingdom which was to be perpetual, and which was to fill the earth, and hence the reference to it here, and the more extended reference in ch. vii. 44. *And in the days of these kings.* Marg., *their.* The reading in the text "*these* kings"—is the more correct. The Vulgate renders this, "in the days of these kingdoms." The natural and obvious sense of the passage is, that during the continuance of the kingdoms above-mentioned, or before they should finally pass away, that is, before the last one should become extinct, another kingdom would be established on the earth which would be perpetual. Before the succession of universal monarchies should have passed away, the new kingdom would be set up that would never be destroyed. Such language is not uncommon. "Thus, if we were to speak of anything taking place in the days of British kings, we should not of course understand it as running through all their reigns, but merely as occurring in some one of them."—Prof. Bush. So it is said in Ruth i. 1 : "It came to pass *in the* days when the judges ruled, that there was a famine in the land ;" that is, the famine occurred sometime under that general administration, or before it had passed away, evidently not meaning that there was a famine in the reign of each one. So it is said of Jephthah, that he was buried *in the cities of Gilead ;* that is, some one of them. Josiah was buried *in the sepulchres of his fathers ;* that is, in some one of them. ¶ *Shall the God of heaven.* The God, who rules in heaven ; the true God. This is designed to show the Divine origin of this kingdom, and to distinguish it from all others. Though the others here referred to were under the Divine control, and were designed to act an important part in preparing the world for this, yet they are not represented as deriving their origin directly from heaven. They were

founded in the usual manner of earthly monarchies, but this was to have a heavenly origin. In accordance with this, the kingdom which the Messiah came to establish is often called, in the New Testament, "the kingdom of heaven," "the kingdom of God," &c. Compare Mic. iv. 7 ; Luke i. 32, 33. ¶ *Set up a kingdom.* "Shall cause to arise or stand up"—קים. It shall not owe its origin to the usual causes by which empires are constituted on the earth—by conquests ; by human policy ; by powerful alliances ; by transmitted hereditary possession—but shall exist because God shall *appoint* and *constitute* it. There can be no reasonable doubt as to what kingdom is here intended, and nearly all expositors have supposed that it refers to the kingdom of the Messiah. Grotius, indeed, who made the fourth kingdom refer to the Seleucidæ and Lagidæ, was constrained by consistency to make this refer to the Roman power; but in this interpretation he stands almost, if not entirely, alone. Yet even he supposes it to refer not to *heathen* Rome only, but to Rome as the perpetual seat of power —the permanent kingdom—the seat of the church: *Imperium Romanum perpetuò mansurum, quod sedes erit ecclesiæ.* And although he maintains that he refers to Rome primarily, yet he is constrained to acknowledge that what is here said is true in a higher sense of the kingdom of Christ: *Sensus sublimior, Christum finem impositurum omnibus imperiis terrestribus.* But there can be no real doubt as to what kingdom is intended. Its distinctly declared Divine origin ; the declaration that it shall never be destroyed ; the assurance that it would absorb all other kingdoms, and that it would stand for ever ; and the entire accordance of these declarations with the account of the kingdom of the Messiah in the New Testament, show beyond a doubt that the kingdom of the Redeemer is intended. ¶ *Which shall never be destroyed.* The others would pass away. The Babylonian would be suc-ceeded by the Medo-Persian, that by the Macedonian, that by the Roman, and that in its turn by the one which the God of heaven would set up. This would be perpetual. Nothing would have power to overthrow it. It would live in the revolutions of all other kingdoms, and would survive them all. Compare Notes on ch. vii. 14; and the summary of the doctrines taught here at the close of the Notes on ver. 45. ¶ *And the kingdom shall not be left to other people.* Marg., *thereof.* Literally, " *Its* kingdom shall not be left to other people ;" that is, the ruling power appropriate to this kingdom or dominion shall never pass away from its rightful possessor, and be transferred to other hands. In respect to other kingdoms, it often happens that their sovereigns are de-posed, and that their power passes into the hands of usurpers. But this can never occur in this kingdom. The government will never change hands. The administration will be perpetual. No foreign power shall sway the sceptre of this kingdom. There *may be* an allusion here to the fact that, in re-spect to each of the other kingdoms mentioned, the power over the same territory *did* pass into the hands of other people. Thus, on the same ter-ritory, the dominion passed from the hands of the Babylonian princes to the hands of Cyrus the Persian, and then to the hands of Alexander the Mace-donian, and then to the hands of the Romans. But this would never occur in regard to the kingdom which the God of heaven would set up. In the region of empire appropriate to it, it would never change hands ; and this promise of perpetuity made this king-dom wholly unlike all its predecessors. ¶ But *it shall break in pieces and con-sume all these kingdoms.* As represent-ed by the stone cut out of the moun-tains without hands, impinging on the image. See Notes on vers. 34, 35.

Two inquiries at once meet us here, of somewhat difficult solution. The first is, How, if this is designed to apply to the kingdom of the Messiah, can the description be true ? The lan-guage here would seem to imply some

violent action; some positive crushing force ; something like that which occurs in conquests when nations are subdued. Would it not appear from this that the kingdom here represented was to make its way by conquests in the same man-ner as the other kingdoms, rather than by a silent and peaceful influence ? Is this language, in fact, applicable to the method in which the kingdom of Christ is to supplant all others ? In reply to these questions, it may be remarked, (1) that the leading idea, as apparent in the prophecy, is not so much that of *violence* as that the kingdoms referred to would be *utterly brought to an end ;* that there would be, under this new kingdom, ultimately an entire cessation of the others ; or that they would be removed or supplanted by this. This is represented (ver. 35) by the fact that the materials composing the other king-doms are represented before this as be-coming like " the chaff of the summer threshing-floors ;" and as "being carried away, so that no place was found for them." The stone cut out of the moun-tain, small at first, was mysteriously enlarged, so that it occupied the place which they did, and ultimately filled the earth. A process of gradual demo-lition, acting on them by constant at-trition, removing portions of them, and occupying their place until they should disappear, and until there should be a complete substitution of the new king-dom in their place, would seem to cor-respond with all that is essential in the prophetic description. See Notes on ver. 34, on the expression, " which *smote* the image upon his feet." But (2) this language is in accordance with that which is commonly used in the predictions respecting the kingdom of the Messiah—language which is de-scriptive of the existence of *power* in subduing the nations, and bringing the opposing kingdoms of the world to an end. Thus in Psal. ii. 9, " Thou shalt break them with a rod of iron: thou shalt dash them in pieces like a potter's ves-sel." Isa. lx. 12, " For the nation and kingdom that will not serve thee shall perish ; yea, those nations shall be utterly wasted." So 1 Cor. xv. 24, 25, " When he shall have put down all rule, and all authority and power.

For he must reign till he hath put all enemies under his feet." These expressions denote that there will be an entire subjection of other kingdoms to that of the Messiah, called in the New Testament " the kingdom of God." They undoubtedly imply that there will be some kind of *force* employed—for this great work cannot be accomplished without the existence of *power;* but it may be remarked (*a*) that it does not necessarily mean that there will be *physical* force, or power like that by which kingdoms have been usually overturned. The kingdom of the Redeemer is a kingdom of *principles*, and those principles will subdue the nations, and bring them into subjection. (*b*) It does not necessarily mean that the effect here described will be accomplished *at once*. It may be by a gradual process, like a continual beating on the image, reducing it ultimately to powder.

The other question which arises here is, How can it be said that the new kingdom which was to be set up would "break in pieces and consume all these kingdoms?" How could the destruction of the image in the Roman period be in fact the destruction of the *three* previous kingdoms, represented by gold, and silver, and brass? Would they not in fact have passed away before the Roman power came into existence? And yet, is not the representation in ver. 35, that the iron, the clay, the brass, the silver, and the gold were broken in pieces together, and were all scattered like the chaff of the summer threshing-floor? Is it supposed that these kingdoms would be all in existence at the same time, and that the action of the symbolical " stone " was to be alike on all of them? To these questions, we may answer, (1.) That the meaning is, undoubtedly, that three of these kingdoms would have passed away at the time of the action of the " stone " referred to. They were to be a *succession* of kingdoms, occupying, to a great extent, the same territory, and not contemporary monarchies occupying distinct territories. (2.) The action of the " stone " was in fact, in a most important sense, to be on them all; that is, it was to be on what *constituted* these successive kingdoms of gold, silver,

brass, and iron. Each was in its turn an universal monarchy. The same territory was substantially occupied by them all. The Medo-Persian sceptre extended over the region under the Babylonian; the Macedonian over that; the Roman over that. There were indeed *accessions* in each successive monarchy, but still anything which affected the Roman empire affected what had *in fact* been the Babylonian, the Medo-Persian, and the Macedonian. A demolition of the image in the time of the Roman empire would be, therefore, in fact, a demolition of the whole. (3.) This interpretation is necessary from the nature of the symbolical representation. The eye of the monarch in the dream was directed to the image as *a splendid whole*. It was necessary to the object in view that he should see it *all at a time*, that he might have a distinct conception of it. This purpose made it impossible to exhibit the kingdoms *in succession*, but they all stood up before him at once. No one can doubt that there *might* have been a different representation, and that the kingdoms might have been made to pass before him in their order, but the representation would have been less grand and imposing. But this design made it necessary that the image should be kept *entire* before the mind until its demolition. It would have been unseemly to have represented the head as removed, and then the shoulders and breast, and then the belly and thighs, until nothing remained but the feet and toes. It was necessary to keep up the representation of *the image of colossal majesty and strength*, until a new power should arise which *would demolish it all*. Nebuchadnezzar is not represented as seeing the parts of the image successively appear or disappear. He does not at first see the golden head rising above the earth, and then the other parts in succession; nor the golden head disappearing, and then the other parts, until nothing was left but the feet and the toes. Such a representation would have destroyed the decorum and beauty of the whole figure; and as it cannot be argued that because Nebuchadnezzar saw the whole image at the outset standing in its complete form, that *therefore* all

45 Forasmuch as thou sawest that the stone was cut out of the

mountain [1] without hands, and that it brake in pieces the iron, the

[1] *which was not in hands.*

these kingdoms must have been simultaneously in existence, so it cannot be argued because he saw the whole image standing when the stone smote upon it, that *therefore* all these kingdoms must have had an existence then. (4.) It may be added, that the destruction of the last was in fact the destruction of all the three predecessors. The whole power had become embodied in that, and the demolition affected the whole series.

45. *Forasmuch as thou sawest that the stone,* &c. On the meaning of the language employed here, see Notes on vers. 34, 35. The word *forasmuch* may be taken either in connection with what precedes, or with what follows. In the former method, there should be a period at the word *gold* in this verse; and then the sense is, "In those days shall the God of heaven set up a kingdom, &c., *forasmuch*, or *because* thou sawest a stone," &c., that is, that was a certain indication of it. According to the other method, the meaning is, "Forasmuch as thou sawest the stone cut out and demolish the image, the great God has made known the certainty of it;" that is, that is a certain indication that it will be done. The Vulgate is, "According to what thou sawest, that the stone was cut out without hands, and reduced the clay, &c., the great God has shown to the king what will be hereafter." The difference in the interpretation is not very material. ¶ *Cut out of the mountain.* This is not inserted in the statement in ver. 34. It seems, however, to be implied there, as there is mention of the stone as "*cut out.*" The representation is evidently that of a stone disengaged from its native bed, the side of a mountain, without any human agency, and then rolling down the side of it and impinging on the image. ¶ *The great God hath made known to the king what shall come to pass hereafter.* Marg., the same as the Chaldee, *after this.* The meaning is simply, in time to come ; in some future period. Daniel claims none of the merit of this discovery to himself,

but ascribes it all to God. ¶ *And the dream is certain, and the interpretation thereof sure.* That is, it is no vain and airy phantom ; no mere working of the imagination. The dream was all that the monarch had supposed it to be—a representation of coming events, and his solicitude in regard to it was well-founded. Daniel speaks with the utmost assurance also as to its fulfilment. He knew that he had been led to this interpretation by no skill of his own ; and his representation of it was such as to satisfy the monarch of its correctness. Two circumstances probably made it appear certain to the monarch, as we learn from the next verse it did : one, that Daniel had recalled the dream to his own recollection, showing that he was under a Divine guidance ; and the other, the plausibility—the verisimilitude—the evident truthfulness of the representation. It was such a manifest *explanation* of the dream that Nebuchadnezzar, in the same manner as Pharaoh had done before him when his dreams were explained by Joseph, at once admitted the correctness of the representation.

Having now gone through with the *exposition* of this important passage respecting the stone cut from the mountain, it seems proper to make a few remarks in regard to the nature of the kingdom that would be set up, as represented by the stone which demolished the image, and which so marvellously increased as to fill the earth. That there is reference to the kingdom of the Messiah cannot be reasonably doubted. The points which are established in respect to that kingdom by the passage now under consideration are the following : —

1. Its superhuman origin. This is indicated in the representation of the stone cut out of the mountain "without hands ;" that is, clearly not by human agency, or in the ordinary course of events. There was to be a superhuman power exerted in detaching it from the mountain, as well as in its future growth. What appeared so marvellous was, that it was cut from its original

brass, the clay, the silver, and the gold; the great God hath made known to the king what shall come to pass [1] hereafter: and the dream *is* certain, and the interpretation thereof sure.

[1] *after this.*

---

resting-place by some invisible power, and moved forward to the consummation of its work without any human agency. That this was designed to be significant of *something* there can be no reasonable doubt, for the result is made to turn on this. I do not see that any special significancy is to be attached to the idea of its being cut from *"a mountain,"* nor that it is required of us to attempt to refine on that expression, and to ascertain whether the mountain means the Roman kingdom, out of which the gospel church was taken, as many suppose; or the Jewish nation, as Augustine supposed; or that "the origin of Christ was sublime and superior to the whole world," as Calvin supposes; or to the mountainous country of Judea in which the Messiah was born, as many others have maintained; or to the tomb of Joseph, as a rock from which the Messiah sprang to life and victory, as others have imagined. All this belongs to a system of interpretation that is trifling in the extreme. The representation of the mountain here is merely for the sake of verisimilitude, like the circumstances in a parable. If a stone was "cut out without hands," it would be natural to speak of it as cut from the mountain or parent-rock to which it was attached. The eye is not here directed to the *mountain* as having anything significant or marvellous about it, but to the *stone* that so mysteriously left its bed, and rolled onward toward the image. The point of interest and of marvel, the mysterious thing that attracted the eye, was that there was no human agency employed; that no hands were seen at work; that none of the ordinary instrumentalities were seen by which great effects are accomplished among men. Now this would properly represent the idea that the kingdom of the Messiah would have a supernatural origin. Its beginnings would be unlike what is usually seen among men. How appropriately this applies to the kingdom of the Messiah, as having its origin not in human power, need not here be stated. Nothing is more apparent; nothing is more frequently dwelt on in the New Testament, than that it had a heavenly origin. It did not owe its beginning to human plans, counsels, or power.

II. Its feebleness in its beginning, compared with its ultimate growth and power. At first it was a stone comparatively small, and that seemed utterly inadequate to the work of demolishing and pulverizing a colossal statue of gold, silver, brass, and iron. Ultimately it grew to be itself of mountain-size, and to fill the land. Now this representation would undoubtedly convey the fair impression that this new power, represented by the stone, would at first be comparatively small and feeble; that there would be comparative weakness in its origin as contrasted with what it would ultimately attain to; and that it would seem to be utterly inadequate to the performance of what it finally accomplished. It is hardly necessary to say that this corresponds entirely with the origin of the Messiah's kingdom. Everywhere it is represented as of feeble beginnings, and, as a system, to human view, entirely inadequate to so great a work as that of bringing other kingdoms to an end, and subduing it to itself. The complete fulfilment of the prophetic statement would be found in such circumstances as the following: (1.) The humble origin of the head of this new power himself —the Messiah—the King of Sion. He was, in fact, of a decayed and dilapidated family; was ranked among the poor; was without powerful friends or political connections; possessed no uncommon advantages of learning, and was regarded with contempt and scorn by the great mass of his countrymen. No one would have supposed that the religion originated by one of so humble an origin would have power to change the destiny of the kingdoms of the earth. (2.) The feebleness of the beginning of his kingdom. His few followers—the little band of fishermen;

the slow progress at first made ; these were circumstances strikingly in accordance with the representation in Daniel. (3.) The absence in that band of all that seemed requisite to accomplish so great a work. They had no arms, no wealth, no political power. They had nothing of that which has commonly been employed to overthrow kingdoms, and the band of fishermen sent forth to this work seemed as little adequate to the undertaking as the stone cut from the mountain did to demolish the colossal image. (4.) All this feebleness in the beginning was wonderfully contrasted with the ultimate results, like the stone, when cut from the mountain, contrasted with its magnitude when it filled the earth. The Saviour himself often referred to the contrast between the feeble origin of his religion, and what it would grow to be. At first it was like a grain of mustard-seed, smallest among seeds ; then it grew to be a tree so large that the fowls of the air lodged in the branches. At first it was like leaven, hidden in meal ; ultimately it would diffuse itself through the mass, so that the whole would be leavened, Mat. xiii. 31–33.

III. It would supplant all other kingdoms. This was clearly indicated by the fact that the " stone " demolished the image, reducing it to powder, and filled the place which that occupied, and all the land. This has been explained (Notes on vers. 34, 35), as meaning that it would not be by sudden violence, but by a continued process of comminution. There would be such an action on the kingdoms of the earth represented by gold, and silver, and brass, and iron, that they would disappear, and the new power represented by the " stone " would finally take their place. As this new power was to be humble in its origin, and feeble to human view ; as it had nothing which, to outward appearance, would seem adequate to the result, the reference would seem to be to the *principles* which would characterize it, and which, as elements of power, would gradually but ultimately secure the changes represented by the demolition of the colossal statue. The only question then would be, whether the principles in the kingdom of the

Messiah had such originality and power as would gradually but certainly change the modes of government that existed in the world, and substitute another kind of reign ; or, what is the influence which it will exert on the nations, causing new methods of government, in accordance with its principles, to prevail on the earth. Though apparently feeble, without arms, or wealth, or civil alliances, it has elements of *power* about it which will ultimately subdue all other principles of government, and take their place. Its work was indeed to be a gradual work, and it is by no means accomplished, yet its effect has been mighty already on the principles that rule among the nations, and will still be more mighty until *the laws of the kingdom of the Messiah shall prevail in all the earth.* This seems to be the idea which it is designed to express by this prophetic image. If one were asked *in what respects* it is to be anticipated that these changes will be wrought, and *in what respects* we can discern the evidences of such changes already, we might say in such points as the following : (1.) In regard to the methods in which governments are founded. Governments were formerly mostly the result of civil or foreign wars. Nearly all the governments of antiquity were originally founded in the *power* of some military leader, and then held by power. Christianity originated new views about wars and conquests ; views that will ultimately prevail. In nothing are the opinions of mankind destined more entirely to be reversed than in regard to *war;* to its glory, its achievements, and the fame of those who have been most celebrated for bloody triumphs. (2.) In regard to the rights of the people. A mighty principle was originated by Christianity in respect to the *rights* of men ; the right of conscience ; the right to the avails of their own labour ; the right to life and liberty. (3.) In regard to oppression. The history of the world has been, to a great extent, a history of oppression. But all this is to be changed by the principles of the true religion ; and when the period shall arrive that there shall be no more occasion to use the word *oppression,* as descriptive of anything that shall have an actual existence on earth, this will be a different world. Then the time will have come, appropriately designated by the demolition of the colossal statue—symbolic of all governments of oppression, and the substitution in its place of that which was at first insignificant, but which had vital energy to supplant all that went before it.

IV. This kingdom will be perpetual. This is asserted in the unequivocal statements that it " shall never be destroyed," and that " it shall not be left to other people;" that is, shall never pass into other hands. There could not be a more positive declaration that the kingdom here referred to will continue through all coming time. Other kingdoms pass away, but this will not; and amidst all the revolutions of other empires this will remain. The lapse of eighteen hundred years since this kingdom was set up, has done not a little to confirm the truth of this prediction. Many other kingdoms during that time have disappeared from the earth, but this remains in its full vigour, and with extending power. It has, at this day, an extent of dominion which it never had before, and there are clearer indications that it will spread over all the earth than ever existed at any previous time. That this kingdom *will* be perpetual may be argued from the following considerations : (1.) From the promises of God. These are absolute; and they are attested by Him who has all power, and who can, with infinite ease, accomplish all that he has spoken. So in Dan. vii. 14, "His dominion is an everlasting dominion, which shall not pass away, and his kingdom that which shall not be destroyed." Luke i. 33, " and he shall reign over the house of Jacob for ever : and of his kingdom there shall be no end." Psa. xlv. 6 (comp. Notes on Heb. i. 8), "Thy throne, O God, is for ever and ever." In Heb. i. 8, it is, "But unto the Son he saith, Thy throne, O God, is for ever and ever." Isa. ix. 7, " Of the increase of his government and peace there shall be no end, upon the throne of David, and upon his kingdom, to order it, and to establish it with judgment and with justice, from henceforth even for ever." (2.) It may be argued, from the fact that the efforts

which have been made to destroy it have shown that this cannot be done by any human power. Eighteen hundred years have now passed away—a period sufficiently long to test the question whether it can be destroyed by force and violence ; by argument and ridicule. The experiment has been fairly made, and if it were possible that it should be destroyed by external force, it would have been done. It cannot be imagined that more favourable circumstances for such a purpose will ever occur. The church of Christ has met every form of opposition that we can conceive could be made against it, and has survived them all. Particularly it has survived the trial which has been made in the following respects :—(a) The Roman power, the whole might of the Roman arms, that had subdued and crushed the world, was brought to bear upon the kingdom of Christ to crush and destroy it, but wholly failed. It cannot be supposed that a new power will ever arise that will be more formidable to Christianity than the Roman was. (b) The power of persecution. That has been tried in every way, and has failed. The most ingenious forms of torture have been devised to extinguish this religion, and have all failed. It has always been found that persecution has only contributed ultimately to the triumph of the cause which it was hoped to crush. (c) The power of philosophy. The ancient philosophers opposed it, and attempted to destroy it by argument. This was early done by Celsus and Porphyry ; but it soon became apparent that the ancient philosophy had nothing that could extinguish the rising religion, and not a few of the prominent philosophers themselves were converted, and became the advocates of the faith. (d) The power of science. Christianity had its origin in an age when science had made comparatively little progress, and in a country where it was almost unknown. The sciences since have made vast advances ; and each one in its turn has been appealed to by the enemies of religion, to furnish an argument against Christianity. Astronomy, history, the discoveries in Egypt, the asserted antiquity of the Hindoos, and geology, have all been employed to overthrow the claims of the Christian religion, and have all been compelled to abandon the field. See this admirably demonstrated in Dr. Wiseman's *Lectures on the Connection between Science and Revealed Religion.* (e) The power of ridicule. At one time it was held that "ridicule is the test of truth," and this has been applied unsparingly to the Christian religion. But the religion still lives, and it cannot be supposed that there will be men endued with the power of sarcasm and wit superior to those who, with these weapons, have made war on Christianity, or that infidelity has any hope from that quarter. It may be inferred, therefore, that there is no *external* source of corruption and decay which will prevent its being perpetual. Other kingdoms usually have; and after a few centuries at most the internal corruption—the defect of the organization—developes itself, and the kingdom falls. But nothing of this kind occurs in the kingdom of Christ. It has lived now through eighteen hundred years, through periods of the world in which there have been constant changes in the arts, in the sciences, in manners, in philosophy, in forms of government. During that time many a system of philosophy has been superseded, and many a kingdom has fallen, but Christianity is as fresh and vigorous, as it meets each coming generation, as it ever was; and the past has demonstrated that the enemies of the gospel have no reason to hope that it will become weak by age, and will fall by its own decrepitude.

V. A fifth characteristic of this kingdom is, that it will universally prevail. This was symbolized by the stone that "became a great mountain, and that filled the whole earth," ver. 35. It is also implied, in the statement in ver. 44, that it "shall break in pieces, and consume all these kingdoms." They will cease, and this will occupy their places. The *principles* of the kingdom of the Messiah, whatever may be the external forms of government that shall exist on the earth, will everywhere prevail. That this will occur may be argued from the following considerations:—(1.) The promises recorded in the Bible. The passage before us is

one. Of the same nature are the following: Psa. ii. 8, "Ask of me, and I shall give thee the heathen for thine inheritance, and the uttermost parts of the earth for thy possession." Mal. i. 11, "For from the rising of the sun even unto the going down of the same, my name shall be great among the Gentiles; and in every place incense shall be offered to my name, and a pure offering." Isa. xi. 9, "The earth shall be full of the knowledge of the Lord, as the waters cover the sea." Comp. Hab. ii. 14; Isa. xlv. 22, and Isa. lx. (2.) The world in its progress *loses* nothing that is of value. Truth is eternal, and when once discovered, society will not let it go. It seizes upon great elements in human nature, and the world will not let it die. Thus it is with discoveries in science, inventions in the arts, and principles in morals. There is no evidence that anything that was known to the ancients which was of permanent value to mankind has been lost; and the few things that *were* lost have been succeeded by that which is better. All that was truly valuable in their science, their philosophy, their arts, their jurisprudence, their literature, we possess still, and the world will always retain it. And what can ever obliterate from the memory of man the printing-press, the steam-engine, the cotton-gin, the telescope, the blow-pipe, the magnetic telegraph! Society ACCUMULATES from age to age all that is truly valuable in inventions, morals, and the arts, and travels with them down to the period when the world shall have reached the highest point of perfectability. This remark is true also of Christianity—the kingdom of Christ. There are *principles* in regard to the happiness and rights of man in that system which cannot be *detached* from society, but which go into its permanent structure, and which "the world will not let die." (3.) Society is thus making constant *advances.* A position gained in human progress is never ultimately lost. "The principles thus accumulated and incorporated into society become permanent. Each age adds something in this respect to the treasures accumulated by all preceding ages, and each one is, in some respects,

46 ¶ Then the king Nebuchadnezzar fell upon his face, and worshipped Daniel, and commanded that they should offer an oblation and sweet odours unto him.

---

an advance on its predecessors, and makes the final triumph of the principles of truth, and liberty, and pure religion more sure." (4.) Christianity, or the kingdom of Christ, is *aggressive*. It makes a steady war on the evil customs, habits, and laws of the world. It is in accordance with its nature to diffuse itself. Nothing can prevent its propagation; and, according to the laws of society, nothing is so certain philosophically in regard to the future, as the final prevalence of the religion of the Redeemer. It may meet with temporary and formidable obstructions. It may be retarded, or extinguished, in certain places. But its general course is onward—like the current of the mighty river towards the ocean. The *only* thing certain in the future is, that the Christian religion will yet spread all over the world; and there is enough in this to gratify the highest wishes of philanthropy, and enough to stimulate to the highest effort to secure so desirable an end.

46. *Then the king Nebuchadnezzar fell upon his face.* This was the common method of signifying profound respect among the Orientals. Comp. Gen. xvii. 3; l. 18; Lev. ix. 24; Numb. xiv. 5; Josh. v. 14; Judg. xiii. 20; Rev. xi. 16. ¶ *And worshipped Daniel.* The word rendered *worshipped* here (סְגִד), in the Chaldee portions of the Bible is uniformly rendered *worship*, Dan. ii. 26; iii. 5–7, 10–12, 14, 15, 18, 28. It occurs nowhere else, and in every instance, except in the one before us, is employed with reference to the homage paid to an idol, all the other cases occurring in the third chapter respecting the image that was set up by Nebuchadnezzar. The corresponding Hebrew word (סָגַד) occurs only in Isa. xliv. 15, 17, 19; xlvi. 6; and is, in every instance, rendered *fall down*, also with reference to idols. The proper idea, therefore, of the word here is, that the monarch meant to render *religious* homage to Daniel, or such adoration as was usually paid to idols. This is confirmed by what is immediately added,

that he commanded that an oblation should be made to him. It is not, however, necessary to suppose that Daniel *received* or *approved* this religious homage of the king, or that he left the impression on his mind that he was *willing* to be honoured as a god. The prostration of the king before him, of course, he could not prevent. The views and feelings which the monarch had in doing it he could not prevent. The command to present an "oblation and sweet odours to him" he could not prevent. But it is not a fair inference that Daniel approved this, or that he did anything to countenance it, or even that he did not, in a proper manner, rebuke it: for (1) we are not to suppose that all that was said was recorded, and no one can prove that Daniel did not express his disapprobation of this religious honour shown to him. (2.) Daniel had in fact, expressed his views, in the clearest manner, on this very point before the monarch. He had, again and again, disclaimed all power to be able to reveal such secrets. He had directed his mind to the true God, as he who alone could disclose coming events, vers. 28, 30, 45. He had taken all possible precaution to prevent any such result, by declaring, in the most emphatic terms (ver. 30), that this secret was not revealed to him "on account of any wisdom which he had more than any living." If now, after all this precaution, and these disclaimers, the king should prostrate himself before him, and, for the moment, feel that he was in the presence of a God, Daniel was not responsible for it, and it should not be inferred that he encouraged or approved it. (3.) It would seem, from the narrative itself, more than probable that Daniel *did* refuse the homage, and direct the thoughts of the monarch to the true God. In the very next verse it is said, "The king *answered* unto Daniel, and said, Of a truth it is, that your God is a God of gods, and a Lord of kings, and a revealer of secrets." *Answered* what? Perhaps something that was said by Daniel. At all events,

47 The king answered unto Daniel, and said, Of a truth *it is,* that your God *is* a God of gods, and a Lord of kings, and a revealer of secrets, seeing thou couldest reveal this secret.

---

it is clear from this that whatever were the momentary expressions of wonder, gratitude, and adoration, on the part of the king, his thoughts soon passed to the proper object of worship—the true God. *And commanded,* &c. The fact that this was *commanded* does not prove that it was *done.* The command was probably given under the excitement of his admiration and wonder. But it does not follow that Daniel received it, or that the command was not recalled on reflection, or that the oblation and odours may not have been presented to the true God. ¶ *That they should offer an oblation.* That is, his attendants, or perhaps the priests to whom pertained the duty of making offerings to the gods. The word rendered *oblation* (מִנְחָה) does not refer to a *bloody* sacrifice, but means a gift or present of any kind. It is applied in the Scriptures to denote (1) *a gift,* or *present,* Gen. xxxii. 13, 18, 20 (14, 19, 21); xliii. 11, 15, 25, 26; (2) *a tribute,* such as was exacted from a subject nation, under the notion of a present, 2 Sam. viii. 2, 6; 1 Kings iv. 21 (v. 1), (3) *an offering* or sacrifice to God, especially a bloodless offering, in opposition to (זֶבַח)—a bloody sacrifice, Lev. ii. 1, 4–6; vi. 14 (7); vii. 9; Psa. xl. 6 (7); Jer. xvii. 26. See the word fully explained in the Notes on Isa. i. 13. There can be no doubt that Nebuchadnezzar *meant* that such an offering should be presented as was usually made in idol worship. ¶ *And sweet odours.* Incense was commonly used in worship (see Notes on Isa. i. 13), and it is not improbable that in the worship of the gods it was accompanied with other fragrant odours. Sweet odours, or " savours," expressed by the same word which is used here, were a part of the prescribed worship in the Hebrew ritual, Lev. i. 9, 13, 17; ii. 2, 9; iii. 5; vi. 21 (14); Numb. xv. 7.

47. *The king answered unto Daniel.* Answered either what he had said in the interpretation of the dream, or *possibly* something that he had said in

regard to the impropriety of offering this homage to him. Comp. Notes on ver. 46. It is certain that, for some cause, whatever might have been the homage which he was disposed to render to Daniel, his thoughts were soon turned from him to the true God, and to an acknowledgment of him as superior to all other beings. He seems, at least, instantly to have reflected on what Daniel had himself said (ver. 30), and to have remembered that religious homage was due, not to Daniel, but to the God who had communicated the secret to him. ¶ *Of a truth* it is. It is truly so. This had been shown by the manner in which this secret was disclosed. ¶ *That your God* is *a God of gods.* Is superior to all other gods; is supreme over all. Comp. Rev. xvii. 14; 1 Tim. vi. 15. The idea is, that whatever subordinate beings there may be, *he* is supreme. ¶ *And a Lord of kings.* Supreme over kings. They are all inferior to him, and subject to his control. ¶ *And a revealer of secrets.* One of the attributes of divinity. See Notes on ver. 28. ¶ *Seeing thou couldest reveal this secret.* A secret which the wisest men of the realm had sought in vain to disclose. The fact that a professed servant of God had been able to do this showed that God was himself supreme, and worthy of adoration. We have here, then, an instance in which a proud and haughty heathen monarch was brought to an acknowledgment of the true God, and was constrained to render him homage. This was a result which it was evidently intended to reach in the whole transaction; in the dream itself; in the fact that the wise men of Babylon could not interpret it; and in the fact that an acknowledged servant of the Most High had been enabled to make the disclosure. The instance is instructive, as showing to what extent a mind clearly not under the influence of any genuine piety—for subsequent events showed that no *permanent* effects were produced on him, and that he was still an idolater (ch. iii.), and a most proud and haughty man (ch. iv.)—may

48 Then the king made Daniel a great man, and gave him many great gifts,[a] and made him ruler over the whole province of Babylon, and

a ver. 6.

chief of the [b] governors over all the wise *men* of Babylon.

49 Then Daniel requested of the king, and [c] he set Shadrach, Meshach,

b ch. 4. 9; 5. 11.   *c* ch. 3. 12.

be brought to acknowledge God. See the remarks at the end of the chapter (7).

48. *Then the king made Daniel a great man.* That is, he gave him an honourable appointment ; he so honoured him that he was regarded as a great man. He was really made great by the grace of God, and the extraordinary favour which God had bestowed upon him, but the estimate which the king had of his greatness was shown by the tokens of the royal favour. ¶ *And gave him many great gifts.* This is a common way of showing esteem in the East. The estimate in which one holds another is evinced by the variety and richness of the presents conferred on him. Hence all persons of distinction expect gifts of those who approach them as expressive of their regard for them, and of the esteem in which they are held. Comp. ver. 6 of this chapter. ¶ *And made him ruler over the whole province of Babylon.* Chald., הַשְׁלֵט—caused him to preside over, or to rule over, from the verb שְׁלַט *shelat, to rule,* and commonly applied to one who rules as a prince, or in an elevated office. From this word the terms *sultan* and *sultana* are derived. ¶ *And chief of the governors over all the wise* men *of Babylon.* This would seem to be an appointment which did not pertain to him as governor of the province of Babylon, or as presiding in the capital, but was a separate appointment, and, therefore, an additional mark of favour. The phrase " chief of the governors " would seem to imply that the magi of Babylon were disposed in certain orders or classes, each of which had its appropriate head, like the head of a college or university. Daniel was placed over the whole as the president, principal, or chancellor. It had been the policy of Nebuchadnezzar to assemble at the capital the principal talent and learning of the realm. Compare Notes, ch. i. 18–20 ; ii. 2. Daniel thus, in both these sta-

tions of honour at an early period of life, though recently an unknown stranger, and a captive, was exalted to the highest honours which could be conferred on a subject, and raised to posts of distinction which would usually be regarded as the highest rewards which could be obtained by a long life of devotedness to the welfare of the country.

49. *Then Daniel requested of the king,* &c. In his own remarkable prosperity, and in the extraordinary honours conferred on him, he did not forget the companions of his humbler days. They were his countrymen ; they had been captives with him ; they had been selected with a view to stand with him before the king (ch. i. 3, 4); they had shared with him in his rules of abstinence (ch. i. 11–17) ; they had all passed an honourable examination before the king (ch. i. 18, 19) ; they had united with him in supplication to God that he would disclose the meaning of the vision (ch. ii. 17, 18) ; and now it was proper that they should be remembered by him who had been so signally honoured. ¶ *Over the affairs of the province of Babylon.* In what particular departments of business they were employed is not mentioned ; but it would seem that all that specially pertained to this province was intrusted to them. Daniel had the general superintendence, but the subordinate duties growing out of the office were intrusted to them. The fact that the king granted the request shows the influence that Daniel had at the court. The reasons which influenced the king in granting the request may have been, not only the favour with which he regarded Daniel, but the fact that the duties of the office conferred on him now were such as to require assistance, and the remembrance of the virtues of these youths when they stood before him. ¶ *But Daniel sat in the gate of the king.* The post of chief honour and dignity as a counsellor of the king. The *gate* of a city in the East, being a

shach, and Abed-nego, over the affairs of the province of Babylon:

but Daniel *sat* ^din the gate of the king.

chief place of concourse, was the place where courts were held, and public business was usually transacted. See Notes on Job xxix. 7. To say, therefore, that he " sat in the gate of the king," is merely to say that he occupied a place with the chief counsellors and dignitaries of the realm. The phrase " Sublime *Porte*," that is, "the Sublime *Gate*," is still employed at Constantinople to denote the government of the sultan; for, in the earlier days of Ottoman rule, the reigning sovereign, as is still the case in some parts of the East, held courts of justice and levees at the entrance of his residence. See Harper's *Magazine*, vol. iv. p. 333. The office of Daniel was, perhaps, not far different from that of the grand vizier of the Turkish government. See Murray's *Ency. Geog.* vol. ii. p. 202.

REMARKS.

Among the lessons of practical value suggested by this chapter, we may notice the following :—

(1.) We have an instance (ver. 1–3) of the methods which were resorted to in early periods of the world to ascertain what the future would be. This great monarch relied on a dream which greatly disturbed him, and on the power which he supposed was intrusted to men to interpret dreams. In common with the prevailing spirit of his times, and of all ancient times (Notes, ver. 1), he believed that dreams might be regarded as prognostics of future events; that they were under Divine direction; and that all that was necessary to make them safe guides in reference to what is to occur, was that they should be properly interpreted. In common, too, with all the people of ancient times, and with most of modern times, the king here referred to had an earnest desire to look into the future. There has been no desire in the human

bosom stronger than this. We are so made that we wish to lift the mysterious veil which shrouds the future; to penetrate the deep darkness which rests on the unseen world. Our great interests are there. The past is fixed, and cannot now affect us, except by the consequences of what we have done, and by teaching us lessons of value derived from our own observation, and that of others. But the future is not yet fixed. Man, so anxious to know what this is to be, finds himself in respect to it peculiarly unendowed. In relation to the past, he is endowed with the faculty of *memory*, but with nothing corresponding to this pertaining to *the future*. He can treasure up what *has* occurred, but he cannot in like manner make the future pass before his mind, that he may become wise by knowing what will take place in far distant times. There can be no doubt that God *could* have endowed the mind with one faculty as well as the other— for he has it himself—but there were obvious reasons why it should not be done. Destitute, then, as man was of this power, one great object of human inquiry has been to see whether the deficiency could be supplied, and whether something might not be found which would be to the future substantially what the memory is to the past. The efforts and results on this subject—one of which we have in the chapter before us—constitute one of the most instructive chapters of the history of our race, and show how effectually God has bounded the limits of human investigation in this respect. Among those methods of attempting to penetrate the future, and of laying open its deep mysteries, may be noticed the following :—

(*a*) Astrology. It was supposed that

the stars might exert an influence over the fates of men, and that by observing their positions, conjunctions, and oppositions, it might be ascertained what would be the destiny of individuals and nations. The belief of this has manifested itself more or less in every age; and in such instances as in the word *lunacy*, and in the common apprehensions about the influence of the moon on health and on vegetation, may be still seen traces of that belief. Even Lord Bacon held that "astrology was a science not to be *rejected*, but reformed;" and in the early periods of the world it was a *fair* subject of investigation whether the heavenly bodies actually exerted such an influence, and whether, if it were so, it was possible to ascertain the laws by which this was done. This was the so-called science of astrology.

(*b*) Necromancy. The belief of this also prevailed in nearly all ancient nations, and we find frequent reference to it in the Scriptures. This consisted in the belief that the dead must be acquainted with the world where they now dwell, so dark to the living, and that it might be possible to make a covenant or compact with them, by which they would be induced to disclose what they knew. It was extensively, if not universally, believed that they re-appeared to men, and that it was not an uncommon occurrence for them to leave their abodes, and to visit the earth again. It was, therefore, not an unnatural and not an unfair subject of inquiry, whether they would not disclose to the more favoured among mortals what they knew of the secrets of the invisible world, and what they knew of events which were to come. Comp. Notes on Isa. viii. 19.

(*c*) The arts of divination. These were founded mainly on the investigations of science. It was at first a fair question whether, amidst the wonders which science was unfolding to the view, it might not contribute to lift the veil from the future, and reveal what was yet to come. It took long to ascertain what *were* the legitimate aims of science, and what might be hoped for from it. Hence it was directed to the inquiry whether some substance might not be found which would transmute all things to gold; whether some elixir might not be discovered which would arrest all disease, and give immortality to man; and whether science would not disclose some means by which the future could be penetrated, and the mysteries of the invisible world be laid open to the view. It required centuries of investigation, a thousand failures, and the results of long and patient thought, to ascertain what *were* the true objects of science, and to convince the world that it was *not* its legitimate purpose to reveal the future to man.

(*d*) Heathen oracles. It was an early inquiry whether God would not, in some way, lift the veil from the future and disclose its secrets to man. The belief that this would be done seems to be natural to the mind of man; and in all ages, and in all countries, he has supposed that the future would be thus disclosed. Hence, among the heathen, certain persons claimed to be divinely inspired; hence such shrines as that at Delphi became celebrated; hence ambiguous responses were uttered, so expressed as to support the credit of the oracle, whatever might be the result; hence men were appointed to observe the flights of birds, to inspect the entrails of animals offered in sacrifice, to interpret any unusual phenomena in the clouds, to mark the direction of meteors, and, in general, to examine any unusual appearances in the heavens or the earth, which would seem to furnish any clew by which the future might be known. Much of all this undoubtedly became mere imposture, and justified the remark of Cicero, that he wondered that one augur could meet another without laughing; but there can be no doubt that by many these inquiries were honestly pursued, and that at first all this seemed to be a legitimate subject of inquiry. What forbade man to pursue it? And who could tell but that in some such ways the secrets of the mysterious future could be found out? It demanded long and patient inquiry and observation to show that this could *not* be so, and that whatever *might* be indicated by any of these things, it was never designed that they should be the means by which man could be made acquainted with the mysteries of the invisible world.

(*e*) Dreams. We have seen (Notes, ver. 1) that it was an early article of belief that through the medium of dreams the Divine will might be made known, and the secrets of the future disclosed. The *theory* on this subject seems to have been, that during sleep the ordinary laws of the mind are suspended; that the soul is abstracted from the visible world; that the thoughts which it has then must be originated by higher beings; and that in this state it has converse with an invisible world, and may be permitted to see much of what is yet to occur. Comp. Intro. to Isaiah, § vii (?).

(*f*) Visions. Men supposed that there might be representations made to certain favoured persons respecting the future, their senses being closed to surrounding objects, and that while in an ecstasy, or trance, the mind might have a view of future events. Such were the visions of Balaam; such, in a remarkable manner, were the visions of the true prophets; and so deeply was

the conviction that this *might* occur engrafted in the human mind, that the belief of it seems to have had a place among the heathen nations. Comp. Intro. to Isaiah, § vii. (4).

Such were some of the ways by which it was supposed that the future might be penetrated by man, and its secrets disclosed. By allowing man to make trial of these methods, and to pursue them through a period of several thousand years, until he himself saw that they were fruitless, God was preparing the race to feel the necessity of direct communications from himself, and to welcome the true revelations which he would make respecting things to come.

(2.) We have in the chapter before us (vers. 4–11) an instance of *the acknowledged failure* of a class of the wisest of men, whose lives were devoted to this employment, in their attempts to disclose the future. This is a fair illustration of all the attempts of the heathen, and it was doubtless permitted in order that it might be seen that all such attempts *must* fail. The magicians, astrologers, and Chaldeans were foiled in a case which fairly came within the province of their art, and when pretenders to this kind of knowledge *ought* to have been able to solve the difficulties of the monarch. Regarding this as a fair illustration of all the attempts of the heathen to penetrate the future, and to discover the great truths which it is desirable for man to know, there are three observations which may be made in regard to it:—I. The trial has been a fair one. (*a*) There was *time* enough allowed for it. It was about four thousand years from the creation of man to the time when the canon of Scripture was completed, and promulgated to the whole world, and it could not be said that man required a longer time to test the question whether he needed a revelation. (b) The trial was a fair one, because it was one which men were at liberty to pursue to any extent, and which was conducted under the best advantages. It was confined to no country or favoured class of men. In all lands, and with every advantage of climate, government, and laws, man has been engaged in the great inquiry; and if it be remembered what immense *numbers* of minds have been employed in these investigations, it cannot be pretended that the utmost desirable freedom has not been allowed to man to test the question whether "by searching he can find out God," and disclose the future. (c) The same thing is true in respect to the *talent* which has been employed in this investigation. It is not too much to say, that the *highest* talent that the world has produced has been engaged in these inquiries, and that the rejecters of revelation cannot hope that higher powers can be brought to bear on it, or that the unaided human intellect can hope to accomplish more in this respect than has been done. The profoundest minds in Egypt and Chaldea were engaged in inquiries of this sort. The very highest talent which Greece produced in its best days was employed on questions of religion; in attempts to find out God, to ascertain the relations of man to him, and to determine what man was to be hereafter. What was true, also, of the ancient heathen, and of the modern heathen, that the best talent has been employed on these questions, is true also of the rejecters of revelation in Christian lands. Men of high powers of intellect have refused to acknowledge the Bible as a revelation, and have chosen to fall back on the unaided resources of their own minds. Aided with all that science and learning can do, they have inquired after a

system of religion that would commend itself to man as true, and as adapted to his wants; and it cannot be pretended that man in *this* respect has not had a fair opportunity to show what the human powers can do. (d) The trial has been a fair one in regard to the field of investigation. Astrology, necromancy, abstruse natural science, oracles, dreams, visions, the observation of the course of events—all these have been open before man, and in one and all of them he has been allowed to pursue his investigations at pleasure. II. There has been an entire *failure* in the attempt. The Chaldeans failed in Babylon, as the magicians had done in Egypt, to explain what was regarded as a prognostic of the future, and in both cases it was necessary to call in the aid of one who had a direct communication from heaven. The same has been the case in *all* attempts to explain the future, and to disclose what man was so desirous of knowing about the invisible world. (a) All reliance on astrology, necromancy, oracles, dreams, and the revelations of the abstruser sciences, has failed. Astrology has ceased to be a science, and the stars are studied for other purposes than to disclose future events; necromancy has ceased to be a science—for no one now hopes to be able to make a compact with the dead, in virtue of which they will disclose the secrets of the invisible world; no one now would consult a heathen oracle with the hope of receiving a response to his inquiries that might be relied on: the abstruser sciences are pursued for other purposes; and no one would repose on dreams to furnish a system of truth which would meet the wants of man. (b) The same thing has been true in regard to the various *systems of religion* on which men have relied. *It is true of the systems of the heathen.* They have been tried in the most ample manner, and have shown that they do not meet the wants of man. The experiment has been fairly made, and the system is becoming worse and worse. It is not adapted to elevate man in the scale of being in regard to the present life; it does not remove the evils which press now upon the race; it does not disclose a certain way by which a sinner may be prepared for the life to come. *It is true in regard to an atonement for sin.* The attempt has been made now for nearly six thousand years, to find some way in which an efficacious sacrifice may be made for sin. Blood has been poured on thousands of altars; animals have been offered, and thousands of human beings have been devoted to the gods, but still there has been no evidence that these bloody offerings have been accepted, or that they have availed to expiate transgression. The experiment has failed. There is no new sacrifice that can be offered now, and it is hopeless for man to attempt to make expiation for his own sins. *The same thing is true of the systems of religion proposed by infidelity.* They are all failures. One system after another is abandoned, and no one is such as the race needs. The best talent that infidelity can hope to produce has been exhausted in this undertaking; for how can it hope to produce men better fitted to propose a system of religion to mankind than Shaftesbury, or Hobbes, or Tindal, or Herbert, or Voltaire, or Hume? Yet, after all that has been done by infidelity in modern times, an intelligent man would prefer trusting his eternal interests to such a system as Socrates would propose, to one proposed by Hume; he would feel safer under the guidance of Cicero or Seneca than under the direction of Voltaire or Gibbon. III. The *reasons* why God has permitted this trial to be made, in such a manner, and with such results, are obvious. In the cases which occurred in the time of Pharaoh in Egypt, and of Nebuchadnezzar in Babylon, the reason evidently was, that when there was an acknowledged failure of the power of the magicians, God might himself, through Joseph and Daniel, get honour to his own name. So the reasons why he has permitted this trial to be made on a large scale, and has suffered it everywhere to fail, are probably these two: (1) to show to man, in such a way as to admit of no doubt, his need of revelation; and (2) to induce him to prize the volume of revealed truth. We should value it the more, and adhere to it the more firmly, in view of the experiment which has been made in all lands. If *that* revelation be rejected, man has *no* resource; he is wholly unable to penetrate the future; he can devise no way of making atonement for sin; he can originate no system that shall alleviate the sorrows under which we groan, or disclose the prospect of happiness beyond the tomb. For if the Bible is taken away, on what shall we fall back to guide us? —on astrology; on necromancy; on heathen oracles and sacrifices; on dreams; on the ravings of priestesses at heathen shrines, or the speculations of infidelity in Christian lands? All these have been tried in vain. The Bible is the only guide on which man can rely to conduct him to heaven: if that fails, all fails, and man is in the midst of impenetrable night.

(3.) We may learn from this chapter (vers. 12–19), that in the perplexities and trials which arise in life, a good man may appeal to God for guidance and help. So Daniel felt, when all human power had failed in complying with the demands of a stern and arbitrary monarch, and when he and his friends, though innocent, were about to be involved in the sweeping sentence which had been issued against the wise men of Babylon. Then it was clear that nothing could save them but Divine interposition; nothing could avert the stroke but such a heavenly influence as would disclose the secret, and thus avert the wrath of the king. In this emergency Daniel felt that he *might* call upon God, and to this service he summoned also his three friends, who were equally interested with him in the issue. In view of this we may observe: I. That *all* good men are liable to meet with similar perplexities and embarrassments; to be placed in circumstances where nothing but the interposition of God can help them. This is true in such respects as the following: (*a*) In reference to the knowledge of the truth. The mind is often perplexed on the subject of religion: reason fails to disclose those truths which it is desirable to know; darkness and obscurity seem to envelope the whole subject; the soul, oppressed with a sense of conscious guilt, seeks to find some way of peace; the heart, entangled in the meshes of unbelief, struggles and pants to be free, and there is no human help—nothing this side the eternal throne on which reliance can be placed to impart the light which is needed. (*b*) In reference to duty. The mind is often perplexed to know what should be done. Though desirous of doing what is right, yet there may be so many conflicting views; there may be such doubt as to what is best and right, that none but God can direct in such an emergency. (*c*) In cases of peril. Daniel and his friends were in danger; and men are often now in such danger that they feel that none but God can save them. On a bed of pain, in a stranded vessel, in a burning house, men often feel that human help is powerless, and that aid can be found

in none but God. Thus the church, in the dark days of persecution, has often been so encompassed with dangers, that it could not but feel that none but God could avert the impending destruction. (*d*) In times when religion declines, and when iniquity abounds. Then the church often is led to feel that there is need of the aid of God, and that none but he can rouse it from its deathlike slumbers, and put back the swelling waves of iniquity. II. In such circumstances it is the privilege of a good man to appeal to God, with the hope that he will interpose. (1.) This was felt by Daniel, and it is an undoubted truth, as revealed in the Bible, that in such circumstances, if we will look to God, we may hope for his guidance and help. Comp. 2 Kings xix. 14, 15; Job xvi. 19–21; Psalm xxv. 9; xlvi. 1, *seq.*; lv. 22; James i. 5, 6. But (2) what kind of interposition and direction may *we* hope for in such perplexities? I answer: (*a*) We may expect the Divine direction by a careful study of the *principles* laid down in the Scriptures. The Bible indeed does not, for it could not, mention the names of individuals, or specify every case which would occur in which Divine direction would be needed, but it lays down great *principles* of truth, applicable to all the circumstances which will ever arise. In this respect there is a wonderful richness and fulness in the Word of God. There is many a rich vein of truth which seems never to have been worked until we are placed in some new and untried situation. When one is thrown into perplexing circumstances; when he is called to pass through trials; when he meets some powerful form of temptation, he is surprised to find how much there is in the Bible adapted to such circumstances that he never saw there before. It seems to be a new book, written to meet just such cases; nor in such circumstances does he ever consult its pages in vain. (b) We may expect direction by his providence. The sparrow falls not to the ground without his direction, and all events are under his control, and as these events occur they may be regarded as so many indications of his will. One of the most interesting and profitable employments in a man's life is to study the indications of Providence in regard to himself, and to endeavour to learn, from what is daily occurring to him, what is the will of God in regard to him. A careful and prayerful observer of the intimations of the Divine will is not in serious danger of error. (c) God guides those who are in perplexity by his Spirit. There is a secret and silent influence on the mind of him who is desirous of being led in the way of duty, suggesting what is true, delivering the mind from prejudice, overcoming opposition to the truth, disposing the heart to charity, peace, and love, prompting to the performance of duty, and gradually elevating the soul to God. If a man would pray when he feels an inward prompting to pray; would read the Bible when some inward voice seems to call him to do it; would do good when the inward monitor urges him to do it; would fix the eye and the heart on heaven when something within seems to lead him toward the skies, he would not be in much danger of error. Such are "spring-times of piety in the soul" —times when the soul may make rapid progress in the knowledge of the truth, and it is not enthusiasm to say that such states of mind are produced by an influence from above.

(4.) In view of this chapter (verses 17, 18), we may observe that it is a privilege to have praying friends—friends on whom we can call to unite with us in prayer in the time of trouble. So Daniel found it when *he* called on his friends to pray; so Esther found it when her whole people were in danger, and when all depended on her successful application to the sovereign (Esther iv. 16), and so the friends of God have found it in all ages. If prayer is heard at all, there are special reasons why it should prevail when many are united in the request. Comp. Matt. xviii. 19. Hence the propriety of worship in the family ; hence the fitness of prayer-meetings ; and hence the appropriateness of prayer offered in the great congregation.

(5.) God should be praised and acknowledged as having supremacy over all things, verses 20–23. Particularly he should be acknowledged (a) in the changes that occur on earth ; in the changes from childhood to youth, and from youth to manhood, and to old age; in the beautiful changes of the seasons, and in all the variety which the seasons bring with them ; in the changes from sickness to health, from poverty to affluence, from oppression and slavery to freedom, from an humble to an exalted condition ; in all the revolutions of empire, and the changes of dynasties. (b) He should be acknowledged in his supremacy over the kings and rulers of the earth. Every monarch reigns by his permission, and every one is designed to accomplish some great purpose in the development of his plans. If a full and correct history of the world could be written, it would be found that God had *some* object to accomplish by the instrumentality of every one whom he has called to a throne, and that as we can now see a distinct design to be accomplished by the reign of Pharaoh, Sennacherib, Cyrus, and Augustus, so we could find some distinct design in reference to every one who has ever reigned. (c) He should be recognized as the source of all knowledge. Particularly (1) he originally endowed every mind, and gave it the capacity which it has for acquiring knowledge ; (2) he preserves the faculties of the mind, and gives them their just balance; (3) he makes the intellect clear and bright, and when it applies itself to the investigation of truth he only can preserve it unclouded; (4) he makes, under the operation of the regular laws of intellect, important *suggestions* to the mind—those pregnant HINTS containing so much "the seeds of things" on which all true progress in knowledge depends—those bright thoughts, those happy conceptions, which come into the soul, and which result in such happy inventions, and such advances in science, art, literature, and law ; and (5) he should be regarded as the original source of those *inventions* which contribute so much to the progress of the race. At the proper time, and the best time, when some new and wonderful discovery is to burst upon the world, he raises up the individual who is to make it, and the discovery takes its place as one of the fixed points of progress, and society, with that as a treasure never to be lost, moves forward on a higher elevation, with greatly accelerated progress. So it was with the invention of alphabetical writing ; the art of printing ; the application of steam to purposes of manufacture and navigation ; the telescope, and the telegraph ; and, in general, in respect to all those great inventions which have contributed to the progress of society. If the whole truth were known, it would be seen that the hand of God was in these things as really as in the "revelation of the deep and secret things to Daniel."

(6.) We may learn from this chapter, as was remarked in the Notes on ver. 30, that for all our attainments in knowledge and wisdom we should ascribe the praise to God alone. In illustration of this we may remark: I. That there is a strong native tendency in man to ascribe the honour of such attainments to himself. It is one of the most difficult of all things to induce man to attribute the praise of whatever excellence he may have, or whatever attainments he may make, to his Creator. This exists universally in regard to talent, rank, and scientific attainments ; and it is even hard for a heart that is endowed with true religion to free itself altogether from self-glorying, as if it were all to be traced to ourselves. II. Yet in our case, as in the case of Daniel, all the honour should be ascribed to God. For (1) it is to him we owe all our original endowments of mind and of body, whatever they may be. In this respect we are as he chose to make us. We have no natural endowment—whether of beauty, strength, genius, aptness for learning, or advantages for distinction in science which he did not confer on us, and which he could not as easily have withheld from us as he did from those less favoured. And why should we be proud of these things ? Shall the oak of Bashan be proud of its far-spreading arms, or its strength ? Shall the cedar of Lebanon be proud of its height, and its vastness, and its beauty? Shall the rose be proud of its beauty or its sweetness, or shall the magnolia boast of its fragrance ? (2.) God has conferred on us all the means of education which we have enjoyed, and all to which the development of our natural powers can be traced. He has preserved our reason ; he has furnished us instructors; he has provided the books which we have read ; he has continued to us the possession of the health which we have enjoyed. At any moment he could have driven reason from the throne ; he could have deprived us of health ; he could have summoned us away. (3.) It is equally owing to him that we have been favoured with any success in the prosecution of our calling in life. Let the merchant who has accumulated great property, apparently by his own industry, suppose that all Divine agency and influence in his case had been withheld, and whatever labour he may have expended, or with whatever skill he may be endowed, he could have met with no such success. Let him reflect how much he owes to favouring gales on the ocean ; to the seasons producing abundant harvests, and to what seems almost to be *chance* or *fortune*, and he will see at once that whatever success he may have been favoured with is to be traced, in an eminent sense, to God. The same thing is true of all the other successful departments of human effort. (4.) This is equally true of all the knowledge which we have of the way of salvation, and all our hopes of eternal life. It is a great principle of religion that we have nothing which we have not received, and that if we have received it, we should not glory as if we had not received it, for it is God who makes us to differ (see 1 Cor. iv. 7). It is God who originally gave us the volume of revealed truth—making us differ from the whole pagan world. It is God who awakened us to see our guilt and danger, making us to differ from the gay and careless world around us. It is God alone who has pardoned our sins, making us to differ from the multitude who are unpardoned in the world. It is God who has given us every hope that we cherish that is well-founded, and all the peace and joy which we have had in communion with himself. For these things, therefore, we should give all the praise to God ; and in our case, as in that of Daniel, it is one of the evidences of our piety when we are disposed to do so.

(7.) We have in this chapter (vers. 46, 47) an instructive instance of the

extent to which an irreligious man may go in showing respect for God. It cannot be supposed that Nebuchadnezzar was a truly pious man. His characteristics and actions, both before and after this, were those of a heathen, and there is no evidence that he was truly converted to God. Yet he evinced the highest respect for one who was a servant and prophet of the Most High (ver. 46), and even for God himself (ver. 47). This was evinced in a still more remarkable manner at a subsequent period (ch. iv.) In this he showed how far it is possible for one to go who has no real piety, and as such cases are not uncommon, it may not be improper to consider them for a moment. I. This respect for God extends to the following things : (1.) An admiration of him, as great, and wise, and powerful. The evidences of his power and wisdom are traced in his works. The mind may be impressed with that which is wise, or overpowered with that which is vast, without there being any real religion, and all this admiration may terminate on God, and be expressed in language of respect for him, or for his ministers. (2.) This admiration of God may be extended to whatever is *beautiful* in religion. The beauty of the works of nature, of the sky, of a landscape, of the ocean, of the setting sun, of the changing clouds, of the flowers of the field, may lead the thoughts up to God, and produce a certain admiration of a Being who has clothed the world with so much loveliness. There is a religion of sentiment as well as of principle ; a religion that terminates on the *beautiful* as well as a religion that terminates on the *holy*. The Greeks, natural admirers of beauty, carried this kind of religion to the highest possible degree ; for their religion was, in all its forms, characterized by the love of the beautiful. So also there is much that is beautiful in

Christianity, as well as in the works of God, and it is possible to be charmed with that without ever having felt any compunction for sin, or any love for pure religion itself. It is possible for one who has a natural admiration for that which is lovely in character, to see a high degree of moral beauty in the character of the Redeemer; for one whose heart is easily moved by sympathy to be affected in view of the sufferings of the injured Saviour. The same eyes that would weep over a well-told tale, or over a tragic representation on the stage, or over a scene of real distress, might weep over the wrongs and woes of Him who was crucified, and yet there might be nothing more than the religion of sentiment—the religion springing from mere natural feeling. (3.) There is much *poetic* religion in the world. It is possible for the imagination to form such a view of the Divine character that it shall *seem* to be lovely, while perhaps there may be scarcely a feature of that character that shall be correct. Not a little of the religion of the world is of this description—where such a God is conceived of as the mind chooses, and the affections are fixed on that imaginary being, while there is not a particle of love to the true God in the soul. So there is a poetic view of man, of his character, of his destiny, while the *real* character of the heart has never been seen. So there is a poetic view of heaven—strongly resembling the views which the ancients had of the Elysian fields. But heaven as a place of holiness has never been thought of, and would not be loved. Men look forward to a place where the refined and the intelligent; the amiable and the lovely; the accomplished and the upright; where poets, orators, warriors, and philosophers will be assembled together. This is the kind of religion which is often manifested in

eulogies, and epitaphs, and in conversation, where those who never had any better religion, and never pretended to any serious piety, are represented as having gone to heaven when they die. There are few who, under the influence of such a religion, are not looking forward to some kind of a heaven; and few persons die, whatever may be their character, unless they are openly and grossly abandoned, for whom the hope is not expressed that they have gone safe to a better world. If we may credit epitaphs, and obituary notices, and funeral eulogiums, and biographies, there are few poets, warriors, statesmen, or philosophers, about whose happiness in the future world we should have any apprehension. II. But in all this there may be no real religion. There is no evidence that there was any in the case of Nebuchadnezzar, and as little is there in the instances now referred to. Such persons may have a kind of reverence for God as great, and powerful, and wise; they may have even a kind of pleasure in looking on the evidence of his existence and perfections in his works; they may have a glow of pleasurable emotion in the mere *poetry* of religion; they may be restrained from doing many things by their consciences; they may erect temples, and build altars, and contribute to the support of religion, and even be zealous for religion, as they understand it, and still have no just views of God, and no true piety whatever. (1.) The mind that is truly religious is not insensible to all this, and may have as exalted notions of God as a great and glorious being, and be as much impressed with the beauty evinced in his works as in the cases supposed. True religion does not destroy the sense of the sublime and beautiful, but rather cultivates this in a higher degree. But (2) there is much besides this that enters into true religion, and without which all these things are vain. (*a*) True religion always arises from just views of God as he is; not from him as an imaginary being. (*b*) True religion must regard God as having *moral* attributes; as benevolent, and just, and true, and holy, and not merely as powerful and great. (*c*) In all these things referred to, there is not necessarily any moral excellence on the part of those who thus admire God and his works. The mere admiration of power implies in us no moral excellence. The admiration of the wisdom which made the worlds and keeps them in their place; of the beauties of poetry, or of a flower, or landscape, though made by God, implies no moral excellence in us, and, therefore, no true religion. There is no more religion in admiring *God* as an architect or painter, than there is in admiring Sir Christopher Wren, or Michael Angelo; and the mere admiration of the works of God as such, implies no more moral excellence in us than it does to admire St. Paul's or St. Peter's. In religion, the heart does not merely admire the beautiful and the grand; it loves that which is pure, and just, and good, and holy. It delights in God as a holy being rather than as a powerful being; it finds pleasure in his moral character, and not merely in his greatness.

(8.) We may learn from this chapter (ver. 49), that when we are favoured with prosperity and honour we should not neglect, or be ashamed of, the companions of our earlier days, and the partakers of our fortune when we were poor and unknown. Joseph, when exalted to the premiership of Egypt, was not ashamed of his aged father, but, though he had been an humble shepherd, presented him, with the deepest feelings of respect towards an aged parent, to Pharaoh; nor was he ashamed of his brethren, though they had done

him so much wrong. Daniel, when in a similar manner advanced to the most honourable post which one could reach, in the most magnificent monarchy of the world, was not ashamed of the youthful friends with whom he had shared the humble and severe lot of bondage. So we, if we are made rich; if we are raised to honour; if we become distinguished for learning or talent; if our names are known abroad, or we are intrusted with a high and honourable office, should not forget the friends and companions of our earlier years.

CHAPTER III.

§ I.—AUTHENTICITY OF THE CHAPTER.

The objections which have been urged against the authenticity of this chapter are much more numerous than those which have been alleged against the two previous chapters.

I. The first which deserves to be noticed is stated by De Wette (p. 383, under the general head of *improbabilities* in the chapter), and Bleek, p. 268, as quoted by Hengstenberg, *die Authentie des Daniel*, p. 83. The objection is, substantially, that if the account in this chapter is true, it would prove that the Chaldeans were inclined to persecution on account of religious opinions, which, it is said, is contrary to their whole character as elsewhere shown. So far as we have any information in regard to them, it is alleged, they were far from having this character, and it is not probable, therefore, that Nebuchadnezzar would make a law which would compel the worship of an idol under severe pains and penalties.

To this objection the following reply may be made :—

(1.) Little is known, on any supposition, of the Chaldeans in general, and little of the character of Nebuchadnezzar in particular, beyond what we find in the book of Daniel. So far, however, as we have any knowledge of either from any source, there is no inconsistency between that and what is said in this chapter to have occurred. It is probable that no one ever perceived any incongruity of this kind in the book itself, nor, if this were all, should we suppose that there was any improbability in the account in this chapter.

(2.) There is properly no account of *persecution* in this narrative, nor any reason to suppose that Nebuchadnezzar designed any such thing. This is admitted by Bertholdt himself (p. 261), and is manifest on the face of the whole narrative. It is indeed stated that Nebuchadnezzar demanded, on severe penalties, a recognition of the god that he worshipped, and required that the reverence should be shown to that god which he thought to be his due. It is true, also, that the monarch intended to be obeyed in what seems to us to be a very arbitrary and unreasonable command, that they should assemble and fall down and worship the image which he had set up. But this does not imply any disposition to persecute on account of religion, or to prevent in others the free exercise of their own religious opinions, or the worship of their own gods. It is well known that it was a doctrine of all ancient idolaters, that respect might be shown to foreign gods—to the gods of other people—without in the least degree implying a want of respect for their own gods, or violating any of their obligations to them. The universal maxim was, that the gods of all nations were to be respected, and hence foreign gods might be introduced for worship, and respect paid to them without in any degree detracting from the honour which was due to their own. Nebuchadnezzar,

therefore, simply demanded that homage should be shown to the idol that *he* had erected; that the god whom *he* worshipped should be acknowledged as *a* god; and that respect should thus be shown to himself, and to the laws of his empire, by acknowledging *his* god, and rendering to that god the degree of homage which was his due. But it is nowhere intimated that he regarded his idol as the *only* true god, or that he demanded that he should be recognized as such, or that he was not willing that all other gods, in their place, should be honoured. There is no intimation, therefore, that he meant to *persecute* any other men for worshipping their own gods, nor is there any reason to suppose that he apprehended that there would be any scruples on religious grounds about acknowledging the image that he set up to be worthy of adoration and praise.

(3.) There is no reason to think that he was so well acquainted with the peculiar character of the Hebrew religion as to suppose that its votaries would have any difficulty on this subject, or would hesitate to unite with others in adoring his image. He knew, indeed, that they were worshippers of Jehovah; that they had reared a magnificent temple to his honour in Jerusalem, and that they professed to keep his laws. But there is no reason to believe that he was very intimately acquainted with the laws and institutions of the Hebrews, or that he supposed that they would have any difficulty in doing what was universally understood to be proper—to show due respect to the gods of other nations. Certainly, if he had intimately known the history of a considerable portion of the Hebrew people, and been acquainted with their proneness to fall into idolatry, he would have seen little to make him doubt that they would readily comply with a command to show respect to the gods worshipped in other lands. There is no reason, therefore, to suppose that he anticipated that the Hebrew exiles, any more than any other people, would hesitate to show to his image the homage which he required.

(4.) The whole account agrees well with the character of Nebuchadnezzar. He was an arbitrary monarch. He was accustomed to implicit obedience. He was determined in his character, and resolute in his purposes. Having once formed the resolution to erect such a magnificent image of his god—one that would correspond with the greatness of his capital, and, at the same time, show his respect for the god that he worshipped — nothing was more natural than that he should issue such a proclamation that homage should be shown to it by all his subjects, and that, in order to secure this, he should issue this decree, that whoever did *not* do it should be punished in the severest manner. There is no reason to suppose that he had any particular class of persons in his eye, or, indeed, that he anticipated that the order would be disobeyed by *any* class of persons. In fact, we see in this whole transaction just one illustration of what usually occurred under the arbitrary despotisms of the East, where, *whatever* is the order that is issued from the throne, universal and absolute submission is demanded, under the threatening of a speedy and fearful punishment. The order of Nebuchadnezzar was not more arbitrary and unreasonable than those which have been frequently issued by the Turkish sultan.

II. A second objection to the chapter is the account of the musical instruments in ver. 5. The objection is, that to some of these instruments *Grecian* names are given, and that this proves that the transaction must have a later date than is attributed to it, or that the account must have been written by one of later times. The objection is, that the whole statement seems to have been derived from the account of some Greek procession in honour of the gods of Greece. See Bleek, p. 259.

To this objection, it may be replied (*a*) that such processions in honour of the gods, or such assemblages, accompanied with musical instruments, were, and are, common among all people. They occur constantly in the East, and it cannot, with any propriety, be said that one is borrowed from another. (*b*) A large part of these instruments have undoubtedly Chaldee names given to them, and the names are such as we may suppose that one living in the times of Nebuchadnezzar would give them. See Notes on ver. 5. (*c*) As to those which are alleged to indicate a Greek origin, it may be observed, that it is quite uncertain whether the origin of the name was Greek or Chaldee. That such names *are* found given to instruments of music by the Greeks is certain ; but it is not certain whence they obtained the name. For anything that can be proved to the contrary, the name may have had an Eastern origin. It is altogether probable that many of the names of things among the Greeks had such an origin ; and if the instrument of music itself—as no one can prove it did not—came in from the East, the *name* came also from the East. (*d*) It may be further stated, that, even on the supposition that the name had its origin in Greece, there is no absolute certainty that the name and the instrument were unknown to the Chaldeans. Who can prove that some Chaldean may not have been in Greece, and may not have borne back to his own country some instrument of music that he found there different from those which he had been accustomed to at home, or that he may not have constructed an instrument resembling one which he had seen there, and given it the same name? Or who can prove that some strolling Greek musician may not have travelled as far as Babylon—for the Greeks travelled everywhere—and carried with him some instrument of music before unknown to the Chaldeans, and imparted to them at the same time the knowledge of the instrument and the name? But until this is shown the objection has no force.

III. A third objection is, that the statement in ver. 22, that the persons appointed to execute the orders of the king died from the heat of the furnace, or that the king issued an order, to execute which perilled the lives of the innocent who were intrusted with its execution, is improbable.

To this it may be said (a) that there is no evidence or affirmation that the king contemplated *their* danger, or designed to peril their lives; but it is undoubtedly a fact that he was intent on the execution of his own order, and that he little regarded the peril of those who executed it. And nothing is more probable than this; and, indeed, nothing more common. A general who orders a company of men to silence or take a battery has no malice against them, and no design on their lives; but he is intent on the accomplishment of the object, whatever may be the peril of the men, or however large a portion of them may fall. In fact, the objection which is here made to the credibility of this narrative is an objection which would lie with equal force against most of the orders issued in battle, and not a few of the commands issued by arbitrary monarchs in time of peace. The fact in this case was, the king was intent on the execution of his purpose—the punishment of the refractory and stubborn men who had resisted his commands, and there is no probability

that, in the excitements of wrath, he would pause to inquire whether the execution of his purpose would endanger the lives of those who were intrusted with the execution of the order or not. (b) There is every probability that the heat *would be* so great as to peril the lives of those who should approach it. It is said to have been made seven times hotter than usual (ver. 19); that is, as hot as it could be made, and, if this were so, it is by no means an unreasonable supposition that those who were compelled to approach it so near as to cast others in should be in danger.

IV. A fourth objection, urged by Griesinger, p. 41, as quoted by Hengstenberg, *Authentie des Daniel*, p. 92, is, that "as Nebuchadnezzar had the furnace already prepared ready to throw these men in, he must have known beforehand that they would not comply with his demand, and so must have designed to punish them; or that this representation is a mere fiction of the writer, to make the delivery of these men appear more marvellous."

To this it may be replied, (a) that there is not the slightest evidence, from the account in Daniel, that Nebuchadnezzar had the furnace prepared beforehand, as if it were expected that some would disobey, and as if he meant to show his wrath. He indeed (ver. 6) threatens this punishment, but it is clear, from ver. 19, that the furnace was not yet heated up, and that the occasion of its being heated in such a manner was the unexpected refusal of these three men to obey him. (b) But if it should be admitted that there was a furnace thus glowing—heated with a view to punish offenders—it would not be contrary to what sometimes occurs in the East under a despotism. Sir John Chardin (*Voy. en Perse.* iv. p. 276) mentions in his time (in the seventeenth century) a case similar to this.

He says that during a whole month, in a time of great scarcity, an oven was kept heated to throw in all persons who had failed to comply with the laws in regard to taxation, and had thus defrauded the government. This was, in fact, strictly in accordance with the character of Oriental despotism. We know, moreover, from Jer. xxix. 22, that this mode of punishment was not unknown in Babylon, and it would seem probable that it was not uncommon in the time of Nebuchadnezzar. Thus Jeremiah says, "And of them shall be taken up a curse by all the captivity of Judah which are in Babylon, saying, The Lord make thee like Zedekiah and like Ahab, whom the king of Babylon roasted in the fire."

V. A fifth objection is stated thus by Bertholdt : "Why did the wonders recorded in this chapter take place ? It was only for this purpose that Nebuchadnezzar might be made to appear to give praise to God, that he is represented as giving commandment that no one should reproach him. But this object is too small to justify such an array of means." To this it may be replied, (a) that it does not appear from the chapter that this was the *object* aimed at. (b) There were other designs in the narrative beside this. They were to show the firmness of the men who refused to worship an idol-god; to illustrate their conscientious adherence to their religion ; to show their confidence in the Divine protection ; to prove that God will defend those who put their trust in him, and that he can deliver them even in the midst of the flames. These things were worthy of record.

VI. It has been objected that "the expression in which Nebuchadnezzar (ver. 28) is represented as breaking out, after the rescue of the three men, is altogether contrary to his dignity, and

to the respect for the religion of his fathers and of his country, which he was bound to defend."—Bertholdt, p. 253. But to this it may be replied, (a) that if this scene actually occurred before the eyes of the king—if God had thus miraculously interposed in delivering his servants in this wonderful manner from the heated furnace, nothing would be more natural than this. It was a manifest miracle, a direct interposition of God, a deliverance of the professed friends of Jehovah by a power that was above all that was human, and an expression of surprise and admiration was in every way proper on such an occasion. (b) It accorded with all the prevailing notions of religion, and of the respect due to the gods, to say this. As above remarked, it was a principle recognized among the heathen to honour the gods of other nations, and if they had interposed to defend their own votaries, it was no more than was admitted in all the nations of idolatry. If, therefore, Jehovah had interposed to save his own friends and worshippers, every principle which Nebuchadnezzar held on the subject would make it proper for him to acknowledge the fact, and to say that honour was due to him for his interposition. In this, moreover, Nebuchadnezzar would be understood as saying nothing derogatory to the gods that he himself worshipped, or to those adored in his own land. All that is *necessary* to be supposed in what he said is, that he now felt that Jehovah, the God whom the Hebrews adored, had shown that he was worthy to be ranked among the gods, and that in common with others, he had power to protect his own friends. To this it may be added (c) that, in his way, Nebuchadnezzar everywhere showed that he was a *religious* man : that is, that he recognized the gods, and was ever ready to acknowledge their interference in human affairs, and to render them the honour which was their due. Indeed, this whole affair grew out of his respect for *religion*, and what here occurred was only in accordance with his general principle, that when any God had shown that he had power to deliver his people, he should be acknowledged, and that no words of reproach should be uttered against him, ver. 29.

VII. A more plausible objection than those which have just been noticed is urged by Lüderwald, Jahn, Dereser, in regard to the account which is given of the image which Nebuchadnezzar is said to have erected. This objection has reference to the *size* of the image, to its proportions, and to the material of which it is said to have been composed. This objection, as stated by Bertholdt (p. 256), is substantially the following :—" That the image had probably a human form, and yet that the proportions of the human figure are by no means observed—the height being represented to have been sixty cubits, and its breadth six cubits—or its height being to its breadth as ten to one, whereas the proportion of a man is only six to one ; that the amount of gold in such an image is incredible, being beyond any means which the king of Babylon could have possessed; and that probably the image here referred to was one that Herodotus says he saw in the temple of Belus at Babylon (I. 183), and which Diodorus Siculus describes (II. 9), and which was only forty feet in height." See Notes on ver. 1. In regard to this objection, we may observe, then—

(*a*) That there is no certainty that this was the same image which is referred to by Herodotus and Diodorus Siculus. That image was *in* the temple ; this was erected on the "plain of Dura." See Notes on ver. 1. But, so far as appears, this may have been erected for a temporary purpose, and the materials may then have been employed for other purposes ; that in the temple was permanent.

(*b*) As to the amount of gold in the image—it is not said or implied that it was of *solid* gold. It is well known that the images of the gods were made of wood or clay, and overlaid with gold or silver, and this is all that is necessarily implied here. See Notes on ver. 1.

(*c*) The *height* of the alleged image can be no real objection to the statement. It is not necessary to assume that it had the human form—though that is probable—but if that be admitted, there can be no objection to the supposition that, either standing by itself, or raised on a pedestal, it may have been as lofty as the statement here implies. The colossal figure at Rhodes was an hundred and five Grecian feet in height, and being made to stride the mouth of the harbour, was a work of much more difficult construction than this figure would have been.

(*d*) As to the alleged *disproportion* in the figure of the image, see Notes on ver. 1. To what is there said may be added : (1.) It is not *necessary* to suppose that it had the human form. Nothing of this kind is affirmed, though it may be regarded as probable. But if it had not, of course the objection would have no force. (2.) If it had the human form, it is by no means clear whether it had a sitting or a standing posture. Nothing is said on this point in regard to the image or statue, and until *this* is determined, nothing can be said properly respecting the proportions. (3.) It is not said whether it stood by itself, or whether it rested on a basis or pediment—and until *this* is determined, no objections can be valid as to the proportion of the statue. It is every way probable that the image was reared on a lofty pedestal, and for anything that appears, the proportions of the *image itself*, whether sitting or standing, may have been well preserved. (4.) But in addition to this it should be said, that if the account here is to be taken literally as stating that the image was ten times as high as it was broad—thus failing to observe the proper human proportions—the account would not be incredible. It is admitted by Gesenius (*Ency. von Ersch und Gruber*, art. *Babylon*, *Th.* vii. p. 24), that the Babylonians had no correct taste in these matters. "The ruins," says he, "are imposing by their colossal greatness, not by their beauty; all the ornaments are rough and barbarian." The Babylonians, indeed, possessed a taste for the colossal, the grand, the imposing, but they also had a taste for the monstrous and the prodigious, and a mere want of *proportion* is not a sufficient argument to prove that what is stated here did not occur.

VIII. But one other objection remains to be noticed. It is one which is noticed by Bertholdt (pp. 251, 252), that, if this is a true account, it is strange that *Daniel* himself is not referred to; that if he was, according to the representation in the last chapter, a high officer at court, it is unaccountable that he is not mentioned as concerned in these affairs, and especially that he did not interpose in behalf of his three friends to save them. To this objection it is sufficient to reply (a) that, as Bertholdt himself (p. 287) suggests, Daniel may have been absent from the capital at this time on some business of state, and consequently the question whether *he* would worship the image may not have been tested. It is probable, from the nature of the case, that he would be employed on such embas-

sies, or be sent to some other part of the empire from time to time, to arrange the affairs of the provinces, and no one can demonstrate that he was not absent on this occasion. Indeed, the fact that he is not mentioned at all in the transaction would serve to imply this; since, if he were at court, it is to be presumed that he himself would have been implicated as well as his three friends. Comp. ch. vi. He was not a man to shrink from duty, or to decline any proper method of showing his attachment to the religion of his fathers, or any proper interest in the welfare of his friends. But (b) it is possible that even if Daniel were at court at that time, and did not unite in the worship of the image, he might have escaped the danger. There were undoubtedly many more Jews in the province of Babylon who did not worship this image, but no formal accusation was brought against them, and their case did not come before the king. For some reason, the accusation was made specific against these three men —*for they were rulers in the province* (ch. ii. 49), and being foreigners, the people under them may have gladly seized the occasion to complain of them to the king. But so little is known of the circumstances, that it is not possible to determine the matter with certainty. All that needs to be said is, that the fact that Daniel was *not* implicated in the affair is no proof that the three persons referred to were not; that it is no evidence that what is said of *them* is not true because nothing is said of *Daniel*.

§ II.—ANALYSIS OF THE CHAPTER.

This chapter, which is complete in itself, or which embraces the entire narrative relating to an important transaction, contains the account of a magnificent brazen image erected by Nebuchadnezzar, and the result of at-

CHAPTER III.

N EBUCHADNEZZAR the
king made *a* an image of gold,
a 2 Ki. 19. 17, 18; Ps. 115. 4, &c.; Is. 40. 19, &c ;
       Je. 16. 20; Ac. 19. 26.

tempting to constrain the conscientious
Hebrews to worship it. The narrative
comprises the following points :—
   I. The erection of the great image in
the plain of Dura, ver. 1.
   II. The dedication of the image in
the presence of the great princes and
governors of the provinces, the high
officers of state, and an immense multitude of the people, accompanied with
solemn music, vers. 2–7.
   III. The complaint of certain Chaldeans respecting the Jews, that they
refused to render homage to the image,
reminding the king that he had solemnly
enjoined this on all persons, on penalty
of being cast into a burning furnace in
case of disobedience, vers. 8–12. This
charge was brought particularly against
Shadrach, Meshach, and Abed-nego.
Daniel escaped the accusation, for reasons which will be stated in the Notes
on ver. 12. The common people of
the Jews also escaped, as the command
extended particularly to the rulers.
   IV. The manner in which Nebuchadnezzar received this accusation, vers.
13–15. He was filled with rage; he
summoned the accused into his presence; he commanded them to prostrate themselves before the image on
penalty of being cast at once into the
fiery furnace.
   V. The noble answer of the accused,
vers. 16–18. They stated to the king
that his threat did not alarm them, and
that they felt no solicitude to answer
him in regard to the matter (ver. 16);
that they were assured that the God
whom they served was able to deliver
them from the furnace, and from the
wrath of the king (ver. 17); but that
even if he did not, whatever might be

whose height *was* threescore cubits,
and the breadth thereof six cubits :
he set it up in the plain of Dura,
in the province of Babylon.

the issue, they could not serve the gods
of the Chaldeans, nor worship the image
which the king had set up.
   VI. The infliction of the threatened
punishment, vers. 19–23. The furnace
was commanded to be heated seven
times hotter than usual; they were
bound and thrown in with their usual
apparel on ; and the hot blast of the
furnace destroyed the men who were
employed to perform this service.
   VII. Their protection and preservation, vers. 24–27. The astonished
monarch who had commanded *three*
men to be cast in *bound,* saw *four* men
walking in the midst of the flames
loose; and satisfied now they had a
Divine Protector, awed by the miracle,
and doubtless dreading the wrath of
the Divine Being that had become their
protector, he commanded them suddenly to come out. The princes, and
governors, and captains were gathered
together, and these men, thus remarkably preserved, appeared before them
uninjured.
   VIII. The effect on the king, vers.
28–30. As in the case when Daniel
had interpreted his dream (ch. ii.), he
acknowledged that this was the act of
the true God, ver. 28. He issued a
solemn command that the God who
had done this should be honoured, for
that no other God could deliver in this
manner, ver. 29. He again restored
them to their honourable command over
the provinces, ver. 30.

   1. *Nebuchadnezzar the king made an
image of gold.* The time when he did
this is not mentioned ; nor is it stated
in whose honour, or for what design,
this colossal image was erected. In
the Greek and Arabic translations, this

is said to have occurred in the eighteenth year of Nebuchadnezzar. This is not, however, in the original text, nor is it known on what authority it is asserted. Dean Prideaux (*Connex. I.* 222) supposes that it was at first some marginal comment on the Greek version that at last crept into the text, and that there was probably some good authority for it. If this is the correct account of the time, the event here recorded occurred B.C. 587, or, according to the chronology of Prideaux, about nineteen years after the transaction recorded in the previous chapter. Hales makes the chronology somewhat different, though not essentially. According to him, Daniel was carried to Babylon B.C. 586, and the image was set up B.C. 569, making an interval from the time that he was carried to Babylon of seventeen years ; and if the dream (ch. ii.) was explained within three or four years after Daniel was taken to Babylon, the interval between that and this occurrence would be some thirteen or fourteen years. Calmet makes the captivity of Daniel 602 years before Christ; the interpretation of the dream 598 ; and the setting up of the image 556—thus making an interval of more than forty years. It is impossible to determine the time with certainty; but allowing the shortest-mentioned period as the interval between the interpretation of the dream (ch. ii.) and the erection of this statue, the time would be sufficient to account for the fact that the impression made by that event on the mind of Nebuchadnezzar, in favour of the claims of the true God (ch. ii. 46, 47), seems to have been entirely effaced. The two chapters, in order that the right impression may be received on this point, should be read with the recollection that such an interval had elapsed. At the time when the event here recorded is supposed by Prideaux to have occurred, Nebuchadnezzar had just returned from finishing the Jewish war. From the spoils which he had taken in that expedition in Syria and Palestine, he had the means in abundance of rearing such a colossal statue ; and at the close of these conquests, nothing would be more natural than that he should wish to rear in his capital

some splendid work of art that would signalize his reign, record the memory of his conquests, and add to the magnificence of the city. The word which is here rendered *image* (Chald. צֵלֵם—Greek εἰκόνα), in the usual form in the Hebrew, means a shade, shadow ; then that which shadows forth anything ; then an image of anything, and then an *idol*, as representing the deity worshipped. It is not necessary to suppose that it was of solid gold, for the amount required for such a structure would have been immense, and probably beyond the means even of Nebuchadnezzar. The presumption is, that it was merely covered over with plates of gold, for this was the usual manner in which statues erected in honour of the gods were made. See Isa. xl. 19. It is not known in honour of whom this statue was erected. Grotius supposed that it was reared to the memory of Nabopolassar, the father of Nebuchadnezzar, and observes that it was customary to erect statues in this manner in honour of parents. Prideaux, Hales, the editor of the *Pict. Bible,* and most others, suppose that it was in honour of Bel, the principal deity worshipped in Babylon. See Notes on Isa. xlvi. 1. Some have supposed that it was in honour of Nebuchadnezzar himself, and that he purposed by it to be worshipped as a god. But this opinion has little probability in its favour. The opinion that it was in honour of Bel, the principal deity of the place, is every way the most probable, and this derives some confirmation from the well-known fact that a magnificent image of this kind was, at some period of his reign, erected by Nebuchadnezzar in honour of this god, in a style to correspond with the magnificence of the city. The account of this given by Herodotus is the following:—"The temple of Jupiter Belus, whose huge gates of brass may still be seen, is a square building, each side of which is two furlongs. In the midst rises a tower, of the solid depth and height of one furlong ; upon which, resting as upon a base, seven other lesser towers are built in regular succession. The ascent is on the outside ; which, winding from the ground, is continued to the highest tower; and in the middle of the whole structure there is a convenient resting-place. In the last tower is a large chapel, in which is placed a couch, magnificently adorned, and near it a table of solid gold; but there is no statue in the place. In this temple there is also a small chapel, lower in the building, which contains a figure of Jupiter, in a sitting posture, with a large table before him; these, with the base of the table, and the seat of the throne, are all of the purest gold, and are estimated by the Chaldeans to be worth eight hundred talents. On the outside of this chapel there are two altars; one is gold, the other is of immense size, and appropriated to the sacrifice of full-grown animals; those only which have not yet left their dams may be offered on the golden altar. On the larger altar, at the anniversary festival in honour of their god, the Chaldeans regularly consume incense to the amount of a thousand talents. There was formerly in this temple a statue of solid gold twelve cubits high; this, however, I mention from the information of the Chaldeans, and not from my own knowledge."—*Clio,* 183.

Diodorus Siculus, a much later writer, speaks to this effect: "Of the tower of Jupiter Belus, the historians who have spoken have given different descriptions; and this temple being now entirely destroyed, we cannot speak accurately respecting it. It was excessively high; constructed throughout with great care; built of brick and bitumen. Semiramis placed on the top of it three statues of massy gold, of Jupiter, Juno, and Rhea. Jupiter was erect, in the

Colossal Figures on the Plain of Thebes, near the Memnonium.
The nearer of the two is known by the name of the Vocal Memnon.

attitude of a man walking; he was forty feet in height; and weighed a thousand Babylonian talents: Rhea, who sat in a chariot of gold, was of the same weight. Juno, who stood upright, weighed eight hundred talents."—B. ii.

The temple of Bel or Belus, in Babylon, stood until the time of Xerxes ; but on his return from the Grecian expedition, he demolished the whole of it, and laid it in rubbish, having first plundered it of its immense riches. Among the spoils which he took from the temple, are mentioned several images and statues of massive gold, and among them the one mentioned by Diodorus Siculus, as being forty feet high. See Strabo, lib. 16, p. 738; Herodotus, lib. 1; Arrian de Expe. Alex. lib. 7, quoted by Prideaux I. 240. It is not very probable that the image which Xerxes removed was the same which Nebuchadnezzar reared in the plain of Dura— comp. the Intro. to this chapter, § I. VII. (a) ; but the fact that such a colossal statue was found in Babylon may be adduced as one incidental corroboration of the probability of the statement here. It is not impossible that Nebuchadnezzar was led, as the editor of Calmet's Dictionary has remarked (Taylor, vol. iii. p. 194), to the construction of this image by what he had seen in Egypt. He had conquered and ravaged Egypt but a few years before this, and had doubtless been struck with the wonders of art which he had seen there. Colossal statues in honour of the gods abounded, and nothing would be more natural than that Nebuchadnezzar should wish to make his capital rival everything which he had seen in Thebes. Nor is it improbable that, while he sought to make his image more magnificent and costly than even those in Egypt were, the views of sculpture would be about the same, and the figure of the statue might be borrowed from what had been seen in Egypt. An illustration of the subject before us is furnished by the preceding engraving, from a photograph, of the two celebrated colossal figures of Amunoph III. standing in the plains of Goorneh, Thebes, one of which is known as the Vocal Memnon. These colossi, exclusive of the pedestals (partially buried), are forty-seven feet high, and eighteen feet three inches wide across the shoulders, and according to Wilkinson are each of one single block, and contain about 11,500 cubic feet of stone. They are made of a

stone not known within several days' journey of the place where they are erected. Calmet refers to these statues, quoting from Norden. ¶ Whose height was threescore cubits. Prideaux and others have been greatly perplexed at the proportions of the image here represented. Prideaux says on the subject (Connex. I. 240, 241), "Nebuchadnezzar's golden image is said indeed in Scripture to have been sixty cubits, that is, ninety feet high ; but this must be understood of the image and pedestal both together ; for that image being said to be but six cubits broad or thick, it is impossible that the image would have been sixty cubits high; for that makes its height to be ten times its breadth or thickness, which exceeds all the proportions of a man, no man's height being above six times his thickness, measuring the slenderest man living at the waist. But where the breadth of this image was measured is not said ; perchance it was from shoulder to shoulder; and then the proportion of six cubits breadth will bring down the height exactly to the measure which Diodorus has mentioned ; for the usual height of a man being four and a half of his breadth between the shoulders, if the image were six cubits broad between the shoulders, it must, according to this proportion, have been twenty-seven cubits high, which is forty and a half feet." The statue itself, therefore, according to Prideaux, was forty feet high; the pedestal fifty feet. But this, says Taylor, the editor of Calmet, is a disproportion of parts which, if not absolutely impossible, is utterly contradictory to every principle of art, even of the rudest sort. To meet the difficulty, Taylor himself supposes that the height referred to in the description was rather proportional than actual height ; that is, if it had stood upright it would have been sixty cubits, though the actual elevation in a sitting posture may have been but little more than thirty cubits, or fifty feet. The breadth, he supposes, was rather the depth or thickness measured from the breast to the back, than the breadth measured from shoulder to shoulder. His argument and illustration may be seen in Calmet, vol. iii. Frag. 156. It is not absolutely

2 Then Nebuchadnezzar the king sent to gather together the princes, the governors, and the captains, the judges, the treasurers, the counsel-

certain, however, that the image was in a sitting posture, and the *natural* construction of the passage is, that the statue was actually sixty cubits in height. No one can doubt that an image of that height could be erected; and when we remember the one at Rhodes, which was 105 Grecian feet in height (see art. "Colossus," in Anthon's *Class. Dict.*), and the desire of Nebuchadnezzar to adorn his capital in the most magnificent manner, it is not to be regarded as improbable that an image of this height was erected. What was the height of the pedestal, if it stood on any, as it probably did, it is impossible now to tell. The length of the *cubit* was not the same in every place. The length originally was the distance between the elbow and the extremity of the middle finger, about eighteen inches. The Hebrew cubit, according to Bishop Cumberland and M. Pelletier, was twenty-one inches; but others fix it at eighteen. — Calmet. The Talmudists say that the Hebrew cubit was larger by one quarter than the Roman. Herodotus says that the cubit in Babylon was three fingers longer than the usual one. — Clio, 178. Still, there is not absolute certainty on that subject. The usual and probable measurement of the cubit would make the image in Babylon about ninety feet high. ¶ And *the breadth thereof six cubits.* About nine feet. This would, of course, make the height ten times the breadth, which Prideaux says is entirely contrary to the usual proportions of a man. It is not known on what *part* of the image this measurement was made, or whether it was the thickness from the breast to the back, or the width from shoulder to shoulder. If the *thickness* of the image here is referred to by the word *"breadth,"* the proportion would be well preserved. "The thickness of a well-proportioned man," says Scheuchzer (*Knupfer Bibel, in loc.*), "measured from the breast to the back is one-tenth of his height." This was understood to be the proportion by Augustine, *Civi. Dei*, l. xv. c. 26. The word which is here rendered *breadth* (רְחַב) occurs nowhere else in

the Chaldean of the Scriptures, except in Ezra vi. 3: "Let the house be builded, the height thereof threescore cubits, and the *breadth* thereof threescore cubits." Perhaps this refers rather to the *depth* of the temple from front to rear, as Taylor has remarked, than to the breadth from one side to another. If it does, it would correspond with the measurement of Solomon's temple, and it is not probable that Cyrus would vary from that plan in his instructions to build a new temple. If that be the true construction, then the meaning here may be, as remarked above, that the image was of that *thickness*, and the breadth from shoulder to shoulder may not be referred to. ¶ *He set it up in the plain of Dura.* It would seem from this that it was set up in an open plain, and not in a temple; perhaps not near a temple. It was not unusual to erect images in this manner, as the colossal figure at Rhodes shows. Where this plain was, it is of course impossible now to determine. The Greek translation of the word is Δεειρᾷ —*Deeira.* Jerome says that the translation of Theodotion is *Deira;* of Symmachus, *Doraum;* and of the LXX. περίβολον—which he says may be rendered *vivarium* vel *conclusum locum.* "Interpreters commonly," says Gesenius, " compare Dura, a city mentioned by Ammian. Marcel. 25. 6, situated on the Tigris ; and another of like name in Polyb. 5, 48, on the Euphrates, near the mouth of the Chaboras." It is not necessary to suppose that this was in the *city* of Babylon ; and, indeed, it is probable that it was not, as the "province of Babylon" doubtless embraced more than the city, and an extensive plain seems to have been selected, perhaps near the city, as a place where the monument would be more conspicuous, and where larger numbers could convene for the homage which was proposed to be shown to it. ¶ *In the province of Babylon.* One of the provinces, or departments, embracing the capital, into which the empire was divided, ch. ii. 48.

2. *Then Nebuchadnezzar the king sent to gather together the princes.* It is difficult now, if not impossible, to

lors, the sheriffs, and all the rulers of the provinces, to come to the dedication of the image which Nebuchadnezzar the king had set up.

determine the exact meaning of the words used here with reference to the various officers designated; and it is not material that it should be done. The general sense is, that he assembled the great officers of the realm to do honour to the image. The object was doubtless to make the occasion as magnificent as possible. Of course, if these high officers were assembled, an immense multitude of the people would congregate also. That this was contemplated, and that it in fact occurred, is apparent from verses 4, 7. The word rendered *princes* (אֲחַשְׁדַּרְפְּנַיָּא) occurs only in Daniel, in Ezra, and in Esther. In Dan. iii. 2, 3, 27, vi. 1-4, 6, 7, it is uniformly rendered *princes;* in Ezra viii. 36, Esther iii. 12, viii. 9, ix. 3, it is uniformly rendered *lieutenants*. The word means, according to Gesenius (*Lex.*), "satraps, the governors or viceroys of the large provinces among the ancient Persians, possessing both civil and military power, and being in the provinces the representatives of the sovereign, whose state and splendour they also rivalled." The etymology of the word is not certainly known. The Persian word *satrap* seems to have been the foundation of this word, with some slight modifications adapting it to the Chaldee mode of pronunciation. ¶ *The governors.* סִגְנַיָּא. This word is rendered *governors* in ch. ii. 48 (see Notes on that place), and in chap. iii. 3, 27; vi. 7. It does not elsewhere occur. The Hebrew word corresponding to this —סְגָנִים—occurs frequently, and is rendered *rulers* in every place except Isa. xli. 25, where it is rendered *princes ·* Ezra ix. 2; Neh. ii. 16; iv. 14 (7); v. 7, 17; vii. 5; Jer. li. 23, 28, 57; Ezek. xxiii. 6, 12, 23, *et al.* The office was evidently one that was inferior to that of the *satrap*, or governor of a whole province. ¶ *And the captains.* פַּחֲוָתָא. This word, wherever it occurs in Daniel, is rendered *captains*, ch. iii. 2, 3, 27; vi. 7; wherever else it occurs it is rendered *governor*, Ezra v. 3, 6, 14; vi. 6, 7, 13. The Hebrew word corres-

ponding to this (פֶּחָה) occurs frequently, and is also rendered indifferently, *governor* or *captain:* 1 Kings x. 15; 2 Chron. ix. 14; Ezra viii. 36; 1 Kings xx. 24; Jer. li. 23, 28, 57, *et al.* It refers to the governor of a province less than a satrapy, and is applied to officers in the Assyrian empire, 2 Kings xviii. 24; Isa. xxxvi. 9; in the Chaldean, Ezek. xxiii. 6, 23; Jer. li. 23; and in the Persian, Esth. viii. 9; ix. 3. The word *captains* does not now very accurately express the sense. The office was not exclusively military, and was of a higher grade than would be denoted by the word *captain* with us. ¶ *The judges.* אֲדַרְגָּזְרַיָּא. This word occurs only here, and in ver. 3. It means properly *great* or *chief judges*—compounded of two words signifying *greatness*, and *judges*. See Gesenius, (*Lex.*) ¶ *The treasurers.* גְּדָבְרַיָּא. This word occurs nowhere else. The word גִּזְבָּר *Gisbâr*, however, the same word with a slight change in the pronunciation, occurs in Ezra i. 8, vii. 21, and denotes *treasurer*. It is derived from a word (גָּנַז) which means to hide, to hoard, to lay up in store. ¶ *The counsellors.* דְּתָבְרַיָּא. This word occurs nowhere else, except in ver. 3. It means one skilled in the law; a judge. The office was evidently inferior to the one denoted by the word *judges*. ¶ *The sheriffs.* A sheriff with us is a county officer, to whom is intrusted the administration of the laws. In England the office is judicial as well as ministerial. With us it is merely ministerial. The duty of the sheriff is to execute the civil and criminal processes throughout the county. He has charge of the jail and prisoners, and attends courts, and keeps the peace. It is not to be supposed that the officer here referred to in Daniel corresponds precisely with this. The word used (תִּפְתָּיֵא) occurs nowhere else. It means, according to Gesenius, persons learned in the law; lawyers. The office had a close relation to that of *Mufti* among the Arabs, the term being derived from the same word, and properly means "a

3 Then the princes, the governors, and captains, the judges, the treasurers, the counsellors, the sheriffs, and all the rulers of the provinces, were gathered together unto the dedication of the image that Nebuchadnezzar the king had set up:

1 *with might,* ch. 4. 14.   2 *they command.*

and they stood before the image that Nebuchadnezzar had set up.

4 Then an herald cried ¹aloud, To you ²it is commanded, O ªpeople, nations, and languages.

5 *That* at what time ye hear the sound of the cornet, flute, harp,

a ch. 4. 1; 6. 25.

wise man; one whose response is equivalent to law." ¶ *And all the rulers of the provinces.* The term here used is a general term, and would apply to any kind of officers or rulers, and is probably designed to embrace all which had not been specified. The object was to assemble the chief officers of the realm. Jacchiades has compared the officers here enumerated with the principal officers of the Turkish empire, and supposes that a counterpart to them may be found in that empire. See the comparison in Grotius, *in loc.* He supposes that the officers last denoted under the title of "rulers of the provinces" were similar to the Turkish *Zangiahos* or *viziers.* Grotius supposes that the term refers to the rulers of cities and places adjacent to cities—a dominion of less extent and importance than that of the rulers of provinces. ¶ *To come to the dedication of the image,* &c. The public setting it apart to the purposes for which it was erected. This was to be done with solemn music, and in the presence of the principal officers of the kingdom. Until it was dedicated to the god in whose honour it was erected, it would not be regarded as an object of worship. It is easy to conceive that such an occasion would bring together an immense concourse of people, and that it would be one of peculiar magnificence.

3. *And they stood before the image.* In the presence of the image. They were drawn up, doubtless, so as at the same time to have the best view of the statue, and to make the most imposing appearance.

4. *Then an herald cried aloud.* Marg., as in Chald., *with might.* He made a loud proclamation. A *herald* here means a public crier. ¶ *To you it is commanded.* Margin, *they commanded.* Literally, "to you command-

ing" (plural); that is, the king has commanded. ¶ *O people, nations, and languages.* The empire of Babylon was made up of different nations, speaking quite different languages. The representatives of these nations were assembled on this occasion, and the command would extend to all. There was evidently no exception made in favour of the scruples of any, and the order would include the Hebrews as well as others. It should be observed, however, that no others *but* the Hebrews would have any scruples on the subject. They were all accustomed to worship idols, and the worship of one god did not prevent their doing homage also to another. It accorded with the prevailing views of idolaters that there were many gods; that there were tutelary divinities presiding over particular people; and that it was not improper to render homage to the god of any people or country. Though, therefore, they might themselves worship other gods in their own countries, they would have no scruples about worshipping also the one that Nebuchadnezzar had set up. In this respect the Jews were an exception. They acknowledged but one God; they believed that all others were false gods, and it was a violation of the fundamental principles of their religion to render homage to any other.

5. That *at what time ye hear the sound of the cornet.* It would not be practicable to determine with precision what kind of instruments of music are denoted by the words used in this verse. They were, doubtless, in many respects different from those which are in use now, though they may have belonged to the same general class, and may have been constructed on substantially the same principles. A full inquiry into the kinds of musical instruments in use

sackbut, psaltery, ¹ dulcimer, and all kinds of music, ye fall down and

¹ *symphony, or, singing.*

among the Hebrews may be found in the various treatises on the subject in Ugolin's *Thesau. Ant. Sacra.* tom. xxxii. Comp. also the Notes on Isa. v. 12. The Chaldee word rendered *cornet*—קַרְנָא—the same as the Hebrew word קֶרֶן *keren*—means a *horn*, as *e.g.*, of an ox, stag, ram. Then it means a wind instrument of music resembling a horn, or perhaps horns were at first literally used. Similar instruments are now used, as the *French horn*, &c. ¶ *Flute.* מַשְׁרוֹקִיתָא *mashrokitha.* Gr., σύριγγός. Vulg., *fistula, pipe.* The Chaldee words occurs nowhere else but in this chapter, ver. 5, 7, 10, 15, and is in each instance rendered *flute.* It probably denoted all the instruments of the pipe or flute class in use among the Babylonians. The corresponding Hebrew word is חָלִיל *hhâlil.* See this explained in the Notes on Isa. v. 12. The following remarks of the Editor of the *Pictorial Bible* will explain the

worship the golden image that Nebuchadnezzar the king hath set up:

usual construction of the ancient pipes or flutes: "The ancient flutes were cylindrical tubes, sometimes of equal diameter throughout, but often wider at the off than the near end, and sometimes widened at that end into a funnel shape, resembling a clarionet. They were always blown, like pipes, at one end, never transversely; they had mouthpieces, and sometimes plugs or stopples, but no keys to open or close the holes beyond the reach of the hands. The holes varied in number in the different varieties of the flute. In their origin they were doubtless made of simple reeds or canes, but in the progress of improvement they came to be made of wood, ivory, bone, and even metal. They were sometimes made in joints, but connected by an interior nozzle which was generally of wood. The flutes were sometimes double, that is, a person played on two instruments at once, either connected or detached; and among the classical ancients the

Sacred Musicians.—Instruments of Music.

player on the double-flute often had a leathern bandage over his mouth to prevent the escape of his breath at the corners. The ancient Egyptians used

the double-flute." Illustrations of the flute or pipe may be seen in the Notes on Isa. v. 12. Very full and interesting descriptions of the musical instruments which were used among the Egyptians may be found in Wilkinson's *Manners and Customs of the Ancient Egyptians*, vol. ii. pp. 222-327. The preceding engraving will furnish an illustration of the usual form of this instrument among the ancients. ¶ *Harp*. On the form of the harp, see Notes on Isa. v. 12. Comp. Wilkinson, as above quoted. The harp was one of the earliest instruments of music that was invented, Gen. iv. 21. The Chaldee word here used is not the common Hebrew word to denote the harp (כִּנּוֹר *kinnor*), but is a word which does not occur in Hebrew—קִיתָרוֹס *kathros*. This occurs nowhere else in the Chaldee, and it is manifestly the same as the Greek κιθάρα, and the Latin *cithara*, denoting a harp. Whether the Chaldees derived it from the Greeks, or the Greeks from the Chaldees, however, cannot be determined with certainty. It has been made an objection to the genuineness of the book of Daniel, that the instruments here referred to were instruments bearing Greek names. See Intro. to ch. § II. IV. (c) (5). ¶ *Sackbut*. Vulg., *Sambuca*. Gr., like the Vulg., σαμβύκη. These words are merely different forms of writing the Chaldee word סַבְּכָא *sabbecha*. The word occurs nowhere else except in this chapter. It seems to have been denoted a stringed instrument similar to the lyre or harp. Strabo affirms that the Greek word σαμβύκη, *sambykē*, is of barbarian, that is, of Oriental origin. The Hebrew word from which this word is not improperly derived—סָבַךְ *sabach*—means, to interweave, to entwine, to plait, as *e.g.*, branches; and it is possible that this instrument may have derived its name from the *intertwining* of the strings. Comp. Gesenius on the word. Passow defines the Greek word σαμβύκη, *sambuca* (*Lat.*), to mean a triangular-stringed instrument that made the highest notes, or had the highest key; but as an instrument which, on account of the shortness of the strings, was not esteemed as very valuable, and had little power. Porphyry and Suidas describe it as a triangular instrument, furnished with cords of unequal length and thickness.

The classical writers mention it as very ancient, and ascribe its invention to the Syrians. Musonius describes it as having a sharp sound; and we are also told that it was often used to accompany the voice in singing Iambic verses. *Pict. Bib.* It seems to have been a species of triangular lyre or harp. ¶ *Psaltery*. The Chaldee is פְּסַנְתֵּרִין *pěsantērin*. Gr., ψαλτήριον; Vulg., *psalterium*. All these words manifestly have the same origin, and it hat been on the ground that this word, among others, is of Greek origin, that the genuineness of this book has been called ed in question. The word occurs nowhere else but in this chapter, vers. 5, 7, 10, 15. The Greek translators often use the word ψαλτήριον, *psaltery*, for נֶבֶל *nēbhěl*, and כִּנּוֹר *kinnor;* and the instrument here referred to was doubtless of the harp kind. For the kind of instrument denoted by the נֶבֶל *nēbhěl*, see Notes on Isa. v. 12. Comp. the illustrations in the *Pict. Bible* on Psa. xcii. 3. It has been alleged that this word is of Greek origin, and hence an objection has been urged against the genuineness of the book of Daniel on the presumption that, at the early period when this book is supposed to have been written, Greek musical instruments had not been introduced into Chaldea. For a general reply to this, see the Intro. § I. II. (d). It may be remarked further, in regard to this objection, (1.) that it is not absolutely certain that the word is derived from the Greek. See Pareau, l. c. p. 424, as quoted in Hengstenberg, *Authentie des Daniel*, p. 16. (2.) It cannot be demonstrated that there were no Greeks in the regions of Chaldea as early as this. Indeed, it is more than probable that there were. See Hengstenberg, p. 16, *seq.* Nebuchadnezzar summoned to this celebration the principal personages throughout the realm, and it is probable that there would be collected on such an occasion all the forms of music that were known, whether of domestic or foreign origin. ¶ *Dulcimer*. סוּמְפֹּנְיָה *sumponya*. This word occurs only here, and in vers. 10 and 15 of this chapter. In the margin it is rendered *symphony* or *singing*. It is the same as the Greek word συμφωνία, *symphony*, and in Italy the same instrument of music is now called by a name of the same origin, *zampogna*, and in Asia Minor *zambonja*. It answered probably to the Hebrew עֻגָב, rendered *organ*, in Gen. iv. 21; Job xxi. 12; xxx. 31; Ps. cl. 4. See Notes on Job xxi. 12. Comp. the tracts on Hebrew musical instruments inscribed *schilte haggibborim* in Ugolin, *Thesau.* vol. xxxii. The word seems to have had a Greek origin, and is one of those on which an objection has been founded against the genuineness of the book. Comp. the Intro. § I. II. (c). The word *dulcimer* means *sweet*, and would denote some instrument of music that was characterized by the sweetness of its tones. Johnson (*Dict.*) describes the instrument as one that is "played by striking brass wires with little sticks." The Greek word would denote properly a concert or harmony of many instruments; but the word here is evidently used to denote a single instrument. Gesenius describes it as a double pipe with a sack; a bagpipe. Servius (on Virg. *Æn.* xi. 27) describes the *symphonia* as a bagpipe: and the Hebrew writers speak of it as a bagpipe consisting of two pipes thrust through a leathern bag, and affording a mournful sound. It may be added, that this is the same name which the bagpipe bore among the Moors in Spain; and all these circumstances concur to show that this was probably the instrument intended here. "The modern Oriental bagpipe is composed of a goatskin, usually with the hair on, and in the natural form, but deprived of the head, the tail, and the feet; being thus of the same shape as that used by the water-carriers. The pipes are usually of reeds, terminating in the tips of cows' horns slightly curved; the whole instrument being most primitively simple in its materials and construction."— *Pict. Bible.* ¶ *And all kinds of music.* All other kinds. It is not probable that all the instruments employed on that occasion were actually enumerated. Only the principal instruments are mentioned, and among them those which showed that such as were of foreign origin were employed on the occasion. From the

following extract from Chardin, it will be seen that the account here is not an improbable one, and that such things were not uncommon in the East:—"At the coronation of Soliman, king of Persia, the general of the musqueteers having whispered some moments in the king's ear, among several other things of lesser importance gave out, that both the loud and soft music should play in the two balconies upon the top of the great building which stands at one end of the palace royal, called *kaisarie*, or palace imperial. No nation was dispensed with, whether Persians, Indians, Turks, Muscovites, Europeans, or others; which was immediately done. And this same *tintamarre*, or confusion of instruments, which sounded more like the noise of war than music, lasted twenty days together, without intermission, or the interruption of night; which number of twenty days was observed to answer to the number of the young monarch's years, who was then twenty years of age," p. 51; quoted in Taylor's *Fragments to Calmet's Dict.* No. 485. It may be observed, also, that in such an assemblage of instruments, nothing would be more probable than that there would be some having names of foreign origin, perhaps names whose origin was to be found in nations not represented there. But if this should occur, it would not be proper to set the fact down as an argument against the authenticity of the history of Sir John Chardin, and as little should the similar fact revealed here be regarded as an argument against the genuineness of the book of Daniel.

[The annexed illustration is a copy of part of the bass-reliefs discovered by Layard at Kouyunjik, and which, in their entire series, represent the triumphal procession of an Assyrian king, returning from conquest with spoils and captives, and accompanied by all the pomp and circumstance of Eastern ceremony. The portion here shown has an especial value in its relation to the Scriptural text, giving, as it does, the form of the harp and other instruments of music from veritable relics, coeval with Biblical events. "We find," says Layard, "from various passages in the Scriptures, that the instruments of music chiefly used on triumphal occasions were the harp, one with ten strings (rendered

viol or lyre in some versions, but probably a kind of dulcimer, the tabor, and the pipe, precisely those represented in the bass-reliefs. First came five men; three carried harps of many strings, which they struck with both hands, dancing at the same time to the measure; a fourth played on the double pipes, such as are seen on the monuments of Egypt, and were used by the Greeks and Romans. They were blown at the end, like the flutes of the modern Yezidis, which they probably resembled in tone and form. The fifth musician carried an instrument not unlike the modern *santour* of the East, consisting of a number of strings stretched over a hollow case or sounding-board. The strings, pressed with the left hand to produce the notes, were struck with a small wand or hammer held in the right. The men were followed by six female musicians, four playing on harps, one on the double pipes, and the sixth on a kind of drum, beaten with both hands, resembling the *tubbul* still used by Eastern dancing-girls. The musicians were accompanied by six women, and nine boys and girls of different ages, singing and clapping their hands to the measure. Some wore their hair in long ringlets, some platted or braided, and others confined in a net. One held her hands to her throat, as the Arab and Persian women still do when they make those shrill and vibrating sounds peculiar to the vocal music of the East." He adds, "it is scarcely possible to determine what these instruments (those named in Daniel) really

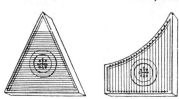

Ancient Musical Instruments.

were: they probably resembled those represented in the bass-reliefs." The sackbut, from its Hebrew name, *Sabca*, has been thought of similar form and character with the Greek *Sambuka*, a triangular instrument, with strings of unequal length and thickness, and which emitted shrill sounds.]

¶ *Ye shall fall down and worship.* That is, you shall render *religious homage.* See these words explained in the Notes on ch. ii. 46. This shows, that whether this image was erected in honour of Belus, or of Nabopolassar, it was designed that he in whose honour

6 And whoso *a*falleth not down and worshippeth, shall the same

a Rev. 13. 15.

hour be cast into the midst of a burning fiery *b* furnace.

b Jer. 29. 22.

it was erected should be worshipped as a god.

6. *And whoso falleth not down and worshippeth*. The order in this verse seems to be tyrannical, and it is contrary to all our notions of freedom of religious opinion and worship. But it was much in the spirit of that age, and indeed of almost every age. It was an act to enforce uniformity in religion by the authority of the civil magistrate, and to secure it by threatened penalties. It should be observed, however, that the command at that time would not be regarded as harsh and oppressive by *heathen* worshippers, and might be complied with consistently with their views, without infringing on their notions of religious liberty. The homage rendered to one god did not, according to their views, conflict with any honour that was due to another, and though they were required to worship this divinity, that would not be a prohibition against worshipping any other. It was also in accordance with all the views of heathenism that all proper honour should be rendered to the particular god or gods which any people adored. The nations assembled here would regard it as no dishonour shown to the particular deity whom they worshipped to render homage to the god worshipped by Nebuchadnezzar, as this command implied no prohibition against worshipping any other god. It was only in respect to those who held that there is but one God, and that all homage rendered to any other is morally wrong, that this command would be oppressive. Accordingly, the contemplated vengeance fell only on the Jews—all, of every other nation, who were assembled, complying with the command without hesitation. It violated *no* principle which they held to render the homage which was claimed, for though they had their own tutelary gods whom they worshipped, they supposed the same was true of every other people, and that *their* gods were equally entitled to respect; but it violated *every* principle on which the Jew acted—

for he believed that there was but one God ruling over all nations, and that homage rendered to any other was morally wrong. Comp. Hengstenberg, *Authentie des Daniel*, pp. 83, 84. ¶ *Shall the same hour*. This accords with the general character of an Oriental despot accustomed to enjoin implicit obedience by the most summary process, and it is entirely conformable to the whole character of Nebuchadnezzar. It would seem from this, that there was an apprehension that some among the multitudes assembled would refuse to obey the command. Whether there was any *design* to make this bear hard on the Jews, it is impossible now to determine. The word which is here rendered *hour* (שָׁעֲתָא) is probably from שְׁעָה—*to look;* and properly denotes a look, a glance of the eye, and then the *time* of such a glance—a moment, an instant. It does not refer to *an hour*, as understood by us, but means *instantly, immediately*—as quick as the glance of an eye. The word is not found in Hebrew, and occurs in Chaldee only in Dan. iii. 6, 15 ; iv. (16, 30), 19, 33 ; v. 5, in each case rendered *hour*. Nothing can be inferred from it, however, in regard to the division of time among the Chaldeans into *hours*—though Herodotus says that the Greeks received the division of the day into twelve parts from them.—Lib. ii., c. 109. ¶ *Be cast into the midst of a burning fiery furnace*. The word here rendered *furnace* (אַתּוּן *attun*) is derived from תְּנַן *tenan, to smoke;* and may be applied to any species of furnace, or large oven. It does not denote the use to which the furnace was commonly applied, or the form of its construction. Any furnace for burning lime—if lime was then burned—or for burning bricks, if they were burned, or for smelting ore, would correspond with the meaning of the word. Nor is it said whether the furnace referred to would be one that would be constructed for the occasion, or one in common use for some other purpose. The editor of Calmet (Taylor) supposes

7 Therefore at that time, when all the people heard the sound of the cornet, flute, harp, sackbut, psaltery, and all kinds of music, all the people, the nations, and the languages, fell down *and* worshipped the golden image that Nebuchadnezzar the king had set up.

8 ¶ Wherefore at that time cer-

tain Chaldeans came near, and accused the Jews.

9 They spake and said to the king Nebuchadnezzar, O king, live for *a* ever.

10 Thou, O king, hast made a decree, that every man that shall hear the sound of the cornet, flute,

<hr>

a ch. 2. 4; 6. 21; Rom. 13. 7.

<hr>

that the "furnace" here referred to was rather a fire kindled in the open court of a temple, like a place set apart for burning martyrs, than a closed furnace of brick. See Cal. *Dict.* vol. iv. p. 330, *seq.* The more obvious representation, however, is, that it was a closed place, in which the intensity of the fire could be greatly increased. Such a mode of punishment is not uncommon in the East. Chardin (vi. p. 118), after speaking of the common modes of inflicting the punishment of death in Persia, remarks that "there are other modes of inflicting the punishment of death on those who have violated the police laws, especially those who have contributed to produce scarcity of food, or who have used false weights, or who have disregarded the laws respecting taxes. The cooks," says he, "were fixed on spits, and roasted over a gentle fire (comp. Jer. xxix. 22), and the bakers were cast into a burning oven. In the year 1668, when the famine was raging, I saw in the royal residence in Ispahan one of these ovens burning to terrify the bakers, and to prevent their taking advantage of the scarcity to increase their gains." See Rosenmüller, *Alte u. neue Morgenland, in loc.*

7. *All the people, the nations, and the languages fell down,* &c. All excepting the Jews. An express exception is made in regard to them in the following verses, and it does not appear that any of them were present on this occasion. It would seem that only the *officers* had been summoned to be present, and it is not improbable that all the rest of the Jewish nation absented themselves.

8. *Wherefore at that time certain Chaldeans came near, and accused the Jews.* It does not appear that they accused the Jews in general, but par-

ticularly Shadrach, Meshach, and Abednego, ver. 12. They were present on the occasion, being summoned with the other officers of the realm (ver. 2), but they could not unite in the idolatrous worship. It has been frequently said that the whole thing was arranged, either by the king of his own accord, or by the instigation of their enemies, with a view to involve the Jews in difficulty, knowing that they could not conscientiously comply with the command to worship the image. But nothing of this kind appears in the narrative itself. It does not appear that the Jews were unpopular, or that there was any less disposition to show favour to them than to any other foreigners. They had been raised indeed to high offices, but there is no evidence that any office was conferred on them which it was not regarded as proper to confer on foreigners ; nor is there any evidence that in the discharge of the duties of the office they had given occasion for a just accusation. The plain account is, that the king set up the image for other purposes, and with no malicious design towards them ; that when summoned to be present with the other officers of the realm at the dedication of the image they obeyed the command ; but that when the order was issued that they should render *religious homage* to the idol, every principle of their religion revolted at it, and they refused. For the probable reasons why Daniel was not included in the number, see Note on ver. 12.

9. *O king, live for ever.* A customary form of address to a monarch, implying that long life was regarded as an eminent blessing. See Notes on ch. ii. 4.

10, 11. *Thou, O king, hast made a decree,* &c. See vers. 4, 5. As the

harp, sackbut, psaltery, and dulcimer, and all kinds of music, shall
fall down and worship the golden
image:

11 And whoso falleth not down
and worshippeth, *that* he should be
cast into the midst of a burning
fiery furnace.

12 There are certain Jews, whom
thou hast set *a* over the affairs of

a ch. 2. 49.

the province of Babylon, Shadrach,
Meshach, and Abed-nego; these
men, O king, have ¹not regarded *b*
thee; they serve not thy gods, nor
worship the golden image which
thou hast set up.

13 ¶ Then Nebuchadnezzar, in
his c rage and fury, commanded to
bring Shadrach, Meshach, and

1 *set no regard upon.*   *b* ch. 6. 13.
          c ver. 19.

decree included "every man" who
heard the sound of the music, it of
course embraced the Jews, whatever
religious scruples they might have.
Whether their scruples, however, were
known at the time is not certain; or
whether they would have been regarded
if known, is no more certain.

12. *There are certain Jews whom
thou hast set over the affairs of the province of Babylon, Shadrach, Meshach,
and Abed-nego.* Ch. ii. 49. It is quite
remarkable that the name of Daniel
does not occur in the record of this
transaction, and that he does not appear to have been involved in the difficulty. *Why* he was not cannot now
be certainly known. We may be sure
that he would not join in the worship
of the idol, and yet it would seem, as
Nebuchadnezzar had summoned all the
high officers of the realm to be present (ver. 2), that he must have been
summoned also. The conjecture of
Prideaux (*Con.* I. 222) is not improbable, that he occupied a place of so
much influence and authority, and enjoyed in so high degree the favour of
the king, that they did not think it
prudent to begin with him, but rather
preferred at first to bring the accusation
against subordinate officers. If *they*
were condemned and punished, consistency might require that he should be
punished also. If he had been involved
at first in the accusation, his high rank,
and his favour with the king, might
have screened them all from punishment. It is possible, however, that
Daniel was absent on the occasion of
the dedication of the image. It should
be remembered that perhaps some eighteen years had elapsed since the transaction referred to in ch. ii. occurred

(see Notes on ch. iii. 1), and Daniel
may have been employed in some remote part of the empire on public business. Comp. Intro. to the chapter, §
I. VIII. ¶ *These men, O king, have
not regarded thee.* Marg., *set no regard upon.* Literally, "they have not
placed towards thee the decree;" that
is, they have not made any account of
it; they have paid no attention to it.
¶ *They serve not thy gods.* Perhaps it
was inferred from the fact that they
would not pay religious homage to *this*
idol, that they did not serve the gods
at all that were acknowledged by the
king; or possibly this may have been
known from what had occurred before.
It may have been well understood in
Babylon, that the Hebrews worshipped
Jehovah only. Now, however, a case
had occurred which was a *test* case,
whether they would on any account
render homage to the idols that were
worshipped in Babylon. In their refusal to worship the idol, it seemed
much to aggravate the offence, and
made the charge much more serious,
that they did not acknowledge *any* of
the gods that were worshipped in Babylon. It was easy, therefore, to persuade the king that they had arrayed
themselves against the fundamental
laws of the realm.

13. *Then Nebuchadnezzar, in* his *rage
and fury.* The word rendered *fury*
means *wrath.* Everything that we
learn of this monarch shows that he
was a man of violent passions, and that
he was easily excited, though he was
susceptible also of deep impressions
on religious subjects. There was much
here to rouse his rage. His command
to worship the image was positive. It
extended to all who were summoned to

Abed-nego. Then they brought these men before the king.

14 Nebuchadnezzar spake, and said unto them, *Is it* [1] true, O Shadrach, Meshach, and Abed-nego, do

[1] or, *of purpose,* as Ex. 21. 13.

its dedication. Their refusal was an act of positive disobedience, and it seemed necessary that the laws should be vindicated. As a man and a monarch, therefore, it was not unnatural that the anger of the sovereign should be thus enkindled. ¶ *Commanded to bring Shadrach,* &c. It is remarkable that he did not order them at once to be slain, as he did the magicians who could not interpret his dream, ch. ii. 12. This shows that he had some respect still for these men, and that he was willing to hear what they could say in their defence. It is proper, also, to recognize the providence of God in inclining him to this course, that their noble reply to his question might be put on record, and that the full power of religious principle might be developed.

14. *Nebuchadnezzar spake and said unto them, Is it true.* Marg., "*of purpose;*" that is, have you done this intentionally? Wintle renders this, "Is it insultingly?" Jacchiades says that the word is used to denote admiration or wonder, as if the king could not believe that it was possible that they could disregard so plain a command, when disobedience was accompanied with such a threat. De Dieu renders it, "Is it a joke?" That is, can you possibly be serious or in earnest that you disobey so positive a command?

Aben Ezra, Theodotion, and Saadias render it as it is in margin, "Have you done this of set purpose and design?" as if the king had regarded it as possible that there had been a misunderstanding, and as if he was not unwilling to find that they could make an apology for their conduct. The Chaldee word (אַרְדָּא) occurs nowhere else. It is rendered by Gesenius, *purpose, design.* That is, "Is it on purpose?" The corresponding Hebrew word (צָדָה) means, *to lie in wait, to waylay,* Exod. xxi. 13; 1 Sam. xxiv. 11, (12). Comp. Numb. xxxv. 20, 22. The true meaning seems to be, "Is it your *determined purpose* not to worship my gods? Have you deliberately made up your minds to this, and do you mean to abide by this resolution?" That this is the meaning is apparent from the fact that he immediately proposes to try them on the point, giving them still an opportunity to comply with his command to worship the image if they would, or to show whether they were finally resolved not to do it. ¶ *Do not ye serve my gods?* It was one of the charges against them that they did not do it, ver. 12.

[A group from Nimroud represents the king and divinities before Baal and the symbolic tree, and illustrates, in part, the service of these gods. At either end is one of the winged divinities,

with the pine, cone, and basket, and in the centre the conventional form of the sacred tree, surmounted by the emblem of Baal. A king stands on each side of the tree, apparently in

not ye serve my gods, nor worship the golden image which I have set up?

15 Now, if ye be ready, that at what time ye hear the sound of the cornet, flute, harp, sackbut, psaltery, and dulcimer, and all kinds of music, ye fall down *a* and worship the image which I have made, *well:* *b* but if ye worship

a Luke 4.7, 8.   *b* Exod. 32. 32; Luke 13. 9.

converse, or in treaty, under the auspices of the god.]

15. *Now, if ye be ready, that at what time,* &c. At the very time; on the very instant. It would seem probable from this that the ceremonies of the consecration of the image were prolonged for a considerable period, so that there was still an opportunity for them to unite in the service if they would. The supposition that such services would be continued through several days is altogether probable, and accords with what was usual on festival occasions. It is remarkable that the king was willing to give them another trial, to see whether they were disposed or not to worship the golden image. To this he might have been led by the apprehension that they had not understood the order, or that they had not duly considered the subject; and possibly by respect for them as faithful officers, and for their countryman Daniel. There seems, moreover, to have been in the bosom of this monarch, with all his pride and passion, a readiness to do justice, and to furnish an opportunity of a fair trial before he proceeded to extremities. See ch. ii. 16, 26, 46, 47. ¶ *And who is that God that shall deliver you out of my hands?* That is, he either supposed that the God whom they worshipped would not be *able* to deliver them, or that he would not be *disposed* to do it. It was a boast of Sennacherib, when he warred against the Jews, that none of the gods of the nations which he had conquered had been able to rescue the lands over which they presided, and he argued from these premises that the God whom the Hebrews worshipped would not be able to defend their country: "Hath any of

not, ye shall be cast the same hour into the midst of a burning fiery furnace; and *c* who *is* that God that shall deliver you out of my hands?

16 Shadrach, Meshach, and Abed-nego answered and said to the king, O Nebuchadnezzar, we *are* not careful *d* to answer thee in this matter.

c Exod. 5. 2; 2 Kings 18. 35.   *d* Matt. 10. 19.

the gods of the nations delivered his land out of the hand of the king of Assyria? Where are the gods of Hamath, and of Arphad? where are the gods of Sepharvaim? and have they delivered Samaria out of my hand? Who are they among all the gods of these lands, that have delivered their land out of my hand, that the Lord should deliver Jerusalem out of my hand?" Isa. xxxvi. 18-20. Nebuchadnezzar seems to have reasoned in a similar manner, and with a degree of vain boasting that strongly resembled this, calling their attention to the certain destruction which awaited them if they did not comply with his demand.

16. *Shadrach, Meshach, and Abed-nego answered and said to the king.* They appear to have answered promptly, and without hesitation, showing that they had carefully considered the subject, and that with them it was a matter of settled and intelligent principle. But they did it in a respectful manner, though they were firm. They neither reviled the monarch nor his gods. They used no reproachful words respecting the image which he had set up, or any of the idols which he worshipped. Nor did they complain of his injustice or severity. They calmly looked at their own duty, and resolved to do it, leaving the consequences with the God whom they worshipped. ¶ *We are not careful to answer thee in this matter.* The word rendered *careful* (חָשַׁח) means, according to Gesenius, *to be needed* or *necessary;* then, *to have need.* The Vulgate renders it, *non oportet nos*—it does not behove us; it is not needful for us. So the Greek, *οὐ χρείαν ἔχομεν* —we have no need. So Luther, *Es ist Nicht noth*—there is no necessity. The

17 If it be *so*, our God, whom *a* we serve, is able to deliver us from the burning fiery furnace ; and he will deliver *us* out of thy hand, O king.

a Psa. 121. 5, 7; Acts 27. 23, 25.

18 But if not,*b* be it known unto thee, O king, that we will not serve thy *c* gods, nor worship the golden image which thou hast set up.

b Job 13. 15; Acts 4. 19.
c Ex. 20. 3–5 ; Lev. 19. 4.

meaning therefore is, that it was not *necessary* that they should reply to the king on that point ; they would not give themselves trouble or solicitude to do it. They had made up their minds, and, whatever was the result, they could not worship the image which he had set up, or the gods whom he adored. They felt that there was no necessity for stating the reasons why they could not do this. Perhaps they thought that argument in their case was improper. It became them to do their duty, and to leave the event with God. They had no need to go into an extended vindication of their conduct, for it might be presumed that their principles of conduct were well known. The *state of mind*, therefore, which is indicated by this passage, is that their minds were made up; that their principles were settled and well understood; that they had come to the deliberate determination, as a matter of conscience, not to yield obedience to the command; that the result could not be modified by any statement which they could make, or by any argument in the case; and that, therefore, they were not anxious about the result, but calmly committed the whole cause to God.

17. *If it be* so. Chald., הֵן אִיתַי — *so it is.* That is, "this is true, that the God whom we serve can save us." The idea is not, as would seem in our translation, "if we are to be cast into the furnace," but the mind is turned on the fact that the God whom they served could save them. Coverdale renders this whole passage, "O Nebuchadnezzar, we ought not to consent unto thee in this matter, for why? our God whom we serve is able to keep us," &c. ¶ *Our God, whom we serve.* Gr., "our God in the heavens, whom we serve." This was a distinct avowal that they were the servants of the true God, and they were not ashamed to avow it, whatever might be the consequences.

¶ *Is able to deliver us from the burning fiery furnace.* This was evidently said in reply to the question asked by the king (ver. 15), "Who is that God that shall deliver you out of my hands?" They were sure that the God whom they worshipped was able, if he should choose to do it, to save them from death. In what way they supposed he could save them is not expressed. Probably it did not occur to them that he would save them in the manner in which he actually did, but they felt that it was entirely within his power to keep them from so horrid a death if he pleased. The state of mind indicated in this verse is that of *entire confidence in God.* Their answer showed (*a*) that they had no doubt of his *ability* to save them if he pleased; (*b*) that they believed he would do what was best in the case; and (*c*) that they were entirely willing to commit the whole case into his hands to dispose of it as he chose. Comp. Isa. xliii. 2.

18. *But if not.* That is, "if he should *not* deliver us; if it should *not* occur that he would protect us, and save us from that heated oven: whatever may be the result in regard to us, our determination is settled." ¶ *Be it known unto thee, O king, that we will not serve thy gods,* &c. This answer is firm and noble. It showed that their minds were made up, and that it was with them a matter of *principle* not to worship false gods. The state of mind which is denoted by this verse is that of a determination to do their duty, whatever might be the consequences. The attention was fixed on what was *right*, not on what would be the result. The sole question which was asked was, what *ought* to be done in the case; and they had no concern about what would follow. True religion is a determined purpose to do right, and not to do wrong, whatever may be the consequences in either case. It matters not what follows—wealth or poverty;

19 ¶ Then was Nebuchadnezzar full ¹ of fury,ᵃ and the form of his visage was changed against Shadrach, Meshach, and Abed-nego : *therefore* he spake, and commanded ᵇ that they should heat the furnace

1 *filled.*   *a* Isa. 51. 13 ; Luke 12. 4, 5.
     b Prov. 16. 14; 21. 24; 27. 3, 4.

honour or dishonour; good report or evil report; life or death ; the mind is firmly fixed on doing right, and not on doing wrong. This is *the religion of principle;* and when we consider the circumstances of those who made this reply ; when we remember their comparative youth, and the few opportunities which they had for instruction in the nature of religion, and that they were captives in a distant land, and that they stood before the most absolute monarch of the earth, with no powerful friends to support them, and with the most horrid kind of death threatening them, we may well admire the grace of that God who could so amply furnish them for such a trial, and love that religion which enabled them to take a stand so noble and so bold.

19. *Then was Nebuchadnezzar full of fury.* Marg., *filled.* He was exceedingly enraged. He evidently was not prepared for a stand so firm and determined on their part, and he did not appreciate their motives, nor was he disposed to yield to them the privilege and right of following their honest convictions. He was deeply excited with anger when the complaint was made that they would not worship his gods (ver. 13), but he had hoped that possibly they had not understood his command, and that what they had done had not been by deliberate purpose (Notes on ver. 14) ; and ho had therefore given them an opportunity to reconsider the subject, and, by complying with his will, to save themselves from the threatened punishment. He now saw, however, that what they had done was done deliberately. He saw that they firmly and intelligently refused to obey, and supposing now that they not only rebelled against his *commands*, but that they disregarded and despised even his *forbearance* (ver. 15), it is not won-

one seven times more than it was wont to be heated.

20 And he commanded the ¹ most mighty men that *were* in his army to bind Shadrach, Meshach, and Abed-nego, *and* to cast *them* into the burning fiery furnace.

1 *mighty of strength.*

derful that he was filled with wrath. What was with them fixed *principle*, he probably regarded as mere *obstinacy*, and he determined to punish them accordingly. ¶ *And the form of his visage was changed.* As the face usually is when men become excited with anger. We may suppose that up to this point he had evinced self-control ; *possibly* he may have shown something like tenderness or compassion. He was indisposed to punish them, and he hoped that they would save him from the necessity of it by complying with his commands. Now he saw that all hope of this was vain, and he gave unrestrained vent to his angry feelings. ¶ *He spake and commanded that they should heat the furnace one seven times more than it was wont to be heated.* Chald., "Than it was *seen* to be heated ;" that is, than it was ever seen. The word *seven* here is a perfect number, and the meaning is, that they should make it as hot as possible. He did not reflect probably that by this command he was contributing to shorten and abridge their sufferings. Wicked men, who are violently opposed to religion, often overdo the matter, and by their haste and impetuosity defeat the very end which they have in view, and even promote the very cause which they wish to destroy.

20. *And he commanded the most mighty men that* were *in his army.* Marg., *mighty of strength.* Chald., "And to mighty men, mighty men of strength who were in his army, he said." He employed the strongest men that could be found for this purpose.

[The two right-hand figures in the annexed sculpture, from Khorsabad, bearing a heavy chariot—a portion of spoil or tribute brought to the Assyrian monarch—represent the *mighty* or strong men who were always in attendance on the person of the king, or in the courts of

21 Then these men were bound in their [1] coats, their hosen, and their [2] hats, and their *other* garments, and were cast into the midst of the burning fiery furnace.

1 or, *mantles.*   2 or, *turbans.*

the palace, to execute the royal commands. At the present day, and especially in the East, men of gigantic proportions are selected for attendants on kings and nobles.]

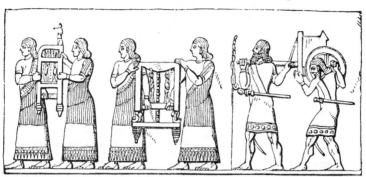

¶ *To bind Shadrach,* &c. Gill supposes that they were probably bound together, as the king afterwards was astonished to see them walking separately in the furnace. But there is no certain evidence of this, and in itself it is not very probable. It is well remarked by Gill, however, that there was no need of binding them at all. They would have made no resistance, and there was no danger that they would make any effort to escape.

21. *Then these men were bound in their coats.* They were seized just as they were. No time was given them for preparation; no change was made in their dress. In *autos-da-fé* of later times, it has been usual to array those who were to suffer in a peculiar dress, indicative of the fact that they were heretics, and that they deserved the flame. Here, however, the anger of the king was so great, that no delay was allowed for any such purpose, and they proceeded to execute the sentence upon them just as they were. The fact that they were thus thrown into the furnace, however, only made the miracle the more conspicuous, since not even their garments were affected by the fire. The word rendered *coats,* is in the margin rendered *mantles.* The Chaldee word (סַרְבָּלִין) means, according to Gesenius, the long and wide pantaloons which are worn by the Orientals, from סַרְבֵּל *sarbel,* to cover. The Greek word used in the translation is derived from this—σαρά-βαρα—and the word σαρβαρίδες is still used in modern Greek. The Chaldee word is used only in this chapter. The Vulgate renders this, *cum braccis suis* —hence the word *breeches,* and *brogues.* The garment referred to, therefore, seems rather to be that which covered the lower part of their person than either a coat or mantle. ¶ *Their hosen.* This word was evidently designed by our translators to denote drawers, or trousers—not stockings, for that was the common meaning of the word when the translation was made. It is not probable that the word is designed to denote *stockings,* as they are not commonly worn in the East. Harmer supposes that the word here used means properly *a hammer,* and that the reference is to a hammer that was carried as a symbol of office, and he refers in illustration of this to the plates of Sir John Chardin of carvings found in the ruins of Persepolis, among which a man is represented with a hammer or mallet in each hand. He supposes that this was some symbol of office. The more common and just representation, however, is to regard this as referring to an article of dress. The Chaldee word (פַּטִּישׁ *pattish*) is from פַּטַשׁ *patash,* to break, to hammer (πατάσσω); to spread out, to expand; and the noun means (1) a ham-

22 Therefore because the king's commandment [1] was urgent, and the furnace exceeding hot, the flame [2] of the fire slew those [a] men

1 *word.*   2 or, *spark.*   a ch. 6. 24.

---

mer; Isa. xli. 7; Jer. xxiii. 29; l. 23; and (2) a garment, probably with the idea of its being *spread out,* and perhaps referring to a tunic or under-garment. Compare Gesenius on the word. The Greek is, *τιάραις,* and so the Latin Vulgate, *tiaris:* the tiara, or covering for the head, turban. The probable reference, however, is to the under-garment worn by the Orientals; the tunic, not a little resembling a shirt with us. ¶ *And their hats.* Marg., or *turbans.* The Chaldee word (כְּרְבְּלָא) is rendered by Gesenius *mantle, pallium.* So the version called the "Breeches" Bible, renders it *clokes.* Coverdale renders it *shoes,* and so the Vulgate, *calceamentis, sandals;* and the Greek, *περικνημίσιν,* greaves, or a garment inclosing the lower limbs; pantaloons. There is

certainly no reason for rendering the word *hats*—as hats were then unknown; nor is there any evidence that it refers to a turban. Buxtorf (*Chald. Lex.*) regards it as meaning a garment, particularly an outer garment, a cloak, and this is probably the correct idea. We should then have in these three words the principal articles of dress in which the Orientals appear, as is shown by the preceding engraving, and from the ruins of Persepolis—the large and loose trou-

that took up Shadrach, Meshach, and Abed-nego.

23 And these three men, Shadrach, Meshach, and Abed-nego,

---

sers; the tunic, or inner garment; and the outer garment, or cloak, that was commonly thrown over all. ¶ *And their* other *garments.* Whatever they had on, whether turban, belt, sandals, &c.

22. *Therefore because the king's commandment was urgent.* Marg., as in Chald., *word.* The meaning is, that the king would admit of no delay; he urged on the execution of his will, even at the imminent peril of those who were intrusted with the execution of his command. ¶ *And the furnace exceeding hot.* Probably so as to send out the flame so far as to render the approach to it dangerous. The urgency of the king would not admit of any arrangements, even if there could have been any, by which the approach to it would be safe. ¶ *The flame of the fire slew those men.* Marg., as in Chald., *spark.* The meaning is, what the fire threw out—the blaze, the heat. Nothing can be more probable than this. It was necessary to approach to the very mouth of the furnace in order to cast them in, and it is very conceivable that a heated furnace would belch forth such flames, or throw out such an amount of heat, that this could not be done but at the peril of life. The Chaldee word rendered *slew* here, means *killed.* It does not mean merely that they were overcome with the heat, but that they actually died. To expose these men thus to death was an act of great cruelty, but we are to remember how absolute is the character of an Oriental despot, and how much enraged this king was, and how regardless such a man would be of any effects on others in the execution of his own will.

23. *And these three men—fell down bound,* &c. That is, the flame did not loosen the cords by which they had been fastened. The fact that they were seen to fall into the furnace *bound,* made the miracle the more remarkable that they should be seen walking loose in the midst of the fire.

In the Septuagint, Syriac, Arabic,

fell down bound into the midst of the burning fiery furnace.

24 Then Nebuchadnezzar the king was astonied, and rose up in haste, *and* spake, and said unto his counsellors, [1] Did not we cast three

1 *or, governors.*

men bound into the midst of the fire ? They answered and said unto the king, True, O king.

25 He answered and said, Lo, I see four men loose, walking *a* in the midst of the fire, and [2] they have

a Isa. 43. 2.   2 *there is no hurt in them.*

and Latin Vulgate, there follow in this place sixty - eight verses, containing "The Song of the Three Holy Children." This is not in the Chaldee, and its origin is unknown. It is with entire propriety placed in the Apocrypha, as being no part of the inspired canon. With some things that are improbable and absurd, the "song" contains many things that are beautiful, and that would be highly appropriate if a song had been uttered at all in the furnace.

24. *Then Nebuchadnezzar the king was astonied.* The word *astonied,* which occurs several times in our translation (Ezra ix. 3 ; Job xvii. 8 ; xviii. 20 ; Ezek. iv. 17 ; Dan. iii. 24 ; iv. 19 ; v. 9), is but another form for *astonished,* and expresses wonder or amazement. The reasons of the wonder here were that the men who were bound when cast into the furnace were seen alive, and walking unbound ; that to them a fourth person was added, walking with them ; and that the fourth had the appearance of a Divine personage. It would seem from this, that the furnace was so made that one could conveniently see into it, and also that the king remained near to it to witness the result of the execution in his own order. ¶ *And rose up in haste.* He would naturally express his surprise to his counsellors, and ask an explanation of the remarkable occurrence which he witnessed. ¶ *And spake, and said unto his counsellors.* Marg., *governors.* The word used (הַדָּבְרִין) occurs only here and in ver. 27 ; ch. iv. 36 ; vi. 7. It is rendered *counsellors* in each case. The Vulgate renders it *optimatibus;* the LXX. μεγιστᾶσιν — his nobles, or distinguished men. The word would seem to mean those who were authorized to *speak* (from דְּבַר) ; that is, those authorized to give counsel ; ministers of state, viziers, cabinet counsellors. ¶ *Did not we cast three men bound,* &c.

The emphasis here is on the words *three,* and *bound.* It was now a matter of astonishment that there were *four,* and that they were all *loose.* It is not to be supposed that Nebuchadnezzar had any doubt on this subject, or that his recollection had so soon failed him, but this manner of introducing the subject is adopted in order to fix the attention strongly on the fact to which he was about to call their attention, and which was to him so much a matter of surprise.

25. *He answered and said, Lo, I see four men loose.* From the fact that he saw these men now loose, and that this filled him with so much surprise, it may be presumed that they had been bound with something that was not combustible—with some sort of fetters or chains. In that case it would be a matter of surprise that they should be *loose,* even though they could survive the action of the fire. The *fourth* personage now so mysteriously added to their number, it is evident, assumed the appearance of *a man,* and not the appearance of a celestial being, though it was the aspect of a man so noble and majestic that he deserved to be called a son of God. ¶ *Walking in the midst of the fire.* The furnace, therefore, was large, so that those who were in it could walk about. The vision must have been sublime ; and it is a beautiful image of the children of God often walking unhurt amidst dangers, safe beneath the Divine protection. ¶ *And they have no hurt.* Marg., *There is no hurt in them.* They walk unharmed amidst the flames. Of course the king judged in this only from appearances, but the result (ver. 27) showed that it was really so. ¶ *And the form of the fourth.* Chaldee, רֵוֵהּ—*his appearance* (from רָאָה

—*to see*) ; that is, he *seemed* to be a son of God ; he *looked* like a son of God. The word does not refer to anything

no hurt ; and the form of the | fourth is like the son *a* of God.

special or peculiar in his *form* or *figure*, but it may be supposed to denote something that was noble or majestic in his mien ; something in his countenance and demeanour that declared him to be of heavenly origin. ¶ *Like the son of God.* There are two inquiries which arise in regard to this expression : one is, what was the idea denoted by the phrase as used by the king, or who did he take this personage to be ? the other, who he actually was ? In regard to the former inquiry, it may be observed, that there is no evidence that the king referred to him to whom this title is so frequently applied in the New Testament, the Lord Jesus Christ. This is clear (1) because there is no reason to believe that the king had *any* knowledge whatever that there would be on earth one to whom this title might be appropriately given; (2) there is no evidence that the title was then commonly given to the Messiah by the Jews, or, if it was, that the king of Babylon was so versed in Jewish theology as to be acquainted with it ; and (3) the language which he uses does not necessarily imply that, even *if* he were acquainted with the fact that there was a prevailing expectation that such a being would appear on the earth, he designed so to use it. The insertion of the article "*the*," which is not in the Chaldee, gives a different impression from what the original would if literally interpreted. There is nothing in the Chaldee to limit it to *any* "son of God," or to designate any one to whom that term could be applied as peculiarly intended. It would seem probable that our translators meant to convey the idea that "*the* Son of God" peculiarly was intended, and doubtless they regarded this as one of his appearances to men before his incarnation ; but it is clear that no such conception entered into the mind of the king of Babylon. The Chaldee is simply, דָּמֵה לְבַר־אֱלָהִין —"like to *a* son of God," or to a son of the *gods*—as the word אֱלָהִין *Elohin* (Chald.), or *Elohim* (Heb.), though often, and indeed usually applied to the

true God, is in the plural number, and in the mouth of a heathen would properly be used to denote the gods that he worshipped. The article is not prefixed to the word "son," and the language would apply to any one who might properly be called a son of God The Vulgate has literally rendered it, "like to a son of God"—*similis filio Dei;* the Greek in the same way — ὁμοία υἱῷ θεοῦ; the Syriac is like the Chaldee ; Castellio renders it, *quartus formam habet Deo nati similem*—"the fourth has a form resembling one born of God ;" Coverdale "the fourth is like an angel to look upon ;" Luther, more definitely, und der vierte ist gleich, als wäre er *ein* Sohn der Götter—"and the fourth as if he might be *a* son of the gods." It is clear that the authors of none of the other versions had the idea which our translators supposed to be conveyed by the text, and which implies that the Babylonian monarch *supposed* that the person whom he saw was the one who afterwards became incarnate for our redemption. In accordance with the common well-known usage of the word *son* in the Hebrew and Chaldee languages, it would denote any one who had a *resemblance* to another, and would be applied to any being who was of a majestic or dignified appearance, and who seemed worthy to be ranked among the gods. It was usual among the heathen to suppose that the gods often appeared in a human form, and probably Nebuchadnezzar regarded this as some such celestial appearance. If it be supposed that he regarded it as some manifestation connected with the *Hebrew* form of religion, the most that would probably occur to him would be, that it was some *angelic* being appearing now for the protection of these worshippers of Jehovah. But a second inquiry, and one that is not so easily answered, in regard to this mysterious personage, arises. Who in fact *was* this being that appeared in the furnace for the protection of these three persecuted men ? Was it an angel, or was it the second person of the Trinity, *the* Son of God ? That this was the Son of

God—the second person of the Trinity, who afterwards became incarnate, has been quite a common opinion of expositors. So it was held by Tertullian, by Augustine, and by Hilary, among the fathers; and so it has been held by Gill, Clarius, and others, among the moderns. Of those who have maintained that it was Christ, some have supposed that Nebuchadnezzar had been made acquainted with the belief of the Hebrews in regard to the Messiah; others, that he spoke under the influence of the Holy Spirit, without being fully aware of what his words imported, as Caiaphas, Saul, Pilate, and others have done.—Poole's *Synopsis.* The Jewish writers Jarchi, Saadias, and Jacchiades suppose that it was an angel, called a son of God, in accordance with the usual custom in the Scriptures. That this latter is the correct opinion, will appear evident, though there cannot be exact certainty, from the following considerations: (1.) The language used implies necessarily nothing more. Though it *might* indeed be applicable to the Messiah—the second person of the Trinity, if it could be determined from other sources that it was he, yet there is nothing in the language which necessarily suggests this. (2.) In the explanation of the matter by Nebuchadnezzar himself (ver. 28), he understood it to be an angel—"Blessed be the God of Shadrach, &c., *who hath sent his angel,*" &c. This shows that he had had no other view of the subject, and that he had no higher knowledge in the case than to suppose that he was an angel of God. The knowledge of the existence of angels was so common among the ancients, that there is no improbability in supposing that Nebuchadnezzar was sufficiently instructed on this point to know that they were sent for the protection of the good. (3.) The belief that it was an angel accords with what we find elsewhere in this book (comp. ch. vi. 22; vii. 10; ix. 21), and in other places in the sacred Scriptures, respecting their being employed to protect and defend the children of God. Compare Psa. xxxiv. 7; xci. 11, 12; Matth. xviii. 10; Luke xvi. 22; Heb. i. 14. (4.) It may be added, that it should not be supposed

that it was the Son of God in the peculiar sense of that term without positive evidence, and such evidence does not exist. Indeed there is scarcely a probability that it was so. If the Redeemer appeared on this occasion, it cannot be explained why, in a case equally important and perilous, he did not appear to Daniel when cast into the lions' den (ch. vi. 22); and as Daniel then attributed his deliverance to the intervention of an angel, there is every reason why the same explanation should be given of this passage. As to the probability that an angel would be employed on an occasion like this, it may be observed, that it is in accordance with the uniform representation of the Scriptures, and with what we know to be a great law of the universe. The weak, the feeble, and those who are in danger are protected by those who are strong; and there is, in itself, no more improbability in the supposition that an *angel* would be employed to work a miracle than there is that a *man* would be. We are not to suppose that the angel was able to prevent the usual effect of fire by any natural strength of his own. The miracle in this case, like all other miracles, was wrought by the power of God. At the same time, the presence of the angel would be a pledge of the Divine protection; would be an assurance that the effect produced was not from any natural cause; would furnish an easy explanation of so remarkable an occurrence; and, perhaps more than all, would impress the Babylonian monarch and his court with some just views of the Divine nature, and with the truth of the religion which was professed by those whom he had cast into the flames. As to the probability that a miracle would be wrought on an occasion like this, it may be remarked that a more appropriate occasion for working a miracle could scarcely be conceived. At a time when the true religion was persecuted; at the court of the most powerful heathen monarch in the world; when the temple at Jerusalem was destroyed, and the fires on the altars had been put out, and the people of God were exiles in a distant land, nothing was more probable than that God would give to his people some

26 ¶ Then Nebuchadnezzar came near to the [1] mouth of the burning fiery furnace, *and* spake, and said, Shadrach, Meshach, and Abednego, ye *a* servants of the most high *b* God, come forth, and come *hither.* Then Shadrach, Meshach, and Abed-nego, came forth of the midst of the fire.

1 *door.*　　*a* Gal. 1. 10.　　*b* Gen. 14. 18.

27 And the princes, governors, and captains, and the king's counsellors, being gathered together, saw these men, upon whose bodies the fire had *c* no power, nor was a hair of their head singed, neither were their coats changed, nor the smell of fire had passed on them.

28 *Then* Nebuchadnezzar spake,

c Isa. 43. 2;　Heb. 11. 34.

manifest tokens of his presence, and some striking confirmation of the truth of his religion. There has perhaps never been an occasion when we should more certainly expect the evidences of the Divine interposition than during the exile of his people in Babylon; and during their long captivity there it is not easy to conceive of an occasion on which such an interposition would be more likely to occur than when, in the very presence of the monarch and his court, three youths of eminent devotedness to the cause of God were cast into a burning furnace, *because* they steadfastly refused to dishonour him.

26. *Then Nebuchadnezzar came near to the mouth,* &c. Marg., *door.* The Chaldee word means door, gate, entrance. The *form* of the furnace is unknown. There was a place, however, through which the fuel was cast into it, and this is doubtless intended by the word *door* or *mouth* here used. ¶ *Ye servants of the most high God.* They had professed to be his servants; he now saw that they were acknowledged as such. The phrase "most high God" implies that he regarded him as supreme over all other gods, though it is probable that he still retained his belief in the existence of inferior divinities. It was much, however, to secure the acknowledgment of the monarch of the capital of the heathen world, that the God whom they adored was supreme. The phrase "most high God" is not often employed in the Scriptures, but in every instance it is used as an appellation of the true God. ¶ *Come forth, and come* hither. The *reasons* which seem to have influenced this·singular monarch to recal the sentence passed on them, and to attempt to punish them no further, seem to have been, that he

had some remains of conscience; that he was accustomed to pay respect to what *he* regarded as God; and that he now saw evidence that a *true* God was there.

27. *And the princes, governors, and captains.* Notes, verse 3. ¶ *And the king's counsellors.* Notes, verse 24. ¶ *Being gathered together, saw these men.* There could be no mistake about the reality of the miracle. They came out as they were cast in. There could have been no trick, no art, no legerdemain, by which they could have been preserved and restored. If the *facts* occurred as they are stated here, then there can be no doubt that this was a real miracle. ¶ *Upon whose bodies the fire had no power.* That is, the usual power of fire on the human body was prevented. ¶ *Nor was a hair of their head singed.* That which would be most likely to have burned. The design is to show that the fire had produced absolutely no effect on them. ¶ *Neither were their coats changed.* On the word *coats,* see Notes on ver. 21. The word *changed* means that there was no change caused by the fire either in their colour or their texture. ¶ *Nor the smell of fire had passed on them.* Not the slightest effect had been produced by the fire; not even so much as to occasion the smell caused by fire when cloth is singed or burned. Perhaps, however, sulphur or pitch had been used in heating the furnace; and the idea may be, that their preservation had been so entire, that not even the smell of the smoke caused by those combustibles could be perceived.

28. Then *Nebuchadnezzar spake, and said, Blessed be the God of Shadrach,* &c. On the characteristic of mind thus evinced by this monarch, see the Notes and practical remarks on ch. ii. 46, 47.

and said, Blessed *be* the God of Shadrach, Meshach, and Abednego, who hath sent his angel, *a* and delivered his servants that trusted in *b* him, and have changed the king's word, and yielded their *c*

a Gen. 19. 15, 16; Ps. 34. 7, 8; 103. 20; Heb. 1. 14.
b ch. 6. 22, 23; Jer. 17. 7.
c Rom. 12. 1; Heb. 11. 37.

¶ *Who hath sent his angel.* This proves that the king regarded this mysterious fourth personage as an angel, and that he used the phrase (ver. 25) "is like the son of God" only in that sense. That an angel should be employed on an embassage of this kind, we have seen, is in accordance with the current statements of the Scriptures. Comp. *Excursus I.* to Prof. Stuart *on the Apocalypse.* See also Luke i. 11–20, 26–38 ; Matt. i. 20, 21 : ii. 13, 19, 20 ; iv. 11 ; xviii. 10 ; Acts xii. 7–15 ; Gen. xxxii. 1, 2 ; 2 Ki. vi. 17 ; Ex. xiv. 19 ; xxiii. 20 ; xxxiii. 2 ; Numb. xx. 16 ; Josh. v. 13 ; Is. lxiii. 9 ; Dan. x. 5–13, 20, 21 ; xii. 1. ¶ *And have changed the king's word.* That is, his purpose or command. Their conduct, and the Divine protection in consequence of their conduct, had had the effect wholly to change his purpose towards them. He had resolved to destroy them ; he now resolved to honour them. This is referred to by the monarch himself as a remarkable result, as indeed it was—that an Eastern despot, who had resolved on the signal punishment of any of his subjects, should be so entirely changed in his purposes towards them. ¶ *And yielded their bodies.* The Greek adds here *εἰς πυρ*—"to the fire." So the Arabic. This is doubtless the sense of the passage. The meaning is, that rather than bow down to worship gods which they regarded as no gods ; rather than violate their consciences, and do wrong, they had preferred to be cast into the flames, committing themselves to the protection of God. It is implied here that they had done this voluntarily, and that they might easily have avoided it if they had chosen to obey the king. He had given them time to deliberate on the subject (vers. 14, 15), and he knew that they had resolved to pursue the course which they did from principle, no matter what might be the

bodies; that they might not serve nor worship any god, except their own God.

29 Therefore ¹ I make a decree, That *d* every people, nation, and language, which speak any ² thing

1 *a decree is made by me.*   d ch. 6. 26, 27.
2 *error.*

results (vers. 16–18). This strength of principle—this obedience to the dictates of conscience—this determination not to do wrong at any hazard—he could not but respect; and this is a remarkable instance to show that a firm and steady course in doing what is right *will* command the respect of even wicked men. This monarch, with all his pride, and haughtiness, and tyranny, had not a few generous qualities, and some of the finest illustrations of human nature were furnished by him. ¶ *That they might not serve nor worship any god, except their own God.* They gave up their bodies to the flame rather than do this.

29. *Therefore I make a decree.* Marg., *A decree is made by me.* Chald., "And from me a decree is laid down," or enacted. This Chaldee word (טְעֵם) means, properly, *taste, flavour;* then *judgment,* the power of *discerning*—apparently as of one who can judge of *wine,* &c., by the taste ; then the sentence, the decree which is consequent on an act of judging—always retaining the idea that the determination or decree is based on a conception of the true merits of the case. The decree in this case was not designed to be regarded as arbitrary, but as being founded on what was right and proper. He had seen evidence that the God whom these three youths worshipped was a true God, and was able to protect those who trusted in him; and regarding him as a real God, he made this proclamation, that respect should be shown to him throughout his extended realm. ¶ *That every people, nation, and language.* This decree is in accordance with the usual style of an Oriental monarch. It was, however, a fact that the empire of Nebuchadnezzar extended over nearly all of the then known world. ¶ *Which speak any thing amiss.* Marg., *error.* The Chaldee word

amiss against the God of Shadrach, Meshach, and Abed-nego, shall be cut [1] in pieces, *a* and their houses shall be made a dunghill : because

1 *made.*   *a* ch. 2. 5.

(שָׁלוּ) means *error, wrong,* and it refers here to anything that would be fitted to lead the minds of men astray in regard to the true character of the God whom these persons worshipped. The Vulgate renders it *blasphemy.* So also it is rendered in the Greek, βλασφημίαν. The intention was, that their God was to be acknowledged as a God of eminent power and rank. It does not appear that Nebuchadnezzar meant that he should be regarded as the *only* true God, but he was willing, in accordance with the prevailing notions of idolatry, that he should take his place among *the* gods, and a most honoured place. ¶*Shall*

¶*And their houses shall be made a dunghill.* Comp. 2 Kings x. 27. The idea is, that the utmost possible dishonour and contempt should be placed on their houses, by devoting them to the most vile and offensive uses. ¶*Because there is no other god that can deliver after this sort.* He does not say that there was no other god at all, for his mind had not yet reached this conclusion, but there was no other one who had equal power with the God of the Hebrews. He had seen a manifestation of his power in the preservation of the three Hebrews, such as no other god had ever exhibited, and he was willing to admit that in this respect he surpassed all other divinities.

30. *Then the king promoted Shadrach,*

there is no other god that can deliver after this sort.

30 Then the king [2] promoted Shadrach, Meshach, and Abed-nego, in the province of Babylon.

2 *made to prosper.*

be cut in pieces. Marg., *made.* This was a species of punishment that was common in many ancient nations. —Gesenius.

[Death by strokes with the sword, or, literally, by hewing in pieces, is still in use in China and in Abyssinia, as we learn from Bruce. The sculpture shown in the engraving is supposed by some to refer only to the breaking up of an idol, but the balance of probabilities is in favour of its being an Assyrian execution. The mutilated figure has none of the attributes of a god, and differs not greatly in costume and appearance from the others. This is one of the sculptures from Khorsabad.]

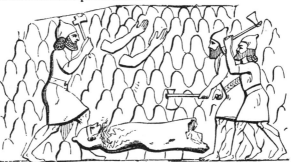

&c. Marg., *made to prosper.* The Chaldee means no more than *made to prosper.* Whether he restored them to their former places, or to higher honours, does not appear. There would be, however, nothing inconsistent with his usual course in supposing that he raised them to more exalted stations. ¶*In the province of Babylon.* See Notes on ch. ii. 49. The Greek and the Arabic add here, " And he counted them worthy to preside over all the Jews that were in his kingdom." But nothing of this is found in the Chaldee, and it is not known by whom this addition was made.

In the Vulgate and the Greek versions, and in some of the critical editions of the Hebrew Scriptures (Walton, Hahn, &c.), the three first verses of the following chapter are subjoined to this. It is well known that the divisions of the chapters are of no authority, but it is clear that these verses belong more appropriately to the following chapter than to this, as the reason there assigned by the monarch for the proclamation is what occurred to himself (ver. 2), rather than what he had witnessed in others. The division, therefore, which is made in our common version of the Bible, and in the Syriac and the Arabic, is the correct one.

PRACTICAL REMARKS.

I. The instance recorded in this chapter (vers. 1–7) is not improbably the first case which ever occurred in the world of an attempt to produce *conformity* in idolatrous worship by penal statute. It has, however, been abundantly imitated since, alike in the heathen and in the nominally Christian world. There are no portions of history more interesting than those which describe the progress of religious liberty; the various steps which have been taken to reach the result which has now been arrived at, and to settle the principles which are now regarded as the true ones. Between the views which were formerly entertained, and which are still entertained in many countries, and those which constitute the Protestant notions on the subject, there is a greater difference than there is, in regard to civil rights, between the views which prevail under an Oriental despotism, and the most enlarged and enlightened notions of civil freedom. The views which have prevailed on the subject are the following:—1. The *general* doctrine among the heathen has been, that there were many gods in heaven and earth, and that all were entitled to reverence. One nation was supposed to have as good a right to worship its own gods as another, and it was regarded as at least an act of courtesy to show respect to the gods that any nation adored, in the same way as respect would be shown to

the sovereigns who presided over them. Hence the gods of all nations could be consistently introduced into the Pantheon at Rome; hence there were few attempts to *proselyte* among the heathen; and hence it was not common to *persecute* those who worshipped other gods. Persecution of idolaters *by* those who were idolaters was, therefore, rarely known among the heathen, and *toleration* was not contrary to the views which prevailed, provided the gods of the country were recognized. In ancient Chaldea, Assyria, Greece, and Rome, in the earliest ages, persecution was rare, and the toleration of other forms of religion was usual. 2. The views which have prevailed leading to persecution, and which are a violation, as we suppose, of all just notions of liberty on the subject of religion, are the following: (*a*) Those among the heathen which, as in the case of Nebuchadnezzar, require *all* to worship a particular god that should be set up. In such a case, it is clear that while all who were *idolaters*, and who supposed that *all* the gods worshipped by others should be respected, could render homage; it is also clear that those who regarded *all* idols as false gods, and believed that *none* of them ought to be worshipped, could *not* comply with the command. Such was the case with the Jews who were in Babylon (vers. 8–18); for supposing that there was but *one* God, it was plain that they could not render homage to any other. While, therefore, every idolater could render homage to *any* idol, the Hebrew could render homage to *none*. (*b*) The views among the heathen *prohibiting* the exercise of a certain kind of religion. According to the prevailing views, no mode of religion could be tolerated which would maintain that *all* the gods that were worshipped were false. Religion was supposed to be identified with the best interests of the state, and was recognized by the laws, and protected by the laws. To deny the claim, therefore, of any and of all the gods that were worshipped; to maintain that all were false alike; to call on men to forsake their idols, and to embrace a new religion—all this was regarded as an attack on the state. This was the attitude which Christianity assumed towards the religions of the Roman empire, and it was this which led to the fiery persecutions which prevailed there. While Rome could consistently tolerate any form of idolatry that would recognize the religion established by the state, it could not tolerate a system which maintained that *all* idolatry was wrong. It would allow another god to be placed in the Pantheon, but it could not recognize a system which would remove every god from that temple. Christianity, then, made war on the system of idolatry that prevailed in the Roman empire in two respects : in proclaiming a *purer* religion, denouncing all the corruptions which idolatry had engendered, and which it countenanced; and in denying altogether that the gods which were worshipped were true gods—thus arraying itself against the laws, the priesthood, the venerable institutions, and all the passions and prejudices of tho people. These views may be thus summed up : (*a*) all the gods worshipped by others were to be recognized; (*b*) new ones might be introduced by authority of the state; (*c*) the gods which the state approved and acknowledged were to be honoured by all; (*d*) if any persons denied their existence, and their claims to homage, they were to be treated as enemies of the state. It was on this last principle that persecutions ever arose under the heathen forms of religion. Infidels, indeed, have been accustomed to charge Christianity with all the persecutions on account of religion, and to

speak in high terms of "the mild tolerance of the ancient heathens;" of "the universal toleration of polytheism;" of "the Roman princes beholding without concern a thousand forms of religion subsisting in peace under their gentle sway."—Gibbon. But it should be remembered that pagan nations required of every citizen conformity to their national idolatries. When this was refused, persecution arose as a matter of course. Stilpo was banished from Athens for affirming that the statue of Minerva in the citadel was no divinity, but only the work of the chisel of Phidias. Protagoras received a similar punishment for this sentence : "Whether there be gods or not, I have nothing to offer." Prodicus, and his pupil Socrates, suffered death for opinions at variance with the established idolatry of Athens. Alcibiades and Æschylus narrowly escaped a like end for a similar cause. Cicero lays it down as a principle of legislation entirely conformable to the laws of the Roman state, that "no man shall have separate gods for himself; and no man shall worship by himself new or foreign gods, unless they have been publicly acknowledged by the laws of the state."—*De Legibus,* ii. 8. Julius Paulus, the Roman civilian, gives the following as a leading feature of the Roman law: "Those who introduced new religions, or such as were unknown in their tendency and nature, by which the minds of men might be agitated, were degraded, if they belonged to the higher ranks, and if they were in a lower state, were punished with death." See M'Ilvaine's *Lectures on the Evidences of Christianity,* pp. 427–429. (*c*) The attempts made to produce conformity in countries where the *Christian* system has prevailed. In such countries, as among the heathen, it has been supposed that religion is an important auxiliary to the purposes of the state, and that it is proper that the state should not only *protect* it, but *regulate* it. It has claimed the right, therefore, to prescribe the form of religion which shall prevail; to require conformity to that, and to punish all who did not conform to the established mode of worship. This attempt to produce conformity has led to most of the persecutions of modern times. 3. The principles which have been settled by the discussions and agitations of past times, and which are recognized in all countries where there are any just views of religious liberty, and which are destined yet to be universally recognized, are the following: (a) There is to be, on the subject of religion, perfect liberty to worship God in the manner that shall be most in accordance with the views of the individual himself, provided in doing it he does not interfere with the rights or disturb the worship of others. It is not merely that men are to be *tolerated* in the exercise of their religion—for the word *tolerate* would seem to imply that the state had some right of control in the matter—but the true word to express the idea is *liberty.* (b) The state is to *protect* all in the enjoyment of these equal rights. Its *authority* does not go beyond this; its *duty* demands this. These two principles comprise all that is required on the subject of religious liberty. They have been in our world, however, principles of slow growth. They were unknown in Greece—for Socrates died because they were not understood; they were unknown in Rome—for the state claimed the power to determine what gods should be admitted into the Pantheon; they were unknown even in Judea—for a national or state religion was established there; they were unknown in Babylon—for the monarch there claimed the right of enforcing conformity to the national religion; they were unknown in Europe in the middle ages—for all the horrors of the Inquisition grew out of the fact that they were not understood; they are unknown in Turkey, and China, and Persia—for the state regards religion as under its control. The doctrine of entire freedom in religion, of perfect liberty to worship God according to our own views of right, is *the last point which society is to reach in this direction.* It is impossible to conceive that there is to be anything *beyond* this which mankind are to desire in the progress towards the perfection of the social organization; and when this shall be everywhere reached, the affairs of the world will be placed on a permanent footing.

II. In the spirit evinced by the three young men, and the answer which they gave, when accused of not worshipping the image, and when threatened with a horrid death, we have a beautiful illustration of the nature and value *of the religion of principle,* vers. 12–18. To enable us to see the force of this example, and to appreciate its value, we are to remember that these were yet comparatively young men; that they were captives in a distant land; that they had no powerful friends at court; that they had had, compared with what we now have, few advantages of instruction; that they were threatened with a most horrid death; and that they had nothing of a worldly nature to hope for by refusing compliance with the king's commands. This instance is of value to us, because it is not only important *to have religion,* but *to have the best kind of religion;* and it is doubtless in order that we *may* have this, that such examples are set before us in the Scriptures. In regard to this kind of religion, there are three inquiries which would present themselves: On what is it founded? what will it lead us to do? and what is its value? (1.) It is founded mainly on two things—an intelligent view of duty, and fixed principle. (*a*) An intelligent view of duty; an acquaintance with what is right, and what is wrong. These young men had made up their minds intelligently, that it was right to worship God, and that it was wrong to render homage to an idol. This was not *obstinacy*. Obstinacy exists where a man has made up his mind, and resolves to act, without any good reason, or without an intelligent view of what is right or wrong, and where he adheres to his purpose not because it is right, but from the influence of mere *will*. The religion of principle is always found where there is an intelligent view of what is right, and a man can give *a reason* for what he does. (*b*) This religion is founded on a determination to *do* what is right, and *not* to do what is wrong. The question is not what is expedient, or popular, or honourable, or lucrative, or pleasant, but what is right. (2.) What will such a religion lead us to do? This question may be answered by a reference to the case before us, and it will be found that it will lead us to do three things: (*a*) To do our *duty* without being solicitous or anxious about the results, ver. 16. (*b*) To put confidence in God, feeling that if he pleases he *can* protect us from danger, ver. 17. (*c*) To do our duty, *whatever may be the consequences—whether he protects us or not*, ver. 18. (3.) What is the *value* of this kind of religion? (*a*) It is the only kind in which there is any fixed and certain standard. If a man regulates his opinions and conduct from expediency, or from respect to the opinions of others, or from feeling, or from popular impulses, there is no standard; there is nothing settled or definite. Now one thing is popular, now another; to-day the feelings may prompt to one thing. to-morrow to another; at one time ex-

pediency will suggest one course, at another a different course. (*b*) It is the only kind of religion on which reliance can be placed. In endeavouring to spread the gospel; to meet the evils which are in the world; to promote the cause of temperance, chastity, liberty, truth, and peace, the only thing on which permanent reliance can be placed is the religion of principle. And (*c*) it is the only religion which is *certainly* genuine. A man may see much poetic beauty in religion; he may have much of the religion of sentiment; he may admire God in the grandeur of his works; he may have warm feelings; easily enkindled on the subject of religion, and may even weep at the foot of the cross in view of the wrongs and woes that the Saviour endured; he may be impressed with the forms, and pomp, and splendour of gorgeous worship, and still have no genuine repentance for his sins, no saving faith in the Redeemer, no real love to God.

III. We have in this chapter (vers. 19-23) an affecting case of an attempt to *punish* men for holding certain opinions, and for acting in conformity with them. When we read of an instance of persecution like this, it occurs to us to ask the following questions:— What is persecution? why has it been permitted by God? and what effects have followed from it? (1.) What is persecution? It is pain inflicted, or some loss, or disadvantage in person, family, or office, on account of holding certain opinions. It has had *two* objects: one to *punish* men for holding certain opinions, as if the persecutor had a right to regard this as an offence against the state; and the other a professed view to reclaim those who are made to suffer, and to save their souls. In regard to the *pain* or *suffering* involved in persecution, it is not material what *kind* of pain is inflicted in order to constitute persecution. *Any* bodily suffering; any deprivation of comfort; any exclusion from office; any holding up of one to public reproach; or any form of ridicule, constitutes the essence of persecution. It may be added, that not a few of the inventions most distinguished for inflicting pain, and known as refinements of cruelty, have been originated in times of persecution, and would probably have been unknown if it had not been for the purpose of restraining men from the free exercise of religious opinions. The Inquisition has been most eminent in this; and within the walls of that dreaded institution it is probable that human ingenuity has been exhausted in devising the most refined modes of inflicting torture on the human frame. (2.) Why has this been permitted? Among the reasons why it has been permitted may be the following: (a) To show the power and reality of religion. It seemed desirable to subject it to *all kinds* of trial, in order to show that its existence could not be accounted for except on the supposition that it is from God. If men had never been called on to *suffer* on account of religion, it would have been easy for the enemies of religion to allege that there was little evidence that it was genuine, or was of value, for it had never been tried. Comp. Job i. 9–11. As it is, it has been subjected to *every form* of trial which wicked men could devise, and has shown itself to be adapted to meet them all. The work of the martyrs has been well done; and religion in the times of martyrdom has shown itself to be all that it is desirable it should be. (b) In order to promote its spread in the world. "The blood of the martyrs" has been "the seed of the church;" and it is probable that religion in past times has owed much of its purity, and of its diffusion, to the fact that it has been persecuted. (c) To

fit the sufferers for an exalted place in heaven. They who have suffered persecution needed trials as well as others, for *all* Christians need them—and *theirs* came in this form. Some of the most lovely traits of Christian character have been brought out in connection with persecution, and some of the most triumphant exhibitions of preparation for heaven have been made at the stake. (3.) What have been the effects of persecution? (a) It has been the *settled* point that the Christian religion cannot be destroyed by persecution. There is no power to be brought against it more mighty than, for example, was that of the Roman empire; and it is impossible to conceive that there should be greater refinements of cruelty than have been employed. (b) The effect has been to diffuse the religion which has been persecuted. The manner in which the sufferings inflicted have been endured has shown that there is reality and power in it. It is also a law of human nature to *sympathize* with the wronged and the oppressed, and we insensibly learn to transfer the sympathy which we have for these *persons* to their *opinions*. When we see one who is *wronged*, we soon find our hearts beating in unison with his, and soon find ourselves taking sides with him in everything.

IV. We have in this chapter (vers. 24–27) an instructive illustration of the *protection* which God affords his people in times of trial. These men were thrown into the furnace on account of their obedience to God, and their refusal to do that which they knew he would not approve. The result showed, by a most manifest miracle, that they were right in the course which they took, and their conduct was the occasion of furnishing a most striking proof of the wisdom of trusting in God in the faithful performance of duty, irrespective of consequences. Similar illustrations were furnished in the case of Daniel in the lions' den (ch. vi. 16–22), and of Peter (Acts xii. 1–10). But a question of much interest arises here, which is, What kind of protection may *we* look for now ? (1.) There are numerous *promises* made to the righteous of every age and country. They are not promises indeed of *miraculous* interference, but they are promises of *an* interposition of some kind in their behalf, which will show that "it is not a vain thing to serve God." Among them are those recorded in the following places:—2 Chron. xvi. 9; Psa. iv. 3; v. 12; xv. 1–5; xxxvii. 3–10, 17–26, 34–40; lviii. 11; lxxxiv. 11; xcii. 12–15; xcvii. 11; cxii. 1–5; Prov. iii. 3, 4, 31–35; x. 2, 3, 6–9, 25–30; xiii. 6, 21, 22; xiv. 30–34; xvi. 7; xx. 7; xxi. 21; Isa. xxxii. 17; xxxiii. 15, 16; Matt. vi. 33; 1 Tim. iv. 8, 9; vi. 6; 1 Pet. iii. 10–13; John xii. 26; Exod. xx. 5, 6; Psal. ix. 9, 10; xxiii. 4; xlvi. 1; lv. 22; Isa. liv. 7, 8; Matt. v. 4; Job v. 19. (2.) In regard to the *kind* of interposition that we may look for now, or the *nature* of the favours implied in these promises, it may be observed : (*a*) That we are not to look for any *miraculous* interpositions in our favour. (*b*) We are not to expect that there will be on earth an *exact adjustment* of the Divine dealings according to the deserts of all persons, or according to the principles of a *completed* moral government, when there will be a perfect system of rewards and punishments. (*c*) We are not to expect that there will be such manifest and open rewards of obedience, and such direct and constant benefits resulting from religion in this world, as to lead men *merely* from these to serve and worship God. If religion were *always* attended with prosperity ; if the righteous were never persecuted, were never

poor, or were never bereaved, multitudes would be induced to become religious, as many followed the Saviour, not because they saw the miracles, but because they did eat of the loaves and fishes, and were filled: John vi. 26. While, therefore, in the Divine administration here it is proper that there should be so many and so marked interpositions in favour of the good as to show that God is the friend of his people, it is *not* proper that there should be so many that men would be induced to engage in his service for the love of the reward rather than for the sake of the service itself; because they are to be happy, rather than because they love virtue. It may be expected, therefore, that while the general course of the Divine administration will be in favour of virtue, there may be much intermingled with this that will appear to be of a contrary kind ; much that will be fitted to *test* the faith of the people of God, and to show that they *love* his service for its own sake.

V. We have, in vers. 28–30, a striking instance of the effect which an adherence to principle will produce on the minds of worldly and wicked men. Such men have no *love* for religion, but they can see that a certain course accords with the views which are professedly held, and that it indicates high integrity. They can see that firmness and consistency are worthy of commendation and reward. They can see, as Nebuchadnezzar did in this case, that such a course will secure the Divine favour, and they will be disposed to honour it on that account. For a time, a tortuous course may seem to prosper, but in the end, solid fame, high rewards, honourable offices, and a grateful remembrance after death, follow in the path of strict integrity and unbending virtue.

CHAPTER IV.

§ I.—AUTHENTICITY OF THE CHAPTER.

To the authenticity of this chapter, as to the preceding, objections and difficulties have been urged, sufficient, in the view of the objectors, to destroy its credibility as a historical narrative. Those objections, which may be seen at length in Bertholdt (pp. 70–72, 285–309), Bleek (*Theol. Zeitscrift, Drittes Heft*, 268, *seq.*), and Eichhorn (*Einlei.* iv. 471, *seq.*), relate mainly to two points—those derived from the want of historical proofs to confirm the narrative, and those derived from its alleged intrinsic improbability.

I. The former of these, derived from the want of historic confirmation of the truth of the narrative, are summarily the following:—(1.) That the historical books of the Old Testament give no intimation that these remarkable things happened to Nebuchadnezzar, that he was deranged and driven from his throne, and made to dwell under the open heaven with the beasts of the field—an omission which, it is said, we cannot suppose would have occurred if these things had happened, since the Hebrew writers, on account of the wrongs which Nebuchadnezzar had done to their nation, would have certainly seized on such facts as a demonstration of the Divine displeasure against him. (2.) There is no record of these events among the heathen writers of antiquity; no writer among the Greeks, or other nations, ever having mentioned them. (3.) It is equally remarkable that Josephus, in his narrative of the sickness of Nebuchadnezzar, makes no allusion to any knowledge of this among other nations, and shows that he derived his information only from the sacred books of his own people. (4.) It is acknowledged by Origen and Jerome that they could find no historical grounds for the truth of this account. (5.) If these things had occurred, as here related, they would not have been thus concealed, for the king himself took all possible measures, by the edict referred to in this chapter, to make them known, and to make a permanent record of them. How could it have happened that all knowledge would have been lost if they had thus occurred? (6.) If the edict was lost, how was it ever recovered again? When, and where, and by whom, was it found? If actually issued, it was designed to make the case known throughout the empire. Why did it fail of producing that effect so as not to have been forgotten? If it was lost, how was the event known? And if it was lost, how could it have been recovered and recorded by the author of this book? Comp. Bertholdt, p. 298.

To these objections, it may be replied, (1) that the silence of the historical books of the Old Testament furnishes no well-founded objection to what is said in this chapter, for none of them pretend to bring down the history of Nebuchadnezzar to the close of his life, or to this period of his life. The books of Kings and of Chronicles mention his invasion of the land of Palestine and of Egypt; they record the fact of his carrying away the children of Israel to Babylon, but they do not profess to make any record of what occurred to *him* after that, nor of the close of his life. The second book of Chronicles closes with an account of the removal of the Jews to Babylon, and the carrying away of the sacred vessels of the temple, and the burning of the temple, and the destruction of the city, but does not relate the history of Nebuchadnezzar any farther, 2 Chron. xxxvi. The silence of the book cannot, therefore, be alleged as an argument against anything that may be said to have occurred after that. As the history closes there; as the design was to give a record of Jewish affairs to the carrying away to Babylon, and not a history of Nebuchadnezzar as such, there is no ground of objection furnished by this silence in regard to anything that might be said to have occurred to Nebuchadnezzar subsequently to this in his own kingdom.

(2) In regard to profane writers, also, nothing can be argued as to the improbability of the account mentioned here from their silence on the subject. It is not remarkable that in the few fragments which are found in their writings respecting the kings and empires of the East, an occurrence of this kind should have been omitted. The general worthlessness or want of value of the historical writings of the Greeks in respect to foreign nations, from which we derive most of our knowledge of those nations, is now generally admitted, and is expressly maintained by Niebuhr, and by Schlosser (see Hengstenberg, *Die Authentie des Daniel*, p. 101), and most of these writers make no allusion at all to Nebuchadnezzar. Even Herodotus, who travelled into the East, and who collected all he could of the history of the world, makes no mention whatever of a conqueror so illustrious as Nebuchadnezzar. How could it be expected that when they have omitted all notice of his conquests, of the great events under him, which exerted so important an effect on the world, there should have been a record of an occurrence like that referred to in this chapter—an occurrence that seems to have exerted no influence whatever on the foreign relations of the empire? It is remarkable that Josephus, who searched for all that he could find to illustrate the literature and history of the Chaldees, says (*Ant.* b. x. ch. xi. § 1) that

he could find only the following "histories as all that he had met with concerning this king: Berosus, in the third book of his Chaldaic history; Philostratus, in the history of Judea and of the Phœnicians, who only mentions him in respect to his siege of Tyre; the Indian history of Megasthenes—'Ινδικά—in which the only fact which is mentioned of him is that he plundered Libya and Iberia; and the Persian history of Diocles, in which there occurs but one solitary reference to Nebuchadnezzar." To these he adds, in his work *against Apion* (b. i. 20), a reference to the "Archives of the Phœnicians," in which it is said that "he conquered Syria and Phœnicia." Berosus is the only one who pretends to give any extended account of him. See *Ant.* b. x. ch. xi. § 1. All those authorities mentioned by Josephus, therefore, except Berosus, may be set aside, since they have made no allusion to many undeniable facts in the life of Nebuchadnezzar, and, therefore, the events referred to in this chapter may have occurred, though they have not related them. There remain two authors who have noticed Nebuchadnezzar at greater length, Abydenus and Berosus. Abydenus was a Greek who lived 268 B.C. He wrote, in Greek, a historical account of the Chaldeans, Babylonians, and Assyrians, only a few fragments of which have been preserved by Eusebius, Cyrill, and Syncellus. Berosus was a Chaldean, and was a priest in the temple of Belus, in the time of Alexander, and having learned of the Macedonians the Greek language, he went to Greece, and opened a school of astronomy and astrology in the island of Cos, where his productions acquired for him great fame with the Athenians. Abydenus was his pupil. Berosus wrote three books relative to the history of the Chaldeans, of which only some fragments are preserved in Josephus and Eusebius. As a priest of Belus he possessed every advantage which could be desired for obtaining a knowledge of the Chaldeans, and if his work had been preserved it would doubtless be of great value. Both these writers professedly derived their knowledge from the traditions of the Chaldeans, and both should be regarded as good authority.

Berosus is adduced by Josephus to confirm the truth of the historical records in the Old Testament. He mentions, according to Josephus, the deluge in the time of Noah, and the account of the resting of the ark on one of the mountains of Armenia. He gives a catalogue of the descendants of Noah, and "at length comes down to Nabolassar, who was king of Babylon and of the Chaldeans." He then mentions the expedition of his son, Nabuchodonosor (Nebuchadnezzar), against the Egyptians; the capture of Jerusalem; the burning of the temple; and the removal of the Jews to Babylon. He then mentions the manner in which Nebuchadnezzar succeeded to the throne; the way in which he distributed his captives in various parts of Babylonia; his adorning of the temple of Belus; his re-building the old city of Babylon, and the building of another city on the other side of the river; his adding a new palace to that which his father had built; and the fact that this palace was finished in fifteen days. After these statements respecting his conquests and the magnificence of his capital, Berosus gives the following narrative:—"Nabuchodonosor, after he had begun to build the forementioned wall, fell sick—ἐμπισὼν εἰς ἀῤῥωστίαν—and departed this life—μιτηλλάξατο τὸν βίον"—[a phrase meaning to die, see Passow on the word μιτάλλασσω] "when he had reigned forty-three years, whereupon his son,

Evil-Merodach, obtained the kingdom." Josephus *against Apion*, b. i. § 20. Now this narrative is remarkable, and goes in fact to confirm the statement in Daniel in two respects: (*a*) It is manifest that Berosus here refers to some sickness in the case of Nebuchadnezzar that was unusual, and that probably preceded, for a considerable time, his death. This appears from the fact, that in the case of the other monarchs whom he mentions in immediate connection with this narrative, no sickness is alluded to as preceding their death. This is the case with respect to Neriglissar and Nabonnedus—successors of Nebuchadnezzar. See Jos. *against Ap.* i. 20. There is no improbability in supposing, that what Berosus here calls *sickness* is the same which is referred to in the chapter before us. Berosus, himself a Chaldean, might not be desirous of stating all the facts about a monarch of his own country so distinguished, and might not be willing to state all that he knew about his being deprived of reason, and about the manner in which he was treated, and yet what occurred to him was so remarkable, and was so well known, that there seemed to be a necessity of alluding to it in some way; and this he did in the most general manner possible. If this were his object, also, he would not be likely to mention the fact that he was restored again to the throne. He would endeavour to make it appear as an ordinary event—a sickness which preceded death—as it *may* have been the fact that he never was wholly restored so far as to be in perfect health. (*b*) This statement of Berosus accords, in respect to *time*, remarkably with that in Daniel. Both accounts agree that the sickness occurred after he had built Babylon, and towards the close of his reign.

The other author which is referred

to is Abydenus. The record which he makes is preserved by Eusebius, *præp. Evang.* ix. 41, and *Chronicon Armeno-latinum,* I. p. 59, and is in the following words: μετὰ ταῦτα δὲ, λέγεται πρὸς Χαλδαίων, ὡς ἀναβὰς ἐπὶ τὰ βασιλήϊα, κατασχεθείη θεῷ ὅτεῳ δὴ, φθεγξάμενος δὲ εἶπεν· οὗτος ἐγὼ Ναβουκοδρόσορος, ὦ Βαβυλώνιοι, τὴν μέλλουσαν ὑμῖν προαγγέλλω συμφορὴν, τὴν ὅτε Βῆλος ἐμὸς πρόγονος, ἤ τε βασίλεια Βῆλτις ἀποτρέψαι Μοίρας πεῖσαι ἀσθενοῦσιν· ἥξει Πέρσης ἡμίονος, τοῖσιν ὑμετέροισι δαίμοσι χρεώμενος συμμάχοισιν· ἐπάξει δὲ δουλοσύνην· οὗ δὴ συναίτιος ἔσται Μήδης, τὸ Ἀσσύριον αὔχημα· ὡς εἴθέ μιν πρόσθεν ἢ δοῦναι τοὺς πολιήτας, Χάρυβδίν τινα, ἢ θάλασσαν εἰσδεξαμένην, ἀϊστῶσαι πρόρριζον· ἢ μιν ἄλλας ὁδοὺς στραφέντα φέρεσθαι διὰ τῆς ἐρήμου, ἵνα οὔτε ἄστεα, οὔτε πάτος ἀνθρώπων, θῆρες δὲ νόμον ἔχουσι, καὶ ὄρνιθες πλάζονται, ἔν τε πέτρῃσι καὶ χαράδρῃσι μοῦνον ἀλώμενον· ἐμέ τε, πρὶν εἰς νόον βαλίσθαι ταῦτα, τέλεος ἀμείνονος κυρῆσαι. Ὁ μὲν θεσπίσας παραχρῆμα ἠφάνιστο. This passage is so remarkable, that I annex a translation of it, as I find it in Prof. Stuart's work on Daniel, p. 122: "After these things" [his conquests which the writer had before referred to], "as it is said by the Chaldeans, having ascended his palace, he was seized by some god, and speaking aloud, he said: 'I, Nebuchadnezzar, O Babylonians, foretell your future calamity, which neither Belus, my ancestor, nor queen Beltis, can persuade the destinies to avert. A *Persian mule* will come, employing your own divinities as his auxiliaries; and he will impose servitude [upon you]. His coadjutor will be the *Mede,* who is the boast of the Assyrians. Would that, before he places my citizens in such a condition, some Charybdis or gulf might swallow him up with utter destruction! Or that, turned in a different direction, he might roam in the desert (where are neither cities, nor

footsteps of man, but wild beasts find pasturage, and the birds wander), being there hemmed in by rocks and ravines! May it be my lot to attain to a better end, before such things come into his mind!' Having uttered this prediction, he forthwith disappeared." This passage so strongly resembles the account in Daniel iv., that even Bertholdt (p. 296) admits that it is identical (*identisch*) with it, though he still maintains that, although it refers to mental derangement, it does nothing to confirm the account of his being made to live with wild beasts, eating grass, and being restored again to his throne. The points of *agreement* in the account of Abydenus and that of Daniel are the following: — (1.) The account of Abydenus, as Bertholdt admits, refers to mental derangement. Such a mental derangement, and the power of prophecy, were in the view of the ancients closely connected, or were identical, and were believed to be produced by the overpowering influence of the gods on the soul. The rational powers of the soul were supposed to be suspended, and the god took entire possession of the body, and through that communicated the knowledge of future events. Compare Dale, *de Oraculis Ethnicorum,* p. 172. Eusebius, *Chron. Arm.-lat.,* p. 61. In itself considered, moreover, nothing would be more natural than that Nebuchadnezzar, in the malady that came upon him, or when it was coming upon him, would express himself in the manner affirmed by Abydenus respecting the coming of the Persian, and the change that would occur to his own kingdom. If the account in Daniel is true respecting the predictions which he is said to have uttered concerning coming events (ch. ii.), nothing would be more natural than that the mind of the monarch would be filled with the anticipation of these events, and that he would give utterance to his anticipations in a time of mental excitement. (2.) There is a remarkable agreement between Abydenus and Daniel in regard to the *time* and the *place* in which what is said of the king occurred. According to Abydenus, the prophetic ecstasy into which he fell was at the close of all his military expeditions, and occurred in the same place, and in the same circumstances, which are mentioned in the book of Daniel—upon his palace—apparently as he walked upon the roof, or upon some place where he had a clear view of the surrounding city which he had built—ἀναβὰς ἐπὶ τὰ βασιλήïα. (3.) The accounts in Abydenus and in Daniel harmonize so far as they relate to the God by whom what occurred was produced. In Daniel it is attributed to the true God, and not to any of the objects of Chaldean worship. It is remarkable that in Abydenus it is not ascribed to an idol, or to any god worshipped by the Chaldees, but to *God* simply, as to a God that was not known—κατασχεθείη θεῷ ὅτεῳ δή. It would seem from this that even the Chaldee tradition did not attribute what was said by Nebuchadnezzar, or what occurred to him, to any of the gods worshipped in Babylon, but to a foreign god, or to one whom they were not accustomed to worship. (4.) In the language which Nebuchadnezzar is reported by Abydenus to have used respecting the return of the Persian king after his conquest, there is a remarkable resemblance to what is said in Daniel, showing that, though the language is applied to different things in Daniel and in Abydenus, it had a common origin. Thus, in the prophecy of Nebuchadnezzar, as reported by Abydenus, it is said, "may he, returning through other ways, be borne through the desert where there are no cities, where

there is no path for men, where wild beasts graze, and the fowls live, wandering about in the midst of rocks and caves." These considerations show that the Chaldean traditions strongly corroborate the account here; or, that there are things in these traditions which cannot be accounted for except on the supposition of the truth of some such occurrence as that which is here stated in Daniel. The sum of the evidence from history is (*a*) that very few things are known of this monarch from profane history ; (*b*) that there is nothing in what *is* known of him which makes what is here stated improbable ; (*c*) that there *are* things related of him which harmonize with what is here affirmed ; and (*d*) that there are traditions which can be best explained by some such supposition as that the record in this chapter is true.

As to the objection that if the edict was promulgated it would not be likely to be lost, or the memory of it fade away, it is sufficient to observe that almost *all* of the edicts, the laws, and the statutes of the Assyrian and Chaldean princes have perished with all the other records of their history, and almost all the facts pertaining to the personal or the public history of these monarchs are now unknown. It cannot be believed that the few fragments which we now have of their writings are all that were ever composed, and in the thing itself there is no more improbability that *this* edict should be lost than any other, or that though it may have been kept by a Hebrew residing among them, it should not have been retained by the Chaldeans themselves. As to the question which has been asked, if this were lost how it could have been recovered again, it is sufficient to remark that, for anything that appears, it never *was* lost in the sense that no one had it in his possession. It would undoubtedly come into the hands of Daniel if he were, according to the account in his book, then in Babylon; and it is not probable that so remarkable a document would be suffered by *him* to be lost. The fact that it was preserved by him is all that is needful to answer the questions on that point. It *may* have been swept away with other matters in the ruin that came upon the Chaldean records in their own country; it has been preserved where it was most important that it should be preserved—in a book where it would be to all ages, and in all lands, a signal proof that God reigns over kings, and that he has power to humble and abase the proud.

II. There is a second class of objections to the credibility of the account in this chapter quite distinct from that just noticed. They are based on what is alleged to be the intrinsic *improbability* that the things which are said to have occurred to Nebuchadnezzar should have happened. It cannot be alleged, indeed, that it is incredible that a monarch should become a maniac —for the kings of the earth are no more exempt from this terrible malady than their subjects; but the objections here referred to relate to the statements respecting the manner in which it is said that this monarch was treated, and that he lived during this long period. These objections may be briefly noticed. (1.). It has been objected, that it is wholly improbable that a monarch at the head of such an empire would, if he became incapable of administering the affairs of government, be so utterly neglected as the representation here would imply:—that he would be suffered to wander from his palace to live with beasts; to fare as they fared, and to become in his whole appearance so *like* a beast. It is indeed admitted by those who make this objection, that there is no improbability that the cala-

mity would befall a king as well as other men; and Michaelis has remarked that it is even more probable that a monarch would be thus afflicted than others (*Anm. Z. Dan.* p. 41; comp. Bertholdt, p. 304), but it is alleged that it is wholly improbable that one so high in office and in power would be treated with the utter neglect which is stated here. "Is it credible," says Bertholdt (p. 300–303), "that the royal family, and the royal counsellors, should have shown so little care or concern for a monarch who had come into a state so perfectly helpless? Would no one have sought him out, and brought him back, if he had wandered so far away? Could he anywhere in the open plains, and the regions about Babylon, destitute of forests, have concealed himself so that no one could have found him? It could only have been by a miracle, that one could have wandered about for so long a time, amidst the dangers which must have befallen him, without having been destroyed by wild beasts, or falling into some form of irrecoverable ruin. What an unwise policy in a government to exhibit to a newly-conquered people so dishonourable a spectacle!"

To this objection it may be replied, (*a*) that its force, as it was formerly urged, may be somewhat removed by a correct interpretation of the chapter, and a more accurate knowledge of the disease which came upon the king, and of the manner in which he was actually treated. According to some views formerly entertained respecting the nature of the malady, it would have been impossible, I admit, to have defended the narrative. In respect to these views, see Notes on ver. 25. It *may* appear, from the fair interpretation of the whole narrative, that nothing more occurred than was natural in the circumstances. (*b*) The supposition that he was left to wander without any kind of oversight or guardianship is entirely gratuitous, and is unauthorized by the account which Nebuchadnezzar gives of what occurred. This opinion has been partly formed from a false interpretation of the phrase in ver. 36—" and my counsellors and my lords *sought unto me*"— as if they had sought him when he was wandering, with a view to find out where he was ; whereas the true meaning of that passage is, that *after* his restoration they sought unto him, or applied to him as the head of the empire, as they had formerly done. (*c*) There is some probability from the passage in ver. 15—"leave the stump of his roots in the earth, *even with a band of iron and brass*"—that Nebuchadnezzar was secured in the manner in which maniacs often have been, and that in his rage he was carefully guarded from all danger of injuring himself. See Notes on ver. 15. (*d*) On the supposition that he was not, still there might have been all proper *care* taken to guard him. All that may be implied when it is said that he "was driven from men, and did eat grass as oxen," &c., may have been that this was his *propensity* in that state ; that he had this roving disposition, and was disposed rather to wander in fields and groves than to dwell in the abodes of men ; and that he was driven *by this propensity*, not *by men*, to leave his palace, and to take up his residence in parks or groves—anywhere rather than in human habitations. This has been not an uncommon propensity with maniacs, and there is no improbability in supposing that this was permitted by those who had the care of him, as far as was consistent with his safety, and with what was due to him as a monarch, though his reason was driven from its throne. In the parks attached to the palace ; in the large pleasure-grounds, that were not improbably stocked with various kinds of animals, as a sort of royal menagerie, there is no improbability in supposing that he may have been allowed at proper times, and with suitable guards, to roam, nor that the fallen and humbled monarch may have found, in comparatively lucid intervals, a degree of pleasant amusement in such grounds, nor even that it might be supposed that this would contribute to his restoration to health. Nor, on *any* supposition in regard to these statements, even admitting that there was a great degree of criminal inattention on the part of his friends, would his treatment have been worse than what has usually occurred in respect to the insane. Up to quite a recent period, and even now in many civilized lands, the insane have been treated with the most gross neglect, and with the severest cruelty, even by their friends. Left to wander where they chose without a protector ; unshaven and unwashed ; the sport of the idle and the vicious ; thrown into common jails among felons ; bound with heavy chains to the cold walls of dungeons ; confined in cellars or garrets with no fire in the coldest weather ; with insufficient clothing, perhaps entirely naked, and in the midst of the most disgusting filth—such treatment, even in Christian lands, and by Christian people, may show that in a heathen land, five hundred years before the light of Christianity dawned upon the world, it is not *wholly* incredible that an insane monarch *might* have been treated in the manner described in this chapter. If the best friends now may so neglect, or treat with such severity, an insane son or daughter, there is no improbability in supposing that in an age of comparative barbarism there may have been as *little* humanity as is implied in this chapter. The following extracts from the Second Annual Report of the Prison Discipline Society (*Boston*) will show what has occurred in the nineteenth century, in this Christian land, and in the old commonwealth of Massachusetts — a commonwealth distinguished for morals, and for humane feeling—and will demonstrate at the same time that what is here stated about the monarch of heathen Babylon is not unworthy of belief. They refer to the treatment of lunatics in that commonwealth before the establishment of the hospital for the insane at Worcester. "In Massachusetts, by an examination made with care, about thirty lunatics have been found in prison. In one prison were found three; in another five; in another six; and in another ten. It is a source of great complaint with the sheriffs and jailers that they must receive such persons, because they have no suitable accommodations for them. Of those last mentioned, one was found in an apartment in which he had been nine years. He had a wreath of rags around his body, and another around his neck. This was all his clothing. He had no bed, chair, or bench. Two or three rough planks were strewed around the room; a heap of filthy straw, like the nest of swine, was in the corner. He had built a bird's nest of mud in the iron grate of his den. Connected with his wretched apartment was a dark dungeon, having no orifice for the admission of light, heat, or air, except the iron door, about two and a half feet square, opening into it from the prison. The other lunatics in the same prison were scattered about in different apartments, with thieves and murderers, and persons under arrest, but not yet convicted of guilt. In the prison of five lunatics, they were confined in separate cells, which were almost dark dungeons. It was difficult after the door was open to see them distinctly.

The ventilation was so incomplete that more than one person on entering them has found the air so fetid as to produce nausea, and almost vomiting. The old straw on which they were laid, and their filthy garments, were such as to make their insanity more hopeless; and at one time it was not considered within the province of the physician to examine particularly the condition of the lunatics. In these circumstances any improvement of their minds could hardly be expected. Instead of having three out of four restored to reason, as is the fact in some of the favoured lunatic asylums, it is to be feared that in these circumstances some who might otherwise be restored would become incurable, and that others might lose their lives, to say nothing of present suffering. In the prison in which were six lunatics their condition was less wretched. But they were sometimes an annoyance, and sometimes a sport to the convicts; and even the apartment in which the females were confined opened into the yard of the men; there was an injurious interchange of obscenity and profanity between them, which was not restrained by the presence of the keeper. In the prison, or house of correction, so called, in which were ten lunatics, two were found about seventy years of age, a male and female, in the same apartment of an upper story. The female was lying upon a heap of straw under a broken window. The snow in a severe storm was beating through the window, and lay upon the straw around her withered body, which was partially covered with a few filthy and tattered garments. The man was lying in the corner of the room in a similar situation, except that he was less exposed to the storm. The former had been in this apartment six, and the latter twenty-one years. Another lunatic in the same prison was found in a plank apartment of the first story, where he had been eight years. During this time he had never left the room but twice. The door of this apartment had not been opened in eighteen months. The food was furnished through a small orifice in the door. The room was warmed by no fire ; and still the woman of the house said *'he had never froze.'* As he was seen through the orifice of the door, the first question was, 'Is that a human being?' The hair was gone from one side of his head, and his eyes were like balls of fire. In the cellar of the same prison were five lunatics. The windows of this cellar were no defence against the storm, and, as might be supposed, the woman of the house said, 'We have a sight to do to keep them from freezing.' There was no fire in this cellar which could be felt by four of these lunatics. One of the five had a little fire of turf in an apartment of the cellar by herself. She was, however, infuriate, if any one came near her. The woman was committed to this cellar seventeen years ago. The apartments are about six feet by eight. They are made of coarse plank, and have an orifice in the door for the admission of light and air, about six inches by four. The darkness was such in two of these apartments that nothing could be seen by looking through the orifice in the door. At the same time there was a poor lunatic in each. A man who has grown old was committed to one of them in 1810, and had lived in it seventeen years. An emaciated female was found in a similar apartment, in the dark, without fire, almost without covering, where she had been nearly two years. A coloured woman in another, in which she had been six years ; and a miserable man in another, in which he had been four years."

(2.) It is asked by Bertholdt, as an objection (p. 301), whether " it is credible that one who had been for so long a time a maniac would be restored again to the throne ; and whether the government would be again placed in his hands, without any apprehension that he would relapse into the same state? Or whether it can be believed that the lives and fortunes of so many millions would be again intrusted to his will and power?" To these questions it may be replied : (*a*) That if he was restored to his reason he had a *right* to the throne, and it might not have been a doubtful point whether he should be restored to it or not. (*b*) It is probable that during that time a *regency* was appointed, and that there would be a hope entertained that he would be restored. Undoubtedly, during the continuation of this malady, the government would be, as was the case during the somewhat similar malady of George III. of Great Britain, placed in the hands of others, and unless there was a revolution, or an usurpation, he would be, of course, restored to his throne on the recovery of his reason. (*c*) To this it may be added, that he was a monarch who had been eminently successful in his conquests ; who had done much to enlarge the limits of the empire, and to adorn the capital ; and that much was to be apprehended from the character of his legal successor, Evil-Merodach (Hengstenberg, p. 113) ; and that if he were displaced, they who were then the chief officers of the nation had reason to suppose that, in accordance with Oriental usage on the accession of a new sovereign, they would lose their places.

(3.) It has been asked also, as an objection, whether " it is not to be presumed that Nebuchadnezzar, on the supposition that he was restored from so fearful a malady, would have employed all the means in his power to suppress the knowledge of it ; or whether, if any communication was made in regard to it, pains would not have been taken to give a colouring to the account by suppressing the real truth, and by attributing the affliction to some other cause?"—Bertholdt, p. 301. To this it may be replied: (a) That if the representation here made of the cause of his malady is correct, that it was a Divine judgment on him for his pride, and that God's design in bringing it on him was that he himself might be made known, it is reasonable to presume that, on his restoration, there would be such a Divine influence on the mind of the monarch, as to lead him to make this proclamation, or this public recognition of the Most High ; (b) that the edict seems to have been made, not as a matter of policy, but under the fresh recollection of a restoration from so terrible a calamity; (c) that Nebuchadnezzar seems to have been a man who had a conscience that prompted him to a decided acknowledgment of Divine interposition; (d) that he had a strong religious propensity (comp. ch. iii.), and was ready to make any public acknowledgment of that which he regarded as Divine ; and (e) that perhaps he supposed that, by stating the truth as it actually occurred, a better impression might be made than already existed in regard to the nature of the malady. It may have been an object, also, with him to convince his subjects that, although he had been deprived of his reason, he was now, in fact, restored to a sound mind.

(4.) Another ground of objection has been urged by Eichhorn, Bertholdt, and others, derived from the character of the edict. It is said that "the narrative represents Nebuchadnezzar at one time as an orthodox Jew, setting forth his views almost in the very words used in the writings of the Jews, and which only a Jew would employ (see vers.

2, 3, 34–37), and then again as a mere idolater, using the language which an idolater would employ, and still acknowledging the reality of idol gods, vers. 8, 9, 18." To this it may be replied, that this very circumstance is rather a confirmation of the truth of the account than otherwise. It is just such an account as we should suppose that a monarch, trained up in idolatry, and practising it all his life, and yet suddenly, and in this impressive manner, made acquainted with the true God, would be likely to give. In an edict published by such a monarch, under such circumstances, it would be strange if there should be no betrayal of the fact that he had been a worshipper of heathen gods, nor would it be strange that when he disclosed his dream to Daniel, asking him to interpret it, and professing to believe that he was under the influence of inspiration from above, he should trace it to the gods in general, vers. 8, 9, 18. And, in like manner, if the thing actually occurred, as is related, it would be certain that he would use such language in describing it as an "orthodox Jew" might use. It is to be remembered that he is represented as obtaining his view of what was meant by the vision from Daniel, and nothing is more probable than that he would use such language as Daniel would have suggested. It could not be supposed that one who had been an idolater all his life would soon efface from his mind all the impressions made by the habit of idolatry, so that no traces of it would appear in a proclamation on an occasion like this ; nor could it be supposed that there would be no recognition of God as the true God. Nothing would be more natural than such an intermingling of false notions with the true. Indeed, there is in fact scarcely any circumstance in regard to this chapter that has more the air of authenticity, nor could there well be anything more probable in itself, than what is here stated. It is just such an intermingling of truth with falsehood as we should expect in a mind trained in heathenism; and yet this is a circumstance which would not be *very* likely to occur to one who attempted a forgery, or who endeavoured to draw the character of a heathen monarch in such circumstances without authentic materials. If the edict was the work of a Jew, he would have been likely to represent its author without any remains of heathenism in his mind : if it were the work of a heathen, there would have been no such recognition of the true God. If it is a mere fiction, the artifice is too refined to have been likely to occur, to attempt to draw him in this state of mind, where there was an intermingling of falsehood with truth ; of the remains of all his old habits of thinking, with new and momentous truths that had just begun to dawn on his mind. The supposition that will best suit all the circumstances of the case, and be liable to the fewest objections, is, that the account is an unvarnished statement of what actually occurred. On the whole subject of the objections to this chapter, the reader may consult Hengstenberg, *Die Authentie des Daniel*, pp. 100-119. For many of the remarks here made, I am indebted to that work. Comp. further the Notes on ver. 25, *seq.* of the chap.

§ II.—ANALYSIS OF THE CHAPTER.

THE chapter professes to be an edict published by Nebuchadnezzar after his recovery from a long period of insanity, which was brought upon him for his pride. The edict was promulgated with a view to lead men to acknowledge the true God. It states, in general, that the approach of his calamity was made known to him in a dream, which was interpreted by Daniel ; that his own heart had been lifted up with pride in view of the splendid city which he had built ; that the predicted malady came suddenly upon him, even while he was indulging in these proud reflections; that he was driven away from the abodes of men, a poor neglected maniac ; that he again recovered his reason, and then his throne ; and that the God who had thus humbled him, and again restored him, was the true God, and was worthy of universal adoration and praise. The edict, therefore, embraces the following parts:—

I. The reason why it was promulgated—to show to all people, dwelling in all parts of the earth, the great things which the high God had done towards him, vers. 1-3.

II. The statement of the fact that he had had a dream which greatly alarmed him, and which none of the Chaldean soothsayers had been able to interpret, vers. 4-7.

III. The statement of the dream in full to Daniel, vers. 8-18.

IV. The interpretation of the dream by Daniel—predicting the fact that he would become a maniac, and would be driven from his throne and kingdom, and compelled to take up his abode with the beasts of the field—a poor neglected outcast, vers. 19-26.

V. The solemn and faithful counsel of Daniel to him to break off his sins, and to become a righteous man, if possibly the terrible calamity might be averted, ver. 27.

VI. The fulfilment of the prediction of Daniel. Nebuchadnezzar was walking on his palace, and, in the pride of his heart, surveying the great city which he had built, and suddenly a voice from heaven addressed him, announcing that his kingdom had departed, and his reason left him, vers. 28-33.

CHAPTER IV.

NEBUCHADNEZZAR the king, unto *a* all people, nations, and languages, that dwell

a ch. 3. 4; 6. 25-27.

VII. At the end of the appointed time, his reason was restored, and he gratefully acknowledged the Divine sovereignty, and was again reinstated on his throne, vers. 34-36.

VIII. For all this, he says that he praised the God of heaven, for he had learned that all his works are truth, and his ways judgment, and that those who walk in pride he is able to abase, ver. 37.

1. *Nebuchadnezzar the king, unto all people*, &c. The Syriac here has, "Nebuchadnezzar the king *wrote* to all people," &c. Many manuscripts in the Chaldee have שְׁלַח *sent*, and some have כְּתַב *wrote;* but neither of these readings are probably genuine, nor are they necessary. The passage is rather a part of the edict of the king than a narrative of the author of the book, and in such an edict the comparatively abrupt style of the present reading would be that which would be adopted. The Septuagint has inserted here a historical statement of the fact that Nebuchadnezzar did actually issue such an edict: "And Nebuchadnezzar the king wrote an encyclical epistle—ἐπιστολὴν ἐγκύκλιον—to all those nations in every place, and to the regions, and to all the tongues that dwell in all countries, generations and generations: 'Nebuchadnezzar the king,'" &c. But nothing of this is in the original. ¶ *Unto all people, nations, and languages that dwell in all the earth.* That is, people speaking all the languages of the earth. Many nations were under the sceptre of the king of Babylon; but it would seem that he designed this as a general proclamation, not only to those who were embraced in his empire, but to all the people of the world. Such a proclamation would be much in accordance with the Oriental style. Comp. Notes on ch. iii. 4. ¶ *Peace be multiplied unto*

in all the earth; Peace *b* be multiplied unto you.

2 I [1] thought it good to show the signs and wonders that the

b 1 Pet. 1. 2.   [1] *it was seemly before me.*

you. This is in accordance with the usual Oriental salutation. Comp. Gen. xliii. 23; Judg. vi. 23; 1 Sam. xxv. 6; Psa. cxxii. 7; Luke x. 5; Eph. vi. 23; 1 Pet. i. 2. This is the salutation with which one meets another now in the Oriental world—the same word still being retained, *Shalom*, or *Salam*. The idea seemed to be, that every blessing was found in peace, and every evil in conflict and war. The expression included the wish that they might be preserved from all that would disturb them; that they might be contented, quiet, prosperous, and happy. When it is said "peace be *multiplied*," the wish is that it might *abound*, or that they might be blessed with the numberless mercies which peace produces.

2. *I thought it good.* Marg., *it was seemly before me.* The marginal reading is more in accordance with the original (שְׁפַר קֳדָמַי). The proper meaning of the Chaldee word (שְׁפַר) is, to be fair or beautiful; and the sense here is, that it seemed to him to be appropriate or becoming to make this public proclamation. It was fit and right that what God had done to him should be proclaimed to all nations. ¶ *To show the signs and wonders.* Signs and wonders, as denoting mighty miracles, are not unfrequently connected in the Scriptures. See Exod. vii. 3; Deut. iv. 34; xiii. 1; xxxiv. 11; Isa. viii. 18; Jer. xxxii. 20. The word rendered *signs* (Heb. אוֹת—Chald. אָת) means, properly, a *sign*, as something significant, or something that points out or designates anything; as Gen. i. 14, "shall be for *signs* and for seasons;" that is, signs of seasons. Then the word denotes an ensign, a military flag, Numb. ii. 2; then a sign of something past, a token or remembrancer, Exod. xiii. 9, 16; Deut. vi. 8; then a sign of something future, a portent, an omen, Isa. viii. 18; then a sign or token of what is visible, as circumcision, Gen. xvii. 11, or the rainbow in the cloud, as a

high *a* God hath wrought toward me.

a ch. 3 26.

token of the covenant which God made with man, Gen. ix. 12; then anything which serves as a sign or proof of the fulfilment of prophecy, Exod. iii. 12; 1 Sam. ii. 34; and then it refers to anything which is a sign or proof of Divine power, Deut. iv. 34; vi. 22; vii. 19, *et al.* The Hebrew word is commonly rendered *signs*, but it is also rendered *token, ensign, miracles.* As applied to what God does, it seems to be used in the sense of anything that is significant of his presence and power; anything that shall manifestly show that what occurs is done by him; anything that is beyond human ability, and that makes known the being and the perfections of God by a direct and extraordinary manifestation. Here the meaning is, that what was done in so remarkable a manner was *significant* of the agency of God; it was that which demonstrated that he exists, and that showed his greatness. The word rendered *wonders* (תְּמַהּ) means, properly, that which is fitted to produce astonishment, or to lead one to wonder, and is applied to miracles as adapted to produce that effect. It refers to that state of mind which exists where anything occurs out of the ordinary course of nature, or which indicates supernatural power. The Hebrew word rendered *wonders* is often used to denote miracles, Exod. iii. 20; vii. 3; xi. 9; Deut. vi. 22, *et al.* The meaning here is, that what had occurred was fitted to excite amazement, and to lead men to wonder at the mighty works of God. ¶ *That the high God.* The God who is exalted, or lifted up; that is, the God who is above all. See ch. iii. 26. It is an appellation which would be given to God as the Supreme Being. The Greek translation of this verse is, "And now I show unto you the deeds—πραξεις— which the great God has done unto me, for it seemed good to me to show to you and your wise men"—τοῖς σοφισταῖς ὑμῶν.

3. *How great* are *his signs!* How great and wonderful are the things by

3 How great *are* his signs! *b* and how mighty *are* his wonders! *c* his

b Deut. 4. 34; Ps. 105. 27; Heb. 2. 4.
c Ps. 72. 18; 86. 10; Isa. 25. 1; 28. 29.

which he makes himself known in this manner! The allusion is doubtless to what had occurred to himself—the event by which a monarch of such state and power had been reduced to a condition so humble. With propriety he would regard this as a signal instance of the Divine interposition, and as adapted to give him an exalted view of the supremacy of the true God. ¶ *And how mighty* are *his wonders!* The wonderful events which he does; the things fitted to produce admiration and astonishment. Comp. Psal. lxxii. 18; lxxxvi. 10; Isa. xxv. 1. ¶ *His kingdom* is *an everlasting kingdom.* Nebuchadnezzar was doubtless led to this reflection by what had occurred to him. He, the most mighty monarch then on earth, had seen that *his* throne had no stability; he had seen that God had power at his will to bring him down from his lofty seat, and to transfer his authority to other hands; and he was naturally led to reflect that the throne of God was the only one that was stable and permanent. He could not but be convinced that God reigned over all, and that his kingdom was not subject to the vicissitudes which occur in the kingdoms of this world. There have been few occurrences on the earth better adapted to teach this lesson than this. ¶ *And his dominion* is *from generation to generation.* That is, it is perpetual. It is not liable to be arrested as that of man is, by death; it does not pass over from one family to another as an earthly sceptre often does. The same sceptre; the same system of laws; the same providential arrangements; the same methods of reward and punishment, have always existed under his government, and will continue to do so to the end of time. There is, perhaps, no more sublime view that can be taken of the government of God than this. All earthly princes die; all authority lodged in the hands of an earthly monarch is soon withdrawn. No one is so mighty that he can prolong his own reign; and no one can make his own

kingdom *is* an everlasting *a* kingdom, and his dominion *b is* from
generation to generation.

a ch. 2. 44; Rev. 11.15.　*b* Job 26.2; 1 Pet. 4.11.

authority extend to the next generation.
Earthly governments, therefore, however mighty, are of short duration ; and
history is made up of the records of a
great number of such administrations,
many of them exceedingly brief, and of
very various character. The sceptre
falls from the hand of the monarch,
never to be resumed by him again ;
another grasps it to retain it also but a
little time, and then he passes away.
But the dominion of God is in all generations the same. This generation is
under the government of the same
Sovereign who reigned when Semiramis or Numa lived; and though the
sceptre has long since fallen from the
hands of Alexander and the Cæsars,
yet the same God who ruled in their
age is still on the throne.

4. *I Nebuchadnezzar was at rest.*
Some manuscripts in the Greek add
here, "In the eighteenth year of his
reign Nebuchadnezzar said." These
words, however, are not in the Hebrew,
and are of no authority. The word
rendered "*at rest*" (שְׁלֵה) means, to be
secure ; to be free from apprehension
or alarm. He designs to describe a
state of tranquillity and security. Gr.,
at peace—εἰρηνεύων : enjoying peace, or
in a condition to enjoy peace. His
wars were over ; his kingdom was tranquil ; he had built a magnificent capital; he had gathered around him the
wealth and the luxuries of the world,
and he was now in a condition to pass
away the remainder of his life in ease
and happiness. ¶ *In mine house.* In
his royal residence. It is possible that
the two words here—*house* and *palace*—
may refer to somewhat different things :
the former—*house*—more particularly
to his own private family—his domestic
relations as a man ; and the latter—
palace—to those connected with the
government who resided in his palace.
If this is so, then the passage would
mean that all around him was peaceful,
and that from no source had he any
cause of disquiet. In his own private

4 ¶ I Nebuchadnezzar was at
rest in mine house, and flourishing
in my palace :
5 I saw a dream which made me

family—embracing his wife and children ; and in the arrangements of the
palace — embracing those who had
charge of public affairs, he had no cause
of uneasiness. ¶ *And flourishing in
my palace.* Gr., εὐθηνῶν ἐπὶ τοῦ θρόνου
μου — literally, "abundant upon my
throne;" that is, he was tranquil, calm,
prosperous on his throne. The Chaldee
word (רַעֲנַן) means, properly, *green;*
as, for example, of leaves or foliage.
Comp. the Hebrew word in Jer. xvii.
8 ; "He shall be as a tree planted by
the waters—her leaf shall be *green.*"
Deut. xii. 2, "Under every *green* tree,"
2 Kings xvi. 4. A green and flourishing tree becomes thus the emblem of
prosperity. See Psal. i. 3 ; xxxvii. 35 ;
xcii. 12–14. The general meaning
here is, that he was enjoying abundant
prosperity. His kingdom was at peace,
and in his own home he had every
means of tranquil enjoyment.

5. *I saw a dream.* That is, he saw
a representation made to him in a dream.
There is something incongruous in our
language in saying of one that he *saw*
a dream. ¶ *Which made me afraid.*
The fear evidently arose from the apprehension that it was designed to disclose some important and solemn event.
This was in accordance with a prevalent belief then (comp. ch. ii. 1), and it
may be added that it is in accordance
with a prevalent belief now. There are
few persons, whatever may be their abstract belief, who are not more or less
disturbed by fearful and solemn representations passing before the mind in
the visions of the night. Comp. Job
iv. 12–17; xxxiii. 14, 15. So Virgil
(*Æn.* iv. 9):—

　"Anna soror, quæ me suspensam insomnia
　　terrent!"

¶ *And the thoughts upon my bed.* The
thoughts which I had upon my bed;
to wit, in my dream. ¶ *And the visions of my head.* What I seemed to
see. The vision seemed to be floating
around his head. ¶ *Troubled me.* Disturbed me ; produced apprehension of

afraid, and the thoughts upon my bed and the visions of my head troubled me.

6 Therefore made I a decree to bring in all the wise *men* of Babylon before me, that they might make known unto me the interpretation of the dream.

7 Then *a* came in the magicians, the astrologers, the Chaldeans, and the soothsayers: and I told the dream before them; but they did not make known unto me the interpretation thereof.

8 ¶ But at the last Daniel came

a ch. 2. 1, 2.

---

what was to come; of some great and important event.

6. *Therefore made I a decree.* The word here rendered *decree* (טְעֵם) means, commonly, *taste, flavour,* as of wine; then *judgment, discernment, reason;* and then a judgment of a king, a mandate, edict. Comp. chap. iii. 10. The primary notion seems to be that of a delicate *taste* enabling one to determine the qualities of wines, viands, &c.; and then a delicate and nice discrimination in regard to the qualities of actions. The word thus expresses a sound and accurate judgment, and is applied to a decree or edict, as declared by one who had the qualifications to express such a judgment. Here it means, that he issued a royal order to summon into his presence all who could be supposed to be qualified to explain the dream. The Greek (Cod. Chisian.) omits vers. 6, 7, 8, and 9. ¶ *To bring in all the wise* men, &c. Particularly such as are enumerated in the following verse. Comp. chap. ii. 12. It was in accordance with his habit thus to call in the wise men who were retained at court to give counsel, and to explain those things which seemed to be an intimation of the Divine will. See Notes on ch. ii. 2. Comp. also Gen. xli. 8.

7. *Then came in the magicians,* &c. All the words occurring here are found in ch. ii. 2, and are explained in the Notes on that verse, except the word rendered *soothsayers.* This occurs in chap. ii. 27. See it explained in the Notes on that verse. All these words refer to the same general class of persons—those who were regarded as endued with eminent wisdom; who were supposed to be qualified to explain remarkable occurrences, to foretell the future, and to declare the will of heaven from portents and wonders. At a time

when there was yet a limited revelation; when the boundaries of science were not determined with accuracy; when it was not certain but that some way *might* be ascertained of lifting the mysterious veil from the future, and when it was an open question whether that might not be by dreams or by communication with departed spirits, or by some undisclosed secrets of nature, it was not unnatural that persons should be found who claimed that this knowledge was under their control. Such claimants to preternatural knowledge are found indeed in every age; and though a large portion of them are undoubted deceivers, yet the existence of such an order of persons should be regarded as merely the *exponent* of the deep and earnest desire existing in the human bosom to penetrate the mysterious future; to find *something* that shall disclose to man, all whose great interests lie *in* the future, what is yet to be. Comp. the remarks at the close of ch. ii. ¶ *And I told the dream before them,* &c. In their presence. In this instance he did not lay on them so hard a requisition as he did on a former occasion, when he required them not only to interpret the dream, but to tell him what it was, ch. ii. But their pretended power here was equally vain. Whether they *attempted* an interpretation of this dream does not appear; but if they did, it was wholly unsatisfactory to the king himself. It would seem more probable that they supposed that the dream might have some reference to the proud monarch himself, and that, as it indicated some awful calamity, they did not dare to hazard a conjecture in regard to its meaning.

8. *But at the last.* After the others had shown that they could not interpret the dream. Why Daniel was not called with the others does not appear;

in before me, whose name ^a was Belteshazzar, according to the name of my god, and in whom is the spirit ^b of the holy gods: and

before him I told the dream, saying,

9 O Belteshazzar, master of the magicians, because I know that the spirit of the holy gods is in thee,

nor is it said in what manner he was at last summoned into the presence of the king. It is probable that his skill on a former occasion (ch. ii.) was remembered, and that when all the others showed that they had no power to interpret the dream, he was called in by Nebuchadnezzar. The Latin Vulgate renders this, Donec collega ingressus est—"until a colleague entered." The Greek, ἕως, until. Aquila and Symmachus render it, "until another entered before me, Daniel." The common version expresses the sense of the Chaldee with sufficient accuracy, though a more literal translation would be, "until afterwards." ¶ Whose name was Belteshazzar. That is, this was the name which he bore at court, or which had been given him by the Chaldeans. See Notes on ch. i. 7. ¶ According to the name of my god. That is, the name of my god Bel, or Belus, is incorporated in the name given to him. This is referred to here, probably, to show the propriety of thus invoking his aid; because he bore the name of the god whom the monarch had adored. There would seem to be a special fitness in summoning him before him, to explain what was supposed to be an intimation of the will of the god whom he worshipped. There is a singular, though not unnatural, mixture of the sentiments of heathenism and of the true religion in the expressions which this monarch uses in this chapter. He had been a heathen all his life; yet he had had some knowledge of the true God, and had been made to feel that he was worthy of universal adoration and praise, ch. ii. That, in this state of mind, he should alternately express such sentiments as were originated by heathenism, and those which spring from just views of God, is not unnatural or improbable. ¶ And in whom is the spirit of the holy gods. It is not easy to determine whom he meant by the holy gods. It would seem probable that this was such language as was dic-

tated by the fact that he had been an idolater. He had been brought to feel that the God whom Daniel worshipped, and by whose aid he had been enabled to interpret the dream, was a true God, and was worthy of universal homage; but perhaps his ideas were still much confused, and he only regarded him as superior to all others, though he did not intend to deny the real existence of others. It might be true, in his apprehension, that there were other gods, though the God of Daniel was supreme, and perhaps he meant to say that the spirit of all the gods was in Daniel; that in an eminent degree he was the favourite of heaven, and that he was able to interpret any communication which came from the invisible world. It is perhaps unnecessary to observe here that the word spirit has no intended reference to the Holy Spirit. It is probably used with reference to the belief that the gods were accustomed to impart wisdom and knowledge to certain men, and may mean that the very spirit of wisdom and knowledge which dwelt in the gods themselves seemed to dwell in the bosom of Daniel. ¶ And before him I told the dream. Not requiring him, as he did before (ch. ii.), to state both the dream and its meaning.

9. O Belteshazzar, master of the magicians. "Master," in the sense that he was first among them, or was superior to them all. Or, perhaps, he still retained office at the head of this class of men—the office to which he had been appointed when he interpreted the former dream, ch. ii. 48. The word rendered master (רַב Rab) is that which was applied to a teacher, a chief, or a great man among the Jews — from whence came the title Rabbi. Comp. ch. ii. 48; v. 11. ¶ Because I know that the spirit of the holy gods is in thee. This he had learned by the skill which he had shown in interpreting his dream on a former occasion, ch. ii.

and no secret troubleth *a* thee, tell me the visions of my dream that I have seen, and the interpretation thereof.

10 Thus *were* the visions of my head in my bed: I ¹ saw, and, behold,

a Isa. 33. 18; 54. 14. 1 *was seeing.*

b tree in the midst of the earth, and the height thereof *was* great.

11 The tree grew, and was strong, and the height thereof reached unto heaven, and the sight thereof to the end of all the earth.

b Ezek. 31. 3, &c.

¶ *And no secret troubleth thee.* That is, so troubles you that you cannot explain it; it is not beyond your power to disclose its signification. The word rendered *secret* (רז) occurs in ch. ii. 18, 19, 27–30, 47. It is not elsewhere found. It means that which is *hidden,* and has reference here to the concealed truth or intimation of the Divine will couched under a dream. The word rendered "*troubleth thee*" (אנס) means, to urge, to press, to compel; and the idea here is, that it did not so *press* upon him as to give him anxiety. It was an easy matter for him to disclose its meaning. Gr., "No mystery is beyond your power"—οὐκ ἀδυνατεῖ σε. ¶ *Tell me the visions of my dream.* The nature of the vision, or the purport of what I have seen. He seems to have desired to know *what sort* of a vision he should regard this to be, as well as its interpretation—whether as an intimation of the Divine will, or as an ordinary dream. The Greek and Arabic render this, "*Hear* the vision of my dream, and tell me the interpretation thereof." This accords better with the probable meaning of the passage, though the word *hear* is not in the Chaldee.

10. *Thus* were *the visions of my head in my bed.* These are the things which I saw upon my bed. When he says that they were the "visions of his *head,*" he states a doctrine which was then doubtless regarded as the truth, that the head is the seat of thought. ¶ *I saw.* Marg., *was seeing.* Chald., "seeing I saw." The phrase would imply attentive and calm contemplation. It was not a flitting vision; it was an object which he contemplated deliberately so as to retain a distinct remembrance of its form and appearance. ¶ *And, behold, a tree in the*

midst of the earth. Occupying a central position on the earth. It seems to have been by itself—remote from any forest: to have stood alone. Its central position, no less than its size and proportions, attracted his attention. Such a tree, thus towering to the heavens, and sending out its branches afar, and affording a shade to the beasts of the field, and a home to the fowls of heaven (ver. 12), was a striking emblem of a great and mighty monarch, and it undoubtedly occurred to Nebuchadnezzar at once that the vision had some reference to himself. Thus in Ezek. xxxi. 3, the Assyrian king is compared with a magnificent cedar: "Behold, the Assyrian was a cedar in Lebanon, with fair branches, and with a shadowing shroud, and of a high stature, and his top was among the thick boughs." Comp. also Ezek. xvii. 22–24, where "the high tree and the green tree" refer probably to Nebuchadnezzar. See Notes on Isa. ii. 13. Comp. Is. x. 18, 19; Jer. xxii. 7, 23. Homer often compares his heroes to trees. Hector, felled by a stone, is compared with an oak overthrown by a thunderbolt. The fall of Simoisius is compared by him to that of a poplar, and that of Euphorbus to the fall of a beautiful olive. Nothing is more obvious than the comparison of a hero with a lofty tree of the forest, and hence it was natural for Nebuchadnezzar to suppose that this vision had a reference to himself. ¶ *And the height thereof was great.* In the next verse it is said to have reached to heaven.

[The symbolic or sacred tree occupies a prominent place in the Assyrian mythology. It is here represented under some variation of its conventional form; and on either side of it is a figure of Nisroch, with the usual attributes. The tree of Nebuchadnezzar's vision may have

12 The leaves thereof *were* fair, and the fruit thereof much, and in it *was* meat for all: the beasts *a* of the field had shadow *b* under it, and the fowls of the heaven dwelt in the boughs thereof, and all flesh was fed of it.

a Ezek. 17. 23.　　　*b* Lam. 4. 20.

been generally suggested to the monarch's mind by the religious emblem with which he was familiar, in the temple of his gods. The sculpture is from the Hall of Nisroch, at Nimroud.]

11. *The tree grew.* Or the tree was *great*—רְבָה. It does not mean that the tree *grew* while he was looking at it so as to reach to the heaven, but that it stood before him in all its glory, its top reaching to the sky, and its branches extending afar. ¶ *And was strong.* It was well-proportioned, with a trunk adapted to its height, and to the mass of boughs and foliage which it bore. The strength here refers to its trunk, and to the fact that it seemed fixed firmly in the earth. ¶ *And the height thereof reached unto heaven.* To the sky; to the region of the clouds. The comparison of trees reaching to heaven is common in Greek and Latin authors.—Grotius. Comp. Virgil's description of Fame.

"Mox sese attollit in auras,
Ingrediturque solo, et caput inter nubila condit."—*Æn.* iv. 176.

¶ *And the sight thereof to the end of all the earth.* It could be seen, or was visible in all parts of the earth. The Greek here for *sight* is κῦτος, breadth, *capaciousness.* Herodotus (*Polymnia*) describes a vision remarkably similar to this, as indicative of a wide and universal monarchy, respecting Xerxes:

"After these things there was a third vision in his sleep, which the magicians (μάγοι) hearing of, said that it pertained to all the earth, and denoted that all men would be subject to him. The vision was this: Xerxes seemed to be crowned with a branch of laurel, and the branches of laurel seemed to extend through all the earth." The vision which Nebuchadnezzar had here, of a tree so conspicuous as to be seen from any part of the world, was one that would be naturally applied to a sovereign having a universal sway.

12. *The leaves thereof* were *fair.* Were beautiful. That is, they were abundant, and green, and there were no signs of decay. Everything indicated a vigorous and healthy growth—a tree in its full beauty and majesty—a striking emblem of a monarch in his glory. ¶ *And the fruit thereof much.* It was loaded with fruit—showing that the tree was in its full vigour. ¶ *And in it* was *meat for all.* Food for all, for so the word *meat* was formerly used. This would indicate the dependence of the multitudes on him whom the tree represented, and would also denote that he was a liberal dispenser of his favours. ¶ *The beasts of the field*

13 I saw in the visions of my head upon my bed, and, behold, a

a vers. 17, 23.

---

had shadow under it. Found a grateful shade under it in the burning heat of noon—a striking emblem of the blessings of a monarchy affording protection, and giving peace to all under it. ¶ *And the fowls of the heaven dwelt in the boughs thereof.* The fowls of the air. They built their nests and reared their young there undisturbed, another striking emblem of the protection afforded under the great monarchy designed to be represented. ¶ *And all flesh was fed of it.* All animals; all that lived. It furnished protection, a home, and food for all. Bertholdt renders this, "all men." In the Greek *Codex Chisian.* there is the following version or paraphrase given of this passage: "Its vision was great, its top reached to the heaven, and its breadth (κῦτος) to the clouds—they filled the things (τὰ) under the heaven—there was a sun and moon, they dwelt in it, and enlightened all the earth."

13. *I saw in the visions of my head upon my bed.* In the visions that passed before me as I lay upon my bed, ver. 10. ¶ *And, behold, a watcher and an holy one.* Or rather, perhaps, "even a holy one;" or, "who was a holy one." He evidently does not intend to refer to *two* beings, a "watcher," *and* "one who was holy;" but he means to designate the character of the watcher, that he was holy, or that he was one of the class of "watchers" who were ranked as holy—as if there were others to whom the name "watcher" might be applied who were *not* holy. So Bertholdt, "not two, but only one, who was both a watcher, and was holy; one of those known as watchers and as holy ones." The copulative (ו) *and* may be so used as to denote not an additional one or thing, but to specify something in addition to, or in explanation of, what the name applied would indicate. Comp. 1 Sam. xxviii. 3: "In Ramah, even (ו) in his own city." 1 Sam. xvii. 40: "And put them in a shepherd's bag which he had, even (ו) in a scrip." Comp. Psa. lxviii. 9 (10); Amos iii. 11; iv. 10; Jer. xv. 13;

watcher *a* and an holy *b* one came down from heaven.

b Matt. 25. 31; Rev. 14. 10.

Isa. i. 13; .xiii. 14; lvii. 11; Eccles. viii. 2.—Gesenius, *Lex.* The word rendered *watcher* (עִיר) is rendered in the Vulgate *vigil;* in the Greek of Theodotion the word is retained without an attempt to translate it—εἷς; the Codex Chisianus has ἄγγελος—"an angel was sent in his strength from heaven." The original word (עִיר) means, properly, *a watcher,* from עִיר, to be hot and ardent; then to be lively, or active, and then to awake, to be awake, to be awake at night, to watch. Comp. Cant. v. 2; Mal. ii. 12. The word used here is employed to denote one who watches, only in this chapter of Daniel, vers. 13, 17, 23. It is in these places evidently applied to the angels, but *why* this term is used is unknown. Gesenius (*Lex.*) supposes that it is given to them as watching over the souls of men. Jerome (*in loc.*) says that the reason why the name is given is because they always *watch,* and are prepared to do the will of God. According to Jerome, the Greek Ἶρις—Iris—as applied to the rainbow, and which seems to be a heavenly being sent down to the earth, is derived from this word. Comp. the *Iliad,* ii. 27. Theodoret says that the name is given to an angel, to denote that the angel is without a body—ἀσώματον—"for he that is encompassed with a body is the servant of sleep, but he that is free from a body is superior to the necessity of sleep." The term *watchers,* as applied to the celestial beings, is of Eastern origin, and not improbably was derived from Persia. "The seven Amhaspands received their name. on account of their great, holy eyes, and so, generally, all the heavenly Izeds watch in the high heaven over the world and the souls of men, and on this account are called the watchers of the world."— Zendavesta, as quoted by Bertholdt, *in loc.* "The Bun-Dehesh, a commentary on the Zendavesta, contains an extract from it, which shows clearly the name and object of the *watchers* in the ancient system of Zoroaster. It runs thus:

14 He cried [1] aloud, and said thus, Hew [a] down the tree, and cut off his branches, shake off his

1 *with might*, ch. 3. 4.
a Matt. 3. 10; Luke 13. 7.

"Ormuzd has set four *watchers* in the four parts of the heavens, to keep their eye upon the host of the stars. They are bound to keep watch over the hosts of the celestial stars. One stands here as the watcher of his circle ; the other there. He has placed them at such and such posts, as watchers over such and such a circle of the heavenly regions ; and this by his own power and might. Tashter guards the east, Statevis watches the west, Venant the south, and Haftorang the north."— Rhode, Die heilige Sage des Zendvolks, p. 267, as quoted by Prof. Stuart, *in loc.* " The epithet *good* is probably added here to distinguish this class of *watchers* from the *bad* ones ; for Ahriman, the evil genius, had *Archdeves* and *Deves*, who corresponded in rank with the Amhaspands and Izeds of the Zendavesta, and who *watched* to do evil as anxiously as the others did to do good."—Prof. Stuart. It is not improbable that these terms, as applicable to celestial beings, would be known in the kingdom of Babylon, and nothing is more natural than that it should be so used in this book. It is not found in any of the books of pure Hebrew.

14. *He cried aloud.* Marg., as in the Chaldee, *with might.* That is, he cried with a strong voice. ¶ *Hew down the tree.* This command does not appear to have been addressed to any particular ones who were to execute the commission, but it is a strong and significant way of saying that it would certainly be done. Or possibly tho command may be understood as addressed to his fellow-watchers (ver. 17), or to orders of angels over whom this one presided. ¶ *And cut off his branches,* &c. The idea here, and in the subsequent part of the verse, is, that the tree was to be utterly cut up, and all its glory and beauty destroyed. It was first to be felled, and then its limbs chopped off, and then these were to be stripped of their foliage, and then the

leaves, and scatter his fruit: let the beasts get away from under it, and the fowls from his branches.

15 Nevertheless, leave the [b] stump

b Job 14. 7-9.

fruit which it bore was to be scattered. All this was strikingly significant, as applied to the monarch, of some awful calamity that was to occur to him *after* he should have been brought down from his throne. A process of humiliation and desolation was to continue, as if the tree, when cut down, were not suffered to lie quietly in its grandeur upon the earth. ¶ *Let the beasts get away,* &c. That is, it shall cease to afford a shade to the beasts and a home to the fowls. The purposes which it had answered in the days of its glory will come to an end.

15. *Nevertheless, leave the stump of his roots in the earth.* As of a tree that is not wholly dead, but which may send up suckers and shoots again. See Notes on Isa. xi. 1. In Theodotion this is, τὴν φυὴν τῶν ῥιζῶν—the nature, germ. Schleusner renders the Greek, " the *trunk* of its roots." The Vulgate is, germen radicum ejus, " the germ of his roots." The *Codex Chis.* has, ῥίζαν μίαν ἄφετε αὐτοῦ ἐν τῇ γῇ—" leave one of his roots in the earth." The original Chaldee word (עִקַּר) means a *stump, trunk* (Gesenius) ; the Hebrew—עִקָּר—the same word with different pointing, means a shrub, or shoot. It occurs only once in Hebrew (Lev. xxv. 47), where it is applied to the stock of a family, or to a person sprung from a foreign family resident in the Hebrew territory: " the *stock* of the stranger's family." The Chaldee form of the word occurs only in Dan. iv. 15, 23, 26, rendered in each place *stump*, yet not meaning *stump* in the sense in which that word is now commonly employed. The word *stump* now means the stub of a tree ; the part of the tree remaining in the earth, or projecting above it after the tree is cut down, without any reference to the question whether it be alive or dead. The word here used implies that it was still alive, or that there was a germ which would send up a new shoot,

of his roots in the earth, even with a band of iron and brass, in the tender grass of the field ; and let it be wet with the dew of heaven, and *let* his portion *be* with the beasts in the grass of the earth :

so that the tree would live again. The idea is, that though the mighty tree would fall, yet there would remain vitality in the root, or the portion that would remain in the earth after the tree was cut down, and that this would spring up again—a most striking image of what would occur to Nebuchadnezzar after he should be cast down from his lofty throne, and be again restored to his reason and to power. ¶ *Even with a band of iron and brass.* This expression may be regarded as applicable either to the cut-down tree, or to the humbled monarch. If applied to the former, it would seem that the idea is, that the stump or root of a tree, deemed so valuable, would be carefully secured by an inclosure of iron or brass, either in the form of a hoop placed round the top of the stump, to preserve it from being opened or cracked by the heat of the sun, so as to admit moisture, which would rot it ; or around the roots, to bind it together, with the hope that it would grow again ; or it may refer to a railing or inclosure of iron or brass, to keep it from being ploughed or dug up as worthless. In either case, it would be guarded with the hope that a tree so valuable might spring up again. If applied to the monarch—an explanation not inconsistent with the proper interpretation of the passage—it would seem to refer to some method of securing the royal maniac in bonds of iron and brass, as with the hope that his reason might still be restored, or with a view to keep him from inflicting fatal injury on himself. That the thing here referred to might be practised in regard to a valuable tree cut down, or broken down, is by no means improbable ; that it might be practised in reference to the monarch is in accordance with the manner in which the insane have been treated in all ages and countries. ¶ *In the tender grass of the field.* Out of doors ; under no shelter ; exposed to dews and rains. The stump would remain in the open field where the grass grew, until it should shoot up again ; and in a condition strongly resembling that, the

monarch would be excluded from his palace and from the abodes of men. For the meaning of this, as applied to Nebuchadnezzar, see Notes on ver. 25. The word which is rendered *tender grass,* means simply young grass or herbage. No emphasis should be put on the word *tender.* It simply means that he would be abroad where the grass springs up and grows. ¶ *And let it be wet with the dew of heaven.* As applied to the tree, meaning that the dew would fall on it and continually moisten it. The falling of the dew upon it would contribute to preserve it alive and secure its growth again. In a dry soil, or if there were no rain or dew, the germ would die. It cannot be supposed that, in regard to the monarch, it could be meant that his remaining under the dew of heaven would in any way contribute to restore his reason, but all that is implied in regard to him is the *fact* that he would thus be an outcast. The word rendered "*let it be wet*"— יִצְטַבַּע from צְבַע—means, to dip in, to immerse ; to tinge ; to dye ; though the word is not found in the latter senses in the Chaldee. In the Targums it is often used for "to dye, to colour." The word occurs only in this chapter of Daniel (vers. 15, 23, 33), and is in each place rendered in the same way. It is not used in the Hebrew scripture in the sense of to dye or tinge, except in the form of a noun—צֶבַע—in Judg. v. 30 : "To Sisera a prey of *divers colours,* a prey of *divers colours* of needlework, of *divers colours* of needlework." In the passage before us, of course, there is no allusion of this kind, but the word means merely that the stump of the tree would be kept moist with the dew ; as applicable to the tree that it might be more likely to sprout up again. ¶ *And let his portion be with the beasts in the grass of the earth.* Here is a change evidently from the *tree* to something represented by the tree. We could not say of a *tree* that its "portion was with the beasts in the grass," though in the confused and in-

16 Let his heart be *a* changed from man's, and let a beast's heart

a Isa. 6. 10.

be given unto him; and let seven times *b* pass over him.

b ch. 12. 7.

---

congruous images of a dream, nothing would be more natural than such a change from a tree to some object represented by it, or having some resemblance to it. It is probable that it was this circumstance that particularly attracted the attention of the monarch ; for though the dream began with a *tree*, it ended with reference to a *person*, and evidently some one whose station would be well represented by such a magnificent and solitary tree. The sense here is, "let him share the lot of beasts ; let him live as they do :" that is, let him live on grass. Comp. ver. 25.

16. *Let his heart be changed from man's, and let a beast's heart be given unto him.* Here the same thing occurs in a more marked form, showing that some *man* was represented by the vision, and indicating some change which was fitted to attract the deepest attention —as if the person referred to should cease to be a man, and become a beast. The word *heart* here seems to refer to *nature*—"let his nature or propensity cease to be that of a man, and become like that of a beast; let him cease to act as a man, and act as the beasts do —evincing as little mind, and living in the same manner." ¶ *And let seven times pass over him.* In this condition, or until he is restored. It is not indeed *said* that he would be restored, but this is implied (*a*) in the very expression "*until* seven times shall pass over him," as if he would then be restored in some way, or as if this condition would then terminate ; and (*b*) in the statement that "the stump of the roots" would be left in the earth as if it might still germinate again. Everything, however, in the dream was fitted to produce perplexity as to what it could mean. The word rendered *times* (עִדָּנִין—sing. עִדָּן) is an important word in the interpretation of Daniel. It is of the same class of words as the Hebrew עַד—to point out, to appoint, to fix ; and would refer properly to time considered as *appointed* or *designated;* then it may mean any stated or designated period, as a year.

The idea is that of time considered as designated or fixed by periods, and the word may refer to *any* such period, however long or short—a day, a month, a year, or any other measure of duration. What measurement or portion is intended in any particular case must be determined from the connection in which the word is found. The word used here does not occur in the Hebrew scripture, and is found only in the book of Daniel, where it is uniformly rendered *time* and *times*. It is found only in the following places : Dan. ii. 8, "that ye would gain *the time;*" ii. 9, "till *the time* be changed;" ii. 21, "and he changeth *the times;*" iii. 5, 15, "at what *time* ye shall hear;" iv. 16, 23, "and let seven *times* pass over him," 25, 32, "seven *times* shall pass over him ;" vii. 12, "for a season and *time;*" vii. 25, "until a *time* and *times* and the dividing of *time*." In the place before us, so far as the meaning of the *word* is concerned, it might mean a day, a week, a month, or a year. The more common interpretation is that which supposes that it was a year, and this will agree better with all the circumstances of the case than any other period. The Greek of Theodotion here is, καὶ ἑπτὰ καιροὶ ἀλλαγήσονται ἐπ' αὐτόν —"And seven times shall change upon him ;" that is, until seven seasons revolve over him. The most natural construction of this Greek phrase would be to refer it to years. The Latin Vulgate interprets it in a similar way—*et septem tempora mutentur super eum*— "And let seven times be changed" or revolve "over him." In the *Cod. Chis.* it is, καὶ ἑπτὰ ἔτη βοσκηθῇ σὺν αὐτοῖς — "and let him feed with them seven years." Luther renders it *times*. Josephus understands by it "*seven years*." —*Ant.* b. x. ch. x. § 6. While the Chaldee word is indeterminate in respect to the length of time, the most natural and obvious construction here and elsewhere, in the use of the word, is to refer it to years. Days or weeks would be obviously too short, and though in this place the word *months*

17 This matter *is* by the ᵃdecree of the watchers, and the demand by the word of the holy ones: to the intent that the living may know ᵇ that the Most High ᶜ ruleth

a vers. 13, 14. *b* Ps. 9. 16, 20. *c* vers. 25, 32, 35.

in the kingdom of men, and giveth it to whomsoever ᵈ he will, and setteth up over it the basest ᵉ of men.

d Ps. 75. 6, 7. *e* Exod. 9. 16; 1 Kings 21. 25; 2 Kings 21. 6, &c.; 2 Chr. 28. 22.

would perhaps embrace all that would be necessary, yet in the other places where the word occurs in Daniel it undoubtedly refers to years, and there is, therefore, a propriety in understanding it in the same manner here.

17. *This matter is by the decree of the watchers.* Notes on ver. 13. They are described here not only as watching over the affairs of men, but as intrusted with the execution of high and important designs of God. The representation is, that one of these heavenly beings was seen by Nebuchadnezzar in his visions, and that this one stated to him that he had come to execute what had been determined on by his associates, or in counsel with others. The idea would seem to be, that the affairs of the kingdom of Nebuchadnezzar had been in important respects placed under the administration of these beings, and that in solemn council they had resolved on this measure. It is not said that this was not in accordance with, and under the direction of, a higher power —that of God; and that is rather implied when it is said that the great design of this was to show to the living that "the *Most High* ruleth in the kingdom of men." In itself considered, there is no improbability in supposing that the affairs of this lower world are in some respects placed under the administration of beings superior to man, nor that events may occur as the result of their deliberation, or, as it is here expressed, by their "decree." If, in any respect, the affairs of the world are subject to their jurisdiction, there is every reason to suppose that there would be harmony of counsel and of action, and an event of this kind might be so represented. ¶ *And the demand.* Or, the matter; the affair; the business. The Chaldee word properly means a question, a petition; then a subject of inquiry, a matter of business. Here it means, that this matter, or this busi-

ness, was in accordance with the direction of the holy ones. ¶ *The holy ones.* Synonymous with the *watchers*, and referring to the same. See Notes on ver. 13. ¶ *To the intent that the living may know.* With the design that those who live on the earth may understand this. That is, the design was to furnish a proof of this, so impressive and striking, that it could not be doubted by any. No more effectual way of doing this could occur than by showing the absolute power of the Most High over such a monarch as Nebuchadnezzar. ¶ *That the Most High.* He who is exalted above all men; all angels; all that pretend to be gods. The phrase here is designed to refer to the true God, and the object was to show that he was the most exalted of all beings, and had absolute control over all. ¶ *Ruleth in the kingdom of men.* Whoever reigns, he reigns over them. ¶ *And giveth it to whomsoever he will.* That is, he gives dominion over men to whomsoever he chooses. It is not by human ordering, or by arrangements among men. It is not by hereditary right; not by succession; not by conquest; not by usurpation; not by election, that this matter is finally determined; it is by the decree and purpose of God. He can remove the hereditary prince by death; he can cause him to be set aside by granting success to a usurper; he can dispose of a crown by conquest; he can cut off the conqueror by death, and transfer the crown to an inferior officer; he can remove one who was the united choice of a people by death, and put another in his place. So the apostle Paul says, "There is no power but of God: the powers that be are ordained of God" (Rom. xiii. 1). ¶ *And setteth up over it the basest of men.* That is, he appoints over the kingdom of men, at his pleasure, those who are of the humblest or lowest rank. The allusion here is not to Nebuchadnezzar as if he

18 This dream I king Nebuchadnezzar have seen. Now thou,
O Belteshazzar, declare the interpretation thereof, forasmuch *a* as all
the wise *men* of my kingdom are
not able to make known unto me
the interpretation: but thou *art*
able; for the spirit of the holy
gods *is* in thee.

19 ¶ Then Daniel, whose name

a ver. 7.

was Belteshazzar, was astonied for
one hour, and his thoughts troubled
him. *b* The king spake and said,
Belteshazzar, let not the dream, or
the interpretation thereof, trouble
thee. Belteshazzar answered and
said, My lord, the dream *be* to
them *c* that hate thee, and the interpretation thereof to thine enemies.

b ver. 9.   *c* 2 Sam. 18.32; Jer. 29.7.

were the *basest* or the *vilest* of men, but
the statement is a general truth, that
God, at his pleasure, sets aside those of
exalted rank, and elevates those of the
lowest rank in their place. There is an
idea now attached commonly to the
word *basest*, which the word used here
by no means conveys. It does not denote the mean, the vile, the worthless,
the illiberal, but those of humble or
lowly rank. This is the proper meaning of the Chaldee word בְּשַׁל—and so
it is rendered in the Vulgate, *humilli-
mum hominem.* The Greek of Theodotion, however, is, "*that which is dises-
teemed among men*"—ἐξουδένωμα ἀνθρώπων. In the latter part of the dream
(vers. 15, 16) we have an illustration
of what often occurs in dreams—their
singular incongruity. In the early part
of the dream, the vision is that of a *tree*,
and the idea is consistently carried out
for a considerable part of it—the height
of the tree, the branches, the leaves,
the fruit, the shade, the stump; then
suddenly there is a *change* to something
that is living and human—the change
of the *heart* to that of a beast; the being
exposed to the dew of heaven; the portion with the beasts of the earth, &c.
Such changes and incongruities, as every
one knows, are common in dreams. So
Shakespeare—

"True, I talk of dreams,
Which are the children of an idle brain,
Begot of nothing but vain fantasy;
Which is as thin of substance as the air,
And more inconstant than the wind, who
woos
Even now the frozen bosom of the North,
And, being anger'd, puffs away from thence,
Turning his face to the dew-dropping South."
Romeo and Juliet.

18. *This dream I king Nebuchadnezzar have seen.* This is the dream
which I saw. He had detailed it at

length as it appeared to him, without
pretending to be able to explain it.
¶ *Forasmuch as all the wise men of my
kingdom,* &c. Ver. 7. ¶ *But thou* art
able, &c. Notes on ver. 9.

19. *Then Daniel, whose name was
Belteshazzar.* Ver. 8. It has been
objected that the mention in this edict
of *both* the names by which Daniel
was known is an improbable circumstance; that a heathen monarch would
only have referred to him by the name
by which he was known in Babylon—
the name which he had himself conferred on him in honour of the god
(*Belus*) after whom he was called. See
Notes on ch. i. 7. To this it may be
replied, that although in ordinary intercourse with him in Babylon, in addressing him as an officer of state under the
Chaldean government, he would undoubtedly be mentioned only by that
name; yet, in a proclamation like this,
both the names by which he was known
would be used—the one to identify him
among his own countrymen, the other
among the Chaldeans. This proclamation was designed for people of all
classes, and ranks, and tongues (ver. 1);
it was intended to make known the
supremacy of the God worshipped by
the Hebrews. Nebuchadnezzar had derived the knowledge of the meaning
of his dream from one who was a Hebrew, and it was natural, therefore, in
order that it might be known by whom
the dream had been interpreted, that he
should so designate him that it would
be understood by all. ¶ *Was astonied.*
Was astonished. The word *astonied*,
now gone out of use, several times occurs in the common version; Ezra ix.
3; Job xvii. 8; xviii. 20; Ezek. iv. 17;
Dan. iii. 24; iv. 19; v. 9. Daniel was

20 The tree *a* that thou sawest, which grew, and was strong, whose height reached unto the heaven, and the sight thereof to all the earth;

a vers. 10-12.

21 Whose leaves *were* fair, and the fruit thereof much, and in it *was* meat for all; under which the beasts of the field dwelt, and upon whose branches the fowls of the heaven had their habitation:

amazed and *overwhelmed* at what was manifestly the fearful import of the dream. ¶ *For one hour.* It is not possible to designate the exact time denoted by the word *hour*—שָׁעָה. According to Gesenius (*Lex.*), it means a moment of time; properly, a look, a glance, a wink of the eye—German, *augenblick.* In Arabic the word means both a moment and an hour. In Dan. iii. 6, 15, it evidently means *immediately.* Here it would seem to mean *a short time.* That is, Daniel was fixed in thought, and maintained a profound silence until the king addressed him. We are not to suppose that this continued during the space of time which we call an hour, but he was silent until Nebuchadnezzar addressed him. He would not seem to be willing even to speak of so fearful calamities as he saw were coming upon the king. ¶ *And his thoughts troubled him.* The thoughts which passed through his mind respecting the fearful import of the dream. ¶ *The king spake and said,* &c. Perceiving that the dream had, as he had probably apprehended, a fearful significancy, and that Daniel hesitated about explaining its meaning. Perhaps he supposed that he hesitated because he apprehended danger to himself if he should express his thoughts, and the king therefore assured him of safety, and encouraged him to declare the full meaning of the vision, whatever that might be. ¶ *Belteshazzar answered and said, My lord, the dream* be *to them that hate thee.* Let such things as are foreboded by the dream happen to your enemies rather than to you. This merely implies that he did not desire that these things should come upon *him.* It was the language of courtesy and of respect; it showed that he had no desire that any calamity should befall the monarch, and that he had no wish for the success of his enemies. There is not, in this, anything necessarily implying a hatred of the

enemies of the king, or any wish that calamity should come upon them; it is the expression of an earnest desire that such an affliction might not come upon *him.* If it must come on any, such was his respect for the sovereign, and such his desire for his welfare and prosperity, that he preferred that it should fall upon those who were his enemies, and who hated him. This language, however, should not be rigidly interpreted. It is the language of an Oriental; language uttered at a court, where only the words of respect were heard. Expressions similar to this occur not unfrequently in ancient writings. Thus Horace, b. iii. ode 27:—

"Hostium uxores puerique cæcos
Sentiant motus orientis Austri."

And Virgil, *Georg.* iii. 513:—

"Di meliora piis, erroremque hostibus illum."

"Such rhetorical embellishments are pointed at no individuals, have nothing in them of malice or ill-will, are used as marks of respect to the ruling powers, and may be presumed to be free from any imputation of a want of charity." —Wintle, *in loc.*

20, 21. *The tree that thou sawest,* &c. In these two verses Daniel refers to the leading circumstances respecting the tree as it appeared in the dream, without any allusion as yet to the order to cut it down. He probably designed to show that he had clearly understood what had been said, or that he had attended to the most minute circumstances as narrated. It was important to do this in order to show clearly that it referred to the king; a fact which probably Nebuchadnezzar himself apprehended, but still it was important that this should be so firmly fixed in his mind that he would not revolt from it when Daniel came to disclose the fearful import of the remainder of the dream. 22. *It is thou, O king.* It is a representation of thyself. Comp. ch. ii. 38. ¶ *That art grown and become*

22 It *is* thou, *a* O king, that art grown and become strong: for thy greatness is grown, and reacheth unto heaven, and thy dominion *b* to the end of the earth.

23 And whereas *c* the king saw a watcher and an holy one coming down from heaven, and saying, Hew the tree down, and destroy it; yet leave the stump of the roots thereof in the earth, even with a band of iron and brass, in the ten-

der grass of the field; and let it be wet with the dew of heaven, and *let* his portion *be* with the beasts of the field, till seven times pass over him;

24 This *is* the interpretation, O king, and this *is* the decree of the Most High, which is come upon my lord the king:

25 That they shall drive *d* thee from men, and thy dwelling shall be with the beasts of the field, and

a ch. 2. 38.   *b* Jer. 27. 6–8.   *c* vers. 13, 14.

d ver. 33.

strong. Referring to the limited extent of his dominion when he came to the throne, and the increase of his power by a wise administration and by conquest. ¶ *For thy greatness is grown.* The majesty and glory of the monarch had increased by all his conquests, and by the magnificence which he had thrown around his court. ¶ *And reacheth unto heaven.* An expression merely denoting the greatness of his authority. The tree is said to have reached unto heaven (ver. 11), and the stateliness and grandeur of so great a monarch might be represented by language which seemed to imply that he had control over all things. ¶ *And thy dominion to the end of the earth.* To the extent of the world as then known. This was almost literally true.

23. *And whereas the king saw a watcher,* &c. See Notes on ver. 13. The recapitulation in this verse is slightly varied from the statement in vers. 14–16, still so as not materially to affect the sense. Daniel seems to have designed to recal the *principal* circumstances in the dream, so as to identify it in the king's mind, and so as to prepare him for the statement of the fearful events which were to happen to him.

24. *This is the decree of the Most High.* Daniel here designs evidently to direct the attention of the monarch to the one living and true God, and to show him that he presides over all. The purpose of the vision was, in a most impressive way, to convince the king of his existence and sovereignty. Hence Daniel says that all this was in accordance with his "decree." It was

not a thing of chance; it was not ordered by idol gods; it was not an event that occurred by the mere force of circumstances, or as the result of the operation of secondary laws: it was a direct Divine interposition—the solemn purpose of the living God that it should be so. Nebuchadnezzar had represented this, in accordance with the prevailing views of religion in his land, as a "decree of the *Watchers*" (ver. 17); Daniel, in accordance with his views of religion, and with *truth*, represents it as the decree of the true God. ¶ *Which is come upon my Lord the king.* The decree had been previously formed; its execution had now come upon the king.

25. *That they shall drive thee from men.* That is, thou shalt be driven from the habitations of men; from the place which thou hast occupied among men. The prophet does not say *who* would do this, but he says that it *would* be done. The language is such as would be used of one who should become a maniac, and bo thrust out of the ordinary society in which he had moved. The Greek of Theodotion here is, καὶ σὶ ἐκδιώξουσιν. The *Codex Chisian.* has, "And the Most High and his angels shall run upon thee— καντα τρίχουσιν — leading thee into prison," or into detention—εἰς φυλακὴν—"and shall thrust thee into a desert place." The general sense is, that he would be in such a state as to be treated like a beast rather than a man; that he would be removed from his ordinary abodes, and be a miserable and neglected outcast. This commences the account of the calamity that was to come upon Nebuchadnezzar, and as there have

they shall make thee to eat *a* grass as oxen, and they shall wet thee with the dew of heaven, and seven times shall pass over thee, till thou

know that the Most High *b* ruleth in the kingdom of men, and giveth it to whomsoever he will.

a Ps. 106. 20. *b* Ps. 83. 18.

been many opinions entertained as to the nature of this malady, it may be proper to notice some of them. Comp. Bertholdt, pp. 286-292. Some have held that there was a real metamorphosis into some form of an animal, though his rational soul remained, so that he was able to acknowledge God and give praise to him. Cedrenus held that he was transformed into a beast, half lion and half ox. An unknown author, mentioned by Justin, maintained that the transformation was into an animal resembling what was seen in the visions of Ezekiel—the Cherubim—composed of an eagle, a lion, an ox, and a man. In support of the opinion that there was a real transformation, an appeal has been made to the common belief among ancient nations, that such metamorphoses had actually occurred, and especially to what Herodotus (iv. 105) says of the *Neuri* (Νευροι): "It is said by the Scythians, as well as by the Greeks who dwell in Scythia, that once in every year they are all of them changed into wolves, and that after remaining in that state for the space of a few days, they resume their former shape." Herodotus adds, however, "This I do not believe, although they swear that it is true." An appeal is also made to an assertion of Apuleius, who says of himself that he was changed into an ass; and also to the *Metamorphoses* of Ovid. This supposed transformation of Nebuchadnezzar some have ascribed to Satan. —Joh. Wier *de Præstigiis Dæmonum*, I. 26, iv. 1. Others have attributed it to the arts of magic or incantation, and suppose that it was a change in appearance only. Augustine (*de Civit. Dei*. lib. xviii. cap. 17), referring to what is said of Diomed and his followers on their return from Troy, that they were changed into birds, says that Varro, in proof of the truth of this, appeals to the fact that Circe changed Ulysses and his companions into beasts; and to the Arcadians, who, by swimming over a certain lake, were changed into wolves,

and that "if they ate no man's flesh, at the end of nine years they swam over the same lake and became men again." Varro farther mentions the case of a man by the name of Dæmonetus, who, tasting of the sacrifices which the Arcadians offered (a child), was turned into a wolf, and became a man again at the end of two years. Augustine himself says, that when he was in Italy, he heard a report that there were women there, who, by giving one a little drug in cheese, had the power of turning him into an ass. See the curious discussion of Augustine how far this could be true, in his work *de Civit. Dei*, lib. xviii. cap. 18. *He* supposes that under the influence of drugs men might be made to *suppose* they were thus transformed, or to have a recollection of what passed in such a state *as if* it were so. Cornelius à Lapide supposes that the transformation in the case of Nebuchadnezzar went only so far that his knees were bent in the other direction, like those of animals, and that he walked like animals. Origen, and many of those who have coincided with him in his allegorical mode of interpreting the Scriptures, supposed that the whole of this account is an allegory, designed to represent the fall of Satan, and his restoration again to the favour of God—in accordance with his belief of the doctrine of universal salvation. Others suppose that the statement here means merely that there was a formidable conspiracy against him; that he was dethroned and bound with fetters; that he was then expelled from the court, and driven into exile; and that, as such, he lived a miserable life, finding a precarious subsistence in woods and wilds, among the beasts of the forest, until, by another revolution, he was restored again to the throne. It is not necessary to examine these various opinions, and to show their absurdity, their puerility, or their falsehood. Some of them are simply ridiculous, and none of them are demanded by any fair interpretation of the chap-

ter. It may seem, perhaps, to be un-
dignified even to *refer* to such opinions
now; but this may serve to illustrate
the method in which the Bible has been
interpreted in former times, and the
steps which have been taken before
men arrived at a clear and rational interpretation of the sacred volume. It
is indeed painful to reflect that such
absurdities and puerilities have been in
any way connected with the interpretation of the Word of God; sad to reflect
that so many persons, in consequence
of them, have discarded the Bible and
the interpretations together as equally
ridiculous and absurd. The *true* account in regard to the calamity of Nebuchadnezzar is undoubtedly the following: (1.) He was a maniac—made
such by a direct Divine judgment
on account of his pride, vers. 30, 31.
The essential thing in the statement
is, that he was deprived of his reason,
and that he was treated *as* a maniac.
Comp. Intro. to the chapter, II.
(1). (2.) The particular *form* of the
insanity with which he was afflicted
seems to have been that he imagined
himself to be a beast; and, this idea
having taken possession of his mind,
he acted accordingly. It may be remarked in regard to this, (*a*) that such
a fancy is no uncommon thing among
maniacs. Numerous instances of this
may be seen in the various works on
insanity—or indeed may be seen by
merely visiting a lunatic asylum. One
imagines that he is a king, and decks
himself out with a sceptre and a diadem; another that he is glass, and is
filled with excessive anxiety lest he
should be broken; others have regarded
themselves as deprived of their proper
nature as human beings; others as having been once dead, and restored to life
again; others as having been dead and
sent back into life without a heart;
others as existing in a manner unlike
any other mortals; others as having no
rational soul. See Arnold *on Insanity*,
I. pp. 176–195. In all these cases, when
such a fancy takes possession of the
mind, there will be an effort on the
part of the patient to act in exact conformity to this view of himself, and his
whole conduct will be adapted to it.
Nothing can convince him that it is

not so; and there is no absurdity in
supposing that, if the thought had
taken possession of the mind of Nebuchadnezzar that he was a beast, he
would live and act *as* a wild beast—
just as it is said that he did. (*b*) In
itself considered, *if* Nebuchadnezzar
was deprived of his reason, and for the
cause assigned—his pride, nothing is
more probable than that he would be
left to imagine himself a beast, and to
act like a beast. This would furnish
the most striking contrast to his former state; would do most to bring down
his pride; and would most effectually
show the supremacy of the Most High.
(3.) In this state of mind, fancying
himself a wild beast, and endeavouring
to act in conformity with this view, it
is probable that he would be indulged
as far as was consistent with his safety.
Perhaps the regency would be induced
to allow this partly from their long
habits of deference to the will of an
arbitrary monarch; partly because by
this indulgence he would be less troublesome; and partly because a painful
spectacle would thus be removed from
the palace. We are not to suppose
that he was permitted to roam in forests
at large without any restraint, and
without any supervision whatever. In
Babylon, attached to the palace, there
were doubtless, as there are all over
the East, royal parks or gardens; there
is every probability that in these parks
there may have been assembled rare
and strange animals as a royal menagerie; and it was doubtless in these
parks, and among *these* animals that
he was allowed to range. Painful as
such a spectacle would be, yet it is not
improbable that to *such* a maniac this
would be allowed, as contributing to his
gratification, or as a means of restoring
him to his right mind. (4.) A king,
however wide his empire, or magnificent his court, would be as *likely* to be
subject to mental derangement as any
other man. No situation in life can
save the human mind from the liability
to so overwhelming a calamity, nor
should we deem it strange that it should
come on a king as well as other men.
The condition of Nebuchadnezzar, as
represented by himself in this edict,
was scarcely more pitiable than that of

George III. of England, though it is not surprising that in the eighteenth century of the Christian era, and in a Christian land, the treatment of the sovereign in such circumstances was different from that which a monarch received in heathen Babylon. (5.) It cannot be shown that this did *not* come upon Nebuchadnezzar, as stated in this chapter (vers. 30, 31), on account of his pride. That he *was* a proud and haughty monarch is apparent from all his history; that God would take some effectual means to humble him is in accordance with his dealings with mankind; that this would be a most effectual means of doing it cannot be doubted. No one can prove, in respect to *any* judgment that comes upon mankind, that it is *not* on account of some sin reigning in the heart; and when it is affirmed in a book claiming to be inspired, that a particular calamity is brought upon men on account of their transgressions, it cannot be demonstrated that the statement is not true. If these remarks are correct, then no well-founded objection can lie against the account here respecting the calamity that came upon this monarch in Babylon. This opinion in regard to the nature of the affliction which came upon Nebuchadnezzar, is probably that which is now generally entertained, and it certainly meets all the circumstances of the case, and frees the narrative from material objection. As a confirmation of its truth, I will copy here the opinion of Dr. Mead, as it is found in his *Medica Sacra:* "All the circumstances of Nebuchadnezzar's case agree so well with a hypochondriacal madness, that to me it appears evident that Nebuchadnezzar was seized with this distemper, and under its influence ran wild into the fields; and that, fancying himself transformed into an ox, he fed on grass after the manner of cattle. For every sort of madness is the result of a disturbed imagination; which this unhappy man laboured under for full seven years. And through neglect of taking proper care of himself, his hair and nails grew to an uncommon length; whereby the latter, growing thicker and crooked, resembled the claws of birds. Now the an-

cients called people affected with this kind of madness, λυκάνθρωποι, *wolf-men* —or κυνάνθρωποι, *dog-men*—because they went abroad in the night imitating wolves or dogs; particularly intent upon opening the sepulchres of the dead, and had their legs much ulcerated, either from frequent falls or the bites of dogs. In like manner are the daughters of Prœtus related to have been mad, who, as Virgil says, *Ecl.* vi. 48,

' ——— implerunt falsis mugitibus agros.'
'With mimic howlings filled the fields.'

For, as Servius observes, Juno possessed their minds with such a species of fury, that, fancying themselves cows, they ran into the fields, bellowed often, and dreaded the plough. Nor was this disorder unknown to the moderns, for Schneckius records a remarkable instance of a husbandman in Padua, who, imagining himself a wolf, attacked and even killed several people in the fields; and when at length he was taken, he persevered in declaring himself a real wolf, and that the only difference consisted in the inversion of his skin and hair." The same opinion as to the nature of the disease is expressed by Dr. J. M. Good, in his *Study of Medicine.* So also Burton (*Anatomy of Melancholy*, Part I. § I. Memb. i. Subs. 4). Burton refers to several cases which would illustrate the opinion. "Wierus," says he, "tells a story of such a one in Padua, 1541, that would not believe the contrary but that he was a wolf. He hath another instance of a Spaniard, who thought himself a bear. Such, belike, or little better, were king Prœtus' daughters, that thought themselves *kine*"—an instance strikingly resembling this case of Nebuchadnezzar, who seems to have imagined himself some kind of beast. Pliny, perhaps referring to diseases of this kind, says, "Some men were turned into wolves in my time, and from wolves to men again," lib. viii. c. 22. See Burton as above. ¶ *And thy dwelling shall be with the beasts of the field.* That is, as above explained, thou wilt imagine thyself to be a beast, and wilt act like a beast. Indulgence will be given to this propensity so as to allow you to range with the beasts in the park, or

26 And whereas they commanded to leave the stump of the tree roots; thy kingdom shall be sure unto thee, after that thou shalt have known that the *a* heavens do rule.

27 Wherefore, O king, let my

a Matt. 5. 34; Luke 15. 18, 21.

---

the royal menagerie. ¶ *And they shall make thee to eat grass as oxen.* That is, this shall be thy propensity, and thou shalt be indulged in it. Fancying himself a beast of some kind—probably, as appears from this expression, *an ox*—nothing would be more natural than that he should attempt to live as oxen do, on grass, that he should be so far indulged that his food would consist of vegetables. Nothing is more common among maniacs than some such freak about food; and it is just as likely that a king would manifest this as any other man. The word *grass* here (עִשְׂבָּא Heb. עֵשֶׂב) means, properly, *herbs; green herbs; vegetables* —represented commonly, as furnishing food for man, Gen. i. 11, 12; ii. 5; iii. 18; Exod. x. 12, 15; Ps. civ. 14. The word *grass*, in our language, conveys an idea which is not *strictly* in accordance with the original. That word would denote only the vegetable productions which cattle eat; the Hebrew word is of a more general signification, embracing all kinds of vegetables —those which man eats, as well as those which animals eat; and the meaning here is, that he would live on vegetable food—a propensity in which they would doubtless indulge a man in such circumstances, painful and humiliating as it would be. The phrase " they shall *make* thee eat grass," rather means, " they shall *permit* thee to do it," or they shall treat thee so that thou wilt do it. It would be his inclination, and they would allow him to be gratified in it. ¶ *And they shall wet thee with the dew of heaven.* Or, shall suffer you to be wet with the dew of heaven; that is, to be out in the open air—no improbable treatment of a maniac, and especially likely to occur in a climate where it was no uncommon thing for all classes of persons to pass the night under the sky. ¶ *And seven times shall pass over thee.* Notes on ver. 16. ¶ *Till thou know,* &c. Until thou shalt effectually learn that the true God rules; that he gives authority to whom he pleases; and that he takes it away when he pleases. Notes on ver. 17. Nothing could be better fitted to teach this lesson than to deprive, by a manifest judgment of heaven, such a monarch of the exercise of reason, and reduce him to the pitiable condition here described.

26. *And whereas they commanded.* The watchers, ver. 15. Comp. ver. 17. ¶ *To leave the stump of the tree roots.* Or, to leave roots to the stump of the tree; that is, it was not to be dug up, or wholly destroyed, but vitality was to be left in the ground. The Chaldee here is the same as in ver. 15, "leave the stump of his roots." ¶ *Thy kingdom shall be sure unto thee.* That is, thou shalt not die under this calamity, but after it has passed away shalt be restored to authority. It *might* have been supposed that this meant that the authority would survive in his family, and that those who were to succeed him would reign—as shoots spring up after the parent tree has fallen; but Daniel was directed to an interpretation which is not less in accordance with the fair meaning of the dream than this would have been. ¶ *After that thou shalt have known that the heavens do rule.* That God rules. This was the great lesson which the event was designed to teach, and when that should have been learned, there would be a propriety that he should be restored to his throne, and should proclaim this to the world.

27. *Wherefore, O king, let my counsel be acceptable unto thee.* Daniel was permitted to see not only the fact that this calamity impended over the king, but the cause of it, and as that cause was his proud and sinful heart, he supposed that the judgment might be averted if the king would reform his life. If the *cause* were removed, he inferred, not unreasonably, that there was a hope that the calamity might be avoided. We cannot but admire here

counsel be acceptable unto thee, and break off *a* thy sins by righteousness, and thine iniquities by

showing mercy to the poor; if *b* it may be ¹ a lengthening of thy tranquillity.

---

a Isa. 55. 7.

b Ps. 41. 1, 2.   1 or, *a healing of thine error.*

---

the boldness and fidelity of Daniel, who not only gave a fair interpretation of the dream, in the case submitted to him, but who went beyond that in a faithful representation to the most mighty monarch of the age, that this was in consequence of his wicked life. ¶ *And break off thy sins by righteousness.* By acts of righteousness or justice ; by abandoning a wicked course of life. It is fairly to be inferred from this that the life of the monarch had been wicked— a fact which is confirmed everywhere in his history. He had, indeed, some good qualities as a man, but he was proud ; he was ambitious ; he was arbitrary in his government ; he was passionate and revengeful ; and he was, doubtless, addicted to such pleasures of life as were commonly found among those of his station. He had a certain kind of respect for religion, whatever was the object of worship, but this was not inconsistent with a wicked life. The word translated *break off* (פְּרֻק) is rendered in the Vulgate *redime*, "*redeem*," and so in the Greek of Theodotion, λύτρωσαι, and in the *Codex Chis.* From this use of the word in some of the versions, and from the fact that the word rendered *righteousness* is often employed in the later Hebrew to denote almsgiving (comp. the margin in Matt. vi. 1, and the Greek text in Tittmann and Hahn where the word δικαιοσύνην is used to denote *alms*), the passage here has been adduced in favour of the doctrine of expiatory merits, and the purchase of absolution by almsgiving—a favourite doctrine in the Roman Catholic communion. But the ordinary and common meaning of the word is not to redeem, but to break, to break off, to abandon. It is the word from which our English word *break* is derived — Germ., *brechen.* Comp. Gen. xxvii. 40, "that thou shalt *break* his yoke ;" Exod. xxxii. 2, "*Break off* the golden ear-rings ;" Exod. xxxii. 3, "And all the people *brake off*

the golden ear-rings ;" Exod. xxxii. 24, "Whosoever hath any gold let them *break it off;*" 1 Kings xix. 11, "A great and strong wind *rent* the mountains;" Zech. xi. 16, "And *tear* their claws in *pieces;*" Ezek. xix. 12, "her strong rods were *broken.*" The word is rendered in our common version, *redeem* once (Psa. cxxxvi. 24), "And hath *redeemed* us from our enemies." It is translated *rending* in Psa. vii. 2, and *deliver* in Lam. v. 8. It does not elsewhere occur in the Scriptures. The fair meaning of the word is, as in our version, to *break off*, and the idea of redeeming the soul by acts of charity or almsgiving is not in the passage, and cannot be derived from it. This passage, therefore, cannot be adduced to defend the doctrine that the soul may be redeemed, or that sins may be expiated by acts of charity and almsgiving. It means that the king was to break off his sins by acts of righteousness ; or, in other words, he was to show by a righteous life that he had abandoned his evil course. The exhortation is, that he would practise those great duties of justice and charity towards mankind in which he had been so deficient, if, perhaps, God might show mercy, and avert the impending calamity. ¶ *And thine iniquities by showing mercy to the poor.* The peculiar "iniquity" of Nebuchadnezzar may have consisted in his oppressing the poor of his realm in the exorbitant exactions imposed on them in carrying on his public works, and building and beautifying his capital. Life, under an Oriental despot, is regarded as of little value. Sixty thousand men were employed by Mohammed Ali in digging the canal from Cairo to Alexandria, in which work almost no tools were furnished them but their hands. A large portion of them died, and were buried by their fellow-labourers in the earth excavated in digging the canal. Who can estimate the number of men that were recklessly employed under the arbitrary monarch of

Egypt on the useless work of building the pyramids? Those structures, doubtless, cost millions of lives, and there is no improbability in supposing that Nebuchadnezzar had employed hundreds of thousands of persons without any adequate compensation, and in a hard and oppressive service, in rearing the walls and the palaces of Babylon, and in excavating the canals to water the city and the adjacent country. No counsel, therefore, could be more appropriate than that he should relieve the poor from those burdens, and do justice to them. There is no intimation that he was to attempt to *purchase* release from the judgments of God by such acts; but the meaning is, that if he would cease from his acts of oppression, it might be hoped that God would avert the threatened calamity. The duty here enjoined of showing mercy to the poor, is one that is everywhere commanded in the Scriptures, Psa. xli. 1; Matt. xix. 21; Gal. ii. 10, *et sæpe.* Its influence in obtaining the Divine favour, or in averting calamity, is also stated. Comp. Psa. xli. 1, "Blessed is he that considereth the poor; the Lord will deliver him in time of trouble." It is a sentiment which occurs frequently in the books of the Apocrypha, and in these books there can be found the progress of the opinion to the point which it reached in the later periods of the Jewish history, and which it has obtained in the Roman Catholic communion, that almsgiving or charity to the poor would be an expiation for sin, and would commend men to God as a ground of righteousness; or, in other words, the progress of the doctrine towards that which teaches that works of supererogation may be performed. Thus in the book of Tobit, iv. 8-10, "If thou hast abundance, give alms accordingly; if thou have little, be not afraid to give according to that little: for thou layest up a good treasure for thyself against the day of necessity. *Because that alms do deliver from death,* and suffereth not to come into darkness." Tobit xii. 9, 10, "For alms *doth deliver from death, and shall purge away all sin.* Those that exercise righteousness and alms shall be filled with life; but they that sin are enemies

to their own life." Tobit xiv. 10, 11, "Manasses gave alms, and escaped the snares of death which they had set for him; but Aman fell into the snare and perished. Wherefore now, my son, consider what alms doeth, and how righteousness doth deliver." Ecclesiasticus xxix. 12, 13, "Shut up alms in thy storehouses; it shall deliver thee from all affliction. It shall fight for thee against thine enemies better than a mighty shield and a strong spear." Ecclesiasticus xl. 24, "Brethren and help are against time of trouble; but alms shall deliver more than them both." In these passages there is evidence of the progress of the sentiment towards the doctrine of supererogation; but there is none whatever that Daniel attributed any *such* efficacy to alms, or that he meant to teach anything more than the common doctrine of religion, that when a man breaks off from his sins it may be hoped that the judgments which impended over him may be averted, and that doing good will meet the smiles and approbation of God. Compare in reference to this sentiment the case of the Ninevites, when the threatening against them was averted by their repentance and humiliation, Jonah iii. 10; the case of Hezekiah, when his predicted death was averted by his tears and prayers, Isa. xxxviii. 1-5; and Jer. xviii. 7, 8, where this principle of the Divine government is fully asserted. ¶ *If it may be a lengthening of thy tranquillity.* Marg., "or, *a healing of thine error.*" The Greek of Theodotion here is, "Perhaps God will be long-suffering toward thy offences." The Greek of the *Codex Chisianus* is, "And thou mayest remain a long time (πολυήμερος γένη) upon the throne of thy kingdom." The Vulgate, "Perhaps he will pardon thy faults." The Syriac, "Until he may remove from thee thy follies." The original word rendered *lengthening* (אַרְכָא) means, properly, as translated here, a prolongation; a drawing out; a lengthening; and the word is here correctly rendered. It has not the meaning assigned to it in the margin of *healing.* It would apply properly to a prolongation of anything—as of life, peace,

28 ¶ All this came upon the king Nebuchadnezzar.

29 At the end of twelve months

he walked ¹ in the palace of the kingdom of Babylon.

1 or, *upon.*

health, prosperity. The word rendered *tranquillity* (שְׁלֵוָה) means, properly, security, safety, quiet; and the reference here is to his calm possession of the throne; to his quietness in his palace, and peace in his kingdom. There is nothing in the text to justify the version in the margin.

28. *All this came upon the king Nebuchadnezzar.* That is, the threatened judgment came upon him in the form in which it was predicted. He did not repent and reform his life as he was exhorted to, and, having given him sufficient time to show whether he was disposed to follow the counsel of Daniel, God suddenly brought the heavy judgment upon him. Why he did *not* follow the counsel of Daniel is not stated, and cannot be known. It may have been that he was so addicted to a life of wickedness that he would not break off from it, even while he admitted the fact that he was exposed on account of it to so awful a judgment—as multitudes do who pursue a course of iniquity, even while they admit that it will be followed by poverty, disgrace, disease and death here, and by the wrath of God hereafter; or it may be, that he did not credit the representation which Daniel made, and refused to follow his counsel on that account; or it may be, that though he purposed to repent, yet, as thousands of others do, he suffered the time to pass on until the forbearance of God was exhausted, and the calamity came suddenly upon him. A full year, it would seem (ver. 29), was given him to see what the effect of the admonition would be, and then all that had been predicted was fulfilled. His conduct furnishes a remarkable illustration of the conduct of sinners under threatened wrath; of the fact that they continue to live in sin when exposed to certain destruction, and when warned in the plainest manner of what will come upon them.

29. *At the end of twelve months.* After the dream, and the interpretation— giving him ample opportunity to re-

pent, and to reform his life, and to avoid the calamity. ¶ *He walked in the palace.* Marg., *upon.* The margin is the more correct rendering. The roofs of houses in the East are made flat, and furnish a common place of promenade, especially in the cool of the evening. See Notes on Mat. ix. 2. The *Codex Chis.* has here, "The king walked upon the walls of the city with all his glory, and went around the towers, and answering, said." The place, however, upon which he walked, appears to have been the roof of his own palace—doubtless reared so high that he could have a good view of the city from it. ¶ *Of the kingdom of Babylon.* Appertaining to that kingdom; the royal residence. As it is to be supposed that this "palace of the kingdom," on the roof of which the king walked, was that which he had himself reared, and as this contributed much to the splendour of the capital of his empire, and doubtless was the occasion, in a considerable degree, of his vainglorious boasting when the judgment of heaven fell upon him (vers. 30, 31), a brief description of that palace seems to be not inappropriate. The description is copied from an article on Babylon in Kitto's *Cyclopædia of Biblical Literature,* vol. i. pp. 270, 271:

"The new palace built by Nebuchadnezzar was prodigious in size, and superb in embellishments. Its outer wall embraced six miles; within that circumference were two other embattled walls, besides a great tower. Three brazen gates led into the grand area, and every gate of consequence throughout the city was of brass. The palace was splendidly decorated with statues of men and animals, with vessels of gold and silver, and furnished with luxuries of all kinds brought thither from conquests in Egypt, Palestine, and Tyre. Its greatest boast were the hanging gardens, which acquired, even from Grecian writers, the appellation of one of the wonders of the world. They are attributed to the gallantry of Nebuchadnezzar, who constructed them

30 The king spake *a* and said, Is not this great Babylon, that I have built for the house of the kingdom,

by the might of my power, and for the honour of my majesty? 31 While *b* the word *was* in the

a Luke 12. 19, 20.

b 1 Thess. 5. 3.

in compliance with a wish of his queen Amytis to possess elevated groves, such as she had enjoyed on the hills around her native Ecbatana. Babylon was all flat, and to accomplish so extravagant a desire, an artificial mountain was reared, four hundred feet on each side, while terraces, one above another, rose to a height that overtopped the walls of the city, that is, above three hundred feet in elevation. The ascent from terrace to terrace was made by corresponding flights of steps, while the terraces themselves were reared to their various stages on ranges of regular piers, which, forming a kind of vaulting, rose in succession one over the other to the required height of each terrace, the whole being bound together by a wall twenty-two feet in thickness. The level of each terrace or garden was then formed in the following manner: the tops of the piers were first laid over with flat stones, sixteen feet in length, and four in width; on these stones were spread beds of matting, then a thick layer of bitumen, after which came two courses of bricks, which were covered with sheets of solid lead. The earth was heaped on this platform, and in order to admit the roots of large trees, prodigious hollow piers were built and filled with mould. From the Euphrates, which flowed close to the foundation, water was drawn up by machinery. The whole, says Q. Curtius (v. 5), had, to those who saw it from a distance, the appearance of woods overhanging mountains. The remains of this palace are found in the vast mound or hill called by the natives *Kasr.* It is of irregular form, eight hundred yards in length, and six hundred yards in breadth. Its appearance is constantly undergoing change from the continual digging which takes place in its inexhaustible quarries for brick of the strongest and finest material. Hence the mass is furrowed into deep ravines, crossing and recrossing each other in every direction."

30. *The king spake and said.* The Chaldee, and the Greek of Theodotion and of the *Codex Chis.*, here is, "the king *answered* and said:" perhaps he replied to some remark made by his attendants in regard to the magnitude of the city; or perhaps the word *answered* is used, as it often seems to be in the Scriptures, to denote a reply to something passing in the mind that is not uttered; to some question or inquiry that the mind starts. He might merely have been thinking of the magnitude of this city, and he gave response to those thoughts in the language which follows. ¶ *Is not this great Babylon, that I have built.* In regard to the situation and the magnitude of Babylon, and the agency of Nebuchadnezzar in beautifying and enlarging it, see the analysis prefixed to the Notes on the thirteenth chapter of Isaiah. He greatly enlarged the city; built a new city on the west side of the river; reared a magnificent palace; and constructed the celebrated hanging gardens; and, in fact, made the city so different from what it was, and so greatly increased its splendour, that he could say without impropriety that he had "*built*" it. ¶ *For the house of the kingdom.* To be considered altogether—embracing the whole city—as a sort of palace of the kingdom. He seems to have looked upon the whole city as one vast palace fitted to be an appropriate residence of the sovereign of so vast an empire. ¶ *And for the honour of my majesty.* To ennoble or glorify my reign; or where one of so much majesty as I am may find an appropriate home.

31. *While the word was in the king's mouth.* In the very act of his speaking—thus showing that there could be no doubt as to the connection between the crime and the punishment. ¶ *There fell a voice from heaven.* There came a voice; or, perhaps, it seemed to *fall* as a thunderbolt. It was uttered above him, and appeared to come from heaven.

king's mouth, there fell a voice from heaven, *saying*, O king Nebuchadnezzar, to thee it is spoken: The kingdom is departed from thee:

32 And *a* they shall drive thee from men, and thy dwelling *shall be* with the beasts of the field:

a vers. 25, 26.

they shall make thee to eat grass as oxen, and seven times shall pass over thee, until thou know that the Most High ruleth in the kingdom of men, and giveth it to whomsoever he will.

33 The same hour was the thing fulfilled upon Nebuchadnezzar : and he was driven from men, and

---

There was an important sense in which it *did* fall from heaven; for it was the voice of God. ¶ *Saying, O king Nebuchadnezzar, to thee it is spoken.* For you it is particularly intended; or what is predicted is now spoken to thee. ¶ *The kingdom is departed from thee.* Thou art about to cease to reign. Up to this time he retained his reason, that he might distinctly understand the source from whence the judgment was to come, and why it was brought upon him, and that he might be prepared, when he should be recovered from his insanity, to testify clearly to the origin and the nature of the judgment. The *Codex Chis.* has an important *addition* to what is said here, which, though of no authority, as having nothing corresponding to it in the original text, yet states what is in itself not improbable. It is as follows: "And at the end of what he was saying, he heard a voice from heaven, To thee it is spoken, O king Nebuchadnezzar, the kingdom of Babylon shall be taken away from thee, and shall be given to another, a man despised or of no rank—ἐξουθενημένῳ ἀνθρώπῳ—in thy house. Behold, I will place him over thy kingdom, and thy power, and thy glory, and thy luxury—τὴν τρυφήν—he shall receive, until thou shalt know that the God of heaven has authority over the kingdom of men, and gives it to whomsoever he will: but until the rising of the sun another king shall rejoice in thy house, and shall possess thy power, and thy strength, and thine authority, and the angels shall drive thee away for seven years, and thou shalt not be seen, and shalt not speak with any man, but they shall feed thee with grass as oxen, and from the herb of the field shall be thy support."

32. *And they shall drive thee from men,* &c. See Notes on ver. 25.

33. *The same hour was the thing fulfilled.* On the word *hour*, see Notes on ver. 19. The use of the word here would seem to confirm the suggestion there made that it means a brief period of time. The idea is clearly that it was done instantly. The event came suddenly upon him, without any interval, as he was speaking. ¶ *Till his hairs were grown like eagles' feathers.* By long neglect and inattention. The Greek version of Theodotion has in this place the word *lions* instead of *eagles:* "till his hairs were grown long like that of lions;" and the passage is paraphrased by Jackson thus, "till his hair was grown long and shagged like the mane of a lion." This would make good sense, but it is not the reading of the Chaldee. The *Codex Chis.* reads it, "and my hairs were like the wings of an eagle. and my nails like those of a lion." The correct idea is, that his hair was neglected until in appearance it resembled the feathers of a bird. ¶ *And his nails like birds' claws.* No unnatural thing, if he was driven out and neglected as the insane have been in much later times, and in much more civilized parts of the world. In regard to the probability of the statement here made respecting the treatment of Nebuchadnezzar, and the objection derived from it against the authenticity of the book of Daniel, see Introduction to the chapter, II. (1). In addition to what is said there, the following cases may be referred to as showing that there is no improbability in supposing that what is here stated actually occurred. The extracts are taken from the *Second Annual Report of the Prison Discipline Society,* and they describe the condition of some

did eat grass as oxen, and his body was wet with the dew of heaven, till his hairs were grown like eagles' *feathers*, and his nails like birds' *claws.*

of the patients before they were admitted into the insane asylum at Worcester. If these things occurred in the commonwealth of Massachusetts, and in the nineteenth century of the Christian era, there is nothing incredible in supposing that a similar thing may have occurred in ancient heathen Babylon. "No. 1. Had been in prison twenty-eight years when he was brought to the Institution. During seven years he had not felt the influence of fire, and many nights he had not lain down for fear of freezing. He had not been shaved for twenty-eight years, and had been provoked and excited by the introduction of hundreds to see the exhibition of his raving. No. 2. Had been in one prison fourteen years: he was naked—his hair and beard grown long—and his skin so entirely filled with the dust of charcoal as to render it impossible, from its appearance, to discover what nation he was of. He was in the habit of screaming so loud as to annoy the whole neighbourhood, and was considered a most dangerous and desperate man. No. 3. An old man of seventy years of age or more; had been *chained for twenty-five years,* and had his chain taken off but once in that time. No. 4. A female: had so long been confined with a *short chain* as wholly to lose the use of her lower limbs. Her health had been materially impaired by confinement, and she was unable to stand, and had not walked for years. No. 8. Had been ten years without clothes: a most inconceivably filthy and degraded being: exceedingly violent and outrageous. No. 9. Another female, exceedingly filthy in her habits, had not worn clothes for two years, during which time she had been confined in a filthy cell, destitute of everything like comfort, tearing everything in pieces that was given her. No. 10. Had been insane eight years: almost the whole of the time in jail and in a cage."

34. *And at the end of the days.* That is, the time designated; to wit, the

34 And at the end of the days I Nebuchadnezzar lifted up mine eyes unto heaven, and mine understanding returned unto me; and I blessed the Most High; and I

"seven times" that were to pass over him. ¶ *I Nebuchadnezzar lifted up mine eyes unto heaven.* Probably the first thing that indicated returning reason. It would not be unnatural, on the supposition that he was deprived of reason *at the very instant* that a voice seemed to speak to him from heaven, and that he continued wholly insane or idiotic during the long interval of seven years, that the first indication of returning reason would be his looking up to the place from whence that voice seemed to come, as if it were still speaking to him. In some forms of mental derangement, when it comes suddenly upon a man, the effect is wholly to *annihilate* the interval, so that, when reason is restored, the individual connects in his recollection the last thing which occurred when reason ceased with the moment when it is restored. A patient had been long an inmate of an insane apartment in Providence, Rhode Island. He was a seaman, and had been injured on the head when his vessel was in a naval engagement, and it was supposed that his brain had been permanently affected. For many years he was idiotic, and no hopes were entertained of his recovery. It was at length suggested that the operation of trepanning should be performed, and the very instant that the bone was raised from its pressure on the brain, he exclaimed, "Has she struck?" The whole interval of time was obliterated from his memory. Similar instances are mentioned by Dr. Abercrombie (*Intellectual Powers,* pp. 252, 253). A man had been employed for a day with a beetle and wedges in splitting pieces of wood for erecting a fence. At night, before going home, he put the beetle and wedges into the hollow of an old tree, and directed his sons, who had been at work in an adjoining field, to accompany him next morning to assist in making the fence. In the night he became maniacal, and continued in a state of insanity for several years, during which time his

praised and honoured him *a* that
liveth for ever, whose dominion *is*
an everlasting *b* dominion, and his

a ch. 12. 7; Rev. 4. 10.   *b* ch. 2. 44; 7. 14;
Ps. 10. 16; Jer. 10. 10; Mic. 4. 7; Luke 1. 33.

mind was not occupied with any of the
subjects with which he had been conversant when in health. After several
years his reason returned suddenly, and
the first question he asked was, whether
his sons had brought home the beetle
and wedges. A lady had been intensely
engaged for some time in a piece of
needlework. Before she had completed
it she became insane, and continued in
that state for seven years; after which
her reason returned suddenly. One of
the first questions she asked related to
her needlework, though she had never
alluded to it, so far as was recollected,
during her illness. Another lady was
liable to periodical paroxysms of delirium, which often attacked her so suddenly that in conversation she would
stop in the middle of a story, or even
of a sentence, and branch off into the
subject of hallucination. On the return
of her reason, she would resume the
subject of her conversation on which
she was engaged at the time of the attack, beginning exactly where she had
left off, though she had never alluded
to it during her delirium; and on the
next attack of delirium she would resume the subject of hallucination with
which she had been occupied at the
conclusion of the former paroxysm. A
similar thing may have occurred to
Nebuchadnezzar. He was deprived of
reason by a sudden voice from heaven.
Nothing was more natural, or would
be more in accordance with the laws
respecting insanity, than that *at the
very instant* when reason returned he
should look up to the place whence the
voice had seemed to come. ¶ *And
mine understanding returned unto me.*
This shows that he regarded himself
as having been a maniac, though doubtless he was ignorant of the manner in
which he had been treated. It would
seem from the narrative, and from the
probabilities of the case, that he found
himself driven out from his palace,
herding with cattle, and in the deplorable condition in regard to personal

kingdom *is* from generation *c* to
generation:
  35 And *d* all the inhabitants of

c Ps. 90. 1.   *d* Isa. 40. 15, 17.

appearance which he here describes.
Seeing this in fact, and recollecting the
prediction, he could not doubt that this
was the way in which he had been
treated during the period of his distressing malady. ¶ *And I blessed the Most
High.* For his recovery, and in an
humble acknowledgment of his dependence. "The acts of praise here referred to are the suitable returns of a
mind truly penitent, and deeply sensible of its faults and of its mercies."—
Winkle. ¶ *And I praised and honoured him.* That is, I *honoured* him
by rendering thanks for his restoring
mercy, by recognizing him as the true
God, and by the acknowledging of the
truth that he has a right to reign, and
that his kingdom is over all. ¶ *That
liveth for ever.* He is the *living* God,
as he is often styled, in contradistinction from all false gods—who have no
life; and he lives *for ever* in contradistinction to his creatures on earth, all of
whom are destined to die. He will
live when all on earth shall have died;
he will live for ever in the future, as he
has lived for ever in the past. ¶ *Whose
dominion is an everlasting dominion.*
His empire extends through all time,
and will continue while eternal ages roll
away. ¶ *And his kingdom is from
generation to generation.* The generations of men pass away. One succeeds
another, and there is no permanency.
Dynasties change, and monarchs die.
No human sovereign can extend his
own power over the next generation,
nor can he secure his authority in the
person of his successors. But the dominion of God is unchanged, while the
generations of men pass away; and
when one disappears from the earth, he
meets the next with the same claim to
the right of sovereignty, with the same
principles of government—carrying forward, through that and successive ages,
the fulfilment of his great and glorious
purposes.
  35. *And all the inhabitants of the
earth are reputed as nothing.* Are re-

the earth *are* reputed as nothing: and he *a* doeth according to his will in the army of heaven, and *among*

a Ps. 115. 3; 135. 6.　　　b Isa. 43. 13.

garded as nothing in comparison with him. Comp. Notes on Isa. xl. 15, 17. Precisely the same sentiment occurs in Isaiah which is expressed here : " All nations before him are as nothing; and they are accounted unto him less than nothing and vanity." ¶ *And he doeth according to his will in the army of heaven.* In the host of heaven— בְּחֵיל —Gr., *in the power of heaven,* ἐν τῇ, δυνάμει. The Chaldee word means properly strength, might, valour ; and it is then applied to an army as possessing strength, or valour, or force. It is here applied to the inhabitants of heaven, probably considered as an army or host, of which God is the head, and which he leads forth or marshals to execute his purposes. In ch. iii. 20, the word is rendered *army.* The sentiment here is, that in respect to the inhabitants of heaven, represented as organized or marshalled, God does his own pleasure. An intimation of his will is all that is needful to control them. This sentiment is in accordance with all the statements in the Scripture, and is a point of theology which must enter into every just view of God. Thus in the Lord's prayer it is implied : " Thy will be done in earth as it is in heaven." So Eph. i. 11—"Who worketh all things after the counsel of his own will." In heaven the will of God is accomplished in the most strict and absolute sense, for his will is law, and the only law to all the dwellers there. The obedience is as entire as if the will of each one of the dwellers there were but a form or manifestation of the will of God itself. ¶ *And among the inhabitants of the earth.* This cannot mean, even as understood by Nebuchadnezzar, that the will of God is actually done among the inhabitants of the earth in the same sense, and to the same extent, as among those who dwell in heaven. His design was, undoubtedly, to assert the supremacy and absolute control of God; a fact that had been so strikingly illustrated in his own case. The sentiment

the inhabitants of the earth : and none can stay *b* his hand, or say unto him, What *c* doest thou ?

c Job 9. 12; Isa. 45. 9; Rom. 9. 20.

expressed by Nebuchadnezzar is *true* in the following respects :—(1.) That man has no power to prevent the fulfilment of the Divine purposes. (2.) That God will accomplish his design in all things, whatever opposition man may make. (3.) That he has absolute control over every human being, and over all that pertains to any one and every one. (4.) That he will overrule all things so as to make them subservient to his own plans. (5.) That he will make use of men to accomplish his own purposes. Comp. Notes on Isa. x. 7. (6.) That there is a great and glorious scheme of administration which God is carrying out by the instrumentality of men. ¶ *And none can stay his hand.* Literally, "none can smite upon his hand" (Gesenius, *Lex.*) ; that is, none can restrain his hand. The language is taken, says Bertholdt, from the custom of striking children upon the hand when about to do anything wrong, in order to restrain them. The phrase is common in the Targums for *to restrain, to hinder.* The Arabs have a similar expression in common use. See numerous instances of the use of the word מְחָא in the sense of *restrain* or *prohibit,* in Buxtorf.—*Lex. Chal.* The truth taught here is, that no one has power to keep back the hand of God when it is put forth to accomplish the purposes which he intends to execute; that is, he will certainly accomplish his own pleasure. ¶ *Or say unto him, What doest thou ?* A similar expression occurs in 2 Sam. xvi. 10: "So let him curse, because the Lord hath said unto him, Curse David. Who shall then say, Wherefore hast thou done so ?" Also in Job ix. 12: "Behold, he taketh away : Who can hinder him ? Who will say unto him, What doest thou ?" See Notes on that passage. The meaning here is plain. God is supreme, and will do his pleasure in heaven and in earth. The *security* that all will be done right is founded on the perfection of his nature ; and that is ample. Mys-

36 At the same time my reason returned unto me; and for the glory of my kingdom, mine honour and brightness returned unto me; and my counsellors and my lords sought unto me; and I was established in my kingdom, and excellent majesty was added *a* unto me.

37 Now I Nebuchadnezzar praise

a Job 42. 12.

terious though his ways may seem to us, yet in that perfection of his nature we have the fullest assurance that no wrong will be done to any of his creatures. Our duty, therefore, is calm submission to his holy will, with the deep conviction that whatever God does will yet be seen to be right.

36. *At the same time my reason returned unto me.* Showing that he regarded himself as having been insane. ¶ *And for the glory of my kingdom.* That is, his restoration to the exercise of his reason contributed to the glory of his kingdom, either by the acts of justice and beneficence which he intended should characterize the remainder of his reign, or by his purpose to reform the abuses which had crept into the government while he was deprived of his reason, or by his determination to complete public works which had been purposed or commenced before his affliction. ¶ *Mine honour and brightness returned unto me.* Evidently referring to his intellect. He was again restored to that strength and clearness of understanding by which, before his affliction, he had been able to do so much for the glory of his kingdom. ¶ *And my counsellors and my lords sought unto me.* As they had done formerly. During his state of mental alienation, of course, the great lords of the empire would not resort to him for counsel. ¶ *And excellent majesty was added unto me.* Majesty and honour appropriate to my state, instead of the treatment incident to the condition of a maniac. Theodotion renders this, "and greater majesty was added to me." It is by no means improbable that additional honour would be conferred on the recovered monarch.

37. *Now I Nebuchadnezzar praise and extol and honour the King of Heaven.* Comp. ch. ii. 47, and vers. 1–3 of this chapter. He felt himself called on, in this public manner, to acknowledge the true God, with whose supremacy he had

been made acquainted in so affecting a manner; to *praise* him that he had preserved him, and restored him to his reason and his throne; to *extol* or exalt him, by recognizing his sovereignty over the mighty kings of the earth, and the power to rule over all; and to *honour* him by making his name and attributes known abroad, and by using all his influence as a monarch to have him reverenced throughout his extended empire. ¶ *All whose works* are *truth.* See Deut. xxxii. 4; Psal. xxxiii. 4; Rev. xv. 3. The meaning is, that all that he does is done in accordance with the true nature of things, or with justice and propriety. It is not based on a false estimate of things, as what is done by man often is. How often are the plans and acts of man, even where there are the best intentions, based on some false estimate of things; on some views which are shown by the result to have been erroneous! But God sees things precisely as they are, and accurately knows what should be done in every case. ¶ *And those that walk in pride he is able to abase.* What had occurred to Nebuchadnezzar might occur to others, and as God had shown that he could reduce the most exalted sovereign of the earth to the lowest condition in which a human being can be, he inferred that he could do the same to all, and that there was no one so exalted in rank, so vigorous in health, and so mighty in intellect, that he could not effectually humble and subdue him. This is indeed an affecting truth which is constantly illustrated in the world. The reverses occurring among men, the sick-bed, the loss of reason, the grave, show how easily God can bring down rank, and beauty, and talent, and all that the world calls great, to the dust.

In the Greek *Codex Chis.* there is at the close of this chapter a beautiful ascription of praise to God, which has nothing to correspond with it in the Chaldee, and the origin of which is un-

and extol and honour the King of heaven, all whose works *a are* truth, and his ways judgment: and those

known. I will translate it, because, although it is not of Divine authority, and is no part of the sacred writings, it contains sentiments not inappropriate to the close of this remarkable chapter. It is as follows :—"To the Most High I make confession, and render praise to Him who made the heaven, and the earth, and the seas, and the rivers, and all things in them ; I acknowledge him and praise him because he is the God of gods, and Lord of lords, and King of kings, for he does signs and wonders, and changes times and seasons, taking away the kingdoms of kings, and placing others in their stead. From this time I will serve him, and from the fear of him trembling has seized me, and I praise all his saints; for the gods of the heathen have not in themselves power to transfer the kingdom of a king to another king, and to kill and to make alive, and to do signs, and great and fearful wonders, and to change mighty deeds, as the God of heaven has done to me, and has brought upon me great changes. I, during all the days of my reign, on account of my life, will bring to the Most High sacrifices for an odour of sweet savour to the Lord, and I and my people will do that which will be acceptable before him—my nation, and the countries which are under my power. And whosoever shall speak against the God of heaven, and whosoever shall countenance those who speak anything, I will condemn to death. Praise the Lord God of heaven, and bring sacrifice and offering to him gloriously. I, king of kings, confess Him gloriously, for so he has done with me ; in the very day he set me upon my throne, and my power, and my kingdom ; among my people I have power, and my majesty has been restored to me. And he sent letters concerning all things that were done unto him in his kingdom; to all the nations that were under him."

Nebuchadnezzar is supposed to have lived but about one year after this (Wintle), but nothing is known of his subsequent deeds. It may be hoped

that walk in pride *b* he is able to abase.

a Deut. 32. 4 ; Ps. 33. 4; Rev. 15. 3.
b Exod. 18. 11; Job 40. 11, 12; ch. 5. 20.

that he continued steadfast in his faith in that God whom he had thus been brought to acknowledge, and that he died in that belief. But of this nothing is known. After so solemn an admonition, however, of his own pride, and after being brought in this public manner to acknowledge the true God, it is to be regarded as not improbable that he looked on the Babylon that he had reared, and over his extended realms, with other feelings than those which he had before this terrible calamity came upon him. "Nebuchadnezzar was succeeded in his kingdom by his son Iloarudam, according to Ptolemy, who is the Evil-Merodach of Jeremiah. After the death of Evil-Merodach, who reigned two years, Niricassolassar, or Neriglissar, who seems to have been the chief of the conspirators against the last king, succeeded him. He had married a daughter of Nebuchadnezzar, and in the course of his reign made a great stand against the growing power of the Medes and Persians ; but at length, after a reign of four years, was killed in a battle with them under the command of Cyrus. His son Laborosoarchod succeeded him, and having reigned only nine months, and not reaching a Thoth, or beginning of an Egyptian year, he is not mentioned by Ptolemy ; but he is said to have been quite the reverse of his father, and to have exercised many acts of wanton cruelty, and was murdered by his own subjects, and succeeded by his son Nabonadius, or Belshazzar."—Wintle.

REMARKS.

(1.) The narrative in this chapter furnishes an illustration of the disposition among men to make arrangements for their own ease and comfort, especially in view of advancing years, ver. 4. Nebuchadnezzar had drawn around him all that it is possible, perhaps, for man to accumulate with this view. He was at the head of the heathen world—the mighty monarch of the mightiest kingdom on the earth. He was at peace—having finished his wars, and having been satiated with the glory of battle and conquest. He had enlarged and beautified his capital, so that it was one of the "wonders of the world." He had built for himself a palace, which surpassed in richness, and elegance, and luxury, all the habitations of man in that age. He had accumulated vast wealth, and there was not a production of any clime which he could not command, nor was there anything that is supposed to be necessary to make man happy in this life which he had not in his possession. All this was the result of arrangement and purpose. He *designed* evidently to reach the point where he might feel that he was "at ease, and flourishing in his palace."

What was true in his case on a large scale is true of others in general, though on a much smaller scale. Most men would be glad to do the same thing; and most men seek to make such an arrangement according to their ability. They look to the time when they may retire from the toils and cares of life, with a competence for their old age, and when they may enjoy life, perhaps, many years, in the tranquillity of honourable and happy retirement. The merchant does not expect always to be a merchant; the man in office to be always burdened with the cares of state. The soldier does not expect always to be in the camp, or the mariner on the sea. The warrior hopes to repose on his laurels; the sailor to find a quiet haven; the merchant to have enough to be permitted to sit down in the evening of life free from care; and the lawyer, the physician, the clergyman, the farmer, each one hopes, after the toils and conflicts of life are over, to be permitted to spend the remainder of his days in comfort, if not in affluence.

This seems to be based on some law of our nature; and it is not to be spoken of harshly, or despised as if it had no foundation in that which is great and noble in our being. I see in this a high and noble truth. It is that our nature looks forward to *rest;* that we are so made as to pant for *repose*—for calm repose when the work of life is over. As our Maker formed us, the law was that we should seek this in the world to come—in that blessed abode where we may be free from all care, and where there shall be everlasting rest. But man, naturally unwilling to look to that world, has abused this law of his being, and seeks to find the rest for which the soul pants, in that interval, usually *very* short, and quite unfitted for tranquil enjoyment, between the period when he toils, and lies down in the grave. The true law of his being would lead him to look onward to everlasting happiness; he abuses and perverts the law, and seeks to satisfy it by making provision for a brief and temporary rest at the close of the present life.

(2.) There is a process often going on in the case of these individuals to *disturb* or *prevent* that state of ease. Thus there was in the case of Nebuchadnezzar, as intimated by the dream. Even then, in his highest state of grandeur, there was a *tendency* to the sad result which followed when he was driven from his throne, and treated as a poor and neglected maniac. This was intimated to him by the dream; and to one who could see all the future, it would be apparent that things were *tending* to this result. The very excitements and agitations of his life, the intoxication of his pride, and the circumstances of ease and grandeur in which he was now placed, all tended by a natural course of things to produce what followed.

And so, in other cases, there is often a process going on, if it could be seen, destined to disappoint all those hopes, and to prevent all that anticipated ease and tranquillity. It is not always visible to men, but could we see things as God sees them, we should perceive that there are causes at work which will blast all those hopes of ease, and disappoint all those expectations of tranquillity. There *may be* (a) the loss of all that we possess : for we hold it by an uncertain tenure, and "riches often take to themselves wings." There *may be* (b) the loss of a wife, or a child—and all our anticipated comforts shall be tasteless, for there shall be none with whom to share them. There *may be* (c) the loss of reason, as in the case of Nebuchadnezzar, for no human precaution can guard against that. There *may be* (d) the loss of health—a loss against which no one can defend himself—which shall render all his preparations for comfort of no value. Or (e) death itself *may* come—for no one has any basis of calculation in regard to his own life, and no one, therefore, who builds for himself a palace can have any security that he will ever enjoy it. Men who build splendid houses for themselves may yet experience sad scenes in their dwellings ; and if they could foresee all that will occur in them, it would so throw a gloom over all the future as to lead them to abandon the undertaking. Who could engage cheerfully in such an enterprise if he saw that he was constructing a house in which a daughter was to lie down and die, or from which his wife and children were soon to be borne forth to the grave ? In this chamber your child may be long sick ; in that one you or your wife may lie down on a bed from which you will never rise; from those doors yourself, your wife, your child, will be borne forth to the grave; and if you *saw* all this now, how could you engage with so much zeal in constructing your magnificent habitation ?

(3.) Our plans of life should be formed with the feeling that this is *possible :* I say not with the gloomy apprehension that these calamities will certainly come, or with no anticipation or hope that there will be different scenes—for then life would be nothing else but gloom ; but that we should allow the *possibility* that these things may occur to enter, as an element, into our calculations respecting the future. Such a feeling will give us sober and just views of life ; will break the force of trouble and disappointment when they come ; and will give us just apprehensions of our dependence on Him in whose hand are all our comforts.

(4.) The dealings of God in our world are such as are eminently fitted to keep up the recognition of these truths. What occurred to Nebuchadnezzar, in the humbling of his pride, and the blighting of his anticipated pleasures, is just an illustration of what is constantly occurring on the earth. What house is there into which trouble, disappointment, and sorrow never come ? What scheme of pride is there in respect to which something does not occur to produce mortification ? What habitation is there into which sickness, bereavement, and death never find their way ? And what abode of man on earth can be made secure from the intrusion of these things ? The most splendid mansion must soon be left by its owner, and never be visited by him again. The most magnificent banqueting-hall will be forsaken by its possessor, and never will he return to it again ; never go into the chamber where he sought repose ; never sit down at the table where he joined with others in revelry.

(5.) The counsel given by Daniel to Nebuchadnezzar (ver. 27), to break off his sins by righteousness, that there might be a lengthening out of his tranquillity, is counsel that may now be given to all sinners, with equal propriety. (I.) For, as in his case, there are certain consequences of sin to which we must look forward, and on which the eye of a sinner should rest. Those consequences are (1) such as spring up in the course of nature, or which are the regular results of sin in the course of events. They are such as can be foreseen, and can be made the basis of calculation, or which a man can know beforehand *will* come upon him if he perseveres in a certain course. Thus he who is intemperate can look upon certain results which will inevitably follow if he perseveres in that course of life. As he looks upon the poverty, and babbling, and woe, and sorrow, and misery, and death of an inebriate, he can see that that lot will be *certainly* his own if he perseveres in his present course, and this can be made with him a matter of definite calculation or anticipation. Or (2) there are all those consequences of sin which are made known in the sacred Scriptures as sure to come upon transgressors. This, too, is a large class; but these consequences are as *certain* as those which occur in the regular course of events. The principal difference between the two is, that revelation has designated *more* sins that will involve the sinner in calamity than can be ascertained in the ordinary course of events, and that it has carried the mind forward, and discloses what will take place in the *future* world as well as what will occur in *this*. But the one is more certain than the other; and alike in reference to what is *sure* to occur in the present life, and what we are *told* will occur in the future state, the sinner should allow himself to be influenced by the anticipation of what is to come. II. Repentance, reformation, and a holy life would, in many cases, go far to arrest these calamities— or, in the language of Daniel, "lengthen out tranquillity." This is true in the following respects : (1.) That impending *temporal* calamities may be often partially or wholly turned away by reformation. An illustration of this thought occurred in the case of Nineveh; and the same thing now occurs. A young man who is in danger of becoming intemperate, and who has already contracted some of the habits that lead to intemperance, could avert a large class of impending ills by so simple a thing as signing the temperance pledge, and adhering to it. *All* the evils of poverty, tears, crime, disease, and an early death, that intemperance produces, he would *certainly* avert; that is, he would make it certain that the large class of ills that intemperance engenders would *never* come upon him. He might experience *other* ills, but he would never suffer those. So it is of the sufferings produced by licentiousness, by gluttony, by the spirit of revenge ; and so it is' of all the woes that follow the violation of human laws. A man may indeed be poor ; he may be sick ; he may be bereaved ; he may lose his reason, but *these* ills he will never experience. But what Daniel here affirms is true in another sense in regard to temporal calamities. A man may, by repentance, and by breaking off from his sins, do much to stay the progress of woe, and to avert the results which he has already begun to experience. Thus the drunkard may reform, and may have restored health, vigour, and prosperity; and thus the licentious may turn from the evil of his ways, and enjoy health and happiness still. On this subject, see Notes on Job xxxiii. 14–25, particularly the Notes on ver. 25. (2.) But by repentance and holy living a man may turn away *all* the results of sin in the future world, and may make it certain that he will never experience a pang beyond the grave. All the woe that sin would cause in the future state may be thus averted, and he who has been deeply guilty may enter the eternal world with the assurance that he will never suffer beyond the grave. Whether, then, we look to the future in the present life, or to the future beyond the grave, we have the highest conceivable motives to abandon the ways of sin, and to lead lives of holiness. If a man were to live *only* on the earth, it would be for his welfare to break off from the ways of transgression; how much higher is this motive when it is remembered that he must exist for ever!

(6.) We have an illustration in the account in this chapter of the evil of *pride*, vers. 29–31. The pride which we may have on account of beauty, or strength, or learning, or accomplishments; which we feel when we look over our lands that we have cultivated, or the houses that we have built, or the reputation which we have acquired, is no less offensive in the sight of a holy God than was the pride of the magnificent monarch who looked out on the towers, and domes, and walls, and palaces of a vast city, and said, "Is not this great Babylon that I have builded?"

(7.) And in view of the calamity that came upon Nebuchadnezzar, and the treatment which he received in his malady, we may make the following remarks: (*a*) We should be thankful for the continuance of *reason*. When we look on such a case as this, or when we go into a lunatic asylum, and see the wretchedness that the loss of reason causes, we should thank God *daily* that we are not deprived of this inestimable blessing. (*b*) We should be thankful for science, and for the Christian religion, and for all that they have done to give comfort to the maniac, or to restore him to a sound mind. When we compare the treatment which the insane

now receive in the lunatic asylums with that which they everywhere meet with in the heathen world, and with that which they have, up to a very recent period, received in Christian lands, there is almost nothing in which we see more marked proof of the interposition of God than in the great change which has been produced. There are few persons who have not, or may not have, some friend or relative who is insane, and there is no one who is not, or may not be, personally interested in the improvement which religion and science have made in the treatment of this class of unfortunate beings. In no one thing, so far as I know, has there been so decided progress in the views and conduct of men; and on no one subject has there been so evident an improvement in modern times, as in the treatment of the insane. (*c*) The possibility of the loss of reason should be an element in our calculations about the future. On this point we can have no security. There is no such vigour of intellect, or clearness of mind, or cultivation of the habits of virtue, and even no such influence of religion, as to make it certain that *we* may not yet be reckoned among the insane; and the *possibility* that this may be so should be admitted as an element in our calculations in regard to the future. We should not jeopard any valuable interest by leaving that undone which *ought* to be done, on the supposition that we may at a future period of life enjoy the exercise of reason. Let us remember that there *may be* in our case, even in youth or middle life, the loss of this faculty; that there *will be*, if we reach old age, in all probability, such a weakening of our mental powers as to unfit us for making any preparation for the life to come, and that on the bed of death, *whenever* that occurs, there is often an entire loss of the mental powers, and commonly so much pain.

distress, or prostration, as to unfit the dying man for calm and deliberate thought ; and let us, therefore, while we *have* reason and health, do all that we know we *ought* to do to make preparation for our eternal state. For what is our reason more certainly given us than to prepare for another world ?

CHAPTER V.

§ I.—AUTHENTICITY OF THE CHAPTER.

Much fewer objections have been made to the authenticity of this chapter, and much fewer difficulties started, than in regard to chapter iv. Those which have been urged may be classed under the following heads :—

I. The first is substantially stated in this manner by Bertholdt, that "Daniel is represented as speaking to the king in such a tone, that if it had actually occurred, he would have been cut to pieces by an arbitrary Babylonian despot; but instead of that, he is not only unpunished, but is suffered to announce to the king the certain destruction of his kingdom by the Medes and Persians ; and not only this, but he is immediately promoted to be a minister or officer of a state of exalted rank,"p. 345.

To this it may be replied, (1.) That the way in which Daniel addressed him was entirely in accordance with the manner in which he addressed Nebuchadnezzar, in which Nathan addressed David, in which Isaiah addressed Ahaz, and Jeremiah the kings in his time. (2.) Belshazzar was overpowered with the remarkable vision of the handwriting on the wall ; his conscience smote him, and he was in deep alarm. He sought the meaning of this extraordinary revelation, and could not but regard it as a communication from heaven. In this state of mind, painful as was the announcement, he would naturally receive it as a Divine communication, and he might fear to treat with indig-

nity one who showed that he had the power of disclosing the meaning of words so mysterious. (3.) It was in accordance with the custom of those times to honour those who showed that they had the power of penetrating the Divine mysteries, and of disclosing the meaning of dreams, prodigies, and omens. (4.) It is not impossible, as Hengstenberg *Authentie des Dan.* 120, suggests, that, smitten with the consciousness of guilt, and knowing that he deserved punishment, he may have hoped to turn away the wrath of God by some act of piety; and that he resolved, therefore, to honour Daniel, who showed that he was a favourite of heaven. The main security of Daniel, however, in these bold and fearful announcements, was undoubtedly to be found in the *smitten conscience* of the trembling monarch, and in the belief that he was a favourite of heaven.

II. The improbability that all this should occur in one night—that so many scenes should have been crowded into so short a time—embracing the feast, the writing, the calling in of the magicians, the investing of Daniel with his new office, the taking of the city, &c. "Why," says Bertholdt, "was not the proclamation in regard to the new minister deferred to the following day? Why did all this occur in the midst of the scenes of revelry which were then taking place?" pp. 345, 346.

To this it may be replied, (1.) That there is, indeed, every appearance of haste and confusion in the transactions. This was natural. But there was assuredly no want of *time* to accomplish all that it is said was accomplished. If it was true that Cyrus broke into the city in the latter part of the night, or if, as historians say was the fact, he had entered the city, and made considerable progress in it before the tidings were communicated to Belshazzar, there is no improbability in supposing that all that is said of the feast, and of the handwriting, and of the calling in of the magicians, and of their failure to decipher the meaning of the writing, and of the summoning of Daniel, and of the interpretation which he gave, actually occurred, for there was time enough to accomplish all this. (2.) As to the other part of the objection, that it is improbable that Daniel would be so soon invested with office, and that a proclamation would be made in the night to this effect, it may be replied, that all that is fairly meant in the chapter (ver. 29) may be that *an order* was made to that effect, with a purpose to carry it into execution on the following day. Bertholdt himself translates the passage (ver. 29), "Then Belshazzar gave command that they should clothe Daniel with scarlet, and put a chain of gold around his neck," &c. Hierauf *gab Belschazar den Befehl* dem Daniel den purpurmantel und den goldenen Halsschmuck umzuhängen, &c. On the one hand, nothing forbids the supposition that the execution of this order might have been deferred; or, on the other, that the order *was* executed at once. But little time would have been necessary to do it. See however, Notes on ver. 29.

III. A third objection or difficulty arises from the writing itself. It is, that it is wholly improbable that Daniel could have had sufficient knowledge to enable him to interpret these words when no one of the Chaldean sages could do it. Where, it is asked, could he have obtained this knowledge? His instruction in reading languages he must have received in Babylon itself, and it is wholly improbable that among so many sages and wise men who were accustomed to the languages spoken in Babylon and in other countries, no one should have been found who was as

able to interpret the words as he.— Bertholdt, p. 346.

To this it is obvious to reply, that the whole narrative supposes that Daniel owed his ability to interpret these words, not to any natural skill, or to any superior advantages of genius or education, but to the fact that he was directly endowed from on high. In other cases, in the times of Nebuchadnezzar, he always disclaimed any power of his own of revealing the meaning of dreams and visions (ch. ii. 27–30), nor did he set up any claim to an ability to do it of himself on this occasion. If he received his knowledge directly from God, all the difficulty in this objection vanishes at once; but the whole book turns on the supposition that he *was* under Divine teaching.

IV. It has been objected that there was no object to be accomplished worthy of such a miracle as that of writing in this mysterious manner on the wall. It is asked by Bertholdt (p. 347), "Is the miracle credible? What purpose was it designed to serve? What end would it accomplish? Was the design to show to Belshazzar that the city was soon to be destroyed? But of what use could this be but a couple of hours before it should occur? Or was it the design to make Belshazzar acquainted with the power of Jehovah, and to punish him for desecrating the vessels of the temple service? But who could attribute to the all-perfect Being such a weakness that he could be angry, and take this method to express his anger, for an act that could not be regarded as so heinous as to be worthy of such an interposition?"

To this it may be replied, (1.) That the objection here made would lie in some degree against almost any single miracle that is recorded in the Scriptures. (2.) That it may have been the intention to warn the king of the impending danger, not so much with a view that the danger should be averted, as to show that it came from God. (3.) Or it may have been the intention to show him the enormity of his sins, and even then to bring him to repentance. (4.) Or it may have been the intention to connect quite distinctly, in the apprehension of all present, and in the view of all future ages, the destruction of Babylon with the crimes of the monarchs, and especially their crimes in connection with the destruction of the city of Jerusalem, the burning of the temple, and the carrying away of the people into a long captivity. There can be no doubt, from many parts of the prophetic writings, that the overthrow of Babylon, and the subversion of the Chaldean power, was in consequence of their treatment of the Hebrew people; and nothing was better fitted to show this than to make the destruction of the city coincident with the desecration of the sacred vessels of the temple. (5.) Or it may have been the intention to recal Daniel into notice, and to give him authority and influence again preparatory to the restoration of his countrymen to their own land. It would seem from the whole narrative that, in accordance with a custom which still prevails in Persia (Chardin, as referred to by Hengstenberg, *Authentie des Daniel*, p. 123), all the magicians and astrologers had been dismissed from court on the death of Nebuchadnezzar, and that Daniel with the others had retired from his place. Yet it may have been important, in order to the restoration of the Hebrew people to their land at the appointed time, that there should be one of their own nation occupying an influential station at court, and Daniel was thus, in consequence of his ability to interpret this mysterious language, restored to his place, and was permitted to keep it until the time of the return of the Hebrews to their country arrived. See ch. vi. 2, 3, 28. (6.) And it may have been the intention to furnish an impressive demonstration that Jehovah is the true God. Other objections it will be more convenient to notice in the course of the exposition of the chapter.

§ II.—BELSHAZZAR.

Of Belshazzar, the closing scene of whose reign is described in this chapter, little more is known than is recorded here. He is mentioned by Daniel as the last king of the Chaldees, under whom Babylon was taken by the Medes and Persians. Herodotus (i. 188) calls this king, and also his father, *Labynetus,* which is undoubtedly a corruption of Nabonnedus, the name by which he was known to Berosus.—Josephus *against Apion,* i. 20. Josephus himself (*Ant.* x. ch. xi. § 2) says that the name of this king, whom he calls Baltasar, among the Babylonians, was Naboandelus. Nabonadius in the canon of Ptolemy, Nabonedus in Eusebius (*Chron. Armen.* i. p. 60), and Nabonnidochus in Eusebius (*Prep. Evang.* ix. 41), are remarked by Winer as only varieties of his name. Winer conjectures that in the name Belshazzar, the element *shazzar* means "the principle of fire." See Kitto's *Cyclopædia.*

The accounts which we have of this king are very meagre, and yet, meagre as they are, they are by no means uniform, and it is difficult to reconcile them. That which is given by Josephus as his own account of the successors of Nebuchadnezzar is in the following language:—"After the death of Nebuchadnezzar Evil-Merodach, his son, succeeded in the kingdom, who immediately set Jeconiah at liberty, and esteemed him among his most intimate friends. When Evil-Merodach was dead, after a reign of eighteen years,

Neglissar, his son, took the government, and retained it forty years, and then ended his life; and after him the succession came to his son, Labosordacus, who continued it in all but nine months; and when he was dead, it came to Baltasar, who by the Babylonians was called Naboandelus; against him did Cyrus the king of Persia, and Darius the king of Media, make war; and when he was besieged in Babylon there happened a wonderful and prodigious vision. He was sat down at supper in a large room, and there were a great many vessels of silver, such as were made for royal entertainments, and he had with him his concubines and his friends; whereupon he came to a resolution, and commanded that those vessels of God which Nebuchadnezzar had plundered out of Jerusalem, and had not made use of, but had put them into his own temple, should be brought out of that temple."—*Ant*. b. x. ch. xi.

§ 2. Josephus then proceeds to give an account of the appearance of the hand, and of the writing, and of the result in the taking of Babylon, substantially the same as that which is found in this chapter of Daniel.

The account which Berosus gives as preserved by Josephus (*against Apion*, b. i. § 20) varies from this in some important particulars. For an account of Berosus, see the Introduction to ch. iv. § I. I. He says, "Nabuchodonosar (Nebuchadnezzar), after he had begun to build the forementioned wall, fell sick and departed this life, when he had reigned forty-three years; whereupon his son, Evil-Merodach, obtained the kingdom. He governed public affairs after an illegal and impure manner, and had a plot laid against him by Neriglissar, his sister's husband, and was slain by him when he had reigned but two years. After he was slain, Neriglissar, the person who plotted against

him, succeeded him in the kingdom, and reigned four years; but his son Laborosoarchad obtained the kingdom, though he was but a child, and kept it nine months; but by reason of the very ill temper, and the ill practices he exhibited to the world, a plot was laid against him also by his friends, and he was tormented to death. After his death the conspirators got together, and by common consent put the crown upon the head of Nabonnedus, a man of Babylon, and one who belonged to that insurrection. In his reign it was that the walls of the city of Babylon were curiously built with burnt brick and bitumen; but when he was come to the seventeenth year of his reign, Cyrus came out of Persia with a great army, and having already conquered the rest of Asia, he came hastily to Babylonia. When Nabonnedus perceived he was coming to attack him, he met him with his forces, and joining battle with him, was beaten, and fled away with a few of his troops with him, and was shut up in the city of Borsippus. Hereupon Cyrus took Babylon, and gave orders that the outer walls of the city should be demolished, because the city had proved very troublesome to him, and cost him a great deal of pains to take it. He then marched away to Borsippus to besiege Nabonnedus; but as Nabonnedus did not sustain the siege, but delivered himself into his hands, he was at first kindly used by Cyrus, who gave him Carmania as a place for him to inhabit in, but sent him out of Babylonia. Accordingly, Nabonnedus spent the rest of his time in that country, and there died."

Roos (*Exposition of Daniel*, p. 65) supposes that Evil-Merodach, who succeeded Nebuchadnezzar, did not reign more than one year, and that this accounts for the reason why he was not mentioned by Daniel; and that Belshazzar was a grandson of Nebuchadnezzar, though, according to the idiom of Scripture, he is called his son, and Nebuchadnezzar his father, Dan. v. 11, 22. Belshazzar, he supposes, must have reigned more than twenty years.

The succession in the Babylonian Chaldean kingdom, according to Dr. Hales, was as follows: "Nabonassar reigned 14 years, from 747 B.C.; Nadius, 2, 733; Chinzirus, 5, 731; Jugaus, 5, 726; Mardok Empad, or Merodach Baladan, 12, 721; Arcianus, 5, 709; first interregnum, 2, 704; Belibus, 3, 702; Aphronadius, 6, 699; Regibelus, 1, 693; Mesessemordach, 4, 692; second interregnum, 8, 688; Asaradin, or Esar-haddon, 13, 680; Saosduchin, 20, 667; Chyneladon, 22, 647; Nabopolassar, or Labynetus I., 21, 625; Nineveh taken by the Babylonians and Medes, 604 B.C. Then follows the Babylonian dynasty, to wit, Nabopolassar, Labynetus I., Boktanser, or, Nebuchadnezzar, who reigned 43 years from 604 B.C.; Ilverodam, or Evil-Merodach, 3, 561 B.C.; Nericassolassar, Neriglissar, or Belshazzar, 5, 558 B.C.; Nabonadius, or Labynetus II., appointed by Darius the Mede, 17, 553 B.C.; Babylon taken by Cyrus, 536 B.C."

Dr. Hales remarks in connection with this, "Nothing can exceed the various and perplexed accounts of the names and reigns of the princes of this dynasty (the Babylonian) in sacred and profane history."

Jahn, following Ptolemy chiefly, thus enumerates the kings of Babylon from the reign of Nebuchadnezzar: "Nabocholassar, or Nebuchadnezzar, 43, 605 B.C.; Iluarodamus, or Evil-Merodach, 2, 562 B.C.; Nerichassolassar, or Neriglissar, 4, 560 B.C; Laborasoarchad, 9 months, 556 B.C.; Nabounned, 17 years, 556 B.C.; Babylon taken by the Medes and Persians, 540 B.C."

In this confusion and discord respect-

ing the chronology of these princes, the following remarks may be made in regard to the credibility of the statements in the book of Daniel: (1.) It is clear that it was not uncommon for the same prince to have more names than one. This has not been unusual, especially among Oriental princes, who seem to have often prided themselves on the number of epithets which they could use as designating their royal state. Since this was the case, it would not be strange if the names of the same kings should be so used by writers, or in tradition, as to leave the impression that there were several; or if one writer should designate a king by one name, and another by another. (2.) It would seem probable, from all the accounts, that Belshazzar was the grandson of Nebuchadnezzar, but little is known of the king or kings whose reign intervened between that of Nebuchadnezzar and Belshazzar. (3.) The testimony of Daniel in the book before us should not be set aside by the statement of Berosus, or by the other confused accounts which have come down to us. For anything that appears to the contrary, the authority of Daniel is as good as that of Berosus, and he is as worthy of belief. Living in Babylon, and through a great part of the reigns of this dynasty; present at the taking of Babylon, and intimate at court; honoured by some of these princes more than any other man in the realm, there is no reason why he should not have had access to the means of information on the subject, and no reason why it should not be supposed that he has given a fair record of what actually occurred. Though the account in regard to the last days of Belshazzar, as given by Berosus, does not agree with that of Daniel, it should not be *assumed* that that of Berosus is correct, and that that of Daniel false. The account in Daniel

CHAPTER V.

BELSHAZZAR the king made a great feast *a* to a thousand

is, to say the least, as probable as that of Berosus, and there are no means of proving that it is false except by the testimony of Berosus. (4.) The statement in Daniel of the manner in which Babylon was taken, and of the death of Belshazzar, is confirmed by Xenophon (*Cyrop.* vii.)—an authority quite equal, at least, to that of Berosus. See Notes on ver. 30 of the chapter. In the record in Daniel of the close of the life of Belshazzar, there is nothing that might not have been supposed to occur, for nothing is more probable than that a king *might* have been celebrating a feast in the manner described, or that the city might be surprised in such a night of revelry, or that, being surprised, the monarch might be slain.

ANALYSIS OF THE CHAPTER.

The chapter comprises a record of the series of events that occurred in Babylon on the night in which it was taken by the Medes and Persians. The scene may be supposed to open in the early evening, at a time when a festival would probably be celebrated, and to continue through a considerable part of the night. It is not known precisely at what time the city was taken, yet it may be supposed that Cyrus was making his approaches while the revel was going on in the palace, and that even while Daniel was interpreting the handwriting on the wall, he was conducting his armies along the channel of the river, and through the open gate on the banks of the river, toward the palace. The order of the events referred to is as follows: (1.) The feast given by Belshazzar in his palace, vers. 1–4; (2.) the mysterious appearance of the part of the hand on the wall, ver. 5; (3.) the summoning of the sooth-

of his lords, and drank wine before the thousand.

a Esth. 1. 3.

sayers to interpret the handwriting, and their inability to do it, vers. 6–9; (4.) the entrance of the queen into the banqueting-hall on account of the trouble of the king, and her reference to Daniel as one qualified to interpret the vision, vers. 10–12; (5.) the summoning of Daniel by the king, and his address to him, vers. 13–16; (6.) the answer of Daniel, declining any rewards for his service, and his solemn address to the king, reminding him of what had occurred to Nebuchadnezzar, and of the fact that he had forgotten the lessons which the Divine dealings with Nebuchadnezzar were adapted to teach, and that his own heart had been lifted up with pride, and that his conduct had been eminently wicked, vers. 17–23; (7.) the interpretation of the words by Daniel, vers. 24–28; (8.) the order to clothe Daniel in a manner appropriate to one of high rank, and the appointment to the third office in the kingdom, ver. 29; and (9.) the taking of the city, and the death of Belshazzar, vers. 30, 31.

1. *Belshazzar the king.* See Intro. to the chapter, § II. In the Introduction to the chapter here referred to, I have stated what seemed to be necessary in order to illustrate the history of Belshazzar, so far as that can be now known. The statements in regard to this monarch, it is well understood, are exceedingly confused, and the task of reconciling them is now hopeless. Little depends, however, in the interpretation of this book, on the attempt to reconcile them, for the narrative here given is equally credible, whichever of the accounts is taken, unless that of Berosus is followed. But it may not be improper to exhibit here the two principal accounts of the successors of Nebuchadnezzar, that the discrepancy may be distinctly seen. I copy from the *Pictorial Bible.* "The common account

we shall collect from *L'Art de Verifier les Dates,* and the other from Hales's | *Analysis,* disposing them in opposite columns for the sake of comparison :—

From *L'Art de Verifier.*	From Hales's *Analysis.*
B.C.	**B.C.**
605 Nebuchadnezzar, who was succeeded by his son	604 Nebuchadnezzar was succeeded by his son
562 Evil-Merodach, who, having provoked general indignation by his tyranny and atrocities, was, after a short reign of about two years, assassinated by his brother-in-law	561 Evil-Merodach, or Ilverodam, who was slain in a battle against the Medes and Persians, and was succeeded by his son
560 Nerigilassar, or Nericassolassar, who was regarded as a deliverer, and succeeded by the choice of the nation. He perished in a battle by Cyrus, and was succeeded by his son	558 Neriglissar, Niricassolassar, or Belshazzar, the common accounts of whom seem to combine what is said both of Neriglissar, and his son, opposite. He was killed by conspirators on the night of the 'impious feast,' leaving a son (a boy),
555 Laborosoarchod, notorious for his cruelty and oppression, and who was assassinated by two nobles, Gobryas and Gadatas, whose sons he had slain. The vacant throne was then ascended by	553 Laborosoarchod, on whose death, nine months after, the dynasty became extinct, and the kingdom came peaceably to 'Darius the Mede,' or Cyaxares who, on the well-known policy of the Medes and Persians, appointed a Babylonian nobleman, named Nabonadius, or Labynetus, to be king, or viceroy. This person revolted against Cyrus, who had succeeded to the united empire of the Medes and Persians. Cyrus could not immediately attend to him, but at last marched to Babylon, took the city, B.C. 536, as foretold by the prophets.
554 Nabonadius, the Labynetus of Herodotus, the Naboandel of Josephus, and the Belshazzar of Daniel, who was the son of Evil-Merodach, and who now succeeded to the throne of his	
538 father. After a voluptuous reign, his city was taken by the Persians under Cyrus, on which occasion he lost his life.	

It will be observed that the principal point of difference in these accounts is, that Hales contends that the succession of Darius the Mede to the Babylonian throne was not attended with war ; that Belshazzar was not the king in whose time the city was taken by Cyrus ; and, consequently, that the events which took place this night were quite distinct from and anterior to that siege and capture of the city by the Persian king

which Isaiah and Jeremiah so remarkably foretold. ¶ *Made a great feast.* On what occasion this feast was made is not stated, but it was not improbably an annual festival in honour of some of the Babylonian deities. This opinion seems to be countenanced by the words of the *Codex Chis.,* "Belshazzar the king made a great festival (ἐν ἡμέρᾳ ἐγκαινισμοῦ τῶν βασιλείων) on the day of the dedication of his kingdom ;" and in ver. 4 it is said that "they praised the gods of gold, of silver, and of brass," &c. ¶ *To a thousand of his lords.* The word *thousand* here is doubtless used as a general term to denote a very large number. It is not improbable, however, that this full number was assembled on such an occasion. "Ctesias says, that the king of Persia furnished provisions daily for fifteen thousand men. Quintus Curtius says that ten thousand men were present at a festival of Alexander the Great; and Statius says of Domitian, that he ordered, on a certain occasion, his guests 'to sit down at a thousand tables.'"—Prof. Stuart, *in loc.* ¶ *And drank wine before the thousand.* The Latin Vulgate here is, "And each one drank according to his age." The Greek of Theodotion, the Arabic, and the Coptic is, "and wine was before the thousand."

The Chaldee, however, is, as in our version, "he drank wine before the thousand." As he was the lord of the feast, and as all that occurred pertained primarily to him, the design is undoubtedly to describe *his* conduct, and to show the effect which the drinking of wine had on him. He drank it in the most public manner, setting an example to his lords, and evidently drinking it to great excess.

[The industrious researches of Layard and Botta have made us familiar with the details of Assyrian life; and we have here sculptured representations of attendants supplying wine to the guests, and of the guests themselves seated at table. For convenience in filling and carrying, the cups have handles; but they are held by the guests in a different manner. The toast is being given, to which all are responding. These remains are from Khorsabad.

"The drinking cups and vessels used on festive occasions (by the Assyrians) were probably of gold, like those of Solomon, or of silver.

When Ahasuerus feasted all the people, both great and small, for seven days, in Shushan the palace, wine was given to them in vessels of

2 Belshazzar, while he tasted the wine, commanded to bring the golden and silver vessels *a* which

a ch. 1. 2; Jer. 52. 19.

his [1] father Nebuchadnezzar had taken[2] out of the temple which *was*

1 or, *grandfather*, as Jer. 27. 7; 2 Sam. 9. 7.;
vers. 11, 18.   2 *brought forth.*

gold, each one differing from the other. The drinking vases of the Assyrians were frequently wrought into the shape of the head and neck of an animal, such as a lion or a bull, and resembled those afterwards in use amongst the Greeks, and found in the tombs of Etruria." The form of cup referred to in the preceding extract is shown in the engraving, copied from the Assyrian remains discovered at Khorsabad.]

2, 3. *Belshazzar, while he tasted the wine.* As the effect of tasting the wine —stating a fact which is illustrated in every age and land, that men, under the influence of intoxicating drinks, will do what they would not do when sober. In his sober moments it would seem probable that he would have respected the vessels consecrated to the service of religion, and would not have treated them with dishonour by introducing them for purposes of revelry. ¶ *Commanded to bring the golden and silver vessels.* These vessels had been carefully deposited in some place as

the spoils of victory (see ch. **i.** 2), and it would appear that they had not before been desecrated for purposes of feasting. Belshazzar did what other men would have done in the same condition. He wished to make a display; to do something unusually surprising; and, though it had not been contemplated when the festival was appointed to make use of these vessels, yet, under the excitement of wine, nothing was too sacred to be introduced to the scenes of intoxication; nothing too foolish to be done. In regard to the vessels taken from the temple at Jerusalem, see Notes on ch. **i.** 2. ¶ *Which his father Nebuchadnezzar had taken.*

[The recent discoveries by Layard and Botta at Nimroud and Khorsabad have revealed to us all the details of Assyrian life, and more particularly all the circumstances attendant on the warlike expeditions and conquests. In the annexed engraving, we have a portion of a bass-relief, in which the spoils of a conquered people are brought together, and an inventory or account taken of them. Amongst other things, a number of vessels are seen of different shapes and capacities; and, from the lavish use of the precious metals in the luxurious East, there can be no doubt that "the golden vessels," whether secular or sacred, would form an important part of the spoils.]

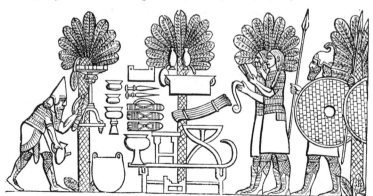

Marg., *grandfather.* According to the best account which we have of Bel-shazzar, he was the son of Evil-Merodach, who was the son of Nebuchad-

in Jerusalem; that the king, and his princes, his wives, and his concubines, might drink therein.

3 Then they brought the golden vessels that were taken out of the

temple of the house of God which *was* at Jerusalem; and the king, and his princes, his wives, and his concubines, drank in them.

4 They drank wine, and praised

---

nezzar (see the Intro. to the chapter, § II.), and therefore the word is used here, as in the margin, to denote grandfather. Compare Jer. xxvii. 7. See Notes on Isa. xiv. 22. The word *father* is often used in a large signification. See 2 Sam ix. 7; also Notes on Matt. i. 1. There is no improbability in supposing that this word would be used to denote a grandfather, when applied to one of the family or dynasty of Nebuchadnezzar. The fact that Belshazzar is here called *the son* of Nebuchadnezzar has been made a ground of objection to the credibility of the book of Daniel, by Lengerke, p. 204. The objection is, that the "last king of Babylon was *not* the son of Nebuchadnezzar." But, in reply to this, in addition to the remarks above made, it may be observed that it is not necessary, in vindicating the assertion in the text, to suppose that he was the *immediate* descendant of Nebuchadnezzar, in the first degree. "The Semitic use of the word in question goes far beyond the first degree of descent, and extends the appellation of *son* to the designation *grandson,* and even of the most remote posterity. In Ezra vi. 14, the prophet Zechariah is called *the son of Iddo;* in Zech. i. 1, 7, the same person is called *the son of Berechiah, the son of Iddo.* So Isaiah threatens Hezekiah (xxxix. 7) that *the sons whom he shall beget* shall be conducted as exiles to Babylon; in which case, however, four generations intervened before this happened. Co in Matt. i. 1, 'Jesus Christ, the son of David, the son of Abraham.' And so we speak every day: 'The sons of Adam, the sons of Abraham, the sons of Israel, the sons of the Pilgrims,' and the like."—Prof. Stuart, *Com. on Dan.* p. 144. ¶ *That the king and his princes, his wives, and his concubines, might drink therein.* Nothing is too sacred to be profaned when men are under the influence of wine. They do not hesitate to desecrate the holiest things, and vessels taken from the altar

of God are regarded with as little reverence as any other. It would seem that Nebuchadnezzar *had* some respect for these vessels, as having been employed in the purposes of religion; at least so much respect as to lay them up as trophies of victory, and that this respect had been shown for them under the reign of his successors, until the exciting scenes of this "impious feast" occurred, when all veneration for them vanished. It was not very common for females in the East to be present at such festivals as this, but it would seem that all the usual restraints of propriety and decency came to be disregarded as the feast advanced. The "wives and concubines" were probably not present when the feast began, for it was made for "his *lords*" (ver. 1); but when the scenes of revelry had advanced so far that it was proposed to introduce the sacred vessels of the temple, it would not be unnatural to propose also to introduce the females of the court. A similar instance is related in the book of Esther. In the feast which Ahasuerus gave, it is said that "on the seventh day, when the heart of the king was merry with wine, he commanded Mehuman, Biztha, &c., the seven chamberlains that served in the presence of Ahasuerus the king, to bring Vashti the queen before the king with the crown royal, to show the people and the princes her beauty," &c. Esth. i.10, 11. Comp. Joseph. *Ant.* b. xi. ch. vi. § 1. The females that were thus introduced to the banquet were those of the harem, yet it would seem that she who was usually called "the queen" by way of eminence, or the queen-mother (comp. Notes on ver. 10), was not among them at this time. The females in the court of an Oriental monarch were divided into two classes; those who were properly concubines, and who had none of the privileges of a wife; and those of a higher class, and who were spoken of as wives, and to whom appertained the privileges of that

the gods of gold, *a* and of silver, of brass, of iron, of wood, and of stone.

a Rev. 9. 20.

5 ¶ In the same hour *b* came forth fingers of a man's hand, and wrote over against the candle-

b ch. 4. 31.

relation. Among the latter, also, in the court of a king, it would seem that there was one to whom properly belonged the appellation of *queen;* that is, probably, a favourite wife whose children were heirs to the crown. See Bertholdt, *in loc.* Comp. 2 Sam. v. 13; 1 Kings xi. 3; Cant. vi. 8.

4. *They drank wine, and praised the gods of gold, and of silver,* &c. Comp. Notes on ver. 1. Idols were made among the heathen of all the materials here mentioned. The word *praised* here means that they spake in praise of these gods; of their history, of their attributes, of what they had done. Nothing can well be conceived more senseless

and stupid than what it is said they did at this feast, and yet it is a fair illustration of what occurs in all the festivals of idolatry. And is that which occurs in more civilized Christian lands, in the scenes of carousal and festivity, more rational than this? It was not much worse to lavish praises on idol gods in a scene of revelry than it is to lavish praises on idol men now; not much less rational to "toast" *gods* than it is to "toast" *men.*

[These various gods are represented in general by the annexed engravings. The three grotesque figures, of which the one to the right hand is shown in front and profile, are copied from remains discovered at Khorsabad; and if

these may be taken as part of the gods in whose honour Belshazzar and his lords drank wine and gave praise, the preceding remarks of our author on their senseless and stupid conduct derive additional force. It is probable that the homage was rather directed to the false divinities which were customarily borne on men's shoulders, on festal occasions, with much pomp and ceremony. Two of these are given, from a bass-relief in the south-west palace at Nimroud; the one to the left is sufficiently identified with the description of Belus or Baal, by Herodotus; and the seated figure has the attributes of the Assyrian Venus, Astarta. In the Epistle of Jeremy, which concludes the apocryphal book of Baruch, there is a remarkable allusion to these idols, which goes far to establish its authenticity.

In the 6th chapter of Baruch, forming Jeremy's Epistle, we read:—

stick upon the plaster of the wall of the king's palace; and the king saw the part of the hand that wrote.

4 v. Now shall ye see in Babylon gods of silver, and of gold, *borne upon shoulders,* which cause the nations to fear.

15 v. He hath also in his right hand a dagger, *and an axe.*

The writer, beyond a doubt, must have witnessed the Assyrian processions, and been familiar with the forms and attributes of the idols borne in them.

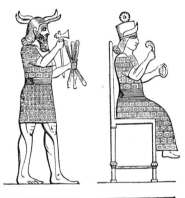

The seated figure, a conventional image of Astarta, comes with peculiar force as an illustration of the character and purpose of Belshazzar's feast. The voluptuous and sensual monarch would naturally direct his homage to a deity in whose service he delighted; and, indeed, it is a very allowable surmise that this feast was made expressly in honour of her: and the impious profanation of the sacred vessels, "taken out of the temple which was in Jerusalem," strengthens this supposition.]

5. *In the same hour.* On the word *hour,* see Notes on ch. iv. 19. ¶ *Came forth fingers of a man's hand.* Not the whole hand, but only the parts usually employed in writing. Not a man writing; not even an arm, but *fingers* that seemed to move themselves. They appeared to come forth from the walls, and were seen before they began to write. It was this that made it so impressive and alarming. It could not be supposed that it was the work of man, or that it was devised by man for the purpose of producing consternation. It was perfectly manifest to all who were there that this was the work of some one superior to man; that it was designed as a Divine intimation of some kind in regard to the scene that was then occurring. But whether as a rebuke for the sin of revelry and dissipation, or for sacrilege in drinking out of the consecrated vessels, or whether it was an intimation of some approaching fearful calamity, would not at once be apparent. It is easy to imagine that it would produce a sudden pause in their revelry, and diffuse seriousness over their minds. The suddenness of the appearance; the fingers, unguided by the hand of man, slowly writing in mysterious characters on the wall; the conviction which must have flashed across the mind that this must be either to rebuke them for their sin, or to announce some fearful calamity, all these things must have combined to produce an overwhelming effect on the revellers. Perhaps, from the prevalent views in the heathen world in regard to the crime of sacrilege, they may have connected this mysterious appearance with the profane act which they were then committing—that of desecrating the vessels of the temple of God. How natural would it be to suppose—recognizing as they did the gods of other nations as *real,* as truly as those which they worshipped—that the God of the Hebrews, seeing the vessels of his worship profaned, had come forth to express his displeasure, and to intimate that there was impending wrath for such an act. The crime of sacrilege was regarded among the heathen as one of the most awful which could be committed, and there was no state of mind in which men would be more likely to be alarmed than when they were, even in the midst of scenes of drunken revelry, engaged in such an act. "The heathen," says Grotius, "thought it a great impiety to convert sacred things to common uses." Numerous instances are on record of the sentiments entertained among the heathen on the subject of sacrilege, and of the calamities which were believed to come upon men as a punishment for it. Among them we may refer to the miser-

6 Then *a* the king's [1] countenance was changed, [2] and his
thoughts troubled him, so that the
joints[3] of his loins were loosed, and
his knees *b* smote one against
another.

a Isa. 21. 2–4.　1 *brightnesses*, ver. 9.
　　　2 *changed it.*

3 *bindings;* or, *knots;* or, *girdles,* Isa. 5. 27.
　　　b Nah. 2. 10.

---

able end of the Phocians, who robbed
the temple of Delphos, and whose act
was the occasion of that war which
was called the Holy War; the destruction of the Gauls in their attempt upon
the same temple; and of Crassus, who
plundered the temple of Jerusalem, and
that of the Syrian goddess.—See Lowth,
in loc. That a conviction of the sin of
sacrilege, according to the prevalent
belief on the subject, may have contributed to produce consternation when
the fingers of the hand appeared at Belshazzar's feast, there is no good reason
to doubt, and we may suppose that the
minds of the revellers were at once
turned to the insult which they had
thus offered to the God of the Hebrews.
¶ *And wrote over against the candlestick.* The candlestick, or lamp-bearer,
perhaps, which had been taken from the
temple at Jerusalem, and which was,
as well as the sacred vessels, introduced
into this scene of revelry. It is probable that as they brought out the vessels of the temple to drink in, they
would also bring out all that had been
taken from the temple in Jerusalem.
Two objects may have been contemplated in the fact that the writing was
" over against the candlestick;" one
was that it might be clearly visible, the
other that it might be more directly intimated that the writing was a rebuke
for the act of sacrilege. On the probable situation where this miracle occurred, the reader may consult Taylor's
Fragments to Calmet's Dictionary, No.
205. He supposes that it was one of
the large inner courts of the palace—
that part of the palace which was prohibited to persons not sent for. See
Notes on ver. 10. ¶ *Upon the plaster
of the wall.* The Chaldee word means
lime, not inappropriately rendered here
plaster. The *manner* of the writing is
not specified. All that is necessary to
suppose is, that the letters were traced
along on the wall so as to be distinctly
visible. Whether they seemed to be

cut into the plaster, or to be traced in
black lines, or lines of light, is not
mentioned, and is immaterial. They
were such as could be seen distinctly
by the king and the guests. Compare,
however, the remarks of Taylor in the
Fragment just referred to. ¶ *And the
king saw the part of the hand that wrote.*
It is not necessary to suppose that the
others did not see it also, but the king
was the most important personage there,
and the miracle was intended particularly for him. Perhaps his eyes were
first attracted to it.

6. *Then the king's countenance was
changed.* The word rendered *countenance* is, in the margin, as in ver. 9,
brightnesses. The Chaldee word means
brightness, splendour (זיו), and the
meaning here is *bright looks, cheerfulness, hilarity.* The word rendered *was
changed,* is in the margin *changed it;*
and the meaning is, that it changed itself: probably from a jocund, cheerful,
and happy expression, it assumed suddenly a deadly paleness. ¶ *And his
thoughts troubled him.* Whether from
the recollection of guilt, or the dread
of wrath, is not said. He would, doubtless, regard this as some supernatural
intimation, and his soul would be
troubled. ¶ *So that the joints of his
loins were loosed.* Marg., *bindings,* or
knots, or *girdles.* The Chaldee word
rendered *joints* (קְטַר) means, properly,
knots; then joints of the bones, as resembling knots, or apparently answering the purposes of knots in the human
frame, as binding it together. The
word *loins* in the Scriptures refers to
the part of the body around which the
girdle was passed, the lower part of the
back; and Gesenius supposes that the
meaning here is, that the joints of his
back, that is, the vertebræ, are referred
to. This part of the body is spoken of
as the seat of strength. When this is
weak the body has no power to stand,
to walk, to labour. The simple idea

7 The king cried ¹ aloud to bring in the astrologers, ᵃ the Chaldeans, and the soothsayers. *And* the king spake, and said to the wise *men* of Babylon, Whosoever shall read this

1 *with might.*   *a* ch. 2. 2; Isa. 47. 13.

writing, and show me the interpretation thereof, shall be clothed with scarlet,² and *have* a chain of gold about his neck, and shall be the third ruler ᵇ in the kingdom.

1 or, *purple.*   *b* ch. 6. 2.

is, that he was greatly terrified, and that under the influence of fear his strength departed. ¶ *And his knees smote one against another.* A common effect of fear (Nah. ii. 10). So Horace, *Et corde et genibus tremit.* And so Virgil, *Tarda trementi genua labant.* "Belshazzar had as much of power, and of drink withal to lead him to bid defiance to God as any ruffian under heaven; and yet when God, as it were, lifted but up his finger against him, how poorly did he crouch and shiver. How did his joints loose, and his knees knock together!" — South's *Sermons*, vol. iv. p. 60.

7. *And the king cried aloud.* Marg., as in the Chaldee, *with might.* This indicates a sudden and an alarming cry. The king was deeply terrified; and, unable himself to divine the meaning of the mysterious appearance of the hand, he naturally turned at once to those whose office it was to explain dreams and supernatural appearances. ¶ *To bring in the astrologers,* &c. See Notes on ch. ii. 2; iv. 7. ¶ *And said to the wise* men *of Babylon.* Those just referred to—the astrologers, &c. Having the power, as was supposed, of interpreting the indications of coming events, they were esteemed as eminently wise. ¶ *Whosoever shall read this writing.* It would seem from this that even the *characters* were not familiar to the king and to those who were with him. Evidently the letters were not in the ordinary Chaldee form, but in some form which to them was strange and unknown. Thus there was a double mystery hanging over the writing—a mystery in regard to the language in which the words were written, and to the meaning of the words. Many conjectures have been formed as to the language employed in this writing (comp. Notes on ver. 24), but such conjectures are useless, since it is impossible now to ascertain what it was.

As the writing, however, had a primary reference to the sacrilege committed in regard to the sacred vessels of the temple, and as Daniel was able to read the letters at once, it would seem not improbable that the words were in the Hebrew character then used—a character such as that found now in the Samaritan Pentateuch—for the Chaldee character now found in the Bible has not improbably been substituted for the more ancient and less elegant character now found in the Samaritan Pentateuch alone. There is no improbability in supposing that even the astrologers and the soothsayers were not familiar with that character, and could not readily read it. ¶ *And show me the interpretation thereof.* The meaning of the words. ¶ *Shall be clothed with scarlet.* The colour worn usually by princes and by persons of rank. The margin is *purple.* So the Greek of Theodotion—*πορφύραν.* So also the Latin Vulgate—*purpurâ.* On the nature and uses of this colour, see Notes on Isa. i. 18. ¶ *And have a chain of gold about his neck.* Also indicative of rank and authority. Comp. Gen. xli. 42. When Joseph was placed over the land of Egypt, the king honoured him in a similar manner, by putting "a gold chain about his neck." This was common in Persia. See Xen. *Cyrop.* I. 3, 2, II. 4, 6, VIII. 5, 18; *Anab.* I. 5, 8. Upon most of the figures in the ruins of Persepolis the same ornament is now found. Prof. Stuart renders this, "a collar of gold." ¶ *And shall be the third ruler in the kingdom.* Of course, the king was first. Who the second was, or why the one who could disclose the meaning of the words should not be raised to the second rank, is not stated. It may be, that the office of prime minister was so fixed, or was held by one whose services were so important to the king, that he could not be at once displaced.

8 Then came in all the king's wise *men :* but they could not read the writing, nor make known to the king the interpretation thereof.

9 Then was king Belshazzar greatly troubled, and his countenance [1] was changed in him, and his lords were astonied.

10 ¶ *Now* the queen, by reason of the words of the king and his lords, came into the banquet-house; *and* the queen spake and said, O king, live for ever; let not thy thoughts trouble thee, nor let thy countenance be changed:

1 *brightnesses,* ver. 6.

Or the meaning may be, that the favoured person who could interpret this would be raised to the third *rank* of dignity, or placed in the third *class* of those who held offices in the realm. The Chaldee is, " and shall rule third in the kingdom," and the idea would seem rather to be that he should be of the third rank or grade in office. So Bertholdt understands it. Grotius understands it as the third person in rank. He says the first was the king ; the second, the son of the king; the third, the prince of the Satraps.

8. *Then came in all the king's wise* men. The classes above referred to, ver. 7. ¶ *But they could not read the writing.* The character was an unknown character to them. It *may* have been a character which was not found in *any* language, and which made the power of Daniel to read it the more remarkable, or it may have been, as suggested in the Notes on ver. 7, a *foreign character* with which they had no acquaintance, though familiar to Daniel.

9. *Then was king Belshazzar greatly troubled.* Not doubting that this was a Divine intimation of some fearful event, and yet unable to understand its meaning. We are quite as likely to be troubled by what is merely *mysterious* in regard to the future—by anything that gives us some undefined foreboding—as we are by that which is really formidable when we know what it is. In the latter case, we know the worst; we can make some preparation for it ; we can feel assured that when *that* is past, *all* is past that we fear—but who can guard himself, or prepare himself, when that which is dreaded is undefined as well as awful; when we know not how to meet it, or how long it may endure, or how terrific and wide may be the sweep of its

desolation ? ¶ *And his countenance was changed in him.* Marg., *brightnesses.* See Notes on ver. 6. ¶ *And his lords were astonied.* Amazed. The Chaldee word means to perplex, disturb, trouble. They were doubtless as much perplexed and troubled as the king himself.

10. *Now the queen.* " Probably the queen-mother, the Nitocris of Herodotus, as the king's wives were at the entertainment."—Wintle. Comp. vers. 2, 3. So Prof. Stuart. The editor of the *Pictorial Bible* also supposes that this was the queen-mother, and thinks that this circumstance will explain her familiarity with the occurrences in the reign of Nebuchadnezzar. * He says, " We are informed above, that the 'wives and concubines ' of the king were present at the banquet. It therefore seems probable that the ' queen ' who now first appears was the *queen-mother;* and this probability is strengthened by the intimate acquaintance which she exhibits with the affairs of Nebuchadnezzar's reign ; at the latter end of which she, as the wife of Evil-Merodach, who was regent during his father's alienation of mind, took an active part in the internal policy of the kingdom, and in the completion of the great works which Nebuchadnezzar had begun in Babylon. This she continued during the reigns of her husband and son, the present king Belshazzar. This famous queen, Nitocris, therefore, could not but be well acquainted with the character and services of Daniel." On the place and influence of the queen-mother in the Oriental courts, see Taylor's *Fragments to Calmet's Dictionary,* No. 16. From the extracts which Taylor has collected, it would seem that she held an exalted place at court, and that it is every way probable that she would be called in, or would come in, on such

11 There *a* is a man in thy kingdom, in whom *is* the spirit of the
holy gods: and, in the days of thy
father,¹ light, and understanding,
and wisdom, like the wisdom of

a ch. 4. 8, 9.

the gods, was found in him ; whom
the king Nebuchadnezzar thy father,¹ the king, *I say,* thy ¹ father,
made master of the magicians, astrologers, Chaldeans, *and* soothsayers ;

1 or, *grandfather,* ver. 2.

an occasion. See also Knolles's *History of the Turks,* as quoted by Taylor, *Fragments,* No. 50. ¶ *By reason
of the words of the king and his lords.*
Their words of amazement and astonishment. These would doubtless be conveyed to her, as there was so much
alarm in the palace, and as there was
a summons to bring in the wise men of
Babylon. If her residence was in some
part of the palace itself, nothing would
be more natural than that she should
be made acquainted with the unusual
occurrence ; or if her residence was, as
Taylor supposes, detached from the palace, it is every way probable that she
would be made acquainted with the
consternation that prevailed, and that,
recollecting the case of Nebuchadnezzar, and the forgotten services of Daniel,
she would feel that the information
which was sought respecting the mysterious writing could be obtained from
him. ¶ And *the queen spake and said,
O king, live for ever.* A common salutation in addressing a king, expressive
of a desire of his happiness and prosperity. ¶ *Let not thy thoughts trouble
thee,* &c. That is, there is a way by
which the mystery may be solved, and
you need not, therefore, be alarmed.
11. *There is a man in thy kingdom.*
To wit, Daniel. As the queen-mother
had lived in the time of Nebuchadnezzar, and recollected the important service which he had rendered in interpreting the dream of the king, it was
natural that her mind should at once
recur to him. It would seem, also,
that though Daniel was no longer employed at court, yet that she still had
an acquaintance with him, so far at
least as to know that he was accessible,
and might be called in on this occasion.
It may be asked, perhaps, how it was
Belshazzar was so ignorant of all this
as to need this information ? For it
is clear from the question which the
king asks in ver. 13, " Art thou that

Daniel ?" that he *was* ignorant of him
personally, and probably even of his
services as an officer in the court of
Nebuchadnezzar. An ingenious and
not improbable solution of this difficulty has been proposed as founded on
a remark of Sir John Chardin : " As
mentioned by the queen, Daniel had
been made by Nebuchadnezzar ' master of the magicians, astrologers, Chaldeans, and soothsayers.' Of this employment Chardin conjectures that he
had been deprived on the death of that
king, and obtains this conclusion from
the fact that when a Persian king dies,
both his astrologers and physicians are
driven from court—the former for not
having predicted, and the latter for not
having prevented, his death. If such
was the etiquette of the ancient Babylonian, as it is of the modern Persian
court, we have certainly a most satisfactory solution of the present difficulty,
as Daniel must then be supposed to
have relinquished his public employments, and to have lived retired in
private life during the eight years occupied by the reigns of Evil-Merodach
and Belshazzar."—Harmer, as quoted
by Rosenmüller (*Morgenland,* on Dan.
v. 13). ¶ *In whom* is *the spirit of the
holy gods.* This is language such as a
heathen would be likely to use when
speaking of one who had showed extraordinary knowledge of Divine things.
See Notes on ch. iv. 9. ¶ *And, in the
days of thy father.* Marg., *grandfather.*
See Notes on vers. 1, 2. ¶ *Light, and
understanding, and wisdom.* Light is
the emblem of knowledge, as it makes
all things clear. The meaning here is,
that he had showed extraordinary wisdom in interpreting the dream of Nebuchadnezzar. ¶ *Like the wisdom of the
gods.* Such as the gods only could
possess. ¶ *Whom the king Nebuchadnezzar thy father, the king,* I say, *thy
father, made master of the magicians,*
&c. See ch. ii. 48. This is repeated

12 Forasmuch as an *a* excellent spirit, and knowledge, and understanding, interpreting ¹ of dreams, and showing of hard sentences, and dissolving ² of doubts,³ were found in the same Daniel, whom the king named Belteshazzar: now let Daniel be called, and he will show the interpretation.

13 Then was Daniel brought in before the king. *And* the king spake and said unto Daniel, *Art*

a ch. 6. 3.   1 or, *of an interpreter.*
2 or, *of a dissolver.*   3 *knots.*

thou that Daniel, which *art* of the children of the captivity of Judah, whom the king my father ⁴ brought out of Jewry ?

14 I have even heard of thee, that the spirit of the gods *is* in thee, and *that* light, and understanding, and excellent wisdom, is found in thee.

15 And now the wise *men*, the astrologers, have been brought in before me, that they should read

4 or, *grandfather*, ver. 2.

here, and dwelt on, in order to call the attention of the king to the fact that Daniel was worthy to be consulted. Though now living in obscurity, there was a propriety that one who had been placed at the very head of the wise men of Babylon by a prince so distinguished as Nebuchadnezzar, should be consulted on the present occasion.

12. *Forasmuch as an excellent spirit.* Not an excellent spirit in the sense in which that phrase is sometimes used now, as denoting a good and pious spirit, but a spirit or mind that *excels;* that is, that is *distinguished* for wisdom and knowledge. ¶ *Interpreting of dreams.* Marg., " or, *of an interpreter.*" This was regarded as a great attainment, and was supposed to prove that one who could do it was inspired by the gods. ¶ *And showing of hard sentences.* The meaning of enigmatical or obscure sentences. To be able to do this was supposed to indicate great attainments, and was a knowledge that was much coveted. Comp. Prov. i. 6: " To understand a proverb, and the interpretation ; the words of the wise, and their dark sayings." ¶ *And dissolving of doubts.* Marg., " or, *a dissolver of knots.*" So the Chaldee. This language is still common in the East, to denote one who has skill in explaining difficult subjects. " In the copy of a patent given to Sir John Chardin in Persia, we find it is addressed ' to the Lords of lords, who have the presence of a lion, the aspect of Deston ; the princes who have the stature of Tahemten-ten, who seem to be in the time of Ardevon, the regents who carry

the majesty of Ferribours. The conquerors of kingdoms. Superintendents *that unloose all manner of knots,* and who are under the ascendant of Mercury,'" &c.—Taylor's *Fragments to Calmet's Dict.*, No. 174. The language used here would be applicable to the explanation of any difficult and perplexing subject. ¶ *Whom the king named Belteshazzar.* That is, the name was given to him by his authority (see Notes on ch. i. 7), and it was by this name that he called him when he addressed him, ch. iv. 9.

13. *Then was Daniel brought in before the king.* From this it is clear that he lived in Babylon, though in comparative obscurity.· It would seem to be not improbable that he was still known to the queen-mother, who, perhaps, kept up an acquaintance with him on account of his former services. ¶ *Art thou that Daniel.* This is a clear proof that Belshazzar was not acquainted personally with him. See Notes on ver. 11. ¶ *Which* art *of the children of the captivity of Judah.* Belonging to those of Judah, or those Jews who were made captives, and who reside in Babylon. See Notes on ch. i. 3. He could not be ignorant that there were Jews in his kingdom, though he was not personally acquainted with Daniel. ¶ *Whom the king my father.* Marg., as in vers. 2, 11, *grandfather.* ¶ *Brought out of Jewry?* Out of Judea. See ch. i. 1–3.

14. *I have even heard of thee,* &c. Ver. 11.

15. *And now the wise* men, &c. Vers. 7, 8.

this writing, and make known unto me the interpretation thereof: but they could not show the interpretation of the thing:

16 And I have heard of thee, that thou canst make ¹ interpretations, and dissolve doubts: now, if thou canst read the writing, and make known to me the interpretation thereof, thou shalt be clothed with scarlet, and *have* a chain of gold about thy neck, and shalt be the third ruler in the kingdom.

¹ *interpret.*

17 ¶ Then Daniel answered and said before the king, Let *a* thy gifts be to thyself, and give thy rewards ² to another; yet I will read the writing *b* unto the king, and make known to him the interpretation.

18 O thou king, the most high God gave Nebuchadnezzar thy father a kingdom, and majesty, and glory, and honour:

a Gen. 14. 23.   2 or, *fee,* as ch. 2 6.
b Psa. 119. 46.

16. *And I have heard of thee,* &c. Ver. 11. ¶ *Canst make interpretations.* Marg., *interpret.* Chald., "interpret interpretations." The meaning is, that he was skilled in interpreting or explaining dreams, omens, &c. ¶ *And dissolve doubts.* Notes on ver. 12. ¶ *Now, if thou canst read the writing,* &c., *thou shalt be clothed with scarlet,* &c. This was the reward which at the first he had promised to any one that was able to do it, and as all others had failed, he was willing that it should be offered to a Jew.

17. *Then Daniel answered and said before the king, Let thy gifts be to thyself.* That is, "I do not desire them; I do not act from a hope of reward." Daniel means undoubtedly to intimate that what he would do would be done from a higher motive than a desire of office or honour. The answer is one that is eminently dignified. Yet he says he would read the writing, implying that he was ready to do anything that would be gratifying to the monarch. It may seem somewhat strange that Daniel, who here disclaimed all desire of office or reward, should so soon (ver. 29) have submitted to be clothed in this manner, and to receive the insignia of office. But, it may be remarked, that when the offer was proposed to him he stated his wishes, and declared that he did not *desire* to be honoured in that way; when he had performed the duty, however, of making known the writing, he could scarcely feel at liberty to resist a command of the king to be clothed in that manner, and to be regarded as an officer in the

kingdom. His intention, in the verse before us, was modestly to decline the honours proposed, and to intimate that he was not influenced by a desire of such honours in what he would do; yet to the king's command afterwards that he should be clothed in robes of office, he could not with propriety make resistance. There is no evidence that he took these honours voluntarily, or that he would not have continued to decline them if he could have done it with propriety. ¶ *And give thy rewards to another.* Marg., "or *fee,* as in ch. ii. 6." Gesenius supposes that the word used here (וּבְזָבָה) is of Persian origin. It means a *gift,* and, if of Persian origin, is derived from a verb, meaning to load with gifts and praises, as a prince does an ambassador. The sense here seems to be, that Daniel was not disposed to interfere with the will of the monarch if he chose to confer gifts and rewards on others, or to question the propriety of his doing so; but that, so far as he was concerned, he had no desire of them for himself, and could not be influenced by them in what he was about to do. ¶ *Yet I will read the writing,* &c. Expressing no doubt that he could do it without difficulty. Probably the *language* of the writing was familiar to him, and he at once saw that there was no difficulty, in the circumstances, in determining its meaning.

18. *O thou king, the most high God gave Nebuchadnezzar thy father a kingdom,* &c. This reference to Nebuchadnezzar is evidently designed to show to Belshazzar the wickedness of his

19 And, for the majesty that he gave him, all *a* people, nations, and languages, trembled and feared before him : whom he would he slew, and whom he would he kept alive, and whom he would he set up, and whom he would he put down.

20 But when his heart was lifted up, and his mind hardened ¹ in pride, he was deposed ² from his kingly throne, and they took his glory from him :

a ch. 4. 22, &c.; Jer. 27. 7.
1 or, *to deal proudly,* Exod. 18. 11.
2 *made to come down.*

21 And he was driven from the sons of men : and his ³ heart was made like the beasts, and his dwelling *was* with the wild asses : they fed him with grass like oxen, and his body was wet with the dew of heaven ; till he knew that the most high God ruled in the kingdom of men, and *that* he appointeth over it whomsoever he will.

22 And thou his son, O Belshazzar, hast not humbled *b* thine

3 or, *he made his heart equal.*
b 2 Chron. 33. 23; 36. 12; Jam. 4. 6.

own course, and the reason which he had to apprehend the Divine vengeance, because he had not learned to avoid the sins which brought so great calamities upon his predecessor. As he was acquainted with what had occurred to Nebuchadnezzar ; as he had doubtless seen the proclamation which he had made on his recovery from the dreadful malady which God had brought upon him for his pride ; and as he had not humbled himself, but had pursued the same course which Nebuchadnezzar did, he had the greater reason to apprehend the judgment of Heaven. See vers. 22, 23. Daniel here traces all the glory which Nebuchadnezzar had to "the most high God," reminding the king that whatever honour and majesty he had he was equally indebted for it to the same source, and that he must expect a similar treatment from him.

19. *And, for the majesty that he gave him.* That is, on account of his greatness, referring to the talents which God had conferred on him, and the power which he had put in his hands. It was so great that all people and nations trembled before him. ¶ *All people, nations, and languages trembled and feared before him.* Stood in awe of him. On the extent of his empire, see Notes on ch. iii. 4; iv. 1, 22. ¶ *Whom he would he slew,* &c. That is, he was an arbitrary—an absolute sovereign. This is exactly descriptive of the power which Oriental despotic monarchs have. ¶ *Whom he would he kept alive.* Whether they had, or had not, been guilty of crime. He had the absolute power of life and death over them.

There was no such instrument as we call a "constitution" to control the sovereign as well as the people ; there was no tribunal to which he was responsible, and no law by which he was bound ; there were no judges to determine on the question of life and death in regard to those who were accused of crime, whom he did not appoint, and whom he might not remove, and whose judgments he might not set aside if he pleased ; there were no "juries" of "peers" to determine on the question of fact whether an accused man was guilty or not. There were none of those safeguards which have been originated to protect the accused in modern times, and which enter so essentially into the notions of liberty now. In an absolute despotism all power is in the hands of one man, and this was in fact the case in Babylon. ¶ *Whom he would he set up.* That is, in places of trust, of office, of rank, &c. ¶ *And whom he would he put down.* No matter what their rank or office.

20. *But when his heart was lifted up.* See ch. iv. 30. ¶ *And his mind hardened in pride.* Marg., *to deal proudly.* The state of mind indicated here is that in which there is no sense of dependence, but where one feels that he has all resources in himself, and need only look to himself. ¶ *He was deposed from his kingly throne.* Marg., *made to come down.* That is, he was so deposed by the providence of God, not by the acts of his own subjects.

21. *And he was driven,* &c. See this fully explained in ch. iv. 25-33.

22. *And thou his son, O Belshazzar,*

heart, though thou knewest all this;

23 But *a* hast lifted up thyself against the Lord of heaven; 'and they have brought the vessels of his house before thee, and thou, and thy lords, thy wives, and thy concubines, have drunk wine in them ;

a vers.3,4.　*b* Judg.16.23.　*c* Ps.115.5-8; Is.37.19

and thou hast praised *b* the gods of silver, and gold, of brass, iron, wood, and stone, which *c* see not, nor hear, nor know : and the God in whose hand thy breath *d is*, and whose *are* all thy ways, *e* hast thou not glorified : *f*

24 Then was the part of the

d Acts 17. 28, 29.　*e* Jer. 10. 23.　*f* Rom. 1. 21.

---

hast not humbled thine heart, &c. As thou shouldst have done in remembrance of these events. The idea is, that we ought to derive valuable lessons from what has taken place in past times ; that, from the events which have occurred in history, we should learn what God approves and what he disapproves ; that we should avoid the course which has subjected others to his displeasure, and which has brought his judgments upon them. The course, however, which Belshazzar pursued has been that of kings and princes commonly in the world, and indeed of mankind at large. How little do men profit by the record of the calamities which have come upon others for their crimes ! How little are the intemperate of one generation admonished by the calamities which have come upon those of another ; how little are the devotees of pleasure ; how little are those in places of power !

23. *But hast lifted up thyself against the Lord of heaven.* The God who had so signally rebuked and humbled Nebuchadnezzar. The monarch had done this, it would seem, during the whole of his reign, and now by a crowning act of impiety he had evinced special disregard of him, and contempt for him, by profaning the sacred vessels of his temple. ¶ *And they have brought the vessels of his house before thee*, &c. See Notes on vers. 2-4. ¶ *And the God in whose hand thy breath* is. Under whose power, and at whose disposal, is thy life. While you have been celebrating the praises of idol gods, who can do you neither good nor evil, you have been showing special contempt for that great Being who keeps you in existence, and who has power to take away your life at any moment. What is here said of Belshazzar is true of all men—

high and low, rich and poor, bond and free, princes and people. It is a deeply affecting consideration, that the breath, on which our life depends, and which is itself so frail a thing, is in the "hand" of a Being who is invisible to us, over whom we can have no control; who can arrest it when he pleases ; who has given us no intimation when he will do it, and who often does it so suddenly as to defy all previous calculation and hope. Nothing is more absolute than the power which God holds over the breath of men, yet there is nothing which is less recognized than that power, and nothing which men are less disposed to acknowledge than their dependence on him for it. ¶ *And whose are all thy ways.* That is, he has power to control thee in all thy ways. You can go nowhere without his permission ; you can never, when abroad, return to your home without the direction of his providence. What is here said, also, is as true of all others as it was of the Chaldean prince. "It is not in man that walketh to direct his steps." "A man's heart deviseth his way, but the Lord directeth his steps." None of us can take a step without his permission; none can go forth on a journey to a distant land without his constant superintending care; none can return without his favour. And yet how little is this recognized! How few feel it when they go out and come in ; when they go forth to their daily employments ; when they start on a voyage or journey ; when they propose to return to their homes ! ¶ *Hast thou not glorified.* That is, thou hast not honoured him by a suitable acknowledgment of dependence on him.

24. *Then was the part of the hand sent from him.* To wit, the fingers. See ver. 5. The sense is, that when it

hand sent from him; and this writing was written.

25 And this *is* the writing that was written, MENE, MENE, TEKEL, UPHARSIN.

26 This *is* the interpretation of

---

was fully perceived that Belshazzar was not disposed to learn that there was a God in heaven; when he refused to profit by the solemn dispensations which had occurred in respect to his predecessor; when his own heart was lifted up with pride, and when he had gone even farther than his predecessors had done by the sacrilegious use of the vessels of the temple, thus showing especial contempt for the God of heaven, then appeared the mysterious handwriting on the wall. It was then an appropriate time for the Most High God, who had been thus contemned and insulted, to come forth and rebuke the proud and impious monarch.

25. *And this is the writing that was written.* The Babylonians, it would seem, were unacquainted with the *characters* that were used, and of course unable to understand the meaning. See ver. 8. The first thing, therefore, for Daniel to do was to read the writing, and this he was able to do without difficulty, probably, as already remarked, because it was in the ancient Hebrew character—a character quite familiar to him, though not known to the Babylonians, whom Belshazzar consulted. It is every way probable that that character *would be* used on an occasion like this, for (*a*) it is manifest that it was intended that the true God, the God of the Hebrews, should be made known, and this was the character in which his communications had been made to men; (*b*) it was clearly the design to honour his own religion, and it is morally certain that there would be something which would show the connection between this occurrence and his own agency, and nothing would do this better than to make use of such a character; and (*c*) it was the Divine intention to put honour on Daniel, and this would be well done by making use of a character which he understood. There have been, indeed, many conjectures respecting the characters which were employed on this occasion, and the reasons of the difficulty of interpreting the words used, but it is most

probable that the above is the true statement, and this will relieve all the difficulties in regard to the account. Prideaux supposes that the characters employed were the ancient Phœnician characters, that were used by the Hebrews, and that are found now in the Samaritan Pentateuch; and that, as above suggested, these might be unknown to the Babylonians, though familiar to Daniel. Others have supposed that the characters were those in common use in Babylon, and that the reason why the Babylonians could not read them was, that they were smitten with a sudden blindness, like the inhabitants of Sodom, Gen. xix. 11. The Talmudists suppose that the words were written in a cabalistic manner, in which certain letters were used to stand for other letters, on the principle referred to by Buxtorf (*Lex. Chal. Rabb. et Talm.* p. 248), and known as אתבש—that is, where the alphabet is reversed, and א (A) is used for ת (T), ב (B) for ש (S), &c., and that on account of this cabalistic transmutation the Babylonians could not read it, though Daniel might have been familiar with that mode of writing. Rabbi Jochanan supposed that there was a change of the order in which the letters of the words were written; other Rabbins, that there was a change merely in the order of the first and second letters; others, that the words were written backwards; others that the words were written, not in the usual horizontal manner, but perpendicularly; and others, that the words were not written in full, but that only the first letters of each were written. See Bertholdt, pp. 349, 350. All these are mere conjectures, and most of them are childish and improbable suppositions. There is no real difficulty in the case if we suppose that the words were written in a character familiar to Daniel, but not familiar to the Babylonians. Or, if this is not admitted, then we may suppose that some mere marks were employed whose signification was made known to Daniel in a miraculous manner.

the thing: MENE; God hath numbered thy kingdom, and finished it.

a Job 31. 6; Ps. 62. 9.

27 TEKEL ; Thou art *a* weighed in the balances, and art found wanting.*b*

b Matt. 22. 11, 12; 1 Cor. 3. 13.

26. *This is the interpretation of the thing.* It may seem not to have been difficult to interpret the meaning of the communication, when one was able to read the words, or when the sense of the words was understood. But, if the words are placed together, and considered in

their abstract form, the whole communication would be so enigmatical that the interpretation would not be likely to occur to any one without a Divine guidance. This will appear more clearly by arranging the words together, as has been done by Hales :—

| MENE, | MENE, | TEKEL, | [PERES] | UPHARSIN. |
| NUMBER, | NUMBER, | WEIGHT, | [DIVISION] | DIVISIONS; |

or, as it is explained more accurately by Bertholdt and Gesenius :—

| *Mene,* | *Mene,* | *Tekel,* | *Upharsin.* |
| *Numbered,* | *Numbered,* | *Weighed,* | *Divided.* |

From this arrangement it will be at once seen that the interpretation proposed by Daniel was not one that would have been likely to have occurred to any one. ¶ *Mene.* מְנֵא. This word is a participle passive from מְנָה—*to number, to review.*—Gesenius, *Lex.* The verb is also written מְנָא.—Buxtorf, *Lex.* It would be literally translated *numbered,* and would apply to that of which an estimate was taken by counting. We use now an expression which would convey a similar idea, when we say of one that " his days are *numbered;*" that is, he has not long to live, or is about to die. The idea seems to be taken from the fact, that the duration of a man's life cannot usually be known, and in the general uncertainty we can form no correct estimate of it, but when he is old, or when he is dangerously sick, we feel that we can with some degree of probability *number* his days, since he cannot now live long. Such is the idea here, as explained by Daniel. All uncertainty about the duration of the kingdom was now removed, for, since the evil had come, an exact estimate of its whole duration—of the number of the years of its continuance —could be made. In the Greek of Theodotion there is no attempt to translate this word, and it is retained in Greek letters— Μανὴ. So also in the *Codex Chis.,* and in the Latin Vulgate. ¶ *God hath numbered thy kingdom.* The word which is used here, and ren-

dered *numbered*—מְנָה—is the verb of which the previous word is the participle. Daniel applies it to the *kingdom* or *reign* of the monarch, as being a thing of more importance than the life of the king himself. It is evident, if, according to the common interpretation of ver. 30, Belshazzar was slain that very night, it *might* have been applied to the king himself, meaning that *his* days were numbered, and that he was about to die. But this interpretation (see Notes) is not absolutely certain, and perhaps the fact that Daniel did *not* so apply the word may be properly regarded as one circumstance showing that such an interpretation is not necessary, though probably it is the correct one. ¶ *And finished it.* This is not the meaning of the word *Mene,* but is the explanation by Daniel of the thing intended. The word in its interpretation fairly implied that; or that might be understood from it. The fact that the " kingdom " in its duration was " *numbered,*" properly expressed the idea that it was now to come to an end. It did actually then come to an end by being merged in that of the Medes and Persians.

27. *Tekel.* This word (תְּקֵל) is also, according to Gesenius, a passive participle (from תְּקַל—*to poise, to weigh*), and means *weighed.* It would be used with reference to anything placed in a balance to ascertain its weight; and hence, like the word *measure,* would

denote that the extent, dimensions, true worth, or character of anything was ascertained. As by the use of scales the weight of anything is known, so the word is applied to any estimate of character or of actions, and a balance becomes the emblem of justice. Thus God, in his judgments of men, is represented as *weighing* their actions. 1 Sam. ii. 3, "The Lord is a God of knowledge, and by him actions are weighed." Comp. Job vi. 2:—

"O that my grief were thoroughly weighed,
And my calamity laid in the balances together."

Job xxxi. 6 :—

"Let me be weighed in an even balance,
That God may know mine integrity."

The balance thus used to denote judgment in this life became also the emblem of judgment in the future state, when the conduct of men will be accurately estimated, and justice dealt out to them according to the strict rules of equity. To illustrate this, I will insert a copy of an Egyptian "Death Judgment," with the remarks of the editor of the *Pictorial Bible* in regard to it:— "The Egyptians entertained the belief that the actions of the dead were so-

lemnly weighed in balances before Osiris, and that the condition of the departed was determined according to the preponderance of good or evil. Such judgment scenes are very frequently represented in the paintings and papyri of ancient Egypt, and one of them we have copied as a suitable illustration of the present subject. One of these scenes, as represented on the walls of a small temple at Dayr-el-Medeeneh, has been so well explained by Mr. Wilkinson, that we shall avail ourselves of his description ; for although that to which it refers is somewhat different from the one which we have engraved, his account affords an adequate elucidation of all that ours contains. ' Osiris, seated on his throne, awaits the arrival of those souls that are ushered into Amenti. The four genii stand before him on a lotus-blossom [ours has the lotus without the genii], the female Cerberus sits behind them, and Harpocrates on the crook of Osiris. Thoth, the god of letters, arrives in the presence of Osiris, bearing in his hand a tablet, on which the actions of the deceased are noted down, while Horus and Arœris are employed in weighing the good deeds * of the judged against

* "This M. Champollion supposes to be the

the ostrich feather, the symbol of truth and justice. A cynocephalus, the emblem of truth, is seated on the top of the balance. At length arrives the deceased, who appears between two figures of the goddess, and bears in his hand the symbol of truth,† indicating his meritorious actions, and his fitness for admission to the presence of Osiris.'

"If the Babylonians entertained a similar notion, the declaration of the prophet, 'Thou art weighed in the balances, and art found wanting!' must have appeared exceedingly awful to them. But again, there are allusions in this declaration to some such custom of literally weighing the royal person, as is described in the following passage in the account of Sir Thomas Roe's embassy to the great Mogul:—' The first of September (which was the late Mogul's birthday), he, retaining an ancient yearly custom, was, in the presence of his chief grandees, weighed in a balance : the ceremony was performed

heart. I still incline to the construction I have put upon it—a type of the good actions of the deceased.

† "Sometimes, instead of the ostrich feather, the deceased bears a vase (which is placed in the other scale), and it has then a similar import."

within his house, or tent, in a fair spacious room, whereinto none were admitted but by special leave. The scales in which he was thus weighed were plated with gold : and so was the beam, on which they hung by great chains, made likewise of that most precious metal. The king, sitting in one of them, was weighed first against silver coin, which immediately afterwards was distributed among the poor ; then was he weighed against gold ; after that against jewels (as they say), but I observed (being there present with my ambassador) that he was weighed against three several things, laid in silken bags in the contrary scale. When I saw him in the balance, I thought on Belshazzar, who was found too light. By his weight (of which his physicians yearly keep an exact account), they presume to guess of the present state of his body, of which they speak flatteringly, however they think it to be.'"

[Annexed is a representation of a pair of scales in the sculptures at Khorsabad. "The Assyrian warriors are seen in the sculptures bearing away in triumph the idols of the conquered nations, or breaking them into pieces, weighing them in scales, and dividing the fragments." The declaration, "Thou art weighed in the balances," takes part of its force from this custom of warfare, intimating, as it does, the entire ruin and overthrow of the monarch. "Lepsius has recently published a bass-relief

from an Egyptian tomb, representing a man weighing rings of gold or silver, with weights in the form of a bull's head, and of a seated lion with a ring on its back, precisely similar to those from Nineveh now in the British Museum."]

The engraving, on the next page, from the sarcophagus of Alexander, will further show how commonly this opinion prevailed, and how natural is the representation here. If the Babylonians entertained such notions in regard to the dead as are here represented, the declaration made by the prophet must have been exceedingly solemn. But whether this were so or not, the language of Daniel in interpreting the word must have been overwhelming to the monarch. It could be understood by him as denoting nothing less than that a solemn sentence had been passed upon his character and conduct by the great Judge of all, and that he was found to have failed in the requirements which had been made of him, and was now condemned. He had no righteousness when his actions came to be estimated as in a balance, and nothing awaited him but an awful condemnation. Who is there now who would not tremble at seeing the word *Tekel*—*weighed*—written on the wall of his chamber at midnight ? ¶ *Thou art weighed in the balances.* That is, this, in the circumstances, is the proper interpretation of this word. It would apply to anything whose value was ascertained by weighing it ; but as the reference here was to the king of Babylon, and as the whole representation

28 PERES ; Thy kingdom is divided, and given *a* to the *b* Medes and Persians.*c*

a Foretold, Isa. 21. 2.   *b* ver. 31.   *c* ch. 6. 28.

was designed for him, Daniel distinctly applies it to him: "*thou* art weighed." On the use and application of this language, see 1 Sam. ii. 3: "The Lord is a God of knowledge, and by him ac-tions are weighed." Comp. also Job xxxi. 6; Prov. xvi. 2, 11. ¶ *And art found wanting.* This is added, like the previous phrase, as an explanation. Even if the *word* could have been read

by the Chaldeans, yet its meaning could not have been understood without a Divine communication, for though it were supposed to be applicable to the monarch, it would still be a question what the result of the weighing or trial would be. That could have been known to Daniel only by a communication from on high.

28. *Peres.* In ver. 25 this is *Uphar-sin.* These are but different forms of the same word—the word in ver. 25 being in the plural, and here in the singular. The verb (פְּרַס) means, *to divide;* and in this form, as in the previous cases, it is, according to Gesenius, a participle meaning *divided.* As it stands here, it would be applicable to anything that was *divided* or *sundered* —whether a kingdom, a palace, a house, a territory, &c. *What* was divided could be known only by Divine revelation. If the *word* had been understood by Belshazzar, undoubtedly it would

have suggested the idea that there was to be some sort of division or sundering, but what that was to be would not be indicated by the mere use of the word. Perhaps to an affrighted imagination there might have been conveyed the idea that there would be a revolt in some of the provinces of the empire, and that a part would be rent away, but it would not have occurred that it would be so rent that the whole would pass under the dominion of a foreign power. Josephus (*Ant.* b. x. ch. xi. § 3) says, that the word "Phares in the Greek tongue means a *fragment,* κλασμα — God will, therefore, break thy kingdom in pieces, and divide it among the Medes and Persians." ¶ *Thy kingdom is divided.* That is, the proper interpretation of this communica-tion is, that the kingdom is about to be rent asunder, or broken into frag-ments. It is to be separated or torn from the dynasty that has ruled over it, and to be given to another. ¶ *And*

29 Then commanded Belshazzar, and they clothed Daniel with scarlet, and *put* a chain of gold about his neck, and made a proclamation concerning him, that *a* he

should be the third ruler in the kingdom.

30 ¶ In that night *b* was Belshazzar the king of the Chaldeans slain.

given to the Medes and Persians. On this united kingdom, see Notes on Isa. xiii. 17. It was *given* to the Medes and Persians when it was taken by Cyrus, and when the kingdom of Babylon became extinct, and thenceforward became a part of the Medo-Persian empire. See Notes on Isa. xiii. 17, 19.

29. *Then commanded Belshazzar.* In compliance with his promise, ver. 16. Though the interpretation had been so fearful in its import, and though Daniel had been so plain and faithful with him, yet he did not hesitate to fulfil his promise. It is a remarkable instance of the result of fidelity, that a proud monarch should have received such a reproof, and such a prediction in this manner, and it is an encouragement to us to do our duty, and to state the truth plainly to wicked men. Their own consciences testify to them that it is the truth, and they will see the truth so

clearly that they cannot deny it. ¶ *And they clothed Daniel with scarlet,* &c. All this, it would seem, was transacted in a single night, and it has been made an objection, as above remarked, to the authenticity of the book, that such events are said to have occurred in so short a space of time, and that Daniel should have been so soon clothed with the robes of office. On this objection, see Intro. to the chapter, § I. II. In respect to the latter part of the objection, it may be here further remarked, that it was not necessary to *fit* him with a suit of clothes made expressly for the occasion, for the loose, flowing robes of the Orientals were as well adapted to one person as another, and in the palaces of kings such garments were always on hand. See Harmer's *Observations on the East,* vol. ii. 392, *seq.* Comp. Rosenmüller, *Morgenland, in loc.* ¶ *That he should be the third ruler,* &c. See Notes on ver. 7.

[The engraving, copied from one of the tablets at Khorsabad, represents a eunuch holding distinguished rank in the Assyrian court; and the chain and other neck ornaments are most probably honorary adornments bestowed upon the wearer by the king, as the rewards of fidelity, or important services rendered.]

30. *In that night was Belshazzar the king of the Chaldeans slain.* On the taking of Babylon, and the consequences, see Notes on Isa. xiii. 17-22, and ch. xlv. 1, 2. The account which Xenophon (*Cyrop.* vii. 5.) gives of the taking of Babylon, and of the death of

31 And Darius *a* the Median took

a ch. 9. 1.   1 *he as the son of.*   2 or, *now.*

the king—though without mentioning his name, agrees so well with the statement here, that it may be regarded as a strong confirmation of its correctness. After describing the preparation made to take the city by draining off the waters of the Euphrates, so as to leave the channel dry beneath the walls for the army of Cyrus, and after recording the charge which Cyrus gave to his generals Gadatas and Gobryas, he adds, "And indeed those who were with Gobryas said that it would not be wonderful if the gates of the palace should be found open, *as the whole city that night seemed to be given up to revelry*"—ὡς ἐν κώμῳ γὰρ δοκεῖ ἡ πόλις πᾶσα εἶναι τῇδε τῇ νυκτί. He then says that as they passed on, after entering the city, "of those whom they encountered, part being smitten died, part fled again back, and part raised a clamour. But those who were with Gobryas also raised a clamour as if they also joined in the revelry, and going as fast as they could, they came soon to the palace of the king. But those who were with Gobryas and Gadatas being arrayed, found the gates of the palace closed, but those who were appointed to go against the guard of the palace fell upon them when drinking before a great light, and were quickly engaged with them in hostile combat. Then a cry arose, and they who were within having asked the cause of the tumult, the king commanded them to see what the affair was, and some of them rushing out opened the gates. As they who were with Gadatas saw the gates open, they rushed in, and pursuing those who attempted to return, and smiting them, they came to the king, and they found him standing with a drawn sabre—ἀκινάκην. And those who were with Gadatas and Gobryas overpowered him, ἐχειροῦντο—and those who were with him were slain—one opposing, and one fleeing, and one seeking his safety in the best way he could. And Cyrus sent certain of his horsemen away, and commanded that they should put to death those whom they found out of their dwellings, but that those who were in their houses,

the kingdom, 1 *being* 2 about threescore and two years old.

and could speak the Syriac language, should be suffered to remain, but that whosoever should be found without should be put to death. "These things they did. But Gadatas and Gobryas came up; and first they rendered thanks to the gods because they had taken vengeance on the impious king—ὅτι τετιμωρημένοι ἦσαν τὸν ἀνόσιον βασιλέα. Then they kissed the hands and feet of Cyrus, weeping with joy and rejoicing. When it was day, and they who had the watch over the towers learned that the city was taken, and *that the king was dead*—τὸν βασιλέα τεθνηκότα—they also surrendered the towers." These extracts from Xenophon abundantly confirm what is here said in Daniel respecting the death of the king, and will more than neutralize what is said by Berosus. See Intro. to the chapter, § II.

31. *And Darius the Median took the kingdom.* The city and kingdom were actually taken by Cyrus, though acting in the name and by the authority of Darius, or Cyaxares, who was his uncle. For a full explanation of the conquests of Cyrus, and of the reason why the city is said to have been taken by Darius, see Notes on Isa. xli. 2. In regard to the question who Darius the Median was, see the Intro. to ch. vi. § II. The name Darius — דָּֽרְיָ֫וֶשׁ, or *Darjavesh* — is the name under which the three Medo-Persian kings are mentioned in the Old Testament. There is some difference of opinion as to its meaning. Herodotus (vi. 98) says, that it is equivalent to ἑρξίης, one who *restrains*, but Hesychius says that it is the same as φρόνιμος — *prudent.* Grotefend, who has found it in the cuneiform inscriptions at Persepolis, as Darheush, or Darjeush (*Heeren's Ideen*, i. 2, p. 350), makes it to be a compound word, the first part being an abbreviation of *Dara*, " *Lord,*" and the latter portion coming from *kshah*, " *king.*" St. Martin reads the name *Dareiousch Vyschtasponea* on the Persepolitan inscriptions; that is, *Darius*, son of *Vishtaspo.* Lassen, however, gives *Darhawus Vistaspaha*, the latter word

being equivalent to the *Gustasp* of the modern Persian, and meaning "one whose employment is about horses." See Anthon's *Class. Dict.*, and Kitto's *Cyclo.*, art. "Darius." Comp. Niehbuhr, *Reisebeschr.*, Part II. Tab. 24, G. and B. Gesenius, *Lex.* This Darius is supposed to be Cyaxares II. (Intro. to ch. vi. § II.), the son and successor of Astyages, the uncle and father-in-law of Cyrus, who held the empire of Media between Astyages and Cyrus, B.C. 569–536. ¶ Being. Marg., "He as *son of.*" The marginal reading is in accordance with the Chaldee—כְּבַר. It is not unusual in the language of the Orientals to denote the age of any one by saying that he is the son of so many years. ¶ *About.* Marg., "or, *now.*" The word, both in the text and the margin, is designed to express the supposed sense of his "being the son of sixty years." The language of the original would, however, be accurately expressed by saying that he was then sixty years old. Though Cyrus was the active agent in taking Babylon, yet it was done in the name and by the authority of Cyaxares or Darius; and as he was the actual sovereign, the name of his general—Cyrus—is not mentioned here, though he was in fact the most important agent in taking the city, and became ultimately much more celebrated than Darius was.

This portion of history, the closing scene in the reign of a mighty monarch, and the closing scene in the independent existence of one of the most powerful kingdoms that has ever existed on the earth, is full of instructive lessons ; and in view of the chapter as thus explained, we may make the following

REMARKS.

(1.) We have here an impressive illustration of the sin of sacrilege (vers. 2, 3). In all ages, and among all people, this has been regarded as a sin of peculiar enormity, and it is quite evident that God in this solemn scene meant to confirm the general judgment of mankind on the subject. Among all people, where any kind of religion has prevailed, there are places and objects which are regarded as set apart to sacred use, and which are not to be employed for common and profane purposes. Though in themselves—in the gold and silver, the wood and stone of which they are made — there is no essential holiness, yet they derive a sacredness from being set apart to Divine purposes, and it has always been held to be a high crime to treat them with indignity or contempt—to rob altars, or to desecrate holy places. This general impression of mankind it was clearly the design of God to confirm in the case before us, when the sacred vessels of the temple—vessels consecrated in the most solemn manner to the worship of Jehovah—were profanely employed for the purposes of carousal. God had borne it patiently when those vessels had been removed from the temple at Jerusalem, and when they had been laid up among the spoils of victory in the temples of Babylon ; but when they were profaned for purposes of revelry — when they were brought forth to grace a heathen festival, and to be employed in the midst of scenes of riot and dissipation, it was time for him to interpose, and to show to these profane revellers that there is a God in heaven.

(2.) We may see the peril of such festivals as that celebrated by Belshazzar and his lords, ver. 1, *seq.* It is by no means probable that when the feast was contemplated and arranged, anything was designed like that which occurred in the progress of the affair. It was not a matter of set purpose to introduce the females of the harem to this scene of carousal, and still less to make use of the sacred vessels dedicated to the worship of Jehovah, to grace the midnight revelry. It is not improbable that they would have been at first shocked at such an outrage on what was regarded as propriety, or what would have been deemed sacred by all people. It was only when the king had "tasted the wine" that these things were proposed ; and none who attend on such a banquet as this, none who come together for purposes of drinking and feasting, can foretell what they may be led to do under the influence of wine and strong drink. No man is certain of *not* doing foolish and wicked things who gives himself up to such indulgences; no man knows what he may do that may be the cause of bitter regret and painful mortification in the recollection.

(3.) God has the means of access to the consciences of men (ver. 5). In this case it was by writing on the wall with his own fingers certain mysterious words which none could interpret, but which no one doubted were of fearful import. No one present, it would appear, had any doubt that somehow what was written was connected with some awful judgment, and the fearfulness of what they dreaded arose manifestly from the consciousness of their own guilt. It is not often that God comes forth in this way to alarm the guilty; but he has a thousand methods of doing it, and no one can be sure that in an instant he will not summon all the sins of his past life to remembrance. He *could* write our guilt in letters of light before us— in the chamber where we sleep; in the hall where we engage in revelry; on the face of the sky at night; or he can make it as plain to our minds *as if* it were thus written out. To Belshazzar, in his palace, surrounded by his lords, he showed this ; to us in society or solitude he can do the same thing. No sinner can have any security that he may not in a moment be overwhelmed with the conviction of his own depravity, and with dreadful apprehension of the wrath to come.

(4.) We have in this chapter (ver. 6) a striking illustration of the effects of a sudden alarm to the guilty. The countenance of the monarch was changed ; his thoughts troubled him ; the joints of his loins were loosed, and his knees smote together. Such effects are not uncommon when a sinner is made to feel that he is in the presence of God, and when his thoughts are led along to the future world. The human frame is so made that these changes occur as indicative of the troubles which the mind experiences, and the fact that it is thus agitated shows the power which God has over us. No guilty man can be secure that he will *not* thus be alarmed when he comes to contemplate the possibility that he may soon be called before his Maker, and the fact that he *may* thus be alarmed should be one of the considerations bearing on his mind to lead him to a course of virtue and religion. Such terror is proof of conscious guilt, for the innocent have nothing to dread; and if a man is sure that he is prepared to appear before God, he is *not* alarmed at the prospect. They who live in sin; they who indulge in revelry; they who are profane and sacrilegious; they who abuse the mercies of God, and live to deride sacred things, can never be certain that in a moment, by the revelation of their guilt to their own souls, and by a sudden message from the eternal world, they may not be overwhelmed with the deepest consternation. Their countenances may become deadly pale, their joints may be loosed, and their limbs tremble. It is only the righteous who can look calmly at the judgment.

(5.) We may see from this chapter one of the effects of the terror of a guilty conscience. It is not said, indeed, that the mysterious fingers on the wall recorded the *guilt* of the monarch. But they recorded *something;* is no one who would not turn pale if they were making some record that he saw a mysterious hand writing all manifestly pertained to him. How his thoughts and purposes — all the natural was it to suppose that it was a deeds of his past life—on the wall of record of his guilt! And who is there his chamber at night, and bringing at that could bear a record made in that once all his concealed thoughts and manner of his own thoughts and pur- all his forgotten deeds before his mind. poses; of his desires and feelings; of And if this is so, how will the sinner what he is conscious is passing within bear the disclosures that will be made the chambers of his own soul? There at the day of judgment?

APPENDIX

I.

EXCURSUS I.

ON THE ALLEGED DISCREPANCY BE-TWEEN DANIEL I. 1, AND JER. XXV. 1, AND SOME OTHER PASSAGES.

THE charge of *historical incorrectness* against the writer of the book of Daniel, rests partly upon some *dates of time*, and partly upon some *historical occurrences*. I shall first examine the allegation of error in respect to the designation of TIME.

In Dan. i. 1, it is said, that Nebuchadnezzar king of Babylon came up against Jerusalem, besieged it, took Jehoiakim captive, and rifled the temple of a part of its furniture, *in the third year of Jehoiakim*. In Jer. xxv. 1, it is explicitly said, that the *first year* of Nebuchadnezzar's reign was the *fourth* year of Jehoiakim's. Moreover, in Jer. xlvi. 2, it is said that king Nebuchadnezzar smote Carchemish on the Euphrates, then in possession of Pharaoh-Necho king of Egypt, in the same *fourth* year of Jehoiakim. Taking all these passages into view, it is alleged that the writer of the book of Daniel could not have lived in the time of Nebuchadnezzar, when the true date of the invasion of Palestine by that king must necessarily have been well known; but at a subsequent period, when the chronology of these events was more obscure, and when he might be misled by erring tradition. That period is placed, by most of the recent critics belonging to the so-called *liberal* school, near to the close of the Maccabean times, with the history of which, as they aver, the book of Daniel concludes.

As this has been, of late, an almost uniform assertion among critics of the new school, and has been placed in the front rank of objections against the genuineness of the book of Daniel, it becomes necessary to give it an attentive examination. Lengerke says of it, in his recent *Commentary* on this book, that "all attempts to remove this objection have to the present hour been frustrated. . . . Not only is the *date* wrong, but the *deportation* [of captives] under Jehoiakim remains at least unproved," p. 2, *seq.*

The documents which must guide our inquiries, are a fragment of Berosus (preserved by Josephus), and several brief passages in the Hebrew Scriptures. These are all the historical data on which we can place any reliance. All subsequent testimony is either a mere repetition of these, or a constructive exegesis of them, or if not, it is mere conjecture. In respect to the original documents, we have evidently the same right of interpretation as Abydenus, Megasthenes, Josephus, Eusebius, and others had. The native Greek historians, whose works are now extant, make no mention at all of Nebuchadnezzar; consequently, Josephus's quotations from the Oriental writers, and the historical notices comprised in the Hebrew Scriptures, are all on which we can place any dependence as legitimate sources of testimony. These consist of the following particulars:—

No. I.—The king of Egypt, Pharaoh-Necho, after having slain Josiah, and deposed his successor, Jehoahaz, made Eliakim (surnamed *Jehoiakim*), the son of Josiah, king over the Hebrews, and treated him as a tributary vassal; 2 Kings xxiii. 29–37. The sacred writer then proceeds thus, in 2 Kings xxiv. 1: "In his days came up Nebuchadnezzar king of Babylon; and Jehoiakim became his servant three years; then he turned and rebelled against him. (2) And Jehovah sent against him bands of the Chaldees, and bands of Syria, and bands of Moab, and bands of the sons of Ammon; yea, he sent them against Judah to destroy him; according to the word of the Lord which he spoke by his servants the prophets."

No. II.—After relating events previous to Jehoiakim's reign, as in the book of Kings, the writer thus proceeds in 2 Chron. xxxvi. 6: "Against him came up Nebuchadnezzar king of Babylon, and he bound him in fetters to convey him to Babylon. (7) And a part of the vessels of the house of the Lord did Nebuchadnezzar take to Babylon, and he put them in his temple at Babylon."

No. III.—Jer. xxv. 1: "The message which was to Jeremiah, concerning all the people of Judah, in the *fourth* year of Jehoiakim the son of Josiah king of Judah; the same was the *first* year of Nebuchadnezzar king of Babylon."

No. IV.—Jer. xlvi. 1, 2: "The word of the Lord . . . against Egypt, against the army of Pharaoh-Necho king of Egypt, which was by the river Euphrates in Carchemish, which Nebuchadnezzar king of Babylon smote, in the *fourth* year of Jehoiakim king of Judah."

No. V.—Dan. i. 1, 2: "In the *third* year of the reign of Jehoiakim king of Judah came Nebuchadnezzar king of Babylon to Jerusalem, and besieged it. And the Lord gave into his hand Jehoiakim king of Judah, and a part of the vessels of the house of God; and he brought them to the land of Shinar, to the house of his God, and the vessels did he bring into the treasure-house of his God."

No. VI.—Berosus, as quoted by Josephus, *Antiq.* X. 11. 1, also *Contra Ap.* I. 19: "When his father Nabopolassar had heard that the satrap, who had been appointed over Egypt and the regions around Coelo-Syria and Phœnicia, had rebelled, not being able himself to endure hardships, he committed to his son Nebuchadnezzar, then in the vigour of life, certain portions of his forces, and sent them against him. And Nebuchadnezzar, falling in with the rebel, and putting his forces in order, gained a victory over him, and the country belonging to his control he brought under his own dominion. Now it came to pass, that Nabopolassar fell sick at that period, and died, *having reigned twenty-one years.* Not long after, having learned the death of his father, he arranged his affairs in Egypt and the other regions, and committed the captives of the *Jews*, the Phœnicians, the Syrians, and the nations in Egypt, to certain of his friends, to conduct them to Babylon, with the most weighty part of his forces, and the remainder of his booty. He himself, accompanied by very few, went to Babylon through the desert. Then taking upon him the affairs which had been managed by the Chaldees, and the kingdom which had been preserved for him by their leader, becoming master of *the whole* (ὁλοκλήρου) of his father's dominion (ἀρχῆς), he assigned to the captives who had arrived, colonial dwelling-places in the most suitable regions of Babylon," &c. The passage goes on to show how Nebuchadnezzar used a part of the spoils as ἀναθήματα, *i.e.,* votive offerings, in the temples of his gods, and the rest in building and adorning the city of Babylon.

Preceding this passage, as quoted from Berosus (*Cont. Apion.* I. 19), Josephus gives a summary of the history of Nebuchadnezzar, as exhibited by the Chaldean historian. In this summary he says, that Berosus has related, "how Nabopolassar sent his son, Nebuchadnezzar, against Egypt and *against our land* [Palestine], with a large force (μετὰ πολλῆς δυνάμεως), who subdued them, burned the temple at Jerusalem, and, transplanting the great mass of the people, carried them away to Babylon." In a part of this summary, he seems to quote the words of Berosus, and represents him as saying, that "the Babylonian conquered Egypt, Syria,

Phœnicia, and Arabia, and exceeded in achievements all of the Chaldean and Babylonian kings, who had reigned before him."

We have now before us all the documents on which any reliance can be safely placed. On these I would make a few remarks which may assist our further inquiries. (a) From a survey of these documents it is plain, at first sight, that no one of them is anything more than a mere *summary* sketch of Jehoiakim's reign ; and so of Nebuchadnezzar's. The particulars of events, and even the order of them, in some respects, are not specified at all. Thus in No. I., *two* invasions of Nebuchadnezzar are made certain ; but no particular time of either is specified. In No. II. only one (probably the final) invasion appears to be mentioned. In Berosus, there is a still more rapid *coup d'œil* of events, without any effort to narrate particulars, much less to make out dates. (b) We are, therefore, at liberty to supply the omissions of one account, by that which another has furnished. An argument against more than one invasion, in the time of Jehoiakim, drawn from the fact that no more than one is mentioned in 2 Chronicles, would amount to nothing ; for it need not be again proved, that the *argumentum a silentio* is in such cases of no value. So an argument drawn from the silence of Berosus as to more than one invasion of Palestine by Nebuchadnezzar, would prove nothing against the united testimony of Kings, Jeremiah, and Daniel, that there was more than one. (c) It follows, that we are at liberty to make out probabilities of time and order of succession in respect to events, from *circumstances* that are narrated, where the writers have omitted formally to make out these in their narrations. This, however, should always be done with caution, and we should keep strictly within the bounds of probability.

In respect to the main subject now before us I would remark, that there are some points so well settled, and of such controlling influence, that nothing can be safely admitted which is inconsistent with them. (1.) It is now a matter of nearly universal agreement, that Nabopolassar, the father of Nebuchadnezzar, in union with the Median king Astyages, destroyed the Assyrian empire, and began his independent reign in Babylon, in 625 B.C. (2.) It seems to be certain, from the testimony of Berosus (No. VI. above) and Syncellus, that he reigned *twenty-one* years. Of course his death was near the close of 605 B.C., or at the beginning of 604. At this period, then, Nebuchadnezzar by inheritance became sole king of Babylon. (3.) *Previously* to this period, Nebuchadnezzar had invaded and subdued Carchemish, and overrun and brought under subjection to himself Syria, Palestine, Moab, the country of the Ammonites, Phœnicia, and Lower Egypt. This is clear from a comparison of No. I. and No. VI. with its sequel above. When these achievements and conquests were completed, Nebuchadnezzar received tidings of his father's death, hastened to Babylon, and left the captives and the booty to be forwarded by his subordinate officers ; No. VI. above. These are *facts* which we must either admit, or else renounce the credit of historical testimony which we are unable fairly to impeach.

The question, then, whether Nebuchadnezzar came into the regions of Hither Asia *before* 604 B.C., is settled. But—how long before? Long enough, at any rate, to overrun and subdue all these countries. Less than some two years for such achievements, no one who looks at the extent of those countries, and knows the slowness with which armies formerly moved in the East, will venture to fix upon. The book of Daniel (i. 1, 2) says, that Nebuchadnezzar came up and besieged Jerusalem in the *third* year of Jehoiakim, *i.e.*, in 607. That this was near the close of that third year, would seem probable from two circumstances ; first, the fast kept by Jehoiakim and his people, on the *ninth* month of the fifth year of this king, *i.e.*, Dec. 605. This was no legal or ritual fast (for none belonged to this period), but one either commemorative of some great evil, *e.g.*, the capture of the city by Nebuchadnezzar (comp. Zech. viii. 19, where four fasts of a like kind are specified); or anticipative of some great and dangerous struggle, *e.g.*,

Jehoiakim's rebellion against Nebuchadnezzar. Moreover, as Nebuchadnezzar is called *king*, while on this expedition, both in Daniel, Kings and Chronicles, and Jeremiah, and as we know (see Nos. III. IV.), that Jehoiakim's *fourth* year corresponded with the *first* year of Nebuchadnezzar, as viewed by the Hebrews, it would seem to follow of course, allowing the historical verity of Daniel, that the invasion by Nebuchadnezzar must have been late in 607. If so, then of course the greater part of his *first* year, as counted by the Hebrews, corresponded to the *fourth* year of Jehoiakim, as Nos. III. IV. declare. Later than the time which Daniel designates, Nebuchadnezzar's expedition could not well have been, if we admit the great extent of his conquests already made at, or a little before, the beginning of 604. Cyrus and Cyaxares were about ten years in subduing Asia Minor; could Nebuchadnezzar have overrun all Hither Asia and Egypt in less than *two?* All those then, who, like Lengerke, Winer, &c., make the fourth year of Nebuchadnezzar and the eighth of Jehoiakim, *i.e.*, 602 or 601, to be the time when the king of Babylon first invaded Palestine, are obliged to dishonour the credit of Berosus, who (No. VI.) says, in so many words, that "when Nebuchadnezzar heard of his father's death, he left the spoil and the captive *Jews*, Syrians, Phœnicians, and Egyptians, to be conducted to Babylon by his officers." The same is also asserted by Alexander Polyhistor, Euseb. *Chron. Arm.* I. p. 45. All agree that this must have been in 604; and scarcely a doubt can remain, that it was near the *commencement* of this year. Lengerke says, in respect to what Berosus asserts, that "it may appear to be doubtful;" p. 6. He refers to Jer. xxix. 10, comp. ver. 2, for proof that the exile of Jeconiah was the *first* deportation of Jews by Nebuchadnezzar. But I can find no proof of such a nature there. The simple truth is, that events are everywhere related, in respect to Jehoiakim's reign, *without any dates* of time, with the exception of Dan. i. 1, 2. But still, these events are plainly such as to show the

entire probability of what is declared by Daniel. "But Nebuchadnezzar took Carchemish in the *fourth* year of Jehoiakim (No. IV. above); how could he do this, and yet send Daniel and his compeers into exile, in the *third* year of the same Jehoiakim?" One may well reply, that there is no impossibility, or even improbability in this. Where is the passage of history to show that Nebuchadnezzar did not besiege and take Jerusalem, *before* he went against Carchemish? Babylon, Carchemish, and Jerusalem, are at the extreme points of a triangle, the shortest side of which is indeed the distance from Babylon to Carchemish? Why then did not Nebuchadnezzar go directly from Babylon to Carchemish? The probable answer seems to me not to be difficult. Jehoiakim was placed on the throne by Pharaoh-Necho, and consequently was his hearty ally and tributary. Nebuchadnezzar, by marching first against him, and then subduing all the countries under Egyptian sway, through which he passed on his march to Carchemish, avoided the possibility of aid from Egypt being given to the city in question, or from the allies of Egypt. Carchemish was the strongest place in all that region; and such a plan showed the expertness of Nebuchadnezzar as a warrior. The whole course of events, in this case, certainly looks as if the assertion in Dan. i. 1, 2, were true. "But how could Jeremiah, then, in the *fourth* year of Jehoiakim (xxv. 1, *seq.*), threaten an invasion of the Chaldees, and seventy years of exile? The exile, according to this view, had already begun." But to this question one may reply, that Nebuchadnezzar's first work, viz., the subjection of Jehoiakim and the making of him a tributary, had indeed already been done; but all of the work which Nebuchadnezzar was to perform, was not yet completed. In his victorious march from Carchemish, where he had been successful, through all the countries of Hither Asia and Lower Egypt, and of course through Palestine, he was still to collect more booty, and to carry away such and so many captives as he thought would effectually prevent insurrection after his departure. It is not probable that he sent away many captives to Babylon, immediately on his first capture of Jerusalem. He could not then spare the troops necessary for such an escort as was required to do this. In all probability, therefore, he contented himself with sending away a sufficient number of *hostages*, belonging to the princes and nobles, to secure the fidelity of Jehoiakim. The book of Daniel (i. 1–3), merely avers, that in the *third* year of Jehoiakim, a part of the vessels of the temple, and *some of the king's seed and of the princes*, were sent to Babylon. Nothing could be more natural or probable than this, under such circumstances. One has only to call to mind, that *hostages*, and those of princely descent, were usually demanded by conquerors, where want of fidelity in the subdued was suspected ; and also, that the booty of gold and silver was one main object, in all such expeditions as that of Nebuchadnezzar's. Hence, in Jer. lii. 27–30, no mention is made of those first hostages as exiles ; first, because they were few in number, and secondly, because their condition was different from that of ordinary exiles. When we find Jeremiah, therefore, in xxv. 1–11, in the *fourth* year of Jehoiakim, threatening subjugation and exile to the Jews, it cannot reasonably be doubted that he did so, because Jehoiakim, the former ally of Egypt, and who moreover had been set on his throne by the Egyptian king, was meditating revolt. Nebuchadnezzar's success at Carchemish was probably as yet unknown in Judea. Jehoiakim, therefore, hoped for a different result, and was ready to join his former master, in case of his success. To prevent this catastrophe, Jeremiah uttered the comminations of chap. xxv. 1–11. And that Jehoiakim's intentions were known to Nebuchadnezzar, seems quite probable from the treatment which, according to Berosus, the Jews experienced at the close of Nebuchadnezzar's expedition, viz., the deportation of Hebrew captives. Still, as this class of exiles is not particularized in Jer. lii. 27–30, they probably consisted mostly of such as might come under the denomination of hostages, *i.e.*, they belonged to the more wealthy and influential families.

That all which has been said of the disposition of Jehoiakim to rebel, is true, seems to be confirmed by the fact, that not long after this period, as soon as Nebuchadnezzar had gone to Babylon and become stationary there, *i.e.*, probably about the end of 604, Jehoiakim did actually rebel, and throw off his allegiance to Babylon. The king of Babylon, however, was so intent on beautifying his capital and his temples, and thus expending the immense wealth which he had collected in his predatory incursions (Berosus in Jos. *Cont. Ap.* i. 19), that he did not immediately undertake to chastise the Jewish king. But at the close of 600 B.C., or early in 599, he again marched up to Jerusalem, and inflicted the penalty that was usual in cases of revolt.

Lengerke and others assert, that Nebuchadnezzar did not invade Judea again, during the life of Jehoiakim, and that this king died and was buried in peace, contrary to the threats of Jeremiah, xxii. 19, and xxxvi. 30, viz., that he should be destroyed by violence, and his dead body be cast out unburied. The appeal for proof of this is to 2 Ki. xxiv. 6, which states, that "Jehoiakim *slept with his fathers,* and that Jehoiachin his son reigned in his stead." Lengerke (p. 7) avers, that the expression *slept* or *rested with his fathers,* means, always and only, that "the person in question descended in quiet to the common grave of his fathers." Surely an entire mistake ! That שָׁכַב of itself merely designates the *death* of an individual, without determining the fact whether it was *peaceful* or *violent,* is clear enough from Hebrew usage. In almost every narration respecting the death of a king, either in the book of Kings or Chronicles, it is said of him, that *he slept with his fathers.* But that this has no concern with indicating his *peaceful burial,* is quite certain from the fact, that in nearly every case of this nature, the burial of the king is the subject of a separate mention, showing of course that this is not involved or implied in the first expression. Nor does שָׁכַב (*slept*) even involve the idea of a *peaceful death;* for it is said of Ahab, who perished of wounds received in battle, that "he slept with his fathers" (1 Ki. xxiv. 40). In ver. 36 is the equivalent expression : *So the king died;* and it is then added : "They buried him in Samaria." In the same way עָצַב alone is used for death, and mostly for the designation of violent death, in Isa. xiv. 8, 17, 43 ; xvii ; Job iii. 13 ; xx. 11, 21 ; xxvi. Not a word is said in 2 Ki. xxiv. 6, of Jehoiakim's *burial;* and of course there is nothing there to show that Jeremiah, in declaring that he should perish *unburied,* had predicted what proved to be untrue. On the other hand ; what are we to make of לְהַאֲבִידוֹ, *to destroy him (i.e.,* Jehoiakim, as Lengerke himself (p. 6) concedes), in 2 Ki. xxiv. 2 ? And what of 2 Chron. xxxvi. 6, which says that the king of Babylon *bound Jehoiakim in fetters to carry him to Babylon,* but makes no mention at all of his being actually sent thither ? That Jeremiah has not given an account of the fulfilment of his own prediction respecting Jehoiakim, is not strange, unless the principle is to be assumed, that prophets are obligated to write full and regular *history,* as well as prediction. I might even argue in favour of the fulfilment of the prediction, from the silence of the prophet. It was an event so well known, one might say with probability, that a special record of it was not needed on his part. Yet I think the books of Chronicles and of Kings, as cited above, have *impliedly* recorded the event in question. Still more express do I find, with Grotius, the recognition of it in Ezek. xix. 9. Here, the preceding context describes the reign and fate of Jehoahaz or Shallum ; comp. 2 Ki. xxiii. 31–33. Then the prophet comes, in his parable, to the *successor* of Shallum, viz., Jehoiakim (in case he means the *immediate* successor), and he says of him, that "the nations set against him . . . . and he was taken in their pit, and they put him in ward *in chains,* and brought him to the king of Babylon ; they brought him into holds, that his voice should no more be heard upon the mountains

of Israel." To interpret all this of Jechoniah, as Rosenmüller, Lengerke, and others have done, seems to me very incongruous. The prophet says of this *lion,* that "he went up and down among the lions . . . . learned to catch prey, and devoured men ; and he knew their desolate places, and laid waste their cities, and the land was desolate, and the fulness thereof, by reason of his roaring." All this now, of a boy *eight* years old, according to 2 Chron. xxxvi. 9, and according to 2 Ki. xxiv. 8, only *eighteen;* and of a child, moreover, who as both records aver, reigned only about *three months!* A most extravagant parable would Ezekiel seem to have written, if all this is to be predicated of such a child, whether aged eight or eighteen, and of only a three months' reign.

There is indeed a difficulty, arising from the extreme brevity of the sacred writers, in finding out the *particulars* in the history of the closing part of Jehoiakim's reign. But certain it is, that nothing against the supposition that he died a violent death, and was left unburied, can be made out from what is recorded. Would Jeremiah have left his predictions standing as they do in his prophecy, if they had not been fulfilled ? Lengerke intimates, that the peaceful accession of Jehoiachin to his father's throne, shows that Nebuchadnezzar was not in Palestine at the time of Jehoiakim's death. But if Nebuchadnezzar had already chastised Jehoiakim on account of his rebellion, and put him into fetters, in which he died through hard usage or violence, may he not have ceded to Jehoiachin the throne of Judea, in consequence of renewed and solemn stipulations to become his vassal ? And specially as he was so young, that little was to be feared from him ? I see nothing of the impossible, or even of the improbable, in all this. The fact that Nebuchadnezzar was very suspicious of Jehoiachin, is clear from the circumstance, that after only three months he returned with his army, and carried off that king and many of his subjects, into exile at Babylon. The phrase לִתְשׁוּבַת הַשָּׁנָה, in 2 Chron. xxxvi. 10, indicates something more, in my apprehension, than has been usually noticed by commentators. In all probability, this *return* or *turning of the year* means the spring of the year, when kings were wont to go out on military expeditions. But still the word *year* here plainly stands related to some other period of time, from which it is reckoned. And what can this be, except the antecedent period when Jehoiakim was deposed and slain? If this were done in the autumn, and Jehoiachin made king either by Nebuchadnezzar himself, or by the people rebelling against Babylon after his departure, he might reign during the three winter months, and in the spring of the year be attacked and carried into exile by Nebuchadnezzar. No doubt this conqueror had large standing garrisons, in all the conquered countries, ready to act at short warning. Hence the shortness of the time, between the first and second invasion at this period, according to the statement made above.

That I have reasoned correctly in regard to the mere *summary* or generic accounts of Jehoiakim's reign, both in the sacred records and in Berosus, I must believe no one will deny who takes due pains minutely to examine them. It follows of course, unless the credibility of these historians can be reasonably impeached, that the omission of particulars by any one of them, is no argument against the verity of another who does state some particulars. This is notably illustrated by Jer. lii. 28, 29. In ver. 28 it is stated, that Nebuchadnezzar carried away captive, in his *seventh* year, 3023 persons. In 2 Ki. xxiv. 12, it is stated, that Jehoiachin and his court gave themselves up to Nebuchadnezzar in the *eighth* year of his reign, who carried him away to Babylon, with 10,000 captives and all the craftsmen and smiths, ver. 14. In Jeremiah, then, the statement refers to what was done one year (*i.e.*, in 599) before that took place which is related in the book of Kings. Both the time and the number of exiles mentioned in the two passages, are discrepant; and consequently we may regard this circumstance as heightening the probability of two invasions, as stated

above, which took place within a small period of time. Again, in Jer. lii. 29 it is stated, that Nebuchadnezzar, in his *eighteenth* year, carried away captive 832 persons. In 2 Ki. xxv. 3–10, it is declared that Nebuchadnezzar, in his *nineteenth* year, took Jerusalem, burned the temple, and carried away captive all except the poor of the land, ver. 12. How many were the captives, is not stated; but there must have been a great many thousands. The same thing is repeated in Jer. lii. 12–16. Here then (in lii. 29) is a statement of deportation, in a different year and in very different numbers from what is stated or implied in the book of Kings. Jer. lii. 29 seems evidently to relate to captives sent away *one year before the siege was completed;* for it lasted some twenty months. Then, again, there is a third deportation mentioned in Jer. lii. 30, in the twenty-third year of Nebuchadnezzar; of which we have no other account. Who will venture now to say, that the books of Jeremiah and of Kings are at variance; or rather, that they are contradictory, in regard to the deportation of exiles? Both may be regarded as true, without doing the least violence to probability.

"But both Daniel and Jeremiah call Nebuchadnezzar *king*, some two or more years before he was king. How can such a mistake be accounted for?"

Easily, I would say; or rather, I would deny that there is any real error in the Jewish historians or prophets, with regard to this matter. Of the father of Nebuchadnezzar, viz., Nabopolassar, the Hebrew Scriptures know nothing. Nebuchadnezzar was generalissimo of the Chaldean invading army. Before he left the country of Palestine, in order to return to Babylon, his father had died, and he had become actual and sole king. The books of Daniel and Jeremiah, written some years afterwards, and also the books of Kings and Chronicles, call him by the name which he had long and universally borne. In the narrations of Jeremiah and Daniel, and also of the other books named, the writers all give him the title of *king*, which was so familiar to them all. The same thing is every day practised, even at the present time.

We speak of Alexander the Great, of the Emperor Augustus, of the Emperor Napoleon, &c., as having done or said this and that, even when we are relating, in a popular way, the things which took place before the sovereignty of these men actually existed. The object of the sacred historians is mainly to designate the leading individual who achieved this or that, not to show in particular how and when he entered on his highest office. The Hebrews, who knew Nebuchadnezzar as the *leader* of the Chaldean army, and also as *king*, before he had actually ended the expedition against them in which he was first engaged, would very naturally of course speak of him as a *king*, when he first invaded Judea. We may easily concede, that he is *anticipatively* so called; for the usage is too common to be either a matter of offence or of stumbling. It cannot fairly be put to the account of error or mistake.

I do not feel, therefore, that we need to resort, as many writers have done, to the expedient of showing that Nebuchadnezzar was constituted by his father a *joint partner* with him of the throne of Babylon, before he set out on the celebrated expedition against Hither Asia, which established an extensive Babylonish empire. Yet this *partnership* is, after all, far from being improbable. Nabopolassar was so enfeebled as to be unable to lead the invading army. Berosus says of him: σύστησας τῷ υἱῷ Ναβουχοδονοσόρῳ, ὄντι ἔτι ἐν ἡλικίᾳ, μέρη τινὰ τῆς δυνάμεως, ἐξέστημψεν ἐπ᾽ αὐτόν, κ. τ. λ. Jos. *Cont. Ap.* I. 19. But δυνάμεως does not here mean *regal power* (as has been maintained), but *military force*. This seems plain from a preceding declaration, in which Berosus states that "Nabopolassar sent his son (Nebuchadnezzar) ἐπὶ τήν ἡμετέραν γῆν—(against Palestine) . . . μετὰ πολλῆς δυνάμεως, *i.e.*, with a large military force." But there is another passage in Berosus, which seems more probably to favour the idea of copartnership in the throne, at the time of Nebuchadnezzar's expedition. After the war is finished, Nebuchadnezzar returns, and is formally installed by the Magi as sole and supreme king. Berosus says of him: "Κυριεύσας ἐξ ὁλοκλήρου

τῆς πατρικῆς ἀρχῆς, *i.e.*, becoming supreme over *the whole* of his father's domain." Is there not a natural implication here, that before this he was in part a κύριος? So Hitzig concedes, (*Begriff der Kritik*, p. 186), and states expressly that Nebuchadnezzar's father made him *co-regent*, before the battle at Carchemish. Knobel (*Prophetism.* II. p. 226) also states this as probable. The like do many others; but I deem it unnecessary to make this a point of any moment. The various sacred writers can be harmonized with each other, and with probable facts, independently of this circumstance. But still, it would be an additional reason for the Hebrew usage, in regard to the appellative *king*, as applied to Nebuchadnezzar previously to his father's death, that he was *co-regent* with his father, from the time that he entered on his first Palestine expedition. The contrary of this cannot be shown. That *Berosus*, a Babylonian, should count dominion as belonging to Nabopolassar until his death, seems to be a matter of course, for such dominion was matter of fact. That Nebuchadnezzar, the appointed heir, then obtained his father's *domain* or *dominion* (ἀρχῆς), was also a matter of course; but that he then obtained it ἐξ ὁλοκλήρου, would seem to imply what has been stated above. Be all this, however, as it may, it seems that all the Hebrew writers, in Kings, Chronicles, Jeremiah, and Daniel, are uniform in regard to the appellative in question. Whatever may have been the state of actual facts, it is a sufficient vindication of the Hebrew historians and prophets, that they have followed the usage of their country in regard to this matter. If they had been writing the particular history of Nebuchadnezzar's life and reign, the matter might then be viewed in a different light, in case a *co-regency* never actually took place.

But we are met, in regard to our views of the *time* of Nebuchadnezzar's *first* invasion, by the allegation of Lengerke, Winer, and others, that in that expedition Nebuchadnezzar did not overrun Judea, nor send away any captives from that country. To confirm this, they appeal to Josephus,

Ant. X. 6. 1, who, after describing the capture of Carchemish, says, that "Nebuchadnezzar then passed over the Euphrates, and took all Syria even to Pelusium, παρὶξ τῆς Ἰουδαίας, *i.e.*, *excepting Judea.*" One is led to wonder, at first view, how Josephus could make this exception; and this wonder is much increased by comparing the declaration in question with what he says in *Cont. Ap.* I. 19. Beyond any reasonable doubt, the two passages are at variance. In the latter passage, he quotes Berosus as saying, that Nebuchadnezzar's father "sent him with an army against Egypt, and against τὴν ἡμιτέραν γῆν, *i.e.*, against Judea." And in the sequel he quotes Berosus as also saying, that, at the close of this expedition, Nebuchadnezzar "sent to Babylon τοὺς αἰχμαλώτους Ἰουδαίων, *the captives of the Jews,* as well as of the Syrians, Phœnicians, and Egyptians." Yet Berosus and the Hebrew Scriptures were, beyond all reasonable question, the only authorities which Josephus had, or at least which he employed, in respect to the history of Nebuchadnezzar. But the source of Josephus's mistake in *Antiq.* X. 6. 1, is in all probability to be found in a passage from Berosus in *Cont. Ap.* I. 19, where, in making a summary in a single sentence of the achievements of Nebuchadnezzar, the Chaldee historian says: "The Babylonian [king] conquered Egypt, Syria, Phœnicia, Arabia, and in his achievements far exceeded all the kings who had before reigned over the Chaldeans and Babylonians." In this mere summary sentence, Berosus omits *Judea*, *i.e.*, the small country of the two tribes, (for this was Judea, at that period); as he also omits Moab, the country of the Ammonites, &c.—omits them evidently because of their comparative smallness. Josephus has unwittingly overlooked this, and so he has *excepted* Judea, in *Antiq.* X. 6. 1, because Berosus has not mentioned it in the passage just quoted. It does not, indeed, much commend his careful accuracy to us, when we find him so doing, because Berosus, as quoted by him, both before and after the sentence in question, has explicitly averred that Nebuchadnezzar came up, in that very first

expedition, to attack *Judea*, and that he carried away captives from that country. But negligences of this kind are somewhat frequent, in this otherwise very valuable historian; *e.g.*, in respect to this same portion of history, Josephus states (*Antiq.* X. 7. 1), that when Nebuchadnezzar took Jehoiachin captive, he carried away with him 10,832 others into exile. Now this statement is palpably made out from combining together 2 Ki. xxiv. 14, and Jer. lii. 29; Josephus having added together the numbers in both passages, without noticing that one deportation is in the *seventh*, and the other in the *eighth* year of Nebuchadnezzar. This discrepancy he does not even notice, much less pretend to reconcile. And so he has not unfrequently done elsewhere. He needs to be closely watched in such matters. Haste, and carelessness of such a kind, may not unfrequently be charged upon him. I cannot think, however, that he meant to make any wrong statements.

It is impossible for me, after having carefully examined all that Berosus of Josephus has to say on these matters, to attach any historical value to the παρὶξ τῆς Ἰουδαίας, which has been quoted above and examined. All things being duly considered, I cannot but think that the evidence of a Babylonian invasion, commencing in the latter part of the third year of Jehoiakim, repeated in 599 at the close of his reign ; renewed against Jehoiachin in 598 ; and then, lastly, at the close of Zedekiah's reign ; are facts as well made out, and as probable, as most facts of such a nature in ancient history. Had there been no gain to be made out of this matter, by warmly enlisted partizans, I do not believe that it would have ever been seriously controverted.

I do not see, then, why Lengerke should be so liberal of his *exclamation points*, when speaking of the intimation of Hengstenberg and Hävernick, that the book of Daniel, by assigning the invasion of Palestine to the *third* year of Jehoiakim, has shown an unusually minute and accurate acquaintance with the history of the Hebrews. Is it not certain, that Nebuchadnezzar's father began his reign, as independent king, in 625 B.C. ? Is it not well established that he died near the end of 605, or at the beginning of 604? Is it not sufficiently established by historical testimony, that Nebuchadnezzar had reduced Carchemish, and overrun all Syria, Phœnicia, Moab, Northern Arabia, Palestine, and Egypt, *before* the death of his father? Was it possible to accomplish all this in less than some *two* years? If not, then Dan. i. 1, 2, seems plainly to be in the right, which assigns Nebuchadnezzar's first invasion of Palestine to the *third* year of Jehoiakim. It could not have been later. Exclamation points, it would be well for Lengerke, and sometimes for his opponents too, to remember, are not arguments, either ratiocinative or historical. The book of Daniel must, as it would seem, be in the right as to the main point in question. Nor does it contradict at all the other books.

The appeal made to Jer. xxxv. 11, in order to show that Nebuchadnezzar had not yet invaded Palestine, in the fourth year of Jehoiakim, is not valid, because there is no note of time in ch. xxxv., and because, as Nebuchadnezzar probably passed through Judea several times during his first invasion, there are no data in this chapter to decide which of his transitions occasioned the flight of the Rechabites to Jerusalem. The fact that Jehoiakim was the known ally and vassal of Pharaoh-Necho, would of itself show that the attitude of Nebuchadnezzar toward Palestine must have been one of hostility. The probability seems to be (comparing this chapter with the following one), that the Rechabites fled from Nebuchadnezzar when he was on his return from Carchemish; for then he was accompanied by troops from the conquered nations mentioned in Jer. xxxv. 11.

I would merely observe, at the close of this difficult and perhaps too long protracted investigation, that no one who has experience in these matters will think of arguing against the actual occurrence of certain particular events, merely because they are not stated in this book of Scripture or in that, since nearly all of the Jewish history in later times is given to us in professed and acknowledged *summaries* only. One writer sometimes sees fit to insert some special particular, which the rest have passed by. *E.g.*, Jer. li. 59, *seq.*, mentions a journey of Zedekiah, with some of his courtiers, to Babylon, in the fourth year of his reign. In 2 Chron. xxxiii. 11, *seq.*, we have an account of Manasseh as having been carried to Babylon, and of his penitence, and his return to Jerusalem. Nowhere else is either of these events even alluded to, so far as I can find. Yet after the recent investigations respecting the books of Chronicles by Movers, Keil, and others, I think no sober critic will be disposed to call in question the position that neither of these accounts is improbable, and that neither can, on any grounds worthy of credit, be fairly controverted. And I would again suggest, that when leading events as to time and place are certain, an assumption of particular circumstances and events attending them, which is built upon the common course of things and supported by probability, is surely neither uncritical nor unsafe. When we suppose, for example, that Daniel and his associates were sent to Babylon as *hostages*, at the time when Jehoiakim first became a vassal to Nebuchadnezzar, and combine this supposition with the declaration in Dan. i. 1, *seq.*, we suppose what seems to be altogether probable, although we cannot establish this particular by any direct testimony, but merely by implication.

It may not be useless to add, that as the Jews evidently called Nebuchadnezzar *king*, from the time that he invaded Palestine, so by a comparison of Dan. i. 1, *seq.*; Jer. xxv. 1; 2 Ki. xxv. 27, we make out forty five years (inclusively) as the period of Nebuchadnezzar's reign, according to the Hebrew method of reckoning. At the same time, Berosus and others make out only forty-three years. Still, there is no real disagreement in the case. The Jews began to reckon two years earlier than Berosus, who counts only upon the *sole* reign of Nebuchadnezzar after the death of his father.

II.

EXCURSUS II.

A second charge of *chronological* error against the book of Daniel is, that it makes an evident mistake in respect to the period when Nebuchadnezzar's dream took place, and Daniel interpreted it. The dream was in the *second* year of Nebuchadnezzar's reign (Dan. ii. 1). Previously to this, Daniel and his fellows had been subjected to a *three* years' discipline, as preparatory to waiting upon the king (Dan. i. 5). That period had passed before Daniel was presented to the king (Dan. i. 18). How, it is asked, could Nebuchadnezzar, as *king*, appoint to Daniel *three* years of discipline, and yet bring in the same Daniel, in the *second* year of his actual reign, to interpret his dream, when it is evident, from the author's own showing, that this Daniel had already completed his three years' course of discipline, and taken his place among the Magi before he was called to interpret the dream? Dan. i. 20; ii. 2, 13.

If the result of the preceding investigation be admitted, then is the solution of this seemingly difficult problem rendered quite easy. Nebuchadnezzar is called king in Dan. i. 1., after the usual manner of the Hebrews (comp. 2 Kin. xxiv. 1; 2 Chron. xxxvi. 6), and in the way of anticipation. In fact he became sole king before that expedition had ended. But when a Jewish writer in Babylon (Daniel) comes to the transactions of his actual reign as reckoned of course in Babylon (for of course the date of his reign there would be from the period when he became *sole* king), the writer dates the events that happened under that reign, in accordance with the Babylonish reckoning. So it seems to be in Dan. ii. 1. According to the result of the preceding examination, Daniel was sent to Babylon in the latter part of 607, or the beginning of 606. Nebuchadnezzar became actual king, by the death of his father, near the end of 605, or at the beginning of 604. Ne-

buchadnezzar's *second* year of actual and sole reign would then be in 603. If we suppose the latter part of this year to be the time when the dream occurred, then we have a period of nearly four years between Daniel's exile and his call to interpret the king's dream. Any part of 603 saves the accuracy of the book of Daniel in respect to this matter. In fact it lies on the very face of this statement in the book of Daniel, that it is scrupulously conformed to historical truth; for how could the writer, after having announced Daniel's deportation as belonging to the *third* year of Jehoiakim, and his discipline as having been completed in *three* years, then declare that Daniel was called upon as one of the Magi, to interpret dreams in the *second* year of Nebuchadnezzar? If Nebuchadnezzar was actual king in the third year of Jehoiakim, he was so when Daniel was carried away to Babylon; and plain enough is it, that Daniel's course of discipline was not complete until the *fourth*, or at least the end of the *third* year of Nebuchadnezzar. The error would, in such a case, be so palpable, that no writer of any intelligence or consistency could fail to notice and correct it. We are constrained to believe, then, that Nebuchadnezzar is named *king* merely in the way of *anticipation*, in Dan. i. 1 (and so in 2 Kings xxiv., 2 Chron. xxxvi., Jer. xxv.); and that the date of his sole and actual reign is referred to in Dan. ii. 1, as the Babylonians reckoned it. Thus understood, all is consistent and probable. We need not resort, as Rosenmüller and others have done, to a *long series* of dreams on the part of Nebuchadnezzar, in which the same thing was repeated; nor to the improbable subterfuge, that, although he dreamed in the *second* year of his reign, he did not concern himself to find out an interpreter of his nocturnal visions, until some considerable time afterwards. Both of these representations seem to me to be contrary to the plain and evident tenor of the whole narration. The agitation was immediate, and the stronger because it was immediate. Procrastination of the matter might, and probably would, have liberated him from his fears, and blunted the edge of his curiosity. That Jeremiah reckons in the Palestine Jewish way, *i.e.*, *anticipatively*, is certain from Jer. xxv. 1; xlvi. 2. That he did not this by mistake, but only in compliance with the usage of the Jews in Palestine seems altogether probable. On the other hand, the state of facts as to Nebuchadnezzar's conquests, as exhibited above, shows that his invasion of Judea must have begun as early as Dan. i. 1 asserts. In truth, facts and events vouch for the writer's minute historical accuracy in this matter, in case it be conceded that Nebuchadnezzar is called king in Dan. i. 1, in the way of *anticipation*, and in accordance with the common Hebrew usage.

III.

EXCURSUS III.

ON THE CHALDEES.

Some Greek writers frequently apply the word *Chaldees* (Χαλδαῖοι) to a fierce people, in the mountainous country bordering on Armenia. Xenophon met with such on his retreat, and he has often made mention of them; *e. g.*, *Anab.* IV. 3, 4; V. 5, 17; VII. 8, 25. Comp. Hab. i. 6, *seq.;* Job i. 17. Strabo notices tribes of the same name, in the country of Pòntus, XII. c. 3, p. 26, 27, 36, Tom. III. edit. Lip. From the Armenian [Assyrian] Chaldees many writers have of late supposed the Babylonian Chaldees to have come; which Isa. xxiii. 13, as interpreted by them, seems to favour: "See! the country of the Chaldeans, this people was not; Assyria assigned it [the country] to the dwellers of the desert; they [the Chaldees] erect their watchtowers, they set in commotion the palaces of it [Tyre], they make it a heap of ruins." As Assyria anciently extended her dominion over all middle Asia, and of course over the Armenian Chaldees, the latter might, under their permission, have emigrated to the plains, and being a courageous and warlike people, they might have obtained pre-eminence wherever they settled, over the feeble inhabitants of the plains. But if the Nomades of Chaldean Armenia were indeed the *predominant* portion of the Babylonish people, so that the country was early named from them, those Nomades must at least have emigrated at an early period of the Assyrian dynasty, *i.e.*, during the one which preceded the invasion of Arbaces, and (according to Ctesias) ended with Sardanapalus, B. C. 747.

The deductions from Isa. xxiii. 13, by Gesenius, Hitzig, Knobel, and others, viz., that the Chaldean power and even name in southern Mesopotamia and Babylon are of *recent* origin, must depend mainly on the correctness of their exegesis of the text in question. But this is far from being made out. On the other hand, substantially with Hupfeld (*Exercitt.*), and Leo (*Allgem. Geschichte*, s. 106), we may with much more probability translate thus: "Behold, the country of the Chaldeans—this people was not [a people]; Assyria—it has assigned it to the beasts of the desert; they erected their towers, they watched her palaces; [but] it has made her a heap of ruins."

In this way we have one main agent, viz., the Chaldean people. The "heap of ruins" is Nineveh, and the "desert" made by invasion, is the Assyrian domain. The prophet is threatening Tyre, and bids her look to what the Chaldeans, their invaders, have already achieved in Assyria. It were easy to vindicate the interpretation just given, but Hupfeld (*Exercitt. Herod.*) has sufficiently done it, and it would be out of place here. The reason why I have now introduced the subject is, because this text is the main dependence of many recent critics for establishing a favourite position of theirs, to which I have already adverted, viz., that the *Chaldean* power, and even name, in southern Mesopotamia and Babylon, is comparatively recent, and that Chaldea was unknown to the biblical writers before the time of Jehoiakim, at least as a national and independent country. *Facts*, strong and (as it seems to me) irresistible, make against this. Schleyer, in his *Würdigung der Einwürfe*, s. 48, *seq.*, 138, *seq.*, has made objections to it which cannot well be met. *Shinar* was the older name of Babylonia, Gen. xi. 2. This had a king (Amraphel) in the days of Abraham, Gen. xiv. 1, 9. That Babylon justly claims a very high antiquity, cannot be denied. Ctesias, Herodotus, Berosus, the Jewish SS., all agree in this. The latter make Nimrod its founder, who was a grandson of Noah (B.C. 2218), Gen. x. 8. Its walls, towers, palaces, bridges, dykes, and architecture of every kind, most of which was on a gigantic scale that rivalled or exceeded that of Egypt, prove incontestably an advanced state of knowledge in Babylon at a very early period, and indicate a metropolis of the highest grandeur. Other facts of much importance are in accordance with this. Simplicius (*Comm. ad Aristot. de Coelo*, p. 123) tells us, that Calisthenes, who accompanied Alexander the Great to Babylon, found astronomical observations there which reached back to 1903 years before that period, and which he sent to Aristotle; and also that the Magi claimed to be in possession of much older ones still. Ptolemy, in his famous *Canon*, plainly allows their astronomical observations to be correct as far back as Nabonassar (about 747 B.C.), and there begins his era from which he dates events. Larcher, and above all Ideler (on the Astronomy of the Chaldees), have shown that the period of 1903 years is neither impossible nor improbable; as Gesenius himself appears to concede, *Comm. in Es.* III. p. 350. But be this as it may, Diodorus Sic. (II. 29) says expressly, that the Chaldean priests (whom, like Daniel, he calls *Chaldeans*), are of *the most ancient Babylonians*, Χαλδαῖοι τοίνυν τῶν ἀρχαιοτάτων ὄντες Βαβυλωνίων. All this seems to show, that the *Chaldees* (both na-

tion and priests) are of the highest antiquity, and that an emigration from the northern mountains, if it ever took place so as to give a name to the country, must have been at a very remote period. Whenever it was, priests and people appear to have come to Babylonia together. There they amalgamated with the population; and the *Magi* (the priests of the fire-worshippers, such as are described by Zoroaster in the Zendavesta), probably engaged in the studies, and united in some of the pursuits, of the native priests in Babylon; the conquerors thus assimilating to the conquered, their superiors in knowledge, like the Goths and Vandals assimilating to the Romans. Hence the mixture of Parsism and gross Polytheism in the religion of Babylon; for plainly the latter contains both elements. In this way, moreover, can we account for that mixture of the Zend and Pehlvi languages with the Semitic, in the composition of many names and offices in Babylon, in the time of Daniel. *Mag* (מַג Jer. xxxix. 3) is the same as the Sanscrit *maha*, Pers. *mogh*, Zend, *meh*, and is equivalent to the Hebrew רַב; and the הַרְטֻמִּין in Daniel are the same as the מָגִים and רַבִּים. But although many, or perhaps even most, of the proper names of men and of *civil* offices among the Chaldeans are best explained from the Zend, or the old Persian, yet the names of their gods and of their *religious* offices are mostly of a *Semitic* origin; *e.g.*, *Belus* = בַּעַל or בֵּעֵל; Mylitta = מוֹלֶדֶת (genetrix); הַרְטֻמִּים from חֶרֶשׁ, Daniel i. 20; ii. 2; and also in Gen. xli. 8; Exod. vii. 11, 22; viii. 3, 14, 15; ix. 11; אַשָּׁף, Dan. i. 20; ii. 2 (Chald.), x. 27; iv. 4; v. 7, 11, 15, = Syr. (incantator) מְכַשֵּׁף, Dan. ii. 2; also Ex. vii. 11; xxii. 17; Deut. xviii. 10; Mal. iii. 5; and so the generic Chaldee word חַכִּים (= *Magus*), Dan. ii. 12, 21; iv. 3; v. 7, 8, is notoriously the same as the Hebrew חָכָם. But many of the names of kings, and of the higher civil officers, seem to be compounds of Semitic with the Parsi, Pehlvi, or Zend; such as Nebuchadnezzar, Belshazzar, &c. (See *Lex.*) The internal evidence, therefore, of a *mixture* of inhabitants in Chaldea, from some quarter or other, appears to be inscribed in high relief upon the language of the Chaldeans, in the time of Nebuchadnezzar. The religion of the Babylonians (as exhibited best of all by Münter in his essay on this subject, and by Gesenius in his Excursus at the end of his *Comm. on Isaiah*), affords striking evidence of Parsism and Polytheism commingled by the union of different nations who retained some of their respective rites, and by the natural progress of the attractive sensual parts of those rites, as the metropolis progressed in riches, and luxury, and debauchery.

This general view of the subject seems necessary, in order to place the reader of the book of Daniel in a position in which he may rightly estimate the various phenomena of the book. There is a mixture throughout of the Assyro-Median and Semitic, both in the names of men and offices, and also in the rites, customs, and opinions of the inhabitants. That the *Assyro-*Chaldean at the time when Daniel lived, was the common spoken language of the court and king, seems to be plainly *negatived*, by Dan. ii. 4, *seq.* The Magi address the king אֲרָמִית *i.e.,* in the *Aramean*, which is substantially the same that we now name *East Aramean* or *Chaldee.* In this language, more than half of the book of Daniel is composed. Doubtless the Jews who lived in that quarter when Daniel wrote the book, could read and understand it; and indeed to the younger part of them, at that period, it must have been vernacular, or nearly so. It is even quite probable, that the history contained in the book of Daniel would thus be more easily read by the younger portion of the Hebrew community in that region than if it had been in the Hebrew; and this, perhaps, might have been the inducement to write it in Aramean.

But to return to the הַכַּשְׂדִּים of our text; I have only to add, that this name, employed to designate a *literary order of men* (equivalent to חַכָּמִים, Chald. חַכִּימִין, and *Magi*), passed into very common use among the Greeks and Romans. So Strabo XV. Tom. III. p. 326, ed. Lips. Diod. Sic. 2. 29, *seq.* Cic. Div. 1. 1, 2. Ammian. Marc. 23. 6. Arrian Alex. 3. 16. In still later times, fortune-tellers and magicians from the East were called *Chaldeans* by European nations. The progress of meaning in regard to the appellation is obvious. First, the Chaldees are conquerors, and offices, or whatever else is eminent, are called Chaldean *par excellence.* Then, as Chaldea abounded in astrologers and soothsayers, it was natural for Greeks and Romans to call these classes of men by the name of *Chaldeans.* Last of all, among the western nations, soothsayers and magicians were called by the same name, without any special regard to the country from which they sprung. One meets, not unfrequently in the classics, with the appellation employed in this manner.

Several questions, of some importance in regard to the genuineness of the book of Daniel, have been recently made, first in regard to the *number* of classes specified in the verse before us, and then in respect to the employment of כַּשְׂדִּים, as designating only one portion of the Magi.

To begin with the latter; Gesenius (*Comm. in Es.* II. s. 355) seems to call in question the limited meaning of the word, and Bleek (on Dan. in *Schleiermacher,* &c., *Zeitschrift,* s. 225) even doubts whether there was any such thing as different classes. Both doubt against the evidence of usage widely extended. Daniel plainly uses the word to denote a *class* of the Magi, in ii. 2, 10; iv. 4 (Engl. Vers. iv. 7); v. 7, 11. And when Gesenius and Hitzig suggest, that in Dan. ii. 4, 10, the name *Chaldeans* is generically employed, Lengerke himself (sufficiently inclined to all which can make against the genuineness of the book), avers very justly that this is only in the way of breviloquence, where one class that is pre-eminent is named instead of recapitulating or particularizing all (*Comm.* s. 50). Decisive, as to the usage of such a method of expression by the writer, is Dan. iii. 24, where only the

הַדָּבְרִין (state-counsellors) are addressed, while ver. 27 shows that they are only one class of the state-officers then and there assembled, to witness the spectacle which is described. Such methods of breviloquence are quite common; and besides all this, we have heathen usage of the same kind as that under discussion; *e. g.*, Herodotus, 1. 181, οἱ Χαλδαῖοι, ἐόντες ἱερέες τούτου τοῦ θεοῦ [*i.e.*, βήλου], compare I. 183, where Χαλδαῖοι occurs three times in the same sense ; Diod. Sic. II. 24, τῶν ἱερέων, οὓς Βαβυλώνιοι καλοῦσι Χαλδαίους, and again in c. 29, Χαλδαῖοι τοίνυν τῶν ἀρχαιοτάτων Βαβυλωνίων . . . παραπλησίαν ἔχουσι τάξιν τοῖς κατ' Αἴγυπτον ἱερεῦσι ; and so Hesychius, Χαλδαῖοι, γένος Μάγων. Ctesias (edit. Bähr, p. 68) seems, indeed, to use *Chaldeans* and *Magi* as synonymes; and so, as we have seen above, later usage among Greeks and Romans often employed the words. But even in Ctesias, the context shows that by *Chaldeans* is there meant the *higher order* of the Magi. So in Dan. ii. 4, 10.

Thus much for the *limited* use of the name *Chaldeans*, which is sufficiently clear and certain. As to the *number* of the classes, with respect to which Lengerke (s. 49 f.) thinks he detects the error of a *later* writer who was not intimately acquainted with Chaldean matters, the question seems not to be one of any great difficulty. He admits, as do nearly all others, that there were *divisions* or *classes* among the Magi. This was notoriously the case as to the priests in Egypt, Ex. vii. 11. Herod. II. 36. 58. Jablonsky, *Panth. Egypt.* Prol. c. 3. The division of priests in India, from the remotest period, is well known. The Medes and Persians admitted the like divisions among their Magi. The author of Daniel, in ii. 2, iv. 4, (Eng. iv. 7), v. 7, 12, appears to name *five* classes of Magi (if indeed the מְכַשְׁפִים of ii. 2 be not merely another name for the גָּזְרִין of the other passages) ; on account of which Lengerke accuses him of mistake; and he declares (p. 47), that "all other ancient writers everywhere acknowledge only *three* classes," and concludes from this

that the writer of the book was some person of a later age and of a remote country, where tradition gave an indistinct and uncertain report. His authorities as to the "united report of all antiquity," are Jerome (*Contra Jovin.* I. p. 55), and Porphyry (*de Abstin.* 4. 16). These are somewhat late writers as to the matter of testifying, "for all antiquity," to a particular usage in Babylon about a thousand years before their time. But in fact neither of these give their own testimony. They both appeal to Eubulus. If Eubulus the philosopher is meant, he lived about 200 B.C. If either the comedian or the orator of the same name be meant (which seems not probable), they lived about 376 B.C. In his history of Mithra, Eubulus asserts, that "the Magi were divided into *three* classes." When? In his time, or at an earlier period ? Among the Persians, or among the Babylonians of Nebuchadnezzar's time? Unquestionably he refers to the *Persians*, inasmuch as the history of *Mithra* concerns them. But even admitting the correctness of the testimony at the time when it was given, it proves nothing in respect to the custom or usage at Babylonia, in the seventh century B.C. Magi indeed there were at Babylonia ; for among the military chieftains of Nebuchadnezzar, at the siege of Jerusalem in Zedekiah's time, was Nergal Sharezer רַב מָג, *chief Magian*. The priesthood, so far from excluding men from civil or military office in those times, was a leading recommendation of them to appointments of this nature, because it implied an unusual degree of knowledge. Thus Ctesias represents Belesys, the leader of the Chaldeans when Nineveh was destroyed, as "the most distinguished of the priests, οὓς Βαβυλώνιοι καλοῦσι Χαλδαίους," Diod. Sic. II. 24. So a Magian was elevated to the throne of Persia, after the death of Cambyses; Ctes. *Persica*, c. 13, *seq.* So, after the death of Nebuchadnezzar's father, while the former was carrying on the war in Judea, the affairs of government, before the return of the prince to Babylon, were administered by priests [ὑπὸ Χαλδαίων], and the supremacy was vested in the *archimagus*, who gave it up, in due time, to Nebuchadnezzar, according to Berosus in Joseph. *Antiq.* X. 11. 1. In fact the Oriental and Egyptian kings, as well as some of the Cæsars, paid the homage to the priesthood of becoming members of their body, if they were not already so when they became kings. It may, I readily concede, have been the usual fact, that the leading divisions of the *Persián* Magi were *three* in number.* But this would be of little avail in showing that such was the custom of the Babylonians, among whom, although the priesthood retained, as it would seem, the honorary name of *Magi*, yet their religion differed in the most striking manner, in many respects, from that of the Parsis. In the rites of the latter there was no temple, no altar, no sacrifice of human victims, no consumption by fire even of any victims, no images of gods, no prostitution-worship of Mylitta ; in a word none of the impurity, cruelty, ridiculous prodigality of expenditure, and abominable rites of the Babylonians. All matters of religion had been changed, by the commingling of the (Assyro-) Chaldean conquerors with the grosser and more sensual heathen of Babylonia, if indeed we concede such an intermixture. How then can testimony about the Magi in a country where pure Parsism prevailed, be applicable to the case of the Babylonian priests and literati, as described by Daniel? But if we must resort, in

the present case, to the testimony of Greek writers, the position of Lengerke is far enough from being confirmed. Diodorus Sic., in speaking περὶ τῶν ἐν Βαβυλῶνι καλουμίνων Χαλδαίων, represents them as practising astrology, soothsaying, magic, incantations, augury from the flight of birds, and the interpretation of dreams and remarkable occurrences, II. 29 ; all of which plainly betokens different classes.†
Strabo, most of all among the Greeks to be relied on in such matters, says (XVI. 1. § 6), " There are, among the Chaldean astronomers, γένη πλείω *many kinds* or *classes*, some are called *Orcheni*, and some *Borsippeni*, besides *many others* (ἄλλοι πλείους), who affirm different things in respect to their doctrines, according to their respective sects." Here then is abundance of room for the four or five classes of Daniel ; and it is indeed quite probable that the subdivisions must have amounted to many more, although it was not to his purpose to name any more than the leading ones. At all events, the testimony of Daniel stands high above any fair

* But this is not established by the *Zendavesta*, as cited by Heeren (*Ideen* I. s. 480, ed. 3d) ; for in Kleuker's edition, II. 261, only *two* classes are spoken of ; viz., *Herbeds* and *Mobeds.* But in *Yesht Sades* (LXXXIII. *ad fin.* II. p. 194), the *Avesta* speaks of the *three* orders of the *Athorne* = priests ; again (*ib.* p. 276), the same thing is mentioned ; once more (p. 156), "the *threefold*, like the Athorne." But in another passage *four* orders of priests seem to be designated. So in *Zendavesta,* III., p. 225, we find *Herbed* (= candidate for the priesthood), *Mobed* (priest), *Destur-Mobed* (teacher-priest), and *Destur Desturan* = (archbishop), a provincial superior. Probably the case is the same in the *Zendavesta* as in Daniel ; *i.e.*, sometimes the leading class only is noted, as in ii. 4, 10 ; then again we have four classes, in ii. 2 ; in v. 7 are three classes (one a new one) ; four classes in iv. 4 ; three in v. 7 ; and four in v. 11. To insist, now, that any one of these passages exhibits the full and exclusive designation of all the classes of the Magi, would be entirely nugatory.

† Certainly this assertion seems very probable, if we turn our attention, for a moment, to the divisions of the priesthood among the Greeks, in relation to such matters. With them every god and goddess had a separate order of priests ; and even the same orders differed from each other in different places. Again, each of these orders had a *high-priest* ; in some places, two ; the Delphians, five. Then there were *assistants* of the sacred order ; viz., the *Parasiti*, or those who provided materials for the celebration of religious rites, and then the Κήρυκες, or *criers*, who also acted the part of cooks and butchers. Besides these classes, there were the νεωκόροι, who kept clean and adorned the temples ; then the ναοφύλακες, who guarded these temples ; and lastly, the πρόπολοι, or general waiters ; Potter's *Gr. Antiq.* I. p. 222, *seq.* Beyond these general divisions, were subordinate ones almost without end ; *e. g.*, as to diviners, μάντεις, χρησμολόγοι, θεομάντεις, of three kinds ; interpreters of dreams, ὀνειροκρίται, ὀνειροσκόποι, ὀνειροπόλοι ; divination by sacrifices employed at least six classes ; by birds, at least as many more ; by lots, at least three ; by ominous words and things, many classes ; by magic and incantation, at least nineteen ; Potter, *ib.* pp. 327, *seq.* We must add to all this, that the priesthood among the Romans was arranged in quite a similar way. I do not aver that the Chaldeans made all of these subdivisions, which are almost endless ; but I may well say, that the offices which Diodorus ascribes to their Magi, involves, from the very nature of the case, something not unlike to this.

exception, in regard to the classification of the Magi. Certainly he has named no improbable class. Nearly all of the classes named, indeed, appertain to the priesthood of the heathen, as elsewhere exhibited in the Scriptures; and if there be a class *sui generis* in Daniel, there can be no good reason to charge him with error; for how can we reasonably suppose, that there was not some one class or more of the priesthood that was peculiar to Babylon?

The suggestion of Gesenius (*Comm.* II. p. 355), that the writer in all probability merely brought together the various designations of such classes of persons as are mentioned elsewhere in the Heb. Scriptures; and the assertion of Lengerke (p. 47), that "he undoubtedly did thus;" seem to have no other basis than an inclination to throw discredit upon the book, and industriously to collect and reckon up everything which may help to show that the writer was lacking as to accurate knowledge. Something more than this, however, seems necessary in order to discredit the book in question.

Equally nugatory seems to be the assertion of Bleek (*Schleierm*, &c., *Zeits.* s. 225), that "it is altogether wonderful, that Nebuchadnezzar should summon all classes of the Magi to interpret his dream, instead of summoning the appropriate class, viz., the ὀνειροσκόποι." It is enough to say in reply, that as Nebuchadnezzar had forgotten all the particulars of his dream, and these were required to be disclosed as well as the interpretation to be given; and moreover, since he knew, as the Magi assert (Da. ii. 10), that "no king or ruler was wont to make such a demand;" the very difficulty and extraordinary nature of the case would naturally induce him to summon all classes of his חַכִּימִין, so that what one class could not accomplish, another perhaps might be able to do. Nothing was more common among the Greeks and Romans, than, where one method of divination failed, to resort to another. Probability, therefore, and consistency are stamped upon the very face of the narrative, in regard to this matter.

One other objection against the pro-

bability of the narration in Dan. ii., has been strongly urged, viz., "the improbability that a *foreigner* should be admitted among the Magi; and above all, that a most rigid Jew could at all be promoted to *supremacy* over the whole order, as it is related of Daniel (ii. 48), that he became כָּל־חֲכִימֵי בָבֶל רַב־סִגְנִין עָל; or if he was promoted, that such a man as Daniel could accept the office, and discharge its duties."

That the Magi had a *supreme head*, is plain from Jer. xxxix. 3, where Nergal Sharezer, a military chieftain of Nebuchadnezzar, is named רַב מַג, *i.e.*, *arch-Magian*. So Sozomen (*Hist. Ecc.* II. 13) speaks of μέγας ἀρχίμαγος. Berosus, as cited by Athenæus (*Deipnos.* XIV. 44), in speaking of the Sakea (*i.e.*, Saturnalian feast) of the Babylonians, mentions the *overseer* as being arrayed in king-like robes, and as called Ζωγάνης (= סְגָן), which means *præfect*. Diodorus Sic. says of the priest Belesys, who led the Babylonians in revolt against Sardanapalus, that he was τῶν ἱερέων ἐπισημότατος. Every large town, province, and kingdom, had an ἀρχίμαγος, Zendav. III. p. 226.

That a foreigner, by special favour of the king, could be introduced among the Magi, seems quite probable from the usage of the Persians, who, although they excluded foreigners in general from that order, did this, as Philostratus (in *Protagora*) asserts, ἦν μὴ ὁ βασιλεύς ἐφῆ, *i.e.*, only in cases where the king did not demand his admission. The Magi, and all others, were at the disposal of the absolute monarch, either in Persia or in Babylon. So Brissonius, *de Regno Pers.* II. § 67, 68. So, likewise, Moses is said to have been "learned in all the wisdom of the Egyptians," being the adopted child of Pharaoh's daughter (Acts vii. 22). Lengerke, however, says: "We know nothing of his being admitted into the order of the priests." But we do at least know, that the Egyptian kings and princes, as a matter of honour and respect, were admitted to this order; nor is there any probability of Moses' being thus instructed, unless he had been admitted into that order.

That Daniel was a *Jew*, would, so far as we know, be no more objection to his promotion, in the eyes of Nebuchadnezzar, than if he had been a foreigner of any other country. This king does not seem to have used the Jews more roughly, than he did all his conquered subjects. That Daniel, as one of the Magi, was made a civil ruler, *i.e.*, Satrap of Babylonia (Dan. ii. 48), as well as Chief Magian, is perfectly in accordance with Oriental usage in general, and with that of Babylon in particular (Jer. xxxix. 3).

"But it must awaken great doubt," it is said, "when Daniel is described as holding the office of chief overseer, over priests who worshipped Bel and Mylitta." (Leng. p. 50). It might, I am ready to concede, if the acceptance of such an office obliged him to the personal performance of heathen rites. But it should be remembered, that *priests* were only a portion of the Magi. I do not say that Daniel's office was a *sinecure;* but I may say, that there was little or no probability, that as *chief* Magian he was subjected to perform the details of priestly rites. He decided cases of appeal; prescribed general rules of order ; participated in the studies of the Literati ; and (which seems to have been the king's special object in promoting him), received the honours and emoluments attached to his high station. Was it not quite possible for an intelligent man, so situated, to avoid participating in the details of heathen worship ? The whole book of Daniel shows him to be both conscientious and fearless. His station must have subjected him, indeed, to severe trials; but it also afforded him great opportunity to aid his exiled countrymen, and to mitigate the severity of their captive state. Reasonably may we suppose, that this was his motive for accepting the office.

Lengerke represents the author of the book of Daniel (who in his view belonged to the period of the Maccabees), as "evidently introducing Daniel among the Magi, that he might, by his interpretation of dreams, elevate the God of Israel above the vanities which the heathen worshipped " (p. 51). That the narration has such a purpose in view, I would readily concede ; but that the whole matter is a mere figment of a sagacious writer in the second century B.C., in order to accomplish such an end, is an assertion which needs some proof. The *ultima ratio*, in all such cases, of this writer, and of others who sympathize in feeling with him, is plain enough. It is simply the denial of all supernatural interposition and occurrences. Against such views, the present volume would not be an appropriate place for argument. The New Testament has given its clear and decided testimony in favour of the truthfulness of this book. A consistent man who renounces the book of Daniel as a record of true history, must also renounce the New Testament. My own belief is, that the God who made the world, *governs* it ; and that he can interpose, and has interposed, in respect to the regular and established order of things, where special purposes were or are to be accomplished that cannot well be brought about in another way.

Notes
on the
Old Testament

Albert Barnes

DANIEL
Volume 2

Baker Books

A Division of Baker Book House Co
Grand Rapids, Michigan 49516

Heritage Edition   Fourteen Volumes 0834-4

When ordering by ISBN (International Standard Book Number), numbers listed above should be preceded by 0-8010-.

Reprinted from the 1853 edition published
by Blackie & Son, London

Reprinted 2001 by Baker Books
a division of Baker Book House Company
P.O. Box 6287, Grand Rapids, MI 49516-6287

ISBN: 0-8010-0841-7

Printed in the United States of America

For information about academic books, resources for Christian
leaders, and all new releases available from Baker Book House,
visit our web site:
http://www.bakerbooks.com/

THE BOOK OF DANIEL.

CHAPTER VI.

§ I.—AUTHENTICITY OF THE CHAPTER.

THIS chapter, like the previous ones, has not escaped serious objections as to its authenticity and credibility. The objections which have been made to it have been derived from what is regarded as incredible in its statements. It is important, as in the previous chapters, to inquire whether the objections are insuperable, or whether this is so free from reasonable objection as to be worthy to be received as a portion of Divine truth. The objections, as urged by Bertholdt (*Daniel aus dem Hebräisch-Aramäischen neu übersetzt*, &c., pp. 72–75, and pp. 357–364) and by Bleek, are capable of being reduced to the four following :—

I. That it is wholly improbable that a monarch, in the circumstances of Darius, would give an order so unreasonable and foolish as that no one of his subjects should present any petition for a month to any one, God or man, but to himself. It is alleged that no good end could have been proposed by it; that it would have perilled the peace of the empire; that among a people who worshipped many gods—who had gods in all their dwellings—it would have been vain to hope that the command could have been carried peaceably into execution; and that, whoever proposed this, it could not have been executed without shaking the stability of the throne. Bertholdt

asks (p. 357, *seq.*), "Can one believe that, among a people so devoted to religion as the Babylonians were, it should have been forbidden them to address their gods for one single day? Is it credible that the counsellors of the king were so irreligious that, without fear of the avenging deities, they would endeavour to enforce such an order as that here referred to—that no petition should be addressed to God or man for a month, except to the king? And was Cyaxares so destitute of religion as not to refuse to sanction such a mandate? And does this agree with the fact that in the issue itself he showed so much respect to a foreign God—the God of the Jews? Under what pretence could the ministers of the king give him this counsel? Could it be under any purpose of deifying his own person? But it remains to be proved that either then, or soon after that time, it was customary in Asia to attribute Divine honours to a monarch, whether deceased or living."

To this objection, Hengstenberg (*Die Authentie des Daniel*, p. 125, *seq.*) replies, by an endeavour to show that it was a common opinion in Persia that the king was regarded "as a representative, and an incarnation of Ormuzd;" and that nothing is more probable than that such a monarch coming to the throne of Babylon would be willing to appear in that character, claiming Divine honours, and early testing the inclination of his new subjects to receive him in that character in which he was recognized in his own land. In confirmation of this, he quotes two passages from Heeren (*Ideen 3te Ausg*. I. i. p. 446, 51) in proof that these ideas thus prevailed. "The person of the king," Heeren says, "is in Asiatic kingdoms the middle point around which all revolves. He is regarded, according to the Oriental notions, not so much the ruler as the actual owner of the people and land. All their arrangements are formed on this fundamental idea, and they are carried to an extent which to Europeans appears incredible and ridiculous." "The idea of citizenship, according to the European nations, is altogether a strange idea to them; all, without exception, from the highest to the lowest, are the servants of the king, and the right to rule over them, and to deal with them as he pleases, is a right which is never called in question." Hengstenberg then remarks, that it is capable of the clearest proof that *the kings of the Medes and Persians were regarded and honoured as the representatives and incarnations of Ormuzd*. In proof of this, he quotes the following passage from Heeren (p. 474), showing that this idea early prevailed among the followers of Zoroaster. "Zoroaster," says he, "saw the kingdom of light and of darkness both developed upon the earth; Iran, the Medo-Bactrish kingdom, under the sceptre of Gustasp, is to him the image of the kingdom of Ormuzd; *the king himself is an image of him;* Turan, the Northern Nomadland, when Afrasiab reigned, is the image of the kingdom of darkness, under the dominion of Ahriman." This idea, says Hengstenberg, the magi made use of when they wished to bring the king to their own interests, or to promote any favourite object of their own. The king was re-

garded as the representative, the visible manifestation of Ormuzd, ruling with power as uncircumscribed as his; the seven princes standing near him were representatives of the seven Amshaspands, who stood before the throne of Ormuzd. The evidence that the Persian kings were regarded as an embodiment of the deity, or that they represented him on earth, Hengstenberg remarks (p. 126), is clear in the classic writings, in the Scriptures, and in the Persian monuments. In proof of this, he appeals to the following authorities among the classic writers:—Plutarch (*Themistocl.* cap. 27); Xenophon (*Agesil.*); Isocrates (*Panegyri de Pers. princ.* p. 17); Arrian (6. 29); Curtius (8. 5). Curtius says, *Persas reges suos inter deos colere.* For the same purpose, Hengstenberg (pp. 128, 129) appeals to the following passage of Scripture, Esth. iii. 4, and the conduct of Mordecai in general, who refused, as he supposes, the respect which Haman demanded as the first minister of the king, on religious grounds, and because more was required and expected of him than mere civil respect—or that a degree of homage was required entirely inconsistent with that due to the true God. In proof of the same thing, Hengstenberg appeals to Persian monuments, pp. 129-132. The proof is too long to be inserted here. These monuments show that the Persian kings were regarded and adored as impersonations of Ormuzd. To this may be added many of their inscriptions. In the work by De Sacy, *Memoires s. divers. Antiq. de la Perse*, Pl. i. p. 27, 31, the Persian kings are mentioned as ἔκγονοι θεῶν, ἐκ γένους θεῶν, and θεοῖ—both as offsprings of the gods, as of the race of the gods, and as gods.

If this is correct, and the Persian kings were regarded as divine—as an impersonation or incarnation of the god that was worshipped—then there is no improbability in the supposition that it might be proposed to the king that for a given space of time he should allow no petition to be presented to any one else, god or man. It would be easy to persuade a monarch having such pretensions to issue such a decree, and especially when he had subjected a foreign people like the Babylonians to be willing thus to assert his authority over them, and show them what respect and homage he demanded. In judging also of the probability of what is here said, we are to remember the arbitrary character of Oriental monarchs, and of the Persian kings no less than others. Assuredly there were as strange things in the character and conduct of Xerxes, one of the successors of this same Darius, as any that are recorded in this chapter of the book of Daniel; and if the acts of folly which he perpetrated had been written in a book claiming to be Divinely inspired, they would have been liable to much greater objection than anything which is stated here. The mere fact that a thing is in itself foolish and unreasonable, and apparently absurd, is no conclusive evidence that a man clothed with absolute authority would not be guilty of it.

To all that has been said on this point, there should be added a remark made by Bertholdt himself (p. 357) respecting Darius, which will show that what is here said of him is really not at all inconsistent with his character, and not improbable. He says, speaking of Darius or Cyaxares, that "from his character, as given by Xenophon, a man of weak mind (*Cyrop.* i. 4, 22; iv. 1, 13); a man passionate and peevish (iii. 3, 29; iv. 5, 8; v. 5; i. 8); a man given to wine and women (iv. 5. 52; v. 5, 44), we are not to ex-

pect much wisdom." There is nothing stated here by Daniel which is inconsistent with the character of such a man.

II. A second objection made to the probability of this statement is drawn from the character of the edict which Darius is said to have proclaimed, commanding that honour should be rendered to Jehovah, vers. 25-27. It is alleged that if such an edict had been published, it is incredible that no mention is made of it in history; that the thing was so remarkable that it must have been noticed by the writers who have referred to Darius or Cyaxares.

To this it may be replied, (1) that, for anything that appears to the contrary, Daniel may be as credible an historian as Xenophon or Herodotus. No one can demonstrate that the account here is not as worthy of belief as if it had appeared in a Greek or Latin classic author. When will the world get over the folly of supposing that what is found in a book claiming to be inspired, should be regarded as suspicious until it is confirmed by the authority of some heathen writer; that what is found in any other book should be regarded as necessarily true, however much it may conflict with the testimony of the sacred writers? Viewed in any light, Daniel is as worthy of confidence as any Greek or Latin historian; what he says is as credible as if it had been found in the works of Sanchoniathon or Berosus. (2.) There are, in fact, few things preserved in any history in regard to Darius the Mede. Comp. § II. The information given of him by Xenophon consists merely of a few detached and fragmentary notices, and it is not at all remarkable that the facts here mentioned, and the proclamation which he made, should be unnoticed by him. A proclamation respecting a foreign god, when it was customary to recognize so many gods, and indeed to regard all such gods as entitled to respect and honour, would not be likely to arrest the attention of a Greek historian even if he knew of it, and, for the same reason, it would be scarcely probable that he would know of it at all. Nothing would be more likely to pass away from the recollection of a people than such an edict, or less likely to be known to a foreigner. So far as the evidence goes, it would seem that the proclamation made no disturbance in the realm; the injunction appeared to be generally acquiesced in by all except Daniel; and it was soon forgotten. If it was understood, as it was not improbable, that this was designed as a sort of *test* to see whether the people would receive the commands of Darius as binding on them; that they would honour him, as the Persian monarch was honoured in his own proper kingdom, it would seem to have been entirely successful, and there was no occasion to refer to it again.

III. A third objection urged by Bertholdt (p. 361), is derived from the account respecting the lions in this chapter. It is alleged by him that the account is so full of improbabilities that it cannot be received as true; that though the fact that they did not fall on Daniel can be explained from the circumstance that they were not hungry, &c., yet that it is incredible that they should have fallen on the enemies of Daniel as soon as they were thrown into the den; that the king should expect to find Daniel alive after being thrown among them; that he should have called in this manner to Daniel, &c.

To all this it is sufficient to reply, that no one can suppose that the facts stated here can be explained by any natural causes. The whole representation is evidently designed to leave

the impression that there was a special Divine interposition—a miracle—in the case, and the only explanation which is admissible here is that which would be proper in the case of any other miracle. The only questions which could be asked, or which would be proper, are these two; whether a miracle is possible; and whether this was a suitable occasion for the miraculous exertion of Divine power. As to the first of these questions, it is not necessary to argue that here—for the objection might lie with equal force against any other miracle referred to in the Bible. As to the second, it may be observed, that it is not easy to conceive of a case when a miracle would be *more* proper. If a miracle was ever proper to protect the innocent; or to vindicate the claims of the true God against all false gods: or to make a deep and lasting impression on the minds of men that Jehovah is the true God, it is not easy to conceive of a more appropriate occasion than this. No situation could be conceived to be more appropriate than when an impression was designed to be made on the mind of the sovereign of the most mighty empire on the earth; or that when, through a proclamation issued from the throne, the nations subject to his sceptre should be summoned to acknowledge him as the true God.

IV. A fourth objection urged by Bleek (*Theologische Zeitschrift*, pp. 262-264) is, substantially, the following: that it is remarkable that there is in this account no allusion to the three companions of Daniel; to those who had been trained with him at the Chaldean court, and had been admitted also to honour, and who had so abundantly shown that they were worshippers of the true God. The whole story, says Bleek, appears to have been designed to produce a moral effect on the mind of the Jews, by the unknown author, to persuade them in some period of persecution to adhere to the God of their fathers in the midst of all persecution and opposition.

To this objection it may be replied, (1.) That it is wholly probable that there were many other pious Jews in Babylon at this time beside Daniel— Jews who would, like him, adhere to the worship of the true God, regardless of the command of the king. We are not to suppose, by any means, that Daniel was the *only* conscientious Jew in Babylon. The narrative evidently does not require that we should come to such a conclusion, but that there was something *peculiar* in regard to Daniel. (2.) As to the three companions and friends of Daniel, it is possible, as Hengstenberg remarks (*Authentie*, &c. p. 135), that they may either have been dead, or may have been removed from office, and were leading private lives. (3.) This edict was evidently aimed at Daniel. The whole narrative supposes this. For some cause, according to the narrative —and there is no improbability that such an opposition *might* exist against a foreigner advanced to honour at court —there was some ground of jealousy against him, and a purpose formed to remove or disgrace him. There does not appear to have been any jealousy of others, or any purpose to disturb others in the free enjoyment of their religion. The aim was to humble Daniel; to secure his removal from office, and to degrade him; and for this purpose a plan was laid with consummate skill. He was known to be upright, and they who laid the plot felt assured that no charge of guilt, no accusation of crime, or unfaithfulness in his office, could be alleged against him. He was known to be a man who would not shrink from the avowal of his opinions, or from the performance of those duties which he owed to his God. He was known to be a man so much devoted to the worship of *Jehovah*, the God of his people, that no law whatever would prevent him from rendering to him the homage which was his due, and it was believed, therefore, that if a law were made, on any pretence, that no one in the realm should ask anything of either God or man, except the king, for a definite space of time, there would be a moral certainty that Daniel would be found to be a violator of that law, and his degradation and death would be certain. What was here proposed was a scheme worthy of crafty and jealous and wicked men; and the only difficulty, evidently, which would occur to their mind would be to persuade the king to enter into the measure so far as to promulgate such a law. As already observed, plausible pretences might be found for that; and when that was done, they would naturally conclude that their whole scheme was successful. (4.) There is no improbability, therefore, in supposing that, as the whole thing was aimed at Daniel, there might have been many pious Jews who still worshipped God in secret in Babylon, and that no one would give information against them. As the edict was not aimed at them, it is not surprising that we hear of no prosecution against them, and no complaint made of them for disregarding the law. If Daniel was found to violate the statute; if he was ensnared and entrapped by the cunning device; if he was humbled and punished, all the purposes contemplated by its authors would be accomplished, and we need not suppose that they would give themselves any trouble about others.

§ II.—THE QUESTION WHO WAS DARIUS
THE MEDE.

Considerable importance is to be
attached to the question who was
" Darius the Mede," as it has been
made a ground of objection to the
Scripture narrative, that no person by
that name is mentioned in the Greek
writers.

There are three Medo-Persian kings
of the name of Darius mentioned in
the Old Testament. One occurs in the
book of Ezra (iv. 5; vi. 1, 12, 15), in
Haggai (i. 1; ii. 10), and in Zechariah
(i. 7), as the king who, in the second
year of his reign, effected the execution
of those decrees of Cyrus which granted
the Jews the liberty of rebuilding the
temple, the fulfilment of which had
been obstructed by the malicious representations which their enemies had
made to his immediate successors. It
is commonly agreed that this king was
Darius Hystaspis, who succeeded the
usurper Smerdis, B.C. 521, and reigned
thirty-six years.

A second is mentioned as " Darius
the Persian," in Nehe. xii. 22. All
that is said of him is, that the succession of priests was registered up to his
reign. This was either Darius Nothus,
B.C. 423, or Darius Codomanus, B.C.
336. See Kitto's Cyclop., art. Darius.

The remaining one is that mentioned
in Daniel only as Darius the Median.
In ch. ix. 1, he is mentioned as Darius
the son of Ahasuerus, of the seed of
the Medes. Much difference of opinion
has prevailed as to the person here intended; but a strict attention to what
is actually expressed in, or fairly deduced from, the terms used in Daniel,
tends to narrow the field of conjecture
very considerably, if it does not decide
the question. It appears from the
passage in ch. v. 30, 31, and vi. 28,
that Darius the Mede obtained the
dominion over Babylon on the death

of Belshazzar, who was the last Chaldean king, and that he was the immediate predecessor of Koresh (Cyrus)
in the sovereignty. The historical
juncture here defined belongs, therefore, to the period when the Medo-
Persian army led by Cyrus took Babylon (B.C. 538), and Darius the Mede
must denote the first king of a foreign
dynasty who assumed the dominion
over the Babylonian empire before
Cyrus. These indications all concur
in the person of Cyaxares the Second,
the son and successor of Astyages [Aha-
suerus], and the immediate predecessor
of Cyrus.—Kitto's Cyclop., art. Darius.

In reference to the question, who
was Darius the Mede, Bertholdt has
examined the different opinions which
have been entertained in a manner that
is satisfactory, and I cannot do better
than to present his views on the subject.
They are found in his Vierter Excurs.
uber den Darius Medus, in his Commentary on Daniel, pp. 843–858. I
will give the substance of the Excursus,
in a free translation :—

" Who was Darius the Mede, the
son of Ahasuerus, of whom mention is
made in the sixth chapter of the book
of Daniel, and again in ch. ix. 1, and
xi. 1? It is agreed on all hands that
he was the immediate successor of
Belshazzar, the king of the Chaldeans
(ch. v. 30). Comp. ch. vi. 1. But,
notwithstanding this, there is uncertainty as to his person, since history
makes no mention of a Median Darius.
It is, therefore, not to be wondered at
that various opinions have been entertained by commentators on the Scriptures, and by historical inquirers.
Conring (Advers. Chronol. c. 13), whom
many have followed, particularly Har-
enberg (Aufklärung des Buchs Daniels,
s. 454, seq.), has endeavoured to show
that Darius the Mede was the fourth
Chaldean monarch, Neriglissar, and

that Belshazzar, his predecessor, was Evil-Merodach. J. Scaliger (*De Emendat. Temporum*, p. 579, *seq.*) recognized in Darius the Mede the last Chaldean king in Babylon, Nabonned, and in Belshazzar, the one before the last, Laborosoarchod, which hypothesis also Calvisius, Petavius, and Buddeus adopted. On the other hand, Syncellus (*Chronogr.* p. 232), Cedrenus (*Chron.* p. 142), the Alexandrine Chronicle, Marsham (*Can. Chron.* p. 604, *seq.*), the two most recent editors of Æschylus, Schütz (in *zweiten Excurs. zu Æschylus's πεϱσαι*), and Bothe (*Æsch. dramata*, p. 671), held that Darius the Mede was the Median king Astyages, the maternal grandfather of Cyrus. Des Vignolles (*Chronologie*, t. 2. p. 495), and Schröer (*Regnum Babyl. Sect.* 6, § 12, *seq.*), held him to be a prince of Media, a younger brother of Astyages, whom Cyrus made king over Babylon. Another opinion, however, deserves more respect than this, which was advanced by Marianus Scotus, a Benedictine monk of the eleventh century, though this hypothesis is not tenable, which opinion has found, in modern times, a warm advocate in Beer (*Kings of Israel and Judah*, p. 22, *seq.*) According to this opinion, it was held that Darius the Mede is the same person as the third Persian king after Cyrus, Darius Hystaspis, and that Belshazzar was indeed the last Chaldean king, Nabonned, but that in the first capture of Babylon under Cyrus, according to the account of Berosus in (*Jos. c. Ap.* i. 20) and Megasthenes (in *Euseb. Præp. Evang.* ix. 44), he was not put to death, but was appointed by Cyrus as a vassal-king; and then in the second taking of Babylon under Darius Hystaspis (*Herod.* iii. 150, *seq.*), from whom he had sought to make himself independent, he was slain. This opinion has

this advantage, that it has in its favour the fact that it has the undoubted name of *Darius*, but it is not conformable to history to suppose that Darius Hystaspis was a son of Ahasuerus the Mede ; for his father, Hystaspis, was a native-born prince of Persia (Xenop. *Cyrop.* iv. 2, 46), of the family of the Achæmenides (*Herod.* i. 209, 210). Darius Hystaspis was indeed remotely related by means of the mother of Cyrus, Mandane, with the royal family ; but this relation could not entitle him to be called a Mede, for, since she was the mother of Cyrus, it is altogether inexplicable that since both were thus connected with each other, that Cyrus should be called *the Persian* (כָּרְסָיָא), and Darius *the Mede* (מָדָיָא), Dan. vi. 28, 29. The supposition, moreover, that Nabonned, after the taking of Babylon, was appointed as a tributary king by Cyrus, is wholly gratuitous ; since Nabonned, according to the express testimony of Xenophon (*Cyrop.* vii. 5, 26, *seq.*), was slain at the taking of Babylon.

"There is yet one other opinion respecting Darius the Mede, to which I will first prefix the following remarks : (1.) Darius the Mede is mentioned in ch. vi. 28 (29) as the immediate predecessor of Cyrus in Babylon. (2.) Belshazzar was the last Babylonish Chaldee king. (3.) The account of the violent death of Belshazzar, with which the fifth chapter closes, stands in direct historical connection with the statement in the beginning of the sixth chapter that Darius the Mede had the kingdom. (4.) Darius the Mede must, therefore, be the first foreign prince after the downfall of the Chaldean dynasty, which directly reigned over Babylon. (5.) The chronological point, therefore, where the history of Belshazzar and of Darius the Mede coincide, developes

itself: the account falls in the time of
the downfall of Babylon through the
Medo-Persian army, and this must be
the occasion as the connecting fact between the fifth and sixth chapters.
According to this, Darius the Mede
can be no other person than the Medish
king Cyaxares II., the son and successor of Astyages, and the predecessor
of Cyrus in the rule over Babylon ;
and Belshazzar is the last Chaldee
monarch, Nabonned, or Labynet.
With this agrees the account of Josephus (*Ant.* x. 11, 4) ; and later, this
opinion found an advocate in Jerome.
"The existence of such a person as
Cyaxares II. has been indeed denied,
because, according to Herodotus (i.
109), and Justin (i. 4, 7), Astyages
had no son. But it should be remarked,
that the latter of these writers only
copies from the former, and what
Herodotus states respecting Astyages
has so much the appearance of fable
that no reliance is to be placed on it.
It has been objected also that Dionysius
of Halicarnassus (b. i. §. 1) says that
the Medish kingdom continued only
through four reigns, so that if we
reckon the names of the reigning kings,
Dejoces, Phraortes, Cyaxares (the contemporary of Nebuchadnezzar), and
Astyages, there will be no place for a
second Cyaxares. But is it not probable
that Dionysius meant, by these words,
only that the Median kingdom came
to an end under the fourth dynasty ?
Finally, it has been objected that,
according to Herodotus (i. 128, *seq.*),
and Ctesias (Περσικ. 2 and 5), no
Median prince sat upon the throne in
Ecbatana after Astyages, but that with
Astyages the kingdom of the Medes
came to an end, and with Cyrus, his
immediate successor, the Persian kingdom took its beginning.   Therewith
agree nearly all the historians of the
following times, Diodorus (ii. 34),

Justin (i. 6, 16, 17, vii. 1), Strabo (ix.
p. 735; xv. p. 1662), Polyän (vii. 7),
and many others. But these writers
only copy from Herodotus and Ctesias,
and the whole rests only on their authority. But their credibility in this
point must be regarded as doubtful,
for it is not difficult to understand the
reasons why they have omitted to make
mention of Cyaxares II. They commenced the history of the reign of
Cyrus with the beginning of his world-
renowned celebrity, and hence it was
natural to connect the beginning of his
reign, and the beginning of the Persian
reign, with the reign of his grandfather
Astyages ; for, so long as his uncle
Cyaxares II. reigned, Cyrus alone
acted, and he in fact was the regent.
But if the silence of Herodotus and
Ctesias is not to be regarded as proof
that no such person as Cyaxares II.
lived and reigned, there are in favour
of that the following positive arguments :—
"(1.) The authority of Xenophon,
who not only says that a Cyaxares
ascended the throne after Astyages,
but that he was a son of Astyages
(*Cyr.* i. 5. 2), and besides relates so
much of this Cyaxares (i. 4, 7 ; iii. 3,
20 ; viii. 5, 19) that his *Cyropædia* may
be regarded as in a measure a history
of him. Yea, Xenophon goes so far
(viii. 7, 1) that he reckons the years of
the reign of Cyrus from the death of
Cyaxares II. Can any one conceive
a reason why Xenophon had a motive
to weave together such a tissue of falsehood as this, unless Cyaxares II.
actually lived? If one should object,
indeed, that he is so far to be reckoned
among fictitious writers that he gives
a moral character to the subjects on
which he writes, and that he has passed
over the difference between Cyrus and
his grandfather Astyages, yet there is
no reason why he should have brought

upon the stage so important a person, wholly from fiction, as Cyaxares. What a degree of boldness it must have required, if he, who lived not much more than a century after the events recorded, had mentioned to his contemporaries so much respecting a prince of whom no one whatever had even heard. But the existence of Cyaxares II. may be proved,

"(2.) From a passage in Æschylus (*Pers.* ver. 762, *seq.*)—

Μῆδος γὰρ ἦν ὁ πρῶτος ἡγεμὼν στρατοῦ
Ἀλλος δ᾽ ἐκείνου παῖς τό δ᾽ ἔργον ἤνυσε·
Τρίτος δ᾽ ἀπ᾽ αὐτοῦ Κῦρος, εὐδαίμων ἀνήρ,
κ.τ.λ.

The first who is here mentioned as the Mede (Μῆδος) is manifestly no other than Astyages, whom, *before* Cyrus, his son succeeded in the government, and who is the same whom we, after Xenophon, call Cyaxares. This testimony is the more important as Æschylus lived before Xenophon, in the time of Darius Hystaspis, and is free from all suspicions from this circumstance, that, according to the public relations which Æschylus sustained, no accounts of the former Persian history could be expected from any doubtful authorities to have been adduced by him. But the existence of Cyaxares II. does not depend solely on the authority of Xenophon, in his *Cyropædia*. For,

"(3.) Josephus (*Ant.* x. 11, 4), who speaks of this person under the name of Darius, adds, ᵗνῆ᾽Ἀστυάγους υἱός, ἕτερον δὲ παρὰ τοῖς Ἕλλησιν ἐκαλεῖτο ονομα—'he was the son of Astyages, but had another name among the Greeks.' This name, which he had among the Greeks, can be found only in their own Xenophon.

"(4.) To all this should be added, that many other data of history, especially those taken from the Hebrew writings, so set out the continuance

of the reign of the Medes over Upper Asia that it is necessary to suppose the existence of such a person as the Medish king, Cyaxares, after the reign of Astyages. Had Cyrus, after the death of Astyages, immediately assumed the government over Upper Asia, how happened it that until the downfall of the Babylonian-Chaldee kingdom mention is made almost always of the Medes, or at least of the Persians, of whom there is special mention? Whence is it that the passage of Abydenus, quoted from Megasthenes, p. 295, speaks of a *Mede*, who, in connection with a Persian, overthrew the Babylonish kingdom? Is not the Mede so represented as to show that he was a prominent and leading person? Is it not necessary to attribute to this fragment a higher authority, and to suppose that a Medish monarch, in connection with a Persian, brought the kingdom of Babylon to an end? Whence did Jeremiah, ch. l. and li., expressly threaten that the Jews would be punished by a Median king? Whence does the author of Isa. xiii. and xiv. mention that the destruction of the Chaldean monarchy would be effected by the Medes? The accession of Cyrus to the throne was no mere change of person in the authority, but it was a change of the reigning nation. So long as a Mede sat on the throne, the Persians, though they acted an important part in the affairs of the nation, yet occupied only the second place. The court was Medish, and the Medes were prominent in all the affairs of the government, as every page of the *Cyropædia* furnishes evidence. Upon the accession of Cyrus, the whole thing was changed. The Persians were now the predominant nation, and from that time onward, as has been remarked, the Persians are always mentioned as having the priority, though before they had but a secondary place. As the reign of Astyages, though he reigned thirty-five years (Herod. i. 130), could not have embraced the whole period mentioned to the accession of Cyrus, so the royal race of the Medes, and the kingdom of the Medes, could not have been extinguished with him, and it is necessary to suppose the existence of Cyaxares II. as his successor, and the predecessor of Cyrus." These considerations, suggested by Bertholdt, are sufficient to demonstrate that such a person as Cyaxares II. lived between the reign of Astyages and Cyrus, and that, after the destruction of Babylon, he was the immediate successor of Belshazzar, or Nabonned, and was the predecessor of Cyrus. He was the first of the foreign princes who reigned over Babylon. It has been made a question why, in the book of Daniel, he is mentioned under the name of *Darius*, and not by his other name Cyaxares. It may be difficult to answer this question, but it will be sufficient to remark (*a*) that it was common for Oriental kings to have many names, and, as we have seen, in regard to the kings of Babylon, one writer might designate them by one name, and another by another. This is indeed the occasion of much confusion in ancient history, but it is inevitable. (*b*) As we have seen, Josephus (*Ant.* x. 11, 4) expressly says that this Darius had another name among the Greeks, and, as Bertholdt remarks, it is natural to seek that name in the writings of their own Xenophon. (*c*) Darius was a common name in Persia, and it may have been one of the names by which the princes of Persia and Media were commonly known. Three of that name are mentioned in the Scriptures, and three who were distinguished are mentioned in profane history—Darius Hystaspis, Darius

Ochus, or Darius Nothus, as he was known among the Greeks, and Darius Codomanus, who was overthrown by Alexander the Great.

An important statement is made by Xenophon respecting Cyaxares II., the son of Astyages, which may account for the fact that his name was omitted by Herodotus and Ctesias. He describes him as a prince given up to sensuality, and this fact explains the reason why he came to surrender all authority so entirely into the hands of his enterprising son-in-law and nephew Cyrus, and why his reign was naturally sunk in that of his distinguished successor.— *Cyrop.* i. 5, viii. 7.

§ III.—ANALYSIS OF THE CHAPTER.

This chapter contains the history of Daniel under the government, or during the reign of Darius the Mede, or Cyaxares II., from a period, it would seem, soon after the accession of Darius to the throne in Babylon, or the conquest of Babylon, till his death. It is not indeed said how soon after that event Daniel was exalted to the premiership in Babylon, but the narrative would lead us to suppose that it was soon after the conquest of Babylon by Cyrus, acting under the authority of Cyaxares. As Daniel, on account of the disclosure made to Belshazzar of the meaning of the handwriting on the wall, had been exalted to high honour at the close of the life of that monarch (ch. v.), it is probable that he would be called to a similar station under the reign of Darius, as it cannot be supposed that Darius would appoint Medes and Persians entirely to fill the high offices of the realm. The chapter contains a record of the following events: (1.) The arrangement of the government after the conquest of Babylon, consisting of one hundred and twenty officers over the kingdom, so divided as to be placed under the care of three superior officers, or "presidents," of whom Daniel held the first place (vers. 1–3). (2.) The dissatisfaction or envy of the officers so appointed against Daniel, for causes now unknown, and their conspiracy to remove him from office, or to bring him into disgrace with the king (ver. 4). (3.) The plan which they formed to secure this, derived from the known piety and integrity of Daniel, and their conviction that, at any hazard, he would remain firm to his religious principles, and would conscientiously maintain the worship of God. Convinced that they could find no fault in his administration; that he could not be convicted of malversation or infidelity in office; that there was nothing in his private or public character that was contrary to justice and integrity, they resolved to take advantage of his well-known piety, and to make that the occasion of his downfall and ruin (ver. 5). (4.) The plan that was artfully proposed was, to induce the king to sign a decree that if any one for thirty days should ask any petition for anything of God or man, he should be thrown into a den of lions—that is, should be, as they supposed, certainly put to death. This proposed decree they apprehended they could induce the king to sign, perhaps because it was flattering to the monarch, or perhaps because it would test the disposition of his new subjects to obey him, or perhaps because they knew he was a weak and effeminate prince, and that he was accustomed to sign papers presented to him by his counsellors without much reflection or hesitation (vers. 6–9). (5.) Daniel, when he was apprised of the contents of the decree, though he saw its bearing, and perhaps its design, yet continued his devotions as usual—praying, as he was known

to do, three times a-day, with his face toward Jerusalem, with his windows open. The case was one where he felt, undoubtedly, that it was a matter of principle that he should worship God in his usual manner, and not allow himself to be driven from the acknowledgment of his God by the fear of death (ver. 10). (6.) They who had laid the plan made report of this to the king, and demanded the execution of the decree. The case was a plain one, for though it had not been intended or expected by the king that Daniel would have been found a violator of the law, yet as the decree was positive, and there had been no concealment on the part of Daniel, the counsellors urged that it was necessary that the decree should be executed (vers. 11–13). (7.) The king, displeased with himself, and evidently enraged against these crafty counsellors, desirous of sparing Daniel, and yet feeling the necessity of maintaining a law positively enacted, sought some way by which Daniel might be saved, and the honour and majesty of the law preserved. No method, however, occurring to him of securing both objects, he was constrained to submit to the execution of the decree, and ordered Daniel to be cast into the den of lions (vers. 14–17). (8.) The king returned to his palace, and passed the night fasting, and overwhelmed with sadness (ver. 18). (9.) In the morning he came with deep anxiety to the place where Daniel had been thrown, and called to see if he were alive (vers. 19, 20). (10.) The reply of Daniel, that he had been preserved by the intervention of an angel, who had closed the mouths of the lions, and had kept him alive (vers. 21, 22). (11.) The release of Daniel from the den, and the command to cast those in who had thus accused Daniel, and who had sought his ruin (vers. 23, 24). (12).

CHAPTER VI.

IT pleased Darius to set *a* over the kingdom an hundred and twenty *b* princes, which should be over the whole kingdom;

a 1 Pet. 2. 14.   *b* Esth. 1. 1.

2 And over these. three presidents, of whom Daniel *was* first; that the princes might give accounts unto them, and the *c* king should have no damage.

c Luke 19. 13, &c.; 1 Cor. 4. 2.

An appropriate proclamation from the king to all men to honour that God who had thus preserved his servant (vers. 25–27). (13.) A statement of the prosperity of Daniel, extending to the reign of Cyrus (ver. 28).

1. *It pleased Darius to set over the kingdom.* Evidently over the kingdom of Babylon, now united to that of Media and Persia. As this was now subject to him, and tributary to him, it would be natural to appoint persons over it in whom he could confide, for the administration of justice, for the collection of revenue, &c. Others, however, suppose that this relates to the whole kingdom of Persia, but as the reference here is mainly to what was the kingdom of Babylon, it is rather to be presumed that this is what is particularly alluded to. Besides, it is hardly probable that he would have exalted Daniel, a Jew, and a resident in Babylon, to so important a post as that of the premiership over the whole empire, though from his position and standing in Babylon there is no improbability in supposing that he might have occupied, under the reign of Darius, a place similar to that which he had occupied under Nebuchadnezzar and Belshazzar. In dividing the kingdom into provinces, and placing officers over each department, Darius followed the same plan which Xenophon tells us that Cyrus did over the nations conquered by him, *Cyrop.* viii. : Ἐδόκει αὐτῷ σατράπας ἤδη πέμπειν ἐπὶ τὰ κατεστραμμένα ἔθνη — "It seemed good to him to appoint satraps over the conquered nations." Compare Esth. i. 1. Archbishop Usher (*Annal.*) thinks that the plan was first instituted by Cyrus, and was followed at his suggestion. It was a measure of obvious prudence in order to maintain so extended an empire in subjection. ¶ *An*

hundred and twenty princes. The word here rendered *princes* (אֲחַשְׁדַּרְפְּנַיָּא) occurs only in Daniel in the Chaldee form, though in the Hebrew form it is found in the book of Esther (iii. 12; viii. 9; ix. 3), and in Ezra (viii. 36); in Esther and Ezra uniformly rendered *lieutenants.* In Daniel (iii. 2, 3, 27; vi. 1–4, 6, 7) it is as uniformly rendered *princes.* It is a word of Persian origin, and is probably the Hebrew mode of pronouncing the Persian word *satrap,* or, as Gesenius supposes, the Persian word was pronounced *ksatrap.* For the etymology of the word, see Gesenius, *Lex.* The word undoubtedly refers to the Persian *satraps,* or governors, or viceroys in the large provinces of the empire, possessing both civil and military powers. They were officers high in rank, and being the representatives of the sovereign, they rivalled his state and splendour. Single parts, or subdivisions of these provinces, were under inferior officers ; the satraps governed whole provinces. The word is rendered *satraps* in the Greek, and the Latin Vulgate.

2. *And over these, three presidents.* סָרְכִין. This word is found only in the plural. The etymology is uncertain, but its meaning is not doubtful. The word *president* expresses it with sufficient accuracy, denoting a high officer that presided over others. It is not improbable that these presided over distinct departments, corresponding somewhat to what are now called "secretaries"—as Secretaries of State, of the Treasury, of Foreign Affairs, &c., though this is not particularly specified. ¶ *Of whom Daniel was first.* First in rank. This office he probably held from the rank which he was known to have occupied under the kings of Babylon, and on account of his reputation for ability and integrity. ¶ *That the princes might give accounts unto*

3 Then this Daniel was preferred above the presidents and princes, because an excellent *a* spirit *was* in him : and the king thought to set him over the whole realm.

a ch. 5. 12; Prov. 17. 27.

4 ¶ Then *b* the presidents and princes sought *c* to find occasion against Daniel concerning the kingdom ; but they could find none occasion nor fault ; foras-

*b.*Eccl. 4. 4.   *c* Ps. 37. 12, &c.

---

them. Be immediately responsible to them ; the accounts of their own administration, and of the state of the empire. ¶ *And the king should have no damage.* Either in the loss of revenue, or in any maladministration of the affairs. Comp. Ezra iv. 13. "They pay not toll, tribute, and custom, and so thou shalt endamage the revenue of the kings." The king was regarded as the source of all power, and as in fact the supreme proprietor of the realm, and any malfeasance or malversation in office was regarded as an injury to him.

3. *Then this Daniel was preferred above the presidents and princes.* That is, he was at their head, or was placed in rank and office over them. ¶ *Because an excellent spirit was in him.* This may refer alike to his wisdom and his integrity—both of which would be necessary in such an office. It was an office of great difficulty and responsibility to manage the affairs of the empire in a proper manner, and required the talents of an accomplished statesman, and, at the same time, as it was an office where confidence was reposed by the sovereign, it demanded integrity. The word "excellent" (יַתִּירָא)

means, properly, that which hangs over, or which is abundant, or more than enough, and then anything that is very great, excellent, pre-eminent. Latin Vulgate, *Spiritus Dei amplior*—"the spirit of God more abundantly." Gr. πνεῦμα περισσόν. It is not said here to what trial of his abilities and integrity Daniel was subjected before he was thus exalted, but it is not necessary to suppose that any such trial occurred at once, or immediately on the accession of Darius. Probably, as he was found in office as appointed by Belshazzar, he was continued by Darius, and as a result of his tried integrity was in due time exalted to the premier-

ship. ¶ *And the king thought to set him over the whole realm.* The whole kingdom over which he presided, embracing Media, Persia, Babylonia, and all the dependent, conquered provinces. This shows that the princes referred to in ver. 1, were those which were appointed over Babylonia, since Daniel (ver. 2) was already placed at the head of all these princes. Yet, in consequence of his talents and fidelity the king was meditating the important measure of placing him over the whole united kingdom as premier. That he should form such a purpose in regard to an officer so talented and faithful as Daniel was, is by no means improbable. The Greek of Theodotion renders this as if it were actually done—καὶ ὁ βασιλεὺς κατέστησεν αὐτὸν, κ.τ.λ.—"And the king placed him over all his kingdom." But the Chaldee (עֲשִׁית) indicates rather a purpose or intention to do it ; or rather, perhaps, that he was actually making arrangements to do this. Probably it was the fact that this design was perceived, and that the arrangements were actually commenced, that aroused the envy and the ill-will of his fellow-officers, and induced them to determine on his ruin.

4. *Then the presidents and princes sought to find occasion against Daniel.* The word rendered *occasion* (עִלָּה) means a pretext or pretence. "The Arabs use the word of any business or affair which serves as a cause or pretext for neglecting another business."—Gesenius, *Lex.* The meaning is, that they sought to find some plausible pretext or reason in respect to Daniel, by which the contemplated appointment might be prevented, and by which he might be effectually humbled. No one who is acquainted with the intrigues of cabinets and courts can have any doubts as to the probability of what is here stated. Nothing has been

much as he *was* faithful, neither was there any error or fault found in him.

5 Then said these men, We shall not find any occasion against this Daniel, except we find *it* against

more common in the world than intrigues of this kind to humble a rival, and to bring down those who are meritorious to a state of degradation. The *cause* of the plot here laid seems to have been mere envy and jealousy—and perhaps the consideration that Daniel was a foreigner, and was one of a despised people held in captivity. ¶ *Concerning the kingdom.* In respect to the administration of the kingdom. They sought to find evidence of malversation in office, or abuse of power, or attempts at personal aggrandizement, or inattention to the duties of the office. This is literally "from the side of the kingdom;" and the meaning is, that the accusation was sought in that quarter, or in that respect. No other charge would be likely to be effectual, except one which pertained to maladministration in office. ¶ *But they could find none occasion nor fault.* This is an honourable testimony to the fidelity of Daniel, and to the uprightness of his character. If there had been any malversation in office, it would have been detected by these men.

5. *We shall not find any occasion,* &c. We shall not find any pretext or any cause by which he may be humbled and degraded. They were satisfied of his integrity, and they saw it was vain to hope to accomplish their purposes by any attack on his moral character, or any charge against him in respect to the manner in which he had discharged the duties of his office. ¶ *Except we find it against him concerning the law of his God.* Unless it be in respect to his religion; unless we can so construe his known conscientiousness in regard to his religion as to make *that* a proof of his unwillingness to obey the king. It occurred to them that such was his well-understood faithfulness in his religious duties, and his conscientiousness, that they might expect that, whatever should occur, he would be found true to his God, and that this might be a basis of calculation in any measure they might propose for his downfall. His habits seem to have

been well understood, and his character was so fixed that they could proceed on this as a settled matter in their plans against him. The only question was, *how* to construe his conduct in this respect as criminal, or *how* to make the king listen to any accusation against him on this account, for his religious views were well known when he was appointed to office; the worship of the God of Daniel was not prohibited by the laws of the realm, and it would not be easy to procure a law directly and avowedly prohibiting that. It is not probable that the king would have consented to pass such a law directly proposed—a law which would have been so likely to produce disturbance, and when no plausible ground could have been alleged for it. There was another method, however, which suggested itself to these crafty counsellors—which was, while they did not seem to aim absolutely and directly to have that worship prohibited, to approach the king with a proposal that would be flattering to his vanity, and that, perhaps, might be suggested as a *test* question, showing the degree of esteem in which he was held in the empire, and the willingness of his subjects to obey him. By proposing a law that, for a limited period, no one should be allowed to present a petition of any kind to any one except to the king himself, the object would be accomplished. A vain monarch could be prevailed on to pass such a law, and this could be represented to him as a measure not improper in order to *test* his subjects as to their willingness to show him respect and obedience; and at the same time it would be certain to effect the purpose against Daniel—for they had no doubt that he would adhere steadfastly to the principles of his religion, and to his well-known habits of worship. This plan was, therefore, crafty in the extreme, and was the highest tribute that could be paid to Daniel. It would be well if the religious character and the fixed habits of all who profess religion were so well understood that it was abso-

him concerning the law of his God.

6 Then these presidents and princes ¹assembled together to the king, and said thus unto him, King Darius, live *a* for ever.

1 or, *came tumultuously.*   *a* ver. 21; Neh. 2. 3.

7 All the presidents of the kingdom, the governors, and the princes, the counsellors, and the captains, have consulted *b* together to establish a royal statute, and to make a firm ²decree, that whoso-

b Ps. 2. 2.   2 or, *interdict.*

---

lutely certain that no accusation could lie against them on any other ground, but that their adherence to their religious principles could be calculated on as a basis of action, whatever might be the consequences.

6. *Then these presidents and princes assembled together.* Marg., *came tumultuously.* The margin expresses the proper meaning of the original word—

רְגַשׁ—*to run together with tumult.* Why they came together in that manner is not stated. Bertholdt suggests that it means that they came in a procession, or in a body, to the king; but there is undoubtedly the idea of their doing it with haste, or with an appearance of great earnestness or excitement. Perhaps they imagined that they would be more likely to carry the measure if proposed as something that demanded immediate action, or something wherein it appeared that the very safety of the king was involved, than if it were proposed in a sedate and calm manner. If it were suggested in such a way as to seem to admit of deliberation, perhaps the suspicion of the king might be aroused, or he might have asked questions as to the ground of the necessity of such a law, which it might not have been easy to answer. ¶ *King Darius, live for ever.* The usual way of saluting a monarch. See Notes on ch. ii. 4.

7. *All the presidents of the kingdom, the governors,* &c. Several functionaries are enumerated here who are not in the previous verses, as having entered into the conspiracy. It is possible, indeed, that all these different classes of officers had been consulted, and had concurred in asking the enactment of the proposed law; but it is much more probable that the leaders merely represented or affirmed what is here said in order to be more certain

of the enactment of the law. If represented as proposed by all the officers of the realm, they appear to have conceived that there would be no hesitation on the part of Darius in granting the request. They could not but be conscious that it was an unusual request, and that it might appear unreasonable, and hence they seem to have used every precaution to make the passing of the law certain. ¶ *Have consulted together to establish a royal statute.* Or, that such a statute might be established. They knew that it could be established only by the king himself, but they were in the habit, doubtless, of recommending such laws as they supposed would be for the good of the realm. ¶ *And to make a firm decree.* Marg., *interdict.* The word used (אֱסָר —from אָסַר—to bind, make fast) means, properly, *a binding;* then anything which is binding or obligatory—as a prohibition, an interdict, a law. ¶ *That whosoever shall ask.* Any one of any rank. The real purpose was to involve Daniel in disgrace, but in order to do this it was necessary to make the prohibition universal—as Herod, in order to be sure that he had cut off the infant king of the Jews, was under a necessity of destroying all the children in the place. ¶ *Of any god or man.* This would include all the gods acknowledged in Babylon, and all foreign divinities. ¶ *For thirty days.* The object of this limitation of time was perhaps twofold: (1) they would be sure to accomplish their purpose in regard to Daniel, for they understood his principles and habits so well that they had no doubt that within that time he would be found engaged in the worship of his God; and (2) it would not do to make the law perpetual, and to make it binding longer than thirty days might expose them to the danger

ever shall ask a petition of any god or man for thirty days, save of

thee, O king, he shall be cast into the den of lions.

of popular tumults. It was easy enough to see that such a law could not be long enforced, yet they seem to have supposed that the people would acquiesce in it for so brief a period as one month. Unreasonable though it might be regarded, yet for so short a space of time it might be expected that it would be patiently submitted to. ¶ *Save of thee, O king.* Perhaps either directly, or through some minister of the realm. ¶ *He shall be cast into the den of lions.* The word *den* (בֹּג) means, properly, a pit, or cistern; and the idea is that the den was underground, probably a cave constructed for that purpose. It was made with so narrow an entrance that it could be covered with a stone, and made perfectly secure, ver. 17. "The inclosures of wild beasts," says Bertholdt, pp. 397, 398, "especially of lions, which the kings of Asia and of North-western Africa formerly had, as they have at the present day, were generally constructed underground, but were ordinarily caves which had been excavated for the purpose, walled up at the sides, inclosed within a wall through which a door led from the outer wall to the space lying between the walls, within which persons could pass round and contemplate the wild beasts." "The emperor of Morocco," says Höst (*Beschreibung von Marokos und Fess*, p. 290, as quoted in Rosenmüller's *Morgenland, in loc.*), "has a cave for lions—Löwengrube— into which men sometimes, and especially Jews, are cast; but they commonly came up again uninjured, for the overseers of the lions are commonly Jews, and they have a sharp instrument in their hands, and with this they can pass among them, if they are careful to keep their faces towards the lions, for a lion will not allow one to turn his back to him. The other Jews will not allow their brethren to remain longer in such a cave than one night, for the lions would be too hungry, but they redeem their brethren out of the cave by the payment of money—which, in fact, is the object of the emperor." In another place (p. 77), he describes one

of these caves. "In one end of the inclosure is a place for ostriches and their young ones, and at the other end towards the mountain is a cave for lions, which stands in a large cavern in the earth that has a division wall, in the midst of which is a door, which the Jews who have the charge of the lions can open and close from above, and, by means of food, they entice the lions from one room into another, that they may have the opportunity of cleaning the cage. It is all under the open sky." Under what pretext the crafty counsellors induced the king to ratify this statute is not stated. Some one or all of the following things may have induced the monarch to sign the decree: (1.) The law proposed was in a high degree flattering to the king, and he may have been ready at once to sign a decree which for the time gave him a supremacy over gods and men. If Alexander the Great desired to be adored as a god, then it is not improbable that a proud and weak Persian monarch would be willing to receive a similar tribute. Xerxes did things more foolish than what is here attributed to Darius. Instances of this are not wanting. Of Holofernes, in Judith iii. 8, it is said that he "had decreed to destroy all the gods of the land, that all nations should worship Nabuchodonosor only, and that all tongues and tribes should call upon him as god." (2.) It may have occurred to him, or may have been suggested, that this was an effectual way to test the readiness of his subjects to obey and honour him. Some such test, it may have been urged, was not improper, and this would determine what was the spirit of obedience as well as any other. (3.) More probably, however, it may have been represented that there was some danger of insubordination, or some conspiracy among the people, and that it was necessary that the sovereign should issue some mandate which would at once and effectually quell it. It may have been urged that there was danger of a revolt, and that it would be an effectual way

8 Now, O king, establish the decree, and sign the writing, that it be not changed, according to the law [a] of the Medes and Persians, which [1] altereth not.

a Esth. 1. 19; 8. 8.   1 *passeth.*

9 Wherefore king Darius signed the writing and the decree.

of preventing it to order that whoever should solicit any favour of any one but the king should be punished, for this would bring all matters at once before him, and secure order. The haste and earnestness with which they urged their request would rather seem to imply that there was a representation that some *sudden* occasion had arisen which made the enactment of such a statute proper. (4.) Or the king may have been in the habit of signing the decrees proposed by his counsellors with little hesitation, and, lost in ease and sensuality, and perceiving only that this proposed law was flattering to himself, and not deliberating on what might be its possible result, he may have signed it at once.

8, 9. *Now, O king, establish the decree.* Ordain, enact, confirm it. ¶ *And sign the writing.* An act necessary to make it the law of the realm. ¶ *That it be not changed.* That, having the sign-manual of the sovereign, it might be so confirmed that it could not be changed. With that sign it became so established, it seems, that even the sovereign himself could not change it. ¶ *According to the law of the Medes and Persians, which altereth not.* Marg., *passeth.* Which does not *pass away;* which is not abrogated. A similar fact in regard to a law of the Medes and Persians is mentioned in Esther viii., in which the king was unable to recal an order which had been given for the massacre of the Jews, and in which he attempted only to counteract it as far as possible by putting the Jews on their guard, and allowing them to defend themselves. Diodorus Siculus (lib. iv.) refers to this custom where he says that Darius, the last king of Persia, would have pardoned Charidemus after he was condemned to death, but could not reverse what the law had passed against him.— Lowth. "When the king of Persia," says Montesquieu (*Spirit of Laws,* as quoted by Rosenmüller, *Morgenland, in loc.*), "has condemned any one to

death, no one dares speak to him to make intercession for him. Were he even drunk when the crime was committed, or were he insane, the command must nevertheless be executed, for the law cannot be countermanded, and the laws cannot contradict themselves. This sentiment prevails throughout Persia." It may seem singular that such a custom prevailed, and that the king, who was the fountain of law, and whose will was law, could not change a statute at his pleasure. But this custom grew out of the opinions which prevailed in the East in regard to the monarch. His will was absolute, and it was a part of the system which prevailed then to exalt the monarch, and leave the impression on the mind of the people that he was more than a man—that he was infallible, and could not err. Nothing was better adapted to keep up that impression than an established principle of this kind—that a law once ordained could not be repealed or changed. To do this would be a practical acknowledgment that there was a defect in the law; that there was a want of wisdom in ordaining it; that all the circumstances were not foreseen; and that the king was liable to be deceived and to err. With all the disadvantages attending such a custom, it was judged better to maintain it than to allow that the monarch could err, and hence when a law was ordained it became fixed and unchanging. Even the king himself could not alter it, and, whatever might be the consequences, it was to be executed. It is evident, however, that such a custom might have *some* advantages. It would serve to prevent hasty legislation, and to give stability to the government by its being known what the laws were, thus avoiding the evils which result when they are frequently changed. It is often preferable to have permanent laws, though not the best that could be framed, than those which would be better, if there were no stability. There is only one Being, how-

10 ¶ Now when Daniel *a* knew that the writing was signed, he went into his house; and his win-

a Luke 14. 26; Acts 4. 17-19.

dows being open in his chamber toward *b* Jerusalem, he kneeled upon his knees three *c* times a day,

b 1 Kings 8. 44, 48; Ps. 5. 7; Jon. 2. 4.
c ver. 13; Ps. 55. 17; Acts 2. 15; 3. 1; 10. 9.

ever, whose laws can be safely unchanging—and that is God, for his laws are formed with a full knowledge of all the relations of things, and of their bearing on all future circumstances and times. It serves to confirm the statement here made respecting the ancient custom in Media and Persia, that the same idea of the inviolability of the royal word has remained, in a mitigated form, to modern times. A remarkable example of this is related by Sir John Malcolm, of Aga Mohammed Khan, the last but one of the Persian kings. After alluding to the present case, and that in Esther, he observes, "The character of the power of the king of Persia has undergone no change. The late king, Aga Mohammed Khan, when encamped near Shiraz, said that he would not move till the snow was off the mountains in the vicinity of his camp. The season proved severe, and the snow remained longer than was expected ; the army began to suffer distress and sickness, but the king said while the snow remained upon the mountain, he would not move; and his word was as law, and could not be broken. A multitude of labourers were collected and sent to remove the snow; their efforts, and a few fine days, cleared the mountains, and Aga Mohammed Khan marched."—*History of Persia*, i. 268, quoted in the *Pict. Bible, in loc.*

10. *Now when Daniel knew that the writing was signed.* Probably there was some proclamation made in regard to that decree. ¶ *He went into his house.* That is, he went in in his usual manner. He made no change in his habits on account of the decree. ¶ *And his windows being open in his chamber.* Open in the usual manner. It does not mean that he took pains to open them for the purpose of ostentation, or to show that he disregarded the decree, but that he took no care to close them with any view to avoid the consequences. In the warm climate of Babylon, the windows probably were commonly open. Houses among the Jews in later times, if not in the time of the exile, were usually constructed with an upper chamber— ὑπερῷον — which was a room not in common use, but employed as a guest chamber, where they received company and held feasts, and where at other times they retired for prayer and meditation. See Notes on Matt. ix. 2. Those "upper rooms" are often the most pleasant and airy part of the house. Dr. Robinson (*Researches*, vol. iii. p. 417), describing the house of the American consular-agent in Sidon, says, "His house was a large one, built upon the eastern wall of the city; the rooms were spacious, and furnished with more appearance of wealth than any I saw in the country. An upper parlour with many windows, on the roof of the proper house, resembled a summer palace; and commanded a delightful view of the country towards the east, full of trees and gardens, and country-houses, quite to the foot of the mountains." ¶ *Toward Jerusalem.* It is not improbable that the windows were open on each side of the chamber, but this is particularly mentioned, because he turned his face toward Jerusalem when he prayed. This was natural to an exile Hebrew in prayer, because the temple of God had stood at Jerusalem, and that was the place where he abode by a visible symbol. It is probable that the Jews in their own country always in their prayers turned the face toward Jerusalem, and it was anticipated when the temple was dedicated, that this would be the case in whatever lands they might be. Thus in the prayer of Solomon, at the dedication, he says, "If thy people go out to battle against their enemy, whithersoever thou shalt send them, and shall pray unto the Lord toward the city which thou hast chosen, and toward the house which I have built for thy name," &c., 1 Ki. viii. 44. And again (vers. 46-49), "If they sin against thee, and thou be angry with

and prayed, and gave ^a thanks | before his God, as he did afore-
            a Phil. 4. 6. | time.

them, and deliver them to the enemy, so that they carry them away captives unto the land of the enemy, far or near; if they shall bethink themselves in the land whither they were carried captives, and repent—and pray unto thee toward their land which thou gavest unto their fathers, the city which thou hast chosen, and the house which I have built for thy name, then hear thou their prayer," &c. Comp. vers. 33, 35, 38. So in Psa. v. 7: "As for me, I will come into thy house in the multitude of thy mercy: and in thy fear will I worship toward thy holy temple." So Jonah ii. 4: "Then I said, I am cast out of thy sight; yet I will look again toward thy holy temple." So in the first book of Esdras (Apocrypha), iv. 58: "Now when this young man was gone forth, he lifted up his face to heaven, toward Jerusalem, and praised the King of heaven." Comp. Intro. § II. V. C. Daniel, therefore, in turning his face toward Jerusalem when he prayed, was acting in accordance with what Solomon had anticipated as proper in just such a supposed case, and with the prevailing habit of his people when abroad. This was not, indeed, particularly prescribed as a duty, but it was recognized as proper; and it was not only in accordance with the instinctive feelings of love to his country and the temple, but a foundation was laid for this in the fact that Jerusalem was regarded as the peculiar dwelling-place of God on earth. In the Koran it *is* enjoined as a duty on all Mussulmen, in whatever part of the earth they may be, to turn their faces towards the Caaba at Mecca when they pray: "The foolish men will say, What hath turned them from their Keblah toward which they formerly prayed? Say, Unto God belongeth the East and the West; he directeth whom he pleaseth to the right way. Thus have we placed you, O Arabians, an intermediate nation, that ye may be witnesses against the rest of mankind, and that the apostle may be a witness against you. We appointed the Keblah, towards which

thou didst formerly pray, only that we might know him who followeth the apostle from him that turneth back on his heels: though this change seem a great matter, unless unto those whom God hath directed. But God will not render your faith of none effect; for God is gracious and merciful unto man. We have seen thee turn about thy face towards heaven with uncertainty, but we will cause thee to turn thyself toward a Keblah that will please thee. Turn, therefore, thy face towards the holy temple of Mecca; and wherever ye be, turn your faces towards that place."—Sale's *Koran*, ch. ii. Wherever Mussulmen are, therefore, they turn their faces towards the temple at Mecca when they pray. Daniel complied with what was probably the general custom of his countrymen, and what was natural in his case, for there was, in the nature of the case, a *reason* why he should turn his face towards the place where God had been accustomed to manifest himself. It served to keep up in his mind the remembrance of his beloved country, and in his case could be attended with no evil. As all visible symbols of the Divine Being are now, however, withdrawn from any particular place on the earth, there is no propriety in imitating his example, and when we pray it is wholly immaterial in what direction the face is turned. ¶ *He kneeled upon his knees three times a day.* In accordance, doubtless, with his usual custom. The amount of the statement is, that he did not vary his habit on account of the command. He evidently neither assumed a posture of ostentation, nor did he abstain from what he was accustomed to do. To have departed from his usual habit in any way would have been a yielding of principle in the case. It is not mentioned at what time in the day Daniel thus kneeled and prayed, but we may presume that it was evening, and morning, and noon. Thus the Psalmist says: "Evening, and morning, and at noon, will I pray, and cry aloud; and he shall hear my voice" (Psa. lv. 17). No one can doubt

11 Then these men assembled, and found Daniel praying and making supplication before his God.

12 Then they came near,*a* and spake before the king concerning the king's decree; Hast thou not signed a decree, that every man that shall ask *a petition* of any god or man within thirty days, save of thee, O king, shall be cast into the den of lions? The king answered

a ch. 3. 8.   *b* ver. 8.
c ch. 5. 13.   *d* ch. 3. 12; Acts 5. 29.

the propriety of thus praying to God; and it would be well for all thus to call upon their God. ¶ *As he did aforetime.* Without making any change. He neither increased nor diminished the number of times each day in which he called upon God; nor did he make any change in the manner of doing it. He did not seek ostentatiously to show that he was a worshipper of God, nor was he deterred by the fear of punishment from doing as he had been accustomed to do. If it should be said that Daniel's habit of worship was ostentatious ; that his praying with his windows open was contrary to the true spirit of retiring devotion, and especially contrary to the spirit required of worshippers in the New Testament, where the Saviour commands us when we pray to "enter into the closet, and to shut the door" (Matt. vi. 6), it may be replied, (1) that there is no *evidence* that Daniel did this for the purpose of ostentation, and the supposition that he did it for that purpose is contrary to all that we know of his character ; (2) as we have seen, this was the customary place for prayer, and the manner of the prayer was that which was usual ; (3) the chamber, or upper part of the house, was in fact the most retired part, and was a place where one would be least *likely* to be heard or seen ; and (4) there is no evidence that it would not have been quite private and unobserved if these men had not gone to his house and listened for the very purpose of detecting him at his devotions. No one could well guard against such a purpose.

11. *Then these men assembled.* &c.

and said, The thing *is* true, according to the law of the Medes and Persians, which altereth *b* not.

13 Then answered they, and said before the king, That Daniel, *c*which *is* of the children of the captivity of Judah, regardeth *d* not thee, O king, nor the decree that thou hast signed, but maketh his petition three times a day.

14 Then the king, when he heard *these* words, was sore *e* displeased

e Mar. 6. 26.

Evidently with a *design* of finding him at his devotions.

12. *Then they came near.* That is, they came near to the king. They had detected Daniel, as they expected and desired to do, in a palpable violation of the law, and they lost no time in apprising the king of it, and in reminding him of the law which he had established. Informers are not apt to lose time. ¶ *The king answered and said, The thing is true,* &c. It is undeniable, whatever may be the consequences. There is no reason to suppose that he as yet had any suspicion of their design in asking this question. It is not improbable that he apprehended there had been some violation of the law, but it does not appear that his suspicions rested on Daniel.

13. *Then answered they — That Daniel, which* is *of the children of the captivity of Judah.* Who is one of the captive Jews. There was art in thus referring to Daniel, instead of mentioning him as sustaining an exalted office. It would serve to aggravate his guilt to remind the king that one who was in fact a foreigner, and a captive, had thus disregarded his solemn commandment. If he had been mentioned as the prime minister, there was at least a possibility that the king would be less disposed to deal with him according to the letter of the statute than if he were mentioned as a captive Jew. ¶ *Regardeth not thee,* &c. Shows open disregard and contempt for the royal authority by making a petition to his God three times a-day.

14. *Then the king, when he heard*

with himself, and set *his* heart on Daniel to deliver him ; and he

laboured till the going down of the sun to deliver him.

---

these *words, was sore displeased with himself.* That is, for having consented to such a decree without deliberation, or with so much haste—or for having consented to it at all. It is remarkable that it is not said that he was displeased with *them* for having proposed it ; but it is clear that he saw that the guilt was his own for having given his assent to it, and that he had acted foolishly. There is no evidence as yet that he saw that the decree had been proposed for the purpose of securing the degradation and ruin of Daniel—though he ultimately perceived it (ver. 24) ; or if he did perceive it, there was no way of preventing the consequences from coming on Daniel—and that was the point that now engrossed his attention. He was doubtless displeased with himself, (1) because he saw that he had done wrong in confirming such a decree, which interfered with what had been tolerated—the free exercise of religion by his subjects ; (2) because he now saw that it was foolish, and unworthy of a king, thus to assent to a law for which there was no good reason, and the consequences of which he had not foreseen ; and (3) because he now saw that he had involved the first officer of the realm, and a man of unsullied character, in ruin, unless some way could be devised by which the consequences of the statute could be averted. It is no uncommon thing for men to be displeased *with themselves* when they experience the unexpected consequences of their follies and their sins. An instance strongly resembling that here stated, in its main features, occurred at a later period in the history of Persia—an instance showing how the innocent may be involved in a general law, and how much perplexity and regret may be caused by the enactment of such a law. It occurred in Persia, in the persecution of Christians, A.D. 344. "An edict appeared, which commanded that all Christians should be thrown into chains and executed. Many belonging to every rank died as martyrs. Among these was an eunuch of the palace, named Azades,

a man greatly prized by the king. So much was the latter affected by his death, that he commanded the punishment of death should be inflicted from thenceforth only on the leaders of the Christian sect ; that is, only on persons of the clerical order."—Neander's *Church History,* Torrey's Translation, vol. iii. p. 146. ¶ *And set* his *heart on Daniel to deliver him.* In what *way* he sought to deliver him is not said. It would seem probable from the representation in the following verse, that it was by an inquiry whether the statute might not properly be changed or cancelled, or whether the penalty might not be commuted—for it is said that his counsellors urged as a reason for the strict infliction of the punishment the absolute unchangeableness of the statute. Perhaps he inquired whether a precedent might not be found for the abrogation of a law enacted by a king by the same authority that enacted it ; or whether it did not come within the king's prerogative to change it ; or whether the punishment might not be commuted without injury ; or whether the evidence of the guilt was perfectly clear ; or whether he might not be pardoned without anything being done to maintain the honour of the law. This is one of the most remarkable instances on record of the case of a monarch seeking to deliver a subject from punishment when the monarch had absolute power, and is a striking illustration of the difficulties which often arise in the administration of justice, where the law is absolute, and where justice seems to demand the infliction of the penalty, and yet where there are strong reasons why the penalty should *not* be inflicted ; that is, why an offender should be pardoned. And yet there is no improbability in this statement about the perplexity of the king ; for (1) there were strong reasons, easily conceivable, why the penalty should *not* be inflicted in this case, because (*a*) the law had been evidently devised by the crafty enemies of Daniel to secure just such a result ; (*b*) Daniel had been guilty of

15 Then these men assembled
unto the king, and said unto the
king, Know, O king, that the law
of the Medes and Persians *is*, That
no decree nor statute which the
king establisheth may be changed.

no *crime*—no moral wrong, but had
done only that which should commend
him more to favour and confidence;
(*c*) his character was every way upright
and pure; (*d*) the very worship which
he had been detected in had been up
to that period allowed, and there was
no reason why it should now be punished, and (*e*) the infliction of the
penalty, though strictly according to
the letter of the law, would be manifestly a violation of justice and equity;
or, in other words, it was every way.
desirable that it should not be inflicted.
(2.) Yet there was great difficulty in
pardoning him who had offended, for
(*a*) the law was absolute in the case;
(*b*) the evidence was clear that Daniel
had done what the law forbade; (*c*) the
law of the realm prohibited any change;
(*d*) the character and government of
the king were involved in the matter.
If he interposed and saved Daniel, and
thus suffered the law to be violated
with impunity, the result would be
that there would be a want of stability
in his administration, and any other
subject could hope that he might violate
the law with the same impunity. Justice, and the honour of the government,
therefore, seemed to demand that the
law should be enforced, and the penalty
inflicted. (3.) It may be added, that
cases of this kind are frequently occurring in the administration of law—
cases where there is a conflict between
justice and mercy, and where one must
be sacrificed to the other. There are
numerous instances in which there can
be no doubt that the law has been
violated, and yet in which strong
reasons exist why the offender should
be pardoned. Yet there are great
difficulties in the whole subject of *pardon*, and there are more embarrassments in regard to this than anything
else pertaining to the administration
of the laws. If an offence is *never*
pardoned, then the government is stern
and inexorable, and its administration
violates some of the finest and most
tender feelings of our nature—for there
are cases when all the benevolent feel-

ings of our nature demand that there
should be the remission of a penalty—
cases, modified by youth, or age, or
sex, or temptation, or previous character, or former service rendered to one's
country. And yet pardon in any instance always does just so much to
weaken the strong arm of the law. It
is a proclamation that in some cases
crime may be committed with impunity. If *often* exercised, law loses its
force, and men are little deterred from
crime by fear of it. If it were *always*
exercised, and a proclamation were
sent forth that *any one* who committed
an offence might be pardoned, the
authority of government would be at
an end. Those, therefore, who are
intrusted with the administration of
the laws, are often substantially in the
same perplexity in which Darius was
in respect to Daniel—all whose *feelings*
incline them to mercy, and who yet
see no way in which it can be exercised consistently with the administration of justice and the prevention of
crime. ¶ *And he laboured.* He sought
to devise some way in which it might
be done. ¶ *Till the going down of the
sun.* Houbigant understands this,
"Till the sun arose;" but the common
rendering is probably the correct one.
Why that hour is mentioned is not
known. It would seem from the following verse that the king was pressed
by his counsellors to carry the decree
into execution, and it is probable that
the king saw that the case was a perfectly clear one, and that nothing could
be hoped for from delay. The law
was clear, and it was equally clear that
it had been violated. There was no
way, then, but to suffer it to take its
course.

15. *Then these men assembled unto
the king.* The Chaldee here is the
same as in ver. 6, "they came tumultuously." They were earnest that the
law should be executed, and they probably apprehended that if the king
were allowed to dwell upon it, the
firmness of his own mind would give
way, and that he would release Daniel.

16 Then the king commanded, and they brought *a* Daniel, and

a Jer. 26.14; Acts 25.11.

cast *him* into the den of lions. *Now* the king spake and said unto Daniel, Thy God, whom thou

---

Perhaps they dreaded the effect of the compunctious visitings which he might have during the silence of the night, and they, therefore, came tumultuously to hasten his decision. ¶ *Know, O king, that the law,* &c. That is a settled matter about which there can be no debate or difference of opinion. It would seem that this was a point so well settled that no question could be raised in regard to it, and, to their minds, it was equally clear that if this were so, it was necessary that the sentence should be executed without delay.

16. *Then the king commanded,* &c. See Notes on ver. 7. Some recent discoveries among the ruins of Babylon have shown that the mode of punishment by throwing offenders against the laws to lions was actually practised there, and these discoveries may be classed among the numerous instances in which modern investigations have tended to confirm the statements in the Bible. Three interesting figures illustrating this fact may be seen in the *Pictorial Bible,* vol. iii. p. 232. The first of those figures, from a block of stone, was found at Babylon near the great mass of ruin that is supposed to mark the site of the grand western palace. It represents a lion standing over the body of a prostrate man, extended on a pedestal which measures nine feet in length by three in breadth. The head has been lately knocked off; but when Mr. Rich saw it, the statue was in a perfect state, and he remarks that "the mouth had a circular aperture into which a man might introduce his fist." The second is from an engraved gem, dug from the ruins of Babylon by

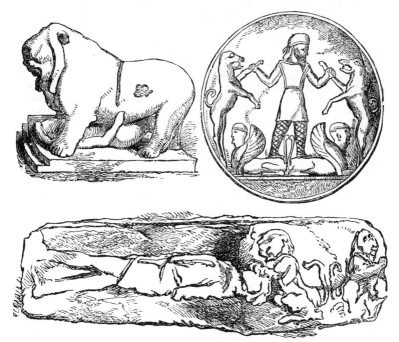

Captain Mignan. It exhibits a man standing on two sphinxes, and engaged with two fierce animals, possibly intended for lions. The third is from a

servest continually, he will *a* deliver thee.

17 And a stone *b* was brought,

a ch. 3. 17; Ps. 37. 39, 40. b Lam. 3. 53.

and laid upon the mouth of the den; and the king sealed *c* it with his own signet, and with the sig-

c Matt. 27. 66.

block of white marble found near the tomb of Daniel at Susa, and thus described by Sir Robert Ker Porter in his *Travels* (vol. ii. p. 416): "It does not exceed ten inches in width and depth, measures twenty in length, and is hollow within, as if to receive some deposit. Three of its sides are cut in bass-relief, two of them with similar representations of a man apparently naked, except a sash round his waist, and a sort of cap on his head. His hands are bound behind him. The corner of the stone forms the neck of the figure, so that its head forms one of its ends. Two lions in sitting postures appear on either side at the top, each having a paw on the head of the man." See *Pict. Bible, in loc.* ¶ Now *the king spake and said unto Daniel, Thy God,* &c. What is here stated is in accordance with what is said in ver. 14, that the king sought earnestly to deliver Daniel from the punishment. He had entire confidence in him, and he expressed that to the last. As to the question of *probability* whether Darius, a heathen, would attempt to comfort Daniel with the hope that he would be delivered, and would express the belief that this would be done by that God whom he served, and in whose cause he was about to be exposed to peril, it may be remarked, (1.) That it was a common thing among the heathen to believe in the interposition of the gods in favour of the righteous, and particularly in favour of their worshippers. See Homer, *passim.* Hence it was that they called on them; that they committed themselves to them in battle and in peril; that they sought their aid by sacrifices and by prayers. No one can doubt that such a belief prevailed, and that the mind of Darius, in accordance with the prevalent custom, might be under its influence. (2.) Darius, undoubtedly, in accordance with the prevailing belief, regarded the God whom Daniel worshipped as *a* god, though not as exclusively *the* true God. He had the

same kind of confidence in him that he had in any god worshipped by foreigners—and probably regarded him as the tutelary divinity of the land of Palestine, and of the Hebrew people. As he might consistently express this belief in reference to *any* foreign divinity, there is no improbability that he would in reference to the God worshipped by Daniel. (3.) He had the utmost confidence both in the integrity and the piety of Daniel; and as he believed that the gods interposed in human affairs, and as he saw in Daniel an eminent instance of devotedness to *his* God, he did not doubt that in such a case it might be hoped that he would save him.

17. *And a stone was brought, and laid upon the mouth of the den.* Probably a large flat stone sufficient to cover the mouth of the cave, and so heavy that Daniel could not remove it from within and escape. It was usual then, as it is now, to close up the entrance to sepulchres with a large stone. See John xi. 38; Matt. xxvii. 60. It would be natural to endeavour to secure this vault or den in the same way —on the one hand so that Daniel could not escape from within, and on the other so that none of his friends could come and rescue him from without. ¶ *And the king sealed it with his own signet.* With his own *seal.* That is, he affixed to the stone, probably by means of clay or wax, his seal in such a way that it could not be removed by any one without breaking it, and consequently without the perpetration of a crime of the highest kind—for no greater offence could be committed against his authority than thus to break his seal, and there could be no greater security that the stone would not be removed. On the manner of sealing a stone in such circumstances, comp. Notes on Matt. xxvii. 66. ¶*And with the signet of his lords.* That it might have all the security which there could be. Perhaps this was at the suggestion of his lords, and the design,

net of his lords, that the purpose might not be changed concerning Daniel.

18 ¶ Then the king went to his palace, and passed the night fast-

ing : neither were ¹ instruments of music brought before him ; and his sleep went from him.

19 Then the king arose very

on their part, may have been so to guard the den that the king should not release Daniel.

[In a chamber, or passage, in the south-west corner of the palace of Kouyunjik, Layard discovered "a large number of pieces of fine clay, bearing the impressions of seals, which, there is no doubt, had been affixed, like modern official seals of wax, to documents written on leather, papyrus, or parchment. Such documents, with seals in clay still attached, have been discovered in Egypt, and specimens are preserved in the British Museum. The writings themselves had been consumed by the fire

which destroyed the building, or had perished from decay." — "The seals most remarkable for beauty of design and skilful execution re-

present horsemen, one, at full speed, raising a spear, the other hunting a stag." But the most noticeable and important are two impressions of a royal signet; the one of Egyptian character, and the other representing a priest ministering before the Assyrian king. An engraved cylinder of translucent green felspar, found near the entrance of the palace, is conjectured to be the signet or amulet of Sennacherib, the presumed builder of the structure. The king stands in an arched frame, with his face to the sacred tree, which is surmounted by the symbol of Baal; and opposite to him is a eunuch. A goat, standing upon the lotus flower, occupies the rest of the cylinder. — *See annexed engravings.*]

¶ *That the purpose might not be changed concerning Daniel.* By the king. Probably they feared that if there was not this security, the king might release him ; but they presumed that he would not violate the seal of the great officers of the realm. It would seem that some sort of *concurrence* between the king and his nobles was required in making and executing the laws.

18. *Then the king went to his palace, and passed the night fasting.* Daniel was probably cast into the den soon after the going down of the sun, ver. 14. It was not unusual to have *suppers* then late at night, as it is now in many places. The great anxiety of the king, however, on account of what had occurred, prevented him from participating in the usual evening meal. As to the *probability* of what is here affirmed, no one can have any doubt who credits the previous statements. In the consciousness of wrong done to a worthy officer of the government ; in the deep anxiety which he had to deliver him ; in the excitement which must have existed against the cunning and wicked authors of the plot to deceive the king and to ruin Daniel ; and in his solicitude and hope that after all Daniel might escape, there is a satisfactory reason for the facts stated that he had no desire for food ; that instruments of music were not brought before him ;

early in the morning, and went in haste unto the den of lions.

20 And when he came to the den, he cried with a lamentable voice unto Daniel; *and* the king spake and said to Daniel, O Daniel, servant of the living God, is thy God, whom thou servest continually, able to deliver thee from the lions?

21 Then said Daniel unto the king, O king, live for ever.

22 My God hath sent his *a*angel,

a ch. 3. 28.

and that he passed a sleepless night. ¶ *Neither were instruments of music brought before him.* It was usual among the ancients to have music at their meals. This custom prevailed among the Greeks and Romans, and doubtless was common in the Oriental world. It should be observed, however, that there is considerable variety in the interpretation of the word here rendered *instruments of music*—דַּחֲוָן.

The margin is *table*. The Latin Vulgate, "He slept supperless, neither was food brought before him." The Greek renders it *food, ἐδέσματα.* So the Syriac. Bertholdt and Gesenius render it *concubines*, and Saadias *dancing girls.* Any of these significations would be appropriate; but it is impossible to determine which is the most correct. The word does not occur elsewhere in the Scriptures.

19. *Then the king arose very early in the morning*, &c. No one can doubt the *probability* of what is here said, if the previous account be true. His deep anxiety; his wakeful night; the remorse which he endured, and his hope that Daniel would be after all preserved, all would prompt to an early visit to the place of his confinement, and to his earnestness in ascertaining whether he were still alive.

20. *He cried with a lamentable voice.* A voice full of anxious solicitude. Literally, "a voice of grief." Such a cry would be natural on such an occasion. ¶ *O Daniel, servant of the living God.* The God who has life; who imparts life; and who can preserve life. This was the appellation, probably, which he had heard Daniel use in regard to God, and it is one which he would naturally employ on such an occasion as this; feeling that the question of *life* was entirely in his hands. ¶ *Whom thou servest continually.* At all times,

and in all circumstances: as a captive in a distant land; in places of honour and power; when surrounded by the great who worship other gods; and when threatened with death for your devotion to the service of God. This had been the character of Daniel, and it was natural to refer to it now.

21. *Then said Daniel unto the king, O king, live for ever.* The common form of salutation in addressing the king. See Notes on ch. ii. 4. There might be more than mere *form* in this, for Daniel may have been aware of the true source of the calamities that had come upon him, and of the innocence of the king in the matter; and he doubtless recalled the interest which the king had shown in him when about to be cast into the den of lions, and his expression of confidence that his God would be able to deliver him (ver. 16), and he could not but have been favourably impressed by the solicitude which the monarch now showed for his welfare in thus early visiting him, and by his anxiety to know whether he were still alive.

22. *My God hath sent his angel.* It was common among the Hebrews to attribute any remarkable preservation from danger to the intervention of an angel sent from God, and no one can demonstrate that it did not occur as they supposed. There is no more absurdity in supposing that God employs an angelic being to defend his people, or to impart blessings to them, than there is in supposing that he employs one human being to render important aid, and to convey important blessings, to another. As a matter of fact, few of the favours which God bestows upon men are conveyed to them directly from himself, but they are mostly imparted by the instrumentality of others. So it is in the blessings of liberty, in deliverance from bondage, in the provision

and hath shut *a* the lions' mouths, that they have not hurt me: forasmuch as before him *b* innocency was found in me; and also before thee, O king, have I done no hurt.

23 Then was the king exceeding glad for him, and commanded that they should take Daniel up out of

the den. So Daniel was taken up out of the den, and no manner of hurt was found upon him, because he believed in his God.

24 ¶ And the king commanded, and they brought those men *c* which had accused Daniel, and they cast *them* into the den of lions, them,

a Heb. 11. 33.   *b* Ps. 18. 20, 24; 26. 6.   *c* Deut. 19. 19.

made for our wants, in the favour bestowed on us in infancy and childhood. As this principle prevails everywhere on the earth, it is not absurd to suppose that it may prevail elsewhere, and that on important occasions, and in instances above the rank of human intervention, God may employ the instrumentality of higher beings to defend his people in trouble, and rescue them from danger. Comp. Psa. xxxiv. 7; xci. 11; Dan. ix. 21; Matt. xviii. 10; Luke xvi. 22; Heb. i. 14. Daniel does not say whether the angel was *visible* or not, but it is rather to be presumed that he was, as in this way it would be more certainly known to him that he owed his deliverance to the intervention of an angel, and as this would be to him a manifest token of the favour and protection of God. ¶ *And hath shut the lions' mouths.* It is clear that Daniel supposed that this was accomplished by a miracle; and this is the only satisfactory solution of what had occurred. There is, moreover, no more objection to the supposition that this was a miracle than there is to any miracle whatever, for (*a*) there is no more fitting occasion for the Divine intervention than when a good man is in danger, and (*b*) the object to be accomplished on the mind of the king, and through him on the minds of the people at large, was worthy of such an interposition. The design was evidently to impress the mind of the monarch with the belief of the existence of the true God, and to furnish in the court of Babylon proof that should be convincing that he is the *only* God. ¶ *Forasmuch as before him innocency was found in me.* (1.) Absolute innocency in reference to the question of guilt on the point in which he had been condemned—he having done only that which God ap-

proved; and (2) general integrity and uprightness of character. We need not suppose that Daniel claimed to be absolutely perfect (comp. ch. ix.), but we may suppose that he means to say that God saw that he was what he professed to be, and that his life was such as he approved. ¶ *And also before thee, O king, have I done no hurt.* That is, he had in no manner violated his duty to the king; he had done nothing that tended to overthrow his government, or to spread disaffection among his subjects.

23. *Then was the king exceeding glad for him.* On account of Daniel. That is, he was rejoiced for the sake of Daniel that he had received no hurt, and that he might be restored to his place, and be useful again in the government.

24. *And the king commanded, and they brought those men which had accused Daniel,* &c. It would seem probable that the king had been aware of their wicked designs against Daniel, and had been satisfied that the whole was the result of a conspiracy, but he felt himself under a necessity of allowing the law to take its course on him whom he believed to be really innocent. That had been done. All that the law could be construed as requiring had been accomplished. It could not be pretended that the law required that any *other* punishment should be inflicted on Daniel, and the way was now clear to deal with the authors of the malicious plot as they deserved. No one can reasonably doubt the *probability* of what is here said in regard to the conspirators against Daniel. The king had arbitrary power. He was convinced of their guilt. His wrath had been with difficulty restrained when he understood the nature of the plot against Daniel. Nothing, there-

their children,^a and their wives; and the lions had the mastery^b of them, and brake all their bones in

a Deut. 24. 16; 2 Kings 14. 6; Esth. 9. 10.

fore, was more natural than that he should subject the guilty to the same punishment which they had sought to bring upon the innocent; nothing more natural than that a proud despot, who saw that, by the force of a law which he could not control, he had been made a tool in subjecting the highest officer of the realm, and the best man in it, to peril of death, should, without any delay, wreak his vengeance on those who had thus made use of him to gratify their own malignant passions. ¶ *Them, their children, and their wives.* This was in accordance with Oriental notions of justice, and was often done. It is said expressly by Ammianus Marcellinus (23, 6, 81), to have been a custom among the Persians: "The laws among them (the Persians) are formidable; among which those which are enacted against the ungrateful and deserters, and similar abominable crimes, surpass others in cruelty, by which, on account of the guilt of one, all the kindred perish"—per quas ob noxam unius omnis propinquitas perit. So Curtius says of the Macedonians: "It is enacted by law that the kindred of those who conspire against the king shall be put to death with them." Instances of this kind of punishment are found among the Hebrews (Josh. vii. 24; 2 Sam. xxi. 5, *seq.*), though it was forbidden by the law of Moses, in judicial transactions, Deut. xxiv. 16. Compare also Ezek. xviii. ; Maurer, *in loc.* In regard to this transaction we may observe (*a*) that nothing is more probable than that this would occur, since, as appears from the above quotations, it was often done, and there was nothing in the character of Darius that would prevent it, though it seems to us to be so unjust. (*b*) It was the act of a heathen monarch, and it is not necessary, in order to defend the Scripture narrative, to vindicate the justice of the transaction. The record may be true, though the thing itself was evil and wrong. (*c*) Yet the same thing **substantially** occurs in the course of

pieces or ever they came at the bottom of the den.
25 ¶ Then^c king Darius wrote

b Ps. 54. 5.   c ch. 4. 1.

Providence, or the administration of justice now. Nothing is more common than that the wife and children of a guilty man should suffer on account of the sin of the husband and father. Who can recount the woes that come upon a family through the intemperance of a father? And in cases where a man is condemned for crime, the consequences are not confined to himself. In shame and mortification, and disgrace; in the anguish experienced when he dies on a gibbet; in the sad remembrance of that disgraceful death; in the loss of one who might have provided for their wants, and been their protector and counsellor, the wife and children *always* suffer; and, though this took another form in ancient times, and when adopted as a principle of punishment is not in accordance with our sense of justice in administering laws, yet it is a principle which pervades the world—for the effects of crime cannot and do not terminate on the guilty individual himself. ¶ *And the lions had the mastery of them.* As the Divine restraint furnished for the protection of Daniel was withdrawn, they acted out their proper nature. ¶ *And brake all their bones in pieces or ever,* &c. Literally "they did not come to the bottom of the den until the lions had the mastery of them, and brake all their bones." They seized upon them as they fell, and destroyed them.

25. *Then king Darius wrote unto all people,* &c. Comp. Notes on ch. ii. 47; iii. 29; iv. 1. If there is a probability that Nebuchadnezzar would make such a proclamation as he did, there is no less probability that the same thing would be done by Darius. Indeed, it is manifest on the face of the whole narrative that one great design of all that occurred was to proclaim the knowledge of the true God, and to secure his recognition. That object was *worthy* of the Divine interposition, and the facts in the case show that God has *power* to induce princes and rulers to

unto all people, nations, and languages, that dwell in all the earth; Peace be multiplied unto you.

26 I make a decree, That in every dominion of my kingdom men*a* tremble and fear before the God of Daniel ; for he *b is* the living God, and stedfast for ever, and his kingdom *c that* which shall not be

a Ps. 99. 1.   b ch. 4. 34.   c ch. 2. 44.
d Ps. 18. 50; 32. 7.   e ch. 4. 3.   1 *hand.*

destroyed, and his dominion *shall be even* unto the end.

27 He delivereth*d* and rescueth, and he worketh signs *e* and wonders in heaven and in earth, who hath delivered Daniel from the power 1 of the lions.

28 So this Daniel prospered in the reign of Darius, and in the reign of Cyrus *f* the Persian.

f ch. 1. 21; Ezra 1. 1, 2.

---

recognize his existence and perfections, and his government over the earth.

26. *I make a decree.* Comp. ch. iii. 29. ¶ *That in every dominion of my kingdom.* Every department or province. The entire kingdom or empire was made up of several kingdoms, as Media, Persia, Babylonia, &c. The meaning is, that he wished the God of Daniel to be honoured and reverenced throughout the whole empire. ¶ *Men tremble and fear before the God of Daniel.* That they honour and reverence him as God. There is no certain evidence that he meant that he should be honoured as the *only* God; but the probability is, that he meant that he should be recognized as a God of great power and glory, and as worthy of universal reverence. How far this heathen monarch might still regard the other deities worshipped in the empire as gods, or how far his own heart might be disposed to honour the God of Daniel, there are no means of ascertaining. It was much, however, that so great a monarch should be led to make a proclamation acknowledging the God of Daniel as having a real existence, and as entitled to universal reverence. ¶ *For he* is *the living God.* An appellation often given to God in the Scriptures, and probably learned by Darius from Daniel. It is not, however, absolutely certain that Darius would attach *all* the ideas to these phrases which Daniel did, or which we would. The attributes here ascribed to God are correct, and the views expressed are far beyond any that prevailed among the heathen; but still it would not be proper to suppose that Darius certainly had all the views of God which these words would convey

to us now. ¶ *And stedfast for ever.* That is, he is always the same. He ever lives; he has power over all; his kingdom is on an immovable foundation. He is not, in his government, to cease to exist, and to be succeeded by another who shall occupy his throne. ¶ *And his kingdom* that *which shall not be destroyed,* &c. See Notes on ch. iv. 3, 34. The similarity between the language used here, and that employed by Nebuchadnezzar, shows that it was probably derived from the same source. It is to be presumed that both monarchs expressed the views which they had learned from Daniel.

27. *He delivereth and rescueth.* As in the case of Daniel. This attribute would of course be prominent in the view of Darius, since so remarkable an instance of his power had been recently manifested in rescuing Daniel. ¶ *And he worketh signs and wonders,* &c. Performs miracles far above all human power. If he had done it on earth in the case of Daniel, it was fair to infer that he did it also in heaven. Comp. Notes, ch. iv. 2, 3. ¶ *The power of the lions.* Marg., *hand.* The hand is the instrument of power. The word *paw* would express the idea here, and would accord with the meaning, as it is usually with the paw that the lion strikes down his prey before he devours it.

28. *So this Daniel prospered in the reign of Darius.* That is, to the end of his reign. It is fairly implied here that he was restored to his honours. ¶ *And in the reign of Cyrus the Persian.* Cyrus the Great, the nephew and successor of Darius. For an account of Cyrus, see Notes on Isa. xli. 2. How *long* during the reign of Cyrus

Daniel "prospered" or lived is not said. During a part of the reign of Darius or Cyaxares, he was occupied busily in securing by his influence the welfare of his own people, and making arrangements for their return to their land; and his high post in the nation to which, under Divine Providence, he had doubtless been raised for this purpose, enabled him to render essential and invaluable service at the court. In the third year of Cyrus, we are informed (ch. x.–xii.), he had a series of visions respecting the future history and sufferings of his nation to the period of their true redemption through the Messiah, as also a consolatory direction to himself to proceed calmly and peaceably to the end of his days, and then await patiently the resurrection of the dead, ch. xii. 12, 13. From that period the accounts respecting him are vague, confused, and even strange, and little or nothing is known of the time or circumstances of his death. Comp. Intro. § I.

From this chapter we may derive the following instructive

PRACTICAL LESSONS.

(1.) We have an instance of what often occurs in the world—of *envy* on account of the excellency of others, and of the honours which they obtain by their talent and their worth, vers. 1–4. Nothing is more frequent than such envy, and nothing more common, as a consequence, than a determination to degrade those who are the subjects of it. Envy always seeks in some way to humble and mortify those who are distinguished. It is the pain, mortification, chagrin, and regret which we have at their superior excellence or prosperity, and this prompts us to endeavour to bring them down to our own level, or below it; to calumniate their characters; to hinder their prosperity; to embarrass them in their plans; to take up and circulate rumours to their disadvantage; to magnify their faults, or to fasten upon them the suspicion of crime. In the instance be-

fore us, we see the effect in a most guilty conspiracy against a man of incorruptible character; a man full in the confidence of his sovereign; a man eminently the friend of virtue and of God.

" Envy will merit, as its shade, pursue;
But, like a shadow, proves the substance true."
—Pope's *Essay on Criticism*

" Base envy withers at another's joy,
And hates that excellence it cannot reach."
—Thomson's *Seasons*.

" Be thou as chaste as ice, as pure as snow,
Thou shalt not escape calumny."
—Shakspeare.

" That thou art blamed shall not be thy defect,
For slander's mark was ever yet the fair:
So thou be good, slander doth yet approve
Thy worth the greater."
—Shakspeare.

(2.) We have in this chapter (vers. 4–9) a striking illustration of the nature and the evils of a *conspiracy* to ruin others. The plan here was deliberately formed to ruin Daniel—the best man in the realm—a man against whom no charge of guilt could be alleged, who had done the conspirators no wrong; who had rendered himself in no way amenable to the laws. A "conspiracy" is a combination of men for evil purposes; an agreement between two or more persons to commit some crime in concert, usually treason, or an insurrection against a government or state. In this case, it was a plot growing wholly out of envy or jealousy; a concerted agreement to ruin a good man, where no wrong had been done or could be pretended, and no crime had been committed. The essential things in this conspiracy, as in all other cases of conspiracy, were two: (*a*) that the purpose was *evil;* and (*b*) that it was to be accomplished by the combined influences of *numbers*. The means on which they relied, or the grounds of calculation on the success of their plot, were the following: (1) that they could calculate on the unwavering integrity of Daniel—on his firm and faithful adherence to the principles of his religion in all circumstances, and in all times of temptation and trial; and (2) that they could induce the king to pass a law, irrepealable from the nature of the case, which Daniel would be certain to violate, and to the penalty of which, therefore, he would be certainly exposed. Now in this purpose there was every element of iniquity, and the grossest conceivable wrong. There were combined all the evils of envy and malice; of perverting and abusing their influence over the king; of secresy in taking advantage of one who did not suspect any such design; and of involving the king himself in the necessity of exposing the best man in his realm, and the highest officer of state, to the certain danger of death. The result, however, showed, as is often the case, that the evil recoiled on themselves, and that the very calamity overwhelmed them and their families which they had designed for another.

(3.) We have here a striking instance of what often occurs, and what should always occur, among the friends of religion, that "no occasion can be found against them except in regard to the law of their God"—on the score of their religion, ver. 5. Daniel was known to be upright. His character for integrity was above suspicion. It was certain that there was no hope of bringing any charge against him that would lie, for any want of uprightness or honesty; for any failure in the discharge of the duties of his office; for any malversation in administering the affairs of the government; for any embezzlement of the public funds, or for any act of injustice towards his fellow-men. It was certain that his character was irreproachable on all these points; and it was equally certain that he did and would maintain unwavering fidelity in the duties of religion. Whatever consequences might follow from it, it was

clear that they could calculate on his maintaining with faithfulness the duties of piety. Whatever plot, therefore, could be formed against him on the basis either of his moral integrity or his piety, it was certain would be successful. But there was no hope in regard to the former, for no law could have been carried prohibiting his doing what was right on the subject of morals. The only hope, therefore, was in respect to his religion; and the main idea in their plot—the thing which constituted the basis of their plan was, *that it was certain that Daniel would maintain his fidelity to his God irrespective of any consequences whatever.* This certainty ought to exist in regard to every good man; every man professing religion. His character ought to be so well understood; his piety ought to be so firm, unwavering, and consistent, that it could be calculated on just as certainly as we calculate on the stability of the laws of nature, that he will be found faithful to his religious duties and obligations. There *are* such men, and the character of every man *should be* such. Then indeed we should know what to depend on in the world; then religion would be respected as it should be.

(4.) We may learn what is our *duty* when we are opposed in the exercise of our religion, or when we are in any way threatened with loss of office, or of property, on account of our religion, ver. 10. *We are to persevere in the discharge of our religious duties, whatever may be the consequences.* So far as the example of Daniel goes, this would involve two things: (*a*) not to swerve from the faithful performance of duty, or not to be deterred from it; and (*b*) not to change our course from any desire of display. These two things were manifested by Daniel. He kept steadily on his way. He did **not** abridge the number of times of his daily devotion; nor, as far as appears, did he change the form or the length. He did not cease to pray in an audible voice; he did not give up prayer in the daytime, and pray only at night; he did not even close his windows; he did not take any precautions to pray when none were near; he did not withdraw into an inner chamber. At the same time, he made no changes in his devotion for the sake of ostentation. He did not open his windows before closed; he did not go into the street; he did not call around him his friends or foes to witness his devotions; he did not, as far as appears, either elevate his voice, or prolong his prayers, in order to attract attention, or to invite persecution. In all this he manifested the true spirit of religion, and set an example to men to be followed in all ages. Not by the loss of fame or money; by the dread of persecution, or contempt of death; by the threatenings of law or the fear of shame, are we to be deterred from the proper and the usual performance of our religious duties; nor by a desire to provoke persecution, and to win the crown of martyrdom, and to elicit applause, and to have our names blazoned abroad, are we to multiply our religious acts, or make an ostentatious display of them, when we are threatened, or when we know that our conduct will excite opposition. We are to ascertain what is right and proper; and then we are modestly and firmly to do it, no matter what may be the consequences. Comp. Matt. v. 16; Acts iv. 16–20; v. 29.

(5.) We have, in the case of Darius, an instance of what often happens, the regret and anguish which the mind experiences in consequence of a rash act, when it cannot be repaired, ver. 14. The act of Darius in making the de-

cree was eminently a rash one. It was done without deliberation at the suggestion of others, and probably under the influence of some very improper feeling—the desire of being esteemed as a god. But it had consequences which he did not foresee, consequences which, if he had foreseen them, would doubtless have prevented his giving a sanction to this iniquitous law. The state of mind which he experienced when he saw how the act involved the best officer in his government, and the best man in his realm, was just what might have been expected, and is an illustration of what often occurs. It was too late now to prevent the effects of the act; and his mind was overwhelmed with remorse and sorrow. He blamed himself for his folly; and he sought in vain for some way to turn aside the consequences which he now deplored. Such instances often occur. (a) Many of our acts are *rash*. They are performed without deliberation; under the influence of improper passions; at the suggestion of others who would be thought to be our friends; and without any clear view of the consequences, or any concern as to what the result may be. (b) As an effect, they often have consequences which we did not anticipate, and which would have deterred us in each instance had we foreseen them. (c) They often produce regret and anguish when too late, and when we cannot prevent the evil. The train of evils which has been commenced it is now too late to retard or prevent, and they now inevitably come upon us. We can only stand and weep over the effects of our rashness and folly; and must now feel that if the evil *is* averted, it will be by the interposition of God alone.

(6.) We have in this chapter an affecting instance of the evils which often arise in a human government from

the want of something like an atonement, ver. 14, *seq.* As has been remarked in the Notes, cases often arise
when it is desirable that pardon should
be extended to the violators of law.
See Notes on ver. 14. In such cases,
some such arrangement as that of an
atonement, by which the honour of the
law might be maintained, and at the
same time the merciful feelings of an
executive might be indulged, and the
benevolent wishes of a community
gratified, would remove difficulties
which are now felt in every administration. The difficulties in the case,
and the advantage which would arise
from an atonement, may be seen by a
brief reference to the circumstances of
the case before us : (*a*) the law was inexorable. It demanded punishment,
as all law does ; for no law in itself
makes any provision for pardon. If
it did, it would be a burlesque on all
legislation. Law denounces penalty ;
it does not pardon or show mercy. It
has become necessary indeed to lodge
a pardoning power with some *man* intrusted with the administration of the
laws, but the pardon is not extended
by the law itself. (*b*) The anxiety of
the king in the case is an illustration
of what often occurs in the administration of law ; for, as above observed,
there *are* cases where, on many accounts, it would seem to be desirable
that the penalty of the law should not
be inflicted. Such a case was that of
Dr. Dodd, in London, in which a petition, signed by thirty thousand names,
was presented, praying for the remission of the penalty of death. Such a
case was that of Major Andrè, when
Washington shed tears at the necessity
of signing the death-warrant of so
young and so accomplished an officer.
Such cases often occur, in which there
is the deepest anxiety in the bosom of

an executive to see if there is not some
way by which the infliction of the penalty of the law may be avoided.
(*c*) Yet there was in the case of Darius
no possibility of a change, and this too
is an illustration of what often occurs.
The law was inexorable. It could not
be repealed. So now there are instances where the penalty of law *cannot* be avoided consistently with the welfare of a community. Punishment *must*
be inflicted, or all law become a nullity.
An instance of this kind was that of
Dr. Dodd. He was convicted of forgery. So important had it been deemed
for the welfare of a commercial community that *that* crime should be prevented, that no one ever had been
pardoned for it, and it was felt that no
one should be. Such an instance was
that of Major Andrè. The safety and
welfare of the whole army, and the
success of the cause, seemed to demand
that the offence should not go unpunished. (*d*) Yet there are difficulties in extending pardon to the guilty ;
(1) if it *is done at all*, it always does so
much to weaken the strong arm of the
law, and if *often* done, it makes law a
nullity ; and (2) if it is *never* done, the
law seems stern and inexorable, and
the finer feelings of our nature, and
the benevolent wishes of the community, are disregarded. (*e*) These difficulties are obviated by an atonement.
The things which are accomplished in
the atonement made under the Divine
government, we think, so far as this
point is concerned, and which distin-
guishes pardon in the Divine administration from pardon everywhere else,
relieving it from all the embarrassments
felt in other governments, are the following: (1.) There is the utmost respect
paid to the *law*. It is honoured (*a*) in
the personal obedience of the Lord
Jesus, and (*b*) in the sacrifice which

he made on the cross to maintain its dignity, and to show that it could not be violated with impunity — *more* honoured by far than it would be by the perfect obedience of man himself, or by its penalty being borne by the sinner. (2.) Pardon can be offered to any extent, or to any number of offenders. All the feelings of benevolence and mercy can be indulged and gratified in the most free manner ; for now that an atonement is made, all proper honour has been shown to the law and to the claims of justice, and no interest will suffer though the most ample proclamation of pardon is issued. There is but one government in the universe that can safely to itself make an unlimited offer of pardon—that is, the government of God. There is not a human government that could safely make the offer which we meet everywhere in the Bible, that *all* offences may be forgiven : that *all* violators of law may be pardoned. If such a proclamation were made, there is no earthly administration that could hope to stand ; no community which would not soon become the prey of lawless plunder and robbery. The reason, and the sole reason, why it can be done in the Divine administration is, that an atonement has been made by which the honour of the law has been secured, and by which it is shown that, while pardon is extended to all, the law is to be honoured, and can never be violated with impunity. (3) The plan of pardon by the atonement secures the observance of the law on the part of those who are pardoned. This can never be depended on when an offender against human laws is pardoned, and when a convict is discharged from the penitentiary. So far as the effect of punishment, or any influence from the act of pardon is concerned, there is no security that the pardoned convict will

not, as his first act, force a dwelling or commit murder. But in the case of *all* who are pardoned through the atonement, it is made certain that they *will be* obedient to the laws of God, and that their lives will be changed from sin to holiness, from disobedience to obedience. This has been secured by incorporating into the plan a provision by which the heart shall be changed *before* pardon is granted : not as the *ground* or *reason* of pardon, but as essential to it. The heart of the sinner is renewed by the Holy Ghost, and he becomes in fact obedient, and is disposed to lead a life of holiness. Thus every hinderance which exists in a human government to pardon is removed in the Divine administration ; the honour of law is secured ; the feelings of benevolence are gratified, and the sinner becomes obedient and holy.

(7.) We have in this chapter (ver. 16) an instance of the confidence which wicked men are constrained to express in the true God. Darius had no doubt that the God whom Daniel served was able to protect and deliver him. The same may be said now. Wicked men know that it is safe to trust in God ; that he is able to save his friends ; that there is more security in the ways of virtue than in the ways of sin ; and that when human help fails, it is proper to repose on the Almighty arm. There is a feeling in the human heart that they who confide in God are safe, and that it is proper to rely on his arm ; and even a wicked father will not hesitate to exhort a Christian son or daughter to serve their God faithfully, and to confide in him in the trials and temptations of life. Ethan Allen, of Vermont, distinguished in the American revolution, was an infidel. His wife was an eminent Christian. When he was about to die, he was asked which of the two he wished his son to imitate in his religious views—his father or his mother. He replied, " His mother."

(8.) The righteous may look for the Divine protection and favour (ver. 22) ; that is, it is an advantage in this world of danger, and temptation, and trial, to be truly religious ; or, in other words, those who are righteous may confidently expect the Divine interposition in their behalf. It is, indeed, a question of some difficulty, but of much importance, to what extent, and in what forms we are authorized now to look for the Divine interposition in our behalf, or what is the real benefit of religion in this world, so far as the Divine protection is concerned; and on this point it seems not inappropriate to lay down a few principles that may be of use, and that may be a proper application of the passage before us to our own circumstances :

(A) There is then a class of Scripture promises that refer to such protection, and that lead us to believe that we may look for the Divine interference in favour of the righteous, or that there is, in this respect, an advantage in true religion. In support of this, reference may be made to the following, among other passages of Scripture :— Psa. xxxiv. 7, 17–22 ; lv. 22 ; xci. 1–8 ; Isa. xliii. 1, 2 ; Luke xii. 6, 7 ; Heb. i. 14 ; xiii. 5, 6.

(B) In regard to the proper interpretation of these passages, or to the nature and extent of the Divine interposition, which we may expect in behalf of the righteous, it may be remarked.

I. That we are *not* to expect now the following things :—

(*a*) The Divine interposition by miracle. It is the common opinion of the Christian world that the age of miracles is past ; and certainly there is nothing in the Bible that authorizes

us to expect that God will *now* interpose for us in that manner. It would be a wholly illogical inference, however, to maintain that there never *has* been any such interposition in behalf of the righteous ; since a reason may have existed for such an interposition in former times which may not exist now.

(*b*) We are not authorized to expect that God will interpose by sending his angels visibly to protect and deliver us in the day of peril. The fair interpretation of those passages of Scripture which refer to that subject, as Psa. xxxiv. 7; Heb. i. 14, does not require us to believe that there will be such interposition, and there is no evidence that such interposition takes place. *This* fact, however, should not be regarded as proof, either (1) that no such visible interposition has ever occurred in former times—since it in no way demonstrates that point; or (2) that the angels may not interpose in our behalf now, though to us invisible. For anything that can be proved to the contrary, it may still be true that the angels may be, invisibly, "ministering spirits to those who shall be heirs of salvation," and that they may be sent to accompany the souls of the righteous on their way to heaven, as they were to conduct Lazarus to Abraham's bosom, Luke xvi. 22.

(*c*) We are not authorized to expect that God will set aside the regular laws of nature in our behalf—that he will thus interpose for us in regard to diseases, to pestilence, to storms, to mildew, to the ravages of the locust or the caterpillar—for this would be a miracle, and all the interposition which we are entitled to expect must be consistent with the belief that the laws of nature will be regarded.

(*d*) We are not authorized to expect that the righteous will never be overwhelmed with the wicked in calamity—that in an explosion on a steam-boat, in a shipwreck, in fire or flood, in an earthquake or in the pestilence, they will not be cut down together. To suppose that God would directly interpose in behalf of his people in such cases, would be to suppose that there would be miracles still, and there is nothing in the Bible, or in the facts that occur, to justify such an expectation.

II. The Divine interposition which we *are* authorized to expect, may be referred to under the following particulars :—

(*a*) All events, great and small, are under the control of the God who loves righteousness—the God of the righteous. Not a sparrow falls to the ground without his notice ; not an event happens without his permission. If, therefore, calamity comes upon the righteous, it is not because the world is without control; it is not because God could not prevent it ; it must be because he sees it best that it should be so.

(*b*) There is a general course of events that is favourable to virtue and religion ; that is, there is a state of things on earth which demonstrates that there is a moral government over men. The essence of such a government, as Bishop Butler (*Analogy*) has shown, is, that virtue, in the course of things, is rewarded as virtue, and that vice is punished as vice. This course of things is so settled and clear as to show that God is the friend of virtue and religion, and the enemy of vice and irreligion—that is, that under his administration, the one, as a great law, has a tendency to promote happiness ; the other to produce misery. But if so, there is an advantage in being righteous; or there is a Divine interposition in behalf of the righteous.

(*c*) There are large classes of evils which a man will certainly avoid by virtue and religion, and those evils are among the most severe that afflict mankind. A course of virtue and religion will make it certain that *those* evils will never come upon him or his family. Thus, for example, by so simple a thing as total abstinence from intoxicating drinks, a man will certainly avoid all the evils that afflict the drunkard—the poverty, disease, disgrace, wretchedness, and ruin of body and soul which are certain to follow from intemperance. By chastity, a man will avoid the woes that come, in the righteous visitation of God, on the debauchee, in the form of the most painful and loathsome of the diseases that afflict our race. By integrity a man will avoid the evils of imprisonment for crime, and the disgrace which attaches to its committal. And by religion—pure religion—by the calmness of mind which it produces—the confidence in God ; the cheerful submission to his will ; the contentment which it causes, and the hopes of a better world which it inspires, a man will certainly avoid a large class of evils which unsettle the mind, and which fill with wretched victims the asylums for the insane. Let a man take up the report of an insane asylum, and ask what proportion of its inmates would have been saved from so fearful a malady by true religion; by the calmness which it produces in trouble ; by its influence in moderating the passions and restraining the desires ; by the acquiescence in the will of God which it produces, and he will be surprised at the number which would have been saved by it from the dreadful evils of insanity. As an illustration of this, I took up the *Report of the Pennsylvania Hospital for the Insane*, for the year 1850, which happened to be lying before me, and looked to see what were the *causes* of insanity in regard to the inmates of the asylum, with a view to the inquiry what proportion of them would probably have been saved from it by the proper influence of religion. Of 1599 patients whose cases were referred to, I found the following, a large part of whom, it may be supposed, would have been saved from insanity if their minds had been under the proper influence of the gospel of Christ, restraining them from sin, moderating their passions, checking their desires, and giving them calmness and submission in the midst of trouble :—

(d) There are cases where God *seems* to interpose in behalf of the righteous directly, in answer to prayer, in times of sickness, poverty, and danger—raising them up from the borders of the grave ; providing for their wants in a manner which appears to be as providential as when the ravens fed Elijah, and rescuing them from danger. There are numerous such cases which cannot be well accounted for on any other supposition than that God does directly interpose in their behalf, and show them these mercies because they are his friends. These are not miracles. The purpose to do this was a part of the original plan when the world was made, and the prayer and the interposition are only the fulfilling of the eternal decree.

(e) God *does* interpose in behalf of his children in giving them support and consolation ; in sustaining them in the time of trial; in upholding them in bereavement and sorrow, and in granting them peace as they go into the valley of the shadow of death. The evidence here is clear, that there *is* a degree of comfort and peace given to true Christians in such seasons, and given in consequence of their religion, which is not granted to the wicked, and to which the devotees of the world are strangers. And if these things are so, then it is clear that there *is* an advantage in this life in being righteous, and that God does now interpose in the course of events, and in the day of trouble, in behalf of his friends.

(9.) God often overrules the malice of men to make himself known, and constrains the wicked to acknowledge him, vers. 25–27. Darius, like Nebuchadnezzar, was constrained to acknowledge him as the true God, and to make proclamation of this throughout his vast empire. So often, by his providence, God constrains the wicked to acknowledge him as the true God, and as ruling in the affairs of men. His interpositions are so apparent; his works are so vast; the proofs of his administration are so clear ; and he so defeats the counsels of the wicked, that they cannot but feel that he rules, and they cannot but acknowledge and proclaim it. It is in this way that from age to age God is raising up a great number of witnesses even among the wicked to acknowledge his existence, and to proclaim the great truths of his government; and it is in this way, among others, that he is constraining the intellect of the world to bow before him. Ultimately all this will be so clear, that the intellect of the world will acknowledge it, and all kings and people will see, as Darius did, that "he is the living God, and steadfast for ever, and his kingdom that which shall not be destroyed, and his dominion shall be unto the end."

CHAPTER VII.

§ I.—ANALYSIS OF THE CHAPTER.

This chapter contains an account of a remarkable prophetic dream which Daniel had in the first year of the reign of Belshazzar, and of the interpretation of the dream. After a brief statement of the contents of the chapter, it will be proper, in order to its more clear exposition, to state the different methods which have been proposed for interpreting it, or the different views of its application which have been adopted. The chapter comprises the following main points : the vision, vers. 1-14 ; and the explanation, vers. 15-28.

I. The vision, vers. 1-14. The dream occurred in the first year of the reign of Belshazzar, and was immediately written out. Daniel is represented as standing near the sea, and a violent wind rages upon the sea, tossing the waves in wild commotion. Suddenly he sees four monsters emerge from the agitated waves, each one apparently remaining for a little time, and then disappearing. The first, in its general form, resembled a lion, but had wings like an eagle. On this he attentively gazed, until the wings were plucked away, and the beast was made to stand upright as a man, and the heart of a man was given to it. Nothing is said as to what became of the beast after this. Then there appeared a second beast, resembling a bear, raising itself up on one side, and having three ribs in its mouth, and a command was given to it to arise and devour much flesh. Nothing is said further of what became of this beast. Then there arose another beast like a leopard, with four wings, and four heads, and to this beast was given wide dominion. Nothing is said as to what became of this animal. Then there arose a fourth beast more remarkable

still. Its form is not mentioned, but it was fierce and strong. It had great iron teeth. It trampled down everything before it, and devoured and brake in pieces. This beast had at first ten horns, but soon there sprang up in the midst of them another—a smaller horn at first, but as this increased three of the ten horns were plucked up by the roots—apparently either *by* this, or in order to give place to it. What was more remarkable still, in this smaller horn there appeared the eyes of a man —emblematic of intelligence and vigilance ; and a mouth speaking great things—indicative of pride and arrogance. Daniel looked on this singular vision till a throne was set up or established, and then the Ancient of days did sit—till the old forms of dominations ceased, and the reign of God was introduced and established. He contemplated it till, on account of the great words which the "horn spake," the beast was slain, and his body was destroyed, and given to the burning flame. In the meantime the dominion was taken away from the other beasts; though their existence was prolonged for a little time. Then appeared in vision one in the form of man, who came to the Ancient of days, and there was given to him universal dominion over all people—a kingdom that should never be destroyed.

II. The interpretation of the vision (verses 15-28). Daniel was greatly troubled at the vision which he had seen, and he approached one who stood near, and asked him the meaning of it, vers. 15, 16. The explanation with which he was favoured was, in general, the following :—That those four beasts which he had seen represented four kings or kingdoms which would exist on the earth, and that the great design of the vision was to state the fact that the saints of the Most High would ultimately possess the kingdom, and would reign for ever, vers. 17, 18. The grand purpose of the vision was to represent the succession of dynasties, and the particular character of each one, until the government over the world should pass into the hands of the people of God, or until the actual rule on the earth should be in the hands of the righteous. The ultimate object, the thing to which all revolutions tended, and which was designed to be indicated in the vision, was the final reign of the saints on the earth. There was to be a time when the kingdom under the whole heaven was to be given to the people of the saints of the Most High; or, in other words, there would be a state of things on the earth, when "all dominions," or all "rulers" (margin, ver. 27), would obey him. This general announcement in reference to the ultimate thing contemplated, and to the three first kingdoms, represented by the three first beasts, was satisfactory to Daniel, but he was still perplexed in regard to the particular thing designed to be represented by the *fourth* beast, so remarkable in its structure, so unlike all the others, and undergoing so surprising a transformation, vers. 19–22. The sum of what was stated to him, in regard to the events represented by the fourth beast, is as follows: (1.) That this was designed to represent a fourth kingdom or dynasty which would arise upon the earth, in many respects, different from the three which would precede it. It was to be a kingdom which would be distinguished for oppressive conquests. It would subdue the whole earth, and it would crush, and prostrate, and trample down those whom it invaded. The description would characterize a dominion that would be stern, and mighty, and cruel, and successful; that would keep the nations which it subdued under its control by the terror of

arms rather than by the administration of just laws, ver. 23. (2.) The ten horns that Daniel saw spring out of its head denoted ten kings that would arise, or a succession of rulers that would sway the authority of the kingdom, ver. 24. (3.) The other horn that sprang up among the ten, and after them, denoted another dynasty that would arise, and this would have peculiar characteristics. It would so far have connection with the former that it would spring out of them. But in most important respects it would differ from them. Its characteristics may be summed up as follows: (*a*) It would spring from their midst, or be somehow attached, or connected with them—as the horn sprang from the head of the beast—and this would properly denote that the new power somehow sprang from the dynasty denoted by the fourth beast — as the horn sprang from the head of that beast; (*b*) though springing from that, it would be "diverse" from it, having a character to be determined, not from the mere fact of its origin, but from something else. (*c*) It would "subdue three of these kings;" that is, it would overcome and prostrate a certain portion of the power and authority denoted by the ten horns—perhaps meaning that it would usurp something like one-third of the power of the kingdom denoted by the fourth beast. (*d*) It would be characterized by arrogance and haughtiness — so much so that the fair construction of its claims would be that of "speaking against the Most High." (*e*) It would "wear out the saints of the Most High"—evidently referring to persecution. (*f*) It would claim legislative authority so as to "change times and laws"—clearly referring to some claim set up over established laws, or to unusual authority, vers. 24, 25. (4.) Into the hand of this new power, all these things would be given for "a time, and times, and half a time:" implying that it would not be permanent, but would come to an end, ver. 25. (5.) After that there would be a judgment—a judicial determination in regard to this new power, and the dominion would be taken away, to be utterly destroyed, ver. 26. (6.) There would come a period when the whole dominion of the earth would pass into the hands of the saints; or, in other words, there would be a universal reign of the principles of truth and righteousness, ver. 27.

In the conclusion of the chapter (ver. 28), Daniel says that these communications deeply affected his heart. He had been permitted to look far into futurity, and to contemplate vast changes in the progress of human affairs, and even to look forward to a period when all the nations would be brought under the dominion of the law of God, and the friends of the Most High would be put in possession of all power. Such events were fitted to fill the mind with solemn thought, and it is not wonderful that he contemplated them with deep emotion.

§ II.—VARIOUS METHODS OF INTERPRETING THIS CHAPTER.

It is hardly necessary to say that there have been very different methods of interpreting this chapter, and that the views of its proper interpretation are by no means agreed on by expositors. It may be useful to refer to some of those methods before we advance to its exposition, that they may be before the mind in its consideration. We shall be the better able to ascertain what is the true interpretation by inquiring which of them, if any, accords with the *fair* exposition of the language employed by the sacred writer. The

opinions entertained may be reduced to the following classes:—

I. Hardt supposes that the four beasts here denote four particular kings —Nebuchadnezzar, Evil-Merodach, Belshazzar, and Cyrus.

II. Ephræm, who is followed by Eichhorn, supposes that the first beast referred to the Babylonish-Chaldean kingdom; the second, the Medish empire under Cyaxares II., the three "ribs" of which denote the Medish, Persian, and Chaldean portions of that empire; the third, the Persian empire, the four heads and wings of which denote the spread of the Persian empire towards the four regions under heaven, or to all parts of the world; the fourth, to the Grecian empire under Alexander and his successors, the ten horns of which denote ten eminent kings among the successors of Alexander, and the "little horn," that sprang up among them, Antiochus Epiphanes. The succeeding state of things, according to Ephræm and Eichhorn, refers to the kingdom of the Messiah.

III. Grotius, representing another class of interpreters, whom Hetzel follows, supposes that the succession of the kingdoms here referred to is the Babylonish-Chaldean; the Persian; the kingdom of Alexander, and his successors. The fifth is the Roman empire.

IV. The most common interpretation which has prevailed in the church is that which supposes that the first beast denotes the Chaldean kingdom; the second, the Medo-Persian; the third, the Greek empire under Alexander and his successors; the fourth, the Roman empire. The dominion of the saints is the reign of the Messiah and his laws. But this opinion, particularly as far as pertains to the fourth and fifth of these kingdoms, has had a great variety of modifications, especially in reference to the signification of the ten horns, and the little horn that sprang up among them. Some who, under the fifth kingdom, suppose that the reign of Christ is referred to, regard the fourth kingdom as relating to Rome under the Cæsars, and that the ten horns refer to a succession of ten regents, and the little horn to Julius Cæsar. Others, who refer the last empire to the personal reign of Christ on the earth, and the kingdom which he would set up, suppose that the ten horns refer to ten kings or dynasties that sprang out of the Roman power—either a succession of the emperors, or those who came in after the invasion of the northern hordes, or certain kingdoms of Europe which succeeded the Roman power after it fell; and by the little horn, they suppose that either the Turkish power with its various branches is designated, or Mahomet, or the Papacy, or Antichrist.

V. The Jews, in general, suppose that the fifth kingdom refers to the reign of the Messiah; but still there has been great diversity of views among them in regard to the application of particular parts of the prophecy. Many of the older interpreters among them supposed that the ten horns denoted ten Roman Cæsars, and that the last horn referred to Titus Vespasian. Most of the later Jewish interpreters refer this to their fabulous Gog and Magog.

VI. Another interpretation which has had its advocates is that which supposes that the first kingdom was the Chaldean; the second, the Persian; the third, that of Alexander; the fourth, that of his successors; and the fifth, that of the Asmonean princes who rose up to deliver the Jewish nation from the despotism of the Syrian kings.

VII. As a specimen of one mode of interpretation which has prevailed to some extent in the church, the opinion of Cocceius may be referred to. He supposes that the first beast, with the eagle's wings, denoted the reign of the Christian emperors in Rome, and the spread of Christianity under them into remote regions of the East and West; the second, with the three ribs in his mouth, the Arian Goths, Vandals, and Lombards; the third, with the four heads and four wings, the Mahometan kingdom with the four Caliphates; the fourth, the kingdom of Charlemagne, and the ten horns in this kingdom, the Carlovingians, Saxons, Salic, Swedish, Hollandish, English, &c., princes and dynasties or people; and the little horn, the Papacy as the actual Antichrist.

The statement of these various opinions, and methods of interpretation, I have translated from Bertholdt, *Daniel*, pp. 419–426. To these should be added the opinion which Bertholdt himself maintains, and which has been held by many others, and which Bertholdt has explained and defended at length, pp. 426–446. That opinion is, substantially, that the first kingdom is the Babylonish kingdom under Nebuchadnezzar, and that the wings of the first beast denote the extended spread of that empire. The second beast, with the three "ribs," or *fangs*, denotes the Median, Lydian, and Babylonish kingdoms, which were erected under one sceptre, the Persian. The third beast, with the four wings and four heads, denotes the Grecian dynasty under Alexander, and the spread of that kingdom throughout the four parts of the world. The fourth beast denotes the kingdom of the Lagidæ and Seleucidæ, under which the Hebrews suffered so much. The statement respecting this kingdom (ver. 7), that "it was diverse from all that went before it," refers to the "plurality of the fourth kingdom," or the fact

CHAPTER VII.

IN the first year of Belshazzar king of Babylon, Daniel [1]had a dream,[a] and visions of his head

1 *saw.*

that it was an *aggregate* made up of many others—a kingdom in a *collective* sense. The "ten horns" denote ten successive princes or kings in that kingdom, and Bertholdt enumerates them in the following order:—1, Seleucus Nicator ; 2, Antiochus Soter ; 3, Antiochus Theos ; 4, Seleucus Kallinicus ; 5, Seleucus Keraunus ; 6, Antiochus the Great ; 7, Seleucus Philopater ; 8, Heliodorus ; 9, Ptolemy Philometer ; 10, Demetrius. The eleventh—denoted by the little horn —was Antiochus Epiphanes, who brought so many calamities upon the Hebrew people. His reign lasted, according to Bertholdt, "a time, and times, and half a time"—or three years and a half; and then the kingdom was restored to the people of God to be a permanent reign, and, ultimately, under the Messiah, to fill the world and endure to the end of time.

The interpretation thus stated, supposing that the "little horn" refers to Antiochus Epiphanes, is also maintained by Prof. Stuart.—*Hints on Prophecy*, 2nd ed., pp. 85–98. Compare also *Commentary on Daniel*, pp. 173–194, and 205–211.

Amidst such a variety of views, the only hope of arriving at any satisfactory conclusion respecting the meaning of this chapter is by a careful examination of the text, and the fair meaning of the symbols employed by Daniel.

1. *In the first year of Belshazzar king of Babylon.* On the character and reign of Belshazzar, see Intro. to ch. v. § II. He was the last of the kings of Babylon, and this fact may cast some light on the disclosures made in the dream. ¶ *Daniel had a dream.*

upon his bed : then he wrote the dream, *and* told the sum of the matters.[2]

a ch. 2. 28 ; Numb. 12. 6 ; Amos 3. 7.
2 or, *words.*

Marg., as in Heb., *saw.* He saw a series of events in vision when he was asleep. The dream refers to that representation, and was of such a nature that it was proper to speak of it as if he saw it. Comp. Notes on ch. ii. 1. ¶ *And visions of his head upon his bed.* Notes on ch. iv. 5. ¶ *Then he wrote the dream.* He made a record of it at the time. He did not commit it to tradition, or wait for its fulfilment before it was recorded, but long before the events referred to occurred he committed the prediction to writing, that when the prophecy was fulfilled they might be compared with it. It was customary among the prophets to record their predictions, whether communicated in a dream, in a vision, or by words to them, that there might be no doubt when the event occurred that there had been an inspired prediction of it, and that there might be an opportunity of a careful comparison of the prediction with the event. Often the prophets were *commanded* to record their predictions. See Isa. viii. 1, 16 ; xxx. 8 ; Hab. ii. 2. Comp. Rev. i. 19 ; xiv. 13 ; xxi. 5. In many instances, as in the case before us, the record was made hundreds of years before the event occurred, and as there is all the evidence that there could be in a case that the record has not been altered to adapt it to the event, the highest proof is thus furnished of the inspiration of the prophets. The meaning here is, that Daniel *wrote out* the dream as soon as it occurred. ¶ And *told the sum of the matters.* Chald., "And spake the head of the words." That is, he spake or told them *by writing.* He made a communication of them in this manner to the world. It is not implied that he made any *oral* communication of them to any one, but that he *communicated* them— to wit, in the way specified. The word *sum* here—שאר—means *head ;* and would properly denote such a record

2 Daniel spake and said, I saw in my vision by night, and, be-hold, the four winds of the heaven strove upon the great sea.

as would be a *heading up*, or a *summary*—as stating in a brief way the contents of a book, or the chief points of a thing without going into detail. The meaning here seems to be that he did not go into detail—as by writing names, and dates, and places ; or, perhaps, that he did not enter into a minute description of *all* that he saw in regard to the beasts that came up from the sea, but that he recorded what might be considered as peculiar, and as having special significancy. The *Codex Chis.* renders this, ἔγραψεν εἰς κεφάλαια λόγων—"He wrote in heads of words," that is, he reduced it to a summary description. It is well remarked by Lengerke, on this place, that the prophets, when they described what was to occur to tyrants in future times, conveyed their oracles in a comparatively dark and obscure manner, yet so as to be clear when the events should occur. The reason of this is obvious. If the meaning of many of the predictions had been understood by those to whom they referred, that fact would have been a motive to them to induce them to defeat them ; and as the fulfilment depended on their voluntary agency, the prophecy would have been void. It was necessary, therefore, in general, to avoid *direct* predictions, and the mention of names, dates, and places, and to make use of *symbols* whose meaning would be obscure at the time when the prediction was made, but which would be plain when the event should occur. A comparison of vers. 4, 9, 11, 14, will show that only a *summary* of what was to occur was recorded. ¶ *Matters.* Marg., as in Chald., *words*. The term *words*, however, is often used to denote *things*.

2. *Daniel spake and said.* That is, he spake and said in the manner intimated in the previous verse. It was by a *record* made at the time, and thus he might be said to *speak* to his own generation and to all future times. ¶ *I saw in my vision by night.* I beheld in the vision ; that is, he saw represented to him the scene which he proceeds to describe. He seemed to see the sea in a tempest, and these monsters come up from it, and the strange succession of events which followed. ¶ *And, behold, the four winds of the heaven.* The winds that blow under the heaven, or that seem to come from the heaven—or the air. Comp. Jer. xlix. 36. The number of the winds is here referred to as *four* as they are now, as blowing mainly from the four quarters of the earth. Nothing is more common now than to designate them in this manner—as the east, the south, the west, the north wind. So the Latins—Eurus, Auster, Zephyrus, Boreas. ¶ *Strove.* מְגִיחָן. Burst, or rushed forth ; seemed to conflict together. The winds burst, rushed from all quarters, and seemed to meet on the sea, throwing it into wild commotion. The Hebrew word (גִּיחַ) means to break or burst forth, as a fountain or stream of waters, Job xl. 23 ; an infant breaking forth from the womb, Job xxxviii. 8 ; a warrior rushing forth to battle, Ezek. xxxii. 2. Hence the Chaldean to break forth ; to rush forth as the winds. The symbol here would naturally denote some wild commotion among the nations, as if the winds of heaven should rush together in confusion. ¶ *Upon the great sea.* This expression would properly apply to *any* great sea or ocean, but it is probable that the one that would occur to Daniel would be the Mediterranean Sea, as that was best known to him and his contemporaries. A heaving ocean—or an ocean tossed with storms—would be a natural emblem to denote a nation, or nations, agitated with internal conflicts, or nations in the midst of revolutions. Among the sacred poets and the prophets, hosts of armies invading a land are compared to overflowing waters, and mighty changes among the nations to the heaving billows of the ocean in a storm. Comp. Jer. xlvi. 7, 8 ; xlvii. 2 ; Isa. viii. 7, 8 ; xvii. 12 ; lix. 19 ; Dan. xi. 40 ; Rev. xiii. 1. The classic reader will be reminded in the description here of

3 And four great beasts ^a came | up from the sea, diverse one from
                                          | another.

the words of Virgil, _Æn._ I. 82, _seq_ :—

"Ac venti, velut agmine facto
Qua data porta ruunt, et terras turbine perflant.
Incubuere mari, totumque a sedibus imis
Una Eurusque, Notusque ruunt, creberque pro-
    cellis.
Africus, et vastos volvunt ad littora fluctus."

Comp. also Ovid, _Trist._ I. 2, 25, _seq._ It was from this agitated sea that the beasts that Daniel saw, representing successive kingdoms, seemed to rise; and the fair interpretation of this part of the symbol is, that there was, or would be, as it appeared in vision to Daniel, commotions among the nations resembling the sea driven by storms, and that from these commotions there would arise successive kingdoms having the characteristics specified by the appearance of the four beasts. We naturally look, in the fulfilment of this, to some state of things in which the nations were agitated and convulsed; in which they struggled against each other, as the winds strove upon the sea; a state of things which _preceded_ the rise of these four successive kingdoms. Without now pretending to determine whether that was the time denoted by this, it is certain that all that is here said would find a counterpart in the period which immediately preceded the reign of Nebuchadnezzar, or the kingdom which he founded and adorned. His rapid and extensive conquests; the agitation of the nations in self-defence, and their wars against one another, would be well denoted by the agitation of the ocean as seen in vision by Daniel. It is true that there have been many other periods of the world to which the image would be applicable, but no one can doubt that it was applicable to _this_ period, and that would be all that would be necessary if the design was to represent a series of kingdoms commencing with that of Nebuchadnezzar.

3. _And four great beasts came up from the sea._ Not at once, but in succession. See the following verses. Their particular form is described in the subsequent verses. The design of mentioning them here, as coming up _from the sea_, seems to have been to

show that this succession of kingdoms sprang from the agitations and commotions among the nations represented by the heaving ocean. It is not uncommon for the prophets to make use of animals to represent or symbolize kingdoms and nations — usually by some animal which was in a manner peculiar to the land that was symbolized, or which abounded there. Thus in Isa. xxvii. 1, leviathan, or the dragon, or crocodile, is used to represent Babylon. See Notes on that passage. In Ezek. xxix. 3–5, the dragon or the crocodile of the Nile is put for Pharaoh; in Ezek. xxxii. 2, Pharaoh is compared to a young lion, and to a whale in the seas. In Psal. lxxiv. 13, 14, the kingdom of Egypt is compared to the dragon and the leviathan. So on ancient coins, animals are often used as emblems of kingdoms, as it may be added, the lion and the unicorn represent Great Britain now, and the eagle the United States. It is well remarked by Lengerke (_in loc._), that when the prophets design to represent kingdoms that are made up of other kingdoms, or that are combined by being brought by conquest under the power of others, they do this, not by any single animal as actually found in nature, but by monsters — fabulous beings that are compounded of others, in which the peculiar qualities of different animals are brought together—as in the case of the lion with eagle's wings. Thus in Rev. xiii. 1, the Romish power is represented by a beast coming out of the sea, having seven heads and ten horns. Comp. ii. Ezra (Apocry.) xi. 1, where an eagle is represented as coming from the sea with twelve powerful wings and three heads. As an illustration of the attempts made in the apocryphal writings to imitate the prophets, the whole of ch. xi. and ch. xii. of the second book of Ezra may be referred to. ¶ _Diverse one from another._ Though they all came up from the same abyss, yet they differed from each other —denoting, doubtless, that though the successive kingdoms referred to would all rise out of the nations represented by the agitated sea, yet that in important respects they would differ from each other.

[We present some illustrations from Assyrian sculptures. They are undoubtedly examples of the symbolical style of representation common in the East; to which Daniel, or the Spirit of God by Daniel, has accommodated himself. See a very full explanation of the subject under Rev. iv. 7, p. 123, where the author has availed himself of the observations of the indefatigable Layard. The reader will recognize as much resemblance between the figures described in the text, and those presented in the illustrations, as will lead him to ascribe both to one and the same principle or style of instruction, which, being common in the time of Daniel, would, therefore, be well understood. The winged and human-headed lion, shown in the

The first beast of the vision "was like a lion, and had eagle's wings," as in the figure before

first engraving, is one of a pair which stood at the entrance to the principal hall at Nimroud.

us; and when the wings were plucked, "and it was lifted up from the earth, and made stand

4 The first *was* like a lion, *a* and had eagle's *b* wings: I beheld till the wings thereof were plucked, and[1] it was lifted up from the

earth, and made stand upon the feet as a man, and a man's heart was given to it.

a Jer.4 7.　　*b* Deut.28.49; Ezek.17.3; Hab.1.8.
1 or, *wherewith.*

upon the feet as a man," it takes a form like that in the second engraving, which represents a lion-headed human figure, also from Nimrud. We need not seek the perfect counterpart of every prophetic beast named by Daniel, and, therefore, leave the remaining four engravings as examples of conventional forms that may be recognized, more or less distinctly, either in D.niel, Ezekiel, or the Apocalypse.]

4. *The first* was *like a lion.* It is to be assumed, in explaining and applying these symbols, that they are *significant* —that is, that there was some adaptedness or propriety in using these symbols to denote the kingdoms referred to; or that in each case there was a *reason* why the particular animal was selected for a symbol rather than one of the others; that is, there was something in the *lion* that was better fitted to symbolize the kingdom referred to than there was in the bear or the leopard, and this was the reason why this particular symbol was chosen in the case. It is to be further assumed that all the characteristics in the symbol were significant, and we are to expect to find them *all* in the kingdom which they were designed to represent; nor can the symbol be fairly applied to any kingdom, unless something shall be found in its character or history that shall correspond alike to the particular circumstances referred to in the symbol, and to the grouping or succession. In regard to the first beast, there were five things that entered into the symbol, all of which it is to be presumed were significant: the lion, the eagle's wings—the fact that the wings were plucked—the fact that the beast was lifted up so as to stand up as a man—and the fact that the heart of a man was given to it. It is proper to consider these in their order, and then to inquire whether they found a fulfilment in any known state of things.

(*a*) The animal that was seen:—*the lion.* The lion, "the king of beasts," is the symbol of strength and courage, and becomes the proper emblem of a

king—as when the Mussulmans call Ali, Mahomet's son-in-law, "The Lion of God, always victorious." Thus it is often used in the Scriptures. Gen. xlix. 9, "Judah is a lion's whelp: from the prey, my son, thou art gone up: he stooped down, he couched as a lion, and as an old lion; who shall rouse him up?" The warlike character, the conquest, the supremacy of that tribe are here undoubtedly denoted. So in Ezek. xix. 2, 3. "What is thy mother? A lioness: she lay down among lions, she nourished her whelps among young lions." Here is an allusion, says Grotius, to Gen. xlix.9. Judea was among the nations like a lioness among the beasts of the forest; she had strength and sovereignty. The lion is an emblem of a hero: 2 Sam. xxiii. 20, "He slew two lion-like men of Moab." Comp. Gesenius *zu Isa.* i. 851. So Hercules and Achilles are called by Homer θυμολέοντα, or λεοντόθυμον—*lionhearted.*—*Il.* **s.** 639, **η.** 228, *Odys.* **λ.** 766. See the character, the intrepidity, and the habits of the lion fully illustrated in Bochart, *Hieroz.* lib. iii. c. 2, pp. 723–745.—Credner, *der Prophet Joel,* s. 100. f. Compare also the following places in Scripture: Psal. vii. 2; xxii. 21; lvii. 4; lviii. 6; lxxiv. 4; 1 Sam. xvii. 37; Job iv. 10; Jer. iv. 7; xlix. 19; Joel i. 6; Isa. xxix. 1, 2. The *proper* notion here, so far as the emblem of *a lion* is concerned, is that of a king or kingdom that would be distinguished for power, conquest, dominion; that would be in relation to other kings and kingdoms as the lion is among the beasts of the forest—keeping them in awe, and maintaining dominion over them—marching where he pleases, with none to cope with him or to resist him.

(*b*) The eagle's wings:—*and had eagle's wings.* Here appears one peculiarity of the emblem—the union of things which are not found joined together in nature—the representation of things or qualities which no one animal would represent. The lion would denote *one* thing, or *one* quality in the kingdom referred to—power, dominion, sovereignty—but there would be some characteristic in that king or kingdom which nothing in the lion would properly represent, and which could be symbolized only by attaching to him qualities to be found in some other animal. The lion, distinguished for his power, his dominion, his keeping other animals in awe—his spring, and the severity of his blow—is not remarkable for his speed, nor for *going forth* to conquest. He does not range far to accomplish his purpose, nor are his movements eminent for fleetness. Hence there were attached to the lion the wings of an eagle. The proper notion, therefore, of this symbol, would be that of a dominion or conquest *rapidly* secured, *as if* a lion, the king of beasts, should move, not as he commonly does, with a spring or bound, confining himself to a certain space or range, but should move as the eagle does, with rapid and prolonged flight, extending his conquests afar. The meaning of the symbol may be seen by comparing this passage with Isa. xlvi. 11, where Cyrus is compared to "a ravenous bird"—"calling a ravenous bird from the east, the man that executeth my counsels from a far country." The eagle is an emblem of *swiftness:* Jer. iv. 13, "His horses are swifter than eagles;" xlviii. 40, "Behold, he shall fly as an eagle, and shall spread his wings over Moab." See also ch. xlix. 22; Lam. iv. 19; Hab. i. 8.

(*c*) The clipping of the wings:—*I beheld till the wings thereof were plucked.* The word used (מְרַט) means, to pluck or pull, as to pull out the beard (comp. Neh. xiii. 25; Isa. l. 6), and would here be properly applied to some process of pulling out the feathers or quills from the wings of the eagle. The obvious and proper meaning of this symbol is, that there was some *check* put to the progress of the conqueror—as there would be to an eagle by plucking off the feathers from his wings; that is, the *rapidity* of his conquests would cease. The prophet says, that he looked on until this was done, imply-

ing that it was not accomplished at once, but leaving the impression that these conquests were extended far. They were, however, checked, and we see the lion again without the wings; the sovereign who has ceased to spread his triumphs over the earth.

(*d*) The lifting up from the earth:— *and it was lifted up from the earth, and made to stand upon the feet as a man.* That is, the lion, with the wings thus plucked off, was made to stand upright on his hind feet—an unusual position, but the meaning of the symbol is not difficult. It was still the lion—the monarch—but changed *as if* the lion was changed to a man; that is, as if the ferocity, and the power, and the energy of the lion had given place to the comparative weakness of a man. There would be as much difference in the case referred to as there would be if a lion so fierce and powerful should be made so far to change his nature as to stand upright, and to walk as a man. This would evidently denote some remarkable change —something that would be unusual— something where there would be a diminution of ferocity, and yet perhaps a change to comparative weakness—as a man is feebler than a lion.

(*e*) The giving to it of a man's heart: —*and a man's heart was given to it.* The word *heart* in the Scriptures often has a closer relation to the intellect or the understanding than it now has commonly with us; and here perhaps it is a general term to denote something like *human nature* — that is, there would be as great a change in the case as if the nature of the lion should be transformed to that of a man; or, the meaning may be, that this mighty empire, carrying its arms with the rapidity of an eagle, and the fierceness of a lion, through the world, would be checked in its career; its ferocity would be tamed, and it would be characterized by comparative moderation and humanity. In ch. iv. 16, it is said of Nebuchadnezzar, "Let his heart be changed from man's, and let a beast's heart be given unto him;" here, if the symbol refers to him, it does not refer to that scene of humiliation when he was compelled to eat grass like a beast, but to the fact that he was brought to look at things as a man should do; he ceased to act like a ravenous beast, and was led to calm reflection, and to think and speak like a man—a rational being. Or, if it refers to the empire of Babylon, instead of the monarch, it would mean that a change had come over the nation under the succession of princes, so that the fierceness and ferocity of the first princes of the empire had ceased, and the nation had not only closed its conquests, but had actually become, to some extent, moderate and rational.

Now, in regard to the application of *this* symbol, there can be but little difficulty, and there is almost no difference of opinion among expositors. All, or nearly all, agree that it refers to the kingdom of Babylon, of which Nebuchadnezzar was the head, and to the gradual diminution of the ferocity of conquest under a succession of comparatively weak princes. Whatever view may be taken of the book of Daniel—whether it be regarded as inspired prophecy composed by Daniel himself, and written at the time when it professes to have been, or whether it be supposed to have been written long after his time by some one who forged it in his name, there can be no doubt that it relates to the head of the Babylonian empire, or to that which the "head of gold," in the image referred to in ch. ii., represents. The circumstances all so well agree with that application, that, although in the explication of the dream (vers. 16-27) this part of it is not explained—for the perplexity of Daniel related particularly to the fourth beast (ver. 19), yet there can be no reasonable doubt as to what was intended. For (*a*) the lion—the king of beasts—would accurately symbolize that kingdom in the days of Nebuchadnezzar—a kingdom occupying the same position among other kingdoms which the lion does among other beasts, and well represented in its power and ferocity by the lion. See the character and position of this kingdom fully illustrated in the Notes on ch. ii. 37, 38. (*b*) The eagle's wings would accurately denote the rapid conquests of that kingdom--its leaving, as it were, its

own native domain, and flying abroad. The lion alone would have represented the character of the kingdom considered as already having spread itself, or as being at the head of other kingdoms; the wings of the eagle, the rapidity with which the arms of the Babylonians were carried into Palestine, Egypt, Assyria, &c. It is true that *this* symbol alone would not designate Babylon any more than it would the conquests of Cyrus, or Alexander, or Cæsar, but it is to be taken in the connection in which it is here found, and no one can doubt that it has a striking applicability to Babylon. (*c*) The clipping or plucking of these wings would denote the cessation of conquest—as if it would extend no farther; that is, we see a nation once distinguished for the invasion of other nations now ceasing its conquests; and remarkable, not for its victories, but as standing at the head of all other nations, as the lion stands among the beasts of the forest. All who are acquainted with history know that, after the conquests of that kingdom under Nebuchadnezzar, it ceased characteristically to be a kingdom distinguished for conquest, but that, though under his successors, it held a pre-eminence or headship among the nations, yet its victories were extended no further. The successors of Nebuchadnezzar were comparatively weak and indolent princes—as if the wings of the monster had been plucked. (*d*) The rising up of the lion on the feet, and standing on the feet as a man, would denote, not inappropriately, the change of the kingdom under the successors of Nebuchadnezzar. See above in the explanation of the symbol. (*e*) The giving of a man's heart to it would not be inapplicable to the change produced in the empire after the time of Nebuchadnezzar, and under a succession of comparatively weak and inefficient princes. Instead of the heart of the lion—of being "lion-hearted"—it had the heart of a man; that is, the character of wildness and fierceness denoted by an untamed beast was succeeded by that which would be better represented by a human being. It is not the character of the lion changed to that of the bear, or the panther, or

5 And, behold, another *a* beast, a second, like to a bear, and it

raised up ¹itself on one side, and

---

the leopard; nor is it man considered as a warrior or conqueror, but man as he is distinguished from the wild and ferocious beast of the desert. The change in the character of the empire, until it ceased under the feeble reign of Belshazzar, would be well denoted by this symbol.

5. *And, behold, another beast, a second, like to a bear.* That is, *after* the lion had appeared, and he had watched it until it had undergone these surprising transformations. There are several circumstances, also, in regard to this symbol, all of which, it is to be supposed, were significant, and all of which demand explication before it is attempted to apply them.

(*a*) The animal seen :—*the bear.* For a full description of the bear, see Bochart, *Hieroz.* lib. iii. c. ix. The animal is well known, and has properties quite distinct from the lion and other animals. There was doubtless some reason why this symbol was employed to denote a particular kingdom, and there was something in the kingdom that corresponded with these peculiar properties, as there was in the case of the lion. The bear might, in some respects, have been a proper representative of Babylon, but it would not in all our its main respects. According to Bochart (*Hieroz.* vol. i. p. 812), the bear is distinguished mainly for two things, cunning and ferocity. Aristotle says that the bear is greedy as well as silly and foolhardy. (Wemyss, *Key to the Symbolic Language of Scripture.*) The *name* in Hebrew is taken from his grumbling or growling. Comp. Isa. lix. 11 :—

"We roar all like bears."

Comp. Horace, *Epod.* 16, 51 :—
"Nec vespertinus circumgemit ursus ovile."

Virgil mentions their ferocity :—
"Atque in præsepibus ursi
Sævire."
    —*Æn.* vii. 17.

The bear is noted as especially fierce when hungry, or when robbed of its whelps. Jerome (on Hos. xiii. 8) remarks, "It is said by those who have

studied the nature of wild beasts, that none among them is more ferocious than the bear when deprived of its young, or when hungry." Compare 2 Sam. xvii. 8; Prov. xvii. 12; Hos. xiii. 8. The characteristics of the kingdom, therefore, that would be denoted by the bear would be ferocity, roughness, fierceness in war, especially when provoked; a spirit less manly and noble than that denoted by the lion; severe in its treatment of enemies, with a mixture of fierce and savage cunning.

(*b*) Its rising up on one of its sides:
—*and it raised up itself on one side.*
The Chaldee word here used (שְׂטַר) occurs nowhere else. It means *side* (Gesenius), and would be applied here to the side of an animal, as if he lifted up one side before the other when he rose. The Latin Vulgate renders it, *in parte stetit.* The Greek (Walton), εἰς μέρος ἓν ἐστάθη—"it stood on one part;" or, as Thompson renders it, "he stood half erect." The *Codex. Chis.*, ἐπὶ τοῦ ἑνὸς πλευροῦ ἐστάθη—"it stood upon one side." Maurer renders this, "on one of its forefeet it was recumbent, and stood on the other," and says that this is the figure exhibited on one of the stones found in Babylon, an engraving of which may be seen in Munter, *Religion d. Babyl.* p. 112. The animal referred to here, as found in Babylon, says Lengerke, "lies kneeling on the right forefoot, and is in the act of rising on the left foot." Bertholdt and Hävernick understand this as meaning that the animal stood on the hindfeet, with the forepart raised, as the bear is said to do; but probably the true position is that referred to by Maurer and Lengerke, that the animal was in the act of raising itself up from a recumbent posture, and rested on one of its forefeet while the other was reached out, and the body on that side was partially raised. This *position* would naturally denote a kingdom that had been quiet and at rest, but that was now rousing itself deliberately for some purpose, as of conquest or war—as the bear that had been couching

it had three ribs in the mouth of it between the teeth of it: and

they said thus unto it, Arise, devour much flesh.

---

down would rise when hungry, or when going forth for prey.

(*c*) The ribs in its mouth:—*and it had three ribs in the mouth of it between the teeth of it.* Bertholdt understands this of fangs or tusks—or fangs crooked or bent like ribs, p. 451. But the proper meaning of the Chaldee עֲלַע is the same as the Hebrew צֵלָע—*a rib.*— Gesenius. The Latin Vulgate is, *tres ordines*—three rows; the Syriac and the Greek, *three ribs.* This would be sufficiently characteristic of a bear, and the attitude of the animal here seems to be that it had killed some other animal, and had, in devouring it, torn out three ribs from its side, and now held them in its mouth. It was slowly rising from a recumbent posture, with these ribs in its mouth, and about to receive a command to go forth and devour much flesh. The number *three,* in this place, Lengerke supposes to be a round number, without any special significancy; others suppose that it denotes the number of nations or kingdoms which the people here represented by the bear had overcome. Perhaps this latter would be the more obvious idea as suggested by the symbol, but it is not necessary, in order to a proper understanding of a symbol, to press such a point too closely. The natural idea which would be suggested by this part of the symbol would be that of a kingdom or people of a fierce and rough character having already subdued some, and then, after reposing, rising up with the trophies of its former conquests to go forth to new victories, or to overcome others. The symbol would be a very striking one to represent a conquering nation in such a posture.

(*d*) The command given to this beast: —*and they said thus unto it, Arise, devour much flesh.* That is, it was said to it; or some one having authority said it. A voice was heard commanding it to go forth and devour. This command is wholly in accordance with the nature of the bear. The bear is called by Aristotle σαρκοφαγῶν, *flesh-eater,* and ζῶον πάμφαγον, *a beast devour-*

ing everything (*Hist. Nat.* viii. 5), and no better description could be given of it. As a symbol, this would properly be applicable to a nation about receiving, as it were, a command from God to go forth to wider conquests than it had already made; to arouse itself from its repose and to achieve new triumphs.

The application of this symbol was not explained by the angel to Daniel; but if the former appertained to Babylon, there can be little difficulty in understanding to what this is to be applied. It is evidently to that which succeeded the Babylonian—the Medo-Persian, the kingdom ruled successively by Cyrus, Cambyses, Smerdis, Darius, Xerxes, Artaxerxes, and Darius Nothus, until it was overthrown by Alexander the Great. The only inquiry now is as to the pertinency of the symbol here employed to represent this kingdom.

(*a*) The symbol of the bear. As already seen, the bear would denote any fierce, rough, overbearing, and arbitrary kingdom, and it is clear that while it *might* have applicability to any such kingdom, it would *better* represent that of Medo-Persia than the *lion* would; for while, in some respects, either symbol would be applicable to either nation, the Medo-Persian did not stand so decidedly at the head of nations as the Babylonian. As to its *character,* however, the bear was not an inappropriate symbol. Taking the whole nation together, it was fierce and rough, and unpolished, little disposed to friendliness with the nations, and dissatisfied while any around it had peace or prosperity. In the image seen in ch. ii., this kingdom, denoted by the breast and arms of silver (ver. 32), is described in the explanation (ver. 39) as "inferior to thee;" that is, to Nebuchadnezzar. For a sufficiently full account of this kingdom—of the mad projects of Cambyses, and his savage rage against the Ethiopians— well represented by the ferocity of the bear; of the ill-starred expedition to Greece under Xerxes—an expedition in its fierceness and folly well represented by the bear, and of the degeneracy of the national character after Xerxes—well represented by the bear as compared with the lion, see Notes on ch. ii. 39. No one acquainted with the history of that nation can doubt the propriety and applicability of the emblem.

(b) The rising up on its side, or from a recumbent posture, as if it had been in a state of repose, and was now arousing itself for action. Different interpretations have been adopted of this emblem as applicable to the Medo-Persians. The ancient Hebrew interpreters, as Jerome remarks, explain it as meaning that that kingdom was "on one side" in the sense of *separate;* that is, that this kingdom kept itself aloof from Judea, or did not inflict injury on it. Thus also Grotius explains it as meaning that it did not injure Judea —"Judea nihil nocuit." Ephræm the Syrian, and Theodoret, explain it as meaning that the empire of the Medo-Persians was situated *on the side* of Judea, or held itself within its proper bounds, in the sense that it never extended its dominion, like Babylon, over the whole earth. Rosenmüller explains it as meaning that in relation to the kingdom represented by the lion, it was *at its side*, both occupying the regions of the East. J. D. Michaelis understands it as denoting that, as the bear was raising itself up, one part being more raised than the other, the Medo-Persian empire was composed of two kingdoms, one of which was more exalted or advanced than the other. Comp. Lengerke. The true meaning however is, that, as seen by Daniel, the nation that had been in a state of repose was now preparing itself for new conquests—a state descriptive of, and in every way quite applicable to the condition of the Medo-Persian empire, after the conquests by Cyrus, as he overran the kingdom of Lydia, &c., then reposing, and *now* about arousing to the conquest and subjugation of Babylon. The precise time, therefore, indicated would be about B.C. 544 (Calmet), when, having overcome the Medes, and having secured the conquest of Lydia, and the dethronement of Crœsus, he is meditating the destruction of Babylon. This interval of re-

pose lasted about a year, and it is at this time that the united empire is seen, under the image of the bear rising on its side, arousing itself to go forth to new conquests.

(c) The ribs in the mouth of the beast. This, as above remarked, would properly refer to some previous conquest —as a bear appearing in that manner would indicate that some other animal had been overcome and slain by him, and torn in pieces. The emblem would be fulfilled if the power here symbolized had been successful in former wars, and had rent kingdoms or people asunder. That this description would apply to the Medo-Persian power before its attack on Babylon, or before extending its dominion over Babylon, and its establishment *as* the Medo-Persian kingdoms, no one can doubt. Compare the Notes on ch. ii. 39. It has been commonly supposed that Cyrus succeeded to the throne of Media without war. But this is far from being the case—though so represented in what may be regarded as the romance of the *Cyropædia*. In the *Anabasis* of Xenophon, however, the fact of his having subdued Media by arms is distinctly admitted, iii. 4, 7, 12. Herodotus, Ctesias, Isocrates, and Strabo, all agree also in the fact that it was so. The Upper Tigris was the seat of one campaign, where the cities of Larissa and Mespila were taken by Cyrus. From Strabo we learn that the decisive battle was fought on the spot where Cyrus afterwards built Pasargardæ, in Persia, for his capital. See Kitto, *Cyclo.*, art. "Cyrus." In addition to this, we are to remember the well-known conquests of Cyrus in Lydia and elsewhere, and the propriety of the emblem will be apparent. It may not be certain that the *number* three is significant in the emblem, but it is *possible* that there may have been reference to the three kingdoms of Persia, Media, and Lydia, that were actually under the dominion of Cyrus when the aggressive movement was made on Babylon.

(d) The command to "arise and devour much flesh." No one can fail to see the appropriateness of this, considered as addressed to the Medo-Persian power—that power which subdued

6 After this I beheld, and, lo, another, like a leopard, which had upon the back of it four wings of a fowl; the beast had also four heads; and ª dominion was given to it.

Babylon; which brought under its dominion a considerable part of the world, and which, under Darius and Xerxes, poured its millions on Greece. The emblem here used is, therefore, one of the most striking and appropriate that could be employed, and it cannot be doubted that it had reference to this kingdom, and that, in all the particulars, there was a clear fulfilment.

6. *After this I beheld, and, lo, another, like a leopard.* That is, as before, after the bear had appeared—indicating that this was to be a succeeding kingdom or power. The beast which now appeared was a monster, and, as in the former cases, so in regard to this, there are several circumstances which demand explanation in order to understand the symbol. It may assist us, perhaps, in forming a correct idea of the symbol here introduced to have before us a representation of the animal as it appeared to Daniel.

(a) The animal itself:—*a leopard.* The word here used—נְמַר—or in Heb. נָמֵר—denotes a panther or leopard, so called from his spots. This is a well-known beast of prey, distinguished for blood-thirstiness and cruelty, and these characteristics are especially applicable to the female panther. The animal is referred to in the Scriptures as emblematic of the following things, or as having the following characteristics: (1.) As next in dignity to the lion—of the same general nature. Compare Bochart, *Hieroz.* P. I. lib. iii. c. vii. Thus the lion and the panther, or leopard, are often united in the Scriptures. Comp. Jer. v. 6; Hos. xiii. 7. See also in the Apocrypha, Ecclesias. xxviii. 23. So also they are united in Homer, *Il. φ* :—

Οὔτε οὖν παρδάλιος τόσσον μένος, οὔτε λέοντος.

"Neither had the leopard nor the lion such strength." (2.) As distinguished for cruelty, or a fierce nature, as contrasted with the gentle and tame animals. Isa. xi. 6, "And the leopard

shall lie down with the kid." In Jer. v. 6, it is compared with the lion and the wolf: "A lion out of the forest shall slay them, and a wolf of the evenings shall spoil them, a leopard shall watch over their cities." Comp. Hos. xiii. 7. (3.) As distinguished for swiftness or fleetness. Habak. i. 8: "Their horses are swifter than the leopards." Comp. also the quotations from the classics in Bochart as above, p. 788. His fleetness is often referred to—the celerity of his *spring* or *bound* especially—by the Greek and Roman writers. (4.) As insidious, or as lying in wait, and springing unexpectedly upon the unwary traveller. Compare Hos. xiii. 7: "As a leopard by the way will I observe them;" that is, I will *watch* (אָשׁוּר) them. So Pliny says of leopards: *Insidunt pardi condensa arborum, occultatique earum ramis in prætereuntia desiliunt.* (5.) They are characterized by their spots. In the general nature of the animal there is a strong resemblance to the lion. Thus, an Arabic writer quoted by Bochart, *defines* the leopard to be "an animal resembling the lion, except that it is smaller, and has a skin marked by black spots." The proper idea in this representation, when used as a symbol, would be of a nation or kingdom that would have more nobleness than the one represented by the bear, but a less decisive headship over others than that represented by the lion; a nation that was addicted to conquest, or that preyed upon others; a nation rapid in its movements, and springing upon others unawares, and *perhaps* in its spots denoting a nation or people made up, not of homogeneous elements, but of various different people. See below in the application of this.

(b) The four wings:—*which had upon the back of it four wings of a fowl.* The first beast was seen with the wings of an eagle, but without any specified number; this appears with wings, but without specifying any particular *kind* of wings, though the *number* is mentioned. In both of them celerity of movement is undoubtedly intended— celerity beyond what would be properly denoted by the animal itself—the lion or the leopard. If there is a difference in the design of the representation, as there would seem to be by mentioning the *kind* of wings in the one case, and the *number* in the other, it is probable that the former would denote a more bold and extended flight; the latter a flight more rapid, denoted by the *four* wings. We should look for the fulfilment of the former in a nation that extended its conquests over a broader space; in the latter, to a nation that moved with more celerity. But there is some danger of pressing these similitudes too far. Nothing is said in the passage about the arrangement of the wings, except that they were on the back of the animal. It is to be supposed that there were two on each side.

(c) The four heads:—*the beast had also four heads.* This representation must have been designed to signify either that the one power or kingdom denoted by the leopard was composed of *four* separate powers or nations now united in one; or that there were four successive kings or dynasties that made up its history; or that the power or kingdom actually appeared, as seen in its prevailing characteristic, *as a* distinct dominion, as having four heads, or as being divided into so many separate sovereignties. It seems to me that either one of these would be a proper and natural fulfilment of the design of the image, though the second suggested would be less proper than either of the others, as the heads appeared on the animal not in succession—as the little horn sprung up in the midst of the other ten, as represented in the fourth beast—but existed simultaneously. The general idea would be, that in some way the one particular sovereignty had four sources of power blended into one, or actually exerted the same kind of dominion, and constituted, in fact, the one kingdom as distinguished from the others.

(d) The dominion given to it:—*and dominion was given to it.* That is, it was appointed to rule where the former had ruled, and until it should be suc-

ceeded by another—the beast with the ten horns.

In regard to the application of this, though the angel did not explain it to Daniel, except in general that a kingdom was represented by it (ver. 17), it would seem that there could be little difficulty, though there has been some variety in the views entertained. Maurer, Lengerke, and some others, refer it to the Medo-Persian empire— supposing that the second symbol referred to the kingdom of Media. But the objections to this are so obvious, and so numerous, that it seems to me the opinion cannot be entertained; for (1) the kingdom of Media did not, in any proper sense, *succeed* that of Babylon; (2) the representation of the bear with three ribs has no proper application to Media; (3) the whole description, as we have seen above, of the second beast, accords entirely with the history of the Medo-Persian empire. If this be so, then we naturally look for the fulfilment of this symbol—the third head—in the kingdom or dynasty that followed directly that of Medo-Persia—the Macedonian dynasty or kingdom founded by Alexander the Great, extending over the same countries before occupied by Babylon and the Medo-Persian empire, and continuing till it was swallowed up in the conquests of Rome. We shall find that all the circumstances agree with this supposition:—

(a) The animal—the leopard. The comparative nobleness of the animal; a beast of prey; the celerity of its movements; the spring or bound with which it leaps upon its prey—all agree well with the kingdom of which Alexander was the founder. Indeed there was no other kingdom among the ancients to which it could be better applied; and it will be admitted that, on the supposition that it was the design of Daniel to choose a symbol that would represent the Macedonian empire, he could not have selected one that was better adapted to it than the leopard. All the characteristics of the animal that have been noticed—(1) as next in dignity to the lion: (2) as distinguished for a fierce nature; (3) as characterized by fleetness; (4) as

7 After this I saw in the night visions, and, behold, a fourth ^a beast,

a ver. 19, 23; ch. 2. 40.

dreadful and terrible, and strong exceedingly; and it had great iron teeth : it devoured and brake in

---

known for lying in wait, and springing suddenly upon its prey; and (5) in the point to be noticed soon—their spots —all agree with the characteristics of Alexander, and his movements among the nations, and with the kingdom that was founded by him in the East. (*b*) The four wings. These represent well the rapidity of the conquests of Alexander, for no more rapid conquests were ever made than were his in the East. It was noticed that the leopard had *four* wings, as contrasted with the first beast, in reference to which the *number* is not mentioned: the one denoting a broader flight, and the other a more rapid one; and the one agrees well with the conquests of Nebuchadnezzar, and the other with those of Alexander. (*c*) The four heads united to one body. It is well known that when Alexander died, his empire was left to four of his generals, and that they came to be at the head of as many distinct dominions, yet all springing from the same source, and all, in fact, out of the Macedonian empire. This fact would not be *so well* represented by four distinct and separate animals, as by *one* animal with four heads; that is, as the head represents authority or dominion, one empire, in fact, now ruling by four distinct authorities. The *one* empire, considered as *Macedonian*, continued its sway till it was swallowed up by the Romans; that is, the Macedonian power or dominion as *distinct* from that of Babylon or Medo-Persia; as having characteristics *unlike* these; as introducing a new order of things, continued, though that power was broken up and exercised under distinct manifestations of sovereignty. The fact was, that, at the death of Alexander, to whom the founding of this empire was owing, "Philip Aridæus, brother of Alexander, and his infant son by Roxana, were appointed by the generals of the army to succeed, and Perdiccas was made regent. The empire was divided into thirty-three governments, distri-

buted among as many general officers. Hence arose a series of bloody, desolating wars, and a period of confusion, anarchy, and crime ensued, that is almost without a parallel in the history of the world. After the battle of Ipsus, 301 B.C., in which Antigonus was defeated, the empire was divided into four kingdoms—Thrace and Bithynia under Lysimachus; Syria and the East under Seleucus; Egypt, under Ptolemy Soter; and Macedonia under Cassander."— Lyman, *Hist. Chart.* It was these four powers, thus springing out of the one empire founded by Alexander, that was clearly represented by the four heads. (*d*) The dominion given to it. No one can doubt that a dominion was given to Alexander and the Macedonian dynasty, which would fully correspond with this. In fact the dominion of the world was practically conceded to that kingdom. (*e*) There is only one other circumstance to be noticed, though perhaps we are not to seek an exact accomplishment for that in any specific events. It is the fact that the leopard is marked by *spots*— a circumstance which many have supposed had a fulfilment in the fact that numerous nations, not homogeneous, were found in the empire of Alexander. So Bochart, *Hieroz.* P. I. lib. iii. c. vii. p. 789, says: "The spots of the leopard refer to the different customs of the nations over which he ruled. Among these, besides the Macedonians, Greeks, Thracians, and Illyrians, in Europe, there were in Africa the Libyans, Egyptians, and Troglodites; in Asia, almost all the nations to the Ganges." But, without insisting on this, no one can compare the *other* particulars which were clearly designed to be symbolical, without perceiving that they had a full accomplishment in the Macedonian empire.

7, 8. *After this I saw in the night visions.* The other beasts were seen also in a dream (ver. 1), and this probably in the same night, though as

pieces, and stamped the residue with the feet of it: and it *was* diverse from all the beasts that *were* before it; and it had ten horns.[a]

a subsequent part of the dream, for the whole vision evidently passed before the prophet in a single dream. The succession, or the fact that he saw one after the other, indicates a sucession in the kingdoms. They were not to be at the same time upon the earth, but one was to arise after another in the order here indicated, though they were in some respects to occupy the same territory. The singular character of the beast that now appears ; the number of the horns ; the springing up of a new horn ; the might and terror of the beast, and the long duration of its dominion upon the earth, attracted and fixed the attention of Daniel, led him into a more minute description of the appearance of the animal, and induced him particularly to ask an explanation of the angel of the meaning of this part of the vision, ver. 19. ¶ *And, behold, a fourth beast.* This beast had peculiar characteristics, all of which were regarded as symbolical, and all of which demand explanation in order that we may have a just view of the nature and design of the symbol.

As in reference to the three former beasts, so also in regard to this, it will be proper to explain first the significance of the different parts of the symbol, and then in the exposition (ver. 19, *seq.*) to inquire into the application. The particulars of this symbol are more numerous, more striking, and more important than in either of the previous ones. These particulars are the following (vers. 7–11):—

(*a*) The animal itself (v. 7):—*a fourth beast, dreadful and terrible, and strong exceedingly.* The form or nature of the beast is not given as in the preceding cases—the lion, the bear, and the leopard—but it is left for the imagination to fill up. It was a beast more terrific in its appearance than either of the others, and was evidently a monster such as could not be designated by a single name. The *terms* which are used here in describing the beast—*dreadful, terrible, exceedingly strong,* are nearly synonymous, and are heaped together in order to give an impressive view of the terror inspired by the beast. There can be no doubt as to the general *meaning* of this, for it is explained (ver. 23) as denoting a kingdom that "should devour the whole earth, and tread it down, and break it in pieces." As a symbol, it would denote some power much more fearful and much more to be dreaded ; having a wider dominion ; and more stern, more oppressive in its character, more severe in its exactions, and more entirely destroying the liberty of others ; advancing more by power and terror, and less by art and cunning, than either. This characteristic is manifest throughout the symbol.

(*b*) The teeth (ver. 7):—*and it had great iron teeth.* Not only teeth or tusks, such as other animals may have, but teeth made of *iron.* This is characteristic of a monster, and shows that there was to be something very peculiar in the dominion that was here symbolized. The teeth are of use to eat or devour ; and the symbol here is that of devouring or rending—as a fierce monster with such teeth might be supposed to rend or devour all that was before it. *This,* too, would denote a nation exceedingly fierce ; a nation of savage ferocity ; a nation that would be signally formidable to all others. For illustration, comp. Jer. xv. 12 ; Mic. iv. 13. As explained in ver. 23, it is said that the kingdom denoted by this would "*devour* the whole earth." Teeth—great teeth, are often used as the symbols of cruelty, or of a devouring enemy. Thus in Prov. xxx. 14: "There is a generation whose teeth are as swords, and their jaw teeth are as knives, to devour the poor from off the earth, and the needy from among men." So David uses the word to denote the cruelty of tyrants: Ps. iii. 7, "Thou hast broken the teeth of the ungodly;" lvii. 4, "whose teeth are spears and arrows;" lviii. 6, "break their teeth in their mouth; break out the great teeth of the young lions."

(c) The stamping with the feet (ver. 7):—*it devoured and brake in pieces, and stamped the residue with the feet of it.* That is, like a fierce monster, whatever it could not devour it stamped down and crushed in tne earth. This indicates a disposition or purpose to destroy, *for the sake of destroying,* or where no other purpose could be gained. It denotes rage, wrath, a determination to crush all in its way, to have universal dominion; and would be applicable to a nation that subdued and crushed others *for the mere sake of doing it,* or because it was unwilling that any other should exist and enjoy liberty—even where itself could not hope for any advantage.

(d) The fact that it was different from all that went before it (ver. 7): —*and it* was *diverse from all the beasts that* were *before it.* The prophet does not specify particularly in what respects it was different, for he does not attempt to give its appearance. It was not a lion, a bear, or a leopard, but he does not say precisely what it was. Probably it was such a monster that there were no animals with which it could be compared. He states some circumstances, however, in which it was different—as in regard to the ten horns, the little horn, the iron teeth, &c., but still the imagination is left to fill up the picture in general. The meaning of this must be, that the fourth kingdom, represented by this beast, would be materially different from those which preceded it, and we must look for the fulfilment in some features that would characterize it by which it would be unlike the others. There must be something *marked* in the difference—something that would be more than the common difference between nations.

(e) The ten horns (ver. 7):—*and it had ten horns.* That is, the prophet saw on it ten horns as characterizing the beast. The *horn* is a symbol of power, and is frequently so used as an emblem or symbol in Daniel (vii. 7, 8, 20, 24; viii. 3–9, 20–22) and Revelation (v. 6; xiii. 1, 11; xvii. 3, 12, 16). It is used as a symbol because the

great strength of horned animals is found there. Thus in Amos vi. 13, it is said:—

"Ye that rejoice in a thing of nought,
That say, Have we not taken *dominion* to
    ourselves by our own strength?"
            (Heb. *horns*.)

So in Deut. xxxiii. 17:—
" His beauty shall be that of a young bull,
  And his horns shall be the horns of a rhinoceros:
With these he shall push the people to the
    extremities of the land:
Such are the ten thousands of Ephraim,
Such the thousands of Manasseh."
            —Wemyss.

So in 1 Kings xxii. 11, we find horns used in a symbolical action on the part of the false prophet Zedekiah. "He made him horns of iron, and said, Thus saith Jehovah, With these shalt thou push the Syrians, until thou have consumed them." In Zech. i. 18, the four horns that are seen by the prophet are said to be the four great powers which had scattered and wasted the Jews. Compare Wemyss on the *Symbolic Language of Scripture,* art. "Horns." There can be no doubt as to the meaning of the symbol here, for it is explained in a subsequent part of the chapter (ver. 24), "the ten horns are the ten kings that shall arise." It would seem also, from that explanation, that they were to be ten kings that would "arise" or spring out of that kingdom at some period of its history. "And the ten horns out of this kingdom are ten kings that shall arise;" that is, not that the kingdom itself would spring out of ten others that would be amalgamated or consolidated into one, but that out of that one kingdom there would spring up *ten* that would exercise dominion, or in which the power of the one kingdom would be ultimately lodged. Though Daniel appears to have seen these horns as appertaining to the beast when he first saw him, yet the subsequent explanation is, that these horns were emblems of the manner in which the power of that one kingdom would be finally exerted; or that ten kings or dynasties would spring out of it. We are, then, naturally to look for the fulfilment of this in some one great kingdom of huge power that would crush the nations, and from which,

8 I considered the horns, and, behold, there came up among them another little horn,^a before whom there were three of the first horns plucked up by the roots : and, behold, in this horn *were* eyes like the eyes of man, ^b and a ^c mouth speaking great things.

a vers. 20, 21, 24.   *b* Rev. 9. 7.   *c* Rev. 13. 5.

while the same general characteristic would remain, there would spring up *ten* kings, or dynasties, or kingdoms, in which the power would be concentrated.

(*f*) The springing up of the little horn (ver. 8):—*I considered the horns, and, behold, there came up among them another little horn.* There are several points to be noticed in regard to this: (1.) The fact that he "considered the horns;" that is, he looked on them until another sprang up among them. This implies that when he first saw the monster, it had no such horn, and that the horn sprang up a considerable time after he first saw it—intimating that it would occur, perhaps, far on in the history of the kingdom that was symbolized. It is implied that it was not an event which would *soon* occur. (2.) It sprang up "among" the others (בֵּינֵיהֵן) — starting from the same source, and appertaining to the same animal, and therefore a development or putting forth of the same power. The language here used does not designate, with any degree of certainty, the precise place which it occupied, but it would seem that the others stood close together, and that this sprang out of the centre, or *from the very midst* of them—implying that the new dominion symbolized would not be a *foreign* dominion, but one that would spring out of the kingdom itself, or that would seem to grow up *in* the kingdom. (3.) It was a little horn ; that is, it was small at first, though subsequently it grew so as to be emblematic of great power. This would denote that the power symbolized would be *small* at first—springing up gradually. The fulfilment of this would be found, neither in conquest nor in revolution, nor in a change of dynasty, nor in a sudden change of a constitution, but in some power that had an obscure origin, and that was feeble and small at the beginning, yet gradually increasing, till, by its own growth, it put aside a portion of the power before exercised and occupied its place. We should naturally look for the fulfilment of this in the increase of some power within the state that had a humble origin, and that slowly developed itself until it absorbed a considerable portion of the authority that essentially resided in the kingdom represented by the monster. (4.) In the growth of that "horn," three of the others were plucked up by the roots. The proper meaning of the word used to express this (אֶתְעֲקַרוּ) is, that they were *rooted out*—as a tree is overturned by the roots, or the roots are turned out from the earth. The process by which this was done seems to have been by *growth.* The gradual increase of the horn so crowded on the others that a portion of them was forced out, and fell. What is fairly indicated by this was not any act of violence, or any sudden convulsion or revolution, but such a gradual *growth* of power that a portion of the original power was removed, and this new power occupied its place. There was no *revolution*, properly so called ; no change of the whole dynasty, for a large portion of the horns remained, but the gradual rise of a new power that would wield a portion of that formerly wielded by others, and that would now wield the power in its place. The number *three* would either indicate that three parts out of the ten were absorbed in this way, or that a considerable, though an indefinite portion, was thus absorbed. (5.) The eyes :—*and behold, in this horn were eyes like the eyes of a man.* Eyes denote intelligence, as we see objects by their aid. The rims of the wheels in Ezekiel's vision were full of eyes (Ezek. i. 18), as symbolic of intelligence. This would denote that the

9 ¶ I beheld till the thrones
were cast down,[a] and the [b]Ancient

a ch. 2. 44; 1 Cor. 15. 24, 25.

power here referred to would be remarkably sagacious. We should naturally look for the fulfilment of this
in a power that laid its plans wisely
and intelligently; that had large and
clear views of policy; that was shrewd
and far-seeing in its counsels and purposes; that was skilled in diplomacy;
or, that was eminent for statesman-
like plans. This part of the symbol,
if it stood alone, would find its fulfilment in *any* wise and shrewd administration; as it stands here, surrounded
by others, it would seem that this, as
contrasted with them, was characteristically shrewd and far-seeing in its
policy. Lengerke, following Jerome,
supposes that this means that the object referred to would be a *man*, "as
the eyes of men are keener and sharper
than those of other animals." But the
more correct interpretation is that
above referred to—that it denotes intelligence, shrewdness, sagacity. (6.)
The mouth:—*and a mouth speaking
great things.* A mouth indicating
pride and arrogance. This is explained in ver. 25, as meaning that
he to whom it refers would "speak
great words against the Most High;"
that is, would be guilty of blasphemy.
There would be such arrogance, and
such claims set up, and such a spirit
evinced, that it would be in fact a
speaking against God. We naturally
look for the fulfilment of this to some
haughty and blaspheming power; some
power that would really blaspheme religion, and that would be opposed to
its progress and prosperity in the
world. The Sept., in the *Cod. Chis.,*
adds here, "and shall make war
against the saints;" but these words
are not found in the original Chaldee.
They accord, however, well with the
explanation in ver. 25. What has
been here considered embraces all that
pertains properly to this symbol—the
symbol of the fourth beast—except
the fact stated in ver. 11, that the
beast was slain, and that his body was
given to the burning flame. The inquiry as to the fulfilment will be ap-

of days did sit, whose [c]garment
was [d] white as snow, and the hair

b ver. 22; Isa. 9. 6. c Psa. 45. 8. d Rev. 1. 14.

propriate when we come to consider
the explanation given at the request
of Daniel, by the angel, in ver. 19-25.
9. *I beheld.* "I continued looking
on these strange sights, and contemplating these transformations." This
implies that some time elapsed before
all these things had occurred. He
looked on till he saw a solemn judgment passed on this fourth beast particularly, *as if* God had come forth in
his majesty and glory to pronounce
that judgment, and to bring the power
and arrogance of the beast to an end.
¶ *Till the thrones were cast down.* The
Chaldee word (כָּרְסָוָן) means, properly,
thrones—seats on which monarchs sit.
So far as the *word* is concerned, it
would apply either to a throne occupied by an earthly monarch, or to the
throne of God. The use of the *plural*
here would seem to imply, at least,
that the reference is not to the throne
of God, but to some other throne.
Maurer and Lengerke suppose that
the allusion is to the thrones on which
the celestial beings sat in the solemn
judgment that was to be pronounced—
the throne of God, and the thrones or
seats of the attending inhabitants of
heaven, coming with him to the solemn
judgment. Lengerke refers for illustration to 1 Kings xxii. 19; Isa. vi. 1;
Job i. 6, and Rev. v. 11, 12. But the
word itself might be properly applied
to the thrones of earthly monarchs as
well as to the throne of God. The
phrase "were cast down" (רְמִיו), in
our translation, would seem to suppose
that there was some throwing down, or
overturning of thrones, at this period,
and that the solemn judgment would
follow this, or be consequent on this.
The Chaldee word (רְמָא) means, as explained by Gesenius, to *cast,* to *throw*
(Dan. iii. 21, 24; vi. 16, 17); to *set,* to
place, e.g., thrones; to *impose* tribute
(Ezra vii. 24). The passage is rendered
by the Latin Vulgate, *throni positi
sunt*—"thrones were placed;" by the

of his head like the pure wool: his

throne ^a *was like* the fiery flame,
and his wheels ^b *as* burning fire.

Greek, ἐτίθησαν—"were placed." So Luther, *stühle gesetzt;* and so Lengerke, *stühle aufgestellt* — the thrones were placed, or set up. The proper meaning, therefore, of the phrase would seem to be—not, as in our translation, that the "thrones would be *cast down*"— as if there was to be an overturning of thrones on the earth to mark this particular period of history—but that there was, in the vision, a setting up, or a placing of thrones for the purpose of administering judgment, &c., on the beast. The use of the plural is, doubtless, in accordance with the language elsewhere employed, to denote the fact that the great Judge would be surrounded with others who would be, as it were, associated in administering justice—either angels or redeemed spirits. Nothing is more common in the Scripture than to represent others as thus associated with God in pronouncing judgment on men. Comp. Matt. xix. 28; Lu. xxii. 30; 1 Cor. vi. 2, 3; 1 Ti. v. 21; Rev. ii. 26; iv. 4. The era, or period, therefore, marked here, would be when a solemn Divine judgment was to be passed on the "beast," or when some events were to take place, *as if* such a judgment were pronounced. The events pertaining to the fourth beast were to be the last in the series preparatory to the reign of the saints, or the setting up of the kingdom of the Messiah, and therefore it is introduced in this manner, *as if* a solemn judgment scene were to occur. ¶ *And the Ancient of days did sit.* Was seated for the purposes of judgment. The phrase "Ancient of days"—עַתִּיק יוֹמִין —is one that denotes an elderly or old person; meaning, *he who is most ancient as to days,* and is equivalent to the French *L'Eternel,* or English, *The Eternal.* It occurs only in this chapter (vers. 9, 13, 22), and is a representation of one venerable in years, sitting down for the purposes of judgment. The appellation does not of itself denote *eternity,* but it is employed, probably, with reference to the fact that God is eternal. God is often repre-

sented under some such appellation, as he that is "from everlasting to everlasting" (Psal. xc. 2), "the first and the last" (Isa. xliv. 6), &c. There can be no doubt that the reference here is to God as a Judge, or as about to pronounce judgment, though there is no necessity for supposing that it will be in a visible and literal form, any more than there is for supposing that all that is here represented by symbols will *literally* take place. If it should be insisted on that the proper interpretation demands that there will be a literal and visible judgment, such as is here described, it may be replied that the same rigid interpretation would demand that there will be a *literal* "slaying of the beast, and a giving of his body to the flame" (ver. 11), and more generally still, that *all* that is here referred to by symbols will literally occur. The fact, however, is, that all these events are referred to by symbols —symbols which have an expressive meaning, but which, by their very nature and design, are not to be literally understood. All that is fairly implied here is, that events would occur in regard to this fourth beast *as if* God should sit in solemn judgment on it, and should condemn it in the manner here referred to. We are, doubtless, in the fulfilment of this, to look for some event that will be of so decisive and marked a character, that it may be regarded *as* a Divine judgment in the case, or that will show the strongly-marked Divine disapprobation — as really *as if* the judgment-seat were formally set, and God should appear in majesty to give sentence. *Sitting* was the usual posture among the ancients, as it is among the moderns, in pronouncing judgment. Among the ancients the judge sat on a throne or bench while the parties stood before him (comp. Zech. iv. 13), and with the Greeks and Romans so essential was the sitting posture for a judge, that a sentence pronounced in any other posture was not valid.—Lengerke. It was a maxim, *Animus sedendo magis sapit;* or, as Servius on the *Æn.* i. 56,

10 A fiery ^a stream issued and came forth from before him: thousand thousands ministered unto him, and ten thousand times ten

a Psa. 50. 3; Isa. 66. 15, 16.

remarks, *Est enim curantis et solliciti sedere.* ¶ *Whose garment* was *white as snow.* Whose robe. The reference here is to the long flowing robe that was worn by ancient princes, noblemen, or priests. See Notes on Isa. vi. 1. Comp. Notes on Rev. i. 13. White was an emblem of purity and honour, and was not an improper symbol of the purity of the judge, and of the justness of the sentence which he would pronounce. So the elder Pitt, in his celebrated speech against employing Indians in the war with the American people, besought the bishops to "interpose the unsullied purity of their lawn." Lengerke supposes, as Prof. Stuart does on Rev. i. 13, that the whiteness here referred to was not the mere colour of the material of which the robe was made, but was a celestial splendour or brightness, as if it were lightning or fire—such as is appropriate to the Divine Majesty. Lengerke refers here to Exod. xix. 18–24; Dan. ii. 22; Matt. xvii. 2; 1 Ti. vi. 16; 2 Esdras vii. 55; *Ascension of Isa.* viii. 21–25; Rev. i. 13, 14; iv. 2–4. But the more correct interpretation is to suppose that this refers to a pure white robe, such as judges might wear, and which would not be an improper symbol of their office. ¶ *And the hair of his head like the pure wool.* That is, for whiteness—a characteristic of venerable age. Compare Notes on Rev. i. 14. The image here set before us is that of one venerable by years and wisdom. ¶ *His throne* was like *the fiery flame.* The seat on which he sat seemed to be fire. That is, it was brilliant and splendid, as if it were a mass of flame. ¶ And *his wheels* as *burning fire.* The wheels of his throne—for, as in Ezek. i., x., the throne on which Jehovah sat appeared to be on wheels. In Ezekiel (i. 16; x. 9), the wheels of the throne appeared to be of the colour of beryl; that is, they were like precious stones. Here, perhaps, they had only the *appearance* of a flame—as such wheels would *seem* to flash flames. So

thousand stood ^b before him: the judgment ^c was set, and the books were opened.

b 1 Kings 22. 19; Psa. 68. 17; Heb. 12. 22.
c Rev. 20. 4, 12.

Milton, in describing the chariot of the Son of God:—

"Forth rush'd with whirlwind sound
The chariot of Paternal Deity,
Flashing thick flames, wheel within wheel undrawn,
Itself instinct with spirit, but convoyed
By four cherubic shapes; four faces each
Had wondrous; as with stars their bodies all,
And wings were set with eyes; with eyes the wheels
Of beryl, *and careering fires between.*"
—*Par. Lost*, b. vi.

10. *A fiery stream issued and came forth from before him.* Streams of fire seemed to burst forth from his throne. Representations of this kind abound in the Scriptures to illustrate the majesty and glory of God. Comp. Rev. iv. 5, "And out of the throne proceeded lightnings, and thunderings, and voices." Exod. xix. 16; Hab. iii. 4; Psal. xviii. 8. ¶ *Thousand thousands ministered unto him.* "A thousand of thousands;" that is, thousands multiplied a thousand times. The mind is struck with the fact that there are thousands present—and then the number seems as great as if those thousands were multiplied a thousand times. The idea is that there was an immense—a countless host. The reference here is to the angels, and God is often represented as attended with great numbers of these celestial beings when he comes down to our world. Deut. xxxiii. 2, "He came with ten thousands of saints;" that is, of holy ones. Psal. lxviii. 17, "The chariots of God are twenty thousand, even thousands of angels." Comp. Jude, ver. 14. The word "ministered" means that they attended on him. ¶ *And ten thousand times ten thousand stood before him.* An innumerable host. These were not to be judged, but were attendants on him as he pronounced sentence. The judgment here referred to was not on the world at large, but on the beast, preparatory to giving the kingdom to the one who was like the Son of man (vers. 13, 14). ¶ *The judgment was set.* That is, all the arrangements for

11 I beheld then, because of the voice of the great words which the horn spake; I beheld, *even* till the beast was slain, *a* and his body destroyed and given to the burning flame.   *a* Rev. 19. 20.

a solemn act of judgment were made, and the process of the judgment commenced. ¶ *And the books were opened.* As containing the record of the deeds of those who were to be judged. Comp. Rev. xx. 12. The great Judge is represented as having before him the record of all the deeds on which judgment was to be pronounced, and to be about to pronounce sentence according to those deeds. The judgment here referred to seems to have been some solemn act on the part of God transferring the power over the world, from that which had long swayed it, to the saints. As already remarked, the necessary interpretation of the passage does not require us to understand this of a literal and visible judgment—of a personal appearing of the "Ancient of days"—of a formal application to him by "one like the Son of man" (ver. 13) —or of a public and visible making over to him of a kingdom upon the earth. It is to be remembered that all this passed in vision before the mind of the prophet; that it is a symbolical representation; and that we are to find the fulfilment of this in some event changing the course of empire—putting a period to the power represented by the "beast" and the "horn," and causing that power to pass into other hands—producing a change as great on the earth *as if* such a solemn act of judgment were passed. The nature of the representation requires that we should look for the fulfilment of this in some great and momentous change in human affairs — some events that would take away the power of the "beast," and that would cause the dominion to pass into other hands. On the fulfilment, see the Notes on ver. 26.

11. *I beheld then, because of the voice of the great words which the horn spake.* I was attracted by these words —by their arrogance, and haughtiness, and pride ; and I saw that it was on account of these mainly that the solemn judgment proceeded against the beast. The attitude of the seer here is this—he heard arrogant and proud words uttered by the "horn," and he waited in deep attention, and in earnest expectation, to learn what judgment would be pronounced. He had seen (ver. 8) that horn spring up and grow to great power, and utter great things ; he had then seen, immediately on this, a solemn and sublime preparation for judgment, and he now waited anxiously to learn what sentence would be pronounced. The result is stated in the subsequent part of the verse. ¶ *I beheld.* I continued beholding. This would seem to imply that it was not done at once, but that some time intervened. ¶ Even *till the beast was slain.* The fourth beast : that which had the ten horns, and on which the little horn had sprung up. This was the result of the judgment. It is evidently implied here that the beast was slain *on account* of the words uttered by the horn that sprang up, or that the pride and arrogance denoted by that symbol were the cause of the fact that the beast was put to death. It is not said *by whom* the beast would be slain ; but the fair meaning is, that the procuring cause of that death would be the Divine judgment, on account of the pride and arrogancy of the "horn" that sprang up in the midst of the others. If the "beast" represents a mighty monarchy that would exist on the earth, and the "little horn" a new power that would spring out of that, then the fulfilment is to be found in such a fact as this— that this power, so mighty and terrible formerly, and that crushed down the nations, would, under the Divine judgment, be ultimately destroyed, on account of the nature of the authority claimed. We are to look for the accomplishment of this in some such state of things as that of a new power springing out of an existing dominion, that the existing dominion still remains, but was so much controlled by the new power, that it would be necessary to destroy the former on account of the arrogance and pride of that which sprang from it. In other words,

12 As concerning the rest of the beasts, they had their dominion taken away: yet [1] their lives

were prolonged for a season and time.

the destruction of the kingdom represented by the fourth beast would be, as a Divine judgment, on account of the arrogancy of that represented by the little horn. ¶ *And his body destroyed.* That is, there would be a destruction of the kingdom here represented as much as there would be of the beast if his body was destroyed. The power of that kingdom, as such, is to come to an end. ¶ *And given to the burning flame. Consumed.* This would represent, in strong terms, that the power here symbolized by the beast would be utterly destroyed. It is not, however, necessary to suppose that this is to be the *mode* in which it would be done, or that it would be by fire. It is to be remembered that all this is *symbol*, and no one part of the symbol should be taken literally more than another, nor is it congruous to suppose there would be a literal consuming *fire* in the case any more than that there would be literally a *beast*, or ten horns, or a little horn, The fair meaning is, that there would be as real a destruction *as if* it were accomplished by fire; or a destruction of which fire would be the proper emblem. The allusion is here, probably, to the fact that the dead bodies of animals were often consumed by fire.

12. *As concerning the rest of the beasts.* They had been superseded, but not destroyed. It would seem that they were still represented in vision to Daniel, as retaining their existence, though their power was taken away, and their fierceness subdued, or that they still seemed to remain alive for a time, or while the vision was passing. They were not cut down, destroyed, and consumed as the fourth beast was. ¶ *They had their dominion taken away.* They were superseded, or they no longer exercised power. They no more appeared exerting a control over the nations. They still existed, but they were subdued and quiet. It was possible to discern them, but they no

longer acted the conspicuous part which they had done in the days of their greatness and grandeur. Their power had passed away. This cannot be difficult of interpretation. We should naturally look for the fulfilment of this in the fact that the nations referred to by these first three beasts were still in being, and could be recognized as nations, in their boundaries, or customs, or languages ; but that the *power* which they had wielded had passed into other hands. ¶ *Yet their lives were prolonged.* Marg., as in Chaldee, " a prolonging in life was given them." That is, they were not utterly destroyed and consumed as the power of the fourth beast was after the solemn judgment. The meaning is, that in these kingdoms there would be energy for a time. They had life still ; and the difference between them and the kingdom represented by the fourth beast was that which would exist between wild animals subdued but still living, and a wild animal killed and burned. We should look for the fulfilment of this in some state of things where the kingdoms referred to by the three beasts were subdued and succeeded by others, though they still retained something of their national character ; while the other kingdom had no successor of a civil kind, but where its power wholly ceased, and the dominion went wholly into other hands—so that it might be said that that kingdom, as such, had *wholly* ceased to be. ¶ *For a season and time.* Comp. Notes on ver. 25. The time mentioned here is not definite. The phrase used (עַד־זְמַן וְעִדָּן) refers to a definite period, both the words in the original referring to a *designated* or *appointed* time, though neither of them indicates anything about the *length* of the time, any more than our word *time* does. Luther renders this, " For there was a time and an hour appointed to them how long each one should continue." Grotius explains this as meaning, " Beyond the time

13 I saw in the night visions, and, behold, *one* like the Son of man *a* came with the clouds of

a Matt.24.30; 25.31; 26.64; Rev.1.7,13; 14.14.

heaven, and came to the *b* Ancient of days, and they brought him near before him.

b ver. 9.

fixed by God they could not continue." The true meaning of the Chaldee is probably this : "For a time, even a definite time." The mind of the prophet is at first fixed upon the fact that they continue to live ; then upon the fact, somehow apparent, that it is for a definite period. Perhaps in the vision he saw them one after another die or disappear. In the words here used, however, there is nothing by which we can determine *how long* they were to continue. The time that the power represented by the little horn is to continue *is* explained in ver. 25, but there is no clue by which we can ascertain how long the existence of the power represented by the first three beasts was to continue. All that is clear is, that it was to be lengthened out for some period, but that that was a definite and fixed period.

13. *I saw in the night visions.* Evidently in the same night visions, or on the same occasion, for the visions are connected. See vers. 1, 7. The meaning is, that he continued beholding, or that a new vision passed before him. ¶ *And, behold, one like the Son of man,* &c. It is remarkable that Daniel does not attempt to represent this by any symbol. The representation by symbols ceases with the fourth beast ; and now the description assumes a literal form—the setting up of the kingdom of the Messiah and of the saints. *Why* this change of form occurs is not stated or known, but the sacred writers seem carefully to have avoided any representation of the Messiah by symbols. The phrase "The Son of Man"—אֱנָשׁ בַּר—does not occur elsewhere in the

Old Testament in such a connection, and with such a reference as it has here, though it is often found in the New, and is, in fact, the favourite term by which the Saviour designates himself. In Dan. iii. 25, we have the phrase "the Son of God" (see Notes on that passage), as applicable to one who appeared with the three "children"

that were cast into the burning furnace ; and in Ezekiel, the phrase "son of man" often occurs as applicable to himself as a prophet, being found more than eighty times in his prophecies, but the expression here used does not elsewhere occur in the Old Testament as applicable to the personage intended. As occurring here, it is important to explain it, not only in view of the events connected with it in the prophecy, but as having done much to mould the language of the New Testament. There are three questions in regard to its meaning : What does it signify ? To whom does it refer ? And what would be its proper fulfilment ? (1.) The phrase is more than a mere Hebrew or Chaldee expression to denote *man*, but is always used with some peculiar significancy, and with relation to some peculiar characteristic of the person to whom it is applied, or with some special design. To ascertain this design, regard should be had to the expression of the original. "While the words אִישׁ and אִשָּׁה are used simply as designations of sex, אֱנוֹשׁ, which is etymologically akin to אָנַשׁ, is employed with constant reference to its original meaning, *to be weak, sick ;* it is the ethical designation of man, but אָדָם denotes man as to his physical, natural condition—whence the use of the word in such passages as Psa. viii. 4; Job xxv. 6, and also its connection with בֶּן, are satisfactorily explained. The emphatic address בֶּן אָדָם—*Son of man*—is therefore [in Ezekiel] a continued admonition to the prophet to remember that he is a man like all the rest."—Hävernick, *Com. on Ezek.* ii. 1, 2, quoted in the *Bibliotheca Sacra*, v. 718. The expression here used is בַּר אֱנוֹשׁ, and would *properly* refer to man as weak and feeble, and as liable to be sick, &c. Applied to any one as "*a* Son of man," it would be used to denote that he partook of the weakness and infirmities of the race ; and, as the phrase *"the* Son of man" is used in the New Testament when applied by the Saviour to himself, there is an undoubted reference to this fact —that he sustained a peculiar relation to our race ; that he was in all respects a man ; that he was one of us ; that he had so taken our nature on himself that there was a peculiar propriety that a term which would at once designate this should be given to him. The phrase here used by Daniel would denote some one (*a*) in the human form ; (*b*) some one sustaining a peculiar relation to man—as if human nature were embodied in him. (2.) The next inquiry here is, *to whom* this refers? Who, in fact, was the one that was thus seen in vision by the prophet? Or who was designed to be set forth by this? This inquiry is not so much, Whom did Daniel suppose or understand this to be? as, Who was in fact designed to be represented ; or in whom would the fulfilment be found? For, on the supposition that this was a heavenly vision, it is clear that it was intended to designate some one in whom the complete fulfilment was to be found. Now, admitting that this was a heavenly vision, and that it was intended to represent what would occur in future times, there are the clearest reasons for supposing that the Messiah was referred to ; and indeed this is so plain, that it may be assumed as one of the indisputable things by which to determine the character and design of the prophecy. Among these reasons are the following : (*a*) The name itself, as a name assumed by the Lord Jesus—the favourite name by which he chose to designate himself when on the earth. This name he used technically ; he used it as one that would be understood to denote the Messiah ; he used it as if it needed no explanation as having a reference to the Messiah. But this usage could have been derived only from this passage in Daniel ; for there is no other place in the Old Testament where the name could refer with propriety to the Messiah, or would be understood to be applicable to him. (*b*) This interpretation has been given to it by the Jewish writers in general, in all ages.

I refer to this, not to say that their explanation is authoritative, but to show that it is the natural and obvious meaning; and because, as we shall see, it is that which has given shape and form to the language of the New Testament, and is fully sanctioned there. Thus, in the ancient book of Zohar it is said, " In the times of the Messiah, Israel shall be one people to the Lord, and he shall make them one nation in the earth, and they shall rule above and below; as it is written, *Behold, one like the Son of man came with the clouds of heaven ;* this is the King Messiah, of whom it is written, *And in the days of these kings shall the God of heaven set up a kingdom which shall never be destroyed,"* &c. So in the Talmud, and so the majority of the ancient Jewish Rabbins. See Gill, *Com. in loc.* It is true that this interpretation has not been uniform among the Jewish Rabbins, but still it has prevailed among them, as it has among Christian interpreters. (*c*) A sanction seems to be given to this interpretation by the adoption of the title "Son of man" by the Lord Jesus, as that by which he chose to designate himself. That title was such as would constantly suggest this place in Daniel as referring to himself, and especially as he connected with it the declaration that "the Son of man would come in the clouds of heaven," &c. It was hardly possible that he should use the title in such a connection without suggesting this place in Daniel, or without leaving the impression on the minds of his hearers that he meant to be understood as applying this to himself. (*d*) It may be added, that it cannot with propriety be applied to any other. Porphyry, indeed, supposed that Judas Maccabeus was intended ; Grotius that it referred to the Roman people; Aben Ezra to the people of Israel; and Cocceius to the people of the Most High (Gill) ; but all these are unnatural interpretations, and are contrary to that which one would obtain by allowing the language of the New Testament to influence his mind. The title—so often used by the Saviour himself ; the attending circumstances of the clouds of heaven ; the *place* which the vision occupies—so immediately preceding the setting up of the kingdom of the saints ; and the fact that that kingdom can be set up only under the Messiah, all point to him as the personage represented in the vision. (3.) But if it refers to the Messiah, the next inquiry is, What is to be regarded as the proper fulfilment of the vision ? To what precisely does it relate ? Are we to suppose that there will be a literal appearing of the Son of man—the Messiah—in the clouds of heaven, and a passing over of the kingdom in a public and solemn manner into the hands of the saints ? In reply to these questions, it may be remarked (a), that this cannot be understood as relating to the last judgment ; for it is not introduced with reference to that at all. The "Son of man" is not here represented as coming with a view to judge the world at the winding-up of human affairs, but for the purpose of setting up a kingdom, or procuring a kingdom for his saints. There is no assembling of the people of the world together ; no act of judging the righteous and the wicked ; no pronouncing of a sentence on either. It is evident that the world is to continue much longer under the dominion of the saints. (b) It is not to be taken literally ; that is, we are not, from this passage, to expect a literal appearance of the Son of man in the clouds of heaven, preparatory to the setting up of the kingdom of the saints. For if one portion is to be taken literally, there is no reason why all should not be. Then we are to expect, not merely the appearing of the Son of man in the clouds, but also the following things, as a part of the fulfilment of the vision, to wit : the literal placing of a throne, or seat ; the literal streaming forth of flame from his throne ; the literal appearing of the "Ancient of days," with a garment of white, and hair as wool ; a literal approach of the Son of man to him as seated on his throne to ask of him a kingdom, &c. But no one can believe that all this is to occur ; no one does believe that it will. (c) The proper interpretation is to regard this, as it was seen by Daniel, as a vision—a representation of a state of things in the world *as if* what is here described would occur. That is, great events were to take place, of which this would be a proper symbolical representation —or *as if* the Son of man, the Messiah, would thus appear ; would approach the "Ancient of days ;" would receive a kingdom, and would make it over to the saints. Now, there is no real difficulty in understanding what is here meant to be taught, and what we are to expect ; and these points of *fact* are the following, viz. :—1. That he who is here called the "Ancient of days " is the source of power and dominion. 2. That there would be some severe adjudication of the power here represented by the *beast* and the *horn*. 3. That the kingdom or dominion of the world is to be in fact given to him who is here called "the Son of man" —the Messiah—a fact represented here by his approaching the "Ancient of days." who is the source of all power. 4. That there is to be some passing over of the kingdom or power into the hands of the saints ; or some setting up of a kingdom on the earth, of which he is to be the head, and in which the dominion over the world shall be in fact in the hands of his people, and the laws of the Messiah everywhere prevail. What will be the essential characteristics of that kingdom we may learn by the exposition of ver. 14, compared with ver. 27. ¶ *Came with the clouds of heaven.* That is, he seemed to come down from the sky encompassed with clouds. So the Saviour, probably intending to refer to this language, speaks of himself, when he shall come to judge the world, as coming in clouds, or encompassed by clouds, Matt. xxiv. 30 ; xxvi. 64 ; Mark xiii. 26 ; xiv. 62. Comp. Rev. i. 7. Clouds are an appropriate symbol of the Divinity. See Psa. xcvii. 2 ; civ. 3. The same symbol was employed by the heathen, representing their deities as appearing covered with a cloud :—

" Tandem venias, precamur,
Nube candentes humeros amictus,
Augur Apollo !"—Horace, *Lyr.* I. 2.

The allusion in the place before us is not to the last judgment, but to the fact that a kingdom on the earth would

14 And *a* there was given him

a Psa. 2. 6-8; Matt. 28. 18; John 3. 35; 1 Cor.
15. 27; Eph. 1. 20, 22.

be passed over into the hands of the Messiah. He is represented as coming sublimely to the world, and as receiving a kingdom that would *succeed* those represented by the beasts. ¶ *And came to the Ancient of days.* Ver. 9. This shows that the passage cannot refer to the final judgment. He comes to the "Ancient of days"—to God as the source of power—as if to ask a petition for a kingdom ; not to pronounce a judgment on mankind. The act here appropriately denotes that God is the source of all power ; that all who reign derive their authority from him, and that even the Messiah, in setting up his kingdom in the world, receives it at the hand of the Father. This is in accordance with all the representations in the New Testament. We are not to suppose that this will occur literally. There is to be no such literal sitting of one with the appearance of age— denoted by the "Ancient of days"— on a throne ; nor is there to be any such literal approaching him by one in the form of a man to receive a kingdom. Such passages show the absurdity of the attempts to interpret the language of the Scriptures literally. All that this symbol fairly means must be, that the kingdom that was to be set up under the Messiah on the earth was received from God. ¶ *And they brought him near before him.* That is, he was brought near before him. Or, it may mean that his attendants brought him near. All that the language necessarily implies is, that he came near to his seat, and received from him a kingdom.

14. *And there was given him dominion.* That is, by him who is represented as the "Ancient of days." The fair interpretation of this is, that he received the dominion from him. This is the uniform representation in the New Testament. Comp. Matt. xxviii. 18 ; John iii. 35 ; 1 Cor. xv. 27. The word *dominion* here means *rule* or *authority*—such as a prince exercises. He was set over a kingdom as a prince or ruler. ¶ *And glory.* That is, the

dominion, and glory, and a kingdom, that all people, nations, and

glory or honour appropriate to one at the head of such an empire. ¶ *And a kingdom.* That is, he would reign. He would have sovereignty. The nature and the extent of this kingdom is immediately designated as one that would be universal and perpetual. What is properly implied in this language as to the question whether it will be literal and visible, will be appropriately considered at the close of the verse. All that is necessary to be noticed here is, that it is everywhere promised in the Old Testament that the Messiah would be a king, and have a kingdom. Comp. Psal. ii. ; Isa. ix. 6, 7. ¶ *That all people, nations, and languages should serve him.* It would be universal ; would embrace all nations. The language here is such as would emphatically denote universality. See Notes on ch. iii. 4 ; iv. 1. It implies that that kingdom would extend over all the nations of the earth, and we are to look for the fulfilment of this only in such a universal reign of the Messiah. ¶ *His dominion is an everlasting dominion,* &c. The others, represented by the four beasts, would all pass away, but this would be permanent and eternal. Nothing would destroy it. It would not have, as most kingdoms of the earth have had, any such internal weakness or source of discord as would be the cause of its destruction, nor would there be any external power that would invade or overthrow it. This declaration affirms nothing as to the *form* in which the kingdom would exist, but merely asserts the *fact* that it would do so. Respecting the kingdom of the Messiah, to which this undoubtedly alludes, the same thing is repeatedly and uniformly affirmed in the New Testament. Compare Matt. xvi. 18 ; Heb. xii. 28 ; Rev. xi. 15. The form and manner in which this will occur is more fully developed in the New Testament ; in the vision seen by Daniel the fact only is stated.

The question now arises, What would be a fulfilment of this prediction respecting the kingdom that will be

languages should serve him: his dominion *is* an everlasting *a* dominion, which shall not pass away, and his kingdom *that* which shall not *b* be destroyed.

15 ¶ I Daniel was grieved in my spirit in the midst of *my* ¹ body, and the visions of my head troubled me.

a Psa.145.13. *b* Heb.12.28. 1 *sheath*, 2 Pet.1.14.

given to the saints ? What, from the language used in the vision, should we be legitimately authorized to expect to take place on the earth ? In regard to these questions, there are but two views which can be taken, and the interpretation of the passage must sustain the one or the other. (*a*) One is that which supposes that this will be literally fulfilled in the sense that the Son of God, the Messiah, will reign personally on earth. According to this, he will come to set up a visible and glorious kingdom, making Jerusalem his capital, and swaying his sceptre over the world. All nations and people will be subject to him ; all authority will be wielded by his people under him. (*b*) According to the other view, there will be a spiritual reign of the Son of God over the earth ; that is, the principles of his religion will everywhere prevail, and the righteous will rule, and the laws of the Redeemer will be obeyed everywhere. There will be such a prevalence of his gospel on the hearts of all—rulers and people ; the gospel will so modify all laws, and control all customs, and remove all abuses, and all the forms of evil ; men will be so generally under the influence of that gospel, that it may be said that *He* reigns on the earth, or that the government actually administered is *his*.

In regard to these different views, and to the true interpretation of the passage, it may be remarked, (1.) That we are not to look for the *literal* fulfilment of this ; we are not to expect that what is here described will literally occur. The whole is evidently a symbolical representation, and the fulfilment is to be found in something that the symbol would properly denote. No one can pretend that there is to be an actual sitting on the throne, by one in the form of an old man— " the Ancient of days "—or that there is to be a literal coming to him by one " like the Son of man," to receive a kingdom. But if one part of the re-

presentation is not to be literally interpreted, why should the other be ? It may be added, that it is nowhere *said* that this would literally occur. (2.) All that is fairly implied here is found in the latter interpretation. Such a prevalence of the principles of the gospel would meet the force of the language, and every part of the vision would find a *real* fulfilment in that. (*a*) The fact that it proceeds from God — represented as "the Ancient of days." (*b*) The fact that it is given by him, or that the kingdom is made over by him to the Messiah. (*c*) The fact that the Messiah would have such a kingdom ; that is, that he would reign on the earth, in the hearts and lives of men. (*d*) The fact that that kingdom would be universal—extending over all people. (*e*) And the fact that it would be perpetual ; that is, that it would extend down to the end of time, or the consummation of all things here, and that it would be then eternal in the heavens. For a very full and ample illustration of this passage—so full and ample as to supersede the necessity of any additional illustration here, see the Notes on ch. ii. 44, 45.

15. *I Daniel was grieved in my spirit.* That is, I was *troubled ;* or my heart was made heavy and sad. This was probably in part because he did not fully understand the meaning of the vision, and partly on account of the fearful and momentous nature of that which was indicated by it. So the apostle John (Rev. v. 4) says, "And I wept much because no man was found worthy to open and to read the book." ¶ *In the midst of my body.* Marg., as in the Chald., *sheath.* The body is undoubtedly referred to, and is so called as the envelope of the mind —or as that in which the soul is *inserted,* as the sword is in the sheath, and from which it is drawn out by death. The same metaphor is employed by Pliny: *Donec cremato co inimici remeanti animæ velut vaginam*

16 I came near unto one of them that stood by, and asked him the truth of all this. So he told me, and made me know the interpretation of the things.

17 These great beasts, which are

1 *high ones, i.e., things or places,* Eph.1.3; 6.12.

four, *are* four kings, *which* shall arise out of the earth.

18 But the saints of the [1]Most High shall take the kingdom, and possess the kingdom *a* for ever, even for ever and ever.

a Rev. 3. 21.

---

ademerint. So, too, a certain philosopher, who was slighted by Alexander the Great on account of his ugly face, is said to have replied, *Corpus hominis nil est nisi vagina gladii in qua anima reconditur.*—Gesenius. Comp. Lengerke, *in loc.* See also Job xxvii. 8, "When God *taketh away* his soul;" or rather *draws out* his soul, as a sword is drawn out of the sheath. Comp. Notes on that place. See also Buxtorf's *Lex. Tal.* p. 1307. The meaning here is plain—that Daniel felt sad and troubled in mind, and that this produced a sensible effect on his body. ¶ *And the visions of my head troubled me.* The head is here regarded as the seat of the intellect, and he speaks of these visions as if they were seen by the head. That is, they seemed to pass before his eyes.

16. *I came near unto one of them that stood by.* That is, to one of the angels who appeared to stand near the throne. ver. 10. Comp. ch. viii. 13 ; Zech. iv. 4, 5 ; Rev. vii. 13. It was natural for Daniel to suppose that the angels who were seen encircling the throne would be able to give him information on the subject, and the answers which Daniel received show that he was not mistaken in his expectation. God has often employed angels to communicate important truths to men, or has made them the medium of communicating his will. Comp. Rev. i. 1 ; Acts vii. 53 ; Heb. ii. 2. ¶ *So he told me, and made me know the interpretation of the things.* He explained the meaning of the symbols, so that Daniel understood them. It would seem probable that Daniel has not recorded *all* that the angel communicated respecting the vision, but he has preserved so much that we may understand its general signification.

17. *These great beasts, which are four, are four kings.* Four kings or four

dynasties. There is no reason for supposing that they refer to individual *kings,* but the obvious meaning is, that they refer to four *dominions* or *empires* that would succeed one another on the earth. So the whole representation leads us to suppose, and so the passage has been always interpreted. The Latin Vulgate renders it *regna ;* the Sept. βασιλεῖαι ; Luther, *Reiche ;* Lengerke, *Königreiche.* This interpretation is confirmed, also, by ver. 23, where it is expressly said that "the fourth beast shall be the fourth *kingdom* upon earth." See also ver. 24. ¶ *Which shall arise out of the earth.* In ver. 2 the beasts are represented as coming up from the *sea*—the emblem of agitated nations. Here the same idea is presented more literally—that they would seem to spring up out of the earth, thus thrown into wild commotion. These dynasties were to be upon the earth, and they were in all things to indicate their earthly origin. Perhaps, also, it is designed by these words to denote a marked contrast between these four dynasties and the one that would follow—which would be of heavenly origin. This was the *general* intimation which was given to the meaning of the vision, and he was satisfied at once as to the explanation, so far as the first three were concerned; but the fourth seemed to indicate more mysterious and important events, and respecting this he was induced to ask a more particular explanation.

18. *But the saints of the Most High shall take the kingdom.* That is, they shall ultimately take possession of the rule over all the world, and shall control it from that time onward to the end. This is the grand thing which the vision is designed to disclose, and on this it was evidently the intention to fix the mind. Everything before was preparatory and subordinate to

19 Then I would know the truth of the fourth beast, which was diverse from all ¹ the others, exceeding dreadful, whose teeth *were of* iron, and his nails *of* brass;

1 *those.*

which devoured, brake in pieces, and stamped the residue with his feet;

20 And of the ten horns that *were* in his head, and *of* the other which came up, and before whom

---

this, and to this all things tended. The phrase rendered *the Most High*—in the margin *"high ones, i.e., things or places"*—עֶלְיוֹנִין—is in the plural number, and means literally *high ones;* but there can be no doubt that it refers here to God, and is given to him as the word *Elohim* is (Gen. i. 1, *et sœpe*), to denote majesty or honour—*pluralis excellentiœ*. The word rendered *saints* means *the holy,* and the reference is undoubtedly to the people of God on the earth, meaning here that they would take possession of the kingdom, or that they would rule. When true religion shall everywhere prevail, and when all offices shall be in the hands of good men—of men that fear God and that keep his commandments—instead of being in the hands of bad men, as they generally have been, then this prediction will be accomplished in respect to all that is fairly implied in it. ¶ *And possess the kingdom for ever, even for ever and ever.* This is a strong and emphatic declaration, affirming that this dominion will be perpetual. It will not pass away, like the other kingdoms, to be succeeded by another one. What is here affirmed, as above remarked, will be true if such a reign should continue on earth to the winding up of all things, and should then be succeeded by an eternal reign of holiness in the heavens. It is not necessary to interpret this as meaning that there would be literally an eternal kingdom on this earth, for it is everywhere taught in the Scriptures that the present order of things will come to a close. But it does seem necessary to understand this as teaching that there will be a state of prevalent righteousness on the earth hereafter, and that when that is introduced it will continue to the end of time.

19. *Then I would know the truth of the fourth beast.* I desired to know

particularly what was symbolized by that. He appears to have been satisfied with the most general intimations in regard to the first three beasts, for the kingdoms represented by them seemed to have nothing very remarkable. But it was different in regard to the fourth. The beast itself was so remarkable—so fierce and terrific; the number of the horns was so great; the springing up of the little horn was so surprising; the character of that horn was so unusual; the judgment passed on it was so solemn; and the vision of one like the Son of man coming to take possession of the kingdom—all these things were of so fearful and so uncommon a character, that the mind of Daniel was peculiarly affected in view of them, and he sought earnestly for a further explanation. In the description that Daniel here gives of the beast and the horns, he refers in the main to the same circumstances which he had before described; but he adds a few which he had before omitted, all tending to impress the mind more deeply with the fearful character and the momentous import of the vision ; as, for instance, the fact that it had nails of brass, and made war with the saints. ¶ *Which was diverse from all the others.* Different in its form and character ;—so different as to attract particular attention, and to leave the impression that something very peculiar and remarkable was denoted by it. Notes, ver. 7. ¶ *Exceeding dreadful.* Notes, ver. 7. ¶ *And his nails* of *brass.* This circumstance is not mentioned in the first statement, ver. 7. It accords well with the other part of the description, that his teeth were of iron, and is designed to denote the fearful and terrific character of the kingdom, symbolized by the beast. ¶ *Which devoured,* &c. See Notes on ver. 7.

20. *And of the ten horns,* &c. See

three fell; even *of* that horn that had eyes, and a mouth that spake very great things, whose look *was* more stout than his fellows.

21 I beheld, and *a* the same horn

a Rev. 13. 7, &c.

Notes on vers. 7, 8. ¶ *Whose look* was *more stout than his fellows.* Literally, "whose aspect was *greater* than that of its companions." This does not mean that its *look* or aspect was more *fierce* or *severe* than that of the others, but that the appearance of the horn was *greater*—רב. In ver. 8, this is described as a "little horn;" and to understand this, and reconcile the two, we must suppose that the seer watched this as it grew until it became the largest of the number. Three fell before it, and it outgrew in size all the others until it became the most prominent. This would clearly denote that the kingdom or the authority referred to by this eleventh horn would be more distinct and prominent than either of the others—would become so conspicuous and important as in fact to concentrate and embody all the power of the beast.

21. *I beheld, and the same horn made war with the saints.* I continued to look on this until I saw war made by this horn with the people of God. This circumstance, also, is not referred to in the first description, and the order of time in the description would seem to imply that the war with the saints would be at a considerable period *after* the first appearance of the horn, or would be only when it had grown to its great size and power. This *"war"* might refer to open hostilities, carried on in the usual manner of war; or to persecution, or to any invasion of the rights and privileges of others. As it is a "war with the *saints,*" it would be most natural to refer it to persecution. ¶ *And prevailed against them.* That is, he overcame and subdued them. He was stronger than they were, and they were not able to resist him. The same events are evidently referred to and in almost similar language—borrowed probably from Daniel—in Rev.

made war with the saints, and prevailed against them;

22 Until the Ancient of days came, and judgment was given to the saints of the Most High; and the time came that the saints possessed the kingdom.

xiii. 5–7: "And there was given him a mouth speaking great things and blasphemies, and power was given unto him to continue forty and two months. And he opened his mouth in blasphemy against God, to blaspheme his name, and his tabernacle, and them that dwell in heaven. And it was given him to make war with the saints, and to overcome them; and power was given him over all kindreds, and tongues, and nations."

22. *Until the Ancient of days came.* Notes, ver. 9. That is, this was to occur *after* the horn grew to its full size, and *after* the war was made with the saints, and they had been overcome. It does not affirm that this would occur *immediately,* but that at some subsequent period the Ancient of days would come, and would set up a kingdom on the earth, or would make over the kingdom to the saints. There would be as real a transfer and as actual a setting up of a peculiar kingdom, *as if* God himself should appear on the earth, and should publicly make over the dominion to them. ¶ *And judgment was given to the saints of the Most High.* That is, there was a solemn act of judgment in the case by which the kingdom was given to their hands. It was as real a transfer as if there had been a judgment pronounced on the beast, and he had been condemned and overthrown, and as if the dominion which he once had should be made over to the servants of the Most High. ¶ *And the time came that the saints possessed the kingdom.* That they ruled on the earth; that good men made and administered the laws; that the principles of religion prevailed, influencing the hearts of all men, and causing righteousness and justice to be done. The universal prevalence of true religion, in controlling the hearts and lives of men, and disposing them to do what in all circumstances *ought*

23 Thus he said, The fourth beast shall be the fourth kingdom upon earth, which shall be diverse from all kingdoms, and shall devour the whole earth, and shall tread it down, and break it in pieces.

---

to be done, would be a complete fulfilment of all that is here said. Thus far the description of what Daniel saw, of which he was so desirous to obtain an explanation. The explanation follows, and embraces the remainder of the chapter.

23–27. *Thus he said,* &c. That is, in explanation of the fourth symbol which appeared—the fourth beast, and of the events connected with his appearing. This explanation embraces the remainder of the chapter; and as the whole subject appeared difficult and momentous to Daniel before the explanation, so it may be said to be in many respects difficult, and in all respects momentous still. It is a question on which expositors of the Scriptures are by no means agreed, to what it refers, and whether it has been already accomplished, or whether it extends still into the future; and it is of importance, therefore, to determine, if possible, what is its true meaning. The two points of inquiry which are properly before us are, first, What do the words of explanation as used by the angel fairly imply—that is, what, according to the fair interpretation of these words, would be the course of events referred to, or what should we naturally expect to find as actually occurring on the earth in the fulfilment of this? and, secondly, To what events the prophecy is actually to be applied—whether to what has already occurred, or what is yet to occur; whether we can find anything in what is now past which would be an accomplishment of this, or whether it is to be applied to events a part of which are yet future? This will lead us into a statement of the *points* which it is affirmed would occur in regard to this kingdom; and then into an inquiry respecting the application.

What is fairly implied in the explanation of the angel? This would embrace the following points:—

(1.) There was to be a fourth kingdom on the earth:—*the fourth beast shall be the fourth kingdom upon earth,* ver. 23. This was to succeed the other three, symbolized by the lion, the bear, and the leopard. No further reference is made to them, but the characteristics of this are fully stated. Those characteristics, which have been explained in the Notes on ver. 7, are, as here repeated, (*a*) that it would be in important respects different from the others; (*b*) that it would devour or subdue the whole earth; (*c*) that it would tread it down and break it in pieces; that is, it would be a universal dynasty, of a fierce and warlike character, that would keep the whole world subdued and subject by power.

(2.) Out of this sovereignty or dominion, ten powers would arise (ver. 24):—*and the ten horns out of this kingdom are ten kings that shall arise.* Comp. Notes on ver. 7. That is, they would spring out of this one dominion, or it would be broken up into these minor sovereignties, yet all manifestly springing from the one kingdom, and wielding the same power. We should not naturally look for the fulfilment of this in a *succession* of kings; for that would have been symbolized by the beast itself representing the entire dominion or dynasty, but rather to a number of contemporaneous powers that had somehow sprung out of the one power, or that now possessed and wielded the power of that one dominion. If the kingdom here referred to should be broken up into such a number of powers, or if in any way these powers became possessed of this authority, and wielded it, such a fact would express what we are to expect to find in this kingdom.

(3.) From the midst of these sovereignties or kingdoms there was to spring up another one of peculiar characteristics, vers. 24, 25. These characteristics are the following: (*a*) That it would spring out of the others, or be, as it were, one form of the administration of the same power—as the eleventh horn sprang from the same source as

24 And the ten horns out of this kingdom *are* ten kings *that* shall arise : and another shall rise after them ; and he shall be diverse from the first, and he shall subdue three kings.

---

the ten, and we are, therefore, to look for the exercise of this power somehow in connection with the same kingdom or dynasty. (*b*) This would not spring up contemporaneously with the ten, but would arise "after them"—and we are to look for this power as in some sense *succeeding* them. (*c*.) It would be small at first—as was the horn (ver. 8), and we are to look for the fulfilment in some power that would be feeble at first. (*d*) It would grow to be a mighty power—for the little horn became so powerful as to pluck up three of the others (ver. 8), and it is said in the explanation (ver. 24), that he would subdue three of the kings. (*e*) It would subdue "three kings ;" that is, three of the ten, and we are to look for the fulfilment in some manifestation of that power by which, either literally three of them were overthrown, or by which about one-third of their power was taken away. The mention of the exact number of "*three*," however, would rather seem to imply that we are to expect some such exact fulfilment, or some prostration of three sovereignties by the new power that would arise. (*f*) It would be proud, and ambitious, and particularly arrogant against God :— "*and he shall speak great words against the Most High*," ver. 25. The Chaldee here rendered *against*—לִצַּד—means, literally, *at*, or *against the part of it*, and then *against*. Vulg. *contra ;* Gr. πρὸς. This would be fulfilled in one who would blaspheme God directly ; or who would be rebellious against his government and authority ; or who would complain of his administration and laws ; or who would give utterance to harsh and reproachful words against his real claims. It would find a fulfilment obviously in an open opposer of the claims and the authority of the true God ; or in one the whole spirit and bearing of whose pretensions might be fairly construed as in fact an utterance of great words against him. (*g*) This

would be a persecuting power :— "*and shall wear out the saints of the Most High*," ver. 25. That is, it would be characterized by a persecution of the real saints—of those who were truly the friends of God, and who served him. (*h*) It would claim legislative power, the power of changing established customs and laws : — "*and think to change times and laws*," ver. 25. The word rendered *think* (סְבַר) means, more properly, to *hope ;* and the idea here is, that he hopes and trusts to be able to change times and laws. Vulg., *Putabit quòd possit mutare tempora*, &c. The state of mind here referred to would be that of one who would *desire* to produce changes in regard to the times and laws referred to, and who would hope that he would be able to effect it. If there was a strong wish to do this, and if there was a belief that in any way he could bring it about, it would meet what is implied in the use of the word here. There would be the exercise of some kind of authority in regard to existing times for festivals, or other occasions, and to existing laws, and there would be a purpose so to change them as to accomplish his own ends. The word *times*—זִמְנִין—would seem to refer properly to some stated or designated times—as times appointed for festivals, &c. Gesenius, "*time*, specially *an appointed time, season :*" Eccles. iii. 1 ; Neh. ii. 6 ; Esth. ix. 27, 31. Lengerke renders the word *Fest-Zeiten*—"festival times," and explains it as meaning *the holy times, festival days*, Lev. xxiii. 2, 4, 37, 44. The allusion is, undoubtedly, to such periods set apart as festivals or fasts—seasons consecrated to the services of religion ; and the kind of jurisdiction which the power here referred to would hope and desire to set up would be to have control of these periods, and so to change and alter them as to accomplish his own purposes—either by abolishing

25 And he shall speak *great* words against the Most High, and shall wear out the saints of the

those in existence, or by substituting others in their place. At all times these seasons have had a direct connection with the state and progress of religion; and he who has power over them, either to abolish existing festivals, or to substitute others in their places, or to appoint new festivals, has an important control over the whole subject of religion, and over a nation. The word rendered *laws* here—חַ—while it might refer to any law, would more properly designate laws pertaining to religion. See Dan. vi. 5, 7, 12 (6, 9, 13); Ezra vii. 12, 21. So Lengerke explains it as referring to the laws of religion, or to religion. The kind of jurisdiction, therefore, referred to in this place would be that which would pertain to the laws and institutions of religion; it would be a purpose to obtain the control of these; it would be a claim of right to abolish such as existed, and to institute new ones; it would be a determination to exert this power in such a way as to promote its own ends. (*i*) It would continue for a definite period:—*and they shall be given into his hands until a time and times and the dividing of time*, ver. 25. *They;* that is, either those laws, or the people, the powers referred to. Maurer refers this to the "saints of the Most High," as meaning that *they* would be delivered into his hands. Though this is not designated expressly, yet perhaps it is the most natural construction, as meaning that he would have jurisdiction over the saints during this period; and if so, then the meaning is, that he would have absolute control over them, or set up a dominion over them, for the time specified—the time, and times, &c. In regard to this expression "a time and times," &c., it is unnecessary to say that there has been great diversity of opinion among expositors, and that many of the controversies in respect to future events turn on the sense attached to this and to the similar expressions which occur in the book of Revelation. The first and main

Most High, and think to change times and laws: and they shall be given into his hand, until a time

inquiry pertains, of course, to its literal and proper signification. The word used here rendered *time, times, time*—עִדָּן עִדָּנִין וּפְלַג—is a word which in itself would no more designate any definite and fixed period than our word *time* does. See ch. ii. 8, 9, 21; iii. 5, 15; iv. 16, 23, 25, 32; vii. 12. In some of these instances, the period *actually referred to* was a year (ch. iv. 16, 23), but this is not necessarily implied in the word used, but the limitation is demanded by the circumstances of the case. So far as the *word* is concerned, it would denote a day, a week, a month, a year, or a larger or smaller division of time, and the period actually intended to be designated must be determined from the connection. The Latin Vulgate is indefinite—*ad tempus;* so the Greek—ἕως καιροῦ; so the Syriac, and so Luther—*eine Zeit;* and so Lengerke—*eine Zeit.* The phrase "for a time" expresses accurately the meaning of the original word. The word rendered *"times"* is the same word in the plural, though evidently with a dual signification.—Gesenius, *Lex.;* Lengerke, *in loc.* The obvious meaning is two such times as is designated by the former "time." The phrase "and the dividing of a time" means clearly *half* of such a period. Thus, if the period denoted by a "time" here be a year, the whole period would be three years and a half. Designations of time like this, or of this same period, occur several times in the prophecies (Daniel and Revelation), and on their meaning much depends in regard to the interpretation of the prophecies pertaining to the future. This period of three years and a half equals forty-two months, or twelve hundred and sixty days—the periods mentioned in Rev. xi. 2; xii. 6, and on which so much depends in the interpretation of that book. The only question of importance in regard to the period of time here designated is, whether this is to be taken literally to denote three years and a half, or whether a symbo-

and times and the dividing of time.

26 But the judgment shall sit, and they shall take away his dominion, to consume and to destroy *it* unto the end.

---

lical method is to be adopted, by making each one of the days represent a year, thus making the time referred to, in fact, twelve hundred and sixty years. On this question expositors are divided, and probably will continue to be, and according as one or the other view is adopted, they refer the events here to Antiochus Epiphanes, or to the Papal power ; or perhaps it should be said more accurately, according as they are disposed to refer the events here to Antiochus or to the Papacy, do they embrace one or the other method of interpretation in regard to the meaning of the days. At this point in the examination of the passage, the only object is to look at it *exegetically;* to examine it *as language* apart from the application, or unbiassed by any purpose of application ; and though absolute certainty cannot perhaps be obtained, yet the following may be regarded as exegetically probable :—(1.) The word *time* may be viewed as denoting *a year :* I mean a year rather than a week, a month, or any other period — because a year is a more marked and important portion of time, and because a day, a week, a month, is so short that it cannot be reasonably supposed that it is intended. As there is no *larger* natural period than a year—no cycle in nature that is so marked and obvious as to be properly suggested by the word *time*, it cannot be supposed that any such cycle is intended. And as there is so much *particularity* in the language used here, "a time, and times, and half a time," it is to be presumed that some definite and marked period is intended, and that it is not time in general. It may be presumed, therefore, that in some sense of the term the period of a *year* is referred to. (2.) The language does not forbid the application to a literal year, and then the actual time designated would be three years and a half. No laws of exegesis, nothing in the language itself, could be regarded as violated, if such an interpretation were given to the language, and so far as

this point is concerned, there would be no room for debate. (3.) The same remark may be made as to the symbolical application of the language—taking it for a much longer period than literally three years and a half; that is, regarding each day as standing for a year, and thus considering it as denoting twelve hundred and sixty years. This could not be shown to be a violation of prophetic usage, or to be forbidden by the nature of prophetic language, because nothing is more common than symbols, and because there are actual instances in which such an interpretation must be understood. Thus in Ezek. iv. 6, where the prophet was commanded to lie upon his right side forty days, it is expressly said that it was symbolical or emblematical : "I have appointed thee each day for a year." No one can doubt that it would be strictly consistent with prophetic usage to suppose that the time here *might* be symbolical, and that a longer time might be referred to than the literal interpretation would require. (4.) It may be added, that there are some circumstances, even considering the passage with reference only to the interpretation of the language, and with no view to the question of its application, which would make this appear *probable*. Among these circumstances are the following: (*a*) The fact that, in the prophecies, it is unusual to designate the *time* literally. Very few instances can be referred to in which this is done. It is commonly by some symbol ; some mark ; some peculiarity of the time or age referred to, that the designation is made, or by some symbol that may be understood when the event has occurred. (*b*) *This* designation of time occurs in the midst of symbols—where all is symbol—the beasts, the horns, the little horn, &c. ; and it would seem to be much more probable that such a method would be adopted as designating the time referred to than a *literal* method. (*c*) It is quite apparent on the mere perusal of the passage here

27 And the kingdom and dominion, and the greatness of the kingdom under the whole heaven, shall be given to the people of the saints of the Most High, whose kingdom *is* an everlasting kingdom, and all

1 or, *rulers.*

dominions[1] shall serve and obey him.

28 Hitherto *is* the end of the matter. As for me Daniel, my cogitations much troubled me, and my countenance changed in me: but I kept the matter in my heart.

---

that the events do actually extend far into the future—far beyond what would be denoted by the brief period of three and a half years. This will be considered more fully in another place in the inquiry as to the meaning of these prophecies. (See also Editor's Preface to volume on Revelation.)

(4.) A fourth point in the explanation given by the interpreter to Daniel is, that there would be a solemn judgment in regard to this power, and that the dominion conceded to it over the saints for a time would be utterly taken away, and the power itself destroyed :—*but the judgment shall sit, and they shall take away his dominion, to consume, and to destroy it unto the end,* ver. 26. That is, it *shall be* taken away ; it shall come entirely to an end. The interpreter does not say *by whom* this would be done, but he asserts the fact, and that the destruction of the dominion would be final. That is, it would entirely and forever cease. This would be done by an act of Divine judgment, or as if a solemn judgment should be held, and a sentence pronounced. It would be *as* manifestly an act of God as if he should sit as a judge, and pronounce sentence. See Notes on vers. 9–11.

(5.) And a fifth point in the explanation of the interpreter is, that the dominion under the whole heaven would be given to the saints of the Most High, and that all nations should serve him ; that is, that there would be a universal prevalence of righteousness on the earth, and that God would reign in the hearts and lives of men, ver. 27. See Notes on vers. 13, 14.

28. *Hitherto* is *the end of the matter.* That is, the end of what I saw and heard. This is the sum of what was disclosed to the prophet, but he still says that he meditated on it with profound interest, and that he had much

solicitude in regard to these great events. The words rendered *hitherto,* mean, *so far,* or *thus far.* The phrase " end of the matter," means " the close of the saying a thing ;" that is, this was all the revelation which was made to him, and he was left to his own meditations respecting it. ¶ *As for me Daniel.* So far as I was concerned ; or so far as this had any effect on me. It was not unnatural, at the close of this remarkable vision, to state the effect that it had on himself. ¶ *My cogitations much troubled me.* My thoughts in regard to it. It was a subject which he could not avoid reflecting on, and which could not but produce deep solicitude in regard to the events which were to occur. Who could look into the future without anxious and agitating thought? These events were such as to engage the profoundest attention ; such as to fix the mind in solemn thought. Compare Notes on Rev. v. 4. ¶ *And my countenance changed in me.* The effect of these revelations depicted themselves on my countenance. The prophet does not say in what way—whether by making him pale, or careworn, or anxious, but merely that it produced a change in his appearance. The Chaldee is *brightness –* ‏זִיו‎ *-* and the meaning would seem to be, that his bright and cheerful countenance was changed ; that is, that his bright looks were changed ; either by becoming pale (Gesenius, Lengerke), or by becoming serious and thoughtful. ¶ *But I kept the matter in my heart.* I communicated to no one the cause of my deep and anxious thoughts. He hid the whole subject in his own mind, until he thought proper to make this record of what he had seen and heard. Perhaps there was no one to whom he could communicate the matter who would credit it ; perhaps there was no one at court who would sympathize with him; perhaps he thought that it might savour of vanity if it were known; perhaps he felt that as no one could throw any new light on the subject, there would be no use in making it a subject of conversation; perhaps he felt so over-powered that he could not readily converse on it.

We are prepared now, having gone through with an exposition of this chapter, as to the meaning of the symbols, the words, and the phrases, to endeavour to ascertain what events are referred to in this remarkable prophecy, and to ask what events it was designed should be pourtrayed. And in reference to this there are but two opinions, or two classes of interpretations, that require notice: that which refers it primarily and exclusively to Antiochus Epiphanes, and that which refers it to the rise and character of the Papal power; that which regards the fourth beast as referring to the empire of Alexander, and the little horn to Antiochus, and that which regards the fourth beast as referring to the Roman empire, and the little horn to the Papal dominion. In inquiring which of these is the true interpretation, it will be proper, first, to consider whether it is applicable to Antiochus Epiphanes; secondly, whether it in fact finds a fulfilment in the Roman empire and the Papacy; and, thirdly, if such is the proper application, what are we to look for in the future in what remains unfulfilled in regard to the prophecy.

I. The question whether it is applicable to the case of Antiochus Epiphanes. A large class of interpreters, of the most respectable character, among whom are Lengerke, Maurer, Prof. Stuart (*Hints on the Interpretation of Prophecy*, p. 86, *seq.;* also *Com. on Daniel*, pp. 205–211), Eichhorn, Bertholdt, Bleek, and many others, suppose that the allusion to Antiochus is clear, and that the primary, if not the exclusive, reference to the prophecy is to him. Professor Stuart (*Hints*, p. 86) says, "The passage in Daniel vii. 25 is so clear as to leave no reasonable room for doubt." "In vers. 8, 20, 24, the rise of Antiochus Epiphanes is described; for the fourth beast is, beyond all reasonable doubt, the divided Grecian dominion which succeeded the reign of Alexander the Great. From this dynasty springs Antiochus, vers. 8, 20, who is most graphically described in ver. 25 'as one who shall speak great words against the Most High,' &c."

The *facts* in regard to Antiochus, so far as they are necessary to be known in the inquiry, are briefly these:—Antiochus Epiphanes (*the Illustrious*, a name taken on himself, Prideaux, iii. 213), was the son of Antiochus the Great, but succeeded his brother, Seleucus Philopator, who died B.C. 176. Antiochus reigned over Syria, the capital of which was Antioch, on the Orontes, from B.C. 176 to B.C. 164. His character, as that of a cruel tyrant, and a most bloodthirsty and bitter enemy of the Jews, is fully detailed in the first and second book of Maccabees. Comp. also Prideaux, *Con.* vol. iii. 213–234. The facts in the case of Antiochus, so far as they are supposed to bear on the application of the prophecy before us, are thus stated by Prof. Stuart (*Hints on the Interpretation of Prophecy*, pp. 89, 90): "In the year 168 before Christ, in the month of May, Antiochus Epiphanes was on his way to attack Egypt, and he detached Apollonius, one of his military confidants, with 22,000 soldiers, in order to subdue and plunder Jerusalem. The mission was executed with entire success. A horrible slaughter was made of the men at Jerusalem, and a large portion of the women and children, being made captives, were sold and treated as slaves. The services of the temple were interrupted, and its joyful feasts were turned into mourning, 1 Mac. i. 37–39. Soon after this the Jews in general were compelled to eat swine's flesh, and to sacrifice to idols. In December of that same year, the temple was profaned by introducing the statue of Jupiter Olympius ; and on the 25th of that month sacrifices were offered to that idol on the altar of Jehovah. Just three years after this last event, viz., December 25, 165 B.C., the temple was expurgated by Judas Maccabeus, and the worship of Jehovah restored. Thus, *three years and a half,* or almost exactly this period, passed away, while Antiochus had complete possession and control of everything in and around Jerusalem and the temple. It may be noted, also, that just three years passed, from the time when the profanation of the temple was carried to its greatest height —viz., by sacrificing to the statue of Jupiter Olympius on the altar of Jehovah, down to the time when Judas renewed the regular worship. I mention this last circumstance in order to account for the *three years* of Antiochus' profanations, which are named as the period of them in Josephus, *Ant.* xii. 7, § 6. This period tallies exactly with the time during which the profanation as consummated was carried on, if we reckon down to the period when the temple worship was restored by Judas Maccabeus. But in *Prœm. ad Bell. Jud.* § 7, and *Bell. Jud.* l. 1, § 1, Josephus reckons three years and a half as the period during which Antiochus ravaged Jerusalem and Judea."

In regard to this statement, while the general facts are correct, there are some additional statements which should be made, to determine as to its real bearing on the case. The act of detaching Apollonius to attack Jerusalem was not, as is stated in this extract, when Antiochus was on his way to Egypt, but was on his return from Egypt, and was just two years after Jerusalem had been taken by Antiochus.—Prideaux, iii. 239. The *occasion* of his detaching Apollonius, was that Antiochus was enraged because he had been defeated in Egypt by the Romans, and resolved to vent all his wrath upon the Jews, who at that time had given him no particular offence. When, two years before, Antiochus had himself taken Jerusalem, he slew forty thousand persons ; he took as many captives, and sold them for slaves ; he forced himself into the temple, and entered the most holy place ; he caused a great sow to be offered on the altar of burnt-offering, to show his contempt for the temple and the Jewish religion ; he sprinkled the broth over every part of the temple for the purpose of polluting it ; he plundered the temple of the altar of incense, the shew-bread table, and the golden candlestick, and then returned to Antioch, having appointed Philip, a Phrygian, a man of a cruel and barbarous temper, to be governor of the Jews.—Prideaux, iii. 231. When Apollonius again attacked the city, two years afterwards, he waited quietly until the Sabbath, and then made his assault. He filled the city with blood, set it on fire, demolished the houses, pulled down the walls, built a strong fortress over against the temple, from which the garrison could fall on all who should attempt to go to worship. From this time, "the temple became deserted, and the daily sacrifices were omitted," until the service was restored by Judas Maccabeus, three years and a half after. The *time* during which this continued was, in fact, just three years and a half, until Judas Maccabeus succeeded in expelling the heathen from the temple and from Jerusalem, when the temple was purified, and was solemnly reconsecrated to the worship of God. See Prideaux, *Con.* iii. 240, 241, and the authorities there cited.

Now, in reference to this interpretation, supposing that the prophecy relates to Antiochus, it must be admitted that there are coincidences which are remarkable, and it is on the ground of these coincidences that the prophecy has been applied to him. These circumstances are such as the following : (*a*) The general character of the authority that would exist as denoted by the "little horn," as that of severity and cruelty. None could be better fitted to represent that than the character of Antiochus Epiphanes. Comp. Prideaux, *Con.* iii. 213, 214. (*b*) His arrogance and blasphemy— "speaking great words against the Most High." Nothing is easier than to find what would be a fulfilment of this in the character of Antiochus— in his sacrilegious entrance into the most holy places ; in his setting up the statue of Jupiter ; in his offering a sow as a sacrifice on the great altar ; in his sprinkling the broth of swine on the temple in contempt of the Hebrews and their worship, and in his causing the daily sacrifice at the temple to cease. (*c*) His making war with the "saints," and "wearing out the saints of the Most High "—all this could be found accomplished in the wars which Antiochus waged against the Jews in the slaughter of so many thousands, and in sending so many into hopeless slavery. (*d*) His attempt to "change times and laws "—this could be found to have been fulfilled in the case of Antiochus—in his arbitrary character, and in his interference with the laws

of the Hebrews. (*e*) The *time*, as above stated, is the most remarkable coincidence. If this is *not* to be regarded as referring exclusively to Antiochus, it must be explained on one of two suppositions—either that it is one of those coincidences which *will* be found to happen in history, as coincidences happen in dreams ; or as having a double reference, intended to refer primarily to Antiochus, but in a secondary and more important sense referring also to other events having a strong resemblance to this ; or, in other words, that the language was designedly so couched as to relate to two similar classes of events. It is not to be regarded as very remarkable, however, that it is possible to find a fulfilment of these predictions in Antiochus, though it be supposed that the design was to describe the Papacy, for some of the expressions are of so general a character that they could be applied to many events which have occurred, and, from the nature of the case, there were strong points of resemblance between Antiochus and the Papal power. It is not absolutely necessary, therefore, to suppose that this had reference to Antiochus Epiphanes ; and there are so many *objections* to this view as to make it, it seems to me, morally impossible that it should have had such a reference. Among these objections are the following :—

(1.) This interpretation makes it necessary to divide the kingdom of the Medes and Persians, and to consider them two kingdoms, as Eichhorn, Jahn, Dereser, De Wette, and Bleek do. In order to this interpretation, the following are the kingdoms denoted by the four beasts—by the first, the Chaldee ; by the second, the Medish ; by the third, the Persian ; and by the fourth, the Macedonian, or the Macedonian-Asiatic kingdom under Alexander the Great. But to say nothing now of any other difficulties, it is an insuperable objection to this, that so far as the kingdoms of the Medes and Persians are mentioned in Scripture, and so far as they play any part in the fulfilment of prophecy, they are always mentioned as *one*. They appear as one; they act as one; they are regarded as one. The kingdom of the Medes does not appear until it is united with that of the Persians, and this remark is of special importance when they are spoken of as *succeeding* the kingdom of Babylon. The kingdom of the Medes was contemporaneous with that of Babylon; it was the Medo-Persian kingdom that was in any proper sense the successor of that of Babylon, as described in these symbols. The kingdom of the Medes, as Hengstenberg well remarks, could in no sense be said to have succeeded that of Babylon any longer than during the reign of Cyaxares II., after the taking of Babylon: and even during that short period of two years, the government was in fact in the hands of Cyrus.—*Die Authentie des Daniel,* p. 200. Schlosser (p. 243) says, "the kingdom of the Medes and Persians is to be regarded as in fact one and the same kingdom, only that in the change of the dynasty another branch obtained the authority." See particularly, Rosenmüller, *Alterthumskunde,* i. 290, 291. These two kingdoms are in fact always blended—their laws, their customs, their religion, and they are mentioned as one. Comp. Esth. i. 3, 18, 19; x. 2; Dan. v. 28; vi. 8, 12, 15.

(2.) In order to this interpretation, it is necessary to divide the empire founded by Alexander, and instead of regarding it as one, to consider that which existed when he reigned as one, and that of Antiochus, one of the successors of Alexander, as another. This opinion is maintained by Bertholdt, who supposes that the first beast represented the Babylonian kingdom; the second, the kingdom of the Medes and Persians; the third, that of Alexander; and the fourth the kingdoms that sprang out of that. In order to this, it is necessary to suppose that the four heads and wings, and the ten horns, equally represent that kingdom, or sprang from it—the four heads, the kingdom when divided at the death of Alexander, and the ten horns, powers that ultimately sprang up from the same dominion. But this is contrary to the whole representation in regard to the Asiatic-Macedonian empire. In ch. viii. 8, 9, where there is an undoubted reference to that empire, it is said "the he-goat waxed very great: and when he was strong, the great horn was broken; and for it came up four notable ones toward the four winds of heaven. And out of one of them came forth a little horn, which waxed exceeding great, toward the south," &c. Here is an undoubted allusion to Alexander, and to his followers, and particularly to Antiochus, but no mention of any such division as is necessary to be supposed if the fourth beast represents the power that succeeded Alexander in the East. In no place is the kingdom of the successors of Alexander divided from his in the same sense in which the kingdom of the Medes and Persians is from that of Babylon, or the kingdom of Alexander from that of the Persians. Comp. Hengstenberg, as above, pp. 203–205.

(3.) The supposition that the fourth beast represents either the kingdom of Alexander, or, according to Bertholdt and others, the successors of Alexander, by no means agrees with the character of that beast as compared with the others. That beast was far more formidable, and more to be dreaded, than either of the others. It had iron teeth and brazen claws; it stamped down all before it, and broke all to pieces, and manifestly represented a far more fearful dominion than either of the others. The same is true in regard to the parallel representation in ch. ii. 33, 40, of the fourth kingdom represented by the legs and feet of iron, as more terrific than either of those denoted by the gold, the silver, or the brass. But this representation by no means agrees with the character of the kingdom of either Alexander or his successors, and in fact would not be true of them. It would agree well, as we shall see, with the Roman power, even as contrasted with that of Babylon, Persia, or Macedon; but it is not the representation which would, with propriety, be given of the empire of Alexander, or his successors, as contrasted with those which preceded them. Comp. Hengstenberg, as above, pp. 205-207. Moreover, this does not agree with what is expressly said of this power that should succeed that of Alexander, in a passage undoubtedly referring to it, in ch. viii. 22, where it is said, "Now that being broken, whereas four stood up for it, four kingdoms shall stand up out of the nation, *but not in his power*."

(4.) On this supposition it is impossible to determine who are meant by the "ten horns" of the fourth beast (ver. 7), and the "ten kings" (ver. 24) that are represented by these. All the statements in Daniel that refer to the Macedonian kingdom (ch. vii. 6; viii. 8, 22) imply that the Macedonian empire in the East, when the founder died, would be divided into four great powers or monarchies—in accordance with what is well known to have been the fact. But who are the ten kings or sovereignties that were to exist under this general Macedonian power, on the supposition that the fourth beast re-

presents this? Bertholdt supposes that the ten horns are "ten Syrian kings," and that the eleventh little horn is Antiochus Epiphanes. The *names* of these kings, according to Bertholdt (pp. 432, 433), are Seleucus Nicator, Antiochus Soter, Antiochus Theos, Seleucus Callinicus, Seleucus Ceraunus, Antiochus the Great, Seleucus Philopator, Heliodorus, Ptolemy Philometor, and Demetrius. So also Prof. Stuart, *Com. on Dan.* p. 208. But it is impossible to make out this exact number of *Syrian* kings from history, to say nothing now of the improbability of supposing that their power was represented by the fourth beast. These kings were not of the same dynasty, of Syria, of Macedonia, or of Egypt, but the list is made up of different kingdoms. Grotius (*in loc.*) forms the catalogue of ten kings out of the lists of the kings of Syria and Egypt—five out of one, and five out of the other; but this is manifestly contrary to the intention of the prophecy, which is to represent them as springing out of one and the same power. It is a further objection to this view, that these are lists of *successive* kings—rising up one after the other; whereas the representation of the ten horns would lead us to suppose that they existed *simultaneously;* or that somehow there were ten powers that sprang out of the one great power represented by the fourth beast.

(5.) Equally difficult is it, on this supposition, to know who are intended by the "three horns" that were plucked up by the little horn that sprang up among the ten, ver. 8. Grotius, who regards the "little horn" as representing Antiochus Epiphanes, supposes that the three horns were his elder brothers, Seleucus, Demetrius, the son of Seleucus, and Ptolemy Philopator, king of Egypt. But it is an insuperable objection to this that the three kings mentioned by Grotius are not all in his list of ten kings, neither Ptolemy Philometor (if Philometor he meant), nor Demetrius being of the number.— Newton *on the Proph.* p. 211. Neither were they plucked up by the roots by Antiochus, or by his order. Seleucus was poisoned by his treasurer, Heliodorus, whose aim it was to usurp the crown for himself, before Antiochus came from Rome, where he had been detained as a hostage for several years. Demetrius lived to dethrone and murder the son of Antiochus, and succeeded him in the kingdom of Syria. Ptolemy Philopator died king of Egypt almost thirty years before Antiochus came to the throne of Syria; or if Ptolemy Philometor, as is most probable, was meant by Grotius, though he suffered much in the wars with Antiochus, yet he survived him about eighteen years, and died in possession of the crown of Egypt.—Newton, *ut supra.* Bertholdt supposes that the three kings were Heliodorus, who poisoned Seleucus Philopator, and sought, by the help of a party, to obtain the throne; Ptolemy Philometor, king of Egypt, who, as sister's son to the king, laid claim to the throne; and Demetrius, who, as son of the former king, was legitimate heir to the throne. But there are two objections to this view; (*a*) that the representation by the prophet is of *actual* kings—which these were not; and (*b*) that Antiochus ascended the throne *peaceably;* Demetrius, who would have been regarded as the king of Syria, not being able to make his title good, was detained as a hostage at Rome. Hengstenberg, pp. 207, 208. Prof. Stuart, *Com. on Dan.*, pp. 208, 209, supposes that the three kings referred to were Heliodorus, Ptolemy Philometor, and Demetrius I.; but in

regard to these it should be observed, that they were mere *pretenders* to the throne, whereas the text in Daniel supposes that they would be *actual* kings. Comp. Hengstenberg, p. 208.

(6.) The *time* here mentioned, on the supposition that literally three years and a half (ver. 25) are intended, does not agree with the actual dominion of Antiochus. In an undoubted reference to him in ch. viii. 13, 14, it is said that "the vision concerning the daily sacrifice, and the transgression of desolation," would be "unto two thousand and three hundred days; then shall the sanctuary be cleansed;" that is, one thousand and forty days, or some two years and ten months more than the time mentioned here. I am aware of the difficulty of explaining this (see Prof. Stuart, *Hints on the Interpretation of Prophecy,* p. 98, *seq.*), and the exact meaning of the passage in ch. viii. 13, 14, will come up for consideration hereafter; but it is an objection of some force to the application of the "time, and times, and dividing of a time" (ver. 25) to Antiochus, that it is not the *same* time which is applied to him elsewhere.

(7.) And one more objection to this application is, that, in the prophecy, it is said that he who was represented by the "little horn" would continue till "the Ancient of days should sit," and evidently till the kingdom should be taken by the one in the likeness of the Son of man, vers. 9, 10, 13, 14, 21, 22, 26. But if this refers to Antiochus, then these events must refer to the coming of the Messiah, and to the setting up of his kingdom in the world. Yet, as a matter of fact; Antiochus died about 164 years before the Saviour came, and there is no way of showing that he *continued* until the Messiah came in the flesh.

These objections to the opinion that this refers to Antiochus Epiphanes seem to me to be insuperable.

II. The question whether it refers to the Roman empire and the Papal power. The fair inquiry is, whether the things referred to in the vision actually find such a correspondence in the Roman empire and the Papacy, that they would fairly represent them if the symbols had been made use of *after* the events occurred. Are they such as we might properly use now as describing the portions of those events that are *past*, on the supposition that the reference was to those events? To determine this, it will be proper to refer to the things in the symbol, and to inquire whether events corresponding to them have actually occurred in the Roman empire and the Papacy. Recalling the exposition which has been above given of the explanation furnished by the angel to Daniel, the things there referred to will find an ample and a striking fulfilment in the Roman empire and the Papal power.

(1.) The fourth kingdom, symbolized by the fourth beast, is accurately represented by the Roman power. This is true in regard to the *place* which that power would occupy in the history of the world, on the supposition that the first three referred to the Babylonian, the Medo-Persian, and the Macedonian. On this supposition there is no need of regarding the Medo-Persian empire as divided into two, represented by two symbols; or the kingdom founded by Alexander—the Asiatic-Macedonian—as distinct from that of his successors. As the Medo-Persian was in fact one dominion, so was the Macedonian under Alexander, and in the form of the four dynasties into which it was divided on his death, and down to the time when the whole was subverted by the Roman conquests. On

this supposition, also, everything in the symbol is fulfilled. The fourth beast —so mighty, so terrific, so powerful, so unlike all the others, armed with iron teeth, and with claws of brass, trampling down and stamping on all the earth—well represents the Roman dominion. The symbol is such a one as we should now use appropriately to represent that power, and in every respect that empire was well represented by the symbol. It may be added, also, that this supposition corresponds with the obvious interpretation of the parallel place in chapter ii. 33, 40, where the same empire is referred to in the image by the legs and feet of iron. See Notes on that passage. It should be added, that this fourth kingdom is to be considered as prolonged through the entire continuance of the *Roman* power, in the various forms in which that power has been kept up on the earth—alike under the empire, and when broken up into separate sovereignties, and when again concentrated and embodied under the Papacy. That *fourth* power or dominion was to be continued, according to the prediction here, until the establishment of the kingdom of the saints. Either, then, that kingdom of the saints has come, or has been set up, or the fourth kingdom, in some form, still remains. The truth is, that in prophecy the entire Roman dominion seems to be contemplated as one—one mighty and formidable power trampling down the liberties of the world; oppressing and persecuting the people of God—the true church; and maintaining an absolute and arbitrary dominion over the souls of men—as a mighty domination standing in the way of the progress of truth, and keeping back the reign of the saints on the earth. In these respects the Papal dominion is, and has been, but a prolongation, in another form, of the influence of heathen Rome, and the entire domination may be represented as one, and might be symbolized by the fourth beast in the vision of Daniel. When that power shall cease, we may, according to the prophecy, look for the time when the "kingdom shall be given to the saints," or when the true kingdom of God shall be set up all over the world.

(2.) Out of this one sovereignty, represented by the fourth beast, ten powers or sovereignties, represented by the ten horns, were to arise. It was shown in the exposition, that these would all spring out of that one dominion, and would wield the power that was wielded by that; that is, that the one great power would be broken up and distributed into the number represented by ten. As the horns all appeared at the same time on the beast, and did not spring up after one another, so these powers would be simultaneous, and would not be a mere succession; and as the horns all sprang from the beast, so these powers would all have the same origin, and be a portion of the same one power now divided into many. The question then is, whether the Roman power was in fact distributed into so many sovereignties at any period such as would be represented by the springing up of the little horn—if that refers to the Papacy. Now, one has only to look into any historical work, to see how in fact the Roman power became distributed and broken up in this way into a large number of kingdoms, or comparatively petty sovereignties, occupying the portions of the world once governed by Rome. In the decline of the empire, and as the new power represented by the "little horn" arose, there was a complete breaking up of the one power that was formerly wielded, and a large number of states and kingdoms sprang out of it. To see that there is no difficulty

in making out the number *ten*, or that some such distribution and breaking up of the one power is naturally suggested, I cast my eye on the historical chart of Lyman, and found the following kingdoms or sovereignties specified as occupying the same territory which was possessed by the Roman empire, and springing from that—viz., the Vandals, Alans, Suevi, Heruli, Franks, Visigoths, Ostrogoths, Burgundians, Lombards, Britons. The Roman empire as such had ceased, and the power was distributed into a large number of comparatively petty sovereignties— well represented at this period by the ten horns on the head of the beast. Even the Romanists themselves admit that the Roman empire was, by means of the incursions of the northern nations, dismembered into ten kingdoms (Calmet on Rev. xiii. 1; and he refers likewise to Berengaud, Bossuet, and Dupin. See Newton, p. 209); and Machiaveli (*Hist. of Flor.* l. i.), with no design of furnishing an illustration of this prophecy, and probably with no recollection of it, has mentioned these names:—1, the Ostrogoths in Mœsia; 2, the Visigoths in Pannonia; 3, the Sueves and Alans in Gascoign and Spain; 4, the Vandals in Africa; 5, the Franks in France; 6, the Burgundians in Burgundy; 7, the Heruli and Turingi in Italy; 8, the Saxons and Angles in Britain; 9, the Huns in Hungary; 10, the Lombards at first upon the Danube, afterwards in Italy. The arrangement proposed by Sir Isaac Newton is the following:—1, The kingdom of the Vandals and Alans in Spain and Africa; 2, the kingdom of the Suevians in Spain; 3, the kingdom of the Visigoths; 4, the kingdom of the Alans in Gallia; 5, the kingdom of the Burgundians; 6, the kingdom of the Franks; 7, the kingdom of the Britons; 8, the kingdom of the Huns;

9, the kingdom of the Lombards ; 10, the kingdom of Ravenna. Comp. also Duffield *on the Prophecies*, pp. 279, 280. For other arrangements constituting the number *ten*, as embracing the ancient power of the Roman empire, see Newton *on the Prophecies*, pp. 209, 210. There is some slight variation in the arrangements proposed by Mr. Mede, Bishop Lloyd, and Sir Isaac Newton ; but still it is remarkable that it is easy to make out that number with so good a degree of certainty, and particularly so, that it should have been suggested by a Romanist himself. Even if it is not practicable to make out the number with strict exactness, or if all writers do not agree in regard to the dynasties constituting the number *ten*, we should bear in remembrance the fact that these powers arose in the midst of great confusion ; that one kingdom arose and another fell in rapid succession ; and that there was not that entire certainty of location and boundary which there is in old and established states. One thing is certain, that there never has been a case in which an empire of vast power has been broken up into small sovereignties, to which this description would so well apply as to the rise of the numerous dynasties in the breaking up of the vast Roman power ; and another thing is equally certain, that if we were now to seek an appropriate symbol of the mighty Roman power—of its conquests, and of the extent of its dominion, and of the condition of that empire, about the time that the Papacy arose, we could not find a more striking or appropriate symbol than that of the terrible fourth beast with iron teeth and brazen claws—stamping the earth beneath his feet, and with ten horns springing out of his head.

(3.) In the midst of these there sprang up a little horn that had re-

markable characteristics. The inquiry now is, if this does not represent Antiochus, whether it finds a proper fulfilment in the Papacy. Now, in regard to this inquiry, the slightest acquaintance with the history and claims of the Papal power will show that there was a striking appropriateness in the symbol—such an appropriateness, that if we desired *now* to find a symbol that would represent this, we could find no one better adapted to it than that employed by Daniel. (*a*) The little horn would spring up among the others, and stand among them — as' dividing the power with them, or sharing or wielding that power. That is, on the supposition that it refers to the Papacy, the Papal power would spring out of the Roman empire; would be one of the sovereignties among which that vast power would be divided, and share with the other ten in wielding authority. It would be an eleventh power added to the ten. And who can be ignorant that the Papal power at the beginning, when it first asserted civil authority, sustained just such a relation to the crumbled and divided Roman empire as this? It was just one of the powers into which that vast sovereignty passed. (*b*) It would not spring up contemporaneously with them, but would arise in their midst, when they already existed. *They* are seen in vision as actually existing together, and this new power starts up among them. What could be more strikingly descriptive of the Papacy—as a power arising when the great Roman authority was broken to fragments, and distributed into a large number of sovereignties ? Then this new power was seen to rise—small at first, but gradually gaining strength, until it surpassed any one of them in strength, and assumed a position in the world which no one of them had.

The representation is exact. It is not a foreign power that invaded them; it starts up in the midst of them—springing out of the head of the same beast, and constituting a part of the same mighty domination that ruled the world. (c) It would be small at first, but would soon become so powerful as to pluck up and displace three of the others. And could any symbol have been better chosen to describe the Papal power than this? Could we find any *now* that would better describe it? Any one needs to have but the slightest acquaintance with the history of the Papal power to know that it was small at its beginnings, and that its ascendency over the world was the consequence of slow but steady growth. Indeed, so feeble was it at its commencement, so undefined were its first appearance and form, that one of the most difficult things in history is to know exactly when it *did* begin, or to determine the exact date of its origin as a distinct power. Different schemes in the interpretation of prophecy turn wholly on this. We see, indeed, that power subsequently strongly marked in its character, and exerting a mighty influence in the world—having subjugated nations to its control; we see causes for a long time at work tending to this, and can trace their gradual operation in producing it, but the exact period when its dominion began, what was the first characteristic act of the Papacy as such, what constituted its precise beginning as a peculiar power blending and combining a peculiar civil and ecclesiastical authority, no one is able with absolute certainty to determine. Who can fix the exact date? Who can tell precisely when it was? It is true that there were several distinct acts, or the exercise of civil authority, in the early history of the Papacy, but what was the precise *beginning* of that power no

one has been able to determine with so much certainty as to leave no room for doubt. Any one can see with what propriety the commencement of such a power would be designated by a little horn springing up among others. (d) It would grow to be mighty, for the "little horn" thus grew to be so powerful as to pluck up three of the horns of the beast. Of the growth of the power of the Papacy no one can be ignorant who has any acquaintance with history. It held nations in subjection, and claimed and exercised the right of displacing and distributing crowns as it pleased. (e) It would subdue "three kings;" that is, three of the ten represented by the ten horns. The prophet saw this at some point in its progress when *three* fell before it, or were overthrown by it. There might have been also other points in its history when it might have been seen as having overthrown more of them—perhaps the whole ten, but the attention was arrested by the fact that, soon after its rise, three of the ten were seen to fall before it. Now, in regard to the application of this, it may be remarked, (1.) That it does *not* apply, as already shown, to Antiochus Epiphanes—there being no sense in which he overthrew three of the princes that occupied the throne in the succession from Alexander, to say nothing of the fact that these were contemporaneous kings or kingdoms. (2.) There is no other period in history, and there are no other events to which it could be applied except either to Antiochus or the Papacy. (3.) In the confusion that existed on the breaking up of the Roman empire, and the imperfect accounts of the transactions which occurred in the rise of the Papal power, it would not be wonderful if it should be difficult to find events *distinctly* recorded that would be in all respects : n accurate and absolute fulfilment of the vision. (4.) Yet it is possible to make out the fulfilment of this with a good degree of certainty in the history of the Papacy. If applicable to the Papal power, what seems to be demanded is, that three of these ten kingdoms, or sovereignties should be rooted up by that power; that they should cease to exist as separate sovereignties; that they should be added to the sovereignty that should spring up; and that, as distinct kingdoms, they should cease to play a part in the history of the world. The three sovereignties thus transplanted, or rooted up, are supposed by Mr. Mede to have been the Greeks, the Longobards, and the Franks. Sir Isaac Newton supposes they were the Exarchate of Ravenna, the Lombards, and the senate and dukedom of Rome. The *objections* which may be made to these suppositions may be seen in Newton *on the Prophecies*, pp. 216, 217. The kingdoms which he supposes are to be referred to were the following:—*First.* The Exarchate of Ravenna. This of right belonged to the Greek emperors. This was the capital of their dominions in Italy. It revolted at the instigation of the Pope, and was seized by Astolphus, king of the Lombards, who thought to make himself master of Italy. The Pope in his exigency applied for aid to Pepin, king of France, who marched into Italy, besieged the Lombards in Pavia, and forced them to surrender the Exarchate and other territories in Italy. These were not restored to the Greek emperor, as they in justice should have been, but, at the solicitation of the Pope, were given to St. Peter and his successors for perpetual possession. "And so," says Platina, "the name of the Exarchate, which had continued from the time of Narses to the taking of Ravenna, one

hundred and seventy years, was extinguished."—*Lives of the Popes.* This, according to Sigonius, was effected in the year 755. See Gibbon, *Dec. and Fall,* vol. ii. 224, iii. 332, 334, 338. From this period, says Bp. Newton, the Popes being now become temporal princes, no longer date their epistles and bulls by the years of the emperor's reign, but by the years of their own advancement to the Papal chair. *Secondly.* The kingdom of the Lombards. This kingdom was troublesome to the Popes. The dominions of the Pope were invaded by Desiderius, in the time of Pope Adrian I. Application was again made to the king of France, and Charles the Great, the son and successor of Pepin, invaded the Lombards; and desirous of enlarging his own dominions, conquered the Lombards, put an end to their kingdom, and gave a great part of their territory to the Pope. This was the end of the kingdom of the Lombards, in the 206th year after their obtaining possessions in Italy, and in the year of our Lord 774. See Gibbon, *Dec. and Fall,* vol. iii. 335. *Thirdly.* The Roman States subjected to the Popes in a civil sense. Though subjected to the Pope spiritually, yet for a long time the Roman people were governed by a senate, and retained many of their old privileges, and elected both the Western Emperors and the Popes. This power, however, as is well known, passed into the hands of the Popes, and has been retained by them to the present time, the Pope having continued to be the civil as well as the ecclesiastical head. See Bp. Newton, pp. 319, 320. All semblance of the freedom of ancient Rome passed away, and this Roman dominion, as such, ceased to be, being completely absorbed in the Papacy. The Saxons, the Franks, &c., continued *their* independence as civil powers; these states passed entirely into the dominion of the Pope, and as independent kingdoms or sovereignties ceased to be. This is the solution in regard to the "three horns" that were to be plucked up, as given by Bp. Newton. Absolute certainty in a case of this kind is not to be expected in the confusion and indefiniteness of that portion of history, nor can it be reasonably demanded. If there were three of these powers planted in regions that became subject to the Papal power, and that disappeared or were absorbed in that one dominion constituting the peculiarity of the Papal dominion, or which entered into the Roman Papal state, considered as a sovereignty by itself among the nations of the earth, this is all that is required. Mr. Faber supposes the three to have been these: the Herulo-Turingic, the Ostrogothic, and the Lombardic, and says of them, that they "were necessarily eradicated in the immediate presence of the Papacy, before which they were geographically standing — and that the temporal principality which bears the name of St. Peter's patrimony, was carved out of the mass of their subjugated dominions."—*Sacred Calendar*, vol. ii. p. 102. Prof. Gaussen (*Discourse on Popery*: Geneva, 1844) supposes that the three kings or kingdoms here referred to were the Heruli, the Ostrogoths, and the Lombards. According to Bower (*Lives of the Popes*, vol. ii. 108, Dr. Cox's edition, note), the temporal dominions granted by Pepin to the Pope, or of which the Pope became possessed in consequence of the intervention of the kings of France, were the following: (1) The Exarchate of Ravenna, which comprised, according to Sigonius, the following cities : — Ravenna, Bologna, Imola, Fienza, Forlimpoli, Forli, Cesena, Bobbio, Ferrara, Commachio,

Adria, Servia, and Secchia. (2.) The Pentapolis, comprehending Rimini, Pesaro, Concha, Fano, Sinigalia, Ancono, Osimo, Umono, Jesi, Fossombrone, Monteferetro, Urbino, Cagli, Lucoli, and Eugubio. (3.) The city and dukedom of Rome, containing several cities of note, which had withdrawn themselves from all subjection to the emperor, had submitted to St. Peter ever since the time of Pope Gregory II, See also Bower, ii. 134, where he says, "The Pope had, by Charlemagne, been put in possession of the Exarchate, the Pentapolis, and the dukedom of Spoleti" [embracing the city and dukedom of Rome]. And again, on the same page (note): "The Pope possessed the Exarchate, the Pentapolis, and the dukedom of Spoleti, with the city and dukedom of Rome." It should be remembered that these statements are made by historians with no reference to any supposed fulfilment of this prophecy, and no allusion to it, but as matters of simple historical fact, occurring in the regular course of history. The *material* fact to be made out in order to show that this description of the "little horn" is applicable to the Papacy is, that at the *commencement* of what was properly the *Papacy* —that is, as I suppose, the *union* of the spiritual and temporal power, or the *assumption* of temporal authority by him who was Bishop of Rome, and who had been before regarded as a mere spiritual or ecclesiastical ruler, there was a *triple* jurisdiction assumed or conceded, a threefold domination ; or a union under himself of what had been three sovereignties, that now disappeared as independent administrations, and whose distinct governments were now merged in the *one* single sovereignty of the Pope. Now, that there was, just at this time, or at the *beginning* of the Papacy, or when it had so increased that it could be recognized as having a place among the temporal sovereignties of the earth, such a united domination, or such a union of three separate powers under one, will be apparent from an extract from Mr. Gibbon. He is speaking of the rewards conferred on the Pope by the Carlovingian race of kings, on account of the favour shown to them in his conferring the crown of France on Pepin, the mayor of the palace—directing in his favour over Childeric, the descendant of Clovis. Of this transaction, Mr. Gibbon observes, in general (iii. 336), that "the mutual obligations of the Popes and the Carlovingian family form the important link of ancient and modern, of civil and ecclesiastical history." He then proceeds (1) to specify the gifts or favours which the Popes conferred on the Carlovingian race; and (2) those which, in return, Pepin and Charlemagne bestowed on the Popes. In reference to the latter, he makes the following statement (iii. 338) :—"The gratitude of the Carlovingians was adequate to these obligations, and their names are consecrated as the saviours and benefactors of the Roman church. Her ancient patrimony of farms and houses was transformed by their bounty *into the temporal dominion of cities and provinces, and the donation of the Exarchate was the first-fruits of the conquests of Pepin.* Astolphus [king of the Lombards] with a sigh relinquished his prey ; the keys and the hostages of the principal cities were delivered to the French ambassador; and in his master's name *he presented them before the tomb of St. Peter.* The ample measure of the Exarchate might comprise all the provinces of Italy which had obeyed the emperor or his vicegerent ; but its strict and proper limits were included in the territories of Ravenna, Bologna, and Ferrara; its inseparable dependency was the Pentapolis, which stretched along the Adriatic from Rimini to Ancona, and advanced into the midland country as far as the ridge of the Apennines. In this transaction, the ambition and avarice of the Popes have been severely condemned. Perhaps the humility of a Christian priest should have rejected an earthly kingdom, which it was not easy for him to govern without renouncing the virtues of his profession. Perhaps a faithful subject, or even a generous enemy, would have been less impatient to divide the spoils of the barbarian ; and if the emperor had intrusted Stephen to solicit in his name the restitution of the Exarchate, I will not absolve the Pope from the reproach of treachery and falsehood. But, in the rigid interpretation of the laws, every one may accept, without inquiry, whatever his benefactor may bestow without injustice. The Greek emperor had abdicated or forfeited his right to the Exarchate ; and the sword of Astolphus was broken by the stronger sword of the Carlovingian. It was not in the cause of the Iconoclast that Pepin had exposed his person and army in a double expedition beyond the Alps ; he possessed, and he might lawfully alienate his conquests : and to the importunities of the Greeks he piously replied, that no human consideration should tempt him to resume the gift which he had conferred on the Roman pontiff for the remission of his sins and the salvation of his soul. The splendid donation was granted in supreme and absolute dominion, *and the world beheld for the first time a Christian bishop invested with the prerogatives of a temporal prince,* the choice of magistrates, the exercise of justice, the imposition of taxes, and the wealth of the palace of Ravenna. In the dissolution of the Lombard kingdom, the inhabitants of the duchy of Spoleti sought a refuge from the storm, shaved their heads after the Ravenna fashion, declared themselves the servants and subjects of St. Peter, *and completed, by this voluntary surrender, the present circle of the Ecclesiastical State.*" The following things are apparent from this extract:—(*a*) That here, according to Mr. Gibbon, was the beginning of the temporal power of the Pope. (*b*) That this was properly, in the view above taken, the commencement of the Papacy as a distinct and peculiar dominion. (*c*) That in this there was a threefold government, or three *temporal* sovereignties united under him, and constituting at that time, in the language of Mr. Gibbon, "the present circle of the ecclesiastical state." There was, *first*, the Exarchate of Ravenna; *secondly*, the Pentapolis, "which," he says, was its "inseparable dependency;" and, *thirdly*, the "duchy of Spoleti," which, he says, "completed the present circle of the ecclesiastical state." This was afterwards, Mr. Gibbon goes on to say, greatly "enlarged;" but this was the form in which the Papal power first made its appearance among the temporal sovereignties of Europe. I do not find, indeed, that the kingdom of the *Lombards* was, as is commonly stated, among the number of the temporal sovereignties that became subject to the authority of the Popes, but I *do* find that there *were* three distinct temporal sovereignties that lost their independent existence, and that were united under that one temporal authority—constituting by the union of the spiritual and temporal power that one peculiar kingdom. In Lombardy the power remained in the possession of the kings of the Lombards themselves, until that kingdom was subdued by the arms of Pepin and Charlemagne, and then it became subject to the crown of France, though for a time under the nominal reign of its own kings. See Gibbon, iii. 334, 335, 338. If it should be said, that in the interpretation of this passage respecting the "three horns" that were plucked up, or the three kingdoms that were thus destroyed, it would be proper to look for them among the *ten* into which the one great kingdom was divided, and that the three above referred to—the Exarchate of Ravenna, the Pentapolis, and the dukedom of Spoleti and Rome—were *not* properly of that number, according to the list above given, it is necessary, in reply to this, to advert only to the two main facts in the case: (1) that the great Roman power was actually divided into a large number of sovereignties that sprang up on its ruins—usually, but not in fact exactly, represented by *ten;* and (2) that the Papacy began its career with a conceded dominion over the three territories above referred to—a part, in fact, of the one great dominion constituting the Roman power, and in the same territory. It is a remarkable fact that the popes to this day wear a triple crown—a fact that exists in regard to no other monarchs—*as if* they had absorbed under themselves three separate and distinct sovereignties; or *as if* they represented three separate forms of dominion. The sum of what is said in the exposition of these verses may be thus expressed: — (1.) That there was originally *one* great sovereignty represented here by the "fourth beast"—the Roman empire. (2.) That, in fact, as is abundantly confirmed by history, this one great and united power was broken up into a large number of separate and independent sovereignties —most naturally and obviously described by *ten*, or such as would appear in a prophetic vision to be *ten*, and such as is actually so represented by historians having no interest in the fulfilment of the prophecy, and no designed reference to what may be symbolized by the "ten horns." (3.) That there was another peculiar and distinct power that sprang out of them, and that grew to be mighty—a power unlike the others, and unlike anything that had before appeared in the world —combining qualities to be found in no other sovereignty—having a peculiar relation at the same time to the *one* original sovereignty, and to the *ten* into which that was divided—the prolongation, in an important sense, of the power of the one, and springing up in a peculiar manner among the others —that peculiar ecclesiastical and civil power—the Papacy—well represented by the "little horn." (4.) That, in fact, this one power absorbed into itself *three* of these sovereignties — annihilating them as independent powers, and combining them into one most peculiar dominion — properly represented by "plucking them up." (5.) That as a proper symbol, or emblem of some such domination, a crown or diadem is still worn, most naturally and obviously *suggesting* such a threefold absorption of dominion. (6.) That all this is actually prefigured by the symbols employed by the prophet, or that the symbols are such as would be naturally employed on the supposition that these events were designed to be referred to. (7.) And that there have been *no other* historical events to which these remarkable symbols could be naturally and obviously applied. And if these things are so, how are they to be explained except on the supposition that Daniel was inspired? Has man any natural sagacity by which such symbols representing the future could be suggested? (*f*) It would be arrogant and proud, "speaking great words against the Most High." No *Protestant* will doubt that this is true of the Papacy; no one acquainted with history will presume to call it in question. The arrogant pretensions of the Papacy have been manifested in all the history of that power, and no one can doubt that its assumptions have been, in fact, by fair construction, "a speaking of great words against God." The Pope has claimed, or allowed to be conferred on him, names and prerogatives which can belong only to God. See this fully shown in the Notes on 2 Thess. ii. 4. The facts there referred to are all that is necessary to illustrate this passage, on the supposition that it refers to the Papacy. Comp. also the *Literalist*, vol. i. pp. 24–27. (*g*) This would be a persecuting power—"making war with the saints," and "wearing out the saints of the Most High." Can any one doubt that this is true of the Papacy? The Inquisition; the "persecutions of the Waldenses;" the ravages of the Duke of Alva; the fires of Smithfield; the tortures at Goa— indeed, the whole history of the Papacy may be appealed to in proof that this is applicable to that power. If anything *could* have "worn out the saints of the Most High"—could have cut them off from the earth so that evangelical religion would have become extinct, it would have been the persecutions of the Papal power. In the year 1208, a crusade was proclaimed by Pope Innocent III. against the Waldenses and Albigenses, in which a million of men perished. From the beginning of the order of the Jesuits, in the year 1540 to 1580, nine hundred thousand were destroyed. One hundred and fifty thousand perished by the Inquisition in thirty years. In the Low Countries fifty thousand persons were hanged, beheaded, burned, or buried alive, for the crime of heresy, within the space of thirty-eight years from the edict of Charles V., against the Protestants, to the peace of Chateau Cam-

bresis in 1559. Eighteen thousand suffered by the hands of the executioner,
in the space of five years and a half,
during the administration of the Duke
of Alva. Indeed, the slightest acquaintance with the history of the Papacy,
will convince any one that what is here
said of "making war with the saints"
(ver. 21), and "wearing out the saints
of the Most High" (ver. 25), is strictly
applicable to that power, and will accurately describe its history. There
have been, indeed, other persecuting
powers, but none to which this language would be so applicable, and none
which it would so naturally suggest.
In proof of this, it is only necessary to
refer to the history of the Papacy, and
to what it has done to extirpate those
who have professed a different faith.
Let any one recal (1) the persecution
of the Waldenses; (2) the acts of the
Duke of Alva in the Low Countries;
(3) the persecution in England under
Mary; (4) the Inquisition; (5) the attempts, too successful, to extinguish all
the efforts at reformation in Italy and
Spain in the time of Luther and Calvin
(see M'Crie), and (6) the attempts to
put down the Reformation in Germany
and Switzerland—all which were either
directly originated or sanctioned by the
Papacy, and all for the same end, and
he will see no reason to doubt that the
language here is *strictly* applicable to
that power, and that there has been no
government on earth which would be
so naturally suggested by it.—Cun-
ninghame, in the *Literalist*, i. 27, 28.
Indeed, who can number up all that
have perished in the Inquisition alone?
(*h*) It would claim legislative power—
"thinking to change times and laws."
The original Chaldee here may be rendered, as is done by Gesenius and De
Wette, *set times, stated times*, or *festival seasons*. The word here, says
Gesenius (*Lex.*), is "spoken of sacred

seasons, festivals," and there can be
no doubt that in this place it refers to
religious institutions. The meaning is,
that he would claim control over such
institutions or festivals, and that he
would appoint or change them at his
pleasure. He would abolish or modify
existing institutions of that kind, or he
would institute new ones, as should
seem good to him. This would be
applicable, then, to some power that
should claim authority to prescribe religious institutions, and to change the
laws of God. No one, also, can fail
to see a fulfilment of this in the claims
of the Papacy, in setting up a jurisdiction over seasons of festival and fast;
and in demanding that the laws of
kingdoms should be so modelled as to
sustain its claims, and modifying the
laws of God as revealed in the Bible.
The right of deposing and setting up
kings; of fixing the boundaries of nations; of giving away crowns and scep-
tres; and of exercising dominion over
the sacred seasons, the customs, the
amusements of nations—all these, as
illustrated under the Papacy, will leave
no doubt that all this would find an
ample fulfilment in the history of that
power. The Pope has claimed to be
the head of the church, and has asserted
and exercised the right of appointing
sacred seasons; of abolishing ancient
institutions; of introducing numberless new festival occasions, practically
abrogating the laws of God on a
great variety of subjects. We need
only refer, in illustration of this, (*a*) to
the claim of infallibility, by which an
absolute jurisdiction is asserted that
covers the whole ground; (*b*) to all the
laws pertaining to image-worship, so
directly in the face of the laws of God;
(*c*) to the celibacy of the clergy, rendering void one of the laws of heaven
in relation to marriage; (*d*) to the
whole doctrine respecting purgatory;

(c) to the doctrine of transubstantiation; (f) to the practical abolition of the Christian Sabbath by appointing numerous saints' days to be observed as equally sacred; (g) to the law withholding the cup from the laity— contrary to the commandment of the Saviour; and (h) in general to the absolute control claimed by the Papacy over the whole subject of religion. Indeed, nothing would better characterize this power than to say that it asserted the right to "change times and laws." And to all this should be added another characteristic (ver. 8), that "it would have the eyes of a man;" that is, would be distinguished for a far-seeing sagacity. Could this be so appropriately applied to anything else as to the deep, the artful, and the far-reaching diplomacy of the court of Rome; to the sagacity of the Jesuit; to the skilful policy which subdued the world to itself?

These illustrations will leave no doubt, it seems to me, that all that is here said will find an ample fulfilment in the Papacy, and that it is to be regarded as having a reference to that power. If so, it only remains,

III. To inquire what, according to this interpretation, we are to expect will yet occur, or what light this passage throws on events that are yet future. The origin, the growth, the general character and influence of this power up to a distant period are illustrated by this interpretation. What remains is the inquiry, from the passage before us, how long this is to continue, and what we are to anticipate in regard to its fall. The following points, then, would seem to be clear, on the supposition that this refers to the Papal power:—

It is to continue a definite period from its establishment, ver. 25. This duration is mentioned as "a time, and times, and the dividing of a time"—

three years and a half—twelve hundred and sixty days—twelve hundred and sixty years. See the Notes on that verse. The only *difficulty* in regard to this, if that interpretation is correct, is to determine the time when the Papacy actually *began*—the *terminus a quo*— and this has given rise to all the diversity of explanation among Protestants. Assuming any one time as the period when the Papal power *arose*, as a date from which to calculate, it is easy to compute *from* that date, and to fix some period—*terminus ad quem*—to which this refers, and which may be looked to as the time of the overthrow of that power. But there is nothing more difficult in history than the determination of the exact time when the *Papacy* properly began: — that is, when the peculiar domination which is fairly understood by that system commenced in the world; or what were its first distinguishing acts. History has not so marked that period that there is no room for doubt. It has not affixed definite dates to it; and to this day it is not easy to make out the *time* when that power commenced, or to designate any one event at a certain period that will surely mark it. It *seems* to have been a gradual growth, and its commencement has not been so definitely characterized as to enable us to demonstrate with absolute certainty the time to which the twelve hundred and sixty years will extend.

Different writers have assigned different periods for the rise of the Papacy, and different acts as the first act of that power; and all the prophecies as to its termination depend on the period which is fixed on as the time of its rise. It is this which has led to so much that is conjectural, and which has been the occasion of so much disappointment, and which throws so much obscurity now over all calcula tions as to the termination of that power. In nothing is the Scripture more clear than that that power shall be destroyed; and if we could ascertain with exactness the date of its origin, there would be little danger of erring in regard to its close. The different *periods* which have been fixed on as the date of its rise have been principally the following: (1.) An edict published by Justinian (A.D. 533), and a letter addressed by him at the same time to the Pope, in which he acknowledged him to be the head of the churches, thus conferring on him a title belonging only to the Saviour, and putting himself and empire under the dominion of the bishop of Rome.—Duffield *on the Prophecies*, p. 281. (2.) The decree of the emperor Phocas (A.D. 606), confirming what had been done by Justinian, and giving his sanction to the code of laws promulgated by him; a code of laws based on the acknowledged supremacy of the Pope, and which became the basis of European legislation for centuries; and conferring on him the title of "Universal Bishop." (3.) The act of Pope Stephen, by which, when appealed to by the claimant to the crown of France, he confirmed Pepin in the kingdom, and set aside Childeric III., and, in return, received from Pepin the Exarchate of Ravenna and the Pentapolis. See Ranke's *Hist. of the Papacy*, vol. i. 23. This occurred about A.D. 752. (4.) The opinion of Mr. Gibbon (iv. 363), that Gregory VII. was the true founder of the Papal power. "Gregory VII.," says he, "who may be adored or detested *as the founder of the Papal monarchy*, was driven from Rome, and died in exile at Salerno." Gregory became Pope A.D. 1073. These different dates, if assumed as the foundation of the Papal power, would, by the addition to each of the period of 1260 years, lead respectively to the years 1793, 1866, 2012, and 2333, as the period of the termination of the Papal dominion. As this is a point of great importance in the explanation of the prophecies, it may be proper to examine these opinions a little more in detail. But in order to this, it is necessary to have a clear conception of what the *Papacy* as a distinct domination is, or what constitutes its peculiarity, as seen by the sacred writers, and as it has in fact existed, and does exist in the world; and in regard to this there can be little difference of opinion. It is not a mere ecclesiastical power—not a mere spiritual domination—not the control of a bishop as such over a church or a diocese—nor is it a mere temporal dominion, but it is manifestly the *union of the two*: that peculiar domination which the bishop of Rome has claimed, as growing out of his primacy as the head of the church, and of a temporal power also, asserted at first over a limited jurisdiction, but ultimately, and as a natural consequence, over all other sovereignties, and claiming universal dominion. We shall not find the Papacy, or the Papal dominion as such, clearly, in the mere spiritual rule of the first bishop of Rome, nor in that mere spiritual dominion, however enlarged, but in that junction of the two, when, in virtue of a pretended Divine right, a temporal dominion grew up that ultimately extended itself over Europe, claiming the authority to dispose of crowns; to lay kingdoms under interdict, and to absolve subjects from their allegiance. If we can find the beginning of this claim—the germ of this peculiar kind of domination—we shall doubtless have found the commencement of the Papacy—the *terminus a quo*—as it was seen by the prophets—the point from which we are to reckon in determining the question of its duration.

With this view, then, of the nature of the Papacy, it is proper to inquire *when* it commenced, or which of the periods referred to, if either, can be properly regarded as the commencement.

I. The edict of Justinian, and the letter to the bishop of Rome, in which he acknowledged him to be the head of the church, A.D. 533. This occurred under John II., reckoned as the fifty-fifth bishop of Rome. The nature of this application of Justinian to the Pope, and the honour conferred on him, was this : On an occasion of a controversy in the church, on the question whether " one person of the Trinity suffered in the flesh," the monks of Constantinople, fearful of being condemned under an edict of Justinian for heresy in denying this, applied to the Pope to decide the point. Justinian, who took great delight in inquiries of that nature, and who maintained the opposite opinion on that subject, also made his appeal to the Pope. Having, therefore, drawn up a long creed, containing the disputed article among the rest, he despatched two bishops with it to Rome, and laid the whole matter before the Pope. At the same time he wrote a letter to the Pope, congratulating him on his election, assuring him that the faith contained in the confession which he sent him was the faith of the whole Eastern church, and entreating him to declare in his answer that he received to his communion all who professed that faith, and none who did not. To add weight to the letter, he accompanied it with a present to St. Peter, consisting of several chalices and other vessels of gold, enriched with precious stones. From this deference to the Pope, on the part of the emperor, and this submitting to him, as the head of the whole church, of an important question to be determined, it has been argued that this was properly the beginning of the Papacy, and that the twelve hundred and sixty years are to be reckoned from that. But against this opinion the objections are insuperable ; for (a) there was here nothing of that which *properly* constitutes the Papacy—the peculiar union of the temporal and spiritual power ; or the peculiar domination which that power has exerted over the world. All that occurred was the mere deference which an emperor showed to one who claimed to be the *spiritual* head of the church, and who had long before claimed that. There was no *change*—no *beginning*, properly so called—no commencement of a new form of domination over mankind, such as the Papacy has been. (b) But, as a matter of fact, there was, after all, little real deference to the Pope in this case. "Little or no account," says Bower, "ought to be made of that extraordinary deference [the deference shown by carrying this question before the Pope]. Justinian paid great deference to the Pope, as well as to all other bishops, when they agreed with him ; but none at all when they did not—thinking himself at least as well qualified as the best of them— and so he certainly was—to decide controversies concerning the faith ; and we shall soon see him entering the lists with his holiness himself."—*Lives of the Popes*, i. 336.

II. The second date which has been assigned to the origin of the Papacy is the decree made by the emperor Phocas (A.D. 606), by which, it is said, he confirmed the grant made by Justinian. This act was the following :—Boniface III., when he had been made bishop of Rome, relying on the favour and partiality which Phocas had shown him, prevailed on him to revoke the decree settling the title of " Universal

Bishop" on the bishop of Constantinople, and obtained another settling that title on himself and his successors. The decree of Phocas, conferring this title, has not indeed come down to us; but it has been the common testimony of historians that such title was conferred. See Mosheim, i. 513; Bower, i. 426. The fact asserted here has been doubted, and Mosheim supposes that it rests on the authority of Baronius. "Still," says he, "it is certain that something of this kind occurred." But there are serious objections to our regarding this as properly the commencement of the Papacy as such. For (a) this was not the beginning of that peculiar domination, or form of power, which the Pope has asserted and maintained. If this title were conferred, it imparted no new power; it did not change the nature of this domination; it did not, in fact, make the Roman bishop different from what he was before. He was still, in all respects, subject to the civil power of the emperors, and had no control beyond that which he exercised in the church. (b) And even *this* little was withdrawn by the same authority which granted it—the authority of the emperor of Constantinople—though it has always since been claimed and asserted by the Pope himself. See Bower, i. 427. It is true that, as a consequence of the fact that this title was conferred on the Popes, they began to *grasp* at power, and aspire to temporal dominion; but still there was no formal grasp of such power growing out of the assumption of this title, nor was any such temporal dominion set up as the immediate result of such a title. The act, therefore, was not sufficiently marked, distinct, and decisive, to constitute an epoch, or the beginning of an era, in the history of the world, and the rise of the Papacy cannot with any

propriety be dated from that. This was undoubtedly one of the *steps* by which that peculiar power rose to its greatness, or which contributed to lay the foundation of its subsequent claims, its arrogance, and its pride; but it is doubtful whether it was so important an event characterizing the Papacy as to be regarded as the origin, or the *terminus a quo* in ascertaining the time of its continuance.* It was, however, in view of this, and with this considered as properly the origin of the Papacy, that the Rev. Robert Fleming, in his work on the *Rise and Fall of the Papacy*, first published in 1701, uttered the following remarkable language, as based on his calculations respecting the continuance of that power:—"If we may suppose that Antichrist began his reign in the year 606, the additional one thousand two hundred and sixty years of his duration, were they *Julian* or ordinary years, would lead down to the year 1866, as the last period of the seven-headed monster. But seeing

* Mr. Hallam (*Middle Ages*, i. 420, note) urges the following arguments substantially against the supposition that the Papal supremacy had its rise from this epoch, and is to be dated from the concession of the title of Universal Bishop made by Phocas to Boniface III., viz.: (1.) Its truth, as commonly stated, appears more than questionable. (2.) "But if the strongest proof could be advanced for the authenticity of this circumstance, we may well deny its importance. The concession of Phocas could have been of no validity in Lombardy, France, and other western countries, where, nevertheless, the Papal supremacy was incomparably more established than in the east." (3.) "Even within the empire it could have had no efficacy after the violent death of that usurper, which occurred soon afterwards." (4.) "The title of Universal Bishop is not very intelligible, but whatever it means the patriarchs of Constantinople had borne it before, and continued to bear it afterwards." (5.) "The preceding Popes, Pelagius II. and Gregory I., had constantly disclaimed the appellation; nor does it appear to have been claimed by the successors of Boniface, at least for some centuries." (6.) "The Popes had undoubtedly exercised a species of supremacy for more than two centuries before this time, which had lately reached a high point of authority under Gregory I." (7.) "There are no sensible marks of this supremacy making a more rapid progress for a century and a half after the pretended grant of this emperor."

they are prophetical years only [of 360 days], we must cast away eighteen years in order to bring them to the exact measure of time that the Spirit of God designs in this book. *And thus the final period of the Papal usurpations (supposing that he did indeed rise in the year* 606) *must conclude with the year* 1848."—[Cobbin's Edition, p. 32.] Whether this be considered as merely a *happy conjecture*—the one successful one among thousands that have failed, or as the result of a proper calculation respecting the future, no one in comparing it with the events of the year 1848, when the Pope was driven from Rome, and when a popular government was established in the very seat of the Papal power, can fail to see that it is remarkable considered as having been uttered a century and a half ago. Whether it is the correct calculation, and that temporary downfall of the Papal government is to be regarded as the first in a series of events that will ultimately end in its destruction, time must determine. The reasons mentioned above, however, and those which will be suggested in favour of a different beginning of that power, make it, at present, more probable that a different period is to be assigned as its close.

III. The third date which has been assigned as the beginning of the Papacy is the grant of Pepin above referred to, A.D. 752. This grant conferred by Pepin was confirmed also by Charlemagne and his successors, and it was undoubtedly at this period that the Papacy began to assume its place among the sovereignties of Europe. In favour of this opinion—that this was properly the rise of the Papacy—the *terminus a quo* of prophecy, the following considerations may be urged: (*a*) We have here a definite act—an act which is palpable and apparent, as characterizing the progress of this domination over men. (*b*) We have here properly the *beginning* of the temporal dominion, or the first acknowledged exercise of that power in acts of temporal sovereignty —in giving laws, asserting dominion, swaying a temporal sceptre, and wearing a temporal crown All the acts before had been of a spiritual character, and all the deference to the Bishop of Rome had been of a spiritual nature. Henceforward, however, he was acknowledged as a temporal prince, and took his place as such among the crowned heads of Europe. (*c*) This is properly the beginning of that mighty domination which the Pope wielded over Europe— a beginning, which, however small at first, ultimately became so powerful and so arrogant as to claim jurisdiction over all the kingdoms of the earth, and the right to absolve subjects from their allegiance, to lay kingdoms under interdict, to dispose of crowns, to order the succession of princes, to tax all people, and to dispose of all newly-discovered countries. (*d*) This accords better with the prophecies than any other one event which has occurred in the world—especially with the prophecy of Daniel, of the springing up of the little horn, and the fact that that little horn plucked up three others of the ten into which the fourth kingdom was divided. (*e*) And it should be added that this agrees with the idea all along held up in the prophecies, that this would be properly *the fourth empire prolonged*. The fifth empire or kingdom is to be the reign of the saints, or the reign of righteousness on the earth ; the fourth extends down in its influences and power to that. As a matter of fact, this *Roman* power was thus concentrated in the Papacy. The form was changed, but it was the *Roman* power that was in the eye of the prophets, and this was contemplated under its various phases, as heathen and nominally Christian, until the reign of the saints should commence, or the kingdom of God should be set up. But it was only in the time of Stephen, and by the act of Pepin and Charlemagne, that this change occurred, or that this dominion of a temporal character was settled in the Papacy—and that the Pope was acknowledged as having this temporal power. This was *consummated* indeed in Hildebrand, or Gregory VII. (Gibbon, iii. 353, iv. 363), but *this* mighty power properly had its *origin* in the time of Pepin.

IV. The fourth date assigned for the origin of the Papacy is the time of Hildebrand, or Gregory VII. This is the period assigned by Mr. Gibbon. Respecting this, he remarks (vol. iv. p. 363), "Gregory the Seventh, who may be adored or detested *as the founder of the Papal monarchy,* was driven from Rome, and died in exile at Salerno." And again (vol. iii. p. 353), he says of Gregory, "After a long series of scandal, the apostolic see was reformed and exalted, by the austerity and zeal of Gregory VII. That ambitious monk devoted his life to the execution of two projects: I. To fix in the college of Cardinals the freedom and independence of election, and forever to abolish the right or usurpation of the emperors and the Roman people. II. To bestow and resume the Western Empire as a fief or benefice of the church, and to extend his temporal dominion over the kings and kingdoms of the earth. After a contest of fifty years, the first of these designs was accomplished by the firm support of the ecclesiastical order, whose liberty was connected with that of the chief. But the second attempt, though it was crowned with some apparent and partial success, has been vigorously resisted

by the secular power, and finally extinguished by the improvement of human reason."

If the views above suggested, however, are correct; or if we look at the Papacy as it was in the time of Hildebrand, it must be apparent that this was not the *rise* or *origin* of that peculiar domination, but was only the carrying out and completing of the plan laid long before to set up a temporal dominion over mankind.

It should be added, that whichever of the three first periods referred to be regarded as the time of the rise of the Papacy, if we add to them the prophetic period of 1260 years, we are *now* in the midst of scenes on which the prophetic eye rested, and we cannot, as fair interpreters of prophecy, but regard this mighty domination as hastening to its fall. It would seem probable, then, that according to the most obvious explanation of the subject, we are at present not far from the termination and fall of that great power, and that events may be expected to occur at about this period of the world, which will be connected with its fall.

(B.) Its power is to be taken away as by a solemn judgment—*as if* the throne was set, and God was to come forth to pronounce judgment on this power to overthrow it, verses 10, 11, 26. This destruction of the power referred to is to be absolute and entire —*as if* the "beast were slain, and the body given to the burning flame"— "and they shall take away his dominion, to consume and destroy it unto the end." This would denote the absolute destruction of this peculiar power—its entire cessation in the world; that is, the absolute destruction of that which had constituted its *peculiarity*—the prolonged power of the beast of the fourth kingdom—concentrated and embodied in that represented by the little horn. If applied to the Roman power, or the fourth kingdom, it means that *that* power which would have been prolonged under the dominion of that represented by the little horn, would wholly cease —as if the body of the beast had been burned. If applied to the power represented by the "little horn"—the Papacy—it means that *that* power which sprang up amidst the others, and which became so mighty—embodying so much of the power of the beast, would wholly pass away *as* an ecclesiastico-civil power. It would cease its dominion, and as one of the ruling powers of the earth would disappear. This would be accomplished by some remarkable Divine manifestation—*as if* God should come in majesty and power to judgment, and should pronounce a sentence; that is, the overthrow would be decisive, and as manifestly the result of the Divine interposition *as if* God should do it by a formal act of judgment. In the overthrow of that power, whenever it occurs, it would be natural, from this prophecy, to anticipate that there would be some scenes of commotion and revolution bearing directly on it, *as if* God were pronouncing sentence on it; some important changes in the nations that had acknowledged its authority, *as if* the great Judge of nations were coming forth to assert his own power and his own right to rule, and to dispose of the kingdoms of the earth as he pleased.

(C.) It is to be anticipated that the power referred to will be destroyed on account of its pride and arrogance. See Notes on ver. 11. That is, whatever power there is upon the earth at the time referred to that shall be properly that of the fourth beast or

kingdom, will be taken away on account of the claims set up and maintained by the "little horn:" "I beheld *because* of the voice of the great words which the horn spake; I beheld till the beast was slain," &c., verse 11. On the supposition that this refers to the Papacy, what is to be expected would be, that the pride and arrogance of that power as such—that is, as an ecclesiastical power claiming dominion over civil things, and wielding civil authority, would be such that the Roman power—the lingering power of the fourth kingdom—would be taken away, and its dominion over the world would cease. That vast Roman domination that once trod down the earth, and that crushed and oppressed the nations, would still linger, like the prolonged life of the beast, until, on account of the arrogance and pride of the Papacy, it would be wholly taken away. If one were to judge of the meaning of this prophecy without attempting to apply it to particular passing events, he would say that it would be fulfilled by some such events as these:—if the people over whom the prolonged Roman civil power would be extended, and over whom the ecclesiastical or papal sceptre would be swayed, should, on account of the pride and arrogance of the Papacy, rise in their might, and demand liberty—*that* would be in fact an end of the prolonged power of the fourth beast ; and it would be on account of the "great words which the horn spake," and would be in all respects a fulfilment of the language of this prophecy. Whether such an end of this power is to occur, time is to determine.

(D.) Simultaneously with this event, as the result of this, we are to anticipate such a spread of truth and righteousness, and such a reign of the saints on the earth, as would be properly symbolized by the coming of the Son of man to the Ancient of days to receive the kingdom, vers. 13, 14. As shown in the interpretation of those verses, this does not necessarily imply that there would be any visible appearing of the Son of man, or any personal reign (see the Notes on these verses), but there would be such a making over of the kingdom to the Son of man and to the saints as would be properly symbolized by such a representation. That is, there would be great changes; there would be a rapid progress of the truth; there would be a spread of the gospel; there would be a change in the governments of the world, so that the power would pass into the hands of the righteous, and they would in fact rule. From that time the "saints" would receive the kingdom, and the affairs of the world would be put on a new footing. From that period it might be said that the reign of the saints would *commence;* that is, there would be such changes in this respect that *that* would constitute an epoch in the history of the world—the proper beginning of the reign of the saints on the earth—the setting up of the new and final dominion in the world. If there should be such changes—such marked progress—such facilities for the spread of truth—such new methods of propagating it—and such certain success attending it, all opposition giving way, and persecution ceasing, as would properly constitute an *epoch* or *era* in the world's history, which would be connected with the conversion of the world to God, this would fairly meet the interpretation of this prophecy; this occurring, all would have taken place which could be fairly shown to be implied in the vision.

(E.) We are to expect a reign of righteousness on the earth. On the character of what we are fairly to expect from the words of the prophecy, see Notes on ver. 14. The prophecy authorizes us to anticipate a time when there shall be a general prevalence of true religion; when the power in the world shall be in the hands of good men—of men fearing God; when the Divine laws shall be obeyed—being acknowledged as the laws that are to control men; when the civil institutions of the world shall be pervaded by religion, and moulded by it; when there shall be no hinderance to the free exercise of religion, and when in fact the reigning power on the earth shall be the kingdom which the Messiah shall set up. There is nothing more certain in the future than such a period, and to that all things are tending. *Such* a period would fulfil all that is fairly implied in this wonderful prophecy, and *to* that faith and hope should calmly and confidently look forward. For that they who love their God and their race should labour and pray; and by the certain assurance that such a period will come, we should be cheered amidst all the moral darkness that exists in the world, and in all that now discourages us in our endeavours to do good.

CHAPTER VIII.

ANALYSIS OF THE CHAPTER.

This chapter contains an account of a vision seen by the prophet in the third year of the reign of Belshazzar. The prophet either was, or appeared to be, in the city of Shushan—afterwards the capital of the Persian empire, in the province of Elam. To that place —then an important town—there is no improbability in supposing that he had gone, as he was then unconnected with the government, or not employed by the government (ch. v.), and as it is not unreasonable to suppose that he would be at liberty to visit other parts of the empire than Babylon. Possibly there may have been Jews at that place, and he may have gone on a visit to them. Or perhaps the scene of the vision may have been laid in Shushan, by the river Ulai, and that the prophet means to represent himself *as if* he had been there, and the vision had seemed to pass there before his mind. But there is no valid objection to the supposition that he was actually there; and this seems to be affirmed in ver. 2. While there, he saw a ram with two horns, one higher than the other, pushing westward, and northward, and southward, so powerful that nothing could oppose him. As he was looking on this, he saw a he-goat come from the west, bounding along, and scarcely touching the ground, with a single remarkable horn between his eyes. This he-goat attacked the ram, broke his two horns, and overcame him entirely. The he-goat became very strong, but at length the horn was broken, and there came up four in its place. From one of these there sprang up a little horn that became exceeding great and mighty, extending itself toward the south, and the east, and the pleasant land—the land of Palestine. This horn became so mighty that it seemed to attack "the host of heaven"—the stars; it cast some of them down to the ground; it magnified itself against the Prince of the host; it caused the daily sacrifice in the temple to cease, and the sanctuary of the Prince of the host was cast down. An earnest inquiry was made by one saint to another how long this was to continue, and the answer was, unto two thousand and three hundred days, and that then the sanctuary would be cleansed. Gabriel is then sent to explain the vision to the prophet, and he announces that the ram with the two horns repre-

sented the kings of Media and Persia; the goat, the king of Greece; the great horn between his eyes, the first king; the four horns that sprang up after that was broken, the four dynasties into which the kingdom would be divided; and the little horn, a king of fierce countenance, and understanding dark sentences, and that would stand up against the Prince of princes, and that would ultimately be destroyed. The effect of this was, that Daniel was overcome by the vision for a certain time; afterward he revived, and attended to the business of the king, but none understood the vision.

This is one of the few prophecies in the Scriptures that are explained to the prophets themselves, and it becomes, therefore, important as a key to explain other prophecies of a similar character. Of the reference to the kingdom of Media and Persia, and to the kingdom of Greece, there is an express statement. The application of a portion of the prophecy to Alexander the Great, and to the four monarchies into which his kingdom was divided at his death, is equally certain. And there can be as little doubt of the application of the remainder to Antiochus Epiphanes, and in this nearly all expositors are agreed. Indeed, so striking and clear is the application to this series of historical events, that Porphyry maintained that this, as well as other portions of Daniel, were written *after* the events occurred. One of two things, indeed, is certain—either that this *was* written after the events here referred to occurred, or that Daniel was inspired. No man by any natural sagacity could have predicted these events with so much accuracy and particularity.

The portion of Daniel which follows is in pure Hebrew. The portion of the book from the fourth verse of the

CHAPTER VIII.

IN the third year of the reign of king Belshazzar a vision appeared unto me, *even unto me*

second chapter to the end of the seventh chapter was written in Chaldee. On this point, see Intro. § IV. III. (1).

1. *In the third year of the reign of king Belshazzar.* In regard to Belshazzar, see Intro. to ch. v. § II. ¶ *A vision appeared unto me.* This vision appears to have occurred to him when awake, or in an ecstasy; the former one occurred when he was asleep, ch. vii. 1. Comp. vers. 17, 18 of this chap., where the prophet represents himself as overpowered, and as falling down to the earth on account of the vision. The representation would seem to have been made to pass before his mind in open day, and when he was fully awake. Comp. the case of Balaam, Num. xxiv. 4: "Which saw the vision of the Almighty, falling into a trance, but having his eyes open." ¶ *After that which appeared unto me at the first.* That occurred in the first year of Belshazzar, ch. vii. 1.

2. *And I saw in a vision.* I looked as the vision appeared to me; or I saw certain things represented to me in a vision. On the word *vision*, see Notes on ch. i. 17. The meaning here would seem to be that a vision appeared to Daniel, and that he contemplated it with earnestness, to understand what it meant. ¶ *That I was at Shushan.* As remarked in the introduction to this chapter, this might mean that he *seemed* to be there, or that the vision was represented to him as being there; but the most natural construction is to suppose that Daniel was actually there himself. *Why* he was there he has not informed us directly—whether he was on public business, or on his own. From ver. 27, however—"Afterward I rose up, and did the king's business"—it would seem most probable that he was then in the service of the king. This supposition will not conflict with the statement in ch. v. 10, 11, in which the queen-mother, when the handwriting appeared on the wall of the palace, informs Belshazzar that there

Daniel, after that which appeared unto me at the first.

2 And I saw in a vision; and it came to pass, when I saw, that I was " a man in his kingdom in whom was the spirit of the holy gods," &c.—from which it might be objected that Daniel was at that time unknown to the king, and could not have been in his employ; for it might have been a fact that he was in the employ of the king as an officer of the government, and yet it may have been forgotten that he had this power of disclosing the meaning of visions. He may have been employed in the public service, but his services to the father of the king, and his extraordinary skill in interpreting dreams and visions may not at once have occurred to the affrighted monarch and his courtiers. Shushan, or Susa, the chief town of Susiana, was the capital of Persia after the time of Cyrus, in which the kings of Persia had their principal residence, Nehem. i. 1; Esther i. 2–5. It was situated on the Eulæus or Choaspes, probably on the spot now occupied by the village Shus.—Rennel, *Geog. of Herodotus;* Kinneir, *Mem. Pers. Emp.;* K. Porter's *Travels,* ii. 4, 11; Ritter, *Erdkunde, Asien,* ix. 294; *Pict. Bib. in loc.* At Shus there are extensive ruins, stretching perhaps twelve miles from one extremity to the other, and consisting, like the other ruins in that country, of hillocks of earth, and rubbish, covered with broken pieces of brick and coloured tile. At the foot of these mounds is the so-called tomb of Daniel, a small building erected on the spot where the remains of Daniel are believed in that region to rest. It is apparently modern, but nothing but the belief that this was the site of the prophet's sepulchre could have led to its being built in the place where it stands.—Malcolm, *Hist. of Persia,* i. 255, 256. The city of Shus is now a gloomy wilderness, inhabited by lions, hyenas, and other beasts of prey.—Kitto's *Cyclo.,* art. "Shushan." Sir John Kinneir says that the dread of these animals compelled Mr. Monteith and himself to take shelter for the night within the walls that encompass

was at Shushan *ᵃ in* the palace, which *is* in the province of Elam; and I saw in a vision, and I was by the river of Ulai.

3 Then I lifted up mine eyes,

a Esth. 1. 2.

and saw, and, behold, there stood before the river a ram, which had *two* horns, and the *two* horns *were* high; but one *was* higher than the other ¹ and the higher came up last.

1 *second.*

Daniel's tomb. Of that tomb Sir John Malcolm says, " It is a small building, but sufficient to shelter some dervishes who watch the remains of the prophet, and are supported by the alms of pious pilgrims, who visit the holy sepulchre. The dervishes are now the only inhabitants of Susa; and every species of wild beast roams at large over the spot on which some of the proudest palaces ever raised by human art once stood." —Vol. i. pp. 255, 256. For a description of the ruins of Susa, see *Pict. Bib. in loc.* This city was about 450 Roman miles from Seleucia, and was built, according to Pliny, 6, 27, in a square of about 120 stadia. It was the summer residence of the Persian kings (*Cyrop.* 8, 6, 10), as they passed the spring in Ecbatana, and the autumn and winter in Babylon. See Lengerke, *in loc.* It was in this city that Alexander the Great married Stateira, daughter of Darius Codomanus. The *name* means a *lily*, and was probably given to it on account of its beauty.— Lengerke. Rosenmüller supposes that the vision here is represented to have appeared to Daniel in this city because it would be the future capital of Persia, and because so much of the vision pertained to Persia. See Maurer, *in loc.* ¶ In *the palace.* This word

(פִּירָה) means a fortress, a castle, a fortified palace.—Gesenius. See Neh. i. 1; Esth. i. 5; ii. 5; viii. 14; ix. 6, 11, 12. It would seem to have been given to the city because it was a fortified place. The word applied not only to the *palace* proper, a royal residence, but to the whole adjacent city. It is not necessary to suppose that Daniel was in the palace proper, but only that he was in the city to which the name was given. ¶ *Which* is *in the province of Elam.* See Notes on Isa. xi. 11. This province was bounded on the east by Persia Proper, on the

west by Babylonia, on the north by Media, and on the south by the Persian Gulf. It was about half as large as Persia, and not quite as large as England.—Kitto's *Cyclo.* It was probably conquered by Nebuchadnezzar, and in the time of Belshazzar was subject to the Babylonian dominion, Shushan had been doubtless the capital of the kingdom of Elam while it continued a separate kingdom, and remained the capital of the province while it was under the Babylonian yoke, and until it was subdued as a part of the empire by Cyrus. It was then made one of the capitals of the united Medo-Persian empire. It was when it was the capital of a province that it was visited by Daniel, and that he saw the vision there. Possibly he may have dwelt there subsequently, and died there. ¶ *And I was by the river of Ulai.* This river flowed by the city of Shushan, or Susa, and fell into the united stream of the Tigris and the Euphrates. It is called by Pliny (*Nat. Hist.* vi. 81) Eulæus; but it is described by Greek writers generally under the name of Choaspes.— Herod. v. 49; Strabo, xv. p. 728. It is now known by the name Kerah, called by the Turks Karasu. It passes on the west of the ruins of Shus (Susa), and enters the Shat-ul-Arab about twenty miles below Korna.—Kinneir, *Geog. Mem. of the Persian Empire,* pp. 96, 97. See Kitto's *Cyclo.*, art. " Ulai."

3. *Then I lifted up mine eyes and saw.* And saw in vision, or there seemed to be before me. ¶ *There stood before the river.* On the bank of the river. ¶ *A ram, which had* two *horns.* There can be no error in explaining the design of this symbol, for in ver. 20 it is expressly said that it denoted the two kings of Media and Persia. The united power of the kingdom was denoted by the ram itself; the fact that

4 I saw the ram pushing west-ward, and northward, and south-ward; so that no beasts might stand before him, neither *was there any* that could deliver out of his

a ch. 5. 19; 11. 3, 16; Isa. 10. 13, 14.

hand; but he did according to his will, *a* and became great.

5 And as I was considering, be-hold, an he-goat *b* came from the west, on the face of the whole earth,

b ver. 21.

there were two powers or kingdoms combined, by the two horns of the ram. ¶ *And the* two *horns* were *high*. Both indicating great power. ¶ *But one* was *higher than the other, and the higher came up last*. The higher horn springing up last denotes Persia, that became the more mighty power of the two, so that the name *Media* became finally almost dropped, and the united kingdom was known in Grecian his-tory as the *Persian*. The Median or Assyrian power was the older, but the Persian became the most mighty.

4. *I saw the ram pushing westward, and northward, and southward*. De-noting the conquests of the united kingdom. The *east* is not mentioned, for none of the conquests of the Medo-Persian empire extended in that direc-tion. Yet nothing could better express the conquests actually made by the Medo-Persian empire than this repre-sentation. On the west the conquests embraced Babylonia, Mesopotamia, Syria, and Asia Minor; on the north, Colchis, Armenia, Iberia, and the re-gions around the Caspian Sea; and on the south, Palestine, Ethiopia, Egypt, and Lybia.—Lengerke. This Medo-Persian power is represented as coming from the east. Isa. xli. 2: "Who raised up the righteous man *from the east*," &c. Isa. xlvi. 11: "Calling a ravenous bird *from the east*," &c. ¶ *He did according to his will, and became great*. This expresses well also the character of the Medo-Persian em-pire. It extended over a great part of the known world, subduing to itself a large portion of the earth. In its early conquests it met with no successful opposition, nor was it stayed until it was subdued by Greece—as at Leuctra and Marathon, and then as it was finally overthrown by Alexander the Great.

5. *And as I was considering*. As I was looking on this vision. It was a vision which would naturally attract

attention, and one which would not be readily understood. It evidently de-noted some combined power that was attempting conquest, but we are not to suppose that Daniel would readily understand what was meant by it. The whole scene was future—for the Medo-Persian power was not yet consolidated in the time of Belshazzar, and the con-quests represented by the ram conti-nued through many years, and those denoted by the he-goat extended still much further into futurity. ¶ *Behold, an he-goat came from the west*. In ver. 21, this is called the " rough-goat." There can be no doubt as to the appli-cation of this, for in ver. 21 it is expressly said that it was "the king of Grecia." The power represented is that of Greece when it was consoli-dated under Alexander the Great, and when he went forth to the subjugation of this vast Persian empire. It may serve to illustrate this, and to show the propriety of representing the Ma-cedonian power by the symbol of a goat, to remark that this symbol is often found, in various ways, in con-nection with Macedon, and that, for some reason, the goat was used as emblematic of that power. A few facts, furnished to the editor of Cal-met's *Dictionary*, by Taylor Combe, Esq., will show the propriety of this allusion to Macedonia under the em-blem of a goat, and that the allusion would be readily understood in after-times. They are condensed here from his account in Taylor's *Calmet*, v. 410–412. (1.) Caranus, the first king of the Macedonians, commenced his reign 814 years before the Christian era. The circumstance of his being led by goats to the city of Edessa, the name of which, when he established there the seat of his kingdom, he con-verted into *Ægæ*, is well worthy of remark: *Urbem Edessam, ob memoriam muneris Ægas, populum Ægeadas.*— Justin, lib. vii. c. 1. The adoption of

and [1] touched not the ground : and
1 or, *none touched* him *in the earth.*
2 *a horn of sight.*

the goat *had* [2]a notable horn between his eyes.

the *goat* as an emblem of Macedon
would have been early suggested by
an important event in their history.
(2.) Bronze figures of a goat have been
found as the symbol of Macedon. Mr.
Combe says, "I have lately had an
opportunity of procuring an ancient
bronze figure of a goat with one horn,
which was the old symbol of Macedon.
As figures representing the types of
ancient countries are extremely rare,
and as neither a bronze nor marble
symbol of Macedon has been hitherto
noticed, I beg leave to trouble you with
the few following observations," &c.
He then says, "The goat which is sent
for your inspection was dug up in Asia
Minor, and was brought, together with
other antiquities, into this country by
a poor Turk." The annexed engraving is a representation of this figure.

The slightest inspection of this figure
will show the propriety of the representation before us. Mr. Combe then
says, "Not only many of the individual towns in Macedon and Thrace
employed this type, but the kingdom
itself of Macedon, which is the oldest
in Europe of which we have any regular and connected history, was represented also by a goat, with this peculiarity, that it had but one horn."
(3.) In the reign of Amyntas the First,

nearly 300 years after Caranus, and
about 547 years before Christ, the
Macedonians, upon being threatened
with an invasion, became tributary to
the Persians. In one of the pilasters
of Persepolis, this very event seems to
be recorded in a manner that throws
considerable light on this subject. A
goat is represented with an immense
horn growing out of the middle of his
forehead, and a man in a Persian dress
is seen by his side, holding the horn
with his left hand, by which is signified
the subjection of Macedon. The subjoined is the figure referred to, and it

strikingly shows how early this symbol was used.   (4.) In the reign of
Archelaus of Macedon, B.C. 413, there

occurs on the reverse of a coin of that king the head of a goat having only one horn. Of this coin, so remarkable for the single horn, there are two varieties, one (No. 1) engraved by Pellerin, and the other (No. 2) preserved in the cabinet of the late Dr. W. Hunter.

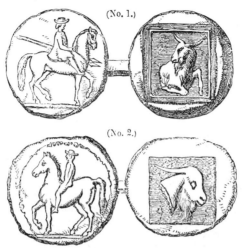

(No. 1.)

(No. 2.)

(5.) "There is a gem," says Mr. Combe, "engraved in the Florentine collection, which, as it confirms what has been already said, and has not hitherto been understood, I think worthy of mention. It will be seen by the drawing of this gem that nothing

more or less is meant by the ram's head with two horns, and the goat's head with one, than the kingdoms of Persia and Macedon, represented under their appropriate symbols. From the circumstance, however, of these characteristic types being united, it is extremely probable that the gem was engraved after the conquest of Persia by Alexander the Great." These remarks and illustrations will show the pro-priety of the symbol used here, and show also how readily it would be understood in after-times. There is no evidence that Daniel understood that this ever had been a symbol of Macedonia, or that, if he had, he could have conjectured, by any natural sagacity, that a power represented by that symbol would have become the conqueror of Media and Persia, and every circumstance, therefore, connected with this only shows the more clearly that he was under the influence of inspiration. It is affirmed by Josephus (*Ant.* b. xi. ch. viii.) that when Alexander was at Jerusalem, the prophecies of Daniel respecting him were shown to him by the high-priest, and that this fact was the means of his conferring important favours on the Jews. If such an event occurred, the circumstances here alluded to show how readily Alexander would recognize the reference to his own country, and to himself, and how probable the account of Josephus is, that this was the means of conciliating him towards the Jewish people. The credibilty of the account, which has been called in question, is examined in Newton *on the Prophecies,* pp. 241–246. ¶ *On the face of*

6 And he came to the ram that had *two* horns, which I had seen standing before the river, and ran unto him in the fury of his power.

7 And I saw him come close unto the ram, and he was moved with choler against him, and smote the ram, and brake his two horns;

the whole earth. He seemed to move over the whole world—well representing the movements of Alexander, who conquered the known world, and who is said to have wept because there were no other worlds to conquer. ¶ *And touched not the ground.* Marg., *none touched* him *in the earth.* The translation in the text, however, is more correct than that in the margin. He seemed to bound along as if he did not touch the ground—denoting the rapidity of his movements and conquests. A similar description of great beauty occurs in Virgil, *Æn.* vii. 806, seq. of Camilla :—

"Cursu pedum prævertere ventos.
Illa vel intactæ segetis per summa volaret
Gramina, nec teneras cursu læsisset aristas,
Vel mare per medium fluctu suspensa tumenti
Ferret iter, celeres nec tingeret æquore plantas."

Nothing would better express the rapid conquests of Alexander the Great than the language employed by Daniel. He died at the early age of thirty-three, and having been chosen generalissimo of the Greeks against the Persians at the age of twenty-one, the whole period occupied by him in his conquests, and in his public life, was but twelve years ; yet in that time he brought the world in subjection to his arms. A single glance at his rapid movements will show the propriety of the description here. In the year 334 B.C., he invaded Persia, and defeated the Persians in the battle of the Granicus ; in the year 333, he again defeated them at the battle of Issus, and conquered Parthia, Bactria, Hyrcania, Sogdiana, and Asia Minor. In the year 332, he conquered Tyre and Egypt, and built Alexandria. In the year 331, he defeated Darius Codomanus, and in 330 completed the conquest of the Persian empire. In the year 328, he defeated Porus, king of India, and pursued his march to the Ganges. In these few years, therefore, he had overrun nearly all the then known world, in conquests more rapid and more decisive than had ever before been made. ¶ *And the goat*

had *a notable horn between his eyes.* The goat represented the Macedonian power, and all this power was concentrated in the person of Alexander—undoubtedly denoted by the single horn —as if all the power of Greece was concentrated in him. The margin is, *a horn of sight.* This corresponds with the Hebrew—the word rendered *notable* (חָזוּת) meaning, properly, *look, appearance,* and then something *conspicuous* or *remarkable.* The literal translation would be, *a horn of appearance;* that is, conspicuous, large.—Gesenius, *Lex.*

6. *And he came to the ram,* &c. Representing the Medo-Persian power. ¶ *And ran unto him in the fury of his power.* Representing the fierceness and fury with which Alexander attacked the Persians at the Granicus, at Issus, and at Arbela, with which he invaded and overthrew them in their own country. Nothing would better express this than to say that it was done in " the fury of power."

[The following is from a medallion of Alexander the Great, in which the ram's horn is allusive to his boast that he was the son of Jupiter-Ammon.]

7. *And I saw him come close unto the ram.* The ram standing on the banks of the Ulai, and in the very heart of the empire. This representa-

and there was no power in the ram to stand before him, but he cast him down to the ground, and stamped upon him : and there was none that could deliver the ram out of his hand.

8 Therefore the he-goat waxed very great : and when he was

---

tion is designed undoubtedly to denote that the Grecian power would attack the Persian in its own dominions. Perhaps the vision was represented at the place which would be the capital of the empire in order to denote this. ¶ *And he was moved with choler against him* [*i.e., the ram*]. With wrath or anger. That is, he acted as if he were furiously enraged. This is not an improper representation. Alexander, though spurred on by ambition as his ruling motive, yet might be supposed without impropriety to represent the concentrated wrath of all Greece on account of the repeated Persian invasions. It is true the Persians had been defeated at Leuctra, at Marathon, and at Salamis, that their hosts had been held in check at Thermopylæ, that they had never succeeded in subduing Greece, and that the Grecians in defending their country had covered themselves with glory. But it is true, also, that the wrongs inflicted or attempted on the Greeks had never been forgotten, and it cannot be doubted that the remembrance of these wrongs was a motive that influenced many a Greek at the battle of the Granicus and Issus, and at Arbela. It would be one of the most powerful motives to which Alexander could appeal in stimulating his army. ¶ *And brake his two horns.* Completely prostrated his power—as Alexander did when he overthrew Darius Codomanus, and subjugated to himself the Medo-Persian empire. That empire ceased at that time, and was merged in that of the son of Philip. ¶ *And there was no power in the ram to stand before him.* To resist him. ¶ *But he cast him down to the ground, and stamped upon him.* An act strikingly expressive of the conduct of Alexander. The empire was crushed beneath his power, and, as it were, trampled to the earth. ¶ *And there was none that could deliver the ram out of his hand.* No auxiliaries that the Persian empire could

call to its aid that could save it from the Grecian conqueror.

8. *Therefore the he-goat waxed very great.* The Macedonian power, especially under the reign of Alexander. ¶ *And when he was strong, the great horn was broken.* In the time, or at the period of its greatest strength. Then an event occurred which broke the horn in which was concentrated its power. It is easy to see the application of this to the Macedonian power. At no time was the empire so strong as at the death of Alexander. Its power did not pine away ; it was not enfeebled, as monarchies are often, by age, and luxury, and corruption ; it was most flourishing and prosperous just at the period when broken by the death of Alexander. Never afterwards did it recover its vigour ; never was it consolidated again. From that time this mighty empire, broken into separate kingdoms, lost its influence in the world. ¶ *And for it came up four notable ones.* In the place of this one horn in which all the power was concentrated, there sprang up four others that were distinguished and remarkable. On the word *notable*, see Notes on ver. 5. This representation would lead us to suppose that the power which had thus been concentrated in one monarchy would be divided and distributed into four, and that instead of that one power there would be four kingdoms that would fill up about the same space in the world, occupy about the same territory, and have about the same characteristics— so that they might be regarded as the succession to the one dynasty. The same representation we have of this one power in ch. vii. 6:—" The beast had also four heads." See also ch. xi. 4: " His kingdom shall be broken, and shall be divided toward the four winds of heaven." This accords with the accounts in history of the effect of Alexander's death, for though the kingdom was not by him divided into

strong, the great horn was broken; and for it came up four *a* notable

a ch. 7. 6, &c.   *b* ch. 11. 25, &c.

four parts, yet, from the confusion and conflicts that arose, the power was ultimately concentrated into four dynasties. At his death, his brother Aridæus was declared king in his stead, and Perdiccas regent. But the unity of the Macedonian power was gone, and disorder and confusion, and a struggle for empire, immediately succeeded. The author of the books of Maccabees (1 Macc. i. 7–9) says: "So Alexander reigned twelve years, and then died. And his servants bare rule every one in his place. And after his death, they all put crowns upon themselves; so did their sons after them many years; and evils were multiplied in the earth." Alexander died B.C. 323; Antipater succeeded Perdiccas, B.C. 321; Ptolemy Lagus the same year took possession of Egypt; Cassander assumed the government of Macedon, B.C. 317; Seleucus Nicator took possession of Syria, B.C. 311; in 305 B.C. the successors of Alexander took the title of kings, and in 301 B.C. there occurred the battle of Ipsus, in which Antigonus, who reigned in Asia Minor, was killed, and then followed in that year a formal division of Alexander's empire between the four victorious princes, Ptolemy, Seleucus, Cassander, and Lysimachus. This great battle of Ipsus, a city of Phrygia, was fought between Antigonus and his son Demetrius on the one side, and the combined forces of these princes on the other. Antigonus had aimed at universal sovereignty; he had taken and plundered the island of Cyprus; had destroyed the fleet of Ptolemy Lagus, and had assumed the crown. Against him and his usurpations, Ptolemy, Cassander, and Lysimachus, combined their forces, and the result was his complete overthrow at the battle of Ipsus. — Lengerke, *in loc.* In this battle, Antigonus lost all his conquests and his life. In the division of the empire, Seleucus Nicator obtained Syria, Babylonia, Media, and Susiana, Armenia, a part of Cappadocia, Cilicia, and his kingdom, in name at least, extended from the Hellespont

ones, toward the four winds of heaven.

9 And *b* out of one of them came

to the Indies. The kingdom of Lysimachus extended over a part of Thrace, Asia Minor, part of Cappadocia, and the countries within the limits of Mount Taurus. Cassander possessed Macedonia, Thessaly, and a part of Greece. Ptolemy obtained Egypt, Cyprus, and Cyrene, and ultimately Cœlo-Syria, Phœnicia, Judea, and a part of Asia Minor and Thrace.— Lengerke, *in loc.* ¶ *Toward the four winds of heaven.* Towards the four quarters of the world. Thus the dominions of Seleucus were in the east; those of Cassander in the west; those of Ptolemy in the south, and those of Lysimachus in the north.

9. *And out of one of them came forth a little horn.* Emblematic of a new power that should spring up. Comp. Notes on ch. vii. 8. This little horn sprang up out of one of the others; it did not spring up in the midst of the others as the little horn, in ch. vii. 8, did among the ten others. This seemed to grow out of one of the four, and the meaning cannot be misunderstood. From one of the four powers or kingdoms into which the empire of Alexander would be divided, there would spring up this ambitious and persecuting power. ¶ *Which waxed exceeding great.* Which became exceedingly powerful. It was comparatively small at first, but ultimately became mighty. There can be no doubt that Antiochus Epiphanes is denoted here. All the circumstances of the prediction find a fulfilment in him; and if it were supposed that this was written *after* he had lived, and that it was the design of the writer to describe him by this symbol, he could not have found a symbol that would have been more striking or appropriate than this. The Syriac version has inserted here, in the Syriac text, the words "Antiochus Epiphanes," and almost without exception expositors have been agreed in the opinion that he is referred to. For a general account of him, see Notes on ch. vii. 24, *seq.* The author of the book of Maccabees, after noticing, in

forth a little horn, which waxed exceeding great, toward the south, and toward the east, and toward the pleasant *a land.*

a Psa. 48. 2; Ezek. 20. 15.

the passage above quoted, the death of Alexander, and the distractions that followed his death, says, "And there came out of them a wicked root, Antiochus, surnamed Epiphanes, son of Antiochus the king, who had been a hostage at Rome, and he reigned in the hundred and thirty and seventh year of the kingdom of the Greeks," 1 Macc. i. 10. A few expositors have supposed that this passage refers to Antichrist—what will not expositors of the Bible suppose? But the great body of interpreters have understood it to refer to Antiochus. This prince was a successor of Seleucus Nicator, who, in the division of the empire of Alexander, obtained Syria, Babylonia, Media, &c. (see above on ver. 8), and whose capital was Antioch. The succession of princes who reigned in Antioch, from Seleucus to Antiochus Epiphanes, were as follows :—

(1.) Seleucus Nicator, B.C. 312–280.

(2.) Antiochus Soter, his son, 280–261.

(3.) Antiochus Theos, his son, 261–247.

(4.) Seleucus Callinicus, his son, 247–226.

(5.) (Alexander), or Seleucus Ceraunus, his son, 226–223.

(6.) Antiochus the Great, his brother, 223–187.

(7.) Seleucus Philopator, his son, 187–176.

(8.) Antiochus Epiphanes, his brother, 176–164.—Clinton's *Fasti Hellenici,* vol. iii. Appendix, ch. iii.

The succession of the Syrian kings reigning in Antioch was continued until Syria was reduced to the form of a Roman province by Pompey, B.C. 63. Seleucus Philopator, the immediate predecessor of Antiochus, having been assassinated by one of his courtiers, his brother Antiochus hastened to occupy the vacant throne, although the natural heir, Demetrius, son of Seleucus, was yet alive, but a hostage at Rome. Antiochus assumed the name of Epiphanes, or *Illustrious.* In **Dan. xi.** 21, it is intimated that he gained the kingdom *by flatteries;* and there can be no doubt that bribery, and the promise of reward to others, was made use of to secure his power. See Kitto's *Cyclo.,* i. 168–170. Of the acts of this prince there will be occasion for a fuller detail in the Notes on the remainder of this chapter, and ch. xi. ¶ *Toward the south.* Toward the country of Egypt, &c. In the year B.C. 171, he declared war against Ptolemy Philometor, and in the year 170 he conquered Egypt, and plundered Jerusalem. 1 Macc. i. 16–19: "Now when the kingdom was established before Antiochus, he thought to reign over Egypt, that he might have the dominion of two realms. Wherefore he entered Egypt with a great multitude, with chariots, and elephants, and horsemen, and a great navy. And made war against Ptolemee king of Egypt: but Ptolemee was afraid of him, and fled; and many were wounded to death. Thus they got the strong cities in the land of Egypt, and he took the spoils thereof." ¶ *And toward the east.* Toward Persia and the countries of the East. He went there—these countries being nominally subject to him—according to the author of the book of Maccabees (1 Macc. iii. 21–37), in order to replenish his exhausted treasury, that he might carry on his wars with the Jews, and that he might keep up the splendour and liberality of his court: "He saw that the money of his treasures failed, and that the tributes in the country were small, because of the dissension and plague which he had brought upon the land, and he feared that he should not be able to bear the charges any longer, nor to have such gifts to give so liberally as he did before; wherefore, being greatly perplexed in his mind, he determined to go into Persia, there to take the tributes of the countries, and to gather much money. So the king departed from Antioch, his royal city, the hundred forty and seventh year; and having passed the river Euphrates, he went through the high countries."

10 And it waxed great, *even* [1] to the *a* host of heaven; and it cast down *b some* of the host and of the

1 or, *against.*   *a* Isa. 14. 13.

¶ *And toward the pleasant* land. The word here used (צְבִי) means, properly, *splendour, beauty,* Isa. iv. 2; xxiv. 16; xxviii. 1, 4, 5. It is applied, in Isa. xiii. 19, to Babylon—"the *glory* of kingdoms." Here it evidently denotes the land of the Israelites, or Palestine —so often described as a land of beauty, as flowing with milk and honey, &c. This is such language as a pious Hebrew would naturally use of his own country, and especially if he was an exile from it, as Daniel was. Nothing more would be necessary to designate the land so as to be understood than such an appellation—as nothing more would be necessary to designate his country to an exile from China than to speak of "the flowery land." Antiochus, on his return from Egypt, turned aside and invaded Judea, and ultimately robbed the temple, destroyed Jerusalem, and spread desolation through the land. See 1 Macc. i.

10. *And it waxed great.* It became **very** powerful. This was eminently true of Antiochus, after having subdued Egypt, &c.   ¶ *Even to the host of heaven.* Marg., *against.* The Hebrew word (צָבָא) means *to* or *unto,* and the natural idea would seem to be that he wished to place himself among the stars, or to exalt himself above all that was earthly. Comp. Notes on Isa. xiv. 13: "For thou hast said in thine heart, I will ascend into heaven, I will exalt my throne above the stars of God." Lengerke supposes that the meaning here is, that he not only carried his conquests to Egypt and to the East, and to the Holy Land in general, but that he made war on the holy army of God—the priests and worshippers of Jehovah, here spoken of as the host of heaven. So Maurer understands it. In 2 Macc. ix. 10, Antiochus is described in this language: "And the man that thought a little afore he could reach the stars of heaven," &c. The *connection* would

stars to the ground, and stamped upon them.

11 Yea, he *c* magnified *himself*

b Rev. 12. 4.   *c* ver. 25.

seem to demand the interpretation proposed by Lengerke and Maurer, for it is immediately said that he cast down some of the host and the stars to the ground. And such an interpretation accords with the language elsewhere used, of the priests and rulers of the Hebrew people. Thus, in Isa. xxiv. 21, they are called "the host of the high ones that are on high." See Notes on that passage. This language is by no means uncommon in the Scriptures. It is usual to compare princes and rulers, and especially ecclesiastical rulers, with the sun, moon, and stars. Undoubtedly it is the design here to describe the pride and ambition of Antiochus, and to show that he did not think anything too exalted for his aspiration. None were too high or too sacred to be secure from his attempts to overthrow them, and even those who, by their position and character, seemed to deserve to be spoken of as suns and stars, as "the host of heaven," were not secure.   ¶ *And it cast down* some *of the host and of the stars to the ground.* The horn seemed to grow up to the stars, and to wrest them from their places, and to cast them to the earth. Antiochus, in the fulfilment of this, cast down and trampled on the princes, and rulers, and people, of the holy host or army of God. All that is implied in this was abundantly fulfilled in what he did to the Jewish people. Comp. 1 Macc. i., and 2 Macc. viii. 2.   ¶ *And stamped upon them.* With indignation and contempt. Nothing could better express the conduct of Antiochus towards the Jews.

11. *Yea, he magnified* himself *even to the prince of the host.* Grotius, Ephræm the Syrian, and others, understand this of Onias the high-priest, as the chief officer of the holy people. Lengerke supposes that it means God himself. This interpretation is the more probable ; and the idea in the phrase "prince of the host" **is, that** as God is the ruler of the host **of**

even ¹ to the prince of the host, and by ² him the daily *ª sacrifice* was taken away, and the place of his sanctuary was cast down.

12 And an ³ host was given *him*

1 or, *against.*   2 or, *from.*   a Exod. 29. 38.
3 or, *the host was given over for the transgression against the daily sacrifice.*

heaven—leading on the constellations, and marshalling the stars, so he may be regarded as the ruler of the holy army here below—the ministers of religion, and his people. Against him *as* the Ruler and Leader of his people Antiochus exalted himself, particularly by attempting to change his laws, and to cause his worship to cease. ¶ *And by him.* Marg., "*from him.*" The meaning is, that the command or authority to do this proceeded from him. ¶ *The daily* sacrifice *was taken away.* The sacrifice that was offered daily in the temple, morning and evening, was suspended. A full account of this may be found in 1 Macc. i. 20-24, 29-32, 44-50. In the execution of the purposes of Antiochus, he "entered the sanctuary, and took away the golden altar, and the candlestick, and all the vessels thereof; and the table of shew-bread, the pouring vessels, &c., and stripped the temple of all the ornaments of gold." After two years he again visited the city, and "smote it very sore, and destroyed much people of Israel, and when he had taken the spoils of the city he set it on fire, and pulled down the walls thereof on every side." Everything in Jerusalem was made desolate. "Her sanctuary was laid waste like a wilderness, her feasts were turned into mourning, her Sabbaths into reproach, her honour into contempt." Subsequently, by a solemn edict, and by more decisive acts, he put a period to the worship of God in the temple, and polluted and defiled every part of it. "For the king had sent letters by messengers unto Jerusalem and the cities of Judah, that they should follow the strange laws of the land, and forbid burnt-offerings, and sacrifices, and drink-offerings in the temple; and that they should profane the Sabbaths and festival days, and pollute the sanctuary and holy people; set up altars, and groves, and chapels of idols, and sacrifice swine's flesh, and unclean beasts; that they

should also leave their children uncircumcised, and make their souls abominable with all manner of uncleanness and profanation; to the end they might forget the laws, and change all the ordinances," 1 Macc. i. 44-49. It was undoubtedly to these acts of Antiochus that the passage before us refers, and the event accords with the words of the prediction as clearly as if what is a prediction had been written afterwards, and had been designed to represent what actually occurred as a matter of historical record. The word which is rendered "*daily*" sacrifice"—the word "sacrifice" being supplied by the translators — תָּמִיד — means, properly, *continuance, perpetuity,* and then that which is continuous or constant—as a sacrifice or service daily occurring. The word *sacrifice* is properly inserted here.—Gesenius, *Lex.* The meaning of the word rendered "was taken away"—

הֻרַם (Hophal from רוּם—to exalt, to lift up)—here is, that it was *lifted up,* and then was taken away ; that is, it was made to cease—*as if* it had been carried away.—Gesenius. ¶ *And the place of his sanctuary.* Of the sanctuary or holy place of the "Prince of the host," that is, of God. The reference is to the temple. ¶ *Was cast down.* The temple was not entirely destroyed by Antiochus, but it was robbed and rifled, and its holy vessels were carried away. The walls indeed remained, but it was desolate, and the whole service then was abandoned. See the passages quoted above from 1 Macc.

12. *And a host was given* him. The Vulgate renders this, "and *strength—robur*—was given him," &c. Theodotion, "and sin was permitted—ἐδόθη— against the sacrifice; and this righteousness was cast on the ground; so he acted and was prospered." Luther renders it, "and such might (or power, *macht*) was given him." The Syriac

against the daily *sacrifice* by reason of transgression, and it cast down the truth to the ground; and it practised, and prospered.

13 ¶ Then I heard one *a* saint

a 1 Pet. 1. 12.

speaking, and another saint ¹ said unto that certain *saint* which spake, How long *shall be* the vision *concerning* the daily *sacrifice*, and the

1 *Palmoni*, or, *the numberer of secrets*, or, *the wonderful numberer.*

renders it, "and strength was given him," &c. Bertholdt renders it, *Statt jenes stellte man den Greuel auf,* "instead of this [the temple] there was set up an abomination." Dathe, "and the stars were delivered to him"—*tradita ei fuerunt astra, seu populus Judaicus.* Maurer understands it also of the Jewish people, and interprets it, "and an army—*exercitus*—the people of the Jews was delivered to destruction, at the same time with the perpetual sacrifice, on account of wickedness, that is, for a wicked thing, or for impure sacrifices." Lengerke renders it, as in our translation, "an host—*ein Heer*—was given up to him at the same time with the daily offering, on account of evil."

The word *host* (צָבָא) is doubtless to be taken here in the same sense as in ver. 10, where it is connected with *heaven* —"the host of heaven." If it refers there to the Jewish people, it doubtless does here, and the appellation is such a one as would not unnaturally be used. It is equivalent to saying "the army of the Lord," or "the people of the Lord," and it should have been rendered here "and *the* host was given up to him;" that is, the people of God, or the holy people were given into his hands. ¶ *Against the daily* sacrifice. This does not convey any clear idea. Lengerke renders it, *sammt den beständigen opfer*—"at the same time with the permanent sacrifice." He remarks that the preposition עַל (rendered in our version *against*), like the Greek ἐπὶ, may denote a connection with anything, or a being with a thing —*Zusammenseyn*—and thus it would denote a union of time, or that the things occurred together, Gen. xxxii. 11 (12); Hos. x. 14; Amos iii. 15. Comp. Gesenius (*Lex.*) on the word עַל,

3. According to this, the meaning is,

that the "host," or the Jewish people, were given to him *at the same time,* or in connection with the daily sacrifice. The conquest over the people, and the command respecting the daily sacrifice, were simultaneous. Both passed into his hands, and he exercised jurisdiction over them both. ¶ *By reason of transgression*—בְּפֶשַׁע. That is, all this was on account of the transgression of the people, or on account of abounding iniquity. God gave up the people, and their temple, and their sacrifices, into the hands of Antiochus, on account of the prevailing impiety. Comp. 1 Macc. i. 11–16. The author of that book traces all these calamities to the acts of certain wicked men, who obtained permission of Antiochus to introduce heathen customs into Jerusalem, and who actually established many of those customs there. ¶ *And it cast down the truth to the ground.* The true system of religion, or the true method of worshipping God—represented here as truth in the abstract. So in Isa. lix. 14, it is said: "Truth is fallen in the street, and equity cannot enter." The meaning here is, that the institutions of the true religion would be utterly prostrate. This was fully accomplished by Antiochus. See 1 Macc. i. ¶ *And it practised.* Hebrew, "it did," or it acted. That is, it undertook a work, and was successful. So in Psa. i. 3, where the same expression occurs: "And whatsoever he doeth shall prosper." This was fully accomplished in Antiochus, who was entirely successful in all his enterprises against Jerusalem. See 1 Macc. i.

13. *Then I heard one saint speaking.* One holy one. The vision was now ended, and the prophet represents himself now as hearing earnest inquiries as to the length of time during which this desolation was to continue. This conversation, or these inquiries, he repre-

transgression[1] of desolation, to give | both the sanctuary and the host to
1 or, *making desolate*; ch. 11. 31; 12. 11. | be trodden under foot?

sents himself as hearing among those whom he calls "saints"—or holy ones —קָדוֹשׁ. This *word* might refer to a saint on earth, or to an angel—to any holy being. As one of these, however, was able to explain the vision, and to tell how long the desolation was to continue, it is more natural to refer it to angels. So Lengerke understands it. The representation is, that one holy one, or angel, was heard by Daniel speaking on this subject, but nothing is recorded of what he said. It is implied only that he was conversing about the desolations that were to come upon the holy city and the people of God. To him thus speaking, and who is introduced as having power to explain it, another holy one approaches, and asks how long this state of things was to continue. The answer to this question (ver. 14) is made, not to the one who made the inquiry, but to Daniel, evidently that it might be recorded. Daniel does not say *where* this vision occurred—whether in heaven or on earth. It was so near to him, however, that he could hear what was said. ¶ *And another saint.* Another holy one—probably an angel. If so, we may conclude, what is in itself every way probable, that one angel has more knowledge than another, or that things are communicated to some which are not to others. ¶ *Unto that certain* saint *which spake.* Marg., *Palmoni*, or, *the numberer of secrets*, or, *the wonderful numberer.* The Hebrew word, פַּלְמוֹנִי *palmoni*, occurs nowhere else in the Scriptures. The similar form, פְּלֹנִי *peloni*, occurs in Ruth iv. 1, "*Ho, such a one, turn aside;*" in 1 Sam. xxi. 2, "appointed my servants to *such* and such a place;" and 2 Kings vi. 8, "In *such* and such a place." The Italic words denote the corresponding Hebrew word. The word, according to Gesenius, means *some one, a certain one;* in Arabic, one who is distinct or definite, whom one points out as with the finger, and not by name. It is

derived from an obsolete noun, פַּלֹון *palon*, from the verb פָּלָה *palá*, to distinguish, and is united commonly with the word אַלְמֹנִי—meaning, properly, one concealed or unknown. It is language, therefore, which would be properly addressed to an unknown person with whom we would desire to speak, or whom we would designate by the finger, or in some such way, without being able to call the name. Thus applied in the passage here, it means that Daniel did not know the names of the persons thus speaking, but simply saw that one was speaking to another. He had no other way of designating or distinguishing them than by applying a term which was commonly used of a stranger when one wished to address him, or to point him out, or to call him to him. There is no foundation in the word for the meaning suggested in the margin. Theodotion does not attempt to translate the word, but retains it— φελμουνί—Phelmouni. The Latin Vulgate well expresses the meaning, *dixit unus sanctus alteri nescio cui loquenti.* The full sense is undoubtedly conveyed by the two ideas, (*a*) that the one referred to was unknown by name, and (*b*) that he wished to designate him in some way, or to point him out. ¶ *How long* shall be *the vision* concerning *the daily* sacrifice? How long is that which is designed to be represented by the vision to continue; that is, how long in fact will the offering of the daily sacrifice in the temple be suspended? ¶ *And the transgression of desolation.* Marg., *making desolate.* That is, the act of iniquity on the part of Antiochus producing such desolation in the holy city and the temple—how long is that to continue? ¶ *To give both the sanctuary.* The temple ; the holy place where God dwelt by a visible symbol, and where he was worshipped. ¶ *And the host.* The people of God— the Jewish people. ¶ *To be trodden under foot.* To be utterly despised and prostrated—as anything which is trodden under our feet.

14 And he said unto me, Unto two thousand and three hundred

1 *evening, morning.*

days;[1] then shall the sanctuary be [2] cleansed.

2 *justified.*

---

14. *And he said unto me.* Instead of answering the one who made the inquiry, the answer is made to Daniel, doubtless that he might make a record of it, or communicate it to others. If it had been made to the inquirer, the answer would have remained with him, and could have been of no use to the world. For the encouragement, however, of the Hebrew people, when their sanctuary and city would be thus desolate, and in order to furnish an instance of the clear fulfilment of a prediction, it was important that it should be recorded, and hence it was made to Daniel. ¶ *Unto two thousand and three hundred days.* Marg., *evening, morning.* So the Hebrew, עֶרֶב בֹּקֶר. So the Latin Vulgate, *ad vesperam et mane.* And so Theodotion—ἕως ἑσπέρας καὶ πρωΐ—"to the evening and morning." The *language* here is evidently that which was derived from Gen. i., or which was common among the Hebrews, to speak of the "evening and the morning" as constituting a day. There can be no doubt, however, that a *day* is intended by this, for this is the fair and obvious interpretation. The Greeks were accustomed to denote the period of a day in the same manner by the word νυχθήμερον (see 2 Cor. xi. 25), in order more emphatically to designate one complete day. See Prof. Stuart's *Hints on Prophecy,* pp. 99, 100. The time then specified by this would be six years and a hundred and ten days. Much difficulty has been felt by expositors in reconciling this statement with the other designations of time in the book of Daniel, supposed to refer to the same event, and with the account furnished by Josephus in regard to the period which elapsed during which the sanctuary was desolate, and the daily sacrifice suspended. The other designations of time which have been *supposed* to refer to the same event in Daniel, are ch. vii. 25, where the time mentioned is three years and a half, or twelve hundred and sixty

days; and ch. xii. 7, where the same time is mentioned, "a time, times, and an half," or three years and an half, or, as before, twelve hundred and sixty days; and ch. xii. 11, where the period mentioned is "a thousand two hundred and ninety days;" and ch. xii. 12, where the time mentioned is "a thousand three hundred and thirty-five days." The time mentioned by Josephus is three years exactly from the time when "their Divine worship was fallen off, and was reduced to a profane and common use," till the time when the lamps were lighted again, and the worship restored, for he says that the one event happened precisely three years after the other, on the same day of the month.—*Ant.* b. xii. ch. vii. § 6. In his *Jewish Wars,* however, b. i. ch. i. § 1, he says that Antiochus "spoiled the temple, and put a stop to the constant practice of offering a daily sacrifice of expiation for three years and six months." Now, in order to explain the passage before us, and to reconcile the accounts, or to show that there is no contradiction between them, the following remarks may be made: (1.) We may lay out of view the passage in ch. vii. 25. See Notes on that passage. If the reasoning there be sound, then that passage had no reference to Antiochus, and though, according to Josephus, there is a remarkable coincidence between the time mentioned there and the time during which the daily sacrifice was suspended, yet that does not demonstrate that the reference there is to Antiochus. (2.) We may lay out of view, also, for the present, the passages in ch. xii. 11, 12. Those will be the subject of consideration hereafter, and for the present ought not to be allowed to embarrass us in ascertaining the meaning of the passage before us. (3.) On the assumption, however, that those passages refer to Antiochus, and that the accounts in Josephus above referred to are correct — though *he* mentions different times, and though different periods are referred to by Daniel, the *variety* may be accounted for by the supposition that separate epochs are referred to at the *starting point* in the calculation—the *terminus a quo*. The truth was, there were several decisive acts in the history of Antiochus that led to the ultimate desolation of Jerusalem, and at one time a writer may have contemplated one, and at another time another. Thus, there was the act by which Jason, made high-priest by Antiochus, was permitted to set up a gymnasium in Jerusalem after the manner of the heathen (Prideaux, iii. 216; 1 Macc. i. 11–15); the act by which he assaulted and took Jerusalem, entering the most holy place, stripping the temple of its treasures, defiling the temple, and offering a great sow on the altar of burnt-offerings (Prideaux, iii. 230, 231; 1 Macc. i. 20–28); the act, just two years after this, by which, having been defeated in his expedition to Egypt, he resolved to vent all his wrath on the Jews, and, on his return, sent Apollonius with a great army to ravage and destroy Jerusalem—when Apollonius, having plundered the city, set it on fire, demolished the houses, pulled down the walls, and with the ruins of the demolished city built a strong fortress on Mount Acra, which overlooked the temple, and from which he could attack all who went to the temple to worship (Prideaux, iii. 239, 240 ; 1 Macc. i. 29–40) ; and the act by which Antiochus solemnly forbade all burnt-offerings, and sacrifices, and drink-offerings in the temple— (Prideaux, iii. 241, 242; 1 Macc. i. 44–51). Now, it is evident that one writing of these calamitous events, and mentioning *how long* they would continue, might at one time contemplate one of these events as the beginning, the *terminus a quo*, and at another time, another of these events might be in his eye. Each one of them was a strongly marked and decisive event, and each one might be contemplated as a period which, in an important sense, determined the destiny of the city, and put an end to the worship of God there. (4.) It seems probable that the time mentioned in the passage be-

fore us is designed to take in the whole series of disastrous events, from the first decisive act which led to the suspending of the daily sacrifice, or the termination of the worship of God there, to the time when the "sanctuary was cleansed." That this is so would seem to be probable from the series of visions presented to Daniel in the chapter before us. The acts of the "little horn" representing Antiochus, as seen in vision, began with his attack on the "pleasant land" (ver. 9), and the things which attracted the attention of Daniel were, that he "waxed great," and made war on "the host of heaven," and "cast some of the host and of the stars to the ground" (ver. 10), and "magnified himself against the prince of the host" (ver. 11)—acts which refer manifestly to his attack on the people of God, and the priests or ministers of religion, and on God himself as the "prince of the host"—unless this phrase should be understood as referring rather to the high-priest. We are then rather to look to the whole series of events as included within the two thousand and three hundred days, than the period in which literally the daily sacrifice was *forbidden* by a solemn statute. It was practically suspended, and the worship of God interrupted during all that time. (5.) The *terminus ad quem*—the conclusion of the period is marked and settled. This was the "cleansing of the sanctuary." This took place, under Judas Maccabeus, Dec. 25, 165 B.C.—Prideaux, iii. 265–268. Now, reckoning *back* from this period, two thousand and three hundred days, we come to August 5, 171 B.C. The question is, whether there were in this year, and at about this time, any events in the series of sufficient importance to constitute *a period* from which to reckon ; events answering to what Daniel saw as the commencement of the vision, when "some of the host and the stars were cast down and stamped upon." Now, as a matter of fact, there commenced in the year 171 B.C. a series of aggressions upon the priesthood, and temple, and city of the Jews on the part of Antiochus, which terminated only with his death. Up to this year, the relations of Antiochus and the Jewish people were peaceful and cordial. In the year 175 B.C. he granted to the Jewish people, who desired it, permission to erect a gymnasium in Jerusalem, as above stated. In the year 173 B.C. demand was made of Antiochus of the provinces of Coelo-Syria and Palestine by the young Philometor of Egypt, who had just come to the throne, and by his mother—a demand which was the origin of the war between Antiochus and the king of Egypt, and the beginning of all the disturbances.—Prideaux, iii. 218. In the year 172 B.C., Antiochus bestowed the office of high-priest on Menelaus, who was the brother of Jason the high-priest. Jason had sent Menelaus to Antioch to pay the king his tribute-money, and while there Menelaus conceived the design of supplanting his brother, and by offering for it more than Jason had, he procured the appointment and returned to Jerusalem.—Prideaux, iii. 220–222. Up to this time all the intercourse of Antiochus with the Jews had been of a peaceful character, and nothing of a hostile nature had occurred. In 171 B.C. began the series of events which finally resulted in the invasion and destruction of the city, and in the cessation of the public worship of God. Menelaus, having procured the high-priesthood, refused to pay the tribute-money which he had promised for it, and was summoned to Antioch. Antiochus being then absent, Menelaus took advantage of his absence, and having, by means of Lysimachus, whom he had left at Jerusalem, procured the vessels out of the temple, he sold them at Tyre, and thus raised money to pay the king. In the meantime, Onias III., the lawful high-priest, who had fled to Antioch, sternly rebuked Menelaus for his sacrilege, and soon after, at the instigation of Menelaus, was allured from his retreat at Daphné, where he had sought an asylum, and was murdered by Andronicus, the vicegerent of Antiochus. At the same time, the Jews in Jerusalem, highly indignant at the profanation by Menelaus, and the sacrilege in robbing the temple, rose in rebellion against Lysimachus and the Syrian forces who defended him, and both cut

off this "sacrilegious robber" (Prideaux), and the guards by whom he was surrounded. This assault on the officer of Antiochus, and rebellion against him, was the commencement of the hostilities which resulted in the ruin of the city, and the closing of the worship of God.—Prideaux, iii. 224–226; Stuart's *Hints on Prophecy*, p. 102. Here commenced a series of aggressions upon the priesthood, and the temple, and the city of the Jews, which, with occasional interruption, continued to the death of Antiochus, and which led to all that was done in profaning the temple, and in suspending the public worship of God, and it is doubtless to this time that the prophet here refers. This is the natural period in describing the series of events which were so disastrous to the Jewish people; this is the period at which one who should now describe them as *history*, would begin. It may not, indeed, be practicable to make out the precise number of *days*, for the exact dates are not preserved in history, but the calculation brings it into the year 171 B.C., the year which is necessary to be supposed in order that the two thousand and three hundred days should be completed. Comp. Lengerke, *in loc.*, p. 388. Various attempts have been made to determine the exact number of the days by historic records. Bertholdt, whom Lengerke follows, determines it in this manner. He regards the time referred to as that from the command to set up heathen altars to the victory over Nicanor, and the solemn celebration of that victory, as referred to in 1 Macc. vii. 48, 49. According to this reckoning, the time is as follows:—The command to set up idol altars was issued in the year 145, on the 15th of the month Kisleu. There remained of that year, after the command was given—

Half of the month Kisleu	15	days.
The month Thebet	30	,,
,, Shebath	29	,,
,, Adar	30	,,
The Year 146	354	,,
,, 147	354	,,
,, 148	354	,,
,, 149	354	,,
,, 150	354	,,
Carry forward,	1874	days.

15 ¶ And it came to pass, when I, *even* I Daniel, had seen the vision, and sought for the meaning, then, behold, there stood before me as the appearance of a man.

16 And I heard a man's voice

Brought over,	1874 days.

The year 151 to the 13th day of the month Adar, when the victory over Nicanor was achieved.................. 337 „

Two intercalary months during this time, according to the Jewish reckoning..................................... 60 „

2271 days.

This would leave but twenty-nine days of the 2300 to be accounted for, and this would be required to go from the place of the battle—between Beth-Horon and Adasa (1 Macc. vii. 39, 40) to Jerusalem, and to make arrangements to celebrate the victory. See Bertholdt, pp. 501–503. The reckoning here is from the time of founding the kingdom of the Seleucidæ, or the era of the Seleucidæ. ¶ *Then shall the sanctuary be cleansed.* Marg., *justified.* The Hebrew word (צָדַק) means, to be right or straight, and then to be just or righteous ; then to vindicate or justify. In the form here used (Niphal), it means to be declared just ; to be justified or vindicated, and, as applied to the temple or sanctuary, to be vindicated from violence or injury ; that is, to be cleansed. See Gesenius, *Lex.* There is undoubtedly reference here to the act of Judas Maccabeus, in solemnly purifying the temple, and repairing it, and re-dedicating it, after the pollutions brought upon it by Antiochus. For a description of this, see Prideaux's *Connexions,* iii. 265–269. Judas designated a priesthood again to serve in the temple ; pulled down the altars which the heathen had erected ; bore out all the defiled stones into an unclean place ; built a new altar in place of the old altar of burnt-offerings which they had defiled ; hallowed the courts ; made a new altar of incense, table of shew-bread, golden candlestick, &c., and solemnly re-consecrated the whole to the service of God. This act occurred on the twenty-fifth day of the ninth month (Kisleu), and the solemnity

between *the banks of* Ulai, which called, and said, Gabriel, [a] make this *man* to understand the vision.

17 So he came near where I stood ; and when he came, I was

[a] Luke 1. 19, 26.

continued for eight days. This is the festival which is called "the feast of dedication" in the New Testament (John x. 22), and which our Saviour honoured with his presence. See 1 Macc. iv. 41–58 ; 2 Macc. x. 1–7 ; Josephus, *Ant.* b. xii. ch. vii. § 6, 7.

15. *And it came to pass,* &c. Daniel saw the vision, but was unable to explain it. ¶ *And sought for the meaning.* Evidently by meditating on it, or endeavouring in his own mind to make it out. ¶ *There stood before me as the appearance of a man.* One having the appearance of a man. This was evidently Gabriel (ver. 16), who now assumed a human form, and who was addressed by the voice from between the banks of the Ulai, and commenced to make known the meaning of the vision.

16. *And I heard a man's voice between* the banks of *Ulai.* Notes on ver. 2. The voice seemed to come from the river, as if it were that of the Genius of the river, and to address Gabriel, who stood near to Daniel on the shore. This was doubtless the voice of God. The speaker was invisible, and this method of explaining the vision was adopted, probably to make the whole scene more impressive. ¶ *Which called, and said, Gabriel.* Gabriel is mentioned in the Scriptures only in Dan. viii. 16 ; ix. 21 ; Luke i. 19, 26. In Luke i. 19, he is mentioned as saying of himself, "I am Gabriel, that stand in the presence of God." The word means, properly, "man of God." Nothing more is known of him, and he is mentioned only as bearing messages to Daniel, to Zacharias the father of John the Baptist, and to Mary. ¶ *Make this* man *to understand the vision.* Explain it to him so that he will understand its meaning.

17. *So he came near where I stood.* He had seen him, evidently, at first in

afraid, and fell upon my face : but he said unto me, Understand, O son of man; for at the time of the end *shall be* the vision.

a ch. 10. 9, 10.

18 Now, as he was speaking with me, I was in a deep sleep *a* on my face toward the ground : but he touched me, and [1] set me upright.

1 *made me stand upon my standing.*

---

the distance. He now drew near to Daniel, that he might communicate with him the more readily. ¶ *And when he came, I was afraid, and fell upon my face.* Doubtless perceiving that he was a celestial being. See Notes on Rev. i. 17. Comp. Ezek. i. 28, and Dan. x. 8, 9. He was completely overpowered by the presence of the celestial stranger, and sank to the ground. ¶ *But he said unto me, Understand, O son of man.* Give attention, that you may understand the vision. On the phrase "son of man," see Notes on ch. vii. 13. It is here simply an address to him as a man. ¶ *For at the time of the end* shall be *the vision.* The *design* of this expression is undoubtedly to cheer and comfort the prophet with some assurance of what was to occur in future times. In what way this was done, or what was the precise idea indicated by these words, interpreters have not been agreed. Maurer explains it, "for this vision looks to the last time ; that is, the time which would immediately precede the coming of the Messiah, which would be a time of calamity, in which the guilt of the wicked would be punished, and the virtue of the saints would be tried, to wit, the time of Antiochus Epiphanes." Lengerke supposes that the end of the existing calamities—the sufferings of the Jews—is referred to; and that the meaning is, that in the time of the Messiah, to which the vision is extended, there would be an end of their sufferings and trials. The design of the angel, says he, is to support and comfort the troubled seer, as if he should not be anxious that these troubles were to occur, since they would have an end, or, as Michaelis observes, that the seer should not suppose that the calamities indicated by the vision would have no end. Perhaps the meaning may be this: "The vision is for the time of the end ;" that is, it has respect

to the closing period of the world, under which the Messiah is to come, and necessarily precedes that, and leads on to that. It pertains to a series of events which are to introduce the latter times, when the kingdom of God shall be set up on the earth. In justification of this view of the passage, it may be remarked that this is not only the most obvious view, but is sustained by all those passages which speak of the coming of the Messiah as "the end," the "last days," &c. Thus 1 Cor. x. 11 : "upon whom the ends of the world are come." Comp. Notes on Isa. ii. 2. According to this interpretation, the meaning is, "the vision pertains to the end, or the closing dispensation of things ;" that is, it has a bearing on the period when the end will come, or will introduce that period. It looks on to future times, even to those times, though now remote (comp. ver. 26), when a new order of things will exist, under which the affairs of the world will be wound up. Comp. Notes on Heb. i. 2.

18. *Now, as he was speaking with me, I was in a deep sleep on my face toward the ground.* Overcome and prostrate with the vision. That is, he had sunk down stupified or senseless. See ch. x. 9. His strength had been entirely taken away by the vision. There is nothing improbable in this, that the sudden appearance of a celestial vision, or a heavenly being, should take away the strength. Compare Gen. xv. 12 ; Job iv. 13, *seq.;* Judg. vi. 22 ; xiii. 20, 22 ; Isa. vi. 5 ; Luke i. 12, 29 ; ii. 9 ; Acts ix. 3, 8. ¶ *But he touched me, and set me upright.* Marg., as in Heb., "made me stand upon my standing." He raised me up on my feet. So the Saviour addressed Saul of Tarsus, when he had been suddenly smitten to the earth, by his appearing to him on the way to Damascus : "Rise, and stand upon thy feet," &c., Acts xxvi. 16.

19 And he said, Behold, I will make thee know what shall be in the last end of the indignation : for at the time appointed *a* the end *shall be.*

20 The ram *b* which thou sawest having *two* horns *are* the kings of Media and Persia.

21 And the rough goat *is* the king of Grecia : and the great horn

that *is* between his eyes *is* the first king.

22 Now that being broken, whereas four stood up for it, four kingdoms shall stand up out of the nation, but not in his power.

23 And in the latter time of their kingdom, when the transgressors are [1] come to the full, a king of fierce countenance, and un-

a Hab. 2. 3 ; Rev. 10. 7.   *b* ver. 3.   [1] *accomplished.*

19. *And he said, Behold, I will make thee know what shall be in the last end of the indignation.* In the future time when the Divine indignation shall be manifest toward the Hebrew people ; to wit, by suffering the evils to come upon them which Antiochus would inflict. It is everywhere represented that these calamities would occur as a proof of the Divine displeasure on account of their sins. Comp. ch. ix. 24; xi. 35; 2 Macc. vii. 33. ¶ *For at the time appointed the end* shall be. It shall not always continue. There is a definite period marked out in the Divine purpose, and when that period shall arrive, the end of all this will take place. See Notes on ver. 17.

20. *The ram which thou sawest,* &c. See Notes on ver. 3. This is one of the instances in the Scriptures in which symbols are explained. There can be no doubt, therefore, as to the meaning.

21. *And the rough goat.* Notes on ver. 5. In ver. 5 he is called a *he-goat.* Here the word *rough* or *hairy*—שָׂעִיר— is applied to it. This appellation is often given to a goat (Lev. iv. 24 ; xvi. 9 ; Gen. xxxvii. 31). It would seem that *either* term—a *he-goat,* or a *hairy-goat*—would serve to designate the animal, and it is probable that the terms were used indiscriminately. ¶ Is *the king of Grecia.* Represents the king of Greece. The word here rendered *Grecia* (יָוָן *Javan*) denotes usually and properly *Ionia,* the western part of Asia Minor; but this name was extended so as to embrace the whole of Greece. See Aristoph. *Acharn.* 504, *ibique Schol.; Æschyl. Pers.* 176, 561; Gesenius, *Lex.* Latin Vulgate and

Theodotion, here render it "the king of the Grecians," and there can be no doubt that the royal power among the Greeks is here referred to. See Notes on ver. 5. ¶ *And the great horn that is between his eyes is the first king.* Alexander the Great. The first that consolidated the whole power, and that was known in the East as the king of Greece. So he is expressly called in 1 Macc. i. 1: "The first over Greece." Philip, his father, was opposed in his attempts to conquer Greece, and was defeated. Alexander invaded Greece, burned Thebes, compelled the Athenians to submit, and was declared generalissimo of the Grecian forces against the Persians.

22. *Now that being broken.* By the death of Alexander. ¶ *Whereas four stood up for it.* Stood up in its place. ¶ *Four kingdoms shall stand up.* Ultimately. It is not necessary to suppose that this would be immediately. If four such should in fact spring out of this one kingdom, all that is implied in the prophecy would be fulfilled. On the fulfilment of this, see Notes on ver. 8. ¶ *But not in his power.* No one of these four dynasties had at any time the power which was wielded by Alexander the Great.

23. *And in the latter time of their kingdom.* When it shall be drawing to an end. All these powers were ultimately absorbed in the Roman power ; and the meaning here is, that taking the time from the period of their formation — the division of the empire after the battle of Ipsus (see Notes on ver. 8), till the time when all would be swallowed up in the Roman dominion, what is here stated—to wit, the rise of Antiochus — would be in

derstanding dark sentences, shall stand up.

24 And his power shall be mighty, *a* but not by his own

Rev. 17. 13, 17.   *b* vers. 10, 12, &c.

power: and he shall destroy wonderfully, and shall prosper, and practise, and *b* shall destroy the mighty and the 1 holy people.

1 *people of the holy ones.*

---

the latter portion of that period. The battle of Ipsus was fought 301 B.C., and the Roman power was extended over all those regions gradually from 168 B.C.—the battle of Pydna, when Perseus was defeated, and Macedonia was reduced to a Roman province, to 30 B.C., when Egypt was subjected— the last of these kingdoms that submitted to the Roman arms. Antiochus began to reign, 175 B.C.—so that it was in the latter part of this period. ¶ *When the transgressors are come to the full.* Marg., *accomplished.* That is, when the state of things—the prevalence of wickedness and. irreligion in Judea—shall have been allowed to continue as long as it. can be—or so that the cup shall be full—then shall appear this formidable power to inflict deserved punishment on the guilty nation. The sacred writers often speak of iniquity as being *full*—of the cup of iniquity as being full—as if there was a certain limit or capacity beyond which it could not be allowed to go. When that arrives, God interposes, and cuts off the guilty by some heavy judgment. Comp. Gen. xv. 16: "The iniquity of the Amorites is not yet full." Matt. xxiii. 32: "Fill ye up then the measure of your fathers." 1 Thess. ii. 16: "To fill up their sins alway." The idea is, that there is a certain measure or amount of sin which can be tolerated, but beyond that the Divine compassion cannot go with safety to the universe, or consistently with the honour of God, and then the punishment may be expected; then punishment must come. This is true, doubtless, of individuals and nations, and this period had arrived in regard to the Jews when Antiochus was permitted to lay their temple, city, and country waste. ¶ *A king of fierce countenance.* Stern and severe. This expression would be applicable to many who have held the kingly office, and no one can doubt that it may be ap-

plied with strict propriety to Antiochus. ¶ *And understanding dark sentences.* Gesenius (*Lex.*) explains the word here rendered "dark sentences" to mean *artifice, trick, stratagem.* This will better agree with the character of Antiochus, who was more distinguished for craft and policy than he was for wisdom, or for explaining enigmas. The meaning seems to be that he would be politic and crafty, seeking to make his way, and to accomplish his purpose, not only by the terror that he inspired, but by deceit and cunning. That this was his character is well known. Comp. Notes on ver. 25. ¶ *Shall stand up.* Shall succeed, or there shall be such a king.

24. *And his power shall be mighty.* He shall be a powerful monarch. Though not *as* mighty as Alexander, yet his conquests of Egypt and other places show that he deserved to be numbered among the mighty kings of the earth. ¶ *But not by his own power.* That is, it shall not be by any strength of his own, but by the power which God gives him. This is true of all kings and princes (comp. John xix. 11; Isa. x. 5, *seq.*), but it seems to be referred to here particularly to show that the calamities which he was about to bring upon the Hebrew people were by Divine direction and appointment. This great power was given him in order that he might be an instrument in the Divine hand of inflicting deserved punishment on them for their sins. ¶ *And he shall destroy wonderfully.* In a wonderful or extraordinary manner shall he spread desolation. This refers particularly to the manner in which he would lay waste the holy city, and the land of Judea. The history in the books of Maccabees shows that this was literally fulfilled. ¶ *And shall prosper.* Antiochus was among the most successful kings in his various expeditions. Particularly was he successful in his enterprises against the

25 And through his policy also
he shall cause craft to prosper in
his hand; and he shall magnify

himself in his heart, and by [1] peace
shall destroy many: he shall also

1 or, *prosperity.*

---

holy land. ¶ *And practise.* Heb., *do.*
That is, he shall be distinguished not
only for *forming* plans, but for *executing* them; not merely for *purposing,*
but for *doing.* ¶ *And shall destroy
the mighty and the holy people.* The
people of God—the Jewish nation. See
Notes on vers. 9–12.

25. *And through his policy.* The
word rendered *policy* here (שֵׂכֶל) means,
properly, intelligence, understanding,
wisdom; and then, in a bad sense, craft,
cunning. So it is rendered here by
Gesenius, and the meaning is, that he
would owe his success in a great measure to craft and subtilty. ¶ *He shall
cause craft to prosper in his hand.* He
shall owe his success in a great measure
to a crafty policy, to intrigue, and to
cunning. This was true in an eminent
sense, of Antiochus. See his history
in Prideaux, above referred to, and the
books of Maccabees. Comp. Notes on
ch. xi. 21. The same character is given
of him by Polybius, *Relig.* lib. xxxi.
c. 5, tom. iv. p. 501, ed. Schweig-
haüser; Appian, *de reb. Syr.* xlv. t. 1,
p. 604, ed. Schweigh. Comp. 2 Macc.
v. 24–26. He came to the kingdom
by deceit (Prideaux, iii. 212), and a
great part of his success was owing to
craft and policy. ¶ *And he shall magnify* himself *in his heart.* Shall be
lifted up with pride, or esteem himself
of great consequence. ¶ *And by peace
shall destroy many.* Marg., *prosperity.*
The Hebrew word (שַׁלְוָה) means, properly, tranquillity, security, ease, carelessness. Here the phrase seems to
mean "in the midst of security" (Gesenius, *Lex.*); that is, while they were
at ease, and regarded themselves as in
a state of safety, he would come suddenly and unexpectedly upon them, and
destroy them. He would make sudden
war on them, invading their territories,
so that they would have no opportunity to make preparation to meet him.
Comp. ch. xi. 21, 24. It would seem
to mean that he would endeavour to

produce the impression that he was
coming in peace; that he pretended
friendship, and designed to keep those
whom he meant to invade and destroy
in a state of false security, so that he
might descend upon them unawares.
This was his policy rather than to declare war openly, and so give his enemies fair warning of what he intended
to do. This description agrees every
way with the character of Antiochus,
a leading part of whose policy always
was to preserve the appearance of
friendship, that he might accomplish
his purpose while his enemies were off
their guard. ¶ *He shall also stand up
against the Prince of princes.* Notes,
ver. 11. Against God, the ruler over
the kings of the earth. ¶ *But he shall
be broken without hand.* That is, without the hand of man, or by no visible
cause. He shall be overcome by a
Divine, invisible power. According
to the author of the first book of Maccabees (ch. vi. 8–16), he died of grief
and remorse in Babylon. He was on
an expedition to Persia, and there laid
siege to Elymais, and was defeated,
and fled to Babylon, when, learning
that his forces in Palestine had been
repulsed, penetrated with grief and
remorse, he sickened and died. According to the account in the second
book of Maccabees (ix.), his death was
most distressing and horrible. Comp.
Prideaux, iii. 272–275. All the statements given of his death, by the
authors of the books of Maccabees,
by Josephus, by Polybius, by Q. Curtius, and by Arrian (see the quotations
in Prideaux), agree in representing it
as attended with every circumstance
of horror that can be well supposed to
accompany a departure from this world,
and as having every mark of the just
judgment of God. The Divine prediction in Daniel was fully accomplished, that his death would be "without hand," in the sense that it would
not be by human instrumentality; but
that it would be by a direct Divine
infliction. When Antiochus died, the

stand up against the Prince of princes; but he shall be broken without hand.

26 And the vision of the evening and the morning which was told

is true: wherefore shut *a* thou up the vision; for it *shall be* for many days.

27 And I Daniel fainted, and

a Rev. 10. 4.

opposition to the Jews ceased, and their land again had peace and rest.

26. *And the vision of the evening and the morning.* That is, of the two thousand three hundred days. See ver. 14, and the margin on that verse. The meaning here is, " the vision pertaining to that succession of evenings and mornings." Perhaps this appellation was given to it particularly because it pertained so much to the evening and morning sacrifice. ¶ *Is true.* Shall be certainly accomplished. This was said by the angel, giving thus to Daniel the assurance that what he had seen (vers. 9–14) was no illusion, but would certainly come to pass. ¶ *Wherefore shut thou up the vision.* Seal it up. Make a record of it, that it may be preserved, and that its fulfilment may be marked. See Notes on Isa. viii. 16. ¶ *For it shall be for many days.* That is, many days will elapse before it will be accomplished. Let a fair record, therefore, be made of it, and let it be sealed up, that it may be preserved to prepare the people for these events. *When* these things would come thus fearfully upon the people of Judea, they would be the better able to bear these trials, knowing the period when they would terminate.

27. *And I Daniel fainted.* Heb., " I was "—נִהְיֵיתִי. Comp. Dan. ii. 1.

The meaning, according to Gesenius (*Lex.*), is, " I was done up, and was sick :"—I was done over, &c. Perhaps the *reason* of his using this verb here is, that he represents himself as *having been sick*, and then as fainting away, as if his life had departed. The Latin Vulgate renders it *langui*. Theodotion, ἐκοιμήθην— " was laid in my bed." The general idea is plain, that he was overcome and prostrate at the effect of the vision. He had been permitted to look into the future, and the scenes were so appalling—the changes that were to occur were so great—the calamities were so

fearful in their character—and, above all, his mind was so affected that the daily sacrifice was to cease, and the worship of God be suspended, that he was entirely overcome. And who of us, probably, could *bear* a revelation of what is to occur hereafter? Where is there strength that could endure the disclosure of what may happen even in a few years? ¶ *And was sick certain days.* The exact time is not specified. The natural interpretation is, that it was for a considerable period. ¶ *Afterwards I rose up, and did the king's business.* Compare Notes on ver. 2. From this it would appear that he had been sent to Shushan on some business pertaining to the government. What it was we are not informed. As a matter of fact, he was sent there for a more important purpose than any which pertained to the government at Babylon—to receive a disclosure of most momentous events that were to occur in distant times. Yet this did not prevent him from attending faithfully to the business intrusted to him—as no views which we take of heavenly things, and no disclosures made to our souls, and no absorption in the duties and enjoyments•of religion, should prevent us from attending with fidelity to whatever secular duties may be intrusted to us. Sickness justifies us, of course, in not attending to them; the highest views which we may have of God and of religious truth should only make us more faithful in the discharge of our duties to our fellow-men, to our country, and in all the relations of life. He who has been favoured with the clearest views of Divine things will be none the less prepared to discharge with faithfulness the duties of this life; he who is permitted and enabled to look far into the future will be none the less likely to be diligent, faithful, and laborious in meeting the responsibilities of the present moment. If a man could see all that there is in heaven, it would

was sick *certain* days : afterward I rose up, and did the king's busi-

ness; and I was astonished at the vision, but none understood *it.*

---

only serve to impress him with a deeper conviction of his obligations in every relation ; if he could see all that there is to come in the vast eternity before him, it would only impress him with a profounder sense of the consequences which may follow from the discharge of the present duty. ¶ *And I was astonished at the vision.* He was stupified—he was overcome—at the splendid appearance, and the momentous nature of the disclosures. Compare Notes on ch. iv. 19. ¶ *But none understood* it. It would seem probable from this, that he communicated it to others, but no one was able to explain it. Its general features were plain, but no one could follow out the details, and tell *precisely* what would occur, before the vision was fulfilled. This is the general nature of prophecy; and if neither Daniel nor any of his friends could explain this vision in detail, are we to hope that we shall be successful in disclosing the full meaning of those which are not yet fulfilled ? The truth is, that in all such revelations of the future, there must be much in detail which is not now fully understood. The general features may be plain—as, in this case, it was clear that a mighty kingdom would rise ; that he would be a tyrant ; that he would oppress the people of God ; that he would invade the holy land; that he would for a time put a period to the offering of the daily sacrifice ; and that this would continue for a definite period ; and that then he would be cut off without human instrumentality : but who from this would have been able to draw out, in detail, all the events which in fact occurred ? Who could have told precisely how these things would come to pass ? Who could have ventured on a biography of Antiochus Epiphanes ? Yet these three things are true in regard to this : (1) that no one by human sagacity could have foreseen these events so as to have been able to furnish these sketches of what was to be ; (2) that these were sufficient to apprise those who were interested particularly of

what would occur ; and (3) that when these events occurred, it was plain to all persons that the prophecy had reference to them. So plain is this—so clear is the application of the predictions in this book, that Porphyry maintained that it was written after the events had occurred, and that the book must have been forged.

CHAPTER IX.

ANALYSIS OF THE CHAPTER.

This chapter is properly divided into three parts, or comprises three things :

I. The inquiry of Daniel into the time that the desolations of Jerusalem were to continue, and his determination to seek the Lord, to pray that his purpose in regard to the restoration of the city and temple might be speedily accomplished, vers. 1–3. Daniel says (ver. 1), that this occurred in the first year of Darius of the seed of the Medes. He was engaged in the study of the books of Jeremiah. He learned from these books that seventy years were to elapse during which the temple, the city, and the land were to be desolate. By a calculation as to the time when this commenced, he was enabled to ascertain the period when it would close, and he found that that period was near, and that, according to the prediction, it might be expected that the time of the restoration was at hand. His mind was, of course, filled with the deepest solicitude. It would seem not improbable that he did not perceive any preparation for this, or any tendency to it, and it could not but be that he would be filled with anxiety in regard to it. He does not appear to have entertained any doubt that the predictions would be fulfilled, and the fact that they were so clear and so positive was a strong reason why he should pray, and was *the* reason why he prayed so earnestly at this time. The prayer which he offered is an illustration of the truth that men will pray more earnestly when they have reason to suppose that God intends to impart a blessing, and that an assurance that an event is to occur is one of the strongest encouragements and incitements to prayer. So men will pray with more faith when they see that God is blessing the means of restoration to health, or when they see indications of an abundant harvest; so they will pray with the more fervour for God to bless his Word when they see evidences of a revival of religion, or that the time has come when God is about to display his power in the conversion of sinners; and so undoubtedly they will pray with the more earnestness as the proofs shall be multiplied that God is about to fulfil all his ancient predictions in the conversion of the whole world to himself. A belief that God intends to do a thing is never any hinderance to real prayer; a belief that he is in fact about to do it does more than anything else can do to arouse the soul to call with earnestness on his name.

II. The prayer of Daniel, vers. 4–19. This prayer is remarkable for its simplicity, its fervour, its appropriateness, its earnestness. It is a frank confession that the Hebrew people, in whose name it was offered, had deserved all the calamities which had come upon them, accompanied with earnest intercession that God would now hear this prayer, and remove the judgments from the people, and accomplish his purpose of mercy towards the city and temple. The long captivity of nearly seventy years; the utter desolation of the city and temple during that time; the numberless privations and evils to which during that period they had been exposed, had demonstrated the

greatness of the sins for which these calamities had come upon the nation, and Daniel now, in the name, and uttering the sentiments, of the captive people, confessed their guilt, and the justness of the Divine dealings with them. Never has there been an instance in which punishment has had more of its designed and appropriate effect than in prompting to the sentiments which are uttered in this prayer: and the prayer, therefore, is just the expression of what we *should* feel when the hand of the Lord has been long and severely laid upon us on account of our sins. The burden of the prayer is confession; the object which he who offers it seeks is, that God would cause the severity of his judgments to cease, and the city and temple to be restored. The particular points in the prayer will be more appropriately elucidated in the exposition of this part of the chapter.

III. The answer to the prayer, vers. 20–27. The principal difficulty in the exposition of the chapter is in this portion; and indeed there is perhaps no part of the prophecies of the Old Testament that is, on some accounts, more difficult of exposition, as there is, in some respects, none more clear, and none more important. It is remarkable, among other things, as not being a direct answer to the prayer, and as seeming to have no bearing on the subject of the petition—that the city of Jerusalem might be rebuilt, and the temple restored; but it directs the mind onward to another and more important event — the coming of the Messiah, and the final closing of sacrifice and oblation, and a more entire and enduring destruction of the temple and city, after it should have been rebuilt, than had yet occurred. To give this information, an angel—the same one whom Daniel had seen before—

was sent forth from heaven, and came near to him and touched him, and said that he was commissioned to impart to him skill and understanding, vers. 20–23. "The speediness of his coming indicates a joyful messenger. The substance of that message is as follows: As a compensation for the seventy years in which the people, the city, and the temple had been entirely prostrate, seventy weeks of years, seven times seventy years of a renewed existence would be secured to them by the Lord; and the end of this period, far from bringing the mercies of God to a close, would for the first time bestow them on the Theocracy in their complete and full measure." — Hengstenberg, *Christology*, ii. 293. The *points* of information which the angel gives in regard to the future condition of the city are these:—

(*a*) That the whole period determined in respect to the holy city, to finish transgression, and to make an end of sins, and to make reconciliation for the people, and to bring in everlasting righteousness, and to seal up the vision and prophecy, and to anoint the Most Holy, was seventy weeks— evidently seventy prophetic weeks, that is, regarding each day as a year, four hundred and ninety years, ver. 24. The time when this period would commence—the *terminus a quo*—is not indeed distinctly specified, but the fair interpretation is, from that time when the vision appeared to Daniel, the first year of Darius, ver. 1. The literal meaning of the phrase "seventy weeks," according to Prof. Stuart (*Hints on the Interpretation of Prophecy*, p. 82), is *seventy sevens*, that is, seventy sevens of years, or four hundred and ninety years. "Daniel," says he, "had been meditating on the accomplishment of the seventy years of exile for the Jews, which Jeremiah had pre-

dicted. At the close of the fervent supplication for the people which he makes, in connection with his meditation, Gabriel appears, and announces to him that '*seventy sevens* are appointed for his people,' as it respects the time then future, in which very serious and very important events are to take place. Daniel had been meditating on the close of the seventy years of Hebrew exile, and the angel now discloses to him a new period of seventy times seven, in which still more important events are to take place."

(*b*) This period of seventy sevens, or four hundred and ninety years, is divided by the angel into smaller portions, each of them determining some important event in the future. He says, therefore (ver. 25), that from the going forth of the command to rebuild the temple, until the time when the Messiah should appear, the whole period might be divided into two portions—one of *seven sevens*, or forty-nine years, and the other of *threescore and two sevens*—sixty-two sevens, or four hundred and thirty-four years, making together four hundred and eighty-three years. This statement is accompanied with the assurance that the "street would be built again, and the wall, even in troublous times." Of these periods of seven weeks, sixty-two weeks, and one week, the close of the first is distinguished by the completion of the rebuilding of the city; that of the second by the appearing of the Anointed One, or the Messiah, the Prince; that of the third by the finished confirmation of the covenant with the many for whom the saving blessings designated in ver. 24, as belonging to the end of the whole period, are designed. The last period of one week is again divided into two halves. While the confirmation of the covenant extends through it, from beginning to end, the cessation of the sacrifice and meat-offering, and the death of the Anointed One, on which this depends, take place in the middle of it.

(*c*) The Messiah would appear after the seven weeks—reaching to the time of completing the rebuilding of the city—and the sixty-two weeks following that (that is, sixty-nine weeks altogether) would have been finished. Throughout half of the other week, after his appearing, he would labour to confirm the covenant with many, and then die a violent death, by which the sacrifices would be made to cease, while the confirmation of the covenant would continue even after his death.

(*d*) A people of a foreign prince would come and destroy the city and the sanctuary. The end of all would be a " flood "—an overflowing calamity, till the end of the desolations should be determined, vers. 26, 27. This fearful desolation is all that the prophet sees in the end, except that there is an obscure intimation that there would be a termination of that. But the design of the vision evidently did not reach thus far. It was to show the series of events *after* the re-building of the city and temple up to the time when the Messiah would come; when the great atonement would be made for sin, and when the oblations and sacrifices of the temple would finally cease ; cease in fact and natu-rally, for the one great sacrifice, super-seding them all, would have been offered, and because the people of a foreign prince would come and sweep the temple and the altar away.

The design of the whole annuncia-tion is, evidently, to produce consola-tion in the mind of the prophet. He was engaged in profound meditation on the present state, and the long-con-tinued desolations of the city and tem-ple. He gave his mind to the study of the prophecies to learn whether these desolations were not soon to end. He ascertained beyond a doubt that the period drew near. He devoted himself to earnest prayer that the desolation might not longer continue ; that God, provoked by the sins of the nation, would no longer execute his fearful judgments, but would graciously inter-pose, and restore the city and temple. He confessed ingenuously and humbly the sins of his people ; acknowledged that the judgments of God were just, but pleaded earnestly, in view of his former mercies to the same people, that he would now have compassion, and fulfil his promises that the city and temple should be restored. An answer is not given *directly,* and in the exact form in which it might have been hoped for ; but an answer *is* given, in which it is *implied* that these blessings so earnestly sought would be bestowed, and in which it is *promised* that there would be far greater bless-ings. It is *assumed* in the answer (ver. 25) that the city would be rebuilt, and then the mind is directed onward to the assurance that it would stand through seven times seventy years— seven times as long as it had now been desolate, and that *then* that which had been the object of the desire of the people of God would be accomplished ; that for which the city and temple had been built would be fulfilled—the Mes-siah would come, the great sacrifice for sin would be made, and all the typical arrangements of the temple would come to an end. Thus, in fact, though not in form, the communication of the angel was an answer to prayer, and that occurred to Daniel which often occurs to those who pray—that the direct prayer which is offered receives a gra-cious answer, and that there accom-panies the answer numberless other mercies which are drawn along in the

CHAPTER IX.

IN the first year of Darius, *a* the son of Ahasuerus, of the seed of the Medes, [1] which was made

a ch. 5. 31.

king over the realm of the Chaldeans ;

2 In the first year of his reign, I Daniel understood by books the

1 or, *in which he.*

train ; or, in other words, that God gives us many more blessings than we ask of him.

1. *In the first year of Darius.* See Notes on ch. v. 31, and Intro. to ch. vi. § II. The king here referred to under this name was Cyaxares II., who lived between Astyages and Cyrus, and in whom was the title of king. He was the immediate successor of Belshazzar, and was the predecessor of Cyrus, and was the first of the foreign princes that reigned over Babylon. On the reasons why he is called in Daniel Darius, and not Cyaxares, see the Intro. to ch. vi. § II. Of course, as he preceded Cyrus, who gave the order to rebuild the temple (Ezra i. 1), this occurred before the close of the seventy years of the captivity. ¶ *The son of Ahasuerus.* Or the son of Astyages. See Intro. to ch. vi. § II. It was no unusual thing for the kings of the East to have several names, and one writer might refer to them under one name, and another under another. ¶ *Of the seed of the Medes.* See as above. ¶ *Which was made king over the realm of the Chaldeans.* By conquest. He succeeded Belshazzar, and was the immediate predecessor of Cyrus. Cyaxares II. ascended the throne of Media, according to the common chronology, B.C. 561. Babylon was taken by Cyrus, acting under the authority of Cyaxares, B.C. 538, and, of course, the reign of Cyaxares, or Darius, over Babylon commenced at that point, and that would be reckoned as the "first year" of his reign. He died B.C. 536, and Cyrus succeeded him ; and as the order to rebuild the temple was in the first year of Cyrus, the time referred to in this chapter, when Daniel represents himself as meditating on the close of the captivity, and offering this prayer, cannot long have preceded that order. He had ascertained that the period of

the captivity was near its close, and he naturally inquired in what way the restoration of the Jews to their own land was to be effected, and by what means the temple was to be rebuilt.

2. *I Daniel understood by books.* By the sacred books, and especially by the writings of Jeremiah. It has been made a ground of objection to the genuineness of Daniel that he mentions " books " in this place (סְפָרִים) as if there were at that time a collection of the sacred books, or as if they had been enrolled together in a volume. The objection is, that the writer speaks as if the canon of the Scriptures was completed, or that he uses such language as the Hebrews did when the canon of the Scriptures was finished, and thus betrays himself. See Bertholdt, *Comm.* p. 78. Comp. De Wette, *Einl.* § 13. This objection has been examined by Hengstenberg, *Beitrag.* pp. 32–35. It is sufficient to reply to it, that there is every probability that the Jews in Babylon would be in possession of the sacred books of their nation, and that, though the canon of the Scriptures was not yet completed, there would exist private collections of those writings. The word here used by Daniel is just such as he would employ on the supposition that he referred to a private collection of the writings of the prophets. Comp. Lengerke, *in loc.* See the Intro., where the objection is examined. ¶ *The number of the years, whereof the word of the Lord came to Jeremiah.* The number of the years in respect to which the word of the Lord came to Jeremiah ; that is, which he had revealed to Jeremiah. The *books* referred to, therefore, were evidently a collection of the writings of Jeremiah, or a collection which embraced his writings. ¶ *That he would accomplish seventy years in the desolations of Jerusalem.* That Jerusalem would so long lie waste. This was

number of the years, whereof the word of the LORD came to Jeremiah the *a* prophet, that he would accomplish seventy years in the desolations of Jerusalem.

3 ¶ And *b* I set my face unto the Lord God, to seek by prayer and supplications, with fasting, and sackcloth, and ashes :

a Jer. 25. 11, 12.
b Neh. 1. 4, &c.; Jer. 29. 10-13.

expressly declared by Jeremiah (ch. xxv. 11, 12): "And this whole land shall be a desolation and an astonishment ; and these nations shall serve the king of Babylon seventy years. And it shall come to pass, when seventy years are accomplished, that I will punish the king of Babylon, and that nation, saith the Lord, for their iniquity," &c. So also Jer. xxix. 10: "For thus saith the Lord, That after seventy years be accomplished at Babylon, I will visit you, and perform my good word toward you, in causing you to return to this place." The time of the desolation and of the captivity, therefore, was fixed and positive, and the only difficulty in determining when it would *close*, was in ascertaining the exact year when it *commenced.* There were several occurrences which might, perhaps, be regarded as the beginning of the desolations and the captivity— the *terminus a quo*—and, according as one or another of them was fixed on, the close would be regarded as nearer or more remote. Daniel, it seems, by close study, had satisfied his own mind on that subject, and had been able to fix upon some period that was undoubtedly the proper beginning, and hence compute the time when it would close. The result showed that his calculation was correct, for, at the time he expected, the order was given by Cyrus to rebuild the city and temple. When he instituted this inquiry, and engaged in this solemn act of prayer, it would have been impossible to have conjectured in what way this could be brought about. The reigning monarch was Cyaxares II., or, as he is here called, Darius, and there was nothing in his character, or in anything that he had done, that could have been a basis of calculation that he would favour the return of the Jews and the rebuilding of the city, and there was then no probability that Cyrus would so soon come

to the throne, and nothing in *his* character, as known, that could be a ground of hope that he would voluntarily interpose, and accomplish the Divine purposes and promises in regard to the holy city. It was probably such circumstances as these which produced the anxiety in the mind of Daniel, and which led him to offer this fervent prayer ; and his fervent supplications should lead us to trust in God that he will accomplish his purposes, and should induce us to pray with fervour and with faith when we see no way in which he will do it. In all cases he can as easily devise a way in answer to prayer, as he could remove Cyaxares from the throne, and incline the heart of Cyrus to undertake the rebuilding of Jerusalem and the temple.

3. *And I set my face unto the Lord God.* Probably the meaning is, that he turned his face toward Jerusalem, the place where God had dwelt; the place of his holy abode on earth. See Notes on ch. vi. 10. The language, however, would not be inappropriate to denote prayer without such a supposition. We turn to one whom we address, and so prayer may be described by "setting the face toward God." The essential idea here is, that he engaged in a set and formal prayer ; he engaged in earnest devotion. He evidently set apart a time for this, for he prepared himself by fasting, and by putting on sackcloth and ashes. ¶ *To seek by prayer and supplications.* To seek his favour ; to pray that he would accomplish his purposes. The words "prayer and supplications," which are often found united, would seem to denote *earnest* prayer, or prayer when *mercy* was implored—the notion of *mercy* or *favour* implored entering into the meaning of the Hebrew word rendered *supplications.* ¶ *With fasting.* In view of the desolations of the city and temple ;

4 And I prayed unto the Lord my God, and made my confession, and said, O Lord, the great *a* and dreadful God, keeping *b* the cove-

nant and mercy to them that love him, and to them that keep his commandments:

a Neh. 9. 32, &c.   *b* Exod. 20. 6.

---

the calamities that had come upon the people; their sins, &c.; and in order also that the mind might be prepared for earnest and fervent prayer. The occasion was one of great importance, and it was proper that the mind should be prepared for it by fasting. It was the purpose of Daniel to humble himself before God, and to recal the sins of the nation for which they now suffered, and fasting was an appropriate means of doing that. ¶ *And sackcloth.* Sackcloth was a coarse kind of cloth, usually made of hair, and employed for the purpose of making sacks, bags, &c. As it was dark, and coarse, and rough, it was regarded as a proper badge of mourning and humiliation, and was worn as such usually by passing or girding it around the loins. See Notes on Isa. iii. 24; Job xvi. 15. ¶ *And ashes.* It was customary to cast ashes on the head in a time of great grief and sorrow. The principles on which this was done seem to have been, (*a*) that the external appearance should correspond with the state of the mind and the heart, and (*b*) that such external circumstances would have a tendency to produce a state of heart corresponding to them—or would produce true humiliation and repentance for sin. Comp. Notes on Job ii. 8. The practical truth taught in this verse, in connection with the preceding, is, that the fact that a thing is certainly predicted, and that God means to accomplish it, is an encouragement to prayer, and will lead to prayer. We could have no encouragement to pray except in the purposes and promises of God, for we have no power ourselves to accomplish the things for which we pray, and all must depend on his will. When that will is known it is the very thing to encourage us in our approaches to him, and is all the assurance that we need to induce us to pray.

4. *And I prayed unto the Lord my God.* Evidently a set and formal

prayer. It would seem probable that he offered this prayer, and then recorded the substance of it afterwards. We have no reason to suppose that we have the whole of it, but we have doubtless its principal topics. ¶ *And made my confession.* Not as an individual, or not of his own sins only, but a confession in behalf of the people, and in their name. There is no reason to suppose that what he here says did *not* express their feelings. They had been long in captivity—far away from their desolate city and temple. They could not but be sensible that these calamities had come upon them on account of their sins; and they could not but feel that the calamities could not be expected to be removed but by confession of their sins, and by acknowledging the justice of the Divine dealings towards them. When we have been afflicted—when we are called to pass through severe trials—and when, borne down by trial, we go to God, and pray that the evil may be removed, the first thing that is demanded is, that we should confess our sins, and acknowledge the justice of God in the judgments that have come upon us. If we attempt to vindicate and justify ourselves, we can have no hope that the judgment will be averted. Daniel, therefore, in the name of the people, began his prayer with the humble and penitent acknowledgment that all that they had suffered was deserved. ¶ *O Lord, the great and dreadful God.* A God great,

and to be feared or venerated—הַנּוֹרָא׃.

This does not mean *dreadful* in the sense that there is anything stern or unamiable in his character, but mainly that he is to be regarded with veneration. ¶ *Keeping the covenant and mercy.* Keeping his covenant and showing mercy. This is often ascribed to God, that he is faithful to his covenant; that is, that he is faithful to his promises to his people, or to those who

5 We *a* have sinned, and have committed iniquity, and have done wickedly, and have rebelled, even by departing from thy precepts, and from thy judgments:

6 Neither *b* have we hearkened

a Ps. 106. 6; Isa. 64. 6, 7.   *b* 2 Chron. 36. 15, 16.

unto thy servants the prophets, which spake in thy name to our kings, our princes, and our fathers, and to all the people of the land.

7 O Lord, righteousness 1 *belongeth* unto thee, *c* but unto us

1 or, *thou hast.*   *c* Psa. 51. 4.

---

sustain a certain relation to him, and who are faithful to *their* covenant vows. If there is alienation and estrangement, and want of faithfulness on either side, it does not begin with him. He is faithful to all his promises, and his fidelity may always be assumed as a basis of calculation in all our intercourse with him. See the word "Covenant," in Cruden's *Concordance.* The word *mercy* seems to be added here to denote that *mercy* enters into his dealings with us even in keeping the covenant. We are so sinful and so unfaithful ourselves, that if *he* is faithful to his covenant, it must be by showing mercy to us. ¶ *To them that love him,* &c. The conditions of the covenant extend no farther than this, since, in a compact of any kind, one is bound to be faithful only while the terms are maintained by the other party. So God binds himself to show favour only while we are obedient, and we can plead his covenant only when we are obedient, when we confess our sins and plead his promises in this sense—that he has assured us that he will restore and receive us if we are penitent. It was this which Daniel pleaded on this occasion. He could not plead that his people had been obedient, and had thus any claims to the Divine favour; but he could cast himself and them on the mercy of a covenant-keeping God, who would remember his covenant with them if they were penitent, and who would graciously pardon.

5. *We have sinned.* Though Daniel was alone, he spake in the name of the people in general—doubtless recounting the long series of crimes in the nation which had preceded the captivity, and which were the cause of the ruin of the city and temple. ¶ *And have committed iniquity,* &c. These varied forms of expression are designed to give *intensity* to what he says. It

is equivalent to saying that they had sinned in every way possible. The mind, in a state of true repentance, dwells on its sins, and recounts the various forms in which iniquity has been done, and multiplies expressions of regret and sorrow on account of transgression. ¶ *From thy precepts.* Thy commands; thy laws. ¶ *Thy judgments.* Thy laws—the word *judgments* in the Scripture denoting what God judges to be right for us to *do,* as well as what it is right for him to *inflict.*

6. *Neither have we hearkened unto thy servants the prophets.* Who called upon us to turn from our sins; who made known the will of God, and who proclaimed that these judgments would come upon us if we did not repent. ¶ *Which spake in thy name to our kings,* &c. To all classes of the people, calling on kings and rulers to turn from their idolatry, and the people to forsake their sins, and to seek the Lord. It was a characteristic of the prophets that they spared no classes of the nation, but faithfully uttered all the word of God. Their admonitions had been unheeded, and the people now saw clearly that these calamities had come upon them because they had *not* hearkened to their voice.

7. *O Lord, righteousness* belongeth *unto thee.* Marg., "or, *thou hast.*" The Hebrew is, "to thee is righteousness, to us shame," &c. The state of mind in him who makes the prayer is that of ascribing righteousness or justice to God. Daniel feels and admits that God has been right in his dealings. He is not disposed to blame him, but to take all the shame and blame to the people. There is no murmuring or complaining on his part as if God had done wrong in any way, but there is the utmost confidence in him, and in his government. This is the true feel-

confusion of faces, as at this day: to the men of Judah, and to the inhabitants of Jerusalem, and unto all Israel, *that are* near, and *that are* far off, through all the countries whither *a* thou hast driven them, because of their trespass that they have trespassed against thee.

8 O Lord, to us *belongeth* *b* confusion of face, to our kings, to our princes, and to our fathers, because we have sinned against thee.

9 To the Lord our God *c belong* mercies and forgivenesses, though we have rebelled against him;

a Lev.26.33,34.   *b* Ezek.16.63.   *c* Psa. 130.4,7.

---

ing with which to come before God when we are afflicted, and when we plead for his mercy and favour. God should be regarded as righteous in all that he has done, and holy in all his judgments and claims, and there should be a willingness to address him as holy, and just, and true, and to take shame and confusion of face to ourselves. Comp. Psa. li. 4. ¶ *But unto us confusion of faces.* Heb., "shame of faces;" that is, that kind of shame which we have when we feel that we are guilty, and which commonly shows itself in the countenance. ¶ *As at this day.* As we actually are at this time. That is, he felt that at that time they were a down‑trodden, an humbled, a contemned people. Their country was in ruins; they were captives in a far distant land, and all on which they had prided themselves was laid waste. All these judgments and humiliating things he says they had deserved, for they had grievously sinned against God. ¶ *To the men of Judah.* Not merely to the *tribe* of Judah, but to the kingdom of that name. After the revolt of the ten tribes—which became known as the kingdom of Ephraim, because Ephraim was the largest tribe, or as the kingdom of Israel— the other portion of the people, the tribes of Judah and Benjamin were known as the kingdom of Judah, since Judah was by far the larger tribe of the two. This kingdom is referred to here, because Daniel belonged to it, and because the ten tribes had been carried away long before and scattered in the countries of the East. The ten tribes had been carried to Assyria. Jerusalem always remained as the capital of the kingdom of Judah, and it is to this portion of the Hebrew people that the prayer of Daniel more

especially appertains. ¶ *And to the inhabitants of Jerusalem.* Particularly to them, as the heaviest calamities had come upon them, and as they had been prominent in the sins for which these judgments had come upon the people. ¶ *And unto all Israel.* All the people who are descendants of Israel or Jacob, wherever they may be, embracing not only those of the kingdom of Judah properly so called, but all who appertain to the nation. They were all of one blood. They had had a common country. They had all revolted, and a succession of heavy judgments had come upon the nation as such, and all had occasion for shame and confusion of face. ¶ That are *near, and* that are *far off.* Whether in Babylon, in Assyria, or in more remote countries. The ten tribes had been carried away some two hundred years before this prayer was offered by Daniel, and they were scattered in far distant lands. ¶ *Through all the countries whither thou hast driven them,* &c. In Babylonia, in Assyria, in Egypt, or in other lands. They were scattered everywhere, and wherever they were they had common cause for humiliation and shame.

8. *O Lord, to us* belongeth *confusion,* &c. To all of us; to the whole people, high and low, rich and poor, the rulers and the ruled. All had been partakers of the guilt; all were involved in the calamities consequent on the guilt. As all had sinned, the judgments had come upon all, and it was proper that the confession should be made in the name of all.

9. *To the Lord our God* belong *mercies and forgivenesses.* Not only does righteousness belong to him in the sense that he has done right, and that he cannot be blamed for what he has done, but mercy and forgiveness be-

10 Neither have we obeyed the voice of the Lord our God, to walk in his laws which he set before us by his servants the prophets.

11 Yea, all ^a Israel have transgressed thy law, even by departing, that they might not obey thy voice; therefore the curse is poured upon us, and the oath that *is* written in

Isa. 1. 4–6.

the law of Moses the servant of God, because we have sinned against him.

12 And he hath confirmed his words, which he spake against us, and against our judges that judged us, by bringing upon us a great evil: for under the whole heaven hath not been done as hath been done upon Jerusalem.

---

long to him in the sense that he only can pardon, and that these are attributes of his nature. ¶ *Though we have rebelled against him.* The word here used and rendered *though* (כִּי) may mean either *though* or *for.* That is, the passage may mean that mercy belongs to God, and we may hope that he will show it, *although* we have been so evil and rebellious; or it may mean that it belongs to him, and he only can show it, *for* we have rebelled against him; that is, our only hope now is in his mercy, *for* we have sinned, and forfeited all claims to his favour. Either of these interpretations makes good sense, but the latter would seem to be most in accordance with the general strain of this part of the prayer, which is to make humble and penitent confession. So the Latin Vulgate *quia.* So Theodotion, ὅτι. So Luther and Lengerke, *denn.* In the same way, the passage in Psa. xxv. 11 is rendered, " For thy name's sake, O Lord, pardon mine iniquity, for (כִּי) it is great "—though this passage will admit of the other interpretation, "*although* it is great."

10. *Neither have we obeyed the voice of the Lord.* The commands of God as made known by the prophets, ver. 6.

11. *Yea, all Israel have transgressed,* &c. Embracing not only the tribe and the kingdom of Judah, but the whole nation. The calamity, therefore, had come upon them all. ¶ *Even by departing.* By departing from thy commandments; or by rebellion against thee. ¶ *That they might not obey thy voice.* By refusing to obey thy voice, or thy commands. ¶ *Therefore the curse is poured upon us.* As rain de-

scends, or as water is poured out. The *curse* here refers to that which was so solemnly threatened by Moses in case the nation did not obey God. See Deut. xxviii. 15–68. ¶ *And the oath that is written in the law of Moses,* &c. The word here rendered *oath* (שְׁבֻעָה) means, properly, a *swearing,* or *an oath;* and hence, either an oath of promise as in a covenant, or an oath of cursing or imprecation—that is, a curse. It is evidently used in the latter sense here. See Gesenius, *Lex.* Daniel saw clearly that the evils which had been threatened by Moses (Deut. xxviii.) had actually come upon the nation, and he as clearly saw that the cause of all these calamities was that which Moses had specified. He, therefore, frankly and penitently confessed these sins in the name of the whole people, and earnestly supplicated for mercy.

12. *And he hath confirmed his words,* &c. By bringing upon the people all that he had threatened in case of their disobedience. Daniel saw that there was a complete fulfilment of all that he had said would come upon them. As all this had been threatened, he could not complain; and as he had confirmed his words in regard to the threatening, he had the same reason to think that he would in regard to his promises. What Daniel here says was true in his time, and in reference to his people will be found to be true at all times, and in reference to all people. Nothing is more certain than that God will " confirm " all the words that he has ever spoken, and that no sinner can hope to escape on the ground that God will be found to be false to his threatenings, or that he has forgotten

13 As *it is* written *a* in the law of Moses, all this evil is come upon us: yet ¹ made we not our prayer before the LORD our God, that we might turn from our iniquities, and understand thy truth.

14 Therefore hath the LORD

a Lev.26.14, &c.; Deut.28.15,&c.; Lam.2.15-17.

watched upon the evil, and brought it upon us: for the LORD our God *is* righteous *b* in all his works which he doeth: for we obeyed not his voice.

15 And now, O Lord our God, that hast brought thy people forth

1 *entreated we not the face of.*   *b* Neh. 9. 33.

---

them, or that he is indifferent to them. ¶ *Against our judges that judged us.* Our magistrates or rulers. ¶ *For under the whole heaven.* In all the world. ¶ *Hath not been done as hath been done upon Jerusalem.* In respect to the slaughter, and the captivity, and the complete desolation. No one can show that at that time this was not literally true. The city was in a state of complete desolation; its temple was in ruins; its people had been slain or borne into captivity.

13. *As* it is *written in the law of Moses.* The word *law* was given to all the writings of Moses. See Notes on Luke xxiv. 44. ¶ *Yet made we not our prayer before the Lord our God.* Marg., *entreated we not the face of.* The Hebrew word here used (חִלָּה) means, properly, *to be polished;* then to be worn down in strength, to be weak; then to be sick, or diseased; then in Piel (the form used here), to rub or stroke the face of any one, to soothe or caress, and hence to beseech, or supplicate. See Gesenius, *Lex.* Here it means, that, as a people, they had failed, when they had sinned, to call upon God for pardon; to confess their sins; to implore his mercy; to deprecate his wrath. It would have been easy to turn aside his threatened judgments if they had been penitent, and had sought his mercy, but they had not done it. What is here said of them can and will be said of all sinners when the Divine judgment comes upon them. ¶ *That we might turn from our iniquities.* That we might seek grace to turn from our transgressions. ¶ *And understand thy truth.* The truth which God had revealed; equivalent to saying that they might be righteous.

14. *Therefore hath the Lord watched upon the evil.* The word here used

and rendered *watched*—שָׁקַד—means, properly, *to wake; to be sleepless; to watch.* Then it means to watch over anything, or to be attentive to it. Jer. i. 12; xxxi. 28; xliv. 27.—Gesenius, *Lex.* The meaning here is, that the Lord had not been inattentive to the progress of things, nor unmindful of his threatening. He had never slumbered, but had carefully observed the course of events, and had been attentive to all that they had done, and to all that he had threatened to do. The practical *truth* taught here—and it is one of great importance to sinners—is, that God is not inattentive to their conduct, though he may seem to be, and that in due time he will show that he has kept an unslumbering eye upon them. See Notes on Isa. xviii. 4. ¶ *For the Lord our God* is *righteous in all his works,* &c. This is the language of a true penitent; language which is always used by one who has right feelings when he reflects on the Divine dealings towards him. God is seen to be righteous in his law and in his dealings, and the only reason why we suffer is that we have sinned. This will be found to be true always; and whatever calamities we suffer, it should be a fixed principle with us to "ascribe righteousness to our Maker," Job xxxvi. 3.

15. *And now, O Lord our God, that hast brought thy people forth out of the land of Egypt.* In former days. The reference to this shows that it is proper to use *arguments* before God when we plead with him (comp. Notes on Job xxiii. 4); that is, to suggest considerations or reasons why the prayer should be granted. Those reasons must be, of course, such as will occur to our own minds as sufficient to make it proper for God to bestow the blessing, and when they are presented before him, it

out of the land of Egypt with a mighty hand, and hast ¹ gotten thee renown, as at this day ; we have sinned, we have done wickedly.

16 ¶ O Lord, according to all thy righteousness, I beseech thee,

1 *made thee a name.*

let thine anger and thy fury be turned away from thy city Jerusalem, thy holy mountain ; because for our sins, and for the iniquities of our fathers, Jerusalem and thy people *are become* a reproach to all *that are* about us.

---

must be with submission to his higher view of the subject. The arguments which it is proper to urge are those derived from the Divine mercy and faithfulness ; from the promises of God ; from his former dealings with his people ; from our sins and misery ; from the great sacrifice made for sin ; from the desirableness that his name should be glorified. Here Daniel properly refers to the former Divine interposition in favour of the Hebrew people, and he pleads the fact that God had delivered them from Egypt as a reason why he should now interpose and save them. The strength of this argument may be supposed to consist in such things as the following: (*a*) in the fact that there was as much reason for interposing now as there was then ; (*b*) in the fact that his interposing then might be considered as a proof that he intended to be regarded as their protector, and to defend them as his people ; (*c*) in the fact that he who had evinced such mighty power at that time must be able to interpose and save them now, &c. ¶ *And hast gotten thee renown.* Marg., *made thee a name.* So the Hebrew. The idea is, that that great event had been the means of making him known as a faithful God, and a God able to deliver. As he was thus known, Daniel prayed that he would again interpose, and would now show that he was *as* able to deliver his people as in former times. ¶ *As at this day.* That is, as God was then regarded. The remembrance of his interposition had been diffused abroad, and had been transmitted from age to age. ¶ *We have sinned*, &c. This turn in the thought shows how deeply the idea of their sinfulness pressed upon the mind of Daniel. The natural and obvious course of thought would have been, that, as God had interposed when his people were de-

livered from Egyptian bondage, he would now again interpose ; but instead of that, the mind of Daniel is overwhelmed with the thought that they had sinned grievously against one who had shown that he was a God so great and glorious, and who had laid them under such obligations to love and serve him.

16. *O Lord, according to all thy righteousness.* The word *righteousness* here seems to refer to all that was excellent and glorious in the character of God. The eye of Daniel is fixed upon what he had formerly done ; upon his character of justice, and mercy, and goodness ; upon the faithfulness of God to his people, and, in view of all that was excellent and lovely in his character, he pleaded that he would interpose and turn away his anger from his people now. It is the character of God that is the ground of his plea—and what else is there that can give us encouragement when we come before him in prayer. ¶ *Let thine anger and thy fury be turned away*, &c. The anger which had come upon the city, and which appeared to rest upon it. Jerusalem was in ruins, and it seemed still to be lying under the wrath of God. The word rendered *fury* is the common one to denote wrath or indignation. It implies no more than anger or indignation, and refers here to the Divine displeasure against their sins, manifested in the destruction of their city. ¶ *Thy holy mountain.* Jerusalem was built on hills, and the city in general might be designated by this phrase. Or, more probably, there is allusion either to Mount Zion, or to Mount Moriah. ¶ *Because for our sins*, &c. There is, on the part of Daniel, no disposition to blame God for what he had done. There is no murmuring or complaining, as if he had been unjust or severe in his dealings with his people.

17 Now, therefore, O our God, hear the prayer of thy servant, and his supplications, and cause thy face to shine upon thy sanctuary that is desolate, for the Lord's sake.

18 O my God, incline thine ear, and hear; open thine eyes, and behold our desolations, and the city which[1] is called by thy name: for we do not [2] present our supplications before thee for our righteousnesses, but for thy great mercies.

19 O Lord, hear; O Lord, forgive; O Lord, hearken, and do; defer not, for thine own sake, O my God; for thy city and thy people are called by thy name.

1 *whereupon thy name is called.* 2 *cause to fall.*

Jerusalem was indeed in ruins, and the people were captives in a distant land, but he felt and admitted that God was just in all that he had done. It was too manifest to be denied that all these calamities had come upon them on account of their sins, and this Daniel, in the name of the people, humbly and penitently acknowledged. ¶ *A reproach to all* that are *about us.* All the surrounding nations. They reproach us with our sins, and with the judgments that have come upon us, as if we were peculiarly wicked, and were forsaken of heaven.

17. *Now, therefore, O our God, hear the prayer of thy servant.* In behalf of the people. He pleaded for his people and country, and earnestly entreated the Lord to be merciful. His argument is based on the confession of sin; on the character of God; on the condition of the city and temple; on the former Divine interpositions in behalf of the people; and by all these considerations, he pleads with God to have mercy upon his people and land. ¶ *And cause thy face to shine upon thy sanctuary.* Upon the temple. That is, that he would look upon it benignly and favourably. The language is common in the Scriptures, when favour and kindness are denoted by lifting up the light of the countenance, and by similar phrases. The allusion is originally, perhaps, to the sun, which, when it shines brightly, is an emblem of favour and mercy; when it is overclouded, is an emblem of wrath. ¶ *For the Lord's sake.* That is, that he would be propitious for his own sake; to wit, that his glory might be promoted; that his excellent character might be displayed; that his mercy and compassion might be shown. All true prayer has its seat in a desire that the glory of God may be promoted, and the excellence of his character displayed. That is of more consequence than *our* welfare, and the gratification of *our* wishes, and that should be uppermost in our hearts when we approach the throne of grace.

18. *O my God, incline thine ear, and hear.* Pleading earnestly for his attention and his favour, as one does to a man. ¶ *Open thine eyes.* As if his eyes had been closed upon the condition of the city, and he did not see it. Of course, all this is figurative, and is the language of strong and earnest pleading when the heart is greatly interested. ¶ *And the city which is called by thy name.* Marg., *whereupon thy name is called.* The margin expresses the sense more literally; but the meaning is, that the city had been consecrated to God, and was called his—the city of Jehovah. It was known as the place of his sanctuary—the city where his worship was celebrated, and which was regarded as his peculiar dwelling-place on the earth. Comp. Psa. xlviii. 1–3; lxxxvii. 3. This is a new ground of entreaty, that the city belonged to God, and that he would remember the close connection between the prosperity of that city and the glory of his own name.

19. *O Lord, hear,* &c. The language in this verse does not require any particular explanation. The repetition—the varied forms of expression—indicate a mind intent on the object; a heart greatly interested; an earnestness that cannot be denied. It is language that is respectful, solemn, devout, but deeply earnest. It is not vain repetition, for its force is not in the *words* employed, but in the manifest fervour, earnestness, and sincerity of spirit which pervade the pleading. It is earnest intercession and supplica-

20 ¶ And whiles I was speaking, and praying, and confessing my sin and the sin of my people Israel, and presenting my supplication

before the LORD my God for the holy mountain of my God;

21 Yea, whiles I *was* speaking in prayer, even the man Gabriel,

---

tion that God would hear—that he would forgive, that he would hearken and do, that he would not defer his gracious interposition. The sins of the people; the desolation of the city; the promises of God; the reproach that the nation was suffering—all these come rushing over the soul, and prompt to the most earnest pleading that perhaps ever proceeded from human lips. And these things justified that earnest pleading—for the prayer was that of a prophet, a man of God, a man that loved his country, a man that was intent on the promotion of the Divine glory as the supreme object of his life. Such earnest intercession; such confession of sin; such a dwelling on arguments why a prayer should be heard, is at all times acceptable to God; and though it cannot be supposed that the Divine Mind needs to be instructed, or that our arguments will convince God or influence him as arguments do men, yet it is undoubtedly proper to urge them as if they would, for it may be only in this way that our own minds can be brought into a proper state. The great argument which *we* are to urge why our prayers should be heard is the sacrifice which has been made for sin by the Redeemer, and the fact that he has purchased for us the blessings which we need; but in connection with that it is proper to urge our own sins and necessities; the wants of our friends or our country; our own danger and that of others; the interposition of God in times past in behalf of his people, and his own gracious promises and purposes. If we have the spirit, the faith, the penitence, the earnestness of Daniel, we may be sure that our prayers will be heard as his was.

20. *And whiles I was speaking*, &c. In the very time when I was thus pleading. ¶ *For the holy mountain of my God.* Notes on ver. 16.

21. *Yea, whiles I* was *speaking in prayer.* How *long* the prayer continued we are not informed. It is probable that we have only the substance

of it, and that Daniel has recorded only the topics on which he dwelt more at length. The subject was of great importance, and it is reasonable to suppose that a day had been devoted to an examination of the prophecies, and to solemn prayer. ¶ *Even the man Gabriel.* Who had the appearance of a man, and hence so called. ¶ *Whom I had seen in the vision at the beginning.* That is, in a *former* vision. See Notes on ch. viii. 16. It cannot refer to what is mentioned in this (the ninth) chapter, for (*a*) he had as yet had no *vision*, but all that is recorded is a prayer; (*b*) there is no intimation that Gabriel had appeared to him at the beginning of the prayer; and (*c*) it is declared that at the beginning of the prayer, Gabriel, then evidently in heaven, had received commandment to go to Daniel, and to communicate the message to him, ver. 23. The meaning undoubtedly is, that the personage who now appeared to him he recognized to be the same who had appeared in a former vision on the banks of the Ulai. The proper meaning of the Hebrew here is, "in a vision at the beginning," as in our translation. So the Vulgate, *à principio;* and so Theodotion—ἐν τῇ ἀρχῇ. The Hebrew word תְּחִלָּה means, properly, *beginning*, Hos. i. 2; Prov. ix. 10; but, in connection with the preposition, as here—בַּתְּחִלָּה—it means also, *before, formerly,* Gen. xiii. 3; xli. 21; xliii. 18, 20; Isa. i. 26. ¶ *Being caused to fly swiftly.* Marg., *with weariness,* or *flight.* On the difficult Hebrew expression here—מֻעָף בִּיעָף— Lengerke may be consulted, *in loc.* The words, according to Gesenius, are derived from יָעַף, to go swiftly, and then, to be wearied, to faint, either with running, Jer. ii. 24, or with severe labour, Isa. xl. 28, or with sorrows, Isa. l. 4. If derived from this word, the meaning in Hophal, the form here used, would be, *wearied with swift running,* and the sense is, that Gabriel had borne the message swiftly to him, and ap-

whom I had seen in the vision at the beginning, being caused to fly swiftly,[1] touched me about the time of the evening oblation.

22 And he informed *me*, and

1 *with weariness, or, flight.*

talked with me, and said, O Daniel, I am now come forth to [2] give thee skill and understanding.

23 At the beginning of thy supplications the [3] commandment came

2 *make thee skilful of.*   3 *word.*

---

peared before him as one does who is wearied with a rapid course. If this be the idea, there is no direct allusion to his *flying*, but the reference is to the rapidity with which he had come on the long journey, as if exhausted by his journey. The Latin Vulgate renders it *cito volans—quickly flying;* Theodotion, πετόμενος — flying; the *Codex Chis.*, τάχει φερόμενος — *borne swiftly.* The Syriac, "with a swift flying he flew and came from heaven." It cannot be determined with certainty, from the words used here, that the coming of Gabriel was by an act of *flying* as with wings. The common representation of the angels in the Old Testament is not with wings, though the Cherubim and Seraphim (Isa. vi. 2, *seq.*) are represented with wings; and in Rev. xiv. 6, we have a representation of an angel flying. Probably the more exact idea here is that of a rapid course, so as to produce weariness, or such as would naturally produce fatigue. ¶ *Touched me.* Daniel was doubtless at this time engaged in prayer. ¶ *About the time of the evening oblation.* The evening sacrifice. This was at the ninth hour of the day, or about three o'clock in the afternoon.

22. *And he informed* me. Heb., Gave me intelligence or understanding. That is, about the design of his visit, and about what would be hereafter. ¶ *And talked with me.* Spake unto me. ¶ *O Daniel, I am now come forth to give thee skill.* Marg., *make thee skilful of.* The Hebrew is, literally, "to make thee skilful, or wise, in understanding." The design was to give him information as to what was to occur.

23. *At the beginning of thy supplications.* We are not informed at what time Daniel began to pray, but as remarked above, it is most natural to suppose that he devoted the day to prayer, and had commenced these solemn acts of devotion in the morning.

¶ *The commandment came forth.* Marg., *word.* That is, the word of God. This evidently means, in heaven; and the idea is, that as soon as he began to pray a command was issued from God to Gabriel that he should visit Daniel, and convey to him the important message respecting future events. It is fair to conclude that he had at once left heaven in obedience to the order, and on this high embassage, and that he had passed over the amazing distance between heaven and earth in the short time during which Daniel was engaged in prayer. If so, and if heaven—the peculiar seat of God, the dwelling-place of angels and of the just—is beyond the region of the fixed stars, some central place in this vast universe, then this may give us some idea of the amazing rapidity with which celestial beings may move. It is calculated that there are stars so remote from our earth, that their light would not travel down to us for many thousand years. If so, how much more rapid may be the movements of celestial beings than even light; perhaps more than that of the lightning's flash—than the electric fluid on telegraphic wires—though *that* moves at the rate of more than 200,000 miles in a second. Compare Dick's *Philosophy of a Future State*, p. 220. "During the few minutes employed in uttering this prayer," says Dr. Dick, "this angelic messenger descended from the celestial regions to the country of Babylonia. This was a rapidity of motion surpassing the comprehension of the most vigorous imagination, and far exceeding even the amazing velocity of light." With such a rapidity it *may be* our privilege yet to pass from world to world on errands of mercy and love, or to survey in distant parts of the universe the wonderful works of God. ¶ *And I am come to show* thee. To make thee acquainted with

forth, and I am come to shew *thee;* for thou *art*[1] greatly beloved: therefore understand the matter, and consider the vision.

1 a man *of desires.*

what will yet be. ¶ *For thou* art *greatly beloved.* Marg., as in Heb., "*a man of desires.*" That is, he was one whose happiness was greatly desired by God; or, a man of God's delight; that is, as in our version, greatly beloved. It was on this account that his prayer was heard, and that God sent to him this important message respecting what was to come. ¶ *Therefore understand the matter.* The matter respecting what was yet to occur in regard to his people. ¶ *And consider the vision.* This vision —the vision of future things which he was now about to present to his view. From this passage, describing the appearance of Gabriel to Daniel, we may learn, (*a*) That our prayers, if sincere, are heard in heaven *as soon* as they are offered. They enter at once into the ears of God, and he regards them at the instant. (*b*) A command, as it were, may be at once issued to answer them—*as if* he directed an angel to bear the answer at once. (*c*) The angels are ready to hasten down to men, to communicate the will of God. Gabriel came evidently with pleasure on his embassage, and to a benevolent being anywhere there is nothing more grateful than to be commissioned to bear glad tidings to others. Possibly that may be a part of the employment of the righteous for ever. (*d*) The thought is an interesting one, if we are permitted to entertain it, that good angels may be constantly employed as Gabriel was ; that whenever prayer is offered on earth they may be commissioned to bring answers of peace and mercy, or despatched to render aid, and that thus the universe may be constantly traversed by these holy beings ministering to those who are "heirs of salvation," Heb. i. 1, 4.

24. *Seventy weeks are determined.* Here commences the celebrated prophecy of the SEVENTY WEEKS—a portion of Scripture which has excited as

24 Seventy weeks *a* are determined upon thy people, and upon thy holy city, to [2] finish the transgression, and to [3] make an end of

a Numb. 14. 34; Ezek. 4. 6.   2 or, *restrain.*
3 or, *seal up.*

much attention, and led to as great a variety of interpretation, as perhaps any other. Of this passage, Professor Stuart (*Hints on the Interpretation of Prophecy,* p. 104) remarks, "It would require a volume of considerable magnitude even to give a history of the ever-varying and contradictory opinions of critics respecting this *locus vexatissimus;* and perhaps a still larger one to establish an exegesis which would stand. I am fully of opinion, that no interpretation as yet published will stand the test of thorough grammatico-historical criticism ; and that a candid, and searching, and thorough *critique* here is still a *desideratum.* May some expositor, fully adequate to the task, speedily appear!" After these remarks of this eminent Biblical scholar, it is with no great confidence of success that I enter on the exposition of the passage. Yet, perhaps, though *all* difficulties may not be removed, and though I cannot hope to contribute anything *new* in the exposition of the passage, something may be written which may relieve it of some of the perplexities attending it, and which may tend to show that its author was under the influence of Divine inspiration. The passage may be properly divided into two parts. The first, in ver. 24, contains a *general* statement of what would occur in the time specified—the seventy weeks ; the second, vers. 25-27, contains a *particular* statement of the manner in which that would be accomplished. In this statement, the whole time of the seventy weeks is broken up into three smaller portions of seven, sixty-two, and one— designating evidently some important epochs or periods (ver. 25), and the last one week is again subdivided in such a way, that, while it is said that the whole work of the Messiah in confirming the covenant would occupy the entire week, yet that he would be cut off in the middle of the week, verse 27.

sins, and to make reconciliation for iniquity, and to bring in everlasting *a* righteousness, and to seal

up the vision and [1] prophecy, and to anoint the Most Holy.

a Heb. 9. 12.   1 *prophet.*

In the *general* statement (ver. 24) it is said that there was a definite time—seventy weeks—during which the subject of the prediction would be accomplished ; that is, during which all that was to be done in reference to the holy city, or in the holy city, to finish the transgression, to make an end of sin, &c., would be effected. The things specified in this verse are *what was to be done,* as detailed more particularly in the subsequent verses. The design in this verse seems to have been to furnish a *general* statement of what was to occur in regard to the holy city—of that city which had been selected for the peculiar purpose of being a place where an atonement was to be made for human transgression. It is quite clear that when Daniel set apart this period for prayer, and engaged in this solemn act of devotion, his design was not to inquire into the ultimate events which would occur in Jerusalem, but merely to pray that the purpose of God, as predicted by Jeremiah, respecting the captivity of the nation, and the rebuilding of the city and temple, might be accomplished. God took occasion from this, however, not only to give an implied assurance about the accomplishment of these purposes, but also to state in a remarkable manner the *whole* ultimate design respecting the holy city, and the great event which was ever onward to characterize it among the cities of the world. In the consideration of the whole passage (vers. 24–27), it will be proper, first, to examine into the literal meaning of the words and phrases, and then to inquire into the fulfilment. ¶ *Seventy weeks.* שָׁבֻעִים שִׁבְעִים. Vulg., *Septuaginta hebdomades.* So Theodotion, Ἑβδομήκοντα ἑβδομάδες. Prof. Stuart (*Hints,* p. 82) renders this "*seventy sevens ;*" that is, seventy times seven years: on the ground that the word denoting *weeks* in the Hebrew is not שָׁבֻעים, but שְׁבֻעוֹת. "The form which is used here," says he, "which is a regular masculine plural, is no doubt

purposely chosen to designate the plural of seven; and with great propriety here, inasmuch as there are many sevens which are to be joined together in one common sum. Daniel had been meditating on the close of the seventy *years* of Hebrew exile, and the angel now discloses to him a new period of *seventy times seven,* in which still more important events are to take place. Seventy sevens, or (to use the Greek phraseology), *seventy heptades,* are determined upon thy people. Heptades of what? Of days, or of years? No one can doubt what the answer is. Daniel had been making diligent search respecting the seventy *years ;* and, in such a connection, nothing but seventy heptades of years could be reasonably supposed to be meant by the angel." The inquiry about the *gender* of the word, of which so much has been said (Hengstenberg, *Chris.* ii. 297), does not seem to be very important, since the same result is reached whether it be rendered *seventy sevens,* or *seventy weeks.* In the former case, as proposed by Prof. Stuart, it means seventy sevens of *years,* or 490 years; in the other, seventy *weeks* of years; that is, as a *week of years* is seven years, seventy such weeks, or as before, 490 years. The usual and proper meaning of the word here used, however—שָׁבוּעַ is *a seven,* ἑβδομάς, *hebdomad, i.e.,* a *week.* — Gesenius, *Lex.* From the *examples* where the word occurs it would seem that the masculine or feminine forms were used indiscriminately. The word occurs only in the following passages, in all of which it is rendered *week,* or *weeks,* except in Ezek. xlv. 21, where it is rendered *seven,* to wit, days. In the following passages the word occurs in the masculine form plural, Dan. ix. 24–26; x. 2, 3; in the following in the feminine form plural, Exod. xxxiv. 22; Numb. xxviii. 26; Deut. xvi. 9, 10, 16; 2 Chron. viii. 13 ; Jer. v. 24 ; Ezek. xlv. 21; and in the following in the singular number, common gender, rendered *week*, Gen. xxix. 27, 28, and in the dual masculine in Lev. xii. 5, rendered *two weeks*. From these passages it is evident that nothing certain can be determined about the meaning of the word from its gender. It would seem to denote *weeks*, periods of seven days—*hebdomads*—in either form, and is doubtless so used here. The fair translation would be, weeks seventy are determined; that is, seventy times seven days, or four hundred and ninety *days*. But it may be asked here, whether this is to be taken literally, as denoting four hundred and ninety days? If not, in what sense is it to be understood? and why do we understand it in a different sense? It is clear that it must be explained literally as denoting four hundred and ninety *days*, or that these days must stand for years, and that the period is four hundred and ninety *years*. That this latter is the true interpretation, as it has been held by all commentators, is apparent from the following considerations: (*a*) This is not uncommon in the prophetic writings. See Notes on ch. vii. 24–28. (See also Editor's Preface to volume on Revelation.) (*b*) Daniel had been making inquiry respecting the seventy *years*, and it is natural to suppose that the answer of the angel would have respect to *years* also; and, thus understood, the answer would have met the inquiry pertinently —"not *seventy* years, but a week of years — seven times seventy years." Comp. Matt. xviii. 21, 22. "In such a connection, nothing but seventy heptades of years could be reasonably supposed to be meant by the angel." — Prof. Stuart's *Hints*, &c., p. 82. (*c*) Years, as Prof. Stuart remarks, are the measure of all considerable periods of time. When the angel speaks, then, in reference to certain events, and declares that they are to take place during *seventy heptades*, it is a matter of course to suppose that he means years. (*d*) The circumstances of the case demand this interpretation. Daniel was seeking comfort in view of the fact that the city and temple had been desolate now for a period of seventy years. The angel comes to bring him consolation, and to give him assurances about the rebuilding of the

city, and the great events that were to occur there. But what consolation would it be to be told that the city would indeed be rebuilt, and that it would continue seventy ordinary weeks —that is, a little more than a year, before a new destruction would come upon it? It cannot well be doubted, then, that by the time here designated, the angel meant to refer to a period of four hundred and ninety years; and if it be asked why this number was not literally and exactly specified in so many words, instead of choosing a mode of designation comparatively so obscure, it may be replied, (1) that the number *seventy* was employed by Daniel as the time respecting which he was making inquiry, and that there was a propriety that there should be a reference to that fact in the reply of the angel—*one* number seventy had been fulfilled in the desolations of the city, there would be *another* number seventy in the events yet to occur; (2) this is in the usual prophetic style, where there is, as Hengstenberg remarks (*Chris.* ii. 299), often a "*concealed* definiteness." It is usual to designate numbers in this way. (3.) The term was sufficiently clear to be understood, or is, at all events, made clear by the result. There is no reason to doubt that Daniel would so understand it, or that it would be so interpreted, as fixing in the minds of the Jewish people the period when the Messiah was about to appear. The meaning then is, that there would be a period of four hundred and ninety years, during which the city, after the order of the rebuilding should go forth (ver. 25), until the entire consummation of the great object for which it should be rebuilt, and that then the purpose would be accomplished, and it would be given up to a greater ruin. There was to be this long period in which most important transactions were to occur in the city. ¶ *Are determined.* The word here used (נֶחְתַּךְ from חָתַךְ) occurs nowhere else in the Scriptures. It properly means, according to Gesenius, to cut off, to divide; and hence, to determine, to destine, to appoint. Theodotion renders it, *συνετμήθησαν*—are cut off, decided, defined. The Vulgate renders it, *abbreviatœ sunt.* Luther, *Sind bestimmet* — are determined. The meaning would seem to be, that this portion of time—the seventy weeks—was *cut off* from the whole of duration, or cut out of it, as it were, and set by itself for a definite purpose. It does not mean that it was cut off from the time which the city would naturally stand, or that this time was *abbreviated*, but that a portion of time—to wit, four hundred and ninety years—was designated or appointed with reference to the city, to accomplish the great and important object which is immediately specified. A certain, definite period was fixed on, and when this was past, the promised Messiah would come. In regard to the construction here—the singular verb with a plural noun, see Hengstenberg, *Christ. in loc.* The true meaning seems to be, that the seventy weeks are spoken of *collectively*, as denoting a period of time; that is, a period of seventy weeks is determined. The prophet, in the use of the singular verb, seems to have contemplated the time, not as separate weeks, or as particular portions, but as one period. ¶ *Upon thy people.* The Jewish people; the nation to which Daniel belonged. This allusion is made because he was inquiring about the close of their exile, and their restoration to their own land. ¶ *And upon thy holy city.* Jerusalem, usually called the holy city, because it was the place where the worship of God was celebrated, Isa. lii. 1; Neh. xi. 1, 18; Matt. xxvii. 53. It is called *"thy holy city"*—the city of Daniel, because he was here making especial inquiry respecting it, and because he was one of the Hebrew people, and the city was the capital of their nation. As one of that nation, it could be called *his.* It was then, indeed, in ruins, but it was to be rebuilt, and it was proper to speak of it as if it were then a city. The meaning of *"upon* thy people and city" (עַל) is, *respecting* or *concerning.*

The purpose respecting the seventy weeks *pertains* to thy people and city;

or there is an important period of four hundred and seventy years determined on, or designated, respecting that people and city. ¶ *To finish the transgression.* The angel proceeds to state what was the object to be accomplished in this purpose, or what would occur during that period. The first thing, *to finish the transgression.* The margin is, *restrain.* The Vulgate renders it, *ut consummetur prævaricatio.* Theodotion, *τοῦ συντελεσθῆναι ἁμαρτίαν*—to finish sin. Thompson renders this, "to finish sin-offerings." The difference between the marginal reading (*restrain*) and the text (*finish*) arises from a doubt as to the meaning of the original word. The common reading of the text is כַּלֵּא, but in 39 Codices examined by Kennicott, it is כלה. The reading in the text is undoubtedly the correct one, but still there is not absolute certainty as to the signification of the word, whether it means to *finish* or to *restrain.* The proper meaning of the word in the common reading of the text (כַּלֵּא) is, to shut up, confine, restrain—as it is rendered in the margin. The meaning of the other word found in many MSS. (כַּלֵּה) is, to be completed, finished, closed—and in Piel, the form used here, to complete, to finish—as it is translated in the common version. Gesenius (*Lex.*) supposes that the word here is *for*—כַּלֵּה—meaning to finish or complete. Hengstenberg, who is followed in this view by Lengerke, supposes that the meaning is to *"shut up* transgression," and that the true reading is that in the text—כלא—though as that word is not used in Piel, and as the Masorites had some doubts as to the derivation of the word, they gave to it not its appropriate *pointing* in this place—which would have been כַּלֵּא—but the pointing of the other word (כַּלֵּה) in the margin. According to Hengstenberg, the sense here of *shutting up* is derived from the general notion of *restraining* or *hindering*, belonging to the word; and he supposes that this will best accord with the other words in this member of the verse—

to cover, and *to seal up.* The idea according to him is, that "sin, which hitherto lay naked and open before the eyes of a righteous God, is now by his mercy *shut up, sealed,* and *covered,* so that it can no more be regarded as existing—a figurative description of the forgiveness of sin." So Lengerke renders it, *Um einzuschliessen [den] Abfall.* Bertholdt, *Bis der Frevel vollbracht.* It seems most probable that the true idea here is that denoted in the margin, and that the sense is not that of *finishing,* but that of *restraining, closing, shutting up,* &c. So it is rendered by Prof. Stuart—"to *restrain* transgression."—*Com. on Daniel, in loc.* The word is used in this sense of *shutting up,* or *restraining,* in several places in the Bible: 1 Sam. vi. 10, " *and shut up* their calves at home;" Jer. xxxii. 3, "Zedekiah *had shut him up;*" Psa. lxxxviii. 8, "I am *shut up,* and I cannot come forth;" Jer. xxxii. 2, "Jeremiah the prophet was *shut up.*" The sense of shutting up, or *restraining,* accords better with the connection than that of *finishing.* The reference of the whole passage is undoubtedly to the Messiah, and to what would be done sometime during the "seventy weeks;" and the meaning here is, not that he would "finish transgression" —which would not be true in any proper sense, but that he would do a work which would *restrain* iniquity in the world, or, more strictly, which would *shut it up*—inclose it—as in a prison, so that it would no more go forth and prevail. The effect would be that which occurs when one is shut up in prison, and no longer goes at large. There would be a restraining power and influence which would check the progress of sin. This does not, I apprehend, refer to the particular transgressions for which the Jewish people had suffered in their long captivity, but sin (הַפֶּשַׁע) in general—the sin of the world. There would be an influence which would restrain and curb it, or which would shut it up so that it would no longer reign and roam at large over the earth. It is true that this might not have been so understood by Daniel at the time,

for the *language* is so general that it *might* have suggested the idea that it referred to the sins of the Jewish people. This language, if there had been no farther explanation of it, might have suggested the idea that in the time specified—seventy weeks— there would be some process—some punishment—some Divine discipline —by which the iniquities of that people, or their propensity to sin, for which this long captivity had come upon them, would be cohibited, or restrained. But the language is not such as necessarily to confine the interpretation to that, and the subsequent statements, and the actual fulfilment in the work of the Messiah, lead us to understand this in a much higher sense, as having reference to sin in general, and as designed to refer to some work that would ultimately be an effectual check on sin, and which would tend to cohibit, or restrain it altogether in the world. Thus understood, the language will well describe the work of the Redeemer—that work which, through the sacrifice made on the cross, is adapted and designed to restrain sin altogether. ¶ *And to make an end of sins.* Marg., *to seal up.* The difference here in the text and the margin arises from a difference in the readings in the Hebrew. The common reading in the text is לְחָתֵם—from חָתַם—*to seal, to seal up.* But the Hebrew marginal reading is a different word—הָתֵם, from תָּמַם—*to complete, to perfect, to finish.* The *pointing* in the text in the word לְחָתֵם is not the proper pointing of that word, which would have been לְחֹתֵם, but the Masorites, as is not unfrequently the case, gave to the word in the text the pointing of another word which they placed in the margin. The marginal reading is found in fifty-five MSS. (Lengerke), but the weight of authority is decidedly in favour of the common reading in the Hebrew text— *to seal,* and not *to finish,* as it is in our translation. The marginal reading, *to finish,* was doubtless substituted by some transcribers, or rather *suggested* by the Masorites, because it seemed to convey a better signification to say

that " sin would be *finished*," than to
say that it would be *sealed*. The
Vulgate has followed the reading in
the margin—*et finem accipiat pec-
catum ;* Theodotion has followed the
other reading, σφραγίσαι ἁμαρτίας. Luther also has it, *to seal.* Coverdale,
" that sin may have an end." The
true rendering is, doubtless, " to seal
sin ;" and the idea is that of removing
it from sight ; to remove it from view.
" The expression is taken," says Lengerke, " from the custom of sealing up
those things which one lays aside and
conceals." Thus in Job ix. 7, " And
sealeth up the stars ;" that is, he so
shuts them up in the heavens as to
prevent their shining—so as to hide
them from the view. They are concealed, hidden, made close—as the
contents of a letter or package are
sealed, indicating that no one is to
examine them. See Notes on that
passage. So also in Job xxxvii. 7,
referring to winter, it is said, " He
sealeth up the hand of every man, that
all men may know his work." That
is, in the winter, when the snow is on
the ground, when the streams are
frozen, the labours of the husbandman
must cease. The hands can no more
be used in ordinary toil. Every man
is prevented from going abroad to his
accustomed labour, and is, as it were,
sealed up in his dwelling. Comp. Jer.
xxxii. 11, 14 ; Isa. xxix. 11 ; Cant.
iv. 12. The idea in the passage before
us is, that the sins of our nature will,
as it were, be sealed up, or closed, or
hidden, so that they will not be seen,
or will not develop themselves ; that
is, " they will be inert, inefficient,
powerless."—Prof. Stuart. The language is applicable to anything that
would hide them from view, or remove
them from sight—as a book whose
writing is so sealed that we cannot
read it ; a tomb that is so closed that
we cannot enter it and see its contents ;
a package that is so sealed that we do
not know what is within it ; a room
that is so shut up that we may not
enter it, and see what is within. It
is not to be supposed that Daniel would
see clearly how this was to be done ;
but we, who have now a full revelation
of the method by which God can re-

move sin, can understand the method
in which this is accomplished by the
blood of the atonement, to wit, that
by that atonement sin is now forgiven,
or is treated *as if* it were hidden from
the view, and a seal, which may not
be broken, placed on that which covers
it. The language thus used, as we are
now able to interpret it, is strikingly
applicable to the work of the Redeemer, and to the method by which
God removes sin. In not a few MSS.
and editions the word rendered *sins* is
in the singular number. The amount
of authority is in favour of the common reading—sins—though the sense
is not materially varied. The work
would have reference to *sin*, and the
effect would be to seal it, and hide it
from the view. ¶ *And to make reconciliation for iniquity.* More literally,
" and to cover iniquity." The word
which is rendered to "make reconciliation "—כָּפַר   *kâphăr,*—properly means
to cover (whence our English word
cover) ; to cover over, to overlay, as
with pitch (Gen. vi. 14) ; and hence to
cover over sin ; that is, to atone for it,
pardon it, forgive it. It is the word
which is commonly used with reference
to atonement or expiation, and seems
to have been so understood by our
translators. It does not necessarily
refer to the means by which sin is
covered over, &c., by an atonement,
but is often used in the general sense
of *to pardon* or *forgive.* Comp. Notes
on Isa. vi. 7, and more fully, Notes on
Isa. xliii. 3. Here there is no necessary allusion to the atonement which
the Messiah would make in order to
cover over sin ; that is, the word is of
so general a character in its signification that it does not necessarily imply
this, but it is the word which would
naturally be used on the supposition
that it had such a reference. As a
matter of fact, undoubtedly, the means
by which this was to be done was by
the atonement, and that was referred
to by the Spirit of inspiration, but this
is not essentially implied in the meaning of the word. In whatever way
that should be done, this word would
be properly used as expressing it. The
Latin Vulgate renders thus, *et deleatur*

iniquitas. Theodotion, ἀπαλεῖψαι τὰς ἀδικίας — "to wipe out iniquities." Luther, "to reconcile for transgression." Here are three things specified, therefore, in regard to sin, which would be done. Sin would be

> *Restrained,*
> *Sealed up,*
> *Covered over.*

These expressions, though not of the nature of a climax, are intensive, and show that the great work referred to pertained to sin, and would be designed to remove it. Its bearing would be on human transgression ; on the way by which it might be pardoned ; on the methods by which it would be removed from the view, and be kept from rising up to condemn and destroy. Such expressions would undoubtedly lead the mind to look forward to some method which was to be disclosed by which sin could be consistently pardoned and removed. In the remainder of the verse, there are three additional things which would be done as necessary to complete the work :—

To bring in everlasting righteousness ;
To seal up the vision and prophecy ; and
To anoint the Most Holy.

¶ *And to bring in everlasting righteousness.* The phrase "to bring in" —literally, "to cause to come"—refers to some direct agency by which that righteousness would be introduced into the world. It would be such an agency as would cause it to exist; or as would establish it in the world. The *mode* of doing this is not indeed here specified, and, so far as the *word* here used is concerned, it would be applicable to any method by which this would be done—whether by making an atonement; or by setting an example; or by persuasion ; or by placing the subject of morals on a better foundation ; or by the administration of a just government ; or in any other way. The term is of the most general character, and its exact force here can be learned only by the subsequently revealed facts as to the way by which this would be accomplished. The essential idea in the language is, that this would be *introduced* by the Messiah ; that is, that he would be its author. The word *righteousness* here

also (פְדֶק) is of a general character. The fair meaning would be, that some method would be introduced by which men would become *righteous.* In the former part of the verse, the reference was to *sin*—to the fact of its existence —to the manner in which it would be disposed of—to the truth that it would be coerced, sealed up, covered over. Here the statement is, that, in contradistinction from that, a method would be introduced by which man would become, in fact, righteous and holy. But the *word* implies nothing as to the method by which this would be done. Whether it would be by a new mode of justification, or by an influence that would make men personally holy— whether this was to be as the result of example, or instruction, or an atoning sacrifice—is not necessarily implied in the use of this word. That, as in the cases already referred to, could be learned only by subsequent developments. It would be, doubtless, understood that there was a reference to the Messiah—for that is specified in the next verse ; and it would be inferred from this word that, under him, righteousness would reign, or that men would be righteous, but nothing could be argued from it as to the methods by which it would be done. It is hardly necessary to add, that, in the prophets, it is constantly said that righteousness would characterize the Messiah and his times ; that he would come to make men righteous, and to set up a kingdom of righteousness in the earth. Yet the exact mode in which it was to be done would be, of course, more fully explained when the Messiah should himself actually appear. The word *"everlasting"* is used here to denote that the righteousness would be permanent and perpetual. In reference to the method of becoming righteous, it would be unchanging—the standing method ever onward by which men would become holy ; in reference to the individuals who should become righteous under this system, it would be a righteousness which would continue for ever. This is the characteristic which is everywhere given of the righteousness which would be introduced by the Messiah. Thus in Isa.

li. 6–8 : "Lift up your eyes to the heavens, and look upon the earth beneath : for the heavens shall vanish away like smoke, and the earth shall wax old like a garment, and they that dwell therein shall die in like manner : but my salvation shall be for ever, and my righteousness shall not be abolished. Hearken unto me, ye that know righteousness, the people in whose heart is my law ; fear ye not the reproach of men, neither be ye afraid of their revilings. For the moth shall eat them up like a garment, and the worm shall eat them like wool : but my righteousness shall be for ever, and my salvation from generation to generation." So Isa. xlv. 17 : "But Israel shall be saved in the Lord with an everlasting salvation ; ye shall not be ashamed nor confounded, world without end." Compare Jer. xxxi. 3. The language used in the passage before us, moreover, is such as could not properly be applied to anything but that righteousness which the Messiah would introduce. It could not be used in reference to the temporal prosperity of the Jews on their return to the holy land, nor to such righteousness as the nation had in former times. The fair and proper meaning of the term is, that it would be *eternal*—that which would *endure for ever*—צֶדֶק עֹלָמִים. It would place righteousness on a permanent and enduring foundation; introduce that which would endure through all changes, and exist when the heavens would be no more. In the plan itself there would be no change; in the righteousness which any one would possess under that system there would be perpetual duration—it would exist for ever and ever. This is the nature of that righteousness by which men are now justified ; this is that which all who are interested in the scheme of redemption actually possess. The *way* in which this "everlasting righteousness" would be introduced is not stated here, but is reserved for future revelations. Probably all that the words would convey to Daniel would be, that there would be some method disclosed by which men would become righteous, and that this would not be temporary or changing,

but would be permanent and eternal. It is not improper that *we* should understand it, as it is explained by the subsequent revelations in the New Testament, as to the method by which sinners are justified before God. ¶ *And to seal up the vision and prophecy.* Marg., as in the Heb., *prophet.* The evident meaning, however, here is *prophecy.* The word *seal* is found, as already explained, in the former part of the verse—"to seal up sins." The word *vision* (for its meaning, see Notes on Isaiah i. 1) need not be understood as referring particularly to the visions seen by Daniel, but should be understood, like the word *prophecy* or *prophet* here, in a general sense—as denoting all the visions seen by the prophets—the series of visions relating to the future, which had been made known to the prophets. The idea seems to be that they would at that time be all *sealed,* in the sense that they would be closed or shut up—no longer open matters—but that the fulfilment would, as it were, close them up for ever. Till that time they would be open for perusal and study ; then they would be closed up as a sealed volume which one does not read, but which contains matter hidden from the view. Comp. Notes on Isa. viii. 16 : "Bind up the testimony ; seal the law among my disciples." See also Dan. viii. 26 ; xii. 4. In Isaiah (viii. 16) the meaning is, that the prophecy was complete, and the direction was given to bind it up, or roll it up like a volume, and to seal it. In Dan. viii. 26, the meaning is, seal up the prophecy, or make a permanent record of it, that, when it is fulfilled, the event may be compared with the prophecy, and it may be seen that the one corresponds with the other. In the passage before us, Gesenius (*Lex.*) renders it, "to complete, to finish"—meaning that the prophecies would be fulfilled. Hengstenberg supposes that it means, that "as soon as the fulfilment takes place, the prophecy, although it retains, in other respects, its great importance, reaches the end of its destination, in so far as the view of believers, who stand in need of consolation and encouragement, is no longer directed to it, to the

146 DANIEL. [B.C. 538.

future prosperity, but to that which has appeared." Lengerke supposes that it means to confirm, corroborate, ratify—*bekräftigen, bestätigen;* that is, "the eternal righteousness will be given to the pious, and the predictions of the prophets will be confirmed and fulfilled." To seal, says he, has also the idea of confirming, since the contents of a writing are secured or made fast by a seal. After all, perhaps, the very idea here is, that of *making fast,* as a lock or seal does—for, as is well known, a seal was often used by the ancients where a lock is with us; and the sense may be, that, as a seal or lock made fast and secure the contents of a writing or a book, so the *event,* when the prophecy was fulfilled, would make it *fast* and *secure.* It would be, as it were, locking it up, or sealing it, forever. It would determine all that seemed to be undetermined about it; settle all that seemed to be indefinite, and leave it no longer uncertain what was meant. According to this interpretation the meaning would be, that the prophecies would be sealed up or settled by the coming of the Messiah. The prophecies terminated on him (comp. Rev. xix. 10); they would find their fulfilment in him; they would be completed in him—and might then be regarded as closed and consummated—as a book that is fully written and is sealed up. All the prophecies, and all the visions, had a reference more or less direct to the coming of the Messiah, and when he should appear they might be regarded as complete. The spirit of prophecy would cease, and the facts would confirm and seal all that had been written. ¶ *And to anoint the Most Holy.* There has been great variety in the interpretation of this expression. The word rendered *anoint*—

מָשַׁח —infinitive from מָשַׁח (whence the word Messiah, ver. 25), means, properly, to strike or draw the hand over anything; to spread over with anything, to smear, to paint, to anoint. It is commonly used with reference to a sacred rite, to anoint, or consecrate by unction, or anointing to any office or use; as, *e.g.,* a priest, Exod. xxviii. 41; xl. 15; a prophet, 1 Kings xix.

16; Isa. lxi. 1; a king, 1 Sam. x. 1; xv. 1; 2 Sam. ii. 4; 1 Kings i. 34. So it is used to denote the consecration of a stone or column as a future sacred place, Gen. xxxi. 13; or vases and vessels as consecrated to God, Exod. xl. 9, 11; Lev. viii. 11; Numb. vii. 1. The word would then denote a setting apart to a sacred use, or consecrating a person or place as holy. Oil, or an unguent, prepared according to a specified rule, was commonly employed for this purpose, but the word may be used in a figurative sense—as denoting to set apart or consecrate in any way *without* the use of oil—as in the case of the Messiah. So far as this *word,* therefore, is concerned, what is here referred to may have occurred without the literal use of oil, by any act of consecration or dedication to a holy use. The phrase, "the Most Holy" (קֹדֶשׁ קָדָשִׁים) has been very variously interpreted. By some it has been understood to apply literally to the most holy place—the holy of holies, in the temple; by others to the whole temple, regarded as holy; by others to Jerusalem at large as a holy place; and by others, as Hengstenberg, to the Christian church as a holy place. By some the thing here referred to is supposed to have been the consecration of the most holy place after the rebuilding of the temple; by others the consecration of the whole temple; by others the consecration of the temple and city by the presence of the Messiah, and by others the consecration of the Christian church, by his presence. The phrase properly means "holy of holies," or most holy. It is applied often in the Scriptures to the *inner sanctuary,* or the portion of the tabernacle and temple containing the ark of the covenant, the two tables of stone, &c. See Notes on Matt. xxi. 12. The phrase occurs in the following places in the Scripture: Exod. xxvi. 33, 34; xxix. 37; xxx. 29, 36; xl. 10; Lev. ii. 3, 10, *et al.*—in all, in about twenty-eight places. See the *Englishman's Hebrew Concordance.* It is not necessarily limited to the inner sanctuary of the temple, but may be applied to the whole house, or to anything that was consecrated to

God in a manner peculiarly sacred. In a large sense, possibly it might apply to Jerusalem, though I am not aware that it ever occurs in this sense in the Scriptures, and in a figurative sense it might be applied undoubtedly, as Hengstenberg supposes, to the Christian church, though it is certain that it is not elsewhere thus used. In regard to the meaning of the expression—an important and difficult one, as is admitted by all—there are five principal opinions which it may be well to notice. The truth will be found in one of them. (1.) That it refers to the consecration by oil or anointing of the temple, that would be rebuilt after the captivity, by Zerubbabel and Joshua. This was the opinion of Michaelis and Jahn. But to this opinion there are insuperable objections: (a) that, according to the uniform tradition of the Jews, the holy oil was wanting in the second temple. In the case of the first temple there might have been a literal anointing, though there is no evidence of that, as there was of the anointing of the vessels of the tabernacle, Exod. xxx. 22, &c. But in the second temple there is every evidence that there can be, that there was no literal anointing. (b) The *time* here referred to is a fatal objection to this opinion. The period is seventy weeks of years, or four hundred and ninety years. This cannot be doubted (see Notes on the first part of the verse) to be the period referred to; but it is absurd to suppose that the consecration of the new temple would be deferred for so long a time, and there is not the slightest evidence that it was. This opinion, therefore, cannot be entertained. (2.) The second opinion is, that it refers to the re-consecration and cleansing of the temple after the abominations of Antiochus Epiphanes. See Notes on ch. viii. 14. But this opinion is liable substantially to the same objections as the other. The cleansing of the temple, or of the sanctuary, as it is said in ch. viii. 14, did *not* occur four hundred and ninety years after the order to rebuild the temple (ver. 25), but at a much earlier period. By no art of construction, if the period here referred to is four hundred and ninety years,

can it be made to apply to the re-dedication of the temple after Antiochus had defiled it. (3.) Others have supposed that this refers to the Messiah himself, and that the meaning is, that he, who was most holy, would then be consecrated or anointed as the Messiah. It is probable, as Hengstenberg (*Christ.* ii. 321, 322) has shown, that the Greek translators thus understood it, but it is a sufficient objection to this that the phrase, though occurring many times in the Scriptures, is never applied to *persons*, unless this be an instance. Its uniform and proper application is to *things*, or *places*, and it is undoubtedly so to be understood in this place. (4.) Hengstenberg supposes (pp. 325–328) that it refers to the Christian church as *a* holy place, or "the New Temple of the Lord," "the Church of the New Covenant," as consecrated and supplied with the gifts of the Spirit. But it is a sufficient refutation of this opinion that the phrase is nowhere else so used; that it has in the Old Testament a settled meaning as referring to the tabernacle or the temple; that it is nowhere employed to denote a collection of *people*, any more than an individual person—an idea which Hengstenberg himself expressly rejects (p. 322); and that there is no proper sense in which it can be said that the Christian church is *anointed*. The language is undoubtedly to be understood as referring to some *place* that was to be thus consecrated, and the uniform Hebrew usage would lead to the supposition that there is reference, in some sense, to the temple at Jerusalem. (5.) It seems to me, therefore, that the obvious and fair interpretation is, to refer it to the temple—as the holy place of God; his peculiar abode on earth. Strictly and properly speaking, the phrase would apply to the inner room of the temple—the sanctuary properly so called (see Notes on Heb. ix. 2); but it might be applied to the whole temple as consecrated to the service of God. If it be asked, then, what anointing or consecration is referred to here, the reply, as it seems to me, is, not that it was then to be set apart anew, or to be dedicated; not that it was literally to be anointed with the consecrating oil, but

25 Know, therefore, and understand, *that* from the going forth of the commandment to ¹ restore and

to build Jerusalem, unto the Messiah the Prince, *shall be* seven weeks

1 or, *build again.*

that it was to be consecrated in the highest and best sense by the presence of the Messiah—that by his coming there was to be a higher and more solemn consecration of the temple to the real purpose for which it was erected than had occurred at any time. It was reared as a holy place ; it would become eminently holy by the presence of him who would come as the anointed of God, and his coming to it would accomplish the purpose for which it was erected, and with reference to which all the rites observed there had been ordained, and then, this work having been accomplished, the temple, and all the rites appertaining to it, would pass away. In confirmation of this view, it may be remarked, that there are repeated allusions to the coming of the Messiah to the second temple, reared after the return from the captivity— as that which would give a peculiar sacredness to the temple, and which would cause it to surpass in glory all its ancient splendour. So in Hag. ii. 7, 9 : " And I will shake all nations, and the desire of all nations shall come : and I will fill this house with glory, saith the Lord of hosts.—The glory of this latter house shall be greater than of the former, saith the Lord of hosts : and in this place will I give peace, saith the Lord of hosts." So Mal. iii. 1, 2 : "The Lord, whom ye seek, shall suddenly come to his temple, even the messenger of the covenant whom ye delight in : behold, he shall come, saith the Lord of hosts. But who may abide the day of his coming ? and who shall stand when he appeareth ? for he is like a refiner's fire, and like fullers' soap," &c. Comp. Matt. xii. 6 : " But I say unto you, That in this place is one greater than the temple." Using the word *anoint*, therefore, as denoting to consecrate, to render holy, to set apart to a sacred use, and the phrase *holy of holies* to designate the temple as such, it seems to me most probable that the reference here is to the highest consecration which could be made of the temple in

the estimation of a Hebrew, or, in fact, the presence of the Messiah, as giving a sacredness to that edifice which nothing else did give or could give, and, therefore, as meeting all the proper force of the language used here. On the supposition that it was designed that there should be a reference to this event, this would be such language as would have been not unnaturally employed by a Hebrew prophet. And if it be so, this may be regarded as the probable meaning of the passage. In this sense, the temple which was to be reared again, and about which Daniel felt so solicitous, would receive its highest, its truest consecration, as connected with an event which was to bring in everlasting righteousness, and to seal up the vision and the prophecy.

25. *Know, therefore, and understand.* Hengstenberg renders this, "and thou wilt know and understand ;" and supposes that the design of Gabriel is to awaken the attention and interest of Daniel by the assurance that, if he would give attention, he would understand the subject by the explanation which he was about to give. So also Theodotion renders it in the future tense. The Hebrew is in the future tense, and would probably convey the idea that he might or would know and understand the matter. So Lengerke renders it, *Und so mögest du wissen*, &c. The object is doubtless to call the attention of Daniel to the subject, with the assurance that he might comprehend the great points of the communication which he was about to make respecting the seventy weeks. In the previous verse, the statement was a general one ; in this, the angel states the time when the period of the seventy weeks was to commence, and then that the whole period was to be broken up or divided into three smaller portions or epochs, each evidently marking some important event, or constituting an important era. The first period of seven weeks was evidently to be characterized by something in which it would be different from

and threescore and two weeks: the street shall ¹be built again,

and the ²wall, even ªin ³ troublous times.

1 *return and be builded.*   2 *or, breach, or, ditch.*   a Neh. 4. 8, &c.; 6. 15.   3 *strait of.*

that which would follow, or it would reach to some important epoch, and then would follow a continuous period of sixty-two weeks, after which, during the remaining one week, to complete the whole number of seventy, the Messiah would come and would be cut off, and the series of desolations would commence which would result in the entire destruction of the city. ¶ That *from the going forth of the command-ment.* Heb., "of the word"—דָּבָר. It is used, however, as in ver. 23, in the sense of commandment or order. The expression "gone forth" (מֹצָא) would properly apply to the *issuing* of an order or decree. So in ver. 23—יָצָא דָבָר—"the commandment went forth." The word properly means a going forth, and is applied to the rising sun, that goes forth from the east, Psa. xix. 6 (7); then a *place* of going forth, as a gate, a fountain of waters, the east, &c., Ezek. xlii. 11; Isa. xli. 18; Psa. lxxv. 6 (7). The word here has undoubted reference to the promulgation of a decree or command, but there is nothing in the words to determine *by whom* the command was to be issued. So far as the *lan-guage* is concerned, it would apply equally well to a command issued by God, or by the Persian king, and no-thing but the circumstances can deter-mine which is referred to. Hengsten-berg supposes that it is the former, and that the reference is to the Divine pur-pose, or the command issued from the "heavenly council" to rebuild Jerusa-lem. But the more natural and obvious meaning is, to understand it of the command actually issued by the Persian monarch to restore and build the city of Jerusalem. This has been the in-terpretation given by the great body of expositors, and the reasons for it seem to be perfectly clear: (*a*) This would be the interpretation affixed to it natur-ally, if there were no theory to support, or if it did not open a chronological difficulty not easy to settle. (*b*) This is the only interpretation which can

give anything like definiteness to the passage. Its purpose is to designate some fixed and certain period from which a reckoning could be made as to the time when the Messiah would come. But, so far as appears, there was no such definite and marked command on the part of God; no period which can be fixed upon when *he* gave command-ment to restore and build Jerusalem; no exact and settled point from which one could reckon as to the period when the Messiah would come. It seems to me, therefore, to be clear, that the al-lusion is to some order to rebuild the city, and as this order could come only from one who had at that time juris-diction over Jerusalem and Judea, and who could command the resources ne-cessary to rebuild the ruined city, that order must be one that would emanate from the reigning power; that is, in fact, the Persian power—for that was the power that had jurisdiction at the close of the seventy years' exile. But, as there were several orders or com-mands in regard to the restoration of the city and the temple, and as there has been much difficulty in ascertaining the exact chronology of the events of that remote period, it has not been easy to determine the precise order referred to, or to relieve the whole subject from perplexity and difficulty. Lengerke supposes that the reference here is the same as in ver. 2, to the promise made to Jeremiah, and that this is the true point from which the reckoning is to be made. The exact edict referred to will be more properly considered at the close of the verse. All that is neces-sarily implied here is, that the time from which the reckoning is to be com-menced is some command or order issued to restore and build Jerusalem. ¶ *To restore.* Marg., *build again.* The Hebrew is, properly, *to cause to return*—לְהָשִׁיב. The word might be applied to the return of the captives to their own land, but it is evidently here used with reference to the city of Jeru-salem, and the meaning must be, *to restore it to its former condition.* It was evidently the purpose to cause it to return, as it were, to its former splendour; to reinstate it in its former condition as a holy city—the city where the worship of God would be celebrated, and it is this purpose which is referred to here. The word, in Hiphil, is used in this sense of restoring to a former state, or to renew, in the following places: Psa. lxxx. 3, " *Turn us again* —הֲשִׁיבֵנוּ —and cause thy face to shine."

So vers. 7, 19, of the same Psalm. Isa. i. 26, "And I will *restore* thy judges as at the first," &c. The meaning here would be met by the supposition that Jerusalem was to be put into its former condition. ¶ *And to build Jerusalem.* It was then in ruins. The command, which is referred to here, must be one to build it up again—its houses, temple, walls; and the fair sense is, that some such *order* would be issued, and the reckoning of the seventy weeks must *begin* at the issuing of this command. The proper interpretation of the prophecy demands that *that* time shall be assumed in endeavouring to ascertain when the seventy weeks would terminate. In doing this, it is evidently required in all fairness that we should not take the time when the Messiah *did* appear— or the birth of the Lord Jesus, assuming that to be the *terminus ad quem*— the point to which the seventy weeks were to extend—and then reckon *backward* for a space of four hundred and ninety years, to see whether we cannot find some event which by a possible construction would bear to be applied as the *terminus a quo*, the point from which we are to begin to reckon; but we are to ascertain when, in fact, the order was given to rebuild Jerusalem, and to make *that* the *terminus a quo*— the starting point in the reckoning. The consideration of the fulfilment of this may with propriety be reserved to the close of the verse. ¶ *Unto the Messiah.* The word *Messiah* occurs but four times in the common version of the Scriptures: Dan. ix. 25, 26: John i. 41; iv. 25. It is synonymous in meaning with the word *Christ*, the Anointed. See Notes on Matt. i. 1.

Messiah is the Hebrew word; Christ the Greek. The Hebrew word (מָשִׁיחַ) occurs frequently in the Old Testament, and, with the exception of these two places in Daniel, it is uniformly translated *anointed*, and is applied to priests, to prophets, and to kings, as being originally set apart to their offices by solemn acts of anointing. So far as the *language* is concerned here, it might be applied to any one who sustained these offices, and the proper application is to be determined from the connection. Our translators have introduced the article — " unto *the* Messiah." This is wanting in the Hebrew, and should not have been introduced, as it gives a definiteness to the prophecy which the original language does not necessarily demand. Our translators undoubtedly understood it as referring to him who is known as the Messiah, but this is not necessarily implied in the original. All that the language fairly conveys is, " until an anointed one." Who *that* was to be is to be determined from other circumstances than the mere use of the language, and in the interpretation of the language it should not be assumed that the reference is to any particular individual. That some eminent personage is designated; some one who by way of eminence would be properly regarded as anointed of God; some one who would act so important a part as to characterize the age, or determine the epoch in which he should live; some one so prominent that he could be referred to as " *anointed*," with no more definite appellation; some one who would be understood to be referred to by the mere use of this language, may be fairly concluded from the expression used—for the angel clearly meant to imply this, and to direct the mind forward to some one who would have such a prominence in the history of the world. The object now is merely to ascertain the meaning of the *language*. All that is fairly implied is, that it refers to some one who would have such a prominence as anointed, or set apart to the office of prophet, priest, or king, that it could be understood that he was referred to by the use of this language. The reference is not to *the* anointed one, as of one who was already known or looked forward to as such—for then the article would have been used; but to some one who, when he appeared, would have such marked characteristics that there would be no difficulty in determining that he was the one intended. Hengstenberg well remarks, "We must, therefore, translate *an anointed one, a prince,* and assume that the prophet, in accordance with the uniform character of his prophecy, chose the more indefinite, instead of the more definite designation, and spoke only of *an* anointed one, *a* prince, instead of *the* anointed one, *the* prince—κατ᾽ ἐξοχήν—and left his hearers to draw a deeper knowledge respecting him, from the prevailing expectations, grounded on earlier prophecies of a future great King, from the remaining declarations of the context, and from the fulfilment, the coincidence of which with the prophecy must here be the more obvious, since an accurate date had been given."—*Christol.* ii. 334, 335. The Vulgate renders this, *Usque ad Christum ducem* — "even to Christ the leader," or ruler. The Syriac, "to the advent of Christ the king." Theodotion, ἕως Χριστοῦ ἡγουμένου — "to Christ the leader," or ruler. The question whether this refers to Christ will be more appropriately considered at the close of the verse. The inquiry will then occur, also, whether this refers to his birth, or to his appearance *as* the anointed one—his taking upon himself publicly the office. The language would apply to either, though it would perhaps more properly refer to the latter—to the time when he should *appear* as such—or should be anointed, crowned, or set apart to the office, and be fully instituted in it. It could not be demonstrated that *either* of these applications would be a departure from the fair interpretation of the words, and the application must be determined by some other circumstances, if any are expressed. What those are in the case will be considered at the close of the verse. ¶ *The Prince.* נָגִיד. This word properly means a leader, a prefect, a prince. It is a word of very general character, and might be applied to *any* leader or ruler. It is applied to an overseer, or, as we should say, a *secretary* of the treasury, 1 Chron. xxvi. 24 ; 2 Chron. xxxi. 12 ; an overseer of the temple, 1 Chron. ix. 11 ; 2 Chron. xxxi. 13 ; of the palace, 2 Chron. xxviii. 7 ; and of military affairs, 1 Chron. xiii. 1 ; 2 Chron. xxxii. 21. It is also used absolutely to denote a prince of a people, any one of royal dignity, 1 Sam. ix. 16 ; x. 1 ; xiii. 14.—Gesenius. So far as this *word*, therefore, is concerned, it would apply to *any* prince or leader, civil or military ; any one of royal dignity, or who should distinguish himself, or make himself a leader in civil, ecclesiastical, or military affairs, or who should receive an appointment to any such station. It is a word which would be as applicable to the Messiah as to any other leader, but which has nothing in itself to make it necessary to apply it to him. All that can be fairly deduced from its use here is, that it would be some prominent leader; some one that would be known without any more definite designation ; some one on whom the mind would naturally rest, and some one to whom when he appeared it would be applied without hesitation and without difficulty. There can be no doubt that a Hebrew, in the circumstances of Daniel, and with the known views and expectations of the Hebrew people, *would* apply such a phrase to the Messiah. ¶ *Shall be seven weeks.* See Notes on ver. 24. The *reason* for dividing the whole period into seven weeks, sixty-two weeks, and one week, is not formally stated, and will be considered at the close of the verse. All that is necessary here in order to an explanation of the language, and of what is to be anticipated in the fulfilment, is this: (*a*) That, according to the above interpretation (ver. 24), the period would be forty-nine years. (*b*) That this was to be the *first* portion of the whole time, not time that would be properly taken out of *any* part of the whole period. (*c*) That there was to be some event at the end of the forty-nine years which would designate a period, or a natural division of the time, or that the portion which was designated by the forty-nine years was to be distinctly characterized from the next period referred to as sixty-two weeks, and the next period as one week. (*d*) No intimation is given in the words as to the nature of this period, or as to what would distinguish one portion from the others, and *what* that was to be is to be learned from subsequent explanations, or from the actual course of events. If one period was characterized by war, and another by peace; one in building the city and the walls, and the other by quiet prosperity; one by abundance, and the other by famine; one by sickness, and the other by health—all that is fairly implied by the *words* would be met. It is foretold only that there would be *something* that would designate these periods, and serve to distinguish the one from the other. ¶ *And threescore and two weeks.* Sixty-two weeks; that is, as above explained (ver. 24), four hundred and thirty-four years. The fair meaning is, that there would be something which would characterize that long period, and serve to distinguish it from that which preceded it. It is not indeed intimated what that would be, and the nature of the case seems to require that we should look *to* the events—to the facts in the course of the history to determine what that was. Whether it was peace, prosperity, quiet, order, or the prevalence of religion as contrasted with the former period, all that the words fairly imply would be fulfilled in either of them. ¶ *The street shall be built again.* This is a general assertion or prediction, which does not seem to have any special reference to the *time* when it would be done. The fair interpretation of the expression does not require us to understand that it should be *after* the united period of the seven weeks and the sixty-two weeks, nor during either one of those periods; that is, the language is not such that we are necessarily required to affix it to any one period. It seems to be a general assurance designed to comfort Daniel with the promise that the walls and streets of Jerusalem, now desolate, would be built again, and that this

would occur some time during this period. His mind was particularly anxious respecting the desolate condition of the city, and the declaration is here made that it would be restored. So far as the language—the grammatical construction is concerned, it seems to me that this would be fulfilled if it were done either at the time of the going forth of the commandment, or during either of the periods designated, or even after these periods. It is, however, most natural, in the connection, to understand it of the *first* period— the seven weeks, or the forty-nine years—since it is said that "the commandment would go forth to restore, and to build Jerusalem;" and since, as the whole subsequent period is divided into three portions, it may be presumed that the thing that would characterize the first portion, or that which would first be done, would be to execute the commandment—that is, to restore and build the city. These considerations would lead us, therefore, to suppose that the thing which would characterize the first period—the forty-nine years— would be the rebuilding of the city; and *the time*—a time which, considering the extent and entireness of the ruins, the nature of the opposition that might be encountered, the difficulty of collecting enough from among the exiles to return and do it, the want of means, and the embarrassments which such an undertaking might be supposed to involve, cannot, probably, be regarded as too long.

The word rendered *street*—רְהֹוב— means *a street*, so called from its *breadth*, and would properly, therefore, be applied to a *wide* street. Then it denotes a market-place, or a forum —the broad open place at the gates of Oriental cities where public trials were held, and things exposed for sale, 2 Chron. xxxii. 6. In Ezra x. 9, the word refers to the area or court before the temple: "And all the people sat in the street (בִּרְהֹוב) of the house of God," &c. Comp. Nehe. viii. 1, 3, 16. The reference in this place, therefore, may be to that area or court; or it may be to any place of concourse, or any thoroughfare. It is such language as would be naturally used to denote that the city would be restored to its former condition. The phrase "shall be built again" is, in the margin, *return and be builded.* This is in accordance with the Hebrew. That is, it would be restored to its former state; it would, as it were, come back and be built up again. Hengstenberg renders it "a street is restored and built." The phrase properly implies that it would assume its former condition, the word *built* here being used in the sense of *made,* as we speak of *making a road.* Lengerke renders it, *wird wieder hergestellt* — "shall be again restored." Theodotion renders it, ἐπιστρέψει — "it shall return," understanding it as meaning that there would be a return, to wit, from the exile. But the more correct meaning undoubtedly is, that *the street* would return to its former state, and be rebuilt. ¶ *And the wall.* Marg., *ditch.* Hengstenberg renders this, "and firmly is it determined;" maintaining that the word

חָרוּץ here means fixed, determined,

resolved on, and that the idea is, the purpose that the city should be rebuilt was firmly resolved on in the Divine mind, and that the *design* of what is here said was to comfort and animate the returned Hebrews in their efforts to rebuild the city, in all the discouragements and troubles which would attend such an undertaking. The common interpretation, however, has been that it refers to a ditch, trench, or wall, that would be constructed at the time of the rebuilding of the city. So the Vulgate, *muri, walls.* So Theodotion, τεῖχος — *wall.* The Syriac renders it, "Jerusalem, and the *villages,* and the streets." Luther, *Mauren, walls.* Lengerke renders it, as Hengstenberg does, "and it is determined." Maurer understands the two expressions, *street* and *wall,* to be equivalent to *within* and *without*—meaning that the city would be thoroughly and entirely rebuilt. The Hebrew

word חָרוּץ means, properly, that which

is cut in, or dug out, from חָרַץ — to cut in. The word is translated *sharppointed things* in Job xli. 30; *gold, fine gold, choice gold,* in Psa. lxviii. 13; Prov. iii. 14; viii. 10, 19; xvi. 16; Zech. ix. 3; *a threshing instrument,* Isa. xxviii. 27; Amos i. 3; *sharp* (referring to a threshing instrument), Isa. xli. 15; *wall,* Dan. ix. 25; and *decision,* Joel iii. 14. It does not elsewhere occur in the Scriptures. The notion of *gold* as connected with the word is probably derived from the fact of its being dug for, or eagerly sought by men. That idea is, of course, not applicable here. Gesenius supposes that it here means a *ditch* or *trench* of a fortified city. This seems to me to be the probable signification. At all events, this has the concurrence of the great body of interpreters; and this accords well with the connection. The word does not properly mean *wall,* and it is never elsewhere so used. It need not be said that it was common, if not universal, in walled cities to make a deep ditch or trench around them to prevent the approach of an enemy, and such *language* would naturally be employed in speaking of the rebuilding of a city. Prof. Stuart renders it, "with broad spaces, and *narrow limits.*" ¶ *Even in troublous times.* Marg., *strait of.* Hengstenberg, "in a time of distress." Lengerke, *Im Druck der Zeiten*—" in a pressure of times." Vulg., *In angustia temporum.* Theodotion, in the Septuagint, renders it, "And these times shall be emptied out" (Thompson)—καὶ ἐκκενωθήσονται οἱ καιροί. The proper meaning of the Hebrew word (צוֹק) is, distress, trouble, anguish; and the reference is, doubtless, to times that would be characterized by trouble, perplexity, and distress. The allusion is clearly to the rebuilding of the city, and the use of this language would lead us to anticipate that such an enterprise would meet with opposition or embarrassment; that there would be difficulty in accomplishing it; that the work would not be carried on easily, and that a considerable time would be necessary to finish it.

Having gone through with an investigation of the meaning of the words and phrases of this verse, we are now prepared to inquire more particularly what things are referred to, and whether the predictions have been fulfilled. The points which it is necessary to examine are the following: —To whom reference is made by the Messiah the Prince; the time designated by the going forth of the commandment—or the *terminus a quo;* the question whether the whole period extends to the *birth* of him here referred to as the Messiah the Prince, or to his assuming the office or appearing as such; the time embraced in the first seven weeks—and the fulfilment —or the question whether, from the time of the going forth of the commandment to the appearing of the Messiah, the period of the four hundred and ninety years can be fairly made out. These are evidently important points, and it need not be said that a great variety of opinions has prevailed in regard to them, and that they are attended with no little difficulty.

I. To whom reference is made as the Messiah the Prince. In the exposition of the meaning of the words, we have seen that there is nothing in the language itself to determine this. It is applicable to *any* one who should be set apart as a ruler or prince, and might be applied to Cyrus, to any anointed king, or to him who is properly designated now as the Messiah —the Lord Jesus. Comp. Notes on Isa. xlv. 1. It is unnecessary to show that a great variety of opinions has been entertained, both among the Jewish Rabbins and among Christian commentators, respecting the question to whom this refers. Among the Jews, Jarchi and Jacchiades supposed that it referred to Cyrus; Ben Gersom, and others, to Zerubbabel; Aben Ezra to Nehemiah; Rabbi Azariah to Artaxerxes. Bertholdt, Lengerke, Maurer, and this class of expositors generally, suppose that the reference is to Cyrus, who is *called* the Messiah, or the "Anointed," in Isa. xlv. 1. According to this interpretation, it is supposed that the reference is to the

seventy years of Jeremiah, and that the meaning is, that "seven weeks," or forty-nine years, would elapse from the desolation of the city till the time of Cyrus. See Maurer, *in loc.* Comp. also Lengerke, pp. 444, 445. As specimens of the views entertained by those who deny the reference of the passage to the Messiah, and of the difficulties and absurdities of those views, we may notice those of Eichhorn and Bertholdt. Eichhorn maintains that the numbers referred to are *round* numbers, and that we are not to expect to be able to make out an exact conformity between those numbers and the events. The "commandment" mentioned in ver. 25 he supposes refers to the order of Cyrus to restore and rebuild the city, which order was given, according to Usher, A.M. 3468. From this point of time must the "seven weeks," or the forty-nine years, be reckoned; but, according to his view, the reckoning must be "backwards and forwards;" that is, it is seven weeks, or forty-nine years, *backward* to Nebuchadnezzar, who is here called "Messiah the Prince," who destroyed the temple and city, A.M. 3416 — or about fifty-two years before the going forth of the edict of Cyrus. From that time, the reckoning of the sixty-two weeks must be commenced. But again, this is not to be computed literally from the time of Nebuchadnezzar; but since the Jews, in accordance with Jeremiah xxv. 11, 12, reckoned *seventy* years, instead of the true time, the point from which the estimate is to begin is the fourth year of the reign of Jehoiakim, and this occurred, according to Usher, A.M. 3397. Reckoning from this point onward, the sixty-two weeks, or 434 years, would bring us to the time of Antiochus Epiphanes (A.M. 3829). At the end of the sixty-two weeks, in the first year of Antiochus Epiphanes, the high-priest, Onias III. (the Messiah of ver. 26), was displaced—"cut off"— וְכָרֵת—and Jason was appointed in his place, and Menelaus the year after removed him. Thus Onias had properly no successor, &c. This absurd opinion Bertholdt (p. 605, *seq.*) attempts to set aside—a task which is very easily performed, and then proposes his own —a hypothesis not less absurd and improbable. According to his theory (p. 613, *seq.*), the seventy years have indeed a historical basis, and the time embraced in them extends from the destruction of Jerusalem by Nebuchadnezzar to the death of Antiochus Epiphanes. It is divided into three periods: (*a*) The seven first hebdomads extend from the destruction of Jerusalem by Nebuchadnezzar to king Cyrus, who gave the exiles permission to return to their land. This is the period during which Jerusalem must lie waste (ver. 2); and after the close of this, by the favour of Cyrus (ver. 25), the promise of Jeremiah (ver. 25 —

—דָּבָר—"commandment"), that Jerusalem shall be rebuilt, goes forth. (*b*) The following sixty-two weeks extend from the return of the exiles to the beginning of the troubles and persecutions under Antiochus. This is the period of the rebuilding of Jerusalem (ver. 25). (*c*) The last period of one week extends from the time of the oppressions and wrongs commenced under Antiochus, to the death of Antiochus. See this view fully explained and illustrated in Bertholdt, *ut supra.* The great mass of Christian interpreters, however, have supposed that the reference is to the Messiah properly so called—the promised Saviour of the world—the Lord Jesus. In support of this opinion, the following considerations may be suggested, which seem to me to be conclusive: (1.) The language itself is such as is properly applicable to him, and such as would naturally suggest him. It is true, as we see in Isa. xlv. 1, that the term Messiah *may* be applied to another, as it is there to Cyrus (see the Notes on the meaning of the word in that place, and in the exposition of this verse), but it is also true that if the term stands by itself, and with no explanation, it would naturally suggest him who, by way of eminence, is known as *the* Messiah. In Isa. xlv. 1, it is expressly limited to Cyrus, and there can be no danger of mistake. Here there is no such limitation, and it is natural, therefore, to apply it in the sense in which among

the Hebrews it would be obviously understood. Even Bertholdt admits the force of this. Thus (p. 563) he says: "That at the words מָשִׁיחַ נָגִיד [Messiah the Prince] we should be led to think of the Messiah, Jesus, and at those, ver. 26, יִכָּרֵת מָשִׁיחַ וְאֵין לוֹ [shall be cut off but not for himself], of his crucifixion, though not absolutely necessary, is still very natural." (2.) This would be the interpretation which would be given to the words by the Jews. They were so much accustomed to look forward to a great prince and deliverer, who would be by way of eminence the Anointed of the Lord, that, unless there was some special limitation or designation in the language, they would naturally apply it to the Messiah, properly so called. Comp. Isa. ix. 6, 7. Early in the history of the Jews, the nation had become accustomed to the expectation that such a deliverer would come, and its hopes were centred on him. In all times of national trouble and calamity; in all their brightest visions of the future, they were accustomed to look to him as one who would deliver them from their troubles, and who would exalt their people to a pitch of glory and of honour, such as they had never known before. Unless, therefore, there was something in the connection which would demand a different interpretation, the language would be of course applied to the Messiah. But it cannot be pretended that there is anything in the connection that demands such a limitation, nor which forbids such an application. (3.) So far as the ancient versions throw any light on the subject, they show that this is the correct interpretation. So the Latin Vulgate, *usque ad Christum ducem.* So the Syriac, "unto Messiah, the most holy" —literally, "*holy* of holies." So Theodotion—ἕως Χριστοῦ—where there can be little doubt that the Messiah was understood to be referred to. The same is found in the Arabic. The *Codex Chis.* is in utter confusion on this whole passage, and nothing can be made of it. (4.) All the circumstances referred to in connection with him who is here called "Messiah the Prince" are such as to be properly applicable to the work which the Lord Jesus came to do, and *not* to Cyrus, or Antiochus, or any other leader or ruler. See the Notes on ver. 24. To no other one, according to the interpretation which the passage in that verse seems to demand, can the expressions there used be applied. In that exposition it was shown that the verse is designed to give a *general* view of what would be accomplished,' or of what is expressed more in detail in the remaining verses of the vision, and that the language there used can be applied properly to the work which the Lord Jesus came to accomplish. Assuredly to no one else can the phrases "to restrain transgression," "to seal up sins," "to cover over iniquity," "to bring in everlasting righteousness," "to seal up the vision and prophecy," and "to consecrate the most holy place," be so well applied. The same is true of the language in the subsequent part of the prophecy, "Messiah shall be cut off," "not for himself," "shall confirm the covenant," "cause the oblation to cease." Any one may see the perplexities in which they are involved by adopting another interpretation, by consulting Bertholdt, or Lengerke on the passage. (5.) The expression here used ("prince"—נָגִיד)—is applied to the Messiah beyond all question in Isa. lv. 4: "I have given him for a witness to the people, a *leader*—נָגִיד—and a commander to the people." (6.) The perplexity attending any other interpretation is an additional proof of this point. In full illustration of this, it is necessary only to refer to the views of Bertholdt and Eichhorn as above exhibited. Whatever may be said about the difficulties on the supposition that it refers to the Lord Jesus—the true Messiah—no one can undertake to reconcile the applications which they have proposed with any belief of the inspiration of the passage. These considerations seem to me to make it clear that the prophecy had reference to the Messiah properly so called—the hope and the expectation of the Jewish people. There can be no doubt that Daniel would so understand it; there

can be no doubt that it would be so applied by the Jews.

II. The next question is, From what point are we to reckon in computing the time when the Messiah would appear—the *terminus a quo?* It is important to fix this, for the whole question of the fulfilment depends on it, and *honesty* requires that it should be determined without reference to the time to which four hundred and ninety years would reach—or the *terminus ad quem*. It is clearly not proper to do as Prideaux does, to *assume* that it refers to the birth of Christ, and then to reckon backward *to* a time which may be made to mean the "going forth of the commandment." The true method, undoubtedly, would be to fix on a time which would accord with the expression here, with no reference to the question of the fulfilment—for in that way only can it be determined to be a true *prophecy*, and in that way only would it be of any use to Daniel, or to those who succeeded him. It need hardly be said, that a great variety of opinions have been maintained in regard to the time designated by the "going forth of the commandment." Bertholdt (pp. 567, 568) mentions no less than *thirteen* opinions which have been entertained on this point, and in such a variety of sentiment, it *seems* almost hopeless to be able to ascertain the truth with certainty. Now, in determining this, there are a few points which may be regarded as certain. They are such as these: (*a*) That the commandment referred to is one that is issued by some prince or king having authority, and not the purpose of God. See Notes above on the first part of the verse. (*b*) That the distinct command would be to "restore and build *Jerusalem*." This is specified, and therefore would seem to be distinguished from a command to build the *temple*, or to restore that from its state of ruin. It is true that the one might appear to be implied in the other, and yet this does not necessarily follow. For various causes it might be permitted to the Jews to rebuild their *temple*, and there might be a royal ordinance commanding that, while there was no purpose to restore the *city* to its former power and splendour, and even while there might be strong objections to it. For the use of the Jews who still resided in Palestine, and for those who were about to return, it might be a matter of policy to permit them to rebuild their temple, and even to aid them in it, while yet it might be regarded as perilous to allow them to rebuild the city, and to place it in its former condition of strength and power. It was a place easily fortified; it had cost the Babylonian monarch much time, and had occasioned him many losses, before he had been able to conquer and subdue it, and, even to Cyrus, it might be a matter of very questionable policy to allow it to be built and fortified again. Accordingly we find that, as a matter of fact, the permission to rebuild the *temple,* and the permission to rebuild the *city,* were quite different things, and were separately granted by different sovereigns, and that the work was executed by different persons. The former might, without impropriety, be regarded as the close of the captivity —or the end of the "seventy years" of Jeremiah—for a permission to rebuild the *temple* was, in fact, a permission to return to their own country, and an implied purpose to aid them in it, while a considerable interval might, and probably would elapse, before a distinct command was issued to restore and rebuild the city itself, and even then a long period might intervene before it would be completed. Accordingly, in the edict published by Cyrus, the permission to rebuild the *temple* is the one that is carefully specified : "Thus saith Cyrus, king of Persia, The Lord God of heaven hath given me all the kingdoms of the earth ; and he hath charged me *to build him an house* at Jerusalem, which is in Judah. Who is there among you of all his people ? his God be with him, and let him go up to Jerusalem, which is in Judah, and *build the house of the Lord God of Israel* (he is the God), which is in Jerusalem," Ezra i. 2, 3. In this order there is nothing said of the restoration of the *city,* and that in fact occurred at a different time, and under the direction of different leaders. The first

enterprise was to rebuild the *temple;* it was still a question whether it would be a matter of policy to allow the *city* to be rebuilt, and that was in fact accomplished at a different time. These considerations seem to make it certain that the edict referred to here was not that which was issued by *Cyrus,* but must have been a subsequent decree bearing particularly on the rebuilding of the city itself. It is true that the command to rebuild *the temple* would imply that either there were persons residing amidst the ruins of Jerusalem, or in the land of Palestine, who were to worship there, and that there would be inhabitants in Jerusalem, probably those who would go from Babylon— for otherwise the temple would be of no service, but still this might be, and there be no permission to rebuild the city with any degree of its ancient strength and splendour, and none to *surround it with walls*—a very material thing in the structure of an ancient city. (*c*) This interpretation is confirmed by the latter part of the verse : "the street shall be built again, and the wall, even in troublous times." If the word rendered *wall* means *trench* or *ditch,* as I have supposed, still it was a trench or ditch which was designed as a *defence* of a city, or which was excavated for making a wall, for the purpose of fortifying a walled city in order to make it stronger, and the expression is one which would not be applied to the mere purpose of rebuilding the *temple,* nor would it be used except in a command to restore the city itself. We are, then, in the fair interpretation of the passage, required now to show that such a command went forth from the Persian king to "restore and rebuild" *the city itself*— that is, a permission to put it into such a condition of strength as it was before.

In order to see how this interpretation accords with the facts in the case, and to determine whether such a period can be found as shall properly correspond with this interpretation, and enable us to ascertain the point of time here referred to—the *terminus a quo*—it is proper to inquire what are the *facts* which history has preserved.

For this purpose, I looked at this point of the investigation into Jahn's *Hebrew Commonwealth*, (pp. 160–177), a work not written with any reference to the fulfilment of this prophecy, and which, indeed, in the portion relating to this period of the world, makes no allusion whatever to Daniel. The inquiry which it was necessary to settle was, whether under any of the Persian kings there was any order or command which would properly correspond with what we have ascertained to be the fair meaning of the passage. A very brief synopsis of the principal events recorded by Jahn as bearing on the restoration of the Jews to their own country, will be all that is needful to add to determine the question before us.

The kings of the Persian universal monarchy, according to Ptolemy, were ten, and the whole sum of their reign two hundred and seven years—from the time of Cyaxares II. to the time of Alexander the Great. But Ptolemy's specific object being chronology, he omitted those who continued not on the throne a full year, and referred the months of their reign, partly to the preceding, and partly to the succeeding monarch. The whole number of sovereigns was in reality fourteen, as appears by the following table :—

B.C.		YEARS.	MONTHS.
538.	Cyaxares II. reigned...	2	—
536.	Cyrus...................	7	—
529.	Cambyses..............	7	5
522.	Smerdis...............	—	7
521.	Darius Hystaspis.......	36	—
485.	Xerxes I...............	21	—
464.	Artaxerxes Longimanus	40	3
424.	Xerxes II..............	—	2
424.	Sogdianus..............	—	7
423.	Darius Nothus..........	19	—
404.	Artaxerxes Mnemon...	46	—
358.	Darius Ochus..........	21	—
337.	Arses.................	—	2
335.	Darius Codomanus....	—	4

Under the reign of this last prince, B.C. 331, the kingdom was entirely subdued by Alexander the Great.

In respect to the question whether any order or command was issued pertaining to the rebuilding of the city of Jerusalem that corresponds with the meaning of the prediction as above explained, the following facts will probably furnish all the knowledge which can be obtained :—

(*a*) *Cyaxares* II. Of course there was nothing in the time of Cyaxares II., the Darius of Daniel (vi. 1 ; ix. 1), as it was under him that Babylon was conquered, and there was no movement towards a restoration of the Jews to their own land commenced by him, the first movement of that kind being under Cyrus.

(*b*) *Cyrus.* What was the nature of the order issued by *him* we have seen above. It was a command to build the *temple*, and was limited to that, and involved no reference to the city. The command, as we have seen above, did not extend to that, and there were probably good reasons why it was not contemplated that it should be rebuilt in its former strength, and fortified as it was before. The purpose to fortify the city, or to encompass it by a wall or ditch, or even to build it at all, could not have been brought within the order of Cyrus, as recorded in Ezra, and that is the only form of the order which we have. The language of Daniel, therefore, seems to have been chosen of design when he says that the command would be issued to rebuild the *city*, not the *temple*. At any rate, such *is* the language, and such was *not* the order of Cyrus.

(*c*) *Cambyses.* After the death of Cyrus the Samaritans wrote to Cambyses (called, by Ezra, Ahasuerus) against the Jews. We are not informed what effect this letter produced, but we can easily judge from the character of this degenerate son of Cyrus, as it is represented in history. He was a "thoughtless, gluttonous, furious warrior, who was considered as raving mad even by his own subjects."—Jahn. He madly invaded Egypt, and on his return learned that Smerdis, his brother, had usurped the throne in his absence ; and died of a wound received from the falling of his sword from its sheath, as he was mounting his horse. No order is mentioned during his reign pertaining to the rebuilding either of the city or the temple.

(*d*) *Smerdis.* He retained the throne about seven months. In the Bible he has the name of Artaxerxes. Comp., respecting him, Ctesias, x. ; Justin, i. 9 ; Herod. iii. 61–67. "To this monarch the Samaritans again addressed themselves, complaining that the Jews were building (that is, *fortifying*) the city of Jerusalem, which they had never thought of doing ; and in consequence of this false accusation, Smerdis issued a positive prohibition of their work."—Jahn. Two things, therefore, may be remarked respecting this reign : —(1) the order or commandment referred to by Daniel could not have been issued during *this* reign, since there was an express "prohibition" against the work of building and fortifying the city ; and (2) this confirms what is said above about the improbability that any order would have been issued by Cyrus to rebuild and fortify the city itself. It could not but have been foreseen that such an order would be likely to excite opposition from the Samaritans, and to cause internal dissensions and difficulties in Palestine, and it is not probable that the Persian government would allow the rebuilding of a city that would lead to such collisions.

(*e*) *Darius Hystaspis.* He reigned thirty-six years. He was a mild and benevolent ruler. "As Smerdis was a mere usurper, his prohibition of rebuilding the temple was of no authority."—Jahn. In the second year of his reign, Haggai and Zechariah appeared, who plied the governor Zerubbabel, the high-priest Joshua, and the whole people, with such powerful appeals to the Divine commands, that the building of the house of God was once more resumed. Upon this, Tatnai, the Persian governor on the west side of the Euphrates, came with his officers to call the Jews to an account, who referred him to the permission of Cyrus, and the Jews were suffered to proceed. The whole matter was, however, made known to Darius, and he caused search to be made among the archives of the state in reference to the alleged decree of Cyrus. The edict of Cyrus was found, which directed that a temple should be built at Jerusalem at the royal expense, and of much larger dimensions than the former. A copy of this was sent to Tatnai, and he was commanded to see that the work should be forwarded, and that the expenses should

be defrayed from the royal treasury, and that the priests should be supplied with whatever was necessary to keep up the daily sacrifice. The work was, therefore, pressed on with renewed vigour, and in the sixth year of his reign the temple was completed and consecrated. The remainder of his reign was spent in unnecessary wars with Scythia, Thrace, India, and Greece. He suffered an overthrow at Marathon, and was preparing for a more energetic campaign in Greece when he died, and left his dominion and his wars to Xerxes. No order was issued during his reign for the rebuilding of the *city* of Jerusalem. All his edicts pertain to the original grant of Cyrus—the permission to build the *temple*.

(*f*) *Xerxes I.* The career of Xerxes is well known. He was distinguished for gluttony, voluptuousness, and cruelty. He is celebrated for his invasion of Greece, for the check which he met at Thermopylæ, and for the overthrow of his naval forces at Salamis by Themistocles. In the twenty-first year of his reign he was murdered by Artabanus, commander of his life-guard. He died in the year 464 B.C. According to Jahn, it is probable that "the Artaxerxes of Ezra, who is mentioned next after Darius Hystaspis, and the Ahasuerus of Esther, are names of Xerxes I." If so, it was under him that the second caravan of Jews went to Judea, under the direction of Ezra (Ezra vii.) Xerxes, if he was the prince referred to, gave Ezra an ample commission in regard to the temple at Jerusalem, granting him full power to do all that was necessary to maintain public worship there, and committing to him the vessels of gold and silver in Babylon, pertaining to the temple, &c. The decree may be found in Ezra vii. 13–26. This decree, however, relates wholly to the temple—the "house of God." There was no order for rebuilding the city, and there is no evidence that anything material was done *in* building the city, or the walls. Respecting this reign, Jahn remarks, "The Hebrew colony in Judea seems never to have been in a very flourishing condition. The administration of justice was particularly defective, and neither civil nor religious institutions were firmly established. Accordingly, the king gave permission anew for all Hebrews to emigrate to Judea," p. 172. Ezra made the journey with the caravan in three months; deposited the precious gifts in the temple, caused the Scriptures to be read and explained; commenced a moral reformation, but did nothing, so far as appears, in reconstructing the city—for his commission did not extend to that.

(g) *Artaxerxes Longimanus.* According to Jahn, he began to reign B.C. 464, and reigned forty years and three months. It was during his reign that Nehemiah lived, and that he acted as governor of Judea. The colony in Judea, says Jahn, which had been so flourishing in the time of Ezra, had greatly declined, in consequence of the fact that Syria and Phœnicia had been the rendezvous of the armies of Artaxerxes. " Nehemiah, the cup-bearer of Artaxerxes, learned the unhappy state of the Hebrews, B.C. 444, from a certain Jew named Hanani, who had come from Judea to Shushan with a caravan. Of the regulations introduced by Esra 478 B.C. there was little remaining, and, amid the confusions of war, the condition of the Jews continually grew worse. This information so affected Nehemiah that the king observed his melancholy, and inquiring its cause, he appointed him governor of Judea, *with full power to fortify Jerusalem,* and thus to secure it from the disasters to which unprotected places are always exposed in time of war. Orders were sent to the royal officers west of the Euphrates *to assist in the fortification of the city,* and to furnish the requisite timber from the king's forest; probably on Mount Libanus, near the sources of the river Kadisha, as that was the place celebrated for its cedars. Thus commissioned, Nehemiah journeyed to Judea, accompanied by military officers and cavalry," pp. 175, 176. Jahn further adds, "as soon as Nehemiah, on his arrival in Palestine, had been acknowledged governor of Judea by the royal officers, he made known his preparations for fortifying Jerusalem to the

elders who composed the Jewish council. All the heads of houses, and the high-priest Eliashib, engaged zealously in the work. The chiefs of the Samaritans, Sanballat, Tobiah, and Geshem, endeavoured to thwart their undertaking by insults, by malicious insinuations that it was a preparation for revolt, by plots, and by threats of a hostile attack. The Jews, notwithstanding, proceeded earnestly in their business, armed the labourers, protected them still further by a guard of armed citizens, and at length happily completed the walls of their city." We have reached a point, then, in the history of the kings of Persia, when there was a distinct order to restore and fortify Jerusalem, and when there was an express expedition undertaken to accomplish this result. In the history of these kings, as reported by Jahn, this is the *first* order that would seem to correspond with the language of Daniel—"the commandment to restore and rebuild Jerusalem," and the assertion that "the street should be built again, and the wall, even in troublous times." It may be well, therefore, to pause here, and to look more distinctly at this order of Artaxerxes Longimanus, and inquire into its conformity with the language of Daniel. The circumstances, then, as stated in the book of Nehemiah, are these: (a) Nehemiah learned from Hanani the state of his brethren in Judea, and the fact that the "walls of the city were broken down, and that the gates were burned with fire," and that the people who were at Jerusalem were in a state of "great affliction and reproach," and gave himself to weeping, and fasting, and prayer, on that account, Neh. i. (b) On coming into the presence of Artaxerxes, to perform the usual duty of presenting the wine to the king, the king saw the sadness and distress of Nehemiah, and inquired the cause, Neh. ii. 1, 2. This, Nehemiah (ii. 1) is careful to remark occurred in the twentieth year of his reign. (c) He states distinctly, that it was because Jerusalem was still in ruins: "Why should not my countenance be sad, when *the city,* the place of my fathers' sepulchres, *lieth waste,* and the gates thereof are consumed with fire?" Neh. ii. 3. (*d*) The *request* of Nehemiah, in accordance with the language in Daniel, was, that he might be permitted to go to Jerusalem and *rebuild the city:* "And I said unto the king, If it please the king, and if thy servant have found favour in thy sight, that thou wouldst send me unto Judah, *unto the city of my fathers' sepulchres, that I may build it,*" Neh. ii. 5. (*e*) The edict of Artaxerxes contemplated the same thing which is foretold by the angel to Daniel: "And a letter unto Asaph the keeper of the king's forest, that he may give me timber to make beams for the gates of the palace which appertained to the house, and *for the wall of the city,*" &c., Neh. ii. 8. (*f*) The work which Nehemiah did, under this edict, was that which is supposed in the prediction in Daniel. His first work was to go forth by night to survey *the state of the city:* "And I went out by night by the gate of the valley, &c., and viewed the walls of Jerusalem, which were broken down, and the gates thereof were consumed with fire," Neh. ii. 13. His next work was to propose to rebuild these walls again: "Then said I unto them, Ye see the distress that we are in, how Jerusalem lieth waste, and the gates thereof are burned with fire: come, and let us build up the wall of Jerusalem, that we be no more a reproach," ver. 17. The next work was to rebuild those walls, a full description of which we have in the third chapter of Nehemiah, vers. 1–32, and in ch. iv. 1–23. The city was thus fortified. It was built again according to the purpose of Nehemiah, and according to the decree of Artaxerxes. It took its place again *as* a fortified city, and the promised work of restoring and rebuilding it was complete. (*g*) The building of the city and the walls under Nehemiah occurred in just such circumstances as are predicted by Daniel. The angel says, "The wall shall be built again, *even in troublous times.*" Let any one read the account of the rebuilding in Nehemiah—the description of the "troubles" which were produced by the opposition of Sanballat and those associated with him (Neh. iv.), and he will see the

striking accuracy of this expression—an accuracy as entire *as if* it had been employed *after* the event in describing it, instead of having been used *before* in predicting it.

It may confirm this interpretation to make three remarks: (1.) *After* this decree of Artaxerxes there was no order issued by Persian kings pertaining to the restoration and rebuilding of the city. Neither Xerxes II., nor Sogdianus, nor Darius Nothus, nor Artaxerxes Mnemon, nor Darius Ochus, nor Arses, nor Darius Codomanus, issued any decree that corresponded at all with this prediction, or any that related to the rebuilding of Jerusalem. There was no occasion for any, for the work was *done.* (2.) A second remark is, that, in the language of Hengstenberg, "Until the twentieth year of Artaxerxes, the new city of Jerusalem was an open, thinly inhabited village, exposed to all aggressions from its neighbours, sustaining the same relation to the former and the latter city as the huts erected after the burning of a city for the first protection from rain and wind do to those which are still uninjured, or which have been rebuilt."—*Christ.* ii. 381. This is quite apparent from the remarks which have been already made respecting the state of the city. The want of any permission to rebuild the city and the walls; the fact that the permission to return extended only to a right to rebuild the temple; the improbabilities above stated, that the rebuilding of the city in its strength would be allowed when they first returned, and the account which Nehemiah gives of the condition of Jerusalem at the time when he asked leave to go and "build" it, all tend to confirm this supposition. See Hengstenberg, as above, pp. 381–386. (3.) A third remark is, that a confirmation of this may be found in the book of Ecclesiasticus, showing how Nehemiah was regarded in respect to the rebuilding of the city: "And among the elect was Neemias, whose renown is great, who raised up for us the walls that were fallen, and set up the gates and the bars, and raised up our ruins again," ch. xlix. 13. On the other hand, Joshua and Zerubbabel are extolled only as rebuilders of the *temple:* " How shall we magnify Zorobabel? even he was as a signet on the right hand:" " so was Jesus the son of Josedec: who in their time builded *the house* and set up *a holy temple* to the Lord," vers. 11, 12. These considerations make the case clear, it seems to me, that the time referred to—the *terminus a quo*—according to the fair interpretation, was the twentieth year of Artaxerxes. To this we are conducted by the proper and necessary exposition of the *language,* and by the orders actually issued from the Persian court in regard to the temple and city.

If it should be objected—the only objection of importance that has been alleged against it—that this would not meet the inquiry of Daniel; that he was seeking for the time when the captivity would cease, and looking for its termination as predicted by Jeremiah; that it would not console him to be referred to a period so remote as is here supposed—the time of the rebuilding of the city; and, still more, that, not knowing that time, the prophecy would afford *him* no basis of calculation as to the appearing of the Messiah, it may be replied: (*a*) That the prediction contained all the consolation and assurance which Daniel sought—the assurance that the city *would be rebuilt,* and that an order *would go forth* for its restoration. (*b*) That the angel does not *profess* to answer the precise point of the inquiry which Daniel had suggested. The prayer of Daniel was the *occasion* of uttering a higher prophecy than the one which he had been contemplating. (*c*) It is not necessary to suppose that the design was that *Daniel* should be able to compute the exact time when the Messiah would appear. It was sufficient for him if he had the assurance that he *would* appear, and if he were furnished with a basis by which it might be calculated when he would appear, after the order to rebuild the city had gone forth. (*d*) At any rate, the prophecy must have appeared to Daniel to have a much more important meaning than would be implied merely by a direct answer to his prayer—per-

taining to the close of the exile. The prophecy indubitably stretched far into future years. Daniel must have seen at once that it contained an important disclosure respecting future events, and, as it implied that the exile *would* close, and that the city would be rebuilt, and as he had already a sufficient intimation *when* the exile would close, from the prophecies of Jeremiah, we may suppose that the mind of Daniel would rest on this as more than he had desired to know—a revelation far beyond what he anticipated when he set apart this day for special prayer.

The only remaining difficulty as to the time referred to as the beginning of the seventy weeks—the *terminus a quo*—is that of determining the exact chronology of the twentieth year of Artaxerxes—the point from which we are to reckon. The time, however, varies only a few years according to the different estimates of chronology, and not so as materially to affect the result. The following are the principal estimates:—

Jahn	414 B.C.
Hengstenberg	454 „
Hales	414 „
Calmet	449 „
Usher	454 „

It will be seen from this, that the difference in the chronology is, at the greatest, but ten years, and in such a matter, where the ancient records are so indefinite, and so little pains were taken to make exact dates, it cannot perhaps be expected that the time could be determined with exact accuracy. Nor, since the numbers used by the angel are in a sense *round* numbers— " seventy weeks," " sixty-two weeks," " one week," is it necessary to suppose that the time could be made out with the exactness of a year, or a month—though this has been often attempted. It is sufficient if the prediction were *so* accurate and determinate that there could be no doubt, in general, as to the time of the appearing of the Messiah, and so that when he appeared it should be manifest that he was referred to. Hengstenberg, however, supposes that the chronology can be made out with literal accuracy. See *Christ.* ii. 394–408.

Taking the dates above given as the *terminus a quo* of the prophecy—the time from which to reckon the beginning of the sixty-nine weeks to the "Messiah the Prince"—or the four hundred and eighty-three years, we obtain, respectively, the following results:—

The period of 444 B.C., the period of Jahn and Hales, would extend to A.D. 39.
That of 454 B.C., the period of Hengstenberg and Usher, to A.D. 29.
That of 449 B.C., the period of Calmet, to A.D. 34.

It is remarkable how all these periods terminate at *about* the time when the Lord Jesus entered on his work, or assumed, at his baptism, the public office of the Messiah—when he was thirty years of age. It is undeniable that, whichever reckoning be correct, or whatever computation we may suppose to have been employed by the Jews, the expectation would have been excited in the public mind that the Messiah was about to appear at that time. Perhaps the real truth may be seen in a stronger light still by supposing that if a sagacious impostor had resolved to take upon himself the office of the Messiah, and had so shaped his plans as to meet the national expectations growing out of this prediction of Daniel, he would have undoubtedly set up his claims at *about* the time when the Lord Jesus publicly appeared as the Messiah. According to the common chronologies, there would not have been a variance of more than nine years in the calculation, and, perhaps, after all, when we consider how little the chronology of ancient times has been regarded or settled, it is much more to be wondered at that there should be so great accuracy than that the time is not more certainly determined. If, notwithstanding the confusion of ancient dates, the time is so *nearly* determined with accuracy, is it not rather to be presumed that if the facts of ancient history could be ascertained, the exact period would be found to have been predicted by the angel?

III. The next point properly is, what is the time referred to by the phrase "*unto* the Messiah the Prince" —the *terminus ad quem*. Here there

can be but two opinions—that which refers it to his birth, and that which refers it to his public manifestation as the Messiah, or his taking the office upon himself. The remarks under the last head have conducted us to the probability that the latter is intended. Indeed, it is morally certain that this is so, if we have ascertained the *terminus a quo* with accuracy. The only question then is, whether this is the fair construction, or whether the language can properly be so applied. We have seen, in the interpretation of the phrase above, that the grammatical construction of the *language* is such as might, without impropriety, be applied to either event. It remains only to look at the probabilities that the latter was the design. It may be admitted, perhaps, that *before* the event occurred, there might have been some uncertainty on the subject, and that with many, on reading the prophecy, the supposition would be that it referred to the birth of the Messiah. But a careful consideration of all the circumstances of the passage might even then have led to different expectation, and might have shown that the probabilities were that it was the public manifestation of the Messiah that was intended. Those may be regarded as stronger now, and may be such as to leave no reasonable doubt on the mind; that is, we may now see what would not be likely to have been seen then— as in the case of all the prophecies. Among these considerations are the following :—(*a*) Such an interpretation may be, after all, the most probable. If we conceive of one who should have predicted the appearance or coming of Jenghis Khan, or Alaric, or Attila, as conquerors, it would not be unnatural to refer this to their public appearing in that character, as to the time when they became known as such, and still more true would this be of one who should be inaugurated or set apart to a public office. If, for example, there had been a prophecy of Gregory the Great, or Leo X., as *Popes*, it would be most natural, unless there was a distinct reference to their birth, to refer this to their election and consecration *as* Popes, for that would in fact be the period when they appeared as such. (b) In the case of this prophecy, there is no allusion to *the birth* of the Messiah. It is not "to his birth," or "to his incarnation," but "unto the Messiah the Prince;" that is, most manifestly, when he appeared *as* such, and was in fact such. In many instances in the prophecies there are allusions to *the birth* of the Messiah; and so numerous and accurate had they become, that there was a general expectation of the event at about the time when he was actually born. But, in the passage before us, the language is that which would be used on the supposition that the designed reference was to his entering as Messiah on the functions of his office, and *not* such as would have been so naturally employed if the reference had been to his birth. (c) His taking upon himself the office of the Messiah by baptism and by the descent of the Holy Spirit on him was, in fact, the most prominent event in his work. Before that, he had passed his life in obscurity. The work which he did *as* Messiah was commenced at that time, and was to be dated from that period. In fact, he was not the Messiah, as such, till he was set apart to the office — any more than an heir to a crown is king until he is crowned, or an elected chief-magistrate is president before he has taken the oath of office. The position which he occupied was, that he was designated or destined for the office of the Messiah, but had not, in fact, entered on it, and could not as yet be spoken of as such. (d) This is the usual method of recording the reign of a king—not from his birth, but from his coronation. Thus, in the table above, respecting the Persian kings, the periods included are those from the beginning of the reign, not from the birth to the decease. So in all statutes and laws, as when we say the first of George III., or the second of Victoria, &c. (e) To these considerations may be added an argument stated by Hengstenberg, which seems to make the proof irrefragable. It is in the following words:—"After the course of seventy weeks shall the whole work of salvation, to be performed by the Mes-

siah, be completed; after sixty-nine weeks, and, as it appears from the more accurate determination in ver, 27, in the middle of the seventieth, he shall be cut off. As now, according to the passage before us, sixty-nine weeks shall elapse before the Messiah, there remains from that event to the completion of salvation only a period of seven, until his violent death, of three and a half years; a certain proof that ' unto the Messiah ' must refer, not to his birth, but to the appearance of the Messiah as such."—*Christ.* ii. 337.

IV. The next question then is, whether, according to this estimate, the time can be made out with any degree of accuracy. The date of the decrees of Artaxerxes are found to be, according to the common reckoning of chronologists, either 444, or 454, or 449 B.C. The addition of 483 years to them we found also to reach, respectively, to A.D. 39, to A.D. 29, and to A.D. 34. One of these (29) varies scarcely at all from the time when the Saviour was baptized, at thirty years of age; another (34) varies scarcely at all from the time when he was put to death; and either of them is so accurate that the mind of any one who should have made the estimate when the command to build the city went forth, would have been directed with great precision to the expectation of the true time of his appearance; and to those who lived when he *did* appear, the time was so accurate that, in the reckoning of any of the prevailing methods of chronology, it would have been sufficiently clear to lead them to the expectation that he was about to come. Two or three remarks, however, may be made in regard to this point. (a) One is, that it is now, perhaps, impossible to determine with *precise* accuracy the historical period of events so remote. Time was not then measured as accurately as it is now; current events were not as distinctly recorded; chronological tables were not kept as they are now; there was no uniform method of determining the length of the year, and the records were much less safely kept. This is manifest, because, even in so important an event as the issuing of the command to rebuild the city in the time of Artaxerxes—an event which it would be supposed was one of sufficient moment to have merited an exact record, at least among the Jews. There is now, among the best chronologists, a difference of ten years as to the computation of the time. (b) There is a variation arising from the difference of the lunar or the solar year—some nations reckoning by the one, and some by the other—and the difference between them, in the period now under consideration, would be greater than that which now occurs in the ordinary reckonings of chronology. (c) Till the exact length of the *year*, as then understood, is ascertained, there can be no hope of fixing the time with the exactness of a month or a day ; and if the usual and general understanding of the length of the year be adopted, then the time here referred to would be so intelligible that there would be no difficulty in ascertaining at about what time the Messiah was to appear, or when he did appear in determining that it was he. This was all that was really necessary in regard to the prophecy. (d) Yet it has been supposed that the time can be made out, even under these disadvantages, with almost entire accuracy. The examination in the case may be seen at length in Hengstenberg, *Chris.* ii. 394–408. It is agreed on all hands that the commencement of the reign of Xerxes occurred in the year 485 before Christ, and that Artaxerxes died in 423. The difference concerns only the beginning of the reign of Artaxerxes. If that occurred in the year 464 B.C., then the problem is solved, for then the decree of the twentieth year of Artaxerxes would occur 444 B.C. ; and if 483 be added to that, the result is A.D. 29—a difference, then, even in reckoning whole years and round numbers, of only one year between that and the time when Jesus was baptized by John. The full proof of this point, about the beginning of the reign of Artaxerxes, may be seen in Hengstenberg, as above. The argument, though long, is so important, and so clear, that it may without impropriety be inserted in this place :—

"According to the prophecy, the terminus a quo, the twentieth year of Artaxerxes, is separated from the *terminus ad quem*, the public appearance of Christ, by a period of sixty-nine weeks of years, or four hundred and eighty-three years. If, now, we compare history with this, it must appear, even to the most prejudiced, in the highest degree remarkable, that, among all the current chronological determinations of this period, not one differs over ten years from the testimony of the prophecy. This wonder must rise to the highest pitch, when it appears from an accurate examination of these determinations, that the only one among them which is correct makes the prophecy and history correspond with each other even to a year.

"Happily, to attain this end, we are not compelled to involve ourselves in a labyrinth of chronological inquiries. We find ourselves, in the main, on sure ground. All chronologists agree, that the commencement of the reign of Xerxes falls in the year 485 before Christ, the death of Artaxerxes, in the year 423. The difference concerns only the year of the commencement of the reign of Artaxerxes. Our problem is completely solved, when we have shown that this falls in the year 474 before Christ. For then the twentieth year of Artaxerxes is the year 455 before Christ, according to the usual reckoning.[*]   = 299 U.C.

Add to this, 483 years.

782 U.C.

"We should probably have been saved the trouble of this investigation, had not the error of an acute man, and the want of independence in his successors, darkened what was in itself clear. According to Thucydides, Artaxerxes began to reign shortly before the flight of Themistocles to Asia. Deceived by certain specious arguments, hereafter to be examined, Dodwell, in the *Annall. Thucyd.*, placed both events in the year 465 before Christ. The thorough refutation of Vitringa, in the cited treatise, remained, strange as it may appear, unknown to the philologians and historians, even as it seems to those of Holland, as Wesseling. The view of Dodwell, adopted also by Corsini in the *Fasta Attica*, became the prevailing one, at which we cannot wonder, when we consider how seldom, in modern times, chronological investigations in general have been fundamental and independent ; when *e.g.*, we observe that Poppo, a generally esteemed recent editor of Thucydides, in a thick volume, entitled, *In Thucydidem Commentarii politici, geograph., chronologici*, furnishes, in reference to the last, nothing more than a reprint of the school edition of the chronological tables collected from Dodwell, excusing himself with an *odio quodam, inveterato totius hujus disciplinæ !* Clinton also (*Fasti Hellenici, lat. vert. Krüger*, Leipz., 1830), though he clearly perceives that Dodwell has confused the whole chronology of this period (comp., *e.g.*, p. 248–253), has not been able to free himself from him in the most important points, though he successfully opposed him in several ; and thus the confusion only becomes still greater, since now neither the actual chronological succession of events, nor the one ingeniously invented by Dodwell, any longer remains. Nevertheless, the truth is advanced by this increased confusion. For now the harmony introduced by Dodwell into the fictitious history is destroyed. The honour, however, of having again discovered the true path, belongs to Krüger alone, who, after more than a hundred years, as an entirely independent inquirer, coincides with Vitringa, in the same result, and in part in the employment of the same arguments. In the acute treatise, *Ueber den Cimonischen Frieden* (in the *Archiv f. Philologie und Pädagog. von Seebode*, I. 2, p. 205, ff.) he places the death of Xerxes in the year 474 or 473, and the flight of Themistocles a year later. This treatise may serve to shame those who reject in the mass the grounds of our opinion (to the establishment of which we now proceed), with the re-

mark, that the author has only found what he sought. Whoever does not feel capable of entering independently upon the investigation, should at least be prevented from condemning, by the circumstance, that a learned man, who has no other design in view than to elucidate a chronologically confused period of Grecian history, gives, for the event which serves to determine the *terminus a quo* of our prophecy, the precise year, which places prophecy and fulfilment in the most exact harmony.

"We examine first the grounds which seem to favour the opinion, that the reign of Artaxerxes commenced in the year 465. (1.) ' The flight of Themistocles must precede the transfer of the dominion of Greece from Athens to Sparta by several years. For this happened during the siege of Byzantium, when the treasonable efforts of Pausanias first commenced ; the flight of Themistocles, however, was a consequence of the complaint, which was raised against him, out of the documents found after the death of Pausanias. But Isocrates says, in the *Panathenaikos*, that the dominion of the Lacedemonians had endured ten years. The expedition of Xerxes, taken as the *terminus a quo*, this transfer falls in the year 470.' But we may spare ourselves the labour which Vitringa takes to invalidate this alleged testimony of Isocrates, since all recent scholars, in part independent of one another, agree that Isocrates speaks of a ten years' dominion, not before, but after that of the Athenians ; compare Coray on *Pan.* c. 19 ; Dahlmann, *Forschungen*, I. p. 45 ; Krüger, p. 221 ; Clinton, p. 250, ff. (2.) That Themistocles in the year 472 was still in Athens, Corsini infers (*Fasti Att.* III. p. 180) from *Æl.* lib. 9, c. 5. According to this, Themistocles sent back Hiero, who was coming to the Olympic games, asserting that, whoever had not taken part in the greatest danger, could not be a sharer of the joy. (The fact is also related by Plutarch.) Now as Hiero, Ol. 75, 3 (478), began to reign, only the Ol. 77 (472) could be intended. But who does not at once perceive that the reference to the games of the Ol. 76 (476) was far more obvious, since the occurrence pre-supposed that the μέγιστος τῶν κινδύνων was still fresh in remembrance? (3.) According to this supposition, Xerxes would reign only eleven years; Artaxerxes, on the contrary, fifty-one. This is in opposition to the testimony of the *Can. Ptolem.* (comp. thereon Ideler, I. p. 109, ff.), which gives to Xerxes twenty-one, and to Artaxerxes forty-one years, and of Ctesias, who gives to Artaxerxes forty-two years, and of some other writers; comp. the passages in Bähr on Ctesias, p. 184. *Ceteris paribus*, this argument would be wholly decisive. But when other weighty authorities are opposed to it, it is not of itself sufficient to outweigh them. The canon has high authority, only where it rests on astronomical observations, which is here not the case. Otherwise it stands on the same ground as all other historical sources. The whole error was committed, as soon as only an ιά in an ancient authority was confounded with a κά; for when a reign of twenty-one years had thus been attributed to Xerxes, the shortening of the reign of Artaxerxes to forty-one years necessarily followed. Wesseling (on Diod. 12, 64) attributes forty-five years to Artaxerxes, thus without hesitation rejecting the authority of the canon. To these arguments, already adduced by others, we subjoin the following. (4.) It seems to be evident from Ctesias, ch. 20, that Artaxerxes was born a considerable time after the commencement of the reign of Xerxes. Ctesias, after relating it, proceeds— γαμεῖ δὲ Ξέρξης Ὀνόφα θυγατέρα Ἄμιστριν καὶ γίνεται αὐτῷ παῖς Δαρειαῖος, καὶ ἕτερος μετὰ δύο ἔτη Ὑστασπης, καὶ ἔτι Ἀρταξέρξης. If he relates the events in the true chronological order, Artaxerxes in the year 474 could at most have been seven years old. On the contrary, however, all accounts agree, that at the death of Xerxes, although still young (comp. Justin, 3, 1), he was yet of a sufficient age to be capable of reigning himself. We must not be satisfied with the answer that it is very improbable that Xerxes, who was born at the beginning of the thirty-sixth year of the reign of Darius (comp. Herod. 7, 2), and was already thirty-four or thirty-five years old at his death, was

not married until so late a period. Ctesias himself frees us from the embarrassment into which we were thrown by his inaccuracy. According to chap. 22, Megabyzus was already married, before the expedition against Greece, with a daughter of Xerxes, who, already mentioned (ch. 20), if Ctesias is there chronologically accurate, could not have been born before that time. According to ch. 28, Megabyzus, immediately after the return of Xerxes from Greece, complained to him of the shameful conduct of this wife of his. (5.) There can be no doubt that the Ahasuerus of the book of Esther is the same as Xerxes. But the twelfth year of this king is there expressly mentioned, ch. iii. 7, and the events related in the following context fall, in part, about the end of the same year. But this difficulty vanishes, as soon as we include the years of the co-regency of Xerxes with Darius. According to the full account in Herodot. 7, ch. 2–4, Xerxes, two years before the death of Darius, was established by him as king: comp. *e.g.* ch. 4—ἀπέδιξε δὲ βασιλῆα Πέρσῃσι Δαρεῖος Ξέρξεα. Of the custom of the Hebrew writers to include the years of a co-regency, where it existed, we have a remarkable example in the account concerning Nebuchadnezzar (comp. Bietr. I. p. 63). But we find even in the book of Esther itself plain indications of this mode of reckoning. The account of the great feast (ch. i.) is placed in its true light by this supposition. The occasion of it was the *actual* commencement of the reign of Xerxes, though we need not on this account exclude, what has hitherto been regarded as the exclusive object, consultations with the nobles respecting the expeditions about to be undertaken. What is related (ch. ii. 16) then falls precisely in the time of the return of Xerxes from Greece, while otherwise, and this is attended with difficulty, about two years after that event.

"We now proceed to lay down the positive grounds for our view; and in the first place, the immediate, and then the mediate proofs, which latter are far more numerous and strong, since they show that the flight of Themistocles, which must precede the reign of Artaxerxes, cannot possibly be placed later than 473 before Christ.

"To the first class belong the following: — 1. It must appear very strange to those who assume a twenty-one years' reign of Xerxes, that the whole period from the eleventh year is a complete *tabula rasa*. The Biblical accounts stop short at the close of the tenth year. Ctesias relates only one inconsiderable event after the Grecian war (ch. 28), which occurred immediately after its termination. No later writer has ventured to introduce anything into the ten years, which, according to our view, the permutation of an ι and κ adds to his age.

"2. We possess a twofold testimony, which places the return of Xerxes from Greece, and his death, in so close connection, that, without rejecting it, we cannot possibly assume a fifteen years' reign after this return, but are rather compelled to place his death not beyond the year 474. The first is that of Ælian, *Var. Hist.* 13, 3: εἴτα ἐπανελθὼν, αἴσχιστα ἀνθρώπων ἀπέθανεν, ἀποσφαγεὶς νύκτωρ ἐν τῇ εὐνῇ ὑπὸ τοῦ υἱοῦ. The second, that of Justin, 3, 1: 'Xerxes rex Persarum, terror antea gentium, bello in Græciam infeliciter gesto, etiam suis contemtui esse cœpit. Quippe Artabanus præfectus ejus, deficiente quotidie regis majestate, in spem regni adductus, cum septem robustissimis filiis,' &c.

"3. The testimonies of Justin, l. c., respecting the age of his sons at his death, are not reconcilable with the twenty-one years' reign of Xerxes: 'Securior de Artaxerxe, puero admodum, fingit regem a Dario, qui erat adolescens, quo maturius regno potiretur, occisum.' If Xerxes reigned twenty-one years, his firstborn, Darius, according to a comparison of Ctesias (ch. 22), could not at his death have been an *adolescens*, but at least thirty-one years old. On the contrary, if eleven years' reign be assumed, these determinations are entirely suitable. Darius was then towards twenty-one years old; Artaxerxes, according to Ctesias (ch. 20), near four years younger than Darius, about seventeen. This determination shows also that it cannot be objected against a fifty-one

years' reign of Artaxerxes that it would give him too great an age. The suggestion can be refuted by the simple remark, that the length of his life remains exactly the same, whether he reigned fifty-one or forty-one years. If he ascended the throne at seventeen, his life terminated at sixty-eight.

"4. According to the most numerous and weighty testimonies, the peace of Cimon was probably concluded after the battle of the Eurymedon (before Christ 470). Now, as all agree that this peace was concluded with Artaxerxes, the commencement of his reign must, in any event, be placed before 470. Comp. Krüger, l. c., p. 218.

"5. The history of Nehemiah is scarcely reconcilable with the supposition that Artaxerxes reigned only forty-seven years. After Nehemiah had accomplished all that is related in ch. i.–xii. of his book, he returned to Persia to discharge the duties of his office, at court. This happened, according to xiii. 6, in the thirty-second year of Artaxerxes. The time of his return is not accurately determined. It says merely, after a considerable time, the לְקֵץ יָמִים. That his absence, however, must have continued a whole series of years, appears from the relation of that which took place in the mean time. The law against marriage with foreign women, to the observance of which the people had bound themselves anew, ch. x. 30, was first violated during his absence; then again, by a decree of the people, executed in all severity, xiii. 1–3; and then again broken, as appears from the fact that Nehemiah, at his return, according to ver. 23, found a great many foreign women in the colony. That these marriages had already existed for some time appears from ver. 24, where it is said that the children of them had spoken half in the language of Ashdod, and could not speak Hebrew. A long absence is also implied in the other abuses which Nehemiah, according to ch. xiii. 10, *seq.*, found on his return. He saw the fruits of the former labours almost destroyed. The same is also evident from the prophecies of Malachi, which were delivered exactly in the time between the two periods of Nehemiah's presence at Jerusalem: comp. Vitringa's excellent *Dissert. de Ætate Mal.*, in his *Obss. ss.* vi. 7, t. 2, p. 353, *seq.* The condition of the people appears here, as it could have been only after they had already been deprived, for a considerable time, of their two faithful leaders, Ezra, who, having arrived thirteen years earlier, had co-operated for a considerable time with Nehemiah, and Nehemiah himself. But, if we consider barely the first-mentioned fact, the marriages with foreign women, it will be evident that a longer period than nine years would be required. For each change there will then only three years be allowed; and as this is undeniably too little for the third, according to ver. 24, the two first must be still more shortened, which is inadmissible. Besides, we do not even have nine years for these events, if the reign of Artaxerxes is fixed at forty-one years. For the relation of Nehemiah pre-supposes that Artaxerxes was yet living at the time of its composition. This, however, cannot be placed in the time immediately after the return of Nehemiah, since it must have been preceded by the abolition of all these abuses. If, however, we are conducted by the authority of Nehemiah, which is liable to no exception, since he was contemporary and closely connected with Artaxerxes, a few years over forty-one, we have gained much. For then the only objection to our determination, the testimony of the canon, is completely set aside.

"We must premise a remark, before we bring forward our indirect proofs, in order to justify the connection in which we place the commencement of the reign of Artaxerxes with the flight of Themistocles. This connection has not, indeed, the unanimous testimony of the ancient writers in its favour. The vouchers for it are, Thucydides (ch. 137), where it is said of Themistocles, who had come into Asia, ἐσπέμπει γράμματα ἐς βασιλέα Ἀρταξέρξην τὸν Ξέρξου, νεωστὶ βασιλεύοντα, and Charon of Lampsacus, who, according to Plutarch (*Them.* ch. 27), makes him in like manner fly to Artaxerxes. On the contrary, others, as Ephorus, Di-

non, Klitarch, and Heraclides (comp. Plut. l. c.), represent him as going to Xerxes. If, now, we examine these testimonies, according to the authorities of the witnesses the decision will unquestionably be in favour of that of Thucydides and Charon. Thucydides was contemporary with Artaxerxes, and was born about the time of the flight of Themistocles. This prince of Greek historians gives (ch. 97) as the cause why he relates the events between the Median and Peloponnesian war, that all his predecessors had passed over these events in silence, and that the only one who touched upon them, Hellanicus, βραχέως τε καὶ τοῖς χρόνοις οὐκ ἀκριβῶς ἐπεμνήσθη them, from which it is evident, first, how little certain are the accounts of this period in later authors, because they can have no credible contemporary voucher, since he could not have been unknown to Thucydides ; and, secondly, that Thucydides himself claims to be regarded as a careful and accurate historian of this period, and therefore must be esteemed such, because so honest a man would assume nothing to himself which did not belong to him. The other witness, Charon, was the less liable to err, since, at the very time of this event, he was a writer of history, and even lived in Asia. On the other hand, the oldest witnesses for the opposite supposition lived more than a century after the event. Ephorus (see on his *Akrisic*, Dahlmann) outlived the dominion of Alexander in Asia; Dinon was father of Klitarch, who accompanied Alexander.

"In weighing these grounds, the authority of Thucydides and Charon was unhesitatingly followed in ancient times. Plutarch (l. c.) does this, with the remark, that the testimony of Thucydides agrees better with the chronological works. Nepos says : '*Scio plerosque ita scripsisse, Themistoclem Xerxe regnante in Asiam transiisse: sed ego potissimum Thucydidi credo, quod ætate proximus de his, qui illorum temporum historias reliquerunt et ejusdem civitatis fuit.*' Suidas, and the Scholiast on *Aristoph. Equites*, from which the former borrowed *verbatim* his second article on Themistocles, makes him flee, πρὸς τὸν Ἀρταξέρξην, τὸν Ξέρξου τοῦ Πέρσου παῖδα, without even mentioning the other supposition. And in this respect, we have the less fear of contradiction, since, as far as we know, all modern critics, without exception, follow Thucydides and Charon. We only still remark that the opposite view can the more easily be rejected, since its origin can so readily be explained, either from the fact that this event fell on the border of the reign of Xerxes and of Artaxerxes, or from a simple confounding of the two names, the assumption of which is more easy the more frequently it occurs; we find it even in Aristotle, the contemporary of those writers, *Pol.* 5, 8, and twice in Ctesias, ch. 35, where Bähr would make a change in opposition to all the manuscripts, and chap. 44. Comp. Bähr on the passage, and Reimarus on *Dio Cass.* II. p. 1370. Finally, the error might arise also from the circumstance that the flight of Themistocles was placed in the right year; but twenty-one years were attributed to Xerxes, from which it necessarily follows that he took refuge with Xerxes. This last opinion is favoured by the coincidence of several contemporary writers in the same error, which presupposes some plausible reason for it.

"We now proceed to lay down our indirect proofs. (1.) We begin with the testimony which gives precisely the year of the flight of Themistocles, that of Cicero, *Læl.* ch. 12. It is true, Corsini, l. c. 3, p. 180, asserts, that Cicero speaks of the year in which Themistocles was banished from Athens; but we need only examine the passage to be convinced of the contrary: '*Themistocles—fecit idem, quod viginti annis ante apud nos fecerat Coriolanus.*' The flight of Coriolanus to the Volci falls in the year 263 U.C., B.C. 492. The flight of Themistocles is accordingly placed by Cicero in the year 472, a year later than by us, which is of no importance, since the round number twenty was the more suitable to the object of Cicero, as the more accurate nineteen, for the chronologists. If Dodwell's view were correct, there would be the space of twenty-seven years between the two events.

"2. Diodorus Siculus, who (11, 55) places the flight of Themistocles in Ol. 77, 2 (B.C. 471), in any event favours our determination, which ascends only two years higher, far more than the opposite one. We remark, however, that he also places in the same year the residence of Themistocles at Magnesia, and his death; and thus it is evident that, whether by mistake or design, he compresses the events in the life of Themistocles, which filled up some years, into the year of his death. If this took place in the year 471, the flight must be dated at least as far back as 473. Our determination differs only a single year from that of Eusebius, who relates the flight of Themistocles in Ol. 77, 1.

"3. But that which forms the chief argument, the whole series of transactions, as they have been recorded in accurate order, especially by Thucydides, compels us without reserve to place the flight of Themistocles not below the year 473. That the expedition of the allied Greeks under the direction of Pausanias, against Cyprus and Byzantium, the capture of the latter city, and the transfer of the supremacy from the Lacedemonians to the Athenians, occasioned by the insolence of Pausanias, fall in the year 477, we may regard as established beyond dispute by Clinton, p. 270, *seq.*[*] The view of O. Müller (*Dorier*, ii. p. 498), who distributes these events into a period of five years, is contradicted by the expression ἐν τῇδε τῇ ἡγεμονίᾳ of Thucydides, ch. 94, whereby the capture of Byzantium is brought into the same year with the expedition against Cyprus. That these words cannot be connected with what follows, without a change of the text in opposition to all critical authority, is shown by Poppo. Moreover, the very last of these events is placed, by the unanimous testimony of antiquity, in the year 477.

---

[*] The grounds are thus briefly summed up by Win., p. 252: "Dodwelli rationi neutiquam favet Isocratis auctoritas. Repugnat rerum gestarum series, repugnat quod Thucyd. significat, Plutarchus et Aristides diserte tradunt, repugnat denique temporis spatium, quod Atheniensium imperio assignant Lysias, Isocrates ipse, Plato, Demosthenes, Aristides, quibus fortasse addendus est Lycurgus."

Clinton shows, p. 249, that all reckonings of the time of the supremacy of
the Athenians, setting out from this
year, differ from one another only in
reference to the assumed termination.
Also, Thucyd. ch. 128, the expedition
against Cyprus, and that against Byzantium, are connected as immediately
succeeding each other. If, however,
Dodwell were compelled by the force
of the arguments to acknowledge that
these events, which he compresses into
one year, do not, as he assumes (p. 61),
belong to the year 470, but to the year
477, he would surely be compelled,
perceiving it to be impossible to lengthen
out the thread of the events until the
year 465, to give up the whole hypothesis. The dissatisfaction of the allies
was followed by the recal of Pausanias.
That this belongs still to the same year
plainly appears, partly from the nature
of the case itself, since it pre-supposes
a continuance of supremacy, partly
from Thucydides, ch. 95: ἐν τούτῳ δὲ οἱ
Λακεδαιμόνιοι μετεπέμποντο Παυσανίαν
ἀνακρινοῦντες ὧν περὶ ἐπυνθάνοντο. Pausanias having come to Sparta, and been
there set at liberty, now betook himself privately in a galley to Byzantium.
This cannot have happened long afterwards, for Thucydides, ch. 128, immediately subjoins it, and what is of
the most importance, Pausanias finds
the fleet still at Byzantium. That his
residence there did not long continue
appears from the account of Thucydides, ch. 131, that he was forcibly expelled thence by the Athenians. He
now retired to the colony in Troas ;
from there he was recalled to Sparta,
after it had been reported that he kept
up an understanding with the barbarians. The Ephori threw him into
prison, but soon after released him.
At this time his intercourse with Themistocles took place, who, being at the
time already expelled from Athens,
resided at Argos, and thence made ex-
cursions into the rest of the Peloponnesus. That Pausanias then for the
first time drew Themistocles into his
plan, when the latter had been driven
from Athens, is asserted by Plutarch,
and a personal intercourse between
them is rendered certain by all accounts.
That there was no considerable period

between this release of Pausanias and
his death is clear. Pausanias was not
condemned, because there was no
certain proof against him. It is,
however, psychologically improbable
that he did not soon afford it, that
he prudently kept himself from giving
open offence for a series of years,
when we consider that he was deprived of all prudence by his haughtiness, arising to madness; that he
himself rendered the execution of his
treasonable plan impossible ; that, according to Thucydides, ch. 130, he
went about in a Median dress, and
caused himself to be accompanied on
a journey through Thrace with Median
and Egyptian satellites, spread a Persian table, made difficult the access to
his person, gave free course to his
passions, of whom Thucydides himself
very significantly remarks, καὶ κατέχειν
τὴν διάνοιαν οὐκ ἠδύνατο ἀλλ' ἔργοις βραχέσι
προυδήλου, ἃ τῇ γνώμῃ μειζόνως ἐπέπειτα
ἔμελλε πράξειν, and of whose senseless
arrogance the same historian, ch. 132,
gives an example, even out of the time
immediately after the battle of Platea.
The discovery was effected by him who
was to bring to Artabazus the last letters to the king. With what haste the
transactions were carried on, and that
by no means a space of four years was
consumed, is evident from the fact
that the king, in order to accelerate
them, had expressly sent Artabazus to
Asia Minor. His death immediately
followed the discovery (comp. Thucyd.
133). We surely do not assume too
little when we give to these events a
period of three years. That we need
not go beyond this is shown by Diodorus, who compresses all these events
into the year 477 (Ol. 75, 4). How
could he have done this, or how could
such an error have arisen, if the beginning and end had been separated
from each other by a period of eight
or nine years? How impossible it
was for him, with his sources, to place
the destruction of Pausanias far beyond this time appears from his fiction,
which can in no other way be explained,
of a twofold accusation of Themistocles. If, now, we must place the death
of Pausanias about the year 474, and
in no event later, the flight of Themis-

tocles cannot be placed farther back than the year 473. For Themistocles, at the death of Pausanias, had already been a considerable time in the Peloponnesus. His accusation followed immediately after the event (comp. Thucydides, I. 135); and the combined interests of the Lacedemonians, to whom nothing could be more desirable than to have the Athenians share their disgrace, and of the enemies of Themistocles at Athens (Plut. *Them.* c. 23: κατεβίων μὲν αὐτοῦ Λακεδαιμόνιοι, κατηγόρουν δ' οἱ φθονοῦντες τῶν πολιτῶν), would cause the decision to be hastened as much as possible. Themistocles, persecuted both by the Athenians and Lacedemonians, now flees from the Peloponnesus to Corcyra. Being denied a residence there, he retires to the opposite continent. In danger of being overtaken by his persecutors (Thucyd. ch. 136: καὶ διωκόμενος ὑπὸ τῶν προστεταγμένων κατὰ πύστιν ἢ χωρείη), he sees himself compelled to flee to Admetus, the king of the Molossians. Nor can he have long resided there, for, according to Thucydides, ch. 137, he was sent forward by Admetus, as soon as his persecutors came. And how can we suppose that they would have been long behind him? How long could his place of residence have remained a secret? It is expressly said by Thucydides, that the coming of his persecutors, and the flight of Themistocles to Asia, very soon happened (ὕστερον οὐ πολλῷ). It is true, that if we could credit the account of Stesimbrotus, in Plut. ch. 24, we must assume that the residence of Themistocles with Admetus continued some months; for he related that his friends brought to him there his wife and children, whom they had secretly conducted out of Athens. But that no dependence is to be placed upon this is evident from the absurd fiction of Stesimbrotus that immediately follows, which, to the surprise even of Plutarch (εἶτ' οὐκ οἶδ' ὅπως ἐπιλαθόμενος τούτων, ἢ τὸν Θεμιστοκλέα ποιῶν ἐπιλαθόμενον, πλεῖσαί φησιν, κ. τ. λ.), he brings forward, without observing that the one fable does away the other —viz., that Themistocles was sent by Admetus to Sicily, and had desired of

Hiero his daughter in marriage, with the promise to bring Greece under subjection to him. Plutarch designates Stesimbrotus as a shameless liar, Pericles, ch. 13. That the sons of Themistocles remained in Athens is manifest from a relation in Suidas, and the testimony of Thucydides, ch. 137, and of Plutarch, that the gold was first sent to Themistocles by his friends after his arrival in Asia, to enable him to reward the service of the captain who brought him to Asia, shows at the same time the incorrectness of the assertion of Stesimbrotus, and confirms the opinion that Themistocles remained in no one place of his flight long enough for his friends to send to him there the necessary gold. Themistocles was conducted by Admetus to Pidna, and from there he betook himself in a boat directly to Asia. This, accordingly, since between the death of Pausanias, and the coming of Themistocles into Asia there could at most be only a year, can at latest have happened in the year 473, perhaps in 474; and even in the former case we are completely justified in placing the beginning of the reign of Artaxerxes, which still cannot have immediately coincided with the coming of Themistocles, in the year 474.

"4. On the supposition that the commencement of the reign of Artaxerxes, and the flight of Themistocles, fall in 465, an extravagant old age must be attributed to Charon of Lampsacus. According to Suidas, he was still flourishing under the first Darius, Ol. 69, 504 B.C. Since now, in his history, he mentions the flight of Themistocles to Artaxerxes, this being placed in 465, he must have been employed in writing history at least forty years. This is not, indeed, absolutely impossible; but, in a doubtful case, it must be rejected as the more improbable alternative. '*Historiæ enim non sunt explicandæ*—says Vitringa (*Proll. in Zach.* p. 29)—*ex raris et insolentibus exemplis, sed ex communi vivendi lege et ordine. Si res secus se habeat, in ipsa historia ascribitur ne fallat incautos.*' Compare his farther excellent remarks on this subject. That this argument is not without force, is evident even from the efforts of some advocates of the false chronology to set it aside by cutting the knot. Suidas, after he has cited the above-mentioned determination of the time of Charon, as he found it in his more ancient authorities, subjoins, μᾶλλον δὲ ἦν ἐπὶ τῶν Περσικῶν. Creuzer, on the *Fragm. Historr. Græc.*, p.95, rejects this date without farther examination, because it gives too great an age to Charon.

"5. According to Thucyd. 1, 136, Themistocles, on his passage to Asia, fell in with the Athenian fleet, which was besieging Naxos. This siege of Naxos, however, according to the testimony of Thucydides, ch. 100, which makes all other arguments superfluous, happened before the great victory of the Athenians on the Eurymedon, which, according to Diodorus, belongs to the year 470, and cannot be placed later, because this was the first considerable undertaking of the Athenians against the Persians, the war with whom formed the only ground for the important requisitions which they made upon their allies. Comp. Thucyd. i. 94. Hitherto, since the supremacy had passed over to the Athenians, scarcely anything had been done against the Persians, except the taking of the unimportant Ægon. Thucydides also leads us to about the same year as that given by Diodorus, who connects the defection of Thasos (467) with χρόνῳ ὕστερον, which cannot stand where events immediately succeed each other. Even for these reasons, the siege of Naxos and the flight of Themistocles, do not fall after 471. If, however, we consider that Naxos was the first confederate city with which the Athenians were involved in discord (comp. Thucyd., p. 1, 98)—which, from the nature of the case, as is rendered especially clear by the remarks of Thucydides and a comparison of the later historians, could scarcely have first happened after seven years—and if we farther consider the way in which Thucydides (ch. 98) connects the events, from the transfer of the supremacy until the capture of Naxos, with one another, we shall, without hesitation, place the latter some years earlier, in the year 474 or 473.

"6. The flight of Themistocles falls at least three years earlier than the battle on the Eurymedon, because in all probability he was dead before the latter event. His death, however, must have been some years subsequent to his coming into Asia (comp. Thucyd. ch. 138). One year passed in learning the language, and some time, in any event, was required for what is implied in ταύτης ἦρχε τῆς χώρας, δόντος, κ. τ. λ. Thucydides relates that, according to the account of some, Themistocles took poison, ἀδύνατον νομίσαντα εἶναι ἐπιτελέσαι βασιλεῖ ἃ ὑπέσχετο. This pre-supposes that Themistocles was compelled to fulfil his promises; and had this not been the case at his death, the report that Thucydides only in this instance relied upon himself could not have arisen. Plutarch expressly connects the death of Themistocles with the expedition of Cimon. This is done by several writers, with the mention of the most special circumstances (compare the passages in Staveren on *Nep. Them.* 10) all of which may be regarded, as they are by Cicero (*Brut.* ch. 11) and Nepos, as fictitious, and yet the historical basis on which alone everything depends, *the fact* that Thucydides died before the battle on the Eurymedon is firmly established.

"7. Krüger (l. c. p. 218) has shown that the account of Plutarch, that Themistocles reached an age of sixty-five years, forbids us to place his death beyond the year 470, and therefore his flight beyond the year 473. According to an account which has internal evidence of credibility, in Ælian, *Var. Hist.* iii. 21, Themistocles, as a small boy coming from school, declined going out of the way of the tyrant Pisistratus. Assuming that this happened in the last year of Pisistratus, B.C. 529, and that Themistocles was at that time six years old, he must have been born in 535, and died in 470. Nor is it a valid objection that, according to Plutarch, Themistocles was still living at the time of the Cyprian expedition of Cimon (449 B.C.), and was still young at the battle of Marathon. For the former rests on a manifest confounding of the former event with the victory over the Persian fleet at Cyprus, which

is supposed to have immediately preceded the victory on the Eurymedon
(comp. Diodor. 11, 60; Dahlmann,
Forschungen, i. p. 69), and the latter
merely on a conclusion drawn from
this error. 'Whoever,' remarks Dahlmann, p. 71, 'reads without prejudice
the passage, Thucyd. 1, 138, will perceive that the death of Themistocles
followed pretty soon after his settle-
ment in Persia; probably in the second
year, if Thucydides is worthy of credit.'
"Until all these arguments are refuted, it remains true that the Messianic interpretation of the prophecy is
the only correct one, and that the alleged pseudo-Daniel, as well as the real
Daniel, possessed an insight into the
future, which could have been given
only by the Spirit of God; and hence,
as this favour could have been shown
to no deceiver, the genuineness of the
book necessarily follows, and the futi-
lity of all objections against it is already
manifest." *

V. The only remaining point of inquiry on this verse is, as to the division
of the whole period of sixty-nine weeks
into two smaller portions of seven weeks
and sixty-two weeks; that is, of the
four hundred and eighty-three years
into one period of four hundred and
thirty-four years, and one of forty-nine
years. This inquiry resolves itself into
another, Whether, after the issuing of
the command in the twentieth year of
Artaxerxes, there was a period of forty-
nine years that was in any manner distinguished from that which followed,
or any *reason* why an epoch should be
made there? If the command in the
twentieth of Artaxerxes was in the year
B.C. 454, then the subtraction of forty-
nine years from this would make the
year 405 B.C. the marked period; that
is, about that time some important
change would occur, or a new series of
affairs would commence which would
properly separate the previous period
from that which followed. Now, the
fair interpretation of this passage respecting the seven weeks, or forty-nine
years, undoubtedly is, that that time
would be required in rebuilding the
city, and in settling its affairs on a

* *Christ.* ii. 394-408.

permanent foundation, and that, from
the close of that time, another period
of sixty-two weeks, or four hundred
and thirty-four years, would elapse to
the appearing of the Messiah. It is true
that this is not distinctly specified in
the text, and true that in the text the
phrase "the street shall be built again,
and the wall, even in troublous times,"
is not limited expressly to either period,
but it is also said in the next verse,
that the period of sixty-two weeks
would be terminated by the appearing
of the Messiah, or by his being cut off,
and, therefore, it is fair to presume
that the previous period of seven
weeks was to be characterized particularly as the "troublous times" in
which the street and the wall were to
be built again. The inquiry now is,
Whether that time was actually occupied in rebuilding and restoring the
city? In regard to this, it may be remarked, (1.) That there is a strong
probability that a considerable time
would be necessary to rebuild the walls
of the city, and to restore Jerusalem
to a condition like that in which it was
before the captivity. We are to remember that it had been long lying in
ruins; that the land was desolate; that
Jerusalem had no commercial importance to make its growth rapid; that
there were few in the city on whom
reliance could be placed in rebuilding
it; that a large portion of the materials
for rebuilding it was to be brought from
a distance; that the work was opposed
with much determination by the Samaritans; that it was necessary, as
Nehemiah informs us, in building the
walls, that the workmen should have a
weapon of defence in one hand whilst
they laboured with the other, and that
those who were engaged on it were
mostly poor. When these things are
considered, it is at least not *improbable*
that the period of forty-nine years
would be required before it could be
said that the work was fully completed.
(2.) A more material question, however, is, whether the *facts* in the case
confirm this, or whether there was
such a termination of the rebuilding of
the city at about that period, that it
could be said that the time occupied
was *seven* weeks rather than, for ex-

ample, six, or five, or nine. It may not be necessary so to make this out as to determine the precise year, or the termination of forty-nine years, but in a general division of the time, it *is* necessary, undoubtedly, so to determine it as to see that *that* time should have been designated, rather than one equally general at the close of *one* week, or two, or six, or nine, or any other number. Now that that *was* the period of the completion of the work contemplated by the decree issued under Artaxerxes, and the work undertaken by Nehemiah, it is not difficult to show: (*a*) It is reasonable to presume that the time referred to in the seven weeks would be the rebuilding of the city, and the restoration of its affairs to its former state—or the completion of the arrangements to restore the nation from the effects of the captivity, and to put it on its former footing. This was the main inquiry by Daniel; this would be a marked period; this would be that for which the "commandment would go forth;" and this would constitute a natural division of the time. (*b*) As a matter of fact, the completion of the work undertaken by Nehemiah, under the command of the Persian kings, reached to the period here designated; and his last act as governor of Judea, in restoring the people, and placing the affairs of the nation on its former basis, occurred at just about the period of the forty-nine years after the issuing of the command by Artaxerxes Longimanus. That event, as is supposed above, occurred B.C. 454. The close of the seven weeks, or of the forty-nine years, would therefore be B.C. 405. This would be about the last year of the reign of Darius Nothus. See the table above. Nehemiah was twice governor of Judea, and the work of restoration which he undertook was not completed until his being the second time in that office. The first time he remained twelve years in office, for he received his commission in the twentieth year of Artaxerxes, and in the thirty-second year he returned again to him, Neh. xiii. 6. This, according to the computation above, would bring it down to B.C. 442. How long he then remained with

the king of Persia he does not definitely state himself, but says it was "certain days," Neh. xiii. 6. After this, he again obtained permission of the king to return to Jerusalem, and went back the second time as governor of Judea, Neh. xiii. 6, 7. The time from his first return to Persia, after the twelve years that he spent in Judea to the year 405 B.C., would be thirty-seven years. According to this, the close of the "seven weeks," and the completion of the enterprise of "rebuilding and restoring" the city, must have been at the end of that thirty-seven years. In reference to this, it may be remarked, (1.) That Nehemiah is known to have lived to a great age (Josephus); yet, supposing he was thirty years old when he was first appointed governor of Judea, and that the time referred to at the close of the "seven weeks," or forty-nine years, was the completion of his work in the restoration of the affairs of Jerusalem, the whole period would only reach to the seventy-ninth year of his age. (2.) The last act of Nehemiah in restoring the city occurred in the fifteenth year of the reign of Darius Nothus—according to Prideaux (*Con.* II. 206, *seq.*)—that is, 408 B.C. This would make, according to the common computation of chronology, a difference from the estimate above of only three years, and, perhaps, considering that the time of "seven weeks" is a reckoning in round numbers, this would be an estimate of sufficient accuracy. But, besides this, it is to be remembered that the exact chronology to a year or a month cannot be made out with absolute certainty; and taking all the circumstances into consideration, it is remarkable that the period designated in the prophecy coincides so nearly with the historical record. The only remaining inquiries, therefore, are, whether the last act of Nehemiah referred to occurred *at* the time mentioned—the 15th of Darius Nothus, or 408 B.C. — and whether that was of sufficient prominence and importance to divide the two periods of the prophecies, or to be a proper closing up of the work of restoring and rebuilding Jerusalem. What he

26 And after threescore and two weeks shall Messiah *a* be cut off, but [1] not for himself: and [2] the

people of the prince that shall come shall destroy the city and the sanc-

a Luke 24. 26, 46.
1 or, *and shall have nothing.* John 14. 30.

2 or, *and they (the Jews) shall be no more his people, Hos.* 1. 9; or, *the prince's (Messiah's,* ver. 25) *future people.*

did in his office as governor of Judea, at his second visitation to Jerusalem, is recorded in Neh. xiii. 7–31. The particular acts which he performed consisted in removing certain abuses which had been suffered to grow up in his absence respecting the temple service, by which the temple had become greatly polluted (ch. xiii. 7–14); in restoring the Sabbath to its proper observance, which had become greatly disregarded (ch. xiii. 15–22); and in constraining those Jews who had contracted unlawful marriages to separate themselves from their wives (ch. xiii. 23–31). These acts were necessary to put the affairs of the temple, and the condition of the city, on their former basis. The *last* of these acts—the separation of those who had contracted unlawful marriages from their wives, is that which designates the close of the "seven weeks," and respecting which the date is to be sought. This is stated in the book of Nehemiah (xiii. 28) to have occurred in the time of "one of the sons of Joiada, the son of Eliashib the high-priest, son-in-law to Sanballat the Horonite." That is, it occurred when Joiada was high-priest. But, according to the *Chron. Alexandrinum*, Joiada succeeded his father in the office in the eleventh year of Darius Nothus, and Prideaux supposes, without improbability, that this event may have occurred as long as four years after he entered on the office of high-priest, which would bring it to the fifteenth of Darius Nothus, or 408 B.C. Comp. Jahn, *Heb. Com.* pp. 179–182; and Prideaux, *Con.* ii. 206–210. The *time,* then, if this be the event referred to, is sufficiently accurate to make it coincide with the prophecy—sufficiently so to divide the previous period from that which succeeded it. The event itself was of sufficient *importance* to have a place here. It was, in fact, *finishing* what was necessary to be done in order to a completion of the purpose to "restore and

rebuild Jerusalem." It was in fact *the restoration of Jewish affairs under the Persian edict,* or what was accomplished in fact under that edict in placing the Jewish affairs on the proper basis—the basis on which they were substantially before the captivity. This was the termination of that captivity in the fullest sense, and divided the past from the future—or constituted a *period* or *epoch* in the history of the Jewish people. It remains only to add, on this verse—and the remark will be equally applicable to the exposition of the two remaining verses of the chapter—that on the supposition that this had been written *after* the coming of the Messiah, and it had been designed to frame what would *seem* to be a prophecy or prediction of these events, the language here would be such as would have been appropriately employed. From the time of the going forth of the command to rebuild the city, the whole duration would have been accurately divided into two great portions—that requisite for the completion of the work of restoring the city, and that extending to the coming of the Messiah, and the former would have been made to terminate where it is now supposed the period of "seven weeks," or forty-nine years, did actually terminate. If this would have been the correct apportionment in a *historic* review, it is correct as *a prophetic* review.

26. *And after threescore and two weeks.* After the completion of the last period of four hundred and thirty-four years. The angel had shown in the previous verse what would be the characteristic of the first period of " seven weeks "—that during that time the wall and the street would be built in circumstances of general distress and anxiety, and he now proceeds to state what would occur in relation to the remaining sixty-two weeks. The particular thing which would characterize that period would

tuary; and the end thereof *shall be*
1 or, *it shall be cut off by desolations.*

with a flood, and unto the end of the
war ¹ desolations are determined.

be, that the Messiah would be cut off,
and that the series of events would
commence which would terminate in
the destruction of the city and the
temple. He does not say that this
would be *immediately* on the termination of the sixty-two weeks, but he
says that it would be "*after*"—אחרי
—*subsequent* to the close of that period.
The word does not mean necessarily
immediately, but it denotes that which
is to succeed—to follow—and would
be well expressed by the word *afterwards:* Gen. xv. 14; xxiii. 19; xxv.
26, *et al.* See Gesenius, *Lex.* The
natural meaning here would be, that
this would be the *next event* in the
order of events to be reckoned; it
would be that on which the prophetic
eye would rest subsequent to the close
of the period of sixty-two weeks.
There are two circumstances in the
prophecy itself which go to show that
it is not meant that this would *immediately* follow :—(*a*) One is, that in the
previous verse it is said that the "sixty-
two weeks" would extend "*unto* the
Messiah;" that is, either to his birth
or to his manifestation as such; and
it is not implied anywhere that he
would be "cut off" *at once* on his appearing, nor is such a supposition reasonable, or one that would have been
embraced by an ancient student of the
prophecies; (*b*) the other is, that, in
the subsequent verse, it is expressly
said that what he would accomplish in
causing the oblation to cease would
occur "in the midst of the week;"
that is, of the remaining one week that
would complete the seventy. This
could not occur if he were to be "cut
off" immediately at the close of the
sixty-two weeks. The careful student
of this prophecy, therefore, would anticipate that the Messiah would appear at the close of the sixty-two
weeks, and that he would continue
during a part, at least, of the remaining one week before he would be cut
off. This point could have been clearly
made out from the prophecy before
the Messiah came. ¶ *Shall Messiah.*

Notes, ver. 25. ¶ *Be cut off.* The
word here used (כָּרַת) means, properly,
to cut, to cut off, as a part of a garment, 1 Sa. xxiv. 5 (6), 11 (12); a
branch of a tree, Numb. xiii. 23; the
prepuce, Exod. iv. 25; the head, 1 Sa.
xvii. 51; v. 4; to cut down trees,
Deut. xix. 5; Isa. xiv. 8; xliv. 14;
Jer. x. 3; xxii. 7. Then it means to
cut off persons, to destroy, Deut. xx.
20; Jer. xi. 19; Gen. ix. 11; Psa.
xxxvii. 9; Prov. ii. 22; x. 31, *et al.*
sæpe. The phrase, "that soul shall
be cut off from his people," "from the
midst of the people," "from Israel,"
"from the congregation," &c., occurs
frequently in the Scriptures (compare
Gen. xvii. 14; Lev. vii. 20, 21; Num.
xv. 30; xix. 13, 20; Exod. xii. 19,
et al.), and denotes the punishment of
death in general, without defining the
manner. "It is never the punishment
of *exile.*"—Gesenius, *Lex.* The proper
notion or meaning here is, undoubtedly,
that of being cut off by death, and
would suggest the idea of a *violent*
death, or a death by the agency of
others. It would apply to one who
was assassinated, or murdered by a
mob, or who was appointed to death
by a judicial decree; or it might be
applied to one who was cut down in
battle, or by the pestilence, or by
lightning, or by shipwreck, but it
would not naturally or properly be
applied to one who had lived out his
days, and died a peaceful death. We
always now connect with the word
the idea of some unusual interposition,
as when we speak of one who is cut
down in middle life. The ancient
translators understood it of a violent
death. So the Latin Vulgate, *occi-
detur Christus;* Syriac, "the Messiah
shall be slain," or put to death. It
need not be here said that this phrase
would find a complete fulfilment in
the manner in which the Lord Jesus
was put to death, nor that this is the
very language in which it is proper
now to describe the manner in which
he was removed. He was cut off by
violence; by a judicial decree: by a

mob; in the midst of his way, &c. If it should be admitted that the angel meant to describe the manner of his death, he could not have found a single word that would have better expressed it. ¶ *But not for himself.* Marg., *and shall have nothing.* This phrase has given rise to not a little discussion, and not a little diversity of opinion. The Latin Vulgate is, *et non erit ejus populus, qui eum negaturus est*—"and they shall not be his people who shall deny him." Theodotion (in the Sept.), καὶ κρίμα οὐκ ἔστιν ἐν αυτῷ—"and there is no crime in him." Syriac, "And it is not with him." The Hebrew is וְאֵין לוֹ—and the interpretation turns on the meaning of the word אֵין. Hengstenberg maintains that it is never used in the sense of לֹא (not), but that it always conveys the idea of *nothing*, or *non-existence*, and that the meaning here is, that, then, "there was nothing to him;" that is, that he ceased to have authority and power, as in the cutting off of a prince or ruler whose power comes to an end. Accordingly he renders it, "and is not to him;" that is, his dominion, authority, or power over the covenant people as an anointed prince, would cease when he was cut off, and another one would come and desolate the sanctuary, and take possession. Bertholdt renders it, *Ohne Nachfolger von den Seinigen zu haben*—"without any successors of his own"—meaning that his family, or that the dynasty would be cut off, or would end with him. He maintains that the whole phrase denotes "a sudden and an unexpected death," and that it here means that he would have no successor of his own family. He applies it to Alexander the Great. Lengerke renders it, *Und nicht ist vorhanden, der ihm angehöret*—and explains the whole to mean, "The anointed one [as the lawful king] shall be cut off, but it shall not then be one who belongs to his family [to wit, upon the throne], but a Prince shall come to whom the crown did not belong, to whom the name *anointed* could not properly belong." Maurer explains it, "There shall be to him no successor or lawful heir." Prof. Stuart renders

it, "One shall be cut off, and there shall be none for it" (the people). C. B. Michaelis, "and not to be will be his lot." Jacch. and Hitzig, "and no one remained to him." Rosch, "and no one was present for him." Our translation—*but not for himself*—was undoubtedly adopted from the common view of the atonement—that the Messiah did not die for himself, but that his life was given as a ransom for others. There can be no doubt of that fact to those who hold the common doctrine of the atonement, and yet it may be doubted whether the translators did not undesignedly allow their views of the atonement to shape the interpretation of this passage, and whether it can be fairly made out from the Hebrew. The ordinary meaning of the Hebrew word אֵין is, undoubtedly, *nothing, emptiness*—in the sense of there being nothing (see Gesenius, *Lex.*); and, thus applied, the sense here would be, that after he was cut off, or in consequence of his being cut off, that which he before possessed would cease, or there would be "nothing" to him; that is, either his life would cease, or his dominion would cease, or he would be cut off as the Prince—the Messiah. This interpretation appears to be confirmed by what is immediately said, that *another* would come and would destroy the city and the sanctuary, or that the possession would pass into his hands. It seems probable to me that this is the fair interpretation. The Messiah would come as a "Prince." It might be expected that he would come to rule—to set up a kingdom. But he would be suddenly cut off by a violent death. The anticipated dominion over the people as a prince would not be set up. It would not pertain to him. Thus suddenly cut off, the expectations of such a ruler would be disappointed and blasted. He would in fact set up no such dominion as might naturally be expected of an anointed prince; he would have no successor; the dynasty would not remain in his hands or his family, and soon the people of a foreign prince would come and would sweep all away. This interpretation does not suppose that the *real* object of his coming would be thwarted, or that he would not set up a kingdom in accordance with the prediction properly explained, but that such a kingdom as would be expected by the people would not be set up. He would be cut off soon after he came, and the anticipated dominion would not pertain to him, or there would be "nothing" of it found in him, and soon after a foreign prince would come and destroy the city and the sanctuary. This interpretation, indeed, will take this passage away as a proof-text of the doctrine of the atonement, or as affirming the design of the death of the Messiah, but it furnishes a meaning as much in accordance with the general strain of the prophecy, and with the facts in the work of the Messiah. For it was a natural expectation that when he came he would set up a kingdom—a temporal reign—and this expectation was extensively cherished among the people. He was, however, soon cut off, and all such hopes at once perished in the minds of his true followers (comp. Luke xxiv. 21), and in the minds of the multitudes who, though not his true followers, began to inquire whether he might not be the predicted Messiah—the Prince to sit on the throne of David. But of such an anticipated dominion or rule, there was "nothing" to him. All these expectations were blighted by his sudden death, and soon, instead of his delivering the nation from bondage and setting up a visible kingdom, a foreign prince would come with his forces and would sweep away everything. Whether this would be the interpretation affixed to these words *before* the advent of the Messiah cannot now be determined. We have few remains of the methods in which the Hebrews interpreted the ancient prophecies, and we may readily suppose that they would not be *disposed* to embrace an exposition which would show them that the reign of the Messiah, as they anticipated it, would not occur, but that almost as soon as he appeared, he would be put to death, and the dominion pass away, and the nation be subjected to the ravages of a foreign power. ¶ *And the people of the prince that shall come.*

Marg., "And they (the Jews) shall be no more his people; or, the Prince's (Messiah's) future people." This seems to be rather an *explanation* of the meaning, than a translation of the Hebrew. The literal rendering would be, "and the city, and the sanctuary, the people of a prince that comes, shall lay waste." On the general supposition that this whole passage refers to the Messiah and his time, the language here used is not difficult of interpretation, and denotes with undoubted accuracy the events that soon followed the "cutting off" of the Messiah.

The word *people* (עַם) is a word that may well be applied to subjects or armies—such a people as an invading prince or warrior would lead with him for purposes of conquest. It denotes properly (*a*) a people, or tribe, or race in general; and then (*b*) the people as opposed to kings, princes, rulers (comp. λαός, the people as opposed to chiefs in Homer, *Il.* ii. 365, xiii. 108, xxiv. 28): and then as soldiers, Judg. v. 2. Hence it may be applied, as it would be understood to be here, to the soldiers of the prince that should come. ¶ *Of the prince that shall come.* The word *prince* here (נָגִיד) is the same which occurs in ver. 25, "Messiah *the prince*." It is clear, however, that another prince is meant here, for (*a*) it is just said that that prince—the Messiah—would be "*cut off*," and this clearly refers to one that was to follow; (*b*) the phrase "that is to come" (הַבָּא) would also imply this. It would naturally suggest the idea that he would come from abroad, or that he would be a foreign prince—for he would "come" for the purposes of destruction. No one can fail to see the applicability of this to the destruction of Jerusalem by the Roman power, after the Lord Jesus was put to death. If that was the design of the prophecy, or if it be admitted that the prophecy contemplated that, the language could not have been better chosen, or the prediction more exact. No one can reasonably doubt that, if the ancient Hebrews had understood the former part of the prophecy, as meaning that the true Messiah would be put to death soon after his appearing, they could not fail to anticipate that a foreign prince would soon come and lay waste their city and sanctuary. ¶ *Shall destroy the city and the sanctuary.* The "holy place" —the temple. This is the termination of the prophecy. It begins with the command to "rebuild and restore" the city, and ends with its destruction. The *time* is not fixed, nor is there in the prophecy any direct intimation when it would occur, unless it be found in the general declaration in ver. 24, that "seventy weeks were determined upon the people and the city." The whole scope of the prophecy, however, would lead to the supposition that this was *soon* to occur after the Messiah should be "cut off." The series of events under the Romans which led to the destruction of the city and temple, in fact, began very soon after the death of the Lord Jesus, and ceased only when the temple was wholly demolished, and the city was rased to its foundations. ¶ *And the end thereof.* Heb., "its end," or "his end"—קצּו. It is not certain as to what the word *it* (וֹ) here refers. It may be either the end of the city, or of the prince, or of the prophecy, so far as the grammatical construction is concerned. As the principal and immediate subject of the prophecy, however, is the city, it is more natural to refer it to that. Hengstenberg renders it, "it will end," supposing, with Vitringa, that it refers to the subject of the discourse : "the thing —the whole affair—all that is here predicted in this series of events— will end with a flood." This accords well with the whole design of the prophecy. ¶ *With a flood.* בַּשֶּׁטֶף. That is, it shall be *like* an overflowing flood. The word here used means a *gushing, outpouring*, as of rain, Job xxxviii. 25 ; of a torrent, Prov. xxvii. 4 ; an overflowing, inundation, flood, Psa. xxxii. 6 ; Nah. i. 8. Hence it would appropriately denote the ravages of an army, sweeping everything away. It would be like a sudden inundation, carrying everything before it. No one can

doubt that this language is applicable in every respect to the desolations brought upon Jerusalem by the Roman armies. ¶ *And unto the end of the war desolations are determined.* Marg., "it shall be cut off by desolations." Hengstenberg renders this, "and unto the end is war, a decree of ruins." So Lengerke—*und bis aufs Ende Krieg und Beschluss der Wüsten.* Bertholdt renders it, "and the great desolations shall continue unto the end of the war." The Latin Vulgate renders it, *et post finem belli statuta desolatio*—"and after the end of the war desolation is determined." Prof. Stuart translates it, "and unto the end shall be war, a decreed measure of desolations." The *literal* meaning of the passage is, "and unto the end of the war desolations are decreed," or determined. The word rendered "determined" (חָרַץ) means, properly, to cut, cut in, engrave ; then to decide, to determine, to decree, to pass sentence. See Notes on ver. 24. Here the meaning naturally is, that such desolations were settled or determined as by a decree or purpose. There was something which made them certain ; that is, it was a part of the great plan here referred to in the vision of the seventy weeks, that there should be such desolations extending through the war. The things which would, therefore, be anticipated from this passage would be, (*a*) that there would be war. This is implied also in the assurance that the people of a foreign prince would come and take the city. (*b*) That this war would be of a *desolating* character, or that it would in a remarkable manner extend and spread ruin over the land. All wars are thus characterized; but it would seem that this would do it in a remarkable manner. (*c*) That these desolations would extend *through* the war, or to its close. There would be no intermission; no cessation. It is hardly necessary to say that this was, in fact, precisely the character of the war which the Romans waged with the Jews after the death of the Saviour, and which ended in the destruction of the city and temple; the overthrow of the whole Hebrew polity; and the re-

27 And he shall confirm ¹ the covenant with many for one week:
and in the midst of the week he

¹ or, *a.*

moval of great numbers of the people to a distant and perpetual captivity. No war, perhaps, has been in its progress more marked by desolation; in none has the purpose of destruction been more perseveringly manifested to its very close. The *language* here, indeed, might apply to many wars—in a certain sense to all wars; to none, however, would it be more appropriate than to the wars of the Romans with the Jews.

27. *And he shall confirm the covenant.* Literally, "he shall make strong"—וְהִגְבִּיר. The idea is that of giving strength, or stability; of making firm and sure. The Hebrew word here evidently refers to the "covenant" which God is said to establish with his people—so often-referred to in the Scriptures as expressing the relation between Him and them, and hence used, in general, to denote the laws and institutions of the true religion—the laws which God has made for his church; his promises to be their protector, &c., and the institutions which grow out of that relation. The margin reads it, more in accordance with the Hebrew, "*a*," meaning that he would confirm or establish "*a* covenant" with the many. According to this, it is not necessary to suppose that it was any existing covenant that it referred to, but that he would ratify what was understood by the word "covenant;" that is, that he would lead many to enter into a true and real covenant with God. This would be fulfilled if he should perform such a work as would bring the "many" into a relation to God corresponding to that which was sustained to him by his ancient people ; that is, bring them to be his true friends and worshippers. The meaning of the expression here cannot be mistaken, that during the time specified, "he" (whoever may be referred to) would, for "one week"—pursue such a course as would tend to establish the true religion ; to render it more stable and firm ; to give it higher sanctions in the approbation of the "many,"

and to bring it to bear more decidedly and powerfully on the heart. Whether this would be by some law enacted in its favour ; or by protection extended over the nation ; or by present example ; or by instruction ; or by some work of a new kind, and new influences which he would set forth, is not mentioned, and beforehand perhaps it could not have been well anticipated in what way this would be. There has been a difference of opinion, however, as to the proper nominative to the verb *confirm*—הִגְבִּיר—whether it is the Messiah, or the foreign prince, or the "one week." Hengstenberg prefers the latter, and renders it, "And one week shall confirm the covenant with many." So also Lengerke renders it. Bertholdt renders it "he," that is, "he shall unite himself firmly with many for one week"—or, a period of seven years, *ein Jahrsiebend lang.* It seems to me that it is an unnatural construction to make the word "week" the nominative to the verb, and that the more obvious interpretation is to refer it to some *person* to whom the whole subject relates. It is not usual to represent *time* as an agent in accomplishing a work. In poetic and metaphorical language, indeed, we personate time as cutting down men, as a destroyer, &c., but this usage would not justify the expression that "time would confirm a covenant with many." That is, evidently, the work of a conscious, intelligent agent ; and it is most natural, therefore, to understand this as of one of the two agents who are spoken of in the passage. These two agents are the "Messiah," and the "prince that should come." But it is not reasonable to suppose that the latter is referred to, because it is said (ver. 26) that the effect and the purpose of his coming would be to "destroy the city and the sanctuary." He was to come "with a flood," and the effect of his coming would be only desolation. The more correct interpretation, therefore, is to refer it to the Messiah, who is the principal subject of the prophecy ;

shall cause the sacrifice and the oblation to cease, and ¹ for the over-

spreading of abominations he shall

1 or, *upon the battlements shall be the idols of the desolator.*

and the work which, according to this, he was to perform was, during that "one week," to exert such an influence as would tend to establish a covenant between the people and God. The effect of his work during that one week would be to secure their adhesion to the *true religion;* to confirm to them the Divine promises, and to establish the principles of that religion which would lead them to God. Nothing is said of the *mode* by which that would be done; and anything, therefore, which would secure this would be a fulfilment of the prophecy. As a matter of fact, if it refers to the Lord Jesus, this was done by his personal instructions, his example, his sufferings and death, and the arrangements which he made to secure the proper effect of his work on the minds of the people — all designed to procure for them the friendship and favour of God, and to unite them to him in the bonds of an enduring covenant. ¶ *With many.*

לָרַבִּים. Or, *for* many; or, *unto* many.

He would perform a work which would pertain to many, or which would bear on many, leading them to God. There is nothing in the word here which would indicate *who* they were, whether his own immediate followers, or those who already were *in* the covenant. The simple idea is, that this would pertain to *many* persons, and it would be fulfilled if the effect of his work were to confirm *many* who were already in the covenant, or if he should bring *many* others into a covenant relation with God. Nothing could be determined from the meaning of the word used here as to which of these things was designed, and consequently a fair fulfilment would be found if *either* of them occurred. If it refers to the Messiah, it would be fulfilled if in fact the effect of his coming should be either by statute or by instructions to confirm and establish those who already sustained this relation to God, or if he gathered other followers, and confirmed them in their allegiance to God. ¶ *For*

one week. The fair interpretation of this, according to the principles adopted throughout this exposition, is, that this includes the space of seven years. See Notes on ver. 24. This is the one week that makes up the seventy — seven of them, or forty-nine years, embracing the period from the command to rebuild the city and temple to its completion under Nehemiah; sixty-two, or four hundred and thirty-four years, to the public appearing of the Messiah, and this one week to complete the whole seventy, or four hundred and ninety years "to finish the transgression, and to make an end of sins, and to make reconciliation for iniquity, and to bring in everlasting righteousness," &c., ver. 24. It is essential, therefore, to find something done, occupying these seven years, that would go to "confirm the covenant" in the sense above explained. In the consideration of this, the attention is arrested by the announcement of an important event which was to occur "in the midst of the week," to wit, in causing the sacrifice and the oblation to cease, showing that there was to be an important change occurring during the "week," or that while he would be, in fact, confirming the covenant through the week in some proper sense, the sacrifice and oblation would cease, and *therefore* the confirming of the many in the covenant must depend on something else than the continuation of the sacrifice and oblation. In regard to this language, as in respect to all the rest of the prophecy, there are, in fact, just two questions: one is, what is *fairly* to be understood by the words, or what is the proper interpretation, independent of anything in the result; the other is, whether anything occurred in that which is regarded as the fulfilment which corresponds with the language so interpreted. (1.) The first inquiry then, is, What is the fair meaning of the language? Or what would one who had a correct knowledge of the proper principles of interpretation understand by this? Now,

make *it* desolate, even until the consummation, and that deter- | mined shall be poured upon [1] the desolate.

in regard to this, while it may be admitted, perhaps, that there would be some liability to a difference of view in interpreting it with no reference to the event, or no shaping of its meaning *by* the event, the following things seem to be clear: (*a*) that the " one week," would comprise seven years, immediately succeeding the appearance of the Messiah, or the sixty-two weeks, and that there was something which he would do in "confirming the covenant," or in establishing the principles of religion, which would extend through that period of seven years, or that that would be, in some proper sense, a *period* of time, having a beginning—to wit, his appearing, and some proper close or termination at the end of the seven years: that is, that there would be some reason why that should be a marked period, or why the whole should terminate *there*, and not at some other time. (*b*) That in the middle of that period of seven years, *another* important event would occur, serving to divide *that* time into two portions, and especially to be known as causing the sacrifice and oblation to cease; in some way affecting the public offering of sacrifice, so that from that time there would be in fact a cessation. (*c*) And that this would be succeeded by the consummation of the whole matter expressed in the words, "and for the overspreading of abomination he shall make it desolate," &c. It is not said, however, that this latter would *immediately* occur, but this would be one of the events that would appertain to the fulfilment of the prophecy. There is nothing, indeed, in the prediction to *forbid* the expectation that this would occur at once, nor is there anything in the words which makes it imperative that we *should* so understand it. It may be admitted that this would be the most *natural* interpretation, but it cannot be shown that that is required. It may be added, also, that this may not have appertained to the direct design of the prophecy—which was to foretell the coming of the Messiah, but that this was *appended* to show the end of the whole thing. When the Messiah should have come, and should have made an atonement for sin, the great design of rebuilding Jerusalem and the temple would have been accomplished, and both might pass away. Whether that would occur *immediately* or not might be in itself a matter of indifference; but it was important to state here that it would occur, for that was properly a completion of the design of rebuilding the city, and of the purpose for which it had ever been set apart as a holy city. (2.) The other inquiry is, whether there was that in what is regarded as the fulfilment of this, which *fairly* corresponds with the prediction. I have attempted above (on ver. 25) to show that this refers to the Messiah properly so called — the Lord Jesus Christ. The inquiry now is, therefore, whether we can find in his life and death what is a fair fulfilment of these reasonable expectations. In order to see this, it is proper to review these points in their order: (*a*) The period, then, which is embraced in the prophecy, is seven years, and it is necessary to find in his life and work something which would be accomplished during these seven years which could be properly referred to as "confirming the covenant with many." The main difficulty in the case is on this point, and I acknowledge that this seems to me to be the most embarrassing portion of the prophecy, and that the solutions which can be given of this are less satisfactory than those that pertain to any other part. Were it not that the remarkable clause " in the midst of the week he shall cause the sacrifice and oblation to cease," were added, I admit that the natural interpretation would be, that he would do this personally, and that we might look for something which he would himself accomplish during the whole period of seven years. That clause, however, looks as if some remarkable event were to occur in the middle of that period; for the fact that he would cause the sacrifice and oblation to cease —that is, would bring the rites of the temple to a close—shows that what is meant by "confirming the covenant" is different from the ordinary worship under the ancient economy. No *Jew* would think of expressing himself thus, or would see how it was practicable to "confirm the covenant" at the same time that all his sacrifices were to cease. The confirming of the covenant, therefore, during that "one week," must be consistent with some work or event that would cause the sacrifice and oblation to cease in the middle of that period. (*b*) The true fulfilment, it seems to me, is to be found in the bearing of the work of the Saviour on the Hebrew people—the ancient covenant people of God—for about the period of seven years after he entered on his work. Then the particular relation of his work to the Jewish people ceased. It may not be practicable to make out the *exact* time of "seven years" in reference to this, and it may be admitted that this would not be understood from the prophecy before the things occurred; but still there are a number of circumstances which will show that this interpretation is not only plausible, but that it has in its very nature strong probability in its favour. They are such as these: (1.) The ministry of the Saviour himself was wholly among the Jews, and his work was what would, in their common language, be spoken of as "confirming the covenant;" that is, it would be strengthening the principles of religion, bringing the Divine promises to bear on the mind, and leading men to God, &c. (2.) This same work was continued by the apostles as they laboured among the Jews. They endeavoured to do the same thing that their Lord and Master had done, with all the additional sanctions, now derived from his life and death. The whole tendency of their ministry would have been properly expressed in this language: that they endeavoured to "confirm the covenant" with the Hebrew people; that is, to bring them to just views of the character of their natural covenant with God; to show them how it was confirmed in the Messiah; to establish the ancient promises; and to bring to bear upon them

the sanctions of their law as it was now fulfilled, and ratified, and enlarged through the Messiah. Had the Saviour himself succeeded in this, or had his apostles, it would have been, in fact, only "confirming the ancient covenant" — the covenant made with Abraham, Isaac, and Jacob; the covenant established under Moses, and ratified by so many laws and customs among the people. The whole bearing of the Saviour's instructions, and of his followers, was to carry out and fulfil the real design of that ancient institution—to show its true nature and meaning, and to impress it on the hearts of men. (3.) This was continued for *about* the period here referred to; at least for a period so long that it could properly be represented in round numbers as "one week," or seven years. The Saviour's own ministry continued about half that time; and then the apostles prosecuted the same work, labouring with the Jews for about the other portion, before they turned their attention to the Gentiles, and before the purpose to endeavour to bring in the Jewish people was abandoned. They remained in Jerusalem; they preached in the synagogues; they observed the rites of the temple service; they directed their first attention everywhere to the Hebrew people; they had not yet learned that they were to turn away from the "covenant people," and to go to the Gentiles. It was a slow process by which they were led to this. It required a miracle to convince Peter of it, and to show him that it was right to go to Cornelius (Acts x.), as a representative of the Gentile people, and it required another miracle to convert Saul of Tarsus, "the apostle of the Gentiles," and to prepare him for the work of carrying the gospel to the heathen world, and a succession of severe persecutions was demanded to induce the apostles to leave Jerusalem, and to go abroad upon the face of the earth to convey the message of salvation. Their first work was among the Jewish people, and they would have remained among them if they had not been driven away by these persecutions, and been thus constrained to go to other lands. It is true that it cannot be shown that this was a period of exactly "half a week," or three years and a half after the ascension of the Saviour, but, in a prophecy of this nature, it was a period that might, in round numbers, be well expressed by that; or the whole might be properly described by "seventy weeks," or four hundred and ninety years, and the last portion after the appearing of the Messiah as *one* of these weeks. There has been much needless anxiety to make out the exact time to a month or a day in regard to this prophecy—not remembering its general design, and not reflecting how uncertain are all the questions in ancient chronology. Compare the sensible remarks of Calvin on ver. 25. (4.) *When* this occurred; *when* the apostles turned away from the Hebrew people, and gave themselves to their labours among the Gentiles, the work of "confirming the covenant" with those to whom the promises had been made, and to whom the law was given, ceased. They were regarded as "broken off" and left, and the hope of success was in the Gentile world. See the reasoning of the apostle Paul in Rom. xi. Jerusalem was given up soon after to destruction, and the whole work, as contemplated in this prophecy, ceased. The object for which the city and temple were rebuilt was accomplished, and here was a proper termination of the *prophecy*. It was not necessary, indeed, that these should be *at once* destroyed, but they were henceforth regarded as having fulfilled the work designed, and as being now left to ruin. The ruin did not at once occur, but the sacrifices thenceforward offered were without meaning, and the train of events was constantly preparing that would sweep away city and temple together. I suppose, therefore, that this last "one week" embraced the period from the beginning of the ministry of the Saviour to that when the direct and exclusive efforts to bring the principles of his religion to bear on the Hebrew people, as carrying out the design of the covenant made by God with their fathers, and confirmed with so many promises, ceased, and the great effort was commenced to evangelize the heathen world. Then was the proper close of the seventy weeks; what is added is merely a statement of the winding up of the whole affair in the destruction of the city and temple. That occurred, indeed, some years after; but at this period all that was material in regard to that city had taken place, and consequently that was all that was necessary to specify as to the proper termination of the design of rebuilding the city and the temple. ¶ *And in the midst of the week.* The word here rendered "in the midst"—יְחֶצִי—means, properly, half, the half part, Exod. xxiv. 6; Numb. xii. 12; then the middle, or the midst, Judg. xvi. 3. The Vulgate renders it, *in dimidio;* the Greek, ἐν τῷ ἡμίσει. Hengstenberg, "the half." So Lengerke, *die Hälfte;* Luther, *mitten.* The natural and obvious interpretation is that which is expressed in our translation, and that will convey the essential idea in the original. It refers to something which was to occur at about the middle portion of this time, or when about half of this period was elapsed, or to something which it would require half of the "one week," or seven years, to accomplish. The meaning of the passage is fully met by the supposition that it refers to the Lord Jesus and his work, and that the exact thing that was intended by the prophecy was his death, or his being "cut off," and thus causing the sacrifice and oblation to cease. Whatever difficulties there may be about the *precise* time of our Lord's ministry, and whether he celebrated three passovers or four after he entered on his public work, it is agreed on all hands that it lasted about three years and a half—the time referred to here. Though a few have supposed that a longer period was occupied, yet the general belief of the church has coincided in that, and there are few points in history better settled. On the supposition that this pertains to the death of the Lord Jesus, and that it was the design of the prophecy here to refer to the effects of that death, this is the very language which would have been used. If the period of "a week" were for any purpose mentioned, then it would be indispensable to suppose that there would be an allusion to the important event—in fact, the *great* event which was to occur in the middle of that period, when the ends of the types and ceremonies of the Hebrew people would be accomplished, and a sacrifice made for the sins of the whole world. ¶ *He shall cause the sacrifice and the oblation to cease.* The word "*he,*" in this place, refers to the Messiah, if the interpretation of the former part of the verse is correct, for there can be no doubt that it is the same person who is mentioned in the phrase "*he* shall confirm the covenant with many." The words "sacrifice" and "oblation" refer to the offerings made in the temple. The former word more properly denotes *bloody* offerings; the latter *offerings* of any kind—whether of flour, fruits, grain, &c. See these words explained in the Notes on Isa. i. 11, 13. The word rendered "cease" (רִשְׁבִּית) means, properly, *to rest* (whence the word *Sabbath*), and then in Hiphil, to cause to rest, or to cause to cease. It conveys the idea of *putting an end to*—as, for example, *war*, Psa. xlvi. 9; *contention*, Prov. xviii. 18; *exultation*, Isa. xvi. 10.— Gesenius. The literal signification here would be met by the supposition that an end would be made of these sacrifices, and this would occur either by their being made wholly to cease to be offered at that time, or by the fact that the object of their appointment was accomplished, and that henceforward they would be useless and would die away. As a matter of fact, so far as the Divine intention in the appointment of these sacrifices and offerings was concerned, they *ceased* at the death of Christ—in the middle of the "week." Then the great sacrifice which they had adumbrated was offered. Then they ceased to have any significancy, no reason existing for their longer continuance. Then, as they never had had any efficacy in themselves, they ceased also to have any propriety as *types*—for the thing which they had prefigured had been accomplished. Then, too, began a series of events and influences which led to their abolition,

for soon they were interrupted by the Romans, and the temple and the altars were swept away to be rebuilt no more. The death of Christ was, in fact, the thing which made them to cease, and the fact that the great atonement has been made, and that there is now no further need of those offerings, is the only philosophical reason which can be given why the Jews have never been able again to rebuild the temple, and why for eighteen hundred years they have found no place where they could again offer a bloody sacrifice. The "sacrifice and the oblation" were made, as the result of the coming of the Messiah, to "cease" *for ever*, and no power of man will be able to restore them again in Jerusalem. Comp. Gibbon's account of the attempt of Julian to rebuild the temple at Jerusalem: *Dec. and Fall*, ii. 35–37. ¶ *And for the overspreading of abominations he shall make it desolate.* The marginal reading here is very different, showing clearly the perplexity of the translators: "Upon the battlements shall be the idols of the desolator." There is great variety, also, in the ancient versions in rendering this passage. The Latin Vulgate is, "And there shall be in the temple the abomination of desolation." The Greek, "And upon the temple shall be an abomination of desolations." The Syriac, "And upon the extremities of the abomination shall rest desolation." The Arabic, "And over the sanctuary shall there be the abomination of ruin." Luther renders it, "And upon the wings shall stand the abomination of desolation." Lengerke and Hengstenberg render it, "And upon the summit of abomination comes the destroyer." Prof. Stuart, "And the water shall be over a winged fowl of abominations." These different translations show that there is great obscurity in the original, and perhaps exclude the hope of being able entirely to free the passage from all difficulties. An examination of the *words*, however, may perhaps enable us to form a judgment of its meaning. The *literal* and *obvious* sense of the original, as I understand it, is, "And upon the wing of the abominations one causing desolation"—וְעַל כְּנַף שִׁקּוּצִים מְשֹׁמֵם. The

word rendered *overspreading* (כְּנַף)
means, properly, *a wing;* so called as
covering, or because it *covers*—from
כָּנַף, to cover, to hide. Then it denotes
anything having a resemblance to a
wing, as an extremity, a corner, as
(*a*) of a garment, the skirt, or flap,
1 Sam. xxiv. 4 (5), 11 (12); Numb.
xv. 38, and hence, as the outer garment was used by the Orientals to wrap
themselves in at night, the word is
used for the extremity or border of a
bed-covering, Deut. xxii. 30 (xxiii. 1);
Ruth iii. 9. (*b*) It is applied to land,
or to the earth—as the earth is compared with a garment spread out, Isa.
xxiv. 16; Job xxxvii. 3; xxxviii. 13.
(*c*) It is used to denote the highest
point, or a battlement, a pinnacle—
as having a resemblance to a wing
spread out. So the word πτερύγιον is
used in Matt. iv. 5. See Notes on
that passage. It would seem most
probable that the allusion by the word
as applied to a building would not be,
as supposed by Gesenius (*Lex.*), and
by Hengstenberg and Lengerke, to the
pinnacle or *summit,* but to some roof,
porch, or piazza that had a resemblance
to the wings of a bird as spread out—
a use of the word that would be very
natural and obvious. The extended
porch that Solomon built on the eastern side of the temple would, not improbably, have, to one standing on
the opposite Mount of Olives, much
the appearance of the wings of a bird
spread out. Nothing certain can be
determined about the allusion here
from the use of this *word,* but the *connection* would lead us to suppose that
the reference was to something pertaining to the city or temple, for the
whole prophecy has a reference to the
city and temple, and it is natural to
suppose that in its close there would
be an allusion to it. The use of the
word "*wing*" here would lead to the
supposition that what is said would
pertain to something in connection
with the temple having a resemblance
to the wings of a bird, and the word
"upon" (עַל) would lead us to suppose
that what was to occur would be somehow *upon* that. The word rendered

abominations (שִׁקּוּצִים) means *abominable things,* things to be held in detes-
tation, as things unclean, filthy garments, &c., and then idols, as things
that are to be held in abhorrence. The
word שִׁקּוּץ *shik-kootz,* is rendered *abomination* in Deut. xxix. 17; 1 Kings
xi. 5, 7; 2 Kings xxiii. 13, 24; Isa.
lxvi. 3; Jer. iv. 1; vii. 30; xiii. 27;
xxxii. 34; Ezek. v. 11; vii. 20; xx. 7,
8, 30; Dan. ix. 27; xi. 31; xii. 11;
Hos. ix. 10; Zech. ix. 7; *abominable
idols* in 2 Chron. xv. 8 (in the margin
abominations); *detestable* in Jer. xvi.
18; Ezek. xi. 18, 21; xxxvii. 23; and
abominable filth in Nah. iii. 6. It does
not occur elsewhere. In most of these
places it is applied to *idols,* and the current usage would lead us so to apply it,
if there were nothing in the connection
to demand a different interpretation.
It *might* refer to anything that was
held in abomination, or that was detestable and offensive. The *word* is
one that might be used of an idol god,
or of anything that would pollute or
defile, or that was from any cause offensive. It is not used in the Old
Testament with reference to a *banner*
or *military standard,* but there can be
no doubt that it might be so applied as
denoting the standard of a foe—of a
heathen—planted on any part of the
temple—a thing which would be particularly detestable and abominable in
the sight of the Jews. The word rendered "he shall make *it* desolate"—
מְשֹׁמֵם—is "he making desolate;" that
is, *a desolator.* It is a Poel participle
from שָׁמֵם—to be astonished, to be laid
waste; and then, in an active sense, to
lay waste, to make desolate.—Gesenius.
The same word, and the same phrase,
occur in ch. xi. 31: "And they shall
place the abomination that maketh desolate," or, as it is in the margin, *astonisheth.* There, also, the expression
is used in connection with "taking
away the daily sacrifices." The word
would be more properly rendered in
this place *desolator,* referring to some
one who would produce desolation.
There is great abruptness in the entire
expression, and it is evident that it was
not the intention to give so clear a pre-

diction in this that it could be fully understood beforehand. The other portions of the prophecy respecting the building of the city, and the coming of the Messiah, and the work that he would accomplish, are much more clear, and their meaning could have been made out with much more certainty. But, in reference to this, it would seem, perhaps, that all that was designed was to throw out suggestions—fragments of thought, that would rather hint at the subject than give any continuous idea. Perhaps a much more *abrupt* method of translation than that which attempts to express it in a continuous grammatical construction capable of being parsed easily, would better express the state of the mind of the speaker, and the language which he uses, than the ordinary versions. The Masoretic pointing, also, may be disregarded, and then the real idea would be better expressed by some such translation as the following :—" He shall cause the sacrifice and the offering to cease. And—upon the wing—the porch of the temple—abominations ! And a desolator !" That is, after the ceasing of the sacrifice and the oblation, the mind is fixed upon the temple where they had been offered. The first thing that arrests the eye is some portion of the temple, here denoted by the word *wing*. The next is something abominable or detestable—an object to be hated and loathed in the very temple itself. The next is a *desolator*— one who had come to carry desolation to that very temple. Whether the "abomination" is connected with the " desolator" or not is not intimated by the language. It might or might not be. The angel uses language as these objects strike the eye, and he expresses himself in this abrupt manner as the eye rests on one or the other. The question then arises, What does this mean? Or what is to be regarded as the proper fulfilment ? It seems to me that there can be no doubt that there is a reference to the Roman standard or banners planted on some part of the temple, or to the Roman army, or to some idols set up by the Romans— objects of abomination to the Jews— as attracting the eye of the angel in the distant future, and as indicating the close of the series of events here referred to in the prophecy. The reasons for this opinion are, summarily, the following :—(*a*) The *place* or *order* in which the passage stands in the prophecy. It is *after* the coming of the Messiah ; *after* the proper cessation of the sacrifice and oblation, and at the close of the whole series of events— the termination of the whole design about rebuilding the city and the temple. (*b*) The *language* is such as would properly represent that. Nothing could be more appropriate, in the common estimation of the Jews, than to speak of such an object as a Roman military standard planted in any part of the temple, as an *abomination ;* and no word would better denote the character of the Roman conqueror than the word *desolator*—for the effect of his coming was to lay the whole city and temple in ruins. (*c*) The language of the Saviour in his reference to this would seem to demand such an interpretation, Matt. xxiv. 15 : "When ye, therefore, shall see the abomination of desolation spoken of by Daniel the prophet stand in the holy place," &c. There can be no reasonable doubt that the Saviour refers to this passage in Daniel (see Notes on Matt. xxiv. 15), or that events occurred in the attack on Jerusalem and the temple that would fully correspond with the language used here. Josephus, for instance, says, that when the city was taken, the Romans brought their ensigns into the temple, and placed them over the eastern gate, and sacrificed to them there. " And now the Romans," says he, " upon the flight of the seditious into the city, and upon the burning of the holy house itself, and all the buildings round about it, brought their ensigns into the temple, and set them over against its eastern gate ; and there they did offer sacrifices to them, and there did they make Titus *Imperator* with the greatest acclamations of joy." —*Jewish Wars,* b. vi. ch. vi. § 1. This fact fully accords with the meaning of the language as above explained, and the reference to it was demanded in order that the purpose of the prophecy should be complete. Its proper termination is the destruction of the city and temple—as its beginning is the order to rebuild them. ¶ *Even until the consummation.* Until the completion—וְעַד־כָּלָה. That is, the series of events in the prophecy shall in fact reach to the completion of everything pertaining to the city and temple. The whole purpose in regard to that shall be completed. The design for which it is to be rebuilt shall be consummated; the sacrifices to be offered there shall be finished, and they shall be no longer efficacious or proper; the whole civil and religious polity connected with the city and temple shall pass away. ¶ *And that determined.* וְנֶחֱרָצָה. See this word explained in the Notes on vers. 24, 26. See also Notes on Isa. x. 23. There seems to be an allusion in the word here to its former use, as denoting that this is the fulfilment of the determination in regard to the city and temple. The idea is, that that which was determined, or decided on, to wit, with reference to the closing scenes of the city and temple, would be accomplished. ¶ *Shall be poured.* תִּתַּךְ The word here used means to pour, to pour out, to overflow—as rain, water, curses, anger, &c. It may be properly applied to calamity or desolation, as these things may be represented as *poured down* upon a people, in the manner of a storm. Compare 2 Sam. xxi. 10; Exod. ix. 33; Psa. xi. 6; Ezek. xxxviii. 22; 2 Chron. xxxiv. 21; xii. 7; Jer. vii. 20; xlii. 18; xliv. 6. ¶ *Upon the desolate.* Marg., *desolator.* The Hebrew word (שֹׁמֵם) is the same, though in another form (*Kal* instead of *Poel*) which is used in the previous part of the verse, and rendered "he shall make it desolate," but which is proposed above to be rendered *desolator.* The verb שָׁמֵם is an intransitive verb, and means, in *Kal,* the form used here, to be astonished or amazed; then "to be laid waste, to be made desolate" (Gesenius); and the meaning in this place, therefore, is that which is desolate or laid waste—the wasted, the perishing, the solitary. The reference is to Jerusalem viewed as desolate or reduced to ruins. The

angel perhaps contemplates it, as he is speaking, in ruins or as desolate, and he sees this also as the termination of the entire series of predictions, and, in view of the whole, speaks of Jerusalem appropriately as *the desolate.* Though it would be rebuilt, yet it would be again reduced to desolation, for the purpose of the rebuilding—the coming of the Messiah—would be accomplished. As the prophecy *finds* Jerusalem a scene of ruins, so it *leaves* it, and the last word *in* the prophecy, therefore, is appropriately the word *desolate.* The intermediate state indeed between the condition of the city as seen at first and at the close is glorious —for it embraces the whole work of the Messiah; but the beginning is a scene of ruins, and so is the close. The sum of the whole in the latter part of the verse may be expressed in a free paraphrase: "He, the Messiah, shall cause the sacrifice and oblation to cease," by having fulfilled in his own death the design of the ancient offerings, thus rendering them now useless, and upon the outspreading—upon the temple regarded as spread out, or some wing or portico, there are seen abominable things—idolatrous ensigns, and the worship of foreigners. A desolator is there, also, come to spread destruction—a foreign army or leader. And this shall continue even to the end of the whole matter—the end of the events contemplated by the prophecy—the end of the city and the temple. And that which is determined on—the destruction decreed—shall be poured out like a tempest on the city doomed to desolation—desolate as surveyed at the beginning of the prophecy—desolate at the close, and therefore appropriately called "*the desolate.*"

After this protracted examination of the meaning of this prophecy, all the remark which it seems proper to make is, that this prediction could have been the result only of inspiration. There is the clearest evidence that the prophecy was recorded long before the time of the Messiah, and it is manifest that it could not have been the result of any natural sagacity. There is not the slightest proof that it was uttered as late as the coming of Christ, and there is nothing better determined in relation to any ancient matter than that it was recorded long before the birth of the Lord Jesus. But it is equally clear that it could have been the result of no mere natural sagacity. How could such events have been fore-seen except by Him who knows all things? How could the order have been determined? How could the time have been fixed? How could it have been anticipated that the Messiah, the Prince, would be cut off? How could it have been known that he would cause the sacrifice and oblation to cease? How could it have been ascer-tained that the period during which he would be engaged in this would be one week—or about seven years? How could it be predicted that a remarkable event would occur in the middle of that period that would in fact cause the sacrifice and oblation ultimately to cease? And how could it be conjec-tured that a foreign prince would come, and plant the standard of abomination in the holy city, and sweep all away —laying the city and the temple in ruins, and bringing the whole polity to an end? These things lie beyond the range of natural sagacity, and if they are fairly implied in this prophecy, they demonstrate that this portion of the book is from God.

CHAPTER X.

ANALYSIS OF THE CHAPTER.

This chapter introduces the last re-velation made to Daniel, and is *merely* introductory to the disclosures made in the two following chapters. The whole extends to the time of the coming of the Messiah, embracing a detail of the principal historical events that would occur, and closes with some

fearful allusions to the ultimate results of human conduct in the day of judg-ment, and to the great principles on which God governs the world. The contents of this introductory chapter are as follows:—(a) The statement of the time when the revelation occurred, ver. 1. This was in the third year of Cyrus king of Persia, subsequently, therefore, to the visions in the previous chapters, and after the order had been given by Cyrus for the restoration of the Jews, Ezra i. 1. (b) The particular period when this occurred was when Daniel was observing a fast that con-tinued through three weeks, vers. 2, 3. This was at the passover, the first month in their ecclesiastical year, and the fast was observed by Daniel, evi-dently, on account of the sins and the calamities of his people. (c) The place where this occurred, ver. 4. He was by the side of the river Hiddekel or Tigris. Why he was there he does not say. But it is to be remembered that he seems to have been employed on some occasions in other parts of the empire than Babylon; and one of his former visions occurred on the banks of a river that flowed into the Tigris —the river Ulai. See Notes on ch. viii. 2. Indeed, it would appear that the banks of rivers were not unfre-quently the places to which the pro-phets resorted, or where they were fa-voured with their visions. They were retired places, and were on many ac-counts favourable for devotion. Comp. Ezek. i. 1; Acts xvi. 13. See also Rev. xxii. 1, 2. (d) While there, en-gaged in his devotions, Daniel saw a man, who suddenly appeared to him, clothed in linen, and girded with a belt of gold. Those who were with him fled astonished, and left him alone to contemplate the vision, and to re-ceive the communication which this glorious stranger had to make to him.

CHAPTER X.

IN the third year of Cyrus king of Persia, a thing was revealed unto Daniel, whose name was called Belteshazzar; and the thing *was* true, but the time appointed *was*

The effect of this vision on himself, however, was wholly to overcome him, to prostrate him to the earth, and to render him insensible, until the angel touched him, and raised him up, vers. 4–10. In all this there is nothing unnatural. The effect is such as would be produced in any case in similar circumstances, and it has a striking resemblance to what occurred to Saul of Tarsus on his way to Damascus (Acts ix. 3, 4; xxii. 7–9; and to John in the visions of Patmos, Rev. i. 10–17. (*e*) He who had thus appeared to Daniel proceeded to state to him the design for which he had come, vers. 11–14. The prayer of Daniel, he said, had been heard the first day in which he had given himself to these solemn acts of devotion. He had himself been commissioned at that time to come to Daniel, and to disclose the events which were to occur. During a period of twenty-one days, however, in which Daniel had been engaged in this season of devotion, he had been withstood by "the prince of the kingdom of Persia," and had been detained until Michael, one of the chief princes, had interposed to release him, and he had now come, at last, to make known to Daniel what would occur to his people in the latter days. The nature of this detention will, of course, be considered in the Notes on ver. 13. (*f*) Daniel then (vers. 15–17) describes the effect which this vision had on him, rendering him unable to converse with him who had thus appeared to him. (*g*) The heavenly messenger then touched him, and bade him be of good courage and be strong (vers. 18, 19), and then said that he would return and fight with the prince

of Persia, after having stated that which was "noted in the Scripture of truth," vers. 20, 21.

1. *In the third year of Cyrus, king of Persia.* In regard to Cyrus, see Notes on Isa. xli. 2. In ch. i. 21, it is said that "Daniel continued even unto the first year of king Cyrus." But it is not necessarily implied in that passage that he *died* then. It may mean only that he continued in authority, and was employed, in various ways, as a public officer, until that time. See Notes on that passage. For anything that appears, he may have lived several years after, though, for causes now unknown, he may have retired from the court after the accession of Cyrus. This vision may have occurred when he was no longer a public officer, though the whole narrative leads us to suppose that he had not lost his interest in the affairs of the Jewish people. He may have retired on account of age, though his declining years would be naturally devoted to the welfare of his people, and he would embrace any opportunity which he might have of doing them good. ¶ *A thing was revealed unto Daniel.* A revelation was made to him. The occasion on which it was done is stated in the next verse. It was when he was earnestly engaged in prayer for his people, and when his mind was deeply anxious in regard to their condition. ¶ *Whose name was called Belteshazzar.* See Notes on ch. i. 7. The name Belteshazzar was probably that by which he was known in Babylon, and as this prophecy was perhaps published in his own time, the use of this name would serve to identify the author. The name *Daniel* would have been sufficient to give it currency and authority among his own countrymen. ¶ *And the thing* was *true*. That is, it would be certainly accomplished. This expresses the deep conviction of the writer that what was revealed in this vision would certainly come to pass. In his own mind there was no

long: [1] and he understood the thing, and had understanding of the vision.

1 *great.*

doubt that it would be so, though the time extended through many years, and though it could not be expected that it would be complete until long after his own death. Perhaps the declaration here is designed to bring the weight of his own authority and his well-known character to pledge his own word, that what is here said would be accomplished; or, as we should say, to stake his veracity as a prophet and a man, on the fulfilment of what he had affirmed. Such an assertion *might* be of great use in consoling the minds of the Jews in the troubles that were to come upon their nation. ¶ *But the time appointed* was *long.* Marg., *great.* There is considerable variety in the translation and interpretation of this passage. The Latin Vulgate renders it, *fortitudo magna.* The Greek, "And the power was great." The Syriac, "And the discourse was apprehended with great effort, but he understood the vision." Luther, "And it was of great matters." Lengerke, "And the misery (*Elend*) is great;" that is, the distress of the people. Bertholdt renders it, "Whose contents pertained to great wars." This variety of interpretation arises from the word rendered in our version "the time appointed"—אָבָצ.

This word properly means an army, host, as going forth to war; then the host of angels, of the stars, and hence God is so often called "Jehovah of hosts." Then the word means warfare, military service, a hard service, a season of affliction or calamity. See Notes on Job vii. 1. It seems to me that this is the meaning here, and that Gesenius (*Lex.*) has correctly expressed the idea: "And true is the edict, and *relates to long warfare;* that is, to many calamities to be endured." It was not a thing to be soon accomplished, nor did it pertain to peaceful and easy times, but it had reference to the calamities, the evils, and the hardships of wars— wars attended with the evils to which they are usually incident, and which were to be conducted on a great scale.

2 In those days I Daniel was mourning three [2] full weeks.

2 *weeks of days.*

This interpretation will accord with the details in the following chapters. ¶ *And he understood the thing,* &c. This seems to be said in contradistinction to what had occurred on some other occasions when the meaning of the vision which he saw was concealed from him. Of this he says he had full understanding. The prophecy was, in fact, more clearly expressed than had been usual in the revelations made to Daniel, for this is almost entirely a historical narrative, and there could be little doubt as to its meaning.

2. *In those days I Daniel was mourning.* I was afflicting myself; that is, he had set apart this time as an extraordinary fast. He was sad and troubled. He does not say on what account he was thus troubled, but there can be little doubt that it was on account of his people. This was two years after the order had been given by Cyrus for the restoration of the Hebrew people to their country, but it is not improbable that they met with many embarrassments in their efforts to return, and possibly there may have sprung up in Babylon some difficulties on the subject that greatly affected the mind of Daniel. The difficulties attending such an enterprise as that of restoring a captured people to their country, when the march lay across a vast desert, would at any time have been such as to have made an extraordinary season of prayer and fasting proper. ¶ *Three full weeks.* Marg., *weeks of days.* Heb., "Three sevens of days." He does not say whether he had designedly set apart that time to be occupied as a season of fasting, or whether he had, under the influence of deep feeling, continued his fast from day to day until it reached that period. Either supposition will accord with the circumstances of the case, and either would have justified such an act at any time, for it would be undoubtedly proper to designate a time of extraordinary devotion, or, under the influence of deep feeling, of domestic trouble, of national affliction, to continue

3 I ate no [1] pleasant bread, neither came flesh nor wine in my mouth, neither did I anoint myself at all, till three whole weeks were fulfilled.

     1 *bread of desires.*

4 And in the four and twentieth day of the first month, as I was by the side of the great river, which *is* Hiddekel;

5 Then I lifted up mine eyes,

---

such religious exercises from day to day.

3. *I ate no pleasant bread.* Marg., *bread of desires.* So the Hebrew. The meaning is, that he abstained from ordinary food, and partook of that only which was coarse and disagreeable. ¶ *Neither came flesh nor wine in my mouth.* That is, he lived on bread or vegetables. It is not to be inferred from this that Daniel ordinarily made use of wine, for it would seem from ch. i. that that was not his custom. What would appear from this passage would be, that he practised on this occasion the most rigid abstinence. ¶ *Neither did I anoint myself.* The use of unguents was common in the East (see Notes on Matt. vi. 17), and Daniel here says that he abstained during these three weeks from that which he ordinarily observed as promoting his personal comfort. He gave himself up to a course of life which would be expressive of deep grief. Nature prompts to this when the mind is overwhelmed with sorrow. Not only do we become indifferent to our food, but it requires an effort *not* to be indifferent to our dress, and to our personal appearance.

4. *And in the four and twentieth day of the first month.* At the close of his season of fasting. Though he had not set apart this season of fasting with any view or expectation that it would be followed by such a result, yet there was a propriety that an occasion like this should be selected as that on which the communication which follows should be made to his mind; for (*a*) his mind was in a prepared state by this extraordinary season of devotion for such a communication; and (*b*) his attention during that period had been turned towards the condition of his people, and it was a fit opportunity to impart to him these extraordinary views of what would occur to them in future days. It may be added, that we shall be more likely to receive

Divine communications to our souls at the close of seasons of sincere and prolonged devotion than at other times, and that, though we may set apart such seasons for different purposes, the Spirit of God may take occasion from them to impart to us clear and elevated views of Divine truth, and of the Divine government. A man is in a better state to obtain such views, and is more likely to obtain them, in such circumstances than he is in others, and he who desires to understand God and his ways should wait upon him with intense and prolonged devotion. The *time* here specified is the "first month"—the month Nisan, answering to a part of our month April. This was the month in which the Passover was celebrated, and was a time, therefore, which a Jew would be likely to select as a season of extraordinary devotion. It was, for some reason, very common for the prophets to record *the very day* on which the visions which they saw appeared to them, or on which Divine communications were made to them. This was often of importance, because it served to determine the time when a prophecy was fulfilled. ¶ *I was by the side of the great river, which is Hiddekel.* That is, the Tigris. The Syriac renders it the Euphrates. The name in the Scriptures, however, denotes the Tigris. *Why* Daniel was there he does not say. He was often away from Babylon (comp. Notes on ch. viii. 2), and he may have been now among some of his people who resided near the Tigris. Possibly he may at that time have ceased to reside at the court in Babylon, and have taken up his residence in some place on the Tigris. See Notes on ver. 1.

5. *Then I lifted up mine eyes, and looked,* &c. While he was engaged in devotion. What is here said would lead us to suppose that he had been occupied in deep thought and meditation, perhaps with his eyes fixed on

and looked, and, behold, [1] a certain
man clothed in linen, whose loins
were girded with fine gold of Uphaz.

1 *one.*

6 His body *a* also *was* like the
beryl, and his face as the appearance of lightning, and his eyes as

a Rev. 1. 13–17.

---

the ground. ¶ *Behold, a certain man
clothed in linen.* One who had the
form and appearance of a man.

[To the same extent that the prophetic beasts
find their types in the conventional forms of
the Assyrian divinities, it is probable that the
"certain man clothed in linen, whose loins
were girded with fine gold of Uphaz," has reference to the gorgeous kingly and sacerdotal
costume shown in the annexed engraving. This
figure forms a tablet or slab, taken from one of
the chambers at Nimroud, and represents the
Assyrian monarch in his twofold character of
king and priest. It is "one of the most carefully sculptured and best preserved in the palace, and is included in the collection sent to
England." The king has one hand on the hilt
of his sword, and with the other grasps a wand,
or staff.]

The subsequent disclosures showed
that he was an angel, but when angels
have appeared on earth they have commonly assumed the human form. The
margin is, "*one.*" So also is the
Hebrew "one man." From ch. xii. 6,
it would seem that two other such
beings appeared in the course of the

vision, but either one only was manifest now to Daniel, or his attention
was particularly directed to him. The
name of this celestial messenger is not
given, but all the circumstances of the
case lead us to suppose that it was the
same who had appeared to him on the
banks of the Ulai (ch. viii. 16), and
the same who had made the revelation
of the seventy weeks, ch. ix. 21, *seq.*
Linen was the common raiment of
priests, because it was supposed to be
more pure than wool, Exod. xxviii. 42;
Lev. vi. 10; xvi. 4, 23; 1 Sam. ii. 18.
It was also worn by prophets, Jer.
xiii. 1, and is represented as the raiment of angels, Rev. xv. 6. The nature of the raiment would suggest the
idea at once that this person thus appearing was one sustaining a saintly
character. ¶ *Whose loins* were *girded
with fine gold of Uphaz.* With a girdle
made of fine gold; that is, probably,
it was made of something in which
fine gold was interwoven, so as to give
it the appearance of pure gold. It
was customary in the East, as it is
now, to wear a girdle around the loins.
See Notes on Matt. v. 38–41. These
girdles are often made of rich material,
and are highly ornamented. Compare
Notes on Rev. i. 13. Nothing is known
of Uphaz, unless, as Gesenius supposes, the word is a corruption of
Ophir, made by a change of a single
letter—ז for ר. Ophir was celebrated
for its gold, but its situation is unknown. See Notes on Job xxii. 24.

6. *His body also* was *like the beryl.*
There is a very striking resemblance
between the description here given and
that of the Saviour as he appeared to
John in Patmos, Rev. i. 13–16. See
Notes on that passage. It contains,
however, no description of the appearance of the *body.* *Beryl* is "a mineral
of great hardness, occurring in green
and bluish-green six-sided prisms. It
is identical with the emerald, except
that the latter has a purer and richer
colour."—Dana, in Webster's *Dic.*
The Hebrew word here used is תַּרְשִׁישׁ

lamps of fire, and his arms and his feet like in colour to polished brass, and the voice of his words like the voice of a multitude.

7 And I Daniel alone saw the vision: for the men that were with me saw not the vision; but a great quaking fell upon them, so that they fled to hide themselves.

8 Therefore I was left alone, and

Tarshish, Tartessus, and properly refers to a country supposed to be on the south of Spain, a place where this mineral was probably found. This was situated between the mouths of the river Bætis, or Guadalquivir, and was a flourishing mart of the Phœnicians, Gen. x. 4; Psa. lxxii. 10; Isa. xxiii. 1, 6, 10, &c.—Gesenius. The name was given to this gem because it was brought from that place. The true meaning of the word, as applied to a gem, is supposed to be the chrysolite, that is, the topaz of the moderns. "Tarshish, the chrysolite," says Rosenmüller (*Mineralogy and Botany of the Bible,* pp. 38, 39), "is a crystalline precious stone of the quartz kind, of a glassy fracture. The prevailing colour is yellowish-green, and pistachiogreen of every variety and degree of shade, but always with a yellow and gold lustre. It is completely diaphanous, and has a strong double refraction. Most commonly the chrysolite is found solid and in grains, or in angular pieces. The Hebrew word *Tarshish* denotes the south of Spain, the Tartessus of the Greeks and Romans, a place to which the Phœnicians traded even in the earliest ages. Probably the Phœnicians first brought the chrysolite from Spain to Syria, and it was on that account called *Tarshish stone.*" ¶ *And his face as the appearance of lightning.* Bright, shining. In Rev. i. 16 it is, "And his countenance was as the sun shineth in his strength." See Notes on that passage. ¶ *And his eyes as lamps of fire.* Keen, penetrating. So in Rev. i. 14: "His eyes were as a flame of fire." ¶ *And his arms and his feet like in colour to polished brass.* So in Rev. i. 15: "And his feet like unto fine brass, as if they burned in a furnace." See Notes on that passage. The meaning is, that they were bright—like burnished metal. The Hebrew here is, "like the *eye* of brass;" then, as the word *eye* comes to denote the *face* or *countenance,* the

meaning is, "like the face or *appearance* of brass." Compare Exod. x. 5, 15; Numb. xxii. 5, 11. It is easy to conceive of the appearance which one would make whose arms and feet resembled burnished brass. ¶ *And the voice of his words like the voice of a multitude.* A multitude of people—loud and strong. So in Rev. i. 15: "And his voice as the sound of many waters."

7. *And I Daniel alone saw the vision.* That is, he only saw it distinctly. The others who were with him appear to have seen or heard something which alarmed them, and they fled. Who those men were, or why they were with him, he does not say. They may have been his own countrymen, engaged with him in the act of devotion, or they may have been Babylonians occupied in the public service; but whoever they were, or whatever was the reason why they were there, they became alarmed and fled. The case was somewhat different with the companions of Saul of Tarsus when the Saviour appeared to him on his way to Damascus. These saw the light; they all fell to the earth together, but Saul only heard the voice of him that spake. Acts xxii. 9.

8. *Therefore I was left alone, and saw this great vision.* That is, I distinctly saw it, or contemplated it. He perceived, doubtless, that it was a heavenly vision; and as he had often been favoured with similar manifestations, he remained to receive the communication which probably he understood was to be made. ¶ *And there remained no strength in me.* He was completely overcome. A similar effect was produced on John when he was in Patmos: "And when I saw him I fell at his feet as dead," Rev. i. 17. That he should be overcome, and his strength taken away, was not an unnatural effect; and what occurred to Daniel and John may demonstrate that there *may* be such views of the Divine character and glory now as to prostrate our phy-

saw this great vision, and there remained no strength in me: for my ¹comeliness was turned in me into corruption, and I retained no strength.

9 Yet heard I the voice of his words: and when I heard the voice of his words, then was I in a deep sleep on my face, and my face toward the ground.

10 ¶ And, behold, an hand touched me, which ²set me upon

1 or, *vigour.*   2 *moved.*

my knees and *upon* the palms of my hands:

11 And he said unto me, O Daniel, a man ³ greatly beloved, understand the words that I speak unto thee, and stand ⁴upright: for unto thee am I now sent. And when he had spoken this word unto me, I stood trembling.

12 Then said he unto me, Fear not, Daniel; for from the first day that thou didst set thine heart to

3 *of desires.*   4 *upon thy standing.*

sical powers. It is certain that such visions as those which appeared to Daniel and John would have this effect; and, though we are not to expect that they will now be vouchsafed to men, no one can doubt that there *may* be such views of God, and heaven, and eternal realities presented to the eye of faith and hope; such joy in the evidence of pardoned sin; such a change from a sense of condemnation to the peace resulting from forgiveness, that the powers of the body may be prostrated, and sink from exhaustion. Indeed, it is not much of the revelation of the Divine character that in our present state we can bear. ¶ *For my comeliness.* Marg., *vigour.* Heb., הוד *hōdh.* The word means, properly, majesty or splendour; then beauty or brightness, as of the complexion. The meaning here is, that his "*bright complexion*" (Gesenius, *Lex.*) was changed upon him; that is, that he turned pale. ¶ *Into corruption.* The phrase here used means literally "into destruction." The sense is, that by the change that came over him, his beauty—his bright or florid complexion was completely *destroyed.* He became deadly pale.

9. *Yet heard I the voice of his words.* What the angel said when he appeared to him Daniel has not recorded. He says (ver. 6) that the voice of his words was "like the voice of a multitude." It is probable that those who were with him had heard that voice, and hearing it, and being struck with the remarkable character of the vision, they had suddenly fled in alarm. Daniel heard more distinctly what he said, though it does not yet appear

that he had heard anything more than the *sound* of his voice. ¶ *And when I heard the voice of his words, then was I in a deep sleep on my face.* Comp. Notes on ch. viii. 18. Lengerke renders this, "I *sank* into a deep sleep," &c. This is undoubtedly the meaning, that when he heard this voice he was overcome, and sank prostrate and senseless upon the earth. The sense of the Hebrew may be thus expressed: "I became (הָיִיתִי) oppressed with sleep," &c.

10. *And, behold, an hand touched me.* The hand of the angel. Comp. ch. viii. 18. ¶ *Which set me upon my knees and* upon *the palms of my hands.* Not "upright," as in ch. viii. 18. That is, he had not strength given him at once to stand erect, but he was partially raised up and enabled to move, though in a feeble and tottering manner. The word here used (נוּעַ) means to move to and fro; to waver; to vacillate; and the sense here, as expressed by Gesenius (*Lex.*) is, "lo, a hand touched me, and caused me to reel (*i.e.*, to stand reeling and trembling) upon my knees and hands." He was gradually restored to strength.

11. *And he said unto me, O Daniel, a man greatly beloved.* That is, in heaven. Marg., as in Heb., *of desires.* See Notes on ch. ix. 23. ¶ *Understand the words that I speak unto thee.* That is, attend to them, implying that he would be able to understand them. ¶ *And stand upright.* Marg., as in Heb., *upon thy standing.* That is, stand erect. See Notes on ch. viii. 18.

12. *Then said he unto me, Fear not.*

understand, and to chasten thyself before thy God, thy words were heard, *a* and I am come for thy words.

13 But the prince of the kingdom of Persia withstood me one and twenty days: but, lo, Michael, [1] one of the chief princes, came to help me; and I remained there with the kings of Persia.

a Acts 10. 30, 31.

1 or, *the first.*   Jude 9; Rev. 12. 7.

Be not alarmed at my presence; do not fear that your devotions are not accepted, and that your prayers are not heard. ¶ *For from the first day that thou didst set thine heart to understand.* That is, by a season of extraordinary devotion. Daniel had devoted three full weeks to such a service (vers. 2, 3), and it would seem from this that one object which he had in view was to make inquiry about the future condition of his people, or to learn what was his own duty in the present circumstances, or what methods he might use to secure the return of his countrymen to their own land. The circumstances of the case were such as to make either of these inquiries proper; and the angel now affirms that, from the first day when he entered on these investigations, he was despatched to come to him, and to assure him that his prayer was heard. The reason why he had not sooner arrived, and why Daniel was left to continue his prayers so long without any answer being returned, is stated in the following verses. Comp. Notes on ch. ix. 23. ¶ *And to chasten thyself before thy God.* That is, by fasting and humiliation. Literally, *to afflict thyself.* ¶ *Thy words were heard.* In heaven. Another proof that prayer is at once heard, though the answer may be long delayed. The instance before us shows that the answer to prayer may *seem* to be delayed, from causes unknown to us, though the prayer ascends at once to heaven, and God *designs* to answer it. In this case, it was deferred by the detention of the messenger on the way (ver. 13); in other cases it may be from a different cause; but it should never be set down as a proof that prayer is not heard, and that it will not be answered, because the answer is not granted at once. Weeks, or months, or years may elapse before the Divine purpose shall be made known, though, so to speak, the messenger may be on his way to us. Something may prevent the answer being borne to us; some "prince of the kingdom of Persia" may withstand the messenger; some cause which we may not know may hinder the immediate answer of our prayer, either in our own hearts, or in outward events which cannot at once be controlled without a miracle, or in the feelings and views of our friends whom we seek to have converted and saved; but the purpose to answer the prayer may have been simultaneous with its being offered, and a train of measures may have been commenced at once to bring about the result, though many weeks or months of delay, of anxiety, of tears, may elapse before we attain the object we desired. Daniel would have been cheered in his days of fasting and service if he had known that an angel was *on his way* to him to comfort him, and to communicate to him an answer from God; often—if not *always*—in our days of deepest anxiety and trouble; when our prayers seem not to penetrate the skies; when we meet with no response; when the thing for which we pray seems to be withheld; when our friends remain unconverted; when irreligion abounds and prevails; when we seem to be doing no good, and when calamity presses upon us, if we saw the arrangement which God was already making to answer the prayer, and could see the messenger on the way, our hearts would exult, and our tears would cease to flow. And why, in our days of trouble and anxiety, should we not believe that it *is* so; and that God, even though the delay may seem to be long, will yet show himself to be a hearer and an answerer of prayer?

13. *But the prince of the kingdom of Persia.* In explaining this very difficult verse, it may be proper (1) to

consider the literal sense of the words; (2) to deduce the fair meaning of the passage as thus explained; and (3) to notice the practical truths taught. The word rendered *prince*—שַׂר *săr*— means, properly, a leader, commander, chief, as of troops, Gen. xxi. 22; of a king's body-guard, Gen. xxxvii. 36; of cup-bearers, Gen. xli. 9; of a prison, Gen. xxxix. 21, 22; of a flock, Gen. xlvii. 6. Then it means a prince, a noble, a chief in the state, Gen. xii. 15. In Dan. viii. 25, in the phrase "Prince of princes," it refers to God. So far as the *word* is concerned in the phrase "prince of the kingdom of Persia," it might refer to a prince ruling over that kingdom, or to a prime minister of the state; but the language also is such that it is applicable to an angelic being supposed to preside over a state, or to influence its counsels. If this idea is admitted; if it is believed that angels *do* thus preside over particular states, this language would properly express that fact. Gesenius (*Lex.*) explains it in this passage as denoting the "chiefs, princes, and angels; *i.e.,* the archangels acting as patrons and advocates of particular nations before God." That this is the proper meaning here as deduced from the words is apparent, for (*a*) it is an angel that is speaking, and it would seem most natural to suppose that he had encountered one of his own rank; (*b*) the mention of Michael who came to his aid—a name which, as we shall see, properly denotes an angel, leads to the same conclusion; (*c*) it accords, also, with the prevailing belief on the subject. Undoubtedly, one who takes into view all the circumstances referred to in this passage would most naturally understand this of an angelic being, having some kind of jurisdiction over the kingdom of Persia. What was the *character* of this "prince," however, whether he was a good or bad angel, is not intimated by the language. It is only implied that he had a chieftainship, or some species of guardian care over that kingdom—watching over its interests and directing its affairs. As he offered resistance, however, to this heavenly messenger on

his way to Daniel, as it was necessary to counteract his plans, and as the aid of Michael was required to overcome his opposition, the fair construction is, that he belonged to the class of evil angels. ¶ *Withstood me.* Heb., "stood over against me." Vulgate, *restitit mihi.* The fair meaning is, that he resisted or opposed him; that he stood over against him, and delayed him on his way to Daniel. In what manner he did this is not stated. The most obvious interpretation is, that, in order to answer the prayers of Daniel in respect to his people, it was necessary that some arrangement should be made in reference to the kingdom of Persia —influencing the government to be favourable to the restoration of the Jews to their own land; or removing some obstacles to such return—obstacles which had given Daniel such disquietude, and which had been thrown in his way by the presiding angel of that kingdom. ¶ *One and twenty days.* During the whole time in which Daniel was engaged in fasting and prayer (vers. 2, 3). The angel had been sent forth to make arrangements to secure the answer to his prayer when he began to pray, but had been delayed during all that time by the opposition which he had met with in Persia. That is, it required all that time to overcome the obstacles existing there to the accomplishment of these purposes, and to make those arrangements which were necessary to secure the result. Meantime, Daniel, not knowing that these arrangements were in a process of completion, or that an angel was employed to secure the answer to his prayers, yet strong in faith, was suffered to continue his supplications with no intimation that his prayers were heard, or that he would be answered. How many arrangements may there be in progress designed to answer our prayers of which we know nothing! How many agents may be employed to bring about an answer! What mighty obstacles may be in a process of removal, and what changes may be made, and what influences exerted, while we are suffered to pray, and fast, and weep, amidst many discouragements, and many trials of our faith and patience!

For a much longer period than Daniel was engaged in his devotions, may we be required often now to pray before the arrangements in the course of Providence shall be so far complete that we shall receive an answer to our supplications, for the things to be done may extend far into future months or years. ¶ *But, lo, Michael, one of the chief princes.* Marg., *the first.* That is, the first in rank of the "princes," or the angels. In other words, "Michael, the archangel." The proper meaning of this name (מִיכָאֵל) is, "Who as God," and is a name given, undoubtedly, from some resemblance to God. The exact reason *why* it is given is not anywhere stated; but may it not be this—that one looking on the majesty and glory of the chief of the angels would instinctively ask, "Who, after all, is like God? Even this lofty angel, with all his glory, cannot be compared to the high and lofty One." Whatever may have been the reason of the appellation, however, the name in the Scriptures has a definite application, and is given to the chief one of the angels. Comp. Notes on Jude 9. The word *Michael*, as a proper name, occurs several times in the Scriptures, Nu. xiii. 13; 1 Ch. v. 13; vi. 40; vii. 3; viii. 16; xii. 20; xxvii. 18; 2 Chron. xxi. 2; Ezra viii. 8. It is used as applicable to an angel or archangel in the following places: Dan. x. 13, 21; xii. 1; Jude 9; Rev. xii. 7. Little more is known of him than (*a*) that he occupied the rank which entitled him to be called an archangel; and (*b*) that he sustained, in the time of Daniel, the relation of patron of Israel before God (ch. x. 21). That an *angel* is referred to here is manifest; for, (1.) It occurs in the account of transactions conducted by an angel. (2.) The use of the word elsewhere leads to this supposition. (3.) What is said to have been done is the appropriate work of an angel. This is apparent, because Gabriel, the speaker, says that what was done was beyond *his* power to accomplish. He was effectually resisted and thwarted by the counsels of Persia, until one of higher wisdom and rank than himself came to his aid. He

could, therefore, have been no less than an angel, and was clearly a being of a higher rank than Gabriel himself. (4.) The phrase "one of the chief princes" sustains this interpretation. It implies that he was one of those who held an exalted rank among those who are called "princes," and if this word in this connection denotes *angels*, then Michael was an angel, and one of the most exalted of the angels. This accords with the appellation given to him by Jude — "the archangel." ¶ *Came to help me.* He does not state in what way this was done, but it is fairly implied that it was by securing better counsels at the court of Persia —counsels more favourable to the Hebrews, and different from those which would have been carried out under the auspices of him who is called "the prince of Persia." There is nothing in the passage to forbid the supposition that it was by so influencing the mind of the king and his ministers as to dispose them to favour the return of the Jews, or to afford them facilities to rebuild their temple, or to remove some of the obstacles which would tend to prevent their restoration. ¶ *And I remained there with the kings of Persia.* The *kings* of Persia here, in the plural, must mean the *rulers*. There was properly but one *king* of that nation, though the name may have been given to subordinate rulers, or perhaps to those who *had been* kings in their own country, and whose countries had been subdued by the Persian arms, and who now resided, with more or less authority, at the Persian court. The phrase "I remained there" has been variously translated. The Vulgate renders it as in our version. The Greek, "And I left him [to wit, Michael] there with the prince of the kingdom of Persia." The Syriac, "And I was hindered there against the prince of the Persians." Luther, "Then obtained I the victory with the kings in Persia." Lengerke, "Then obtained I the ascendency (Vorrang) among the kings of Persia." That is, as he explains it, "I obtained the victory; I secured this result that my counsel in behalf of the Jewish people prevailed," p. 503. The same explanation is given by Geier,

Gesenius, De Wette, Hävernick. The word רָתַי (*Yáthar*) properly means, to hang out and over ; to be redundant ; to remain or be left ; to be over and above ; to excel, &c. Hence the notion in Niphal, of excelling others, of getting the ascendency, of obtaining a victory. This is, undoubtedly, the meaning here, for he was not *left* with the kings of Persia ; he did not *remain* there. The true idea is, that by the help of Michael, who came to his aid, he was enabled so far to influence the Persian counsels against the purposes of him who is called the "prince of Persia," as to secure the favours for the Hebrew people which Daniel sought by prayer; and having done this, he came at once to him. The only delay in the case was that which was caused by the purposes of the Persian court, and by the difficulty of securing such arrangements there as to favour the Hebrew people, and to facilitate their return to their own country. Having done this, he came at once to Daniel to announce the long series of events which would follow pertaining to his people, and in reference to which his mind had been so much affected during his protracted period of devotion.

Such is the explanation of the literal meaning of this difficult passage. Now, in reference to the second point suggested as necessary to its proper interpretation — its real meaning — the exact truth taught in it, the following remarks may be made :—(1.) There was early a prevailing opinion that special angels had the charge of individuals, as their guardians ; and the same idea existed respecting nations, that their affairs were assigned to particular celestial beings. This notion among the Hebrews was found in *this* form—that they were *angels*, or *created* beings of exalted rank who thus presided over the affairs of men. Among the Greeks, and other heathen nations, the form which it took was, that they were *gods* or tutelary divinities, and hence each people, each class, each family, each house, had its own god. The Hebrews never approximated to this opinion so far as to suppose that these beings were divine, or that they occupied

the place of the supreme God—JEHO-VAH — who was peculiarly their covenant God, and who was the only true God. They did admit the supposition, however, that there might be guardian angels of their own nation, and the same idea seems to have prevailed among them in regard to other nations. This is clearly the idea in the passage before us, that while Michael was, in a peculiar sense, intrusted with the affairs of the Hebrew people, there were intelligent invisible beings of angelic rank who presided over other nations, and who influenced their counsels. It does not appear by any means that it was supposed that in all cases these were *good* beings, for the counsels of the nations were too often malignant and evil to admit of this supposition. In the case before us, it is evidently supposed that the influence of the presiding angel of Persia was adverse to that which was right, and such as should be counteracted by one who came from heaven. Comp. Notes on Eph. ii. 2. (2.) No one can demonstrate that this is *not* so. The existence of wicked angels is no more incredible in itself than the existence of wicked men, and that they should influence nations and rulers is in itself no more improbable than that distinguished statesmen should. There may be, indeed, no foundation for the opinion that particular angels are *assigned* to particular individuals or nations as peculiar *guardians ;* but it may be true, notwithstanding, that some one of these fallen spirits—for if there are *any* such beings at all, they are numerous—may have special influence over a particular individual or nation. If it be said that we know too little about this to enable us to make any positive statements in *favour* of this opinion, it should also be said that we know too little to enable us to make any positive statements *against* it ; and for aught any one can prove, it *may* be so. No one has a right to assume that it is not so ; no one can demonstrate that it is not so. It may be said further, that things look *as if* this were so. There are many influences on nations and individuals; many things that occur that can be most easily accounted for on the supposition that there is such an agency from some invisible quarter. If we admit the reality of such influence, and such interpositions, the things which occur are more easily explained than if we deny it. There are measures taken; plans proposed; influences exerted; schemes adopted—there are things from an unseen quarter to give prosperity, or to thwart the best laid plans, that cannot be well explained without the supposition of such an interference; things which perplex all philosophers and all historians in accounting for them; things which cannot be anticipated or explained on any known principles of human nature. If we admit the reality of the influence of invisible beings, as in the case before us, the solution becomes comparatively easy; at least we find phenomena just such as we should expect on such a supposition. (3.) It may be added, also, in regard to the particular case before us (*a*) that the counsels *against* the Jews to prevent their return to their own land, and to embarrass them, were such as we should anticipate on the supposition that an evil angel—an enemy of God and his people—had influenced the Persian rulers; and (*b*) that the changes wrought *in* those counsels in favour of the Jews, facilitating their return to their own land, were such as we should expect to find on the supposition that those counsels and plans were overruled and changed by the interposition say of Gabriel and Michael. And similar events often happen. There are such changes in the counsels of nations, and in the minds of rulers, as *would* occur on the supposition that superior beings were engaged in thwarting evil plans, and influencing those who have the power to do right. In reference to the Jews in their exile, there had been a long series of acts of opposition and oppression pursued by the governments of the East, *as if* under the direction of some malignant spirit; then a series of acts in their favour followed, *as if* the change had been brought about by the interposition of some benignant angel. These facts are the historical basis on which the representation is here made.

In reference to the third point suggested pertaining to this passage—the practical truths taught that may be of use to us—it may be remarked that the *great* truth is, that the answer to prayer is often delayed, not by any indisposition on the part of God to answer it, and not by any purpose *not* to answer it, and not by the mere intention of trying our faith, but *by the necessary arrangements to bring it about*. It is of such a nature that it *cannot* be answered at once. It requires *time* to make important changes; to influence the minds of men; to remove obstacles; to raise up friends; to put in operation agencies that shall secure the thing desired. There is some obstacle to be overcome. There is some plan of evil to be checked and stayed. There is some agency to be used which is not now in existence, and which is to be created. The opposition of the "prince of Persia" could not be overcome at once, and it was necessary to bring in the agency of a higher power—that of Michael—to effect the change. This could not be done in a moment, a day, or a week, and hence the long delay of three "full weeks" before Daniel had an assurance that his prayers would be answered. So it often happens now. We pray for the conversion of a child; yet there may be obstacles to his conversion, unseen by us, which are to be patiently removed, and perhaps by a foreign influence, before it can be done. Satan may have already secured a control over his heart, which is to be broken gradually, before the prayer shall be answered. We pray for the removal of the evils of intemperance, of slavery, of superstition, of idolatry; yet these may be so interlocked with the customs of a country, with the interests of men, and with the laws, that they cannot be at once eradicated except by miracle, and the answer to the prayer seems to be long delayed. We pray for the universal spread of the gospel of Christ; yet how many obstacles are to be overcome, and how many arrangements made, before this prayer can be fully answered; and how many tears are to be shed, and perils encountered, and lives sacrificed, before the prayer of the church shall be

14 Now I am come to make thee understand what shall befall thy people in the latter *a* days: for *b* yet the vision *is* for *many* days.

15 And when he had spoken such words unto me, I set my face toward the ground, and I became dumb.

16 And, behold, *one* like the

similitude of the sons of men touched *c* my lips: then I opened my mouth and spake, and said unto him that stood before me, O my lord, by the vision my sorrows are turned upon me, and I have retained no strength.*d*

17 For how can ¹ the servant of this my lord talk with this my lord?

a Gen. 49. 1; 2 Tim. 3. 1.
b ch. 8. 26; Hab. 2. 3.

c Isa. 6. 7; Jer. 1. 9.
d ver. 8.　　　　1 or, *this servant of.*

---

fully answered, and the earth shall be filled with the knowledge of the Lord. The *duty*, then, which is taught, is that of patience, of perseverance, of faith in God, of a firm belief that he is true to all his promises, and that he is a hearer of prayer—though the blessing seems long delayed.

14. *Now I am come to make thee understand*, &c. After these long delays, and after the arrangements have been made necessary to bring about the objects sought by your prayers. ¶ *In the latter days.* In future times—extending down to the last period of the world. See Notes on Isa. ii. 2. ¶ *For yet the vision* is *for* many *days.* Extends far into future time. It is probable that the prayer of Daniel referred more particularly to what he desired should soon occur—the restoration of the people to their own land; the angel informs him that the disclosures which he was to make covered a much more extended period, and embraced more important events. So it is often. The answer to prayer often includes much more than we asked for, and the abundant blessings that are conferred, beyond what we supplicate, are vastly beyond a compensation for the delay.

15. *And when he had spoken such words*, &c. Daniel was naturally overcome by the communication which had been made to him. The manner in which the prayer was answered seems to have been entirely different from what he had expected. The presence of a heavenly being; the majesty of his appearance; the assurance that he gave that he had come to answer his prayer; and the fact that he had important revelations to make respecting

the future, overcame him, and he laid his face upon the ground in silence. Is there any one of us who would *not* be awed into profound silence if a heavenly messenger should stand before us to disclose what was to occur to us, to our families, to our friends, to our country, in far-distant years ?

16. *And, behold,* one *like the similitude of the sons of men touched my lips.* In the form of a man. The reference here is undoubtedly to Gabriel appearing to Daniel in human form. Why he does not *name* him is unknown; nor is there any intimation whether he changed his form as he now approached the prophet. It would seem not improbable that, seeing the effect of his presence and his words on Daniel, he laid aside some of the manifestations of awe and majesty in which he had at first appeared to him, and approached him as a man, and placed his hands on his lips—as a sign that he should speak, or as imparting power to him to speak. See Notes on Isa. vi. 6, 7. ¶ *I opened my mouth, and spake.* His fear was removed, and he was now able to address the heavenly messenger. ¶ *O my lord.* A title of respectful address, but without indicating the rank of him to whom it is applied. ¶ *By the vision my sorrows are turned upon me.* The word rendered *sorrows* (צִירִים) means, properly, *writhings, throes, pains,* as of a woman in travail, Isa. xiii. 8; xxi. 3; 1 Sam. iv. 19; and then *any* deep pain or anguish. Here it refers to *terror* or *fright,* as so great as to prostrate the strength of Daniel. The word rendered *are turned* (נֶהֶפְכוּ—from הָפַךְ)

for as for me, straightway there remained no strength in me, neither is there breath left in me.

18 Then there came again and touched me *one* like the appearance of a man, and he strengthened me,

19 And said, O man greatly beloved, fear not; peace *be* unto thee; be strong, yea, be strong. And when he had spoken unto me, I was strengthened, and said, Let my lord speak; for *ᵃ* thou hast strengthened me.

20 Then said he, Knowest thou wherefore I come unto thee? and

a 2 Cor. 12. 9.

means, in Niphal, to turn one's self about, to turn back. The same phrase which is here used occurs also in 1 Sam. iv. 19, "her pains turned upon her;" that is, came upon her. Perhaps *we* should express the idea by saying that they *rolled* upon us, or over us—like the surges of the ocean.

17. *For how can the servant of this my lord.* Acknowledging his humble and lowly condition and rank in the presence of an angel—a messenger now sent from heaven. ¶ *Neither is there breath left in me.* That is, he was utterly overcome and prostrate. He felt that he was incapable of speaking in the presence of one who had descended from God.

18. *Then there came again and touched me,* &c. The same one is here referred to doubtless who is mentioned in ver. 16—the angel. He came to him again in this condescending and familiar manner in order to allay his fears, and to prepare him to receive his communications with entire calmness.

19. *And said, O man greatly beloved.* See Notes on ch. ix. 23. ¶ *Fear not.* Neither at my presence, nor at what I have to say. There was nothing in the visitation of an angel that could be a ground of dread to a good man; there was nothing in what he had to communicate that could be a reasonable cause of alarm. ¶ *Be strong, yea, be strong.* These are words of encouragement such as we address to those who are timid and fearful. We exhort them not to yield; to make a vigorous effort to meet danger, difficulty, or trial. ¶ *Let my lord speak.* That is, I am now prepared to receive what you have to communicate. ¶ *For thou hast strengthened me.* By your encouraging words, and by the kindness of your manner.

20. *Then said he, Knowest thou*

wherefore I come unto thee? This was known by what the angel had said in ver. 14. He seems to have called his attention to it, and to have proposed the question, because Daniel had been so overcome by his fright that it might be doubtful whether he had understood him distinctly when he had told him the object of his coming. He therefore proposes the question here; and as the silence of Daniel seems to have been construed as a declaration that he *did* understand the purpose of the visit, he proceeds to unfold fully the purport of his message. ¶ *And now will I return.* That is, evidently, after he had made known to him the message which he came to deliver. He cannot mean that he would *then* leave Daniel, and return immediately to Persia, for he proceeds at length (ch. xi., xii.) to deliver his message to him, and to state what would occur in the world in future times. ¶ *To fight with the prince of Persia.* In ver. 13, he says that he had had a contest with that "prince," and that in consequence of that he had been delayed on his journey to Daniel. By the interposition of Michael, the affairs of Persia had been so arranged that the opposition to what was desired by Daniel had been in part removed—so far, at least, as to make it certain that his prayers would be answered. See Notes on that verse. But still it would seem that the difficulty was not entirely overcome, and that it would be desirable for him to return, and to complete the arrangements which had been commenced. There were still causes in existence in Persia which might tend to frustrate all these plans unless they were counteracted, and his presence might still be necessary there to secure the safe return of the exiles to their own land, and the means re-

now will I return to fight with the prince *a* of Persia: and when I am

a ver 13.

quired to rebuild the city and temple. The simple meaning of this is, that it would be necessary to exert a farther influence at the Persian court in order to bring about the object desired; and this fact is expressed in language derived from the belief that angelic beings, good and bad, have much to do in controlling the minds of men. ¶ *And when I am gone forth.* Literally, "and I go forth." The meaning seems to be, that he would return to Persia, and would so direct affairs there that the welfare of the Jews would be promoted, and that protection would be extended to them. This, he says, he would continue as long as it was necessary, for when *he* should have gone forth, the king of Greece would come, and the affairs of Persia would be put on a new footing, but on such a footing as not to require *his* presence—for the government would be of itself favourable to the Jews. The sense is, that up to the time when this "king of Grecia" should come, there would be a state of things in the Persian court that would demand the presence of some being from heaven—exerting some constant influence to prevent an outbreak against the Jews, and to secure their peace and prosperity; but that when the "king of Grecia" should come, he would himself favour their cause, and render the presence of the angel unnecessary. No one can prove that this is *not* a correct representation, or that the favour shown to the Jews at the Persian court during all the time of the rebuilding of the city and the temple, was not to be traced to some presiding influence from above, or that that was not put forth in connection with the ministration of an angelic being. Indeed, it is in accordance with all the teachings of the Bible that the disposition of kings and princes to show favour to the people of God, like all else that is good in this world, is to be traced to an influence from above; and it is not contrary to any of the laws of analogy, or anything with which we are ac-

gone forth, lo, the prince of Grecia shall come.

21 But I will show thee that

quainted pertaining to the spiritual world, to suppose that angelic interposition may be employed in any case in bringing about that which is good ¶ *Lo, the prince of Grecia shall come* Hebrew, *Javan*—יָוָן. There can be no doubt that Greece is intended. The word properly denotes Ionia (derived from this word), "the name of which province," says Gesenius, "as being adjacent to the East, and better known, was extended so as to comprehend the whole of Greece, as is expressly said by Greek writers themselves."—*Lex.* By the "prince of Greece" here, there can be no doubt that there is reference to Alexander the Great, who conquered Persia. See ch. xi. 1-4. The meaning here is, that when he should come, and conquer Persia, the opposition which the Hebrews had encountered from that country would cease, and there would then be no need of the interposition of the angel at the Persian court. The matter of fact was, that the Hebrews were favoured by Alexander the Great, and that whatever there was in the Persian or Chaldean power which they had had reason to dread was then brought to an end, for all those Eastern governments were absorbed in the empire of Alexander—the Macedonian monarchy.

21. *But I will show thee that which is noted in the scripture of truth.* The word *noted* here means *written*, or *recorded.* The *scripture of truth* means the *true writing*, and the reference is doubtless to the Divine purposes or decrees in this matter—for (*a*) there is no other writing where these things were then found; (*b*) the angel came to make known what could be known in no other way, and therefore what was not yet found in any book to which man had access; (*c*) this language accords with common representations in the Scriptures respecting future events. They are described as written down in a book that is in the hands of God, in which are recorded

which is noted in the scripture of truth: and *there is* none that [1] *strengtheneth himself.*

holdeth[1] with me in these things, but Michael [a] your prince.

[a] ver. 13.

---

all future events—the names of those that shall be saved—and all the deeds of men. Comp. Deut. xxxii. 34; Mal. iii. 16; Ps. cxxxix. 16; Rev. v. 1. The representation is figurative, of course; and the meaning is, that, in the view of the Divine mind, all future events are as certain as if they were actually recorded as history, or as if they were now all written down. The angel came that he might unfold a portion of that volume, and disclose the contents of its secret pages; that is, describe an important series of events of great interest to the Jewish people and to the world at large. ¶ *And there is none that holdeth with me in these things.* Marg., *strengtheneth himself.* So the Hebrew. The idea is, that there was none that rendered aid in this matter, or that stood by him, and would accomplish the designs which he was meditating in their behalf pertaining to Persia. The angel saw that there were powerful influences against the interests of the Hebrew people at work in the court of Persia; that it was necessary that they should be counteracted; that unless this were done, fearful calamities would come upon the Jewish people, and they would be subjected to great embarrassments in their efforts to rebuild their city and temple, and he says that there was no one whose aid could be permanently and certainly relied on but that of Michael. He himself was to return to the court of Persia to endeavour to counteract the influence of the "prince of Persia," but, as in the former case when on his way to Daniel (ver. 13), he would not have been able to counteract the machinations of that prince if it had not been for the interposition of Michael, so he felt now that reliance was still to be placed on his assistance in the matter. ¶ *But Michael your prince.* See Notes on ver. 13. The patron, or guardian of your people, and of their interests. The idea intended to be conveyed here undoubtedly is, that Michael was a guardian angel for the Jewish people; that he had special charge of their affairs; that his interposition might be depended on in the time of trouble and danger, and that, under him, their interests would be safe. No one can prove that this is *not* so; and as on earth some of the most important favours that we enjoy are conferred by the instrumentality of others; as we are often defended when in danger by them; as we are counselled and directed by them; as God raises up for the orphan, and the widow, and the insane, and the sorrowful, and the feeble, those of wealth, and power, and learning, who can better guard their interests than they could themselves, and as these relations are often sustained, and these favours conferred by those who are invisible to the recipients, so it gives, in a higher sense, a new beauty to the arrangements of the universe to suppose that this benevolent office is often undertaken and discharged by angelic beings. Thus they may defend us from danger; ward off the designs of our enemies; defeat their machinations, and save us from numberless evils that would otherwise come upon us. This view receives additional confirmation, if it be admitted that there are *evil* angels, and that they seek the ruin of mankind. They are malignant; they tempt the race of man; they have power far superior to our own; they can set in operation a train of evil influences which we can neither foresee nor counteract; and they can excite the minds of wicked men to do us injury in a way which we cannot anticipate, and against which we cannot defend ourselves. In these circumstances, any one can perceive that there is concinnity and propriety in the supposition that there are good beings of a higher order who feel an interest in the welfare of man, and who come to us, on their benevolent errand, to defend us from danger, and to aid us in our efforts to escape from the perils of our fallen condition, and to reach the kingdom of heaven.

CHAPTER XI.

ANALYSIS OF THE CHAPTER.

This chapter contains a portion of those things which the angel said were written in "the scripture of truth," and which he came to disclose to Daniel. The revelation also embraces the twelfth chapter, and the two comprise the last recorded communication that was made to Daniel. The revelation which is made in these chapters not only embraces a large portion of history of interest to the Jewish people of ancient times, and designed to give instruction as to the important events that would pertain to their nation, but also, in its progress, alludes to important *periods* in the future as marking decisive eras in the world's history, and contains hints as to what would occur down to the end of all things.

The chapter before us embraces the following definitely marked periods:—

I. The succession of kings in Persia to the time of a mighty king who should **arouse** all the strength of his kingdom to make war on Greece — referring doubtless to Xerxes, vers. 1, 2. Of those kings in Persia there would be three—three so prominent as to deserve notice in the rapid glance at future events—Cambyses, Smerdis, and Darius Hystaspis.

II. After this succession of kings, one would stand up or appear who would be characterized as ruling "with great dominion," and "according to his will," ver. 3. The dominion evidently would pass into his hand, and he would be distinguished from all that went before him. There can be no doubt, from the connection, and from what is said in ver. 4, that the reference here is to Alexander the Great.

III. The state of the empire after the death of this mighty king, ver. 4. His kingdom would be broken, and would be divided into four parts—referring doubtless to the division of the empire of Alexander after his death.

IV. The history then proceeds to notice the events that would pertain to *two* of these portions of the empire —the conflicts between the king of the south, and the king of the north—or between Egypt and Syria, vers. 5-19. This portion of the history embraces, in detail, an account of the policy, the negotiations, and the wars of Antiochus the Great, till the time of his death. These kingdoms are particularly referred to, probably because their conflicts would affect the holy land, and pertain ultimately to the history of religion, and its establishment and triumph in the world. In the notice of these two sovereignties, there is considerable detail—so much so that the principal events could have been readily anticipated by those who were in possession of the writings of Daniel. The destiny of the other two portions of the empire of Alexander did not particularly affect the history of religion, or pertain to the holy land, and therefore they are not introduced. In a particular manner, the history of Antiochus the Great is traced with great minuteness in this portion of the prophecy, because his doings had a special bearing on the Jewish nation, and were connected with the progress of religion. The commentary on this portion of the chapter will show that the leading events are traced *as* accurately as would be a summary of the history made out *after* the transactions had occurred.

V. A brief reference to the successor of Antiochus the Great, Seleucus IV., ver. 20. As he occupied the throne, however, but for a short period, and as his doings did not particularly affect the condition of the Hebrew people, or the interests of religion, and his

CHAPTER XI.

ALSO I, in the first *a* year of Darius the Mede, *even* I stood

to confirm and to strengthen him.

2 And now will I show *a* thee

a ch. 9. 1.   *a* Amos 3. 7.

reign was, in every respect, unimportant, it is passed over with only a slight notice.

VI. The life and acts of Antiochus Epiphanes, vers. 21–45. There can be no doubt that this portion of the chapter refers to Antiochus, and it contains a full detail of his character and of his doings. The account here, though without naming him, is just such as would have been given by one who should have written *after* the events had occurred, and there is no more difficulty in applying the description in this chapter to him now than there would have been in such a historical narrative. The revelation is made, evidently, to prepare the Jewish people for these fearful events, and these heavy trials, in their history; and also to assure them that more glorious results would follow, and that deliverance would succeed these calamities. In the troubles which Antiochus would bring upon the Hebrew people, it was important that they should have before them a record containing the great outlines of what would occur, and the assurance of ultimate triumph—just as it is important for us now in the trials which we have reason to anticipate in this life, to have before us in the Bible the permanent record that we shall yet find deliverance. In the twelfth chapter, therefore, the angel directs the mind onward to brighter times, and assures Daniel that there would be a day of rejoicing.

1. *Also I.* I the angel. He alludes here to what he had done on a former occasion to promote the interests of the Hebrew people, and to secure those arrangements which were necessary

for their welfare—particularly in the favourable disposition of Darius the Mede towards them. ¶ *In the first year of Darius the Mede.* See Notes on ch. v. 31. He does not here state the things contemplated or done by Darius in which he had confirmed or strengthened him, but there can be no reasonable doubt that it was the purpose which he had conceived to restore the Jews to their own land, and to give them permission to rebuild their city and temple. Comp. ch. ix. 1. It was in that year that Daniel offered his solemn prayer, as recorded in ch. ix.; in that year that, according to the time predicted by Jeremiah (see Dan. ix. 2), the captivity would terminate; and in that year that an influence from above led the mind of the Persian king to contemplate the restoration of the captive people. Cyrus was, indeed, the one through whom the edict for their return was promulgated; but as he reigned under his uncle Cyaxares or Darius, and as Cyaxares was the source of authority, it is evident that *his* mind must have been influenced to grant this favour, and it is to this that the angel here refers. ¶ *I stood to confirm and to strengthen him.* Comp. Notes on ch. x. 13. It would seem that the mind of Darius was not wholly decided; that there were adverse influences bearing on it: that there were probably counsellors of his realm who advised against the proposed measures, and the angel here says that *he* stood by him, and confirmed him in his purpose, and secured the execution of his benevolent plan. Who can prove that an angel may not exert an influence on the heart of kings? And what class of men is there who, when they *intend* to do good and right, are more likely to have their purposes changed by evil counsellors than kings; and who are there that more need a heavenly influence to confirm their design to do right?

2. *And now will I show thee the truth.* That is, the truth about events that are to occur in the future, and which

the truth. Behold, there shall stand up yet three kings in Persia; and the fourth shall be far richer than *they* all: and by his strength

---

will accord with what is written in "the scripture of truth," chap. x. 21. ¶ *Behold, there shall stand up yet three kings in Persia.* The phrase "stand up," means that there would *be* so many kings in Persia; that is, there would be three *before* the fourth which he mentions. The same Hebrew word here rendered *stand up* (עָמַד) occurs in vers. 3, 4, 6–8, 14–16 (twice), 17, 20, 21, 25, 31; also in ch. xii. 1, 13. In ver. 8 it is rendered *continue;* in ver. 15, *withstand;* in the other cases, *stand up,* or simply *stand.* Gesenius says it is a word used particularly of a new prince, as in Dan. viii. 23; xi. 2, 3, 20. He does not say that there would be none afterwards, but he evidently designs to touch on the great and leading events respecting the Persian empire, so far as they would affect the Hebrew people, and so far as they would constitute prominent points in the history of the world. He does not, therefore, go into all the details respecting the history, nor does he mention all the kings that would reign. The prominent, the material points, would be the reign of those three kings; then the reign of the fourth, or Xerxes, as his mad expedition to Greece would lay the real foundation for the invasion of Persia by Alexander, and the overthrow of the Persian empire; then the life and conquests of Alexander, and then the wars consequent on the division of his empire at his death. The "three kings" here referred to were Cambyses, Smerdis, and Darius Hystaspis. As this communication was made in the third year of Cyrus (ch. x. 1), these would be the next in order; and by the fourth is undoubtedly meant Xerxes. There were several kings of Persia *after* Xerxes, as Artaxerxes Longimanus, Darius Nothus, Artaxerxes Mnemon, Ochus, and Darius Codomanus, but these are not enumerated because the real ground of the invasion of Alexander, the thing which connected him with the affairs of Persia, did not oc-

cur in their reign, but it was the invasion of Greece by Xerxes. ¶ *And the fourth shall be far richer than* they *all.* That is, Xerxes—for he was the fourth in order, and the description here agrees entirely with him. He would of course inherit the wealth accumulated by these kings, and it is here implied that he would increase that wealth, or that, in some way, he would possess more than they all combined. The *wealth* of this king is here mentioned probably because the magnificence and glory of an Oriental monarch was estimated in a considerable degree by his possessions, and because his riches enabled him to accomplish his expedition into Greece. Some idea of the treasures of Xerxes may be obtained by considering, (*a*) That Cyrus had collected a vast amount of wealth by the conquest of Lydia, and the subjugation of Crœsus, its rich king, by the conquest of Asia Minor, of Armenia, and of Babylon—for it is said respecting him, "I will give thee the treasures of darkness, and hidden riches of secret places," Isa. xlv. 3: see Notes on that passage. (*b*) That Cambyses increased that wealth which he inherited from Cyrus by his victories, and by his plundering the temples wherever he came. A single case occurring in his conquests may illustrate the amount of wealth which was accumulated. On his return from Thebes, in Egypt, he caused all the temples in that city to be pillaged and burnt to the ground. But he saved from the flames gold to the amount of three hundred talents, and silver to the amount of two thousand and five hundred talents. He is also said to have carried away the famous circle of gold that encompassed the tomb of king Ozymandias, being three hundred and sixty-five cubits in circumference, on which were represented all the motions of the several constellations.—*Universal History,* iv. 140. (*c*) This was further increased by the conquests of Darius Hystaspis, and by his heavy taxes on the people. So burdensome were these taxes, that he was called

through his riches he shall stir up all against the realm of Grecia.

3 And a mighty king shall stand up, that shall rule with great do-

by the Persians, ὁ κάπηλος—the "merchant," or "hoarder." One of the first acts of Darius was to divide his kingdom into provinces for the purpose of raising tribute. "During the reign of Cyrus, and indeed of Cambyses, there were no specific tributes; but presents were made to the sovereign. On account of these and similar innovations, the Persians call Darius a merchant, Cambyses a despot, but Cyrus a parent."—Herodotus, b. iii. lxxxix. A full account of the taxation of the kingdom, and the amount of the revenue under Darius, may be seen in Herodotus, b. iii. xc.–xcvi. The sum of the tribute under Darius, according to Herodotus, was fourteen thousand five hundred and sixty talents. Besides this sum received from regular taxation, Herodotus enumerates a great amount of gold and silver, and other valuable things, which Darius was accustomed to receive annually from the Ethiopians, from the people of Colchis, from the Arabians, and from India. All this vast wealth was inherited by Xerxes, the son and successor of Darius, and the "fourth king" here referred to. Xerxes was full four years in making provision for his celebrated expedition into Greece. Of the amount of his forces, and his preparation, a full account may be seen in Herodotus, b. vii. Of his *wealth* Justin makes this remark: *Si regem spectes, divitias, non ducem, laudes: quarum tanta copia in regno ejus fuit, ut cum flumina multitudine consumerentur, opes tamen regiæ superessent.—Hist.* ii. 10. Comp. Diod. Sic. x. c. 3; Pliny, *Hist. Nat.* xxiii. 10; Æl. xiii. 3; Herod. iii. 96; vii. 27–29. In the city of Celænæ, Herodotus says, there lived a man named Pythius, son of Atys, a native of Lydia, who entertained Xerxes and all his army with great magnificence, and who farther engaged to supply the king with money for the war. Xerxes on this was induced to inquire of his Persian attendants who this Pythius was, and what were the resources which enabled him to make these offers. "It is the same," they replied, "who presented your father Darius with a plane-tree and a vine of gold, and who, next to yourself, is the richest of mankind."—Herod. vii. 27. ¶ *And by his strength through his riches he shall stir up all against the realm of Grecia.* That is, all his kingdom. He was enabled to do this by his great wealth—collecting and equipping, probably, the largest army that was ever assembled. The expedition of Xerxes against Greece is too well known to need to be detailed here, and no one can fail to see the applicability of this description to that invasion. Four years were spent in preparing for this expedition, and the forces that constituted the army were gathered out of all parts of the vast empire of Xerxes, embracing, as was then supposed, all the habitable world except Greece. According to Justin, the army was composed of seven hundred thousand of his own, and three hundred thousand auxiliaries. Diodorus Siculus makes it to be about three hundred thousand men; Prideaux, from Herodotus and others, computes it to have amounted, putting all his forces by sea and land together, to two millions six hundred and forty-one thousand six hundred and ten men; and he adds that the servants, eunuchs, suttlers, and such persons as followed the camp, made as many more, so that the whole number that followed Xerxes could not have been less than five millions.—*Connexions*, pt. i. b. iv. vol. i. p. 410. Grotius reckons his forces at five millions two hundred and eighty-two thousand. These immense numbers justify the expression here, and show with what propriety it is applied to the hosts of Xerxes. On the supposition that this was written *after* the event, and that it was *history* instead of *prophecy*, this would be the very language which would be employed.

3. *And a mighty king shall stand up.* So far as the *language* here is concerned, it is not said whether this would be in Persia, as a successor of the "fourth king" (ver. 2), or whether

minion, and do according to his will.

4 And when he shall stand up,

his kingdom ^a shall be broken, and shall be divided toward the four

it would be in some other part of the world. The next verse, however, shows that the reference is to Alexander the Great—for to no other one is it applicable. There were several monarchs of Persia, indeed, that succeeded Xerxes before the kingdom was invaded and subdued by Alexander (see Notes on ver. 2), and these are here entirely passed over without being alluded to. It must be admitted, that one who should have read this prophecy before the events had occurred would have inferred naturally that this "mighty king that should stand up" would appear immediately *after* the "fourth," and probably that he would be his successor in the realm; but it may be remarked, (*a*) that the *language* here is not inconsistent with the facts in the case—it being literally true that such a "mighty king" did "stand up" who "ruled with great dominion, and according to his will;" (*b*) that there was no necessity in the prophetic history of referring to the acts of these intermediate kings of Persia, since they did not contribute at all to the result—it being well known that the reason alleged by Alexander for his invasion of the Persian empire was not anything which *they* had done, but the wrongs sustained by Greece in consequence of the invasion by Xerxes and his predecessor. The real *succession* of events in the case was that last invasion of Greece by Xerxes, and the consequent invasion of the Persian empire by Alexander. It was these transactions which the angel evidently meant to connect together, and hence all that was intermediate was omitted. Thus Alexander, in his letter to Darius, says: "Your ancestors entered into Macedonia, and the other parts of Greece, and did us damage, when they had received no affront from us as the cause of it; and now I, created general of the Grecians, provoked by you, and desirous of avenging the injury done by the Persians, have passed over into Asia." —Arrian, *Exped. Alex.* i. 2. ¶ *That shall rule with great dominion.* That

shall have a wide and extended empire. The *language* here would apply to any of the monarchs of Persia that succeeded Xerxes, but it would be more strictly applicable to Alexander the Great than to any prince of ancient or modern times. The whole world, except Greece, was supposed to be subject to the power of Persia; and it was one of the leading and avowed purposes of Darius and Xerxes in invading Greece, by adding that to their empire, to have the earth under their control. When, therefore, Alexander had conquered Persia, it was supposed that *he* had subdued the world; nor was it an unnatural feeling that, having done this, he, whose sole principle of action was ambition, should sit down and weep because there were no more worlds to conquer. In fact, he then swayed a sceptre more extended and mighty than any before him had done, and it is with peculiar propriety that the language here is used in regard to him. ¶ *And do according to his will.* Would be an arbitrary prince. This also was true of the Persian kings, and of Oriental despots generally; but it was eminently so of Alexander—who, in subduing kingdoms, conquering mighty armies, controlling the millions under his sway, laying the foundations of cities, and newly arranging the boundaries of empires, seemed to consult only his own will, and felt that everything was to be subordinate to it. It is said that this passage was shown to Alexander by the high-priest of the Jews, and that these prophecies did much to conciliate his favour towards the Hebrew people.

4. *And when he shall stand up.* In the might and power of his kingdom. When his power shall be fully established. I understand this, with Rosenmüller and Hävernick, as meaning, when he shall be at the height of his authority and power, then his kingdom would be broken up. The reference is, undoubtedly, to the sudden death of Alexander; and the sense

winds of heaven; and not to his posterity, nor according to his dominion which he ruled: for his kingdom shall be plucked up, even for others beside those.

5 ¶ And the king of the south

is, that his empire would not *gradually* diminish and decay, but that some event would occur, the effect of which would be to rend it into four parts. ¶ *His kingdom shall be broken.* To wit, by his death. The language is such as is properly applicable to this, and indeed implies this, for it is said that it would not be "to his posterity" —an event which might be naturally expected to occur; or, in other words, the allusion to his posterity is such language as would be employed on the supposition that the reference here is to his death. ¶ *And shall be divided toward the four winds of heaven.* Into four parts. For the remarkable fulfilment of this prediction, see the Notes on ch. viii. 8. ¶ *And not to his posterity.* See also the Notes on ch. viii. 8. ¶ *Nor according to his dominion which he ruled.* This was literally true of the division of the empire. No one of his successors ever obtained as wide a dominion as he did himself. ¶ *For his kingdom shall be plucked up.* By his death. This does not naturally mean that it would be by *conquest,* for it is said that it would be "divided towards the four winds of heaven"— language which is not properly expressive of conquest. All that is implied is met by the supposition, that at his decease the kingdom which had been founded by him, and which had been sustained by his valour and political wisdom, would fall to pieces. ¶ *Even for others beside those.* That is, to others beside those to whom it should be at first divided. Literally, *exclusively,* or *to the exclusion of*—מִלְּבַד.

The word *those* refers to his posterity; and the meaning is, that the process of division would not stop with them, or that the four portions of the empire, as thus divided, would not remain in their hands, or pass to their posterity. There would be other changes and other divisions; and it was not to be expected that just four, and no more, empires would grow out of the one which had been founded, or that when

that one should be divided into four parts, that partition would always continue. There would be other divisions, and other princes besides those who first obtained the empire would come in, and the process of division would ultimately be carried much farther. It is unnecessary to say that this occurred in the empire founded by Alexander. It was, soon after his death, separated into four parts, but at no distant period this arrangement was broken up, and all traces of the empire, as established by him, or as divided among his four successors, wholly disappeared.

5. *And the king of the south.* The angel here leaves the general history of the empire, and confines himself, in his predictions, to two parts of it— the kingdom of the south, and the kingdom of the north; or the kingdoms to the north and the south of Palestine—that of Syria and that of Egypt; or that of the Seleucidæ, and that of the Ptolemies. The reason why he does this is not stated, but it is, doubtless, because the events pertaining to these kingdoms would particularly affect the Jewish people, and be properly connected with sacred history. Comp. Notes on chap. viii. 7, 8. The "king of the south" here is, undoubtedly, the king of Egypt. This part of the empire was obtained by Ptolemy, and was in the hands of his successors until Egypt was subdued by the Romans. Between the kingdoms of Egypt and Syria long and bloody wars prevailed, and the prospective history of these wars it is the design of the angel here to trace. As the remainder of the chapter refers to these two dynasties, till the death of the great persecutor, Antiochus Epiphanes, and as the events referred to were very important in history, and as introductory to what was to follow in the world, it may be useful here, in order to a clear exposition of the whole chapter, to present a list of these two lines of princes. It is necessary only to premise, that the death of Alexan-

shall be strong, and *one* of his princes; and he shall be strong above him, and have dominion;

his dominion *shall be* a great dominion.

der the Great occurred B.C. 323; that of his brother, Philip Aridæus, B.C. 316; that of his son, Alexander Ægus, by Roxana, B.C. 309 ; and that a short time after this (about B.C. 306), the chief Macedonian governors and

princes assumed the royal title. The following list of the succession of the Seleucidæ and the Ptolemies—or the kings of the north and the south—of Syria and Egypt, is copied from Elliott *on the Apocalypse*, iv. 123 :—

The Ptolemies.

B.C.
323 Ptolemy Soter, son of Ptolemy Lagus, governor of Egypt.

306 ——————— takes the title of king of Egypt.
284 Ptolemy Philadelphus. (It was under him that the Septuagint Greek translation of the Old Testament was made.)

246 Ptolemy Euergetes.

221 Ptolemy Philopator.
204 Ptolemy Epiphanes.

180 Ptolemy Philometor.

The Seleucidæ.

B.C.
323 Seleucus Nicator, governor of Babylon.
312 ——————— recovers Babylon, and the Æra of the Seleucidæ begins.

280 Antiochus Soter.
261 Antiochus Theus.
246 Seleucus Callinicus.
226 Seleucus Ceraunus.
225 Antiochus the Great.

187 Seleucus Philopator.

175 Antiochus Epiphanes.
164 Antiochus Eupator, of whom the *Romans* assume the guardianship.

"After this, fourteen more *Syrian* kings reigned, in reigns of short and uncertain power, till Syria was occupied and formed into a Roman province under Pompey, at which time the era of the Seleucidæ properly ends; and six more *Egyptian* princes, to the death of Ptolemy Auletes, who dying B.C. 51, left his kingdom and children to Roman guardianship—one of these children being the *Cleopatra* so famous in the histories of Cæsar and Anthony." —Elliott, *ut supra.* ¶ *Shall be strong.* This is in accordance with the well-known fact. One of the most powerful of those monarchies, if not *the* most powerful, was Egypt. ¶ *And* one *of his princes; and he shall be strong above him.* The meaning of this passage is, that there would be "one of his princes," that is, of the princes of Alexander, who would be more mighty than the one who obtained Egypt, or the

south, and that he would have a more extended dominion. The reference is, doubtless, to Seleucus Nicator, or the conqueror. In the division of the empire he obtained Syria, Babylonia, Media, Susiana, Armenia, a part of Cappadocia, and Cilicia, and his kingdom stretched from the Hellespont to the Indus. See Notes on ch. viii. 8. Comp. Arrian, *Exp. Alex.* vii. 22; Appian, p. 618 ; and Lengerke, *in loc.* The proper translation of this passage probably would be, "And the king of the south shall be mighty. But from among his princes [the princes of Alexander] also there shall be [one] who shall be mightier than he, and he shall reign, and his dominion shall be a great dominion." It was of these two dominions that the angel spake, and hence follows, through the remainder of the chapter, the history pertaining to them and their successors.

6 And in the end of years they shall ¹ join themselves together; for the king's daughter of the south shall come to the king of the north to make an ² agreement: but she shall not retain the power of the

1 *associate.*

2 *rights.*

Seleucus Nicator reigned from B.C. 312 to B.C. 280—or thirty-two years. In his time lived Berosus and Megasthenes, referred to in the Introduction to ch. iv.

6. *And in the end of years.* In the future periods of the history of these two kingdoms. The event here referred to did not occur during the lives of these two kings, Seleucus Nicator and Ptolemy Soter, but in the reign of their successors, Ptolemy Philadelphus and Antiochus Theos or Theus. The phrase "the end of years" would well denote such a future period. The Vulgate renders it, "after the end of years ;" that is, after many years have elapsed. The meaning is "after a certain course or lapse of years." The word *end* in Daniel (קֵץ) often seems to refer to a time when a predicted event would be fulfilled, whether near or remote ; whether it would be really the *end* or *termination* of an empire or of the world, or whether it would be succeeded by other events. It would be the end of that matter—of the thing predicted ; and in this sense the word seems to be employed here. Compare chap. viii. 17, ver. 13 of this chapter (margin), and ch. xii. 13. ¶ *They shall join themselves together.* Marg., *associate.* The meaning is, that there would be an alliance formed, or an attempt made, to unite the two kingdoms more closely by a marriage between different persons of the royal families. The word "they" refers to the two sovereigns of Egypt and Syria—the south and the north. ¶ *For the king's daughter of the south shall come to the king of the north to make an agreement.* Marg., *rights.* The Hebrew word properly means rectitudes or rights (in the plural מֵישָׁרִים) ; but here it seems to be used in the sense of *peace,* or an alliance. The act of making peace was regarded as an act of *justice,* or doing *right,* and hence the word came to be used in the sense of making an alliance or compact. This idea we should now express by saying that the design was "to make things right or straight"— as if they were wrong and crooked before, giving occasion to discord, and misunderstanding, and wars. The intention now was to establish peace on a permanent basis. The compact here referred to was one formed between Berenice, the daughter of Ptolemy Philadelphus, king of Egypt, and Antiochus Theos, king of Syria. Ptolemy, in order to bring a war in which he was engaged to an end, and to restore peace, gave his daughter in marriage to Antiochus, in hopes of establishing a permanent peace and alliance between the two kingdoms. One of the conditions of this alliance was, that Antiochus should divorce his former wife Laodice, and that the children of that former wife should be excluded from the succession to the throne. In this way Ptolemy hoped that the kingdom of Syria might become ultimately attached to that of Egypt, if there should be children by the marriage of Berenice with Antiochus. Ptolemy, however, died two years after this marriage was consummated, and Antiochus restored again his former wife Laodice, and put away Berenice, but was himself murdered by Laodice, who feared the fickleness of her husband. The officers of the court of Syria then planned the death of Berenice and her children, but she fled with them to Daphné, and was there put to death, with her children.—Appian, c. lxv. ; Lengerke, *in loc.* She was put to death by poison. See Gill, *in loc.* ¶ *But she shall not retain the power of the arm.* The word *retain* here is the same as in ch. x. 8, "I retained no strength." The word *arm* is a word of frequent use in the Old Testament, both in the singular and plural, to denote *strength, power,* whether of an individual or an army. So Job xxii. 8, "A man of *arm,*" that is, *strength;* Gen. xlix. 24, "The arms [power] of his hands were made strong by the God

arm; neither shall he stand, nor his arm: but she shall be given up, and they that brought her, and [1] he that begat her, and he that strengthened her in *these* times.

1 or, *whom she brought forth.*

7 But out of a branch of her roots shall *one* stand up in his estate, [2] which shall come with an army, and shall enter into the fortress of the king of the north,

2 *place,* or, *office,* ver. 20.

of Jacob." Comp. Isa. li. 9, and lxii. 8. It is frequently used in this chapter in the sense of *strength,* or *power.* See vers. 15, 22, 31. This alliance was formed with the hope that the succession might be in her. She was, however, as stated above, with her children, put to death. While queen of Syria, she, of course, had power, and had the prospect of succeeding to the supreme authority. ¶ *Neither shall he stand.* The king of the south; to wit, Egypt. That is, he would not prosper in his ambitious purpose of bringing Syria, by this marriage alliance, under his control. ¶ *Nor his arm.* What he regarded as his strength, and in which he placed reliance, as one does on his arm in accomplishing any design. The word "arm" here is used in the sense of *help,* or *alliance;* that is, that on which he depended for the stability of his empire. ¶ *But she shall be given up.* That is, she shall be given up to death, to wit, by the command of Laodice. ¶ *And they that brought her.* That is, those who conducted her to Daphné; or those who came with her into Syria, and who were her attendants and friends. Of course they would be surrendered or delivered up when she was put to death. ¶ *And he that begat her.* Marg., "or, *whom she brought forth.*" The margin expresses the sense more correctly. The Latin Vulgate is, *adolescentes ejus.* The Greek, ἡ νεάνις. So the Syriac. The Hebrew (וְהִילְדָהּ) will admit of this construction. The article in the word has the force of a relative, and is connected with the suffix, giving it a relative signification. See Ewald, as quoted by Lengerke, *in loc.* According to the present pointing, indeed, the literal meaning would be, "and he who begat her;" but this pointing is not authoritative. Dathe, Bertholdt, Dereser, De Wette, and Rosenmüller suppose that the reading

should be וְהִילְדָהּ. Then the sense would be, "her child," or "her offspring." Lengerke and Ewald, however, suppose that this idea is implied in the present reading of the text, and that no change is necessary. The obvious meaning is, that she and her child, or her offspring, would be thus surrendered. The matter of fact was, that her little son was slain with her. See Prideaux's *Connexions,* iii. 120. ¶ *And he that strengthened her in* these *times.* It is not known who is here referred to. Doubtless, on such an occasion, she would have some one who would be a confidential counsellor or adviser, and, whoever that was, he would be likely to be cut off with her.

7. *But out of a branch of her roots.* Comp. Notes on Isa. xi. 1. The meaning is, that as a branch or shoot springs up from a tree that is decayed and fallen, so there would spring up some one of her family who would come to avenge her. That is, a person is indicated who would be of a common stock with her; or, in other words, if taken strictly, a brother. The phrase "branch of her roots" is somewhat peculiar. The words "her roots" must refer to her family; that from which she sprang. We speak thus of the root or *stem* of a family or house; and the meaning here is, not that one of her *descendants,* or one that should *spring from her,* would thus come, but a branch of the same family; a branch springing from the same root or stem. The fact in the case—a fact to which there is undoubted reference here—is, that her revenge was undertaken by Ptolemy Euergetes, her brother. As soon as he heard of the calamities that had come upon her, he hastened with a great force out of Egypt to defend and rescue her. But it was in vain. She and her son were cut off before he could arrive for her help, but, in con-

and shall deal against them, and shall prevail :

8 And shall also carry captives into Egypt their gods, with their princes, *and* with [1] their precious vessels of silver and of gold ; and

1 *vessels of their desire.*   2 or, *war.*

he shall continue *more* years than the king of the north.

9 So the king of the south shall come into *his* kingdom, and shall return into his own land.

10 But his sons shall [2] be stirred up, and shall assemble a multitude

nection with an army which had come from Asia Minor for the same purpose, he undertook to avenge her death. He made himself master not only of Syria and Cilicia, but passed over the Euphrates, and brought all under subjection to him as far as the river Tigris. Having done this, he marched back to Egypt, taking with him vast treasures. See Prideaux, *Con.* iii. 120, 121. ¶ *Shall* one *stand up.* Shall one arise. See Notes, ver. 2. That is, there shall *be* one who shall appear for that purpose. ¶ *In his estate.* Marg., *place,* or *office.* The word ‎כֵּן means, properly, stand, station, place; then base, pedestal. Comp. vers. 20, 21, 38. See also Gen. xl. 13: "Within three days shall Pharaoh restore thee to *thy place.*" And again, Gen. xli. 13, "to my *office.*" Here it means, in his place or stead. That is, he would take the place which his father would naturally occupy—the place of protector, or defender, or avenger. Ptolemy Philadelphus, her father, in fact died before she was put to death ; and his death was the cause of the calamities that came upon her, for as long as he lived his power would be dreaded. But when he was dead, Ptolemy Euergetes stood up in his place as her defender and avenger. ¶ *Which shall come with an army.* As Ptolemy Euergetes did. See above. He came out of Egypt as soon as he heard of these calamities, to defend her. ¶ *And shall enter into the fortress of the king of the north.* His strongholds. In fact, he overran Syria and Cilicia, and extended his ravages to the Euphrates and the Tigris. Polybius (*Hist.* l. 5) says that he entered into the fortified cities of Syria, and took them. In the passage before us, the singular—*fortress*—is put for the plural. ¶ *And shall deal against them.* Shall *act* against them. Literally,

" shall do against them." ¶ *And shall prevail.* Shall overcome, or subdue them. As seen above, he took possession of no small part of the kingdom of Syria. He was recalled home by a sedition in Egypt; and had it not been for this (Justin says), he would have made himself master of the whole kingdom of Seleucus.

8. *And shall also carry captives into Egypt their gods,* &c. That is, their idols. Jerome (*in loc.*) says that Ptolemy took with him, on his return, forty thousand talents of silver, a vast number of precious vessels of gold, and images to the number of two thousand four hundred, among which were many of the Egyptian idols, which Cambyses, on his conquering Egypt, had carried into Persia. These Ptolemy restored to the temple to which they belonged, and by this much endeared himself to his people. It was on account of the service which he thus rendered to his country that he was called Euergetes, that is, the Benefactor.—Prideaux, iii. 121. In 1631, an inscription on an ancient marble in honour of this action of Euergetes was published by Allatius : *Sacris quæ ab Egypto Persæ abstulerant receptis, ac cum reliquâ congestâ gazâ in Egyptum relatis.* — Wintle. ¶ *And he shall continue* more *years than the king of the north.* Ptolemy Euergetes survived Seleucus about four years.—Prideaux, iii. 122. He reigned twenty-five years.

9. *So the king of the south shall come into* his *kingdom.* That is, into the kingdom of the north, or the kingdom of Syria. This verse seems to be a summary of what had been said about his invading Syria. He would come, on account of the wrongs done to his sister, into the kingdom of the north, and would then return again to his own land.

10. *But his sons shall be stirred up.*

of great forces: and *one* shall certainly come, and overflow,*a* and
pass through; then shall he ¹return,
and be stirred up, *even* to his fortress.*b*

11 And the king of the south
shall be moved with choler, and
shall come forth and fight with
him, *even* with the king of the
north: and he shall set forth a

Marg., "or, *war.*" The Hebrew word
(יִתְגָּרוּ—from גָּרָה) means, to be rough;
then, in Piel, to excite, stir up; and
then, in Hithpa, to excite one's self,
to be stirred up to anger, to make war
upon, &c. Here it means, according
to Gesenius (*Lex.*), that they would
be excited or angry. The reference
here, according to Lengerke, Maurer,
Gill, and others, is to the son of the
king of the north, Seleucus Callinicus.
He was killed, according to Justin
(lib. xxvii. c. 3), by a fall from his
horse. The war with Egypt was continued by his two sons, Seleucus Ceraunus and Antiochus the Great, until
the death of the former, when it was
prosecuted by Antiochus alone. See
Prideaux, iii. 136. Seleucus Ceraunus
succeeded his father—assuming the
name of Ceraunus, or the Thunderer;
but, dying soon, he left the crown to
his brother, Antiochus the Great, then
only fifteen years of age, by whom the
war with Egypt was successfully prosecuted. ¶ *And shall assemble a multitude of great forces.* Against Egypt.
In such a war they would naturally
summon to their aid all the forces
which they could command. ¶ *And
one shall certainly come.* There is a
change here in the Hebrew from the
plural to the singular number, as
is indicated in our translation by the
insertion of the word *one.* The fact
was, that the war was prosecuted by
Antiochus the Great alone. Seleucus
died in the third year of his reign, in
Phrygia; being slain, according to one
report (Jerome), through the treachery
of Nicanor and Apaturius, or, according to another, was poisoned. See
Prideaux, iii. 137. Antiochus succeeded to the empire, and prosecuted
the war. This was done for the purpose of recovering Syria from the dominion of Ptolemy of Egypt, and was
conducted with various degrees of suc-

cess, until the whole was brought under
the control of Antiochus. See Prideaux,
Con. iii. 138, *seq.* ¶ *And overflow.*
Like a torrent. ¶ *And pass through.*
Through the land—not the land of
Egypt, but every part of Syria. ¶ *Then
shall he return.* Marg., *be stirred
up again.* The margin is the more
correct rendering—the Hebrew word
being the same as that which is used
in the first part of the verse. The idea
would seem to be, that he would be
aroused or stirred up after a defeat,
and would on the second expedition
enter into the strongholds or fortresses
of the land. This was literally true.
Ptolemy marched into Syria with an
army of seventy thousand foot, five
thousand horse, and seventy-three elephants, and was met by Antiochus
with an army of sixty-two thousand
foot, six thousand horse, and one hundred and two elephants. In a great
battle, Antiochus was defeated, and
returned to Antioch (Prideaux, *Con.*
iii. 151–153); but the following year
he again rallied his forces, and invaded
Syria, took Gaza and the other strongholds, and subdued the whole country
of Syria (including Palestine) to himself.—Prideaux, *Con.* iii. 176, 177.
¶ *Even to his fortress.* The singular
for the plural; perhaps using the word
"fortress" by way of eminence, as
denoting his *strongest* fortress, and,
therefore, including all the others.

11. *And the king of the south shall
be moved with choler.* With anger.
That is, that his provinces were invaded,
and his strongholds taken—referring
particularly to the invasion of Syria
and Palestine as mentioned in the
previous verse, and the attempt to
wrest them out of the hands of the
king of Egypt. Nothing would be
more natural than that this should
occur. ¶ *And shall come forth and
fight with him,* even *with the king
of the north.* There were frequent

great multitude; but *a* the multitude shall be given into his hand.

12 *And* when he hath taken

a Psa. 33. 16; Eccl. 9. 11, 12.

away the multitude, his heart shall be lifted up; and he shall cast down *many* ten thousands: but he shall not be strengthened *by it.*

---

and almost constant wars between these two kingdoms. Yet the reference here is to Ptolemy Philopator, who succeeded Ptolemy Euergetes in Egypt, and who was exasperated at the conduct of Antiochus in invading Syria and Palestine. He assembled an army, and marched with it to Raphia, where he met Antiochus, and a battle was fought. ¶ *And he shall set forth a great multitude.* This army of Ptolemy, according to Polybius, ch. 86, was led through Arabia Petræa, and consisted of seventy thousand infantry, and five thousand cavalry, and seventy-three elephants. The army of Antiochus consisted of sixty-two thousand foot, six thousand horse, and a hundred and two elephants. — Prideaux, *Con.* iii. 151. ¶ *But the multitude shall be given into his hand.* That is, the multitude of the army of Antiochus. In the battle that was fought at Raphia, Ptolemy gained the victory. Ten thousand of the army of Antiochus were slain, four thousand taken prisoners, and with the remainder of his forces Antiochus retreated to Antioch.—Prideaux, iii. 152, 153. Perhaps also the expression "the multitude shall be given into his hand" may refer not only to the army, and his victory over it, but to the fact that the inhabitants of Cœlo-Syria and Palestine would hasten to submit themselves to him. After this great battle at Raphia, and the retreat of Antiochus, we are told that the cities of Cœlo-Syria and Palestine vied with each other in submitting themselves to Ptolemy. They had been long under the government of Egypt, and preferred that to the government of Antiochus. They had submitted to Antiochus only by force, and that force now being removed, they returned readily to the authority of their old masters. Had Ptolemy possessed energy and capacity for government, it would have been easy to have retained the control over these countries.

12. And *when he hath taken away*

the multitude. When he has subdued them. Lengerke, however, renders this, "And the multitude shall lift themselves up," supposing it to refer to the fact that the people as well as the king would be excited. But the more natural interpretation is that in our common version, and the same sense of the word (נשא) occurs in Amos iv. 2. ¶ *His heart shall be lifted up.* That is, he will be proud and self-confident. The reference is to the effect which would be produced on him after his defeat of Antiochus. He was a man naturally indolent and effeminate — a most profligate and vicious prince. —Prideaux, *Con.* iii. 146. The effect of such a victory would be to lift him up with pride. ¶ *And he shall cast down many ten thousands.* Or, rather, the meaning is, "he *has* cast down many myriads." The object seems to be to give a reason why his heart was lifted up. The fact that he had been thus successful is the reason which is assigned, and this effect of a great victory has not been uncommon in the world. ¶ *But he shall not be strengthened* by it. He was wholly given up to luxury, sloth, and voluptuousness, and returned immediately after his victory into Egypt, and surrendered himself up to the enjoyment of his pleasures. The consequence was, that he, by his conduct, excited some of his people to rebellion, and greatly weakened himself in the affections and confidence of the rest. After the victory, he concluded a truce with Antiochus; and the result was, that his people, who expected much more from him, and supposed that he would have prosecuted the war, became dissatisfied with his conduct, and broke out into rebellion. As a matter of fact, he was less strong in the confidence and affections of his people, and would have been less able to wage a war, after his triumph over Antiochus than he was before. See Prideaux, *Con.* iii. 155, *seq.*

13 For the king of the north shall return, and shall set forth a multitude greater than the former, and shall certainly come ¹ after certain years with a great army and with much riches.

14 And in those times there shall many stand up against the king of the south: also the ² robbers of thy people shall exalt themselves

1 *at the end of times*, even *years:* ch. 4. 16; 12. 7.
2 *children of robbers.*

13. *For the king of the north shall return.* That is, he shall come again into the regions of Cœlo-Syria and Palestine, to recover them if possible from the power of the Egyptian king. ¶ *And shall set forth a multitude greater than the former.* Than he had in the former war when he was defeated. The fact was, that Antiochus, in this expedition, brought with him the forces with which he had successfully invaded the East, and the army had been raised for that purpose, and was much larger than that with which he had formerly attacked Ptolemy. See Prideaux, iii. 163–165. ¶ *And shall certainly come after certain years with a great army.* This occurred B.C. 203, fourteen years after the former war.—Prideaux, iii. 19. ¶ *With much riches.* Obtained in his conquests in Parthia and other portions of the East. See Prideaux, *ut supra.* The *history* of Antiochus corresponds precisely with the statement here.

14. *And in those times there shall many stand up against the king of the south.* Against the king of Egypt. That is, not only Antiochus the Great, who was always opposed to him, and who was constantly waging war with him, but also others with whom he would be particularly involved, or who would be opposed to him. The reference is especially to Philip, king of Macedon, and to Agathocles, who excited a rebellion against him in Egypt. See Jerome on Dan. xi.; Polybius, xv. 20; Lengerke, *in loc.;* and Prideaux, iii. 198. Antiochus and Philip of Macedon entered into an agreement to invade the dominions of Ptolemy Epiphanes, and to divide them between themselves. At the same time a treasonable plot was laid against the life of Ptolemy by Scopas the Ætolian (Polyb. xvii.), who had under his command the army of the Egyptians, and who designed to take advantage of the

youth of the king, and seize upon the throne. This project was defeated by the vigilance of Aristomenes, the prime minister.—Prideaux, iii. 181. See also the account of the conspiracy of Agathocles, and his sister Agathoclea, against Ptolemy, when an infant, in Prideaux, iii. 168, *seq.* These facts fully accord with what is said in the passage before us. ¶ *Also the robbers of thy people shall exalt themselves.* The angel here turns to Daniel, and states what would be done in these circumstances by his own people—the Jews. It is to be remembered that, in these times, they were alternately under the dominion of the Egyptian and the Syrian monarchs—of Ptolemy and of Antiochus. The principal seat of the wars between Syria and Egypt was Palestine — the border land ·between them and Judea, therefore, often changed masters. Ptolemy Philopator had subdued Cœlo-Syria and Palestine, and Ptolemy Epiphanes came into possession of them when he ascended the throne. But the angel now says that a portion of his people would take occasion, from the weakness of the youthful monarch of Egypt, and the conspiracies in his own kingdom, and the foreign combinations against him, to attempt to throw off his authority, and to become independent. That part of the people who would attempt to do this is designated in the common translation as "the robbers of thy people." This, however, is scarcely a correct version, and does not properly indicate the persons that would be engaged in the plot. The marginal reading is, *children of robbers.* The Latin Vulgate, *filii quoque prævaricatorum populi tui.* The Greek renders it οἱ υἱοὶ τῶν λοιμῶν τοῦ λαοῦ σοῦ—"the sons of the pests of thy people." Lengerke renders it, "the most powerful people of thy nation"—*die gewaltsamsten Leute deines Volkes.* The Hebrew

to establish the vision; but they shall fall.*a*

15 So the king of the north shall come, and cast up a mount, and take the ¹ most fenced cities; and

the arms of the south shall not withstand, neither ² his chosen people, neither *shall there be any* strength to withstand.

a Rev 17. 17.

1 *city of munitions.*   2 *the people of his choices.*

word (פָּרִיץ) means, properly, *rending, ravenous*—as of wild beasts, Isa. xxxv. 9 ; and then *violent, rapacious; an oppressor, robber.*—Gesenius, *Lex.* The reference here seems to be to the mighty ones of the nation; the chiefs, or rulers —but a name is given them that would properly denote their character for oppression and rapacity. It would seem —what is indeed probable from the circumstances of the case — that the nation was not only subject to this foreign authority, but that those who were placed over it, under that foreign authority, and who were probably mainly of their own people, were also themselves tyrannical and oppressive in their character. These subordinate rulers, however, preferred the authority of Antiochus to that of Ptolemy, and on the occasion of his return from the conquests of Cœlo-Syria and Samaria, they met him, and professed submission to him.—Josephus, *Ant.* b. xii. ch. iii. § 3. "The Jews," says Josephus, "of their own accord, went over to him, and received him into the city [Jerusalem], and gave plentiful provision to his army, and to his elephants, and readily assisted him when he besieged the garrison which was in the citadel of Jerusalem." On this occasion, Josephus says that Antiochus bestowed many favours on the Jews; wrote letters to the generals of his armies commending their conduct; published a decree respecting the piety of the Jewish people, and sent an epistle to Ptolemy, stating what he had done for them, and what he desired should be further done. See these statements and letters in Josephus, *ut supra.* ¶ *To establish the vision.* That is, to bring to pass what is seen in the vision, and what had been predicted in regard to the Hebrew people. Their conduct in this matter shall have an important bearing on the fulfilment of the prophecy pertaining

to that people—shall be one of the links in the chain of events securing its accomplishment. The angel does not say that it was a part of their *design* to "establish the vision," but that that would be the *result* of what they did. No doubt their conduct in this matter had a great influence on the series of events that contributed to the accomplishment of that prediction. Lengerke supposes that the "vision" here refers to that spoken of in ch. ix. 24. ¶ *But they shall fall.* They shall not succeed in the object which they have in view. Their conduct in the affair will indeed promote the fulfilment of the "vision," but it will not secure the ends which *they* have in view— perhaps their own aggrandizement; or the favour of Antiochus towards themselves; or the permanent separation of the nation from the Egyptian rule, or the hope that their country might become independent altogether. As a matter of fact, Antiochus subsequently, on his return from Egypt (B.C. 198), took Jerusalem, and slew many of the party of Ptolemy, who had given themselves up to him, though he showed particular favour to those who had adhered to the observance of their own law, and could not be prevailed on by the king of Egypt to apostatize from it.—Prideaux, iii. 198 ; Jos. *Ant.* b. xii. ch. v. § 3.

15. *So the king of the north.* Antiochus the Great. ¶ *Shall come.* Shall come again into these provinces. This occurred after he had vanquished the army of the Egyptians at Paneas. He then took Sidon and Patara, and made himself master of the whole country. —Prideaux, iii. 198. This happened B.C. 198. Scopas, a general of Ptolemy, had been sent by him into Cœlo-Syria and Palestine, with a view of subjecting those countries again to Egyptian rule. He was met by Antiochus at Paneas, near the sources of the Jordan, and defeated, and fled with ten thousand men to Sidon, where he

16 But he that cometh against him shall do according to his own will, and none shall stand before him; and he shall stand in ¹ the

glorious land, which by his hand shall be consumed.

¹ *the land of ornament,* or, *goodly land,* vers. 41, 45.

---

fortified himself, but from whence he was expelled by Antiochus. ¶ *And cast up a mount.* A fortification. That is, he shall so entrench himself that he cannot be dislodged. The reference does not seem to be to any particular fortification, but to the general fact that he would so entrench or fortify himself that he would make his conquests secure. ¶ *And take the most fenced cities.* Marg., *city of munitions.* Heb., "city of fortifications." The singular is used here in a collective sense; or perhaps there is allusion particularly to Sidon, where Scopas entrenched himself, making it as strong as possible. ¶ *And the arms of the south shall not withstand.* Shall not be able to resist him, or to dislodge him. The power of the Egyptian forces shall not be sufficient to remove him from his entrenchments. The Hebrew is, "shall not *stand;*" that is, shall not stand against him, or maintain their position in his advances. The word *arms* (זְרֹעוֹת) is used here in the sense of *heroes, warriors, commanders,* as in Ezek. xxx. 22, 24, 25. ¶ *Neither his chosen people.* Marg., "the people of his choices." Those whom he had selected or chosen to carry on the war—referring, perhaps, to the fact that he would deem it necessary to employ picked men, or to send the choicest of his forces in order to withstand Antiochus. Such an occurrence is in every way probable. To illustrate this, it is only necessary to say that the Egyptians sent three of their most distinguished generals, with a select army, to deliver Sidon—Eropus, Menocles, and Damoxenus.—Lengerke, *in loc.* ¶ *Neither* shall there be any *strength to withstand.* No forces which the Egyptians can employ. In other words, Antiochus would carry all before him. This is in strict accordance with the history. When Scopas was defeated by Antiochus at Paneas, near the sources of the Jordan, he fled and

entrenched himself in Sidon. There he was followed and besieged by Antiochus. The king of Egypt sent the three generals above named, with a choice army, to endeavour to deliver Scopas, but they were unable. Scopas was obliged to surrender, in consequence of famine, and the chosen forces returned to Egypt.

16. *But he that cometh against him shall do according to his own will.* That is, Antiochus, who "came against" Scopas, the Egyptian general, sent out by Ptolemy. The idea is, that Antiochus would be entirely successful in the countries of Cœlo-Syria and Palestine. As a matter of fact, as stated above, he drove Scopas out of those regions, and compelled him to take refuge in Sidon, and then besieged him, and compelled him to surrender. ¶ *And none shall stand before him.* That is, neither the forces that Scopas had under his command, nor the choice and select armies sent out from Egypt for his rescue, under Eropus, Menocles, and Damoxenus. ¶ *And he shall stand in the glorious land.* Marg., "the land of ornament, or, goodly land." The Hebrew word צְבִי means, properly, *splendour, beauty,* and was given to the holy land, or Palestine, on account of its beauty, as being a land of beauty or fertility. Compare Ezek. xx. 6, 15; xxvi. 12; Jer. iii. 19, and Dan. xi. 45. The meaning here is, that he would obtain possession of the land of Israel, and that no one would be able to stand against him. By the defeat of Scopas, and of the forces sent to aid him when entrenched in Sidon, this was accomplished. ¶ *Which by his hand shall be consumed.* As would be natural when his invading army should pass through it. The angel does not seem to refer to any *wanton* destruction of the land, but only to what would necessarily occur in its invasion, and in securing provision for the wants of an

17 He shall also set his face ^ato enter with the strength of his

a Prov. 19. 21.

army.   As a matter of fact, Antiochus did many things to conciliate the favour of the Jews, and granted to them many privileges. See Josephus, *Ant.* b. xii. ch. iii. § 3.   But, according to Josephus, these favours were granted subsequently to the wars with Scopas, and as a compensation for the injuries which their country had suffered in the wars which had been waged between him and Scopas within their borders.   The following language of Josephus respecting the effect of these wars will justify and explain what is here said by the angel: "Now it happened that, in the reign of Antiochus the Great, who ruled over all Asia, the Jews, as well as the inhabitants of Cœlo-Syria, suffered greatly, and their land was sorely harassed; for while he was at war with Ptolemy Philopator, and with his son who was called *Epiphanes*, it fell out that these nations were equally sufferers, both when he was beaten, and when he beat the others; so that they were like to a ship in a storm, which is tossed by the waves on both sides; and just thus were they in their situation in the middle between Antiochus's prosperity and its change to adversity."—*Ant.* b. xii. ch. iii. § 3.   When Antiochus was successful against Scopas, however, the Jews "went over to him," says Josephus, "of their own accord," and received him into Jerusalem; and as a consequence of the aid which they rendered him, he granted them the favours and privileges mentioned by Josephus.   The immediate consequence of the wars, however, was extended desolation; and it is this to which the passage before us refers. Lengerke, however, supposes that the meaning of the passage is, that the whole land would be subdued under him.   The Hebrew word rendered " shall be consumed"—כָּלָה—means, properly, *to be completed, finished, closed;* then to be *consumed, wasted, spent, destroyed;* Gen. xxi. 15 ; 1 Kings xvii. 16 ; Jer. xvi. 4; Ezek. v. 13.   The destruction

whole kingdom, and ¹ upright ones with him; thus shall he do: and

1 or, *much uprightness,* or, *equal conditions.*

caused by invading and conflicting armies in a land would answer to all that is properly implied in the use of the word.

17. *He shall also set his face.* Antiochus.   That is, he shall resolve or determine.   To set one's face in any direction is to determine to go there. The meaning here is, that Antiochus, flushed with success, and resolved to push his conquests to the utmost, would make use of all the forces at his disposal to overcome the Egyptians, and to bring them into subjection to his sway.   He had driven Scopas from Cœlo-Syria, and from Sidon; had subjected the land of Palestine to his control; and now nothing seemed to prevent his extending his conquests to the utmost limits of his ambition. The reference here is to a *purpose* of Antiochus to wage war with Egypt, and to invade it.   From that purpose, however, he was turned, as we shall see, by his wars in Asia Minor; and he endeavoured, as stated in the subsequent part of the verse, if not to subdue Egypt and to bring it under his control, at least to neutralize it so that it would not interfere with his wars with the Romans.   If his attention had not been diverted, however, by more promising or more brilliant prospects in another direction, he would undoubtedly have made an immediate descent on Egypt itself.   ¶ *With the strength of his whole kingdom.* Summoning all the forces of his empire. This would seem to be necessary in invading Egypt, and in the purpose to dethrone and humble his great rival. The armies which he had employed had been sufficient to drive Scopas out of Palestine, and to subdue that country; but obviously stronger forces would be necessary in carrying the war into Egypt, and attempting a foreign conquest.   ¶ *And upright ones with him.* Marg., " or, *much uprightness,* or, *equal conditions.*"   The Hebrew word here used (יְשָׁרִים) means, properly, *straight, right;* then that which is straight or

he shall give him the daughter of women, ¹ corrupting her: but she

shall not stand *on his side*, neither be for him.   1 *to corrupt.*

---

upright—applied to persons, denoting their righteousness or integrity, Job i. 1, 8; Psal. xi. 7. By way of eminence it is applied to the Jewish people, as being a righteous or upright people— the people of God—and is language which a Hebrew would naturally apply to his own nation. In this sense it is undoubtedly used here, to denote not the *pious* portion, but the nation as such; and the meaning is, that, in addition to those whom he could muster from his own kingdom, Antiochus would expect to be accompanied with large numbers of the Hebrews—the "upright" people—in his invasion of Egypt. This he might anticipate from two causes, (*a*) the fact that they had already rendered him so much aid, and showed themselves so friendly, as stated by Josephus in the passage referred to above; and (*b*) from the benefits which he had granted to them, which furnished a reasonable presumption that they would not withhold their aid in his further attempts to subdue Egypt. The Jews might hope at least that if Egypt were subjected to the Syrian sceptre, their own country, lying between the two, would be at peace, and that they would no more be harassed by its being made the seat of wars— the battle-field of two great contending powers. It was not without reason, therefore, that Antiochus anticipated that in his invasion of Egypt he would be accompanied and assisted by not a few of the Hebrew people. As this is the natural and obvious meaning of the passage, and accords entirely with the sense of the Hebrew word, it is unnecessary to attempt to prove that the marginal reading is not correct. ¶ *Thus shall he do.* That is, in the manner which is immediately specified. He shall adopt the policy there stated—by giving his daughter in marriage with an Egyptian prince—to accomplish the ends which he has in view. The reference here is to another stroke of policy, made necessary by his new wars with the Romans, and by the diversion of his forces, in consequence, in a new direction. The *natural* step, after the

defeat of the Egyptian armies in Palestine, would have been to carry his conquests at once into Egypt, and this he appears to have contemplated. But, in the meantime, he became engaged in wars in another quarter—with the Romans; and, as Ptolemy in such circumstances would be likely to unite with the Romans against Antiochus, in order to bind the Egyptians to himself, and to neutralize them in these wars, this alliance was proposed and formed by which he connected his own family with the royal family in Egypt by marriage. ¶ *And he shall give him.* Give to Ptolemy. Antiochus would seek to form a matrimonial alliance that would, for the time at least, secure the neutrality or the friendship of the Egyptians. ¶ *The daughter of women.* The reference here is undoubtedly to his own daughter, Cleopatra. The historical facts in the case, as stated by Lengerke (*in loc.*), are these: —After Antiochus had subdued Cœlo-Syria and Palestine, he became involved in wars with the Romans in Asia Minor, in order to extend the kingdom of Syria to the limits which it had in the time of Seleucus Nicator. In order to carry on his designs in that quarter, however, it became necessary to secure the neutrality or the co-operation of Egypt, for Ptolemy would naturally, in such circumstances, favour the Romans in their wars with Antiochus. Antiochus, therefore, negotiated a marriage between his daughter Cleopatra and Ptolemy Epiphanes, the son of Ptolemy Philopator, then thirteen years of age. The valuable consideration in the view of Ptolemy in this marriage was, that, as a dowry, Cœlo-Syria, Samaria, Judea, and Phœnicia were given to her.—Josephus, *Ant.* b. xii. ch. 4, § 1. This agreement or contract of marriage was entered into immediately after the defeat of Scopas, B.C. 197. The contract was, that the marriage should take place as soon as the parties were of suitable age, and that Cœlo-Syria and Palestine should be given as a dowry. The marriage took place B.C. 193, when Antiochus

18 After this shall he turn his face unto the isles, and shall take many: but a prince for [1] his own

[1] *him.*

---

was making preparation for his wars with the Romans.—Jahn, *Heb. Commonwealth,* ch. ix. § 89, p. 246. In this way the neutrality of the king of Egypt was secured, while Antiochus prosecuted his work against the Romans. The appellation here bestowed on Cleopatra—*daughter of women*—seems to have been given to her by way of eminence, as an heiress to the crown, or a princess, or as the principal one among the women of the land. There can be no doubt of its reference to her. ¶ *Corrupting her.* Marg., as in Hebrew, *to corrupt.* There has been some doubt, however, in regard to the word *her,* in this place, whether it refers to Cleopatra or to the kingdom of Egypt. Rosenmüller, Prideaux, J. D. Michaelis, Bertholdt, Dereser, and others, refer it to Cleopatra, and suppose that it means that Antiochus had instilled into her mind evil principles, in order that she might betray her husband, and that thus, by the aid of her arts, he might obtain possession of Egypt. On the other hand, Lengerke, Maurer, De Wette, Hävernick, Elliott (*Apocalypse,* iv. 130), and others, suppose that the reference is to Egypt, and that the meaning is, that Antiochus was disposed to enter into this alliance with a view of influencing the Egyptian government not to unite with the Romans and oppose him; that is, that it was on his part an artful device to turn away the Egyptian government from its true interest, and to accomplish his own purposes. The latter agrees best with the connection, though the Hebrew will admit of either construction. As a matter of fact, *both* these objects seem to have been aimed at—for it was equally true that in this way he sought to turn away the Egyptian government and kingdom from its true interests, and that in making use of his daughter to carry out this project, it was expected that she would employ artifice to influence her future husband. This arrangement was the more necessary, as, in consequence of the fame which the Romans had acquired in overcoming Hannibal,

the Egyptians had applied to them for protection and aid in their wars with Antiochus, and offered them, as a consideration, the guardianship of young Ptolemy. This offer the Romans accepted with joy, and sent M. Æmilius Lepidus to Alexandria as guardian of the young king of Egypt.—Polybius, xv. 20; Appian, *Syriac.* i. 1; Livy, xxxi. 14; xxxiii. 19; Justin, xxx. 2, 3; xxxi. 1. The whole was, on the part of Antiochus, a stroke of policy; and it could not be accomplished without that which has been found necessary in political devices—the employment of bribery or corruption. It accords well with the character of Antiochus to suppose that he would not hesitate to instil into the mind of his daughter all his own views of policy. ¶ *But she shall not stand* on his side, *neither be for him.* That is, she would become attached to her husband, and would favour his interests rather than the crafty designs of her father. On this passage, Jerome remarks: "Antiochus, desirous not only of possessing Syria, Cilicia, and Lycia, and the other provinces which belonged to Ptolemy, but of extending also his own sceptre over Egypt itself, betrothed his own daughter Cleopatra to Ptolemy, and promised to give as a dowry Cœlo-Syria and Judea. But he could not obtain possession of Egypt in this way, because Ptolemy Epiphanes, perceiving his design, acted with caution, and because Cleopatra favoured the purposes of her husband rather than those of her father." So Jahn (*Heb. Commonwealth,* p. 246) says:—"He indulged the hope that when his daughter became queen of Egypt, she would bring the kingdom under his influence; but she proved more faithful to her husband than to her father."

18. *After this shall he turn his face unto the isles.* The islands of the Mediterranean, particularly those in the neighbourhood of and constituting a part of Greece. This he did in his wars with the Romans, for the Roman power then comprehended that part of the world, and it was the design of

behalf shall cause [1] the reproach offered by him to cease; without

his own reproach he shall cause *it* to turn upon him.   1 *his reproach.*

Antiochus, as already remarked, to extend the limits of his empire as far as it was at the time of Seleucus Nicator. This occurred after the defeat of Scopas, for, having given his daughter in marriage to Ptolemy, he supposed that he had guarded himself from any interference in his wars with the Romans from the Egyptians, and sent two of his sons with an army by land to Sardis, and he himself with a great fleet sailed at the same time into the Ægean Sea, and took many of the islands in that sea. The war which was waged between Antiochus and the Romans lasted for three years, and ended in the defeat of Antiochus, and in the subjugation of the Syrian kingdom to the Roman power, though, when it became a Roman province, it continued to be governed by its own kings. In this war, Hannibal, general of the Carthaginians, was desirous that Antiochus should unite with him in carrying his arms into Italy, with the hope that together they would be able to overcome the Romans; but Antiochus preferred to confine his operations to Asia Minor and the maritime parts of Greece; and the consequence of this, and of the luxury and indolence into which he sank, was his ultimate overthrow. Comp. Jahn's *Heb. Commonwealth*, pp. 246–249. ¶ *And shall take many.* Many of those islands; many portions of the maritime country of Asia Minor and Greece. As a matter of fact, during this war which he waged, he became possessed of Ephesus, Ætolia, the island of Eubœa, where, in the year 191 B.C. he married Eubia, a young lady of great beauty, and gave himself up for a long time to festivity and amusements—and then entrenched himself strongly at the pass of Thermopylæ. Afterwards, when driven from that stronghold, he sailed to the Thracian Chersonesus, and fortified Sestos, Abydos, and other places, and, in fact, during these military expeditions, obtained the mastery of no inconsiderable part of the maritime portions of Greece. The prophecy was strictly fulfilled, that he should "take

many" of those places. ¶ *But a prince for his own behalf.* A Roman prince, or a leader of the Roman armies. The reference is to Lucius Cornelius Scipio, called Scipio Asiaticus, in contradistinction from Publius Cornelius Scipio, called Africanus, from his conquest over Hannibal and the Carthaginians. The Scipio here referred to received the name *Asiaticus*, on account of his victories in the East, and particularly in this war with Antiochus. He was a brother of Scipio Africanus, and had accompanied him in his expedition into Spain and Africa. After his return he was rewarded with the consulship for his services to the state, and was empowered to attack Antiochus, who had declared war against the Romans. In this war he was prosperous, and succeeded in retrieving the honour of the Roman name, and in wiping off the reproach which the Roman armies had suffered from the conquests of Antiochus. When it is said that he would do this *"for his own behalf,"* the meaning is, doubtless, that he would engage in the enterprise for his own glory, or to secure fame for himself. It was not the love of justice, or the love of country, but it was to secure for himself a public triumph— perhaps hoping, by subduing Antiochus, to obtain one equal to that which his brother had received after his wars with Hannibal. The motive here ascribed to this "prince" was so common in the leaders of the Roman armies, and has been so generally prevalent among mankind, that there can be no hesitation in supposing that it was accurately ascribed to this conqueror, Scipio, and that the enterprise in which he embarked in opposing Antiochus was primarily "on his own behalf." ¶ *Shall cause the reproach offered by him to cease.* The reproach offered by Antiochus to the Roman power. The margin is, *"his reproach."* The reference is to the disgrace brought on the Roman armies by the conquests of Antiochus. Antiochus had seemed to mock that power; he had engaged in war with the conquerors of nations;

19 Then he shall turn his face toward the fort of his own land:

a Psa. 37. 36.

but he shall stumble and fall, and not *a* be found.

20 Then shall stand up in his

---

he had gained victories, and thus appeared to insult the majesty of the Roman name. All this was turned back again, or caused to cease, by the victories of Scipio. ¶ *Without his own reproach.* Without any reproach to himself—any discomfiture—any imputation of want of skill or valour. That is, he would so conduct the war as to secure an untarnished reputation. This was in all respects true of Scipio. ¶ *He shall cause* it *to turn upon him.* The reproach or shame which he seemed to cast upon the Romans would return upon himself. This occurred in the successive defeats of Antiochus in several engagements by water and by land, and in his final and complete overthrow at the battle of Magnesia (B.C. 190) by Scipio. After being several times overcome by the Romans, and vainly sueing for peace, "Antiochus lost all presence of mind, and withdrew his garrisons from all the cities on the Hellespont, and, in his precipitate flight, left all his military stores behind him. He renewed his attempts to enter into negotiations for peace, but when he was required to relinquish all his possessions west of the Taurus, and defray the expenses of the war, he resolved to try his fortune once more in a battle by land. Antiochus brought into the field seventy thousand infantry, twelve thousand cavalry, and a great number of camels, elephants, and chariots armed with scythes. To these the Romans could oppose but thirty thousand men, and yet they gained a decisive victory. The Romans lost only three hundred and twenty-five men; while, of the forces of Antiochus, fifty thousand infantry, four thousand cavalry, and fifteen elephants were left dead on the field, fifteen hundred men were made prisoners, and the king himself with great difficulty made his escape to Sardis. He now humbly sued for peace, and it was granted on the terms with which he had formerly refused compliance—that he should

surrender all his possessions west of the Taurus, and that he should defray the expenses of the war. He further obligated himself to keep no elephants, and not more than twelve ships. To secure the performance of these conditions, the Romans required him to deliver up twelve hostages of their own selection, among whom was his son Antiochus, afterwards surnamed Epiphanes."—Jahn's *Hebrew Commonwealth,* pp. 248, 249.

19. *Then he shall turn his face toward the fort of his own land.* The strong fortifications of his own land—for the Hebrew word is in the plural. This he would do, of course, for protection. He would cease his attempts at conquest, and endeavour to find security in his own fortresses. As a matter of fact, after this defeat, Antiochus, in order to replenish his exhausted coffers, and to find the means of meeting the claims of the Romans, went into certain provinces of his empire. He attempted no other foreign wars, but sought security in his own dominions. ¶ *But he shall stumble and fall, and not be found.* He died in an attempt to plunder the temple of Elymaïs. In this he provoked the people to an insurrection, and was slain, together with the soldiers who were with him. What was his *motive* for plundering that temple is uncertain, whether it was to meet the demands of the Romans, or whether it was avarice (Justin, xxxiii. 2); but it was in this way that he "stumbled and fell," and passed away.—Jerome, *Com. in loc.*; Diod. Sic., *Fragmenta,* xxvi. 30, 49; Justin, xxxii. 2; Strabo, p. 744. The prophecy respecting him terminates here, and the particulars specified are as minute and accurate as if it had been written *after* the event. Indeed, the whole account is just such as one would prepare now who should undertake to express in a brief compass the principal events in the life of Antiochus the Great.

20. *Then shall stand up in his estate.*

estate,[1] a [2]raiser of taxes *in* the glory of the kingdom: but within

few days he shall be destroyed, neither in [3]anger, nor in battle.

1 or, *place*, ver. 7.

2 *one that causeth an exacter to pass over.*

3 *angers.*

Marg., "or, *place*." The word used — קֵן — means, properly, *a stand, station, place* (see Notes on verse 7), and the idea here is simply that he would be succeeded in the kingdom by such an one. His successor would have the character and destiny which the prophecy proceeds to specify. ¶ *A raiser of taxes.* One who shall be mainly characterized for this; that is, whose government would be distinguished eminently by his efforts to wring money out of the people. The Hebrew word נֹגֵשׂ means, properly, to urge, to drive, to impel, and it is then applied to one who urges or presses a debtor, or who exacts tribute of a people. The word is used with reference to *money* exactions in Deut. xv. 2, 3: "Every creditor that lendeth aught unto his neighbour, he shall not *exact* it of his neighbour or of his brother. Of a foreigner thou mayest *exact* it again." So in 2 Kings xxiii. 35, Jehoiakim taxed the land " to give the money according to the commandment of Pharaoh: he *exacted* the silver and the gold of the people of the land." In Zech. ix. 8—"And no *oppressor* shall pass through them any more"— the same word is used. Here it denotes one who would be mainly characterized by his extorting tribute of his people, or using means to obtain money. ¶ In *the glory of the kingdom*. The word "*in*" here is supplied by our translators. Lengerke renders it, "who shall suffer the tax-gatherer (eintreiber) to go through the glory of the kingdom." This is evidently the meaning. He would lay the richest and most productive parts of his kingdom under contribution. This might be either to pay a debt contracted by a former monarch; or to carry on war; or to obtain the means of luxurious indulgence; or for purposes of magnificence and display. ¶ *But within few days.* A comparatively brief period. Comp. Gen. xxvii. 44; xxix. 20. It is impossible from this to determine

the precise period which he would live, but the language would leave the impression that his would be a short reign. ¶ *He shall be destroyed.* Heb., *shall be broken.* That is, his power shall be broken; he shall cease to reign. It would not be certainly inferred from this that he would be put to death, or would die at that time, but that his reign then would come to an end, though it might be in some peaceful way. ¶ *Neither in anger.* Heb., *angers.* Not in any tumult or excitement, or by any rage of his subjects. This would certainly imply that his death would be a peaceful death. ¶ *Nor in battle.* As many kings fell. The description would indicate a reign of peace, and one whose end would be peace, but who would have but a brief reign. The reference here is, undoubtedly, to Seleucus Philopator, the eldest son of Antiochus the Great, and his immediate successor. The fulfilment of the prediction is seen in the following facts in regard to him: (*a*) As an exactor of tribute. He was bound to pay the tribute which his father had agreed to pay to the Romans. This tribute amounted to a thousand talents annually, and consequently made it necessary for him to apply his energies to the raising of that sum. The Jewish talent of silver was equal to about 1505 dollars of our money [about £339], and, consequently, this thousand talents, of the Jewish talent of silver here referred to, was equal to about a million and a half of dollars. The Greek talent of silver was worth 1055 dollars of our money [about £238], and, if this was the talent, the sum would be about a million dollars. To raise this, in addition to the ordinary expenses of the government, would require an effort, and, as this was continued from year to year, and as Seleucus was known for little else, it was not unnatural that he should be characterized as the "raiser of taxes." (*b*) Especially would this be true in the estimation of the Jews,

21 And in his [1] estate shall stand up a vile person, to whom they shall not give the honour of the kingdom: but he shall come in peaceably, and obtain the kingdom by flatteries.　　　1 or, *place*, ver. 7.

---

for no small part of these taxes, or this revenue, was derived from Palestine. Seleucus, taking advantage of the disturbances in Egypt, had re-united to the Syrian crown the provinces of Cœlo-Syria and Palestine, which his father Antiochus the Great had given in dowry to his daughter Cleopatra, who was married to Ptolemy Epiphanes. — Jahn, *Heb. Commonwealth*, p. 255. In the year 176 B.C., Simon, a Benjamite, who became governor of the temple at Jerusalem, the farmer of the revenues of the Egyptian kings, attempted to make some innovations, which were steadily resisted by the high-priest Onias III. Simon, in anger, went to Apollonius, governor of Cœlo-Syria under Seleucus, and informed him of the great treasures contained in the temple. "The king," says Jahn (*Heb. Commonwealth*, p. 255), "though a friend to the Jews, and though he had regularly made disbursements, according to the directions of his father, towards sustaining the expenses of the sacrifices at Jerusalem, determined to apply to his own use the treasures of the temple; for the annual payment of one thousand talents to the Romans had reduced his finances to a very low ebb. With the design, therefore, of replenishing his exhausted treasury, he sent Heliodorus to Jerusalem to plunder the temple." Comp. Appian, *Syriac.* xlv. 60–65. See also Prideaux, *Con.* iii. 208; 2 Macc. iii. Besides this, the necessity of raising so much revenue would give him the character of a "raiser of taxes." (c) This was done in what might properly be termed "the glory of his kingdom," or in what would, in the language of an Hebrew, be so called—Cœlo-Syria and Palestine. To the eye of a Hebrew this was the glory of all lands, and the Jewish writers were accustomed to designate it by some such appellation. Comp. Notes on ver. 16. (d) His reign continued but a short time — answering to what is here said, that it would be for a "few days." In fact,

he reigned but eleven or twelve years, and that, compared with the long reign of Antiochus his father—thirty-seven years—was a brief period. (e) The manner of his death. He did not fall in battle, nor was he cut off in a popular tumult. He was, in fact, poisoned. In the eleventh year of his reign, he sent his only son Demetrius as hostage to Rome, and released his brother Antiochus, who had resided twelve years in that city. As the heir to the crown was now out of the way, Heliodorus sought to raise himself to the royal dignity, and for this purpose he destroyed the king by poison. He attached a large party to his interests, and finally gained over those who were in favour of submitting to the king of Egypt. Antiochus Epiphanes received notice of these transactions while he was at Athens on his return from Rome. He applied himself to Eumenes, king of Pergamos, whom, with his brother Attalus, he easily induced to espouse his cause, and they, with the help of a part of the Syrians, deprived Heliodorus of his usurped authority. Thus, in the year 175 B. C., Antiochus Epiphanes quietly ascended the throne, while the lawful heir, Demetrius, was absent at Rome. — Appian, *Syriac.* xlv. 60–65; Jahn, *Heb. Commonwealth*, ch. ix. § 91. The remainder of this chapter is occupied with a detail of the crimes, the cruelties, and the oppressions of Antiochus Epiphanes, or Antiochus IV.

21. *And in his estate.* In his place. Notes on vers. 7, 20. ¶ *Shall stand up a vile person.* There shall succeed to the throne. The reference here is to Antiochus Epiphanes, who reigned from B.C. 175 to B.C. 163. The epithet "*vile*" here given him was one which his subsequent history showed was eminently appropriate to him in all respects, as a man and as a prince. The Hebrew word rendered "vile"—נִבְזֶה—properly means one despised or held in contempt, Isa. xlix. 7; Psa.

xxii. 6 (7). The meaning here is, that he was one who deserved to be despised, and who would be held in contempt— a man of a low, base, contemptible character. Vulg., *despectus;* Gr. ἐξου-δενώθη; Luther, *ein ungeachteter.* Never were terms better applied to a man than these to Antiochus Epiphanes— both before and after his ascension to the throne. The manner of his seizing upon the crown is stated above. He was surnamed Epiphanes (Ἐπιφανής), *the Illustrious,* because, if we believe Appian, he vindicated the claims of the royal family against the usurpations of the foreigner Heliodorus. He also bore the name Θεός, *God,* which is still seen upon his coins. But by his subjects he was called Epimanes (Ἐπιμανής), *the Insane,* instead of *Epiphanes* —a name which he much more richly deserved. The following statement from Jahn (*Heb. Commonwealth,* ch. x. § 92) will show with what propriety the term "*vile*" was applied to him: " He often lounged like a mere idler about the streets of Antioch, attended by two or three servants, and not deigning to look at the nobles; would talk with goldsmiths and other mechanics in their workshops, engage in idle and trifling conversation with the lowest of the people, and mingle in the society of foreigners and men of the vilest character. He was not ashamed to go into the dissipated circles of the young, to drink and carouse with them, and to assist their merriment by singing songs and playing on his flute. He often appeared in the public baths among the common people, engaging in every kind of foolish jest, without the least regard to the dignity of his station and character. Not unfrequently he was seen drunk in the streets, when he would throw his money about, and practise various other fooleries equally extravagant. He would parade the streets of his capital in a long robe, and with a garland of roses upon his head: and if any attempted to pass by or to follow him, he would pelt them with stones, which he carried concealed under his garments," &c. See also Appian in *Syriacis,* xlv. 70–75 ; Eusebius in *Chronicon;* Athenæus, lib. v. p. 193 ;

x. p. 438 ; Livy, xli. 20 ; Diod. Sic. *Frag.* xxvi. 65 ; xxxi. 7, 8 ; Prideaux, *Con.* iii. 212–214 ; 1 Macc. i. 9. ¶ *To whom they shall not give the honour of the kingdom.* That is, the people. Or, in other words, it should not be conferred on him by any law or act of the nation, or in any regular succession or claim. The true heir to the crown was Demetrius, who was absent at Rome. On him the crown would have regularly devolved ; but in his absence it was obtained by Antiochus by arts which he practised, and not by any voluntary grant of the nation. ¶ *But he shall come in peaceably.* Quietly ; without war or force ; by art rather than by arms. Gesenius (*Lex.*) renders the phrase here used " in the midst of security ;" that is, unexpectedly, suddenly. The idea seems to be, that he would do it when the nation was not expecting it, or apprehending it ; when they would be taken off their guard, and he would " steal a march upon them." All this accorded with fact. The nation seemed not to have anticipated that Antiochus would attempt to ascend the throne on the death of his brother. But he quietly left Rome—while Demetrius, his nephew, the true heir to the crown, remained there ; came to Athens, and learned what was the state of things in Syria, where Heliodorus had usurped the authority ; made an agreement with the king of Pergamos to aid him, and, by the assistance of a part of the Syrians who were opposed to the usurper Heliodorus, deprived him of the authority, and himself took possession of the crown. No one seemed to suspect that this was his aim, or to doubt that his object was to remove an usurper that his nephew might be placed on the throne. ¶ *And obtain the kingdom by flatteries.* בַּחֲלַקְלַקּוֹת—*lubricitates, blanditiæ.* "The word," says Elliott (*Apoc.* iv. 133), " has a double sense, being applied both to the slipperiness of a path, and the slipperiness or flattering and deceit of the tongue." In the former sense it occurs in Psa. xxxv. 6, "Let their way be dark and slippery ;" in the latter, its originating verb, Prov. ii. 16. vii. 5, " The stranger that flattereth or dis-

22 And *a* with the arms of a flood shall they be overflown from before him, and shall be broken ; yea, also the prince of the covenant.

a ver. 10. Fulfilled, 170 B C.

23 And after the league *made* with him he shall work deceitfully: *b* for he shall come up, and shall become strong with a small people.

b ch. 8. 25.

---

sembleth with his words ;" and Prov. xxix. 5, "A man that flattereth [or dissembleth to] his neighbour." In this latter sense the verbal seems to be used both here and in the verses (32, 34) below : "arts of dissimulation."—Gesenius. The probable meaning here is, that he would obtain the throne by acts of dissembling, and by promises of rewards and offices. Such promises he would probably make to Eumenes, king of Pergamos, and to the Syrian nobles and people who espoused his cause. It would not be difficult to secure the aid of multitudes in this way, and the character of Antiochus was just such as to permit him to use any of these arts to accomplish his ends. Perhaps, also, he might hold out the hope of aid from the Romans, with whom he had long lived. It was no uncommon thing for an usurper to make his way by flattering certain classes of a people, and by promises of largesses, of offices, and of the removal of oppressive burdens. Comp. Prideaux, *Con.* iii. 212. See also the case of Absalom in 2 Sam. xv. 1–6

22. *And with the arms of a flood.* The reference here is to some mighty invasion of some country by Antiochus, which would sweep everything before him. There seems to be some confusion of metaphor in the phrase, "the *arms* of a flood." The idea in the mind of the writer appears to have been this : He saw an invasion of some country by hosts of men under the command of Antiochus. This it was not unnatural to compare with an *inundation of waters* spreading over a land. See Isa. viii. 8. Nor was it altogether unnatural to speak of an inundation as having *arms* extending far and near; sweeping everything to itself, or carrying it away. Thus we speak of an arm of the sea, an arm of a river, &c. In this manner the inundation—the invasion—seemed to

spread itself out like waters, sweeping all away. ¶ *Shall they be overflown from before him.* The prophet does not specify *who* they would be that would thus be overthrown. Some have supposed that the reference is to the Hebrews, but the more correct interpretation is that which refers it to Egypt, See Notes on ver. 25. As a matter of fact, the forces of Heliodorus, the forces of the Hebrews, and the forces of the Egyptians, were alike broken and scattered before him. The eye of the prophet, however, seems rather here to be on the invasion of Egypt, which was one of the earliest and most prominent acts of Antiochus, and into the history of which the prophet goes most into detail. ¶ *Yea, also the prince of the covenant.* He also shall be broken and overcome. There has been some diversity of opinion as to who is meant by "the prince of the covenant" here. Many suppose that it is the high priest of the Jews, as being the chief prince or ruler under the "covenant" which God made with them, or among the "covenant" people. But this appellation is not elsewhere given to the Jewish high priest, nor is it such as could with much propriety be applied to him. The reference is rather to the king of Egypt, with whom a covenant or compact had been made by Antiochus the Great, and who was supposed to be united, therefore, to the Syrians by a solemn treaty. See Lengerke, *in loc.* So Elliott, *Apoc.* iv. 133.

23. *And after the league* made *with him.* A treaty of peace and concord. The great subject of contention between the kings of Syria and Egypt was the possession of Cœlo-Syria and Palestine. This they often endeavoured to settle by conquest, as each of them claimed that in the original partition of the empire of Alexander this portion of the empire fell to him.

self; and often they endeavoured to settle it by treaty. Consequently this region was constantly passing from one to the other, and was also the seat of frequent wars. The "league" here referred to seems to have been that respecting this country—the successive promises which had been made to the king of Egypt that Cœlo-Syria and Palestine should be made over to him. These provinces had been secured to Ptolemy Lagus by the treaty made 301 B.C., and they had been again pledged by Antiochus the Great, in dowry, when his daughter Cleopatra should be made queen of Egypt.—Jahn, *Heb. Commonwealth*, p. 260. Antiochus Epiphanes, however, was by no means disposed to confirm this grant, and hence the wars in which he was involved with the Egyptians. ¶ *He shall work deceitfully.* In reference to the covenant or treaty above referred to. He shall endeavour to evade its claims; he shall refuse to comply with its conditions; he shall not deliver up the provinces according to the terms of the compact. The history accords exactly with this, for he did not intend to comply with the terms of the treaty, but sought every means to evade it, and finally waged a succession of bloody wars with Egypt. In reference to the terms of this treaty, and to secure their respective interests, both parties sent ambassadors to Rome to urge their claims before the Roman Senate.—Polybius, *Legat.* § 78, 82 ; Jerome, *Com. in loc.* As soon as Ptolemy Philometor had reached his fourteenth year, he was solemnly invested with the government; and ambassadors from all surrounding countries came to congratulate him on his accession to the throne. "On this occasion Antiochus sent to Egypt Apollonius, the son of Mnestheus, apparently to congratulate the king on his coronation, but with the real intention of sounding the purposes of the Egyptian court. When Apollonius, on his return, informed Antiochus that he was viewed as an enemy by the Egyptians, he immediately sailed to Joppa to survey his frontiers towards Egypt, and to put them in a state of defence."—Jahn, *Heb. Commonwealth,*

p. 260 ; 2 Macc. iv. 21. The purpose of Antiochus was undoubtedly not to surrender Cœlo-Syria and Palestine according to the treaties which had been made ; and yet he designed to secure them if possible without an open rupture, and hence his arts of diplomacy, or his efforts to evade compliance with the terms of the compact. Even when he had invaded Egypt, and had obtained possession of the king, Ptolemy Philometor, he still "pretended that he had come to Egypt solely for the good of king Ptolemy, to set the affairs of his kingdom in order for him; and Ptolemy found it expedient to act as though he really thought him his friend. But he must have seen," says Jahn, "that Antiochus, with all his professions of friendship, was not unmindful of spoil, for he plundered Egypt in every quarter."—*Heb. Commonwealth*, p. 263. ¶ *For he shall come up.* Come upon Egypt. The result would be war. Rather than surrender the provinces according to the treaty, he would ultimately invade Egypt, and carry war into its borders. ¶ *And shall become strong with a small people.* The meaning of this seems to be, that at first his own forces would be small; that he would go up in such a way as not to excite suspicion, but that, either by an increase of his forces there, by uniting himself to confederates, by alluring the people by the promise of rewards, or by gradually taking one town after another and adding them to his dominions, he would become strong. Jahn (*Heb. Commonwealth,* p. 263) says, "*with a small body of troops* he made himself master of Memphis, and of all Egypt as far as Alexandria, almost without striking a blow." Compare Diod. Sic. xxvi. 75, 77; Jos. *Ant.* xii. 5, 2. The fact in the case was, that Antiochus pretended in his invasion of Egypt to be the friend of the Egyptian king, and that he came to aid him, and to settle him firmly on the throne. By degrees, however, he became possessed of one town after another, and subdued one place after another, until he finally became possessed of the king himself, and had him entirely in his power.

24 He shall enter [1] peaceably even upon the fattest places of the province; and he shall do *that* which his fathers have not done, nor his fathers' fathers; he shall scatter

[1] or, *into the peaceable and fat.*

among them the prey, and spoil, and riches; *yea,* and he shall forecast [2] his devices against the strong holds, even for a time.

25 And he shall stir up his power

[2] *think his thoughts.*

24. *He shall enter peaceably even upon the fattest places of the province.* The margin is, " or, *into the peaceable and fat.*" The version in the text, however, is the more correct, and the sense is, that he would do this *unexpectedly* (Lengerke, *unvermuthet*); he would make gradual and artful approaches until he had seized upon the best portions of the land. Comp. Gen. xxvii. 28, 39. The history is, that he went there with different professions than those of conquest, and one after another he took possession of the principal towns of Egypt. In his first invasion of that country, Diodorus Siculus and Josephus both say that Antiochus "availed himself of a mean artifice," without specifying what it was. Jahn says that probably it was that he pretended to come as the friend of Ptolemy. It was to this that the allusion is here, when it is said that he would "enter *peaceably*"—that is, with some pretence of peace or friendship, or with some false and flattering art. Josephus (*Ant.* xii. ch. v. § 2) says of Antiochus, that "he came with great forces to Pelusium, and circumvented Ptolemy Philometor *by treachery,* and seized upon Egypt." The fact stated by Diodorus and Josephus, that he took possession of Memphis and of all Egypt, as far as Alexandria, fully illustrates what is said here, that he would "enter upon the fattest places of the province." These were the most choice and fertile portions of Egypt." ¶ *And he shall do that which his fathers have not done, nor his fathers' fathers.* Which none of his predecessors have been able to do ; to wit, in the conquest of Egypt. No one of them had it so completely in his possession ; no one obtained from it so much spoil. There can be no doubt that such was the fact. The wars of his predecessors with the Egyptians had been mostly waged in Cœlo-Syria and Palestine, for the possession of

these provinces. Antiochus Epiphanes, however, at first took Pelusium, the key of Egypt, and then invaded Egypt itself, seized upon its strongest places, and made the king a captive.—Jahn, *Heb. Commonwealth,* p. 263. Comp. 1 Macc. i. 16. ¶ *He shall scatter among them the prey,* &c. Among his followers. He shall reward them with the spoils of Egypt. Comp. 1 Macc. i. 19 : "Thus they got the strong cities in the land of Egypt, and he took the spoils thereof. ¶ *And he shall forecast his devices.* Marg., " *think his thoughts.*" The margin is in accordance with the Hebrew. The meaning is, that he would form plans, or that this would be his aim. He would direct the war against the strongly-fortified places of Egypt. ¶ *Against the strongholds.* Antiochus took possession of Pelusium, the key of Egypt ; he seized upon Memphis, and he then laid siege to Alexandria, supposing that if that were reduced, the whole country would be his.—Jos. *Ant.* b. xii. ch. v. § 2. ¶ *Even for a time.* Josephus (*ut sup.*) says that he was driven from Alexandria, and out of all Egypt, by the threatenings of the Romans, commanding him to let that country alone. There were other reasons also which, combined with this, induced him to retire from that country. He was greatly enraged by the effect which a report of his death had produced in Judea. It was said that all the Jews rejoiced at that report, and rose in rebellion ; and he therefore resolved to inflict revenge on them, and left Egypt, and went to Jerusalem, and subdued it either by storm or by stratagem.

25. *And he shall stir up his power and his courage against the king of the south with a great army.* This must refer to a subsequent invasion of Egypt by Antiochus. In the course of his reign he four times invaded that country with various degrees of success. In

and his courage against the king of the south with a great army; and the king of the south shall be stirred up to battle with a very great and mighty army; but he shall not stand: for they shall forecast devices against him.

26 Yea, they that feed of the portion of his meat shall destroy him, and his army shall overflow; and many shall fall down slain.

27 And both these kings' 1 hearts *shall be* to do mischief, and they

1 *their hearts.*

the first, he took Pelusium, and having placed a garrison there, retired into winter-quarters to Tyre. In the second, above referred to, he took Memphis and laid siege to Alexandria. The third invasion here referred to was after he had taken Jerusalem, and was caused by the fact that, as Ptolemy Philometor was in the hands of Antiochus, the Egyptians had raised Ptolemy Physcon (*the Gross*) to the throne. This prince assumed the name of Euergetes II. The pretended object of Antiochus in this invasion (B.C. 168) was to support the claims of Ptolemy Philometor against the usurpation of his brother, but his real purpose was to subject the whole country to his own power. He defeated the Alexandrians by sea near Pelusium, and then drew up his land forces before the city of Alexandria. Ptolemy Physcon sent an embassy to Rome to solicit the protection of the Senate, and at the same time entered into negotiations of peace with Antiochus. The proposals were rejected; but when Antiochus perceived that the conquest of Alexandria would be difficult, he retired to Memphis, and pretended to deliver up the kingdom to Ptolemy Philometor, and having left a strong garrison at Pelusium, he returned to Antioch. This invasion is thus described by the author of the book of Maccabees (1 Macc. i. 17); "Wherefore he entered Egypt with a great multitude, with chariots, and elephants, and horsemen, and a great navy."— Porphyry, as quoted by Scaliger; Polybius, *Legat*, §§ 81, 82, 84; Livy, xliv. 19; xlv. 11; Justin, xxxiv. 2; Prideaux, *Con.* iii. 232–235. ¶ *And theking of the south.* Ptolemy Physcon, king of Egypt. ¶ *Shall be stirred up to battle with a very great and mighty army.* To oppose Antiochus. ¶ *But he shall not stand.* He shall not be able to resist him. His navy was defeated; Antiochus still held possession

of Memphis, and laid siege to Alexandria. ¶ *For they shall forecast devices against him.* Heb., "shall think thoughts" (see Notes on ver. 24); that is, they shall form plans against him to defeat him. The reference here is to the invading forces, that they would form sagacious plans for the overthrow of the king of Egypt.

26. *Yea, they that feed of the portion of his meat shall destroy him.* They of his own family; they who are nourished at his table; they who are his cabinet counsellors, and professed and confidential friends. The meaning is, that they would prove treacherous and unfaithful. This is by no means improbable. Antiochus was powerful, and had seized upon Pelusium, and upon Memphis, and upon the fairest portions of Egypt. He was also in possession of the person of the lawful king, and had a fair prospect of subduing the whole country. In these circumstances, nothing would be more natural than that the very inmates of the palace—the persons around the reigning king—should begin to doubt whether he could hold out, and should be disposed to make terms with the invader. ¶ *And his army shall overflow.* The connection here requires us to understand this of the army of the king of Egypt. The meaning seems to be, that his forces would be great, and would spread themselves out like overflowing waters, but that notwithstanding this many of them would be slain. ¶ *And many shall fall down slain.* In battle. Notwithstanding the army would be numerous, and would, as it were, spread over the land, still it would not be sufficient to keep out the invaders, but many of them would fall in the field. The account in 1 Macc. i. 18 is, that "Ptolemy was afraid of him [Antiochus] and fled; *and many were wounded to death.*"

27. *And both these kings' hearts* shall

shall speak lies at one table; but it shall not prosper: *a* for yet the end *shall be* at the time appointed.

a vers. 29, 35, 40; ch. 8. 19.

be *to do mischief*. Marg., *their hearts*. The meaning is, that their hearts were set on some evil or unjust purpose. The reference here is, evidently, to Antiochus and Ptolemy Philometor, and the time alluded to is when Ptolemy was in the possession of Antiochus, and when they were together forming their plans. Antiochus invaded the country under pretence of aiding Ptolemy and establishing him in the government, and for the same reason, under pretence of protecting him, he had him now in his possession. At first, also, it would seem that Ptolemy coincided with his plans, or was so far deceived by the acts of Antiochus as to believe in his friendship, and to unite with him in his schemes, for it is expressly said by the historians, as quoted above, that when Antiochus left Egypt, leaving Ptolemy at Memphis, and a strong garrison in Pelusium, Ptolemy began to see through his crafty designs, and to act accordingly. Until that time, however, he seems to have regarded the professions of Antiochus as sincere, and to have entered fully into his plans. To that fact there is allusion here; and the meaning is, that they were forming united schemes of evil—of conquests, and robbery, and oppression. The guiding spirit in this was undoubtedly Antiochus, but Ptolemy seems to have concurred in it. ¶ *And they shall speak lies at one table*. At the same table. Ptolemy was a captive, and was entirely in the possession of Antiochus, but it was a matter of policy with the latter to hide from him as far as possible the fact that he was a prisoner, and to treat him as a king. It is to be presumed, therefore, that he would do so, and that they would be seated at the same table; that is, that Ptolemy would be treated outwardly with the respect due to a king. In this familiar condition—in this state of apparently respectful and confidential intercourse — they would form their plans. Yet the devices of both would

28 Then shall he return into his land with great riches; and his heart *shall be* against the holy covenant; and he shall do *exploits*, and return to his own land.

be *false*—or would be, in fact, *speaking lies*. Antiochus would be acting perfidiously throughout, endeavouring to impose on Ptolemy, and making promises, and giving assurances, which he knew to be false; and Ptolemy would be equally acting a deceitful part —entering into engagements which, perhaps, he did not intend to keep, and which would, at any rate, be soon violated. It is impossible now to know *how* he came into the hands of Antiochus—whether he surrendered himself in war; or whether he was persuaded to do it by the arts of his courtiers; or whether he was really deceived by Antiochus and supposed that he was his friend, and that his protection was necessary. On any of these suppositions it cannot be supposed that he would be very likely to be sincere in his transactions with Antiochus. ¶ *But it shall not prosper*. The scheme concocted, whatever it was, would not be successful. The plan of Antiochus was to obtain possession of the whole of Egypt, but in this he failed; and so far as Ptolemy entered into the scheme proposed by Antiochus, on pretence for the good of his country, it also failed. Whatever the purpose was, it was soon broken up by the fact that Antiochus left Egypt, and made war on Jerusalem. ¶ *For yet the end* shall be *at the time appointed*. See ver. 29. The end—the result—shall not be now, and in the manner contemplated by these two kings. It shall be at the time "appointed," to wit, by God, and in another manner. The whole case shall issue differently from what they design, and at the time which an overruling Providence has designated. The *reason* implied here why they could not carry out their design was, that there was an "appointed time" when these affairs were to be determined, and that no purposes of theirs could be allowed to frustrate the higher counsels of the Most High.

28. *Then shall he return into his*

29 At the time appointed he shall return, and come toward the

land with great riches. Enriched with the spoils of Egypt. Having taken Memphis, and the fairest portions of Egypt, he would, of course, carry great wealth to his own country on his return. Thus it is said in 1 Macc. i. 19: "Thus they got the strong cities in the land of Egypt, and he took the spoils thereof." The meaning here is, that he would *set out* to return to his own land. As a matter of fact, on his way he would pause to bring desolation on Jerusalem, as is intimated in the subsequent part of the verse. ¶ *And his heart* shall be *against the holy covenant.* The words "holy covenant" are a technical expression to denote the Jewish institutions. The Hebrew people were called the "covenant people," as being a people with whom God had entered into covenant. All their privileges were regarded as the result of that covenant, and hence the word came to be applied to all the institutions of the nation. When it is said that his heart was against that covenant, the meaning is, that he was enraged against it; and determined to bring calamity upon the place and people connected with it. The reason of this was the following: When he was in Egypt, a report was spread abroad that he was dead. In consequence of this rumour, Jason took the opportunity of recovering the office of high-priest from his brother Menelaus, and with a thousand men took Jerusalem, drove Menelaus into the castle, and slew many whom he took for his enemies. Antiochus, hearing of this, supposed that all the Jews had revolted, and determined to inflict summary chastisement on them on his way to his own land. See Jahn, *Hebrew Commonwealth,* p. 263. ¶ *And he shall do* exploits, *and return to his own land.* The word "exploits" is supplied by the translators. The Hebrew is, simply, "he shall do;" that is, he shall accomplish the purpose of his heart on the covenant people. In this expedition he took Jerusalem, whether by storm or by stratagem is not quite certain. Diodorus Siculus, and the author of the second book of Macca-

south: but it shall not be as the former, or as the latter.

bees, and Josephus (*Jewish Wars,* i. 1, 2, and vi. 10, 1), say that it was by storm. The account which he gives in his *Antiquities* (b. xii. ch. v. § 3) is, that he took it by stratagem, but the statement in the *Jewish Wars* is much more probable, for Antiochus plundered the city, slew eighty thousand persons, men, women, and children, took forty thousand prisoners, and sold as many into slavery, 2 Macc. v. 5, 6, 11–14. As if this were not enough, under the guidance of the high-priest Menelaus, he went into the sanctuary, uttering blasphemous language, took away all the gold and silver vessels he could find there, the golden table, altar, and candlestick, and all the great vessels, and that he might leave nothing behind, searched the subterranean vaults, and in this manner collected eighteen hundred talents of gold. He then sacrificed swine on the altar, boiled a piece of the flesh, and sprinkled the whole temple with the broth, 2 Macc. v. 15–21; 1 Macc. i. 21–28; Diodorus Sic. xxxiv. 1; Jahn, *Hebrew Commonwealth,* p. 264.

29. *At the time appointed.* In the purposes of God. See Notes on ver. 27. That is, at the time when God shall design to accomplish his own purposes in regard to him. The idea is, that there was a definite period in the Divine Mind in which all this was to be done, and that when this should occur Antiochus would return again to invade Egypt. ¶ *He shall return, and come toward the south.* With an intention of invading Egypt. The occasion of this invasion was, that after the departure of Antiochus, leaving Ptolemy in possession of Egypt, or having professedly given up the kingdom to him, Ptolemy suspected the designs of Antiochus, and came to an agreement with his brother Physcon, that they should share the government between them, and resist Antiochus with their united power. To do this, they hired mercenary troops from Greece. Antiochus, learning this, openly threw off the mask, and pre-

30 ¶ For the ships *a* of Chittim shall come against him; therefore he shall be grieved, and return, and have indignation against the

holy covenant: so shall he do; [1] he shall even return, and have intelligence with them that forsake the holy covenant.

a Nu. 24. 24.

1 Fulfilled, 168, 169, **B.C.**

pared to invade Egypt again, B.C. 167. He sent his fleet to Cyprus to secure possession of that island, and led his army towards Egypt to subdue the two brothers, designing to annex the whole country to his dominions. ¶ *But it shall not be as the former, or as the latter.* At the first invasion or the second. In these he was successful; in this he would not be. The reason of his want of success is stated in the following verse—that by the aid which the two brothers had obtained from abroad, as expressed in the next verse, they would be able to oppose him.

30. *For the ships of Chittim shall come against him.* The word rendered *Chittim*—כִּתִּים—according to Gesenius, properly means *Cyprians,* so called from a celebrated Phœnician colony in the island of Cyprus. In a wider acceptation the name came to comprehend the islands and coasts of the Mediterranean Sea, especially the northern parts, and therefore stands for the islands and coasts of Greece and the Ægean Sea. See Gesenius, *Lex.,* and comp. Josephus, *Ant.* b. i. ch. vi. 1. The Egyptian government had called in the aid of the Romans, and Antiochus, therefore, was threatened with a war with the Romans if he did not abandon his enterprise against Egypt. The reference in the passage before us is to the embassage which the Romans sent to Antiochus in Egypt, requiring him to desist from his enterprise against Egypt. "When he had arrived at Leusine, about four miles from Alexandria, he met Caius Popilius Lænas, Caius Decimius, and Caius Hostilius, ambassadors, whom the Roman Senate had sent to him at the earnest request of Ptolemy Physcon. They were instructed to assure Antiochus that he must leave the kingdom of Egypt and the island of Cyprus in peace, or expect a war with the Romans. When Antiochus said that he would lay the

affair before his council, Popilius, the head of the legation, with his staff drew a circle about the king in the sand on which they stood, and exclaimed, 'Before you leave that circle, you must give me an answer which I can report to the Senate.' Antiochus was confounded, but on a little reflection, he said he would do whatever the Senate required."— Jahn, *Heb. Commonwealth,* pp. 265, 266; Polyb. *Legat.* §§ 90, 92; Livy, xliv. 14, 29; 41–46; xlv. 10, 12. These ambassadors came by the way of Greece, and in Grecian vessels, and their coming might properly be described as "ships from Chittim." They went from Rome to Brundusium, and then passed over to the Grecian shore, and from thence by the way of Chalcis, Delos, and Rhodes, to Alexandria.—Prideaux, iii. 237. ¶ *Therefore he shall be grieved.* The word here used—כָּאַה—means, properly, to become faint-hearted; to be frightened; to be dejected, sad, humbled, Job xxx. 8; Ezek. xiii. 22; Psa. cix. 16. The meaning here is, that he became dispirited, dejected, cast down, and abandoned his purpose. He saw that it would be vain to attempt to contend with the Romans, and he was constrained reluctantly to relinquish his enterprise. ¶ *And return.* Set out to return to his own land. ¶ *And have indignation against the holy covenant.* See Notes on ver. 28. That is, he would be filled with wrath against Jerusalem and the Jews. Polybius says that he left Egypt in great anger, because he was compelled by the Romans to abandon his designs. In this condition he was, of course, in a state of mind to become irritated against any other people, and, if an occasion should be given, would seek to vent his wrath in some other direction. This habitual state of feeling towards Jerusalem and the Jews would make him ready to seize upon the slightest pretext to

31 And arms shall stand on his part, and they shall pollute the sanctuary of strength, and shall take away the daily *sacrifice*, and they shall place the abomination that maketh [1] desolate.   1 or, *astonisheth*.

---

wreak his vengeance on the holy land. What was the immediate occasion of his taking this opportunity to attack Jerusalem is not certainly known, but in his marching back through Palestine, he detached from his army twenty-two thousand men, under the command of Apollonius, and sent them to Jerusalem to destroy it.—Prideaux, iii. 239; Jahn, *Heb. Commonwealth*, p. 266.   Apollonius arrived before Jerusalem B. C. 167, just two years after the city had been taken by Antiochus himself.   ¶ *So shall he do.* That is, in the manner described in this and the following verses.   ¶ *He shall even return.* On his way to his own land.   ¶ *And have intelligence with them that forsake the holy covenant.* Have an understanding with them; that is, with a portion of the nation—with those who were disposed to cast off the religion of their fathers. There was a considerable part of the nation that was inclined to do this, and to introduce the customs of the Greeks (comp. Jahn, *Heb. Commonwealth*, pp. 258–260); and it was natural that Antiochus should seek to have an understanding with them, and to make use of them in accomplishing his designs.   It was very probably at the solicitation of this infidel and disaffected party of the Hebrew people that Antiochus had interfered in their affairs at all. Comp. 1 Macc. i. 11–15.

31. *And arms shall stand on his part.* Up to this verse there is a general agreement among commentators, that the reference is to Antiochus Epiphanes. From this verse, however, to the end of the chapter, there is no little diversity of opinion. One portion suppose that the description of Antiochus and his deeds continues still to be the design of the prophet ; another, that the Romans are here introduced, and that a part of the predictions in the remainder of this chapter are yet to be fulfilled ; another, as Jerome, and most of the Christian fathers, suppose that the reference is to Antiochus as the type of Antichrist, and that the description passes from the type to the antitype.   In this last class are found Bishop Newton, Gill, Calvin, Prideaux, Wintle, Elliott (*Apocalypse*, iv. 137, *seq.*), and others ; in the former, Grotius, Lengerke, Bertholdt, Maurer, &c. In this same class is found the name of Porphyry—who maintained that the whole referred to Antiochus, and that the allusion was so clear as to prove that this portion of the book was written *after* the events had occurred. The reason suggested for the change in the supposed reference, as alleged by Bishop Newton *on the Prophecies*, p. 296, is, substantially, that what follows can be applied only in part to Antiochus. Whether this portion of the chapter can be shown to refer to him, we shall be able to determine as we proceed. Nothing can be clearer than the allusion up to this point.   The word rendered *arms*, in the verse before us (זְרֹעִים — sing. זְרוֹעַ), means, properly, the arm — especially the lower arm below the elbow ; and then comes to denote strength, might, power ; and thence is applied to a military force, or an army.   See ver. 15.   Such is undoubtedly the meaning here, and the reference is to the military force which Antiochus would employ to wreak his vengeance on the Jews—particularly by the instrumentality of Apollonius. Others would apply this to the Romans, and suppose that they are introduced here ; but this construction is forced and unnatural, for (*a*) the reference in the previous verses was, undoubtedly, to Antiochus, and the narrative seems to proceed as if there were no change.   (*b*) There is nothing in the statement which does not agree with what was done by Antiochus. As a matter of fact, as attested by all history, he detached Apollonius with twenty-two thousand men, on his mortified return to his own land, to attack and lay waste Jerusalem, and Apollonius did all that is here said would be done.   Bishop Newton concedes (p. 294) that " this interpretation might be ad-

mitted, if the other parts were equally applicable to Antiochus; but," says he, "the difficulty, or rather impossibility of applying them to Antiochus, or any of the Syrian kings, his successors, obliges us to look out for another interpretation." Accordingly, he says that Jerome and the Christians of his time contend that these things apply to Antichrist; and he himself adopts the view proposed by Sir Isaac Newton, that it refers to the Romans, and that the allusion is to the fact that, at the very time when Antiochus retreated out of Egypt, the Romans conquered Macedonia, "putting an end to the reign of Daniel's third beast," and that the prophet here leaves off the description of the actions of the Greeks, and commences a description of those of the Romans in Greece. As, however, all that is *here* said is strictly applicable to what was done by Antiochus, such an interpretation is unnecessary. ¶ *And they shall pollute the sanctuary of strength.* The "sanctuary *of strength*" seems to refer to the fortifications or defences that had been set up to protect Jerusalem, or the temple. At various points the temple was defended in this manner, not only by the walls of the city, but by fortifications erected within, and so as to prevent an army from approaching the temple, even if they should penetrate the outer wall. Comp. 1 Macc. i. 36. The temple itself might thus be regarded as fortified, or as a place of strength—and, as a matter of fact, when Titus ultimately destroyed the city, the chief difficulty was to obtain possession of the temple—a place that held out to the last. When it is said that they would "*pollute* the sanctuary of strength," the reference is to what was done by Apollonius, at the command of Antiochus, to profane the temple, and to put an end to the sacrifices and worship there. Comp. 1 Macc. i. 29, 37–49; Jos. *Ant.* b. xii. ch. v. § 4. The account in the book of Maccabees is as follows: "Thus they shed innocent blood on every side of the sanctuary and defiled it, insomuch that the inhabitants of Jerusalem fled because of them, wherefore the city was made a habitation of strangers,

and became strange to those who were born in her, and her own children left her. Her sanctuary was laid waste like a wilderness, and her feasts were turned into mourning, her sabbaths into reproach, her honour into contempt. As had been her glory, so was her dishonour increased, and her excellency was turned into mourning. Moreover, king Antiochus wrote to his whole kingdom that all should be one people, and every one should leave his laws; so all the heathen agreed, according to the commandment of the king. Yea, many Israelites consented to his religion, and sacrificed unto idols, and profaned the Sabbath. For the king had sent letters by messengers unto Jerusalem and the cities of Judah, that they should follow the strange laws of the land, and forbid burnt-offerings, and sacrifices, and drink-offerings, in the temple; and that they should profane the sabbaths and festival days, and pollute the sanctuary and holy people; set up altars, and groves, and chapels of idols, and sacrifice swine's flesh and unclean beasts; that they should also leave their children uncircumcised, and make their souls abominable with all manner of uncleanness and profanation, to the end they might forget the law, and change all the ordinances." ¶ *And shall take away the daily* sacrifice. That is, shall forbid it, and so pollute the temple and the altar as to prevent its being offered. See the quotation above. This occurred in the month of June, B.C. 167. See Jahn, *Heb. Commonwealth*, p. 267. ¶ *And they shall place the abomination that maketh desolate.* Marg., or, *astonisheth.* The Hebrew word מְשֹׁמֵם will bear either interpretation, though the usage of the word is in favour of the translation in the text. The passage will also admit of this translation—"the abomination of desolation *of him* who makes desolate," or of *the desolater.* See Gesenius, *Lex.* 3. The idea is, that somehow the thing here referred to would be connected with the *desolation*, or the laying waste of the city and temple; and the sense is not materially varied whether we regard it as "the abomination that makes

32 And such as do wickedly against the covenant shall he [1] corrupt by flatteries: but the people that do know their God shall be strong, and do *exploits*.

1 or, *cause to dissemble.*

desolate," that is, that *indicates* the desolation, or, "the abomination *of the desolater*," that is, of him who has laid the city and temple waste. On the meaning of the phrase "abomination of desolation," see Notes on ch. ix. 27. The reference here is, undoubtedly, to something that Antiochus set up in the temple that was an indication of desolation, or the result of his having laid the temple in ruins. The very expression occurs in 1 Macc. i. 54: "Now, the fifteenth day of the month Casleu, in the hundred and forty-fifth year, they set up *the abomination of desolation* upon the altar, and builded idol-altars throughout the cities of Judah on every side." This would seem, from ver. 59, to have been an idol-altar erected *over* or *upon* the altar of burnt-offerings. "They did sacrifice upon the idol-altar, which was upon the altar of God." "At this time an old man, by the name of Athenæus, was sent to Jerusalem to instruct the Jews in the Greek religion, and compel them to an observance of its rites. He dedicated the temple to Jupiter Olympius; and on the altar of Jehovah he placed a smaller altar, to be used in sacrificing to the heathen god." — Jahn, *Heb. Commonwealth*, pp. 267, 268. The reference here is, probably, to this altar, as being in itself and in the situation where it was located an "abominable" thing in the eyes of the Hebrews, and as being placed there by a *desolater*, or *waster*. The same *language* which is here used is applied in ch. ix. 27, and in the New Testament, with great propriety to what the Romans set up in the temple as an indication of its conquest and profanation; but that fact does not make it certain that it is so to be understood *here*, for it is as applicable to what Antiochus did as it is to what was done by the Romans. See Notes on ch. ix. 27.

32. *And such as do wickedly against the covenant*. That is, among the Jews.

33 And they that understand among the people shall instruct many; yet they shall fall by the sword, and by flame, by captivity, and by spoil, *many* days.

They who apostatized, and who became willing to receive the religion of foreigners. There *was* such a party in Jerusalem, and it was numerous. See Jahn, *Heb. Commonwealth*, pp. 258, 259. Comp. 1 Macc. i. 52: "Then many of the people were gathered unto them, to wit, every one that forsook the law; and so they committed evils in the land." ¶ *Shall he corrupt by flatteries*. By flattering promises of his favour, of office, of national prosperity, &c. See Notes on ver. 21. The margin is, "or, *cause to dissemble*." The meaning of the Hebrew word חָנֵף is, rather, *to profane, to pollute, to defile;* and the idea here is, that he would cause them to become defiled; that is, that he would seduce them to impiety and apostasy. ¶ *But the people that do know their God*. They who adhere to the service and worship of the true God, and who are incapable of being seduced to apostasy and sin. The reference here is, undoubtedly, to Judas Maccabeus and his followers— a full account of whose doings is to be found in the books of the Maccabees. See also Prideaux, *Con.* iii. 245, *seq.*, and Jahn, *Heb. Commonwealth*, pp. 268, *seq.* ¶ *Shall be strong*. Shall evince great valour, and shall show great vigour in opposing him. ¶ *And do* exploits. The word "*exploits*," as in ver. 28, is supplied by the translators, but not improperly. The meaning is, that they would show great prowess, and perform illustrious deeds in battle. See Prideaux, *Con.* iii. pp. 262, 263.

33. *And they that understand among the people*. Among the Hebrew people. The allusion is to such as, in those times of so general corruption and apostasy, should have a proper understanding of the law of God and the nature of religion. There were such in the days of Judas Maccabeus, and it is reasonable to suppose that they would endeavour to inculcate just

34 Now when they shall fall, they shall be holpen with a little help: but many shall cleave to them with flatteries.

views among the people. ¶ *Shall instruct many.* In the nature of religion; in their duty to their country and to God. See Prideaux, *Con.* iii. 265. ¶ *Yet they shall fall by the sword.* They shall not be immediately nor always successful. Their final triumph would be only after many of them had fallen in battle, or been made captives. Mattathias, the father of Judas Maccabeus, who began the opposition to Antiochus (1 Macc. ii. 1), having summoned to his standard as many as he could induce to follow him, retired for security to the mountains. He was pursued, and refusing to fight on the Sabbath, his enemies came upon him, and slew many of his followers, 1 Macc. ii. 14–37. The author of the book of Maccabees (1 Macc. ii. 38) says of this: "So they rose up against them in battle on the sabbath, and they slew them, with their wives and children, and their cattle, to the number of a thousand people." ¶ *And by flame.* By fire. That is, probably, their dwellings would be fired, and they would perish in the flames, or in caves where they fled for shelter, or by being cast into heated caldrons of brass. See 2 Macc. vi. 11: "And others that had run together into caves near by" (when Antiochus endeavoured to enforce on them the observance of heathen laws and customs), "to keep the sabbath-day secretly, being discovered to Philip, were all burnt together, because they made a conscience to help themselves for the honour of the most sacred day." 2 Macc. vii. 3–5: "Then the king, being in a rage, commanded pans and caldrons to be made hot: which forthwith being heated, he commanded to cut out the tongue of him that spake first, and to cut off the utmost parts of his body, the rest of his brethren and his mother looking on. Now when he was thus maimed in all his members, he commanded him, being yet alive, to be brought to the fire, and to be fried in the pan," &c. ¶ *By captivity.* 1 Macc. i. 32: "But the women and children took they captive." See also 2 Macc. v. 24. ¶ *And*

by spoil. By plunder, to wit, of the temple and city. See 1 Macc. i. 20–24. ¶ *Many days.* Heb., *days.* The time is not specified, but the idea is that it would be for a considerable period. Josephus says it was three years.— *Ant.* b. xii. ch. vii. §§ 6, 7 ; 1 Macc. i. 59; iv. 54 ; 2 Macc. x. 1–7.

34. *Now when they shall fall, they shall be holpen with a little help.* By small accessions to their forces. The armies of the Maccabees were never *very* numerous ; but the idea here is, that when they should be persecuted, there would be accessions to their forces, so that they would be able to prosecute the war. At first the numbers were very few who took up arms, and undertook to defend the institutions of religion, but their numbers increased until they were finally victorious. Those who first banded together, when the calamities came upon the nation, were Mattathias and his few followers, and this is the little help that is here referred to. See 1 Macc. ii. ¶ *But many shall cleave to them.* As was the case under Judas Maccabeus, when the forces were so far increased as to be able to contend successfully with Antiochus. ¶ *With flatteries.* Perhaps with flattering hopes of spoil or honour; that is, that they would not unite sincerely with the defenders of the true religion, but would be actuated by prospect of plunder or reward. For the meaning of the word, see Notes on ver. 21. The sense here is not that Judas would flatter them, or would secure their co-operation by flatteries, but that this would be what they would propose to their own minds, and what would influence them. Comp. 1 Macc. v. 55–57: "Now what time as Judas and Jonathan were in the land of Galaad, and Simon his brother in Galilee before Ptolemais, Joseph the son of Zacharias, and Azarias, captains of the garrisons, heard of the valiant acts and warlike deeds which they had done. Wherefore they said, Let us also get us a name, and go fight against the heathen round about us." Comp. 2 Macc. xii. 40; xiii. 21.

35 And *some* of them of understanding shall fall, to *a* try *1* them, and to purge, and to make *them* white, *even* to the time of the end:

a 2 Chron. 32. 31.   1 or, *by them.*

There can be no doubt that many might join them from these motives. Such an event would be likely to occur anywhere, when one was successful, and where there was a prospect of spoils or of fame in uniting with a victorious leader of an army.

35. *And* some *of them of understanding shall fall.* Some of those who have a correct understanding of religion, and who have joined the army from pure motives. The idea seems to be that on some occasion they would meet with a temporary defeat, in order that the sincerity of the others might be tested, or that it might be seen who adhered to the cause from principle, and who from selfish purposes. If they should not always be successful; if they should be temporarily defeated; if some of the most eminent among them should fall among the slain; and if the cause should at any time look dark, this would serve to try the sincerity of the remainder of the army, and would be likely to *thin it off* of those who had joined it only from mercenary motives. ¶ *To try them.* Marg., "or, *by them.*" So the Hebrew—בָהֶם. The meaning perhaps is, that it would be *by* them, as it were, that the army would be tried. As they would fall in battle, and as the cause would seem to be doubtful, this would test the fidelity of others. The word *try* here (צָרַף) means, properly, *to melt, to smelt*—as metals; then to prove any one; and then to purify. ¶ *And to purge.* To purify; to test the army and to make it pure. ¶ *And to make* them *white.* To wit, by thus allowing those who had joined the army from mercenary motives to withdraw. Comp. 2 Macc. xii. 39–41. ¶ *Even to the time of the end.* The end of the war or the conflict. There would be an end of these persecutions and trials, and this process had reference to that, or tended to bring it about. The act of freeing the army

because *it is* yet for a time appointed.*b*

36 And the king shall do according to his will; and *c* he shall

b Hab. 2. 3.   *c* Isa. 14. 13, 14; Rev. 13, 5. 6.

from false friends—from those who had joined it from mercenary motives, would have a tendency to accomplish the result in the best way possible, and in the speediest manner. ¶ *Because* it is *yet for a time appointed.* See Notes on ver. 27. This seems to be designed for an assurance that the calamity would come to an end, or that there was a limit beyond which it could not pass. Thus it would be an encouragement to those who were engaged in the struggle, for they would see that success must ultimately crown their labours.

36. *And the king shall do according to his will.* Shall be absolute and supreme, and shall accomplish his purposes. This refers, it seems to me, beyond question, to Antiochus Epiphanes, and was exactly fulfilled in him. He accomplished his purposes in regard to the city and temple in the most arbitrary manner, and was, in every respect, an absolute despot. It should be said, however, here, that most Christian interpreters suppose that the allusion here to Antiochus ceases, and that henceforward it refers to Antichrist. So Jerome, Gill, Bp. Newton, and others; and so Jerome says many of the Jews understood it. The only reason alleged for this is, that there are things affirmed here of the "king" which could not be true of Antiochus. But, in opposition to this, it may be observed (*a*) that the allusion in the previous verses is undoubtedly to Antiochus Epiphanes. (*b*) There is no indication of any *change*, for the prophetic narrative seems to proceed as if the allusion to the same person continued. (*c*) The word "*king*" is not a word to be applied to Antichrist, it being nowhere used of him. (*d*) Such a transition, without any more decided marks of it, would not be in accordance with the usual method in the prophetic writings, leaving a plain prediction in the very midst of the description, and passing on at once to a representation of one who would arise

exalt himself, and magnify himself above every god, and shall speak marvellous things against the God of gods, and shall prosper till the in-

dignation be accomplished: for that that is determined *a* shall be done.

37 Neither shall he regard the

a ch. 9. 27.

after many hundred years, and of whom the former could be considered as in no way the type. The most obvious and honest way, therefore, of interpreting this is, to refer it to Antiochus, and perhaps we shall find that the difficulty of applying it to him is not insuperable. ¶ *And he shall exalt himself.* No one can doubt that *this* will agree with Antiochus Epiphanes—a proud, haughty, absolute, and stern monarch, the purpose of whose reign was to exalt himself, and to extend the limits of his empire. ¶ *And magnify himself above every god.* That is, by directing what gods should or should not be worshipped; attempting to displace the claim of all those who were worshipped as gods at his pleasure, and establishing the worship of other gods in their place. Thus he assumed the right to determine what god should be worshipped in Jerusalem, abolishing the worship of Jehovah, and setting up that of Jupiter Olympius in the stead; and so throughout his whole dominion, by a proclamation, he forbade the worship of any god but his, 1. Macc. i. 44–51; Jos. *Ant.* b. xii. ch. v. § § 4, 5. One who assumes or claims the right to forbid the adoration of any particular god, and to order divine homage to be rendered to any one which he chooses, exalts himself *above* the gods, as he in this way denies the right which *they* must be supposed to claim to prescribe their own worship. ¶ *And shall speak marvellous things.* The Hebrew word נִפְלָאֹות would properly denote things wonderful, or fitted to excite astonishment; things that are unusual and extraordinary: and the meaning here is, that the things spoken would be so impious and atrocious—so amazing and wonderful for their wickedness, as to produce amazement. ¶ *Against the God of gods.* The true God, Jehovah; he is supreme, and is superior to all that is called God, or that is worshipped as such. Nothing could be better descrip-

tive of Antiochus than this; nothing was ever more strikingly fulfilled than this was in him. ¶ *And shall prosper till the indignation be accomplished.* Referring still to the fact that there was an appointed time during which this was to continue. That time might well be called a time of "indignation," for the Lord seemed to be angry against his temple and people, and suffered this heathen king to pour out *his* wrath without measure against the temple, the city, and the whole land. ¶ *For that that is determined shall be done.* What is purposed in regard to the city and temple, and to all other things, must be accomplished. Comp. ch. x. 21. The angel here states a general truth—that all that God has ordained will come to pass. The application of this truth here is, that the series of events must be suffered to run on, and that it could not be expected that they would be arrested until all that had been determined in the Divine mind should be effected. They who would suffer, therefore, in those times must wait with patience until the Divine purposes should be brought about, and when the period should arrive, the calamities would cease.

37. *Neither shall he regard the God of his fathers.* The god that his fathers or ancestors had worshipped. That is, he would not be bound or restrained by the religion of his own land, or by any of the usual laws of religion. He would worship any God that he pleased, or none as he pleased. The usual restraints that bind men—the restraints derived from the religion of their ancestors—would in this case be of no avail. See Notes on ver. 36. This was in all respects true of Antiochus. At his pleasure he worshipped the gods commonly adored in his country, or the gods worshipped by the Greeks and Romans, or no gods. And, in a special manner, instead of honouring the god of his fathers, and causing the image of that god to be placed in the temple at Jerusalem, as it might have been

God of his fathers, nor the desire
of women, nor regard any god: for

he shall magnify himself above
all.ᵃ

ᵃ 2 Thess. 2. 4.

supposed he would, he caused the altar of Jupiter Olympius to be set up there, and his worship to be celebrated there. In fact, as Antiochus had been educated abroad, and had passed his early life in foreign countries, he had never paid much respect to the religion of his own land. The attempt to introduce a foreign religion into Judea was an attempt to introduce the religion of the Greeks (Jahn, *Heb. Commonwealth*, p. 267); and in no instance did he endeavour to force upon them the peculiar religion of his own nation. In his private feelings, therefore, and in his public acts, it might be said of Antiochus, that he was characterized in an eminent degree by a want of regard for the faith of his ancestors. The language used here by the angel is that which would properly denote great infidelity and impiety. ¶ *Nor the desire of women.* The phrase " the desire of women" is in itself ambiguous, and may either mean what *they* desire, that is, what is agreeable to them, or what they commonly seek, and for which they would plead; or it may mean *his own* desire—that is, that he would not be restrained by the desire of women, by any regard for women, for honourable matrimony, or by irregular passion. The phrase here is probably to be taken in the former sense, as this best suits the connection. There has been great variety in the interpretation of this expression. Some have maintained that it cannot be applicable to Antiochus at all, since he was a man eminently licentious and under the influence of abandoned women. Jerome, *in loc.*, J. D. Michaelis, Dereser, Gesenius, and Lengerke suppose that this means that he would not regard the beautiful statue of the goddess Venus whose temple was in Elymaïs, which he plundered. Stäudlin and Dathe, that he would not regard the weeping or tears of women—that is, that he would be cruel. Bertholdt, that he would not spare little children, the object of a mother's love—that is, that he would be a cruel tyrant. Jerome renders it, *Et erit in concupiscentiis*

fœminarum, and explains it of unbridled lust, and applies it principally to Antiochus. Elliott, strangely it seems to me (*Apocalypse*, iv. 152), interprets it as referring to that which was so much the object of desire among the *Hebrew* women—the Messiah, the promised seed of the woman; and he says that he had found this opinion hinted at by Faber *on the Prophecies* (Ed. 5), i. 380–385. Others expound it as signifying that he would not regard honourable matrimony, but would be given to unlawful pleasures. It may not be practicable to determine with certainty the meaning of the expression, but it seems to me that the design of the whole is to set forth the impiety and hard-heartedness of Antiochus. He would not regard the gods of his fathers; that is, he would not be controlled by any of the principles of the religion in which he had been educated, but would set them all at defiance, and would do as he pleased; and, in like manner, he would be unaffected by the influences derived from the female character—would disregard the objects that were nearest to their hearts, their sentiments of kindness and compassion; their pleadings and their tears; he would be a cruel tyrant, alike regardless of all the restraints derived from heaven and earth—the best influences from above and from below. It is not necessary to say that this agrees exactly with the character of Antiochus. He was sensual and corrupt, and given to licentious indulgence, and was incapable of honour able and pure love, and was a stranger to all those bland and pure affections produced by intercourse with refined and enlightened females. If one wishes to describe a high state of tyranny and depravity in a man, it cannot be done better than by saying that he disregards whatever is attractive and interesting to a virtuous female mind. ¶ *Nor regard any god.* Any religious restraints whatever—the laws of any god worshipped in his own land or elsewhere—in heaven or on earth. That is, he would be utterly irreligious

38 But ¹in his ²estate shall he honour the God of ³forces; and a god whom his fathers knew not shall he honour with gold, and silver, and with precious stones, and ⁴pleasant things.

1 *as for the Almighty God, in his seat, he shall honour, yea, he shall honour a god*, &c.
2 or, *stead.*

3 *Mauzzim*, or, *gods protectors*, or, *munitions.*
4 *things desired;* Isa. 44. 9.

in heart, and where it conflicted with his purposes would set at nought every consideration derived from reverence to God. This harmonizes well with the previous declaration about women. The two commonly go together. He that is unrestrained by the attractive virtues of the female mind and character; he that has no regard for the sympathies and kindnesses that interest virtuous females; he that sees nothing lovely in what commonly engages their thoughts; and he that throws himself beyond the restraints of their society, and the effects of their conversation, is commonly a man who cuts himself loose from all religion, and is at the same time a despiser of virtuous females and of God. No one will expect piety towards God to be found in a bosom that sees nothing to interest him in the sympathies and virtues of the female mind; and the character of a woman-hater and a hater of God will uniformly be found united in the same person. Such a person was Antiochus Epiphanes; and such men have often been found in the world. ¶ *For he shall magnify himself above all.* Above all the restraints of religion, and all those derived from the intercourse of virtuous social life—setting at nought all the restraints that usually bind men. Comp. Notes on ch. viii. 10, 11.

38. *But in his estate.* The marginal reading here is, "*As for the Almighty God, in his seat he shall honour, yea, he shall honour a god,*" &c. The more correct rendering, however, is that in the text, and the reference is to some god which he would honour, or for which he would show respect. The rendering proposed by Lengerke is the true rendering, "But the god of forces [firm places, fastnesses—*der Vesten*] he shall honour in their foundation" [*auf seinem Gestelle*]. The Vulgate renders this, "But the god Maozim shall he honour in his place." So also the Greek. The phrase "in his estate"

—עַל־כַּנּוֹ—means, properly, "upon his base," or foundation. It occurs in vers. 20, 21, where it is applied to a monarch who would succeed another—occupying the same place, or the same seat or throne. See Notes on ver. 2. Here it seems to mean that he would honour the god referred to in the place which he occupied, or, as it were, on his own throne, or in his own temple. The margin is, "or *stead;*" but the idea is not that he would honour this god *instead* of another, but that he would do it in his own place. If, however, as Gesenius and De Wette suppose, the sense is, "in his place, or stead," the correct interpretation is, that he would honour this "god of forces," in the stead of honouring the god of his fathers, or any other god. The general idea is clear, that he would show disrespect or contempt for all other gods, and pay his devotions to this god alone. ¶ *Shall he honour.* Pay respect to; worship; obey. This would be *his* god. He would show no respect to the god of his fathers, nor to any of the idols usually worshipped, but would honour *this* god exclusively. ¶ *The God of forces.* Marg., *Mauzzim*, or *gods protectors;* or, *munitions.* Heb., מָעֻזִּים *Mauzzim;* Latin Vulg., *Maozim;* Gr., Μαωζεὶμ; Syriac, "the strong God;" Luther, *Mausim;* Lengerke, *der Vesten*—fastnesses, fortresses. The Hebrew word מָעוֹז means, properly, a strong or fortified place, a fortress; and Gesenius (*Lex.*) supposes that the reference here is to "the god of fortresses, a deity of the Syrians obtruded upon the Jews, perhaps *Mars.*" So also Grotius, C. B. Michaelis, Stäudlin, Bertholdt, and Winer. Dereser, Hävernick, and Lengerke explain it as referring to the Jupiter Capitolinus that Antiochus had learned to worship by his long residence in Rome, and whose worship he transferred to his own country. There has been no little speculation as to the meaning of this passage, and as to the god here referred to; but it would seem that the general idea is plain. It is, that the only god which he would acknowledge would be *force*, or *power*, or *dominion*. He would set at nought the worship of the god of his fathers, and all the usual obligations and restraints of religion; he would discard and despise all the pleadings of humanity and kindness, as if they were the weaknesses of women, and he would depend solely on force. He would, as it were, adore only the "god of force," and carry his purposes, not by right, or by the claims of religion, but by arms. The meaning is not, I apprehend, that he would formally set up this "god of forces," and adore him, but that this would be, in fact, the *only* god that he would practically acknowledge. In selecting such a god as would properly represent his feelings he would choose such an one as would denote *force* or *dominion*. Such a god would be the god of war, or the Roman Jupiter, who, as being supreme, and ruling the world by his mere power, would be a fit representative of the prevailing purpose of the monarch. The general sentiment is, that all obligations of religion, and justice, and compassion, would be disregarded, and he would carry his purposes by mere power, with the idea, perhaps, included, as seems to be implied in the remainder of the verse, that he would set up and adore such a foreign god as would be a suitable representation of this purpose. It is hardly necessary to say that this was eminently true of Antiochus Epiphanes; and it may be equally said to be true of all the great heroes and conquerors of the world. Mars, the god of war, was thus adored openly in ancient times, and the devotion of heroes and conquerors to that idol god, though less open and formal, has not been less real by the heroes and conquerors of modern times; and, as we say now of an avaricious or covetous man that he is a worshipper of mammon, though he in fact formally worships no god, and has no altar, so it might be affirmed of Antiochus, and

may be of heroes and conquerors in general, that the only god that is honoured is the god of war, of power, of force; and that setting at nought all the obligations of religion, and of worship of the true God, they pay their devotions to this god alone. Next to mammon, the god that is most adored in this world is the "god of force"— this *Mauzzim* that Antiochus so faithfully served. In illustration of the fact that seems here to be implied, that he would introduce such a god as would be a fit representative of this purpose of his life, it may be remarked that, when in Rome, where Antiochus spent his early years, he had learned to worship the Jupiter of the Capitol, and that he endeavoured to introduce the worship of that foreign god into Syria. Of this *fact* there can be no doubt. It was one of the characteristics of Antiochus that he imitated the manners and customs of the Romans to a ridiculous extent (Diod. Sic. *Frag.* xxvi. 65); and it was a fact that he sent rich gifts to Rome in honour of the Jupiter worshipped there (Livy, lxii. 6), and that he purposed to erect a magnificent temple in honour of Jupiter Capitolinus in Antioch—Livy, xli. 20. This temple, however, was not completed. It will be remembered, also, that he caused an altar to Jupiter to be erected over the altar of burnt-sacrifice in Jerusalem. It should be added, that they who apply this to Antichrist, or the Pope, refer it to idol or image worship. Elliott (*Apocalypse*, iv. 153) supposes that it relates to the homage paid to the saints and martyrs under the Papacy, and says that an appellation answering to the word *Mahuzzim* was actually given to the departed martyrs and saints under the Papal apostasy. Thus he remarks: "As to what is said of the wilful king's honouring the god *Mahuzzim* (a god whom his fathers knew not) in place of his ancestors' god, and the true God, it seems to me to have been well and consistently explained, by a reference to those *saints*, and their *relics* and *images*, which the apostasy from its first development regarded and worshipped as the *Mahuzzim*, or *fortresses* of the places where they were depo-

39 Thus shall he do in the [1] most strong holds with a strange god, whom he shall acknowledge *and*

1 *fortresses of munitions.*

increase with glory: and he shall cause them to rule over many, and shall divide the land for [2] gain.

2 *a price.*

---

sited."—*Apoc.* iv. 157. But all this appears forced and unnatural; and if it be not supposed that it was designed to refer to Antichrist or the Papacy, no application of the *language* can be found so obvious and appropriate as that which supposes that it refers to Antiochus, and to his reliance on *force* rather than on justice and right. ¶ *And a god whom his fathers knew not.* This foreign god, Jupiter, whom he had learned to worship at Rome. ¶ *Shall he honour with gold, and silver, and with precious stones,* &c. That is, he shall lavish these things on building a temple for him, or on his image. This accords with the account which Livy gives (xli. 20) of the temple which he commenced at Antioch in honour of Jupiter. Livy says that, although in his conduct he was profligate, and although in many things it was supposed that he was deranged—"Quidam haud dubie insanire aiebant"—yet that in two respects he was distinguished for having a noble mind—for his worship of the gods, and for his favour towards cities in adorning them : " In duabus tamen magnis honestisque rebus vere regius erat animus, in urbium donis, et deorum cultu." He then adds, in words that are all the commentary which we need on the passage before us : " Magnificentiæ vero in deos vel Jovis Olympii templum Athenis, unum in terris inchoatum pro magnitudine dei, potest testis esse. Sed et Delon aris insignibus statuarumque copia exornavit ; et Antiochiæ Jovis capitolini magnificum templum, non laqueatum auro tantum, sed parietibus totis lamina inauratum, et alia multa in aliis locis pollicita, quia perbreve tempus regni ejus fuit, non perfecit." ¶ *And pleasant things.* Marg., *things desired.* That is, with ornaments, or statuary, or perhaps pictures. Comp. Notes on Isa. ii. 16. He meant that the temple should be beautified and adorned in the highest degree. This temple, Livy says, he did not live to finish.

39. *Thus shall he do in the most strong holds.* Marg., *fortresses of munitions.* The reference is to strongly fortified places ; to those places which had been made strong for purposes of defence. The idea is, that he would carry on his purposes against these places, as it were, under the auspices of this strange god. It was a fact, that in his wars Antiochus came into possession of the strong places, or the fortified towns of the nations which he attacked—Jerusalem, Sidon, Pelusium, Memphis — then among the strongest places in the world. ¶ *With a strange god.* A foreign god whom his fathers did not acknowledge ; that is, according to the supposition above, and according to the fact, with the god whom he had adored at Rome, and whose worship he was ambitious to transfer to his own empire—the Jupiter of the Capitol. He seemed to be acting under the auspices of this foreign god. ¶ *Whom he shall acknowledge.* By building temples and altars to him. ¶ *And increase with glory.* That is, with honour. He would seem to *increase* or extend his dominion in the world, by introducing his worship in his own country and in the lands which he would conquer. Before, his dominion appeared to be only at Rome; Antiochus sought that it might be extended farther, over his own kingdom, and over the countries that he would conquer. ¶ *And he shall cause them to rule over many.* That is, the foreign gods. Mention had been made before of only one god ; but the introduction of the worship of Jupiter would be naturally connected with that of the other gods of Rome, and they are, therefore, referred to in this manner. The conquests of Antiochus would seem to be a setting up of the dominion of these gods over the lands which he subdued. ¶ *And shall divide the land for gain.* Marg., *a price.* The reference here is, probably, to the Holy Land, and the idea is that it would be partitioned out among his followers for

40 And at the time of the end shall the king of the south push at him: and the king of the north shall come against him like a

a price, or with a view to gain; that is, perhaps, that it would be "farmed out" for the purpose of raising revenue, and that with this view, as often occurred, it would be set up for sale to the highest bidder. This was a common way of raising revenue, by "farming out" a conquered province; that is, by disposing of the privilege of raising a revenue in it to the one who would offer most for it, and the consequence was, that it gave rise to vast rapacity in extorting funds from the people. Comp. 1 Macc. iii. 35, 36, where, speaking of Lysias, whom Antiochus had "set to oversee the affairs of the king from the river Euphrates unto the borders of Egypt," it is said of Antiochus that he " gave him [Lysias] charge of all things that he would have done, as also concerning them that dwelt in Judea and Jerusalem : to wit, that he should send an army against them, to destroy and root out the strength of Israel, and the remnant of Jerusalem, and to take away their memorial from that place ; and that he should place strangers in all their quarters, *and divide their land by lot.*"

40. *And at the time of the end.* See ver. 35. The "time of the end" must properly denote the end or consummation of the series of events under consideration, or the matter in hand, and properly and obviously means here the end or consummation of the transactions which had been referred to in the previous part of the vision. It is equivalent to what we should say by expressing it thus · "at the winding up of the affair." In ch. xii. 4, 9, 13, the word "end," however, obviously refers to *another* close or consummation—the end or consummation of the affairs that reach far into the future—the final dispensation of things in this world. It has been held by many that this could not be understood as referring to Antiochus, because what is here stated did not occur in the close of his reign. Perhaps at first sight the most obvious interpretation of what is said in this and the

subsequent verses to the end of the chapter would be, that, after the series of events referred to in the previous verses ; after Antiochus had invaded Egypt, and had been driven thence by the fear of the Romans, he would, in the close of his reign, again attack that country, and bring it, and Libya, and Æthiopia into subjection (ver. 43) ; and that when there, tidings out of the north should compel him to abandon the expedition and return again to his own land. Porphyry (see Jerome, *in loc.*) says that this was so, and that Antiochus actually invaded Egypt in the "eleventh year of his reign," which was the year before he died ; and he maintains, therefore, that all this had a literal application to Antiochus, and that *being* so literally true, it must have been written *after* the events had occurred. Unfortunately the fifteen books of Porphyry are lost, and we have only the fragments of his works preserved which are to be found in the Commentary of Jerome on the book of Daniel. The statement of Porphyry, referred to by Jerome, is contrary to the otherwise universal testimony of history about the last days of Antiochus, and there are such improbabilities in the statement as to leave the general impression that Porphyry in this respect falsified history in order to make it appear that this must have been written *after* the events referred to. If the statement of Porphyry were correct, there would be no difficulty in applying this to Antiochus. The common belief, however, in regard to Antiochus is, that he did *not* invade Egypt after the series of events referred to above, and after he had been required to retire by the authority of the Roman ambassadors, as stated in the Notes on ver. 30. This belief accords also with all the probabilities of the case. Under these circumstances, many commentators have supposed that this portion of the chapter (vers. 40–45) could not refer to Antiochus, and they have applied it to Antichrist, or to the Roman power. Yet how forced and unnatural such an

whirlwind, *a* with chariots, and with horsemen, and with many

a Zech. 9. 14.

application must be, any one can perceive by examining Newton *on the Prophecies*, pp. 308–315. The obvious, and perhaps it may be added the *honest*, application of the passage must be to Antiochus. This is that which would occur to any reader of the prophecy; this is that which he would obviously hold to be the true application; and this is that only which would occur to any one, unless it were deemed necessary to *bend* the prophecy to accommodate it to the *history*. Honesty and fairness, it seems to me, require that we should understand this as referring to the series of events which had been described in the previous portion of the chapter, and as designed to state the ultimate issue or close of the whole. There will be no difficulty in this if we may regard these verses (40–45) as containing a recapitulation, or a summing up of the series of events, with a statement of the manner in which they would close. If so interpreted all will be clear. It will then be a general statement of what would occur in regard to this remarkable transaction that would so materially affect the interests of religion in Judea, and be such an important chapter in the history of the world. This summing up, moreover, would give occasion to mention some circumstances in regard to the conquests of Antiochus which could not so well be introduced in the narrative itself, and to present, in few words, a summary of all that would occur, and to state the manner in which all would be terminated. Such a summing up, or recapitulation, is not uncommon, and in this way the impression of the whole would be more distinct. With this view, the phrase "and at the time of the end" (ver. 40) would refer, not so much to the "time of the end" of the reign of Antiochus, but to the "time of the end" of *the whole series* of the transactions referred to by the angel as recorded "in the scripture of truth" (ch. x. 21), from the time of Darius the Mede (ch. xi. 1)

ships; and he shall enter into the countries, and shall overflow and pass over.

to the close of the reign of Antiochus —a series of events embracing a period of some three hundred and fifty years. Viewed in reference to this long period, the whole reign of Antiochus, which was only eleven years, might be regarded as "the time of the end." It was, indeed, the most disastrous portion of the whole period, and in this chapter it occupies more space than all that went before it—for it was to be the time of the peculiar and dreadful trial of the Hebrew people, but it was "*the end*" of the matter—the winding up of the series—the closing of the events on which the eye of the angel was fixed, and which were so important to be known beforehand. In these verses, therefore (40–45), he sums up what would occur in what he here calls appropriately "the time of the end"—the period when the predicted termination of this series of important events should arrive—to wit, in the brief and eventful reign of Antiochus. ¶ *Shall the king of the south.* The king of Egypt. See vers. 5, 6, 9. ¶ *Push at him.* As in the wars referred to in the previous verse—in endeavouring to expel him from Cœlo-Syria and Palestine, and from Egypt itself, vers. 25, 29, 30. See Notes on those verses. ¶ *And the king of the north shall come against him.* The king of Syria—Antiochus. Against the king of Egypt. He shall repeatedly invade his lands. See the Notes above. ¶ *Like a whirlwind.* As if he would sweep everything before him. This he did when he invaded Egypt; when he seized on Memphis, and the best portion of the land of Egypt, and when he obtained possession of the person of Ptolemy. See Notes on vers. 25–27. ¶ *With chariots, and with horsemen, and with many ships.* All this literally occurred in the successive invasions of Egypt by Antiochus. See the Notes above. ¶ *And he shall enter into the countries.* Into Cœlo-Syria, Palestine, Egypt, and the adjacent lands. ¶ *And shall overflow and pass over.* Like a flood he shall

41 He shall enter also into the glorious [1] land, [a] and many *countries* shall be overthrown; but these shall escape out of his hand, *even* Edom, [b] and Moab, and the chief of the children of Ammon.

1 *land of delight*, or *ornament*, or *goodly land*.

a vers. 16, 45. *b* Isa. 11. 14, 15.

spread his armies over these countries. See Notes on ver. 22.

41. *He shall enter also into the glorious land.* Marg., *land of delight*, or *ornament*, or *goodly land.* The Hebrew is, "land of ornament;" that is, of beauty, to wit, Palestine, or the Holy Land. The same word is used in ver. 16. See Notes on that place. As to the *fact* that he would invade that land, see Notes on vers. 28, 31–33. ¶ *And many* countries *shall be overthrown.* The word *countries* here is supplied by the translators. The Hebrew word רַבּוֹת may denote "many things," and might refer to cities, dwellings, institutions, &c. The meaning is, that he would produce wide devastation, which was true of Antiochus, when, either personally or by his generals, he invaded the land of Palestine. See the Notes above. ¶ *But these shall escape out of his hand*, &c. Intent on his work in Palestine, and having enough there to occupy his attention, the neighbouring lands of Edom, Moab, and Ammon shall not be molested by him. The wrath of Antiochus was particularly against the Jews, and it is not a little remarkable that no mention is made of his invading these adjacent countries. The route which he pursued was to Egypt, along the shores of the Mediterranean, and though he turned from his course to wreak his vengeance on the Jews, yet it does not appear that he carried his arms farther from the main line of his march. Antiochus was principally engaged with the Egyptians and the Romans; he was also engaged with the Jews, for Palestine had been the battle-field—the main place and object of contention between the king of Syria and the king of Egypt. Moab, and Edom, and Ammon were comparatively remote from the scene of conflict, and were left unmolested. It would seem most probable, also, that these nations were friendly to Antiochus, and were in alliance with him, or at least it is certain that they were hostile to the Jews, which, for the purposes of Antiochus, amounted to the same thing. Judas Maccabeus is represented as engaged with them in war, and consequently they must have either been in alliance with Antiochus, or in some other way promoting his interests. See 1 Macc. iv. 61; v. 3, 6–9. These countries were, therefore, in fact, secure from the invasions of Antiochus, and so far the prophecy was literally fulfilled. It may be added (*a*), that no occurrence *since* that time has taken place to which the prophecy can with propriety be applied; and (*b*), that no natural sagacity could have foreseen this, and that, therefore, if the prediction was uttered *before* the days of Antiochus, it must have been the result of Divine inspiration. As to the former of these remarks (*a*), if any one is desirous of seeing how forced and unnatural must be any attempt to apply this to any other times than those of Antiochus, he has only to consult Bishop Newton *on the Prophecies* (pp. 311–313), who explains it as referring to the Ottoman empire, and to the fact that though the Turks have been able to take Jerusalem, they have never been able to subdue the Arabians, the Moabites, or the Ammonites. Aleppo, Damascus, and Gaza, says he, were forced to submit, but these other places "escaped out of the hands" of the Turks. As to the other remark (*b*), if one, writing *after* the events, had intended to give a brief and striking view of what Antiochus did, he could not find better language to express it than to say in the words of the passage before us, "He shall enter also into the glorious land, and many *countries* shall be overthrown; but these shall escape out of his hand, *even* Edom, and Moab, and the chief of the children of Ammon." But it is clear that there is no natural sagacity by which this could

42 He shall ¹ stretch forth his hand also upon the countries; and the land of Egypt shall not escape.

43 But he shall have power

¹ *send forth.*

over the treasures of gold and of silver, and over all the precious things of Egypt; and the Libyans and the Ethiopians *shall be* at his steps.

be foreseen. There was nothing in the character of those nations, or in the nature of the case, which would lead one to anticipate it—for the presumption would be, that if a desolating war were waged on Palestine by a cruel conqueror, his ravages would be extended to the neighbouring countries also.

42. *He shall stretch forth his hand also upon the countries.* Marg., *send forth.* Significant of war and conquest. The idea is, that he would be an invader of foreign lands—a characteristic which it is not necessary to show appertained to Antiochus. ¶ *And the land of Egypt shall not escape.* Moab and Edom, and the land of Ammon would escape, but Egypt would not. We have seen in the exposition of this chapter (Notes on vers. 25–28) that he, in fact, subdued Memphis and the best portions of Egypt, and even obtained possession of the person of the king.

43. *But he shall have power over the treasures of gold and of silver.* See Notes on ver. 28. Having seized upon the most important places in Egypt, and having possession of the person of the king, he would, of course, have the wealth of Egypt at his disposal, and would return to his land laden with spoils. ¶ *And over all the precious things of Egypt.* The rich lands, the public buildings, the contents of the royal palace, the works of art, and the monuments, and books, and implements of war. All these would, of course, be at the disposal of the conqueror. ¶ *And the Libyans.* The word *Libyans,* in the Hebrew Scriptures, is everywhere joined with the Egyptians and Ethiopians. They are supposed to have been a people of Egyptian origin, and their country bordered on Egypt in the west. See Tanner's *Ancient Atlas.* A conquest of Egypt was almost in itself a conquest of Libya. ¶ *And the Ethiopians.* Heb., *Cushites—כֻּשִׁים.* On the general meaning of the word *Cush* or *Ethiopia* in the Scriptures, see Notes on Isa xi.

11. The reference here, undoubtedly, is to the African Cush or Ethiopia, which bounded Egypt on the south. This country comprehended not only Ethiopia above Syene and the Cataracts, but likewise Thebais or Upper Egypt. A subjugation of Egypt would be, in fact, almost a conquest of this land. ¶ Shall be *at his steps.* Gesenius renders this, "in his company." The word means properly *step,* or *walk.* Comp. Psa. xxxvii. 23 ; Prov. xx. 24. The Vulgate renders this, "And he shall pass also through Libya and Ethiopia." The Greek, "and he shall have power over all the secret treasures of gold and of silver, and over all the desirable things of Egypt, and of the Libyans, and of the Ethiopians, in their strongholds." Lengerke renders it, "And the Libyans and Ethiopians shall follow his steps." The proper sense of the Hebrew would be, that they accompanied him ; that they marched with him or followed him ; and the phrase would be applicable either to those who were allies, or who were led captive. The more probable idea would be that they were allies, or were associated with him, than that they were captives. I do not know that there are any distinct historical facts which show the truth of what is here predicted respecting Antiochus, but it cannot be considered as improbable that the prophecy was fulfilled ; for (*a*), as already observed, these nations, naturally allied to Egypt as being a part of the same people, bounded Egypt on the west and on the south ; (*b*) in the days of Ezekiel (Ezekiel xxx. 4, 5), we find that they were actually confederated with Egypt in a "league," and that the calamity which fell upon Egypt, also fell directly upon Ethiopia and Libya ; and (*c*) the possession of Egypt, therefore, would be naturally followed with the subjugation of these places, or it might be presumed that they would seek the alliance and friendship of one who had subdued it.

44 But tidings out of the east and out of the north shall trouble him: therefore he shall go forth with great fury to destroy, and utterly to make away many. 45 And he shall plant the taber-

---

44. *But tidings out of the east and out of the north shall trouble him.* Shall disturb him, or alarm him. That is, he will hear something from those quarters that will disarrange all his other plans, or that will summon him forth in his last and final expedition—on that expedition in which "he will come to his end" (ver. 45), or which will be the end of this series of historical events. The reference here is to the winding up of this series of transactions, and, according to the view taken on ver. 40 (see Notes on that place), it is not necessary to suppose that this would happen immediately after what is stated in ver. 43, but it is rather to be regarded as a statement of what would occur *in the end*, or of the manner in which the person here referred to would finally come to an end, or in which these events would be closed. As a matter of fact, Antiochus, as will be seen in the Notes on ver. 45, was called forth in a war-like expedition by tidings or reports from Parthia and Armenia — regions lying to the east and the north, and it was in this expedition that he lost his life, and that this series of historical events was closed. Lengerke says, Antiochus assembled an army to take vengeance on the Jews, who, after the close of the unfortunate campaign in Egypt, rose up, under the Maccabees, against Antiochus, 1 Macc. iii. 10, *seq.* Then the intelligence that the Parthians in the east, and the Armenians in the north, had armed themselves for war against him, alarmed him. So Tacitus (*Hist.* v. 8) says [Antiochus Judæis], *Demere superstitionem et mores Græcorum dare adnixus, quominus teterrimam gentem in melius mutaret, Parthorum bello prohibitus est, nam ea tempestate Arsaces defecerat.* In the year 147 B.C., Antiochus went on the expedition to Persia and Armenia, on the return from which he died. The occasions for this were these: (*a*) Artaxias, the king of Armenia, who was his vassal, had revolted from him, and (*b*) he sought to replenish his exhausted treasury, that he might wage the war with Judas Maccabeus. See 1 Macc. iii. 27–37 ; Jos. *Ant.* b. xii. ch. vii. § 2 ; Appian, *Syriac.* xlvi. 80 ; Porphyry, in Jerome, *in loc.* ¶ *Therefore he shall go forth with great fury to destroy,* &c. Great fury at the revolt of Artaxias, and especially at this juncture when he was waging war with the Jews ; and great fury at the Jews, with a determination to obtain the means utterly to destroy them. 1 Macc. iii. 27: "Now when king Antiochus heard these things [the successes of Judas Maccabeus], he was full of indignation." In every way his wrath was kindled. He was enraged against the Jews on account of their success; he was enraged against Artaxias for revolting from him; he was enraged because his treasury was exhausted, and he had not the means of prosecuting the war. In this mood of mind he crossed the Euphrates (1 Macc. iii. 37) to prosecute the war in the East, and, as it is said here, "utterly to make away many." Everything conspired to kindle his fury, and in this state of mind, he went forth on his last expedition to the East. Nothing, in fact, could better describe the state of mind of Antiochus than the language here used by the angel to Daniel.

45. *And he shall plant the tabernacles of his palace.* The royal tents ; the military tents of himself and his court. Oriental princes, when they went forth even in war, marched in great state, with a large retinue of the officers of their court, and often with their wives and concubines, and with all the appliances of luxury. Comp. the account of the invasion of Greece by Xerxes, or of the camp of Darius, as taken by Alexander the Great. The military stations of Antiochus, therefore, in this march, would be, for a time, the residence of the court, and would be distinguished for as great a degree of royal luxury as the circumstances would allow. At the same time, they would consist of *tabernacles* or *tents,* as those stations were not designed to be permanent. The meaning is, that

nacles of his palace between the seas in the ¹ glorious holy moun-

tain; yet *a* he shall come to his end, and none shall help him.

1 or, *goodly;* Heb. *mountain of delight of holiness.*

a 2 Thess. 2. 8.

the royal temporary residence in this expedition, and previous to the close —the end of the whole matter, that is, the death of Antiochus—would be in the mountain here referred to. ¶ *Between the seas.* That is, between some seas in the "east," or "north"—for it was by tidings from the east and north that he would be disturbed and summoned forth, ver. 44. We are, therefore, most naturally to look for this place in one of those quarters. The *fact* was, that he had two objects in view—the one was to put down the revolt in Armenia, and the other to replenish his exhausted treasury from Persia. The former would be naturally that which he would first endeavour to accomplish, for if he suffered the revolt to proceed, it might increase to such an extent that it would be impossible to subdue it. Besides, he would not be likely to go to Persia when there was a formidable insurrection in his rear, by which he might be harassed either *in* Persia, or on his return. It is most probable, therefore, that he would first quell the rebellion in Armenia on his way to Persia, and that the place here referred to where he would pitch his royal tent, and where he would end his days, would be some mountain where he would encamp before he reached the confines of Persia. There have been various conjectures as to the place here denoted by the phrase "between the seas," and much speculation has been employed to determine the precise location. Jerome renders it, "And he shall pitch his tent in Apadno between the seas"— regarding the word which our translators have rendered *his palaces* (אַפַּדְנוֹ)

as a proper name denoting a place. So the Greek, ἐφαδανῷ. The Syriac renders it, " in a plain, between the sea and the mountain." Theodoret takes it for a place near Jerusalem ; Jerome says it was near Nicopolis, which was formerly called Emmaus, where the mountainous parts of Judea began to rise, and that it lay between the Dead Sea

on the east, and the Mediterranean on the west, where he supposes that Antichrist will pitch his tent; Porphyry and Calmet place it between the two rivers, the Tigris and Euphrates—the latter supposing it means "Padan of two rivers," that is, some place in Mesopotamia ; and Dr. Goodwin supposes that the British Isles are intended, "which so eminently stand 'between the seas.' " Prof. Stuart understands this of the Mediterranean Sea, and that the idea is, that the encampment of Antiochus was in some situation between this sea and Jerusalem, mentioned here as "the holy and beautiful mountain." So far as the *phrase* here used— "between the seas "—is concerned, there can be no difficulty. It might be applied to any place lying between two sheets of water, as the country between the Dead Sea and the Mediterranean, or the Dead Sea, and Persian Gulf ; or the Caspian and Euxine Seas ; or the Caspian Sea and the Persian Gulf, for there is nothing in the *language* to determine the exact locality. There is no reason for taking the word אַפַּדְנוֹ (*apadno*) as a proper name—the literal meaning of it being *tent* or *tabernacle;* and the simple idea in the passage is, that the transaction here referred to—the event which would close this series, and which would constitute the "end" of these affairs — would occur in some mountainous region situated between two seas or bodies of water. *Any such place*, so far as the meaning of the word is concerned, would correspond with this prophecy. ¶ *In the glorious holy mountain.* That is, this would occur (*a*) in a mountain, or in a mountainous region ; and (*b*) it would be a mountain to which the appellation here used—"glorious holy"—would be properly given. The most obvious application of this phrase, it cannot be doubted, would be Jerusalem, as being the "holy mountain," or "the mountain of holiness," and as the place which the word "glorious" (צְבִי) would most naturally suggest. Comp. vers. 16, 41. Bertholdt and Dereser propose a change in the text here, and understand it as signifying that "he would pitch his tent between a sea and a mountain, and would seize upon a temple (קֹדֶשׁ) there." But there is no authority for so changing the text. Rosenmüller, whom Lengerke follows, renders it, "between some sea and the glorious holy mountain;" Lengerke supposes that the meaning is, that Antiochus, on his return from Egypt, and *before* he went to Persia, "pitched his tents in that region, somewhere along the coasts of the Mediterranean, for the purpose of chastising the Jews," and that this is the reference here. But this, as well as the proposed reading of Dereser and Bertholdt, is a forced interpretation. Gesenius (*Lex.*) supposes that the phrase means, "mount of holy beauty," *i.e.*, Mount Sion. There are some things which are clear, and which the honest principles of interpretation demand in this passage, such as the following: (*a*) What is here stated was to occur *after* the rumour from the east and the north (ver. 44) should call forth the person here referred to on this expedition. (*b*) It would not be long before his "end,"—before the close of the series, and would be connected with that; or would be the place where that would occur. (*c*) It would be on some mountainous region, to which the appellation "glorious holy" might with propriety be applied. The only question of difficulty is, whether it is necessary to interpret this of Jerusalem, or whether it may be applied to some other mountainous region where it may be supposed Antiochus "pitched his tents" on his last expedition to the East, and near the close of his life. Jerome renders this, *Supermontem inclytum et sanctum;* the Greek, "on the holy mountain Sabaein"—σαβαεὶν. The Syriac, "in a plain, between a sea and a mountain, and shall preserve his sanctuary." The *literal* meaning of the passage may be thus expressed, "on a mountain of beauty that is holy or sacred." The essential things are, (*a*) that it would be on a mountain,

or in a mountainous region ; (*b*) that this mountain would be celebrated or distinguished for *beauty*—צְבִי—that is, for the beauty of its situation, or the beauty of its scenery, or the beauty of its structures—or that it should be *regarded* as beautiful ; (*c*) that it would be held as sacred or holy—קֹדֶשׁ—that is, as sacred to religion, or regarded as a holy place, or a place of worship. Now it is true that this language *might* be applied to Mount Sion, for *that* was a mountain ; it was distinguished for beauty, or was so regarded by those who dwelt there (comp. Psa. xlviii. 2) ; and it was holy, as being the place where the worship of God was celebrated. But it is also true, that, so far as the language is concerned, it might be applied to any other mountain or mountainous region that was distinguished for beauty, and that was regarded as sacred, or in any way consecrated to religion. I see no objection, therefore, to the supposition, that this may be understood of some mountain or elevated spot which was held as sacred to religion, or where a temple was reared for worship, and hence it *may* have referred to some mountain, in the vicinity of some temple dedicated to idol worship, where Antiochus would pitch his tent for the purpose of rapine and plunder. ¶ *Yet he shall come to his end.* Evidently in the expedition referred to, and in the vicinity referred to. Though he had gone full of wrath ; and though he was preparing to wreak his vengeance on the people of God ; and though he had every prospect of success in the enterprise, yet he would come to an end there, or would die. This would be the end of his career, and would be at the same time the end of that series of calamities that the angel predicted. The assurance is more than once given (vers. 27, 35); that there was an "appointed" time during which these troubles would continue, or that there would be an "end" of them at the appointed time, and the design was, that when these inflictions came upon the Jews they should be permitted to comfort themselves with the assurance that they would have a termination—that is, that the institutions of religion in their land would not be utterly overthrown. ¶ *And none shall help him.* None shall save his life; none shall rescue him out of his danger. That is, he would certainly die, and his plans of evil would thus be brought to a close.

The question now is, whether this can be applied to the closing scenes in the life of Antiochus Epiphanes. The materials for writing the life of Antiochus are indeed scanty, but there is little doubt as to the place and manner of his death. According to all the accounts, he received intelligence of the success of the Jewish arms under Judas Maccabeus, and the overthrow of the Syrians, at Elymaïs or Persepolis (2 Macc. ix. 2), in Persia; and as he was detained there by an insurrection of the people, occasioned by his robbing the celebrated Temple of Diana (Jos. *Ant.* b. xii. ch. ix. § 1), in which his father, Antiochus the Great, lost his life; his vexation was almost beyond endurance. He set out on his return with a determination to make every possible effort to exterminate the Jews; but during his journey he was attacked by a disease, in which he suffered excessive pain, and was tormented by the bitterest anguish of conscience, on account of his sacrilege and other crimes. He finally died at Tabæ in Paratacene, on the frontiers of Persia and Babylon, in the year 163 B.C, after a reign of eleven years. See the account of his wretched death in 2 Macc. ix.; Jos. *Antiq.* b. xii. ch. ix.; § 1; Prideaux, *Con.* iii. pp. 272, 273; Polybius in *Excerpta Valesii de Virtutibus et Vitiis,* xxxi., and Appian, *Syriac.* xlvi. 80. Now this account agrees substantially with the prediction in the passage before us in the following respects:—(*a*) The circumstances which called him forth. It was on account of "tidings" or rumours out of the east and north that he went on this last expedition. (*b*) The place specified where the last scenes would occur, "between the seas." Any one has only to look on a map of the Eastern hemisphere to see that the ancient Persepolis, the capital of Persia, where the rumour of the success of the Jews

reached him which induced him to return, is "between the seas"—the Caspian Sea and the Persian Gulf—lying not far from midway between the two. (*c*) The "glorious holy mountain," or, as the interpretation above proposed would render it, "the mountain of beauty," sacred to religion or to worship. (1.) The whole region was mountainous. (2.) It is not unlikely that a temple would be raised on a mountain or elevated place, for this was the almost universal custom among the ancients, and it may be assumed as not improbable, that the temple of Diana, at Elymaïs, or Persepolis, which Antiochus robbed, and where he "pitched his tent," was on such a place. Such a place would be regarded as "holy," and would be spoken of as "an ornament," or as beautiful, for this was the language which the Hebrews were accustomed to apply to a place of worship. I suppose, therefore, that the reference is here to the closing scene in the life of Antiochus, and that the account in the prophecy agrees in the most striking manner with the facts of history, and consequently that it is not necessary to look to any other events for a fulfilment, or to suppose that it has any secondary and ultimate reference to what would occur in far-distant years.

In view of this exposition, we may see the force of the opinion maintained by Porphyry, that this portion of the book of Daniel must have been written *after* the events occurred. He could not but see, as any one can now, the surprising accuracy of the statements of the chapter, and their applicability to the events of history as they had actually occurred; and seeing this, there was but one of two courses to be taken—either to admit the inspiration of the book, or to maintain that it was written *after* the events. He chose the latter alternative; and, so far as can be judged from the few fragments which we have of his work in the commentary of Jerome on this book, he did it solely on the ground of the *accuracy* of the description. He referred to no external evidence; he adduced no historical proofs that the book was written subsequent to the events; but he maintained simply that an account so minute and exact could not have been written *before* the events, and that the very accuracy of the alleged predictions, and their entire agreement with history, was full demonstration that they were written *after*. The testimony of Porphyry, therefore, may be allowed to be a sufficient proof of the correspondence of this portion of the book of Daniel with the facts of history; and if the book was written before the age of Antiochus Epiphanes, the evidence is clear of its inspiration, for no man will seriously maintain that these historic events could be drawn out, with so much particularity of detail, by any natural skill, three hundred and seventy years before they occurred, as must have been the case if written by Daniel. Human sagacity does not extend its vision thus far into the future with the power of foretelling the fates of kingdoms, and giving in detail the lives and fortunes of individual men. Either the infidel must dispose of the testimony that Daniel lived and wrote at the time alleged, or, as an honest man, he should admit that he was inspired.

CHAPTER XII.

ANALYSIS OF THE CHAPTER.

There are several general remarks which may be made respecting this, the closing chapter of the book of Daniel.

I. It is a part, or a continuation of the general prophecy or vision which was commenced in ch. x., and which embraces the whole of the eleventh chapter. Except for the *length* of the prophecy there should have been no division whatever, and it should be read as a continuous whole; or if a division were desirable, that which was made by Cardinal Hugo in the 13th century, and which occurs in our translation of the Bible, is one of the most unhappy. On every account, and for every reason, the division should have been at the close of the fourth verse of this chapter, and the first four verses should have been attached to the pre-

vious portion. That the beginning of this chapter is a continuation of the address of the angel to Daniel, is plain from a mere glance. The address ends at ver. 4; and then commences a colloquy between two angels who appear in the vision, designed to cast further light on what had been said. It will contribute to a right understanding of this chapter to remember, that it is a part of the one vision or prophecy which was commenced in ch. x., and that the whole three chapters (x., xi., xii.) should be read together. If ch. xi., therefore, refers to the historical events connected with the reign of Antiochus, and the troubles under him, it would seem to be plain that this does also, and that the angel meant to designate the time when these troubles would close, and the indications by which it might be known that they were about to come to an end.

II. At the same time that this is true, it must also be admitted that the *language* which is used is such as is applicable to other events, and that it supposed that there was a belief in the doctrines to which that language would be naturally applied. It is not such language as would have been originally employed to describe the historical transactions respecting the persecutions under Antiochus, nor unless the doctrines which are obviously conveyed by that language were understood and believed. I refer here to the statements respecting the resurrection of the dead and of the future state. This language is found particularly in ver. 2, 3: "And many of them that sleep in the dust of the earth shall awake, some to everlasting life, and some to shame and everlasting contempt. And they that be wise shall shine as the brightness of the firmament; and they that turn many to righteousness, as the stars for ever and ever." This language is appropriate to express such doctrines as the following: (*a*) that of the resurrection of the dead—or a being raised up out of the dust of the earth ; (*b*) that of retribution *after* the resurrection : a part being raised to everlasting life, and a part to everlasting shame; (*c*) that of the eternity of future retribution, or the eternity of rewards and punishments: awaking to *everlasting* life, and to *everlasting* shame ; (*d*) that of the high honours and rewards of those who would be engaged in doing good, or of that portion of mankind who would be instrumental in turning the wicked from the paths of sin: " they that turn many to righteousness, as the stars for ever and ever." It is impossible to conceive that this language would have been used unless these doctrines were known and believed, and unless it be supposed that they were so familiar that it would be readily understood. Whatever may have been the particular thing to which it was applied by the angel, it is such language as could have been intelligible only where there was a belief of these doctrines, and it may, therefore, be set down as an indication of a prevalent belief in the time of Daniel on these subjects. Such would be understood now if the same language were used by us, to whatever we might apply it, for it would not be employed unless there was a belief of the truth of the doctrines which it is naturally adapted to convey.

III. If the angel intended, therefore, primarily to refer to events that would occur in the time of Antiochus —to the arousing of many to defend their country, as if called from the dust of the earth, or to their being summoned by Judas Maccabeus from caves and fastnesses, and to the honour to which many of them might be raised, and the shame and con-tempt which would await others, it seems difficult to doubt that the mind of the speaker, at the same time, glanced onward to higher doctrines, and that it was the intention of the angel to bring into view far-distant events, of which these occurrences might be regarded as an emblem, and that he meant to advert to what would literally occur in the time of the Maccabees as a beautiful and striking illustration of more momentous and glorious scenes when the earth should give up its dead, and when the final judgment should occur. On these scenes, perhaps, the mind of the angel ultimately rested, and a prominent part of the design of the entire vision may have been to bring them into view, and to direct the thoughts of the pious onward, far beyond the troubles and the triumphs in the days of the Maccabees, to the time when the dead should arise, and when the retributions of eternity should occur. It was no uncommon thing among the prophets to allow the eye to glance from one object to another lying in the same range of vision, or having such points of resemblance that the one would suggest the other; and it often happened, that a description which commenced with some natural event terminated in some more important spiritual truth, to which that event had a resemblance, and which it was adapted to suggest. Comp. Intro. to Isaiah, § VII. 3. (3) (4) (5). Three things occur often in such a case : (1) language is employed in speaking of what is to take place, which is derived from the secondary and remote event, and which naturally suggests that; (2) ideas are intermingled in the description which are appropriate to the secondary event only, and which should be understood as applicable to that ; and

(3) the description which was *commenced* with reference to one event or class of events, often passes over entirely, and *terminates* on the secondary and ultimate events. This point will be more particularly examined on the Notes on the chapter.

IV. The contents of the chapter are as follows :—

(1.) The concluding statement of what would occur at the time referred to in the previous chapter, ver. 1–3. This statement embraces many particulars : that Michael, the guardian angel, would stand up in behalf of the people ; that there would be great trouble, such as there had not been since the time when the nation began to exist ; that there would be deliverance for all whose names were recorded in the book ; that there would be an awakening of those who slept in the dust—some coming to life and honour, and some to shame and dishonour ; and that distinguished glory would await those who turned many to righteousness.

(2.) At this stage of the matter, all having been disclosed that the angel purposed to reveal, Daniel is commanded to shut and seal the book ; yet with the encouragement held out that more would yet be known on the subject, ver. 4. The matter was evidently involved still in mystery, and there were many points on which it could not but be desired that there should be fuller information—points relating to the time when these things would happen, and a more particular account of the full meaning of what had been predicted, &c. On these points it is clear that many questions might be asked, and it is probable that the mind of Daniel would be left still in perplexity in regard to them. To meet this state of mind, the angel says to Daniel that "many would run to

and fro, and that knowledge would be increased ;" that is, that by intercourse with one another in future times ; by spreading abroad the knowledge already obtained ; by diffusing information, and by careful inquiry, those of coming ages would obtain much clearer views on these points ; or, in other words, that time, and the intercourse of individuals and nations, would clear up the obscurities of prophecy.

(3.) In this state of perplexity, Daniel looked and saw two other personages standing on the two sides of the river, and between them and the angel who had conversed with Daniel a colloquy or conversation ensues, respecting the time necessary to accomplish these things, ver. 5–7. They are introduced as interested in the inquiry as to the *time* of the continuance of these things—that is, how long it would be to the end of these wonders. These were evidently angels also, and they are represented (*a*) as ignorant of the future—a circumstance which we must suppose to exist among the angels ; and (*b*) as feeling a deep interest in the transactions which were to occur, and the period when it might be expected they would have their completion. To this natural inquiry, the angel who had conversed with Daniel gives a solemn answer (ver. 7), that the period would be "a time, and times, and an half ;" and that all these things would be accomplished, when he to whom reference was made had finished his purpose of scattering the holy people.

(4.) Daniel, perplexed and overwhelmed with these strange predictions, hearing what was said about the time, but not understanding it, asks with intense interest when the end of these things should be, ver. 8. He had heard the reply of the angel, but it conveyed no idea to his mind. He was deeply solicitous to look into the

CHAPTER XII.

AND at that time shall *a*Michael stand up, the great prince which standeth for the children of thy people; and *b* there shall be a

a ch. 10. 13, 21; Jude 9.   *b* Matt. 24. 21.

future, and to ascertain *when* these events would end, and *what* would be their termination. The answer to his anxious, earnest inquiry, is contained in vers. 9–13, and embraces several points—giving some further information, but still evidently designed to leave the matter obscure in many respects. (*a*) The matter was sealed up, and his question could not be definitely answered, ver. 9. When the time of the end should come, it is implied the matter would be clearer, and might be understood, but that all had been communicated substantially that could be. (*b*) A statement is made (ver. 10) of the general result of the trials on two classes of persons: the things that would occur would tend to make the righteous more holy, but the wicked would continue to do wickedly, notwithstanding all these heavy judgments. The latter too would, when these events took place, fail to understand their design ; but the former would obtain a just view of them, and would be made wiser by them. Time, to the one class, would disclose the meaning of the Divine dealings, and they would comprehend them ; to the other they would still be dark and unintelligible. (*c*) A statement is, however, made as to the *time* when these things would be accomplished, but still so obscure as to induce the angel himself to say to Daniel that he must go his way till the end should be, vers. 11–13. Two periods of time are mentioned, both different from the one in ver. 7. In one of them (ver. 11) it is said that from the time when the daily sacrifice should be taken away, and the abomination that maketh desolate should be set up, would be a thousand two hundred and ninety days. In the other (ver. 12) it is said that he would be blessed or happy who should reach a certain period mentioned—a thousand three hundred and thirty-five days. What these different periods of time refer to will of course be the subject of inquiry in the Notes on the chapter. (*d*) The whole closes, therefore (ver. 13), with a direction to Daniel that, for the present, he should go his way. Nothing additional would be disclosed. Time would reveal more ; time would explain all. Meanwhile there is an assurance given that, as for himself, he would have "rest," and would "stand in his lot at the end of the days." This seems to be a gracious assurance to him that he had nothing to fear from these troubles personally, and that whatever should come, he would have peace, and would occupy the position in future times which was due to him. His lot would be happy and peaceful; his name would be honoured; his salvation would be secured. It seems to be implied that, with this pledge, he ought to allow his mind to be calm, and not suffer himself to be distressed because he could not penetrate the future, and foresee all that was to occur; and the truth, therefore, with which the book closes is, that, having security about our own personal salvation—or having no ground of solicitude respecting that— or having that matter made safe—we should calmly commit all events to God, with the firm conviction that in his own time his purposes will be accomplished, and that being then understood, he will be seen to be worthy of confidence and praise.

1. *And at that time.* At the period

time of trouble, such as never was since there was a nation *even* to that same time: and at that time

a Jer. 30. 7; Rom. 11. 26.

thy *a* people shall be delivered, every one that shall be found written *b* in the book.

b Rev. 13. 8.

referred to in the preceding chapter. The fair construction of the passage demands this interpretation, and if that refers to Antiochus Epiphanes, then what is here said must also; and we are to look for the direct and immediate fulfilment of this prediction in something that occurred under him, however it may be supposed to have an ultimate reference to other and more remote events. The phrase "at that time," however, does not limit what is here said to any one part of his life, or to his death, but to the general period referred to in the time of his reign. That reign was but eleven years, and the fulfilment must be found somewhere during that period. ¶ *Shall Michael.* On the meaning of this word, and the being here referred to, see Notes on ch. x. 13. ¶ *Stand up.* That is, he shall interpose; he shall come forth to render aid. This does not mean necessarily that he would *visibly* appear, but that he would *in fact* interpose. In the time of great distress and trouble, there would be supernatural or angelic aid rendered to the people of God. No man can prove that this would not be so, nor is there any inherent improbability in the supposition that good angels may be employed to render assistance in the time of trouble. Comp. Notes on ch. x. 13. ¶ *The great prince which standeth for the children of thy people.* See Notes as above on ch. x. 13. The meaning is, that he had the affairs of the Hebrew people, or the people of God, especially under his protection, or he was appointed to watch over them. This doctrine is in accordance with the notions that prevailed at that time; and no one can demonstrate that it is not true. There is no authority for applying this to the Messiah, as many have done, for the term *Michael* is not elsewhere given to him, and all that the language fairly conveys is met by the other supposition. The simple meaning is, that he who was the guardian angel of that nation, or who was appointed to watch over its interests, would at that time of great trouble interpose and render aid. ¶ *And there shall be a time of trouble.* Under Antiochus Epiphanes. See Notes on ch. xi. 21–45. Comp. the books of the Maccabees, *passim.* ¶ *Such as never was since there was a nation* even *to that same time.* This *might* be construed with reference to the Jewish nation, as meaning that the trouble would be greater than any that had occurred during its history. But it may also be taken, as our translators understand it, in a more general sense, as referring to any or all nations. In either sense it can hardly be considered as the language of hyperbole. The troubles that came upon the land under the persecutions of Antiochus probably surpassed any that the Hebrew nation ever experienced, nor could it be shown that, for the same period of time, they were surpassed among any other people. The Saviour has employed this language as adapted to express the intensity of the trials which would be brought upon the Jews by the Romans (Matt. xxiv. 21), but he does not say that as used in Daniel it had reference originally to that event. It was language appropriate to express the thought which he wished to convey, and he, therefore, so employed it. ¶ *And at that time.* When these troubles are at their height. ¶ *Thy people shall be delivered.* To wit, by the valour and virtues of the Maccabees. See the accounts in the books of the Maccabees. Comp. Prideaux, *Con.* iii. 257, *seq.* ¶ *Every one that shall be found written in the book.* Whose names are enrolled; that is, enrolled as among the living. The idea is, that a register was made of the names of those who were to be spared, to wit, by God, or by the angel, and that all whose names were so recorded would be preserved. Those not so enrolled would be cut off under the persecutions of Antiochus. The language here does not refer to the book of eternal life or salvation, nor is it implied that

2 And many of them that sleep in the dust of the earth shall awake, some to everlasting life,[a] and some to [b] shame *and* everlasting contempt.

they who would thus be preserved would necessarily be saved, but to their preservation from death and persecution, *as if* their names were recorded in a book, or were enrolled. We frequently meet with similar ideas in the Scriptures. The idea is, of course, poetical, but it expresses with sufficient clearness the thought that there was a Divine purpose in regard to them, and that there was a definite number whom God designed to keep alive, and that these would be delivered from those troubles, while many others would be cut off. Comp. Notes on ch. x. 21.

2. *And many of them.* The natural and obvious meaning of the word *many* (רַבִּים) here is, that a large portion of the persons referred to would thus awake, but not all. So we should understand it if applied to other things, as in such expressions as these — "many of the people," "many of the houses in a city," "many of the trees in a forest," "many of the rivers in a country," &c. In the Scriptures, however, it is undeniable that the word is sometimes used to denote the whole considered *as* constituted of many, as in Rom. v. 15, 16, 19. In these passages no one can well doubt that the word *many* is used to denote *all*, considered as composed of the "*many*" that make up the human race, or the "*many*" offences that man has committed. So if it were to be used respecting those who were to come forth from the caves and fastnesses where they had been driven by persecution, or those who sleep in their graves, and who will come forth in a general resurrection, it *might* be used of them considered as the many, and it might be said "the many" or "the multitude" comes forth. Not a few interpreters, therefore, have understood this in the sense of *all*, considered as referring to a multitude, or as suggesting the idea of a multitude, or keeping up the idea that there would be great numbers. If this is the proper interpretation, the word "many" was used instead of the word "all" to suggest to the mind the idea that there would be a *multitude*, or that there would be a *great number*. Some, as Lengerke, apply it to all the Israelites who "were not written in the book" (ver. 1), that is, to a resurrection of all the Israelites who had died; some, as Porphyry, a coming forth of the multitudes out of the caves and fastnesses who had been driven there by persecution; and some, as Rosenmüller and Hävernick, understand it as meaning *all*, as in Rom. v. 15, 19. The sum of all that can be said in regard to the meaning of the word, it seems to me, is, that it is so far ambiguous that it *might* be applied (*a*) to "*many*" considered as a large portion of a number of persons or things; (*b*) or, in an absolute sense, to the whole of any number of persons or things considered as a multitude or great number. As used here in the visions of the future, it would seem to denote that the eye of the angel was fixed on a great multitude rising from the dust of the earth, without any particular or distinct reference to the question whether all arose. There would be a vast or general resurrection from the dust; so much so that the mind would be interested mainly in the contemplation of the *great hosts* who would thus come forth. Thus understood, the language might, of itself, apply either to a general arousing of the Hebrew people in the time of the Maccabees, or to a general resurrection of the dead in the last day. ¶ *That sleep.* This expression is one that denotes either natural sleep, or anything that resembles sleep. In the latter sense it is often used to denote death, and especially the death of the pious—who calmly slumber in their graves in the hope of awaking in the morning of the resurrection. See Notes on 1 Thess. iv. 14. It cannot be denied that it might be applied to those who, for any cause, were inactive, or whose energies were not aroused—as we often employ the word sleep or slumber—and that it might be thus

used of those who seemed to slumber in the midst of the persecutions which raged, and the wrongs that were committed by Antiochus; but it would be most natural to understand it of those who were *dead*, and this idea would be particularly suggested in the connection in which it stands here. ¶ *In the dust of the earth.* Heb., "In the ground, or earth of dust"—אַדְמַת־עָפָר.

The language denotes the ground or earth considered as composed of dust, and would naturally refer to those who are dead and buried—considered as sleeping there with the hope of awaking in the resurrection. ¶ *Shall awake.* This is language appropriate to those who are asleep, and to the dead considered as being asleep. It might, indeed, be applied to an arousing from a state of lethargy and inaction, but its most obvious, and its full meaning, would be to apply it to the resurrection of the dead, considered as an awaking to life of those who were slumbering in their graves. ¶ *Some.* One portion of them. The relative number is not designated, but it is implied that there would be two classes. They would not all rise to the same destiny, or the same lot. ¶ *To everlasting life.* So that they would live for ever. This stands in contrast with their "sleeping in the dust of the earth," or their being dead, and it implies that that state would not occur in regard to them again. Once they slept in the dust of the earth; now they would live for ever, or would die no more. Whether in this world or in another is not here said, and there is nothing in the passage which would enable one to determine this. The single idea is that of living for ever, or never dying again. This is language which *must* have been derived from the doctrine of the resurrection of the dead, and of the future state, and which must imply the belief of that doctrine in whatever sense it may be used here. It is such as in subsequent times was employed by the sacred writers to denote the future state, and the rewards of the righteous. The most common term employed in the New Testament, perhaps, to describe true religion, is

life, and the usual phrase to denote the condition of the righteous after the resurrection is *eternal* or *everlasting life.* Comp. Matt. xxv. 46. This language, then, would most naturally be referred to that state, and covers all the subsequent revelations respecting the condition of the blessed. ¶ *And some to shame.* Another portion in such a way that they shall have only shame or dishonour. The Hebrew word means *reproach, scorn, contumely;* and it may be applied to the reproach which one casts on another, Job xvi. 10; Psa. xxxix. 8 (9); lxxix. 12; or to the reproach which rests on any one, Josh. v. 9; Isa. liv. 4. Here the word means the reproach or dishonour which would rest on them for their sins, their misconduct, their evil deeds. The word itself would apply to any persons who were subjected to disgrace for their former misconduct. If it be understood here as having a reference to those who would be aroused from their apathy, and summoned from their retreats in the times of the Maccabees, the meaning is, that they would be called forth to public shame on account of their apostasy, and their conformity to heathen customs; if it be interpreted as applying to the resurrection of the dead, it means that the wicked would rise to reproach and shame before the universe for their folly and vileness. As a matter of fact, one of the bitterest ingredients in the doom of the wicked will be the shame and confusion with which they will be overwhelmed in the great day on account of the sins and follies of their course in this world. ¶ And *everlasting contempt.* The word " everlasting " in this place is the same which in the former part of the verse is applied to the other portion that would awake, and like that properly denotes eternal; as in Matt. xxv. 46, the word translated " everlasting " [punishment] is the same which is rendered "eternal" [life], and means that which is to endure forever. So the Greek here, where the same word occurs, as in Matt. xxv. 46—" some to everlasting life," εἰς ζωὴν αἰώνιον, "and some to everlasting contempt," εἰς αἰσχύνην αἰώνιον—is one which would denote a strict and proper eternity.

3 And they that be [1] wise shall shine [a] as the brightness of the firmament; and they that turn many to righteousness, as the [b] stars for ever and ever.

1 or, *teachers.*   a Matt.13.43.   b 1 Cor.15.41,42.

The word "contempt" (דְּרָאוֹן) means, properly, *a repulse;* and then *aversion, abhorrence.* The meaning here is aversion or abhorrence—the feeling with which we turn away from that which is loathsome, disgusting, or hateful. Then it denotes the state of mind with which we contemplate the vile and the abandoned; and in this respect expresses the emotion with which the wicked will be viewed on the final trial. The word *everlasting* completes the image, meaning that this feeling of loathing and abhorrence would continue for ever. In a subordinate sense this language *might* be used to denote the feelings with which cowards, ingrates, and apostates are regarded on earth; but it cannot be doubted that it will receive its most perfect fulfilment in the future world—in that aversion with which the lost will be viewed by all holy beings in the world to come.

3. *And they that be wise.* This is the language which, in the Scriptures, is employed to denote the pious, or those who serve God and keep his commandments. See the book of Proverbs, *passim.* True religion is wisdom, and sin is folly, and they who live for God and for heaven are the truly wise. The meaning is, that they have chosen the path which true wisdom suggests as that in which man should walk, while all the ways of sin are ways of folly. The language here used is expressive of a general truth, applicable in itself to all the righteous at all times, and nothing can be inferred from the term employed as to what was designed by the angel. ¶ *Shall shine as the brightness of the firmament.* As the sky above us. The image is that of the sky at night, thick set with bright and beautiful stars. No comparison could be more striking. The meaning would seem to be, that each one of the righteous will be like a bright and beautiful star, and that, in their numbers, and order, and harmony, they would resemble the heavenly constellations at night. Nothing can be more sublime than to look on the heavens in a clear night, and to think of the number and the order of the stars above us as an emblem of the righteous in the heavenly world. The word rendered *firmament* means, properly, *expanse,* or that which is spread out, and it is applied to the sky as it *appears* to be spread out above us. ¶ *And they that turn many to righteousness.* Referring to those who would be instrumental in converting men to the worship of the true God, and to the ways of religion. This is very general language, and might be applied to any persons who have been the means of bringing sinners to the knowledge of the truth. It would apply in an eminent degree to ministers of the gospel who were successful in their work, and to missionaries among the heathen. From the mere language, however, nothing certain can be argued as to the original reference as used by the angel, and it seems to have been his intention to employ language so general that it might be applied to *all,* of all ages and countries, who would be instrumental in turning men to God. ¶ *As the stars.* As the stars that are distinguished by their size and lustre in the firmament. In the former part of the verse, when speaking of those who were "wise," the design seems to be to compare them to the sky as it appears, set over with innumerable stars, and in their numbers and groupings constituting great beauty; in this member of the sentence the design seems to be to compare those who are eminent in converting men, to the particular beautiful and bright stars that strike us as we look on the heavens—those more distinguished in size and splendour, and that seem to lead on the others. The meaning is, that amidst the hosts of the saved they will be conspicuous, or they will be honoured in proportion to their toils, their sacrifices, and their success. ¶ *For ever and ever.* To all eternity. This refers to those who shall turn many to righteousness; and the meaning is, that they shall continue thus to be distinguished and honoured to all eternity.

4 But thou, O Daniel, shut *a* up the words, and seal the book, *even*

a Rev. 10. 4.

to the time of the end ; many shall run to and fro, and knowledge shall be increased.

---

4. *But thou, O Daniel, shut up the words.* To wit, by sealing them up, or by closing the book, and writing no more in it. The meaning is, that all has been communicated which it was intended to communicate. The angel had no more to say, and the volume might be sealed up. ¶ *And seal the book.* This would seem to have been not an unusual custom in closing a prophecy, either by affixing a seal to it that should be designed to confirm it as the prophet's work—as we seal a deed, a will, or a contract ; or to secure the volume, as we seal a letter. Comp. Notes on chap. viii. 26 ; Isa. viii. 16. ¶ Even *to the time of the end.* That is, the period when all these things shall be accomplished. Then (*a*) the truth of the prediction now carefully sealed up will be seen and acknowledged ; (*b*) and then, also, it may be expected that there will be clearer knowledge on all these subjects, for the facts will throw increased light on the meaning and the bearing of the predictions. ¶ *Many shall run to and fro.* Shall pass up and down in the world, or shall go from place to place. The reference is clearly to those who should thus go to impart knowledge ; to give information ; to call the attention of men to great and important matters. The *language* is applicable to any methods of imparting important knowledge, and it refers to a time when this would be the characteristic of the age. There is nothing else to which it can be so well applied as to the labours of Christian missionaries, and ministers of the gospel, and others who, in the cause of Christian truth, go about to rouse the attention of men to the great subjects of religion ; and the natural application of the language is to refer it to the times when the gospel would be preached to the world at large. ¶ *And knowledge shall be increased.* To wit, by this method. The angel seems to mean that in this way there would be an advance in knowledge on all the subjects of reli-

gion, and particularly on the points to which he had referred. This would be one of the characteristics of these times, and this would be the means by which it would be accomplished. Our own age has furnished a good *illustration* of the meaning of this language, and it will be still more fully and strikingly illustrated as the time approaches when the knowledge of the Lord shall fill the whole world.

Having thus gone through with an exposition of these, the closing words of the vision (vers. 1 4), it seems proper that we should endeavour to ascertain the meaning of the angel in what is here said, and the bearing of this more particularly on what he had said before. With this view, therefore, several remarks may be made here. (1.) It seems clear that there was in some respects, and for some purpose, a *primary* reference to Antiochus, and to the fact that in his times there would be a great rousing up of the friends of God and of religion, *as if* from their graves. (*a*) The connection demands it. If the close of the last chapter refers to Antiochus, then it cannot be denied that this does also, for it is introduced in immediate connection with that, and as referring to that time: "And at that time." (*b*) The facts referred to would require the same interpretation. Thus it is said that it would be a time of trouble, such as there had never been since the nation existed—a state of things which clearly refers to the calamities which would be brought upon them by the persecutions of Antiochus Epiphanes. (*c*) This interpretation seems to be in accordance with the purpose of the angel to give the assurance that these troubles would come to an end, and that in the time of the greatest calamity, when everything seemed tending to ruin, God would interpose, and would secure the people, and would cause his own worship to be restored. Porphyry then, it appears to me, was so far right as to apply this to the times of Antiochus, and to the events that occurred under the Maccabees. "Then," says he, "those who, as it were, sleep in the dust of the earth, and are pressed down with the weight of evils, and, as it were, hid in sepulchres of misery, shall rise from the dust of the earth to unexpected victory, and shall raise their heads from the ground—the observers of the law rising to everlasting life, and the violators of it to eternal shame." He also refers to the history, in which it is said that, in the times of the persecutions, many of the Jews fled to the desert, and hid themselves in caves and caverns, and that after the victories of the Maccabees they came forth, and that this was metaphorically (μεταφορικῶς) called a resurrection of the dead.—Jerome, *in loc.* According to this interpretation, the meaning would be, that there would be a general uprising of the people ; a general arousing of them from their lethargy, or summoning them from their retreats and hiding-places, *as if* the dead, good and bad, should arise from their dust.

(2.) This *language*, however, is derived from the doctrine of the literal resurrection of the dead. It implies the belief of that doctrine. It is such language as would be used only where that doctrine was known and believed. It would convey no proper idea *unless* it were known and believed. The passage, then, may be adduced as full proof that the doctrine of the resurrection of the dead, both of the just and the unjust, was understood and believed in the time of Daniel. No one can reasonably doubt this. Such language is *not* used in countries where the doctrine of the resurrection of the dead is not believed, and where used, as it is in Christian lands, is full proof, even when employed for illustration, that the doctrine of the resurrection is a common article of belief. Compare Notes on Isa. xxvi. 19. This language is not found in the Greek and Latin classic writers ; nor in heathen writings in modern times ; nor is it found in the earlier Hebrew Scriptures ; nor is it used by infidels even for illustration ; and the proof, therefore, is clear that as employed in the time of Daniel

the doctrine of the resurrection of the dead was known and believed. If so, it marks an important fact in the progress of theological opinion and knowledge in his times. How it came to be known is not intimated here, nor explained elsewhere, but of the fact no one can have any reasonable doubt. Even now, so clear and accurate is the language, that if we wish to express the doctrine of the resurrection of the dead, we cannot do it better than by employing the language of the angel in addressing Daniel. (See Editor's Preface to volume on Job.)

(3.) The *full* meaning of the language is not met by the events that occurred in the times of the Maccabees. As figurative, or, as Porphyry says, *metaphorical*, it might be used to describe those events. But what then occurred would not come up to the proper and complete meaning of the prediction. That is, if nothing *more* was intended, we should feel that the event fell far short of the full import of the language ; of the ideas which it was fitted to convey; and of the hopes which it was adapted to inspire. If that was all, then this lofty language would not have been used. There was nothing in the *facts* that adequately corresponded with it. In the obvious and literal sense, there was nothing which could be called a resurrection to "*everlasting* life ;" nothing that could be called an awaking to "*everlasting* shame and contempt." There was nothing which would justify literally the language " they shall shine as the brightness of the firmament, and as the stars *for ever and ever.*" The language naturally has a higher signification than this, and even when employed for illustration, that higher signification should be recognized and would be suggested to the mind.

(4.) The passage looks onward to a higher and more important event than any that occurred in the times of the Maccabees—to the general resurrection of the dead, of the just and the unjust, and to the final glory of the righteous. The order of thought in the mind of the angel would seem to have been this : he designed primarily to furnish to Daniel an assur-

5 ¶ Then I Daniel looked, and, behold, there stood other two, the one on this side of the ¹ bank of the river, and the other on that side of the bank of the river.

¹ lip.

ance that deliverance would come in the time of the severe troubles which were to overwhelm the nation, and that the nation would ultimately be safe. In doing this his mind almost unconsciously glanced forward to a final deliverance from death and the grave, and he expressed the thought which he designed to convey in the well-known and familiar language used to describe the resurrection. Commencing the description in this manner, by the laws of prophetic suggestion (comp. Intro. to Isa. § VII. III.), the mind finally rested on the ultimate event, and that which *began* with the deliverance in the times of the Maccabees, *ended* in the full contemplation of the resurrection of the dead, and the scenes beyond the last judgment.

(5.) If it be asked what would be the *pertinency* or the *propriety* of this language, if this be the correct interpretation, or what would be its bearing on the design of the angel, it may be replied: (*a*) that the assurance was in this way conveyed that *these* troubles under Antiochus would cease—an assurance as definite and distinct as though all that was said had been confined to that; (*b*) that a much more important, and more cheering *general* truth was thus brought to view, that ultimately the people of God would emerge from all trouble, and would stand before God in glory—a truth of great value then, and at all times ; (*c*) that this truth was of so universal a nature that it might be applied in *all* times of trouble—that when the church was assailed ; when the people of God were persecuted ; when they were driven away from their temples of worship, and when the rites of religion were suspended ; when the zeal of many should grow cold, and the pious should be disheartened, they might look on to brighter times. There was to be an end of all these troubles. There was to be a winding up of these affairs. All the dead were to be raised from their graves, the good and the bad, and

thus the righteous would triumph, and would shine like the brightness of the firmament, and the wicked would be overwhelmed with shame and contempt.

(6.) From all this it follows that this passage may be used to prove the doctrine of the resurrection of the dead, and the doctrine of eternal retribution. Not, indeed, the primary thing in the use of the language as applied by the angel, it is, nevertheless, based on the *truth* and the *belief* of these doctrines, and the mind of the angel ultimately rested on these great truths as adapted to awe the wicked, and to give consolation to the people of God in times of trouble. Thus Daniel was directed to some of the most glorious truths that would be established and inculcated by the coming of the Messiah, and long before he appeared had a glimpse of the great doctrine which he came to teach respecting the ultimate destiny of man.

5. *Then I Daniel looked.* My attention was attracted in a new direction. Hitherto, it would seem, it had been fixed on the angel, and on what he was saying. The angel now informed him that he had closed his communication, and Daniel was now attracted by a new heavenly vision. ¶ *And, behold, there stood other two.* Two other angels. The connection requires us to understand this of angels, though they are not expressly called so. ¶ *The one on this side of the bank of the river.* Marg., as in Heb., *lip.* The word is used to denote the bank of the river from its resemblance to a lip. The river referred to here is the Hiddekel or Tigris, Notes on ch. x. 4. These angels stood on each side of the river, though it does not appear that there was any special significancy in that fact. It perhaps contributed merely to the majesty and solemnity of the vision. The names of these angels are not mentioned, and their appearing is merely an indication of the interest which they take in the affairs of men, and in the Divine purposes and doings. They came here as if they had been deeply interested lis-

6 And *one* said to the man clothed in linen, which *was* [1] upon the waters of the river, How long *shall it be to* the end of these wonders?   1 or, *from above.*   a Rev. 10. 5-7.

7 And I heard the man clothed in linen, which *was* upon the waters of the river, when he [a] held up his right hand and his left hand unto heaven, and sware by him that

---

teners to what the angel had been saying, and for the purpose of making inquiry as to the final result of all these wonderful events. The angel which had been addressing Daniel stood *over* the river, ver. 6.

6. *And one said.* One of these angels. It would seem that, though before unseen by Daniel, they had been present, and had listened with deep interest to the communication respecting the future which the angel had made to him. Feeling a deep concern in the issue of these wonderful events—thus evincing the interest which we are taught to believe the heavenly beings take in human affairs (see Notes on 1 Pet. i. 12)—one of them now addressed him who had been endowed with so much ability to disclose the future, as to the termination of these events. Such an inquiry was natural, and accords with what we should suppose an angel would make on an occasion like this. ¶ *To the man clothed in linen.* The angel. Notes on ch. x. 5. ¶ *Which was upon the waters of the river.* Marg., *from above.* So the Hebrew. The meaning is, the man seemed to stand *over* the river. Comp. ch. viii. 16. Lengerke supposes that by this was intimated the fact that the Divine control was over the waters as well as over the land—in other words, over the whole earth. ¶ *How long* shall it be to *the end of these wonders?* Nothing had been said on this point that could determine it. The angel had detailed a succession of remarkable events which must, from the nature of the case, extend far into future years; he had repeatedly spoken of an end, and had declared that that series of events would terminate, and had thus given the assurance to Daniel that these troubles would be succeeded by brighter and happier times, but he had said nothing by which it could be determined when this would be. It was natural to start this inquiry, and as well for the sake of Daniel as him-

self, the angel here puts the question when this would be.

7. *And I heard the man,* &c. That is, he replied to the question at once, and in a most solemn manner, as if he were communicating a great and momentous truth respecting the future. ¶ *When he held up his right hand and his left hand unto heaven.* Towards heaven; as if appealing to heaven for the sincerity and truth of what he was about to utter. The act of swearing or taking an oath was often accompanied with the lifting up of the hand to heaven, usually the right hand (comp. Gen. xiv. 22; Exod. vi. 8; Deut. xxxii. 40; Ezek. xx. 5; Rev. x. 5); but here the angel stretched *both* hands towards heaven, as if he were about to make the affirmation in the most solemn manner conceivable. ¶ *And sware by him that liveth for ever.* By the eternal God. That is, he made to him: he made the solemn asseveration in his presence; he called him to witness to the truth of what he said. The occasion; the manner; the posture of the angel; the appeal to the Eternal One—all give great sublimity to this transaction, and all imply that the answer was to be one of great consequence in regard to future times. ¶ *That* it shall be *for a time, times, and an half.* Marg., or, *a part.* The word הֲצִי means, properly, *half, the half part,* that which is *divided* (חָצָה —to divide), *s.c.,* in the middle. The word "*times*" means *two* times, for it is dual in its form, and the expression means three times, or periods, and a half. See the meaning of the language fully considered and explained in the Notes on ch. vii. 24-28. (See Editor's Essay on Year-day Principle, prefixed to vol. on Revelation.) ¶ *And when he shall have accomplished.* When he shall have finished his purpose in the matter; when he shall have done all that he could do. ¶ *To scatter the*

liveth for ever, that *it shall be* for a time, times, and ¹ an half; and

¹ or, *a part.*

when he shall have accomplished to scatter the power of the holy people, all these *things* shall be finished.

power. All that constituted the power —their armies, means of defence, &c.

The word rendered *power* (יָד) means, properly, *hand*, but it is sometimes used to denote *a part* of a thing—as a portion that we take up by the hand—a handful; that is, a part of a thing taken up at once in dividing,—Gesenius, *Lex.* See Jer. vi. 3; 2 Kings xi. 7; Gen. xlvii. 24. In accordance with this, Gesenius, Lengerke, and De Wette suppose that the reference here is to the scattering of a *portion* or *part* of the Hebrew people in other lands, and to the hope that they would be restored again to their own country; and that the meaning of the angel is, that when these dispersions were ended, all this would have been accomplished. The word has also the sense of *power, might, strength* (Ges., *Lex.*), the hand being regarded as the seat of strength, Isa. xxviii. 2; Job xxvii. 11; Psa. lxxvi. 5 (6). Thus employed, it may denote whatever *constituted* their strength; and then the idea in the passage before us is, that all this would be *scattered.* When that should have been done; when that dispersion should have been ended; when these scattered forces and people should have been again restored, then all this that was predicted would be accomplished, and these troubles cease. This would be in the period designated by the "time, and times, and an half." If it refers to Antiochus, it means that the scattered forces and people of the Hebrews would be rallied under the Maccabees, and that on their return victory would crown their efforts, and the land would be again at peace. If it has a higher and an ultimate signification, it would seem to imply that when the scattered Hebrew people should be gathered into the Christian church—when their dispersions and their wanderings should come to an end by their returning to the Messiah, and, under him, to the true God, then the series of predictions will have received their complete fulfilment—for then religion will triumph

in the world, and the kingdom of God be set up over all the nations, agreeably to Rom. xi. 15-25. In reference, then, to the *meaning* of the passage as used by the angel here, the following remarks may be made: (1.) It *had* an applicability to the times of Antiochus, and to the duration of the calamities that would come upon the Hebrew people under his reign. If there had been nothing further intended than this, the mere language employed would have found a literal fulfilment in these events, and there can be no reasonable doubt that the primary reference of the angel was to them. See this point fully considered and illustrated in the Notes on ch. vii. 24-28. (2.) Yet there are circumstances which lead us to suppose that, at the same time, and by the laws of prophetic suggestion (see Intro. to Isa. § VII. III.), more important events were also referred to, and were designed to be connected with this statement. Those circumstances are (*a*) the manner in which the angel introduces the subject—by a solemn appeal, with outstretched arms, to heaven. This would look as if he regarded the answer as of momentous importance, and as if he were contemplating vast movements in the future. (*b*) The fact that the language here had a *settled meaning* —referring, as used elsewhere, to future events deeply affecting the welfare of the world. The language is so couched, indeed, that it *would express* the fact in regard to the duration of the troubles under Antiochus; but it was also of such a nature that in its higher signification it would describe the duration of more momentous transactions, and would designate a period when the true religion would begin its universal reign; when the evils of a vast Antichristian power would come to an end, and when the kingdom of the saints would be set up in the world. See the Notes on ch. vii. 24-28. (3.) The full meaning of the language would then seem to be, that the angel designed to include *all* in the future to which those

8 And I heard, but I understood not; then said I, O my Lord, what *shall be* the end of these *things?*

9 And he said, Go thy way,

Daniel; for the words *are* closed up and sealed till the time of the end.

10 Many shall be purified, and

words, as intended by the Divine Spirit, would be applicable. The period designated by the phrase, "a time, and times, and an half," was most momentous. *In* that time the troubles introduced by Antiochus would end, and a state of peace and prosperity would succeed; and *in* that time, also, far greater troubles and woes—those connected with a most fearful apostasy from the true religion, and the setting up of a kingdom of oppression and wrong over the people of God, of which the oppressions and wrongs under Antiochus would be but an emblem, would also come to an end, and there would be a state of peace—a reign of righteousness—a prevalence of religion—and a far-diffused happiness in the world, at which the joy at the dedication of the temple, and the triumphs over Antiochus, would be but a symbol. The ultimate reference, therefore, I suppose, is to the downfall of that great Antichristian power, the Papacy, and the spread and triumphs of the true religion subsequent to that, and consequent on that in the world. These were events that justified the solemn asseveration of the angel, and that made it proper for him, in referring to them, to stretch out both his hands in this sublime manner to heaven.

8. *And I heard, but I understood not.* He understood not the full significance of the language employed— "a time, and times, and an half." This would make it probable that there was something more intended than merely three years and a half as the period of the continuation of these troubles. Daniel saw, apparently from the manner of the angel, as well as from the terms which he used, that there was something mystical and unusual in those terms, and he says, therefore, that he could not understand their full import. ¶ *Then said I, O my Lord.* A term of civil address. The language is such as would be used by an inferior when respectfully addressing one of superior rank. It is

not a term that is peculiarly appropriate to God, or that implies a Divine nature, but is here given to the angel as an appellation of respect, or as denoting one of superior rank. ¶ *What* shall be *the end of these* things ? Indicating great anxiety to know what was to be the termination of these wonders. The "end" had been often referred to in the communication of the angel, and now he had used an enigmatical expression as referring to it, and Daniel asks, with great emphasis, when the end *was* to be.

9. *And he said, Go thy way, Daniel.* That is, make no further inquiries. All has been disclosed that is to be. At the close of his communication (ver. 4), he had told Daniel to shut up, and seal the book, for his revelations were ended. He here repeats substantially the same thing, and he assures him that no more could be imparted on the subject. ¶ *For the words* are *closed up and sealed till the time of the end.* He had finished his communication, and had directed Daniel to close up the record which he made of it, and to affix a seal to the volume, ver. 4. He regarded the whole, therefore, as closed and sealed, until the "end" should come. The events themselves would unfold the meaning of the prediction more fully, and would confirm its truth by their exact correspondence with it. Yet, though the revelation was closed, and all that the angel had designed to say had been said, he does, in the subsequent verses, throw out some suggestions as to the *time,* or as to some important events which were to mark the termination of the wonders referred to. They are bare hints, however, the meaning of which was to be reserved till the time when the predictions would be accomplished, and they are not of such a nature that they can be supposed to have furnished any additional light to Daniel, or to have done anything to relieve the perplexity of his mind in the case.

10. *Many shall be purified.* In fu-

made white, and tried; but *a* the wicked shall do wickedly: and

a Rev. 22. 11.

none of the wicked shall understand; but the wise shall understand.

ture times. That is, as the connection would seem to require, there will be a system introduced by which many will become purified, and made holy. Daniel might hope and expect that under the arrangements which God would make, many of the human race would be cleansed from sin. To what *he* would apply this we cannot determine, but it is a great truth of immense importance in regard to the human family, that, before the "end," or the consummation, "*many*" will be made holy. ¶ *And made white.* White is the emblem of innocence or purity, and hence the term is so often applied to the righteous. "They have washed their robes, and made them *white* in the blood of the Lamb," "they shall walk before me in *white*," &c. Hence the angels are represented as appearing in white raiment. The meaning here is, that many on the earth would be made *holy* before the end would come. The mind of Daniel was thus directed onward to one of the most glorious truths pertaining to future times—that multitudes of the human race would be redeemed, and would be prepared for a holy heaven. ¶ *And tried.* Tried as in a furnace; that is, they will be subjected to persecutions, and to various other forms of suffering, that will test the strength of their faith, and the nature of their religion. This language, also, is of a general character, and would in itself apply to the times of Antiochus, but it is also fitted to describe what would occur in other ages. Perhaps the meaning is, that it would be *a prominent thing* in the future, in introducing the triumphs of religion; and in preparing the people of God for heaven, that they would be subjected to various forms of trial. There have been facts enough of this kind in the history of the church to justify this description, and to show that it would be a marked feature in spreading religion on the earth, that its friends would be persecuted. ¶ *But the wicked shall do wickedly.* They will continue to do wickedly. Not-

withstanding all the judgments that will come upon men; notwithstanding all that will be done to purify the people of God, and, notwithstanding the fact that "*many*" will be of a different character—will be "purified and made white, and tried," yet it will be a truth still, that there will be wicked men upon the earth, and that they will act out their nature. This remark seems to have been thrown in by the angel to prevent the impression which Daniel might possibly get from what was said, not only that the true religion would generally prevail, but that wickedness would *wholly* cease in the earth. Such a time, perhaps, we are not authorized to look for; while we may hope and believe that there will be a period when the worship of God will pervade the world, and will supersede all other forms of worship, yet we have no reason to expect that every individual of the human family at any one time will be converted, and that none of the remains of the apostasy will be seen on the earth. There will be wicked men still, and they will act out their nature, despite all that is done to save them, and despite the fact that religion will have the ascendency in the hearts and lives of the great mass of mankind. For an illustration of this, see Notes on Rev. ix. 20, 21, and xx. 7. ¶ *And none of the wicked shall understand.* This, also, is a general declaration. It means, that none of the wicked would understand the import of these prophecies, or the true nature of religion. Their depravity of heart would prevent it; their purpose to lead a wicked life would so cloud their understandings, and pervert their moral judgments, that they would have no correct appreciation of the government of God, and the nature of the Divine plans and dispensations. Comp. Notes on 1 Cor. ii. 14. The fact here asserted has been always true, and always will be, that sin prevents a clear perception of Divine truth, and that wicked men have no appropriate views of the plans and

11 And from the time *that* the daily *sacrifice* shall be taken away,

1 *to set up the abomination.*

and 1 the abomination that 2 maketh desolate set up, *there shall be* a

2 or, *astonisheth.*

purposes of God. To comprehend religion aright a man needs a pure heart; and no one under the influence of depraved feelings, and corrupt propensities and appetites, can expect to have a just appreciation of that which is good. Doubtless it will be found to be true in the days of millennial glory, when the true religion shall spread over the world, and when the earth shall be filled with light, that there will be wicked men who will have no correct understanding of the nature of religion, and whose minds will be blind to all the evidences of the truth of revelation which shall be diffused around them. No man, unless he is converted, has any proper conception of the beauty of religion. ¶ *But the wise shall understand.* They who serve God and love him, and who, therefore, come under the denomination of the truly *wise.* Notes on ver. 3. The meaning is, that religion—the love of God and a pure heart—will qualify them to perceive the import of Divine truth; to appreciate what is revealed, and to obtain a just view of passing events—or to " understand the signs of the times." Humble and sincere piety—a heart and mind made pure and clear by the influence of Divine truth—is the best preparation for understanding the works and ways of God. Comp. Notes on 1 Cor. ii. 9-12, 14, 15.

11. *And from the time.* Though the angel had said (vers. 4, 9) that his communication was closed, and that he imparted all that he was *commissioned* to communicate to Daniel, yet, as it would seem, in reply to the earnest request of Daniel, he volunteers an additional statement, in regard to certain important *periods* that were to occur in the future. The language, however, is *very* obscure; and it would appear, from ver. 13, that the angel scarcely expected that Daniel would understand it. The statement relates to certain *periods* that would succeed the time when the daily sacrifice would be taken away. Two such periods are mentioned as marking important epochs

in the future. ¶ That *the daily* sacrifice *shall be taken away.* This is the point of reckoning—the *terminus a quo.* The "taking away of the daily sacrifice" refers, undoubtedly, to some act, or some state of things, by which it would be made to cease; by which the daily offerings at Jerusalem would be either temporarily suspended or totally abolished. See Notes on ch. viii. 11; ix. 27; xi. 31. The *language* here is applicable to either of two events :— to the act of Antiochus, causing the daily sacrifice to cease in Jerusalem (ch. viii. 11; xi. 31), or to the final closing of those sacrifices by the death of the Messiah as the great offering to whom they referred, and the destruction of the temple and the altar by the Romans, ch. ix. 27. The view taken in the interpretation of this passage will depend on the question to *which* of these there is allusion here by the angel, or whether there is an allusion to *both.* The *language* evidently is applicable to both, and might be employed with reference to either. ¶ *And the abomination that maketh desolate set up.* See these words explained in the Notes on ch. viii. 13; ix. 27; xi. 31. The same remark may be made here which was made respecting the previous expression — that the *language* is applicable to two quite distinct events, and events which were separated by a long interval of time : to the act of Antiochus in setting up an image of Jupiter in the temple, and to a similar act on the part of the Romans when the temple was finally destroyed. The view which is taken of the *time* referred to here will depend on the question which of these is to be regarded as the *stand-point* or the *terminus a quo,* or whether the language is *designedly* so used that an important epoch was to occur in *both* cases within a specified period *after* these events. On these points there has been great diversity of opinion. ¶ There shall be *a thousand two hundred and ninety days.* If this is to be taken literally, it would be three years and two hun-

thousand two hundred and ninety days.

12 Blessed *is* he that waiteth, and cometh to the thousand three

dred and ten days, reckoning the year at 360 days, and is thirty days more than the three years and a half referred to in ver. 7. Prof. Stuart, who supposes that the time is to be taken literally, and that the passage refers exclusively to Antiochus Epiphanes, explains the application of the language in the following manner: "Antiochus took away the daily sacrifice as is here declared. This was in the latter part of May, B.C. 168. Profane history does not indeed give us the *day*, but it designates the year and the season. As we have already seen [compare the extract copied from Prof. Stuart on ch. vii. 24–28], about three and a half years elapsed, after the temple worship was entirely broken up, before Judas Maccabeus expurgated the temple and restored its rites. The *terminus ad quem* is not mentioned in the verse now before us; but still it is plainly implied. The end of the 1290 days must, of course, be marked by some signal event, just as the commencement of them is so marked. And as the *suppression* of the temple rites constitutes the definitive mark of the commencement, so it would seem plain that the *restoration* of the same rites must mark the conclusion of the period which is designated. The 'time of the end,' *i.e.*, the period at the close of which the persecutions of Antiochus would cease, is distinctly adverted to in ch. vii. 25; xi. 30–35; and xii. 7. The nature of the case, in the verse before us, shows that the same period is tacitly referred to in the words of the speaker. No doubt remains that his march [the march of Antiochus] from Antioch to Egypt, for hostile purposes, was in the spring of the year 168 B.C. He was delayed for some time on this march by ambassadors from Egypt, who met him in Cœlo-Syria. Very naturally, therefore, we may conclude that he arrived opposite Jerusalem in the latter part of May, and that there and then he commissioned Apollonius to rifle and profane the temple. The exact time from the period when this was done, down to the time of the expurga-

tion, seems to have been, and is designated as being, 1290 days."—*Hints on Prophecy*, pp. 94, 95. It is evident, however, that there is here no clear making out of the exact time by any historical records, though it is in itself not improbable. Still the great difficulty is, that in the supposition that the "time, and times, and an half" refers to Antiochus, as denoting the period of his persecutions, thus limiting it to three years and a half—a period which can be made out without material difficulty (comp. Notes on ch. vii. 24–28)—that *another* time or period should be mentioned here of *thirty* days more, concerning which there is no corresponding event in the historical facts, or at least none that can now be demonstrated to have occurred. See the remarks at the close of the next verses.

12. *Blessed* is *he that waiteth.* This indicates a patient expectation of an event that was to occur, and the happy state of him who would reach it. The angel refers to another period different from the "time, and times, and an half," and different also from the twelve hundred and ninety days. He speaks of *this* as the consummation—as the desirable time; and pronounces him blessed who shall be permitted to see it. The idea here is, that of one looking out for this as a happy period, and that he would be regarded as a happy man who should live in that age. ¶ *And cometh to.* Literally, "touches." That is, whose life would reach to that time; or who would not be cut off before that period. ¶ *The thousand three hundred and five and thirty days.* The *article* is not used in the original, and its insertion here seems to make the period more distinct and definite than it is necessarily in the Hebrew. There is much apparent abruptness in all these expressions; and what the angel says in these closing and additional communications has much the appearance of a fragmentary character —of hints, or detached and unexplained thoughts thrown out on which he was not *disposed* to enlarge, and which, for

hundred and five and thirty days.

13 But go thou thy way till the

end *be*, for [1] thou shalt rest, and stand in thy lot at the end of the days. [1 or, *and*.]

---

some reason, he was not inclined to explain. In respect to this period of 1335 days, it seems to stand by itself. Nothing is said of the time when it would occur; no intimation is given of its commencement, as in the former cases—the *terminus a quo;* and nothing is said of its characteristics further than that he would be blessed who should be permitted to see it—implying that it would be, on some accounts, a happy period.

13. *But go thou thy way till the end* be. See vers. 4, 9. The meaning is, that nothing more would be communicated, and that he must wait for the disclosures of future times. When that should occur which is here called *"the end,"* he would understand this more fully and perfectly. The language implies, also, that *he* would be present at the development which is here called *"the end;"* and that then *he* would comprehend clearly what was meant by these revelations. This is such language as would be used on the supposition that the reference was to far-distant times, and to the scenes of the resurrection and the final judgment, when Daniel would be present. Comp. Notes on vers. 2, 3. ¶ *For thou shalt rest.* Rest now; and perhaps the meaning is, shalt enjoy a long season of repose before the consummation shall occur. In ver. 2, he had spoken of those who *"sleep* in the dust of the earth;" and the allusion here would seem to be the same as applied to Daniel. The period referred to was far distant. Important events were to intervene. The affairs of the world were to move on for ages before the "end" should come. There would be scenes of revolution, commotion, and tumult—momentous changes before that consummation would be reached. But during that long interval Daniel would *"rest."* He would quietly and calmly *"sleep* in the dust of the earth"—in the grave. He would be agitated by none of these troubles—disturbed by none of these changes; for he would peacefully

slumber in the hope of being awaked in the resurrection. This also is such language as would be employed by one who believed in the doctrine of the resurrection, and who meant to say that he with whom he was conversing would repose in the tomb while the affairs of the world would move on in the long period that would intervene between the time when he was then speaking and the "end" or consummation of all things—the final resurrection. I do not see that it is possible to explain the language on any other supposition than this. The word rendered "shalt rest"—תָּנוּחַ—would be well applied to the *rest* in the grave. So it is used in Job iii. 13, "Then had I been *at rest;"* Job iii. 17, "There the weary be *at rest."* ¶ *And stand in thy lot.* In thy place. The language is derived from the lot or portion which falls to one—as when a lot is cast, or anything is determined by lot. Comp. Judg. i. 3; Isa. lvii. 6; Psa. cxxv. 3; xvi. 5. Gesenius (*Lex.*) renders this, "And arise to thy lot in the end of days; *i.e.,* in the Messiah's kingdom." Comp. Rev. xx. 6. The meaning is, that he need have no apprehension for himself as to the future. That was not now indeed disclosed to him; and the subject was left in designed obscurity. He would "rest," perhaps a long time, in the grave. But in the far-distant future he would occupy his appropriate place; he would rise from his rest; he would appear again on the stage of action; he would have the lot and rank which properly belonged to him. What idea this would convey to the mind of Daniel it is impossible now to determine, for he gives no statement on that point; but it is clear that it is such language as would be appropriately used by one who believed in the doctrine of the resurrection of the dead, and who meant to direct the mind onward to those far-distant and glorious scenes when the dead would all arise, and when each one of the righteous would stand up in his appropriate place or lot. ¶ *At the end of the days.* After the close of the periods referred to, when the consummation of all things should take place. It is impossible not to regard this as applicable to *a* resurrection from the dead; and there is every reason to suppose that Daniel would so understand it, for (*a*) if it be interpreted as referring to the close of the persecutions of Antiochus Epiphanes, it must be so understood. This prophecy was uttered about 534 years B.C. The death of Antiochus occurred 164 B.C. The *interval* between the prophecy and that event was, therefore, 370 years. It is impossible to believe that it was *meant* by the angel that Daniel would continue to live during all that time, so that he should then "stand in his lot," not having died; or that he *did* continue to live during all that period, and that at the end of it he "stood in his lot," or occupied the post of distinction and honour which is referred to in this language. But if this *had* been the meaning, it would have implied that he would, at that time, rise from the dead. (*b*) If it be referred, as Gesenius explains it, to the times of the Messiah, the same thing would follow—for that time was still more remote; and, if it be supposed that Daniel understood it as relating to those times, it must also be admitted that *he* believed that there would be a resurrection, and that he would then appear in his proper place. (*c*) There is only one other supposition, and that directly involves the idea that the allusion is to the general resurrection, as referred to in ver. 3, and that Daniel would have part in that. This is admitted by Lengerke, by Maurer, and even by Bertholdt, to be the meaning, though he applies it to the reign of the Messiah. No other interpretation, therefore, can be affixed to this than that it implies the doctrine of the resurrection of the dead, and that the mind of Daniel was directed onward to that. With this great and glorious doctrine the book appropriately closes. The hope of such a resurrection was fitted to soothe the mind of Daniel in view of all the troubles which he then experienced, and of all the darkness which rested on the future; for what we most want in the troubles and in the darkness of the present life is the assurance that, after having "rested" in the grave—in the calm sleep of the righteous—we shall "awake" in the morning of the resurrection, and shall "stand in our lot"—or in our appropriate place, as the acknowledged children of God, "at the end of days"—when time shall be no more, and when the consummation of all things shall have arrived.

In reference to the application of this prophecy, the following general remarks may be made:—

I. One class of interpreters explain it literally as applicable to Antiochus Epiphanes. Of this class is Prof. Stuart, who supposes that its reference to Antiochus can be shown in the following manner:—"The place which this passage occupies shows that the *terminus a quo,* or period from which the days designated are to be reckoned, is the same as that to which reference is made in the previous verse. This, as we have already seen, is the period when Antiochus, by his military agent Apollonius, took possession of Jerusalem, and put a stop to the temple worship there. The author of the first book of Maccabees, who is allowed by all to deserve credit as an historian, after describing the capture of Jerusalem by the agent of Antiochus (in the year 145 of the Seleucidæ—168 B.C.), and setting before the reader the widespread devastation which ensued, adds, respecting the invaders: 'They shed innocent blood around the sanctuary, and defiled the holy place; and the inhabitants of Jerusalem fled away: the sanctuary thereof was made desolate; her feasts were turned into mourning, her sabbaths into reproach, and her honour into disgrace;' 1 Macc. i. 37–39. To the period when this state of things commenced we must look, then, in order to find the date from which the 1335 days are to be reckoned. Supposing now that Apollonius captured Jerusalem in the latter part of May, B.C. 168, the 1335 days would expire about the middle of February, in the year B.C. 164. Did any event take place at this period which would naturally call forth the congratulations of the prophet, as addressed in the text before us to the Jewish people?

"History enables us to answer this question. Late in the year 165 B.C., or at least very early in the year 164 B.C., Antiochus Epiphanes, learning that there were great insurrections and disturbances in Armenia and Persia, hastened thither with a portion of his armies, while the other portion was commissioned against Palestine. He was victorious for a time; but being led by cupidity to seek for the treasures that were laid up in the temple of the Persian Diana at Elymaïs, he undertook to rifle them. The inhabitants of the place, however, rose *en masse* and drove him out of the city; after which he fled to Ecbatana. There he heard of the total discomfiture by Judas Maccabeus of his troops in Palestine, which were led on by Nicanor and Timotheus. In the rage occasioned by this disappointment, he uttered the most horrid blasphemies against the God of the Jews, and threatened to make Jerusalem the burying-place of the nation. Immediately he directed his course toward Judea; and designing to pass through Babylon, he made all possible haste in his journey. In the meantime he had a fall from his chariot which injured him; and soon after, being seized with a mortal sickness in his bowels (probably the cholera), he died at Tabæ, in the mountainous country, near the confines of Babylonia and Persia. Report stated, even in ancient times, that Antiochus was greatly distressed on his death-bed by the sacrilege which he had committed.

"Thus perished the most bitter and bloody enemy which ever rose up against the Jewish nation and their worship. By following the series of events, it is easy to see that his death took place some time in February of the year 164 B.C. Assuming that the commencement or *terminus a quo* of the 1335 days is the same as that of the 1290 days, it is plain that they terminate at the period when the death

of Antiochus is said to have taken place. 'It was long before the commencement of the spring,' says Frœlich, 'that Antiochus passed the Euphrates, and made his attack on Elymaïs:' so that no more probable time can be fixed upon for his death than at the expiration of the 1335 days; *i.e.*, some time in February of 164 B.C. No wonder that the angel pronounced those of the pious and believing Jews to be *blessed* who lived to see such a day of deliverance."—*Hints on Prophecy*, pp. 95–97.

There are, however, serious and obvious difficulties in regard to this view, and to the supposition that this is all that is intended here—objections and difficulties of so much force that most Christian interpreters have supposed that something further was intended. Among these difficulties and objections are the following:—

(*a*) The air of *mystery* which is thrown over the whole matter by the angel, as if he were reluctant to make the communication; as if something more was meant than the words expressed; as if he shrank from disclosing all that he knew, or that might be said. If it referred to Antiochus alone, it is difficult to see why so much mystery was made of it, and why he was so unwilling to allude further to the subject — *as if* it were something that did not pertain to the matter in hand.

(*b*) The *detached* and *fragmentary* character of what is here said. It stands aside from the main communication. It is uttered after all that the angel had intended to reveal had been said. It is brought out at the earnest request of Daniel, and then only in *hints*, and in enigmatical language, and in such a manner that it would convey no distinct conception to his mind. This would seem to imply that it referred to something else than the main point that had been under consideration.

(*c*) The difference of *time* specified here by the angel. This relates to two points:—

1. To what would occur *after* the "closing of the daily sacrifice, and the setting up of the abomination of deso-

lation." The angel *now* says that what he here refers to would extend to a period of twelve hundred and *ninety* days. But in the accounts before given, the time specified had uniformly been "a time, and times, and half a time;" that is, three years and a half, or twelve hundred and *sixty* days—differing from this by thirty days. Why should this thirty days have been added here if it referred to the time when the sanctuary would be cleansed, and the temple worship restored? Professor Stuart (*Hints on Prophecy*, pp. 93, 94) supposes that it was in order that the *exact* period might be mentioned. But this is liable to objections. For (*a*) the period of three and a half years was sufficiently exact; (*b*) there was no danger of mistake on the subject, and no such error had been made as to require correction; (*c*) this was not of sufficient importance to justify the manifest anxiety of the angel in the case, or to furnish any answer to the inquiries of Daniel, since so small an item of information would not relieve the mind of Daniel. The allusion, then, would *seem* to be something else than what had been referred to by the "three and a half years."

2. But there is a greater difficulty in regard to the other period—the 1335 days; for (*a*) that stands wholly *detached* from what had been said. (*b*) The *beginning* of that period—the *terminus a quo*—is not specified. It is true that Prof. Stuart (*Hints on Prophecy*, p. 95) supposes that this must be the same as that mentioned in the previous verse, but this is not apparent in the communication. It is an isolated statement, and would *seem* to refer to some momentous and important period in the future which would be characterized as a glorious or "blessed" period in the world's history, or of such a nature that he ought to regard himself as peculiarly happy who should be permitted to live then. Now it is true that with much probability this may be shown, as Prof. Stuart has done in the passage quoted above, to accord well with the time when Antiochus died, as that was an important event, and

would be so regarded by those pious Jews who would be permitted to live to that time; but it is true also that the *main* thing for rejoicing was the conquest of Judas Maccabeus and the cleansing of the sanctuary, and that the death of Antiochus does not seem to meet the fulness of what is said here. If that were all, it is not easily conceivable why the angel should have made so much a mystery of it, or why he should have been so reluctant to impart what he knew. The whole matter, therefore, appears to have a higher importance than the mere death of Antiochus and the delivery of the Jews from his persecutions.

II. Another class, and it may be said Christian interpreters generally, have supposed that there was here a reference to some higher and more important events in the far-distant future. But it is scarcely needful to say, that the opinions entertained have been almost as numerous as the writers on the prophecies, and that the judgment of the world has not settled down on any one particular method of the application. It would not be profitable to state the opinions which have been advanced; still less to attempt to refute them—most of them being fanciful conjectures. These may be seen detailed in great variety in Poole's *Synopsis*. It is not commonly pretended that these opinions are based on any exact interpretation of the words, or on any certain mode of determining their correctness, and those who hold them admit that it must be reserved to future years—to their fulfilment—to understand the exact meaning of the prophecy. Thus Prideaux, who supposes that this passage refers to Antiochus, frankly says: "Many things may be said for the probable solving of this difficulty [the fact that the angel here refers to an additional thirty days above the three years and a half, which he says can neither be applied to Antiochus nor to Antichrist], but I shall offer none of them. Those that shall live to see the extirpation of Antichrist, which will be at the end of those years, will best be able to unfold these matters, it being of the nature of these prophecies not thoroughly to be understood till they are thoroughly fulfilled."—Vol. iii. 283, 284. So Bishop Newton, who supposes that the setting up of the abomination of desolation here refers to the Mahometans invading and devastating Christendom, and that the religion of Mahomet will prevail in the East for the space of 1260 years, and then a great revolution—"perhaps the restoration of the Jews, perhaps the destruction of Antichrist" —indicated by the 1290 years, will occur; and that this will be succeeded by another still more glorious event— perhaps "the conversion of the Gentiles, and the beginning of the millennium, or reign of the saints on the earth"—indicated by the 1335 years —says, notwithstanding, "What is the precise time of their beginning, and consequently of their ending, as well as what are the great and signal events which will take place at the end of each period, we can only conjecture; time alone can with certainty discover."—*Prophecies*, p. 321. These expressions indicate the *common* feeling of those who understand these statements as referring to future events; and the reasonings of those who have attempted to make a more specific application have been such as to demonstrate the wisdom of this modesty, and to make us wish that it had been imitated by all. At all events, such speculations on this subject have been so wild and unfounded; so at variance with all just rules of interpretation; so much the fruit of mere fancy, and so incapable of solid support by reasoning, as to admonish us that no more conjectures should be added to the number.

III. The sum of all that it seems to me can be said on the matter is this:—

(1.) That it is probable, for the reasons above stated, that the angel referred to *other* events than the persecutions and the death of Antiochus, for if that was all, the additional information which he gave by the specification of the period of 1260 days, and 1290 days, and 1335 days, was quite too meagre to be worthy of a formal and solemn revelation from God. In other words, if this was all, there was no correspondence between the importance of the events and the solemn manner in which the terms of the communication were made. There was no such *importance* in these three periods as to make these separate disclosures necessary. If this were all, the statements were such indeed as might be made by a *weak man* attaching importance to trifles, but not such as would be made by an *inspired angel* professing to communicate great and momentous truths.

(2.) Either by design, or because the language which he would employ to designate higher events happened to be such as would note those periods also, the angel employed terms which, in the main, would be applicable to what would occur under the persecutions of Antiochus, while, at the same time, his eye was on more important and momentous events in the far-distant future. Thus the three years and a half would apply with sufficient accuracy to the time between the taking away of the daily sacrifice, and the expurgation of the temple by Judas Maccabeus; and then, also, it so happens that the *thirteen hundred and thirty-five* days would designate with sufficient accuracy the death of Antiochus, but there is nothing in the history to which the period of *twelve hundred and ninety* days could with particular propriety be applied, and there is no reason in the history why reference should have been made to that.

(3.) The angel had his eye on three great and important epochs lying apparently far in the future, and constituting important periods in the history of the church and the world. These were, respectively, composed of 1260, 1290, and 1335 prophetic days, that is, years. Whether they had the same beginning or point of reckoning—*termini a quo*— and whether they would, as far as they would respectively extend, cover the same space of time, he does not intimate with any certainty, and, of course, if this is the correct view it would be impossible now to determine, and the development is to be left to the times specified. One of them, the 1260 years, or the three years and a half, we can fix, we think, by applying it to the Papacy. See Notes on ch. vii. 24–28. But in determining even this, it was necessary to wait until the time and course of events should disclose its meaning ; and in reference to the other two periods, doubtless still future, it may be necessary now to wait until events, still to occur, shall disclose what was intended by the angel. The first has been made clear by history : there can be no doubt that the others in the same manner will be made equally clear. That this is the true interpretation, and that this is the view which the angel desired to convey to the mind of Daniel, seems to be clear from such expressions as these occurring in the prophecy : " Seal the book *to the time of the end*," ver. 4 ; "many shall run to and fro, *and knowledge shall be increased*," ver. 4 ; "the words are closed up and sealed *till the time of the end*," ver. 9 ; "many shall be made *white*," ver. 10 ; "the wise *shall understand*," ver. 10 ; "go thou thy way *till the end be*," ver. 13. This language seems to imply that these things could not then be understood, but that when the events to which they refer should take place they would be plain to all.

(4.) Two of those events or periods —the 1290 days and the 1335 days— seem to lie still in the future, and the full understanding of the prediction is to be reserved for developments yet to be made in the history of the world. Whether it be by the conversion of the Jews and the Gentiles, respectively, as Bishop Newton supposes, it would be vain to conjecture, and time must determine. That such *periods*—marked and important periods—*are* to occur in the future, or in some era now commenced but not yet completed, I am constrained to believe ; and that it will be possible, in time to come, to determine what they are, seems to me to be *as* undoubted. But where there is nothing certain to be the basis of calculation, it is idle to add other conjectures to those already made, and it is wiser to leave the matter, as much of the predictions respecting the future must of necessity be left to time and to events to make them clear.

Let me add, in the conclusion of the exposition of this remarkable book :—

(*a*) That the mind of Daniel is left at the close of all the Divine communications to him looking into the far-distant future, ver. 13. His attention is directed onward. Fragments of great truths had been thrown out, with little apparent connection, by the angel ; hints of momentous import had been suggested respecting great doctrines to be made clearer in future ages. A time was to occur, perhaps in the far-distant future, when the dead were to be raised ; when all that slept in the dust of the earth should awake ; when the righteous should shine as the brightness of the firmament, and when he himself should " stand in his lot "— sharing the joys of the blessed, and occupying the position which would be appropriate to him. With this cheering prospect the communications of the angel to him are closed. Nothing could be better fitted to comfort his heart in a land of exile : nothing better fitted to elevate his thoughts.

(*b*) In the same manner it is proper that *we* should look *onward*. All the revelations of God terminate in this manner ; all are designed and adapted to direct the mind to far-distant and most glorious scenes in the future. We have all that Daniel had ; and we have what Daniel had not—the clear revelation of the gospel. In that gospel are stated in a still more clear manner those glorious truths respecting the future which are fitted to cheer us in time of trouble, to elevate our minds amidst the low scenes of earth, and to comfort and sustain us on the bed of death With much more distinctness than Daniel saw them, we are permitted to contemplate the truths respecting the resurrection of the dead, the scenes of the final judgment, and the future happiness of the righteous. We have now knowledge of the resurrection of the Redeemer, and, through him, the assurance that all his people will be raised up to honour and glory ; and though, in reference to the resurrection of the dead, and the future glory of the righteous, there is much that is still obscure, yet there is all that is necessary to inspire us with hope, and to stimulate us to endeavour to obtain the crown of life.

(c) It is not improper, therefore, to close the exposition of this book with the expression of a wish that what was promised to Daniel may occur to us who read his words—that "we may stand in our lot at the end of days;" that when all the scenes of earth shall have passed away in regard to us, and the end of the world itself shall have come, it may be our happy portion to occupy a place among the redeemed, and to stand accepted before God. To ourselves, if we are truly righteous through our Redeemer, we may apply the promise made to Daniel; and for his readers the author can express no higher wish than that this lot may be theirs. If the exposition of this book shall be so blessed as to confirm any in the belief of the great truths of revelation, and lead their minds to a more confirmed hope in regard to these future glorious scenes; if by dwelling on the firm piety, the consummate wisdom, and the steady confidence in God evinced by this remarkable man, their souls shall be more established in the pursuit of the same piety, wisdom, and confidence in God; and if it shall lead the minds of any to contemplate with a more steady and enlightened faith the scenes which are yet to occur on our earth, when the saints shall reign, or in heaven, when all the children of God shall be gathered there from all lands, the great object of these studies will have been accomplished, and the labour which has been bestowed upon it will not have been in vain. To these high and holy purposes I now consecrate these reflections on the book of Daniel, with an earnest prayer that He, from whom all blessings come, may be pleased so to accept this exposition of one of the portions of his revealed truth, as to make it the means of promoting the interests of truth and piety in the world; with a grateful sense of his goodness in allowing me to complete it, and with thankfulness that I have been permitted for so many hours, in the preparation of this work, to contemplate the lofty integrity, the profound wisdom, the stern and unyielding virtue, and the humble piety of this distinguished saint and eminent statesman of ancient times. He is under a good influence, and he is likely to have his own piety quickened, and his own purposes of unflinching integrity and faithfulness, and of humble devotion to God strengthened, who studies the writings and the character of the prophet Daniel.

APPENDIX

THE books of Maccabees are the titles of certain Jewish histories, containing principally the details of the heroic exploits of the family of that name. The first book contains a lucid and authentic history of the undertakings of Antiochus Epiphanes against the Jews, from the year B.C. 175 to the death of Simon Maccabeus B.C. 135. This history is confessedly of great value. It is on the whole entitled to credit, chronologically accurate, and advantageously distinguished above all other historical productions of this period. It is the second book in order of time. Of the author nothing is known; but he must have been a Palestinian Jew, who wrote some considerable time after the death of Simon Maccabeus, and even of Hyrcanus, and made use of several written, although chiefly of traditionary, sources of information. At the same time, it is not impossible that the author was present at several of the events which he so graphically describes.

The second book of Maccabees is a work of very inferior character to the first. It is an abridgment of a more ancient work, written by a Jew named Jason, who lived at Cyrene in Africa, comprising the principal transactions of the Jews which occurred during the reigns of Seleucus IV., Antiochus Epiphanes, and Antiochus Eupator. It partly goes over the same ground with the first book, but commences ten or twelve years earlier, and embraces in all a period of fifteen years. It does not appear that the author of either saw the other's work. This history supplies some blanks in the first book, but the letters prefixed to it contradict some of the facts recorded in the body of the work, and are not considered genuine. A different account, too, is given of the place and manner of the death of Antiochus Epiphanes from that contained in the first book.—*Kitto Abridged.*

FIRST BOOK OF THE MACCABEES.

CHAP. I.

14 Antiochus gave leave to set up the fashions of the Gentiles in Jerusalem, 22 and spoiled it, and the temple in it, 57 and set up therein the abomination of desolation, 63 and slew those that did circumcise their children.

AND it happened, after that Alexander *son* of Philip, the Macedonian, who came out of the land of Chettiim, had smitten Darius king of the Persians and Medes, that he reigned in his stead, the first over Greece,

2 And made many wars, and won many strong holds, and slew the kings of the earth,

3 And went through to the ends of the earth, and took spoils of many nations, insomuch that the earth was quiet before him; whereupon he was exalted, and his heart was lifted up.

4 And he gathered a mighty strong host, and ruled over countries, and nations, and kings, who became tributaries unto him.

5 And after these things he fell sick, and perceived that he should die.

6 Wherefore he called his servants, such as were honourable, and had been brought up with him from his youth, and parted his kingdom among them, while he was yet alive.

7 So Alexander reigned twelve years, and *then* died.

8 And his servants bare rule every one in his place.

9 And after his death they all put crowns *upon themselves;* so did their sons after them many years: and evils were multiplied in the earth.

10 And there came out of them a wicked root, Antiochus *surnamed* Epiphanes, son of Antiochus the king, who had been an hostage at Rome, and he reigned in the hundred and thirty and seventh year of the kingdom of the Greeks.

11 In those days went there out of Israel wicked men, who persuaded many, saying, Let us go and make a covenant with the heathen that are round about us: for since we departed from them we have had much sorrow.

12 So this device pleased them well.

13 Then certain of the people were so forward herein, that they went to the king, who gave them licence to do after the ordinances of the heathen:

14 Whereupon they built a place of exercise at Jerusalem according to the customs of the heathen:

15 And made themselves uncircumcised, and forsook the holy covenant, and joined themselves to the heathen, and were sold to do mischief.

16 Now when the kingdom was established before Antiochus, he thought to reign over Egypt, that he might have the dominion of two realms.

17 Wherefore he entered into Egypt with a great multitude, with chariots, and elephants, and horsemen, and a great navy,

18 And made war against Ptolemee king of Egypt: but Ptolemee was afraid of him, and fled; and many were wounded to death.

19 Thus they got the strong cities in the land of Egypt, and he took the spoils thereof.

20 And after that Antiochus had smitten Egypt, he returned again in the hundred forty and third year, and went up against Israel and Jerusalem with a great multitude,

21 And entered proudly into the sanctuary, and took away the golden altar, and the candlestick of light, and all the vessels thereof,

22 And the table of the shewbread, and the pouring vessels, and the vials, and the censers of gold, and the veil, and the crowns, and the golden ornaments that were before the temple, all which he pulled off.

23 He took also the silver and the gold, and the precious vessels: also he took the hidden treasures which he found.

24 And when he had taken all away, he went into his own land, having made a great massacre, and spoken very proudly.

25 Therefore there was great mourning in Israel, in every place where they were;

26 So that the princes and elders mourned, the virgins and young men were made feeble, and the beauty of women was changed.

27 Every bridegroom took up lamentation, and she that sat in the marriage chamber was in heaviness.

28 The land also was moved for the inhabitants thereof, and all the house of Jacob was covered with confusion.

29 And after two years fully expired the king sent his chief collector of tribute unto the cities of Judah, who came unto Jerusalem with a great multitude,

30 And spake peaceably words unto them, but *all was* deceit: for when they had given him credence, he fell suddenly upon the city, and smote it very sore, and destroyed much people of Israel.

31 And when he had taken the spoils of the city, he set it on fire, and pulled down the houses and walls thereof on every side.

32 But the women and children took they captive, and possessed the cattle.

33 Then builded they the city of David with a great and strong wall, *and* with mighty towers, and made it a strong hold for them.

34 And they put therein a sinful nation, wicked men, and fortified *themselves* therein.

35 They stored it also with armour and victuals, and when they had gathered together the spoils of Jerusalem, they laid them up there, and so they became a sore snare:

36 For it was a place to lie in wait against the sanctuary, and an evil adversary to Israel.

37 Thus they shed innocent blood on every side of the sanctuary, and defiled it:

38 Insomuch that the inhabitants of Jerusalem fled because of them: whereupon *the city* was made an habitation of strangers, and so came strange to those that were born in her; and her own children left her.

39 Her sanctuary was laid waste like a wilderness, her feasts were turned into mourning, her sabbaths into reproach, her honour into contempt.

40 As had been her glory, so was her dishonour increased, and her excellency was turned into mourning.

41 Moreover king Antiochus wrote to his whole kingdom, that all should be one people,

42 And every one should leave his laws: so all the heathen agreed according to the commandment of the king.

43 Yea, many also of the Israelites consented to his religion, and sacrificed unto idols, and profaned the sabbath.

44 For the king had sent letters by messengers unto Jerusalem and the cities of Judah, that they should follow the strange laws of the land,

45 And forbid burnt-offerings, and sacrifice, and drink-offerings, in the temple; and that they should profane the sabbaths and festival days:

46 And pollute the sanctuary and holy people:

47 Set up altars, and groves, and chapels of idols, and sacrifice swine's flesh, and unclean beasts:

48 That they should also leave their children uncircumcised, and make their souls abominable with all manner of uncleanness and profanation:

49 To the end they might forget the law, and change all the ordinances.

50 And whosoever would not do according to the commandment of the king, he said, he should die.

51 In the selfsame manner wrote he to his whole kingdom, and appointed overseers over all the people, commanding the cities of Judah to sacrifice, city by city.

52 Then many of the people were gathered unto them, to wit, every one that forsook the law; and so they committed evils in the land;

53 And drove the Israelites into secret places, even wheresoever they could flee for succour.

54 Now the fifteenth day of the month Casleu, in the hundred forty and fifth year, they set up the abomination of desolation upon the altar, and builded idol altars throughout the cities of Juda on every side;

55 And burnt incense at the doors of their houses, and in the streets.

56 And when they had rent in pieces the books of the law which they found, they burnt them with fire.

57 And wheresoever was found with any the book of the testament, or if any consented to the law, the king's commandment was, that they should put him to death.

58 Thus did they by their authority unto the Israelites every month, to as many as were found in the cities.

59 Now the five and twentieth day of the month they did sacrifice upon the idol altar, which was upon the altar of God.

60 At which time according to the commandment they put to death certain women,

that had caused their children to be circumcised.

61 And they hanged the infants about their necks, and rifled their houses, and slew them that had circumcised them.

62 Howbeit many in Israel were fully resolved and confirmed in themselves not to eat any unclean thing.

63 Wherefore they chose rather to die, that they might not be defiled with meats, and that they might not profane the holy covenant: so then they died.

64 And there was very great wrath upon Israel.

CHAP. II.

6 Mattathias lamenteth the case of Jerusalem. 24 He slayeth a Jew that did sacrifice to idols in his presence, and the king's messenger also. 34 He and his are assailed upon the sabbath, and make no resistance. 50 He dieth, and instructeth his sons; 66 and maketh their brother Judas Maccabeus general.

IN those days arose Mattathias *the son* of John, *the son* of Simeon, a priest of the sons of Joarib, from Jerusalem, and dwelt in Modin.

2 And he had five sons, Joannan, called Caddis:

3 Simon, called Thassi:

4 Judas, who was called Maccabeus:

5 Eleazar, called Avaran: and Jonathan, whose surname was Apphus.

6 And when he saw the blasphemies that were committed in Judah and Jerusalem,

7 He said, Woe is me! wherefore was I born to see this misery of my people, and of the holy city, and to dwell there, when it was delivered into the hand of the enemy, and the sanctuary into the hand of strangers?

8 Her temple is become as a man without glory.

9 Her glorious vessels are carried away into captivity, her infants are slain in the streets, her young men with the sword of the enemy.

10 What nation hath not had a part in *her* kingdom, and gotten of her spoils?

11 All her ornaments are taken away; of a free woman she is become a bondslave.

12 And, behold, our sanctuary, even our beauty and our glory, is laid waste, and the Gentiles have profaned it.

13 To what end therefore shall we live any longer?

14 Then Mattathias and his sons rent their clothes, and put on sackcloth, and mourned very sore,

15 In the mean while the king's officers, such as compelled the people to revolt, came into the city Modin, to make them sacrifice.

16 And when many of Israel came unto them, Mattathias also and his sons came together.

17 Then answered the king's officers, and said to Mattathias on this wise, Thou art a ruler, and an honourable and great man in this city, and strengthened with sons and brethren :

18 Now therefore come thou first, and fulfil the king's commandment, like as all the heathen have done, yea, and the men of Judah also, and such as remain at Jerusalem: so shalt thou and thy house be in the number of the king's friends, and thou and thy children shall be honoured with silver and gold, and many rewards.

19 Then Mattathias answered and spake with a loud voice, Though all the nations that are under the king's dominion obey him, and fall away every one from the religion of their fathers, and give consent to his commandments :

20 Yet will I and my sons and my brethren walk in the covenant of our fathers.

21 God forbid that we should forsake the law and the ordinances.

22 We will not hearken to the king's words, to go from our religion, either on the right hand, or the left.

23 Now when he had left speaking these words, there came one of the Jews in the sight of all to sacrifice on the altar which was at Modin, according to the king's commandment.

24 Which thing when Mattathias saw, he was inflamed with zeal, and his reins trembled, neither could he forbear to show his anger according to judgment: wherefore he ran, and slew him upon the altar.

25 Also the king's commissioner, who compelled men to sacrifice, he killed at that time, and the altar he pulled down.

26 Thus dealt he zealously for the law of God, like as Phinees did unto Zambri the son of Salom.

27 And Mattathias cried throughout the city with a loud voice, saying, Whosoever is zealous of the law, and maintaineth the covenant, let him follow me.

28 So he and his sons fled into the mountains, and left all that ever they had in the city.

29 Then many that sought after justice and judgment went down into the wilderness, to dwell there :

30 Both they, and their children, and their wives, and their cattle; because afflictions increased sore upon them.

31 Now when it was told the king's servants,

and the host that was at Jerusalem, in the city of David, that certain men, who had broken the king's commandment, were gone down into the secret places in the wilderness,

32 They pursued after them a great number, and having overtaken them, they camped against them, and made war against them on the sabbath day.

33 And they said unto them, Let that which ye have done hitherto suffice; come forth, and do according to the commandment of the king, and ye shall live.

34 But they said, We will not come forth, neither will we do the king's commandment, to profane the sabbath day.

35 So then they gave them the battle with all speed.

36 Howbeit they answered them not, neither cast they a stone at them, nor stopped the places where they lay hid;

37 But said, Let us die all in our innocency: heaven and earth shall testify for us, that ye put us to death wrongfully.

38 So they rose up against them in battle on the sabbath, and they slew them, with their wives and children, and their cattle, to the number of a thousand people.

39 Now when Mattathias and his friends understood hereof, they mourned for them right sore.

40 And one of them said to another, If we all do as our brethren have done, and fight not for our lives and laws against the heathen, they will now quickly root us out of the earth.

41 At that time therefore they decreed, saying, Whosoever shall come to make battle with us on the sabbath day, we will fight against him; neither will we die all, as our brethren that were murdered in the secret places.

42 Then came there unto him a company of Assideans, who were mighty men of Israel, even all such as were voluntarily devoted unto the law.

43 Also all they that fled for persecution joined themselves unto them, and were a stay unto them.

44 So they joined their forces, and smote sinful men in their anger, and wicked men in their wrath : but the rest fled to the heathen for succour.

45 Then Mattathias and his friends went round about, and pulled down the altars :

46 And what children soever they found within the coast of Israel uncircumcised, those they circumcised valiantly.

47 They pursued also after the proud men, and the work prospered in their hand.

48 So they recovered the law out of the hand of the Gentiles, and out of the hand of kings, neither suffered they the sinner to triumph.

49 Now when the time drew near that Mattathias should die, he said unto his sons, Now hath pride and rebuke gotten strength, and the time of destruction, and the wrath of indignation:

50 Now therefore, my sons, be ye zealous for the law, and give your lives for the covenant of your fathers.

51 Call to remembrance what acts our fathers did in their time; so shall ye receive great honour and an everlasting name.

52 Was not Abraham found faithful in temptation, and it was imputed unto him for righteousness?

53 Joseph in the time of his distress kept the commandment, and was made lord of Egypt.

54 Phinees our father in being zealous and fervent obtained the covenant of an everlasting priesthood.

55 Jesus for fulfilling the word was made a judge in Israel.

56 Caleb for bearing witness before the congregation received the heritage of the land.

57 David for being merciful possessed the throne of an everlasting kingdom.

58 Elias for being zealous and fervent for the law was taken up into heaven.

59 Ananias, Azarias, and Misael, by believing were saved out of the flame.

60 Daniel for his innocency was delivered from the mouth of lions.

61 And thus consider ye throughout all ages, that none that put their trust in him shall be overcome.

62 Fear not then the words of a sinful man: for his glory shall be dung and worms.

63 To-day he shall be lifted up, and to-morrow he shall not be found, because he is returned into his dust, and his thought is come to nothing.

64 Wherefore, ye my sons, be valiant, and shew yourselves men in the behalf of the law; for by it shall ye obtain glory.

65 And, behold, I know that your brother Simon is a man of counsel, give ear unto him alway : he shall be a father unto you.

66 As for Judas Maccabeus, he hath been mighty and strong, even from his youth up: let him be your captain, and fight the battle of the people.

67 Take also unto you all those that observe the law, and avenge ye the wrong of your people.

68 Recompense fully the heathen, and take heed to the commandments of the law.

69 So he blessed them, and was gathered to his fathers.

70 And he died in the hundred forty and sixth year, and his sons buried him in the sepulchres of his fathers at Modin, and all Israel made great lamentation for him.

CHAP. III.

1 *The valour and fame of Judas Maccabeus.* 10 *He overthroweth the forces of Samaria and Syria.* 27 *Antiochus sendeth a great power against him.* 44 *He and his fall to fasting and prayer,* 58 *and are encouraged.*

THEN his son Judas, called Maccabeus, rose up in his stead.

2 And all his brethren helped him, and so did all they that held with his father, and they fought with cheerfulness the battle of Israel.

3 So he gat his people great honour, and put on a breastplate as a giant, and girt his warlike harness about him, and he made battles, protecting the host with his sword.

4 In his acts he was like a lion, and like a lion's whelp roaring for his prey.

5 For he pursued the wicked, and sought them out, and burnt up those that vexed his people.

6 Wherefore the wicked shrunk for fear of him, and all the workers of iniquity were troubled, because salvation prospered in his hand.

7 He grieved also many kings, and made Jacob glad with his acts, and his memorial is blessed for ever.

8 Moreover he went through the cities of Juda, destroying the ungodly out of them, and turning away wrath from Israel:

9 So that he was renowned unto the utmost part of the earth, and he received unto him such as were ready to perish.

10 Then Apollonius gathered the Gentiles together, and a great host out of Samaria, to fight against Israel.

11 Which thing when Judas perceived, he went forth to meet him, and so he smote him, and slew him: many also fell down slain, but the rest fled.

12 Wherefore Judas took their spoils, and Apollonius' sword also, and therewith he fought all his life long.

13 Now when Seron, a prince of the army of Syria, heard say that Judas had gathered unto him a multitude and company of the faithful to go out with him to war;

14 He said, I will get me a name and honour in the kingdom ; for I will go fight with Judas and them that are with him, who despise the king's commandment.

15 So he made him ready to go up, and there went with him a mighty host of the ungodly to help him, and to be avenged of the children of Israel.

16 And when he came near to the going up of Bethhoron, Judas went forth to meet him with a small company:

17 Who, when they saw the host coming to meet them, said unto Judas, How shall we be able, being so few, to fight against so great a multitude and so strong, seeing we are ready to faint with fasting all this day?

18 Unto whom Judas answered, It is no hard matter for many to be shut up in the hands of a few; and with *the God of* heaven it is all one, to deliver with a great multitude, or a small company:

19 For the victory of battle standeth not in the multitude of an host; but strength cometh from heaven.

20 They come against us in much pride and iniquity to destroy us, and our wives and children, and to spoil us:

21 But we fight for our lives and our laws.

22 Wherefore the Lord himself will overthrow them before our face: and as for you, be ye not afraid of them.

23 Now as soon as he had left off speaking, he leapt suddenly upon them, and so Seron and his host was overthrown before him.

24 And they pursued them from the going down of Bethhoron unto the plain, where were slain about eight hundred men of them ; and the residue fled into the land of the Philistines.

25 Then began the fear of Judas and his brethren, and an exceeding great dread, to fall upon the nations round about them:

26 Insomuch as his fame came unto the king, and all nations talked of the battles of Judas.

27 Now when king Antiochus heard these things, he was full of indignation: wherefore he sent and gathered together all the forces of his realm, even a very strong army.

28 He opened also his treasure, and gave his soldiers pay for a year, commanding them to be ready whensoever he should need them.

29 Nevertheless, when he saw that the money of his treasures failed, and that the tributes in the country were small, because of the dissension and plague, which he had brought upon the land in taking away the laws which had been of old time;

30 He feared that he should not be able to bear the charges any longer, nor to have such gifts to give so liberally as he did before: for he had abounded above the kings that were before him.

31 Wherefore, being greatly perplexed in his mind, he determined to go into Persia, there to take the tributes of the countries, and to gather much money.

32 So he left Lysias, a nobleman, and one of the blood royal, to oversee the affairs of the king from the river Euphrates unto the borders of Egypt:

33 And to bring up his son Antiochus, until he came again.

34 Moreover he delivered unto him the half of his forces, and the elephants, and gave him charge of all things that he would have done, as also concerning them that dwelt in Juda and Jerusalem:

35 *To wit,* that he should send an army against them, to destroy and root out the strength of Israel, and the remnant of Jerusalem, and to take away their memorial from that place;

36 And that he should place strangers in all their quarters, and divide their land by lot.

37 So the king took the half of the forces that remained, and departed from Antioch, his royal city, the hundred forty and seventh year; and having passed the river Euphrates, he went through the high countries.

38 Then Lysias chose Ptolemee the *son* of Dorymenes, and Nicanor, and Gorgias, mighty men of the king's friends:

39 And with them he sent forty thousand footmen, and seven thousand horsemen, to go into the land of Juda, and to destroy it, as the king commanded.

40 So they went forth with all their power, and came and pitched by Emmaus in the plain country.

41 And the merchants of the country, hearing the fame of them, took silver and gold very much, with servants, and came into the camp to buy the children of Israel for slaves: a power also of Syria and of the land of the Philistines joined themselves unto them.

42 Now when Judas and his brethren saw that miseries were multiplied, and that the forces did encamp themselves in their borders; for they knew how the king had given commandment to destroy the people, and utterly abolish them;

43 They said one to another, Let us restore the decayed estate of our people, and let us fight for our people and the sanctuary.

44 Then was the congregation gathered together, that they might be ready for battle, and that they might pray, and ask mercy and compassion.

45 Now Jerusalem lay void as a wilderness, there was none of her children that went in or

out: the sanctuary also was trodden down, and aliens kept the strong hold; the heathen had their habitation in that place; and joy was taken from Jacob, and the pipe with the harp ceased.

46 Wherefore the Israelites assembled themselves together, and came to Maspha, over against Jerusalem; for in Maspha was the place where they prayed aforetime in Israel.

47 Then they fasted that day, and put on sackcloth, and cast ashes upon their heads, and rent their clothes,

48 And laid open the book of the law, wherein the heathen had sought to paint the likeness of their images.

49 They brought also the priests' garments, and the firstfruits, and the tithes: and the Nazarites they stirred up, who had accomplished their days.

50 Then cried they with a loud voice toward heaven, saying, What shall we do with these, and whither shall we carry them away?

51 For thy sanctuary is trodden down and profaned, and thy priests are in heaviness, and brought low.

52 And, lo, the heathen are assembled together against us to destroy us: what things they imagine against us, thou knowest.

53 How shall we be able to stand against them, except thou, O God, be our help?

54 Then sounded they with trumpets, and cried with a loud voice.

55 And after this Judas ordained captains over the people, *even* captains over thousands, and over hundreds, and over fifties, and over tens.

56 But as for such as were building houses, or had betrothed wives, or were planting vineyards, or were fearful, those he commanded that they should return, every man to his own house, according to the law.

57 So the camp removed, and pitched upon the south side of Emmaus.

58 And Judas said, Arm yourselves, and be valiant men, and see that ye be in readiness against the morning, that ye may fight with these nations, that are assembled together against us to destroy us and our sanctuary:

59 For it is better for us to die in battle, than to behold the calamities of our people and our sanctuary.

60 Nevertheless, as the will *of God* is in heaven, so let him do.

CHAP. IV.

6 *Judas defeateth the plot,* 14 *and forces of Gorgias,* 23 *and spoileth their tents,* 34 *and overthroweth Lysias.* 45 *He pulleth down*

the altar which the heathen had profaned, and setteth up a new: 60 *and maketh a wall about Sion.*

THEN took Gorgias five thousand footmen, and a thousand of the best horsemen and removed out of the camp by night;

2 To the end he might rush in upon the camp of the Jews, and smite them suddenly. And the men of the fortress were his guides.

3 Now when Judas heard thereof, he himself removed, and the valiant men with him, that he might smite the king's army which was at Emmaus,

4 While as yet the forces were dispersed from the camp.

5 In the mean season came Gorgias by night into the camp of Judas: and when he found no man there, he sought them in the mountains: for said he, These fellows flee from us.

6 But as soon as it was day, Judas shewed himself in the plain with three thousand men, who nevertheless had neither armour nor swords to their minds.

7 And they saw the camp of the heathen, that it was strong and well harnessed, and compassed round about with horsemen; and these were expert of war.

8 Then said Judas to the men that were with him, Fear ye not their multitude, neither be ye afraid of their assault.

9 Remember how our fathers were delivered in the Red sea, when Pharaoh pursued them with an army.

10 Now therefore let us cry unto heaven, if peradventure the Lord will have mercy upon us, and remember the covenant of our fathers, and destroy this host before our face this day:

11 That so all the heathen may know that there is one who delivereth and saveth Israel.

12 Then the strangers lifted up their eyes, and saw them coming over against them.

13 Wherefore they went out of the camp to battle; but they that were with Judas sounded their trumpets.

14 So they joined battle, and the heathen being discomfited fled into the plain.

15 Howbeit all the hindmost of them were slain with the sword: for they pursued them unto Gazera, and unto the plains of Idumea, and Azotus, and Jamnia, so that there were slain of them upon a three thousand men.

16 This done, Judas returned again with his host from pursuing them,

17 And said to the people, Be not greedy of the spoils, inasmuch as there is a battle before us,

18 And Gorgias and his host are here by us

in the mountain: but stand ye now against our enemies, and overcome them, and after this ye may boldly take the spoils.

19 As Judas was yet speaking these words, there appeared a part of them looking out of the mountain:

20 Who when they perceived that the Jews had put their host to flight, and were burning the tents; for the smoke that was seen declared what was done:

21 When therefore they perceived these things, they were sore afraid, and seeing also the host of Judas in the plain ready to fight,

22 They fled every one into the land of strangers.

23 Then Judas returned to spoil the tents, where they got much gold, and silver, and blue silk, and purple of the sea, and great riches.

24 After this they went home, and sung a song of thanksgiving, and praised the Lord in heaven: because it is good, because his mercy *endureth* for ever.

25 Thus Israel had a great deliverance that day.

26 Now all the strangers that had escaped came and told Lysias what had happened:

27 Who, when he heard thereof, was confounded and discouraged, because neither such things as he would were done unto Israel, nor such things as the king commanded him were come to pass.

28 The next year therefore following Lysias gathered together threescore thousand choice men *of foot*, and five thousand horsemen, that he might subdue them.

29 So they came into Idumea, and pitched their tents at Bethsura, and Judas met them with ten thousand men.

30 And when he saw that mighty army, he prayed and said, Blessed art thou, O Saviour of Israel, who didst quell the violence of the mighty man by the hand of thy servant David, and gavest the host of strangers into the hands of Jonathan the son of Saul, and his armour-bearer;

31 Shut up this army in the hand of thy people Israel, and let them be confounded in their power and horsemen:

32 Make them to be of no courage, and cause the boldness of their strength to fall away, and let them quake at their destruction:

33 Cast them down with the sword of them that love thee, and let all those that know thy name praise thee with thanksgiving.

34 So they joined battle; and there were slain of the host of Lysias about five thousand men, even before them were they slain.

35 Now when Lysias saw his army put to flight, and the manliness of Judas' soldiers, and how they were ready either to live or die valiantly, he went into Antiochia, and gathered together a company of strangers, and having made his army greater than it was, he purposed to come again into Judea.

36 Then said Judas and his brethren, Behold, our enemies are discomfited: let us go up to cleanse and dedicate the sanctuary.

37 Upon this all the host assembled themselves together, and went up into mount Sion.

38 And when they saw the sanctuary desolate, and the altar profaned, and the gates burned up, and shrubs growing in the courts as in a forest, or in one of the mountains, yea, and the priests' chambers pulled down;

39 They rent their clothes, and made great lamentation, and cast ashes upon their heads,

40 And fell down flat to the ground upon their faces, and blew an alarm with the trumpets, and cried toward heaven.

41 Then Judas appointed certain men to fight against those that were in the fortress, until he had cleansed the sanctuary.

42 So he chose priests of blameless conversation, such as had pleasure in the law:

43 Who cleansed the sanctuary, and bare out the defiled stones into an unclean place.

44 And when as they consulted what to do with the altar of burnt-offerings, which was profaned;

45 They thought it best to pull it down, lest it should be a reproach to them, because the heathen had defiled it: wherefore they pulled it down,

46 And laid up the stones in the mountain of the temple in a convenient place, until there should come a prophet to shew what should be done with them.

47 Then they took whole stones according to the law, and built a new altar according to the former;

48 And made up the sanctuary, and the things that were within the temple, and hallowed the courts.

49 They made also new holy vessels, and into the temple they brought the candlestick, and the altar of burnt-offerings, and of incense, and the table.

50 And upon the altar they burned incense, and the lamps that were upon the candlestick they lighted, that they might give light in the temple.

51 Furthermore they set the loaves upon the table, and spread out the veils, and finished all the works which they had begun to make.

52 Now on the five and twentieth day of the ninth month, which *is called* the month Casleu,

in the hundred forty and eighth year, they rose up betimes in the morning,

53 And offered sacrifice according to the law upon the new altar of burnt-offerings, which they had made.

54 Look, at what time and what day the heathen had profaned it, even in that was it dedicated with songs, and citherns, and harps, and cymbals.

55 Then all the people fell upon their faces, worshipping and praising the God of heaven, who had given them good success.

56 And so they kept the dedication of the altar eight days, and offered burnt-offerings with gladness, and sacrificed the sacrifice of deliverance and praise.

57 They decked also the forefront of the temple with crowns of gold, and with shields; and the gates and the chambers they renewed, and hanged doors upon them.

58 Thus was there very great gladness among the people, for that the reproach of the heathen was put away.

59 Moreover Judas and his brethren with the whole congregation of Israel ordained, that the days of the dedication of the altar should be kept in their season from year to year by the space of eight days, from the five and twentieth day of the month Casleu, with mirth and gladness.

60 At that time also they builded up the mount Sion with high walls and strong towers round about, lest the Gentiles should come and tread it down, as they had done before.

61 And they set there a garrison to keep it, and fortified Bethsura to preserve it; that the people might have a defence against Idumea.

CHAP. V.

3 *Judas smiteth the children of Esau, Bean, and Ammon.* 17 *Simon is sent into Galilee.* 25 *The exploits of Judas in Galaad.* 51 *He destroyeth Ephron, for denying him to pass through it.* 56 *Divers, that in Judas' absence would fight with their enemies, are slain.*

NOW when the nations round about heard that the altar was built, and the sanctuary renewed as before, it displeased them very much.

2 Wherefore they thought to destroy the generation of Jacob that was among them, and thereupon they began to slay and destroy the people.

3 Then Judas fought against the children of Esau in Idumea at Arabattine, because they besieged Israel: and he gave them a great over-throw, and abated their courage, and took their spoils.

4 Also he remembered the injury of the children of Bean, who had been a snare and an offence unto the people, in that they lay in wait for them in the ways.

5 He shut them up therefore in the towers, and encamped against them, and destroyed them utterly, and burned the towers of that *place* with fire, and all that were therein.

6 Afterward he passed over to the children of Ammon, where he found a mighty power, and much people, with Timotheus their captain.

7 So he fought many battles with them, till at length they were discomfited before him; and he smote them.

8 And when he had taken Jazar, with the towns belonging thereto, he returned into Judea.

9 Then the heathen that were at Galaad assembled themselves together against the Israelites that were in their quarters, to destroy them; but they fled to the fortress of Dathema,

10 And sent letters unto Judas and his brethren, The heathen that are round about us are assembled together against us to destroy us:

11 And they are preparing to come and take the fortress whereunto we are fled, Timotheus being captain of their host.

12 Come now therefore, and deliver us from their hands, for many of us are slain:

13 Yea, all our brethren that were in the places of Tobie are put to death: their wives and their children also they have carried away captives, and borne away their stuff; and they have destroyed there about a thousand men.

14 While these letters were yet reading, behold, there came other messengers from Galilee with their clothes rent, who reported on this wise,

15 And said, They of Ptolemais, and of Tyrus, and Sidon, and all Galilee of the Gentiles, are assembled together against us to consume us.

16 Now when Judas and the people heard these words, there assembled a great congregation together, to consult what they should do for their brethren, that were in trouble, and assaulted of them.

17 Then said Judas unto Simon his brother, Choose thee out men, and go and deliver thy brethren that are in Galilee, for I and Jonathan my brother will go into the country of Galaad.

18 So he left Joseph the *son* of Zacharias, and Azarias, captains of the people, with the remnant of the host in Judea to keep it.

19 Unto whom he gave commandment, saying, Take ye the charge of this people, and see that ye make not war against the heathen until the time that we come again.

20 Now unto Simon were given three thousand men to go into Galilee, and unto Judas eight thousand men for the country of Galaad.

21 Then went Simon into Galilee, where he fought many battles with the heathen, so that the heathen were discomfited by him.

22 And he pursued them unto the gate of Ptolemais; and there were slain of the heathen about three thousand men, whose spoils he took.

23 And those that were in Galilee, and in Arbattis, with their wives and their children, and all that they had, took he away *with him*, and brought them into Judea with great joy.

24 Judas Maccabeus also and his brother Jonathan went over Jordan, and travelled three days' journey in the wilderness,

25 Where they met with the Nabathites, who came unto them in a peaceable manner, and told them every thing that had happened to their brethren in the land of Galaad:

26 And how that many of them were shut up in Bosora, and Bosor, and Alema, Casphor, Maked, and Carnaim; all these cities are strong and great:

27 And that they were shut up in the rest of the cities of the country of Galaad, and that against to-morrow they had appointed to bring their host against the forts, and to take them, and to destroy them all in one day.

28 Hereupon Judas and his host turned suddenly by the way of the wilderness unto Bosora; and when he had won the city, he slew all the males with the edge of the sword, and took all their spoils, and burned the city with fire.

29 From whence he removed by night, and went till he came to the fortress.

30 And betimes in the morning they looked up, and, behold, there was an innumerable people bearing ladders and other engines of war, to take the fortress: for they assaulted them.

31 When Judas therefore saw that the battle was begun, and that the cry of the city went up to heaven, with trumpets, and a great sound,

32 He said unto his host, Fight this day for your brethren.

33 So he went forth behind them in three companies, who sounded their trumpets, and cried with prayer.

34 Then the host of Timotheus, knowing that it was Maccabeus, fled from him: wherefore he smote them with a great slaughter; so that there were killed of them that day about eight thousand men.

35 This done, Judas turned aside to Maspha; and after he had assaulted it, he took it, and slew all the males therein, and received the spoils thereof, and burnt it with fire.

36 From thence went he, and took Casphon, Magad, Bosor, and the other cities of the country of Galaad.

37 After these things gathered Timotheus another host, and encamped against Raphon beyond the brook.

38 So Judas sent *men* to espy the host, who brought him word, saying, All the heathen that be round about us are assembled unto them, even a very great host.

39 He hath also hired the Arabians to help them, and they have pitched their tents beyond the brook, ready to come and fight against thee. Upon this Judas went to meet them.

40 Then Timotheus said unto the captains of his host, When Judas and his host come near the brook, if he pass over first unto us, we shall not be able to withstand him; for he will mightily prevail against us:

41 But if he be afraid, and camp beyond the river, we shall go over unto him, and prevail against him.

42 Now when Judas came near the brook, he caused the scribes of the people to remain by the brook: unto whom he gave commandment, saying, Suffer no man to remain in the camp, but let all come to the battle.

43 So he went first over unto them, and all the people after him: then all the heathen, being discomfited before him, cast away their weapons, and fled unto the temple that was at Carnaim.

44 But they took the city, and burned the temple with all that were therein. Thus was Carnaim subdued, neither could they stand any longer before Judas.

45 Then Judas gathered together all the Israelites that were in the country of Galaad, from the least unto the greatest, even their wives, and their children, and their stuff, a very great host, to the end they might come into the land of Judea.

46 Now when they came unto Ephron, (this was a great city in the way as they should go, very well fortified) they could not turn from it, either on the right hand or the left, but must needs pass through the midst of it.

47 Then they of the city shut them out, and stopped up the gates with stones.

48 Whereupon Judas sent unto them in peaceable manner, saying, Let us pass through your land to go into our own country, and none

shall do you any hurt; we will only pass through on foot: howbeit they would not open unto him.

49 Wherefore Judas commanded a proclamation to be made throughout the host, that every man should pitch his tent in the place where he was.

50 So the soldiers pitched, and assaulted the city all that day and all that night, till at the length the city was delivered into his hands:

51 Who then slew all the males with the edge of the sword, and rased the city, and took the spoils thereof, and passed through the city over them that were slain.

52 After this went they over Jordan into the great plain before Bethsan.

53 And Judas gathered together those that came behind, and exhorted the people all the way through, till they came into the land of Judea.

54 So they went up to mount Sion with joy and gladness, where they offered burnt-offerings, because not one of them were slain until they had returned in peace.

55 Now what time as Judas and Jonathan were in the land of Galaad, and Simon his brother in Galilee before Ptolemais,

56 Joseph the *son* of Zacharias, and Azarias, captains of the garrisons, heard of the valiant acts and warlike deeds which they had done.

57 Wherefore they said, Let us also get us a name, and go fight against the heathen that are round about us.

58 So when they had given charge unto the garrison that was with them, they went toward Jamnia.

59 Then came Gorgias and his men out of the city to fight against them.

60 And so it was, that Joseph and Azarias were put to flight, and pursued unto the borders of Judea: and there were slain that day of the people of Israel about two thousand men.

61 Thus was there a great overthrow among the children of Israel, because they were not obedient unto Judas and his brethren, but thought to do some valiant act.

62 Moreover these men came not of the seed of those, by whose hand deliverance was given unto Israel.

63 Howbeit the man Judas and his brethren were greatly renowned in the sight of all Israel, and of all the heathen, wheresoever their name was heard of;

64 Insomuch as the people assembled unto them with joyful acclamations.

65 Afterward went Judas forth with his brethren, and fought against the children of Esau in the land toward the south, where he

smote Hebron, and the towns thereof, and pulled down the fortress of it, and burned the towers thereof round about.

66 From thence he removed to go into the land of the Philistines, and passed through Samaria.

67 At that time certain priests, desirous to shew their valour, were slain in battle, for that they went out to fight unadvisedly.

68 So Judas turned to Azotus in the land of the Philistines, and when he had pulled down their altars, and burned their carved images with fire, and spoiled their cities, he returned into the land of Judea.

CHAP. VI.

8 *Antiochus dieth,* 12 *and confesseth that he is plagued for the wrong done to Jerusalem.* 20 *Judas besiegeth those in the tower at Jerusalem.* 28 *They procure Antiochus the younger to come into Judea.* 51 *He besiegeth Sion,* 60 *and maketh peace with Israel ;* 62 *yet overthroweth the wall of Sion.*

ABOUT that time king Antiochus travelling through the high countries heard say, that Elymais in the country of Persia was a city greatly renowned for riches, silver, and gold;

2 And that there was in it a very rich temple, wherein were coverings of gold, and breastplates, and shields, which Alexander, *son* of Philip, the Macedonian king, who reigned first among the Grecians, had left there.

3 Wherefore he came and sought to take the city, and to spoil it ; but he was not able, because they of the city, having had warning thereof,

4 Rose up against him in battle : so he fled, and departed thence with great heaviness, and returned to Babylon.

5 Moreover there came one who brought him tidings into Persia, that the armies, which went against the land of Judea, were put to flight:

6 And that Lysias, who went forth first with a great power, was driven away of the Jews ; and that they were made strong by the armour, and power, and store of spoils, which they had gotten of the armies, whom they had destroyed :

7 Also that they had pulled down the abomination, which he had set up upon the altar in Jerusalem, and that they had compassed about the sanctuary with high walls, as before, and his city Bethsura.

8 Now when the king heard these words, he was astonished and sore moved : whereupon he laid him down upon his bed, and fell sick for grief, because it had not befallen him as he looked for.

9 And there he continued many days : for

his grief was ever more and more, and he made account that he should die.

10 Wherefore he called for all his friends, and said unto them, The sleep is gone from mine eyes, and my heart faileth for very care.

11 And I thought with myself, Into what tribulation am I come, and how great a flood *of misery* is it, wherein now I am! for I was bountiful and beloved in my power.

12 But now I remember the evils that I did at Jerusalem, and that I took all the vessels of gold and silver that were therein, and sent to destroy the inhabitants of Judea without a cause.

13 I perceive therefore that for this cause these troubles are come upon me, and, behold, I perish through great grief in a strange land.

14 Then called he for Philip, one of his friends, whom he made ruler over all his realm,

15 And gave him the crown, and his robe, and his signet, to the end he should bring up his son Antiochus, and nourish him up for the kingdom.

16 So king Antiochus died there in the hundred forty and ninth year.

17 Now when Lysias knew that the king was dead, he set up Antiochus his son, whom he had brought up being young, to reign in his stead, and his name he called Eupator.

18 About this time they that were in the tower shut up the Israelites round about the sanctuary, and sought always their hurt, and the strengthening of the heathen.

19 Wherefore Judas, purposing to destroy them, called all the people together to besiege them.

20 So they came together, and besieged them in the hundred and fiftieth year, and he made mounts for shot against them, and *other* engines.

21 Howbeit certain of them that were besieged got forth, unto whom some ungodly men of Israel joined themselves:

22 And they went unto the king, and said, How long will it be ere thou execute judgment, and avenge our brethren?

23 We have been willing to serve thy father, and to do as he would have us, and to obey his commandments;

24 For which cause they of our nation besiege the tower, and are alienated from us: moreover as many of us as they could light on they slew, and spoiled our inheritance.

25 Neither have they stretched out their hand against us only, but also against all their borders.

26 And, behold, this day are they besieging the tower at Jerusalem, to take it: the sanctuary also and Bethsura have they fortified.

27 Wherefore if thou dost not prevent them quickly, they will do greater things than these, neither shalt thou be able to rule them.

28 Now when the king heard this, he was angry, and gathered together all his friends, and the captains of his army, and those that had charge of the horse.

29 There came also unto him from other kingdoms, and from isles of the sea, bands of hired soldiers.

30 So that the number of his army was an hundred thousand footmen, and twenty thousand horsemen, and two and thirty elephants exercised in battle.

31 These went through Idumea, and pitched against Bethsura, which they assaulted many days, making engines of war; but they *of Bethsura* came out, and burned them with fire, and fought valiantly.

32 Upon this Judas removed from the tower, and pitched in Bathzacharias, over against the king's camp.

33 Then the king rising very early marched fiercely with his host toward Bathzacharias, where his armies made them ready to battle, and sounded the trumpets.

34 And to the end they might provoke the elephants to fight, they showed them the blood of grapes and mulberries.

35 Moreover they divided the beasts among the armies, and for every elephant they appointed a thousand men, armed with coats of mail, and with helmets of brass on their heads; and beside this, for every beast were ordained five hundred horsemen of the best.

36 These were ready at every occasion: wheresoever the beast was, and whithersoever the beast went, they went also, neither departed they from him.

37 And upon the beasts were there strong towers of wood, which covered every one of them, and were girt fast unto them with devices: there were also upon every one two and thirty strong men, that fought upon them, beside the Indian that ruled him.

38 As for the remnant of the horsemen, they set them on this side and that side at the two parts of the host, giving them signs what to do, and being harnessed all over amidst the ranks.

39 Now when the sun shone upon the shields of gold and brass, the mountains glistered therewith, and shined like lamps of fire.

40 So part of the king's army being spread upon the high mountains, and part on the valleys below, they marched on safely and in order.

41 Wherefore all that heard the noise of their multitude, and the marching of the company,

and the rattling of the harness, were moved: for the army was **very** great and mighty.

42 Then Judas **and** his host drew near, and entered into battle, and there were slain of the king's army six hundred men.

43 ¶ Eleazar also, *surnamed* Savaran, perceiving that one of the beasts, armed with royal harness, was higher than all the rest, and supposing that the king was upon him,

44 Put himself in jeopardy, to the end he might deliver his people, and get him a perpetual name:

45 Wherefore he ran upon him courageously through the midst of the battle, slaying on the right hand and on the left, so that they were divided from him on both sides.

46 Which done, he crept under the elephant, and thrust him under, and slew him: whereupon the elephant fell down upon him, and there he died.

47 Howbeit *the rest of the Jews* seeing the strength of the king, and the violence of his forces, turned away from them.

48 ¶ Then the king's army went up to Jerusalem to meet them, and the king pitched his tents against Judea, and against mount Sion.

49 But with them that were in Bethsura he made peace: for they came out of the city, because they had no victuals there to endure the siege, it being a year of rest to the land.

50 So the king took Bethsura, and set a garrison there to keep it.

51 As for the sanctuary, he besieged it many days: and set there artillery with engines and instruments to cast fire and stones, and pieces to cast darts and slings.

52 Whereupon they also made engines against their engines, and held them battle a long season.

53 Yet at the last, their vessels being without victuals, (for that it was the seventh year, and they in Judea, that were delivered from the Gentiles, had eaten up the residue of the store;)

54 There were but a few left in the sanctuary, because the famine did so prevail against them, that they were fain to disperse themselves, every man to his own place.

55 At that time Lysias heard say, that Philip, whom Antiochus the king, whiles he lived, had appointed to bring up his son Antiochus, that he might be king,

56 Was returned out of Persia and Media, and the king's host also that went with him, and that he sought to take unto him the ruling of the affairs.

57 Wherefore he went in all haste, and said to the king and the captains of the host and the company, We decay daily, and our victuals are but small, and the place we lay siege unto is strong, and the affairs of the kingdom lie upon us;

58 Now therefore let us be friends with these men, and make peace with them, and with all their nation;

59 And covenant with them, that they shall live after their laws, as they did before: for they are therefore displeased, and have done all these things, because we abolished their laws.

60 So the king and the princes were content: wherefore he sent unto them to make peace; and they accepted thereof.

61 Also the king and the princes made an oath unto them: whereupon they went out of the strong hold.

62 Then the king entered into mount Sion; but when he saw the strength of the place, he brake his oath that he had made, and gave commandment to pull down the wall round about.

63 Afterward departed he in all haste, and returned unto Antiochia, where he found Philip to be master of the city: so he fought against him, and took the city by force.

SECOND BOOK OF THE MACCABEES.

CHAP. I.

1 *A letter of the Jews from Jerusalem to them of Egypt, to thank God for the death of Antiochus.* 19 *Of the fire that was hid in the pit.* 24 *The prayer of Neemias.*

THE brethren, the Jews that be at Jerusalem and in the land of Judea, wish unto the brethren, the Jews that are throughout Egypt, health and peace:

2 God be gracious unto you, and remember his covenant that he made with Abraham, Isaac, and Jacob, his faithful servants;

3 And give you all an heart to serve him, and to do his will, with a good courage and a willing mind;

4 And open your hearts in his law and commandments, and send you peace,

5 And hear your prayers, and be at one with you, and never forsake you in time of trouble.

6 And now we be here praying for you.

7 What time as Demetrius reigned, in the hundred threescore and ninth year, we the Jews wrote unto you in the extremity of trouble that came upon us in those years, from the time that Jason and his company revolted from the holy land and kingdom,

8 And burned the porch, and shed innocent blood: then we prayed unto the Lord, and were heard; we offered also sacrifices and fine flour, and lighted the lamps, and set forth the loaves.

9 And now see that ye keep the feast of tabernacles in the month Casleu.

10 In the hundred fourscore and eighth year, the people that were at Jerusalem and in Judea, and the council, and Judas, sent greeting and health unto Aristobulus, king Ptolemeus' master, who was of the stock of the anointed priests, and to the Jews that were in Egypt:

11 Insomuch as God hath delivered us from great perils, we thank him highly, as having been in battle against a king.

12 For he cast them out that fought within the holy city.

13 For when the leader was come into Persia, and the army with him that seemed invincible, they were slain in the temple of Nanea by the deceit of Nanea's priests.

14 For Antiochus, as though he would marry her, came into the place, and his friends that were with him, to receive money in name of a dowry.

15 Which when the priests of Nanea had set forth, and he was entered with a small company into the compass of the temple, they shut the temple as soon as Antiochus was come in:

16 And opening a privy door of the roof, they threw stones like thunderbolts, and struck down the captain, hewed them in pieces, smote off their heads, and cast them to those that were without.

17 Blessed be our God in all things, who hath delivered up the ungodly.

18 Therefore whereas we are now purposed to keep the purification of the temple upon the five and twentieth day of *the month* Casleu, we thought it necessary to certify you thereof, that ye also might keep *it, as the feast* of the tabernacles, and of the fire, *which was given us* when Neemias offered sacrifice, after that he had builded the temple and the altar.

19 For when our fathers were led into Persia, the priests that were then devout took the fire of the altar privily, and hid it in an hollow place of a pit without water, where they kept *it* sure, so that the place was unknown to all men.

20 Now after many years, when it pleased God, Neemias, being sent from the king of Persia, did send of the posterity of those priests that had hid it to the fire: but when they told us they found no fire, but thick water;

21 Then commanded he them to draw it up, and to bring it; and when the sacrifices were laid on, Neemias commanded the priests to sprinkle the wood and the things laid thereupon with the water.

22 When this was done, and the time came that the sun shone, which afore was hid in the cloud, there was a great fire kindled, so that every man marvelled.

23 And the priests made a prayer whilst the sacrifice was consuming, *I say,* both the priests, and all *the rest,* Jonathan beginning, and the rest answering thereunto, as Neemias did.

24 And the prayer was after this manner; O Lord, Lord God, Creator of all things, who art fearful and strong, and righteous, and merciful, and the only and gracious King,

25 The only giver of all things, the only just, almighty, and everlasting, thou that deliverest Israel from all trouble, and didst choose the fathers, and sanctify them:

26 Receive the sacrifice for thy whole people Israel, and preserve thine own portion, and sanctify it.

27 Gather those together that are scattered from us, deliver them that serve among the heathen, look upon them that are despised and abhorred, and let the heathen know that thou art our God.

28 Punish them that oppress us, and with pride do us wrong.

29 Plant thy people again in thy holy place, as Moses hath spoken.

30 And the priests sung psalms of thanksgiving.

31 Now when the sacrifice was consumed. Neemias commanded the water that was left to be poured on the great stones.

32 When this was done, there was kindled a flame: but it was consumed by the light that shined from the altar.

33 So when this matter was known, it was told the king of Persia, that in the place, where the priests that were led away had hid the fire, there appeared water, and that Neemias had purified the sacrifices therewith.

34 Then the king, inclosing the place, made it holy, after he had tried the matter.

35 And the king took many gifts, and bestowed thereof on those whom he would gratify.

36 And Neemias called this thing Naphthar, which is as much as to say, a cleansing: but many men call it Nephi.

CHAP. II.

1 *What Jeremy the prophet did.* 5 *How he hid the tabernacle, the ark, and the altar.* 15 *What Neemias and Judas wrote.* 20 *What Jason wrote in five books:* 25 *and how those were abridged by the author of this book.*

IT is also found in the records, that Jeremy the prophet commanded them that were carried away to take of the fire, as it hath been signified:

2 And how that the prophet, having given them the law, charged them not to forget the commandments of the Lord, and that they should not err in their minds, when they see images of silver and gold, with their ornaments.

3 And with other such speeches exhorted he them, that the law should not depart from their hearts.

4 It was also contained in the same writing, that the prophet, being warned of God, commanded the tabernacle and the ark to go with him, as he went forth into the mountain, where Moses climbed up, and saw the heritage of God.

5 And when Jeremy came thither, he found an hollow cave, wherein he laid the tabernacle, and the ark, and the altar of incense, and so stopped the door.

6 And some of those that followed him came to mark the way, but they could not find it.

7 Which when Jeremy perceived, he blamed them, saying, As for that place, it shall be unknown until the time that God gather his people again together, and receive them unto mercy.

8 Then shall the Lord shew them these things, and the glory of the Lord shall appear, and the cloud also, as it was shewed under Moses, and as when Solomon desired that the place might be honourably sanctified.

9 It was also declared, that he being wise offered the sacrifice of dedication, and of the finishing of the temple.

10 And as when Moses prayed unto the Lord, the fire came down from heaven, and consumed the sacrifices; even so prayed Solomon also, and the fire came down from heaven, and consumed the burnt-offerings.

11 And Moses said, Because the sin-offering was not to be eaten, it was consumed.

12 So Solomon kept those eight days.

13 The same things also were reported in the writings and commentaries of Neemias; and how he founding a library gathered together the acts of the kings, and the prophets, and of David, and the epistles of the kings concerning the holy gifts.

14 In like manner also Judas gathered together all those things that were lost by reason of the war we had, and they remain with us.

15 Wherefore if ye have need thereof, send some to fetch them unto you.

16 Whereas we then are about to celebrate the purification, we have written unto you, and ye shall do well, if ye keep the same days.

17 We hope also, that the God, that delivered all his people, and gave them all an heritage, and the kingdom, and the priesthood, and the sanctuary,

18 As he promised in the law, will shortly have mercy upon us, and gather us together out of every land under heaven into the holy place: for he hath delivered us out of great troubles, and hath purified the place.

19 Now as concerning Judas Maccabeus, and his brethren, and the purification of the great temple, and the dedication of the altar,

20 And the wars against Antiochus Epiphanes, and Eupator his son,

21 And the manifest signs that came from heaven unto those that behaved themselves manfully to their honour for Judaism: so that, being but a few, they overcame the whole country, and chased barbarous multitudes,

22 And recovered again the temple renowned all the world over, and freed the city, and up-

held the laws which were going down, the Lord being gracious unto them with all favour:

23 *All these things, I say,* being declared by Jason of Cyrene in five books, we will assay to abridge in one volume.

24 For considering the infinite number, and the difficulty which they find that desire to look into the narrations of the story, for the variety of the matter,

25 We have been careful, that they that will read may have delight, and that they that are desirous to commit to memory might have ease, and that all into whose hands it comes might have profit.

26 Therefore to us, that have taken upon us this painful labour of abridging, it was not easy, but a matter of sweat and watching;

27 Even as it is no ease unto him that prepareth a banquet, and seeketh the benefit of others: yet for the pleasuring of many we will undertake gladly this great pains;

28 Leaving to the author the exact handling of every particular, and labouring to follow the rules of an abridgement.

29 For as the master builder of a new house must care for the whole building; but he that undertaketh to set it out, and paint it, must seek out fit things for the adorning thereof: even so I think it is with us.

30 To stand upon every point, and go over things at large, and to be curious in particulars, belongeth to the first author of the story:

31 But to use brevity, and avoid much labouring of the work, is to be granted to him that will make an abridgement.

32 Here then will we begin the story: only adding thus much to that which hath been said, that it is a foolish thing to make a long prologue, and to be short in the story itself.

CHAP. III.

1 *Of the honour done to the temple by the kings of the Gentiles.* 4 *Simon uttereth what treasures are in the temple.* 7 *Heliodorus is sent to take them away.* 24 *He is stricken of God, and healed at the prayer of Onias.*

NOW when the holy city was inhabited with all peace, and the laws were kept very well, because of the godliness of Onias the high priest, and his hatred of wickedness,

2 It came to pass that even the kings themselves did honour the place, and magnify the temple with their best gifts;

3 Insomuch that Seleucus king of Asia of his own revenues bare all the costs belonging to the service of the sacrifices.

4 But one Simon of the tribe of Benjamin, who was made governor of the temple, fell out with the high priest about disorder in the city.

5 And when he could not overcome Onias, he gat him to Apollonius *the son* of Thraseas, who then was governor of Celosyria and Phenice,

6 And told him that the treasury in Jerusalem was full of infinite sums of money, so that the multitude of their riches, which did not pertain to the account of the sacrifices, was innumerable, and that it was possible to bring all into the king's hand.

7 Now when Apollonius came to the king, and had showed him of the money whereof he was told, the king chose out Heliodorus his treasurer, and sent him with a commandment to bring him the foresaid money.

8 So forthwith Heliodorus took his journey, under a colour of visiting the cities of Celosyria and Phenice, but indeed to fulfil the king's purpose.

9 And when he was come to Jerusalem, and had been courteously received of the high priest of the city, he told him what intelligence was given of the money, and declared wherefore he came, and asked if these things were so indeed.

10 Then the high priest told him that there was such money laid up for the relief of widows and fatherless children:

11 And that some of it belonged to Hircanus son of Tobias, a man of great dignity, and not as that wicked Simon had misinformed: the sum whereof in all was four hundred talents of silver, and two hundred of gold:

12 And that it was altogether impossible that such wrongs should be done unto them, that had committed it to the holiness of the place, and to the majesty and inviolable sanctity of the temple, honoured over all the world.

13 But Heliodorus, because of the king's commandment given him, said, That in any wise it must be brought into the king's treasury.

14 So at the day which he appointed he entered in to order this matter: wherefore there was no small agony throughout the whole city.

15 But the priests, prostrating themselves before the altar in their priests' vestments, called unto heaven upon him that made a law concerning things given to be kept, that they should safely be preserved for such as had committed them to be kept.

16 Then whoso had looked the high priest in the face, it would have wounded his heart: for his countenance and the changing of his colour declared the inward agony of his mind.

17 For the man was so compassed with fear and horror of the body, that it was manifest to

them that looked upon him, what sorrow he had now in his heart.

18 Others ran flocking out of their houses to the general supplication, because the place was like to come into contempt.

19 And the women, girt with sackcloth under their breasts, abounded in the streets, and the virgins that were kept in ran, some to the gates, and some to the walls, and others looked out of the windows.

20 And all, holding their hands toward heaven, made supplication.

21 Then it would have pitied a man to see the falling down of the multitude of all sorts, and the fear of the high priest, being in such an agony.

22 They then called upon the Almighty Lord to keep the things committed of trust safe and sure for those that had committed them.

23 Nevertheless Heliodorus executed that which was decreed.

24 Now as he was there present himself with his guard about the treasury, the Lord of spirits, and the Prince of all power, caused a great apparition, so that all that presumed to come in with him were astonished at the power of God, and fainted, and were sore afraid.

25 For there appeared unto them an horse with a terrible rider upon him, and adorned with a very fair covering, and he ran fiercely, and smote at Heliodorus with his forefeet, and it seemed that he that sat upon the horse had complete harness of gold.

26 Moreover two other young men appeared before him, notable in strength, excellent in beauty, and comely in apparel, who stood by him on either side, and scourged him continually, and gave him many sore stripes.

27 And Heliodorus fell suddenly unto the ground, and was compassed with great darkness: but they that were with him took him up, and put him into a litter.

28 Thus him, that lately came with a great train and with all his guard into the said treasury, they carried out, being unable to help himself with his weapons: and manifestly they acknowledged the power of God:

29 For he by the hand of God was cast down, and lay speechless without all hope of life.

30 But they praised the Lord, that had miraculously honoured his own place; for the temple, which a little afore was full of fear and trouble, when the Almighty Lord appeared, was filled with joy and gladness.

31 Then straightway certain of Heliodorus' friends prayed Onias, that he would call upon the most High to grant him his life, who lay ready to give up the ghost.

32 So the high priest, suspecting lest the king should misconceive that some treachery had been done to Heliodorus by the Jews, offered a sacrifice for the health of the man.

33 Now as the high priest was making an atonement, the same young men in the same clothing appeared and stood beside Heliodorus, saying, Give Onias the high priest great thanks, insomuch as for his sake the Lord hath granted thee life:

34 And seeing that thou hast been scourged from heaven, declare unto all men the mighty power of God. And when they had spoken these words, they appeared no more.

35 So Heliodorus, after he had offered sacrifice unto the Lord, and made great vows unto him that had saved his life, and saluted Onias, returned with his host to the king.

36 Then testified he to all men the works of the great God, which he had seen with his eyes.

37 And when the king asked Heliodorus, who might be a fit man to be sent yet once again to Jerusalem, he said,

38 If thou hast any enemy or traitor, send him thither, and thou shalt receive him well scourged, if he escape with his life: for in that place, no doubt, there is an especial power of God.

39 For he that dwelleth in heaven hath his eye on that place, and defendeth it; and he beateth and destroyeth them that come to hurt it.

40 And the things concerning Heliodorus, and the keeping of the treasury, fell out on this sort.

CHAP. IV.

1 *Simon slandereth Onias.* 7 *Jason, by corrupting the king, obtaineth the office of the high priest.* 24 *Menelaus getteth the same from Jason by the like corruption.* 34 *Andronicus traitorously murdereth Onias.* 36 *The king being informed thereof, causeth Andronicus to be put to death.* 39 *The wickedness of Lysimachus, by the instigation of Menelaus.*

THIS Simon now, of whom we spake afore, having been a bewrayer of the money, and of his country, slandered Onias, as if he had terrified Heliodorus, and been the worker of these evils.

2 Thus was he bold to call him a traitor, that had deserved well of the city, and tendered his own nation, and was so zealous of the laws.

3 But when their hatred went so far, that by one of Simon's faction murders were committed,

4 Onias seeing the danger of this contention, and that Apollonius, as being the governor of

Celosyria and Phenice, did rage, and increase Simon's malice,

5 He went to the king, not to be an accuser of his countrymen, but seeking the good of all, both publick and private:

6 For he saw that it was impossible that the state should continue quiet, and Simon leave his folly, unless the king did look thereunto.

7 But after the death of Seleucus, when Antiochus, called Epiphanes, took the kingdom, Jason the brother of Onias laboured underhand to be high priest,

8 Promising unto the king by intercession three hundred and threescore talents of silver, and of another revenue eighty talents:

9 Beside this, he promised to assign an hundred and fifty more, if he might have licence to set him up a place for exercise, and for the training up of youth in the fashions of the heathen, and to write them of Jerusalem *by the name of* Antiochians.

10 Which when the king had granted, and he had gotten into his hand the rule, he forthwith brought his own nation to the Greekish fashion.

11 And the royal privileges granted of special favour to the Jews by the means of John the father of Eupolemus, who went ambassador to Rome for amity and aid, he took away; and putting down the governments which were according to the law, he brought up new customs against the law:

12 For he built gladly a place of exercise under the tower itself, and brought the chief young men under his subjection, and made them wear a hat.

13 Now such was the height of Greek fashions, and increase of heathenish manners, through the exceeding profaneness of Jason, that ungodly wretch, and no high priest;

14 That the priests had no courage to serve any more at the altar, but despising the temple, and neglecting the sacrifices, hastened to be partakers of the unlawful allowance in the place of exercise, after the game of Discus called them forth;

15 Not setting by the honours of their fathers, but liking the glory of the Grecians best of all.

16 By reason whereof sore calamity came upon them: for they had them to be their enemies and avengers, whose custom they followed so earnestly, and unto whom they desired to be like in all things.

17 For it is not a light thing to do wickedly against the laws of God: but the time following shall declare these things.

18 Now when the game that was used every

fifth year was kept at Tyrus, the king being present,

19 This ungracious Jason sent special messengers from Jerusalem, who were Antiochians, to carry three hundred drachms of silver to the sacrifice of Hercules, which even the bearers thereof thought fit not to bestow upon the sacrifice, because it was not convenient, but to be reserved for other charges.

20 This money then, in regard of the sender, was appointed to Hercules' sacrifice; but because of the bearers thereof, it was employed to the making of gallies.

21 Now when Apollonius the *son* of Menestheus was sent into Egypt for the coronation of king *Ptolemeus* Philometor, Antiochus, understanding him not to be well affected to his affairs, provided for his own safety: whereupon he came to Joppe, and from thence to Jerusalem:

22 Where he was honourably received of Jason, and of the city, and was brought in with torch light, and with great shoutings: and so afterward went with his host unto Phenice.

23 Three years afterward Jason sent Menelaus, the aforesaid Simon's brother, to bear the money unto the king, and to put him in mind of certain necessary matters.

24 But he being brought to the presence of the king, when he had magnified him for the glorious appearance of his power, got the priesthood to himself, offering more than Jason by three hundred talents of silver.

25 So he came with the king's mandate, bringing nothing worthy the high priesthood, but having the fury of a cruel tyrant, and the rage of a savage beast.

26 Then Jason, who had undermined his own brother, being undermined by another, was compelled to flee into the country of the Ammonites.

27 So Menelaus got the principality: but as for the money that he had promised unto the king, he took no good order for it, albeit Sostratus the ruler of the castle required it:

28 For unto him appertained the gathering of the customs. Wherefore they were both called before the king.

29 Now Menelaus left his brother Lysimachus in his stead in the priesthood; and Sostratus *left* Crates, who was governor of the Cyprians.

30 While those things were in doing, they of Tarsus and Mallos made insurrection, because they were given to the king's concubine, called Antiochis.

31 Then came the king in all haste to appease matters, leaving Andronicus, a man in authority, for his deputy.

32 Now Menelaus, supposing that he had gotten a convenient time, stole certain vessels of gold out of the temple, and gave some of them to Andronicus, and some he sold into Tyrus and the cities round about.

33 Which when Onias knew of a surety, he reproved him, and withdrew himself into a sanctuary at Daphne, that lieth by Antiochia.

34 Wherefore Menelaus, taking Andronicus apart, prayed him to get Onias into his hands; who being persuaded thereunto, and coming to Onias in deceit, gave him his right hand with oaths; and though he were suspected *by him,* yet persuaded he him to come forth of the sanctuary: whom forthwith he shut up without regard of justice.

35 For the which cause not only the Jews, but many also of other nations, took great indignation, and were much grieved for the unjust murder of the man.

36 And when the king was come again from the places about Cilicia, the Jews that were in the city, and certain of the Greeks that abhorred the fact also, complained because Onias was slain without cause.

37 Therefore Antiochus was heartily sorry, and moved to pity, and wept, because of the sober and modest behaviour of him that was dead.

38 And being kindled with anger, forthwith he took away Andronicus his purple, and rent off his clothes, and leading him through the whole city unto that very place, where he had committed impiety against Onias, there slew he the cursed murderer. Thus the Lord rewarded him his punishment, as he had deserved.

39 Now when many sacrileges had been committed in the city by Lysimachus with the consent of Menelaus, and the bruit thereof was spread abroad, the multitude gathered themselves together against Lysimachus, many vessels of gold being already carried away.

40 Whereupon the common people rising, and being filled with rage, Lysimachus armed about three thousand men, and began first to offer violence; one Auranus being the leader, a man far gone in years, and no less in folly.

41 They then seeing the attempt of Lysimachus, some of them caught stones, some clubs, others taking handfuls of dust, that was next at hand, cast them all together upon Lysimachus, and those that set upon them.

42 Thus many of them they wounded, and some they struck to the ground, and all *of them* they forced to flee : but as for the churchrobber himself, him they killed beside the treasury.

43 Of these matters therefore there was an accusation laid against Menelaus.

44 Now when the king came to Tyrus, three men that were sent from the senate pleaded the cause before him:

45 But Menelaus, being now convicted, promised Ptolemee the *son* of Dorymenes to give him much money, if he would pacify the king toward him.

46 Whereupon Ptolemee taking the king aside into a certain gallery, as it were to take the air, brought him to be of another mind:

47 Insomuch that he discharged Menelaus from the accusations, who notwithstanding was cause of all the mischief: and those poor men, who, if they had told their cause, yea, before the Scythians, should have been judged innocent, them he condemned to death.

48 Thus they that followed the matter for the city, and for the people, and for the holy vessels, did soon suffer unjust punishment.

49 Wherefore even they of Tyrus, moved with hatred of that wicked deed, caused them to be honourably buried.

50 And so through the covetousness of them that were of power Menelaus remained still in authority, increasing in malice, and being a great traitor to the citizens.

CHAP. V.

2 *Of the signs and tokens seen in Jerusalem.* 6 *Of the end and wickedness of Jason.* 11 *The pursuit of Antiochus against the Jews.* 15 *The spoiling of the temple.* 27 *Maccabeus fleeth into the wilderness.*

ABOUT the same time Antiochus prepared his second voyage into Egypt:

2 And then it happened, that through all the city, for the space almost of forty days, there were seen horsemen running in the air, in cloth of gold, and armed with lances, like a band of soldiers,

3 And troops of horsemen in array, encountering and running one against another, with shaking of shields, and multitude of pikes, and drawing of swords, and casting of darts, and glittering of golden ornaments, and harness of all sorts.

4 Wherefore every man prayed that that apparition might turn to good.

5 Now when there was gone forth a false rumour, as though Antiochus had been dead, Jason took at the least a thousand men, and suddenly made an assault upon the city; and they that were upon the walls being put back, and the city at length taken, Menelaus fled into the castle:

6 But Jason slew his own citizens without mercy, not considering that to get the day of

them of his own nation would be a most un-happy day for him; but thinking they had been *his* enemies, and not *his* countrymen, whom he conquered.

7 Howbeit for all this he obtained not the principality, but at the last received shame for the reward of his treason, and fled again into the country of the Ammonites.

8 In the end therefore he had an unhappy return, being accused before Aretas the king of the Arabians, fleeing from city to city, pursued of all men, hated as a forsaker of the laws, and being had in abomination as an open enemy of his country and countrymen, he was cast out into Egypt.

9 Thus he that had driven many out of their country perished in a strange land, retiring to the Lacedemonians, and thinking *there* to find succour by reason of his kindred:

10 And he that had cast out many unburied had none to mourn for him, nor any solemn funerals at all, nor sepulchre with his fathers.

11 Now when this that was done came to the king's ear, he thought that Judea had revolted: whereupon removing out of Egypt in a furious mind, he took the city by force of arms,

12 And commanded his men of war not to spare such as they met, and to slay such as went up upon the houses.

13 Thus there was killing of young and old, making away of men, women, and children, slaying of virgins and infants.

14 And there were destroyed within the space of three whole days fourscore thousand, whereof forty thousand were slain in the conflict; and no fewer sold than slain.

15 Yet was he not content with this, but presumed to go into the most holy temple of all the world; Menelaus, that traitor to the laws, and to his own country, being his guide:

16 And taking the holy vessels with polluted hands, and with profane hands pulling down the things that were dedicated by other kings to the augmentation and glory and honour of the place, he gave them away.

17 And so haughty was Antiochus in mind, that he considered not that the Lord was angry for a while for the sins of them that dwelt in the city, and therefore his eye was not upon the place.

18 For had they not been formerly wrapped in many sins, this man, as soon as he had come, had forthwith been scourged, and put back from his presumption, as Heliodorus was, whom Seleucus the king sent to view the treasury.

19 Nevertheless God did not choose the people for the place's sake, but the place for the people's sake.

20 And therefore the place itself, that was partaker with them of the adversity that happened to the nation, did afterward communicate in the benefits sent from the Lord: and as it was forsaken in the wrath of the Almighty, so again, the great Lord being reconciled, it was set up with all glory.

21 So when Antiochus had carried out of the temple a thousand and eight hundred talents, he departed in all haste unto Antiochia, weening in his pride to make the land navigable, and the sea passable by foot: such was the haughtiness of his mind.

22 And he left governors to vex the nation: at Jerusalem, Philip, for his country a Phrygian, and for manners more barbarous than he that set him there;

23 And at Garizim, Andronicus; and besides, Menelaus, who worse than all the rest bare an heavy hand over the citizens, having a malicious mind against his countrymen the Jews,

24 He sent also that detestable ringleader Apollonius with an army of two and twenty thousand, commanding him to slay all those that were in their best age, and to sell the women and the younger sort:

25 Who coming to Jerusalem, and pretending peace, did forbear till the holy day of the sabbath, when taking the Jews keeping holy day, he commanded his men to arm themselves.

26 And so he slew all them that were gone to the celebrating of the sabbath, and running through the city with weapons slew great multitudes.

27 But Judas Maccabeus with nine others, or thereabout, withdrew himself into the wilderness, and lived in the mountains after the manner of beasts, with his company, who fed on herbs continually, lest they should be partakers of the pollution.

CHAP. VI.

1 *The Jews are compelled to leave the law of God.* 4 *The temple is defiled.* 8 *Cruelty upon the people and the women.* 12 *An exhortation to bear affliction, by the example of the valiant courage of Eleazarus, cruelly tortured.*

NOT long after this the king sent an old man of Athens to compel the Jews to depart from the laws of their fathers, and not to live after the laws of God:

2 And to pollute also the temple in Jerusalem, and to call it the temple of Jupiter Olympius; and that in Garizim, of Jupiter the Defender of strangers, as they did desire that dwelt in the place.

3 The coming in of this mischief was sore and grievous to the people:

4 For the temple was filled with riot and revelling by the Gentiles, who dallied with harlots, and had to do with women within the circuit of the holy places, and besides that brought in things that were not lawful.

5 The altar also was filled with profane things, which the law forbiddeth.

6 Neither was it lawful for a man to keep sabbath days or ancient feasts, or to profess himself at all to be a Jew.

7 And in the day of the king's birth every month they were brought by bitter constraint to eat of the sacrifices; and when the feast of Bacchus was kept, the Jews were compelled to go in procession to Bacchus, carrying ivy.

8 Moreover there went out a decree to the neighbour cities of the heathen, by the suggestion of Ptolemee, against the Jews, that they should observe the same fashions, and be partakers of their sacrifices:

9 And whoso would not conform themselves to the manners of the Gentiles should be put to death. Then might a man have seen the present misery.

10 For there were two women brought, who had circumcised their children; whom when they had openly led round about the city, the babes hanging at their breasts, they cast them down headlong from the wall.

11 And others, that had run together into caves near by, to keep the sabbath day secretly, being discovered to Philip, were all burnt together, because they made a conscience to help themselves for the honour of the most sacred day.

12 Now I beseech those that read this book, that they be not discouraged for these calamities, but that they judge those punishments not to be for destruction, but for a chastening of our nation.

13 For it is a token of his great goodness, when wicked doers are not suffered any long time, but forthwith punished.

14 For not as with other nations, whom the Lord patiently forbeareth to punish, till they be come to the fulness of their sins, so dealeth he with us.

15 Lest that, being come to the height of sin, afterwards he should take vengeance of us.

16 And therefore he never withdraweth his mercy from us: and though he punish with adversity, yet doth he never forsake his people

17 But let this that we have spoken be for a warning unto us. And now will we come to the declaring of the matter in few words.

18 Eleazar, one of the principal scribes, an aged man, and of a well favoured countenance, was constrained to open his mouth, and to eat swine's flesh.

19 But he, choosing rather to die gloriously, than to live stained with such an abomination, spit it forth, and came of his own accord to the torment,

20 As it behoved them to come, that are resolute to stand out against such things, as are not lawful for love of life to be tasted.

21 But they that had the charge of that wicked feast, for the old acquaintance they had with the man, taking him aside, besought him to bring flesh of his own provision, such as was lawful for him to use, and make as if he did eat of the flesh taken from the sacrifice commanded by the king;

22 That in so doing he might be delivered from death, and for the old friendship with them find favour.

23 But he began to consider discreetly, and as became his age, and the excellency of his ancient years, and the honour of his gray head, whereunto he was come, and his most honest education from a child, or rather the holy law made and given by God: therefore he answered accordingly, and willed them straightways to send him to the grave.

24 For it becometh not our age, *said he*, in any wise to dissemble, whereby many young persons might think that Eleazar, being fourscore years old and ten, were now gone to a strange religion;

25 And so they through mine hypocrisy, and desire to live a little time and a moment longer, should be deceived by me, and I get a stain to mine old age, and make it abominable.

26 For though for the present time I should be delivered from the punishment of men: yet should I not escape the hand of the Almighty, neither alive, nor dead.

27 Wherefore now, manfully changing this life, I will shew myself such an one as mine age requireth,

28 And leave a notable example to such as be young to die willingly and courageously for the honourable and holy laws. And when he had said these words, immediately he went to the torment:

29 They that led him changing the good will they bare him a little before into hatred, because the foresaid speeches proceeded, as they thought, from a desperate mind.

30 But when he was ready to die with stripes, he groaned, and said, It is manifest unto the Lord, that hath the holy knowledge, that whereas I might have been delivered from death, I *now* endure sore pains in body by being beaten: but in soul am well content to suffer these things, because I fear him.

31 And thus this man died, leaving his death

for an example of a noble courage, and a memorial of virtue, not only unto young men, but unto all his nation.

CHAP. VII.

The constancy and cruel death of seven brethren and their mother in one day, because they would not eat swine's flesh at the king's commandment.

IT came to pass also, that seven brethren with their mother were taken, and compelled by the king against the law to taste swine's flesh, and were tormented with scourges and whips.

2 But one of them that spake first said thus, What wouldest thou ask or learn of us? we are ready to die, rather than to transgress the laws of our fathers.

3 Then the king, being in a rage, commanded pans and chaldrons to be made hot:

4 Which forthwith being heated, he commanded to cut out the tongue of him that spake first, and to cut off the utmost parts of his body, the rest of his brethren and his mother looking on.

5 Now when he was thus maimed in all his members, he commanded him being yet alive to be brought to the fire, and to be fried in the pan: and as the vapour of the pan was for a good space dispersed, they exhorted one another with the mother to die manfully, saying thus,

6 The Lord God looketh upon us, and in truth hath comfort in us, as Moses in his song, which witnessed to their faces, declared, saying, And he shall be comforted in his servants.

7 So when the first was dead after this manner, they brought the second to make him a mocking stock: and when they had pulled off the skin of his head with the hair, they asked him, Wilt thou eat, before thou be punished throughout every member of thy body?

8 But he answered in his own language, and said, No. Wherefore he also received the next torment in order, as the former did.

9 And when he was at the last gasp, he said, Thou like a fury takest us out of this present life, but the King of the world shall raise us up, who have died for his laws, unto everlasting life.

10 After him was the third made a mocking stock: and when he was required, he put out his tongue, and that right soon, holding forth his hands manfully,

11 And said courageously, These I had from heaven; and for his laws I despise them; and from him I hope to receive them again.

12 Insomuch that the king, and they that were with him, marvelled at the young man's courage, for that he nothing regarded the pains.

13 Now when this man was dead also, they tormented and mangled the fourth in like manner.

14 So when he was ready to die he said thus, It is good, being put to death by men, to look for hope from God to be raised up again by him: as for thee, thou shalt have no resurrection to life.

15 Afterward they brought the fifth also, and mangled him.

16 Then looked he unto the king, and said, Thou hast power over men, thou art corruptible, thou doest what thou wilt; yet think not that our nation is forsaken of God;

17 But abide a while, and behold his great power, how he will torment thee and thy seed.

18 After him also they brought the sixth, who being ready to die said, Be not deceived without cause: for we suffer these things for ourselves, having sinned against our God: therefore marvellous things are done unto us.

19 But think not thou, that takest in hand to strive against God, that thou shalt escape unpunished.

20 But the mother was marvellous above all, and worthy of honourable memory: for when she saw her seven sons slain within the space of one day, she bare it with a good courage, because of the hope that she had in the Lord.

21 Yea, she exhorted every one of them in her own language, filled with courageous spirits; and stirring up her womanish thoughts with a manly stomach, she said unto them,

22 I cannot tell how ye came into my womb; for I neither gave you breath nor life, neither was it I that formed the members of every one of you;

23 But doubtless the Creator of the world, who formed the generation of man, and found out the beginning of all things, will also of his own mercy give you breath and life again, as ye now regard not your own selves for his laws' sake.

24 Now Antiochus, thinking himself despised, and suspecting it to be a reproachful speech, whilst the youngest was yet alive, did not only exhort him by words, but also assured him with oaths, that he would make him both a rich and a happy man, if he would turn from the laws of his fathers; and that also he would take him for his friend, and trust him with affairs.

25 But when the young man would in no case hearken unto him, the king called his mother, and exhorted her that she would counsel the young man to save his life.

26 And when he had exhorted her with many

words, she promised him that she would counsel her son.

27 But she bowing herself toward him, laughing the cruel tyrant to scorn, spake in her country language on this manner; O my son, have pity upon me that bare thee nine months in my womb, and gave thee suck three years, and nourished thee, and brought thee up unto this age, and endured the troubles of education.

28 I beseech thee, my son, look upon the heaven and the earth, and all that is therein, and consider that God made them of things that were not; and so was mankind made likewise.

29 Fear not this tormentor, but, being worthy of thy brethren, take thy death, that I may receive thee again in mercy with thy brethren.

30 Whiles she was yet speaking these words, the young man said, Whom wait ye for? I will not obey the king's commandment: but I will obey the commandment of the law that was given unto our fathers by Moses.

31 And thou, that hast been the author of all mischief against the Hebrews, shalt not escape the hands of God.

32 For we suffer because of our sins.

33 And though the living Lord be angry with us a little while for our chastening and correction, yet shall he be at one again with his servants.

34 But thou, O godless man, and of all other most wicked, be not lifted up without a cause, nor puffed up with uncertain hopes, lifting up thy hand against the servants of God:

35 For thou hast not yet escaped the judgment of Almighty God, who seeth all things.

36 For our brethren, who now have suffered a short pain, are dead under God's covenant of everlasting life: but thou, through the judgment of God, shalt receive just punishment for thy pride.

37 But I, as my brethren, offer up my body and life for the laws of our fathers, beseeching God that he would speedily be merciful unto our nation; and that thou by torments and plagues mayest confess, that he alone is God;

38 And that in me and my brethren the wrath of the Almighty, which is justly brought upon all our nation, may cease.

39 Then the king, being in a rage, handled him worse than all the rest, and took it grievously that he was mocked.

40 So this man died undefiled, and put his whole trust in the Lord.

41 Last of all after the sons the mother died.

42 Let this be enough now to have spoken concerning the idolatrous feasts, and the extreme tortures.

CHAP. VIII.

1 *Judas gathereth an host.* 9 *Nicanor is sent against him: who presumeth to make much money of his prisoners.* 16 *Judas encourageth his men, and putteth Nicanor to flight,* 28 *and divideth the spoils.* 30 *Other enemies are also defeated,* 35 *and Nicanor fleeth with grief to Antioch.*

THEN Judas Maccabeus, and they that were with him, went privily into the towns, and called their kinsfolks together, and took unto them all such as continued in the Jews' religion, and assembled about six thousand men.

2 And they called upon the Lord, that he would look upon the people that was trodden down of all; and also pity the temple profaned of ungodly men;

3 And that he would have compassion upon the city, sore defaced, and ready to be made even with the ground; and hear the blood that cried unto him,

4 And remember the wicked slaughter of harmless infants, and the blasphemies committed against his name; and that he would shew his hatred against the wicked.

5 Now when Maccabeus had his company about him, he could not be withstood by the heathen: for the wrath of the Lord was turned into mercy.

6 Therefore he came at unawares, and burnt up towns and cities, and got into his hands the most commodious places, and overcame and put to flight no small number of his enemies.

7 But specially took he advantage of the night for such privy attempts, insomuch that the bruit of his manliness was spread every where.

8 So when Philip saw that this man increased by little and little, and that things prospered with him still more and more, he wrote unto Ptolemeus, the governor of Celosyria and Phenice, to yield more aid to the king's affairs.

9 Then forthwith choosing Nicanor the *son* of Patroclus, one of his special friends, he sent him with no fewer than twenty thousand of all nations under him, to root out the whole generation of the Jews; and with him he joined also Gorgias a captain, who in matters of war had great experience.

10 So Nicanor undertook to make so much money of the captive Jews, as should defray the tribute of two thousand talents, which the king was to pay to the Romans.

11 Wherefore immediately he sent to the cities upon the sea coast, proclaiming a sale of the captive Jews, and promising that they should have fourscore and ten bodies for one

talent, not expecting the vengeance that was to follow upon him from the Almighty God.

12 Now when word was brought unto Judas of Nicanor's coming, and he had imparted unto those that were with him that the army was at hand,

13 They that were fearful, and distrusted the justice of God, fled, and conveyed themselves away.

14 Others sold all that they had left, and withal besought the Lord to deliver them, being sold by the wicked Nicanor before they met together:

15 And if not for their own sakes, yet for the covenants he had made with their fathers, and for his holy and glorious name's sake, by which they were called.

16 So Maccabeus called his men together unto the number of six thousand, and exhorted them not to be stricken with terror of the enemy, nor to fear the great multitude of the heathen, who came wrongfully against them; but to fight manfully,

17 And to set before their eyes the injury that they had unjustly done to the holy place, and the cruel handling of the city, whereof they made a mockery, and also the taking away of the government of their forefathers:

18 For they, said he, trust in their weapons and boldness; but our confidence is in the Almighty God, who at a beck can cast down both them that come against us, and also all the world.

19 Moreover he recounted unto them what helps their forefathers had found, and how they were delivered, when under Sennacherib an hundred fourscore and five thousand perished.

20 And he told them of the battle that they had in Babylon with the Galatians, how they came but eight thousand in all to the business, with four thousand Macedonians, and that the Macedonians being perplexed, the eight thousand destroyed an hundred and twenty thousand because of the help that they had from heaven, and so received a great booty.

21 Thus when he had made them bold with these words, and ready to die for the laws and the country, he divided his army into four parts.

22 And joined with himself his own brethren, leaders of each band, *to wit*, Simon, and Joseph, and Jonathan, giving each one fifteen hundred men.

23 Also *he appointed* Eleazar to read the holy book: and when he had given them this watchword, The help of God; himself leading the first band, he joined battle with Nicanor.

24 And by the help of the Almighty, they slew above nine thousand of their enemies, and wounded and maimed the most part of Nicanor's host, and so put all to flight;

25 And took their money that came to buy them, and pursued them far: but lacking time they returned:

26 For it was the day before the sabbath, and therefore they would no longer pursue them.

27 So when they had gathered their armour together, and spoiled their enemies, they occupied themselves about the sabbath, yielding exceeding praise and thanks to the Lord, who had preserved them unto that day, which was the beginning of mercy distilling upon them.

28 And after the sabbath, when they had given part of the spoils to the maimed, and the widows, and orphans, the residue they divided among themselves and their servants.

29 When this was done, and they had made a common supplication, they besought the merciful Lord to be reconciled with his servants for ever.

30 Moreover of those that were with Timotheus and Bacchides, who fought against them, they slew above twenty thousand, and very easily got high and strong holds, and divided among themselves many spoils more, and made the maimed, orphans, widows, yea, and the aged also, equal in spoils with themselves.

31 And when they had gathered their armour together, they laid them up all carefully in convenient places, and the remnant of the spoils they brought to Jerusalem.

32 They slew also Philarches, that wicked person, who was with Timotheus, and had annoyed the Jews many ways.

33 Furthermore at such time as they kept the feast for the victory in their country they burnt Callisthenes, that had set fire upon the holy gates, who had fled into a little house; and so he received a reward meet for his wickedness.

34 As for that most ungracious Nicanor, who had brought a thousand merchants to buy the Jews,

35 He was through the help of the Lord brought down by them, of whom he made least account; and putting off his glorious apparel, and discharging his company, he came like a fugitive servant through the midland unto Antioch, having very great dishonour, for that his host was destroyed.

36 Thus he, that took upon him to make good to the Romans their tribute by means of the captives in Jerusalem, told abroad, that the Jews had God to fight for them, and therefore they could not be hurt, because they followed the laws that he gave them.

CHAP. IX.

1 *Antiochus is chased from Persepolis.* 5 *He is stricken with a sore disease,* 14 *and promiseth to become a Jew.* 28 *He dieth miserably.*

ABOUT that time came Antiochus with dishonour out of the country of Persia.

2 For he had entered the *city* called Persepolis, and went about to rob the temple, and to hold the city; whereupon the multitude running to defend themselves with their weapons put them to flight; and so it happened, that Antiochus being put to flight of the inhabitants returned with shame.

3 Now when he came to Ecbatane, news was brought him what had happened unto Nicanor and Timotheus.

4 Then swelling with anger, he thought to avenge upon the Jews the disgrace done unto him by those that made him flee. Therefore commanded he his chariotman to drive without ceasing, and to dispatch the journey, the judgment of God now following him. For he had spoken proudly in this sort, That he would come to Jerusalem, and make it a common burying-place of the Jews.

5 But the Lord Almighty, the God of Israel, smote him with an incurable and invisible plague: for as soon as he had spoken these words, a pain of the bowels that was remediless came upon him, and sore torments of the inner parts;

6 And that most justly: for he had tormented other men's bowels with many and strange torments.

7 Howbeit he nothing at all ceased from his bragging, but still was filled with pride, breathing out fire in his rage against the Jews, and commanding to haste the journey: but it came to pass that he fell down from his chariot, carried violently; so that having a sore fall, all the members of his body were much pained.

8 And thus he that a little afore thought he might command the waves of the sea, (so proud was he beyond the condition of man) and weigh the high mountains in a balance, was now cast on the ground, and carried in an horselitter, showing forth unto all the manifest power of God.

9 So that the worms rose up out of the body of this wicked man, and whiles he lived in sorrow and pain, his flesh fell away, and the filthiness of his smell was noisome to all his army.

10 And the man, that thought a little afore he could reach to the stars of heaven, no man could endure to carry for his intolerable stink.

11 Here therefore, being plagued, he began to leave off his great pride, and to come to the knowledge *of himself* by the scourge of God, his pain increasing every moment.

12 And when he himself could not abide his own smell, he said these words, It is meet to be subject unto God, and that a man that is mortal should not proudly think of himself, as if he were God.

13 This wicked person vowed also unto the Lord, who now no more would have mercy upon him, saying thus,

14 That the holy city (to the which he was going in haste, to lay it even with the ground, and to make it a common burying-place,) he would set at liberty:

15 And as touching the Jews, whom he had judged not worthy so much as to be buried, but to be cast out with their children to be devoured of the fowls and wild beasts, he would make them all equals to the citizens of Athens:

16 And the holy temple, which before he had spoiled, he would garnish with goodly gifts, and restore all the holy vessels with many more, and out of his own revenue defray the charges belonging to the sacrifices:

17 Yea, and that also he would become a Jew himself, and go through all the world that was inhabited, and declare the power of God.

18 But for all this his pains would not cease: for the just judgment of God was come upon him: therefore despairing of his health, he wrote unto the Jews the letter underwritten, containing the form of a supplication, after this manner:

19 Antiochus, king and governor, to the good Jews his citizens wisheth much joy, health, and prosperity:

20 If ye and your children fare well, and your affairs be to your contentment, I give very great thanks to God, having my hope in heaven.

21 As for me, I was weak, or else I would have remembered kindly your honour and good will. Returning out of Persia, and being taken with a grievous disease, I thought it necessary to care for the common safety of all:

22 Not distrusting mine health, but having great hope to escape this sickness.

23 But considering that even my father, at what time he led an army into the high countries, appointed a successor,

24 To the end that, if any thing fell out contrary to expectation, or if any tidings were brought that were grievous, they of the land, knowing to whom the state was left, might not be troubled:

25 Again, considering how that the princes that are borderers and neighbours unto my

kingdom wait for opportunities, and expect what shall be the event, I have appointed my son Antiochus king, whom I often committed and commended unto many of you, when I went up into the high provinces; to whom I have written as followeth:

26 Therefore I pray and request you to remember the benefits that I have done unto you generally, and in special, and that every man will be still faithful to me and my son.

27 For I am persuaded that he understanding my mind will favourably and graciously yield to your desires.

28 Thus the murderer and blasphemer having suffered most grievously, as he entreated other men, so died he a miserable death in a strange country in the mountains.

29 And Philip, that was brought up with him, carried away his body, who also fearing the son of Antiochus went into Egypt to Ptolemeus Philometor.

CHAP. X.

1 *Judas recovereth the city, and purifieth the temple.* 14 *Gorgias vexeth the Jews.* 16 *Judas winneth their holds.* 29 *Timotheus and his men are discomfited.* 35 *Gazara is taken, and Timotheus slain.*

NOW Maccabeus and his company, the Lord guiding them, recovered the temple and the city:

2 But the altars which the heathen had built in the open street, and also the chapels, they pulled down.

3 And having cleansed the temple they made another altar, and striking stones they took fire out of them, and offered a sacrifice after two years, and set forth incense, and lights, and shewbread.

4 When that was done, they fell flat down, and besought the Lord that they might come no more into such troubles; but if they sinned any more against him, that he himself would chasten them with mercy, and that they might not be delivered unto the blasphemous and barbarous nations.

5 Now upon the same day that the strangers profaned the temple, on the very same day it was cleansed again, even the five and twentieth day of the same month, which is Casleu.

6 And they kept eight days with gladness, as in the feast of the tabernacles, remembering that not long afore they had held the feast of the tabernacles, when as they wandered in the mountains and dens like beasts.

7 Therefore they bare branches, and fair boughs, and palms also, and sang psalms unto

him that had given them good success in cleansing his place.

8 They ordained also by a common statute and decree, That every year those days should be kept of the whole nation of the Jews.

9 And this was the end of Antiochus, called Epiphanes.

10 Now will we declare the acts of Antiochus Eupator, who was the son of this wicked man, gathering briefly the calamities of the wars.

11 So when he was come to the crown, he set one Lysias over the affairs of his realm, and *appointed him* chief governor of Celosyria and Phenice.

12 For Ptolemeus, that was called Macron, choosing rather to do justice unto the Jews for the wrong that had been done unto them, endeavoured to continue peace with them.

13 Whereupon being accused of *the king's* friends before Eupator, and called traitor at every word, because he had left Cyprus, that Philometor had committed unto him, and departed to Antiochus Epiphanes, and seeing that he was in no honourable place, he was so discouraged, that he poisoned himself and died.

14 But when Gorgias was governor of the holds, he hired soldiers, and nourished war continually with the Jews:

15 And therewithal the Idumeans, having gotten into their hands the most commodious holds, kept the Jews occupied, and receiving those that were banished from Jerusalem, they went about to nourish war.

16 Then they that were with Maccabeus made supplication, and besought God that he would be their helper; and so they ran with violence upon the strong holds of the Idumeans,

17 And assaulting them strongly, they won the holds, and kept off all that fought upon the wall, and slew all that fell into their hands, and killed no fewer than twenty thousand.

18 And because certain, who were no less than nine thousand, were fled together into two very strong castles, having all manner of things convenient to *sustain* the siege,

19 Maccabeus left Simon and Joseph, and Zaccheus also, and them that were with him, who were enough to besiege them, and departed himself unto those places which more needed his help.

20 Now they that were with Simon, being led with covetousness, were persuaded for money through certain of those that were in the castle, and took seventy thousand drachms, and let some of them escape.

21 But when it was told Maccabeus what was done, he called the governors of the people together, and accused those men, that they had sold

their brethren for money, and set their enemies free to fight against them.

22 So he slew those that were found traitors, and immediately took the two castles.

23 And having good success with his weapons in all things he took in hand, he slew in the two holds more than twenty thousand.

24 Now Timotheus, whom the Jews had overcome before, when he had gathered a great multitude of foreign forces, and horses out of Asia not a few, came as though he would take Jewry by force of arms.

25 But when he drew near, they that were with Maccabeus turned themselves to pray unto God, and sprinkled earth upon their heads, and girded their loins with sackcloth,

26 And fell down at the foot of the altar, and besought him to be merciful to them, and to be an enemy to their enemies, and an adversary to their adversaries, as the law declareth.

27 So after the prayer they took their weapons, and went on further from the city : and when they drew near to their enemies, they kept y themselves.

28 Now the sun being newly risen, they joined both together; the one part having together with their virtue their refuge also unto the Lord for a pledge of their success and victory : the other side making their rage leader of their battle.

29 But when the battle waxed strong, there appeared unto the enemies from heaven five comely men upon horses, with bridles of gold, and two of them led the Jews,

30 And took Maccabeus betwixt them, and covered him on every side with their weapons, and kept him safe, but shot arrows and lightnings against the enemies: so that being confounded with blindness, and full of trouble, they were killed.

31 And there were slain *of footmen* twenty thousand and five hundred, and six hundred horsemen.

32 As for Timotheus himself, he fled into a very strong hold, called Gazara, where Chereas was governor.

33 But they that were with Maccabeus laid siege against the fortress courageously four days.

34 And they that were within, trusting to the strength of the place, blasphemed exceedingly, and uttered wicked words.

35 Nevertheless upon the fifth day early twenty young men of Maccabeus' company, inflamed with anger because of the blasphemies, assaulted the wall manly, and with a fierce courage killed all that they met withal.

36 Others likewise ascending after them, whiles they were busied with them that were within, burnt the towers, and kindling fires, burnt the blasphemers alive; and others broke open the gates, and, having received in the rest of the army, took the city,

37 And killed Timotheus, that was hid in a certain pit, and Chereas his brother, with Apollophanes.

38 When this was done, they praised the Lord with psalms and thanksgiving, who had done so great things for Israel, and given them the victory.

HISTORICAL SYNCHRONISMS,

THE EMPIRES OF PROPHECY

THE historical portions of the Book of DANIEL make extensive reference to the principal ancient nations of the East; and the prophecies are universally interpreted as Divine predictions concerning the great monarchies that were to succeed in order, after the Chaldæo-Babylonian empire had passed away. It is desirable, therefore, to state in few words, what were the condition and circumstances of the countries in the time of the prophet, and in what order of succession the several empires arose, to what extent they attained, and how they merged the one into the other, until Rome, the last and greatest, absorbed the most valuable states and kingdoms which had appertained to the nations that preceded her.

When Daniel was chief minister in the court of Nebuchadnezzar (B.C. 560), that monarch had founded the Chaldæo-Babylonian empire, by the conquest of Nineveh, and the subjugation of Phœnicia, Syria, Judah, and other countries of the East. At this time, Babylon was the centre of a monarchy that claimed superiority of place and power over every other kingdom then existent. The extensive rule and absolute authority of Nebuchadnezzar, are expressively stated in Daniel ii. 37, 38; and iii. 22; and in other passages.

The kingdom of Israel had ceased for nearly a century and a half, and its people had been transplanted into Media. The Assyrian monarch, Esar-haddon, about 711 B.C. established in Samaria colonies from Babylon and neighbouring countries, and these people, afterwards known as Samaritans, were regarded with bitter animosity by the Jews, at the end of the Captivity, on account of their idolatrous practices, and their erection of a rival temple on Mount Gerizim.

Judah had been subjected by Nebuchadnezzar, who had carried the people captive to Babylon, and destroyed the temple in Jerusalem. To this event, the pathetic lamentation in the 137th Psalm refers.

Media, a country of ten tribes, of which the chief was the Magians, had become great in arms, and had aided Nebuchadnezzar in the overthrow of Nineveh. Astyages, the successor of the warlike Cyaxares, was dethroned by Cyrus in the time of Belshazzar. At an earlier period, Media was a country of nomadic people, unpossessed of much political importance.

Egypt, a few years before the coming of Daniel to Babylon, was under the government of Pharaoh-Necho, an enterprising sovereign, who endeavoured to connect the Mediterranean and Red Seas by a canal, but abandoned the undertaking after a loss of 120,000 men.

Greece was rejoicing in the wise legislation of Solon.

Rome was under the rule of the first Tarquin, by whom the walls of the city were built of stone, also the Cloacæ and Circus Maximus, and the foundations of the Capitol laid.

In Magna Græcia, or Southern Italy, the city of Sybaris, on the Bay of Tarentum, was in its prosperity. This city, which was then a seat of luxury, became afterwards a centre of effeminate and sensual pleasures, and its name passed into a proverb as a synonyme for immorality.

Asia Minor was governed by the rich Lydian king, Crœsus, whose name has also become a proverb for wealth.

Cyrus having dethroned Astyages, 559 B.C., and thus become master of Media, next directed his power against Babylon, at that time subject to Belshazzar, and by its conquest laid the foundation of the Persian empire, which gradually comprehended Media, Persia proper, Assyria, Babylonia, Asia Minor, Syria, Phœnicia, and Palestine. Cambyses, the successor of Cyrus, besieged and took Memphis, and added Egypt, Libya, and Cyrene, to the empire. Darius I. was unsuccessful in an expedition against Scythia, but rendered Macedonia and Thrace tributaries, and also the countries north of the Indus. The Persians were led into quarrels with the Greeks on account of the loss of Macedonia, and their after-history is a record of continual wars between the two peoples, which eventually resulted in the destruction of the Persian monarchy. The Greeks obtained decisive victories at Marathon, Thermopylæ, Salamis, Platæa, and Mycale, in the time of Xerxes; and the overthrow of Darius by Alexander of Macedon, known in history as Alexander the Great, put an end to the Persian empire, which thereafter became part of the great Macedonian monarchy. The royal palaces of Persia were at Babylon, Susa, and Ecbatana; and the mausoleum of the kings at Persepolis. The reference of the prophetic beasts to the preceding empires, and those which follow, is discussed in the notes of our author.

Macedonia, the nucleus of Alexander's empire, goes back to about 800 B.C. Its early history records continual wars with the Persians and Illyrians. It became subject to Persia, but was set free by the battle and victory of Platæa. After many vicissitudes it came under the government of Philip of Macedon, whose son and successor Alexander, overthrew Darius III. at Arbela, and by the subjugation of Persia, laid the foundation of the Macedonian empire, B.C. 333. This vast monarchy included Media, Persia, Thrace, Macedonia, Greece, Syria, Phœnicia, Palestine, Egypt, and provinces beyond the Indus to the river Hyphasis. Still seeking fresh conquests, Alexander arrived in Babylon, where he died either by poison, or intemperate excess, B.C. 323. His dominions were then dismembered, and partitioned amongst his generals and his family, who, for twenty-two years were in deadly contest with each other, before their several claims were adjusted.

The Roman empire, about 200 B.C. had become the dictator of all the nations from the Atlantic to the Euphrates. Passing through many vicissitudes, sometimes subject to internal strife and the war of factions, at others, enlarging the boundaries of her rule and consolidating her power, she at length reached the age of Augustus, under whom she extended her sway over the principal countries of the then known world. Her possessions in Europe were Spain, Gaul, Britain, Rhœtia, Vindelicia, Noricum, Pannonia, Illyria, Greece, Thrace, Mœsia, and Daria; in Asia, Asia Minor, Syria, Phœnicia, Palestine, the north-eastern coasts of the Black Sea, Armenia, Mesopotamia, and Assyria; and in Africa, Egypt and the whole of the northern coast. After Augustus, and to the reign of Vitellius, Rome was subject to the arbitrary will of tyrants, noticeable for little beyond their vices and luxurious effeminacy. From Vitellius to Antoninus she enjoyed a period of happiness and prosperity; but from Commodus to Diocletian the power was in the hands of a military despotism. The Roman spirit became thoroughly enervated by luxury and vicious indulgence, and the empire gradually tottered to its fall. The removal of the seat of government from Rome to Constantinople by Constantine, hastened on the crisis, and the subsequent divisions of the empire divided and weakened its power. The German tribes began to make bolder incursions, and effected permanent settlements. At length, A.D. 476, the Western empire, of which Rome was the capital, fell under the power of the Heruli. The Eastern empire survived for centuries, and after many alternations of grandeur and declension, finally terminated A.D. 1453, when the Ottoman power became triumphant. The Gothic kingdoms which arose out of the ruins of the Roman empire are considered to be pointed at in Daniel vii. 20, and denoted by the ten horns of the fourth beast.

On the ruins of the Western empire, arose the temporal power of the Papacy. The barbarian conquerors of Rome, not less superstitious than ferocious and cruel, submitted themselves to the designs of an ambitious hierarchy, which sought to establish an universal empire, on the basis of an infallible spiritual authority. To effect this, the Roman church threw aside the simplicity of the Gospel system, and amalgamated with Truth the various forms of idolatry, which prevailed amongst the peoples over whom she sought to lay her rule. Following out this line of policy, she at length succeeded in her designs, and secured an absolute and arbitrary power, both in temporal and spiritual matters; but every step in her advance to this point degraded her more and more as a church of Christ; and when her ambitious views were at length realized, she had reached the bad eminence in idolatry and all wickedness that identifies her with the Antichrist of prophecy.

Dec, 25 2002
Harley C. Headley -

June 19 2004
Harley C. Headley

Feb. 20 2005
Harley C. Headley